The Rorschach: A Comprehensive System, in two volumes
by John E. Exner, Jr.
Theory and Practice in Behavior Therapy
by Aubrey J. Yates
Principles of Psychotherapy
by Irving B. Weiner

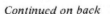
P9-CSE-447

Psychoactive Drugs and Social Judgment: Theory and Research
edited by Kenneth Hammond and C. R. B. Joyce
Clinical Methods in Psychology
edited by Irving B. Weiner
Human Resources for Troubled Children
by Werner I. Halpern and Stanley Kissel
Hyperactivity
by Dorothea M. Ross and Sheila A. Ross
Heroin Addiction: Theory, Research and Treatment
by Jerome J. Platt and Christina Labate
Children's Rights and the Mental Health Profession
edited by Gerald P. Koocher
The Role of the Father in Child Development
edited by Michael E. Lamb
Handbook of Behavioral Assessment
edited by Anthony R. Ciminero, Karen S. Calhoun, and Henry E. Adams
Counseling and Psychotherapy: A Behavioral Approach
by E. Lakin Phillips
Dimensions of Personality
edited by Harvey London and John E. Exner, Jr.
The Mental Health Industry: A Cultural Phenomenon
by Peter A. Magaro, Robert Gripp, David McDowell, and Ivan W. Miller III
Nonverbal Communication: The State of the Art
by Robert G. Harper, Arthur N. Wiens, and Joseph D. Matarazzo
Alcoholism and Treatment
by David J. Armor, J. Michael Polich, and Harriet B. Stambul
A Biodevelopmental Approach to Clinical Child Psychology: Cognitive Controls and
Cognitive Control Theory
by Sebastiano Santostefano
Handbook of Infant Development
edited by Joy D. Osofsky
Understanding the Rape Victim: A Synthesis of Research Findings
by Sedelle Katz and Mary Ann Mazur
Childhood Pathology and Later Adjustment: The Question of Prediction
by Loretta K. Cass and Carolyn B. Thomas
Intelligent Testing with the WISC-R
by Alan S. Kaufman
Adaptation in Schizophrenia: The Theory of Segmental Set
by David Shakow
Psychotherapy: An Eclectic Approach
by Sol L. Garfield
Handbook of Minimal Brain Dysfunctions
edited by Herbert E. Rie and Ellen D. Rie
Handbook of Behavioral Interventions: A Clinical Guide
edited by Alan Goldstein and Edna B. Foa
Art Psychotherapy
by Harriet Wadeson
Handbook of Adolescent Psychology
edited by Joseph Adelson
Psychotherapy Supervision: Theory, Research and Practice
edited by Allen K. Hess

Continued on back

CLINICAL METHODS
IN PSYCHOLOGY

CLINICAL METHODS IN PSYCHOLOGY

Second Edition

Edited by
IRVING B. WEINER
University of Denver

A WILEY-INTERSCIENCE PUBLICATION

JOHN WILEY & SONS

New York · Chichester · Brisbane · Toronto · Singapore

Library of Congress Cataloging in Publication Data:

Main entry under title:

Clinical methods in psychology.

(Wiley series on personality processes)
"A Wiley-Interscience publication."
Includes bibliographies and indexes.
1. Clinical psychology. I. Weiner, Irving B.
II. Series. [DNLM: 1. Psychology, Clinical. 2. Psycho-
therapy. WM 100 C639]

RC467.C577 1983   157'.9   83-6825
ISBN 0-471-88896-6

Printed in the United States of America

10 9 8 7 6 5 4 3 2 1

To David Shakow (1901–1981)
With appreciation for his contributions
to clinical psychology
as a science and
as a profession

Contributors

THOMAS J. BOLL, PH.D., Professor of Psychology, Pediatrics, and Neurological Surgery; Director, Medical Psychology Program, University of Alabama in Birmingham; Diplomate, American Board of Professional Psychology

EDWARD S. BORDIN, PH.D., Professor of Psychology, University of Michigan; Diplomate, American Board of Professional Psychology

JAMES N. BUTCHER, PH.D., Professor and Director of Graduate Education in Clinical Psychology, Department of Psychology, University of Minnesota

EMORY L. COWEN, PH.D., Professor of Psychology, University of Rochester

JOHN E. EXNER, JR., PH.D., Professor of Psychology, Long Island University; Executive Director, Rorschach Workshops; Diplomate, American Board of Professional Psychology

RONALD E. FOX, PH.D., Professor and Dean, School of Professional Psychology, Wright State University; Diplomate, American Board of Professional Psychology

MARVIN R. GOLDFRIED, PH.D., Professor of Psychology and Psychiatry, State University of New York at Stony Brook; Diplomate, American Board of Professional Psychology

MALCOLM D. GYNTHER, PH.D., Professor of Psychology, Auburn University; Diplomate, American Board of Professional Psychology

RUTH A. GYNTHER, M.A., formerly Instructor in Psychology, University of Missouri at St. Louis

ALAN S. KAUFMAN, PH.D., Professor of Psychology, California School of Professional Psychology, San Diego

JAMES W. LANGENBUCHER, doctoral candidate in clinical psychology, Rutgers University

BERNARD LUBIN, PH.D., Professor and Chairman, Department of Psychology, University of Missouri at Kansas City; Diplomate, American Board of Professional Psychology

GAIL R. MAUDAL, PH.D., Clinical Psychologist, Dakota County Mental Health Center, Minneapolis, Minnesota

PETER E. NATHAN, PH.D., Professor and Chairman, Department of Clinical Psychology, Graduate School of Applied and Professional Psychology, Rutgers University

CECIL R. REYNOLDS, PH.D., Associate Professor and Director, School Psychology Training Program, Texas A & M University

ZIGFRIDS T. STELMACHERS, PH.D., Director, Crisis Intervention Center and Chief Psychologist, Hennepin County Medical Center, Minneapolis, Minnesota; Diplomate, American Board of Professional Psychology

IRVING B. WEINER, PH.D., Vice Chancellor for Academic Affairs and Professor of Psychology, University of Denver; Diplomate, American Board of Professional Psychology

ARTHUR N. WIENS, PH.D., Professor and Director of Training, Department of Medical Psychology, University of Oregon Medical School; Diplomate, American Board of Professional Psychology

GEOREGANN WITTE, doctoral candidate in clinical psychology, Rutgers University

Series Preface

This series of books is addressed to behavioral scientists interested in the nature of human personality. Its scope should prove pertinent to personality theorists and researchers as well as to clinicians concerned with applying an understanding of personality processes to the amelioration of emotional difficulties in living. To this end, the series provides a scholarly integration of theoretical formulations, empirical data, and practical recommendations.

Six major aspects of studying and learning about human personality can be designated: personality theory, personality structure and dynamics, personality development, personality assessment, personality change, and personality adjustment. In exploring these aspects of personality, the books in the series discuss a number of distinct but related subject areas: the nature and implications of various theories of personality; personality characteristics that account for consistencies and variations in human behavior; the emergence of personality processes in children and adolescents; the use of interviewing and testing procedures to evaluate individual differences in personality; efforts to modify personality styles through psychotherapy, counseling, behavior therapy, and other methods of influence; and patterns of abnormal personality functioning that impair individual competence.

IRVING B. WEINER

University of Denver
Denver, Colorado

Preface

This second edition of *Clinical Methods in Psychology,* like the first edition, surveys the major methods of assessment and intervention currently employed in the practice of clinical psychology. The contributing authors delineate theoretical, research, and applied aspects of the methods with which clinicians work and seek to address the needs and interests of both beginning and experienced practitioners.

To this end, each chapter discusses the historical development of a particular method of assessment or intervention, identifies theoretical similarities and differences among its leading proponents, summarizes findings bearing on its utility, and provides specific recommendations for putting it into practice in clinical settings. Although the authors approach their task in somewhat different ways, they all write both as practitioners concerned with helping people in psychological distress and as scientists concerned with systematic, empirical investigation of clinical methods.

For beginning clinicians each chapter offers an introduction to the central concepts, techniques, and lines of research on which the particular method of assessment or intervention is based. For more experienced readers the chapters also appraise the present state of the literature, offer guidelines for future directions in practice and research, and include extensive bibliographies useful for reference purposes.

Although compiled for the same purpose and along the same lines as its 1976 predecessor, this second edition is substantially revised and updated. Three chapters and their authors are entirely new. Thomas Boll has prepared a chapter on neuropsychological assessment (Chapter 6), and Emory Cowen has written on community mental health and primary prevention (Chapter 12). Neither of these topics was covered in the first edition, and the Boll and Cowen chapters provide a solid overview and comprehensive reference source on these two relatively new methods. The third entirely new contribution replaces the chapter "Measures of Intelligence and Conceptual Thinking" from the first edition. It is a chapter by Alan Kaufman and Cecil Reynolds entitled "Clinical Evaluation of Intellectual Function" (Chapter 3). Drawing on their authoritative knowledge of recent developments in the areas of intelligence testing and educational assessment, Kaufman and Reynolds cast a modern light on this traditional topic.

As another major change from the first edition, Chapter 2 by Exner has been completely rewritten, and its title has been changed from "Projective Techniques" to "Rorschach Assessment." There are two main reasons for this change in emphasis. First, although the distinction between "projective" and "objective" tests has a long history in clinical psychology and has served some purposes as well, it no longer fits current knowledge about the Rorschach. Recent formulations and abundant research data, which Exner elaborates, indicate that the Rorschach is best conceived as a problem-solving task on which subjects bring to bear their preferred modes of perceptual–cognitive operation, with "projection" playing only a peripheral role in shaping certain aspects of the response process. Moreover, the precision and interscorer reliability of numerous scorable dimensions of cognitive operation on the Rorschach, combined with extensive normative data, make these features of the test as objective as those of many "objective" tests.

Whether this observation applies to other tests traditionally labeled projective techniques is difficult to determine, which is the second reason for the changed focus of Exner's chapter. In contrast to abundant new information in an expanding Rorschach literature, there have been few advances in theory or research since 1976 concerning the other projective tests covered in the previous version. Hence, aside from some limited updating that Exner provides on these measures, the first edition still offers as full an introduction to them as could have been included in the present volume.

The other chapters concerned with methods of assessment—by Wiens on the clinical interview (Chapter 1), by Gynther and Gynther on personality inventories (Chapter 4), and by Goldfried on behavioral assessment (Chapter 5)—have been carefully updated and expanded to include some emerging topics not covered in the first edition. Among these are recently developed multidimensional personality scales, techniques for automated assessment, and measures of cognitive and physiological components of behavior.

In the other chapters on methods of intervention Weiner and newly added coauthor Edward Bordin bring up to date the status of outcome research in individual psychotherapy (Chapter 7); Lubin in his chapter on group psychotherapy (Chapter 8) adds material on self-help groups; Fox, in a largely rewritten contribution on family therapy (Chapter 9), includes information on behavioral approaches with families; Nathan, in another rewritten chapter assisted by two new coauthors, Georgeann Witte and James Langenbucher, expands his previous discussion of behavior therapy to include sections on ethical issues, evaluation, cognitive perspectives, and health psychology (Chapter 10); and Butcher and Maudal in their chapter on crisis intervention, with the addition of Zigfrids Stelmachers as coauthor, introduce new material on assessing danger and on the organization and management of crisis intervention programs (Chapter 11).

As in any revised text, a reliable index of how much new information is provided is the number of references to literature that has appeared since the previous edition was published. The chapters of this revision of the 1976 *Clinical Methods in Psychology* include approximately 2,400 references, of which approximately 950, or just under 40%, have publication dates of 1976 or later. Inasmuch as each chapter includes a historical introduction and a review of basic concepts, which require repeating references to older literature, the total of 40% new citations confirms that this second edition is a substantially new book and a guide to practice for the 1980s.

The authors wish to express their sincere appreciation to the many colleagues who read portions of the manuscript in draft form and to the many persons who contributed clerical assistance. We also gratefully acknowledge permission from the following publishers to reprint copyrighted material: CBA College Publishing, Pergamon Press, Prentice-Hall, and Syracuse University Press.

IRVING B. WEINER

Denver, Colorado
August 1983

Contents

PART ONE

Methods of Assessment

CHAPTER 1

The Assessment Interview

ARTHUR N. WIENS

In the opening sentence of the first edition of this chapter (Wiens, 1976) the observation was made that there are many fields in which interviewing is an important professional skill, and many areas of research that contribute knowledge regarding interviewing. The student of the interview—and that includes all clinical psychologists—is well advised to be knowledgeable about this research, which is being presented in a great variety of professional journals and books. Again, as then, review of some aspects of interviewing practice and research is done with the keen awareness that even as this chapter is being written new findings are being reported.

When psychologists speak of assessment they are usually referring to a range of assessment procedures, including the interview, various paper-and-pencil self-report measures, intelligence tests, personality tests, standardized test or interaction situations, and so on. In arriving at clinical decisions, the clinician–assessor brings together data from different sources and judgmentally arrives at a summary recommendation and/or description of the individual being evaluated. In a clinical setting, there is typically an individual assessor, whereas in many business settings assessment centers have been utilized. In the assessment center method, each participant is given the same opportunity to demonstrate his or her abilities in standardized situations, and each participant is observed by more than one judge. Multiple observers, multiple sources of information, and specifically defined objective dimensions of performance all add to the objectivity of the process. One thousand or more organizations throughout the world are making use of the assessment center method, and at least 30,000 individuals are assessed yearly, mostly in business organizations (Moses & Byham, 1977). These centers are accumulating a great deal of data and information that needs to be incorporated into our general assessment knowledge base.

In the clinical setting assessment information may be gathered for diagnostic or treatment planning purposes. In fact, there is great deal of overlap between the diagnostic and psychotherapeutic interview. In many instances the assessment interview may be the first in a sequence of treatment interviews. In both situations there is two-person interaction, and there are many similarities in the two interviews, both in objectives and process. Research findings on the interview originate in studies of the psychotherapeutic process as well as in study of the assessment process, and the student of the interview should be aware of the research literature in both areas. Furthermore, the concern for the patient that is expressed in the psychotherapeutic interview must also be present in the assessment interview. An interview that is only "diagnostic" will probably make the patient feel like some kind of specimen of psychopathology and actually make it difficult for him or her to share concerns with the interviewer. The importance of the relationship established between interviewer and interviewee will be discussed at some length in this chapter.

Through recorded history the interview has been used professionally by philosophers, physicians, priests, and attorneys. In this century many new professionals have been added to this interviewer list. These include psychologists, psychiatrists, social workers, sociologists, anthropologists, nurses, economists, newspaper reporters, salespeople, welfare caseworkers, finance company interviewers, and so on. A listing of interview situations would be almost endless. The novice interviewer can learn about interviewing from many different sources and should by no means limit study to psychology textbooks or psychology instructors. Interviewing can be observed daily on national and local television, and one might profit from paying close attention to the skills of television interviewers as they try to elicit verbal responses from a variety of interviewees, some of whom are presumably motivated to be frank, open, and expressive and others of whom are quite reticent. One such television interviewer has published her thoughts and experiences on how to talk with practically anybody about practically anything (Walters, 1970).

A great variety of professionals and lay persons have excellent talent and skill in interviewing. Some people assume that one either has this skill or does not, and that it cannot be explicitly learned. A related assumption that is often made is that interviewing skills cannot be taught but can only be gradually acquired through personal professional experience and through observation and imitation of a more experienced interviewer. I would certainly not disagree that important interviewing skills are learned through observation and modeling. I would, however, call the reader's attention to society's increasing interest in interpersonal communication skills, and to the development of numerous formal courses on interviewing for both lay and professional individuals in almost all of our communities. R. G. Matarazzo (1978) has discussed various of these in her presentation of research on the teaching and learning of psychotherapeutic skills. A parallel development has been the publication of considerable material on interviewing. Among these publications are a book on the mental health interview by Pope (1979); a chapter on basic interviewing skills by Johnson (1981); a chapter on behavioral interviewing by Morganstern and Tevlin (1981); a book on clinical interviewing with children by Greenspan (1981); and a chapter on interviewing strategies in child assessment by Kanfer, Eyberg, and Krahn (1982). The content of some of these publications will be referred to later in this chapter.

The assumption that interviewing skills cannot be taught must certainly be questioned as one reviews the current interviewing research literature in which behavioral scientists report on their efforts to study specific aspects of the interview interaction. With a specification of interview behaviors, it becomes possible to assess the interview effects of a variety of interviewer and interviewee characteristics and tactics. It is also reasonable to assume that the beginning interviewer can study and should know various aspects of the psychological forces at work in the interview. Such knowledge can then be a basis for acquiring and using insightfully the specific techniques of interviewing.

Some characteristics of a skillful interviewer may seem like plain common sense, whereas others may appear more subtle and nonverbal. Eric G. Anderson (1981) describes an old Scottish doctor who, many years ago, was instructing his new assistant in the ways of his rural practice in Britain. "Pay attention tae the way yer patient comes in, laddies," he said. "You've got tae give them value for their money. If the man is wearing a clean shirt, it means he expects tae get his chest examined." During the past several decades, research in nonverbal communication has generated convincing evidence that facial expressions, body posture and movements, and styles of speaking can serve as valuable sources of information in the interview (Harper, Wiens, & Matarazzo, 1978). The development of sophisticated audio and video equipment permits the recordings of interviews for later and more detailed analyses. New developments in computer technology are further facilitating such detailed analyses.

Accurate and reliable description that differentiates and predicts is the basis of hypothesis formation and testing in science. Placing an object or organism or a set of behaviors into a certain class allows us to infer certain characteristics without needing to demonstrate each characteristic anew each time. In clinical personality assessment this description and classification process is called *diagnosis*. Since the first edition of this chapter, hospitals, clinics, and virtually all health care settings have become even more insistent that a carefully developed diagnosis be assigned to each patient. Social service agencies and third-party payers such as Blue Cross have diagnostic requirements with which the assessment interviewer must be familiar. The development of the third edition of the *Diagnostic and Statistical Manual of Mental Disorders* (APA, 1980) has been helpful to diagnosticians. The diagnostic criteria in DSM-III are not the general descriptions found in the earlier editions (DSM-I and DSM-II), but are instead specific, denotable features designed to assist clinicians in making a diagnosis. The DSM-III diagnoses do not assume any particular etiology for the dysfunction the patient is experiencing, unless the mechanism is included in the definition of the disorder (e.g., organic pathology). Rather, the general approach can be said to be descriptive in that definitions of the disorders consist by and large of descriptions of the clinical features. The reliability of these diagnoses and a description of some standardized diagnostic interviewing schedules will be presented later in this chapter.

This chapter is organized under the following headings: General Considerations in Assessment Interviews; Research on the Anatomy of the Interview; Studies in Nonverbal Communication; Roles and Tactics in the Interview Interaction; and Specific Considerations in the Initial Clinical Interview. An attempt is made in each instance to refer to specific research programs to allow the reader to identify additional sources of review and study. An attempt is also made to evaluate the research findings for possible clinical implications that can provide a basis for developing specific clinical interview guidelines.

GENERAL CONSIDERATIONS IN ASSESSMENT INTERVIEWS

Both participants share actively in the process of interviewing, and both participants are influenced by each other; the end product of the interview is a result of this interaction. This assumption of mutual interaction is also referred to as the relationship aspect of the interview and, in this chapter, is viewed as a most critical consideration for the interview. The relationship established between the interviewer and interviewee determines whether or not the purposes of the interview can be achieved. Relationship considerations hold from the first interview encounter and thus make artificial any attempt to distinguish between assessment and therapy interviews.

Rapport and Relationship

All interviewers make some estimate of the degree to which the interviewee has cooperated and actively participated in the interview. It is almost universally assumed that the establishment of good rapport between the interviewer and interviewee is important in interviewee participation and has the highest priority in an initial interview as well as in subsequent interviews, as for example in interview therapy. Research interviewers, as well as clinical interviewers, assume that the emotional interaction between themselves and their interviewees affects the pattern of communication between them. In research assessment interviewing, the research interviewer endeavors to obtain community acceptance and support for the research project and is careful not to become identified with any community group. For example, in an industrial interview study support is sought from union as well as company officials. Typically an appointment time is set so that the interviewee is relatively free. The nature and purpose of the study and the interview are explained, with care taken not to give too long or complex an introduction; brief introductions usually work best. If the personal needs (including altruism), of the interviewee can be met in some way, such an explanation can help to induce rapport. Finally, interviewers who are confident and expect to obtain interviewee cooperation usually do elicit active interviewee participation.

Clinical interviewers have long assumed that the relationship is the communication bridge between people. If the relationship is positive, each person is likely to be more receptive to the message being sent. A positive relationship might be characterized by feelings such as relaxation, comfort, trust, respect, harmony, warmth, or psychological safety. If the relationship is negative, there is less desire and readiness to hear what is being said. A negative relationship may be characterized by feelings such as hostility, defensiveness, unease, mistrust, disrespect, discordance, or psychological danger. A positive relationship frees the interviewee to reveal thoughts and feelings without defensiveness or distortion, because of the implied promise of acceptance and understanding and freedom from punishing criticism, rejection, or reprisal. Motivation to participate in the interview may also be derived from the interviewee's opportunity to talk fully about topics of interest.

From the standpoint of the interviewer, a positive relationship has the effect of intensifying his or her influence, thus making suggestions more appealing and techniques more effective. A good relationship also makes the interviewer a more attractive model of behavior for the interviewee to imitate. Another effect of a good relationship is that the positive atmosphere created acts as a counterconditioning context. In a relationship context that counters anxiety, discussion of problems and situations that normally evoke anxiety may lead to the evocation of less anxiety by these problems and situations in the future. This phenomenon is very similar to the counterconditioning seen in behaviorally oriented relaxation and desensitization procedures.

An exellent discussion of the essential qualities of an interviewer counselor is offered by Tyler (1969), who notes that it is often quite difficult to analyze what good interviewers do because the essential qualities involved in a good relationship are attitudes rather than skills. Essential attitudes include acceptance, understanding, and sincerity. The interviewer quality of acceptance involves a thoroughgoing basic regard for the worth of human individuals and particularly for the interviewee sitting in the office. The accepting interviewer does not view the interviewee with cynicism or contempt. In fact, it has been suggested that if the interviewer has not discovered something about the interviewee to like by the end of an initial interview, the session has not been successful for the establishment of a relationship.

The quality of understanding (or *empathy)* involves the effort to grasp clearly and completely the meaning the interviewee is trying to convey. Understanding is a sharing process in which the interviewer tries to assume the client's place and tries to see the circumstances as they appear to the interviewee.

The quality of sincerity, which has been called *congruence,* refers to interviewer consistency, or the harmony that must exist between what an interviewer says and does and what he or she really is. Gilmore (1973) makes an interesting distinction between acceptance and understanding on the one hand and sincerity on the other. You can *accept* or *understand* somebody, but you cannot *sincere* somebody. The interviewer can only *be sincere,* and, although this quality is hard to define, it might be considered an interviewer characteristic to the extent to which the interviewer communicates a valid and reliable picture of what he or she is really like inside. The reader is urged to study the extended discussion on this topic by Gilmore (1973, pp. 178–225), in which she also makes some suggestions on the development of greater personal sincerity.

A practical implication of this discussion is the implicit conclusion that no one interviewer can be all these things to all people. There is no evidence to support a belief that interviewers can function equally well with all types of interviewees. A somewhat related question might be whether there are some assessment and therapeutic intervention procedures that are less dependent on the nature of the relationship between the participants. Behavior therapists, for example, might appear to minimize the importance of the relationship, treating it as a general rather than a specific condition for therapy. Patterson (1968) discusses this issue in considerable detail and marshals both evidence and arguments to suggest that the behavior therapist is highly interested in, concerned about, and devoted to helping the client. The behavior therapist has the same interviewer characteristics as those referrred to above. In short, behavior therapists are involved in relationship with their clients and behavior therapists are human; they are nice people, not machines.

Communication

In any clinical interview situation, and in any interpersonal situation, as well, communication takes place between the participants. If one examines the many forms communication can take (both verbal and nonverbal), it becomes impossible to conceive of a two-person interaction that does not involve communication. Obviously, some forms of communication are more effective than others, and perhaps some are not consciously intended at all. Communication includes more than the factual content of the client's statements; it extends to, and perhaps most importantly includes, feelings that are often hard to put into words.

There are great individual differences in communication styles, and there are also changes within each interviewer from one client to the next. It is probably not possible yet, if it ever will be, to suggest very specific rules of good communication. Yet, as Tyler (1969) has outlined, there are some general communication practices among experienced interviewers that are worth noting. For example, an interviewee often makes a series of comments that may involve both facts and feelings of some variety. When the interviewee pauses, the interviewer decides how to respond. The most often preferred response is a brief interviewer comment that can put together several of the feelings or attitudes that have been expressed. Short of a brief summarizing comment, the interviewer should at least indicate understanding of some one feeling by responding to it. If the interviewee's comments involve several people, it behooves the interviewer to respond to the interviewee's side of the relationship.

In this regard, Tyler (1969, p. 19) offers the example of a client talking about difficulties with an unreasonable police officer. The interviewer could comment, "He must have been a very unpleasant person," and expect to obtain more information about the officer's attitutdes and motives. Or the interviewer could comment, "You seem to dislike people of that sort intensely," and expect to gain a better understanding of how the interviewee reacts.

The specific words the interviewer uses to achieve the interview purpose are important. A basic communication consideration is the use of words for which both participants in the interview have a common definition. It is difficult to know whether this is the case without frequently exploring the meaning both parties assign to words. In addition to the obvious consideration of a common definition, it is important for the interviewer to consider whether the choice of words is likely to put the interviewee on the defensive. Words such as *coward, stupid, effeminate* (with a male), or *masculine* (with a woman) are best not used unless the interviewee has introduced them. Tact is desirable in all interpersonal situations, including the interview.

The interviewer also finds that some personal anxieties, struggles, and aspirations are being stimulated, and that he or she feels an impulse to talk about himself or herself. This impulse is best resisted in favor of keeping the focus of the discussion on the interviewee, this being one of the differences between an interview and a conversation. It is furthermore not good interviewing practice for the interviewer to recount personal experiences with the interviewee, even though the problem situations appear to be similar. The interviewee will likely see differences in the situations and question whether the interviewer's solution really applies. Also, a basic assumption about any interpersonal partner is that what that person has done to someone else, he or she is likely to do to the person being addressed.

Another task of the interviewer is to decide how to respond to silence. The interviewee should be allowed the opportunity to reflect on what has been said. But if the silence is based on some aspect of duress or confrontation, the interviewer is best advised to break the silence and reestablish communication. It is highly unlikely that communication will be enhanced or a positive relationship furthered by an interviewer's insisting on waiting out the interviewee. It should be repeated that many different words can be used to convey understanding and acceptance, and phraseology does not have to be elegant. Good interviewing does require careful listening, however, both for the words and statements of the interviewee and for themes that may recur. In Tyler's (1969) words, "Listen, think, respond. It is the hardest kind of work, but worth the effort" (p. 42).

Interview versus Conversation

The term *interview* has a history of usage going back for centuries. It was used originally to designate a face-to-face meeting of individuals for a formal conference on some point. Later the term became familiar in its journalistic usage as reporters interviewed people to obtain statements for publication. Virtually all current definitions of the interview include reference to a face-to-face verbal exchange in which one person, the interviewer, attempts to elicit information or expressions of opinion or belief from another person, the interviewee.

An interview resembles a conversation in several ways. They both typically involve a face-to-face verbal exchange of information, ideas, attitudes, or feelings and contain messages exchanged through nonverbal as well as verbal modes of expression. However, a crucial characteristic that distinguishes an interview from a conversation is that the interview is designed to achieve a consciously selected purpose. There may be no central theme in a conversation, but in an interview the content is directed toward a specific purpose and is likely to have unity, progression, and thematic continuity. If the purpose of the interview is to be achieved, one participant must assume and maintain responsibility for directing the interaction (asking questions) toward the goal, and the other participant must facilitate achievement of the purpose by following the direction of the interaction (answering questions). There are no comparable status terms or selected role behaviors in a conversation.

The nonreciprocal roles of the two participants in an interview relationship result from the fact that, in one form or another, the purpose of the interview is to give some benefit to the interviewee. The interviewer has a professional obligation to perform clearly defined services for the client. Whereas interviewees may reveal a great deal about themselves from wide segments of their lives, interviewers typically limit their revelations to their professional lives.

Furthermore, whereas in conversation a person may respond in a spontaneous and unplanned manner, an interviewer deliberately and consciously plans actions to further the purpose of the interview. The interview itself is planned to occur at a definite time and place, and, unlike a conversation, which can be started and terminated at will, an interview once initiated must be continued until its purpose has been achieved or until it is clear that the purpose cannot be achieved. An interview requires exclusive attention to the interaction, and for the interviewer to become bored or to terminate the contract for personal reasons may be a dereliction of professional responsibility. Finally, because an interview has a purpose other than amusement, unpleasant facts and feelings are not avoided. It may actually be necessary to introduce unpleasant facts and feelings if doing so will be of help. For a fuller exposition of these points, the interested reader should consult Kadushin (1972). Weiner and Bordin in Chapter 7 of this book also touch on these considerations in distinguishing between a formal psychotherapy relationship and interpersonal relationships that may inadvertently be psychotherapeutic.

Interview Validity

Researchers and clinicians need to have some idea of the extent to which the interview constitutes a valid measuring instrument. More specifically, one might ask about the validity of a particular interview technique, interview topic, or interview situation or context. A question that must be considered is whether answers in an interview have any relationship to the interviewee's actual behavior, the underlying attitudes that govern behavior, or the factual events which the interviewee is reporting (Maccoby & Maccoby, 1954). For example, it has often been recorded that eyewitness reports are notoriously unreliable and that omissions and distortions in such reports become more pronounced with the passage of time. It is also well known that interviewees typically want to put themselves in a favorable light before the interviewer and may therefore distort or conceal attitudes and behavior. Likewise, research on psychological assessment indicates that answers to items on personality tests may be affected by a person's tendency to give what he or she believes to be the proper or socially desirable answer. Rosenthal (1966) has shown that even in very carefully controlled experimental research studies experimenters tend in subtle ways to influence their subjects' behavior toward support of the experimental hypotheses. The results of verbal conditioning studies clearly show the necessity of paying careful attention to the interviewer's behavior and the clinical setting as determinants of the obtained interview material. Matarazzo and Wiens (1972) have reviewed a series of studies in which it was demonstrated that slight changes in interviewer verbal behavior clearly modified interviewee speech output. Hence it cannot simply be assumed that an interviewee's behavior is determined solely by conscious thought.

Kahn and Cannell (1961) point out that the concept *true value* becomes very obscure when one wishes to assess and measure attitudes. An interviewee's response to solicitation of feelings about a supervisor might be influenced by public and private sentiments on this topic. It is also more than likely that there is not a single enduring or true opinion about a supervisor, but that the attitude depends on the immediate situation. For example, different attitudes would probably be expressed in such different situations as being recommended for a promotion, being reprimanded for a mistake, having just heard an eloquent sermon on brotherly love, and sitting together in a union meeting to promote demands for a wage increase. Each attitude would, however, have a validity of its own, and in a sense each would be true because each existed. The problem for the interviewer is to decide which of these attitudes to measure and which has target value. Once the objective has been defined, there is then a true value that constitutes the target.

Some researchers have attempted to assess accuracy of interview data by comparing results obtained through personal interviews with information obtained from independent objective sources (see Kahn & Cannell, 1961; Maccoby & Maccoby, 1954). For example, victims of auto accidents tend to exaggerate the amount of work time and pay they lost, and as many as 40% of respondents may inaccurately report charitable contributions, 17% inaccurately report age, and 2% inaccurately report possession of a telephone. Problems of validity of self-report seem to be especially prevalent in studies of human sexual behavior.

Finally, one must consider how aware interviewees are of their own behavior and motives. It has been suggested that in the spheres of behavior where repression and other defense mechanisms are at work it becomes most important to check interview findings against overt behavior. There is the celebrated interview of a mother concerning her child-rearing practices. During the interview she held her small son on her lap. The child began to play with his genitals. The mother, without looking directly at the child, moved his hand away and held it securely for a while as she continued to talk to the interviewer. Later in the interview the mother was asked what she ordinarily did when her child played with himself. She replied that he never did—he was a very "good" boy. She was evidently entirely unaware of what had occurred in the very presence of the interviewer. Similarly, people may be unconscious of the ways in which they express aggression or the ways in which they attempt to obtain approval from others.

Kanfer and Phillips (1970) have written an excellent discussion of the methodological problems involved in using a person's self-report as an indicator of actual experience. They too conclude that, when a person describes an experience or internal state in an interview, care must be taken to recognize this behavior as a response that is under the control of both the person's history and the interview situation and not to accept it as a true record of past or internal events. The interview must be considered a measurement device that is fallible and subject to substantial sources of error and bias. This does not mean, however, that the interview should be discarded as a means of collecting information. The interview, like other measurement techniques, has great value and unique advantages. What it does mean is that more must be learned about sources of interview bias and influence, and that methods of eliminating or accounting for them must be developed.

Recording Interview Data

A question that arises in the minds of most novice interviewers has to do with how to record or report interview findings. Many interviews are summarized from memory, the interviewer attempting to remember as much as possible of what the interviewee has said and to make notes on the content after the interview. Arguments advanced in favor of recording from memory are that taking notes in the interview might upset the interviewee, destroy confidence in the anonymity of the interview, or produce an unnatural atmosphere (Maccoby & Maccoby, 1954). However, recording from memory has the disadvantage of permitting more distortion due to the interviewer's biases than does immediate recording. Furthermore, points that were significant or dramatic to the interviewer are likely to be sharpened, and other points dropped out. Aside from memory distortion, a considerable amount of interview content is inevitably lost, and it is also essentially inevitable that the temporal sequences of the interview will be rearranged. In particular, points are likely to be brought into conjunction and made to seem related that were separated and unrelated in the actual interview.

Experienced interviewers who take notes during the interview report few instances in which the note taking impaired rapport. Not infrequently interviewees may comment on the note taking, sometimes to ask that a given point not be recorded, but more often to ask if they are going too fast for the interviewer to keep up. Some interviewees are flattered that someone finds their comments important enough to write down, and perhaps most give a bit more consideration to their responses. Probably the majority of interviewees regard it as perfectly natural that the interviewer take notes.

At times it is useful to tape-record interviews. Professional ethics requires that such recordings be made only with the knowledge and consent of both participants. Fortunately, experience shows that the presence of a microphone is seldom a deterrent to the interview. When there is some reaction to the recording, the interviewer is much more likely to remain aware of and nervous about the microphone than the interviewee. The interviewee is usually willing to accept the recording apparatus on the interviewer's explanation of its importance. If the subject matter of the interview is likely to be very personal, it is advisable to tell the interviewee that if he or she wants to speak "off the record" the microphone will be turned off. Experience indicates that interviewees seldom avail themselves of this opportunity, but that it helps them to feel somewhat freer. Rating from recordings also permits researchers to study emphasis, intonation, pitch, and pauses, cues that are valuable for some data analysis purposes.

Richardson, Dohrenwend, and Klein (1965) emphasize the importance of visual information as well in understanding interview data. They use as an example an analysis of interview transcripts in terms of the number of lines of type used respectively by the interviewer and interviewee. One interviewer–interviewee ratio revealed that the interviewer said almost nothing compared to other interviewers. On observing this interviewer, however, the authors noticed that she offered the interviewee an almost continuous nonverbal commentary by nodding her head, gesturing with hands and arms, and changing her facial expression and posture. This commentary indicated her knowledge of the subject matter and her interest, support, and understanding.

In 1946 a course for Veterans Administration personal counselors was planned by the staff of the University of Chicago Counseling Center. The course lasted for six weeks, and Blocksma and Porter (1947) measured some differences in counselor interview behavior before and after intruction. This was the first objective research on attitudes and behaviors of counselors before and after training. The specifics of the training course are not reviewed here, but it is of interest to note that the trainees took a paper-and-pencil test that required them to select a response to given client statements. In every case the student selected from among five different response classes assumed to communicate different intentions of the counselor: moralization or evaluation; diagnosis or formulation; interpretation or explanation; support or encouragement; and reflection or understanding.

Blocksma and Porter's data indicated very little relationship between what the students *said* they would do on the paper-and-pencil test and what they actually *did* in interviews with clients. For example, during the pretraining evaluation they selected 89% reflection responses in the written test, but only 11% reflection responses in the interview. Marked changes took place in the students' interview behavior over the 6 weeks of training. In their pretraining interviews the students' comments were 84% directive and 11% nondirective, whereas in the posttraining interview their responses were 30% directive and 59% nondirective. These investigators also found that on the pretest 60% of the responses suggested that the student was thinking *about* the client and evaluating him or her, whereas on the posttest 61% of the responses indicated that the student was thinking *with* the client and allowing self-evaluation. Of particular interest here is the finding that the students could not reliably predict their actual interview behavior. There seems to be no substitute for actual observation and recording if interview data are to be faithfully retained.

RESEARCH ON THE ANATOMY OF THE INTERVIEW

Researchers of the interview have examined many different aspects of dyadic interaction. Traditionally, investigators have focused on *what* the interview participants say, that is, on the content aspects of speech. Research on content analysis has included the study of variables such as frequency of usage of grammatical units (verbs, pronouns, adjectives, and other grammatical units) and themes (references to parents or other significant humans), distress–relief words, past- or future-tense usage, affectionate or hostile words, so-called manifest or latent meanings, degree of inferred empathy toward the conversational partner, and anxiety-laden versus neutral themes and topics.

Other investigators have studied human speech and interview interaction with a focus on *how* something is said. Physicists, electronic engineers, experts on acoustics, students of high-fidelity sound recording, and others have recorded speech and played it into oscilloscopes and other electronic equipment in order to analyze its formal components such as its frequencies, intensities, timbre, and related acoustical qualities. Pope (1979) has used the term *style* to refer to various paralinguistic and nonverbal aspects of communication, describing style as imparting coloration to what is said. Matarazzo and Wiens (1972) and Harper, Wiens, and Matarazzo (1978) have reviewed various aspects of the research just referred to and have presented references for more detailed review for the interested reader.

Temporal Characteristics of Interview Speech

Another area of noncontent interview research (research on the formal properties of speech) is the study of the different rates (timing) of verbal interaction. It is easily recognized that some interviewees talk and act rapidly, whereas others are slow and deliberate. One can also observe that in many cases people whom one does not like or cannot get along with say exactly the same things as the people whom one likes. Actors may take a short play, play it first as a tragedy and then, using the same words, play it as a comedy. Here the language is seen as unimportant, and the timing is the factor that makes the difference in its effect on the audience (Chapple & Arensberg, 1940, p. 33).

My colleagues and I have for many years conducted research concerned with the reliability and validity of inferences based on structural–temporal dimensions of the interview, that is, frequency and duration of single units of speech and silence. Three major speech variables have been studied in many different situations: duration of utterance (DOU), reaction time latency (RTL), and percentage of interruptions. The mean speech duration (DOU) is defined as the total time the interviewee (or interviewer) speaks divided by that person's total number of speech units. RTL is defined similarly. The percentage of interruptions is defined as the total number of times the interviewee (or interviewer) speaks divided into the number of these same speech units that were interruptions of the interview partner. The interested reader should consult Matarazzo and Wiens (1972) for a detailed definition of a speech unit, which is the basic datum in this interview research.

Minimal but significant interviewer standardization was introduced so that it would be possible to compare interview findings from one interview to the next. Specifically, the interviewer is asked to use open-ended questions and a nondirective interviewing style, that is, to follow the discussion topics as the interviewee introduces them. In clinical research interviews, however, the general topic areas are constant across interviews (e.g., topic areas such as family, occupation, education). In addition to using the prescribed speaking style, the interviewer is asked to speak in utterances of 5 seconds' duration, to respond to the interviewee with less than 1-second response latencies, and to refrain from interrupting the interviewee.

A series of reliability studies of the interviewing procedures is summarized by Saslow and Matarazzo (1959). In the first of these studies two different interviewers examined the same new patient in an outpatient psychiatry clinic using the standardized interview format described above. These two male interviewers had no knowledge of the content of each other's interviews, and each talked about what he would typically discuss in such an initial assessment interview. The two interviews (of approximately 35 minutes' duration) were conducted 5 minutes apart. The product–moment coefficient of correlation between the interviewees' DOUs in the two different interviews was .91. The correlations for the other speech variables were equally high. This study was replicated using intervals between interviews of 1 week, 5 weeks, and 8 weeks. These studies suggested that the verbal interaction measures employed reflected stable and invariant behavior characteristics under the real-life, minimally standardized interview conditions in which these patients were studied. It was also apparent that there were wide individual differences in speech, silence, and interruption behavior.

Modifiability of Temporal Speech Characteristics

Subsequent studies revealed that despite this high test–retest reliability planned changes in the interviewer's own speech behavior during any single interview could produce striking corresponding changes in the speech behavior of the interviewee. These planned changes in the interviewer's own speech behavior have included increases and decreases in the average DOU, increases and decreases in RTL, and increases and decreases in speech interruptions.

In one series of studies it was found that, by doubling or halving the duration of each of the interviewer's speech units (from a mean of 5.3 to 9.9 to 6.1 seconds, respectively, in each of the three 15-minute periods of a 45-minute interview), the interviewer was able to influence the mean DOU of interviewees in the three comparable periods of the interview (24.3, 46.9, and 26.6 seconds, respectively). The positive results of this study were cross-validated in two additional studies in which the interviewer unobtrusively controlled his single speech unit durations to approximately 10-5-10 seconds and 5-15-5 seconds in the three parts of his planned interview.

That such interviewer-control effects are not limited to face-to-face employment interviews was revealed in another study (Matarazzo, Wiens, Saslow, Dunham, & Voas, 1964) in which it was demonstrated that the DOUs of an orbiting astronaut were correlated with changes in the DOUs of ground communicators. In an ingenious extension of this last study, Ray and Webb (1966) showed that how much or how little President Kennedy talked in response to a reporter's questions in his press conferences was related to the length of the questions posed by the reporter. Such effects are clearly out of the realm of conscious awareness.

Planned changes in the interviewer's own RTL (reaction time before responding to the interviewee), utilizing preplanned interviewer RTLs of 1-1-1, 1-5-1, 5-1-5, 1-10-1, and 1-15-1 seconds in separate studies, also produced the predicted increases and decreases in the corresponding RTLs of the interviewee. The frequency of an interviewer's interruption of the interviewee likewise revealed that the interviewee's interruption rate covaried with that of the interviewer with surprising regularity.

One possible implication of these findings for clinical interviews is that interviewers could conceivably induce depressed patients to talk in longer utterances or manic patients to talk in shorter utterances by modifying their own DOUs. Another possible implication of these findings for an ongoing interview series would be the deliberate pairing of interviewers and interviewees whose speech characteristics presumably could combine to create an effective interviewer–interviewee combination.

Other speech modifiability studies have employed head nodding and saying "mm-hmm" during the experimental periods of a standardized interview and have demonstrated that these are powerful tactics that can increase interviewee DOUs. In other work, an experimentally induced set in which interviewees were led to believe that they would talk to either "cold" or "warm" interviewers was found to influence markedly the interviewee's RTLs.

Individual Differences among Groups

An early question in this research program was whether the highly reliable average DOUs for each interviewee could be useful for differential diagnosis. This question was examined in a study of the interview speech behavior of five different groups of interviewees: 19 state hospital, back-ward, chronic psychotic patients (schizophrenics); 40 neurotic and acutely psychotic patients from the inpatient and outpatient psychiatric services of a general hospital; 60 outpatient clinic neurotics; 40 normals (applicants for sales positions at a Boston department store); and 17 normals (applicants for sales positions at a Chicago department store). The results revealed clear differences among these five groups. Whereas the two normal groups did not differ from each other, each of them differed significantly from each of the three patient groups. Specifically, although the range of individual differences in each diagnostic group was very large, the median value for DOUs increased steadily from the presumably most disturbed group (the back-ward schizophrenic patients), in which it was the shortest, to the neurotic and acutely psychotic group, the outpatient neurotics, and finally to the presumably best adjusted (the two normal) groups, in which it was the longest. As noted, the variability within each group was too large to allow accurate individual diagnosis by DOU alone. Nevertheless, the results are encouraging to those investigators who wish to develop objective indices to aid in differential diagnosis.

Nathan, Schneller, and Lindsley (1964) have reported comparable data from assessment interviews they conducted with mental hospital patients. Their patients talked less when discussing personally related, stressful content than when discussing presumably neutral content, and less severely ill patients had a higher rate of talking than more severely ill patients. Kanfer (1960) reported that female mental patients talked at a 25% slower rate when talking with an interviewer about relationships with men than when talking about their present illness. Craig (1966) reported differences in the DOUs and RTLs of mental patients related to whether an interviewer gave them personality interpretations that were congruent with their own perceptions or interpretations that were incongruent. Kanfer (1960) and Pope, Blass, Siegman, and Raher (1970), studying psychosomatic patients and recording periodic free-speech monologues, found differences in speech and silence behavior associated with whether the patient was clinically rated as being in a state of anxiety or rated as being in a state of depression. In another study, based on interview data from normal subjects, Pope, Siegman, and Blass (1970) demonstrated similar differences in speech behavior under anxiety-stimulated and under neutral conditions.

Two studies in this area have examined individual differences among groups of nurses. In the first study, Wiens, Matarazzo, Saslow, Thompson, and Matarazzo (1965) interviewed groups of staff nurses, head nurses, and supervising nurses. Standardized interview procedures were used, and the interviewers were asked to start each interview with a request that the interviewee describe her nursing activities on a typical working day. Beyond this, the interviewers were asked to keep their comments nonchallenging, open-ended, and limited to the interviewee's past comments or to some new, general topic that followed naturally from her past comments. In general, the supervising and head nurses did not differ significantly from each other, but the staff nurses differed significantly from both of these groups in their speech and interruption characteristics. Specifically, the staff nurses interrupted the interviewer fewer times, spoke in shorter speech units (and consequently talked more often than members of the other two groups), and utilized less of the total interview time for their own speech. This research did not answer the question of whether the differentiating interaction characteristics were inherent in the individual nurses and had led to the appointment of some but not others to administrative positions, or whether the appointment to an administrative position stimulated the development of the verbal interaction patterns that characterized the supervising and head nurses.

In a second study with nurses, Molde and Wiens (1968) investigated the temporal verbal behavior of two groups of nurses, psychiatric and surgical, engaged in widely different work settings. As was predicted, the psychiatric nurses had a greater verbal output in the standardized interview than did the surgical nurses. The latter group was found to interrupt the interviewer more frequently and to exhibit a shorter RTL in responding to the interviewer's comments than did their psychiatric counterparts. It seemed likely that some of these observed differences could be accounted for on the basis of occupational demands on the nurses' verbal behavior, although it is not clear what interrelationships exist between innate or idiosyncratic factors and environmental influences on speech behavior, or how they interact.

Some Relationships between Noncontent Speech Variables and Interview Content

An early attempt to study the relationship of the content of an interview to the concurrent noncontent speech behavior of the interviewee was reported by Kanfer,

Phillips, Matarazzo, and Saslow (1960). In this study the interviewers were asked to vary their style of speaking from neutral to interpretive while discussing relatively standardized content with two groups of student nurse interviewees. In one part of the interview the interviewers used neutral statements, and in another part, continuing with similar content, they made interpretations about the student nurse interviewees' motivations and life styles. The results indicated a significant drop in the interviewees' mean DOUs under the interpretation conditions as compared to the neutral condition.

In related work, Manaugh, Wiens, and Matarazzo (1970) attempted experimentally to induce a momentary motivational state in two of four college groups studied. The experimental but not the control groups were instructed by a research assistant, through a brief set of written instructions, to attempt to deceive an interviewer about their education by stating initially that they had completed 1 year more of college than in fact they had, and subsequently to answer all other questions in this content area so as to be consistent with this initial deception. The data analysis revealed a significant effect on the speech behavior of these college student interviewees in the education content area for *both* the control and experimental groups; that is, all groups talked with a longer mean DOU and a shorter RTL when discussing education content. Thus, even if the education-deception set influenced behavior in the two deception groups, the empirically recorded effect of education content itself, as found in the two control groups, was so powerful as to have masked what otherwise might have been a successful experimentally introduced motivational set in the two deception groups.

In a follow-up study, Matarazzo, Wiens, Jackson, and Manaugh (1970a) selected two topic areas (college major and living setting) that were assumed to be equally salient among a sample of undergraduate college students. However, again transcending the effort to induce motivational states, it was found in both control and experimental groups that college major was a content topic of apparent higher intrinsic saliency for the 80 subjects than was living setting. The differential saliency was clearly revealed in differences in their temporal speech behavior, specifically, longer DOU and shorter RTL when discussing college major. Concurrent with this study, large numbers of job applicants were being interviewed for the civil service position of police patrolman. These interviews, of 45 minutes' duration, were unobtrusively divided into three 15-minute segments during each of which a different content area (education, occupation, family) was discussed. The results confirmed further that the temporal dimensions of speech can be differentially affected by the content topics under discussion (Matarazzo, Wiens, Jackson, & Manaugh, 1970b). Specifically, these job applicants spoke with a shorter RTL and a longer mean DOU while discussing their occupational histories than at other times. These results were cross-validated and were interpreted to mean that occupation was a more salient topic for these interviewees, in this particular situation, than education and family. The outcome of these studies suggested that an aspect of these subjects' motivational or personality-emotional state was being revealed in their noncontent interview speech behavior.

It has been suggested that as the complexity of a verbal task increases, whether the greater complexity is based on cognitive or on emotional factors, speech may become more internalized, and external speech (DOU) consequently decreases and internal thought processes increase (reflected in longer RTL). In this regard, Goldman-Eisler (1968) studied silence and hesitation phenomena in speech and concluded that silence is used for higher cognitive activity. In an interesting cross-cultural study with Dutch subjects, Ramsay (1968) showed that there are significant differences between extroverts and introverts in the length of silences between their utterances. His view of introverts is that such people are thoughful, think before speaking, and weigh their words more carefully than extroverts; in this way, he concludes, introverts' speech patterns are consistent with other aspects of their behavior. Siegman and Pope (1965) similarly found a significant negative correlation between extroversion and duration of silence in an interview situation.

Aronson and Weintraub (1972) and Weintraub (1981) report verbal styles associated with different pathological behavioral patterns such as impulsive outbursts, delusional symptom formation, and depression. Whereas they score speech behavior along many dimensions, of particular interest here is that depressed patients can be differentiated by their low rate and quantity of speech (the exception being the agitated depressive patient). By contrast the impulsive patient is likely to have a high speech rate.

Siegman and Pope (1972) studied the effects of anxiety on speech. They acknowledge that anxiety is generally assumed to have a disruptive effect on speech, inasmuch as speech is a finely coordinated behavior and anxiety is expected to disrupt such behavior. They also argue that if anxiety is regarded as a drive state it might be expected that an increase in anxiety level increases verbal output at the same time as it produces an increase in speech disturbances (e.g., corrections, repetitions). Anxiety, in other words, may have both a facilitating and a disruptive effect on speech. The Siegman and Pope research data supported their reasoning, and they concluded that in normal subjects both low- and high-anxiety arousal are associated with speech productivity, speech disruptions, and an accelerated speech tempo.

There is of course great interest in assessing whether the speech variables discussed above relate to such interpersonal interview characteristics as empathy, transference, warmth, unconditional positive regard, experiencing, and other variables. Matarazzo and Wiens (1972) conclude that there is preliminary evidence that this may be the case. For example, it has been demonstrated that a modest increase in an interviewer's DOU produces a significant increase in the interviewee's speech output, or DOU. One possible dynamic underlying this phenomenon may be a greater satisfaction that the interviewee feels with the longer DOUs of the interviewer. Truax (1970) has reported finding a similar relationship between duration of therapist talk and the therapist's independently rated level of accurate empathy. Therapists who talked more per session were rated as showing higher levels of accurate empathy, and their patients showed greater degrees of overall improvement than patients of therapists who talked less. The studies cited above, illustrating a somewhat larger body of literature, serve as evidence relating *noncontent* speech behaviors to a variety of interview variables traditionally assessed from the *content* of the same interview.

STUDIES IN NONVERBAL COMMUNICATION

The challenge of assessing reliably the presence of identifiable human attitudes, motivational states, and other personality characteristics has attracted investigators in many branches of social and psychological sciences since the turn of the century. Personality tests (objective and projective), a variety of self-report questionnaires, attitude surveys, and the like have all been used with a modest degree of utility and common acceptance (see Chapters 2 and 4). There has been general recognition that the efficacy of all of these procedures is highly dependent on the cooperation, personal awareness, and active participation of the individuals to be assessed. Faced with these limitations, behavioral and social scientists have looked for clues to individual personality and motivational states in overt behaviors that are not typically under the conscious control of the individual. Of particular interest in this respect has been the question of how valid are inferences of an individual's attitudinal or motivational state from more or less subtle nonverbal behaviors emitted during social interactions and, especially, psychological interviews. Specifically, psychologists and others have attempted to identify channels of information other than the consciously controlled channel of verbal content. In recent years research in nonverbal communication has generated convincing evidence that facial expressions, body posture and movements, and styles of speaking can serve as valuable sources of information (Harper, Wiens, & Matarazzo, 1978; Druckman, Rozelle, & Baxter, 1982). The development of sophisticated audio and video recording equipment has been necessary to record interviewees adequately for later and more detailed analyses.

Psycholinguistics and Paralanguage

Perhaps many persons would say that it is of obvious importance to study language in order to understand human behavior. It appears that psychologists have come to this realization somewhat belatedly, although the growing prominence of the field of psycholinguistics suggests that there may now be a major interest in language. One psychologist who has greatly increased our awareness of the importance of language is George A. Miller (1973), who writes:

> There presently exists a behavioral procedure that can exert powerful control over people's thoughts and actions. This technique of control can cause you to do things you would never think of doing otherwise. It can change opinions and beliefs. It can be used to deceive you. It can make you happy or sad. It can put ideas into your head. It can make you want things you don't have. You can even use it to control yourself. It is

an enormously powerful tool with a universal range of application. . . . Far from thinking of it as an evil or threatening thing, most people regard this particular kind of control as one of the greatest triumphs of the human mind, indeed, as the very thing that raises man above all other animals. [pp. 4–5]

Miller was, of course, talking about human language, which is a basic essential for much human communication.

Language among humans is characterized by many individual differences. A major source of difference is that people speak different languages and come from diverse cultural backgrounds. Within countries there are many regional and ethnic language differences that must be understood for effective communication. The study of intercultural communication is obviously imperative, for example, for the businessperson or the politican who wants to conduct business overseas.The study of ethnic language characteristics may be equally imperative for the psychologist who wants to communicate with members of ethnic miniority groups. One statistical aspect of language that has been widely explored is the size of the vocabulary. Most of us are sensitive about the number of words we recognize and use, and psychologists who measure intelligence typically find that estimates of vocabulary size are among the most dependable indicators they possess. Many assessment interviewers actually utilize a selection of test vocabulary words for a quick, general estimate of intelligence. For example, the vocabulary list from the Stanford-Binet Test of Intelligence or the Wechsler Adult Intelligence Scale is easily used for this purpose because the number of words correctly defined can be readily translated into an equivalent IQ score (see Chapter 3).

However, it is not easy to obtain a reliable estimate of the number of words a person knows. As Miller (1969) has pointed out, people have multiple vocabularies, one for talking, one for reading, one for writing, and so on. The differences in the size of the several vocabularies within one person are sometimes larger than the differences in the size of same vocabulary among different people. It is a general rule of verbal learning that recognition is easier than recall; a word may be recognized by a person even though he or she cannot use it effectively. A large recognition vocabulary despite relatively small talking and writing (recall) vocabularies allows people to understand a wide range of speakers even though they could not have used their words. Intelligence, age, and education are major factors correlated with differences in the size of vocabulary.

The person with a large vocabulary is likely to have a more diversified speaking style than one who is restricted to a small vocabulary. A person with a limited vocabulary reuses a word sooner, on the average, than a person who has a large vocabulary. It is possible simply to count the number of words that intervene between the successive use of a common word such as *the*. On the average, more words intervene between successive uses of the word *the* if the speaker has a diverse vocabulary. A closely related index is called the type–token *ratio* (TTR), which provides a more direct measure of diversification. The TTR is the ratio of the number of different words (types) to the total number of words (tokens) in the passage.

Typically, a total sample can be divided into subsamples of equal word length, and the TTR for each segment can then be determined and these several values averaged together for a mean segmental TTR.

Other statistical measures of verbal style include sentence length, styles in punctuation, and verbal–adjective ratios. Regarding the latter, the verb–adjective ratio is usually higher for spoken than for written language. The more time one has to produce the symbols, the more qualification one puts on them. The comparison of different kinds of writing shows the largest variations. As noted by Miller (1969), for example, the dialogue in plays shows a ratio of 9 verbs per adjective, whereas scientific writings show only 1.3 verbs per adjective. Legal statutes, which deal with the acts of human beings, have 5 verbs per adjective, and fiction about 3 verbs per adjective. Theses written for the master's degree have 1.5 verbs for each adjective, but by the time candidates reach the Ph.D. level, the ratio is reduced to 1.1. verbs per adjective. In one Ph.D. thesis a cautious writer was found to use two qualifications for every construction, a verb–adjective ratio of 0.5. It is important here to note that this indicator of statistical style changes with the type of writing, and this ratio cannot be used to indicate changes in emotional stability, for example, unless the verbal tasks are carefully equated.

Kasl and Mahl (1965) have urged attention to what might seem to be irrelevant or nonlexical aspects of speech, particularly speech disturbances. Under the heading of flustered or confused speech they include a number of distinct speech disturbance categories. These include the familiar *ah* or some of its variants such as *eh, uh,* or *uhm.* Also included are sentence changes that consist of a correction or change in the content of expression and that must be sensed by the listener as interruptions in the flow of the sentence. Repetitions, stutters, word omissions, sentence incompletions, slips of the tongue, and intruding incoherent sounds rounded out a total of eight speech dysfluency categories that Kasl and Mahl scored in their research. In terms of absolute frequency, they found that a disturbance occurred, on the average, for every 16 "words" spoken, which is equivalent to 1 disturbance for every 4.6 seconds an individual spends talking.

Kasl and Mahl also reported that under conditions of manipulated anxiety the frequency of all speech disturbances except for *ah* showed a sizable increase. An additional interesting finding was that the non-*ah* ratio of speech disturbance was not affected by whether the experimenter was present in the room or was in a monitor room, whereas the *ah* ratio of speech disturbance was distinctly affected. This led them to speculate that various facial expressions, movements of the head, and so on are cues that may give feedback to a speaker. When the experimenter was in the monitor room, then, providing no listener feedback to the speaker, perhaps more uncertainty was introduced about the effects of his or her speaking on the listener, and the use of *ah* enabled the subject to pause briefly to determine what to say next. This hypothesis is consistent with the work of Goldman-Eisler, who has suggested that silent pauses in speech become lengthened with greater cognitive activity.

Voice is generally thought of as a purely individual matter, yet one can ask whether the voice has a social quality as well as an individual one. Intuitively, people probably attach a great deal of importance to voices and to the speech behavior they carry. For example, if a speaker's voice can be characterized as raucous, it is difficult not to infer automatically some negative personal attributes of that person. Two research approaches to attempting to differentiate verbal content from voice quality have been to ask speakers to convey emotion while speaking meaningless content (e.g., reciting the alphabet or saying only numbers), and to use electronic filtering techniques to mask meaningful speech frequencies while preserving affective tone. Employing the first approach, Davitz and Davitz (1974) showed that reading the alphabet can carry affective meaning when subjects are instructed to instill such meaning into their reading. In their study all feelings were identified more consistently than chance alone would predict. Additionally, some errors in identification were consistent; that is, fear was most commonly misidentified as nervousness, love as sadness, and pride as satisfaction.

Fascinating clinical extensions of these observations are found in two studies, one by Milmoe, Rosenthal, Blane, Chafetz, and Wolf (1974) on the doctor's voice, and the other by Milmoe, Novey, Kagan, and Rosenthal (1974) on the mother's voice. In the first study, doctors whose voices were rated as less angry and more anxious were more successful in referring alcoholic patients for further treatment than were doctors with angry, nonanxious voices. Alcoholic patients were used as subjects on the assumption that, being sensitized to rejection, they would be especially aware of the subtle, unintended cues conveyed by the doctor, whether cues of sympathy and acceptance or cues of anger and disgust. The positive relationship between inferred anxiety in the voice and effectiveness with alcoholic patients may relate to the notion that an effectively functioning healer whose manner of speech is perceived by others to have an anxious, nervous quality may be seen by the patients as showing marked concern. The second study indicated that mothers whose voices were rated high on dimensions of anxiety and anger had children who showed various signs of irritability such as crying and becoming upset at separation. Other examples of voice quality communication are the familiar modifications in voice level, tone of voice, speed of communication, and the like that are appropriate for funerals, weddings, receptions, formal interviews, and so on.

The interview situation is almost invariably one in which the participants listen to each other talk and can also hear their own voices. Mahl (1972) reported research in which he studied interviewees who were talking but unable to hear the sound of their own voices. Reviewing a variety of studies on delayed auditory feedback, partial deafness, temporary hearing loss, and the like, he called attention to the deterioration of speech quality in the deafened person and the corresponding importance of continual auditory feedback in the preservation of developed speech patterns. Mahl's study involved interviewing college students in four conditions: (a) sitting in the usual face-to-face arrangement; (b) facing the interviewer but being unable to hear themselves because sound was masked through earphones they were wearing; (c) being unable to see the interviewer who sat behind them; and (d) being able neither to see the interviewer nor to hear themselves talk. Students were interviewed three times, so that novelty of the situation was not a factor. In the noise condition, the masking noise was administered at all times except when the interviewer spoke.

A variety of linguistic changes was observed in this study. The masking noise produced louder speech, flattening of intonation, a shift toward lower-social-status dialect, prolongation of sounds, changes in pitch, various vocal noises, slurring, change in rate, and fragmentation of phrasing. Significant behavioral–psychological changes were also observed, including greater affective expression without auditory feedback (this also involved more direct emotional response to the interviewer); freer associative responses, indicated by increased verbal productivity and increased spontaneity in the communication of highly personal information; increased cognitive confusion; and "thinking aloud." The latter phenomenon was infrequent but very striking when it occurred, because it involved unintended and unconscious utterance of content. In one instance a subject disclaimed even the thoughts involved.

Mahl concluded that the disinhibition shown was related to the feedback deficit and that normal auditory feedback plays an important role in the regulation of many *vocal* dimensions of language behavior, in the control of the vocal expression of affects and thought, and in the maintenance of a sense of self and reality. Possible implications of this study for the interviewing situation include the observation that people are less aware of cues emanating from their speech partners when they are talking than when they are silent, and also that when people are talking they are less aware of stimulation arising from within themselves than when they are silent.

There are many other situations in which the study of paralinguistic characteristics is important, and an excellent overview of these situations is provided by Duncan (1969) in a discussion of various nonlanguage or nonverbal communicative functions. Weitz (1972) has suggested that in interracial situations the paralinguistic channel may carry more accurate information than the more socially controlled verbal channel. Her informal discussions with blacks have confirmed the observation that tone is often closely attended to as reliably indicating whether the interviewer's attitude is hostile, patronizing, or genuinely friendly. Weitz also concludes that there is individual variation in sensitivity to such paralinguistic and nonverbal channels, with the more dependent member of the dyad having the most to gain by being attuned to the other's emotional state and to the affective tone of the interaction.

The importance of noncontent (tonal or vocal) characteristics of speech is also suggested in the findings of a study by Mehrabian and Wiener (1967). In that study, single-word contents with three degrees of attitude (positive, neutral, and negative) each were combined with three degrees of attitude (positive, neutral, and negative) communicated in tones of voice. Stimulus words used were *honey, thanks,* and *dear* (positive content); *maybe, really,* and *okay* (neutral content); and *don't, brute,* and *terrible* (negative content). Different subjects were instructed so they would attend to (a) both the content and tone of the stimulus words, (b) the content only, or (c) the tone only. The findings indicated that the independent effects of tone generally were stronger than the independent effects of content. Interestingly, the responses of subjects who were instructed to attend to all the information (tone plus content) showed no differences related to content. The variability of response to tone and content combined was determined primarily by variations in tone. These results demonstrate the relative importance of noncontent variables, in this case tone, when assessing the emotional meaning of verbal behavior. A familiar example to the reader will be the use of the phrase *that's just great,* which can only be interpreted if one knows the vocal characteristics of its utterance.

Mehrabian (1972) also introduced and explicated the concept of *immediacy* as broadly describing the extent to which communication reflects closeness of interaction. Generally speaking, a face-to-face discussion is more immediate than one via videotape, which in turn is more immediate than a telephone conversation, which is more immediate than a letter, and so on. Verbal examples of variations in immediacy are personal pronouns *I* and *we,* which are verbally closer than *he, she,* or *it,* and phrases such as *my country, our country,* or *their country,* or *I feel, I think,* or *it is my opinion.* As Mehrabian has defined immediacy, it refers to the degree of intensity and directness of interaction between a speaker and the object about which he speaks. Generally, there is more immediacy in statements about persons one likes than in statements about those one dislikes. More immediate statements are also generally judged to be more positive in tone or to reflect a more positive speaker feeling.

An interesting related topic is the form of address people use when speaking to each other. This varies with the language being spoken; consider, for example, the use of such second-person pronouns as *du* and *sie* in German or, in English, the choice between second- and third-person use in directives such as *one should not* or *you should not.* Also, of course, the form of address varies in terms of the use of honorifics, title and last name, or first name. Slobin, Miller, and Porter (1972) have pointed out that it is apparently a sociolinguistic universal that the address term exchanged between intimates (familiar pronoun, first name, etc.) is the same term used in addressing social inferiors, and that the term exchanged between nonintimates (polite pronoun, title, and last name, etc.) is also used to address social superiors (p. 263). Slobin et al. showed that status is unequal in a business setting where nonreciprocal address patterns occur. Age is also a factor in this regard, but apparently it is not as important as achievement. In most dyads in which the superior person is the younger, naming is symmetric; that is, there is mutual use of either title and last name or first names. An interesting additional finding was that, although the person of higher status is the pace-setter in linguistic address, the person of lower status might take the lead in self-disclosure in an effort to increase intimacy.

Selzer (1973) reminds interviewers that all interview behavior should be for the benefit of the patient, and that any interviewer behavior that does not meet this criterion has no place in a clinical situation. He then goes on to suggest possible emotional meanings for the interviewer of addressing a patient by first name, beginning with the need to feel superior. This need may arise particularly in the insecure therapist who fears the patient may be more intelligent, more successful, or better endowed in some way. The use of first names may also minimize the patient's difficulties. That is, a need to assume that the patient is suffering a temporary child-like disturbance may be implemented by addressing the patient as if he or she were a child. The use of first names may also avoid therapeutic commitment by conveying to the patient that he or she and the interviewer are merely chatting.

The use of first names may also imply an offer of friendship that can carry with it the implied demand that the patient reciprocate. However, friendship relationships may pose a problem for the patient, both in general and with specific reference to the feeling that one must not do or say anything to jeopardize friendship with the interviewer. The interviewee might then hesitate to discuss topics that might offend or alienate the interviewer. Finally, the status differential implied by the use of first names may push the patient into a greater state of dependence or regression at the expense of working toward greater maturity and reliance on his or her own judgment. Selzer acknowledges that these are speculative concerns and that the use of first names may be warranted in some instances. He also makes the good point that interviewers should have a good reason for addressing their patients in the manner they choose.

Facial Expression and Visual Interaction

It has been suggested (Weitz, 1972) that nonverbal behavior can be seen in some sense as predating verbal behavior and perhaps as being a more primitive system. For example, under stress people often resort to nonverbal signs, such as screaming or crying with accompanying facial expressions, rather than undertaking a complex verbal analysis of the situation. Comparative psychologists and ethologists have been interested in facial communication among animals, and social scientists within the fields of anthropology, sociology, and psychology have been interested in possible cross-cultural universals in facial expression. For example, the "eybrow flash" of recognition on greeting seems to be characteristic of all studied cultures and primate groups. The work of Ekman and Friesen (see, e.g., their 1969 publication) is frequently referred to in reviews of facially displayed affect. In their human cross-cultural research, Ekman and Friesen demonstrated that there is consistent recognition of facial expressions of such primary affects as happiness, surprise, fear, sadness, anger, disgust, and interest. They have also developed a Facial Affect Scoring Technique (FAST) to study more systematically the identification of affect and the various aspects of the face that contribute to an observer's judgment of expressed affect.

There are various facial phenomena to which interviewer and interviewee pay attention. This chapter has already called attention to some effects of interviewer head nods. Another very common behavior is the smile, which to many interviewees can communicate such acceptance messages as "I like you," or "This is enjoyable." Or a smile can indicate the opposite, as noted by Birdwhistell (1970):

> My mother took great pride in her role of gracious hostess. She would say firmly, "No matter how much I disagree with a guest I never allow an unchristian word to cross my

lips. I just smile." Well, my mother's thin-lipped smile, which could be confined to her mouth, when accompanied by an audible input of air through her tightened nostrils required no words—Christian or otherwise—to reveal her attitude. [p. 52]

Very likely, most interviewers would think first of visual interaction, or looking into an interviewee's eyes, if asked to say what they attend to in facial expression. It is interesting to note, for example, the emotional reaction produced when one person in a dyad is wearing dark glasses. Almost automatically, the person wearing the dark glasses becomes the observer and the other person becomes the observed, even though the person without the dark glasses might ostensibly be the interviewer. The reader can note for himself or herself the personal discomfort when an interviewee does not offer to remove dark glasses; it is as if he or she is on the other side of a one-way screen.

Argyle and Kendon (1967) and Exline (1974) have presented excellent overviews of gaze behavior, as well as reports on their own research on this topic. The act of looking (what a person is looking at) can be easily identified by most people and is often the start of some focused interaction. Eye contact has an important role in signaling verbal interaction. The listener signals attention by looking at the talker's mouth or eyes. When the time comes for the talker to be a listener, there will usually be an eye signal. The talker will look toward the listener, and the latter will signal readiness to talk by glancing away. Once a discussion is underway, each person looks at the other's eye region in glances of varying lengths, usually between 1 and 7 seconds. The person listening gives longer glances than the one talking and tends to look considerably more.

Typically, the person in a small group who receives the most looking time by an experimenter, for example, is judged as the person toward whom the experimenter feels the most positive. In group discussions, power coalitions are likely to be signaled by the pattern of looking behavior among the members of the discussion group. The mutual look is a well-recognized signal of involvement with each other and, other things being equal, the longer the periods of eye contact, the greater the level of mutual involvement. Conversely, people who avert their gazes may be signaling a "walling off" of themselves, a fear of rejection, or generally a wish not to be seen. Autistic children typically avert their gazes. Exline (1974) calls attention to a study in which members of a dyad were looking at each other when they received the signal to speak. Dominant subjects were the first to break the gaze, perhaps because they realized that to continue looking was a cue for the other to speak and it was assumed that the dominant subjects would not give the floor to their partners. It may also be suggested that with increased cognitive difficulty with the topic under discussion there is a decrease in the amount of time speakers look at their listeners.

As Miller (1973) points out, even the pupils of the eyes communicate. When a person becomes excited or interested in something, the pupils will increase in size. In one study subjects were asked to state which one of two pictures of a pretty girl preferred; the only difference in the pictures was the dilation of the eyes. The preference judgments clearly favored the picture in which the girl's eyes were dilated, although the judges did not consciously realize what the difference in the pictures was or what stimulus cue determined their preference.

Gestures, Body Movement, and Spatial Relations

Writings on gestures and body movements in oratory, mime, and dance date back to early Greece and Rome. One modern-day example of communication in body and hand movement is Hawaiian dancing: "Watch the hands." Many researchers working in this area of nonverbal communication have tried to introduce some kind of grammar to record, note, and study these phenomena experimentally. Prominent among these researchers are Birdwhistell (1970), Ekman and Friesen (1969), Scheflen (1972), and Mehrabian (1972). An excellent overview of gestures and body movements in interviews has been presented by Mahl (1968).

The use of the hands may be a relatively independent channel of communication, as it is in the signs and finger spelling used by the deaf. Typically, however, such movements occur outside the awarenes of conscious intention of the interview participants. A wide range of individual differences in body movement can be observed among interviewees (and interviewer). For example, Mahl (1969) describes such interviewee behaviors as patting and stroking hair, fingering mouth, playing with ring, keeping a coat on or off, crossing legs, rotating foot and ankle, tapping fingers, shaking head, shrugging shoulders, putting palms up and out, folding arms, and many more. The language of body movements has a large vocabulary. Some gestures, of course, are ritualized and, in a sense, serve as a direct substitute for the verbal meaning associated with them: the bow, shrug, smile, wink, military salute, pointed finger, thumbed nose, stuck-out tongue, and so on. Other gestures are more culturally specific, such as the handshake or the slap on the back, which are gestures of intimacy and friendship to an American but might be highly offensive to an individual of another culture who does not wish to be touched. There are probably more than 200 such mannerisms and gestures that can be studied.

Some clinicians have suggested that postural rigidity or tension may be an important measure of how difficult it will be to induce changes in a client. The reader might also imitate the changing positions of a client to try intuitively to infer unverbalized feelings. Some typical positions that have been interpreted in this way include the forward lean, which is generally viewed as being an attentive, approach posture; drawing back or turning away, which is viewed as a negative or withdrawal posture; the expanded chest, erect head, and raised shoulders, which may suggest pride or arrogance; and the dejected posture, typically characterized by forward-leaning trunk, bowed head, drooping shoulders, and sunken chest. Relaxation is often conveyed by asymmetry in posture. Generally, people assume more of an approach position with another person they like than with one they do not like. Higher-status members in a dyad usually show more relaxation than lower-status members, and moderate relaxation often accompanies the emotion of liking or approach. Extreme relaxation in posture is likely to be assumed in talking with persons who are disliked or not respected. Very tense posture is typically seen with persons in situations that are threatening.

Hall (1966), an anthropologist, has studied the spatial relations he found in various kinds of interaction among people in different cultures. Each culture appears to have its own implicit norms regarding permissible proximity between two speakers. For Americans, Hall has distinguished four zones: 0 to 6 inches for intimate interaction; 1½ to 4 feet for personal; 4 to 10 feet for social-consultative; and 10 feet and over for public interaction. For example, two strangers will converse impersonally at a distance of about 4 feet. If one of them moves closer, the other will back away. Hall suggests that communicators who violate these implicit distance limits will elicit negative feelings from the persons to whom they are talking.

Regarding cultural and group differences in these norms, several studies have shown that persons greeting each other maintain different distances. For example, in one study Mexicans stood closest to each other, whites next closest, and blacks farthest apart. Typically, Latin Americans have a closer impersonal distance than North Americans, and it is virtually impossible for a North and South American both to be comfortable when they talk to each other unless one can adopt the zones normal for the other. Among two North Americans a personal conversation can be shifted to an impersonal one by the simple procedure of moving back to a distance of 4 or 5 feet. If the discussion partner cannot follow, he or she will probably find it quite impossible to maintain a personal discussion at that distance. There also appear to be some sex and age differences in regard to spatial proximity, with male–female pairs assuming the closest positions, then female–female, and finally male–male pairs. Children seem to assume the closest positions to each other, then adolescents, and finally adults. It has also been found that interviewees who come into the office expecting a negative evaluation are more likely to select chairs farther removed from the interviewer than those expecting a positve evaluation.

Kinzel (1970) has extended the concept of spatial proximity to the idea of a body buffer zone in violent prisoners. In comparing the measurement of the body buffer zones of eight violent and six nonviolent prisoners, he found the zones of the violent group to be almost four times larger. In the violent group the rear zones were larger than the front zones; in the nonviolent group the front zones were larger. He suggested, on the basis of daily clinical observations of prisoners, that physical proximity to another inmate was at least as powerful a trigger of violence as were threats, thefts, or other more overt provocations. Violent inmates spoke of their victims as "messing with me" or "getting up to my face" when they were actually at conversational distances. Kinzel poses such possible clinical implications as distinguishing violent from nonviolent individuals by body buffer zone measurements and using periodic zone measurements to document the effect of psychotropic medication, need for incarceration, evidence for change or improvement, and so on.

Obviously, to become conversant in the language of nonverbal communication, one would have to become aware of how the various channels of communication relate to each other. Some interesting research in this regard has been reported by Mehrabian (1972). He demonstrated that tone of voice (positive, neutral, or negative) was less potent than facial expression depicted on photographs (positive, neutral, or negative). Each of the subjects in his study heard neutral content words expressed with one of the three degrees of attitude while seeing a photograph with one of the three degrees of attitude. Analysis indicated that the facial component had a stronger effect than the vocal component. Estimating relative weighting in message communication, he concluded that the message received was weighted 55% by the facial expression, 38% by the tone, and only 7% by the content. If these results have any generality for real-life communication situations, they suggest the importance of careful observation of nonverbal components, especially if these components are inconsistent with the verbal content component.

Another study that demonstrates how the various channels of nonverbal communication can be used is reported by Hetherington (1973). In this study, observations of nonverbal behavior were used in combination with other information to discover the effects of the loss of a father on adolescent girls. Hetherington found that the absence of a father, especially if it occurred before the girl was 5 years old, resulted in social awkwardness with men. If the absence was due to the death of the father, the girls tended to be frightened of men; absence due to a divorce was related to being clumsily erotic with men. With respect to nonverbal behaviors, girls whose fathers had died, when interviewed by a man, tended to choose a seat far away from the interviewer, keep silent, sit stiffly upright, turn their shoulders away from the interviewer, establish little eye contact, and smile rarely. Girls who were fatherless as a result of divorce, when compared to the preceding group or control subjects from intact families, tended more often to choose a seat close to the interviewer, be talkative, assume an open, sometimes sprawling posture, lean forward, look into the interviewer's eyes, and smile. Fatherless girls in general, when compared to girls from intact families, tended to show mannerisms such as plucking at their clothes, pulling and twirling their hair, and pulling at their fingers.

Friedman (1969) presents an interesting extension of concern with nonverbal behavior into the area of physical diagnosis. According to him, one of the most lethal causes of coronary artery disease is a behavior pattern he calls Type A. He claims that almost all people under 60 who have heart attacks are Type A personalities and, unless the behavior patterns associated with this personality type can be altered, none of the other precautions against it can forestall the disease.

What behavior do Type A personalities show? They are ambitious, competitive, impatient, and aggressive, and they are involved in an incessant struggle against time and/or other people. Their sense of time urgency is perhaps their most dominant trait. Almost always punctual, they are greatly annoyed if kept waiting. They usually feel dreadfully behind in doing all the things they think they should; they worry inordinately about meeting deadlines. Delays in restaurants, at airports, or in traffic irritate them. Similarly, they are impatient with people who do not come to the point quickly in conversation. They tend to talk rapidly and eat rapidly, rarely remaining long at the table. Type A personalities do not usually spare the time to indulge in hobbies and, when they do, they prefer competitive games or gambling. They dislike doing routine jobs at home because they feel their time can be spent more profitably. In fact, they often try to do several things simultaneously (reading while eating or shaving, for example), and frequently engage in two lines of thought at once with the result that they listen inattentively—particularly when they deem the conversation insignificant. They generally strive frantically for things worth having (a beautiful home, a better job, a bigger bank balance) at the expense of things worth being (well read, knowledgeable about art, appreciative of nature). Often they pay little more than lip service to the human values of love, affection, and friendship. And they are chronically dissatisfied with their socioeconomic status, no matter how relatively high. Finally, and most devastatingly to their depersonalization, they are obsessed by numbers—billings per month, clients served, merchandise sold, money earned—and tend to judge their lives by these number values.

Over the years Friedman and his colleagues have devised a structured oral interview, administered by trained personnel, as the best approach to behavioral typing. Whereas in broad terms they distinguish the Type A personality from Type B (who tends to be calm, relaxed, and patient even though he or she may also work hard and long), their scale actually has five categories. Their interview queries the subject about work and leisure habits and about attitudes toward time and pressures, but it is analyzed more for the intensity and emotional overtone of the responses than for the actual verbal answers. Emphatic, often explosive, replies are typical of Type A personalities; their voices, for example, are often loud or even hostile. Also, because their impatience makes them anticipate what others will say, they frequently interrupt the interviewer to answer questions before they are fully asked. The Type A personality's motor behavior (gestures, grimaces, and other body language) is also analyzed (table pounding and fist clenching are typical Type A gestures). Additional description of the Type A personality is probably beyond our purpose here, as is how to change from Type A to Type B. This research does indicate again, however, the importance and possible diagnostic utility of careful observation of nonverbal behavior.

Other authors have noted the importance of careful interviewing in patient diagnosis and treatment. Wolf and Goodell (1976) call attention to an old dictum in medicine that it is important to know what kind of patient has the disease, perhaps even more important than knowing what kind of disease the patient has. They offer various suggestions on talking with patients. Friedman (1979) suggests that effective nonverbal communication is essential for successful patient–practitioner interaction and that there are major aspects of nonverbal communication that are of direct relevance to health care. These include touch, facial expression, voice tone, and so on. DiMatteo has been researching nonverbal communication and physician–patient rapport for some years. DiMatteo and Taranta (1976) reported two factors contributing significantly to patient satisfaction with the physician–patient relationship: (a) the ability of the physician to understand the emotions of others apparent in their body movement and posture cues, and (b) the physician's skill at detecting emotional messages to others through nonverbal channels of facial expression and voice tone. In a recent book, DiMatteo and DiNicola (1982) discuss the communication of information between practitioner and patient and its importance in achieving patient compliance with specific treatment recommendations. Their thoughtful observations and recommendations should be carefully reviewed by readers interested in practitioner–patient relationships.

As noted repeatedly in this section, verbal communication uses only one of the many kinds of signals that people can exchange; other signals can reinforce or contradict the verbal message. These subtle signals are especially important in psychotherapy, where a patient tries to communicate emotional troubles but may find it difficult to express in words the real sources of distress. A good therapist (and interviewer) learns to listen for more than the content of words alone, and learns how to use nonverbal signals to help interpret the verbal signals. Unfortunately, no one has yet put together all the research findings reviewed above so that the novice interviewer could systematically use them in behavioral assessment. Each interviewer probably uses some aspects of nonverbal evaluation and interpretation with semiawareness. Perhaps by more conscious concern we can make our intuition even more reliable. Nonverbal communication is not to be denied; actions speak louder than words.

ROLES AND TACTICS IN THE INTERVIEW INTERACTION

The interview interaction can be viewed as a dynamic process that is constantly changing throughout the course of an interview. Furthermore, it should be kept in mind that this dynamic state of affairs holds true for the interviewer, and that influence between the interviewer and interviewee is a reciprocal relationship constantly being modified in response to cues each receives from the other. Most novice interviewers readily admit that the interviewer has an influence on the interviewee, but it is less frequently recognized that the interviewer's behavior depends in significant measure on the interviewee's behavior. For example, when it is assumed that patients in psychotherapy engage in inner-determined free association to arrive ultimately at the causal bases for behavior, it may also be assumed that what the interviewer does has little effect in determining the nature of these associations. In this framework the recognition of reciprocal interaction and influence may be disquieting, because it eliminates the simple expedient of assigning blame to the client if the interview does not achieve its purpose. It is difficult to assert that the client's defensiveness, wish not to get well, transference problems, and the like are the entire basis of an interview's being stalled if the interviewer and interviewee are assumed to share the credit or blame for what is or is not accomplished.

Ideally, in a mutual interview relationship both participants feel some responsibility for a successful interview outcome, and both feel some personal autonomy and responsibility for their own behavior. The kind of mutual interaction that develops in this situation has been popularized in Berne's (1964) ideas and writing on the "games people play," in which it is always assumed that there have to be two players. These games are often highly ritualized, and they may be either complementary, mutually satisfying transactions or transactions with explicit and implicit meanings that involve incompatible behavioral demands. In contrast to Berne's games, however, in most assessment and therapy interviews every effort is made to achieve game-free authenticity. Viewed from the standpoint of the interviewer, this means that he or she is active in motivating a full interviewee response and making clear to the interviewee that any points of view on relevant topics, and any degrees of enthusiasm or hostility, are equally acceptable. As has been previously asserted in this chapter, the interview interaction has a purpose, and the interviewer has the major responsibility in keeping the interview on target. Discussing counseling interviews, Gilmore (1973) has aptly stated in this regard that "failure to discern the difference between communicating as a means to an end and communication as an end in itself can block the forward movement of counseling and lock the client and counselor into a race track course of endless circular laps" (p. 230).

Interviewer Role

Despite the assertion that the interview involves reciprocal interaction, it is helpful to look at interviewer and interviewee roles separately. Kahn and Cannell (1961) call attention to two major functions of the interviewer role, communication and measurement. The measurement or assessment role requires the interviewer to direct and control the communication process toward specific objectives. The interviewer must be clear about assessment objectives and, through careful formulation of major questions, ensure that the flow of communication is directed to these specific objectives. In most instances the interviewer probably teaches the interviewee what the latter's role involves. This is done in part by communicating to the interviewee, either directly or in some subtle fashion, when an inquiry has been responded to completely. Additionally, the interviewer remains nonresponsive to irrelevant interviewee responses or digressions, until the interviewee recognizes and adapts to this pattern in the interaction. This description of interviewer behavior assumes a situation in which the two participants have established a purpose for the interview that is mutually understood and accepted.

Invariably (see Maccoby & Maccoby, 1954) the interviewee places the interviewer in a role with status implications; in a medical school setting, for example, the interviewer typically is placed in the role of an expert, the doctor. In this regard it is of interest to recall that people are generally more eager to communicate to those above them in the social status hierarchy than to those below them. For example, a young interviewer may exert less status influence in an interview with someone older than with an interviewee of the same age or younger. Sex and social status effects are equally relative. This also includes the matter of the interviewer's personal appearance. The interviewee's confidence in the interviewer will be enhanced if the latter is well groomed and dressed appropriately for the setting in which he or she works. Johnson (1981) has pointed out that even though everyone has the right to personal standards it is well to remember that the professional engages in a special relationship with another person and therefore has a special responsibility to that person. The interviewer demonstrates respect for himself or herself and for the patient by dressing in a professional manner. It is important that the interviewer not stimulate a negative reaction in the patient by his or her own inappropriate appearance or behavior.

The interviewee has legitimate expectations of the interviewer, including the expectation that the interviewer is able to convey warmth and acceptance and is sincere in interpersonal relationships. An additional legitimate expectation is that the interviewer is competent in interview skills and familiar with a variety of methods for starting an interview and keeping it moving. Beyond this, the interviewer is expected to have expert knowledge related to the purpose of the interview. If the interviewer appears naive, the interviewee will have cause to doubt whether his or her statements will be understood. However, if the interviewer is overbearingly expert, he or she may come across as knowing everything, which can also block communication. Ideally, the interviewer should be seen as an expert seeking additional information from an informed person who has detailed knowledge or opinions to contribute, and who is more informed about the interviewee than he or she is about himself or herself.

Assessment interviews require in particular a thorough knowledge of normative expectations (see Kadushin, 1972). If a child is toilet-trained at 20 months, is this late or early? If talking starts at 15 months, is this indicative of developmental lag or normal development? To know what is unusual, unexpected, or atypical, one needs to know the usual and typical. A background of knowledge is very important to the clinician's task, and it is to be lamented that the emphasis on feeling and doing in psychology has introduced in some quarters an anti-intellectual downgrading of interviewer knowledgeability. Good interviewing is impossible without a considerable amount of knowing and thinking.

It must also be asserted that the professional interviewer needs to maintain a degree of emotional neutrality toward those whom he or she serves. It has long been recognized that physicians should refrain from treating other than minor illnesses in their own families because of the possibility that their emotional involvement would affect their judgment and the quality of their treatment. So it should be in psychological practice, although emotional neutrality is not easy to achieve and is not to be equated with coldness. The term means, rather, that the interviewer's subjective feelings are under sufficient control so that he or she is free to focus on the patient's needs. One of the consequences of an overly close relationship with clients is that it becomes increasingly improbable that difficult questions will be asked. Furthermore, accepting the potential for social or personal relationships with patients is likely to accentuate the interviewer's tendency to like or dislike some kinds of interviewees. Sometimes these likes or dislikes can be based on generalized prejudice and thus lead to denial of a given client's individuality.

There are also several potential personal satisfactions that the interviewer must guard against. One of these is simple narcissism, or using the power and control one has in an interview to impress the client with how much knowlege or experience one has in the area of discussion. A related danger is seeking testimonials from interviewees as to how helpful and gratifying the interview has been. Novice or unsure interviewers are particularly prone to act in this way, and they may also be tempted to induce such flattery by allying themselves with the client against the institution the interviewer represents, whether a particular agency or "the establishment" more generally. Interviewers may also curry favor by engaging in a conspiracy to withhold information or by failing to follow up worrisome or debatable questions. In general, certain areas may remain unexplored because of fear that the attempt to introduce the material will evoke hostility toward the interviewer. Because of the possibility of these and similar negative consequences, social contacts between interviewers and interviewees are not to be encouraged. It is likewise desirable for interviewers to be outside the power hierarchy of interviewees, lest interviewees avoid topics for fear they might discredit themselves.

It should also be noted that the typical interview situation is one in which the interviewee becomes to some extent dependent on the expert knowledge of the interviewer. This dependency usually consists of a partial suspension of personal judgment in deference to the interviewer, heightened susceptibility to the interviewer's influence, and willingness to disclose personal information that would otherwise be kept private. It is accordingly incumbent on the interviewer to be loyal to clients and to respect the professional ethic of confidentiality. The professional interviewer expects and receives a higher level of trust from those served than do most other professionals. Because of the high expectations the public holds for the professional psychological interviewer, lay people are particularly outraged when they believe a given professional places monetary or other personal rewards and satisfactions (including sexual relationships) above humanitarian concerns. Furthermore, as Adler (1972) has pointed out, the professional interviewer's work is rarely subject to evaluation and regulation by others. The implied self-responsibility for interviewers' work with patients and the responsibility to their profession and colleagues must not be taken lightly.

To turn briefly to some research reports regarding the effect of role expectations, Kanfer and Phillips (1970) note that the flow of communication in an interview is heavily determined by role assignment. Kanfer asked female nurses to discuss personal experiences in dyads. When they acted as peers in these discussions, the nurses spent about the same amount of time talking and listening. When he asked them to adopt complementary patient and therapist roles, however, he found a significant shift in relative speaking time. Specifically, the subjects talking as patients talked abut 60% of the time as contrasted with 30% talking time in the therapist role.

Heller (1972) studied extensively the effects of various interviewer and interviewee behaviors. His method was to have previously instructed clients interviewed by experimentally naive interviewers who were asked to adopt various interview tactics. One interesting finding was that, with subjects who had a prior set toward admitting personal inadequacies and weaknesses, interviewers instructed to be passive, friendly, or silent were particularly successful in eliciting open problem discussion. The more ambiguous situations, providing least feedback, seemed most to facilitate these clients' self-disclosure. In a follow-up study Heller found that more reserved interviewers, as contrasted with more open and friendly interviewers, elicited more subject self-disclosure. He interpreted the reserved interview situation as mildly stressful and suggested that this mild stress facilitated expression in those subjects who were ready to talk about themsleves.

With interviewees in general, however, active-friendly interviewers are probably clearly preferred over passive-hostile interviewers. The latter's passivity, lack of communication, and lack of orientation cues tend to be felt by most interviewees as presenting a somewhat punishing situation. However, whereas interviewer control, structure, and activity have generally favorable effects on the interview, this is so only up to the point at which an interviewer becomes overly dominating, inflexible, and unresponsive to the interviewee's needs. By and large, more structure may be needed in early portions of the interview, as naive interviewees learn what is expected of them, and less structure after they have become familiar with their role.

Certainly there are great interviewee individual differences, including age, intelligence, and experience in the interviewee role. Assessment interviews, which require that certain content areas be covered, may require more interview directness than therapy interviews. Firm interview direction may also be needed in times of crisis when emergency action is necessary. Heller has pointed out in this regard that greater verbal productivity has been observed under friendly and "warm" interview conditions than under reserved and "cold" interview conditions, provided that the warm and friendly conditions were first in the sequence. Productivity was not recovered if the sequence of the conditions was reversed. Kadushin (1972) has also reported that a high degree of extroversion and sociability is not related to high interviewer competence. Greater interviewer competence tends to be associated with an interest in people that is scientific and objective rather than highly emotional or personal. Higher intelligence, variety of interests, and a wide range of experiences seem also to be associated with the capacity to empathize with a greater range of people.

Interviewee Role

The person in the interviewee role, if he or she is to be successful, has to have some capacity to communicate, to translate feelings and thoughts into words, and to organize his or her communication. Given these abilities and a competent interviewer, the interviewee will gain satisfaction from the interview through an increase in his or her sense of personal adequacy. It can also be noted that there are some interviewees who are so dogmatic or socially insensitive that it is difficult for them to recognize and perceive interviewer expressions of desirable attitudes. Given interviewee preferences, however, it is likely for them to choose interviewers who do not show disrespect by being insincere or in a hurry, or by interrupting, yawning, or being late for interviews. Further individual interviewee preferences tend to vary with the problems involved. For example, in the area of personal problems, the interviewee might be concerned most with the interviewer's affective characteristics, whereas in areas of educational–occupational problems, focus might be on the interviewer's cognitive skills and knowledge. Clients from deprived social backgrounds may show initial preference for interviewers with strong political power who command access to jobs, housing, or an increase in income (Kadushin, 1972).

Interviewee variables such as social class, verbal facility, and intelligence have been related to the probability of an interviewee's being referred for or continued in psychotherapy. With reference to a continued series of interviews such as in psychotherapy, Strupp (1963) has suggested a greater probability for success if the interviewer and patient have mutually congruent expectations of what is expected and if the patient is intelligent, well educated, and able to communicate feelings, and recognizes problems as psychological and wants psychological help.

Pope has discussed possible strain that can develop in an interview as a consequence of a lack of value congruence between lower-class clients and middle- and upper-class interviewers. He presents the following comparison of values between these groups (Pope, 1979, pp. 499–500):

Middle-Class Values	Lower-Class Values
a) Self-reliance, because of the opportunity for progress through individual attainment.	Group solidarity, because progress through individual attainment is not feasible.
b) The delay of immediate gratification in favor of future attainment and pleasure. Saving and investment are the methods of attaining future security.	The rejection of gratification delay because income is too low to permit saving for future security.
c) The responsible budgeting of time, as part of the delay of immediate gratification.	The view of time budgeting and saving for future security as equally pointless.
d) The inhibition and control of immediate aggressive impulse. Such control is congruent with a value system that stresses delay of gratification and a future time orientation.	The indulgence of aggressive impulse, as a means of asserting immediate social control, particularly during adolescence. This impulsiveness is congruent with the rejection of gratification delay and a present time rather than a future time orientation.
e) The emphasis, rather early in life, on verbal communication as a means of settling differences with others. This is consistent with the value placed on the control of aggressive impulse.	The positive evaluation of action and impulse rather than a primary emphasis on communication.
f) The choice of introspection as the major means of coping with problems that are perceived as basically internal.	A primary emphasis on coping with the environment, because external pressures are a relatively more demanding than internal conflicts.

Pope asserts that when interviewers are not sensitive to the value differences with lower-class clients the latter are likely to feel misunderstood and pressured in a direction that conflicts with their survival needs. Clinicians may feel that they are formulating goals for a patient that meet mental health criteria, when in fact they are using the mental health code to reinforce values that are rewarding to middle-class patients but not to those from the working class. There is no easy way to mitigate this type of culture conflict; the reader would be well advised, however, to read the thoughtful discussion that Pope presents on this topic.

Heller (1972) suggests that specific kinds of interviewee behavior evoke predictable interviewer behaviors. For example, in a study in which clients enacted specific roles, he found that interviewers who were faced with dominant or dependent client behavior responded, respectively, with either passive or hyper-responsible behavior; when faced with hostile or friendly client behavior, they responded, respectively, with hostile or likable, agreeable behavior. Matarazzo, Wiens, Matarazzo, and Saslow (1968) have noted variations in the verbal output of patients that appeared related to the level of interviewer verbal output. That is, when patients talked little, the interviewers talked more, hoping to stimulate them; when patients were more verbally active, the interviewers' tendency was to talk less, so as not to impede the patients' productivity.

Interviewees vary widely in the ease with which they can establish a new relationship. The person who has grown up in a small family, or in an urban setting, or who has moved frequently, or whose work involves dealing with many people may have had a great deal of experience in forming new interpersonal relationships. Conversely, the person who has lived only in a small community, or has essentially only long-time associates, or does not work in a setting where he or she meets new people may experience more difficulty in forming a new relationship. Similarly, the assessment interviewer will soon learn that there are assessment cues that can be gleaned from the nature of the relationship (or verbal interaction) with different interviewees. Some verbal and vocal characteristics are seen rather commonly with certain diagnostic groups; for example, the depressed patient typically demonstrates short DOUs and long RTLs.

Interviewees also approach the interview with a great variety of motivations. Some interviewees may have sought the appointment, whereas others may have been instructed to appear. The adolescent delinquent may be an involuntary interviewee, as may also the parents of a child when there is concern over possible child abuse. In all cases the interview has been affected by the events that have preceded it. Additional interviewee attitudes are shaped by immediate determinants associated with the interview situation itself, such as waiting for long periods in noisy, unattractive waiting rooms on uncomfortable, hard benches. The highly anxious patient may find even a short wait quite intolerable. These and many other interviewee variables may occur to readers as they consider the stimulus qualities that different interviewees present.

Interview Tactics

There are extensive published sources and supervisor opinions that the interested reader can consult regarding questions about interview tactics. Assessment interviews are done for a great variety of purposes, and different tactics may be appropriate for each of them. The theoretical or conceptual framework the interviewer chooses is also a major determinant of how the interviewer will structure the interview. Additionally, the broad literature on psychotherapy can be profitably reviewed for a host of suggestions on interview tactics (see Chapters 7, 8, and 9).

An excellent text on client-centered counseling and interviewing was written by Porter (1950), and the novice interviewer is encouraged to go back to this early text for a clear exposition of assumptions about personality and of interviewer tactics derived from these assumptions. A central hypothesis in Porter's presentation is that people have within themselves the capacities to order and reorder behavior without external manipulation by others. The interview aim that follows from this assumption is to keep the client expressing and exploring attitudes as freely as possible. If interviewers utilize some sort of reassurance, persuasion, moralization, instruction, or coercion, they are making an assumption as to limiting factors in the capacity of clients to continue on their own. When an interviewer attempts to *understand* a client as the latter perceives the situation, however, he or she operates on an assumption that the client does not need energizing from an external source but has the capacity to continue on his or her own. In this frame of reference, the interviewer is forced to deal with the reality the client holds no matter how much insight the interviewer may have into the errors of perception the client makes, and it is the meanings that the client has come to assign to life experiences that constitute the reality to which he or she responds.

By contrast, a behavorial orientation or social learning approach places emphasis on external variables shown to exercise control over behavior. The assumption then is that psychological functioning involves a reciprocal interaction between behavior and its controlling environment. Ideally, every interviewer question should have the sole purpose of a more thorough functional analysis of the problem behavior. Morganstern and Tevlin (1981) recognize that the beginning interviewer may know what information to seek but still be quite unclear as to the manner in which the necessary information is to be obtained. Although they recognize the importance of a "complete" functional analysis of a problem behavior, they do assert that an interview should be focused only on content relevant to treatment. This protects the patient's right to minimal intrusion, however interesting other aspects of the patient's life might be to the interviewer and patient. Discussion of the relationship variables in the interview is much the same as with any other theoretical orientation. That is, the interviewer must be genuinely compassionate and must have the capacity to listen to his or her patients. This would imply that the interviewer does not interrupt with premature questions, does not prematurely reassure or explain away the patient's concerns, and so on. The patient needs to know and to feel that the interviewer is making every effort to understand the problem as the former is experiencing it. Of course, the skillful behavioral interviewer will explicitly define the patient's statements within a behavioral framework. The interviewer-therapist is expected both to model and to shape a behavioral language.

According to Kanfer and Phillips (1970), behavior assessment serves four main purposes:

> 1) identification of therapeutic target responses and their maintaining stimuli; 2) assessment of functional relationships among response classes and among discriminative and reinforcing stimuli; 3) determination of available social resources, personal assets, and skills for use in a therapeutic program, as well as of limitations and obstacles in the person and in the environment; and 4) availability of specific therapeutic strategies or behavioral techniques most consonant with the personal and environmental factors in the patient's life situation. [p. 504]

Kanfer and Phillips indicate that in their approach to behavioral assessment they nevertheless make use of a wide range of historical, social, cognitive, and biological factors in addition to directly observable behavior. The approach by social learning theorists has been to construct a model of assessment that includes attention to etiology, assessment, and therapy and effectively links these three facets of the total situation. Behavioral approaches to assessment are elaborated by Goldfried in Chapter 5 of this book.

A general categorization of interviewer comments consists of classifying them as open-ended or closed-ended questions. Open-ended questions ask the interviewee to recall something or to produce it spontaneously. Closed-ended questions ask the interviewee to recognize something. As noted in the earlier discussion of vocabulary skills, a recall task is more difficult than a recognition task, but at the same time it is usually more productive in eliciting interviewee attitudes. The open-ended question encourages the interviewee to say more and does not overly limit the area or topic to be discussed. A typical open-ended question might be "What brings you to see me?" In contrast, a closed-ended question might be "Did your doctor send you to see me?"

An open-ended question is designed to encourage the spontaneous flow of information from the patient with as little direct interviewer questioning as possible. It is assumed that if interviewees are allowed to describe their problems in their own words and in their own way, more of their total situation will be revealed. As the interviewer listens carefully, he or she gradually pieces together a total picture. Closed-ended or yes-or-no questions are not necessarily to be avoided altogether; in fact, they are often the most efficient means of determining whether something is or is not the case. However, they typically do not contribute to a spontaneous flow of communication from the interviewee.

In addition to open- and closed-ended questions, many other interviewer verbal tactics have been described in the literature. An excellent review of several of these appears in Gilmore's book (1973), including misused questions, paraphrasing, describing behaviors and feelings, perception checking, verbatim playback, summarizing, formulating a choice point, facilitating transitions, gaining a figure–ground perspective, requesting a contrast, and introducing concrete examples. The interested reader is encouraged to review Gilmore's descriptions of these tactics. She also includes excellent discussions of alternative ways of obtaining information. For example, information abut friendships or meaningful relationships might well be obtained by asking such questions as "Who takes care of you? . . . Whom do you take care of? . . . Who could get in touch with you any time of the day or night? . . . Who knows if your head aches? . . ." (Gilmore, 1973, p. 11).

There are also some ways of asking questions that are almost guaranteed to elicit some negative feeling in response. For example, a question such as "According to your record you have not lost any weight—why do you keep eating so much?" will almost surely antagonize a patient and stimulate defensiveness. The problem with putting patients on the defensive is that they will probably say very little, and they may not reveal what they really think. Asking *why* questions typically antagonizes patients, because they call on them to account for their behavior. It is difficult to begin a question with "why" and still avoid overtones of accusation. It is usually better for interviewers to indicate that they do not yet understand and wish more information. The novice interviewer is encouraged to experiment with beginning questions with the word *how* rather than *why*. "How did this happen to come about?" is a question more likely to elicit an informative response than the same question begun with the word *why*.

It is of course necessary for the interviewer to use words that the interviewee understands. Thus questions should be brief, simple, and clear. It may be necessary to rephrase a question several times before the desired flow of communication is established. Along with this verbal interaction, the interviewer should maintain good eye contact with the interviewee while they are talking to each other. Good eye contact consists of spontaneous glances that express an interest and desire to communicate. Poor eye contact can comprise never looking at interviewees, staring at them fixedly, or looking away from them as soon as they look at you. Likewise, a desirable postural position involves sitting with one's body facing another person, hands gesturing occasionally, being facially responsive (e.g., smiling and frowning as appropriate), and occasionally leaning toward the interviewee to emphasize a verbal point or to indicate a nonverbal positive approach.

Ivey (1971) and his associates have emphasized particularly the notions of *attention* and *attending behavior,* which are defined behaviorally as eye contact, physical attention, and verbal following behavior. This concept makes use of the observation that interviewees talk about what the interviewer attends or listens to, both verbally and nonverbally. Once attending behavior is learned, the interviewer can then pay selective attention to emotional aspects of the interviewee's comments; that is, he or she can reinforce emotional components of the interviewee's behavior. Tyler (1969), among others, emphasizes this same kind of interviewer behavior.

Standardized and Nonstandardized Interviews

An essential feature of the standardized or *structured* interview is that the interviewer asks questions that have been decided on in advance and are repeated with the same wording and in the same order from one interview to the next. This form of interview can be used when the same or nearly the same information is to be elicited from each interviewee. It can also be used on successive occasions with the same interviewee. The interview data collected are usually fairly easy to quantify. Standardized interviews typically allow information to be compared from case to case; they are more reliable than unstandardized interviews, and they minimize errors of question wording. Usually they are not used in exploratory research or initial interviews or before the data to be collected have been carefully defined and articulated.

Unstandardized or *unstructured* interviews allow interviewers freedom to reword questions, to introduce new questions or to modify question order, and generally to follow interviewees' spontaneous sequences of ideas. It is often assumed that such spontaneous discussion allows interviewees to follow more nearly their natural train of thought and may allow them to bring out interview material that is more predictive of what they would say or do in real-life situations. The flexibility of the unstructured interview may also allow interviewers to adapt their techniques to the interviewees' particular situations. In some cases they may omit topics that do not seem applicable, and in other cases they may introduce related topics not originally planned for.

Actually, it seems that most experienced clinical psychologists probably have adopted a semistandardized interviewing style or format. Listening to a clinician interviewing a series of patients, one can probably soon discern topic areas that he or she routinely introduces and questions that he or she asks in almost the same way of every interviewee. Without a semistandardized format or interview guide, interviewers are very likely to overlook topics they should cover. However, experienced clinicians are also aware that they can best maintain rapport with interviewees by formulating questions in words that are familiar to interviewees and habitually used by them, and by taking up topics when interviewees indicate a readiness and willingness to discuss them. The semistandardized interview gives more discretion to the interviewer in formulating the wording and sequence of questions in this way, and it accordingly requires a higher level of experience, skill, and training than is required in following a more standardized interview format. Required in particular are an overall conceptual grasp of theoretical context and considerable prior knowledge of the subject matter of the interview.

Peterson (1968) suggests that most clinical interviewing should involve an intermediate degree of structure. With total client spontaneity it is essentially impossible to define, teach, use, test, or improve interview strategy, and with a rigid interview structure the interviewer may cover the questions in a predefined schedule but remain totally ignorant of what matters to the client. Peterson suggests that the assessment needs to determine specifically what the person is doing (both thought and behavior) and then to examine in fine detail the antecedent, concurrent, and consequent conditions under which the behavior to be changed occurs. The actions and reactions of other people in the client's environment are important, including both what the patient does to and with others and what others do to and with him or her.

Finding out what people are doing to each other can be a difficult and time-consuming task, but such systematic inquiry in relation to possible treatment modalities is an essential task for the clinician to pursue. With this purpose in mind, Peterson describes an interview strategy involving an initial *scanning* operation that consists of asking the patient and referral sources about the nature of the problem behavior and the circumstances that precede and follow it. The scanning operation is followed by an extended *inquiry* that includes a more detailed and individualized study of the client and others most centrally involved. The third phase of the interview sequence consists of *periodic appraisal* following introduction of treatment measures. The fourth phase is a *follow-up* study. It is clear that he does not propose or utilize a single initial interview as his assessment procedure.

Peterson (1968, pp. 121–122) presents the basic content of one possible guided interview outline, which the interested reader should consult for details. The outline includes two major headings: Definition of Problem Behavior and Determinants of Problem Behavior. The definition of problem behavior includes assessment of the nature of the problem as defined by the client, of the severity of the problem, and of the generality of the problem. The determinants of problem behavior include identifying conditions that intensify problem behavior, conditions that alleviate problem behavior, and the perceived origins, specific antecedents, and specific consequences of problem behavior. Suggested changes and suggested leads for further inquiry are also noted. The novice interviewer will be glad to know that possible wordings of questions for assessment of these different interview areas are included in Peterson's presentation.

Diagnostic Interview Schedules

For many clinical psychologists and psychiatrists the most used methods of diagnostic study in the past have been relatively open-ended history taking and the Mental Status Examination. The Mental Status Examination introduces some organization into the diagnostic interview and into the classification and reporting of the information that is offered by the interviewee. While certain information is to be obtained, the interviewer is not expected to follow a rigid interview outline. A description of the examination can be found in many psychiatry and neurology textbooks, in many abnormal psychology texts, and in various assessment manuals. The examination outlines a thorough exploration of the following topics: appearance and behavior of the patient; sensorium, or functioning of the central nervous system; thought processes; thought content and intellect; perceptual disturbances; emotional regulation; volition, or ability to follow willfully a course of action; and somatic functions.

It would seem clear that reliability in diagnosis would be enhanced by using more structured interviews than has often been the case in the past. As clinical psychologists who emphasize the use of psychological tests are especially aware, open-ended history taking is likely to omit important questions and leave significant aspects of patient functioning without review. Furthermore, individual clinicians are likely to have their individual biases and to over- or underemphasize certain aspects of history taking. Related to this is the fact that an initial impression may lead one to miss diagnostic cues that are contrary to the expectations established on the basis of that first impression. All of us must be aware of how likely we are to see and observe what we are looking for in a clinical interview or any other interaction situation.

Spitzer, Endicott, and Robins (1975) noted five sources of unreliability and then determined that two of these contributed most heavily to diagnostic unreliability. The first source of unreliability they noted was *subject variance,* which occurs when patients actually have different conditions at different times. They gave the example of the patient who may show acute alcohol intoxication on admission to a hospital but develop delirium tremens several days later. A second source of unreliability is *occasion variance,* which occurs when patients are in different stages of the same condition at different times. An example of this would be a patient with a bipolar disorder who is depressed during one period of illness and manic during another.

A third source of unreliability is *information variance,* which occurs when clinicians have different sources of information about their patients. Examples here include clinicians who talk with patients' families and those who do not, or interviewers who question patients about areas of functioning and symptoms about which other interviewers do not. A fourth area of unreliability is *obervation vari-*

ance, which occurs when clinicians notice different things although presumably observing the same patient behavior. Clinicians may disagree on whether a patient was tearful, hard to follow, or hallucinating. A fifth source of unreliability is *criterion variance,* which occurs when clinicians use varying diagnostic criteria (e.g., whether a formal thought disorder is necessary for the diagnosis of schizophrenia or precludes a diagnosis of affective disorder). Spitzer et al. (1975) concluded that the largest source of diagnostic variability, by far, was criterion variance. Their efforts on behalf of the development of the DSM-III diagnostic criteria obviously reflected their confidence in this conclusion.

In their research they tried particularly to reduce criterion variance and information variance, the second major source of unreliability. Their efforts to control for varying interviewing styles and coverage led to the development of the Research Diagnostic Criteria (RDC), which provide sets of specific inclusion and exclusion criteria for a large number of functional disorders, with particular emphasis on the subtyping of affective disorders (Spitzer, Endicott, & Robins, 1978). In using the RDC, clinicians are required to use these criteria regardless of their own personal concepts of the disorder. With this approach, the clinician's task is (a) to determine the presence or absence of specific clinical phenomena, and (b) to apply the comprehensive rules provided for making a diagnosis. A given patient can be categorized in different ways, for instance, by the presence or absence of endogenous psychopathology, situational stressors, psychotic features, and so on. The Kappa values for the RDC were usually above .70 and frequently above .80 (Endicott & Spitzer, 1978) and represent impressive levels of agreement.

The RDC has some limitations, however. For example, its use to date has been with adult inpatients only, so that its usefulness with adult outpatients and with children remains to be demonstrated (Meier, 1979). The RDC has also been used mainly by researchers trying to obtain homogeneous patient samples, and patients who did not fit the criteria were left undiagnosed. The clinician, however, often does not have the latitude to allow patients to go undiagnosed. The proper use of the RDC criteria also depends on experience and knowledge of psychopathology, because the criteria involve clinical concepts rather than a mere listing of complaints. Meier (1979) suggests that despite some limitations the RDC remains one of the best tools available to a researcher who wishes to study homogeneous patient groups and that the clinician can also use it to good advantage.

Another structured interview guide is the Schedule of Affective Disorders and Schizophrenia (SADS) described by Endicott and Spitzer (1978). The SADS is an interview schedule that interviewers use to ensure adequate coverage of critical areas of psychopathology and functioning. Part I of the SADS includes items that are used to describe the features of the current episode of illness when they were most severe, as well as the patient's functioning during the week prior to the interview. Part II of the SADS focuses primarily on past history and past illness. The organization of the SADS is similar to that of a clinical interview focused on differential diagnosis. The SADS provides for a progression of questions, items, and criteria that systematically rule in and out specific diagnoses. Eight summary scale scores can be generated with the SADS: depressive mood and ideation; endogenous features; depressive-associated features; suicidal ideation and behavior; anxiety; manic syndrome; delusions–hallucinations; and formal thought disorder.

Both the items and the summary scales of the SADS show high interjudge reliability for test–retest evaluations as well as for joint interviews. Coefficients of reliability for the joint interviews across the eight summary scales range from .82 to .99, and for the test–retest interviews across the eight summary scales, they ranged from .49 to .93 (Endicott & Spitzer, 1978). The authors point out that in the test–retest condition it is possible that both subject variance and information variance will be introduced. Patients may be in different stages of illness at the time of a second interview and may also show different behavior or tell one interviewer something they don't tell the other. Even so, these coefficients of reliability are very impressive. Interviewers who use the SADS and the RDC can relate their findings to the diagnostic categories in DSM-III. Many of the DSM-III diagnostic categories are virtually identical with thsoe contained in the RDC.

The Clinical Record

A clinical record (patient or client file) should be opened immediately after an initial interview. Generally, the clinical record should contain sufficient information to identify the patient clearly, to justify the diagnosis and treatment, and to document the results accurately. Some interviewers may feel impatient with this time-consuming paperwork until their efforts with a patient are challenged and they recognize that the patient record can be a clinician's best friend or worst enemy. In malpractice or general liability suits the content and quality of the patient record are pivotal. Such other factors as the clinician's credentials, personality, and reputation pale in comparison with the quality of the patient record; juries tend to believe the record.

More positively stated, a well-documented patient record is the mark of a true professional who does things thoroughly and painstakingly because they are important. A carefully developed record is a means of communication among health care personnel who are involved in providing appropriate care to the patient. Third-party payers often scrutinize records thoroughly for documentation before bills are certified for payment; thus the record can assure reimbursement of costs for the patient. The patient record is both a public and a legal document, and many different persons may gain access to it; it is a critical and potent defense against malpractice and general liability suits. It is also the basis for such additional activities as patient care audits, continuous monitoring activities, utilization review, credentialing, education, risk management, research, management statistics, and so on.

The patient record is the patient's other self, and it must faithfully mirror or reproduce the patient and the patient's experiences. The record must be intelligible, timely, complete, clear, concise, and objective; it must also be legible. Generalizations in a record are to be avoided; for example, a generalization such as "patient uncooperative" is not as meaningful to a reader as a statement such as "The patient refused to answer questions about. . . ." It is usually better to state facts than to state conclusions. One criterion to be kept in mind in record keeping is that the record should be such that if the first clinician were suddenly to disappear, a second clinician could, from the record alone, immediately continue the assessment and treatment of the patient.

The patient record should also describe the clinician's reasoning, keeping in mind especially the bridging between facts and observations and decisions about the patient. A problem list is often developed and treatment methods and goals formulated for each problem on this list. One method of record keeping is to outline and structure chart entries systematically; a useful system is to "soap" a record. The acronym SOAP stands for:

Subjective element: the patient's expression of his or her condition, pain, complaints, reactions, and so on or what the spouse or family say about the problem

Objective element: test or laboratory findings or the results of direct observations regarding the problem

Assessment: the clinician's evaluation; formulation of the problem and evaluation of treatment effectiveness

Plan: treatment plan; what is to be done to solve the problem

The value of this approach or some other such formula is that it jogs the memory, disciplines the record keeper, and provides an outline for logical progression and completeness in his or her thought processes. It leads clinicians to disclose their reasoning and to justify their actions.

There are many other details about record keeping that a clinician will have to learn about which will not be reviewed further here. There is one more issue, however, that should be addressed, and that is the issue of confidentiality. A breach of confidentiality can be considered to be one kind of invasion of privacy. Privacy laws in early times were probably enacted to protect people from physical interference with life and property. These laws generally became extended to include the right to be let alone and to the protection of one's inviolate personality. Presently a person is assumed to occupy a certain emotional, cognitive, or psychological space, the use, management, or control of which properly resides with the person. The concept of privacy is important to psychologists who feel that their effectiveness, whether in assessment or psychotherapy, is contingent on the capacity of the patient to work with his or her most private thoughts and feelings, and that anything that impairs the confidentiality of the treatment situation thereby lessens its effectiveness.

Generally speaking, all patient records are confidential, and a clinician–interviewer should not disclose any information acquired in attending the patient in a professional capacity. It is usually good practice to refuse to give out any information with respect to a patient without written permission from the patient or compulsory court process, such as a subpoena or notice of disposition. This procedure will protect the clinician from an invasion of privacy suit by the patient, while at the same time complying with the law. Confidentiality extends to the admission of nonessential persons into the presence of the patient, or the taking of unauthorized pictures of the patient without the specific consent of the patient, which should be in written form.

SPECIFIC CONSIDERATIONS IN THE INITIAL CLINICAL INTERVIEW

In a very real sense, the initial clinical interview begins with the telephone call that sets up the office appointment. This call may be from the office of another professional, but often patients are asked to take the initiative and arrange their own appointments. It is then important to convey to patient callers that their call was expected and that you are pleased to hear from them. In most instances such a telephone call is a personal acknowledgement of psychopathology made with considerable trepidation, and the initial interview should not be arranged for some time in the distant future. The interviewer must convey interest in the patient by availability. In fact, if the interviewer has a long waiting list, the patient should be offered the option of referral to another professional.

Before the initial meeting with the patient, the interviewer must do such preparatory work as carefully studying the referral letter or other available patient data. Some patients directly express their annoyance at being asked questions that have already been answered for the record, and probably most patients feel lack of interest on the part of an interviewer who did not bother to review their chart. Interviewer preparation should also involve the study necessary to become informed about the probable symptom or problem areas the patient may present, for example, bed wetting, alcoholism, or ulcers. If possible, the interviewer should try to imagine what the patient may be thinking or wishing to accomplish in the interview, and how to respond. Similarly, interviewers should have clearly in mind what they hope to accomplish, so that they can convey clear expectations to their patients. If psychological testing is to be recommended, there should be initial arrangements for time commitments, consulting, and so on. The general idea here is to have a plan of procedure. Such a plan facilitates the interview and provides a frame of reference for the patient's comments and for observations of behavior in the office.

There are many theoretical frameworks from which to observe and categorize interview behavior with respect to its emphasis or focus, and a host of initial interview situations call for different interview behaviors. The focus here is on the clinical–psychological interview that has as one of its functions the assessment of psychopathology. Although a review of the various definitions of psychopathology is beyond the scope of the present discussion, Spitzer and Endicott (1973) have proposed a useful conceptualization in which they suggest that the essential quality of all psychopathological behavior is that it is judged to be undesirable either to the person experiencing it (e.g., a painful emotion) or to other persons with whom the patient interacts. They emphasize that the focus of observation in identifying psychopathology is on behavior, but this includes private experience (thoughts and feelings) as well as directly observable behavior. The interested reader is encouraged to study Spitzer and Endicott's extended discussion of psychopathology and the manner in which they differentiate it from behavior that is deviant merely in the sense of being statistically infrequent.

The interview framework proposed by Spitzer and Endicott includes observation of subjective distress, impaired thought processes, impaired relations with other people, abnormal motor behavior, inappropriate behavior or affect, impaired ability to carry out goal-directed activities, and impaired ability to test reality adequately (Spitzer & Endicott, 1973, pp. 398–399). The assessment of these psychopathological characteristics involves attention to all the interview interactions discussed in this chapter. For example, in the assessment of subjective distress the interviewer should pay attention to verbal content and also to facial expression and bodily posture. The interviewer could also do content analysis of a segment of the interviewee's speech and note any dysfluencies that occur.

In this last regard, impairment of an interviewee's thought processes may be clearly demonstrated in speech that is unintelligible because it is disorganized. Even in instances of mild impairment, there may be juxtaposition of statement, excessive or unnecessary details, inability to proceed directly to a goal idea, and so on. At times the interviewee, although not showing these obvious speech problems, may report that he or she feels unable to concentrate or that his or her thoughts are racing. Objective and subjective correlates of these kinds are reviewed by Spitzer and Endicott (1973) for each of the psychopathological characteristics they identify. Also noteworthy are the structured interview schedules they have developed for use in research and clinical assessments.

The interviewer must recognize that his or her effect can be psychotherapeutic or psychonoxious. Interviewers must give thought to the personal and professional code of ethics that guides behavior with patients. They must be clear in their minds about the ethical limitations of social, physical, or business contact with patients and about such issues as confidentiality and other patient and institutional rights. They must be aware of personal limitations, inasmuch as no interviewer or therapist has the techniques or the know-how to be successful with all patients, and some should best be referred to other clinicians. Interviewers should have learned to listen carefully with full attention, so that their comments will follow directly from what the interviewees have been saying. The interviewee must be allowed an opportunity to have his or her full say, which usually means an uninterrupted opportunity to review the presenting complaint. It is also imperative to know how the interviewee is using specific words and to obtain precise descriptions of disturbances and complaints, so that it is possible to have behavioral referents for the patient's expressed feelings.

In summarizing the purposes of the initial clinical interview, it should be noted that they are to gather information about the patient and the patient's problems that is not available from other sources, to establish a relationship with the patient that will facilitate assessment and treatment, to give the patient an understanding of his or her psychopathological behavior, and to support and direct the patient in his or her search for relief.

The Patient Approaches the Interview

Most patients probably have some stereotyped concept of the interviewer as a "shrink," "mind reader," or something else more or less flattering. It is important to assess sensitively the patient's attitudes from initial behaviors, such as whether the patient is eager, distrustful, vigorous, feeling coerced, or whatever. Often it is useful to ascertain what the patient was told when referred and with what expectations or preparatory set he or she has come in. Many patients coming to see a psychologist implicitly or explicitly have concerns that they may be judged to be "crazy." In addition, each patient probably has his or her own enduring readiness for certain interview behavior; for example, the self-pitying neurotic may talk endlessly about bad luck, illnesses, and the overwhelming nature of his or her problems.

By and large the interviewer should assume that there is no such person as an unmotivated patient; it is better to view the task as that of attempting a match of interviewer and interviewee motivations. There is always a reason (motivation) for the patient's having appeared to be interviewed. Admittedly, there are times when the only definable motivation appears to be curiosity about what the psychologist will say or do, but it is up to the interviewer to nurture whatever motivation is present. Not infrequently the patient tries to shift responsibility for further treatment or change to the interviewer, in which case it is useful to stress the concept of mutual participation. Some interviewers and therapists even model, sometimes by film, the appropriate role behaviors of a patient in the interview. Such a procedure certainly calls attention to the fact that roles are learned; in fact, there seem to be few inherent or instinctive "patient behaviors."

The Interviewer Approaches the Interview

There are perhaps a few people who still think that what the patient does is independent of the stimulus value of the interviewer, but probably not very many. It behooves each interviewer to know the usual patient responses he or she elicits. Knowing their own stimulus value, interviewers can better focus full attention on their patients and take every opportunity to observe their patients rather than themselves. There can be role problems for the interviewer, particularly with regard to personal curiosity, decision making, judging, being the saintly helper, and so forth. Above all, however, objectivity must be maintained. interviewers must constantly keep one foot in reality and not become completely caught up in the terrors or delights of the patient's world. If the patient has an emotional outburst, it is up to the interviewer to remember or try to understand what precipitated the emotional outburst, including whatever stimulus he or she presented.

It is not uncommon in an interview situation for the patient to cry while giving personal history. This may embarrass the interviewer and make him or her sufficiently uncomfortable to want to move to another area of discussion. Crying, however, signals in most patients an important area for discussion, and the patient should be helped to conduct further exploration in this area. As Enelow and Adler (1972) point out, a time when it is mandatory for the interviewer to remain silent is when the patient has stopped speaking because he or she is overwhelmed or about to be overwhelmed by emotion. Appropriate interviewer silence may allow patients to express the emotion and then go ahead to discuss things they could not bring themselves to discuss before. If, however, patients wish to withhold their feelings, they have the opportunity to do so.

There are instances in which it may be helpful to give patients permission to cry, in a sense, by a comment recognizing how bad they feel or by the nonverbal communication of offering a tissue. The extent to which a patient is helped or the interview facilitated by such a show of emotion depends on the interviewer's ability to facilitate it and on what happens after the emotion has subsided. A supportive response is almost always helpful. For the interviewer not to acknowledge crying and make some accepting comment about it is quite devastating; in the absence of interviewer acknowledgment and acceptance, patients almost always feel that they have made fools of themselves. However, a supportive attitude at such a time with a comment such as "I understand," or "I know that was upsetting" is very helpful in furthering the development of rapport and a working relationship.

Like crying, anger furnishes a valuable clue in the total picture of a patient's response to life stress. This is a situation in which it is highly important for the interviewer not to become angry in return. It is important for the interviewer to recognize the emotion and to consider whether he or she in some way stimulated the anger, or whether it reflects some difficulty or personality trait of the patient. It may be useful for the interviewer in the latter case to recognize that he or she is not the personal target of the patient's anger. It is then easier for the interviewer to avoid retaliating or responding angrily. This restraint in turn facilitates the patient's examination of what he or she is saying and the meaning of his or her feelings in the particular situation. Giving information and accepting the patient's anger are two methods for containing it. It is important for the interviewer not to take it as a personal affront and respond in kind.

The Interview

The initial clinical interview is in many respect the most important encounter between patient and interviewer. In the first place, if it does not fulfill the patient's expectations to some degree, it is likely to be the only interview. It can generally be assumed that this interview should allow the patient maximum spontaneity in self-presentation. Interviewers who ask opening questions such as "What is the situation that brings you here today?" tell patients that they are interested in them and their problems and encourage them to discuss anything they feel may be important. As a rule of thumb, the fewer the interviewer's utterances to keep the patient talking, the better, especially early in the interview. You cannot hear what the patient is saying when you are talking. An open-ended-question approach allows the interviewer to learn quickly which problems the patient considers most important and generates information about the way the patient approaches problems. If the patient can express himself or herself well, very few questions may be necessary.

Allen and Allen (1978), writing for psychiatrists and other health professionals, suggest that the practitioner has five interrelated and overlapping tasks at the first meeting. First, the interviewer must carefully observe the patient to pick up signals as to feelings that the patient is not putting into words. Second, there must be interpersonal contact, that is, responsiveness to each other. Third, the interviewer must try to integrate the available information from the patient and formulate why this particular patient is having this particular kind of problem now. Fourth, the interviewer must arrive at a diagnosis to help describe the patient to himself or herself and others, and to act as a guide to appropriate care. Fifth, the final task is agreement on a treatment plan with the patient and the forging of a therapeutic alliance between patient and interviewer.

Allen and Allen (1978) have many helpful suggestions for the novice (and experienced) interviewer. Regarding observation of the anxious patient, they note that such patients are likely to sit leaning forward, head up, eyes wide open, and eyebrows raised, looking as if they are ready to run. Characteristicaly, anxious patients speak after a short inspiration. When they walk into the examining room, they will probably walk erectly, head pulled up and back, shoulders and torso perpendicular to the floor. Shaking hands, their palms may be cold and wet, their fingers tremulous.

Probably the most common emotional distress that a psychologist is asked to help with is anxiety and depression. Lipp (1977) has suggested that there are four questions that can be used to evaluate anxiety and depression. The first question is "What do *you* think is wrong with you?" It is important to discover what the patient thinks is wrong, and how serious it is thought to be. Although some patients may insist that the interviewer is supposed to have the answer to that question, it is safe to assume that the patient has formulated some answers or hypotheses, and it is important to know what these are to begin to have some ideas about potential sources of anxiety or depression in the patient. The second question to ask is "How much does this condition interfere with your life or your future plans?" For example, if the condition is expected to interfere with the patient's job, what other sources of self-esteem can the patient rely on? It is important to try to understand the personal meaning the presenting problem has for the patient. The third question is "How upsetting is this illness and/or hospitalization for you?" It may be necessary to point out to the patient that coping responses are demanded with his or her condition. This reassurance may be especially needed with patients who may be reluctant to acknowledge their distress. It is important to develop some idea of the patient's level of distress and coping resources. The fourth question is "How much has this gotten you down?" The language of all of these questions can, of course, be tailored to the individual patient. With this last question the interviewer may be able to assess depth of depression, suicidal ideation, and the like. With each of these questions the interviewer's goal is to assess the levels of anxiety and depression and balance them against the patient's coping abilities and resources. All four questions lend themselves to use with virtually all patients the interviewer is likely to encounter (Lipp, 1977, pp. 23–25).

An important behavioral attitude for the interviewer is to encourage patient specificity by frequently asking for examples of the problem situations the patient is describing. If a male patient talks about arguing frequently with his wife, the interviewer does not begin to understand the real nature of the problem until he or she obtains specific examples of two or three actual arguments. If the patient claims to be "nervous." the interviewer should not accept the statement as sufficient but should inquire how he or she experiences this nervousness. An especially useful source of data on functional impairment is to ask the patient for a detailed account of a present typical day and compare this with a detailed typical day before the onset of symptoms. It may be necessary to ask the patient to start this description from the time he or she arises and continue in a step-by-step fashion throughout the day until retiring. Tenacity and firmness are frequently necessary in order to obtain the exact sequence of activities, the time consumed by each, whether this was a solitary time or with whom it was shared, and so forth. It is best to ask about a specific day, usually the one before the day of the interview, as this is often the day most easy to recall.

After completing a review of the chief complaint, the interviewer may profitably ask for an outline of landmarks in life development. This can include such matters as early family circumstances and relationships and the patient's role in the family; illnesses and accidents, especially as they may have affected the patient's relationship to family or peers or his or her self-concept; friendships, separations, and loss of significant others through death or geographical moves; educational successes and failures; marriages, divorces, and children; and work successes and failures. All these events, in outline up to and including the present, can help the interviewer to grasp the kind of major stresses to which the patient has been subjected, the behaviors consistently rewarded or punished, and characteristic methods of fulfilling needs for security, self-esteem, affection, and approval. It should help the interviewer to understand what factors maintain the present maladaptive behaviors, and also help to determine whether there is sufficient variety and challenge in the patient's life situation. Throughout the interview there should be careful attention to possible recurrent themes, because there are usually predictably recurrent, unique problem situations that arise from the patient's pathological life style. In many instances interviewees probably cannot define such themes clearly on their own and have to depend on the interviewers to recognize them and call them to their attention.

Given a conceptual framework, it is generally easier for the interviewer to follow, as they come up, the leads the patient presents for discussion. Given a framework for data collection, the interviewer can conceptually fit information where it belongs, even though it may emerge in random sequence. Maintaining the flow of discussion can involve many of the interviewer tactics discussed in this chapter, including various verbal comments (see, for example, Gilmore, 1973) as well as vocal or nonverbal behaviors. An essential aspect of all of these interviewer tactics is the conveying of empathy, understanding, and sincere interest.

Finally, the patient must be able to anticipate termination of the interview; practically, this is easy to accomplish by the interviewer's pointing out when time is running short (approximately 10 minutes before the end of the interview). This gives opportunity for the patient to bring up any additional topics he or she wants to discuss in that session. Although the interviewer has been summing up periodically during the course of the interview, there needs to be a final summation. Each person who consults an expert expects and is entitled to an expert opinion about his or her situation. Interviewers must summarize with patients their perceptions of the main aspects of the problems that have been presented, including both expressions of emotion and descriptive content, and their recommendations for therapeutic programs or other potentially helpful courses of action. The interviewer and patient should make every effort to achieve a common understanding of the diagnostic formulation and treatment recommendations. If this congruence is not achieved, there is less likelihood of the patient's following through on the recommendations. Part of the summing-up process is to elicit patients' reactions and to stress the importance of their perceptions and feelings and the need for mutuality in planning a therapeutic program.

REFERENCES

Adler, L. M. The social context of the clinical interview. In A. J. Enelow & S. N. Swisher (Eds.), *Interviewing and patient care.* New York: Oxford University Press, 1972.

Allen, J. R., & Allen, B. A. *Guide to psychiatry: A handbook on psychiatry for health professionals.* Garden City, N. Y.: Medical Examination Publishing Company, 1978.

American Psychiatric Association. *Diagnostic and statistical manual of mental disorders: DSM-III.* Washington, D.C.: Authors, 1980.

Anderson, E. G. The seven deadly sins in patient care. *Behavioral Medicine,* 1981, **8,** 16–18.

Argyle, M., & Kendon, A. The experimental analysis of social performance. In L. Berkowitz (Ed.), *Advances in experimental social psychology* (Vol. 3). New York: Academic Press, 1967.

Aronson, H., & Weintraub, W. Personal adaptation as reflected in verbal behavior. In A. W. Siegman & B. Pope (Eds.), *Studies in dyadic communication.* New York: Pergamon Press, 1972.

Berne, E. *Games people play.* New York: Grove Press, 1964.

Birdwhistell, R. L. *Kinesics and context: Essays on body motion communication.* Philadelphia: University of Pennsylvania Press, 1970.

Blocksma, D. D., & Porter, E. H., Jr. A short-term training program in client-centered counseling. *Journal of Consulting Psychology,* 1947, **11,** 55–60.

Chapple, E. D., & Arensberg, C. M. Measuring human relations: An introduction to the study of the interaction of individuals. *Genetic Psychology Monographs,* 1940, **22,** 3–147.

Craig, K. D. Incongruencies between content and temporary measures of patients' responses to confrontation with personality descriptions. *Journal of Consulting Psychology,* 1966, **30,** 550–554.

Davitz, J. R., & Davitz, L. J. The communication of feelings by content-free speech. In S. Weitz (Ed.), *Nonverbal communication.* New York: Oxford University Press, 1974.

DiMatteo, M. R., & DiNicola, D. D. *Achieving patient compliance: The psychology of the medical practitioner's role.* New York: Pergamon Press, 1982.

DiMatteo, M. R., & Taranta, A. Nonverbal communication and physician–patient rapport: An empirical study. *Professional Psychology,* 1976, **10,** 540–547.

Druckman, D., Rozelle, R. M., & Baxter, J. C. *Nonverbal communication: Survey, theory, and research.* Beverly Hills, Calif.: Sage Publications, 1982.

Duncan, S. Nonverbal communication. *Psychological Bulletin,* 1969, **72,** 118–137.

Ekman, P., & Friesen, W. V. The repertoire of nonverbal behavior: Categories, origins, usage, and coding. *Semiotica,* 1969, **1,** 49–98.

Endicott, J., & Spitzer, R. L. A diagnostic interview: The schedule for affective disorders and schizophrenia. *Archives of General Psychiatry,* 1978, **35,** 837–844.

Enelow, A. J., & Adler, L. M. Basic interviewing. In A. J. Enelow & S. N. Swisher (Eds.), *Interviewing and patient care.* New York: Oxford University Press, 1972.

Exline, R. Visual interaction: The glances of power and preference. In S. Weitz (Ed.), *Nonverbal communication.* New York: Oxford University Press, 1974.

Friedman, H. R. Nonverbal communication between patients and medical practitioners. *Journal of Social Issues,* 1979, **35,** 82–99.

Friedman, M. *Pathogenesis of coronary artery disease.* New York: McGraw-Hill, 1969.

Gilmore, S. K. *The counselor-in-training.* New York: Appleton-Century-Crofts, 1973.

Goldman-Eisler, F. *Psycholinguistics: Experiments in spontaneous speech.* New York: Academic Press, 1968.

Greenspan, S. I. *The clinical interview of the child.* New York: McGraw-Hill, 1981.

Harper, R. G., Wiens, A. N., & Matarazzo, J. D. *Nonverbal communication: The state of the art.* New York: Wiley, 1978.

Hall, E. T. *The hidden dimension.* New York: Doubleday, 1966.

Heller, K. Interview structure and interview style in initial interviews. In A. W. Siegman & B. Pope (Eds.) *Studies in dyadic communication.* New York: Pergamon Press, 1972.

Hetherington, E. M. Girls without fathers. *Psychology Today,* 1973, **3,** 46–52.

Ivey, A. E. *Microcounseling: Innovations in interning.* Springfield, Ill.: Charles C. Thomas, 1971.

Johnson, W. R. Basic interviewing skills, In C. E. Walker (Ed.). *Clinical practice of psychology.* New York: Pergamon Press, 1981.

Kadushin, A. *The social work interview.* New York: Columbia University Prress, 1972.

Kahn, R. L., & Cannell, C. F. *The dynamics of interviewing: Theory, technique, and cases.* New York: Wiley, 1961.

Kanfer, F. H. Verbal rate, eyeblink and content in structured psychiatric interviews. *Journal of Abnormal and Social Psychology,* 1960, **61,** 341–347.

Kanfer, F. H., & Phillips, J. S. *Learning foundations of behavior therapy.* New York: Wiley, 1970.

Kanfer, F. H., Phillips, J. S., Matarazzo, J. D., & Saslow, G. Experimental modification of interviewer content in standardized interviews. *Journal of Consulting Psychology,* 1960, **24,** 528–536.

Kanfer, R., Eyberg, S. M., & Krahn, G. L. Interviewing strategies in child assessment. In C. E. Walker & M. C. Roberts (Eds.), *Handbook of clinical child psychology.* New York: Wiley, 1982.

Kasl, S. V., & Mahl, G. F. The relationship of disturbances and hesitations in spontaneous speech to anxiety. *Journal of Personality and Social Psychology,* 1965, **1,** 425–433.

Kinzel, A. F. Body-buffer zone in violent prisoners. *American Journal of Psychiatry,* 1970, **127,** 59–64.

Lipp, M. R. *Respectful treatment: The human side of medical care.* Hagerstown: Harper & Row, 1977.

Maccoby, E. E., & Maccoby, N. The interview: A tool of social science. In G. Lindzey (Ed.), *Handbook of social psychology.* Reading, Mass.: Addison-Wesley, 1954.

Mahl, G. F. Gestures and body movements in interviews. In J. Schlien, H. Hunt, J. D. Matarazzo, & C. Savage (Eds.), *Research in psychotherapy* (Vol. 3). Washington, D.C.: American Psychological Association, 1968.

Mahl, G. F. People talking when they can't hear their voices. In A. W. Siegman & B. Pope (Eds.). *Studies in dyadic communication.* New York: Pergamon Press, 1972.

Manaugh, T. S., Wiens, A. N., & Matarazzo, J. D. Content saliency and interviewee speech behavior. *Journal of Clinical Psychology,* 1970, **26,** 17–24.

Matarazzo, J. D., & Wiens, A. N. *The interview: Research on its anatomy and structure.* Chicago:Aldine-Atherton, 1972.

Matarazzo, J. D., Wiens, A. N., Jackson, R. H., & Manaugh, T. S. Interviewee speech behavior under conditions of endogenously-present and exogenously-induced motivational states. *Journal of Clinical Psychology,* 1970, **26,** 141–148.(a)

Matarazzo, J. D., Wiens, A. N., Jackson, R. H., & Manaugh, T. S. Interviewee speech behavior under different content conditions. *Jounral of Applied Psychology,* 1970, **54,** 15–26.(b)

Matarazzo, J. D., Wiens, A. N., Matarazzo, R. G., & Saslow, G. Speech and silence behavior in clinical psychotherapy and its laboratory correlates. In J. Shlien, H. Hunt, J. D. Matarazzo, & C. Savage (Eds.), *Research in psychotherapy* (Vol. 3). Washington, D.C.: American Psychological Association, 1968.

Matarazzo, J. D., Wiens, A. N., Saslow, G., Dunham, R. M., & Voas, R. B. Speech durations of astronaut and ground communicator. *Science,* 1964, **143,** 148–150.

Matarazzo, R. G. Research on the teaching and learning of psychotherapeutic skills. In S. L. Garfield & A. E. Bergin (Eds.), *Handbook of psychotherapy and behavior change: An empirical analysis* (2nd ed.) New York: Wiley, 1978.

Mehrabian, A. *Nonverbal communication.* Chicago: Aldine-Atherton, 1972.

Mehrabian, A., & Wiener, M. Decording of inconsistent communication. *Journal of Personality and Social Psychology,* 1967, **6,** 109–114.

Meier, A. The research diagnostic criteria: Historical background, development, validity, and reliability. *Canadian Journal of Psychiatry,* 1979, **24,** 167–178.

Miller, G. A. Statistical indicators of style. In N. N. Markel (Ed.), *Psycholinguistics: An introduction to the study of speech and personality.* Homewood, Ill.: Dorsey Press, 1969.

Miller, G. A. *Communication, language, and meaning.* New York: Basic Books, 1973.

Milmoe, S., Novey, M. S., Kagan, J., & Rosenthal, R. The mother's voice: Postdictor of her baby's behavior. In S. Weitz (Ed.), *Nonverbal communication.* New York: Oxford University Press, 1974.

Milmoe, S., Rosenthal, R., Blane, H. T., Chafetz, M. E., & Wolf, I. The doctor's voice: Postdictor of successful referral of alcoholic patients. In S. Weitz (Ed.), *Nonverbal communication.* New York: Oxford University Press, 1974.

Molde, D. A., & Wiens, A. N. Interview interaction behavior of nurses with task versus person orientation. *Nursing Research,* 1968, **17,** 45–51.

Morganstern, K. P., & Tevlin, H. E. Behavioral interviewing. In M. Hersen & A. S. Bellack (Eds.), *Behavioral assessment: A practical handbook* (2nd ed.). New York: Pergamon Press, 1981.

Moses, J. L., & Byham, W. C. *Applying the assessment center method.* New York: Pergamon Press, 1977.

Nathan, P. E., Schneller, P., & Lindsley, O. R. Direct measurement of communication during psychiatric admission interviews. *Behavior Research and Therapy,* 1964, **2,** 49–57.

Patterson, C. H. Relationship therapy and/or behavior therapy. *Psychotherapy: Theory, Research, and Practice,* 1968, **5,** 226–233.

Peterson, D. R. *The clinical study of social behavior.* New York: Appleton-Century-Crofts, 1968.

Pope, B. *The mental health interview: Research and application.* New York: Pergamon Press, 1979.

Pope, B., Blass, T., Siegman, A. W., & Raher, J. Anxiety and depression in speech. *Journal of Consulting and Clinical Psychology,* 1970, **35,** 128–133.

Pope, B., Siegman, A. W., & Blass, T. Anxiety and speech in the initial interview. *Journal of Consulting and Clinical Psychology.* 1970. **35,** 233–238.

Porter, E. H. *An introduction to therapeutic counseling.* Boston: Houghton-Mifflin, 1950.

Ramsay, R. W. Speech patterns and personality. *Language and Speech,* 1968, **11,** 54–63.

Rankin, P. T. The importance of listening ability. *The English Journal,* 1928, **27,** 623–630.

Ray, M. L., & Webb, E. J. Speech duration effects in the Kennedy news conferences, *Science,* 1966, **153,** 899–901.

Richardson, S. A., Dohrenwend, B. S., & Klein, D. *Interviewing: Its forms and functions.* New York: Basic Books, 1965.

Rosenthal, R. *Experimenter effects in behavioral research.* New York: Appleton-Century-Crofts, 1966.

Saslow, G., & Matarazzo, J. D. A technique for studying changes in interview behavior, In E. A. Rubenstein & M. B. Parloff (Eds.), *Research in psychotherapy* (Vol. 1) Washington, D.C.: American Psychological Association, 1959.

Scheflen, A. E. *Body language and social order: Communication as behavioral control.* Englewood Cliffs, N.J.: Prentice-Hall, 1972.

Selzer, M. L. The use of first names in psychotherapy. In H. M. Ruitenbeek (Ed.), *The analytic situation: How patient and therapist communicate.* Chicago: Aldine, 1973.

Siegman, A. W., & Pope, B. Personality variables associated with productivity and verbal fluency in the initial interview. *Proceedings of the 73rd Annual Convention of the American Psychological Association,* 1965, 273.

Siegman, A. W., & Pope, B. The effects of ambiguity and anxiety on interviewee verbal behavior. In A. W. Siegman & B. Pope (Eds.), *Studies in dyadic communication.* New York: Pergamon Press, 1972.

Slobin, D. I., Miller, S. H., & Porter, L. W. Forms of address and social relations in a business organization. In S. Moscovici (Ed.), *The psychosociology of language.* Chicago: Markham, 1972.

Spitzer, R. L., & Endicott, J. The value of the interview for the evaluation of psychopathology. In M. Hammer, K. Salzinger, & S. Sutton (Eds.) *Psychopathology: Contributions from the social, behavioral, and biological sciences.* New York: Wiley, 1973.

Spitzer, R. L., Endicott, J., & Robins, E. Clinical criteria for diagnosis and DSM-III. *American Journal of Psychiatry,* 1975, **132,** 1187–1192.

Spitzer, R. L., Endicott, J., & Robins, E. Research diagnostic criteria rationale and reliability. *Archives of General Psychiatry,* 1978, **35,** 773–782.

Strupp, H. Psychotherapy revisited: The problem of outcome. *Psychotherapy: Theory, Research and Practice,* 1963, **1,** 1–13.

Truax, C. B. Length of therapist response, accurate empathy and patient improvement. *Journal of Clinical Psychology.* 1970, **26,** 539–541.

Tyler, L. E. *The work of the counselor* (3rd ed.). New York: Appleton-Century-Crofts, 1969.

Walters, B. *How to talk with practically anybody about practically anything.* New York: Dell, 1970.

Weintraub, W. *Verbal behavior: Adaptation and psychopathology.* New York: Springer Publishing, 1981.

Weitz, S. Attitude, voice, and behavior: A repressed affect model of interacial interaction. *Journal of Personality and Social Psychology,* 1972, **24,** 14–21.

Wiens, A. N. The assessment interview. In I. B. Weiner (Ed.), *Clinical methods in psychology.* New York: Wiley, 1976.

Wiens, A. N., Matarazzo, J. D., Saslow, G., Thompson, S. M., & Matarazzo, R. G. Interview interaction behavior of supervisors, head nurses and staff nurses. *Nursing Research,* 1965, **14,** 322–329.

Wolf, S., & Goodell, H. Behavioral science in clinical medicine. Springfield, Ill.: Charles C. Thomas, 1976.

CHAPTER 2

Rorschach Assessment

JOHN E. EXNER, JR.

The 10 Swiss inkblots that constitute the stimuli of the Rorschach test were first unveiled to the professional public in 1921, with the release of Rorschach's classic monograph, *Psychodiagnostik*. Since that time the test has stimulated great interest, extensive use, and considerable research. For at least two decades, the 1940s and 1950s, its name was almost synonomous with the term *clinical psychology*. Those were years when the primary role of the clinician focused on assessment or psycho-diagnostics. But even as the role of the clinician broadened and diversified during the 1960s and 1970s, the Rorschach remained among the most commonly used psychological tests in the clinical setting, as it continues to be today. It is a test from which considerable information about a subject can be derived, if it is properly administered and interpreted. Some of this information is relevant to diagnostic decisions; some can be important to intervention planning; some may be used to make predictions; but most provides descriptive information about the psychologi-cal characteristics of the subject.

Although the test has become an integral part of clinical psychology, its develop-ment has frequently been marked by controversy. It has often proved to be baffling to the researcher and an irritant to those who have advocated the stringent applica-tion of psychometric principles to any psychological test. The ranks of those critical of the test swelled considerably through the 1950s and 1960s, and many urged its abandonment as a test in the clinical setting (Jensen, 1958; Zubin, Eron, & Schumer, 1965). Some of the criticisms leveled at the Rorschach and its use were clearly justified. Many Rorschach advocates had overestimated its usefulness, and some had even likened it to a magical X-ray of the mind in spite of an increasing number of publications concerning the test that reported negative findings for such important issues as diagnostic accuracy, reliability, and validity. On the other hand, many of the criticisms of the test were unjust, often springing from bias, ignorance, or misunderstanding. Considerable research published during the 1970s and 1980s has served to shed new light on the test that has diminished criticism of it and led to some resurgence in its use as an important clinical tool. Much of this newer research has focused on what the test is and what it is not, as well as on the psychological operations or processes that it evokes. It may seem strange that nearly 60 years elapsed after the publication of Rorschach's monograph before these important issues began to be addressed in some depth, but in effect, that is what happened, and for many reasons.

HISTORY OF THE RORSCHACH

Rorschach did not conceive of his work, published in *Psychodiagnostik,* as having yielded a test per se. Instead, he regarded this monograph as a report of his findings from an investigation in perception that he believed might ultimately lend itself to a sophisticated diagnostic approach. Although he used inkblots as his stimulus figures, this idea was not original with him. There had been many attempts to use inkblots as some form of test well before Rorschach began his experiments. Binet and Henri had tried to incorporate them into their early efforts to develop an intelligence test (1895, 1896). They believed that the inkblot stimuli might be useful in studying visual imagination, but they abandoned their effort because of problems they encountered in group administration. Several other investigators, in both the United States and Europe, wrote about the use of inkblot stimuli to study imagination and creativeness (Dearborn, 1897, 1898; Kirkpatrick, 1900; Rybakov, 1911; Pyle, 1913, 1915; Whipple, 1914; Parsons, 1917).

It is doubtful that any of this work stimulated Rorschach's original study, but it is very probable that he became familiar with much of it before he wrote his monograph. Nevertheless the seed of his idea developed somewhat serendipitously. As a young psychiatric resident in 1911, he found himself besieged with patient management problems. On a day away from work, he visited a long-time friend who had become a teacher at a local intermediate school. The friend, Konrad Gehring, was teaching a class of adolescent boys who were somewhat obstreperous. Gehring found that if he contracted with his students to work for a period of time and then be permitted to play a very popular game, his management problems were reduced significantly. The game which was called Blotto, had been flourishing in Europe for nearly 100 years by that time and was popular with both children and adults. Inkblots could be purchased easily in many stores, or they could be and often were created by players of the game. Sometimes the game was played by creating poems to go with the blots. In other variations the blots were used in the game of charades, or people would simply describe what they could see in the blots.

It was the patient management potential that caused Rorschach to hang blots on his ward and encourage patients to play the game. This was the same year in which Eugen Bleuler published his famous work *Dementia Praecox,* in which the term *schizophrenia* was first coined. Bleuler's concepts were very intriguing to the professional community and they posed the important issue of how to differentiate schizophrenics from patients with an organically induced dementia. As almost a passing matter, Rorschach noted that many of the patients on his ward who had been identified as schizophrenic seemed to respond to the Blotto game quite differently from other patients. He made a brief report on this to a local psychiatric society, but little interest was expressed in his apparent finding. He did not pursue the matter for several years. He married and after completing his residency practiced for a short time in Moscow and then returned to Switzerland.

It was not until 1917 that Rorschach decided on a systematic collection of data using inkblots as the stimuli. It seems probable that his decision was influenced by a publication of Hens (1917), who reported on the use of inkblots with children, normal adults, and patients. Hens suggested a classification system for the content of inkblot responses that might be diagnostically useful; this approach was very different from the approach that Rorschach had conceived. It seems clear that he was familiar with the literature on perception and intrigued with the concepts of Ach, Mach, Loetze, and Helmholtz, especially with the notion of an *apperceptive mass*. This notion is pervasive in much of his writing concerning his findings.

Rorschach used about 40 blots in his investigation and ultimately collected data on 405 subjects, of whom 117 were nonpatients that he subdivided into "educated" and "noneducated" groups. The sample also included 188 schizophrenics, who were really his target population. In accord with his 1911 observations, the schizophrenic group did respond very differently while playing the Blotto game. Rorschach was very creative in his awareness of the need to show some statistical differentiation across his groups, and, following largely from the work of the Gestaltists (mainly Wertheimer), he decided to establish codes that would reveal some of the differences in responding. One set of codes, or scores as they have come to be called, was used to reflect the area of the blot that was used in the response; for instance, *W* stands for the whole blot, *D* for large detail areas of the blot, and *Dd* for small or unusual blot areas. A second set of codes concerned the features of the blot that were mainly responsible for creating the image perceived, for instance, *F* for form, *C* for color, *M* for the impression of movement, and so on. The third set of codes comprised abbreviations for the content of the answer, such as *H* for human, *A* for animal, *An* for anatomy, and so on.

By early 1921 the sample sizes of Rorschach's groups were sufficient for him to demonstrate that his inkblot method could be diagnostically useful, especially in identifying schizophrenic disorder. He had also discovered that clusterings or high frequencies of certain kinds of responses, mainly movement or color responses, appeared to relate to distinctive kinds of psychological and/or behavioral characteristics. Thus the method seemed to have both a diagnostic potential and the potential for detecting features of the person that in contemporary psychological terminology would be called personality traits or styles.

Many of Rorschach's colleagues were enthusiastic about his experiment, particularly its diagnostic potential, and encouraged him to publish his findings in a form which others could use to learn the method. This encouragement led to the writing of his monograph, but two events were to blunt the impact of this brilliant research effort. First, no one wanted to publish the monograph. It was only through the extensive effort of one of Rorschach's close psychiatric colleagues, Walter Morgenhaler, that a publisher, the House of Bircher, was located. Bircher agreed to do the monograph, but he rebelled at the notion of reproducing all of the blots with which Rorschach had experimented. A compromise was struck. The monograph would focus only on the 10 blots that Rorschach had used most frequently and consistently in his data collection. It does seem certain that Rorschach had faith that these 10 had the greatest stimulus value to provoke the sorts of differentiations that he had discovered. But then a second problem occurred. For reasons unknown, the 10 blots were reproduced with very marked differences in the saturation levels of the coloring. These differences in shading made the stimulus figures very different from the fully saturated blots that Rorschach had been using. Rorschach's own creativeness solved the problem. He was intrigued with the stimulus properties of the multishaded blots and decided to use them in his further experimentation.

Rorschach decided to call his method a Form Interpretation Test, but he always cautioned that his findings were preliminary and required much more experimentation. And so the monograph was published, together with inkblots different from those about which it was written. But Rorschach was not at all discouraged by a new set of blots. Quite the contrary, he was truly excited with them, as they added another stimulus dimension that might broaden the range of differentiating responses. He was eager to set forth collecting more data, but then tragedy struck. He developed acute appendicitis complicated by peritonitis and died in April 1922, only 8 months after the monograph was released. He was only 37 years old and had devoted less than 4 years to his experiment. Had he lived to extend his work, the nature of the test and the direction of its development might have been much different.

The publication of the monograph was a financial disaster. Only a few copies were sold before Rorschach died and before the House of Bircher was to enter bankruptcy. Fortunately, the subsequent auction of Bircher goods left the monograph and the 10 plates in the hands of Verlag Hans Huber, a large and highly respected publishing house in Bern. Huber continued to produce the monograph and the blots, and still does today. However, the fact that Rorschach was no longer alive as well as the fact that there was a new set of 10 blots posed significant problems for those who would try to continue his work. And that was only the beginning of the difficulties surrounding Rorschach's work.

THE RORSCHACH SYSTEMS

Although Rorschach's colleagues continued to use his method after his death, none followed the systematic empirical approach to data collection as Rorschach had. Instead, the focus was on clinical applications and differential diagnosis. Rorschach deliberately avoided theorizing about the nature of his method and cautioned repeatedly in the monograph about the limitations of content analysis.

However, this did not deter many users of the test from trying to apply it more directly to the increasingly popular Freudian theory, which at that time was probably the most compelling innovation in psychiatry.

Three of Rorschach's close friends and colleagues became the strongest advocates of the Form Interpretation Test, which they began to call Rorschach's Test. They were Walter Morgenthaler, who had been instrumental in finding a publisher for the monograph, Emil Oberholzer, and Georgi Roemer. Originally, they based their advocacy on the premise that the method was well suited for the differentiation of schizophrenia, but, like many others in that contemporary psychiatric community, they felt that Rorschach's work was basically incomplete because of the lack of content interpretation. Roemer tried to extend Rorschach's work by using a new set of blots and ultimately formulated many interesting but not well-received positions concerning the test. Morgenthaler and Oberholzer remained faithful to Rorschach's blots and to his method for scoring, but each sought to extend Rorschach's contribution by giving far greater emphasis to the use of the content. Oberholzer in particular was to play an important role in the ultimate expansion of the use and understanding of the test.

Actually, none of the early European Rorschachers exploited the use of content interpretation inordinately, but at the same time none seemed equipped, by reason of understanding or motive, to extend Rorschach's postulates concerning the perceptual properties of the method. No new scores were added to the format until 1932, when Hans Binder published a rather elaborate scheme for scoring the achromatic and shading responses. Unlike Rorschach, however, Binder did not develop his format empirically. Instead it evolved somewhat intuitively and when finally published included a conceptual scheme that was to influence Bruno Klopfer to a considerable extent. But that is getting slightly ahead of the story.

Many people and events were to conspire to determine the expansion and growth of the Rorschach Test. Emil Oberholzer was to become a very central figure during the first phase of that growth. By the mid-1920s he had become a widely recognized psychoanalyst who specialized in work with children. Because of his reputation, a young American psychiatrist, David Levy, petitioned for and received a grant to study with Oberholzer for one year. During his year with Oberholzer, Levy learned about the Rorschach Test and on his return to the United States brought several copies of the blot photos (they were not yet mounted on cardboard) with him with the intent of exploring their use further. Other interests deterred Levy from his intent to use and study the Rorschach Test, but he did publish a translation of one of Oberholzer's papers about it in 1926. At that time Levy had accepted a post as a staff psychiatrist with the Institute of Guidance in New York City. The institute was interdisciplinary and was used as a resource by the New York City schools to serve the needs of children, mainly those whose academic performances were substandard, but it also provided psychiatric consultation and service to disturbed children from the greater New York area. Therefore, it was a natural training facility for students in psychiatry and psychology. What followed would be an effort by five psychologists to extend Rorschach's work.

Samuel J. Beck

In 1927, Samuel J. Beck, who was a graduate student at Columbia University, was awarded a student fellowship at the institute. Typically he worked a few hours a week, learning to administer various tests of intelligence, aptitude, and achievement. By early 1929, Beck was actively searching for a research topic that might be appropriate for a dissertation. In a casual conversation one afternoon, Levy mentioned to Beck that he had brought the Rorschach blots with him when he returned from his studies in Switzerland. Beck became intrigued with the test and, with Levy's encouragement, broached the idea of a standardization study to his dissertation advisor, the famous experimental psychologist Robert S. Woodworth. Woodworth was not aware of Rorschach's work but was familiar with some of the experiments of the Gestaltists, particularly Wertheimer, in which inkblots were used as part of the stimulus field. After reviewing the test with Beck, Woodworth agreed that a standardization study using children might be a valuable contribution to the literature on individual differences. Thus, nearly 7 years after Rorschach's death, the first systematic investigation concerning his test was initiated, and Beck was to find himself launched on a career that was to make him one of the truly great figures in the Rorschach Test story.

Marguerite R. Hertz

It took Beck nearly 3 years to complete his study, which involved testing almost 150 children. During that period he maintained contact with two close friends whom he had first met while working as a newspaper reporter in Cleveland some 10 years earlier. They were Ralph and Marguerite Hertz. It was shortly after Beck began his investigation that the Hertzes visited New York. At that time Marguerite Hertz was a psychology graduate student, studying at Western Reserve University. Beck shared some of his notions about the Rorschach test, and Hertz was quick to recognize the enormous potential that the method held. As a result, she also petitioned to do her dissertation about the test, and her study, which was similar to Beck's but with several variations in sampling, earned her the first doctorate in psychology granted by Western Reserve. The Beck and Hertz studies were completed by 1932. After graduating, Hertz became involved in a very elaborate multidisciplinary study of children at the Brush Foundation in Cleveland, while Beck accepted a joint position at the Boston Psychopathic Hospital and Harvard Medical School.

If at that time one were to have attempted to predict the future of the Rorschach Test it is doubtful that one would have foreseen any controversy. Both Beck and Hertz were trained in empirically oriented psychology programs, and many of the findings of their studies were very similar, as were most of their conclusions. But events of the world would ultimately alter this harmonious situation, the most significant event being the rise to power of Adolf Hitler in Germany and the chaos and destruction that would ensue.

Bruno Klopfer

During the early 1930s, one of those who was markedly affected by the power of the Nazis in Germany was Bruno Klopfer. Klopfer had completed his Ph.D. degree in 1922 at the University of Munich. He was a specialist in children and focused much of his work on the emotional problems of children as related to their academic progress or lack thereof. He ultimately became a senior staff member at the Berlin

Information Center for Child Guidance, a unit very similar to the Institute for Child Guidance in New York where Beck did most of his research. Unlike Beck, who by 1932 had become deeply interested in the test and its use, Klopfer had no interest in the Rorschach. His training and subsequent orientation were essentially phenomenological, and his abiding interest was in Freudian and Jungian psychoanalytic theories. In fact, he had begun personal analysis in 1927 and training analysis in 1931 with the intent of becoming a practicing analyst. By 1933 the many directives from the government to the Berlin Information Center for Child Guidance concerning studies on and services for Aryan and non-Aryan children, as well as the ever-increasing pressures on Jews, led Klopfer to decide to flee the country. Klopfer's analyst, Werner Heilbrun, contacted many professionals outside Germany, seeking assistance for him. One who was willing to help was Carl Jung, who promised a position for Klopfer if he could reach Zurich, which he did during 1933.

The position that Jung found for Klopfer was that of a technician at the Zurich Psychotechnic Institute, a facility committed mainly to psychological testing, much of which was administered to candidates for various types of employment. The Rorschach Test was among those used routinely, and Klopfer was therefore taught how to administer and score it by another technician, Alice Garbasky. During that time he also became intrigued with some of the postulates offered by Rorschach in the monograph *Psychodiagnostik,* but he did not become strongly interested in teaching or using the method; his first love remained psychoanalysis. His stay in Zurich gave him the opportunity for considerable personal experience with Jung, but the position of a technician was a far cry from the more prestigious appointments he had held previously. After many letters to many places, Klopfer was finally offered and accepted at Columbia University. He immigrated to the United States in early 1934. Interestingly, this was just shortly after Beck had gone to Switzerland under a Rockefeller Fellowship to study for a year with Emil Oberholzer. Beck hoped that his journey would lead him to a better understanding of Rorschach's work and especially of his thinking concerning the use of the multi-shaded blots that had been produced with the publication of the monograph.

By 1934, Beck had already published nine articles concerning the Rorschach Test describing its potential merits for the study of personality organization and individual differences. The first three of these appeared before Beck completed his dissertation, so that by 1934 considerable interest had developed about the test in both psychology and psychiatry in the United States. Interest here had now begun to parallel that which had evolved in Europe during the first decade after Rorschach's death. But whereas on most of the European continent the test had gradually gained widespread use, the American student of the test was faced with two problems. First, Rorschach's monograph was not easily available, and, if it was located, knowledge of German was required, as it was not to be translated into English until 1941. The second and more difficult obstacle was the fact that there were very few opportunities to learn the tactics of administration and scoring and the principles of interpretation. Hertz did some training in Cleveland as did Beck at Harvard, and when Levy left New York to head the children's unit at Michael Reese Hospital in

Chicago in 1933, he trained a few technicians to administer the test, but still, it was not uncommon for the interested student to experience frustration in his or her attempts to learn to use it. This situation would have a major impact on Bruno Klopfer and ultimately cause him to become one of the most significant Rorschach figures.

In 1934, some of the graduate students at Columbia learned that Klopfer had gained considerable experience with the test in Zurich, and they petitioned their department chairman, Woodworth, for a seminar about the test to be conducted by this new research associate in anthropology. Woodworth was reluctant to undertake the administrative complexities of arranging a joint appointment for a relative unknown to his department, and he suggested that he would try instead to arrange for some training by Beck after Beck's return from Switzerland. But the students were not be be deterred from their interest, and they enticed Klopfer to begin an informal seminar in his apartment two evenings each week. Klopfer agreed to do so with the proviso that at least seven students would participate, each paying a very small stipend for the 6 weeks of seminar.

It was Klopfer's intention to provide the fundamentals of administration and scoring during the first informal seminar, but that objective was subverted by the incompleteness of Rorschach's work. At almost every meeting, when participants discussed various responses that they had collected in their practice with the test, the lack of precise designations for various blot areas and the lack of a more elaborate set of scores or codes to differentiate the variety of answers that emphasized the shading of the blots led to debates that might last well into the night. Klopfer readily perceived that the future of the test could hinge on the resolution of these kinds of problems. Fortunately, he was a masterful teacher and an excellent organizer, and his own rekindled excitement about the test and the challenge posed by its incompleteness soon spread to those around him. The first seminar led to a second and a third, and by 1935 Klopfer was devoting most of his time to the test.

It is very important to note that Klopfer manifested his commitment to the test at a time in which the profession was, at best, cautious about innovations. American psychology looked askance on phenomenology in those years, having established itself as closely allied with the demanding traditions of "pure science." Behaviorism was the byword, and anyone willing to depart from the rigors of empiricism or unwilling to accept its tenets would be regarded with a somewhat jaundiced eye. This was to create a problem for Klopfer, but even more so for the development of the test.

Klopfer was quick to recognize the need to disseminate information about the Rorschach, especially as in each of his seminars new scores were adopted or new formulations about the test evolved. In 1936, he began to publish a mimeographed newsletter that he called *Rorschach Research Exchange,* which was later to become the *Journal of Projective Techniques* and ultimately the *Journal of Personality Assessment.* Although its basic purpose was to provide updates concerning the test development going on in the many seminars that he conducted, Klopfer also hoped that it could serve as a vehicle to share data, ideas, and experiences about the test.

He invited Beck, Levy, Hertz, and Oberholzer to contribute and anticipated that a dialogue among those who were experienced in using and researching the test would stimulate much more rapid development. But this was not to be.

Early Controversy

Shortly before the first issue of the *Exchange* appeared, an article was published by Beck (1936) in another journal that was highly critical of some of the Swiss psychiatrists who were applying Rorschach's test in ways that Beck felt were far too subjective. As he had done in previous articles, Beck pointed to the need for careful, systematic investigation that would lead to fixed standards for administration, scoring, and interpretation. It is not surprising, in light of his firm position, that Beck reacted to Klopfer's movement to expand the scoring format for the test with marked coolness. There is no question that the scoring format that the Klopfer group developed, which was presented in the first issue of the *Exchange* (Klopfer & Sender, 1936), was well organized and carefully thought through. But the absence of any data base, plus the fact that the format diversified the scoring well beyond points that Rorschach had defined and/or that Beck had explored, made the new format's acceptance at best difficult and at worst impossible for anyone with an empirical interest in the test.

Things went from bad to potentially disastrous in early 1937 when Beck's first book on the Rorschach, *Introduction to the Rorschach Method,* was released. Beck arranged for Klopfer to receive a prepublication copy of the book, which was the first monograph of the American Orthopsychiatric Association and was later to become known as Beck's Manual. Klopfer decided to devote a major segment of an article that he wrote for a later issue of the first volume of the *Exchange* (Klopfer, 1937) to a review of Beck's Manual. As might be expected, it was more negative than positive, and it naturally provoked a reply from Beck that was published in the second volume of the *Exchange* (Beck, 1937). That article, "Some Rorschach Problems," was very critical of the Klopfer approach and clearly documented the fact that a major schism existed between the two orientations. In the next issue of the *Exchange* a series of comments on the Beck article was published, most of which were written by followers of Klopfer or by those who favored his orientation. Obviously, most were highly critical of Beck and some were openly hostile, and collectively they only served to strengthen Beck's resolve.

Marguerite Hertz was dismayed by the Beck–Klopfer controversy, but she could not avoid being caught up in it. Her initial enthusiasm for the test never waned after her first contact with it, and, like Beck, she was among the earliest to identify the need for further development of the test. She responded positively to Klopfer's first efforts to create a consolidated approach to studying the test, but, like Beck, she was strongly committed to careful investigation. Thus, when the Beck–Klopfer schism was brought out in the *Exchange,* she attempted to take the role of a mediator by publishing an article in one of the 1937 issues that cited the limited data base from which Beck had drawn conclusions and at the same time criticized the Klopfer group for "refining scoring to the extent of becoming involved in a maze of symbols." Hertz quickly found herself unable to agree fully with Beck's conservatism but also unable to commit herself to the more intuitive approach to Klopfer. Periodically, she would issue pleas for reconciliation and compromise (Hertz, 1939, 1941, 1952).

By the late 1930s, the schism between Beck and Klopfer had become irreconcilable, and no further communication, verbal or written, was to occur. After his return from Switzerland, Beck decided to join his old mentor, David Levy, at the Michael Reese Hospital in Chicago, and he also accepted a position on the faculty at the University of Chicago. Klopfer remained in New York, at Columbia and the City Univeristy of New York, and at the end of World War II moved to California, eventually taking a professorship at the University of California in Los Angeles. Hertz remained in Cleveland as a professor at Western Reserve University. In effect, they went their own ways and developed the Rorschach in accord with their particular theoretical and/or empirical biases. As a consequence, the Rorschach became fragmented into three separate systems. But that was not the end of the diversification of the test.

Zygmunt Piotrowski

One of the participants in Klopfer's first seminar was a young postdoctoral fellow from the Neuropsychiatric Institute in New York.

He had been trained as an experimental psychologist, receiving his Ph.D. in 1927 from the University of Poznan in Poland. This was Zygmunt Piotrowski. He had intended to broaden his education by studying at various schools throughout the scientific world and, after obtaining his degree, had studied at the Sorbonne in Paris and then accepted a position as an instructor at the Columbia University College of Physicians and Surgeons. A subject for someone learning to administer the Rorschach while still a graduate student, he had a vague idea of the context of the test but little interest in it. His main purpose in coming to the United States was to learn more about neurology, since he was very interested in the development of symbolic logic. Thus it was a somewhat casual decision that took him to Klopfer's first Rorschach seminar. The subject matter intrigued him, but he was less interested in the development of the test than he was in how the test data might differentiate creative from uncreative people and how those with neurological dysfunction might perform on this seemingly ambiguous task. Piotrowski continued a close relationship with Klopfer until the Beck criticisms called his attention to the lack of research about the method. Gradually, he backed away from the Klopfer group and devoted himself to studies of the neurologically impaired under the tutelage of Kurt Goldstein, with the intent of returning to his homeland in 1939. The invasion of Poland by Germany altered his course, and he accepted a position at the Jefferson Medical School in Philadelphia where he was able to continue his studies of the neurologically impaired and at the same time pursue much of his own thinking about the Rorschach. By 1957 he had developed an elaborate framework with which to approach the test, published in his well-known book, *Perceptanalysis,* in which he attempted to integrate his own hard-won wisdoms concerning perceptual interpretation into an understanding and interpretive approach to the test. Thus a fourth approach to the Rorschach came into being.

David Rapaport

There was still one more figure who would have a significant impact on the development of the Rorschach in the United States. This was David Rapaport. Like so many others of his time, Rapaport fled Europe in 1938, shortly after completing his Ph.D. at the Royal Hungarian Petrus at Pazmany. He had studied under Paul von Schiller and consequently had a very strong psychoanalytic orientation. He had had some limited training with the Rorschach in Hungary, but he had no strong commitment to it or to other psychological tests. His forte was theory, and primary among his professional dreams was to augment contemporary thinking about the function of the ego in the classic analytic model. After coming to the United States, he worked briefly at the Mount Sinai in New York and then took a position at a state hospital in Oswatomie, Kansas. He accepted the position in Kansas partly because he needed to work but also because it brought him close to the mecca of psychoanalytic thinking and practice in the United States, the Menninger Foundation. His position at Oswatomie afforded him frequent contact with Menninger's, and when Karl Menninger decided to expand a small research unit at the foundation, Rapaport applied for the post and was appointed head of the unit.

Menninger wanted this research unit to focus on issues of diagnosis, especially the use of psychological testing for that purpose. Hence Rapaport put to one side his theoretical interests and devoted himself faithfully during a 5–7 year period to the study of tests, including the Rorschach. He was admittedly ill-equipped for psychometric research, but he had an acute awareness of his own limitations and surrounded himself with a brilliant young staff, most of them psychology graduate students at the University of Kansas, one of whom was Roy Schafer. Rapaport was also aware of the Beck–Klopfer dispute and, being careful to avoid taking sides, he proceeded to study each of several tests using his own logic plus the rapidly increasing bank of knowledge that he gained after arriving in the United States. Ultimately, he was the senior author in a masterfully produced two-volume series, *Diagnostic Psychological Testing* (1946), which focused on the clinical applications of eight psychological tests.

Rapaport's approach to the Rorschach resembled Klopfer's in many ways but was much more influenced by his allegiance to psychoanalytic propositions. Thus, although the two volumes were filled with charts and graphs that highlighted data, the conclusions often neglected or went well beyond those data. Had the Rapaport and Klopfer groups merged their efforts the results might have been much more striking, and some of Rapaport's original methodology might have been thwarted. But this was not to be, and by 1946 the seeds of a fifth approach to the test, one which was markedly incompatible with each of the other four approaches, had been sown. After the publication of the two volumes, Rapaport was to drift away from psychological testing and back to his first love, developing a more detailed theoretical model of ego functioning. However, the system that he had developed was to be reflected in a classic book published in 1954 by his disciple, Roy Schafer. That work, *Psychoanalytic Interpretation in Rorschach Testing* (1954), added considerably to the basic Rapaport approach by focusing extensively on the applications of content analysis to derive a broader picture of the dynamics of the personality.

And so, in a period of slightly more than 20 years (1936 to 1957), five American Rorschach systems had developed. Most of the similarities among them consisted of the features that each had incorporated from Rorschach's original work. Going beyond those features, the systems were very different, so much so in some respects that they defied comparison with respect to many issues of scoring and approaches to interpretation (Exner, 1969). In spite of this, the Rorschach *method* flourished as one of the mainstays in psychodiagnostics. Practitioners and researchers alike tended to ignore the existence of five distinctly different approaches to the method. Either they were not fully cognizant of the breadth of the differences, or they unrealistically minimized them. Most preferred to think that a single test, the Rorschach, existed and could be described in laudatory or critical terms depending on one's perspective. That trend proabably persisted for so long because of another thread that was to tie the systems together by altering the way in which the method was characterized—the notion of *projective* techniques.

THE ISSUE OF PROJECTION AND PROJECTIVE TECHNIQUES

During the first three decades of the twentieth century, applied psychology centered mainly on the use of tests to study intelligence and operations related to intelligence, such as aptitudes, achievement, motor coordination, and the like. Methods devised to study features of personality usually concentrated on single traits, such as introversion, dominance, and flexibility. In instances in which a personality description or diagnosis was called for, a thorough interview and social history provided the bulk of the data (Louttit, 1936). The tests that were used were generally constructed on traditional psychometric principles wherein specific scores could be judged against group means with little or no regard for the contents of responses. Rorschach tried to use that format in his experiment, and those principles clearly marked the early investigations of Beck and Hertz.

At about the same time that Klopfer was beginning his first seminar, Morgan and Murray (1935) introduced the Thematic Apperception Test (TAT), which was based in part on the premise that people reveal something of their own personalities when confronted with an ambiguous social situation. Three years later, Murray (1938) offered an elegant description of how the process of projection operates in an ambiguous stimulus situation. That concept of projection was derived essentially from Freud's (1894, 1896, 1911) basic postulate that a commonly used ego defense is the translation of internally experienced dangers into external dangers, making them easier to deal with. Whereas Freud concentrated on the defensive characteristic of this process, Murray described it as a more "natural" process in which defense, as such, may or may not be relevant. Thus, projection was conceptualized as the tendency of people to be influenced in the cognitive mediation of perceptual inputs by their needs, interests, and overall psychological organization. This concept was neatly crystallized by Frank (1939) in a classic paper in which he coined the term *projective hypothesis* and suggested the label *projective methods* for a variety of techniques useful to the clinician in evoking this kind of action. Obviously, the Rorschach was cited as one technique with this potential.

The *Zeitgeist* of psychology and psychiatry was ripe for this movement, and very quickly the availability of methods such as the Rorschach and TAT began to swing clinicians from an orientation based almost exclusively on nomothetic comparisons toward a more intensive study of the idiography of the person. Psychodynamic theory was gaining ever increasing popularity, and this change in direction, emphasizing the unique needs, interests, conflicts, and styles of the individual, afforded the clinician a new status among professionals. By the early 1940s, case studies, research papers, opinions, and arguments concerning projective techniques were developed. Louttit and Brown (1947) reported that between 1935 and 1946 a 60% turnover occurred among the 20 most frequently used tests in clinical settings. Sundberg (1961), repeating the Louttit and Browne survey with data through 1959, found that between 1935 and 1959 the turnover rate among the 20 most frequently used tests had reached 76%.

In the Louttit and Browne survey the Rorschach and TAT ranked among the 10 most frequently used instruments, ranking fourth and fifth respectively. In the Sundberg survey, they ranked first and fourth respectively. In a more extensive survey by Lubin, Wallis, and Paine (1971), the Rorschach ranked third and the TAT seventh.

Although the data from these surveys provide an indication of the popularity of the Rorschach and of projective techniques in general, they fail to reflect that extensive controversy that has swirled around projective methodology. This long and frequently bitter controversy created a schism among many psychologists interested in measurement, individual differences, and personality assessment, and one of its unfortunate byproducts was a tendency to categorize psychological tests as either objective or projective. This classification scheme implies that objective tests have been developed in accord with fundamental measurement principles and are therefore scorable, have been standardized, and have been demonstrated to have credible reliability and validity. Conversely, the implications regarding projective tests are that they lack some or all of these measurement features and that data derived from them are interpreted more subjectively.

Although there is some truth to these implications, the objective–projective dichotomy itself is grossly oversimplified. Theoretically, any stimulus situation that evokes or facilitates the process of projection, as defined by Murray and Frank, can be considered to be a projective method. This is quite independent of whether or not basic rules of measurement have been employed in developing or establishing the test. In other words, any stimulus situation that *is not structured* to elicit a specific class of response, as are an arithmetic test, true–false inventories, and the like, may be considered a projective technique. For instance, intelligence tests are usually regarded as objective tests because they are well structured and have been developed within a basic measurement framework. However, some intelligence tests include items that permit a relatively open-ended form of response. The comprehension subtest of the Wechsler scales is a good example. The best answer to the question "Why does the state require people to get a license before they get married?" is that it is for purposes of record keeping. "To prevent the scourge of VD from being inflicted on unsuspecting women" is not only a less than satisfactory response but also conveys something about the peculiar interests of the respondent.

Some psychological tests have been deliberately designed to permit a wide latitude of responses. The TAT is obviously one of these. The original Morgan and Murray format for its use included a technique of scoring for needs and presses as they appear in each story, on a scale of 1 to 5. But over the nearly 50 years since its publication, approaches to the use and interpretation of the TAT have proliferated widely. By the late 1940s, at least 20 different approaches had been published, ranging from the strictly qualitative, which emphasizes content analysis, to those that are more score oriented. Unfortunately, none has been pursued to the point of establishing a sturdy empirical basis for the test. Thus it is probably correct to identify the TAT being primaily a projective technique. Conversely, some sentence completion tests that were designed to evoke the process of projection, such as that of Rotter and Rafferty (1950), have included an elaborate format for objective scoring and have been sufficiently researched to establish extensive normative data and address the issues of reliability and validity very successfully. It is a projective test, yet it is also a very objective test, and to force it into one or the other of these categories would be misleading.

As noted earlier, the Rorschach was *not* designed as a projective technique nor developed as such during its first two decades of use. However, the ambiguity of its stimuli does permit a broad range of responses, and often the elaboration of these responses becomes highly revealing about the subject. It is therefore not surprising that it was hailed as an important test in the projective movement of the early 1940s and was to become among those conspicuously categorized as such. This does not mean that efforts to establish psychometric credibility for the test were abandoned. Beck and Hertz remained in the forefront among many researchers studying the test and its wide array of variables, and they were joined by many others seeking to demonstrate its efficacy as a projective method.

By 1950, some of that research had a positive yield. Beck had published some useful normative data, both Beck and Hertz had published actuarially based tables for the discrimination of adequate form-fit of responses, and several hundred sound research articles had appeared offering data related to the meaning of many of the Rorschach scoring variables. Yet all of this work constituted only a small segment of the Rorschach literature, which by that time had burgeoned to more than 3000 books and articles. Many were clinical case studies, and many others were research works offering negative or contradictory findings. Critics of projective methods often cited the latter as evidence that the test itself was of little use and had little or no scientific merit.

With the rush into the projective movement, the fact had been overlooked that there were still five different approaches to the test (or *technique* as some now preferred to call it). Both advocates and critics ignored or downplayed those differences as irrelevant to the larger issue of whether the method had merit. Many of the critics of the Rorschach and of projective methods in general were also critics of psychoanalytic theory and naively linked the two. The erroneous presumption was that the process of projection is a manifestation of the unconscious as defined in Freudian theory (Lindzey, 1961; Sargent, 1945; Symonds, 1946; Wiggins, Renner, Clore, & Rose, 1971). In point of fact, very few projective methods are theory based, and certainly not the Rorschach, even though many clinicians trained during the 1940s and 1950s were strongly imbued with psychodynamic concepts and analytic models for understanding personality. Thus it was natural for them to interpret data from any tests in that framework.

In 1954, Paul Meehl published an important work, *Clinical versus Statistical Prediction,* that served to define and possibly even broaden the schism that had come to exist between those favoring a stringent psychometric approach and those aligned with the more global approach to assessment. Meehl reviewed 20 validity studies, all but one of which showed that the actuarial method was equal to or better than the "clinical" technique, which customarily included the use of projective methods. He argued for the abandonment of the clinical approach to assessment in favor of less time-consuming actuarial techniques such as the MMPI, to allow clinicians more time for other important work, especially therapy. Later Gough (1963) and Sawyer (1966) published surveys of predictive studies that appear to support Meehl's argument, although Gough observed that no adequate test of the clinician's forecasting skills had yet been carried out.

Holt (1958, 1970), in two excellent rejoinders to the Meehl argument, pointed out that many of the studies cited by Meehl used extremely inadequate and even contaminated criteria. In his 1970 paper, Holt called attention to the fact that another survey of predictive studies, by Korman (1968) reported very positive findings for the clinical method. Holt noted with some sense of dismay that the Sawyer and Korman studies were published within 2 years of each other but that their respective bibliographies showed absolutely no overlap. This probably illustrates the extreme state of the dichotomy and also how a selective use of literature could be used to support almost any bias on the subject. As both Holt (1970) and Weiner (1972) have pointed out, the focus of the argument of Meehl et al. was prediction, whereas the major focus of the diagnostician has been to describe and understand the person.

As noted earlier, the use of the Rorschach continued to be very widespread during the era of this controversy and even into the 1960s and 1970s, during which time the very character of clinical psychology was to change considerably. Through the 1950s, the major role of the clinician was psychodiagnosis. But then times changed, and the profession broadened its scope and role. New models of behavior and intervention were introduced, and many clinicians found themselves much more involved in planning and conducting intervention. Some universities reduced or even discontinued training for assessment; in clinical settings, however, assessment (a term that had come to replace *psychodiagnosis*) continued as a routine way of life for the professional, and the Rorschach method remained one of the standards. But to some extent, it also remained in a state of developmental limbo. All of the systems were firmly in place by 1957, and none of the systematizers was oriented toward integration or compromise. Research concerning the Rorschach continued to be published at a fairly substantial rate, and much of it was system specific. However, it was commonplace for authors and readers alike to interpret findings, whether positive or negative, as applicable to *the* Rorschach, thereby disregarding or minimizing as unimportant the considerable differences that existed among the systems.

DEVELOPMENT OF THE COMPREHENSIVE SYSTEM

In *The Rorschach System,* a comparative analysis of the five approaches, this author illustrated the enormous magnitude of the differences among them (Exner, 1969). Only two of the five systems used the same seating arrangement. None of the five used instructions to the subject that were identical or even particularly similar to those used by the other four. Fifteen different codes or scores had been developed among the five systems to identify the *location* or area of the blot used in a response. Not one of those scores was defined in the same way across all systems. All five included Rorschach's scoring symbol *F* to denote that the *form* or shape of the blot or blot area was important to the response, but each of the systems used a different criterion to decide whether the form had been used accurately.

All five scored the perception of movement differently, and all even defined the presence of movement differently. Sixteen different symbols evolved across the systems to be used when the response included reference to *chromatic color,* but even when the same symbol was used in more than one system, mainly those derived from Rorschach's original scores, the criteria for its application differed markedly.

The greatest disagreement among the systems occurred for the scoring of those answers that included the use of *shading* or *achromatic* color. The scoring symbols were basically unique for each system, as were the criteria for their application. This is not surprising, since Rorschach's original work included no mention of such features because of the fact that his blots were not shaded until after his monograph was published.

The differences among the systems extended well beyond the issues of scoring symbols and scoring criteria. The five systems differed markedly with respect to which scores should be calculated in a quantitative summary of a record and which relationships among scores might be important to interpretation. As might be expected, the systems also differed substantially about the approach to interpretation and the interpretive meaningfulness of many variables and configurations of variables. However, in spite of their very marked differences, the systematizers tended to offer many similar kinds of interpretive hypotheses. For the most part, these reflected postulates offered by Rorschach, and to the casual observer their presence in all or most all of the systems could have suggested much greater agreement among the systematizers than was truly the case. Interpretive differences have remained very considerable across the systems on most matters in which Rorschach was not definitive in his postulates or offered no hypotheses.

One conclusion from the comparative analysis presented in *The Rorschach Sys-*

tems was that the lack of agreement among the five systems in the basic areas of administration, scoring, and interpretation had, in effect, created five uniquely different Rorschach tests, similar only in that each used the same stimulus figures and that some or all had incorporated several of Rorschach's basic interpretive postulates. But even some of the latter had been uniquely embellished by each of the systematizers.

Two questions were implicit in the comparison presented in *The Rorschach System:* (a) which of the five systems demonstrate the greatest empirical sturdiness? and (b) Which of the five systems has the greatest clinical utility? In 1968, following the completion of the comparative analysis, the Rorschach Research Foundation was created to address these issues. One of the first projects completed by the foundation was to determine how clinicians were actually using the Rorschach. The findings were very striking (Exner & Exner, 1972). Approximately 22% of 395 clinicians surveyed had abandoned scoring altogether. Moreover, three out of four who continued to score the responses did so in a personalized way; that is, they did not follow any one system consistently. In other words, one might administer the Rorschach using the Rapaport face-to-face seating, give the Klopfer instructions, score responses using various criteria from Beck, Klopfer, and Piotrowski, and draw from at least as many sources in trying to interpret the resulting data. It appeared that more often than not, clinicians who were using the Rorschach method tended to piece together an assortment of features from the several systems and from their own experience with the test to generate a final product that they identified as *the* Rorschach. Thus the five major approaches had proliferated into almost as many different tests as there were test users. These findings, while striking, were not very surprising. An earlier survey of university instructors of the Rorschach had revealed that 12% did not teach scoring and that the variability of methods taught for administration, scoring, and interpretation was extremely wide (Jackson & Wohl, 1966). Obviously, the divergence of Rorschach methodology into five major approaches and the subsequent proliferation of those approaches did little to promote a more thorough understanding of the method as a test or to enhance its development.

Another major project completed at the Rorschach Research Foundation in 1970 involved a careful review of all published Rorschach research. The objective of the project was to categorize and cross-reference studies as they related to the variables of administration, scoring, and interpretation as they had evolved in each of the five systems. At that time the Rorschach literature consisted of more than 4000 articles and 29 books, plus Rorschach's original monograph. In spite of that voluminous literature, a surprisingly large number of basic variables had not been systematically researched. For instance, the issue of seating arrangements had never been subjected to experimental manipulation, and only one study had ever compared the effects of differences in instructions, and that for only two of the systems. No research had been published on 12 of the scoring variables, and only a handful of studies had appeared concerning six other scores. Similarily, many interpretive postulates had not been addressed experimentally, and for many others the findings were at best equivocal because of inadequacies in research design or data analysis. In fact, problems in research design and/or data analysis marked a very large number of the published articles concerning the Rorschach.

About 2100 of the more than 4000 articles that had appeared concerning Rorschach were purportedly research works. However, when scrutinized against *contemporary* standards for adequacy of design and/or data analysis, more than 600 were judged to be seriously flawed, and nearly 800 others were found to be questionable value. This should not be interpreted to mean that most Rorschach research was incompetent, careless, or illogical. The majority of these studies were conducted between 1935 and 1955, an era in which the tactics of research design and data analysis were often considerably less sophisticated than presently, particularly in the clinical field. For instance, 24 studies had been published addressing the issue of blind analysis in Rorschach interpretation; using contemporary design standards, no more than 9 of the 24 would be judged as having been adequate tests of the issue. Twenty-six studies had been published focusing on the stimulus characteristics of the blots; only 10 of the 26 were not marked by serious design flaws.

The literature review did yield nearly 700 research works that were judged methodologically adequate. These studies provided an initial data bank for evaluating elements of the various Rorschach systems. Although many of these studies reported positive findings, others reported negative or equivocal results, and in some instances two or more seemingly adequate investigations reported contradictory results. In addition to these previous data, 835 Rorschach protocols were collected for the foundation by 157 examiners, including records of more than 200 nonpatients. These new records provided a data source for the study of specific issues on which previously reported findings were equivocal, contradictory, incomplete, or based on very small samples. Moreover the training of the examiners, all of whom were Ph.D.s in clinical psychology, embraced all five systems. Some had been trained to use the Beck system, some the Klopfer system, some the Hertz system, and so on. Thus records they obtained permitted the comparison of Rorschach yields among the five different methods of administration.

By late 1970, the data accumualted by the Foundation tended to support three broad conclusions. First, the five different methods of administration produced five relatively different kinds of records. Second, scores, scoring criteria, and interpretive postulates existed within each of the five systems for which no empirical support existed or for which negative findings had been reported. Third, each of the systems included many empirically sturdy elements which, if applied faithfully for administration, scoring, and interpretation, could yield a considerable positive result. At the same time, some of that positive yield was likely to be offset in most cases by the flaws in the system, either in scoring or interpretation.

Keep in mind, however, that in the survey of Rorschach users mentioned earlier it was found that most tended to mix systems. Actually, fewer than 20% faithfully followed any single system. The fact, plus the finding that each system was significantly limited to flaws, led to a decision to alter the objective of the foundation. The thrust was changed from studying each system for its merits and liabilities to integrating the features of all systems for which empirically defensible data existed or could be established.

During the next 3½ years, the pool of protocols was increased to nearly 1200, and more than 150 investigations were completed concerning the array of elements involved in the use of the Rorschach. In the early phases of the project, many fundamental issues were addressed, such as seating, instructions, recording and inquirying responses, and the selection of codes or the scores to be used. Some of that early research also yielded findings from which new scores or revised scoring criteria evolved. In addition, the issue of interscorer reliability was tackled, and no scoring category was included in the "new" system unless a minimum 0.85 level was achieved. Interestingly, this caused the initial rejection of many seemingly useful scores that have later been added to the system using a revision of the criterion for application. Each of dozens of interpretive postulates was explored, and no procedure or score was included in the new system unless it met the fundamental requirements for validation. In the course of this research, several new approaches to coding or scoring of answers evolved that subsequently met the required criterion for interscorer reliability and the more important criterion of validation for meaningfulness in interpretation. The use of computer technology aided this effort enormously. It permitted very complex analyses to be performed quickly and easily whereas only a decade earlier such analyses of data would have been inordinately time-consuming.

The final product was published in its first form in 1974 as the Rorschach Comprehensive System. Consistent with this name, it reflected an integration of the hard-won, empirically demonstrable wisdoms that had marked the growth of the Rorschach from the time of Rorschach's monograph in 1921 to the early 1970s. It also represented the works of all of the systematizers, plus the findings of the many dedicated researchers who, in their own ways, had studied this very complex tactic for generating information about personality functioning.

Interestingly, as more information about the Rorschach method has emerged, a fundamental reality has remained pervasive (Exner, 1978; Exner & Weiner, 1982). The method, as a test, has not changed very much if at all. The 10 Swiss inkblots constitute the primary elements of the test as they did more than 60 years ago. If there is a major difference, it is that some psychometric properties of the test have been satisfactorily explored and some of the other basic requirements of a sound psychological test have been met. Much of the research that has appeared clearly illustrates that the Rorschach is not a magical X-ray of the mind, as some have thought it to be, but is rather a very complex procedure that elicits a subject's preferred modes of coping with experience. There is no question that the process of projection occurs in the test, as in many other psychological tests, but it is misleading to identify the method as a projective technique. It is much more than that, and, as the data concerning the test have expanded through more extensive research, it has become increasingly clear how the test stimuli, when approached in the context of the task at hand, provoke a very complex set of psychological operations into action.

THE NATURE OF THE RORSCHACH AND THE RESPONSE PROCESS

Cattell (1951) may have been one of the first to describe the fundamental nature of the Rorschach. He did so, somewhat unwittingly, in attempting to define the *projec-*

tive situation. He correctly noted that in the projective situation the subject is asked or required to provide something that is not really there. In other words, the nature of the task requires subjects to misperceive the stimulus and through this misperception to "project" something of themselves into the response. In reality, Cattell was only partially correct in his description of the projective sutuation as it applies to the Rorschach. Although the Rorschach situation does require subjects to misperceive inkblots and define them as being something they are not, this is really a *problem-solving process* that does not necessarily force subjects to project (Exner, 1980).

In effect, the instructions to the subject ("Tell me, what might this be?") call for scanning the stimulus carefully and ultimately making some decision about which of several answers that might be given would be "best" or "most appropriate" for the situation. There is no encouragement to project oneself into the answer, as might be the case if the instructions included reference to feelings or thoughts about the answer delivered. However, subjects often do embellish their responses in a highly personalized manner that does reflect much of their own idiography. For instance, one of the most common answers to the first blot is "a bat," which occurs in approximately 55 of every 100 records taken from nonschizophrenic adult males. The high frequency identifies it as a *Popular* response. The majority of such answers are very simply stated, such as "It looks like a bat," or "It could be a bat," with little or no embellishment to the response. It is a rather straightforward identification of the stimulus, given that the subject cannot identify the stimulus as an inkblot and thus must identify it as something else. There is probably no element of projection involved in these kinds of responses. They are based simply on the process of classification. However, if the subject responds, "This is a very angry bat searching out some prey to attack," the simple classification response of "bat" has been embellished considerably. The response goes well beyond simple perceptual identification and probably does include projected material. Although the Rorschach method does therefore permit projection to occur, its basic nature is to provoke the *perceptual–cognitive* operations of the subject that might ordinarily occur in most problem-solving or coping situations.

As Rorschach suspected, it is the manner in which responses are coded or scored that best reflects the kinds of perceptual–cognitive operations that have occurred. This is not to suggest that the embellishments or projections are unimportant to the interpretation of the record. Quite the contrary, they are often critically important in fleshing out a more complete understanding of the subject. However, the bulk of empirically sturdy data that have emerged regarding the Rorschach as a test centers around the scoring, especially the frequencies, proportions, and relationships that appear among scores.

The Comprehensive System currently includes 116 scores and score-related variables, such as score derivations, proportions, and ratios. These are illustrated in Figure 2.1, which is a Structural Summary Blank used with the system (Exner, 1976). The upper portion of the blank shows the individual scores, of which nine are used to code the location of the responses and provide information about whether the area is discrete or whether an integration of areas may have occurred and whether a specific contour demand is present in the response. Twenty-three

STRUCTURAL SUMMARY

R = Zf = ZSum = P = (2) =

Location Features		Determinants (Blends First)		Contents			Contents (Idiographic)

Location Features

W =

D =

Dd =

S =

DW =

DQ		M Quality	
+	=	+	=
o	=	o	=
v	=	w	=
—	=	—	=
		NO FORM	=

Form Quality

FQx		FQf	
+	=	+	=
o	=	o	=
w	=	w	=
—	=	—	=
NO FORM	=		

Determinants (Blends First)

M =
FM =
m =
C =
Cn =
CF =
FC =
C' =
C' F =
FC' =
T =
TF =
FT =
V =
VF =
FV =
Y =
YF =
FY =
rF =
Fr =
FD =
F =

Contents

H	=	Bl	=
(H)	=	Bt	=
Hd	=	Cg	=
(Hd)	=	Cl	=
A	=	Ex	=
(A)	=	Fi	=
Ad	=	Fd	=
(Ad)	=	Ge	=
Ab	=	Hh	=
Al	=	Ls	=
An	=	Na	=
Art	=	Sx	=
Ay	=	Xy	=

Contents (Idiographic)

....

....

....

....

....

....

....

....

S-CONSTELLATION (Adult)

....FV + VF + V + FD > 2

....Col-Shd Bl > 0

....3r + (2)/R < .30

....Zd > ± 3.5

....ep > EA

....CF + C > FC

....X + % < .70

....S > 3

....P < 3 or > 8

....H < 2

....R < 17

........TOTAL

Special Scorings

DV =

INCOM =

FABCOM =

ALOG =

CONTAM =

————

CP =

MOR =

PER =

PSV =

RATIOS, PERCENTAGES, AND DERIVATIONS

ZSum-Zest =

Zd =

EB =   EA =

eb =   ep =

(FM=   m=   T=   C'=   V=   Y=   )

Blends:R =

a:p =

Ma:Mp =

FC:CF+C =

W:M =

W:D =

L =

F+% =

X+% =

A% =

Afr =

3r+(2)/R =

Cont:R =

H+Hd:A+Ad =
(H)+(Hd):(A)+(Ad) =

H+A:Hd+Ad =

XRT Achrom =

XRT Chrom =

Figure 2.1. Structural summary blank for the comprehensive system.

scores are available to identify what characteristics of the blot have contributed to the formation of the precept, such as F for form, C for chromatic color, and T for the use of shading features to imply a textural quality. There are 26 different codes used to classify the content of responses; 1 to indicate whether a "pair" of the same object is perceived because of the blot symmetry; a table of weighted values that are assigned to responses in which some organizational action has occurred; 1 code to reflect the fact that a response is very common; and 9 for the coding of answers in which special kinds of verbalizations occur. The following illustrates the scoring for the response, "A bat flying at night with his hands out like ready to grab something," elaborated later during the Inquiry segment of the test to indicate that the entire blot was used; that the main features of the response are based on its shape; and that the fact the blot is dark provided the notion that it was "at night."

Location	Determinants and Form Quality	Content	Popular	Organized	Special
Wo	$FM^a.F\acute{C}o$	*A*	*P*	1.0	INCOM

Once all responses are scored, the frequencies for each kind of score are entered in the Structural Summary and the various ratios, derivations, and proportions are calculated, following which the interpretation proceeds. Before turning to the matter of interpretation, however, it is important to consider the response process more fully.

Sometimes it is difficult to appreciate fully the capacities of the human being to process information. The Rorschach blots are, of course, a form of visual stimulation. Figure 2.2 is a facsimile of the third blot of the test that shows the eye-movement activity of a 24-year-old nonpatient female viewing the blot for the first time in an investigation on stimulus input time (Exner & Martin, 1980). The subject's head was held in a retainer to minimize random head movement, and the blots were presented on a screen directly in front of her. The arrows in Figure 2.2 approximate focal points of the eye as the blot was scanned during a 900-millisecond tachistoscopic presentation. If the input from peripheral vision is considered in addition to the focal points, it appears that the subject had scanned essentially the entire stimulus figure during this very brief interval.

The thoroughness of the scanning pattern in Figure 2.2 is very similar to that found in other subjects for about the same amount of stimulus exposure. These kinds of data are important because they suggest that for most subjects, on most of the blots, the stimulus is scanned sufficiently to permit encoding in a second or less. Yet the average reaction time for a first response is typically 6 seconds or longer, depending on the complexity of the blot stimuli. For instance, on Card III (the third blot) the average reaction time for the first answer is nearly 7 seconds. Thus for most subjects an interval of 5 seconds or more occurs between input and output. The issue of what happens between input and output becomes very important to the understanding of the Rorschach method. Apparently, several operations or processes go on during this relatively brief time lapse.

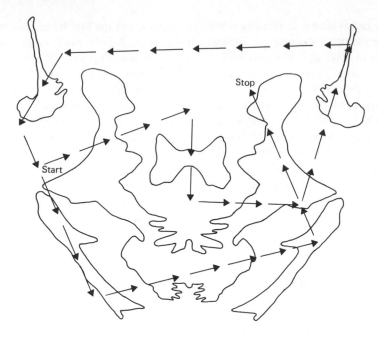

Figure 2.2.   Eye-scanning activity of Card III by a 24-year-old nonpatient female during a 900-ms interval.

Classification

It seems reasonably clear that one of the first operations that occurs during and/or after the encoding of the stimulus relates to classification. In other words, the input is held in some form of short-term storage while data from long-term storage are generated from which to make comparisons. Whereas the number of potential "reality-based" classifications of an entire blot is probably limited, the potential number of classifications of parts of blots seems astronomical. Whatever the actual number of potential classifications, it has been fairly well established that subjects can generate a large number of answers to each blot when required to do so by an instructional set (Exner, Armbruster, & Mittman, 1978). More important is the fact that when large numbers of answers are given by nonschizophrenic subjects, the overwhelming majority do reflect an appropriate "fit" to the contours of the blot or blot area. Thus it does not seem very difficult for most subjects to stretch their imaginations a bit and find that the blots or blot areas are similar to many objects that they have encountered in life.

The process of classifying seems to take place quickly. Colligan (1983) has demonstrated that both schizophrenics and nonpatients can form and deliver answers with only very brief exposures to the blots, and allowing less than 1 second after exposure before the first answer is articulated. She exposed the blots tachistoscopically to several groups of subjects for either 200, 400, or 600 milliseconds, and allowed a 900-millisecond interval before the response was required. The composite of the Exner, Armbruster, and Mittman and the Colligan studies indicates that most subjects do classify and are prepared to deliver a relatively large number of answers for each blot rapidly. Certainly within the range of 5 to 10 seconds following exposure, most subjects have formulated several potential answers.

Censoring

Then, however, a second process or operation seems to occur. The instructions used by Rorschach and Klopfer and in the Comprehensive System are deliberately vague: "Tell me, what might this be? What does it look like?" These instructions are less structured than those used by some of the systematizers, such as Beck, who would include: ". . . and tell me everything you see there." The decision to use Rorschach's original instructions was based on the premise that the procedure should afford the subject the greatest possible latitude in offering answers. The early research of the Rorschach Research Foundation revealed that the Rorschach instructions typically yielded a record of between 18 and 23 answers, whereas, the instructions of the other systems yielded an average of 10 more answers. However, when the potential interpretive yields of those instructional methods were compared, it was found that the shorter records included as much interpretive richness as the longer records, and in some instances were more interpretively rich.

The vagueness of the instructions permits the subject to become selective. In the Exner, Armbruster, and Mittman study, all subjects gave at least 50 responses to the 10 blots. Under standardized procedures of administration, the average number of responses is about 22, with a standard deviation of about 5. Interestingly, that average appears universally consistent. Several cross-cultural studies have been reported that show this to be the case (Exner,1978; Exner & Weiner, 1982).

In light of these findings, it seems reasonable to assume that some process of censoring or discrimination takes place after many potential responses have been classified. Exner (1978) and Exner et al. (1978) have demonstrated that the elements of set and social desirability are both influential in determining how many answers will be given and what kinds of potential responses might be censored out. There are at least two other processes or operations that contribute very significantly to the determination of which answers will be delivered and which will be discarded or withheld.

Psychological Styles

The first of these processes is especially significant in establishing the Rorschach *method* as the Rorschach *Test*. It is the tendency of people to adopt certain psychological habits or styles in dealing with the world. These are the features that are often described when the term *personality* is employed. Some early authors identified these features as *habits*, and later they became known as *traits*. Much of contemporary psychology identifies these features as *styles*. Whatever term is used, the features being identified are those that are relatively enduring in the behaviors of the person. They are features that afford psychologists the luxury of predicting behavior, and for most people they are simply descriptions of redundancies that mark a person as being consistently similar to or different from others in certain respects. It would be wrong to reduce Rorschach responses to simplistic behavioral notions, and yet Rorschach responses are samples of behavior. Hence if some characteristic of a person is pervasive, it should become manifest in some way in this problem-solving operation. And it does!

Much of the early criticism of the Rorschach focused on the lack of hard validation data for various postulates, and much also focused on the premise that the Rorschach was not a psychometrically reliable test. Several authors had attempted to study the issue of reliability using a *split-half* technique to study the internal consistency of the test. Since the 10 blots do not represent equivalent stimuli, this approach was doomed from the start, but many critics of the test were delighted by the nonsignificant findings. Only a few of the early Rorschach researchers, led by Hertz, attempted a temporal consistency (test–retest) method of studying the reliability of the test. Although these studies did yield much more positive findings than the split-half method, most were also criticized for involving small samples. Following the establishment of the basic format for the Comprehensive System (Exner, 1974), many temporal consistency studies were completed. The most elaborate of these involved the retesting of 100 nonpatient subjects 3 years after they had taken the test for the first time (Exner, Armbruster, & Viglione, 1978). The results indicate that most of the Rorschach scores, and especially the many score derivations, ratios, and proportions that are so important to interpretation, are highly consistent over that very long interval. These findings are reflected in Table 2.1, which also includes retest correlations for two groups of children retested after lengthy intervals (Exner & Weiner, 1982).

Whereas the data in Table 2.1 indicate that most Rorschach scores and score derivations are very stable for adults over long periods, they also signify that the same is not true for children. Obviously, Rorschach data should not be used to make long-term predictions about the still-developing child. This does not mean that the test has a more limited usefulness with children. In fact, if the stability of test results is reviewed by retesting over briefer intervals, consistently high retest correlations are found for both adults and children. The data in Table 2.2 show the retest correlations for 35 nonpatient adults and 35 nonpatient 9-year-old fourth graders, when the retesting was done after a period of 18 to 21 days (Thomas, Alinsky, & Exner, 1982).

Further research indicates that it is very difficult to alter or interfere with the basic psychological operations that are represented in the scores and score-related derivations, even in young children. In one study (Thomas & Exner, 1980) 60 8-year-olds were randomized into two groups of 30 each and administered the test twice, with the second testing only 3 or 4 days after the first, and by a different examiner. The 30 children in the control group were retested just as in a routine temporal consistency study, but the children in the experimental group were asked to give *different* answers in their second test from those they had given in the first and were offered a reward for being cooperative. The retest correlations for the two

Table 2.1.   Correlation Coefficients for Two Testings with Two Groups of Children, One Group Retested after 24 Months, and the Second Group Retested after 30 Months, Compared with Retest Data for 100 Adults Retested after 36 to 39 Months

		First Test Age 6—Retest after 24 months $N=30$	First Test Age 9—Retest after 30 months $N=25$	100 Adults Retested after 36 to 39 months
		r	r	r
Variable	*Description*			
R	Response	.67	.61	.79
P	Popular	.77	.74	.73
Zf	Z frequency	.55	.68	.83
F	Pure Form	.51	.69	.70
M	Human Movement	.48	.62	.87
FM	Animal Movement	.49	.60	.72
m	Inanimate Movement	.13	.09	.31
a	Active Movement	.86	.81	.86
P	Passive Movement	.42	.29	.75
FC	Form Color	.38	.34	.86
CF + C + Cn	Color Dominant	.27	.35	.79
Sum C	Sum Weighted Color	.41	.58	.86
Sum SH	Sum of all Achromatic and Shading	.08	.29	.66
Percentage	*Ratio*			
L	Lambda	.18	.39	.82
X + %	Extended good form	.84	.86	.80
Afr	Affective Ratio	.51	.79	.90
3r + (2)/R	Egocentricity Index	.78	.74	.87
EA	Experience Actual	.19	.45	.85
ep	Experience Potential	.20	.57	.72

groups were very similar to each other and closely resembled those for the 9-year-old subjects represented in Table 2.2. In fact, the two groups differed for only two basic variables, (a) the frequency of *F* responses and (b) the sum of the achromatic and shading variables. The subjects in the experimental group gave significantly fewer *F* responses in their second test, and more responses that included the achromatic or shading feature, than did the control group.

This same design has been repeated recently using two groups of randomly selected inpatient depressives (Sudik, 1983). A similar result occurred, although these adult depressives did tend to show greater change for the *F* and shading variables than did the nonpatient children, and they also showed more variability for some of the variables related to emotional control.

A major question in this kind of study is whether the experimental subjects really

Table 2.2.   Correlation Coefficients for Two Testings for Two Groups of 35 Subjects Each with the Second Test Administered 18 to 21 Days after the First Test

		35 Adults	35 9-year-olds
		r	r
Variable	*Description*		
R	Response	.84	.87
P	Popular	.81	.89
Zf	Z frequency	.89	.92
F	Pure Form	.76	.80
M	Human Movement	.83	.87
FM	Animal Movement	.72	.78
m	Inanimate Movement	.34	.20
a	Active Movement	.87	.91
p	Passive Movement	.85	.88
FC	Form Color	.92	.84
CF + C + Cn	Color Dominant	.83	.92
Sum C	Sum Weighted Color	.83	.87
T	Texture	.96	.92
C'	Achromatic Color	.67	.74
Y	Diffuse Shading	.41	.17
V	Vista	.89	.93
FD	Form Dimension	.86	.81
Percentage	*Ratio*		
L	Lambda	.76	.84
X + %	Extended good form	.87	.92
Afr	Affective Ratio	.85	.91
3r + (2)/R	Egocentricity Index	.90	.86
EA	Experience Actual	.84	.87
ep	Experience Potential	.59	.70

do give different answers in the second test. In the study with children, controls repeated about 86% of their responses, while the experimentals repeated only about 15%. The depressive controls repeated about 70%, while the experimentals repeated about 32%.

The accumulated data concerning the temporal consistency of Rorschach scores suggest that people, even children over brief periods, do give the same kinds of answers. This does not mean that they give the same responses, however; when instructed not to do so, they generally will follow that instruction. But in spite of giving new and/or different answers, they tend to produce the same configurations of scores. This becomes even more apparent when ratios between certain scores and certain score percentages are reviewed. In effect, people tend to be redundant in their behaviors, and this tendency to replicate behaviors when in a coping situation is a process that affords the Rorschach method, as a test, much of its empirical sturdiness.

Psychological States

A fourth process that influences the censoring and discriminating operations and also affects the redundancy of response behaviors is the psychological state of the person at the time the test is administered. This should not be interpreted to mean that the entire test performance is influenced by the state of the person; however, some situational conditions can alter some kinds of responses very significantly. A review of Tables 2.1 and 2.2 will call attention to the fact that a few of the listed variables have very low or at best modest retest correlations. This considerable variation from one test to another illustrates the impact of "state" conditions and influences.

This phenomenon is possibly best illustrated in the Rorschach response by a classic study. Card I is most commonly reported to be either a bat or a butterfly. In fact, there is a clear sex difference between these two answers. Both are considered common or Popular, but the bat response appears significantly more often among male subjects whereas the butterfly response appears significantly more often in the protocols of female subjects. Exner (1959) produced several different forms of Card I, each with the blot changed in color from the standard grey-black to some chromatic color. In 400 male subjects the frequency of the bat response decreased significantly in comparison to the control group who were administered the standard grey-black version of the card.

These data did not seem especially important at the time of the study. However, in later research it was found that inpatient depressive subjects who give the Popular "bat" response tend to articulate the presence of the achromatic or shading features, whereas most other subjects who report a bat do not. In fact, the differences are very striking. Slightly more than 1 in 100 nondepressed subjects who report a bat on Card I also articulate the presence of the grey-black features as being relevant to that percept. Slightly more than 22 in 100 inpatient depressives giving the same answer include some direct reference to those features in their answer or in their clarification of it in the Inquiry. This issue of articulation becomes even more intriguing when the retest data for depressives are reviewed. If the retest is done at a time when the depression has subsided significantly, the subjects who gave a bat response to Card I in their first test tend to do so again; however, the frequency with which they articulate grey-black features of the blot as being relevant to the percept is now reduced to slightly more than 4 in 100.

Some Rorschach variables such as m (Inanimate Movement) and Y Diffuse Shading) are very unstable over time. Nevertheless, the data concerning their interpretive meaningfulness seems unequivocal. They tend to defy an old psychometric axiom that something cannot be valid unless it is also reliable. In this instance, both correlate with external criteria indicating the presence of situational stress (Exner, 1978; Exner & Weiner, 1982). Thus in some instances it is possible to use

Rorschach findings to detect the presence of state phenomena, which is especially important to the understanding of crisis conditions.

In summary, then, during that few-second interval between the time of the stimulus input and the first response, several operations have probably occurred that influence the answer given. The subject has (a) classified the blot and many of its parts, (b) rejected or censored some potential answers because they do not seem acceptable, (c) been strongly influenced by psychological habits, traits, or styles in the classification and censoring process, and (d) also been strongly influenced by current psychological states in these decision operations. Ultimately responses are delivered, and the accumulation of these answers as they are scored and studied provides the data bank from which the test is interpreted.

INTERPRETATION OF THE RORSCHACH

The main purpose for personality assessment is to gain a broad understanding of the person. Information concerning both assets and liabilities permits the formulation of a description of the psychological and behavioral features that characterize the individual. Such an understanding can contribute significantly to important issues such as intervention planning and intervention evaluation. In some cases differential diagnosis is also important, as it may contribute to the formulation of a treatment plan. This is most common when questions concerning serious psychological disturbances, such as major affective disorders or schizophrenia, have been raised. Diagnosis, if necessary, can usually be achieved once a thorough understanding of the subject has been developed. Diagnostic conclusions are not always easily generated, however, because almost every diagnostic grouping will include subjects who vary considerably in many personality characteristics. Nevertheless, some types of disturbances are marked by considerable homogeneity among subjects, and this does tend to appear in Rorschach data. Schizophrenia and depression are good illustrations.

Indices of Schizophrenia and Depression

Table 2.3 shows agreements between Rorschach-based diagnoses of schizophrenia and final diagnostic decisions based on the Research Diagnostic Criteria (Spitzer, Endicott, & Robins, 1976). This study involved 85 first-admission patients all of whom had exhibited psychotic-like features at the time of admission. Rorschachs were administered to these patients 4 to 10 days after admission and were subjected to four different "sorts" regarding the presence of schizophrenia (Exner, 1981). Two of the sorts were done by a computer programmed to identify schizophrenia using a combination of five structural variables that have been shown to appear with substantial frequency among schizophrenics and with much lower frequency among nonschizophrenic subjects. The remaining two sorts were done by six clinical psychologists, each of whom had considerable Rorschach training and experience.

Table 2.3. Agreements for the Diagnosis of Schizophrenia between the Research Diagnostic Criteria and Four Rorschach-Based Sorting Procedures for 85 First-Admission Patients

	RDC-Based Diagnoses			
	Schizophrenic $N=46$		Nonschizophrenic $N=39$	
Sort Procedures	N Correct	False Positives	N Correct	False Positives
Computer sort #1 $= X+\%$ <.70 plus three of four variables[a]	40	5	34	6
Computer sort #2 $= X+\%$ <.70 plus four variables positive[a]	35	0	39	11
Computer sort #3 $=$ unanimous agreement among three judges working with the complete Rorschach	39	2	37	7
Computer sort #4 $=$ unanimous agreement among three judges working with the Rorschach plus brief history	42	1	38	4

[a] The four variables used in computer sorts are:

1. *Sum FQx minus* greater than *Sum FQx weak*
2. *Sum* 5 Critical Special Scores 4 or more
3. *Sum* FABCOM + ALOG + CONTAM greater than *Sum* DV + INCOM
4. *Sum M-* responses greater than 0

Three of these six judges made their decisions based on the total Rorschach, which had been completely scored by whoever administered the test. The remaining three judges also used the total Rorschach, but they additionally had access to a brief one-page history about the subject. All of the judges made their decisions independently.

It will be noted from Table 2.3 that all four sorting procedures yield a fairly substantial "correct" rate. Computer sort #1 correctly identified 87% of each group, but the issue of false positives is important, as five nonschizophrenic subjects were erroneously identified as being schizophrenic. Computer sort #2, using a more stringent selection criterion to identify schizophrenia, correctly selected 76% of the schizophrenic subjects and all of the nonschizophrenics, but misidentified 11 schizophrenic subjects.

A comparison of the results of the two computer sorts with the two sorts by trained clinicians using the complete Rorschachs reveals that a substantial reduction in errors concerning the presence of schizophrenia occurs when the element of human judgment is injected. In sort #3, the three judges working only with the total test correctly identified 85% of the schizophrenics and 95% of the nonschizophrenics. More important, they misidentified only two nonschizophrenic subjects as being schizophrenic. The addition of a brief history makes for further improvement in accuracy. The three judges who had the advantage of the brief history plus the complete Rorschach were able to identify correctly 91% of the schizophrenics and 97% of the nonschizophrenics. Not shown in Table 2.3 is a sort done by three other experienced clinicians for the same 85 cases, working only from the brief history. They unanimously agreed on the correct identification of 29 schizophrenics but also misidentified 27 of the nonschizophrenics as being schizophrenic. Their decisions were no better than a chance sort.

Similar findings to these occur in attempting to differentiate major depressive disturbances accurately. An often important differential diagnostic issue is whether reports by a subject of depression represent the presence of a sustained or chronic form of depression or depressive personality, or whether such reports represent a more chronic sense of helplessness, or a situationally related reactive phenomenon. The data presented in Table 2.4 reflect the efficacy of the Rorschach for resolving this issue. This study involved evaluation of 80 first-admission patients who presented features of and/or acknowledgement of depression (Exner, Murillo, & McGuire, 1981).

As in the study concerning schizophrenia, the sorts involving the use of the complete Rorschach by experienced clinicians yielded good overall accuracy, but less so than in the schizophrenia study. In fact, the three judges working with the whole Rorschach did not do as well as computer sort #1 for correct identification of major depressive disturbances (72% vs. 83%), and the judges working with the total Rorschach plus a brief history performed only about as well as computer sort #2 (86% each). These findings suggest that the Structural (scoring) variables related to major depressive disturbances as defined in DSM-III are more discretely represented by the perpetual–cognitive operations reflected in Rorschach scoring than is true for schizophrenia. This is clearly the case if the data regarding discrimination of major depressive disorders are contrasted with other efforts at differential diagnoses that have more subtle demands.

As noted earlier, most diagnostic classifications incorporate subjects with considerable heterogeneity in personality features. Then too, some subclassifications of a single major category include many homogeneous features. For instance, it is possible to differentiate most situationally related depressions from those that are more chronic or endogenous. This holds true because most reactive depressions do not include those elements that correlate with the low self-esteem, confusion of feelings, morbidity in thinking, and internalization of feelings that mark the more chronically depressed person. Conversely, it is very difficult if not impossible to differentiate the chronic unipolar depressive from the bipolar (manic-depressive) using Rorschach data alone, as the latter often includes the same kinds of features as the former.

Diagnostic differentiation of the less severe disturbances is even more difficult, although not always impossible. Typically, however, the critical elements leading to diagnostic and other kinds of conclusions extend beyond Structural (scoring) features, such as those used in Tables 2.3 and 2.4, and include broad descriptions of

Table 2.4.   Agreements Between Four Rorschach-based Sorts and DSM-III Criteria for the Diagnosis of Major Depressive Disorder for 80 Patients

| | DSM-based Decisions | | | |
| | Major Depressive Disorder N=43 | | Other N=37 | |
Sort Procedures	N Correct	False Positives	N Correct	False Positives
Computer sort #1 = any five of seven variables positive[a]	35	9	28	8
Computer sort #2 = any four of variables 1–5 positive	37	2	35	6
Computer sort #3 = unanimous agreement among three judges using total Rorschach	31	8	29	12
Computer sort #4 = unanimous agreement among three judges using total Rorschach plus brief history	37	3	34	6

[a] The seven variables used in computer sort #1 are:

1. *Sum* Vista responses greater than 0
2. *Sum* Color-Shading Blends greater than 0
3. $3r + (2)/R$ less than 0.30
4. *Sum* MOR greater than 3
5. *Sum* C' responses greater than 3
6. *Afr* less than 0.45
7. *Sum FM* greater than *Sum m*

personality structure and dynamics based on many varied aspects of a subject's responses. All of the principles for conducting such Rorschach interpretations cannot be fully outlined within the limits of this chapter, and the reader is referred to the three volumes on the Comprehensive System for an elaboration of them (Exner, 1974, 1978; Exner & Weiner, 1982). However, this chapter concludes with one protocol, which, together with the kinds of interpretive statements that would be generated by Structural and Content analyses of the data, should help to illustrate how the total Rorschach, including the "projected" material, can be used in the assessment process.

Case Illustration

The subject is a 29-year-old unemployed female school teacher. She is single, a college graduate with a major in history. She has taught (in grammar school) for 3 years. Her parents are living. She has one sister, 32 years old. She is being evaluated in connection with frequent visits to her physician with complaints of headaches, upset stomach, and occasional insomnia. The physician has raised the question of possible psychosomatic features and seeks advice regarding the need for psychotherapy.

Interpretation of a Rorschach protocol should always begin with the quantitative or Structural data. The reason for this is that these are the features for which the greatest empirical sturdiness has been established. Consequently, interpretations derived from these data have a much greater likelihood of being correct than those derived from a more qualitative analysis of the record. Nonetheless, qualitative analysis is also critically important, since it touches on those projected elements that are not usually captured in the scoring.

The first two issues to be addressed using Structural data are those of schizophrenia and/or major depressive disturbance. With reference to the findings reported in Tables 2.3 and 2.4, this subject offers no substantial evidence for schizophrenia or major depressive disturbance. Therefore, any diagnostic conclusions will probably be derived from the description that results using both the Structural and Content analyses.

A review of the data in the Structural Summary indicates the following, with the data source and the data for each interpretation shown in parentheses at the end of the statement:

1. This is a person who has never developed a consistent style of coping or problem solving. Consequently, she is less predictable than most people and more prone to vacillation in those situations. People of this kind are often at a disadvantage because they tend to make more errors than people who have a more well-established coping style, and they tend to repeat these errors with greater frequency. ($EB = 2:2:5$)

2. This is also a person who does not modulate emotional discharge as effectively as most adults. When she releases emotion, it tends to become overly intense and to influence her thinking, decisions, and behavior more than is usually the case among adults. ($FC:CF + C = 1:2$)

3. At the same time, she seems as willing to process emotional stimuli as are most adults. The processing of emotional stimuli often increases the need for some exchange. In that she does not modulate her emotions as effectively as do most adults, it is likely that some of her emotional exchanges will be marked by limited self-control. ($Afr = .67$)

4. The picture is made more complex by several other factors. When she does delay making responses, using the option to "think things over," she tends to avoid doing just that. Instead she has the habit of fleeing into a fantasy life whereby she can exert greater control over what is happening than if she responded directly to a situation. In other words, she is not very prone to confront problems directly. Most of the time she prefers to let others initiate solutions. ($M^a:M^p = 0:2$)

5. Even though she is not very efficient in many of her coping styles, she does make a distinct effort to organize each new stimulus field carefully. In fact, she

devotes more time to this process than most people and prefers to defer decision making until she has an abundance of information available. This can be an asset for her, although people such as this usually do not function very well under time pressure. ($Zd = 4:5$; $Zf = 9$)

6.   She tends to set goals for herself that are slightly beyond her functional capabilities. Although this may be an admirable objective, the composite of her inefficient coping styles, limited effective use of her thinking, and marginal emotional control makes for a higher probability of failure in many goal-directed behaviors. Failure often leads to disappointment and/or frustration. ($W:M = 7:2$)

7.   The latter is especially important, since her tolerance for stress is somewhat marginal. She is not really as mature as most adults, and she consequently has more limited resources available to her with which to contend with unexpected stress situations. This creates the potential for her being thrown into an "overload" situation more easily than is true for most adults, and in such a situation she can become quite disorganized. ($EA:ep = 4.5:6$)

8.   Currently, she is experiencing more stimulation from unmet need states than should be the case for an adult. ($eb = 4:2$; $ep = 6$; $FM = 4$)

9.   Her immaturity and inefficiency are made more complex by the fact that she is much more self-centered than most people and seems to harbor a naive and child-like tendency toward self-gratification. This will have a marked impact on her interpersonal relations. ($3r + (2)/R = .67$; $Fr = 1$)

10.   She is very interested in people and would like to be dependent upon them. However, her immaturity and excessive self-centeredness tend to reduce the likelihood of deep or sustained relations with others. (H Cont $= 4$; Pure $H = 2$; $FD = 1$)

11.   Her perceptual accuracy is good, and she is very aware of conventionality. ($X + \% = .80$; $P = 7$)

A sequential review of the Contents of her responses adds the following, more speculative, postulates:: While she tends to be excessively self-centered, her self-concept is more diffuse than would be expected for an adult female. She is probably highly defensive in most of her interpersonal contacts. She often tries to intellectualize rather than be open about her feelings. This has probably occurred because of an enduring sense of vulnerability, and as a way to exert greater control over her emotions. She feels precarious in her world and is very concerned about unwanted intrusions or demands from it.

Overall, then, this is a rather immature and inadequate individual whose psychological growth appears to have been thwarted, or at least not appropriately facilitated, by factors that are not clear from the test data. She does not have a well-developed or mature self-image; she is not consistent or efficient in much of her coping behavior; and she is naively self-centered, which contributes significantly to interpersonal difficulties. She would like to be close to people, especially in some kind of passive-dependent relationship. Unfortunately, she does not have a very good understanding of people and is often overly influenced by her need to guard herself against her perceived sense of vulnerability. The end product tends to be a kind of chronic helplessness and more limited adaptation.

Protocol 1. A 29-Year-Old Female

Card		Free Association		Inquiry	Scoring
I	8"	1. It ll sk of insect, a bf	E:	(Rpts S's response)	Wo FMᵃo A P 1.0
			S:	It has it wgs stretched out like it was in flight	
			E:	Can u show me where it is?	
			S:	Oh, yes, its all of it, ths r the wgs & ths wld b the body	
		2. Ths prt down here mite be prt of a H body, the legs	E:	(Rpts S's response)	Do Fo Hd
			S:	(U can just c the outlin of it in here, just legs like from the waist dwn	
II	17"	3. It ll 2 bears in a circus balancing a ball on thr noses	E:	(Rpts S's response)	W+ FMᵃ.CFo (2) A P 4.5
			S:	Ths cntr thg is the ball & ths r the bears, u can c thr heads here & their bodies	
			E:	U mentioned that thy wer in a circus	
			S:	Well yes, ther doing an act w the ball & all the red color repres.. the circus atmosphr	
III	13"	4. Oh, ths is a pic of 2 male dancers, thr bodies r bent over in the mdl of a danc holdg s.t. betw thm	E:	(Rpts S's response)	D+ Mᵖo (2) H P 3.0
			S:	Thyr rite here (points) & theyr holdg ths pot. It ll thy hav big mittens on to hold the pot	
			E:	Mittens?	
			S:	U can't c hands thr, just mittens	
IV	4"	5. Oh, thts 1 of ths African voodoo rites	E:	(Rpts S's response)	W+ Mᵖo H 4.0
			S:	Its an African witch Dr, he seems to hav a mask on & he's sittg on a chair	
			E:	I'm not sure I see it as u do	
			S:	Her r his ft & ths is the mask so it must be s.s. of voodoo thg	
V	3"	6. It ll a big bat w its wgs strchd out, like it mite b flyg	E:	(Rpts s's response)	Wo FMᵃo A P 1.0
			S:	Oh yes, all of it here ll that, ths r the wgs & the feelers here	
		7. Ths thgs on the end cld b dead tree limbs or branches	E:	(Rpts S's response)	Do Fw Bt MOR
			S:	Thy just re me of that, just dead lookg, lik thy were brkn off just laying ther	

Card	Time	No.	Response and Inquiry	Scoring
VI	5"	8.	A bearskin rug, not ths top tho E: (Rpts S's response) S: Well yes it does 11 that, it has that shape to it & u can almost feel the fur	Do FTo Ad P
VII	10"	9.	Ths 11 a bunch of fried shrimp E: (Rpts S's response) S: It just 11 pieces of fried shrimp to me E: I'm not sure I c it as u do S: Well I guess u cld say ther r 4 pieces, c ths wld be tails on ths 2 pieces & it all looks breaded w meal E: Breaded w meal? S: It all grainy looking	W + FTo (2) Fd 2.5
VIII	15"	10.	Well the pink object cld b a lion & ths wld b a piece of wood & he's tyg to cross, its a tree stump & stones & he can c his reflection as he goes E: (Rpts S's response) S: U c here is the lion & ths r the stump here & the stones, they r very colorful, like the sun was hitting on them to bring the C's out.	W + FMa FC.Fro A,Ls, P 4.5
IX	10"	11.	Mayb thts a 3 tier bowl of s.s E: (Rpts S's response) S: Yes like u'd c at a luncheon w 3 very different sections like an abstract, very colorful w each color setting off the sections	Wo CFo Hh 5.5
		12.	Ths wht prt in the midl cld b a goblet E: (Rpts S's response) S: It has that goblet shape about it u c, its rite here (points)	DSo Fo Hh
X	14"	13.	Oh dear, I can't seem to make a.t. out of all of it but ths blue thgs 11 lobsters to me E: (Rpts S's response) S: Here, the blu, all the legs, like lobster 11	DO Fo (2) A P
		14.	Ths grey thg up above the lobsters cld b crabs E: (Rpts S's response) S: Yes, thr r 2 of them, u c, here & here, thy hav the unusual short legs & a fat body like a crab	Do Fw (2) A
		15.v	I c a face in here too w funny glasses or more correctly, a nose piece bec the eyes wld b here & u can't c glasses there E: (Rpts S's response) S: U c ths yellow thgs r eyes & the blue is the nose piece like on glasses except its a rather unusual one & 1 suppose ths is a small mouth & mayb even a beard dwn here. A funny looking man, ths green prt up here doesn't count tho	DdS- F- Hd 6.0

PROTOCOL I

CARD	RT	NO.	LOCATION	DETERMINANTS (S)		CONTENT (S)	POP	Z SCORE	SPECIAL
I	8"	1.	Wo	$FM^a o$		A	P	1.0	
		2.	Do	Fo		Hd			
II	17"	3.	W+	$FM^a.CFo$	(2)	A	P	4.5	
III	13"	4.	D+	$M^p o$	(2)	H	P	3.0	
IV	4"	5.	W+	$M^p o$		H		4.0	
V	3"	6.	Wo	$FM^a o$		A	P	1.0	
		7.	Do	Fw		Bt			MOR
VI	5"	8.	Do	FTo		Ad	P		
VII	10"	9.	W+	FTo	(2)	Fd		2.5	
VIII	15"	10.	W+	$FM^a.FC.Fro$		A,Ls	P	4.5	
IX	10"	11.	Wo	CFo		Hh		5.5	
		12.	DSo	Fo		Hh			
X	14"	13.	Do	Fo	(2)	A	P		
		14.	Do	Fw	(2)	A			
		15.	DdS-	F-		Hd			

Protocol 1. (Continued)

STRUCTURAL SUMMARY

= 15   Zf = 9   ZSum = 32.0   P = 7   (2) = 5

cation Features

= 7

= 7

= 1

= 2

√ =

DQ	**M Quality**
= 5	+ = 0
= 8	o = 2
= 1	w = 0
= 1	— = 0
	NO FORM =

m Quality

FQf

= 0	+ = 0
= 12	o = 3
= 2	w = 2
= 1	— = 1
= 0	

Determinants
(Blends First)

FM.FC.Fr = 1

FM.CF = 1

M	= 2
FM	= 2
m	=
C	=
Cn	=
CF	=
FC	= 1
C'F	=
FC'	=
T	=
TF	=
FT	= 2
V	=
VF	=
FV	=
Y	=
YF	=
FY	=
rF	=
Fr	=
FD	=
F	= 6

Contents

H	= 2	Bl	=	
(H)	=	Bt	= 1	
Hd	= 2	Cg	=	
(Hd)	=	Cl	=	
A	= 6	Ex	=	
(A)	=	Fi	=	
Ad	= 1	Fd	= 1	
(Ad)	=	Ge	=	
Ab	=	Hh	= 2	
Al	=	Ls	= 0,1	
An	=	Na	=	
Art	=	Sx	=	
Ay	=	Xy	=	

Contents
(Idiographic)

.... =

.... =

.... =

.... =

.... =

.... =

S-CONSTELLATION (Adult)

....FV+VF+V+FD > 2

....Col-Shd Bl > 0

....3r+(2)/R < .30

....Zd > ± 3.5

....ep > EA

....CF+C > FC

....X+% < .70

....S > 3

....P < 3 or > 8

....H < 2

....R < 17

........TOTAL

Special Scorings

DV	=
INCOM	=
FABCOM	=
ALOG	=
CONTAM	=
CP	=
MOR	= 1
PER	=
PSV	=
	=

RATIOS, PERCENTAGES, AND DERIVATIONS

m-Zest = 32.0−27.5

= +4.5

= 2:2.5   EA = 4.5

= 4:2   ep = 6

=4 m= 0 T= 2 C'= 0 V= 0 Y= 0)

ds:R = 2:15

= 4:12

Mp = 0:2

FC:CF+C = 1:2

W:M = 7:2

W:D = 7:7

L = .67

F+% = .50

X+% = .80

A% = .47

Afr = .67

3r+(2)/R = .53

Cont:R = 5:15

H+Hd:A+Ad = 4:7
(H)+(Hd):(A)+(Ad) = 0:0

H+A:Hd+Ad = 8:3

XRT Achrom = 6.0"

XRT Chrom = 13.8"

Protocol 1. (Continued)

A diagnostic label would probably not contribute very much to treatment planning. Some might suggest that she is a borderline personality disorder, but she is not really as susceptible to severe disorganization as that label implies. Others might more correctly consider her an inadequate or immature personality with some passive-dependent features. Regardless of the label, treatment must focus on development, with special attention to broadening accessible resources, developing greater consistency in coping, reducing self-centeredness, and creating effective interpersonal skills, the composite of which should promote a more distinct and age-appropriate self-image.

CONCLUSION

This then is the current status of the Rorschach, what it is, and how it is used. In spite of the fact that more than 60 years have passed since Rorschach presented his findings, many questions about the test remain unanswered. Information about the processes involved is accumulating slowly, but much more is needed. Similarly, matters of diagnostic and descriptive efficacy need much more investigation. Nonetheless, even without those added data, the Rorschach stands as a test that can make a valuable contribution to the assessment process.

REFERENCES

Beck, S. J. Autism in Rorschach scoring. *American Journal of Orthopsychiatry*, 1936, **6,** 83–85.

Beck, S. J. Some present Rorschach problems. *Rorschach Research Exchange*, 1937, **2,** 15–22.(a)

Beck, S. J. Introduction to the Rorschach method: A Manual of personality study. *American Orthopsychiatric Association Monograph*, 1937, No. 1(b)

Beck, S. J. *Rorschach's Test*. I. *Basic Processes*. New York: Grune & Stratton, 1944.

Beck, S. J. *Rorschach's Test*. II. *A variety of personality pictures*. New York: Grune & Stratton, 1945.

Beck, S. J. *Rorschach's Test*. III. *Advances in interpretation*. New York: Grune & Stratton, 1952.

Binder, H. Die Helldunkeldeutungen in psychodiagnostischen experiment von Rorschach. *Schweiz Archives Neurologie und Psychiatrie*, 1932, **30,** 1–67.

Cattell, R. B. Principles of design in "projective" or misperceptive tests of personality. In H. Anderson & G. Anderson (Eds.), *Projective techniques*. New York: Prentice-Hall, 1951.

Colligan, S. *Information processing and the Rorschach response*. Doctoral dissertation, Long Island University, 1983.

Dearborn, G. Blots of ink in experimental psychology. *Psychological Review*, 1897, **4,** 390–391.

Dearborn, G. A study of imaginations. *American Journal of Psychology*, 1898, **9,** 183–190.

Exner, J. E. The influence of chromatic and achromatic color in the Rorschach. *Journal of Projective Techniques*, 1959, **23**, 418–425.

Exner, J. E. *The Rorschach systems*. New York: Grune & Stratton, 1969.

Exner, J. E. *The Rorschach: A comprehensive system*. (Vol. 1). New York: Wiley, 1974.

Exner, J. E. *Structural Summary Blank*. Bayville, N.Y.: Rorschach Workshops, 1976.

Exner, J. E. *The Rorschach: A comprehensive system*. (Vol. 2). *Recent research and advanced interpretation*. New York: Wiley, 1978.

Exner, J. E. But it's only an inkblot. *Journal of Personality Assessment,* 1980, **44**, 562–577.

Exner, J. E. *The response process and diagnostic efficacy*. Paper presented at the 10th International Rorschach Congress, Washington D.C., 1981.

Exner, J. E., Armbruster, G. L., & Mittman, B. The Rorschach response process. *Journal of Personality Assessment*, 1978, **42**, 27–38.

Exner, J. E., Armbruster, G. L., & Viglione, D. The temporal stability of some Rorschach features. *Journal of Personality Assessment*, 1978, **42**, 474–482.

Exner, J. E., & Exner, D. E. How clinicians use the Rorschach. *Journal of Personality Assessment*, 1972, **36**, 403–408.

Exner, J. E., & Martin, L. S. Eye movement for Cards II and III by nonpatient adults. Workshops Study 301 (unpublished), Rorschach Workshops, 1980.

Exner, J. E., Murillo, L. G., & McGuire, H. L. Rorschach based differentiation of sustained versus reactive depression. Workshops Study 347 (unpublished), Rorschach Workshops, 1981.

Exner, J. E., & Weiner, I. B. *The Rorschach: A comprehensive system*. (Vol. 3). *Assessment of children and adolescents*. New York: Wiley, 1982.

Frank, L. K. Projective methods for the study of personality. *Journal of Psychology*, 1939, **8**, 343–389.

Freud, S. (1894) The anxiety neurosis. *Collected papers* (Vol. 1). London: Hogarth Press, 1953. Pp. 76-106.

Freud, S. (1896) Further remarks on the defense of neuropsychoses. *Collected papers* (Vol. 1). London: Hogarth Press, 1953. Pp. 155-182.

Freud, S. (1911) Psychoanalytic notes on an autobiographical account of a case of paranoia. *Collected papers* (Vol. 3). London: Hogath Press, 1953. Pp. 387-396

Gough, H. G. Clinical versus statistical prediction in psychology. In L. Postman (Ed.), *Psychology in the making*. New York: Knopf, 1963.

Hens, S. *Phantasieprufung mit formlosen Klecksen be, schulkindern, normalen erwachseuen und genteskranken*. Doctoral dissertation, University of Zurich, 1917.

Hertz, M. R. Discussion on "Some recent Rorschach problems." *Rorschach Research Exchange*, 1937, **2**, 53–65.

Hertz, M.R. On the standardization of the Rorschach method. *Rorschach Research Exchange*, 1939, **3**, 120–133.

Hertz, M. R. Rorschach: Twenty years after. *Rorschach Research Exchange*, 1941, **5**, 90–129.

Hertz, M. R. The Rorschach: Thirty years after. In D. Brower & L.E. Abt (Eds.), *Progress in clinical psychology*. New York: Grune & Stratton, 1952.

Holt, R. R. Clinical and statistical prediction: A reformulation and some new data. *Journal of Abnormal and Social Psychology*, 1958, **56**, 1–12.

Holt, R. R. Yet another look at clinical and statistical prediction: Or, is clinical psychology worthwhile? *American Psychologist*, 1970, **25**, 337–349.

Jensen, A. R. Personality. *Annual Review of Psychology*, 1958, **9**, 395–422.

Jackson, C. W., & Wohl, J. A survey of Rorschach teaching in the university. *Journal of Projective Techniques and Personality Assessment*, 1966, **30**, 115–134.

Kirkpatrick, E. A. Individual tests of school children. *Psychological Review*, 1900, **7**, 274–280.

Klopfer, B. The present status of the theoretical development of the Rorschach method. Rorschach Research Exchange, 1937, **1**, 142–147.

Klopfer, B., Ainsworth, M. D., Klopfer, W. G., & Holt, R. R. *Developments in the Rorschach technique.* (Vol. I). *Technique and theory.* Yonkers-on-Hudson, N.Y.: World Book, 1954.

Klopfer, B., et al., *Developments in the Rorschach technique.* (Vol. II). *Fields of application.* Yonkers-on-Hudson, N.Y.: World Book, 1956.

Klopfer, B., & Kelley, D. *The Rorschach technique.* Yonkers-on-Hudson, N.Y.: World. Book, 1942.

Klopfer, B., & Sender, S. A system of refined scoring symbols. *Rorschach Research Exchange*, 1936, **1**, 19–22.

Korman, A. K. The prediction of managerial performance: A review. *Personnel Psychology*, 1968, 21, 295-322.

Lindzey, G. *Projective techniques and crosscultural research.* New York: Appleton-Century-Crofts, 1961.

Louttit, C. M. *Clinical psychology.* New York: Harper, 1936.

Louttit, C. M., & Browne, C. G. Psychometric instruments in psychological clinics. *Journal of Consulting Psychology*, 1947, **11**, 49–54.

Lubin, B., Wallis, R. R., & Paine, C. Patterns of psychological test usage in the United States: 1935–1969. *Professional Psychology*, 1971, **2**, 70–74.

Meehl, P. E. *Clinical versus statistical prediction.* Minneapolis: University of Minnesota Press, 1952.

Morgan, C., & Murray, H. A. A method for investigating phantasies: The Thematic Apperception Test. *Archives of Neurology and Psychiatry*, 1935, **34**, 289–306.

Murray, H. A. *Explorations in personality.* New York: Oxford University Press, 1938.

Parsons, C.J. Children's interpretation of inkblots (A study on some characteristics of children's imagination). *British Journal of Psychology*, 1917, **9**, 74–92.

Piotrowski, Z. *Perceptanalysis.* New York: Macmillan, 1957.

Pyle, W. H. *Examination of school children.* New York: Macmillan, 1913.

Pyle, W. H. A psychological study of bright and dull children. *Journal of Educational Psychology*, 1915, **17**, 151–156.

Rapaport, D., Gill, M., & Schafer, R. *Diagnostic psychgological testing* (2 vols.). Chicago: Yearbook Publishers, 1945, 1946.

Rorschach, H. *Psychodiagnostik.* Bern: Bircher, 1921. (Trans. Hans Huber Verlag, 1942.)

Rotter, J. B., & Rafferty, J. E. *Manual: The Rotter Incomplete Sentences Blank.* New York: Psychological Corporation, 1950.

Rybakov, T. *Atlas for experimental research on personality.* Moscow: University of Moscow, 1911.

Sargent, H. Projective methods: Their origins, theory, and application in personality research. *Psychological Bulletin*, 1945, **42**, 257–293.

Sawyer, J. Measurement and prediction, clinical and statistical. *Psychological Bulletin*, 1966, **66**, 178–200.

Schafer, R. *Psychoanalytic interpretation in Rorschach testing*. New York: Grune & Stratton, 1954.

Sudik, N. *The temporal stability of Rorschach scores among major depressive disorders*. Doctoral dissertation, United States International University, 1983.

Sundberg, N. D. The practice of psychological testing in clinical services in the United States. *American Psychologist*, 1961, **16**, 79–83.

Symonds, P. M. *The dynamics of human adjustment*. New York: Appleton-Century-Crofts, 1946.

Thomas, E. E., Alinsky, D., & Exner, J. E. *The stability of some Rorschach variables in 9 year olds as compared with nonpatient adults*. Workshop Study 441 (unpublished), Rorschach Workshops, 1982.

Thomas, E. E., & Exner, J. E. The effects of instructions to give different responses during retest on the consistency of scores for eight year olds. Workshop Study 372, Rorschach Workshops, 1980. In J.E. Exner, But its only an inkblot. *Journal of Personality Assessment*, 1980, **44**, 562–577.

Weiner, I. B. Does psychodiagnosis have a future? *Journal of Personality Assessment*, 1972, **36**, 534–546.

Whipple, G. M. *Manual of mental and physical tests* (2 Vols.). Baltimore: Warwick & York, 1914.

Wiggins, J. S., Renner, K. E., Clore, J. L., & Rose, R. J. *The psychology of personality*. Reading, Mass.: Addison-Wesley, 1971.

Zubin, J., Eron, L. D., & Schumer, F., *An experimental approach to projective techniques*. New York: Wiley, 1965.

CHAPTER 3

Clinical Evaluation of Intellectual Function

ALAN S. KAUFMAN AND CECIL R. REYNOLDS

The evaluation of intellectual integrity and the level of intellectual functioning of the individual has been the metier, and in many cases the raison d'être, of psychologists in applied settings since the earliest attempts to apply the special methods of psychology to the human condition. Though the role of the psychologist has expanded considerably since World War II, assessment of intelligence remains an integral component of the psychologist's function, whether he or she is in private practice or working in the public sector. The uses of intelligence tests are many and quite varied, ranging from predicting future academic levels to distinguishing organic from psychiatric syndromes to the projective evaluation of personality. Intelligence tests are among the most frequently administered of all tests by clinical psychologists (Korchin, 1976);and school psychologists, who spend more than 60% of their time engaged in testing activities (Hughes, 1979), administer intelligence batteries more frequently than any other category of tests (Goh, Teslow, & Fuller, 1981). Despite the controversy over their use, the commercial development and publication of intelligence tests have significantly increased in recent years (Reynolds & Elliott, 1982). Even though psychologists are increasingly engaging in roles that are far removed from the assessment of intelligence, it seems clear that the clinical evaluation of mental functioning will remain an important aspect of clinical psychology for some time.

This chapter begins with a brief history of inteligence testing followed by a review of the development of a philosophy of intelligent testing. Screening techniques for the brief appraisal of general intellectual level are addressed next, and then we turn to methods of intelligence test interpretation. The Wechsler scales are featured throughout the chapter because of their immense popularity and their generally superior psychometric characteristics and broad research base. Applications of the Wechsler scales to diagnosis and evaluation of learning disabilities are discussed next, followed by a treatment of issues and methods in the estimation of premorbid levels of intellectual functioning. Following these discussions, the problem of potential cultural bias in intelligence tests is treated.

A BRIEF HISTORY OF INTELLIGENCE TESTING

The roots of the study of intelligence and its measurement can be traced to physicians, educators, and psychologists who were deeply involved with populations at the extremes of the intellectual continuum. Esquirol (1838) and Seguin (1866) were committed to the study of mentally retarded individuals, and Galton (1869) was fascinated by the mental abilities of men of genius. The separate contributions of these pioneers have been profoundly felt in the field of intelligence testing; however, it has been the innovative research investigations of Binet (1903), who focused on the mental abilities of typical or average children at each age, which have had the longest lasting and most direct effect on individual intelligence testing as we know it today.

Esquirol made several important contributions, most notably distinguishing "between the idiot, whose intelligence does not develop beyond a very low level, and the demented person" (Peterson, 1925, p. 163). This distinction between mental retardation and emotional disturbance reflected a vital breakthrough for assessment and indicates the primitive state of the art in the early nineteenth century. Esquirol also described a hierarchy of retardation (or feeble-mindedness, as it was known in earlier times) with idiots occupying the bottom rung, followed by imbeciles, and peaking with morons (Peterson, 1925). He was well ahead of his time in concluding that the use of language was the most dependable criterion for inferring a retarded individual's intelligence level (Anastasi, 1976), and Esquirol (1828) is also credited with developing a precursor of the mental age concept by pointing out that "an idiot is incapable of acquiring the knowledge common to other persons of his own age" (Peterson, 1925, p. 183).

Seguin was heavily influenced in his work with mentally retarded individuals by Itard, of *Wild Boy of Aveyron* fame. Like Esquirol, Seguin tried to establish criteria for distinguishing between different levels of retardation, although Seguin (1866) focused on sensory discrimination and motor control. Optimism regarding treatment of retarded individuals characterized Seguin's approach, and he instituted a comprehensive program of sense-training and muscle-training techniques, much of which lives on in institutions for the mentally retarded (Anastasi, 1976). Tests developed by Seguin such as the Seguin Form Board—which requires the rapid placement of various wooden geometric shapes into their proper holes—are still included in nonverbal performance tests, such as the Arthur Point Scale (Arthur, 1947).

Not only were Esquirol and Seguin pioneers in individual intellectual assessment, but their efforts helped bring the world out of the dark ages, instilling more humane treatment of retarded and insane people. Prior to the nineteenth century, "neglect, ridicule, and even torture had been the common lot of these unfortunates" (Anastasi, 1976, p. 5). However, one conceivably negative consequence of their focus on the differentiation of levels of retardation is the prevalent practice of labeling individuals in various special education categories. The Esquirol tradition has produced euphemisms for terms like *imbecile,* as evidenced by the American Association on Mental Deficiency's (AAMD) classification scheme which features mild, moderate, severe, and profound levels of retardation. To this day, occasional case reports in folders of retarded individuals will include offensive and archaic labels such as *low-grade moron*. Whether a person is considered to suffer from idiocy or profound retardation, the use of unpleasant, pigeonholing labels remains an unfortunate byproduct of the great contributions of the pioneers in the field of retardation.

Francis Galton channeled his enthusiasm for gifted men of genius and the study of the genetics of intelligence into the development of what was apparently the first comprehensive individual intelligence test. Galton's tests, administered for a small fee in the Anthropometric Laboratory he first established in 1884 in Kensington, England, required sensory discrimination and sensory-motor coordination. In accordance with Galton's (1883) belief that intelligence must be intimately related to sensory abilities because environmental knowledge comes to us via the senses, Galton developed a series of tests such as weight discrimination, reaction time, visual discrimination, steadiness of hand, keenness of sight, and strength of squeeze. His empirical justification for this test battery came from comparisons between gifted and retarded individuals which, not surprisingly, showed obvious superiority in favor of the gifted (Peterson, 1925). Galton's influence spread far beyond his laboratory as tests like his were developed throughout Europe and in the United States as well. James McKeen Cattell, an assistant at Galton's Anthropometric Laboratory, set up a laboratory in 1890 at the University of Pennsylvania and moved it to Columbia University the following year. Cattell coined the term *mental tests;* Galton's influence was clearly evidenced in Cattell's 40-to-60 minute individual examination as the tests included keenness of hearing, reaction time, afterimages, color vision, sensitivity to pain, and the like (Peterson, 1925). However, Cattell's (1890) work was not merely an imitation of Galton's tests. Cattell elaborated upon and improved his mentor's methodology by emphasizing the vital notion that administration procedures must be standardized to obtain results that are strictly comparable from person to person and time to time.

In the meantime, a challenge was being issued to the Galton view of sensory and motor intelligence by Alfred Binet of France. In collaboration with Simon and Henri, Binet conducted numerous investigations of complex mental tasks, rejecting the Galton notion that performance on simple, elementary sensory discrimination and motor coordination tasks equates to intelligent behavior. Although Binet and his co-workers developed numerous tests of higher mental processes not long after the time that Galton's laboratory was founded, these tasks of memory, imagination, comprehension, moral sentiments, and so forth did not have an immediate impact on the field of intellectual measurement. In fact, Cattell considered carefully the arguments for "tests of a strictly psychological nature" put forth by Binet and others, but rejected these arguments in favor of "more definite and simple tests" since "measurements of the body and of the senses come as completely within our scope as the higher mental processes" (Cattell & Farrand, 1896; Peterson, 1925, p. 79).

The downfall of the Galton-Cattell approach, and the concomitant upswing of the Binet methodology, came oddly enough as the result of two very flawed investigations. Stella Sharp (1898–99) directly compared sensory discrimination tests with tests of complex mental functions and concluded that the simplest mental processes yielded comparatively unimportant information, whereas the tests of Binet and

Henri showed much value in assessing "individual psychical differences." However, these well-respected conclusions of Sharp were based on a sample of only seven advanced college students in psychology along with a "control group" of less advanced undergraduates in an experimental psychology course. Apart from the small and homogeneous nature of the sample, the methodology was weak and quantified only partially.

The second study that spelled doom for the Galton approach was Wissler's (1901) correlational analysis at Barnard College based on data for 250 freshmen and 35 seniors. The tests and anthropometric measures obtained at Cattell's laboratory "showed little more than a mere chance relation" when correlated with each other or when correlated with academic marks (Wissler, 1901). However, the highly selected groups evaluated were extremely restricted in range, which would have depressed coefficients for any tests, including highly complex ones. It is ironical that studies with serious methodological shortcomings would help mark the downfall of the Galton movement. A further irony is that Galton developed a statistical method that was the forerunner of the coefficient of correlation, perfected by his friend Karl Pearson; as indicated, low Pearsonian correlations obtained by Wissler were instrumental in a swing toward the Binet tests.

Even though initial reaction to the two studies was predominantly anti*testing*, causing a lack of enthusiasm for the Galton-Cattell as well as for the Binet-Henri approach in the United States, the methodology of Binet eventually triumphed, first throughout Europe and finally in America (Peterson, 1925). Thus, support was finally given to the claims we now know axiomatically to be true, the claims repeatedly made by Binet and his collaborators in his own journal *(L'Année Psychologique)*, founded in 1895: that efficiency in simple sensory-motor tests bears only a small relationship to other criteria of intellect (Binet used teachers' estimates of ability), and that the tests of higher mental processes, though they give more variable and unstable results than simple tests, are more significant and therefore distinguish among the everyday activities of different individuals (Binet & Henri, 1896; Binet & Simon, 1905). Indeed, the willingness of Binet to accept *error* in measurement as a necessity for proper intellectual assessment constitutes one of his most dynamic contributions to the field (Kaufman, 1983).

Interestingly, recent research by Jensen (1979) and his students (e.g., Vernon, 1981) has revitalized the early work of Galton to some extent. While confirming that simple reaction-time measures contribute little to variation in intellectual function, these researchers have found substantial relationships between intelligence and complex reaction time, especially coupled with intraindividual variability in complex reaction time over repeated trials of the same task. Thus adaptations of Galton's work might yet be found to impact upon objective intellectual assessment in the future.

Alfred Binet's Legacy in the United States

In addition to recognizing the inevitability of some variability in test performance, Binet "discarded the specific test for the specific ability and took a group of tests which seemed to cover in general the chief psychological characteristics that go to make up intelligence. And, furthermore, as the norm or standard of intelligence he took what the average child at each age could do" (Pintner & Paterson, 1925, p. 7). The age-level approach characterizes the Stanford-Binet Intelligence Scale (Terman & Merrill, 1973) to this day, and the tasks developed by Binet and his colleagues are extremely similar to the specific tasks constituting every major intelligence test in current use (Kaufman, 1983).

The Binet-Simon scale, including the 1911 revision that extended through adulthood, were welcomed in Europe and the United States, and its translation and adaptation were begun almost immediately. Town directly translated the Binet-Simon scale into English by 1913; early revisions and adaptations were developed by Bobertag in Germany, by Johnston and also Winch in England, and by several investigators in the United States, including Goddard, Kuhlmann, Wallin, Terman, and Yerkes (Pintner & Paterson, 1925).

Terman's (1916) Stanford Revision and Extension of the Binet-Simon Intelligence Scale, later shortened to Stanford-Binet, emerged victorious despite the earlier appearance of pretenders to the throne such as the Goddard-Binet (Goddard, 1911) and the Kuhlman-Binet (Kuhlman, 1912). Terman's success was not due to luck or coincidence. After publishing a revision of the Binet scale that he termed "tentative" (Terman & Childs, 1912), he spent years painstakingly and thoroughly standardizing the scale. He was specifically trying to meet the needs of the growing number of practitioners in the field whose demand "for more and more accurate diagnoses . . . raised the whole question of the accurate placing of tests in the scale and the accurate evaluation of the responses made by the child" (Pintner & Paterson, 1925, p. 11). Terman also introduced the term *IQ* in his 1916 scale, borrowing Stern's (1914) concept, and making his revised Binet even more attractive to individual mental examiners.

Despite the many advantages of Terman's scale over its competitors, there was still much room for improvement; adult intelligence was not adequately measured, standardization was not representative enough, directions for administering and scoring some tasks were unclear, and too many of the tasks were verbal (Sattler, 1982). The 1937 revision of the Binet (Terman & Merrill, 1937) produced two forms (L and M) and corrected many of the problems with the earlier version; for examples, more nonverbal tests were added at the preschool levels, the standardization was much improved, and levels were added at the lower and upper ends of the scale.

The two most recent Binet revisions have been gross disappointments. In 1960 Forms L and M were combined into the present Form L-M, and the deviation IQ (a standard score with a mean of 100 and standard deviation of 16) replaced the ratio IQ (Terman & Merrill, 1937). Astonishingly, there was no restandardization of the 1960 Stanford-Binet. Instead, data from a nonrepresentative sample of 4498 children, tested in the early 1950s, were used to determine changes in item difficulties obtained in the 1930s. This technique was less than satisfactory as a substitution for a new standardization (Berger, 1970).

The 1972 Stanford-Binet represented a restandardization of the instrument, but there were no modifications of existing items (except for a couple of trivial substitutions) or switching of tasks from one level to another. Consequently, tests that are placed at year level V (for example) are now solved by the average 4 1/2-year-old for reasons such as the impact of mass media on the mental function of preschool children. The result is the misplacement of numerous tasks and the total loss of meaning of the mental age (MA) concept. For example, a child of 4 who earns an MA of 4 obtains an IQ of 88 instead of the expected 100! It is ironical that Terman's rigor in determining accurate placements for tasks in his 1916 scale was instrumental in the triumph of his Binet revision over the versions developed by his competitors; the lack of rigor in this same important endeavor, conducted more than 50 years after Terman's initial work and about 15 years after his death, has been instrumental in the diminished usage of the once-venerated Stanford-Binet. To be sure, the Binet is still used by practitioners throughout the country (Goh, Teslow, & Fuller, 1981), but this one-score, unrevised battery has clearly been superseded in everyday practice by Wechsler's scales, notably the Wechsler Intelligence Scale for Children—Revised (WISC-R; Wechsler, 1974) for school-age youngsters.

Although Terman and Merrill's battery will continue to be of major historical importance and central to the understanding of the heritage of intelligence testing, for the practicing psychologist the Stanford-Binet is best eschewed in favor of more contemporary methods. Indeed, the Stanford-Binet is not a clinical scale to be discussed in later parts of this chapter because of its many antiquated characteristics; perhaps it is best to accept Friedes' (1972) kind offering: *Requiescat in pace*. The impact of the Binet tradition will not be forgotten, however. It is felt whenever an intelligence test is administered, for as new scales and procedures are developed, the prototypical tasks of Binet and Terman repeatedly appear.

David Wechsler's Contributions to Intellectual Evaluation

The biggest challenge to the Stanford-Binet monopoly came from David Wechsler in 1939 when he published the Wechsler-Bellevue Scale (Wechsler, 1939). Present-day instruments which trace their heritage to Form I and Form II of the Wechsler-Bellevue are the WISC-R, Wechsler Preschool and Primary Scale of Intelligence (WPPSI; Wechsler, 1967), and Wechsler Adult Intelligence Scale—Revised (WAIS-R; Wechsler, 1981). All Wechsler scales include 10 to 12 separate subtests with about half included on a Verbal Scale and half on a Performance Scale; three IQs are yielded, a Verbal IQ, a Performance IQ, and a Full Scale IQ. The yielding of a global IQ, despite the separate subtests and scales, is consistent with Wechsler's (1958) notion about the existence of the construct of global intelligence. He stated:

> The grouping of subtests into Verbal . . . and Performance . . . , while intending to emphasize a dichotomy, as regards possible types of ability called for by the individual tests, does not imply that these are the only abilities involved in the tests. Nor does it presume that there are different kinds of intelligence, e.g., verbal, manipulative, etc. It merely implies that these are different ways in which intelligence may manifest itself.

The subtests are different measures of intelligence, not measures of different kinds of intelligence, and the dichotomy into Verbal and Performance areas is only one of several ways in which the tests could be grouped. [Wechsler, 1958, p. 64]

Wechsler was thus basically accepting the Terman/Binet *definition* of intelligence as a global entity, but he used a different type of *methodology* to measure it. Rather than employ a plethora of brief tasks organized by age level such that any individual would get an arbitrary sampling of these tasks based on his or her age and ability level, Wechsler limited his scale to a smaller number of reliable tasks, predetermining that all people are administered all tasks. He selected nonverbal tests, conspicuously absent at most age levels of the Stanford-Binet, to constitute fully half of his intelligence scale.

Wechsler followed four procedures before selecting 11 subtests for his original 1939 Wechsler-Bellevue scale: (a) careful analysis of all existing standardized tests regarding functions measured and reliability; (b) empirical assessment of each test's validity claims; (c) subjective judgment of each test's clinical value; and (d) tryout data collected over a two-year period on individuals with "known" levels of intelligene (Wechsler, 1958, p. 63). By limiting his tests to those already in existence, Wechsler selected the best measurement tools available in the mid-1930s; in actuality all of his tasks were developed not later than the early 1920s.

Many Wechsler tasks were taken directly from the work of Binet and the Americans who adapted the Binet scales during the first 10 or 15 years of the twentieth century. These include several direct analogs, that is, Comprehension, Similarities, Vocabulary, Digit Span, and Picture Completion, and some that are closely similar to Binet tasks: for example, Arithmetic (Making Change) and Object Assembly (Patience Pictures). Other than Binet's work, the main sources of Wechsler subtests were the army examinations developed during World War I. Extremely similar versions of Wechsler's Information, Arithmetic, and Comprehension subtests appeared in Army Group Examination Alpha; close analogs of Mazes, Digit Symbol (Coding), and Picture Completion appeared on Army Group Examination Beta; and the direct ancestors of Object Assembly, Digit Symbol (Coding), Mazes, Picture Arrangement, and Picture Completion constituted half of the Army Individual Performance Scale Examination (Yoakum & Yerkes, 1920). Whereas a cousin of Wechsler's Block Design subtest appeared on the Army Individual Test (Cube Construction), Wechsler's task follows directly from the test originated by Kohs (1923).

Thus all of the subtests in the WISC-R and WAIS-R were developed and used at least 60 years ago. They were constructed without benefit of a theoretical model at a time when diverse and comprehensive theories of learning, cognition, and intelligence had not yet germinated. Since the 1920s, impressive theories and research investigations have emerged from separate disciplines such as cognition, learning, child development, and neuropsychology, many of which relate directly to the measurement of intelligence. The work of Piaget, Cattell-Horn, Guilford, Gagne, Luria, Bruner, Sperry, Hebb, and so many others has been blatantly ignored by the publishers of individual tests of intelligence. The tradition *and* the tasks of Alfred Binet and World War I psychologists are alive and well in all popular present-day individual assessment tools for measuring the intelligence of adults and also of preschool, elementary school, and high school students.

These assertions are not intended to diminish the genius of Alfred Binet and David Wechsler. Binet was a man of vision and a true innovator and pioneer. Wechsler, whose death in May 1981 was a deep loss to psychology, had the clinical insight to provide verbal and nonverbal scales and the empirical sophistication to select and standardize tasks with exceptional psychometric properties. Many others had developed primarily verbal scales (the Binet adaptions) or performance scales (Cornell & Coxe, 1934; Pintner & Paterson, 1925), but Wechsler was the one who realized just how clinically valuable a verbal/nonverbal comparison would be for all individuals if derived from well-standardized scales.

Binet and Wechsler were both courageous. Binet dared to speak out strongly against the sensory-motor view of intelligence that had attained almost worldwide acceptance. Wechsler was bold enough to challenge the Stanford-Binet monopoly in the United States; to many psychologists a Binet age scale was synonymous with an intelligence test. Both men ultimately triumphed.

Binet's victory, with an assist from Terman, led to supremacy in the United States for about 50 years. Wechsler settled for second place for many years. However, while the Stanford-Binet failed to respond to a changing environment, Wechsler did, indeed, try harder. The two forms of the Wechsler-Bellevue were replaced by improved models known as the WISC and WAIS. As these scales became outmoded, they were replaced by the WPPSI, WISC-R, and WAIS-R, test batteries with better and more representative norms, updated content, and greatly improved psychometric properties.

With the increasing stress on the psychoeducational assessment of learning disabilities in the 1960s, and on neuropsychological evaluation in the 1970s, the V–P IQ discrepancies and subtest profiles yielded by Wechsler's scales were waiting and ready to overtake the one-score Binet. The Wechsler scales have been used widely with exceptional populations, and their value has been documented in hundreds of research investigations.

A PHILOSOPHY OF INTELLIGENT TESTING

Conventional intelligence tests and even the entire concept of intelligence testing are currently the focus of considerable controversy. Always the subject of scrutiny, intelligence tests in the past decade have been placed on trial in the federal courts (*Larry P.*, 1979; *PASE*, 1980), state legislatures (New York's "truth-in-testing" legislation), the lay press, and open scholarly forums (Reynolds & Brown, in press; Sattler, Hilliard, Lambert, Albee, & Jensen, 1981). Albee, Hilliard, and Williams, who contend the IQ tests are inherently unacceptable measurement devices with no real utility, represent one extreme; at the other extreme are such well-known figures as Herrnstein and Jensen who believe the immense value of intelligence tests is by now clearly self-evident. Whereas critics of testing demand a moratorium on their use with children, psychologists are often forced to adhere to rigid administrative rules that require the use of *precise* obtained IQs when making placement or diagnostic decisions, with no consideration permitted for measurement error, the influence of behavioral variables on performance, or appropriate sensitivity to the child's cultural or linguistic heritage.

A middle ground is sorely needed. Tests need to be preserved, along with their rich clinical heritage and their prominent place in the neurological, psychological, and educational literature. Yet the proponents of tests need to be less defensive and more open to rational criticisms of the current popular instruments. Knowledge of the weaknesses as well as the strengths of individually administered intelligence tests can serve the dual functions of (a) improving examiners' ability to interpret profiles of any given instrument and (b) enabling them to select pertinent supplementary tests and subtests so as to secure a thorough assessment of the intellectual abilities of any child, adolescent, or adult referred for evaluation. The quality of individual mental assessment is no longer simply a question answered in terms of an instrument's empirical or psychometric characteristics. High reliability and validity coefficients, a meaningful factor structure, and normative data obtained by stratified random sampling techniques do not ensure that an intelligence test is valuable for all or even most assessment purposes. The skills and training of the psychologist engaged in using intelligence tests will certainly interact with the utility of intelligence testing beyond the level of simple actuarial prediction of academic performance.

Indeed, with low-IQ children the primary role of the intelligent tester is to use the test results to develop a means of intervention that will "beat" the prediction made by global IQs. Considerable research during this century has amply demonstrated that children with very low IQs show concomitantly low levels of academic attainment. The purpose of administering an intelligence test to a low-IQ child then is at least twofold: (a) to determine that the child is indeed at high risk for academic failure, and (b) to articulate a set of learning circumstances that defeat the prediction. For individuals with average or high IQs, the specific tasks of the intelligent tester may change, but the philosophy remains the same. When evaluating a learning-disabled child, for example, the task is primarily one of fulfilling the prediction made by the global IQs. Most LD children exhibit average or better general intelligence yet have a history of academic performance significantly below what would be predicted from their intelligence test performance. The intelligent tester then takes on the responsibility of preventing the child from becoming an outlier in the prediction; that is, he or she must design a set of environmental conditions that cause the child to achieve and learn at the level predicted by the intelligence test.

When engaged in intelligent testing, the child or adult becomes the primary focus of the evaluation and the tests fade into the background as only a vehicle to understanding. The test setting becomes completely oriented to the examinee. Interpretation and communication of test results in the context of the individual's particular background, referral behaviors and approach to performance on diverse tasks constitute the crux of competent evaluation. Global test scores are deemphasized; flexibility, a broad base of knowledge in psychology, and insight on the part of the psychologist are demanded; and the intelligence test becomes a dynamic helping agent, not an instrument for labeling, placement in dead-end programs, or disillusionment of eager, caring teachers and parents. Intelligent testing through individualization becomes the key to accomplishment and is antithetical to the development of computerized or depersonalized form reporting for individually administered cognitive tests such as espoused by Alcorn and Nicholson (1975) and Vitelli and Goldblatt (1979). (See reviews by Reynolds, 1980, 1981f.) For the intelligent tester it is imperative to be sensitive and socially aware and to heed Halpern's (1974) plea to "recognize that intelligence and cognition do not comprise the total human being!"

Intelligent testing urges the use of contemporary measures of intelligence as necessary to achieve a true understanding of the individual's intellectual functioning. The approach to test interpretation adopted under this philosophy has been likened to that of a psychological "detective" (Kaufman, 1979a) and requires a melding of clinical skill, mastery of psychometrics and measurement, and extensive knowledge of differential psychology, especially those aspects related to theories of cognitive development and intelligence. A far more extensive treatment of this approach to test interpretations appears in the book *Intelligent Testing with the WISC-R* (Kaufman, 1979a). Discussion of applications of this philosophy to preschool children may be found in Kaufman and Kaufman (1977) and Reynolds and Clark (1983).

Clinical skills with children are obviously important to the intelligent tester in building rapport and maintaining the proper ambience during the actual testing setting. Although adhering to standardized procedure and obtaining valid scores are very important, the child must remain the lodestar of the evaluation. Critical to the dynamic understanding of the child's performance are close, insightful observation and recording of behavior during the testing period. Fully half of the important information to be gathered during the administration of an intelligence test comes from observing behavior under a set of standard conditions. Behavior at various points in the course of the assessment will often dictate the proper interpretation of test scores. Many individuals earn IQs of 100, but each in a different manner, with infinite nuances of behavior interacting directly with a person's test performance.

Knowledge and skill in psychometrics and measurement are requisite to intelligent testing. The clinical evaluation of test performance must be directed by careful analyses of the statistical properties of the test scores, the internal psychometric characteristics of the test, and the data regarding the test's relationship to external factors. As one example, difference scores have long had inherent interest for psychologists, especially between subparts of an intelligence scale. Difference scores are unreliable, and small discrepancies between levels of performance may be best attributed to measurement error. If large enough, however, difference scores can provide valuable information regarding the choice of an appropriate remedial or therapeutic program. The psychometric characteristics of the tests in question dictate the size of the differences needed for statistical confidence in their reflecting real rather than chance fluctuations. Interpretation of subscale differences often requires integrating clinical observations of the child's behaviors with data on the relationship of the test scores to other factors and with theories of intelligence, *but only after first establishing that they are real and not based on error.*

One of the major limitations of most contemporary intelligence tests is their lack of foundation in theories of intelligence, whether these theories be based on research in neuropsychology, cognitive information processing, factor analysis, learning theory, or other domains. Nevertheless, many profiles obtained by children and adults on intelligence tests are interpretable from diverse theoretical perspectives and can frequently be shown to display a close fit to one or another theoretical approach to intelligence. Theories then become useful in developing a full understanding of the individual. Competing theories of intelligence abound (see Reynolds, 1981b; Vernon, 1979; White, 1979). Well-grounded, empirically evaluated models of intellectual functioning enable one to reach a broader understanding of the examinee and to make specific predictions regarding behavior outside of the testing situation itself. One will not always be correct; however, the intelligent tester has an excellent chance of making sense out of the predictable individual variations in behavior, cognitive skills, and academic performance by invoking the nomothetic framework provided by theory. The alternative often is to be stymied or forced to rely on trial-and-error or anecdotal, illusory relationships when each new set of profile fluctuations is encountered. Theories, even speculative ones, are more efficient guides to developing hypotheses for understanding and treating problems than are purely clinical impressions or armchair speculations.

Intelligent testing requires the combination of clinical skill, psychometric sophistication, and a broad base of knowledge of theories of individual differences. Alone, none is sufficient; yet, when properly implemented, these elements engage in a synergistic interaction to produce the greatest possible understanding. Obviously, all of these factors cannot be presented here and occur only as the product of extensive training. The remaining portions of this chapter will focus on providing the psychometric groundwork for intelligent testing. Though the focus will be on the Wechsler scales, the conceptual nature of the methods described is applicable to most standardized tests, including intellectual, neuropsychological (Reynolds, 1982), and perhaps even personality scales.

SCREENING FOR INTELLECTUAL DISORDERS

Comprehensive evaluation of intellectual functioning, though highly desirable and recommended when questions of cognitive function arise, realistically is time-consuming, expensive, and not always necessary. Hence a variety of brief measures of intelligence have been developed over the years. When deciding to use a brief measure of intelligence, one must recognize and accept a considerable loss of clinical information and much material potentially relevant to diagnosis and treatment. Before turning to a discussion of screening methods, it is useful to review the purpose of screening and to evaluate the use of screening techniques. More detailed discussions of the issues to follow can be found in several sources (Kaufman, 1979a; Kaufman & Kaufman, 1977; Reynolds, 1979, 1981d; Stangler, Huber, & Routh, 1980).

Although nearly all individuals with intellectual disorders will ultimately be identified during their public school careers, it is during the early years that corrective, habilitative efforts have the greatest probability of eventual success. Additionally, parents, teachers, and pediatricians, though good sources of referral, cannot be relied upon entirely to identify these children; consequently, numerous brief screening measures of intelligence have been developed. In the course of comprehensive psychological assessments of children or adults, a brief screening measure of intelligence will sometimes be sufficient to meet the clinician's need for information. With young children, brief screening measures are more likely to be used to evaluate large numbers of children in a short time period. In this instance screening has as its direct goal identifying children who are most likely to develop learning, behavior, or other problems that can interfere with appropriate social, emotional, or academic development.

Screening is conducted on a probability basis and reduces the cost of identifying handicapped children by selecting out (or screening out) those children *most likely* to have problems. A screening test is not a criterion measure. No matter how poorly a child performs on a screening test, it does not necessarily mean the child is handicapped. In fact, a good screening test has a built-in pathological bias. Because it is usually considered less tolerable to miss locating a handicapped child than to recommend comprehensive evaluation of a nonhandicapped child, whenever a screening test is "in doubt" about a child, it should identify the child as potentially handicapped. This can be accomplished most directly by setting cutting scores to identify the largest number of children that can receive comprehensive evaluations.

Children identified as potentially handicapped through a screening test (or other process) can then be referred for a thorough individual evaluation intended to (a) determine that the child was incorrectly identified and is not in need of therapeutic intervention, special assistance, or placement in a special education program, or (b) confirm and appraise more accurately the child's specific difficulties. The latter appraisal is multifaceted and involves determination of an appropriate classification and delineation of an individual educational program or plan of therapy that capitalizes on children's assets, limits the effects of their liabilities, and makes treatment as palatable and successful as possible. Even in the comprehensive individual assessment, however, one must remember that tests are nothing more than methods for obtaining quantifiable samples of behavior.

Screening tests, as a rule, provide very limited, restrictive samples of behavior and are all but useless with respect to diagnostic decision making and the development of instructional plans. Screening tests are usually less reliable measures of a child's skills that are designed to detect areas of deficit or handicap; hence they do not typically allow for the identification of a child's strengths. From a legal standpoint, neither do the vast majority of screening tests meet the requirements of P.L. 94-142 for use in educational placement. The results of a screening test cannot substitute for comprehensive individual assessment information, and screening-test information certainly cannot be allowed to override the results of the individual assessment of the referred pupil. However, when used appropriately, screening tests can enhance economically a clinician's or school district's ability to identify and to serve the handicapped. Used in an attempt to circumvent, stunt, or substitute for a comprehensive individual evaluation, screening tests can lead to major errors in the identification–programming process and provide a great disservice to the teachers, parents, and other individuals involved. Not all intellectual screening tests are group administered. Some of the best screening tests are individually administered, although individual administration does not elevate the status of a screening measure within the total evaluation process.

Group Screening of Intellectual Function

A number of well-designed group tests are available for use in intellectual screening with youngsters who are at least at the beginning kidergarten stage. One need only review Buros' (1974) *Tests in Print* and the most recent volume of his yearbook series, *The Eighth Mental Measurements Yearbook* (Buros, 1978), to locate nearly all tests available for the group testing of cognitive skill. In addition to descriptive information on each test, comprehensive reviews of the technical adequacy and general quality of the measures are provided in the yearbooks. There are far too many of these tests to be reviewed here, and the reader is thus referred to these sources for information on group tests for intellectual screening and to Ebel (1982) for a more general discussion of the evaluation and selection of group tests.

Group tests are typically not available for use with children below age 5, who are far less accustomed to formal environments and do not have the necessary attentional, visual–motor, perceptual, and social skills to allow them to sit and concentrate on the test materials for the necessary amount of time without close supervision. Such close supervision and attention are readily available under the circumstances of individual asssessment. Individual assessment of children should be the rule below age 5 and is recommended for elderly persons as well. The use of group tests further removes the clinician from the process and takes away the possibility of obtaining good observational data.

Individual Screening of Intellectual Function

The use of individually administered screening tests need not be an extremely expensive or time-consuming enterprise. Individual screening instruments are available that are valid, reliable, informative, and require only 20 to 30 minutes for administration. Of these, the most reasonable seem to be the carefully developed short forms of the major individually administered intelligence tests. These short forms are typically at least as reliable as other brief tests, have more validity information available, are more familiar to educational and psychological personnel, and are traditionally better normed than nearly all other brief tests of intelligence. Short forms of the major scales have an added advantage: If an individual is noted to be at risk on the screening measure, the remainder of the scale can be administered without a duplication of effort. The development of short forms of the Wechsler scales has been a popular topic in the psychometric literature for some time, and several short forms of the WISC-R have been proposed. Of these, the most useful appears to be the short form proposed by Kaufman (1976).

Previously, short forms have been developed typically on purely empirical grounds without regard to rational and psychological bases for the inclusion of specific subtests. Although empirical development is necessary, it seems insufficient as the sole method of choosing subtests for a short form. Kaufman's (1976) four-test short form of the WISC-R was developed on the basis of empirical and rational psychological characteristics of the various subtests using data gleaned from the large national standardization sample of the test with careful delineation of the short form's psychometric properties.

In choosing subtests for the short form, Kaufman determined that two Verbal and two Performance tests would be included and that each dyad should be truly representative of its respective scale. For the Verbal dyad, the Arithmetic and Vocabulary subtests were chosen. For the 10 possible dyads, the range of correlations with Verbal IQ was but .88 to .93; thus any combination was about equally empirically adequate. The Arithmetic-Vocabulary combination was chosen because (a) the tests tap diverse mental skills, (b) the verbal–numerical combination is known to be an excellent predictor of school or academic attainment, (c) Vocabulary is the best single measure of general intelligence (customarily referred to as g) on the WISC-R, and (d) the inclusion of Arithmetic ensures that the Freedom from Distractibility factor (see later discussion of factor analysis of the WISC-R) is represented.

For the 10 possible Performance Scale dyads, the range of correlations was again very restrictive, though smaller on the average than the Verbal dyad–Verbal Scale correlations. Kaufman (1976) selected the Picture Arrangement–Block Design dyad to represent the Performance Scale. It had the largest correlation with the Performance IQ (0.89) and has considerable intuitive and rational appeal. Block Design is the best measure of g for the entire battery and is the most reliable of all Performance Scale tests. Block Design and Picture Arrangement measure diverse sets of mental skill, and Picture Arrangement is more complex than the remaining Performance tasks in addition to being one of the clinically most interesting of all Wechsler tasks. Once chosen from results with the even age groups of the standardization sample, both dyads were cross-validated using the odd age groups.

Using a method of linear equating described by Tellegen and Briggs (1967), Kaufman generated conversion equations for the estimation of Full Scale IQ from short-form scores at each age level. Since the equations were all so similar, a single equation determined from the intercorrelation matrix of all 11 age groups was used to convert short-form scores to estimate Full Scale IQs. The equation, applicable to the entire age range of the WISC-R, is:

$$\text{Estimated WISC-R Full Scale IQ} = 1.64X_{SF} + 34.1 \tag{1}$$

where X_{SF} is the sum of the child's *scaled* scores on the four component subtests. Although this equation is easy to use, Kaufman (1976, Table 3, p. 185) also provides a conversion table for estimating Full Scale IQs based on it.

The psychometric characteristics of the Kaufman WISC-R short form are admirable given its brevity. The split-half reliability ranges from .89 to .93 across the age range while short-term test–retest reliability estimates range from .83 to .91. At every age, the short form correlates above .90 with the Full Scale IQ. At the appropriate age levels, the WISC-R short-form IQs correlate .80 with the WPPSI and .89 with the WAIS. The short-form estimates of WISC-R Full Scale IQs, on the average, are within 3 points of the Full Scale IQ obtained from administration of the total scale (Kaufman, 1976). The standard error of estimate of the short-form estimated Full Scale IQs is about 5 points.

Short forms of other individual intelligence tests have also been developed but are not featured here. For adults, Reynolds, Willson, and Clark (in press) have recently developed a short form of the WAIS-R (Wechsler, 1981). For young children, short forms of the WPPSI (Kaufman, 1972) and the McCarthy Scales of Children's Abilities (Kaufman, 1977) are the most appropriate individual screening methods (see Reynolds & Clark, 1983, for discussion of various proposed short forms of these scales). When choosing or developing short forms of existing or new intelligence tests, psychologists would be wise to adhere to the blend of psychological, clinical, and psychometric considerations proposed by Kaufman (1972, 1976, 1977).

INDIVIDUAL DIAGNOSIS OF INTELLECTUAL DISORDERS

Before proceeding with a formal cognitive assessment, it is essential to understand the legal requirements. As of September 1, 1978, all handicapped children ages 3 to 18 must receive a "free, appropriate public education." Under the provision of P.L. 94-142 (Education for All Handicapped Children Act of 1975), before a child can be identified as handicapped, he or she must be provided with a "full and individual evaluation." This evaluation has to be conducted according to specific requirements: (a) The tests must be presented in the child's native language or mode of communication; (b) the tests must be well normed and used specifically for the purposes for which they were intended (validated); (c) the tests must be administered by an individual trained in their usage as they were designed by the producer; (d) no single instrument can be used for appropriate programming; and (e) a multidisciplinary team must conduct the evaluation, consisting of at least one specialist in the area of difficulty. Section 504 of the Vocational Rehabilitation Act of 1973 extends these requirements to the handicapped of all ages.

Obviously, to be consistent with federal law and good psychological sense, evaluation procedures must adhere to strict qualifications. For instance, the stipulation in P.L. 94-142 that "tests and other evaluation materials include those tailored to assess specific areas of educational needs and not merely which are designed to provide a single intelligence quotient" should be nothing new to competent psychologists who are accustomed to performing comprehensive child studies. Even though this chapter focuses on the use of the major individual intelligence scales, the days should be far behind us when the diagnosis of mental retardation, for example, was made on the basis of a single score from an IQ test. It is imperative that a variety of techniques be employed in the diagnosis of any cognitive disorder at any age, but especially during childhood when the plasticity of the central nervous system is so great and development so rapid.

In addition, it is mandated that "tests are selected and administered so as best to ensure that, when a test is administered to a student with impaired sensory, manual, or speaking skill, the test results accurately reflect the student's aptitude or achievement level or whatever other factor the test purports to measure rather than reflecting the student's impaired sensory, manual, or speaking skills (except where those skills are the factors that the test purports to measure)." Most psychological tests are not standardized for use with sensory-impaired populations, nor are examiners routinely trained in the skills necessary to communicate effectively with these children. Without specific training in the evaluation and assessment of sensory-impaired children, most psychologists would do well to refer such children to an appropriate specialist. Although one continues to hear horror stories regarding the wrongful diagnosis of hearing-impaired and visually impaired children based on low levels of performance on standardized intelligence scales, the limitations of tests standardized on normal children for such populations are now better understood and such acts of incompetence are rare. At the preschool level, slight visual or hearing impairments may be less readily apparent, and young children suspected of having cognitive disorders should routinely have hearing and visual examinations.

Many factors influence the outcome of a cognitive assessment, and all must be considered when evaluating the performance of an individual. Factors influencing the assessment process are reviewed elsewhere by Kaufman (1979a), Lutey and Copeland (1982), and Matarazzo (1972); readers are cautioned to pay particular attention to external and situational factors when evaluating preschoolers.

It is frequently necessary to arrive at a specific diagnosis when evaluating handicapped individuals. Several systems for the classification of mental and cognitive disorders are available, with which the examiner should be familiar (e.g.., the diagnostic criteria of P.L. 94-142, the DSM-III, the International Classification of Diseases, and several actuarial systems reviewed in McDermott, 1982). Psychologists and other diagnostic personnel will typically be restricted to the use of a particular system as a function of the location of their employment. In public school settings the categories and criteria of P.L. 94-142 are almost universally employed, whereas hospitals and mental health centers most often adopt the DSM-III. Diagnostic personnel in settings where no single system is given exclusive preference should adopt one system and use it consistently, so as to foster accurate communication among the different types and levels of personnel who may encounter the individual in question. Accurate diagnostic decision making is difficult and requires hands-on exposure to the many handicapping conditions that can affect children and adults, in addition to thorough academic training regarding the characteristics of these handicaps.

TRADITIONAL NORMATIVE APPROACHES TO TEST INTERPRETATION

The first line of attack in test interpretation is the evaluation of the individual's performance relative to the performance of an appropriate reference group. In the vast majority of cases this will be the individual's age peers. For the Wechsler scales, the three global IQs would first be examined and compared to the mean level of performance of the standardization samples. Since the Wechsler IQs are standardized within separate age levels and assume an essentially normal distribution, the normative evaluation of performance is relatively simple and straightforward. Given the constant mean (100) and standard deviation (15) of the Verbal, Performance, and Full Scale IQs, the relative standing of the individual with regard to age peers is readily revealed from tables in the test manual or a table of the normal curve. However, Wechsler grouped tasks into these three IQ scales on a purely intuitive basis; before making direct interpretations of the scales, evidence for the reality of their existence must be examined. Such evidence comes most directly from factor analysis.

Factor Analysis of the Wechsler Scales

One of the most frequent avenues of research with the Wechsler scales has been factor analysis. A striking consistency of results has occurred across a number of ages and populations that has implications for test interpretation. Some major differences occur across the three Wechsler scales (WPPSI, WISC-R, WAIS-R) that are important to note as well.

Three consistent and pervasive factors emerged for each of the 11 age groups in the WISC-R standardization sample, regardless of whether orthogonal or oblique rotational procedures were employed: Verbal Comprehension, Perceptual Organization, and Freedom from Distractibility (Kaufman, 1975). Each of the 12 WISC-R subtests was found to have a *primary* loading on one and only one of these factors, as shown below:

Verbal Comprehension	Perceptual Organization	Freedom from Distractibility
Information	Picture Completion	Arithmetic
Similarities	Picture Arrangement	Digit Span
Vocabulary	Block Design	Coding
Comprehension	Object Assembly	
	Mazes	

The first two factors bear an obvious relationship to the Verbal and Performance Scales, respectively. The third factor was labeled Freedom from Distractibility, to follow the historical precedent established by Cohen (1952, 1959) for other Wechsler batteries, and because of research with hyperactive children showing that drug therapy leads to decreased distractibiltiy and improved memory and arithmetic skills in these youngsters (Wender, 1971).

Tables 3.1 through 3.3 show the median varimax loadings obtained for the 11 age groups between 6 ½ and 16 ½ years in the normative sample, along with results from a series of replications with various groups of normal and clinical groups. Note that Information had a substantial loading on the third factor for the standardization

Table 3.1.   Factor Loadings on the Verbal Comprehension Factor for a Variety of Normal and Clinical Samples

	WISC-R Subtest													
	(1)	(2)	(3)	(4)	(5)	(6)	(7)	(8)	(9)	(10)	(11)	(12)	(13)	Median
Verbal														
Information	63	63	72	66	70	73	82	59	84	71	76	69	73	71
Similarities	64	59	66	67	59	67	75	69	77	69	68	70	66	67
Arithmetic	37	43	65	40	42	41	44	43	66	48	39	43	62	43
Vocabulary	72	74	76	67	74	57	82	81	82	70	76	82	82	76
Comprehension	64	64	74	61	71	53	65	77	82	55	56	72	64	64
Digit Span	18	35	46	33	31	46	23	28	38	14	—	—	44	33
Performance														
Picture														
Completion	35	20	36	32	22	16	30	31	16	24	28	29	37	29
Picture														
Arrangement	33	20	39	17	2	46	38	30	48	18	23	25	41	30
Block Design	27	17	23	20	14	27	37	32	23	22	31	20	33	23
Object Assembly	21	07	09	14	09	04	20	20	23	28	−10	25	20	20
Coding	15	12	35	14	21	26	27	20	07	14	21	11	38	20
Mazes	12	18	30	06	16	10	—	08	—	—	—	—	23	14

Note. Decimal points are omitted. Loadings of .35 and above are italicized. The groups are as follows:
1. Standardization sample, ages 6½–16½ (N = 2200), 85% white, 15% nonwhite, median varimax loadings for 11 age groups are shown in table. Source: Kaufman (1975).
2. Anglos, grades 1–9 (N = 252). Source: Reschly (1978).
3. Blacks, grades 1–9 (N = 235). Source: Reschly (1978).
4. Chicanos, grades 1–9 (N = 223). Source: Reschly (1978).
5. Native-American Papagos, grades 1–9 (N = 240). Source: Reschly (1978).
6. Mentally retarded sample, ages 6–16½ (N = 80), mean WISC-R IQ = 50.6, 82% white, 18% nonwhite. Source: Van Hagen and Kaufman (1975).
7. Adolescent psychiatric sample, ages 10½–16 (N = 100), 68% white, 32% nonwhite. Source: De Horn and Klinge (1978).
8. Sample of children referred because of concerns about intellectual ability, ages 7–16 (N = 164), mean WISC-R IQ = 85.9, 63% white, 24% black, 13% Latino. Source: Swerdlik and Schweitzer (1978).
9. Sample of children referred for learning and/or behavior problems, ages 6–13 (N = 106). 90% Spanish surname, 8% white, 2% black. Source: Stedman, Lawlis, Cortner, and Achterberg (1978).
10. Sample of Chicano children referred for school-related problems, mean age = 10½ (N = 142). Source: Gutkin and Reynolds (1980).
11. Sample and Anglo children referred for learning difficulties, mean age = 11 (N – 109). Source: Dean (1979).
12. Sample of learning-disabled children, mean age = 10½ (N = 275). Source: Schooler, Beebe, and Koepke (1978).
13. Sample of low-SES children from the WISC-R standardization sample (N = 782). Source: Carlson, Reynolds, and Gutkin (in press).

sample (Mdn = .41). However, this relationship was not obtained for two oblique rotations of the WISC-R factors, so it was concluded that the distractibility factor was composed only of Arithmetic, Digit Span, and Coding. This conclusion has received additional support from the results of factor analyses of supplementary populations. A distractibility dimension emerged for mentally retarded children and adolescents (Van Hagen & Kaufman, 1975), adolescent psychiatric patients (De

Table 3.2.   Factor Loadings on the Perceptual Organization Factor for a Variety of Normal and Clinical Samples

	WISC-R Subtest													
	(1)	(2)	(3)	(4)	(5)	(6)	(7)	(8)	(9)	(10)	(11)	(12)	(13)	Median
Verbal														
Information	25	32	32	20	26	12	29	33	10	13	09	11	29	25
Similarities	34	26	30	15	34	08	*45*	22	23	33	*39*	30	34	30
Arithmetic	20	26	*37*	13	*37*	16	*40*	*39*	13	31	–23	*37*	27	27
Vocabulary	24	23	19	26	14	27	31	23	30	27	22	23	26	24
Comprehension	30	22	16	20	13	*48*	*38*	25	18	33	–12	15	34	22
Digit Span	12	02	32	14	*36*	06	10	26	23	22	—	—	19	19
Performance														
Picture Completion	*57*	*49*	*44*	*52*	*54*	*83*	*68*	*59*	*83*	*56*	*66*	*47*	*59*	*57*
Picture Arrangement	*41*	*53*	*47*	*38*	*43*	*41*	*58*	*52*	31	*72*	*59*	*56*	*44*	*47*
Block Design	*66*	*60*	*66*	*59*	*68*	*62*	*71*	*70*	*75*	*64*	*73*	*70*	*74*	*68*
Object Assembly	*65*	*59*	*57*	*58*	*56*	*70*	*76*	*76*	*68*	*51*	*69*	*80*	*73*	*68*
Coding	20	16	27	16	25	*45*	30	*44*	05	*37*	29	*43*	19	27
Mazes	*47*	*42*	*47*	*47*	*56*	*67*	—	*55*	—	—	—	—	*52*	*50*

Note. Decimal points are omitted. Loadings of .35 and above are italicized. See the Note to Table 3.1 for a description of the 13 groups and for the data sources.

Horn & Klinge, 1978), normal groups of Anglos and Chicanos (Reschly, 1978), blacks (Gutkin & Reynolds, 1981), and children referred to school or clinical psychologists for suspected learning and/or behavioral disorders (Lombard & Reidel, 1978; Stedman, Lawlis, Cortner, & Achterberg, 1978; Swerdlik & Schweitzer, 1978). As indicated in Table 3.3, the median loadings for these samples on the distractibility factor were above .40 for Arithmetic, Digit Span, and Coding, but only .30 for Information. Thus the existence of the WISC-R Freedom from Distractibility factor and its composition have been cross-validated for an impressive variety of normal and clinical groups.

Even more striking than the cross-validational evidence for the third factor is the evidence for the first two factors. Verbal Comprehension and Perceptual Organization dimensions have emerged for every sample whose WISC-R subtest scores were subjected to factor analysis, including two groups that did not produce a distractibility factor (the blacks and native American Papagos investigated by Reschly, 1978). Furthermore, when hierarchical factor solutions have been applied to WISC-R data, clear verbal and perceptual dimensions are yielded even after the extraction of a large general intelligence factor (Vance & Wallbrown, 1978; Wallbrown, Blaha, Wallbrown, & Engin, 1975). Tables 3.1 and 3.2 present the median varimax loadings for 13 samples on the Verbal Comprehension and Perceptual Organization factors. The median loadings for these cross-validation samples on the nonverbal

Table 3.3.   Factor Loadings for the Freedom from Distractibility Factor for a Variety of Normal and Clinical Samples

	WISC-R Subtest									
	(1)	(2)	(4)	(6)	(7)	(8)	(9)	(11)	(13)	Median
Verbal										
Information	*41*	26	33	24	14	*38*	16	−19	*42*	26
Similarities	28	26	22	23	22	27	04	−26	28	23
Arithmetic	*58*	*45*	*45*	*54*	*49*	*49*	*40*	*52*	*58*	*49*
Vocabulary	33	12	30	02	17	17	03	20	33	17
Comprehension	24	21	06	12	*45*	16	09	*21*	26	21
Digit Span	*56*	*40*	31	29	*37*	*65*	*42*	—	*56*	*41*
Performance										
Picture Completion	11	09	12	12	−01	19	01	27	13	12
Picture Arrangement	12	00	*39*	*45*	12	*43*	21	−17	24	21
Block Design	28	22	16	05	23	17	04	*47*	30	22
Object Assembly	12	18	09	09	13	12	*36*	24	11	12
Coding	*42*	*40*	*37*	*43*	*57*	19	*94*	*44*	*38*	*42*
Mazes	22	10	20	24	—	22	—	—	23	22

Note. Decimal points are omitted. Loadings of .35 and above are italicized. See the Note to Table 3.1 for a description of the nine groups and for the data sources. Groups 3 and 5 are omitted from this table because a Freedom from Distractibility factor did not emerge for those two samples. Hence, the loadings shown in Tables 3.1 and 3.2 reflect data obtained from Reschly's (1978) two-factor solutions for blacks and Native-American Papagos, but not from his three-factor solutions for white and Chicanos. Groups 10 and 12 are also omitted from this table because Gutkin and Reynolds (1980) only identified two meaningful factors, and Schooler et al. (1978) did not even investigate three-factor solutions.

dimension are very close to the medians for the standardization sample on the Perceptual Organization factor. The Verbal Comprehension factors for the standardization sample and the supplementary populations are also close in composition. The main difference concerns the Arithmetic and Digit Span subtests: For the standardization sample, these tasks were far more associated with the third than the first factor; for the cross-validation groups, they loaded almost equally on the verbal and distractibility dimensions. Examination of data for the separate supplementary populations revealed that the approximately equal loadings by Arithmetic and Digit Span on the first and third factors characterized the normal as well as the clinical samples.

One important inference to be drawn from the various factor analyses is that the empirical results support the construct validity of the WISC-R. The Verbal Comprehension factor reflects the construct purported by Wechsler to be measured by the Verbal Scale. Four Verbal subtests have very high loadings on this factor, and, although arithmetic is a distant fifth, it is clearly associated with the Verbal Comprehension dimension. The fact that Digit Span was the sixth best measure of Verbal Comprehension for the cross-validation samples (but not for the standardization groups) offers tentative support for its placement by Wechsler on the Verbal Scale. Equally good evidence is provided by factor analysis for the construct validity of the

Performance Scale. The pattern of loadings on the Perceptual Organization factor suggests that this dimension corresponds to a unitary ability underlying the Performance Scale. Only Coding among the six nonverbal subtests receives no empirical support for its inclusion on the Performance Scale.

Review of the WISC-R factor-analytic literature has thus shown that three factors are typically isolated—two that relate closely to Wechsler's Verbal–Performance dichotomy and a third that may correspond to a behavioral attribute. These factors are remarkably similar in composition from age to age and across sex (Reynolds & Gutkin, 1980) throughout the entire range serviced by the WISC-R and also from group to group, whether normal or exceptional populations are tested. The three factors have been isolated for Spanish-speaking as well as English-speaking children (Gutkin & Reynolds, 1980; Reschly, 1978; Stedman et al., 1978). Furthermore, the factors do not fragment and split into highly specific factors when four or five factors are rotated (Kaufman, 1975).

The robust nature of the various WISC-R factors is important for clinicians to understand because of the implications that these data hold for competent interpretation of the WISC-R. More so than profiles on the old WISC, children's WISC-R profiles should be attacked by featuring the Verbal and Performance Scales and subserving fluctuations in the pattern of subtest scores. The large, omnipresent Verbal Comprehension and Perceptual Organization factors suggest that the Verbal and Performance IQs correspond to real, unitary dimensions of ability in children. As such, profile interpretation should begin by focusing on these global verbal and nonverbal skill areas. This suggestion seems simple enough, but so many methods of interpretation tend to focus on the individuality of the 10 to 12 subtests, as if the WISC-R were a mixed bag of about a dozen separate and diverse skills, each assessing a finite aspect of a child's intellect (see, for example, the interpretive procedures of Banas & Wills, 1977, 1978; Vitelli & Goldblatt, 1979; or Reynolds, 1981f, for a brief critique). Even a table such as the one appearing in the *WISC-R Manual* (Wechsler, 1974, Table 12), which presents the differences between *pairs* of scaled scores for statistical significance, can impel examiners to focus off target. The pairwise technique places a stress on the *subtests* (taken two at a time), rather than on the two major *scales;* furthermore, this procedure offers clinicians a series of statements about a child's strong and weak abilities, but fails to provide a succinct overview of his or her skills.

Later we will present logical and statistical methods for the very necessary look beyond the IQ scales, but intelligent test interpretation begins by viewing overall performance on *g* (as estimated by the Full Scale IQ) and the Verbal and Performance Scales. The third factor will also need to be examined for many children. Gutkin (1979) provides a formula for estimating a deviation IQ with a mean of 100 and standard deviation of 15 for the Freedom from Distractibility factor.

The third WISC-R factor, which may be a measure of attention/distractibility, anxiety, symbolic ability, sequential processing, or memory, is a particularly intriguing one. Its pervasivenesss and robustness on the WISC-R are not matched in factor analyses of other Wechsler batteries. Recent factor-analytic studies of the

WAIS-R show a large general factor accompanied by strong Verbal Comprehension and Perceptual Organization factors that correspond to the Full Scale, Verbal, and Performance IQ Scales (Gutkin, Reynolds, & Galvin, in press). When WAIS-R distractibility factors do appear for the various adult age groups, they are much smaller in magnitude than their WISC-R counterparts; indeed, for some groups the WAIS-R distractibility dimensions have such small eigenvalues that they are of questionable significance (Naglieri & Kaufman, 1982). Finally, numerous studies of the preschool version of the Wechsler, the WPPSI, have repeatedly located only a large general factor and the two factors corresponding to the a priori–determined IQ scales (e.g., Carlson & Reynolds, 1981; Kaufman &Hollenbeck, 1974).

Normative Evaluation of the IQs

Once the IQs have been derived, some judgment of the individual's level of intellectual function relative to age peers is appropriate. Probably the most readily understandable approach is the reporting of a percentile rank with a descriptive classification. Wechsler IQs are essentially normally distributed, and tables of percentile ranks, expressing the percentage of the population scoring above and below a given score, are available in a variety of sources including Reynolds (1981a), Sattler (1982), and many measurement texts. When reporting the IQ it is helpful to give a descriptive classification in addition to the percentile rank. Wechsler (1974) and others (e.g., Kaufman & Kaufman, 1977) present various descriptive classification schemes.

The terminology of certain systems can be offensive, and care must be given to choosing an appropriate descriptor. The term *mentally defective* to describe persons having Wechsler or Binet IQs below 70, though perhaps accurate, seems unduly harsh. On the other hand, accuracy is an important concern. For these reasons, a system for descriptive classification of IQ level adapted from Kaufman and Kaufman (1977) is presented for use in Table 3.4 (and originally adapted by these authors from Wechsler, 1974).

When reporting IQs, percentile ranks, and descriptive classifications of performance level, we also feel that it is important to make some statement regarding measurement error. Even though the three Wechsler scales have Full Scale IQs with reliability coefficients in the mid-.90s, considerable error can still be present for individuals. From the reliability estimates, a very practical statistic known as the *standard error of measurement* (SE_m) can be derived, which allows the establishment of a confidence interval around the reported IQ. Though varying somewhat from scale to scale, the SE_m of the Wechsler Full Scale IQs is around 3 IQ points. Since the SE_m is normally distributed about the true score of the individual, we can band the obtained score to represent any given level of confidence desired, simply by multiplying the SE_m by the necessary value of z from a table of the normal curve. For example, 1 SE_m will capture about 68% of a child's score and 2 SE_m about 95%. We feel that the 85%-to-90% level of confidence is appropriate for most clinical purposes; for the Wechsler scales, this requires banding the reported Full

Table 3.4.   Descriptive Classification Corresponding to Various Levels of
IQ on the Wechsler Scales

IQ Range	Percentile Ranks	Descriptive Classification
130 and above	98 and above	Very superior
120 to 129	91 to 97	Superior
110 to 119	75 to 90	High average
90 to 109	25 to 73	Average
80 to 89	9 to 23	Low average
70 to 79	3 to 8	Borderline
69 and below	2 and below	Cognitively deficient

Scale IQ with about 5 points on each side. The primary purpose of such reporting is to highlight the concept of error and guard against overinterpretation and rigidity in the use of cutoff scores.*

Normative evaluation of levels of performance is crucial to intelligent testing. Performance on IQ tests is related to a variety of factors, the most important for children being school attainment. The IQ test makes a good prediction of the child's future level of academic performance, and can help to explain current levels of academic functioning (extensive reviews of predictive studies with IQ tests may be found in Lutey, 1977; and Sattler, 1982). Important information is gleaned for adults as well, including predictions of success in certain jobs, response to various psychotherapies, and the probability of recovery from neurological insult. However crucial, normative interpretation is insufficient for intelligent testing. Much more information lies beyond comparisons of individuals to their peers. Intraindividual differences can be important in altering the predictions made by the IQs, for those predictions assume no major changes occurring in the environment. One must look past the IQs to generate hypotheses for intervention.

* Note that the SE_m is symmetrical only about the true score, which is obtained by regressing the obtained score to the mean of the distribution via the reliability coefficient where the true score (X_∞) becomes $X_\infty = X + r_{xx}(X_i - X)$. Our recommendation for banding obtained scores is thus technically in error but seems appropriate for several reasons: Banding X_i instead of $X\infty$ avoids considerable confusion when interpreting scores to a psychometrically unsophisticated audience; as long as r_{xx} is above .90, the differences between the two methods are very small, within 3 SDs of the mean; the primary purpose of reporting the confidence interval in test interpretation is not to convey detailed technical information regarding the test, but rather to highlight the fact that there is error present in the IQ and help avoid reifying the obtained numbers.

IPSATIVE EVALUATION OF TEST PERFORMANCE

Normative assessment of performance on the Wechsler scales proceeds from the assumptions that g is primarily the determinant of the Full Scale IQ, that verbal comprehension ability is the primary determinant of scores on the Verbal Scale, that perceptual organization ability is the determinant of scores on the Performance Scale, and, where applicable, that some unitary trait or ability underlies performance on the distractibility factor. A corollary assumption is that fluctuations in a child's or adult's profile are due to chance error. Fortunately, statistics and formulas are available to permit clinicians to test these important assumptions. When the assumptions cannot be refuted by the simple empirical procedures, then examiners should not ordinarily go beyond a normative interpretation of the Wechsler profile. However, when fluctuations between scales and among subtest scores are statistically significant, causing the examiners to reject some or all of the assumptions, then ipsative (intraindividual) evaluation takes over and the clinical "detective work" predominates.

Verbal–Performance IQ Differences

During ipsative assessment of scores, the individual's own mean level of performance becomes the normative standard against which scores are held for comparison. The first step in the process is to examine the Verbal and Performance IQs (VIQ & PIQ) to determine whether use of the Full Scale IQ (FSIQ) is justifiable. To do this, the examiner first compares the VIQ with the PIQ to find the difference between these scores. For the WISC-R a difference in these two scores of 12 points is statistically significant at $p \leq .05$ and 15 points at $p \leq .01$; for the WAIS-R the comparable values are 10 and 13, respectively, and for the WPPSI, the corresponding values are closer to 11 and 14. What does it mean if these scores differ significantly? First of all, it renders the FSIQ inadequate as a summary statistic representing the general level of ability for the individual. It means that the levels of performance on the Verbal and Performance Scales are different to the extent that we can be reasonably confident that the differences are real, not due to chance or the error inherent in all tests. It also, by inference, tells us that this individual does not think, reason, or express himself or herself at an equivalent level through the verbal modality of language as through more concrete, nonverbal methods. The existence of the difference does not, however, tell us why it is there.

Many explanations of V–P IQ differences are possible. Factor analysis is a group data analysis procedure; as noted earlier, this technique provides strong support for interpretation of distinct Verbal and Performance Scales, but it does not explain why a child or adult might score substantially higher on one scale than the other. Kaufman (1979a) has offered a variety of potential explanations for VIQ–PIQ differences on the WISC-R that in most instances are equally applicable to the WPPSI and the WAIS-R. Kaufman suggests that VIQ–PIQ differences for individuals may reflect (a) sensory deficits, (b) differences in verbal and nonverbal intelligence, (c) differences in fluid versus crystallized intelligence, (d) psycholinguistic deficiencies, (e) bilingualism, (f) effects of black dialect, (g) motor coordination problems, (h) reactions to time pressures on the Performance Scale, (i) differences in field dependence/independence, (j) differences on Guilford's operation of evaluation, or (k) socioeconomic influences. Proper interpretation of V–P IQ discrepancies requires close observation of children or adults while they perform the various tasks making up the Wechsler scales, in addition to a comprehensive understanding of contemporary theories of intelligence. Once the best explanation of a child's reliable Verbal–Performance difference has been found, this explanation will almost invariably contribute to the development of appropriate teaching methods for the child that reflect strengths in his or her methods and preferences for learning. For adults, VIQ–PIQ differences can assist in localization of neurological trauma as well as the evaluation of differences in learning. Attempts have been made to link V–P differences to personality characteristics and such factors as obsessive–compulsive tendencies (e.g., Blatt & Allison, 1981), but as yet no satisfactory data-based support for these interpretations is available.

Another factor to consider in evaluating the meaning of VIQ–PIQ differences is the frequency of occurrence of a difference score of a given magnitude. For a VIQ–PIQ difference to have *diagnostic* significance, it should be relatively infrequent in the normal population. Large discrepancies between Verbal and Performance IQs have commonly been associated with a variety of abnormalities, such as neurological impairment (e.g., Holroyd & Wright, 1965). However, these clinical assumptions have usually been made in the absence of hard data on *normal* individuals. How can inferences be made relating interscale or intrascale scatter on a Wechsler battery to *abnormalities,* without first considering *normal* VIQ–PIQ discrepancies?

Wechsler (1974) reports the magnitude of VIQ–PIQ differences required for statistical significance at various levels. About 9 points are required for significance at p < .15, about 12 points are needed for p <.05, and about 15 points between the VIQ and PIQ are necessary for p <.01. These values reflect the degree to which the VIQs and PIQs must differ in order for the discrepancies to be meaningful, as opposed to being due merely to chance error, and they are based on the reliability coefficients of the VIQs and PIQs. The probabilities translate into the amount of confidence one should have that the V–P IQ discrepancy stands for a true difference in the individual's verbal and nonverbal intelligence. However, even though statistical significance provides important information for determining whether a child has "real" differences in the abilities underlying the Verbal and Performance Scales, the meaningfulness of the discrepancy does not translate to the *frequency of occurrence* of a given V–P difference. Yet it is the frequency of occurrence among a normal population that is most pertinent for understanding abnormal conditions.

In a study of the WISC-R standardization sample, the average child aged 6½ to 16½ years had a VIQ–PIQ discrepancy, regardless of direction, equal to 9.7 points (SD = 7.6) (Kaufman, 1976c). The mean discrepancy was approximately the same for each of the 11 age groups. Similarly, discrepancies were unrelated to the variables of sex and race. In contrast, a trend was noted with regard to socioeconomic status. The mean discrepancy was nearly 11 points for children of professional parents and decreased to a mean of about 9 points for children of unskilled workers. For all youngsters in the normative sample it was observed that one out of two normal children had a significant VIQ–PIQ difference at the 85% level of confidence (9-point discrepancy or higher); one out of three had a significant discrepancy at the 95% level of confidence (12+ points); and one out of four had a significant discrepancy at the 99% level of confidence (15+ points). Thus 25% of normal school-age children have a V–P difference of a magnitude that Wechsler (1974, p. 34) claims "is important and calls for further investigation."

The V–P IQ discrepancies for the WISC-R seem to surprise many clinicians, even though analogous data have been available for years on the 1949 WISC (Seashore, 1951) and the Wechsler Adult Intelligence Scale (WAIS) (Matarazzo, 1972). If earlier studies have been ignored to some extent by clinicians and researchers, it is essential for the WISC-R data to be internalized by test users—particularly in view of current controversy over labeling and legal definitions of various exceptionalities. Recently, results for the WISC-R and WAIS have been replicated for the WPPSI (Reynolds & Gutkin, 1981c).

Kaufman (1979a) has provided a table summarizing the distribution of VIQ–PIQ differences on the WISC-R that is reproduced here as Table 3.5. The table shows the magnitude of V–P discrepancies occurring at different frequencies within the normal population. These values provide an index of "unusualness" or "abnormality" of various V–P discrepancies. From the far-right column of Table 3.5, it is evident that discrepancies of 15 or more points occur less than 25% of the time among normal children; discrepancies of 19 points occur less than 15% of the time; discrepancies of 30 points occur less than 2% of the time; and so forth. These values enable examiners to evaluate every significant ($p < .05$)VIQ–PIQ discrepancy they observe and determine whether the difference in the child's verbal and nonverbal abilities is unusual or abnormal; they are, therefore, worthy of considerable attention. Separate norms are presented in Table 3.5 for five different socioeconomic categories, because, as noted above, VIQ–PIQ discrepancies were a function of socioeconomic background, with larger differences associated with the higher occupational groups. Clinicians have the option of using the basal rates for the total group or those for the separate parental occupation categories, based on their personal preferences. Similarly, they may choose any degree of abnormality that makes sense for a given purpose. When merely attempting to describe in a case report whether a child's V–P discrepancy is rare or typical, then a criterion such as "less than 15%" seems adequate. However, when examiners are intending to base a diagnosis of an exceptionality in part upon the degree of interscale scatter, then a more conservative criterion, such as "less than 5%" or "less than 2%," should be employed.

Whereas tables of these values for the WAIS (Matarazzo, 1972) and the WPPSI (Reynolds & Gutkin, 1981c) are available, Kaufman's (1979a) WISC-R table corresponds almost exactly to the distributions of difference scores for the other scales. Comparable data for the WAIS-R are not yet available, but the WAIS-R distributions will undoubtedly resemble closely the WISC-R distributions given the similar

Table 3.5. Percentage of Normal Children Obtaining WISC-R V–P Discrepancies of a Given Magnitude or Greater, by Parental Occupation

Size of V–P Discrepancy (Regardless of Direction)	Parental Occupation					
	Professional and Technical	Managerial, Clerical, Sales	Skilled Workers	Semiskilled Workers	Unskilled Workers	Total Sample
9	52	48	48	46	43	48
10	48	44	43	41	37	43
11	43	40	39	36	34	39
12	40	35	34	31	29	34
13	36	33	31	28	26	31
14	32	29	29	25	24	28
15	29	25	26	21	22	24
16	26	22	22	19	19	22
17	24	19	18	15	16	18
18	20	16	16	14	15	16
19	16	15	13	12	14	14
20	13	13	12	10	13	12
21	11	11	8	9	10	10
22	10	9	7	7	9	8
23	8	8	6	6	8	7
24	7	7	5	5	6	6
25	6	6	4	4	5	5
26	5	5	3	3	4	4
27	4	4	2	2	3	3
28–30	3	3	1	1	2	2
31–33	2	2	<1	<1	1	1
34+	1	1	<1	<1	<1	<1

correlation between the Verbal and Performance Scales and the constant SD. (The distribution of difference scores is a direct function of these variables.)

The focus in this section on the abnormality of profile fluctuations is not intended to minimize the importance of statistically significant differences in a person's abilities. V–P IQ discrepancies that are large enough to be significant are highly valuable, even if they are not large enough to be termed "rare." These significant differences indicate real discrepancies in the individual's abilities and therefore provide valuable input for making educational and other practical recommendations. The key distinction here is between diagnosis and treatment. When differences are both significant and rare, they may be used as one piece of evidence in formulating diagnostic hypotheses, *and* they are likely to be translatable to remedial action. However, differences that are significant but not unusual in their occurrence have *only* remedial implications; diagnosis of an abnormality should not be based, even partially, on deviations that occur with reasonable frequency among normal individuals unless they form part of a carefully delineated syndrome.

Fluctuations in Performance on Individual Subtests

The next line of attack for interpreting the Wechsler Scales requires the examiner to evaluate a person's performance on each subtest of the Verbal and Performance

Scales. There must, of course, be statistical and psychometric justification for the interpretation of any individual subtest. First of all, the subtest must deviate from the mean of all subtests on the same scale by a statistically significant amount, and secondly, the subtest must have at least adequate *specificity* (reliable unique variance). Both conditions must be met prior to interpretation of a child's performance on any single subtest.

To determine whether a person's performance on any subtest deviates significantly from the mean of all subtests, the Verbal and Performance Scales should be considered separately. Using the Verbal Scale as an example, the person's mean scaled score on the Verbal Scale should be calculated and then subtracted from each subtest scaled score. Exact values are available in Sattler (1982) for determining whether a subtest's deviation is statistically significant; however, the values are all very close to 3.0 to 4.0 scaled-score points for the WISC-R and WAIS-R and 3.0 for the WPPSI. These are the recommended values for determining whether a difference is real or most likely due to measurement error or other uncontrolled, random factors. Thus any subtest deviating from the mean of all subtests by the designated number of points (or more) on the Verbal Scale should be considered a candidate for individual interpretation that may reflect a significant strength or weakness in the child's ability spectrum. This procedure is then repeated for the Performance Scale.

Once it has been ascertained that a significant discrepancy exists, one must evaluate the amount of specific variance (or subtest specificity) that the subtest possesses and judge whether or not it is adequate to support interpretation of the subtest independent of the general factor. Subtest specificity refers to the amount of variance in a score that is both reliable and unique to that subtest, that is, not shared or held in common with other subtests of the same scale. Subtest specificity is readily calculated as a byproduct of factor analysis and is the percentage of reliable variance minus either the multiple correlation of all other subtests with the subtest or the communality estimate from the factor analysis. Kaufman (1979a), Carlson and Reynolds (1981), and Gutkin, Reynolds, and Galvin (in press) have calculated the specific variances of the WISC-R, WPPSI, and WAIS-R subtests, respectively, and classified each as possessing ample, adequate, or inadequate specificity. Table 3.6 summarizes the classifications of each of the sources. From the table it can be seen that there exists adequate specificity to allow the interpretation of most of the Wechsler subtests at most ages. However, some significant fluctuations do occur, and Table 3.6 should be a useful guide. The classifications in Table 3.6 are based on the following criteria: For ample specificity, the subtest must display specific variance of at least 25% and specific variance must exceed error variance; for adequate specificity, there must be 15% to 24% specific variance and specific greater than error variance; and tests with inadequate specificity must fall below 15% and typically show error variance in excess of specific variance.

Once a subtest has been identified as deviating significantly from the mean and as having at least adequate specificity, one still must determine just what interpretation is appropriate for this finding. Behavioral observations taken during the testing may strongly influence this interpretation. It is also necessary to know just what is measured by the subtest(s) in question. This can be determined by making a content

Table 3.6. Classification of Wechsler Scale Subtests According to Relative Proportion of Subtest Specific Variance

	Ample	Adequate	Inadequate
WPPSI			
	Vocabulary	Arithmetic	Information
	Similarities	Geometric Design	Comprehension
	Sentences	Animal House (age 4)	
	Animal House		
	(except at age 4)		
	Picture Completion		
	Mazes		
	Block Design		
WISC-R			
	Information	Vocabulary	Similarities
	Similarities	Comprehension	(ages 9½ to 16½)
	(ages 6½ to 8½)	Picture Completion	Object Assembly
	Arithmetic	(ages 9½ to 16½)	
	Digit Span		
	Picture Completion		
	(ages 6½ to 8½)		
	Picture Arrangement		
	Block Design		
	Coding		
	Mazes		
WAIS-R[a]			
	Digit Span	Information	Vocabulary
	Arithmetic	Comprehension	Comprehension
	Picture Completion	(ages 25 to 74)	(ages 16 to 24)
	Picture Arrangement	Similarities	Object Assembly
	Digit Symbol	Block Design	

[a] Only major age trends noted.

analysis of the mental operations necessary to perform the tasks called for by the subtest and by reviewing the primary correlates of the subtest in the research literature. Kaufman (1979a), Lutey (1977), and Sattler (1982) are excellent sources of information on the skills tapped by the various subtests, but the examiner must meld this information with his or her own observations of the child's performance. It is also preferable to look for trends in abilities across multiple subtests that appear as strengths or weaknesses not only on each scale but also across scales than to become too excited about a single subtest that deviates from the child's mean subtest score. It is always appropriate to apply logic, intuition, and good common sense to test interpretation along with one's statistical and psychometric expertise. For individual assessment neither is totally adequate, especially when attempting to devise appropriate instructional programs for a special needs learner or gain significant insights into the cognitive structure and function of the individual.

Just as with VIQ–PIQ discrepancies, it is useful to examine the range of subtest scatter on the Wechsler scales. Both the range of subtest scores obtained by an individual and the number of subtests deviating from the mean of the subtests are of interest. It is frequently quite surprising to clinicians to learn of the results of such investigations with *normal* children, since the notion of scatter has long been associated with a variety of *abnormal* conditions. Kaufman (1976b) has reported on the degree of subtest scatter characterizing the 2200 normal children of the WISC-R standardization sample.

For each normal child aged 6½ to 16½ years, scaled scores on the 10 regular subtests were rank-ordered from high to low. Then the lowest score was subtracted from the highest score, yielding a scaled-score range for each youngster. Whereas the informally obtained estimates of these ranges from clinicians with years of experience tend to cluster around 3 to 4 points, the actual ranges computed for the standardization group averaged an astonishing 7 points (SD = 2) (Kaufman, 1976b). This mean range spans more than two standard deviations; furthermore, a mean scaled-score range on the Full Scale of 7 ± 2 characterized each of the 11 age groups, male and female, black and white, and children from each of five parental occupation categories.

In practical terms, a scaled-score range of 7 means that the average child's subtest scores ranged from about 6 to 13 or 7 to 14. Since normality is often defined as ± 1 standard deviation from the mean, even a scaled-score range as large as 9 points (i.e., 7 + 2) can be considered normal. Thus a range of scaled scores from 3 to 12, from 6 to 15, or from 8 to 17 can legitimately be termed normal when empirical guidelines are used. One has to wonder how many times ranges such as these have been interpreted as indicative of marked scatter, and how many times youngsters have been assigned a label such *learning disabled,* at least in part because of the so-called scatter in their WISC-R profiles.

Table 3.7 provides a summary of the results of Kaufman's (1976b) analysis of scaled-score ranges for this group of children and should serve as a guide to interpreting the range of subtest performance for individual children. To use Table 3.7, compute the child's ranges on the Verbal, Performance, and Full Scales. Subtract the child's lowest scaled score from his or her highest scaled score for each of the three scales. Then enter these values into the pertinent columns in Table 3.7, to determine whether the child's intrascale scatter is rare or fairly typical. Suppose only the 10 regular subtests are administered, and a girl obtains a Verbal range of 5, a Performance range of 10, and a Full Scale range of 11. Her Verbal scaled-score range of 5 reflects normal variability, because a range of 7 is required to occur less than 15% of the time in the normal population. However, her Performance range of 10 and the Full Scale range of 11 are both reasonably rare, each occurring less than 10% of the time. As with VIQ–PIQ discrepancies, clinicians may select any degree of abnormality that makes sense to them; and they would probably be wise to adapt the specific level to the circumstances surrounding the evaluation and the purposes for which the test scores are intended.

Kaufman (1976b) has also provided results from an analysis of the WISC-R standardization data with regard to the number of subtests deviating significantly from the mean of all subtests on the same scale. More than half of the children showed at least one subtest deviating significantly from the scale mean; nearly one-fourth showed at least three significant deviations from the mean of all subtests. These analyses are not restrictive to the WISC-R. Reynolds and Gutkin (1981c) reported values nearly identical to those published by Kaufman (1976b) for scaled-score range and number of deviant subtests for the WPPSI sample of 4- to 6½-year-olds. Comparable data for the WAIS-R are not yet available. However, clinicians would certainly not be far afield if they applied the WISC-R data on scatter, summarized in Table 3.7, directly to WAIS-R profiles. When doing so, they should eliminate Digit Span from the computations for the Full Scale score, since this subtest is optional on the WISC-R.

Table 3.7.   Degree of Abnormality of an Index of Subtest Scatter (Scaled-Score Range)[a]

| Frequency of Occurrence in Normal Population | Size of Scaled-Score Range | | | | | |
| | Verbal Scale | | Performance Scale | | Full Scale | |
	5 Subtest	6 Subtest	5 Subtest	6 Subtest	10 Subtest	12 Subtest
< 15%	7	8	9	9	10	11
< 10%	8	9	10	10	11	12
< 5%	9	10	11	11	12	13
< 2%	10	11	12	13	13	14
< 1%	11	12	13	13	14	14

[a] Scaled-score range equals a child's highest scaled score minus his or her lowest scaled score.

The fact that it is normal for children to show peaks and valleys in their ability spectrum has vital implications for assessment. Clinicians and researchers working with exceptional populations should routinely consult the baseline data for the standardization sample in order to interpret the profiles of the children they test. No diagnosis of exceptionality should be based in any way on Wechsler scatter, unless the degree of interscale or intrascale scatter in the child's profile is demonstrated by empirical comparisons to be rare within the normal population. Furthermore, no clinical sample should be claimed to exhibit considerable scatter unless there is empirical evidence to show that the indices of scatter, VIQ–PIQ discrepancy, and scaled-score ranges for the clinical group are significantly greater than the indices for normal children.

Results of studies with the WISC-R and WPPSI standardization groups have challenged the stereotype that normal children have "flat" profiles. Now it is time to investigate empirically the stereotypes pertaining to the considerable scatter that supposedly characterizes the Wechsler profiles of samples of individuals with emotional, neurological, and school-related disorders. Fortunately, a number of these studies have been conducted; the interesting results of these investigations are reviewed in the next section.

Subtest scatter and the specific fluctuations occurring for individuals should also be evaluated from the standpoint of theory. Neuropsychological, componential, cognitive, factor, and psychometric models of intelligence all have contributions to make to intelligent test interpretation. Although space limits reviews of such models and their application to intelligence testing, discussions may be found in Kaufman (1979a), Reynolds (1981b), and White (1979). Kaufman (1979a) in particular provides a thorough discussion of the theoretical underpinnings and meaning of the trait or ability underlying the third WISC-R factor (Freedom from Distractibility).

THE WECHSLER SCALES AND LEARNING DISABILITIES ASSESSMENT: A BRIEF REVIEW *

Researchers and practitioners concerned with learning-disabled (LD) populations or with those referred to variously as having minimal brain damage, minimal brain dysfunction, hyperactive child syndrome, attention deficit disorder, dyslexia, or other neurologically based learning disorders have always had an affinity for the Wechsler scales. The WISC and now the WISC-R have been especially intriguing to these workers as the instruments of choice in evaluating LD children.

The aims of this section are to examine the state of the art of the utility of the WISC-R for LD assessment and to chart some appropriate pathways for future study. Three main areas will be treated: (a) *factor analysis* of the WISC-R, as related to LD populations; (b) *recategorizations* of the WISC-R subtest scores according to Bannatyne's (1971, 1974) system, an approach that has apparctly produced a characteristic group profile for LD samples; and (c) evaluations of *scatter* in WISC-R profiles for LD youngsters since they are frequently stereotyped as having much interscale and intrascale variability.

Learning Disabilities and Factor Analysis of the WISC-R

A generation ago it was an impressive psychometric feat to conduct a factor analysis of a multiscore test battery; the accomplishment of such a task was frequently rewarded by the granting of a doctoral degree. Cohen's (1959) landmark factor-analytic investigation was not published until a decade after the 1949 WISC first appeared. Today the push-button psychometrics of computer technology have resulted in a landslide of factor analyses of the WISC-R.

Pertinent Research Findings.   As we have noted, every study conducted to date has supported the construct validity of the Verbal and Performance Scales. Robust Verbal Comprehension and Perceptual Organization factors have emerged for children across a host of demographic characteristics and for a variety of exceptional populations: clinic referrals (Lombard & Riedel, 1978; Swerdlik & Schweitzer, 1978), mentally retarded (Schoole, Beebe & Koepke, 1978; Van Hagen & Kaufman, 1975), gifted (Karnes & Brown, 1980), learning disabled (Blaha & Vance,

* This section represents an abridged and otherwise modified version of Kaufman, A. S., "The WISC-R and LD assessment: state of the art," from *Journal of Learning Disabilities,* 1981, *14,* 520–526.

1979; Peterson & Hart, 1979; Schooler et al., 1978), and emotionally or behaviorally disordered (DeHorn & Klinge, 1978; Finch, Kendall, Spirito, Entin, Montgomery, & Schwartz, 1979; Peterson & Hart, 1979; Reynolds & Streur, 1981).

Some have not investigated three-factor solutions (e.g., Schooler et al., 1978), but most researchers have explored the third factor and have typically found a dimension labeled Freedom from Distractibility. This factor, not hypothesized by Wechsler in his dichotomous treatment of the WISC-R subtests, usually has significant loadings by at least two of the following three tasks: Arithmetic, Digit Span, Coding. Occasionally other subtests join in, such as Picture Arrangement (Swerdlik & Schweitzer, 1978; Van Hagen & Kaufman, 1975), Picture Completion (Karnes & Brown, 1980), or Block Design (Dean, 1979; Peterson & Hart, 1979), but the overwhelming consistency from sample to sample is clearly limited to the Arithmetic–Digit Span–Coding triad.

Reevance to LD Assessment.   The emergence of solid Verbal Comprehension and Perceptual Organization factors for learning-disabled groups would seem to bode well for the meaningful interpretation of the VIQ and PIQ and the difference between them. For most groups the latter generalization tends to be true, but there is a mitigating circumstance for learning-disabled children: the consistent findings of the ACID profile—low scores in *A*rithmetic, *C*oding, *I*nformation, and *D*igit Span—for diverse groups of this exceptional population (Ackerman, Dykman, & Peters, 1976; Kaufman, 1979a). Relatively low scores on Information and Arithmetic (both directly related to school achievement) will often distort the meaning of the IQ, and a weakness on Coding will likewise render the IQ an inefficient estimate of nonverbal intelligence. Despite the factor-analytic construct validity support for Wechsler's VIQ–PIQ dichotomy, there is thus reason to doubt the practical value of the simple VIQ–PIQ discrepancy for assessing learning-disabled or potentially learning-disabled children. Since three-quarters of the ACID profile (i.e., ACD) corresponds precisely to the Freedom from Distractibility factor, it is evident that the third factor may hold the key to competent LD asessment.

Avenues for Future Research.   We now understand the factor structure of the WISC-R and do not need to know more about the slight differences in the two or three factors for various ethnic or exceptional groups. Small differences in factorial composition from sample to sample cannot be attributed to ethnic membership or type of exceptionality; they are just as likely to be due to an irrelevant uncontrolled variable or, most likely of all, to the chance fluctuations that are known to characterize correlation matrices.

Future research in this area should focus on what the factors *mean* in either a theoretical or clinical sense. Does the Verbal Comprehension factor measure so-called general intelligence, or is it more aligned to school achievement or to Guilford's semantic content dimension? Does Perceptual Organization reflect conventional nonverbal intelligence, fluid ability from the Cattell-Horn approach, spatial ability from Bannatyne's regrouping, the cognitive style of field independence, or simultaneous processing? Does Freedom from Distractibility assess what its label claims, or is the third factor more related to successive processing, Guilford's symbolic ability, memory, automatic processing, stimulus trace (Baumeister & Bartless, 1962), attention–concentration, anxiety, or Bannatyne's sequencing ability?

The needed research could be factor-analytic or correlational in nature, for instance, by analyzing WISC-R data in conjunction with other instruments that are known to measure constructs such as manifest anxiety, successive versus simultaneous processing, and fluid versus crystallized intelligence. However, better still would be well-designed experimental research in which groups known to differ on various constructs could be compared on their WISC-R factor scores. Conducting such construct validation studies for various homogenously defined populations such as learning-disabled children may show that the factors measure different constructs for different groups and subgroups, or that the factors have to be interpreted differently for individuals under varied circumstances. Regardless of the outcome of such studies, the cumulative results would enhance the interpretation of the WISC-R from a theoretical and clinical base and might shed light on the dynamics underlying the ACID profile in groups of learning-disabled children.

Bannatyne Recategorizations

The preceding discussion of WISC-R factor analyses and LD populations leads directly to the topic of recategorizing Wechsler's subtests into Bannatyne's four categories: Conceptual (Similarities, Vocabulary, Comprehension), Spatial (Picture Completion, Block Design, Object Assembly), Sequencing (Arithmetic, Digit Span, Coding), and Acquired Knowledge (Information, Arithmetic, Vocabulary). The relationship to the factor-analytic section is twofold. First, the three WISC-R factors could easily be labeled totally in accordance with the Bannatyne model, namely Conceptual (Verbal Comprehension), Spatial (Perceptual Organization), and Sequencing (Freedom from Distractibility). Second, the characteristic LD profile of low scores on the ACID subtests makes much more sense when interpreted from Bannatyne's four-category approach than from Wechsler's two-scale system.

Pertinent Research Findings.   A seemingly characteristic Wechsler profile of Spatial > Conceptual > Sequencing has been found for groups of reading-disabled (Rugel, 1974) and learning-disabled (Clarizio & Bernard, 1981; Smith, Coleman, Dokecki, & Davis, 1977) children. However, the consistency of this finding, which has almost come to be accepted as fact, has been challenged on several grounds by recent investigations. Some studies have simply not produced the expected relationships among the three Bannatyne categories for LD samples (Thompson, 1981) or failed to find significant differences among the group means (Vance & Singer, 1979). Other investigations have shown different Bannatyne patterns when a variable is introduced in addition to the presence of learning disabilities: Mexican-American LD children showed a Spatial > Sequential > Conceptual pattern (Gutkin, 1979a), and LD youngsters with superior intelligence displayed Conceptual > Spatial > Sequential (Schiff, Kaufman, & Kaufman, 1981).

Furthermore, despite mean differences in Bannatyne categories for *groups*, the proportions of *individuals* in the group displaying the characteristic pattern have generally been very small. Gutkin's (1979a) Caucasian sample of 53 LD children had substantial differences in the group means of Spatial (25.85), Conceptual (21.47), and Sequential (19.66) abilities; however, only 30% of the individuals in this group displayed the predicted pattern, a value that dropped to a mere 2% when statistical criteria ($p < .05$) were imposed on the comparisons. Similarly, less than half of 60 Israeli LD children displayed the predicted pattern, despite striking differences in the mean scores on the Spatial (27.48), Conceptual (23.33), and Sequential (18.88) categories (Raviv, Margalith, Raviv, & Sade, 1981).

Of equal concern to the negative findings cited above is the emergence of Spatial > Conceptual > Sequential group patterns for exceptionalities other than learning disabilities. Groups such as juvenile delinquents, emotionally handicapped, and even nonimpaired referrals displayed the identical Bannatyne patterning and could not be differentiated significantly from learning-disabled children on the basis of the latter group's so-called characteristic pattern (Clarizio & Bernard, 1981; Groff & Hubble, 1981; Henry & Wittman, 1981; Thompson, 1981).

Relevance to LD Assessment.   The above findings virtually speak for themselves regarding LD diagnosis.What was once considered an optimistic, exciting approach for diagnosis of learning disabilities has come to a grinding halt. It is reasonable to conclude that differential diagnosis of learning disabilities will not be aided by application of knowledge about the so-called characteristic Bannatyne pattern. One should not conclude, however, that Bannatyne's recategorizations are irrelevant to LD assessment; that would be far from the truth. Although the groupings do not facilitate differential diagnosis, they still provide a convenient framework for understanding the learning disabled child's assets and deficits. As indicated earlier, the VIQ–PIQ dichotomy is not sufficient for understanding the fluctuations that characterize the profiles of LD samples. The four-category system espoused by Bannatyne still succeeds in making more sense out of many WISC-R profiles, especially those of LD children, than does a simple VIQ–PIQ split or even the three-way factor-analytic division. The more that WISC-R profiles can be systematized and understood, the easier it is to translate test results to educational action. Brief discussions and statistics for applying Bannatyne's recategorization to the performance of individual children on the WISC-R can be found in Reynolds (1981c) and Reynolds and Gutkin (1981b).

Another potentially valuable categorization scheme has been proposed by Witkin, Dyk, Faterson, Goodenough, and Karp (1974): Verbal–Comprehension (Information, Vocabulary, Comprehension), Analytic–Field–Approach (Object Assembly, Picture Completion, Block Design), and Attention–Concentration (Arithmetic, Digit Span, Coding). The first category is a variant of the Verbal Comprehension factor and of Bannatyne's Conceptual triad. The latter two categories are identical in composition to Bannatyne's Spatial and Sequencing groups, respectively, but are assigned quite different interpretations by Witkin. Stevenson (1979) applied this approach to a group of 55 learning-disabled children and found a depressed score in attention–concentration, agreeing with the bulk of Bannatyne LD research. The interpretations given the groupings by Witkin are important and worthy of consideration when analyzing the profile of any learning-disabled child. However, Bannatyne's four-category approach is still superior to Witkin's for LD assessment because (a) Information is included in Witkin's Verbal Comprehension grouping, (b) LD children typically score low on this subtest, and (c) Bannatyne offers an Acquired Knowledge grouping, invaluable for interpreting LD profiles.

Avenues for Future Research.   It is surely time to stop looking at Bannatyne scores in the Conceptual, Spatial, and Sequencing categories for heterogeneous groups of learning-disabled children. This approach seems to have no future for differential diagnosis and no longer will be contributing new knowledge to the field. However, the results of Schiff et al. (1981) with superior-IQ learning-disabled children suggest that it is possible to find a profile that characterizes not only a group, but also substantial proportions of individuals within the group. Perhaps the key variable is to investigate LD populations that are defined rather homogeneously.

A second area of needed research is that of the utility of Bannatyne's Acquired Knowledge category, frequently forgotten in WISC-R studies. Logically, LD youngsters of average intelligence should perform relatively poorly in the achievement-oriented WISC-R subtests, and this has been borne out in the studies which have utilized all four Bannatyne categories (Smith et al., 1977; Thompson, 1981; Vance & Singer, 1979). Longitudinal investigations of a potential decline in the Acquired Knowledge scores (and, hence, in the IQs) of learning-disabled children would be of special value; any such decline would imply the VIQ becomes a less valid estimate of verbal intelligence as LD children mature from the primary grades to high school. Indeed, there is certainly a question of whether the VIQ is valid for any learning-disabled child who performs poorly on the Acquired Knowledge subtests, regardless of age. That, too, is an important and researchable issue.

The final avenue of research in this area, and undoubtedly the most important, is the theoretical and clinical meaning of strengths and weaknesses exhibited by LD children in the Bannatyne categories—which brings us full circle to the suggested line of research in the area of factor analysis. Once again, the recommendation is to conduct construct validity investigations of the abilities, traits, processes, or behaviors underlying each Bannatyne category. Whether an LD child's elevated scores in the Picture Completion–Block Design–Object Assembly triad, for example, reflect good spatial ability, perceptual organization, simultaneous processing, or analytic–field-approach is a question that can be answered by well-designed research studies.

Scatter

The stereotype of the learning-disabled child as having a WISC-R profile replete with subtest scatter and a large VIQ–PIQ difference still persists in many assessment circles, despite the findings presented earlier. For years, these notions were accepted as clinical axioms; now a body of research has accumulated to challenge this stereotype.

Pertinent Research Findings.   As we have noted, normal children have substantial VIQ–PIQ discrepancies, averaging about 10 points (regardless of direction), and it is not unusual for normal youngsters to have differences of 15 or more points. Similarly, considerable subtest scatter characterizes the profiles of normal youngsters.

Numerous studies have now been published comparing the VIQ–PIQ discrepancies and subtest scatter of learning-disabled and other exceptional groups to the basal levels found in the normal population. Table 3.8 summarizes these studies. The VIQ–PIQ discrepancies for learning disabled children have tended to be significantly (but not overwhelmingly) larger than normal values, although some studies have shown no difference at all (Stevenson, 1979; Thompson, 1980). A similar finding has emerged for subtest scatter. Of the 436 learning-disabled children listed in Table 3.8 (spread across seven studies and excluding the group with superior IQ), the mean scaled-score range for the 10 regular WISC-R subtests equals 7.8. This value is not consequentially larger than the 7.0 for normal children. Interestingly, Naglieri's (1979) learning-disabled sample had significantly more subtest scatter than the normative population, but *not* more than a local control group. In fact, Naglieri's normal control group had the fourth highest index of subtest scatter among all groups listed in Table 3.8.

The findings with the conventional WISC-R reported in Table 3.8 have received some cross-cultural validation. Using a Hebrew translation of the WISC-R, Raviv et al. (1981) compared the scatter for a group of 60 Israeli LD children with a sample of 60 matched controls. The mean VIQ–PIQ discrepancy of 11.6 for the LD sample did not differ significantly from the mean of 10.8 for the normals. Although the mean scatter index of 7.5 for the LDs was significantly greater than the value of 6.8 for the controls, the magnitude of the difference is of little practical consequence.

Only Schiff et al.'s (1981) group of LD children with superior IQs showed an impressively high VIQ–PIQ discrepancy and subtest scatter index, suggesting that certain homogeneously defined exceptional samples may have characteristic amounts of inter- and intrascale variability of potential diagnostic value. Otherwise, conventional learning-disabled, emotionally disturbed, juvenile delinquent, mentally retarded, and clinic referral populations tend to be close to "normal" in their profile fluctuations.

Relevance to LD Assessment.   Despite the existing stereotype, children with learning disabilities do not seem to be characterized by abnormal scatter in their WISC-R profiles. The small difference between LD and normal scatter that has been observed in previous investigations may, in fact, represent a selection bias stemming from the stereotype; other things being equal, children with apparent WISC-R scatter are more likely to be labeled LD than those with flatter profiles. The data presented in Table 3.8 strongly imply that the magnitude of VIQ–PIQ discrepancy and the size of scaled-score range are not likely to be very useful in the diagnosis of LD or in its differential diagnosis. Nevertheless, significant strengths or weaknesses

Table 3.8.   WISC-R VIQ–PIQ Discrepancies and Subtest Scatter Indices for a Variety of Samples

Source	N	Description of Sample	Mean VIQ–PIQ Discrepancy (Regardless of Sign)	Mean Scaled-Score Range (High Minus Low Scaled Score—10 Subtests)
Kaufman (1976a, 1976b)	2200	Normal standardization sample	9.7	7.0
Anderson, Kaufman, and Kaufman (1976)	41	Learning disabled	12.5	7.5
Gutkin (1979b)	51	Learning disabled	11.9	7.7
Naglieri (1979)	20	Learning disabled	13.6	8.5
Stevenson (1979)	55	Learning disabled	10.1	7.2
Tabachnick (1979)	105	Learning disabled	—	7.6
Thompson (1980)	64	Learning disabled	10.0	7.6
Ryckman (1981)	100	Learning disabled	—	8.2
Schiff et al. (1981)	30	Learning disabled (superior IQ)	18.6	9.3
Gutkin (1979b)	23	Minimally brain injured	11.8	7.3
Weiner and Kaufman (1979)	46	Referrals for learning and/or behavior problems	9.2	7.3
Stritchart and Love (1979)	40	Referrals for learning disabilities	9.8	7.3
Moore and Wielan (1981)	434	Referrals for reading problems	11.2	—
Naglieri (1979)	20	Mentally retarded	9.6	6.6
Thompson (1980)	14	Mentally retarded	7.6	5.9
Gutkin (1979b)	10	Mentally retarded	8.5	6.0
Gutkin (1979b)	17	Emotionally disturbed	12.9	7.8
Thompson (1980)	51	Psychological or behavioral disorder	8.4	7.2
Ollendick (1979)	121	Juvenile delinquents	—	7.3
Naglieri (1979)	20	Normal control group	12.6	8.0

in a WISC-R profile are potentially valuable, even when the overall scatter is within normal limits, when planning educational interventions for LD youngsters.

Avenues for Future Research.   Many samples of handicapped children have been analyzed for WISC-R scatter, and the results clearly imply that future research along this line will contribute only minimally to knowledge in this area. Perhaps very homogeneously defined groups such as the LD sample with superior IQs should continue to be examined to determine the diagnostic utility of scatter indexes; heterogeneous or loosely defined samples, however, should be left alone. A more fruitful line for research would be to reverse the procedure; to identify samples of children with abnormally large VIQ–PIQ discrepancies and/or scaled-score ranges and examine the characteristics of these empirically defined samples. What proportion of these children with unusual profiles are brain injured, LD, emotionally disturbed, language disordered, normal, and so forth? By working "backward," we should be able to determine whether much WISC-R profile variability is, indeed, diagnostic of LD, and whether this information contributes significantly to differential diagnosis.

Whenever researchers do evaluate samples of known exceptional children, future studies should meet two criteria besides a homogeneous definition: (a) They should be large in size, preferably at least 200, to reduce errors inherent in sampling procedures; and (b) a local control group of normal individuals, similar to the experimental group in background variables but necessarily smaller in size, should be tested to provide an additional pertinent comparison. Naglieri's (1979) study shows the advisability of using a local control in addition to the standardization sample for effective evaluation of abnormal profile variability.

Conclusions

Research since the WISC-R's arrival in 1974, and especially since 1979, has greatly added to our understanding of the role of the WISC-R in LD assessment. We know that the factor structure is rather stable for a variety of normal and exceptional samples, including LD and LD referrals, and that the three-factor solution corresponds reasonably well to the group profiles of childen with learning disabilities. Research with Bannatyne's recategorizations has shown that this four-category approach seems to fit LD data even better than the three factors and certainly better than the simple two-scale approach advocated by Wechsler. Unfortunately, the initial optimism of the diagnostic utility of the Bannatyne regroupings has been dampened by a stream of studies which militate against its use for differential diagnosis.

Finally, we have learned that normal children do not have flat WISC-R profiles and that virtually all exceptional samples do not possess the stereotypical high VIQ–PIQ discrepancies or large amounts of intersubtest variability. As with the Bannatyne categories, the utility of scatter indexes for diagnosis is suspect.

Although the main thrust of the research results seems depressing and pessimistic, there is also reason for hope. The studies have taught us much about learning disabilities and have broken some persistent and long-enduring axioms. If assessment procedures can be improved substantially by the bulk of knowledge gained from the studies reviewed here, then that improvement represents an important advance in the field. Also, the recategorizations have permitted and encouraged the application of psychological theory to WISC-R interpretation. By departing from a simplistic VIQ–PIQ dichotomy, the regroupings have fostered analysis in terms of simultaneous and sequential processing from the neuropsychological and cognitive literature, analytic–field-approach from the cognitive style literature, and so forth. This application of theory fosters a deeper and more meaningful understanding of the WISC-R profile, leading to a more process-oriented treatment of LD children's strengths and weaknesses. If future researchers succeed in uncovering the constructs underlying each LD child's test profile, then the translation of these processes, traits, or abilities into educational intervention becomes a logical outcome of the investigations.

ESTIMATING PREMORBID LEVELS OF INTELLECTUAL FUNCTIONING

In the neuropsychological assessment of children or adults with head injury or other sudden neurological trauma, premorbid intellectual status may prove to be an important consideration. Frequently, premorbid levels of functioning are estimated clinically from the history, parental background, and teacher reports of academic functioning. Attempts to use "hold" versus "don't hold" marker subtests from the Wechsler scales have been made in an effort to place such estimation on a more empirical and thereby less subjective footing. These methods frequently prove to be inaccurate (e.g., Lezak, 1976; Matarazzo, 1972), leaving the clinician with few alternatives other than subjective (i.e., clinical) impressions.

Recently, more objective methods have been proposed based on regression modeling from demographic data. Wilson, Rosenbaum, Brown, Rourke, Whitman, and Grisell (1978) have provided formulas for estimating the premorbid IQs of adults on the WAIS given knowledge of their age, race, sex, educational level, and occupational status. Using a regression model and the standardization data as a source, Wilson et al. reported impressive results, obtaining R^2 values ranging from .42 to .54 between those variables and the Wechsler IQs. Unfortunately, the formulas reported will not in any way be accurate for the WAIS-R, and new formulas to allow such estimation with adults have yet to be determined.

Following up on the Wilson et al. (1978) approach with adults, Reynolds and Gutkin (1979) generated regression equations for predicting the premorbid intellectual status of children using demographic variables, with the WISC-R standardization sample providing the data source. For adults, age and number of years of education were good estimators in the multiple regression; for children, however, the method of standardization eliminates the use of these two variables. The relevant and available demographic variables for children were socioeconomic status (as determined by parents' occupation), race, sex, geographic region, and urban versus rural residence. All five of these variables were found to contribute significantly to estimation of the WISC-R Verbal and Full Scale IQs, while geographic region dropped out of the equation for the Performance IQ.

The actual regression equations and standard errors of estimate obtained were as follows:

Estimated Verbal IQ = 127.85 − 3.7 (SES) − 8.86 (race) − 2.40 (sex) − 0.68 (region) − 1.16 (residence)
   Standard error of estimate VIQ = 13.47

Estimated Performance IQ = 121.08-9.18 (race) − 2.80 (SES) − 1.07 (residence) − 0.64 (sex)
   Standard error of estimate PIQ = 13.07

Estimated Full Scale IQ = 126.9 − 3.65 (SES) − 9.72 (race) − 1.79 (sex) − 1.20 (residence) − 0.41 (region)
   Standard error of estimate FSIQ = 13.50

For each equation, demograpic variables take the following values (descriptions for making these classifications are available in Wechsler, 1974):

Sex: male = 1, female = 2

Race: white = 1, black = 2, other = 3

SES (based on father's occupational group): upper = 1, upper middle = 2, middle = 3, lower middle = 4, lower = 5

Region: Northeast = 1, North Central = 2, South = 3, West = 4

Residence: urban = 1, rural = 1

These equations essentially provide a shortcut to developing tables to display the mean IQs of groups of children with the same demographic characteristics. Their utility in clinical diagnosis and decision making remains to be tested adequately. The multiple Rs obtained for the children were not large, ranging from .37 to .44. However, this method has certain advantages over clinical estimation. The regression equations provide a standardized quantitative procedure for estimating premorbid IQs. Being systematic and quantifiable are major advantages, and the necessary data are typically easily and readily available to the clinician and can quickly be evaluated. Reynolds and Gutkin (1979) provide an example of how this technique might be applied and discuss its limitations and further research needs in more detail. Though much remains to be done, regression modeling to estimate premorbid levels of function appears to be superior to other purely clinically derived estimates.

THE PROBLEM OF CULTURAL BIAS IN INTELLIGENCE TESTING

The issue of potential cultural bias in educational and psychological tests has been with psychology since at least the early 1920s. The past two decades, characterized by an insurgence of support and concern for individual liberties, civil rights, and social justice, have seen the subject of test bias become the focus of interest for psychologists, educators, and the lay public alike. Lawmakers and the courts have shown increasing concern, as witnessed by the recent passage of the so-called truth-in-testing legislation in New York state and similar forthcoming efforts in the federal legislature. Two directly opposing major federal district court decisions have recently been handed down on the question whether intelligence tests are culturally biased against black children (*Larry P.,* 1979, *PASE,*. 1980). The issues are many and have been hotly contested, even in the scholarly literature (see Reynolds & Brown, in press).

Much of the furor over bias in testing, as well as the court cases, has centered around the use of intelligence tests to evaluate minority children suspected of mental retardation. Even though definitions and conceptualizations of mental retardation have been modified over the last decade to add emphasis to children's adaptive behavior (ability to function independently within their own culture and within the larger society) and social maturity, level of intellectual functioning remains an important consideration in the diagnosis of mental retardation. Since black children as a group earn a lower mean score on intelligence tests (Reynolds & Gutkin, 1981a), a significantly larger portion of black than white children are diagnosed as mildly mentally retarded. Although the true cause of the mean difference in performance of blacks and whites on intelligence tests is not known, one (among many) proposed explanations is that the tests are faulty. This explanation, which has become known as the cultural test bias hypothesis, contends that minority children earn lower scores on intelligence tests not because of less ability but rather because of an inherent cultural bias of the tests that makes them artifactually more difficult for minority children. These biases are generally stated to stem from the white middle-class orientation of test authors and publishers and the lack of relevant experience of taking such tests among black and other minority children. Although psychologists have been aware of the potential for such problems since the early days of testing (Reynolds & Brown, in press), most significant research on bias in testing is relatively recent.

The Association of Black Psychologists' early efforts to raise the consciousness of the psychological community were successful in spurring much empirical research on the various issues involved and also resulted in the appointment of an American Psychological Association committee to study the issues (Cleary, Humphreys, Kendrick, & Wesman, 1975). At its 1969 annual meeting, the Association of Black Psychologists adopted the following official policy statement on educational and psychological testing:

> The Association of Black Psychologists fully supports those parents who have chosen to defend their rights by refusing to allow their children and themselves to be subjected to achievement, intelligence, aptitude and performance tests which have been and are being used to A. Label black people as uneducable. B. Place black children in "special" classes and schools. C. Perpetuate inferior education of blacks. D. Assign black children to educational tracks. E. Deny black children higher educational opportunities. F. Destroy positive growth and development of black people.

Many quite possibly legitimate objections to the use of educational and psychological tests with minorities have been raised by black and other minority psychologists. Too frequently the objections of these groups are viewed as fact without a review of any empirical evidence (e.g., CEC, 1978; Hilliard, 1979). The problems most often cited in the use of tests with minorities typically fall into the following categories as described by Reynolds (1982):

1. *Inappropriate content.*   Black or other minority children have not been exposed to the material involved in the test questions or other stimulus materials. The tests are geared primarily toward white middle-class homes and values.

2. *Inappropriate standardization samples.*   Ethnic minorities are underrepresented in the collection of normative reference group data. Williams (Wright & Isenstein, 1977) has criticized the WISC-R standardization sample for including blacks only in proportion to the United States total population. Out of 2200 children

in the WISC-R standardization sample, 330 were minority. Williams contends that such small actual representation has no impact on the test. In earlier years it was not unusual for standardization samples to be all white (e.g., the 1949 WISC).

3. *Examiner and language bias.*   Since most psychologists are white and primarily speak only standard English, they intimidate blacks and other ethnic minorities. They are also unable to communicate accurately with minority children. Lower test scores for minorities, then, are said to reflect only this intimidation and difficulty in the communication process, not lowered ability levels.

4. *Inequitable social consequences.*   As a result of bias in educational and psychological tests, minority-group members, who are already at a disadvantage in the educational and vocational markets because of past discrimination, are disproportionately relegated to dead-end educational tracks and thought unable to learn. Labeling effects also fall under this category.

5. *Measurement of different constructs.*   Related to 1. above, this position asserts that the tests are measuring significantly different attributes when used with children from other cultures than the white middle class. Mercer (1979), for example, contends that, when IQ tests are used with minorities, they are measuring only the degree of Anglocentrism of the home.

6. *Differential predictive validity.*   Although tests may accurately predict a variety of outcomes for white middle-class children, they fail to predict at an acceptable level any relevant criteria for minority-group members. Corollary to this objection is a variety of competing positions regarding the selection of an appropriate, common criterion against which to validate tests across cultural groupings. Scholastic or academic attainment levels are considered by a variety of black psychologists to be biased as criteria.

There is today a considerable body of research in each of the above areas of potential bias in assessment that did not exist a decade ago. To the extent that the cultural test bias hypothesis is a scientific question, as it must be to receive rational consideration, it must be evaluated via a thorough consideration of carefully conceived research. As with other scientific questions, one must be guided by the data. Recently the evidence regarding the cultural test bias hypothesis has been reviewed extensively (Jensen, 1980; Reynolds, 1981e, 1982) and debated (Reynolds & Brown, in press). Empirical research into the question of bias has failed to substantiate the existence of cultural bias in well-constructed, well-standardized educational and psychological tests when used with members of American ethnic minority groups born in the United States. The internal psychometric characteristics of intelligence and other aptitude tests behave in essentially the same manner across ethnic groupings, and the tests predict later and concurrent academic performance equivalently for all groups. Although most of this research has focused on adults and school-age children, recent studies have also dealt with preschool tests. Across the age span, with a variety of tests and criteria, the results have been quite consistent. Whatever intelligence tests are measuring for white middle-class children, be it scholastic aptitude, learning potential, or intelligence, they are most likely measuring the same construct when used with American-born ethnic minorities.

The issues regarding cultural bias in psychological and educational assessment are complex and not given to simple resolution. The fervent feelings displayed by otherwise calm, competent, objective professionals are a further indication of the complexity of the issues of bias. The controversy over bias will likely remain with psychology and education for at least as long as the nature/nurture controversy, despite the existence of a convincing body of evidence failing to support cultural test-bias hypotheses. Bias in intelligence testing will remain in the spotlight for some time to come as well, especially now that the *Larry P.* (1979) and *PASE* (1980) decisions have been appealed and given their propensity to elicit polemic emotional arguments.

The empirical evidence regarding test bias does not support the contentions of minority spokespersons. Nevertheless, bias is not merely an empirical issue (Flaugher, 1978), and the results of research investigations should not make psychologists any less sensitive to the needs and feelings of minority group members. Instruments should be chosen as supplements to IQ tests that are known to include tasks on which blacks have consistently performed well. An example of a good supplement is the Torrance Test of Creative Thinking (Torrance, 1974), which measures skills such as figural fluency and flexibility; blacks have been shown to outperform whites on some nonverbal creative skills (Kaltsounis, 1974).

Furthermore, it is incumbent on new test developers to include tasks that call upon skills believed to be well developed among minority group members. That was one goal in the development of the Kaufman-Assessment Battery for Children (K-ABC; Kaufman & Kaufman, 1983), an intelligence and achievement test for 2½ to 12½-year-olds derived from neuropsychological theory. This battery includes tasks such as Gestalt Closure and Face Recognition that resemble tests in the literature that have been shown to be far less culturally dependent (Bogen, DeZure, Tenhouten, & Marsh, 1972; Kagan & Klein, 1973) than most traditional tasks of intelligence tests.

In the meantime, clinicians would be wise to follow these guidelines in order to ensure nonbiased assessment: (a) Assessment should be conducted with the most reliable instrumentation available; and (b) multiple abilities should be assessed. In other words, psychologists need to view multiple sources of accurately derived data prior to making decisions concerning children. It is hoped that this is not too far from what has actually been occurring in the practice of psychological assessment, though one continues to hear isolated stories of grossly incompetent placement decisions. This is not to say that psychologists should be blind to a child's environmental background. Information concerning the home, community, and school environment must all be evaluated in the individualized decision-making process. Some would deny services to minority children, claiming that they are not handicapped but only artificially appear so on culturally biased tests. However, the psychologist cannot ignore the data demonstrating that *low-IQ, ethnic, disadvantaged children are just as likely to fail academically as are white, middle-class, low-IQ children, provided that their environmental circumstances remain constant.* Indeed, recall that it is the purpose of the assessment *process* to beat the prediction, to provide insight into hypotheses for environmental interventions that will prevent the predicted failure. Low-IQ minority children have the same entitlements to remedial, compensatory, and preventive programs as white middle-class low-IQ children, and ethnic minorities should not be denied services on unfounded assumptions that the test caused the low score and not a deficiency or dysfunction on the part of the child or the child's environment. These issues and the empirical research with children to date are reviewed in detail in Reynolds (1981e, 1982) and Reynolds and Brown (in press). Properly executed, intelligent testing by sensitive, well-trained professionals can prevent conflicts over bias, since testing is conceptualized entirely as a vehicle for understanding that leads to the betterment of the individual in multiple areas of functioning.

REFERENCES

Ackerman, P. T., Dykman, R. A., & Peters, J. E. Hierarchical factor patterns on the WISC as related to area of learning deficit. *Perceptual and Motor Skills,* 1976, **42,** 381–386.

Alcorn, C. L., & Nicholson, C. L. *A technique for programming interpretations and educational recommendations based on the WISC-R.* Paper presented to the annual meeting of the National Association of School Psychologists, Atlanta, April 1975.

Anatasi, A. *Psychological testing* (4th ed.). New York: Macmillan, 1976.

Anderson, M., Kaufman, A. S., & Kaufman, N. L. Use of the WISC-R with a learning disabled population: Some diagnostic implications. *Psychology in the Schools,* 1976, **13,** 381–386.

Arthur, G. *A Point Scale of Performance, revised form II: Manual for administering and scoring the tests.* New York: Psychological Corporation, 1947.

Banas, N., & Wills, I. H. Prescriptions from WISC-R patterns, *Academic Therapy,* 1977, **13,** 241–246.

Banas, N., & Wills, I. H. Prescription from WISC-R patterns, *Academic Therapy,* 1978, **13,** 365–370.

Baumeister, A. A., & Bartlett, C. J. A comparison of the factor structure of normals and retardates on the WISC. *American Joural of Mental Deficiency,* 1962, **66,** 641–646.

Berger, M. The third revision of the Stanford-Binet (Form L-M): Some methodological limitations and their practical implications. *Bulletin of the British Psychological Society,* 1970, **23,** 17–26.

Binet, A. *L'étude expérimental de l'intelligence.* Paris: Schleicher, 1903.

Binet, A., & Henri, V. La psychologie individuelle. *L'Année Psychologique,* 1896, **2,** 411–465.

Binet, A., & Simon, T. Methodes nouvelles pour le diagnostic du niveau intellectual des anormaux. *L'Année Psychologique,* 1905, **11,** 191–244.

Blaha, J., & Vance, H. The hierarchical factor structure of the WISC-R for learning disabled children. *Learning Disabilities Quarterly,* 1979, **2,** 71–75.

Blatt, S. J., & Allison, J. The intelligence test in personality asessment. In A. Rabin (Ed.), *Assessment with projective techniques: A concise introduction,* New York: Springer-Verlag, 1982.

Bogen, J. E., DeZure, R., Tenhouten, N., & Marsh, J. The other side of the brain IV: The A/P ratio. *Bulletin of the Los Angeles Neurological Society,* 1972, **37,** 49–61.

Buros, O. K. (Ed.) *The eighth mental measurements yearbook.* Highland Park, NJ: Gryphon Press, 1978.

Carlson, L. C., & Reynolds C. R. Factor structure and specific variance of the WPPSI subtests at six age levels. *Psychology in the schools,* 1981, **18,** 48–54.

Carlson, L. C., Reynolds, C. R., & Gutkin, T. B. Comparative structure of the WISC-R for upper and lower SES groups. *Journal of School Psychology,* in press.

Cattell, J. M. Mental tests and measurements. *Mind,* 1890, **15,** 373ff.

Cattell, J. M., & Farrand, L. Physical and mental measurements of the students of Columbia University. *Psychological Review,* 1896, **3,** 618–648.

Clarizio, H., & Bernard, R. Recategorized WISC-R scores of learning disabled children and differential diagnosis. *Psychology in the Schools,* 1981, **18,** 5–12.

Cleary, T. A., Humphreys, L. G., Kendrick, S. A., & Wesman, A., Educational uses of tests with disadvantaged students. *American Psychologist,* 1975, **30,** 15–41.

Cohen, J. A factor-analytically based rationale for the Wechsler Bellevue. *Journal of Consulting Psychology,* 1952, **16,** 272–277.

Cohen, J. The factorial structure of the WISC at ages 7–6, 10–6, and 13–6. *Journal of Consulting Psychology,* 1959, **23,** 285–299.

Cornell, E. L., & Coxe, W. W. *A performance ability scale: Examination manual.* New York: World Book, 1934.

Council for Exceptional Children (CEC). Minorities position policy statements. *Exceptional Children,* 1978, **45,** 57–64.

Dean, R. S. *WISC-R factor structure for Anglo and Hispanic children.* Paper presented at the meeting of the American Psychological Association, New York, September 1979.

DeHorn, A., & Klinge, V. Correlations and factor analysis of the WISC-R and the Peabody Picture Vocabulary Test for an adolescent psychiatric sample. *Journal of Consulting and Clinical Psychology,* 1978, **46,** 1160–1161.

Ebel, R. Evaluation and selection of group measures. In C. R. Reynolds & T. B. Gutkin (Eds.), *The handbook of school psychology,* New York: Wiley, 1982.

Esquirol, J. E. D. Observations pour servir a l'histoire de l'idiotie. *Les maladies mentales,* 1828.

Esquirol, J. E. D. *Des maladies mentales considerées sous les rapports médical, hygiénique, et médico-légal.* (2 vols.) Paris: Baillière, 1838.

Finch, A. J., Kendall, P. C., Spirito, A., Entin, A., Montgomery, L. E., & Schwartz, D. J. Short form and factor-analytic studies of the WISC-R with behavior problem children. *Journal of Abnormal Child Psychology,* 1979, **7,** 337–344.

Flaugher, R. L. The many definitions of test bias. *American Psychologist,* 1978, **33,** 671–679.

Friedes, D. Review of the Stanford-Binet Intelligence Scale. In O. K. Buros (Ed.), *The seventh mental measurements yearbook,* Highland Park, N.J.: Gryphon Press,1972.

Galton, F. *Hereditary genius: An inquiry into its laws and consequences.* London: Macmillan, 1869.

Galton, F. *Inquiries into human faculty and its development.* London: Macmillan, 1883.

Goddard, H. H. A revision of the Binet scale. *Training school,* 1911, **8,** 56–62.

Goh, D. S., Teslow, C. J., & Fuller, G. B. The practice of psychological assessment among school psychologists. *Professional Psychology,* 1981, **12,** 696–706.

Groff, M., & Hubble, L. Recategorized WISC-R scores of juvenile delinquents. *Journal of Learning Disabilities,* 1981, **14,** 515–516.

Gutkin, T. B. Bannatyne patterns of Caucasian and Mexican-American learning disabled children. *Psychology in the School,* 1979, **16,** 178–183. (a)

Gutkin, T. B. WISC-R scatter indices: Useful information for differential diagnosis? *Journal of School Psychology,* 1979, **17,** 368–371. (b)

Gutkin, T. B. The WISC-R Verbal Comprehension, Perceptual Organization, and Freedom from Distractibility deviation quotients: Data for practitioners. *Psychology in the Schools,* 1979, **16,** 356–360. (c)

Gutkin, T. B., & Reynolds, C. R. Factorial similarity of the WISC-R for Anglos and Chicanos referred for psychological services. *Journal of School Psychology,* 1980, **18,** 34–39.

Gutkin, T. B., & Reynolds, C. R. Factorial similarity of the WISC-R for white and black children from the standardization sample. *Journal of Educational Psychology,* 1981, **73,** 227–231.

Gutkin, T. B., Reynolds, C. R., & Galvin, G. A. Factor analysis of the Wechsler Adult Intelligence Scale—Revised (WAIS-R): An examination of the standardization sample. *Journal of School Psychology,* in press.

Halpern, F. C. Clinicians must listen. In G. J. Williams & Sol Gordon (Eds.), *Clinical child psychology,* New York: Behavioral Publications, 1974.

Henry, S. A., & Wittman, R. D. Diagnostic implications of Bannatyne's, recategorized WISC-R scores for identifying learning disabled children. *Journal of Learning Disabilities,* 1981, **14,** 517–520.

Herring, J. P. *Herring Revision of the Binet-Simon Tests: Examination manual—Form A.* London: World Book, 1922.

Hilliard, A. G. Standardization and cultural bias as impediments to the scientific study and validation of ''intelligence.'' *Journal of Research and Development in Education,* 1979, **12,** 47–58.

Holroyd, J., & Wright, F. Neurological implications of WISC Verbal-Performance discrepancies in a psychiatric setting. *Journal of Consulting Psychology,* 1965, **29,** 206–212.

Hughes, J. Consistency of administrators' and psychologists' actual and ideal perceptions of school psychologists' activities. *Psychology in the schools,* 1979, **16,** 234–239.

Jensen, A. R. *g:* Outmoded theory or unconquered frontier? *Creative Science and Technology,* 1979, **2,** 16–29.

Jensen, A. R. *Bias in mental testing.* New York: The Free Press, 1980.

Jensen, A. R., & Reynolds, C. R. Race, social class, and ability patterns on the WISC-R. *Personality and Individual Differences,* in press.

Kagan, J., & Klein, R. E. Cross-cultural perspectives on early development. *American Psychologist,* 1973, **28,** 947–961.

Kaltsounis, W. Race, socioeconomic status, and creativity. *Psychological Reports,* 1974, **35,** 164–166.

Karnes, F. A., & Brown, K. E. Factor analysis of the WISC-R for the gifted. *Journal of Educational Psychology*, 1980, **72**, 197–199.

Kaufman, A. S. A short form of the Wechsler Preschool and Primary Scale of Intelligence. *Journal of Consulting and Clinical Psychology*, 1972, **39**, 361–369.

Kaufman, A. S. Factor analysis of the WISC-R at eleven age levels between 6½ and 16½ years. *Journal of Consulting and Clinical Psychology*, 1975, **43**, 135–147.

Kaufman, A. S. Do normal children have "flat" ability profiles? *Psychology in the Schools*, 1976, **13**, 284–285. (a)

Kaufman, A. S. A new approach to the interpretation of test scatter on the WISC-R. *Journal of Learning Disabilities*, 1976, **9**, 160–168. (b)

Kaufman, A. S. Verbal-Performance IQ discrepancies on the WISC-R. *Journal of Consulting and Clinical Psychology*, 1976, **9**, 160–168. (c)

Kaufman, A. S. A four-test form of the WISC-R. *Contemporary Educational Psychology*, 1976, **1**, 180–196. (d)

Kaufman, A. S. A McCarthy short form for rapid screening of preschool, kindergarten, and first-grade children. *Contemporary Educational Psychology*, 1977, **2**, 149–157.

Kaufman, A. S. *Intelligent testing with the WISC-R*. New York: Wiley-Interscience, 1979. (a)

Kaufman, A. S. Cerebral specialization and intelligence testing. *Journal of Research and Development in Education*, 1979, **12**, 96–107. (b)

Kaufman, A. S. The WISC-R and LD assessment: State of the art. *Journal of Learning Disabilities*, 1981, **14**, 520–526.

Kaufman, A. S. The impact of WISC-R research for school psychologists. In C. R. Reynolds & T. B. Gutkin (Eds.), *The handbook of school psychology*. New York: Wiley, 1982.

Kaufman, A. S. Intelligence: Old concepts, new perspectives. In G. Hynd (Ed.), *The school psychologist: An introduction*, Syracuse: Syracuse University Press, 1983.

Kaufman, A. S., & Hollenbeck, G. P. Comparative structure of the WPPSI for blacks and whites. *Journal of Clinical Psychology*, 1974, **30**, 316–319.

Kaufman, A. S., & Kaufman, N. L. *Clinical evaluation of young children with the McCarthy Scales*. New York: Grune & Stratton, 1977.

Kaufman, A. S., & Kaufman, N. L. *Kaufman assessment battery for children*. Circle Pines, Minn. American Guidance Services, 1983.

Kohs, S. C. *Intelligence measurement*. New York. Macmillan, 1923.

Korchin, S. J. *Modern clinical psychology*. New York: Basic Books, 1976.

Kuhlman, F. A revision of the Binet-Simon system for measuring the intelligence of children. *Journal of Psych-Asthenics Monograph Supplement*, 1912, **1**, 1–41.

Larry P. et al. v. Riles et al. United States District Court for the Northern District of California, C-71-2270RFP, October 1979, slip opinion.

Lezak, M. *Neuropsychological assessment*. New York: Oxford University Press, 1976.

Lombard, T. J., & Reidel, R. G. An analysis of the factor structure of the WISC-R and the effect of color on the Coding subtest. *Psychology in the Schools*, 1978, **15**, 176–179.

Lutey, C. *Individual intelligence testing: A manual and sourcebook* (2nd & enlarged ed.). Greeley, Colo.: Carol L. Lutey, 1977.

Lutey, C., & Copeland, E. Cognitive assessments of the school aged child. In C. R. Reynolds & T. B. Gutkin (Eds.), *The handbook of school psychology,* New York: Wiley, 1982.

Matarazzo, J. D. *Wechsler's measurement and appraisal of adult intelligence* (5th ed.). Baltimore: Williams & Wilkins, 1972.

McDermott, P. Actuarial assessment systems for the grouping and classification of school children. In C. R. Reynolds & T. B. Gutkin (Eds.), *The handbook of school psychology,* New York: Wiley, 1982.

McDermott, P. Diagnosis and classification of childhood disorders. In R. T. Brown & C. R. Reynolds (Eds.), *Psychological perspectives on childhood exceptionality.* New York: Wiley-Interscience, in press.

Mercer, J. R. In defense of racially and culturally nondiscriminatory assessment. *School Psychology Digest,* 1979, **3,** 89–95.

Moore, D. W., & Wielan, O. P. WISC-R scatter indices of children referred for reading diagnosis. *Journal of Learning Disabilities,* 1981, **14,** 416–418.

Naglieri, J. A. *A comparison of McCarthy GCI and WISC-R IQ scores for educable mentally retarded, learning disabled and normal children.* Unpublished doctoral dissertation, University of Georgia, 1979.

Naglieri, J. A., & Kaufman, A. S. *Determining the number of WAIS-R. factors using several methods.* Paper presented at the annual meeting of the American Psychological Association, Washington, D.C., August 1982.

Ollendick, T. H. Discrepancies between verbal and performance IQs and subtest scatter on the WISC-R for juvenile delinquents. *Psychological Reports,* 1979, **45,** 563–568.

PASE: Parents in Action on Special Education et al. v. Hannon et al. United States District Court for the Northern District of Illinois, Eastern Division, C-74-3586RFP, July 1980, slip opinion.

Peterson, C. R., & Hart, D. H. Factor structure of the WISC-R for a clinic-referred population and specific subgroups. *Journal of Consulting and Clinical Psychology,* 1979, **47,** 643–645.

Peterson, J. *Early conceptions and tests of intelligence.* Chicago: World Book, 1925.

Pintner, R., & Paterson, D. G. *A scale of performance tests.* New York: Appleton, 1925.

Raviv, A., Margalith, M., Raviv, A., & Sade, E. The cognitive pattern of Israeli learning disabled children as reflected in the Hebrew version of the WISC-R. *Journal of Learning Disabilities,* 1981, **14,** 411–415.

Reschly, D. J. WISC-R factor structures among Anglos, Blacks, Chicanos, and Native-American Papagos. *Journal of Consulting and Clinical Psychology,* 1978, **46,** 417–422.

Reynolds, C. R. Should we screen preschoolers? *Contemporary Educational Psychology,* 1979, **4,** 175–181.

Reynolds, C. R. Two commercial interpretive systems for the WISC-R. *School Psychology Review,* 1980, **9,** 385–386.

Reynolds, C. R. The fallacy of "two years below grade level for age" as a diagnostic criterion for reading disorders. *Journal of School Psychology,* 1981, **19,** 350–358. (a)

Reynolds, C. R. The neuropsychological basis of intelligence. In G. Hynd & J. Obrzut (Es.), *Neuropsychological assessment and the school-aged child: Issues and procedures.* New York: Grune & Stratton, 1981. (b)

Reynolds, C. R. A note on determining significant discrepancies among category scores on

Bannatyne's regrouping of WISC-R subtests. *Journal of Learning Disabilities,* 1981, **14,** 468–469. (c)

Reynolds, C. R. Screening tests: Problems and promises. In N. Lambert (Ed.), *Special education assessment matrix,* Monterey, Calif.: CTB/McGraw-Hill, 1981. (d)

Reynolds, C. R. *Test bias: In God we trust, all others must have data.* Invited address to the annual meeting of the American Psychological Association, Los Angeles, August 1981. (e)

Reynolds, C. R. Review of the TARDOR Interpretive Scoring System for the WISC-R. *Measurement and Evaluation in Guidance,* 1981, **14,** 46–48. (f)

Reynolds, C. R. The problem of bias in psychological assessment. In C. R. Reynolds & T. B. Gutkin (Eds.), *The handbook of school psychology,* New York: Wiley, 1982.

Reynolds, C. R. Determining statistically reliable strengths and weaknesses in the performance of single individuals on the Luria-Nebraska Neuropsychological Battery. *Journal of Consulting and Clinical Psychology,* 1982, **50,** 525–529.

Reynolds, C. R., & Brown, R. T. (Eds.) *Perspectives on bias in mental testing.* New York: Plenum, in press.

Reynolds, C. R., & Clark, J. H. Cognitive assessment of the preschool child. In K. Paget & B. Bracken (Eds.), *Psychoeducational assessment of preschool and primary aged children,* New York: Grune & Stratton, 1983.

Reynolds, C. R., & Elliott, S. N. *Trends in test development and test publishing.* Paper presented to the annual meeting of the National Council on Measurement in Education, New York, March 1982.

Reynolds, C. R., & Gutkin, T. B. Predicting the premorbid intellectual status of children using demographic data. *Clinical Neuropsychology,* 1979, **1,** 36–38.

Reynolds, C. R., & Gutkin, T. B. Stability of the WISC-R factor structure across sex at two age levels. *Journal of Clinical Psychology,* 1980, **36,** 775–777.

Reynolds, C. R., & Gutkin, T. B. A multivariate comparison of the intellectual performance of blacks and whites matched on four demographic variables. *Personality and Individual Differences,* 1981, **2,** 175–180. (a)

Reynolds, C. R., & Gutkin, T. B. Statistics for the interpretation of Bannatyne recategorizations of WPPSI subtests. *Journal of Learning Disabilities,* 1981, **14,** 464–467. (b)

Reynolds, C. R., & Gutkin, T. B. Test scatter on the WPPSI: Normative analyses of the standardization sample. *Journal of Learning Disabilities,* 1981, **14,** 460–464. (c)

Reynolds, C. R., & Streur, J. *Factor structure of the WISC-R for emotionally disturbed children.* Paper presented to the annual meeting of the National Association of School Psychologists, Houston, April 1981.

Reynolds, C. R., Willson, V. L., & Clark, P. L. A WISC-R short form for clinical screening. *Clinical Neuropsychology,* in press.

Rugel, R. P. The factor structure of the WISC in two populations of disabled readers. *Journal of Learning Disabilities,* 1974, **7,** 581–585.

Sattler, J. M. *Assessment of children's intelligence and special abilities* (2nd ed.). Boston: Allyn & Bacon, 1982.

Sattler, J., Hilliard, A., Lambert, N., Albee, G., & Jensen, A. *Intelligence tests on trial: Larry P. and PASE.* Symposium presented at the annual meeting of the American Psychological Association, Los Angeles, August 1981.

Schiff, M. M., Kaufman, A. S., & Kaufman, N. L. Scatter analysis of WISC-R profiles for learning disabled children with superior intelligence. *Journal of Learning Disabilities,* 1981, **14,** 426–430.

Schooler, D. L., Beebe, M. C., & Koepke, T. Factor analysis of WISC-R scores for children identified as learning disabled, educable mentally impaired, and emotionally impaired. *Psychology in the Schools,* 1978, **15,** 478–485.

Seashore, H. G. Differences between verbal and performance IQs on the WISC. *Journal of Consulting Psychology,* 1951, **15,** 62–67.

Seguin, E. *Idiocy: Its treatment by the physiological method* (Reprinted from original edition of 1866). New York: Bureau of Publications, Teachers College, Columbia University, 1907.

Sharp, S. E. Individual psychology: A study in psychological method. *American Journal of Psychology,* 1898–99, **10,** 329–391.

Smith, M. D., Coleman, J. M., Dokecki, P. R., & Davis, E. E. Recategorized WISC-R scores of learning disabled children. *Journal of Learning Disabilities,* 1977, **10,** 437–443.

Stangler, S. R., Huber, C. J., & Routh, D. K. *Screening growth and development of preschool children.* New York: McGraw-Hill, 1980.

Stedman, J. M., Lawlis, G. F., Cortner, R. H., & Achterberg, G. Relationships between WISC-R factors, Wide-Range Achievement Test scores, and visual-motor maturation in children referred for psychological evaluation. *Journal of Consulting and Clinical Psychology,* 1978, **46,** 869–872.

Stern, W. *The psychological methods of testing intelligence.* Baltimore: Warwick and York, 1914.

Stevenson, L. P. *WISC-R analysis: Implications for diagnosis and educational intervention of LD children.* Paper presented at the meeting of the Council for Exceptional Children, Dallas, April 1979.

Strichart, S. S., & Love, E. WISC-R performance of children referred to a university center for learning disabilities. *Psychology in the Schools,* 1979, **16,** 183–188.

Swerdlik, M. E., & Schweitzer, J. A comparison of factor structures of the WISC and WISC-R. *Psychology in the Schools,* 1978, **15,** 166–172.

Tabachnick, B. G. Test scatter on the WISC-R. *Journal of Learning Disabilities,* 1979, **12,** 626–628.

Tellegen, A., & Briggs, P. F. Old wine in new skins: Grouping Wechsler subtests into new scales. *Journal of Consulting Psychology,* 1967, **31,** 499–506.

Terman, L. M. *The measurement of intelligence.* Boston: Houghton-Mifflin, 1916.

Terman, L. M., & Childs, H. G. A tentative revision and extension of the Binet-Simon Measuring Scale of Intelligence. *Journal of Educational Psychology,* 1912, **3,** 61–74; 133–143; 198–208; 277–289.

Terman, L. M., & Merrill, M. A. *Measuring intelligence.* Boston: Houghton-Mifflin, 1937.

Terman, L. M., & Merrill, M. A. *Stanford-Binet Intelligence Scale: 1972 Norms edition.* Boston: Houghton-Mifflin, 1973.

Thompson, R. J. The diagnostic utility of WISC-R measures with children referred to a developmental evaluation center. *Journal of Consulting and Clinical Psychology,* 1980, **48,** 440–447.

Thompson, R. J. The diagnostic utility of Bannatyne's recategorized WISC-R scores with children referred to a developmental evaluation center. *Psychology in the Schools,* 1981, **18,** 43–47.

Torrance, E. P. *Torrance tests of creative thinking: Directions manual and scoring guide.* Lexington, Mass.: Ginn, 1974.

Vance, H. B., & Singer, M. G. Recategorization of the WISC-R subtest scaled scores for learning disabled children. *Journal of Learning Disabilities,* 1979, **12,** 487–491.

Vance, H. B., & Wallbrown, F. H. The structure of intelligence for black children: A hierarchical approach. *Psychological Record,* 1978, **28,** 31–39.

Van Hagen, J., & Kaufman, A. S. Factor analysis of the WISC-R for a group of mentally retarded children and adolescents. *Journal of Consulting and Clinical Psychology,* 1975, **43,** 661–667.

Vernon, P. A. *Intelligence: Heredity and environment.* San Francisco: W. H. Freeman, 1979.

Vernon, P. A. *Speed of information processing and general intelligence.* Unpublished doctoral dissertation. University of California, Berkeley, 1981.

Vitelli, R., & Goldblatt, R. *The TARDOR interpretive scoring system for the WISC-R.* Manchester, Conn.: TARDOR Publishers, 1979.

Wallbrown, F., Blaha, J., Wallbrown, J., & Engin, A. The hierarchical factor structure of the Wechsler Intelligence Scale for Children—Revised. *Journal of Psychology,* 1975, **89,** 223–235.

Wechsler, D. *Measurement of adult intelligence.* Baltimore: Williams and Wilkins, 1939.

Wechsler, D. *Measurement and appraisal of adult intelligence* (4th ed.). Baltimore: Williams and Wilkins, 1958.

Wechsler, D. *Manual for the Wechsler Preschool and Primary Scale of Intelligence (WPPSI).* New York: Psychological Corporation, 1967.

Wechsler, D. *Manual for the Wechsler Intelligence Scale for Children—Revised (WISC-R).* New York: Psychological Corporation, 1974.

Wechsler, D. *Manual for the Wechsler Adult Intelligence Scale—Revised (WAIS-R).* New York: Psychological Corporation, 1981.

Weiner, S. G., & Kaufman, A. S. WISC-R vs. WISC for black children suspected of learning or behavioral disorders. *Journal of Learning Disabilities,* 1979, **12,** 100–105.

Wender, P. H. *Minimal brain dysfunction in children.* New York: Wiley-Interscience, 1971.

White, W. (Ed.) Intelligence. Special issue of *Journal of Research and Development in Education,* 1979, **12**(1).

Wilson, R. S., Rosenbaum, G., Brown G., Rourke, D., Whitman, D., & Grisell, J. An index of premorbid intelligence. *Journal of Consulting and Clinical Psychology,* 1978, **46,** 1554–1555.

Wissler, C. The correlation of mental and physical tests. *Psychological Review,* 1901, **3** (Monograph Supplement 16).

Witkin, H. A., Dyke, R. B., Faterson, H. G., Goodenough, D. R., & Karp, S. A. *Psychological differentiation.* Potomac, Md.: Erlbaum, 1974.

Wright, B. J., & Isenstein, V. R. *Psychological tests and minorities.* Rockville, Md.: NIMH, DHEW Publication # (ADM) 78-482, 1977.

Yoakum, C. S., & Yerkes, R. M. *Army Mental Tests.* New York: Henry Holt, 1920.

CHAPTER 4

Personality Inventories

MALCOLM D. GYNTHER AND RUTH A. GYNTHER

Personality develops in an interpersonal context. Whether this construct is defined in terms of the mutual relations among superego, ego, and id (Freud, 1933), prediction of what a person will do in a given situation (Cattell, 1950), or what lies behind specific acts and within the individual (Allport, 1937), it is clear that from the lay person's point of view personality is "what makes Johnny run" (or cheat or steal or create). People are probably more interested in understanding other people (and themselves) than they are in anything else. Crises on the local and international scene come and go, but concerns about getting along with one's wife, outwitting or otherwise adapting to one's boss or supervisor, and keeping up with one's children are perennial. Courses that offer to teach one how to win friends and influence people are always popular, and books that offer solutions to interpersonal dilemmas (e.g., Dyer's *Pulling Your Own Strings*) frequently become best sellers.

One often hears someone refer to another as having a terrific personality, or as not having much personality, or as simply a rotten personality. Sometimes there is consensus, and sometimes objections are made to the generalization offered. Nonetheless, one gets the impression that the lay person has a handle on personality description. Furthermore, one often hears comments to the effect that "Joe will come to a bad end," or "Mary has a bright future ahead of her," or "George is certain to make a pile of money." Here it appears that lay people also have the ability to predict future events, a skill that has tended to elude behavioral scientists.

What kinds of data are lay people working with? Are their generalizations and predictions accurate? What is it that professionals in this field are trying to accomplish over and above what everyone else does every day?

It appears that lay concepts of another's personality are primarily determined by the social stimulus value of others—what impact they have, and how they affect people who come in contact with them. First impressions seem to be formed very rapidly as we select friends, fall in love, choose candidates for political office, or size up customers. These judgments are, however, subject to many kinds of error. Observers may be influenced by hearsay and perceive people as someone else has described them. They may produce a halo effect by finding one characteristic that turns them on or off and then generalizing to other aspects of a person's behavior. They may use a stereotype based on characteristics believed to be universal in the group to which a person belongs. Furthermore, the people being judged may behave in such a way as to create a false impression. They may be putting their best foot forward. They may be making a deliberate effort to deceive by assuming a temporary role that is not characteristic of them. Or they may come from backgrounds so different from that of the observer that they are hard to understand.

We should not conclude from this list of potential errors that lay people are bound to be wrong in their impressions or predictions. Every group or community seems to have a member or two who have great insight into the behavior of others. Taft (1955) concluded that accurate judgment occurs when the judge possesses appropriate judgmental norms, has high judging ability (a combination of general and social intelligence), and is motivated and free to make accurate judgments about the subject. More recent studies (e.g., Cline, 1964) provide modest but positive evidence for the generality of judgmental accuracy. For our purposes, the point is that none of the dimensions posited by Taft that relate to making judgments of others excludes the possibility that lay people can be experts. Indeed, there are a host of studies (e.g., Goldberg, 1959; Goldberg, 1965; Johnston & McNeal, 1967) showing that the amount of professional training and the experience of a judge are unrelated to his or her judgmental accuracy.

If, then, it may be conceded that certain lay people are good or even excellent judges of personality, what are professional personologists attempting to do? Hundreds or indeed thousands of individuals would not be spending their careers in the fields of personality theory or assessment if there were satisfaction with the notion that our "wise" men and women or Delphic oracles could solve the perplexities of human nature. One clear distinction is that the professional is interested in quantification. Mathematical procedures underlie the advances in physical sciences. Unless one can make explicit the bases of his or her predictions, the area of study is apt to remain an art. Another feature that is likely to elude lay people is the need for systematic verification. Dramatic predictive "hits" are often remembered, but the many other predictions that were not borne out are forgotten. Generalization is also a goal of scientific endeavor. To be able to say something relevant about one individual is interesting but not really adequate for developing "laws" of behavior. One needs to establish relationships that will hold, to a greater or lesser degree, for a class of individuals. Furthermore, methods or instruments for evaluating personality must be devised. There are so many occasions where assessment is called for—in education, clinical, business and industrial, legal, and research settings—that one can't possibly solve the logistical problems of seeing that a few of the sages among us make contact with these hundreds of thousands or, more probably, millions of clients per year. These instruments should possess qualities that enable those who use them to avoid those errors which are characteristic of informal appraisals of personality (i.e., halo effect, stereotyping, etc.).

The material to follow will attempt to elucidate some principles of formal personality assessment, describe how base rates and selection ratios affect decision making, indicate what approaches are used in objective personality assessment, give a historical sketch of the development of personality inventories, and review some of the most important inventories available today. These reviews will include the aims of the test constructor, the strategy used to accomplish those goals, the resulting scales, the psychometric properties of the instrument, and the most salient research related to clinical interpretation of the scales or profiles. Evaluations of the current status of the inventories will also be given. Three newly developed inventories will be briefly reviewed. Some discussion of controversial issues will also be offered. The major purpose of this chapter is to give the reader a view of what psychologists are doing to bring order into a very complex area. Although some consideration will necessarily be given to psychometric issues, the major focus will be applied, in keeping with the clinical orientation of this book.

KEY STEPS IN ASSESSMENT: THE PREDICTION PARADIGM

This section will outline and briefly illustrate the basic steps in the prediction process. Although earlier writers described the process to a greater or lesser degree, we are following here the discussion presented in Wiggins' *Personality and Prediction* (1973), an excellent book that is highly recommended for a more extensive treatment of these and related issues. The following six steps constitute the basic prediction paradigm:

1. *Criterion analysis.*   The criterion is that aspect of human behavior to be predicted in a given assessment problem. When it is stated boldly in that fashion, one might say, "Fine, let's get on with it." But closer examination reveals unexpected complexities. Suppose you are interested in predicting successful response to psychotherapy. By *successful* in this instance, you mean that the client—let us say the client is male—will be able to handle his family, work, financial, and other responsibilities competently. But what exactly does that statement mean? Following therapy, the client may feel so liberated from his doubts and fears that he resigns from his safe, secure job to seek a more challenging one, or he may discover that his wife is not compatible with his "new" self. Are these behaviors classifiable under the heading of "family and work competency"? Perhaps these are academic questions, because ultimate criteria of this type are rarely employed in practice. Obviously one would have to spend years collecting the relevant data. Such time-consuming procedures are very expensive. Consequently, most assessment studies focus on intermediate criteria of performance that are presumed to be related to ultimate criteria. In our example we might substitute "improvement" at the end of 30 weekly treatment sessions on whatever measures we are interested in for the more distant "successful handling" of real-life responsibilities. Other assessment studies might choose instead to focus on immediate criteria of performance. In the example used, that might be defined as the client's appearing for his first therapy session on time, being responsive verbally, seeming reluctant to leave, and asking to return the next week. Whether these particular indicators are relevant to the intermediate and ultimate criteria is a matter for conjecture, but assessors should select immediate criteria that they have reason to believe are relevant to the more long-term values.

2. *Selection of instruments.*   The next step in the process involves the selec-

tion of instruments to be used in the prediction of criterion scores. Ideally, the instrument should be relevant to the criterion, as in the job sample technique: If one wants to hire an auto mechanic, that individual might be asked to tune an engine to allow evaluation of his or her proficiency. This approach is difficult to apply to personality assessment problems in which criteria are often complex or imprecisely defined. Great care should be taken to select or develop instruments that have predictive capability. Continuous evaluation to improve the instruments is essential. Considerations of convenience and economy often enter into the choice of instruments, but one must not allow these practical considerations to take precedence over criterion relevance. A short, inexpensive, objective procedure that has no predictive power may be worse than previous highly informal unstructured interviewing, since some people (those who instituted it) will insist on using the numerical "results" of the invalid procedure for decision making.

3. *Development of predictor battery.*   After the instruments have been chosen, it is necessary to obtain empirical information concerning the relationships between predictors and criteria. Ideally, one gives the instruments to all candidates for the treatment in question and accepts all candidates into the program, regardless of where their scores fall. Later, measures of response to treatment are obtained and relations between predicted and actual criterion scores are computed. When the criterion standard is of an intermediate or ultimate nature, it is often not practical to wait until such measures become available. Under these conditions, the battery of instruments may be administered to patients currently in treatment on whom intermediate or ultimate criterion data already exist.

4. *Combination of data.*   Predictor measures must be combined so as to yield the most accurate forecast of criterion scores. The multiple-regression model is often used for this purpose. The question of how much weight to give human (or more narrowly, clinical) judgment must also be considered.

5. *Cross validation of predictor weights.*   The multiple-regression equation derived for a given sample cannot be assumed to hold for other similar samples. A frequent solution to this problem is to divide randomly a group of patients for whom both predictor and criterion measures are available into a derivation sample and a cross-validation sample. A set of regression weights is determined for the derivation sample and then also used for prediction of the criterion in the cross-validation sample. The correlation between predicted and obtained scores in the cross-validation sample is then assumed to be a reasonably accurate estimate of the predictive validity of a fixed set of predictors. Although there are disagreements as to optimal cross-validation procedures, there is agreement that some kind of cross-validation is essential if one is to make accurate predictions.

6. *Application of predictor battery.*   The final step of the prediction process involves the application of the assessment battery for purposes of selection and/or classification. Testing under standard conditions, scoring of the inventories or tests, applying cross-validated regression weights to the test scores—all this is done to obtain a predicted criterion score for each subject. Individuals may then be rank-ordered in terms of their predicted criterion scores, which represent, let us say, their probable favorable response to parole. If the parole board wishes to achieve the best

possible record, it may then select only those individuals in the top quartile of scores for release to the community. This latter point has to do with decision making, which after all is the overriding concern of personality assessment.

DISCRIMINATIVE EFFICIENCY OF PSYCHOLOGICAL TESTS: BASE RATES AND SELECTION DATA

Cronbach and Gleser's *Psychological Tests and Personnel Decisions* (1957) directed attention to the outcomes of decisions and their consequences for individuals and institutions, whereas traditional assessment psychologists have emphasized measurement and prediction. The decision theory orientation raises questions about the classical procedures for determining the worth of a psychological test or assessment procedure. For example, the validity coefficient tells us the degree of association that exists between predicted and obtained criterion scores. However, from a practical standpoint, the number of correct decisions resulting from use of a given cutoff score seems more important than knowledge of the validity coefficient.

The following discussion represents only a small part of the area mapped out by Cronbach and Gleser. For a comprehensive view of this contribution, the interested reader should consult the original monograph (Cronbach & Gleser, 1957) or the revised edition (Cronbach & Gleser, 1965).

There are four possible outcomes of a prediction that, let us say, has to do with success in college (i.e., graduation). When success is predicted and success in fact occurs, the individuals so classified are called *valid positives*. When success is predicted but failure results, the individuals are referred to as *false positives*. When failure is predicted and failure occurs, the individuals are described as *valid negatives*. When failure is predicted but success takes place, these individuals are known as *false negatives*. All these conditions involve cutoff scores on the predictor variable (e.g., an equation from the California Psychological Inventory) and cutoff classification on the criterion (in this instance, graduation vs. failure to graduate from college). The extent to which a predictor score or set of scores is able to separate and classify outcomes accurately (valid positives and valid negatives) is referred to as the *discriminative efficiency* of the score or set of scores. The probability of occurrence of any of the subtypes mentioned above is determined by dividing the frequency of a given outcome by the total number of people in the sample.

Perhaps a simple illustration will elucidate the usefulness of this approach. Gynther and Mayer (1960) asked if a brief IQ test (the Kent-EGY) could serve as a substitute for the WAIS, which takes about an hour to administer and some 15 to 20 minutes to score properly. The literature indicated that correlations of .60 to .65 had been found between the two tests, but that information in no way answered the question. So both Wechslers and Kent-EGYs were given to 47 patients referred to a psychology service with a question of mental deficiency. They were classified as either defective or nondefective on the basis of cutoff scores established by the text constructors. The Wechsler classifications were considered as the criterion measures, and the Kent-EGY scores as predictor variables. Analysis of the results by means of the usual fourfold contingency table showed that the Kent-EGY predicted deficiency correctly 46% (13/28) of the time, while it identified nondefectives with 95% (18/19) accuracy. With respect to correct classification of all subjects, this test was accurate in 66% [(18 + 13)/47)] of the cases. The original question can now be answered. If the Kent-EGY score is 19 or above, mental deficiency is essentially ruled out; if the score obtained is 18 or less, one must proceed with the WAIS to get an accurate "diagnosis."

Two other terms need to be mentioned: *base rate* and *selection ratio*. Base rate, which refers to the proportion of actual positives (i.e., potential college graduates) that exist in the total sample, has been a very well-known term since Meehl and Rosen published an influential article on it in 1955. More generally, it refers to the frequency of occurrence of any event (e.g., suicide attempts) in a given sample. Selection ratio, which refers to the proportion of predicted positives selected in relation to the total number of subjects, has probably been more widely used in industrial or military circles than in clinical settings. A less technical definition has been given by Cronbach (1970): The selection ratio is the proportion of persons tested who are accepted.

A helpful example of the influence of the base rate can be drawn from Meehl and Rosen (1955). Men being inducted into the military service were given an inventory to detect "those men who would not complete basic training because of psychiatric disability or AWOL recidivism." All those given the inventory were allowed to undergo basic training regardless of their test scores. Samples of individuals who made a good adjustment (N = 415) and a poor adjustment (N = 89) to basic training were selected for a study of predictive validity. The base rates for good and poor adjustment were 82% and 18%, respectively. The most effective scale for screening out misfits picked up, at a given cutting point, 55% of the poor adjustment group (valid positives) and 19% of the good adjustment group (false positives). Meehl and Rosen asked, given these facts, how good this cutting score is for the purpose stated. They assumed that 5% of all inductees would fall into the poor adjustment group and 95% would make a good adjustment. If one casts 10,000 cases into a fourfold contingency table (on the basis of the four percentages just given), it will be found that the cutoff score is actually no good for screening out misfits. Only $275/2080$ or 13% of those predicted to make a poor adjustment would actually fall in that category. The decisions for 1805 or 87% would be incorrect! (If one were to use the original base rates of 82% and 18%, decisions for "only" 62% of the predicted "poors" would be incorrect.)

Cronbach (1970, p. 540) has supplied an illustration that shows even more clearly than Meehl and Rosen's data how changes in the base rate influence the predictive accuracy of a cutoff score. In this case, the problem has to do with the number of patients coming to a clinic who are depressed. When that frequency (i.e., base rate) is 50%, use of a given cutting score on a psychological inventory correctly classifies 80% of these individuals. However, if only 20% are depressed, use of the same cutting score results in only 50% correct identification. If only 5% are depressed, use of this cutting score correctly identifies only 15 to 20% of these patients. Finally, if the base rate for depression is 2%, the cutting score accurately identifies less than 10% of the depressed patients. There are conditions where the base rate is known to be less than 10% (e.g., suicide in psychiatric inpatients); the reader can imagine the probability of correct test predictions (and the tremendous number of false positives) that is likely to occur using a cutoff score obtained from any test with less than perfect validity.

As stated earlier, the concept of selection ratio has been applied more in industrial than clinical settings. Cronbach (1970) has said, "There are no quotas in clinical diagnosis; every person tested can be called 'normal' or every one called 'schizophrenic' if such uniform classification appears correct" (p. 446). However, it is possible to conceive of situations in which this concept might be relevant to the clinical or counseling psychologist, especially one who is interested in understanding outcomes of prediction. One might, for example, wish to consider assigning patients to treatment under conditions in which there are not enough therapists to handle every patient. Or one might wish to consider the relationship between test scores and admission to two kinds of colleges, the state university and a highly selective private university. Those in academic work certainly are familiar with differences between the number of applicants and the number of admissions to graduate school in psychology.

When most applicants for a position or treatment are accepted, the selection ratio is considered to be high. Such a ratio would be in effect in most state universities. When only a small fraction of applicants is accepted, the selection ratio is said to be low. At the present time, that type of ratio is characteristic of acceptances to graduate programs in clinical psychology.

Selection becomes increasingly efficient as the selection ratio becomes smaller. This is true even when the test being used possesses very modest validity. We are not referring to the overall proportion of correct decisions, but rather to the proportion of applicants selected who are subsequently judged to have performed well. This orientation ignores the outcomes of rejection. In industrial settings it may be appropriate to display little interest in the applicant who is not hired, but in clinical settings the proportion of false negatives who do not receive the required treatment is of great importance. If the selection ratio is set very low (e.g., 5%) for some specialized, expensive brain surgery, the vast majority of patients who could benefit from it will not receive it.

Base rates and selection ratios markedly affect the predictive power of cutoff scores derived from psychological tests. Indices developed under one set of circumstances cannot be expected to work equally well in other situations where these parameters have different values. Individuals who are interested in developing new test indices or applying well-established ones cannot ignore the constraints these variables place on predictive accuracy.

THE NATURE OF OBJECTIVE PERSONALITY MEASURES

What kind of instrument might be used to carry out "objective personality assessment"? One often hears that projective tests (e.g., Rorschach) are characterized by ambiguous stimuli, whereas objective measures (e.g., MMPI) are noted for their unambiguous structured stimuli. However, if one were to give 20 students tracing paper and pencils and ask them to reproduce Card I of the Rorschach, it is likely that great correspondence would be found in the resulting drawings. Structured inventories typically make use of statements containing qualifiers such as "usually," "sometimes," or "seldom." Simpson (1944) has shown that such ratings are interpreted quite differently by different subjects. For example, 25% of his subjects said they applied "usually" only to behaviors that occurred at least 90% of the time; another 25% said that "usually" included frequencies below 70%. Many other examples could be given to demonstrate that classification into "objective–projective" or "structured–unstructured" cannot be done on the basis of stimulus properties.

What does differentiate the two types of measurement techniques is the restriction placed on the response option. Objective personality measuring devices are commonly designed so that the subject must answer "true" or "false," whereas tests such as the Rorschach allow a multitude of responses. Wiggins (1973) also emphasized the nearly perfect scoring reliability that results from a true–false response option procedure. Subjects' test-taking attitudes and the examiner's set have also been considered as distinguishing features between structured and unstructured techniques. It would be difficult to improve on Kelly's (1958) comment: "When the subject is asked to guess what the examiner is thinking, we call it an objective test; when the examiner tries to guess what the subject is thinking, we call it a projective device" (p. 332). Exner in Chapter 2 of this volume provides some additional perspectives on the nature of "projective" tests.

Although graduate students frequently identify objective personality assessment courses as MMPI courses, the types of data available for this kind of assessment are far broader than even the self-report inventory approach in general. Cronbach (1970) offered three general categories: observations in representative situations, reports from others and from the subject, and performance tests. Cattell (1946) has described the same basic sources of information somewhat differently: life-record data (L data), questionnaire date (Q data), and objective test data (T data). L data are obtained from observations of subjects in everyday life situations (e.g., by peers or trained observers) or by the analysis of life-history documents or biographies. Q data are obtained from the self-reports of subjects. T data are obtained from the behavioral responses (physiological, motoric, verbal) to a wide assortment of provocative physical, pictorial, or verbal stimuli. Performance tests are intended to get distortion-free information on overt behavior; it is assumed that the subject cannot perceive the relationship between his responses and the variable (e.g., persistence) being assessed. Cattell and Warburton (1967) have published a volume containing hundreds of examples of tests of this type.

Although other chapters of this book cover L data and T data in detail (see Chapters 1, 2, 3, 5, and 6), it may be appropriate to give some examples of the instruments being used in these areas. The life-history approach often takes the form of rating scales for evaluating the current mental status of psychiatric patients. Among the best known of these endeavors are the DIAGNO system (see Spitzer & Endicott, 1969), the Inpatient Multidimensional Psychiatric Scale (see Lorr &

Klett, 1970), and the Brief Psychiatric Rating Scale (Overall & Gorham, 1962). As an illustration that L data need not take the form of rating scales, Overall's study (1971) of the relationship between marital status and psychopathology can be mentioned.

T data come in many forms. One of the most detailed analyses of such data has been presented by Cattell, Schmidt, and Bjerstedt (1972). Their monograph deals with Cattell's Objective–Analytic Personality Test Battery and examines the relationship between objective tests and clinical diagnoses. Another set of instruments that has also been investigated extensively is the Halstead Neuropsychological Test Battery. This battery has been used to differentiate among brain-damaged, schizophrenic, and medical patients (Levine & Feirstein, 1972), as well as to study the cognitive functioning of neurological patients (Reitan & Boll, 1971). Other investigators (e.g., Overall & Gorham, 1972) have employed the Holtzman Inkblot Test and measures of digit copying and synonym learning (Kendrick, 1972) for similar purposes.

For extended general presentations of objective personality assessment, the reader is referred to the following texts: *Objective Personality Assessment* (Butcher, 1972), *Assessment of Persons* (Sundberg, 1977), *Personality and Psychological Assessment* (Kleinmuntz, 1982), and *Personality Assessment* (Lanyon & Goodstein, 1982). Goodstein and Lanyon (1971) have also edited *Readings in Personality Assessment,* which starts with selections from Galton and Jung and concludes with articles on such topics as computer interpretation of psychological tests. McReynolds' (Vol. IV, 1978) series called *Advances in Psychological Assessment* also contain many interesting and authoritative articles. A promising new series named *Advances in Personality Assessment* (Spielberger & Butcher, 1982) is also under way. As the major focus of this chapter is self-report personality inventories (Q data), we will now turn to that topic.

DEVELOPMENT OF PERSONALITY INVENTORIES:
A HISTORICAL SKETCH

One writer has traced the beginnings of assessment back to the Chinese civil service examinations of 4000 years ago (DuBois, 1970) while another (Hathaway, 1965) cited a Biblical episode concerning a method of personnel selection. For our purposes, Galton appears to be a good starting point, inasmuch as he might be designated the father of the scientific study of individual differences, and he actually devised a questionnaire concerning imagery. Interest in individual differences could be traced through the writings of such men as J. McKeen Cattell and G. Stanley Hall up to the present, and the academic endeavors of these psychologists constitute one of two major influences leading to the development of personality inventories. The other major influence consisted of demands by society for help in dealing with such pressing problems as the education of slow learners and the classification and treatment of mental disorders, demands responded to by Binet, Kraepelin, Jung, and others.

These academic and pragmatic lines of investigation merged in World War I. Hundreds of thousands of men were being inducted into military service as rapidly as possible. Some evaluation of their emotional fitness for warfare was desired, but too few qualified people were available for interviewing them all. Woodworth and Poffenberger responded to this need by developing the Personal Data Sheet (Woodworth, 1920), which is generally considered the first personality inventory. Psychiatric texts were examined for symptoms of psychological disturbance in order to develop a paper-and-pencil version of the psychiatric interview. The final scale (which was never actually used during the war) contained 116 items of the following kind: "Have you failed to get a square deal in life?" "Are you happy most of the time?" "Does the sight of blood make you sick or dizzy?" The respondent was to answer "yes" or "no" to each item. Recruits who reported many symptoms were detained for further questioning, and the Personal Data Sheet, by that criterion, seemed an impressive predictor of maladjustment. The item content of this inventory was chosen on the basis of face validity; that is, items were included if the test developer thought they would elicit different responses from well-adjusted and poorly adjusted subjects.

Although many people tried to adapt Woodworth's questionnaire to groups such as school children, juvenile delinquents, and college students, the next substantive advance in item selection procedures was made by Strong (1927). The Strong Vocational Interest Blank was designed by means of an empirical approach to item selection. Unlike a priori, rational, or face-validity approaches, in which the test constructor tries to select items that seem adequately to sample the relevant domain, *criterion keying* (another term for the empirical strategy) is a technique that makes few theoretical assumptions about an item included on a personality test. Strong's procedure was to compare the responses given to test items by persons of one occupation with those given by people in general. For example, several thousand engineers took his test. He tabulated their answers item by item to determine for which items the difference in responses between engineers and people in general was statistically significant, and these items were retained for the engineer scoring key. A high score on this scale would then lead to two interrelated predictions: (a) This individual's pattern of interests is very similar to that of practicing engineers; and (b) this individual is more likely to enjoy a career in engineering than people with lower scores.

In the early 1930s two inventories that deserve comment were published. Bernreuter's Personality Inventory (1931) was notable in that it was one of the first adjustment questionnaires that was multidimensional (unlike the Personal Data Sheet, which yielded a single global measure of adjustment). Bernreuter combined items from earlier inventories measuring neurotic tendencies, ascendance–submission, and introversion–extroversion with his own Self-Sufficiency scale. The other questionnaire, the Allport-Vernon Study of Values (1931), was novel in that it was the first popular inventory to be derived from a theory, namely, Spranger's (1928) typology of the religious man, aesthetic man, economic man, and so forth, and it required forced-choice responding.

The next important development was the application of an external strategy to the construction of adjustment scales. The Humm-Wadsworth Temperament Schedule (1935) was probably the first of this type to be published (and to use psychiatric patients for criterion groups), although for various reasons it never was employed very much in clinical settings. One reason might be that the Minnesota Multiphasic Personality Inventory   (MMPI) was "announced" in 1940 (Hathaway & McKinley, 1940) and published 3 years later (Hathaway & McKinley, 1943). This inventory became popular almost immediately, probably in large part because of the demand for assessment and classification associated with screening of personnel for military duty in World War II.

Several other trends emerged in the 1940s and 1950s, including (a) more concentrated efforts to develop inventories by factor-analytic methods, (b) the use of criterion keying to develop an inventory to describe normal personalities, and (c) another application of the forced-choice method, this time derived from a different theory. Guilford and his associates published a number of inventories (STDCR, Guilford, 1940; GAMIN, Guilford & Martin, 1943; the Temperament Survey, Guilford & Zimmerman, 1949), all based on one version of the internal (i.e., factor-analytic) strategy of test construction. Basically, this is a statistical procedure for identifying clusters of items that are relatively highly correlated with each other. Cattell utilized a somewhat different approach from Guilford's in that he assembled personality trait names rather than inventory items. He published the Sixteen Personality Factor Questionnaire (16 PF) in 1949 and other inventories [e.g., the IPAT Anxiety Scale Questionnaire (Cattell & Scheier, 1963)] later. Eysenck, the third of the major figures associated with the factor-analytic approach, published the Maudsley Personality Inventory in 1959 and the Eysenck Personality Inventory four years later (Eysenck & Eysenck, 1963). Gough (1957) applied the empirical strategy to construction of an inventory [i.e., the California Psychological Inventory (CPI)], which was designed to tap important dimensions of normal functioning not being measured by any of the then-existing adjustment inventories. The other well-known inventory published in the 1950s was the Edwards Personal Preference Schedule (EPPS, Edwards, 1954). In some respects this inventory resembled the Study of Values, but Edwards derived his items from Murray's (1938) personality need theory.

We will conclude this highly selective review by briefly describing three of the more recent inventories to appear on the scene: Edwards' (1967) Personality Inventory (EPI), Jackson's (1967) Personality Research Form (PRF), and Millon's (1977) Clinical Multiaxial Inventory (CMI). All three instruments were constructed using a mixed intuitive–internal strategy plus, in Millon's case, an external validation step to produce the final version of his inventory. The EPI is notable for including about 1200 items to measure 53 scales; it represents the farthest departure yet from Woodworth's simple global index of adjustment. This inventory no longer uses the forced-choice format of the earlier EPPS, but is administered with unusual instructions: "Predict how people who know you best would mark each statement if they were asked to describe you." The PRF is yet another attempt to measure Murray's constructs. The inventory consists of 20 scales with such familiar names as Achievement, Affiliation, Aggression, and Autonomy. Jackson in particular has been guided by the multitrait model (Campbell & Fiske, 1959), which emphasizes the necessity of demonstrating both convergent and discriminant validity of a personality scale. Millon's CMI is noteworthy in that its scales are coordinated directly with the official psychiatric nomenclature for mental disorders, the DSM-III. Scales are divided into patterns of personality disorder (e.g., Avoidant Personality) and clinical symptom and syndrome categories (e.g., Dysthymic, Paranoid).

For the reader who wishes a comprehensive historical review of personality scales and inventories, Goldberg's (1971) article is recommended. We now turn to a brief discussion of the rationale used for selecting the inventories that receive fuller review in the remainder of this chapter.

CRITERIA FOR MAJOR REVIEWS

The principal criteria used for selecting personality inventories for discussion at length are (a) clinical (adjustment–maladjustment) emphasis, (b) multidimensionality (as opposed to single-scale approaches), (c) importance as determined by the amount of research activity, (d) importance as determined by degree of usage, and (e) the wish to exemplify the different strategies of test construction. The first criterion applies to such excellent inventories as the Strong-Campbell Interest Inventory (Campbell, 1977) which has been around for 55 years and is probably more popular than ever before, but is rarely used for clinical evaluation. The second criterion raises questions concerning the wisdom of including a questionnaire such as the Eysenck Personality Inventory (Eysenck & Eysenck, 1963), which measures only two traits. The third criterion can be applied by examining the lists of references in the Personality section of the *Eighth Mental Measurements Yearbook* (Buros, 1978). The top 10 in amount of research activity are the MMPI (Hathaway & McKinley, 1967) (first), EPPS (Edwards, 1959), 16 PF (Cattell, Eber, & Tatsuoka, 1970), CPI (Gough, 1975), Study of Values (Allport, Vernon, & Lindsey, 1970), Eysenck Personality Inventory (Eysenck & Eysenck, 1969), Personal Orientation Inventory (Shostrom, 1966), Tennessee Self Concept Scale (Fitts, 1965), the Adjective Check List (Gough & Heilbrun, 1965), and Omnibus Personality Inventory (OPI, Heist & Yonge, 1968) (tenth). The MMPI has nearly 1200 references listed for the approximately 6 to 7 years reviewed, which is almost four times the number of studies reported for the EPPS, and nine times the number reported for the OPI.

The most recent source for considering the fourth criterion is a survey of psychological test usage in the United States being conducted by Bernard Lubin and his associates. This survey is much more restrictive than that published by Lubin, Wallis, and Paine in 1971. In the earlier study, the authors drew up a list of 149 tests and asked respondents how often they used them. In this new study, only the 30 most frequently used tests from the 1971 list were asked about. Since the CPI, 16 PF, Study of Values, and other well-known inventories ranked thirty-first or higher 12 years ago, no information is currently available on their usage.

The MMPI and Edwards's PPS were the only objective personality inventories in the top 30. Results (B. Lubin, Note 5), based on a 48% return rate of the 458 mental health agencies sampled, show that the MMPI is first and the EPPS seventeenth in weighted score ranks. The ranks of the MMPI in VA stations and state hospitals were third and second, respectively, which suggests little change in usage from the first and fourth ranks obtained in 1971.

Two new samples were obtained on this occasion: military centers and private practitioners. More than half of the air force, navy, and army units responded, while only 31% of the 739 private practitioners furnished the requested data. MMPI usage is very high in these settings, ranking first in the military centers and fourth in private practice. The EPPS is used considerably less frequently by these psychologists.

The final criterion has to do with strategy of scale construction. Our thought here was to attempt to include at least one example of each approach to inventory development if, in so doing, we could also reasonably satisfy the other criteria. There is some disagreement on what the strategies are. Goldberg (1974) has divided them into three categories: *intuitive, intuitive–internal,* and *external.* On other occasions, the same author (Goldberg, 1972) has used the terms *factor-analytic, contrasted groups, rational,* and *theoretical.* We find the latter set more meaningful, but this is probably a matter of taste. In any case, the inventories that best seem to fulfill the five criteria are the MMPI, the CPI, the 16 PF, and Jackson's PRF. The first two of these were developed primarily by the contrasted-groups strategy, the 16 PF was constructed by means of the factor-analytic strategy, and the PRF represents a sophisticated combination of rational and theoretical strategies.

THE MINNESOTA MULTIPHASIC PERSONALITY INVENTORY (MMPI)

Aims

This inventory was developed "as an aid in differential psychiatric diagnosis" (Hathaway & McKinley, 1940). Twenty-five years later, Hathaway (1965) stated that the instrument was developed "as an objective aid in the routine psychiatric case work-up of adult patients and as a method for determining the severity of the conditions" (p. 463). Thus the inventory constructors had two assessment objectives in mind: type and degree of maladjustment.

Strategy of Test Construction

The method of contrasted groups was used. A set of 504 items, derived from earlier inventories, clinical reports, psychiatric interviewing manuals, and other sources, was administered to normal subjects and carefully diagnosed psychiatric groups. The normative sample consisted of 724 visitors to the University of Minnesota hospitals. Potential subjects who said they were currently under the care of a physician were excluded. This sample corresponded well in age, sex, and marital status to the overall Minnesota population. According to Dahlstrom, Welsh, and Dahlstrom (1972), a normal Minnesota adult, circa 1940, was "about thirty-five years old, . . . married, lived in a small town or rural area, . . . had eight years of general schooling, and worked at a skilled or semiskilled trade (or was married to a man with such an occupational level)" (p. 8).

The psychiatric patients available to the test constructors numbered over 800, although far fewer than that served as members of the final criterion groups. For the derivation of eight clinical scales of the instrument the following kinds of criterion groups were used: (a) patients who showed an abnormal concern for their bodily functions; (b) patients who showed relatively uncomplicated depressive disorders; (c) patients who demonstrated conversion reactions; (d) cases in a psychiatric setting being studied at the request of courts because of delinquent actions (no capital offenders were included); (e) patients whose most prominent clinical features were ideas of reference, persecutory delusions, and grandiosity; (f) patients who showed obsessive ruminations, compulsive rituals, abnormal fears, and guilt feelings; (g) patients who displayed apathy, bizarre mentation, delusions and/or hallucinations, and autism; and (h) patients who showed overactivity, emotional excitement, and flight of ideas. For three other empirically derived scales, one used as a criterion group psychiatric patients whose profiles were all within normal limits on the clinical scales; a second used several criterion groups, including male sexual inverts relatively free from neurosis, normal males as distinguished from normal females, and feminine males identified by means of an attitude interest inventory (items added in this analysis brought the total up to 550); and the third used college students who scored high and low on a social introversion–extroversion inventory.

The typical item-selection procedure involved contrasting the responses to the 504 items of the criterion groups listed above with the normative sample. Items that had true–false endorsement frequencies that differed at or beyond the .05 level of significance were retained for the final scales. In many cases derivation of the final scale actually progressed through several stages, so the outline just given is simpler than what actually occurred.

Although the MMPI has been described as the "prototypic example of empirical test construction in the realm of personality" (Wiggins, 1973, p. 389), it also includes two scales that were not derived by the method of contrasted groups. One of these scales, the Lie scale, might be described as rationally derived, in that it essentially duplicates items devised by Hartshorne and May (1928) for their studies of deceit in school children. The other scale, the Frequency scale, was statistically derived; its items were those answered by no more than 10% (and often less than 5%) of the normative sample in a particular direction.

Prior to presenting the scales that resulted from the analyses described above, we should point out that shifts in thinking about the meaning of MMPI scale scores and profiles had occurred by the time the current form of the inventory was published (Hathaway & McKinley, 1951). Meehl (cited by Cronbach, 1970) had the following to say in 1951: "These days we are tending to start with the test, sort people on the basis of it, and then take a good look at the people to see what kind of people they are. This, of course, is different from the way in which the test was built. . . . The primary function of psychometrics is (not) . . . to prophesy what the psychiatrist is going to say about somebody" (p. 534).

These remarks were based on nearly 10 years of research and clinical experience with the inventory and are included to show how and why the MMPI was transformed (by what has been called the bootstraps effect) from a psychiatric inventory into a personality questionnaire.

The MMPI Scales

Table 4.1 gives the scales, number of items on the scales, and brief interpretations of high scale scores. The scales are listed by name (e.g., Schizophrenia), abbreviation (e.g., Sc), and number (e.g., 8) to reflect prevalent usage in the 1940s, the 1950s, and after 1960, respectively. Whereas scales once were referred to as Depression or Paranoia, or as D or Pa, one seldom hears any designation but 2 or 6 now. The word *classical* has been used to describe the terms given in the right-hand column. Many more correlates than these are now available and will be described later in this section. Numerous correlates have also been identified for patterns or profiles of scale elevations, which are typically referred to in terms of the two highest scale scores (e.g., a 2–7 or a 4–9 profile). Sometimes three-point high scores are used (e.g., a 2–7–4).

Psychometric Properties

The method of item selection for the MMPI resulted in the inclusion of many items on more than one scale. For a summary of the amount and direction of item overlap, the reader should see Dahlstrom, Welsh, and Dahlstrom (1972, p. 232). Their table shows that some items appear on as many as six scales. Typically only a small fraction of the items identified with a scale appear just on that scale. Of the 78 items making up Scale 8, for example, only 16 are unique to that scale.

The true–false keying balance is also of interest. Examination of the basic scales shows that few have an approximately equal split of true–false answers. Scales L and K are the worst offenders; 100% of L's items are keyed false and 29 of K's 30 items are keyed false. Scales 7, 8, and 9 each have a true–false keying ratio of more than 3:1, whereas Scale 3's is less than 1:3. The only scales that one could call relatively well balanced are 4, 5 (for males and females), and 0.

Intercorrelations among the basic scales are reported in Dahlstrom, Welsh, and Dahlstrom (1975, pp. 261–263). The correlations were obtained from four different investigations using normal and patient (both medical and psychiatric) subjects and they indicate that several of the scales are highly correlated. For example, the correlations between Scales 7 and 8 vary from .77 to .87 across the different samples, and two of the correlations between Scales 1 and 3 exceed .70. Some of the scales are negatively correlated with each other; for example, the values between Scales K and 8 vary from − .54 to − .66. In some cases the correlations are moderate (e.g., between Scales 3 and 6) and in other instances the relationships are minimal (e.g.,

Table 4.1.   Standard MMPI Scales

Scale Name	Scale Abbreviation	Scale Number	Number of Items	Classical Interpretation of Elevated Scores
Lie	L	—	15	Denial of common frailties
Frequency	F	—	64	Invalidity of profile
Correction	K	—	30	Defensive, evasive
Hypochondriasis	Hs	1	33	Emphasis on somatic complaints
Depression	D	2	60	Unhappy, depressed
Hysteria	Hy	3	60	Hysterical symptomatology
Psychopathic Deviancy	Pd	4	50	Lack of social conformity; often in trouble with law
Masculinity–Femininity	Mf	5	60	Effeminate (males); masculine orientation (females)
Paranoia	Pa	6	40	Suspicious
Psychasthenia	Pt	7	48	Worried, anxious
Schizophrenia	Sc	8	78	Withdrawn; bizarre mentation
Hypomania	Ma	9	46	Impulsive; expansive
Social Introversion–Extroversion	Si	0	70	Introverted, shy

between Scales 3 and 9). Generally speaking, the intercorrelations are positive, often significant, undoubtedly due in part to the item overlap.

Scales so obviously intercorrelated naturally draw the interest of factor-analytically oriented investigators, who ask whether the variance associated with the 10 or 13 scales can be explained more parsimoniously. Dahlstrom, Welsh, and Dahlstrom (1975, pp. 122–125) have summarized the factor-analytic findings through 1974. The findings of Welsh (1956) are typical. His analyses disclosed that nearly all the variance across the scale scores can be identified by two factors, which he labeled A (anxiety) and R (repression). Other investigators have given these factors different labels, ranging from substantive (e.g., introversion) to stylistic (e.g., social desirability) designations. A later study by Block (1965), which attempted to control for various response biases, obtained factors that were called ego-resiliency and ego-control. Although not everyone would agree on the meaning of the dimensions, there is consensus that two virtually independent factors account for most of the MMPI scale variance.

The final psychometric feature of the MMPI we wish to mention is the reliability of the scales (cf. Dahlstrom, Welsh, & Dahlstrom, 1975, pp. 253–260). The short-term (i.e., 1 to 2 weeks) stability figures for psychiatric patients range from .59 to .89 with a median value of about .80. As retesting intervals become longer, the stability coefficients drop considerably. For high school students retested 3 years after the first test, the values range from .32 to .61 with a median in the low .40s. For college students with an 8-month interval between tests, the values range from .42 to .76 with a median in the mid-.50s. Values for the longest retest interval (1 year) that has been examined for psychiatric patients range from .34 to .76 with median values in the .50s. Since reliability coefficients limit validity coefficients, some writers have expressed concern about the size of these reliability figures.

However, it is difficult to see how an inventory that, at least in part, is measuring mood can display the level of reliability coefficients found with intelligence tests.

As for split-half estimates of reliability, Dahlstrom, Welsh, and Dahlstrom (1975) report several investigations with psychiatric patients but only one involving a normal group. The obtained coefficients over all samples range from $-.05$ to $.96$ with median values in the .70s. Many of the values would be considered unacceptable for inventories constructed by internal consistency analyses. Perhaps the reason that so few internal consistency studies of the MMPI have been done is that they do not make much sense. For example, in splitting the scale one might find nearly all the true-keyed statements in one half and nearly all the false-keyed statements in the other half.

Many psychometrically sophisticated psychologists have expressed dismay concerning the properties of the MMPI that we have briefly reviewed above. The heterogeneity of the scales, the relatively high scale intercorrelations, the item overlap, the imbalance in true–false keying, and the moderate stability coefficients have all been criticized. However, the intent of the test constructors was to produce an instrument that could help make judgments and decisions. Hathaway (1972, p. xiv) acknowledges the MMPI's "lack of constructural quality" but feels that it "affords some independent security for insecure personal judgments." In the next section we will review the principal work that undergirds Hathaway's guarded optimism about the utility of the inventory.

Research on the Interpretation of Scales and Profiles

The MMPI has been investigated more thoroughly than any other personality inventory. Approximately 6000 studies are cited in a 1975 handbook on the instrument (Dahlstrom, Welsh, & Dahlstrom, 1975). A classified bibliography prepared by Butcher (1979) indicates that major attention has focused on psychometric characteristics and identification of medical and psychiatric disorders. Other areas of research are more specific and include such diverse focuses as aging, automated interpretation, locus of control, pharmacological studies, and occupational groups. An attempt to review a representative sample of these studies or to concentrate on the most important among them might produce some worthwhile generalizations, but would not serve the applied aims of this chapter. Hence the emphasis here will fall on empirical findings most relevant to the clinical interpretation of the MMPI.

Much of the early work investigated relationships between scale scores and either self-ratings or ratings by others (friends or experts). The investigators obtained correlates of high scale scores, low scale scores, and high-point scale scores by the method of contrasted groups. The distinction between the first and third of these terms is that *high* means that the scale score has a T value greater than 60, 65, or possibly 70, whereas *high-point* means that the scale so designated has the highest T score in the profile. These two kinds of high score definitions have been termed *nomothetic* and *idiographic*, respectively; correlates arising from each method are presented by Dahlstrom, Welsh, and Dahlstrom (1972, Chapters 6 and 7).

The problem with high scale analysis is that *high* is defined in different ways by different investigators. Therefore, the correlates obtained are not very useful for MMPI interpretation. High-point correlates, however, do have an immediate application, since anyone can look at an MMPI and determine the peak score. Guthrie (1949), for example, found that medical patients with peak scores on Scale 1 presented a wide variety of symptoms and complaints, little manifest anxiety, and a marked tendency to consult with doctors frequently. Black (1953) found only one term significantly related to an MMPI peak score on Scale 2 in a group of college women: shy. However, ratings of these women by others significantly omitted such adjectives as cheerful, kind, energetic, relaxed, and self-confident and painted a general picture of self-depreciation and inadequacy. Guthrie's (1949) medical patients with high-points 2s showed a high incidence of depression with some physical symptoms.

Meehl (1956), in a widely cited paper titled "Wanted—A Good Cookbook," stressed the need for a complete collection of test-defined code types with empirically derived descriptive data. It is generally agreed that the first real "cookbook," to use Meehl's term, was produced by Marks and Seeman (1963). These investigators examined hundreds of MMPIs obtained from psychiatric patients admitted to the University of Kansas Medical Center. Eventually 16 high-frequency code types, which accounted for 78% of the total sample, were selected. Two-point or 3-point high codes and many additional rules were used to specify each profile type.

The primary source of descriptor data for these profile types was a 108-item Q deck containing both descriptive and dynamic items. Professional staff familiar with the patient sorted each Q item into one of nine categories on the basis of how well it fit the patient's behavior. For each profile type the five patients whose descriptions were most similar were selected as a defining group. The mean placement of each Q item was then computed on the five patients in each of the 16 profile types. Demographic data and descriptive data from case histories, hospital records, and therapy notes were also analyzed and are included in the correlates offered. Frequency of occurrence of descriptor data for a given code type was compared to base rates derived from the entire sample. Although males were included in the study, the profile type descriptors are for women only. It should also be noted that the average amount of education for the final sample of 320 patients (20 per code type) was 13 years and the average IQ was 112. The patients were almost all voluntary admissions, preference having been given to those likely to benefit from short-term treatment.

So many differentiating correlates were found for each code type that it is not possible to illustrate the richness and complexity of this system in the limited space available. Perhaps an example would be helpful. Five "most descriptive" and five "least descriptive" Q-item characteristics are given for a profile that fit Marks and Seeman's 8-9/9-8 code type. The most descriptive characteristics are: the genotype has schizoid features; delusional thinking is present; spends a good deal of time in personal fantasy and daydreams; tends to be ruminative and overideational; and utilizes regression as a defense mechanism. The least descriptive characteristics include: is normal, healthy, symptom-free; has the capacity for forming close interpersonal relationships; has a resilient ego-defense system; has a safe margin of integration; and would be organized and adaptive when under stress or trauma. Response to treatment, prognosis, school history, relations with father, and many other correlates are also given for this and the other 15 code types.

Psychologists in Idaho, Maine, or Texas who obtain a profile that fits one of Marks and Seeman's 16 code types should, in principle, be able to describe their patient in terms of the significant correlates given in the "cookbook." In practice, this has not worked very well. The code types, which accounted for about 80% of the derivation sample, have shown classification rates of only 15 to 28% in other samples (e.g., Gynther, Altman, Warbin, & Sletten, 1972; Pauker, 1966; Shultz, Gibeau, & Barry, 1968). The difficulty is caused by the numerous criteria used to define the code types. Furthermore (and somewhat surprisingly considering the empirical nature of this enterprise), there have been very few attempts to cross-validate Marks and Seeman's findings. In the 20 years that have passed since the cookbook's publication, very few investigators have attempted to check out the accuracy of these correlates in other settings. Gynther and Brilliant (1968) showed that diagnoses and certain demographic characteristics ascribed to the MMPI $K +$ profile did not hold up in a public mental health center. Palmer (1970), in a much more comprehensive study, examined the validity of all the code types developed by Marks and Seeman in 2119 subjects available to him. He secured "perfect matches" only for the 3-2-1, 4-8-2, 8-9, 2-8, and $K +$ code types. Of these, he found that the 3-2-1 code type had moderate, the 4-8-2 and 8-9 fair, and the 2-8 and $K +$ poor generalizability to his sample.

The next effort to establish empirical correlates of MMPI code types was carried out by Gilberstadt and Duker (1965). These investigators selected profiles for detailed analysis not on the basis of high-frequency codes, but to represent cardinal types of disturbed patients with classical case-history characteristics. As Wiggins (1973) said, "Although the Gilberstadt-Duker system is primarily actuarial in method, it is clearly clinical in spirit" (p. 113). The profiles used were those of males tested in a Veterans Administration Hospital setting. Specifications for defining the profiles were built up by reading many case records and gradually refining the rules on the basis of continuous input of this type. Nineteen profile types based on 266 cases were finally defined; the number of subjects representing each type ranged from 6 to 36, with a median of 11. The primary source of descriptors was a 131-item checklist from which three judges independently rated each case-history record for the presence or absence of these items. An item was counted if two of the three judges agreed on its presence in the case-history material. Comparisons were then made between the code type sample and a general abnormal (control) sample of 100 patients. Items that appeared significantly more often ($p < .05$) in the code-type sample were listed as profile correlates.

As an illustration of the Gilberstadt and Duker findings, they list the following correlates as being significantly associated with the 4-3 code type: assaultive, father alcoholic, financial status poor, headache, heavy drinking, hostile, impulsive, moodiness, and suicide attempt. Diagnosis, alternative diagnoses, and other salient characteristics are also listed for each profile.

Application of the Gilberstadt and Duker system to MMPIs obtained elsewhere has unfortunately resulted in the same problem of limited applicability that has plagued the Marks and Seeman system. Whereas approximately 80% of the MMPIs in the Minneapolis VA Hospital were classifiable into one of the 19 code types in the system, workers elsewhere have typically been able to classify only about 25% of their profiles. Validity studies have also been rare. Fowler and Athey (1971) found good validity generalization of Gilberstadt and Duker's 1-2-3-4 code type, as did Palmer (1970). However, it is probably no coincidence that 1-2-3-4 is based on the largest derivation group (36 subjects) of any of the 19 code types. Less favorable were the validity generalization results for 7 other Gilberstadt and Duker code types that Palmer was able to test: 2-7-4 and 8-6 were classed as only moderate in generalizability; 2-7, 2-7-8, and 8-1-2-3 as fair; and 4 and 4-3 as poor.

Four other sets of investigations have been published that follow the empirical tradition pioneered by Guthrie (1949), Hathaway and Meehl (1952), Black (1953), and others. All share one significant feature not included in any of the multicode studies reviewed: Replication was an intrinsic part of the design. Lewandowski and Graham (1972) randomly divided MMPI profiles of 588 hospitalized psychiatric patients into two samples. Profiles were classified according to 19 frequently occurring reciprocal 2-point code types (i.e., $1\frac{2}{3}$-1). For each subsample, each code type was compared with all other profiles on 68 behavioral and demographic variables. Although more than 300 significant differences were found for the comparisons in each subsample, in only 66 instances were the same differences significant in both subsamples. This finding is very suggestive when one recalls that Marks and Seeman's and Gilberstadt and Duker's correlates are based on the derivation samples only.

As an example of Lewandowski and Graham's (1972) findings, correlates for their $2\frac{2}{3}$-2 code type include the following: has to be reminded what to do, more somatic concern, less conceptually disorganized, less unusual mannerisms and posturing, less suspicious, less hallucinatory behavior, and less unusual thought content. The modifiers *more* and *less* in this list reflect comparisons of the frequency of the behavior for this code type with the frequency for all other code types. Although 588 MMPIs may seem a large number, replication procedures of this kind require even larger samples. For example, 10 of Lewandowski and Graham's 19 code types had fewer than 10 profiles in one or another of their samples, and 6 of these 10 had just one replicated descriptor or none at all.

Gynther, Altman, and Sletten (1973) carried out a similar study with much larger samples. They analyzed 16 2-point code types, plus a high F code type, which accounted for 76% of all MMPIs obtained from patients in several public mental health facilities. Positive cross-validating results were obtained for 11 code types, marginal results for 3 code types, and negative results for 3 code types. As an illustration of their findings, part of the interpretation of the $F > 25$ profile is given: "This type of patient usually appears to be confused. . . . In an interview situation, patients . . . tend to be withdrawn and verbally unproductive. . . . Delusions of reference and hallucinations, particularly auditory hallucinations may be present. . . . Despite the frequency of symptoms of confusion, organic diagnoses are not more common than for other patients. A diagnosis of alcoholism is relatively infrequent" (p. 272). These investigators conducted several additional analyses of their data indicating (a) 3-point codes seem to have correlates essentially similar to those found for the parent 2-point codes; (b) absolute elevation seems to have little effect on correlates; (c) sex does not seem to affect code-type correlates, although results for 2-4/4-2 were an exception to this generalization; (d) reciprocal code types have very similar correlates, although differential results for 2-8 and 8-2 were found; and (e) descriptors that apply to profiles given by whites do not seem to hold for blacks.

As a third set of additional data, a 1974 revision by Marks, Seeman, and Haller of their 1963 book included some new features. The adult section is very similar to the earlier version; however, 12 of the 16 code types are now defined by high points rather than by several contingency rules, and the interpretive output is a narrative statement rather than an enumeration of significant descriptors. Both modifications should make this system more useful to clinicians.

Even more important, the book had a new adolescent section that reflected numerous improvements based on the authors' experience with their adult study. The abnormal sample was much more representative of disturbed youth than the adult sample was of adults with problems; over 1200 descriptors were used; profiles were grouped by the two highest scales; and correlates were derived for 29 of the 45 2-point combinations. The authors also replicated their findings for 18 of the 29 code types and presented the output in narrative form.

Many more adolescent profiles will be classifiable than was the case for adults' profiles. Indeed, Marks, Seeman, and Haller estimated the coverage at 90%. The procedure used should result in reliable and valid findings, especially for the replicated code types. The narrative reports are rich in detail, so much so that an example of the output unfortunately cannot be given (the reports run from one to two and one-half book pages in length). In our opinion, this opus represents the acme of code-type correlate research. Regretfully, it must be added that very few, if any, studies have been conducted to demonstrate the validity generalization of their findings.

The most recent series of studies in this tradition has been carried out by Kelley and King. So far this team has published results on about five different code types. University students seen as outpatients at a student mental health service served as subjects. In the case of the 2-7-8 code type (Kelley & King, 1979), both the split-sample replication procedure and the single-sample method were used to analyze their data. Males with 2-7-8 were found to be depressed and withdrawn, with impaired affect and disordered thinking, symptoms consistent with a diagnosis of schizophrenia. Females with 2-7-8 were also depressed but displayed no impairment in affect or thinking and were usually viewed as neurotic. Sex differences tended to crop up throughout the Kelley and King studies of different code types. Fewer descriptors emerged from the split-sample technique; however, both procedures produced a generally similar picture. The authors concluded that the single-sample method "is probably more consistent with the theoretical intent of cross-validation than is the split replication method" (p. 685). For a theoretical discussion of this issue the reader is referred to a recent article by Green (1982).

Three other developments unrelated to such actuarial studies should be brought to the attention of clinicians who wish to use the MMPI for applied purposes. One of these developments allows psychologists to get different information from the MMPI, another offers temptingly shorter versions of the inventory, and the third evaluates so-called critical items.

Wiggins (1969) was concerned with clarifying the content of the MMPI item pool. He developed 13 mutually exclusive scales that were "internally consistent, moderately independent, and representative of the major substantive clusters of the MMPI" (p. 144). These scales are labeled Social Maladjustment, Depression, Feminine Interest, Poor Morale, Religious Fundamentalism, Authority Conflict, Psychoticism, Organic Symptoms, Family Problems, Manifest Hostility, Phobias, Hypomania, and Poor Health. Although some of these scales appear to be measuring much the same dimensions as the standard scales measure, others clearly give new information. In our opinion, these scales can profitably be used to supplement interpretation of an MMPI profile.

For many years neophytes in MMPI administration were told to give the first 375 items (plus the 7 additional K items) if giving the whole inventory was not feasible. This so-called abbreviated version amounted to omitting the unscored items and yielded full scale scores (except for Scale 0). Then in 1968 Kincannon published a 71-item inventory called the Mini-Mult. This major modification was designed to be given orally and take not more than 10 to 15 minutes. Other versions soon followed: Dean's (1972) Midi-Mult, Faschingbauer's Abbreviated MMPI (FAM; 1974), and Overall and Gomez-Mont's (1974) MMPI-168. Short- to standard-form correlations between scale scores have generally been high, typically ranging from .75 to .95. However, success in predicting the code type has been modest. Hoffmann and Butcher (1975) found hit rates of 36.7% for the Mini-Mult, 40.4% for the MMPI-168, and 49.4% for the FAM, and concluded that clinical use of the short forms could not be recommended. Newmark, Ziff, Finch, and Kendall (1978) compared the same three instruments with direct measures of pathology obtained from the Brief Psychiatric Rating Scale. Multiple correlations among the ratings and the different MMPI forms were significantly high and comparable. These authors therefore concluded that the abbreviated forms are an accurate substitute for the standard MMPI in predicting objective measures of pathology. Butcher, Kendall, and Hoffman (1980), however, raised serious questions about these findings. They reanalyzed the data, compared them to similar investigations, concluded that the unusually high agreement percentages were "improbable," and recommended that the study be replicated using a sample not so extremely atypical. Obviously this is a lively area of research with mixed results and differences of opinion. Most knowledgeable persons appear to agree that if short forms are to be used, empirical correlates derived specifically for those forms are needed. Simple comparisons between short and standard forms no longer constitute sophisticated methodology.

MMPI critical items are those statements which, if answered in the keyed direction, are supposed to alert the clinician to serious problems bothering the patient. Examples are: "Evil spirits possess me at times" (T) and "I have never indulged in any unusual sex practices" (F). This 38-item list was selected by Grayson (1951) on an intuitive basis. Most of the automated interpretive systems print these items on their reports, and there is little doubt that many of the psychiatrists, physicians, and psychologists subscribing to these services take these endorsements at face value. Dahlstrom (1969) has referred to this acceptance of the content of test responses as descriptive of the subject's personality and behavior as the first level of conceptualization about the validity of inventory item endorsements. (The acceptance of this position was explicit in Woodworth's Personal Data Sheet.) Constructors of the MMPI took quite a different stance. Hathaway and McKinley (1940) considered that what a true or false endorsement of an item signifies is unknown, but can be discovered by empirical means.

Given this context, it is curious that the critical items were accepted so uncritically for so long a time. Apparently the first investigators to ask how well they work were Koss and her colleagues (Koss & Butcher, 1973; Koss, Butcher, & Hoffman, 1976). To examine this issue, samples of approximately 100 psychiatric patients characterized by one of six specified crisis states (e.g., threatened assault) were compared to a control sample of 300 patients admitted under noncrisis circumstances. Results showed that 29 of the 38 Grayson items differentiated some crisis group from the controls. The 29 items were mainly related to crises of psychotic proportions and not to less serious crises. Twenty-three of the Grayson items were judged to be relevant to the various crises. Of this number, 15 (70%) were valid. Lachar and Wrobel (1979) recently conducted a similar study and found that 26 of the 33 relevant Grayson items were empirically valid. Between the two studies, 19 of the 38 Grayson items were found to be unreliable as samples of behavior.

Identification of crisis states is an important clinical activity, as Butcher et al. elaborate in Chapter 11 of this volume. The Koss-Butcher and the Lachar-Wrobel lists have been validated empirically and are recommended to replace the Grayson and other rationally developed lists. However, the following limitations are still present in these newer lists: The degree of Scale *F* and/or Scale 8 overlap is relatively high; the proportion of items with "true" as the deviant response is very large; certain frequent crises are not represented in the MMPI and hence cannot be detected (e.g., marital discord); and single items are more vulnerable to mismarking or misinterpretation by the patient than scales. For further information on this topic, as well as other MMPI approaches to identifying crisis states, see Koss (1980).

Comment

The MMPI has never lacked for critics (e.g., Norman, 1972), but nonetheless rolls merrily along, piling up new records for clinical usage and research activity with each passing year. Approximately one new study is completed each workday; the grand total is now between 7500 and 8000 references. Books also have been appearing more frequently than in the past. Notable examples from the mid-1970s to the present are the second volume of the revised *Handbook* (Dahlstrom, Welsh, & Dahlstrom, 1975); *A Handbook of Cross-National MMPI Research* (Butcher & Pancheri, 1976); Graham's (1977) *The MMPI: A Practical Guide;* Faschingbauer and Newmark's (1978) *Short Forms of the MMPI; New Developments in the Use of the*

MMPI (Butcher, 1979); a revised version of the *Basic Readings* (Dahlstrom & Dahlstrom, 1980); and Greene's (1980) *The MMPI: An Interpretive Manual.* Graham's and Greene's books are particularly useful to the practicing clinician, since they focus on profile interpretation. The latter may be favored by academicians since it is more up-to-date and contains many more references.

In this review we have emphasized research that produces empirical correlates of various MMPI profiles (e.g., Marks, Seeman, & Haller, 1974). These data appear to us to be the most valid available to the clinician. However, none of these efforts has yielded reports or even significant descriptors on all of the 2-point or 3-point code types a clinician may encounter. One apparent solution to this frustrating state of affairs is the automated report. Such reports have been available for several years, but it is clear that a bandwagon effect is now taking place. New scoring and interpretive services pop up with almost every issue of the APA *Monitor.* These commercial operations provide a report for every MMPI submitted. We take up this enterprise later in the chapter.

The MMPI, despite its well-known faults, continues to dominate the field of objective assessment of personality and psychopathology. This state of affairs will continue until a better inventory appears. Occasional contenders are touted, as in Goldberg's (1974) comment on Jackson's Differential Personality Inventory, but they usually fade away. In a later section of this chapter, we will discuss three instruments—Delhees and Cattell's Clinical Analysis Questionnaire, Millon's Clinical Multiaxial Inventory, and Jackson's Basic Personality Inventory—which may be viewed as the latest challengers.

If one looks back (with some nostalgia) at the *Mental Measurement Yearbook* reviews written by such eminent individuals as Arthur Benton, Albert Ellis, Hans Eysenck, and Julian Rotter, a common thread of respect can be discerned for the effort that has been put forth on behalf of the MMPI, coupled with doubt concerning its usefulness for individual assessment. This early ambivalence is still present today, but one gets the impression from the numbers involved (i.e., tests given, studies published) that a kind of functional autonomy has been achieved. The next chapter in this remarkable history is the development of new national norms to replace the 40-year-old ones still in use (Butcher, Note 1).

THE CALIFORNIA PSYCHOLOGICAL INVENTORY (CPI)

Aims

The goal of the constructor of this inventory was to devise an instrument to diagnose and evaluate individuals, with emphasis upon interpersonal behavior and dispositions relevant to social interactions. "The purpose of each scale is to predict what an individual will do in a specified context, and/or to identify individuals who will be described in a certain way" (Gough, 1968, p. 56). To achieve this end Gough selected so-called folk concepts, that is, attributes of interpersonal behavior that are found in all cultures and societies. Advantages of this approach, according to

Gough, are that such scales should be valid cross-culturally, readily comprehended by the user, and of value in forecasting longitudinal criteria as well as immediate and current behavior.

Strategy of Inventory Construction

The primary test construction strategy was the method of contrasted groups, although four of the CPI scales were rationally derived and one was defined statistically. The external criteria used varied considerably from scale to scale. For two scales friends and acquaintances were asked to nominate members of their group who were high or low on the trait in question. The friends (judges) were provided with a written description of the behavior patterns considered to be relevant. The number of nominations received by each person in the group was tallied, and the group rank ordered. Then responses to individual items of the inventory were correlated with these nominations.

For several scales Gough used scores obtained on other tests or scales—IQ, California Fascism and Ethnocentrism, Sims score cards (social status)—to select criterion groups for subsequent item analysis. For other scales more objective criteria were used. One scale contrasted the responses of males to those of females, as well as responses of homosexual to those of heterosexual males. Another scale was based on the number of extracurricular activities in which student subjects participated. Another scale was derived by contrasting the item responses of delinquents and nondelinquents. Two scales were constructed by using grade-point averages, one at the high school level and the other at the college level. Two other scales were developed by comparing protocols obtained from psychiatric patients with responses of subjects trying to feign anxiety and distress and protocols obtained from high school students responding either to standard or "fake good" instructions. The final scale derivation using the method of contrasted groups compared 25 able young psychologists with subjects in other fields and training programs. Items that distinguished these groups were then correlated with instructors' ratings of the competence and potential of 50 psychology graduate students, and items correlated with this second criterion were retained.

Four of the scales were derived rationally to tap other dimensions that Gough felt were important in social interactions, including poise, rigidity, a sense of personal worth, and freedom from impulsivity. Although there were some differences in the exact procedures used to derive these scales, internal consistency analyses were prominent.

The remaining scale was developed by surveying response frequencies obtained in a number of samples. Those items answered in a particular way by 95% or more of all respondents make up this scale.

The CPI Scales

The scales resulting from these many analyses are presented in Table 4.2. The scales are grouped in four classes, partially on the basis of factor-analytic findings

Table 4.2.   CPI Scales

Class	Scale	Abbreviation	Number of Items
I	Dominance	*Do*	46
	Capacity for Status	*Cs*	32
	Sociability	*Sy*	36
	Social Presence	*Sp*	56
	Self-Acceptance	*Sa*	34
	Sense of Well-Being	*Wb*	44
II	Responsibility	*Re*	42
	Socialization	*So*	54
	Self-Control	*Sc*	50
	Tolerance	*To*	32
	Good Impression	*Gi*	40
	Communality	*Cm*	28
III	Achievement via Conformance	*Ac*	38
	Achievement via Independence	*Ai*	32
	Intellectual Efficiency	*Ie*	52
IV	Psychological-Mindedness	*Py*	22
	Flexibility	*Fx*	22
	Femininity	*Fe*	38

and partially on the basis of interpretational considerations. According to Gough (1968), Class I scales pertain to "interpersonal effectiveness, style, and adequacy"; Class II scales emphase "intrapersonal controls, values, styles, and beliefs"; Class III scales "are of basic relevance to academic counseling and guidance"; and Class IV scales "reflect broad and far reaching attitudes toward life" (p. 76). Although all the scales in the inventory have now been shown to have some personological meaning, it should be noted that *Wb, Gi,* and *Cm* were originally constructed as validity scales. Thus these scales now serve a dual purpose. In addition to saying something about individuals' intra- and interpersonal behavior, low scores on *Wb* and *Cm* and either very low or very high scores on *Gi* raise questions about the validity of the profile.

Psychometric Properties

Gough was an undergraduate at the University of Minnesota in the late 1930s and a graduate student in the late 1940s. As might be expected for a student at Minnesota at that time, he worked with the MMPI and developed some of his scales from MMPI items. For other scales, however, he found the MMPI item pool lacking in relevant questions and therefore turned to new items addressed more explicitly to interpersonal behavior and constructive achievement. The result is that approximately 178 of the 480 CPI items are virtually identical to MMPI items and 35 others are very similar (cf. Megargee, 1972). Megargee also notes that "the proportion of MMPI items on the various CPI scales ranges from a low of 4% for the Communality (*Cm*) scale, to a high of 91% for the Well-Being (*Wb*) scale" (p. 25). Thorn-dike (1959) reacted to these similarities by calling the CPI "the sane man's MMPI," but he obviously failed to appreciate the remarkably different philosophies underlying construction of the two inventories.

Item overlap among the CPI scales is extensive, although less so than on such other inventories as the Strong Vocational Interest Blank. From 1 to 6 of *Do*'s 46 items, for example, appear on every other scale except *Cm* and *Fx*. Thirteen of *Sc*'s 50 items are members of *Gi* and ten, scored in the opposite direction, belong to *Sp*. The number of unique or pure items per scale ranges from 2 out of 50 for *Sc*, 3 out of 34 for *Sa*, and 6 out of 56 for *Sp*, to 28 out of 28 for *Cm* and 22 out of 22 for *Fx*. Perhaps surprisingly, Rogers and Shure (1965) found that the factorial structure of the CPI was almost entirely unaffected by the item overlap problem.

True–false keying on the scales ranges from balanced to almost completely imbalanced. *Sa* and *Cm*, for example, are perfectly balanced. *Do, Sy, Sp, Re, So, Ie,* and *Fe* are reasonably well balanced. *Fx* (1T, 21F), *To* and *Ai* (both 3T, 29F), and *Wb* (5T, 39F) are least well balanced. Of the 18 scales, 14 have more false- than true-keyed responses, and the total item T–F ratio is approximately 1:2.

Gough's (1975) revised manual contains intercorrelation matrices, for males and females separately, for the 18 CPI scales. These values are based on more than 9000 subjects from many different sources. The correlations vary from − .30 to + .78, with the vast majority being positive. Some examples might be instructive. *Re* (females) correlates .60 with *Ac* and .58 with *To*, yet only .06 with *Sp* and .09 with *Sa*. *Py*'s correlations with the other scales are all low to moderate, whereas *Gi*'s correlations range from − .13 to .78. The scales with the lowest correlations with the other scales appear to be *Fx, Fe,* and *Cm*.

The intercorrelations just briefly described have stimulated a host of factor-analytic studies. Megargee (1972) reported 20 such investigations and noted that nearly all were performed from 1960 to 1964. According to Gough, the best of these studies is one by Nichols and Schnell (1963), and Levin and Karni's (1970) demonstration of cross-cultural invariance of the CPI is also worth special study. In general the same basic factors, usually five in number, have been found. Factor 1, the largest factor, appears to be a measure of impulse management and socialization. *Sc* has shown loadings as high as .93 on this factor. *Gi, Wb, To, Ac,* and *Re* also typically have high loadings on it. This factor resembles Gough's Class II (see Table 4.2), with the addition of *Wb* and *Ac*. Factor 2, the second largest factor extracted, appears to be a measure of interpersonal effectiveness (some psychologists refer to this cluster as a measure of extraversion). *Do, Cs, Sy, Sp,* and *Sa* all load highly on this factor. Clearly, these variables represent Gough's Class I, excluding *Wb*

The other three factors account for considerably less variance than the first two factors. Factor 3 is usually defined by high loadings from *Ai* and *Fx;* sometimes secondary loadings from *To* and *Ie* are present. Each investigator has labeled this factor differently, but adaptive flexibility seems to be an important common feature. Factor 4 has high loadings on *Cm* and *So* and may be regarded as reflecting the internalization of conventional values. The label *superego strength* has also been applied to it (Mitchell & Pierce-Jones, 1960). Factor 5 is invariably defined, when it appears, by a high loading on the *Fe* scale. Consequently, it has been labeled *femininity*.

Stability coefficients over 1 to 4 weeks have been shown to range from .49 to .87 for prisoners and .71 to .90 for first-year college women. In the former sample *Fx, Py,* and *Cm* were the only correlations below .70, and the median value was .80. In the latter study, which only included 11 scales, the median was .83. Test–retest reliability coefficients obtained from studies using a 1-year interval have ranged from .38 for *Cm* to .77 for *Ie* with a median value in the middle .60s. Internal consistency coefficients have also been calculated. Several sets are presented in Megargee's (1972) *Handbook*. KR-21 values computed on over 7500 high school students ranged from .22 to .94. The lowest coefficient was obtained for *Py;* only one other coefficient was less than .50. In fact, the median value was in the .70s. *Sc, Gi, Ie,* and *Wb* were among the scales with the highest coefficients. Split-half coefficients are also given for 500 men and women. Uncorrected values ranged from .45 to .77. As usual, *Py* was among the lowest coefficients.

Research on the Interpretation of Scales and Profiles

Before reporting research relevant to CPI interpretation, it is appropriate to give Gough's and Megargee's recommendations concerning the task of interpretation. Assuming the inventory is valid (i.e., by checking *Cm, Gi,* and *Wb* scores), the interpreter should consider overall profile height. Scores above the mean suggest positive adjustment, whereas those below the mean indicate problem areas. Next, one should look at the relative elevations of the different homogeneous groups of scales. Gough recommended examining the four classes of scales, as they are divided on the profile sheet, whereas Megargee suggested that the five factors discussed earlier be considered next. The next step is to look at the scores on the individual scales. Listing the highest and lowest scales is helpful. Finally, one integrates the data into "an overall CPI portrait. Here configural analysis of scale interactions is of primary importance" (Megargee, 1972, p. 145). The overall approach is obviously clinical, and Gough himself teaches students by engaging "in free-wheeling clinical interpretations . . . specifying whenever possible the test cues to which he is responding" (Megargee, 1972, p. 129). Gough obviously feels that there is no substitute for the master interpreter, a position that is at some odds with Meehl's and Hathaway's hopes for an actuarially derived master cookbook.

Despite his emphasis on the subjective aspects of interpretation, Gough has carried out many studies to furnish empirical correlates of high and low scores on the various CPI scales. His primary technique for accomplishing this goal has been comparison of Adjective Check List (ACL) (Gough & Heilbrun, 1965) and Q-sort (Block, 1961) findings with scale scores. A convenient method for making such comparisons is to correlate scale scores with the number of times an ACL item is checked by a panel of observers or with the mean placement a panel of observers gives to a *Q*-sort description. The aim of these analyses is to reveal what others tend to say about subjects with higher or lower scores on a certain scale or variable. The methodology is applicable not only to scale scores, but also to signs, clusters, and regression equations. For the rationale underlying these procedures, see Gough (1965).

This technique can be illustrated with reference to the derivation of correlates for the *Do* scale, for which 101 fraternity men and 92 sorority members at the University of California served as subjects. Each subject was described on the ACL by five peers.

> If an adjective was checked by one observer, a score of one was assigned to the subject on that attribute; if three checked the word, the subject's score became three. If all five observers checked the word, and if in addition three of these observers double-checked the word (to indicate its centrality in characterizing the subject), then the score became eight . . . in the way indicated each student was given a score on each of the 300 descriptions in the Check List. . . . By correlating the . . . descriptions with the *Do* scale, for males and females separately, patterns of relationships were specified. [Gough, 1968, p. 60]

High- and low-scoring males were described as ambitious, dominant, and forceful or as apathetic, indifferent, with narrow interests, respectively. Among females the high and low scorers were characterized as aggressive, bossy, and conceited or as cautious, gentle, and inhibited, respectively. *Do* correlates for males and females thus appear to be somewhat different. As Gough (1968) pointed out, "The high scoring female is equally strong, but more likely to be coercive" (p. 60).

Clusters of differentiating attributes have been derived for each of the 18 CPI scales and may be found in Gough (1968, 1975) or Megargee (1972). Space does not permit us to list all these correlates here, but perhaps one other set would be of interest. These are the descriptors derived for *Cm,* which, it will be recalled, is a statistically derived validity scale. High and low male scorers on *Cm* have been characterized as cautious, conscientious, and deliberate or as attractive, careless, and courageous, respectively. Female high scorers have been described as clear-thinking, confident, and energetic, and female low scorers as appreciative, artistic, and awkward.

Gregory and Morris (1978) subsequently correlated scores on the CPI scales with peer-rated adjectives from the Adjective Check List for 95 college sorority members in what they describe as a "direct replication" of Gough's (1968) study. They found confirmation for many of the correlates established earlier. Some differences were also found. For example, high scores on *Do* were no longer associated with aggressive, bossy, and conceited attributes among females. The authors concluded that low scores reflect general maladjustment rather than the polar opposite of high scores (e.g., impulsivity was not correlated with low *Sc* scores as expected). High scores for the most part were associated with the designated trait; however, *Wb, To,* and *Ai* did not demonstrate satisfactory relationships. Gregory and Morris indicated that the poorest results overall were found for *Cm* and *Fx.* Validity generalization seems satisfactory for a study carried out more than 10 years later in a very different college setting with individuals whose background characteristics vary in unspecified ways from the earlier Berkeley group.

These kinds of data obviously permit an interpreter to make numerous comments about a subject's CPI scale scores. Are there equivalent empirical data to assist with interpretation of the other elements—profile elevations, factors, homogeneous clusters, combination of scales—considered important by Gough and Megargee?

The answer is: some, but not as much as one might expect. Goodstein, Crites, Heilbrun, and Rempel (1961) compared overall CPI profile elevation of personal adjustment clients, vocational–educational clients, and nonclients and found a definite ordering of the groups in the expected direction; that is, the nonclients had higher average profiles than the second group, who in turn had higher average profiles than the first group. Enthusiasm for this type of analysis has been tempered, however, by indications that some scales appear to have a curvilinear relation with behavior. Megargee (1966), for example, found that very high Sc scores are associated with episodic aggressive acts, whereas moderate elevations on this scale contraindicate such acting out.

Megargee (1972) has also provided adjectives presumably descriptive of high and low scorers on the different factors, but it appears that these descriptions were obtained via inspection of the adjectives in the different scales making up the factors rather than by empirical analyses. Megargee (1972) states in this regard, "Some of the redundancy to be found in the Factor 1 scales is evident in the adjectival descriptions. One would be hard put to differentiate from one another those individuals high on Re, So, and Sc" (p. 125). His specific comments about factor correlates will not be reported here.

Concerning correlates of classes or combination of scales, Megargee (1972) remarks: "Scale configuration patterns are thus part of the psychological folklore, one step beyond the realm of well-validated test-behavior relationships . . . only a minuscule percentage of the 153 possible pairs of CPI scales has been investigated; no studies . . . have attempted systematic validation of triads or larger combinations of scales" (p. 146). In other words, studies such as those of Marks and Seeman (1963) or Gilberstadt and Duker (1965) with the MMPI have still to be done with the CPI.

However, some CPI investigations have featured the "combinations of scales" approach. For example, Gough (1968) obtained behavioral correlates for Do–Re and Ac–Ai interactions. His procedure was to select the 36 subjects, half male and half female, who were most extreme on the bisecting diagonal of the quadrant for a combination of these two scales and then perform t-tests of the mean scores on the ACL items for this subgroup versus the remainder of the sample. High Do–high Re students selected in this way were (to name three of ten adjectives given) dominant, ambitious, and responsible; high Do–low Re students, on the other hand, were touchy, dominant, and aggressive. Low Do–high Re students were quiet, calm, and peaceable, whereas low Do–low Re students were irresponsible, suggestible, and careless. It appears that some of these quadrant correlates are predictable from what is known of the two scales taken alone, while others take on "added meaning."

A technique has also been devised to obtain what might be called very specialized interpretations. What kind of women, for example, make good airline stewardesses? Those with a sexy, "fly me" air? Gough (1968) reported deriving a four-variable equation that correlated .40 with ratings of stewardess inflight performance. He then correlated the adjectival descriptions in the sample of 92 sorority girls mentioned earlier with scores on the "airline stewardess" equation ($64.293 + .227\,So - 1.902\,Cm + 1.226\,Ac - .398\,Ai$). Adjectives used most frequently to describe college women with relatively high scores on the equation were modest, reserved, and feminine, whereas adjectives such as adventurous, pleasure-seeking, and uninhibited were associated with lower scores. Hence the "coffee, tea, or me" image of stewardesses is not consistent with the data.

Burger and Cross (1979) used a Q-technique factor analysis to identify modal CPI profiles. Three profiles accounting for 57% of the cases were replicated in each of three samples. Profile type 1 could be characterized as aggressively ascendant, type 2 as constructively conventional, and type 3 as interpersonally ineffective. The authors suggested that "the raw score profile of an individual subject can be correlated with each of the modal profiles and described in terms of its similarity to them" (p. 69). They also pointed out that interpretation of individual profiles can be enriched when nontest correlates of the modal types are identified. Computer assistance would be necessary for the clinician to take advantage of Burger and Cross' typology, which resembles a complex approach to MMPI profile analysis developed by Sines (1966).

Moderator variables have been shown to affect interpretation of MMPIs, but the same factors have been somewhat neglected by CPI researchers. Cross, Barclay, and Burger (1978) demonstrated that ethnicity, gender, and socioeconomic status are related both singly and pairwise to scores on most of the CPI scales. Jones (1978), using a pool of 361 items drawn from the CPI and MMPI, found that 80% of them discriminated between blacks and whites. Martin, Blair, Dannenmaier, Jones, and Asako (1981) showed that age affects scores on 12 of the 18 CPI scales. More work is needed to clarify what adjustments to interpretation may be needed to deal with clients differing significantly from the norms on these factors.

A new orientation to interpretation is being provided by Gough (Note 3). He has developed three nonoverlapping and uncorrelated scales to measure role (internalizing–externalizing), character (norm maintaining vs. norm questioning), and competence. By cutting at the midpoint on each of the first two of these scales, everyone can be located in one of four quadrants (to oversimplify: leaders, rebels, followers, and equivocators). Then seven levels of competence are defined according to scores on that measure. Thus a norm-questioning, externalizing person at a high level of competence would be described as creative, and such a person at a low level of competence would be viewed as antisocial. Norm-maintaining, internalizing individuals at high, average, and low levels of competence are seen as responsible, conventional, and conforming, respectively. Gough points out that this method allows the linking of the normal to the abnormal in one continuum and thus avoids the "A vs. non-A Aristotelian difficulties of much clinical thinking." This theoretical model will be presented in a new manual that is scheduled to appear in 1984.

Although they are not relevant to scale or profile interpretation for the individual client, any sketch of CPI findings is incomplete without reference to a vast number of studies concerned with predicting academic achievement. As Megargee (1972) pointed out, "The CPI could not have come on stage at a more propitious time" (p. 161). Sputnik had just been launched by the Soviet Union, and throughout the United States there was great concern with locating talented, highly motivated young people. Research with the CPI was addressed to predicting achievement in secondary school and college; achievement in student teaching, medicine, dentistry, and police and military training; and success in leadership roles. Generally speaking, it proved possible to develop multiple regression equations that could make significant and noteworthy improvements over more traditional techniques in selection and classification for such purposes.

Finally, we should note that the CPI, in keeping with Gough's folk-concept philosophy, has been applied to other cultures both more frequently and more successfully than any other personality inventory. Either the full inventory or selected scales have been evaluated in studies involving translations into Chinese (Mandarin and Cantonese), Ceylonese, Portuguese, Norwegian, Dutch, Italian, Polish, and French. The *So* scale in particular has been administered in the native language to offenders and nonoffenders in countries as diverse as Austria, Costa Rica, India, Israel, Japan, South Africa, and Taiwan. In every nation tested thus far, highly significant differences between delinquent and nondelinquent groups have been found.

There are other research areas as well in which the CPI is now being used. In health psychology Bayer, Whissell-Buechy, and Honzik (1980) have shown that teenage personality traits as measured by the California *Q*-sort are related to health ratings at midlife. Subjects who had provided the *Q*-sort data as adolescents filled out the CPI once in their thirties and again in their forties. For males *Ac* and *So* correlated in the .40s with health ratings, and for females *Wb* and *Ie* were in the same range. Multiple correlations were not reported, but would obviously be in the .50s or low .60s. In life-span psychology Brooks (1981), using the Berkeley and Oakland growth and guidance samples, demonstrated that for both sexes intellectual effectiveness, impulse control, and broad interests during adolescence are significantly predictive of Social Maturity Index scores at ages 40 to 48. In addition, behavioral qualities often attributed to the opposite sex emerged as predictive (e.g., boys described as nurturant and girls as ambitious tend to be socially mature in their forties.

The field of occupational and professional behavior is also attracting increased attention. Police officers' CPI scores and work ratings have been compared in at least six studies (see Mills & Bohannon, 1980), and the resulting data have pointed to integrity, good judgment, decisiveness, and ability to control aggression as key concomitants of good performance. Professionals working in managerial capacities in industrial settings, both with and without a background in engineering, can be differentiated from those working as engineers (Grant & Patton, 1981).

The CPI has also begun to enter the laboratory. Waid, Orne, and Wilson (1979) have shown that subjects classified as unsocialized by *So* scores can lie more successfully to experienced polygraph examiners than subjects classified as socialized.

This effect is due at least partially to the fact that high *So* subjects are more responsive electrodermally than low *So* subjects. Genetic–heritability work has also been undertaken, as reviewed by Loehlin & Nichols (1976). Carey, Goldsmith, Tellegen, and Gottesman (1978), for example, showed that correlations are higher for monozygotic than dizygotic twins on every scale.

Numerous studies involving the *Fe* scale and sex-role typology have also been done (e.g., Baucom, 1980; Betz & Bander, 1980). This very popular research topic appears to have a not-very-hidden agenda, namely that androgyny is the desirable and sex typing the undesirable state of affairs for the individual and for society. Supporting evidence for this assumption in the form of behavioral correlates or adjustment measures is not compelling, however.

Comment

In the course of reviewing the CPI for the *Eighth Mental Measurements Yearbook,* the senior author recommended that empirical correlates of common configurations be developed. No such work has been carried out. One gets the distinct impression that the shakers and movers of this inventory are satisfied with their ability to deal with clinical interpretation on the basis of the scale–descriptor relationships already established. However, these aides to interpretation need updating and cross-validation, as Gregory and Morris' (1978) results make clear.

Another recommendation was that more effort be expended to determine the relations between moderator variables and CPI scale scores. Some work is emerging on these lines. Not unexpectedly, gender, ethnicity, age, and other variables affect scores and item endorsement patterns as well. How these findings might modify interpretation needs further clarification.

Despite these reservations, the CPI continues to thrive. New research areas crop up and old ones are reexamined in greater depth. The *Eighth Mental Measurements Yearbook* (1978) lists some 450 studies conducted over a 5-year period. Some 75 to 80 investigations are carried out each year, counting master's theses and doctoral dissertations. For those who wish to obtain the "same" information in less time, a short form has been developed (Burger, 1975). Given the difficulties with MMPI short forms discussed previously, however, we question the advisability of using this format.

The quarter-century-old CPI is about to have a face-lift. Gough (Note 3) has announced that he is adding two scales: Empathy and Independence. Both are best defined by the interpersonal factor and will be located in that region of the profile sheet. The present 18 scales will all be retained, although the longer ones will be shortened and the shorter ones lengthened. Item overlap among scales will be reduced. Also, offensive items will be dropped. All these changes will result in a new edition of about 450 items.

We asked in our review what the CPI is useful for and how useful it is compared to other tests purporting to measure similar dimensions. One study (Hall & McKinnon, 1969) compared the predictive power of the SVIB, CPI, MMPI, Firo-B, and other tests with regard to creativity in architects. The cross-validated correlation of

.47 for the CPI was superior to every measure but the SVIB. With regard to the first part of the question, the answer appears to be that it is useful (a) as a source of research inspiration to generations of scholars and (b) as an instrument for counseling "normal" individuals. Providing feedback to clients from the CPI is a much easier task than providing it from the MMPI, since the latter requires translation from psychiatric/personological terminology to lay language.

Abnormal behavior has received more professional attention than normal behavior despite the fact that deviance is meaningless without normative baselines. By the same token, the MMPI is used far more frequently clinically and in research than the CPI, reflecting a similar imbalance of priorities. The CPI has potentials and validities beyond those most psychologists recognize. Gough has declined to push his instrument through workshops and annual meetings. Perhaps he needs a Boswell to bring it more forcefully to the attention of the psychological community. One book in 25 years is not enough to accomplish this feat.

THE SIXTEEN PERSONALITY FACTORS QUESTIONNAIRE (16 PF)

Aims

Raymond B. Cattell (Note 2) stated his goal in personality research very simply: "to define and measure objectively the basic components of personality demonstrated factor analytically to be unitary in nature." The 16 PF was devised as one of the measures of these basic components, and Cattell describes it as "not a questionnaire composed of arbitrary scales, but one which consists of scales carefully oriented and groomed to basic concepts in human personality structure research. Its publication was undertaken to meet the demand of research psychologists for a personality measuring instrument duly validated with respect to the primary personality factors and rooted in basic concepts in general psychology" (Cattell, Eber, & Tatsuoka, 1970, p. 13).

Strategy of Construction

In developing his concept of the "total personality," Cattell turned to what he designated the "language personality sphere," which "captures all the particularity of behavior accumulated in our speech and dictionaries" (Cattell, 1957, p. 71). Allport and Odbert had already catalogued all trait names appearing in an unabridged dictionary and reduced the list to 4504 "real traits." From this list Cattell culled 171 terms that he felt, on the basis of semantic meaning, represented "synonym groups." College students rated their acquaintances using these 171 terms, the results were intercorrelated, and on the basis of cluster analysis approximately 36 surface traits were identified. Thus surface traits are clusters of observable attributes that are encoded in the ordinary language of personality. These 36 dimensions plus others that Cattell felt needed to be represented served as the basis for bipolar rating scales that were used in a series of peer-rating studies conducted in college, military, and clinical settings. Factorial study of these data led Cattell to conclude that there were approximately 15 distinct factors (plus intelligence) that accounted for the intercorrelations among rating variables, and he designated these the *primary personality factors*.

Eighteen hundred items were then written to represent (a) the surface trait variables identified by the rating method, (b) marker variables suggested by previous factorial studies of temperament, and (c) several areas of interest and values that were thought to represent general personality dimensions. A series of factor-analytic studies revealed at least 16 source traits in the questionnaire realm, 4 of which had not appeared in rater descriptions. Items for the 16 PF were selected that correlated highly with the source traits they were designed to measure, and the 1967–68 edition contains only those items which continued to have significant validity for the factors after 10 successive factor analyses on different samples (Cattell, 1973a).

As this brief account indicates, trait definition via factor analysis is the most distinctive aspect of Cattell's theory of personality. Cattell is interested in factor analysis not as a technique for reducing a number of variables to a simpler mathematical form, but as a procedure that, when used properly, permits the direct identification and measurement of primary source traits that account for observable covariation among surface traits (Wiggins, 1973, pp. 496–498). Cattell rotates factors obliquely to a position uniquely defined by simple structure in the data themselves and therefore having "general scientific meaningfulness." Incidentally, it should be noted that even if factoring is to orthogonal solutions, as in Guilford's analyses, the scales themselves come out substantially correlated, but not in the way that represents the natural complexity of human nature (Cattell, Eber, & Tatsuoka, 1970).

There are five forms of the 16 PF: Forms A and B for "newspaper literate" adults consisting of 187 items each; Forms C and D with a somewhat less demanding vocabulary and consisting of 105 items each; and Form E, which has 128 items with a very simple vocabulary for the educationally disadvantaged. Forms A through D use a three-choice response including an "in between" alternative. Form E has only two choices. A tape recording is available for Form E so that it may be given orally. Cattell strongly recommends the use of more than one form in evaluating a subject, and for crucial assessments he advocates using four forms (e.g., A, B, C, and D) and breaking up the testing time (Cattell, Eber, & Tatsuoka, 1970, p. 3). Four editions of the test were published between 1949 and 1969. Unfortunately, data in articles other than those of Cattell, Eber, and Tatsuoka are often reported without reference to the form and/or edition used.

Standardization data are generally available for American adults, university undergraduates, and high school seniors. Norms are provided for each of these groups for males alone, females alone, and the total population. Significant differences between males and females on 12 of the 16 scales are noted, and age correction tables (recommended especially for research) are provided for those scales that show a significant change with age.

All editions of Form A and the latest editions of the other forms have norms based on samples stratified according to geographic area, population density, age, family income, and (in the 1967–68 edition) race in proportions indicated by the U.S. Census Bureau. More than 10,000 individuals were tested to establish the 1967–68 norms for Forms A and B, and more than 5000 for Forms C and D.

The 16 PF Scales

The primary factors of the 16 PF are shown in Table 4.3. Each factor is designated by a letter, and the high and low poles of each factor are designated by both a technical name and a popularly descriptive label. The alphabetical order is based on evidence of diminishing contribution to behavioral variance (Cattell, Eber, & Tatsuoka, 1970, p. 15). In several cases the technical terms are acronymic names given

Table 4.3.   The 16 PF Factors

	Primaries	
Factor	Low Sten Score Description	High Sten Score Description
A	Reserved, Sizothymia[a]	Outgoing, Affectothymia
B	Dull, Low Intelligence	Bright, High Intelligence
C	Affected by Feelings, Lower Ego Strength	Emotionally Stable, Higher Ego Strength
E	Humble, Submissiveness	Assertive, Dominance
F	Sober, Desurgency	Happy-Go-Lucky, Surgency
G	Expedient, Weaker Superego Strength	Conscientious, Stronger Superego Strength
H	Shy, Threctia	Venturesome, Parmia
I	Tough-Minded, Harria	Tender-Minded, Premsia
L	Trusting, Alaxia	Suspicious, Protension
M	Practical, Praxernia	Imaginative, Autia
N	Forthright, Artlessness	Astute, Shrewdness
O	Self-Assured, Untroubled Adequacy	Apprehensive, Guilt Proneness
Q_1	Conservative, Conservativism of Temperament	Experimenting, Radicalism
Q_2	Group Dependent, Group Adherence	Self-Sufficient, Self-Sufficiency
Q_3	Undisciplined Self-Conflict, Low Self-Sentiment Integration	Controlled, High Strength of Self-Sentiment
Q_4	Relaxed, Low Ergic Tension	Tense, High Ergic Tension
	Secondaries	
Symbol	Technical Title	Popular Label
Q_I	Exvia–Invia	Extraversion–Introversion
Q_{II}	Adjustment–Anxiety	Low Anxiety–High Anxiety
Q_{III}	Pathemia–Cortertia	Sensitivity, Emotionalism vs. Tough Poise
Q_{IV}	Subduedness–Independence	Dependence–Independence

[a] The second term given for each of the primaries is Cattell's technical term.

to factors in an attempt to increase precision and to distinguish them from surface traits of ordinary language. Many research articles present evidence tied to these precise, technical designations on such matters as degree of inheritance of the traits, age curves, physiological associations, achievement, and clinical criteria. However, such terms as Premsia, Parmia, and Threctia make communication difficult with those not immersed in the system, as would polonium, propionic acid, or uranium 238 with nonchemists.

Although eight second-stratum factors may be scored from the 16 PF, only four are as yet considered sufficiently defined to be generally useful. The primary factors involved with Q_I, Extraversion, include Affectothymia (A), Dominance (E), Surgency (F), Venturesomeness (H), and Group Adherence (Q_2-). Q_{II}, Anxiety, is made up of Low Ego Strength ($C-$), High Guilt Proneness (O), High Ergic Tension (Q_4), Suspiciousness (L), Shyness ($H-$), and Low Self-Sentiment Integration (Q_3). This factor possesses high constancy of pattern across cultures (Cattell & Nichols, 1972). Q_{III}, Cortertia, is related to Reserve ($A-$), Tough-Mindedness ($I-$), and Practicality ($M-$). Q_{IV}, Independence, involves Dominance (E), Suspiciousness (L), and Imaginativeness (M). This factor has shown considerable variability with respect to sex and culture. Men score significantly higher on it than women, and both psychotic and neurotic persons score low on it.

Psychometric Properties

In contrast to the MMPI and CPI, there is no item overlap among the 16 PF scales. Keying is balanced between responses *a* and *c* with the keyed response contributing 2 points to the scale raw score (except for scale *B*, Intelligence, on which each keyed response is worth 1 point). The intermediate response, *b,* contributes 1 point. In order to minimize distortion, items were chosen to be as neutral in social desirability as possible. Also of note, items that are not "face valid" were used whenever possible. Motivational Distortion scales have been built into Forms C and D—the forms more commonly used in personnel selection—and involve items showing maximum shift from an anonymous to a job-seeking situation.

A test–retest of 146 American adults and undergraduates with an intervening time of 4 to 7 days produced correlations ranging from .65 on Intelligence to .93 on Venturesomeness with a median value of .87 for all scales. This study used the 1961 edition of Forms A and B combined. The lower figure for Intelligence is explained by the fact that subjects attempted to solve the intelligence items between sessions. The other factors that typically have low stability coefficients are Imaginativeness (M), Shrewdness (N), and Self-Sentiment (Q_3). These factors, according to Cattell, Eber, and Tatsuoka (1970), seem relatively likely to fluctuate with psychological state and to be affected by conditions of text administration, as when rapport is not properly established or when the subject is uncooperative or physically uncomfortable.

When the test–retest interval has been extended to 2 months, the range of coefficients for Forms A plus B has been from .63 for Intelligence to .88 for Venturesomeness, with a median coefficient of .78. A 4-year retesting interval produced stability coefficients for Form A ranging from .21 for females on Shrewdness to .64 for females on Venturesomeness (*H*). It is suggested that in order to cancel out reversible state changes in evaluating a trait, one might retest two or three times over a month or so and average the results (Cattell, Eber, & Tatsuoka, 1970, p. 31).

Equivalency coefficients for Form A correlated with B (1967–68 edition) ranged from .21 for Shrewdness (*N*) to .71 for Venturesomeness (*H*). The median value reflecting the degree to which these forms parallel each other over all scales was .51. The equivalency coefficient for C with D (1961–62 edition) ranged from .16 for Shrewdness (*N*) and Suspiciousness (*L*) to .55 for Venturesomeness (*H*), with a median of .38. The Forms A and C combination correlated with Forms B and D yielded coefficients between .35 (Shrewdness—*N*) and .79 (Venturesomeness—*H*). with a median of .60.

As indicated earlier, the 16 PF factors are correlated with each other. The intercorrelation matrix provided in the Cattell et al. handbook indicates that the highest correlations (.70 to .75) exist among scales *C* − (Low Ego Strength), *O* (Guilt Proneness), and Q_4 (Tenseness), which make up the second-order factor Anxiety. The intelligence scale has very low correlations with other scales as does *I* (Tender-Minded). Approximately 20% of the intercorrelations are greater than ± .30.

Other researchers have subjected the 16 PF scales to factor analysis, frequently in conjunction with the MMPI, CPI, and EPPS scales. Kear-Colwell (1973) factor-analyzed the scores of 174 psychiatric hospital admissions on the 16 PF and the EPPS. He found second-order factors on the 16 PF that closely matched those reported by Cattell and Nichols (1972) and, as expected, found only limited relationships between information provided by the 16 PF and results from the need-oriented EPPS. LaForge (1962) factor-analyzed the responses of 178 undergraduate students to the 16 PF and the MMPI. A large fraction of the variance of the 16 PF (excluding *B*) was derivable from four components that LaForge designated Anxiety, Extraversion, Unbroken Success, and Sensitivity. O'Dell and Karson (1969) also factored combined 16 PF and MMPI scales and reported the following factors: MMPI Pathology, Anxiety versus Dynamic Integration, Exvia–Invia, Cortical Alertness, and Independence–Dependence. In spite of the investigators changing the original technically chosen names, there is very high convergence of findings on the patterns of these second orders.

Research on the Interpretation of Scales and Profiles

Cattell, Eber, and Tatsuoka (1970) provide two approaches to interpretation and diagnosis: profile matching and criterion estimation using specification equations. As an example of the first of these approaches, the mean profile of neurotic subjects tested in the midwestern and eastern United States and in Canada, Australia, and Britain shows poor ego strength (*C* −), lack of independence of mind and capacity to solve problems forcefully (*E* −), greater than average inhibition (*F* −), and below average superego expression (*G* −). The average neurotic also tends to be shy (*H* −), overprotected (*I* +), and dominated by high anxiety and a sense of guilty unworthiness (Q_4 and *O*). With the use of formulas and tables the similarity between an individual subject's profile and this typical profile can be determined, as a basis for drawing a diagnostic conclusion.

The second approach involves the application of a Neuroticism specification equation for which weights have been determined by comparison of the scores of consensually diagnosed neurotics with those of normal control subjects. The equation for Neuroticism is:

$$6.27 - .07B - .26C - .17E - .38F - .10G + .10H + .22I + .26O - .09Q_1 + .35Q_4$$

The higher a profile's score on this equation, the more similar it is to profiles of neurotic individuals.

Mean profiles are provided by Cattell et al. (1970) for many different subject groups, including delinquents, attempted suicides, homosexuals, addicts, and patients with psychosomatic disorders. Profiles and specification equations are also presented for many different occupational groups, including academicians, accountants, artists, miners, the police, social workers, and writers, and there are also specification equations for variables relevant to educational and vocational guidance, such as freedom from accidents, salesmanship, teaching effectiveness, and creativity.

Profile matching and specification equations thus permit classification by the 16 PF, but what about behavioral correlates? The most extensive and systematic presentation of "natural history" and criterion associates appears in Cattell's compendium *Personality and Mood by Questionnaire* (1973b). There is empirical evidence, for example, that a high-*A* person is relatively likely to be a "joiner," be generous in interpersonal relationships, be unafraid of criticism, and be casual in meeting obligations. Low *C* is the most general pathological indicator and tends to characterize neurotic, psychotic, alcoholic, and drug-addicted individuals. In neurotics it is associated with poor muscle tone and posture and a long history of symptoms which increase under stress. As further examples of 16 PF correlates, a change toward surgence (*F* +) might be found in successful psychotherapy and with mild intoxication. High *F* is associated with conversion hysteria and low *F* with headaches, worrying, irritability, depression, and phobias. For more information regarding each of the factors, the reader is referred to Chapter 9 in the *Handbook* (Cattell, Eber, & Tatsuoka, 1970).

Two major aids to interpreting the 16 PF have been published in recent years. Karson and O'Dell (1976) wrote what they described as a "simple, elementary guide." The book briefly discusses administration, scoring, and construction of the test, but the major focus is on interpretation of high and low scores on the basic scales and the second-order factors. The interpretive guidelines were written by Karson on the basis of his extensive clinical and research experience with the instrument. Adjectives used to define each factor and materials from Cattell's writings are also used to give additional meaning to the scores. The authors often use nicknames to personalize the factors (e.g., Errol Flynn, for *H* +, Walter Mitty for *M* +), which is consistent with their belief that one reason the 16 PF has not been as popular as it deserves to be is the forbidding nature of the trait names.

Following their description of the 16 PF factors, the authors give their general approach to interpretation. First, indices of faking and random answering are examined. Winder, O'Dell, and Karson (1975) developed scales for detection of "faking good" and "faking bad." They report that if one uses a cutting score of 6, 85% of those who faked good and 94% of those who faked bad are detected. Only 10% of those who answered honestly are erroneously classified in the first instance, whereas none of the honest responders is misclassified in the fake bad selection process. The Random scale (O'Dell, 1971) consists of 31 infrequent answers. Use of the appropriate cutting score results in detection rates similar to those found for the faking good scale.

Karson and O'Dell recommend looking next at the second-order scores, especially Anxiety and Extraversion, to get an overall feel for the profile. Then the highest and lowest scores are interpreted, using the adjectives or statements that are applicable. Next, *complex cognitions* take place in an attempt to integrate the findings. Finally, a summary featuring a specific psychiatric diagnosis or the principal psychodynamics is given.

The last third of this guide is devoted to the presentation of 15 case studies. The profile is given and followed by the presenting problem (when known), an in-depth interpretation, and follow-up information, if available. The authors point out that they frequently do not follow the steps recommended (because random and faking bad scores were not available in the older cases); nevertheless, sufficient details are given to show the neophyte how they achieve a portrait of the personality. On the final page of the book, one is advised that a computer analysis, the Karson Clinical Report, is now available.

More recently, Krug (1981) has written a manual that features interpretation of the profile itself rather than the scale-by-scale approach we have been discussing. After briefly describing the clinical significance of and relevant research findings for each scale, he discusses different ways the 16 PF can be coded. He points out that the 2-point high-score system used with the MMPI is not appropriate, because of the bipolar nature of the 16 PF factors. He argues that primary scores cannot be used either, since this practice would result in far too many configurations. He concludes that coding must depend on second-order factors, which represent a condensation of information supplied by the primaries.

If one splits the scores on the first four second-order factors into high, average, and low categories, 81 patterns are generated. Krug provides data on the distribution of these codes for 17,381 normals, sex distribution within types, and a comparison with distributions among some 2500 psychiatric patients. Patterns vary greatly in frequency. The 2222 pattern (average scores on Extraversion, Anxiety, Tough Poise, and Independence) is most frequent for all samples and accounts for 12% to 13% of the cases. The 1111 type (low on all four factors) is extremely rare, being found in only 1 or 2 cases out of 1000. Some codes are generated by males or females more than 10 times as often as by the other sex, whereas others faithfully reflect the base rates for gender. Frequencies for psychiatric as compared to normal samples are significantly different for nearly half the 81 patterns.

Modal profiles were generated for each of the second-order factor subtypes by taking frequency counts of the primary scale scores falling into each type. Thus, for pattern 1111, factor *A* appears as 6, factor *B* as 5, factor *C* as 10, and so on. Sten scores are also presented for the occupational scales (e.g., Accountant, 5.0; Electrician, 9.4; Production Manager, 2.8), career theme scales (cf. Walter, 1979), clinical scales, and other scales (e.g., Leadership). A narrative report ties these various bits of data together. Krug believes that this material will be an ongoing resource for individual interpretation and a means for sharpening interpretive skills. Although clinicians will probably find Krug's presentation helpful, it should be noted that his types do not actually add any predictive value to that which can be obtained from specification equations from primaries on whatever criterion is wanted.

The publications just reviewed are major contributions to the individual who wishes to use the 16 PF for applied purposes. However, much additional empirical work is currently in process. A sampling of these studies will be presented to give an idea of the areas in which the 16 PF is attracting research attention. Howe and Helmes (1980), for example, found that this instrument was unsuitable for discriminating among psychiatric groups; Bolton (1980) showed that subtest and IQ scores from the WAIS are correlated with the second-order factors; the same author's (1977) factor analysis of items, parcels, and scales from 16 PF-E provided strong confirmation of the eight 16 PF secondaries; Stroup and Manderscheid's (1977) analysis of the CPI and 16 PF disclosed a high degree of congruence across samples and methods, with five factors common to both instruments; Ward, Cunningham, and Wakefield (1976) found three pairs of related factors between Holland's VPI and the 16 PF; Burger and Kabacoff (1982) derived four modal profiles which successfully classified about two-thirds of all the 16 PF protocols; and Goldberg, Norman, and Schwartz' (1980) comparison of the Objective–Analytic Battery with the 16 PF led them to conclude that one should be cautious concerning claims about the superiority of the battery. Many other studies have examined such diverse areas as automated test interpretation, predictive validity of the 16 PF in traffic violations and military performance, differences between Americans and New Zealanders, subclinical affective disorders, astrological signs and personality, anorexia nervosa, adjustment of the blind, physical fitness, and success in athletics.

It is important to note that the 16 PF is one of a series of tests. The same source traits can be measured by the High School Personality Questionnaire, the Children's Personality Questionnaire, and the Early School Personality Questionnaire. Obviously these instruments would be useful to those interested in developmental issues. What further differentiates these tests from others is that they deal with concepts embedded in general personality theory, for instance, by known life age curves, by studies of early influence, by heritability values. Also, although there are definitely differences at the trait level, the same factor structure has been demonstrated for the 16 PF cross-nationally, in Germany, France, the United Kingdom, Brazil, and India.

Comment

Three reviews of the 16 PF appeared in the *Eighth Mental Measurements Yearbook* (Buros, 1978). The evaluations range from positive ("the 16 PF compares favorably with any other inventory") through guarded ("the 16 PF should not be used . . . unless certain precautions are taken") to negative ("it is impossible to recommend the 16 PF in an unqualified manner for any use, from the most basic research to the most pragmatically oriented applications"). Although the reviewers focus on a variety of shortcomings, all agree that the evidence for validity is, at best, difficult to evaluate and, at worst, not available for many important criteria.

However, in the same source one notes that over 600 studies have been done in the 6-year period covered and that, indeed, the 16 PF is now third (replacing the CPI) in terms of total number of references for an objective personality assessment device. Furthermore, it appears that this 1949-based instrument is moving into high gear among clinicians as well. This resurgence can be traced to the publication of the handbook in 1970 with additional momentum provided by the two interpretive manuals produced recently. The availability of a computer-generated report that can be adjusted to focus on clinical issues, career development, and marriage counseling also undoubtedly plays a role.

Cattell himself is still active in research involving one or the other of his many instruments. For example, Cattell, Price, and Patrick (1981) showed that selected subtests from the O-A Kit differentiated clinically depressed samples from controls in the directions hypothesized across different ethnic groups. However, his major current contributions are toward integrative linkages of areas often treated separately. His two-volume opus, *Personality and Learning Theory* (1979, 1980), relates personality, traits, and states to the stimuli, environment, and observer, and it unravels the learning principles by which personality structures are acquired. The *Inheritance of Personality and Ability* (Cattell, 1981) links genetics and learning theory. Procedures (e.g., path coefficients) to relate learning increments of a trait to measured environmental features are given, as well as analyses of heritability of source traits in Q and T data. Spectrad theory (Cattell, 1982) is offered as a model for solving the problems associated with attribution theory. This new theory encompasses the estimation of traits as well as the causal action of situations and permits the prediction of the deviation of a perception from the true value.

For the most part, it seems that second- and even third-generation 16 PFers have taken over the applied use and commercial exploitation of this test. Although a great deal of empirical data have been generated over the years (e.g., Cattell, Eber, & Tatsuoka, 1970; Cattell, 1973b), it should be pointed out that the new interpretive manuals go considerably beyond established correlates of scales and/or configurations. So does the software that animates the automated reports. One hopes that research will soon be undertaken to supply the additional facts needed to support these new developments.

THE PERSONALITY RESEARCH FORM (PRF)

Aims

The goals in constructing the PRF were"to develop sets of personality scales and an item pool which might be useful in personality research" and "to provide an instrument for measuring broadly relevant personality traits in settings such as schools and colleges, clinics and guidance centers, and in business and industry" (Jackson, 1967, p. 4).

Strategy of Test Construction

The methodology used to construct the PRF was a mixed intuitive–internal strategy. Prior to describing the procedures employed, it is important to recognize Jackson's guiding principles, which were (a) the importance of psychological theory, (b) the necessity for suppressing response style variance, (c) the importance of scale homogeneity as well as generalizability, and (d) the importance of enhancing convergent and discriminant validity from the beginning of the test construction program (see Jackson, 1970, for further details). Murray's (1938) need system was selected as the theoretical substructure for the instrument, since the variables give comprehensive coverage of the domain of needs, states, and dispositions and have been defined carefully and researched extensively.

The first step in scale construction was a careful study of Murray's 20 traits. Mutually exclusive, specific definitions of each of the traits were developed. The next task—according to Jackson, the most difficult of all—was to create an item pool. Some 3000 items, over 100 for each trait, were written. These items had to be relatively short and free from ambiguity and also conceptually linked to the relevant trait and conceptually distinct from each irrelevant trait. Following critical review by two or more judges, these items were administered to over 1000 college students. Biserial correlations were computed between each item and (a) the provisional scale of which it was a member, (b) related scales, and (c) a large set of items scaled for desirability (the provisional Desirability scale). Items that showed endorsement rates of less than 5% or over 95% were eliminated, as were items showing higher correlations with the Desirability scale or related scales than with the scale to which they were assigned.

In order to maximize content saturation and keep desirability variance within manageable limits, items were next ranked in terms of the magnitude of the Differential Reliability Index within each scale. The Differential Reliability Index for each item was calculated by obtaining the square root of the difference between an item's squared biserial correlation with its own scale and its squared biserial correlation with Desirability. No absolute value was required. If Desirability variance was relatively low, an item of moderately high content saturation was considered satisfactory. If Desirability variance was relatively high, on the other hand, correlation with content had to be very high for the item to be retained. Items that survived these hurdles were assigned to parallel forms by pairing items in terms of similarity of endorsement proportions and item–scale correlations and reassigning each member of the paired items to alternate forms until these forms were maximally similar in summary statistics. Finally, each scale was reviewed to evaluate the generalizability and representativeness of scale content. As Jackson (1967) said,"An exhibition scale containing a majority of items solely concerned with interest in public speaking . . . may not adequately reflect the broader construct of exhibition" (p. 17).

The description given above outlines what is clearly an elaborate series of sequential strategies faithfully based on the principles enunciated earlier. Validity scales for the PRF were conceived somewhat differently. The emphasis here was upon assessment of general styles of responding, rather than upon specific content dimensions. Means for detecting nonpurposeful responding and the tendency to respond desirably or undesirably were considered essential. To identify nonpurposeful responding, items were written that, although neither bizarre nor particularly undesirable, would be highly unlikely to be endorsed (e.g., "I learned to repair watches in Switzerland."). Sixty-five provisional items were given to over 300 subjects, and those that correlated higher with the scale than with any of the other scales, including Desirability, were retained. The Desirability scale was developed by selecting about 60 items from each extreme of the distribution of Desirability scale values, eliminating those which showed substantial content homogeneity, and giving the remaining 107 items to over 300 college students. The responses were subjected to the same item analysis routine used with content scales, except that desirability was not suppressed. The surviving items for Desirability were then assigned to one of the two parallel forms.

The PRF is available in four formats, two 300-item parallel forms and two 440-item parallel forms. Forms A and B are divided into 15 20-item scales; Forms AA and BB contain the same scales plus 7 different 20-item scales. The PRF is also available in a Form E, which comprises all 22 scales with 16 items for each. Form E was based on an additional analysis and comprises the best items from Forms AA and BB, selected on the basis of high content saturation and mutual minimum redundancy. In the following section the scales included on the longer forms will be labeled and briefly defined.

The PRF Scales

Table 4.4 provides the names of the scales and two of the 15 defining trait adjectives given in the manual (Jackson, 1967). Although the definitions are unipolar, it should be pointed out that all these dimensions were conceived as bipolar. For every scale, half of the items were written in terms of one pole of the dimension, and half in terms of the other. As Jackson (1967) notes, "Rather than calling one scale Dominance, it would have been equally correct to label it Submissiveness" (p. 11). Thus low scores as well as high scores on PRF scales are interpretable in terms of personality characteristics.

Psychometric Properties

As in the 16 PF, there is no item overlap among scales, and response keying is balanced. Each scale contains 10 items keyed true and 10 items keyed false. Questions could be raised concerning the rational or intuitive selection of items, but Jackson (1970) has provided a persuasive argument in defense of this procedure. The argument draws attention to studies in which judges (given descriptions of hypothetical people) were asked to rate the probability that these people would endorse certain personality items. Multidimensional successive intervals scaling

Table 4.4.   PRF Scales

Scale	Abbreviation	Two Trait Adjectives
Abasement	Ab	Self-blaming, humble
Achievement	Ac	Industrious, ambitious
Affiliation	Af	Warm, cooperative
Aggression	Ag	Aggressive, irritable
Autonomy	Au	Self-reliant, individualistic
Change	Ch	Unpredictable, vacillating
Cognitive Structure	Cs	Perfectionistic, rigid
Defendence	De	Defensive, touchy
Dominance	Do	Domineering, persuasive
Endurance	En	Steadfast, jealous
Exhibition	Ex	Spellbinding, ostentatious
Harmavoidance	Ha	Fearful, cautious
Impulsivity	Im	Reckless, excitable
Nurturance	Nu	Comforting, charitable
Order	Or	Neat, methodical
Play	Pl	Playful, carefree
Sentience	Se	Aware, sensuous
Social Recognition	Sr	Approval seeking, courteous
Succorance	Su	Trusting, dependent
Understanding	Un	Curious, reflective
Desirability[a]	Dy	
Infrequency[a]	In	

[a] Validity scales.

was then applied to appraise the degree to which each item was considered relevant to a hypothetical item universe. For further details, see Jackson (1970, pp. 68–71).

Intercorrelations among the basic scales for Form A are reported in the manual (Jackson, 1967). These correlations, which are based on the normative sample of 1029 males and 1002 females, range from +.64 to −.63. Achievement and Endurance are highly positively correlated in both samples, as are Cognitive Structure and Order. Succorance and Autonomy are highly negatively related in both samples. However, these examples are exceptions. Only 15 out of the 462 correlations are as large as ±.50. The vast majority of the values are between ±.30. Lack of item overlap, plus suppression of a Desirability factor, no doubt accounts for the relative independence of the scales from each other. As Jackson pointed out, Desirability variance can be totally eliminated from content scale scores on the longer PRF forms by partial regression techniques.

Jackson (1970) also reports factor-analytic findings for the PRF. Traditional linear components factor analysis was rejected because of interactions between trait and method factors, and a technique called multimethod factor analysis, which considers only trait variance, was developed. Variance unique to a single method is eliminated with this procedure, which Jackson and Guthrie (1968) used to factor correlations among PRF scales, self-ratings, and peer behavior ratings. Eighteen factors appeared for the 20 PRF content scales. The factor loadings provided strong evidence for convergent and discriminative properties of the PRF scales. As an example, Dominance as measured by self-ratings, peer ratings, and PRF scores loaded .76, .64, and .60 on Factor II, respectively; equivalent correlations for Abasement on the same factor were $-.52$, $-.38$, and $-.56$, respectively.

Other studies have used more traditional factor-analytic procedures to describe the inventory's structure. Stricker (1974), for example, found six oblique factors (i.e., conscientiousness, hostility, ascendance, dependence, imagination, and carefreeness) in a principal axis analysis of the content scales. Stricker also found that response bias measures were only moderately related to the PRF scales and did not define any of the factors. Helmes and Jackson (1977) performed a factor analysis of PRF Form E items. Of the 352 items, only 2 failed to load in the keyed direction. The mean loading of items on their scale factor was .38. These results indicate that the factor structure of this inventory is reliable and consistent.

Studies of PRF test–retest reliability have been undertaken. Bentler (1964), for example, administered Form AA to college students on two occasions 1 week apart. Stability coefficients for the 20 content scales ranged from .69 for Change to .90 for Harmavoidance. Most correlations were in the .80s. The stability coefficient for Infrequency was only .46, but this kind of result seems unavoidable for scales with very small means and markedly skewed distributions. Another study evaluated parallel form reliability over two testing sessions separated by two weeks. In this instance values reflect not only stability but also degree of similarity between forms. Subjects took either Form AA or BB first, then the other long form on the second occasion. Corrected odd–even reliability coefficients of Form AA content scales ranged from .48 for Defendence to .86 for Dominance and Order, with a median value in the mid .70s. Infrequency, again, had the lowest coefficient, .33. No long-term test–retest studies have been reported in the literature.

Internal consistency estimates are also reported in the manual (Jackson, 1967). For the original item pool KR-20 coefficients for the content scales ranged from .80 for Defendence to .94 for six of the scales. The median value was .925, which is remarkably high for any test and almost unbelievable for personality scales. The KR-20 estimates for the final 20 item scales are naturally not as high as for the 100 +-item original scales. In a sample of 202 subjects Form AA scale coefficients, excluding Infrequency, ranged from .54 for Change to .85 for Dominance and Order, with a median in the low .70s.

Research on the Interpretation of Scales and Profiles

The PRF was developed many years after the MMPI, CPI, and 16 PF, and Jackson's major concern appears to have been to construct the best possible inventory on the basis of available psychometric knowledge. Any practical utility of the instrument, one gathers, was a hoped-for byproduct of the construction program. If this evaluation is correct, one might not expect an immediate focus on applied concerns. Examination of the studies conducted by Jackson and others from 1965 to 1970 tends to confirm this impression. Several studies (e.g., Braun & Asta, 1969; Braun

& Costantini, 1970; Hoffman, 1968) were concerned with the effects of "fake good" or "fake bad" instructions on PRF performance. Other authors (e.g., Acker, 1967; Bither, 1969; Kusyszyn & Greenwood, 1970) used from two to eight PRF scales to examine postulated relationships between pairs of variables such as need achievement and academic performance, decision making and needs for exhibition and dominance, and defensiveness and a tendency to distort responses to personality items in a favorable direction.

Other studies, although primarily concerned with construct validation, do contain material of some interest to applied psychologists. The manual (1967), for example, reports correlations of the PRF with 37 occupational scales from the Strong Vocational Interest Blank and also with the CPI scales. Careful perusal of these tables helps to clarify what the PRF scales measure. To give a few examples, PRF Achievement correlates .62 with CPI Achievement via Conformance, but only .27 with Achievement via Independence. PRF Exhibition correlates .69 with CPI Self-Acceptance, .68 with Social Presence, and .67 with Sociability. The highest correlation reported is .78 for PRF Dominance and CPI Dominance, which is good evidence for convergent validity. PRF Cognitive Structure, which is unlikely to be familiar to most psychologists, correlates − .70 with CPI Flexibility and − .48 with Capacity for Status. Turning to the PRF–SVIB correlations, some interesting relationships emerge. Clinical Psychologist correlates .40 with Exhibition, whereas Experimental Psychologist correlates − .37 with this scale. Biological Scientist correlates .49 with Understanding, whereas Banker correlates − .51 with the same scale. Banker also correlates .36 with Harmavoidance, whereas Army Officer correlates − .38. Engineer correlates .32 with Endurance, whereas Real Estate Sales correlates − .35. Most of these correlations make intuitive sense and add additional meaning to scores on both instruments.

Edwards and Abbott (1973) compared scores on the Edwards Personality Inventory (EPI), the EPPS, and the PRF. Fairly large correlations were found between the PRF and EPI scales. PTF scales having the highest correlation with an EPI scale were Achievement with Is a Hard Worker (.74), Affiliation with Makes Friends Easily (.70), Aggression with Critical of Others (.64), Cognitive Structure with Plans and Organizes Things (.66), Dominance with Assumes Responsibility (.80), Exhibition with Enjoys Being the Center of Attention (.69), Nurturance with Helps Others (.64), Order with Plans and Organizes Things (.70), and Succorance with Dependent (.73). These relations offer evidence that traits with similar names on the different inventories appear to be measuring the same substantive dimensions.

Trott and Morf (1972) compared college students' responses to the PRF and MMPI by means of multimethod factor analysis. A number of interesting relationships emerged. One factor, for example, included MMPI *F* (loaded − .68) and PRF Achievement (loaded .80) as salient variables. The authors suggested that the negative pole of this factor might reflect a genuine and pathological inability to marshal resources to compete effectively. Another factor included MMPI Scale 3 (*Hy*) (.79) and PRF Harmavoidance (.42) and Understanding (− .38). The caution and fearfulness and lack of curiosity and of reflective thought indicated by the PRF variables were considered to be consistent with the clinical description of the hysterical personality. Another factor, which was interpreted as reflecting difficulty in the control of hostile impulses, included PRF Aggression (.43) and MMPI K ($-$.68). The authors concluded that high scores on many PRF scales, especially Dominance and Affiliation, are contraindictions of pathology and, more broadly, that psychopathological behavior is intimately linked with interpersonal behavior in general.

The major evidence for external validity of the scales is based on comparisons of PRF scores with behavior ratings of the various traits (see Jackson, 1967, pp. 23–24). Judges were asked to rate on a 9-point scale the degree to which each trait was present or absent. Pooled ratings of peers served as the principal criterion measures, although comparisons of PRF scores and self-ratings were also done. Validity coefficients were based on cross-validational data with no cases excluded. The values ranged from .16 to .64 with a median of .27 to .30. All these values were probably attenuated by the very small number of judges. If one considers only the 14 content scales included in the shorter PRF forms, the results were more impressive. These validity coefficients ranged from .16 to .64 with a median of .36 to .38. The highest coefficients were found for Order and Harmavoidance; the lowest for Understanding, Cognitive Structure, and Abasement. Kusyszyn (1968) also used the same procedures to establish the validity of 8 of the PRF scales (*Ac, Ag, Au, Ex, Im, Nu, Or,* and *Pl*). Subjects were members of fraternities. Coefficients ranged from .24 for Autonomy to .58 for Play for the total sample. For that portion of the sample who shared common living quarters and would be expected to be better acquainted, the coefficients ranged from .35 to .71 with a median of .47.

More recently, Harris (1980) investigated the relationships among PRF scores and self- and peer ratings of PRF variables. Subjects were first-year graduate students in clinical psychology. Median correlations among the three measures ranged from .61 to .81. Solomon (1981) had subjects complete the PRF and then rate each other on the interpersonal dimensions of the Bales system. PRF scales Dominance and Exhibitionism correlated .42 with peer ratings of dominance–submissiveness. Other scales also were significantly related to Bales' factors in a meaningful way. Klockars and Walkup (1980), on the other hand, found very low (.02 to .15) correlations between PRF scores and peer ratings. These investigators focused on criteria thought to be relevant to the subject's potential to be an effective resident advisor. Overall, these data suggest that PRF scales do, in fact, measure those traits whose labels they bear, although it is clear that an interpreter of the PRF should place more confidence on results associated with some scales (e.g., Order) than on data obtained from others (e.g., Abasement).

A sampling of the most recent research shows a continuation of the same trends noted earlier, that is, examinations of the internal structure of the test, comparisons of one group with another, evaluations of test–nontest relationships, and investigations of convergence between PRF scales and those of other personality inventories. Examples of studies in the first of these categories are Abbott's (1975) demonstration that PRF scales correlate only slightly with Social Desirability scores, and Helmes, Reed, and Jackson's (1977) findings that only 5% of the PRF items have extreme Desirability values as compared to 24% of CPI items and 22% of MMPI items. Illustrations of work in the second category are Pihl and Spiers' (1977) analysis of personality differences among psychologists, social workers, physiotherapists, and vocational therapists, and Worell and Worell's (1977) comparison of supporters and nonsupporters of the Women's Liberation Movement.

The third category includes Knudson and Golding's (1974) finding that the PRF predicts such behavior as organizations joined, leadership activities, and dating frequency; Maudal, Butcher, and Mauger's (1974) study showing that the PRF can discriminate college persisters from college dropouts; Laosa, Swartz, and Witzke's (1975) demonstration that PRF scale scores are related to grade-point averages and teacher ratings; Green, Burkhart, and Harrison's (1979) results indicating that the PRF is more highly correlated with paper-and-pencil assertiveness measures than it is with behavioral measures of assertiveness; and Bridgwater's (1981) study with ski instructors in which PRF scores were correlated with age, amount of education, and overall teaching effectiveness. The fourth category is illustrated by Lorr's (1975) examination of the convergences in constructs of the PRF, Comrey Personality Scale, Interpersonal Style Inventory, and Edwards PPS. He found that 14 of the PRF's 20 content scales were also measured by the other three inventories in combination. Goldberg (1977) showed that scores on the CPI could be predicted from PRF scores and vice versa, with one exception: PRF Sentience could not be predicted by any CPI scale or combination of scales.

In addition to this list, other interesting studies with the PRF are being conducted on correspondence between self-ratings and PRF scores (Merrens, 1975); classification and selection of military applicants (Skinner & Jackson, 1977); development of the PRF Androgyny scale (Berzins, Welling, & Welter, 1978); predictive utility of subtle and obvious items (Holden & Jackson, 1981); use of PRF scales to measure therapy outcome (Mungas, Trontel, Winegardner, Brown, Sweeney, & Walters, 1979); identification of alcoholic subtypes (Nerviano, 1976); examination of the validity of implicit personality theory (Jackson, Chan, & Stricker, 1979); relations between A–B therapist type and therapeutic effectiveness (Barnes & Berzins, 1978); and interactions among personality, sexual attitudes, and experiences (Zuckerman, Tushup, & Finner, 1976).

Comment

The publication of the PRF was followed by many laudatory reviews, but there was something of a wait-and-see attitude exemplified by Wiggins' (1972) cautionary remark: "Whether these scale construction efforts, and particularly the attention paid to substantive considerations, will guarantee significant incremental validities in applied settings is another question" (p. 303). Our summary in the 1976 edition of the present volume suggested that the PRF had not proved itself vis-à-vis other inventories, but argued that insufficient time had passed for a judgment to be made.

In a later review Hogan (1978) stated that this test's empirical validity had yet to be demonstrated, but that "one would expect that validational evidence would be forthcoming in the future" (p. 1008). He was referring to empirical evidence for descriptions of high scorers, relations between PRF scales and real-life criteria, and correlates of profiles, all of which would function as aides in interpretation.

Another 5 years have passed and we still find very little of the validational evidence that Hogan anticipated. We have cited articles comparing peer ratings to PRF scores and noted the studies correlating scale scores with nontest data. Yet no systematic efforts to supply correlates for scales or configurations in the manner of Marks or Gough have been published or, to our knowledge, are under way. If this state of affairs continues, one would have to agree with Hogan's (1978) assessment that the instrument "is likely to be of more interest to psychometricians and personality researchers than it is to test users in practical or applied situations" (p. 1007).

There is some evidence that even research interest in the PRF is waning. The *Eighth Mental Measurements Yearbook* (1978) and several other bibliographic sources seem to concur that 1972 and 1973 were the years of peak activity, references appearing at a rate of about 30 per year. More recently, studies have been appearing at the annual rate of 10 to 15. In our opinion, Jackson himself is probably responsible for this declining research activity, in that the similar Jackson Personality Inventory he published in 1976 has drawn attention away from its stable mate.

In the first edition of this volume we said that admirers (and detractors) of the PRF should be patient because it takes so long for a test to reach maturity. Now that the test is in its mid-teens, one is tempted to predict a future involving continuation in academia but little likelihood of a sudden shift to the clinic or counseling center.

NEW MULTIDIMENSIONAL ASSESSMENT INSTRUMENTS

In the first edition of *Clinical Methods in Psychology* we reviewed three popular inventories—the Allport-Vernon-Lindsey Study of Values, the Edwards Personal Preference Schedule, and the Eysenck Personality Inventory—that had already been in use for many years. These reviews could have been updated for this second edition, but we felt that the reader might appreciate learning about some relatively new tests, rather than hearing more about old ones. Hence we decided to present briefly Millon's Clinical Multiaxial Inventory, Jackson's Basic Personality Inventory, and the Clinical Analysis Questionnaire, which bears a close relation to Cattell's 16 PF. Each of these inventories has been considered by its originators as at least in part a replacement of the aging MMPI.

The Millon Clinical Multiaxial Inventory (MCMI)

The MCMI was constructed in 1977 to help clinicians make assessment and treatment decisions about persons with emotional and interpersonal difficulties. The scales reflect Millon's views of personality and psychopathology, as described in his books, *Modern Psychopathology* (1969) and *Disorders of Personality* (1981), and also the basic personality patterns and clinical symptom syndromes described in DSM-III. This correspondence is not surprising, since the author was a member of the DSM-III Task Force Committee of the American Psychiatric Association.

The initial item pool for this instrument was prepared on the basis of theoretically derived definitions of each provisional scale. These approximately 3500 items were reduced to 1100 items on rational grounds such as clarity, simplicity, and scale relevance. Items not achieving their highest correlation with their substantively designated scale and those with less than .15 or over .85 endorsement frequencies were dropped, which reduced the 1100 to 440. Other screening procedures reduced the total further to 271 clinical and 18 correction items. This 289-item Research Form was subjected to two external validation studies that resulted in the elimination (and addition) of numerous other items.

The normal group involved in constructing the MCMI consisted of 297 subjects drawn from colleges, personnel offices, and industrial plants. They were approximately evenly divided by gender and ranged in age from 18 to 66. A patient population used in this preliminary work included 1591 persons, 58% males and 42% females from 18 to 66 years of age, of whom about 70% were outpatients and 30% inpatients. The data on these patients were obtained from over 200 clinicians from 27 states and Great Britain. The ethnic–racial distribution was white, 81%; black, 14%; Latino, 3%; Oriental, 1%; other, 1%. Their socioeconomic class distribution accurately reflected population figures. Ninety-six percent of their primary diagnoses fell into the following categories: neurosis (15%), personality disorder (11%), alcohol-drug problem (16%), affective disorder (24%), schizophrenic disorder (19%), and paranoid disorder (11%).

The final clinical version of the instrument contains 175 items. There are scales for eight basic personality patterns: Schizoid, Avoidant, Dependent, Histrionic, Narcissistic, Antisocial, Compulsive, and Passive–Aggressive. Three other scales assess pathological personality disorders: Schizotypal, Borderline (Cycloid), and Paranoid; and nine scales evaluate clinical symptom syndromes: Anxiety, Somatoform, Hypomanic, Dysthymic, Alcohol Abuse, Drug Abuse, Psychotic Thinking, Psychotic Depression, and Psychotic Delusions. The number of keyed items for each of these scales ranges from 30 to 47, except for Psychotic Delusions with 16 and Psychotic Depression with 24 items. Examination of the scales shows that the preponderance of items are keyed true. The Borderline (Cycloid), Paranoid, and three psychotic syndrome scales contain no items keyed false. Detection and/or control of distortion tendencies is handled by means of a weight factor, an adjustment score, and a four-item validity index.

As one might anticipate, item overlap is substantial. Twenty of the 190 scale-by-scale comparisons show a percent overlap of 40 or more. The range is from 0 to 65%. Intercorrelation of MCMI scales is even more striking; 53 of the 190 comparisons yield coefficients of .60 or greater. The range is from .01 to .96, and nine of the coefficients are .90 or higher. Factor analysis of these matrices, using a general psychiatric sample, discloses three major factors: depressive and emotional lability, paranoid behavior and thinking, and schizoid behavioral detachment and thought. Test–retest reliability coefficients for a 4- to 6-week period are in the .80s for the basic personality scales, in the .70s for scales measuring pathological personality disorders, and in the .60s for scales assessing clinical symptoms. Internal consistency estimates have a median value of .88 with a range of .58 to .95.

So much for derivation of items, norms, scales, and internal structure of this instrument. The question is: How well does it work in fulfilling its aim to provide clinicians with useful information for assessing and treating patients? Several pieces of relevant data are provided by Millon, who gives correlations among the MCMI, the MMPI (basic and content scales), the Psychological Screening Inventory (Lanyon, 1973), and the Symptom Distress Checklist (Derogatis, Lipman, & Covi, 1973). Examination of these data shows evidence of convergent validity among the new MCMI scales and these other established scales. For example, the correlations are .64 between the Schizoid scale and MMPI Scale 0, .51 between Compulsive and MMPI Scale K, and .66 between Hypomania and MMPI scale 9. A more direct response to the question asked above is a comparison of the MCMI report with those generated from the MMPI by Psychological Corporation and Roche Psychiatric Institute in terms of information provided, descriptive accuracy, and report format and utility. Twenty-three clinicians rated the three programs on 100 cases with which they were very familiar. Results showed that the MCMI fared much better than the Psychological Corporation output (which is not surprising in view of the very limited capacity of this program) and as good as or slightly better than the Roche product. This kind of study should not be viewed as indicating that the MCMI (or the Roche) report is valid. However, the results suggest that clinicians find the MCMI narrative at least as accurate as the Roche narrative. The utilities of these reports were not at issue, since the clinicians had already seen the patients for 17 sessions on the average.

All of the preceding information has been taken from the revised version of the MCMI manual (Millon, 1982). We hesitate to base our description and critique of a measure solely on a product of the author, no matter how complete or well prepared it may be, except perhaps when the inventory is brand new. The MCMI is 5 years old, but much to our surprise we were unable to find any references to it in *Psychological Abstracts* or the *Social Science Citation Index.*The author (Millon, Note 6) stated that a substantial number of publications will be forthcoming in the near future, but he was able to refer us to only one article using his instrument, by Gilbride and Hebert (1980).

Given this distressing limitation, our evaluation can only be tentative at this time. In some ways it seems that Millon has attempted the "impossible dream," that is, to construct a relatively brief inventory (the same length as the short forms of the MMPI) that can assess personality and psychopathology relatively independently and also provide differential diagnoses and guidelines for treatment planning. Some psychometricians would be upset with the resulting instrument because of its substantial item overlap, high intercorrelations among scales, and imbalanced true–false keying. However, Millon offers a persuasive justification for these characteristics. The instrument deserves an extensive field trial, keeping in mind that it was designed to be used with psychiatric patients over 17 years old with eighth-grade reading skills. It is not recommended for evaluating medical patients or for assessing general personality traits among college students (but will obviously be used in that manner just as the MMPI has been). An automated scoring and interpretive report is available through National Computer Systems, Inc. It is unfortunate that templates for hand scoring are not available. The author offers what appear to be good reasons for this decision, but researchers may be put off by their inability to "play" with the data.

The manual is impressive. We invite psychologists to study this inventory so we can see how good the MCMI really is.

Basic Personality Inventory (BPI)

The manual for this instrument was not available at the time of this writing, although Jackson (Note 4) predicts that it will be prepared later this year. The following information was obtained from an unofficial users' manual prepared by two of Jackson's former students and from Ronald Holden's dissertation. Both sets of data were supplied by Jackson, whom we thank for his courtesy in this regard.

The BPI is designed primarily to indicate areas of personality maladjustment or psychopathology. However, given the bipolar nature of the scale definitions, it is also possible for the inventory to indicate areas of personality strength. The 12 scales on this 240-item instrument are Hypochondriasis (*Hyp*), Depression (*Dep*), Denial (*Den*), Interpersonal Problems (*IPs*), Alienation (*Ali*), Persecutory Ideas (*PId*), Anxiety (*Axy*), Thinking Disorder (*ThD*), Impulse Expression (*ImE*), Social Introversion (*SoI*), Self Depreciation (*SDp*), and Deviation (*Dev*). Each 20-item scale has 10 true-keyed and 10 false-keyed items, except for the Deviation scale which has 20 true-keyed items.

The constructs underlying the BPI are based on a multimethod factor analysis of the Differential Personality Inventory (DPI, Jackson & Messick, 1975) and the MMPI. These constructs were developed with a sample of 282 white male psychiatric patients who were administered the standard MMPI and the 28 DPI scales (Hoffman, Jackson, & Skinner, 1975). A complete components analysis of the MMPI was performed, and the factor loadings were rotated so that only one scale loaded on each orthogonal factor. Then a principal components analysis of the DPI was undertaken. The 11 factors extracted were rotated to a pattern based on theoretical links of the DPI constructs to individual MMPI scales. Finally, an intercorrelation matrix between the 13 MMPI and 11 DPI factors was calculated and factored. The first 11 factors served as the constructs underlying the BPI scales. Once the constructs were defined, a minimum-redundancy item analysis was employed as the criterion for selecting DPI items to develop new scales. Items were then rewritten to enhance their substantive relationships to the underlying constructs, to simplify them, and to eliminate item overlap with the DPI.

With the emphasis on high relevant item–factor correlations for item selection, one would expect the scales of the BPI to show substantial internal consistencies. KR-20 values for a variety of samples range from .56 to .88 with a median in the low .70s. Test–retest stability values over a one-month interval range from .63 to .87 with a median in the high .70s. Analyses of the mean absolute factor loading in the targeted direction and the degree of congruence between the rotated item factors and their respective targets demonstrate both convergent and discriminant validity at the item level.

The current normative samples for the BPI are 278 male and 538 female junior and senior high school students enrolled in 16 schools in London, Ontario, and 168 male and 251 female undergraduate and graduate students at the University of Western Ontario. Tables of raw score means, standard deviations, and T-score equivalents are available. Analyses of the adolescent data reveal that males obtain significantly higher scores than females on *Den, IPs, Ali,* and *Sol,* while females obtain higher scores on *Hyp, Axy,* and *ThD.* A similar pattern was found in a large sample of teenage delinquents.

Fifth-grade reading level is required to understand the BPI. Scoring may be done manually using the templates available. The BPI can also be administered and scored immediately by a TRS-80 microcomputer. If this procedure is used, the profile is also printed, as well as a narrative description for each scale, depending on T-score elevation and the critical items on the Deviation scale endorsed by the client. Before any detailed interpretation is done, checks for validity must be carried out. To check random responding, raw scores are examined. If all scores are approximately 10 (the score by chance), the test is considered invalid. Faking good may be detected by elevations on the Denial scale. Faking bad will result in an elevated profile (except for Denial), especially on the Deviation scale.

The scales can be organized into five broad categories to emphasize some of the psychosocial and psychometric clusterings: (a) measures of antisocial orientation, which include *IPs, Ali,* and *ImE;* (b) measures of personal emotional adjustment, which include *Dep, Axy,* and *Hyp;* (c) measures of personal cognitive adjustment, which include *PId* and *ThD;* (d) measures of social and self-perception, which include *SDp* and *Sol;* and (e) the validity measures *Den* and *Dev.* Elevations often occur in the clusters indicated and tend to define the problem area. Low scores may be considered positive signs. A very low score on *ImE,* for example, may be given by an individual who carefully plans activities and is basically self-controlled. A low score on *Den* may be indicative of a person who is very open concerning thoughts and feelings.

Three sets of data bear on the validity of the BPI scales. Jackson (1975) used peer-rated item responses, self-adjective ratings, and peer adjective ratings as critcria for a university undergraduate sample of roommate pairs. Results are not reported in terms of scale–criteria correlation coefficients, but in the form of a multimethod factor analysis. Examination of these findings shows that the BPI scales define factors that are also delineated by relevant and only by relevant criteria.

Holden, Helmes, Jackson, and Fekken (1981) examined the validity of the BPI in terms of diagnostic efficiency. Using 352 psychiatric inpatients, they attempted to predict each patient's diagnosis on the basis of scores from the 12 BPI scales. The rate of accurate predictions ranged from 3.2% for psychotics to 59.1% for neurotics, and the total hit rate over the seven diagnostic categories was 33.2%. This rate may appear to be low, but it does represent a significant increase over the unadjusted chance rate of 14.3%.

No authors are mentioned by Jackson for the other study cited, which involved multiple discriminant analysis. Here it was shown that overall the BPI differentiated male and female delinquent and nondelinquent groups to a very significant degree. Furthermore, the first three discriminant functions and 11 of 12 univariate F tests for scales considered singly were significant. To facilitate substantive interpretation, correlations between BPI scales and discriminant function composite scores were computed. The first dimension accounted for 69% of the between group dispersion. This dimension is bipolar with *Dev* (.58), *Ali* (.38), *Den* (.33), *SDp* (.30), and *Dep* (.28) loading the positive pole, while *Hyp* ($-.32$) and *IPs* ($-.27$) are representative of the negative end. With the delinquent samples at the positive pole, this dimension clearly distinguished the normal samples from the delinquent groups.

Jackson and other workers with the BPI recommend its use in the assessment of psychopathology with the general population and, in particular, with adolescents in conflict with the law. An obvious reservation concerning its general use is that the adult norms are based on college students between 20 and 25 years of age. How older and less educated adults would perform is not known at this time. However, given Jackson's demonstrated ability to construct tests with many praiseworthy qualities, this new instrument deserves not only research attention but also clinical trials. In that manner, we can determine whether it is as good as its proponents claim.

The Clinical Analysis Questionnaire (CAQ)

Delhees and Cattell (1971) constructed this instrument to assess depression and psychosis more adequately than was possible with the 16 PF. Sometimes one gets the impression that CAQ refers just to 12 new clinical scales it introduces; on other occasions CAQ seems to refer to the 16 PF plus these 12 additional scales. According to the manual (Krug, 1980), the latter interpretation is correct. We will therefore include some remarks about the 16 PF subsection in our description of the test, but will concentrate primarily on the 12 pathology scales, since we have already discussed the 16 PF at length.

The CAQ has 272 items, 128 in scales covering the normal personality structure (8 per scale) and 144 in scales covering pathological traits (12 per scale). The principal source of items for the first part was Form A of the 16 PF. Half of the CAQ Part I items are identical with 16 PF Form A items. Ten percent are slightly modified from their original appearance, another 20% of the items were drawn from Forms B, C, and D of the 16 PF, and the final 20% consist of previously unpublished or drastically modified items.

The initial pool of Part II items for the CAQ was developed from abnormal behaviors reported in various studies of depression, schizophrenia, and MMPI configurations, not from psychiatric conceptions. Refinements and improvements were made as a consequence of successive factor-analytic validity studies. Items were also checked for clarity and screened for potentially offensive content.

The CAQ was designed for use with adults and should ordinarily be given to clients age 16 or older. The test requires an average reading level of grade 6.7. It can be scored by hand, and computer scoring services are available. Norm tables are available for normal adult men and women, and special norms for college students, prisoners, psychiatric patients, and clinically diagnosed adolescents are also presented in the manual. These data are based on 3249 protocols (including 965 normals, 888 students, 446 convicts, and 950 clinical cases) tested at more than 60 locations in the United States and Canada. Sampling considerations included location, occupation, community size, race, and age. When cell frequencies differed from ideal proportions, a weighting procedure was used to achieve a statistical balance.

Test-taking attitude can be evaluated by scoring the V scale (Krug, 1979), which consists of 10 dichotomously scored items with very infrequently endorsed alternatives. Scores of 0 to 2 indicate that the profile is valid. Since the normal 16 PF personality traits have been discussed earlier in the chapter, we will now turn to the clinical scales, which include seven varieties of Depression (Hypochondriasis, Suicidal Depression, Agitation, Anxious Depression, Low Energy Depression, Guilt and Resentment, and Boredom and Withdrawal) and Paranoia, Psychopathic Deviation, Schizophrenia, Psychasthenia, and Psychological Inadequacy (formerly called General Psychosis). The last five scales were initially identified in factor-analytic studies of the MMPI.

Intercorrelations among CAQ scale scores for normal and clinical samples are presented in the manual (Krug, 1980). Examination of these data shows relationships in line with expectations. That is, subareas of Depression are substantially (.60 to .80) correlated with each other, except for Agitation. Psychotic scales are also highly intercorrelated, except for Psychopathic Deviation. Differences between scale correlations of normals and patients are minor. Second-order factors reflecting the content of these 12 scales are depression, psychoticism, and neuroticism.

Reliabilities of the CAQ Part II scales for a one-day interval range from .67 for Boredom and Withdrawal to .90 for Schizophrenia. The clinical scales are more reliable than the normal personality scales on both test–retest and internal consistency measures. This finding seems odd; why should enduring traits be less consistent than clinical symptoms? Factor pattern matrices reported in the manual show that, across four independent analyses, 97% of the loadings are in agreement with the underlying factor model. Validity coefficients (factor structure values) range from .45 for Psychopathic Deviance to .86 for Hypochondriasis. These figures are not likely to be duplicated in an external criterion study, but they do represent the theoretical upper limit of predictive potential for any single scale.

Criterion-related validity studies with schizophrenics, neurotics, personality disorders, substance abusers, convicts, child abusers, battered women, and homosexuals have provided results consistent with the scales' designated names. For instance, schizophrenics' peak score is frequently on the Schizophrenia scale, neurotics peak on Hypochondriasis or Anxious Depression, and personality disorders are apt to be highest on Psychopathic Deviation or on Agitation. Females score higher than males on all but the two clinical scales just named. Correlations ranging from − .07 to − .28 show a decrease over all these scales with increasing age.

The manual (Krug, 1980) also presents correlations between CAQ and MMPI clinical scales. As examples, Hypochondriasis is most highly correlated (.48) with Scale 1, Suicidal Depression is most highly correlated (.37) with Scale 7, Boredom and Withdrawal with Scale 0 (.60), and Psychopathic Deviation with Scale 0 (−.42). Correlations between the CAQ and the Motivation Analysis Test are also given. The manual concludes by presenting and interpreting eight profiles selected to illustrate applications of the CAQ in clinical evaluation, forensic examination, marriage counseling, and employment screening.

Empirical studies of the CAQ have included work on subjective helplessness and depression (Donovan, O'Leary, & Walker, 1979), schizophrenics (Deathrage, 1977), escape attempts and early release of convicts (Eber, 1975), child abusers (Cardillo & Sahd, 1977), battered women (Star, Clark, Goetz, & O'Malia, 1979), and couples involved in open-ended marriages (Knapp, 1974). Equations have been derived to predict proneness to alcohol and narcotic addiction. It is interesting to note that the Guilt and Resentment score is prominent among the former group, whereas the Psychopathic Deviation score plays an important role in the latter group.

A review of this instrument by McNair (1978) focused mostly on the inadequacies of the temporary manual, which was first issued in 1971 and later appeared with a 1975 copyright. He was so upset by the fact that correlations among the pathology factors, second-order factor solutions, and primary factor analyses were not included ("an insult to potential users' intelligence") that it is difficult to guess how he might react to the present manual, in which these pieces of information are supplied. Despite his irritation with the omissions, McNair did characterize the items as "interesting, even appealing" and the test as "intriguing, innovative."

McNair (1978) stated that "the CAQ should be restricted to research." Obviously this warning, which may no longer be justified, is not being followed. Brochures from the Institute of Personality and Ability Testing indicate that the "CAQ will help you (i.e., busy professionals) develop meaningful insights into individual problems and solutions to those problems." We hope that those who are using the instrument will also provide empirical data, above and beyond single case examples, to bolster these claims.

None of the constructors of these new instruments depended on the contrasted-group strategy to develop their scales. It is probably no coincidence that each inventory is much shorter than the cumbersome MMPI. It is also worth noting that two of these three questionnaires include scales to measure basic personality traits as well as clinical symptomatology.

CONTROVERSIAL TOPICS

When this chapter was originally written, we listed a number of areas in which researchers and theorists had been unable to agree on explanations of the phenomena involved. These topics included clinical versus statistical prediction, traits versus states, invasion of privacy, and others. Many had been discussed on numerous previous occasions, so they were simply designated with relevant references cited. Others were somewhat less familiar and were treated in some detail, including the adequacy of clinical judgment, the relations between moderator variables and test performance, and the impact of the Barnum effect on statements and reports.

When one peruses this list now, one wonders whatever happened to some of the controversies. For example, concern over whether tests can be interpreted in terms of their named scales (content) or whether in fact response styles or sets were responsible for patterns of responding generated hundreds of articles in the 1950s and 1960s. Was the disagreement resolved? Not exactly. Rather, "it just kind of dried up and blew away," as Meehl (1978) said about concepts and theories in such soft areas of psychology as personality.

Given this sobering evidence about the relatively brief half-life of certain kinds of controversies, one hesitates to depict any area as problematic in a general or enduring sense. It may be more realistic to speak in terms of topics that are currently generating some research and are also of interest to the writers. From that more modest perspective, the following three issues are offered. Readers of the earlier edition will recognize one that was discussed in detail then and another referred to in passing. The third topic is new to this volume.

Moderator Variables and Test Performance

The purpose of this mini-essay is to present interrelations between demographic factors and responses to the MMPI. Emphasis will be placed on recent research. Implications for interpretation will be given when possible. MMPI research is used to illustrate these relationships because far more research has been done with this instrument than with any other personality inventory. However research conducted with other inventories shows that none is free of such effects.

Gender.   Aaronson's (1958) work with scale scores and Webb's (1970) study of code types showed clearly that male and female psychiatric patients describe themselves differently on the MMPI. Yet these findings in and of themselves do not indicate that the same profile has a different interpretive significance for men and women. Gynther, Altman, and Sletten's (1973) analysis of 17 code types for psychiatric cases indicated that there were sex differences only for 2-4/4-2. Alcoholism and various associated descriptors were found for males and females; however, women als displayed depressed mood, crying, and suicidal attempts or gestures. Ritzema's (1974) findings for an inpatient sample were similar in that only minor differences were demonstrated for most code types. However, the classic 4-9/9-4 had different implications for males and females. When women obtained this profile, they were described as irritable, hostile, grandiose, and uncooperative; male 4-9/9-4s, on the other hand, deviated in the other direction from the base rates; they were less anxious and displayed fewer guilt feelings and a less depressed mood. Women classified as 7-8/8-7 and 4-8/8-4 were also described as more deviant than men with those code types.

Although sex differences were relatively uncommon in the investigations just reported, Kelley and King, who have obtained their subjects in a college counseling center, have typically found such differences in the code types they have studied. For example, males classified as 2-7-8s displayed depression, withdrawal, impaired affect, and disordered thinking, whereas females with this code type were seen as basically neurotic with anxiety, insomnia, and obsessive ruminations (Kelley & King, 1979). Males who obtained a normal profile when evaluated at the center were of three types: those with psychotic disorders in remission, those with marital problems, or those who had abused drugs. Females' complaints were due to situational problems; none had previous hospitalization for psychosis (Kelley & King, 1978). These actuarial findings suggest that correlates may be similar for some profiles by gender, but that the clinician cannot take this for granted.

Age.   Early work showed that MMPI scale scores and code types differed as a function of age. Both Aaronson (1958) and Webb (1970) interpreted their findings as indicating problems of impulse control for the young and concerns about physical and/or mental functioning in older subjects. Swenson, Pearson, and Osborne (1973) collected MMPIs on 50,000 medical patients. They found the most dramatic age differences on Scales 2 and 9. Only 6% of subjects younger than 20 obtained peaks on Scale 2, whereas 23% of subjects older than 70 peaked on that scale alone. In contrast, about 21% of the younger patients peaked on Scale 9, whereas fewer than 5% of the elderly peaked on that scale.

Ritzema (1974) found that many of the code types had very similar interpretive significance for younger and older psychiatric patients. However, younger patients classified as 8-9/9-8s displayed far more deviant behavior—tension, grandiosity, conceptual disorganization—than older patients with that code type.

Adolescent norms have been developed to deal with clients aged 14 to 17 inclusive. Marks, Seeman, and Haller (1974) have shown that employing these norms can lead to substantially different results from the use of standard norms. Scale scores, especially *F*, 8, and 9, are often reduced. Lachar, Klinge, and Grisell (1976) demonstrated that this adjustment resulted in more accurate interpretations, according to clinicians who knew the patients well.

Special norms are also available for evaluating the profiles of elderly clients. Adjustments on Scales 1 and 2 are most striking. Greene's (1980) review of this literature led him to conclude that "aged persons may elevate Scales 1, 2, and 3 about 10 T-score points, elevate Scale 0 about 5 T-score points, and lower Scale 9 about 3 T-score points compared to the original Minnesota normative group" (pp. 213–214). More investigation of code-type correlates is needed, but it seems apparent that age affects MMPI scale scores.

Ethnicity.   More than 40 studies have been published concerning black–white differences on the MMPI. Scales *F*, 8, and 9 most frequently differentiate the racial groups. Except for the special case of drug abusers, blacks invariably obtain higher scores (in the range of 5 to 8 T points) on these scales.

Scale score differences have obvious implications if cutting scores are used for classification purposes, but are any data directly relevant to the interpretation of a black person's MMPI? Gynther, Altman, and Warbin (1973b) obtained replicated correlates (e.g., poor recent memory) for whites with highly elevated profiles, but none for blacks with the same kind of profile. Smith and Graham (1981) recently confirmed these findings with an entirely different sample of psychiatric patients. Gynther, Altman, and Warbin (1973a) also failed to find any replicated correlates associated with the familiar 4-9/9-4 code type for blacks.

Ritzema (1974) found some similarities between code-type correlates of blacks and those of whites, notably for 6-8/8-6, but more differences. For instance, whites classified as 1-3/3-1s displayed somatic concern, anxiety, and tension, whereas blacks having the same profile had no descriptors different from base rate values. Black 2-4/4-2s were suspicious, hostile, anxious, and hallucinatory, whereas whites in this category displayed none of those behaviors.

White (1974) devised a Race-Sensitive scale, scores on which can be used to adjust blacks' scores on Scales F, 4, 8, and 9. His corrections are intended to reduce overinterpretation of pathology. Validity studies have yet to be done to demonstrate that such corrected profiles are more accurate descriptions of blacks than uncorrected profiles.

Relatively few studies of other ethnic groups have been conducted. However, the available evidence (e.g., Bull, 1976; Penk, Robinowitz, Roberts, Dolan, & Atkins, 1981; Sue & Sue, 1974) suggests that Latinos, American Indians, and Asian-Americans respond differently than the normative group. In summary, then, ethnicity is related to test performance at the item, scale, and configural level.

Education, Occupation, and Intelligence.   Miller (1978) has shown that scores on Scales L and 1 decrease as education increases, whereas Scale K scores increase with greater education. For males Scale 5 scores also increase with years of education. For both sexes 1-2/2-1s and 1-3/3-1s are twice as frequent among the less educated clients.

Ritzema's (1974) data showed that both more and less educated 6-8/8-6s manifested psychotic behavior. However, no correlates were obtained for the more educated 2-3/3-2s, whereas less educated patients with this code type displayed somatic concern and depressive mood. The more educated 4-9/9-4s also had no correlates, whereas the less educated displayed several including uncooperativeness.

Other investigations have demonstrated that there are distinctive relationships between intelligence and occupation and between validity and clinical scale scores. Code-type correlates of various levels of these factors have yet to be developed. However, the available information does indicate that these interrelationships should be considered by an MMPI interpreter.

Miscellaneous.   Religious affiliation and involvement, place of residence in the United States, and location in rural and urban settings have also been examined with regard to their possible effects on profiles. In brief, place of residence and religious affiliation seem unrelated, whereas religious involvement and rural–urban residence seem related to MMPI responding.

Skeptics might point to the 5-to-8 T-point differences associated with the various demographic variables and argue that this difference is insufficient to affect profile configuration and, hence, the meaning of the MMPI generated by a client. However, the variables usually occur in combination, for instance, youthfulness, member of a minority group, not well educated. Under those conditions, T-score differences increase to the point where profiles and code types are changed with concurrent changes in meaning.

Individual clinicians would have difficulty keeping these complex relationships in mind (if indeed they are ever fully worked out). Computers are up to the challenge. Branching statements can be added to software to handle these contingencies, and, as will be seen in the next section, the newest commercial interpretive system has included such statements in its program. It will be interesting to see if users detect the hoped-for increase in interpretive accuracy.

Automated Psychological Reports

Automation/Computer-Generated Reports.   These terms evoke images from the movies *Modern Times* and *2001 A.D.,* in which machines ran the show and the only role for humans was to oil the machinery or punch the buttons at prearranged times. A very different, far from glamorous picture is suggested by the phrase "Garbage in, garbage out," which makes fun of and puts down computers for their lack of "intelligence" and "wisdom." These two notions seem to reflect people's love–hate relations with devices that can outperform them, yet are still under their control.

Computers entered the field of personality assessment 20 years ago when Mayo Clinic personnel devised a method for interpreting MMPI validity and clinical scales in terms of different phrases for different absolute elevations. Output involved brief sentences for each scale, and we are told that the medical staff, for whom this report was constructed, was pleased. By the mid-1960s several other enterprising psychologists had put together more sophisticated systems for interpreting MMPIs, and a similar program was also devised for the 16 PF.

The post-Mayo MMPI systems—Roche Psychiatric Service Institute, Institute of Clinical Analysis, OPTIMUM (now Behaviordyne), Clinical Psychological Services (now Caldwell Report)—produced reports resembling those written by an individual clinician. Typically they begin by evaluating test-taking attitude as inferred from validity scale scores, then discuss personality characteristics and pathological symptoms derived from clinical scale scores and configurations, and then give diagnostic impression and treatment considerations. Raw and T scores are often printed out for supplementary scales (e.g., Wiggins' content scales, Ego Strength, Low Back Pain, etc.), and the Grayson critical items are usually included. One system prints a variety of different reports, including one for the client, and the others print only one.

There are numerous advantages to the users of these systems. They save professional time, cost relatively little (although that is less true now than it used to be), and produce interpretations more reliably than a clinician can. Also, as Fowler (1979) has pointed out, "They offer an alternative to the endless cycle of training new personnel, generation after generation, to do approximately the same thing with test data as their predecessors did" (p. 351). Furthermore, a report can be produced for every profile since all these systems are nonactuarial; that is, the statement library is based on the codebook builder's clinical skill and interpretation rather than on empirically determined code type correlates (although such findings, of course, may be included in the library). The actuarial approach would not work for commercial systems, since numerous MMPIs would have to be returned to the sender marked "no interpretation available."

Are there any disadvantages? Yes, there is the very serious problem of not knowing whether any (or which ones) of these reports are valid. Very few studies have been done due to the proprietary nature of the software of all systems mentioned except the Mayo Clinic one, which is handled commercially by Psychological Corporation. Hedlund, Morgan, and Master (1972) compared a modified form of these statements with independent clinical information on army psychiatric inpatients and found concordance on only 2 out of 38 items, an outcome that implies that this version of the Mayo program has little validity generalization. Ordinarily user acceptance studies have been presented as evidence for the quality of the reports. These investigations are surveys asking if the user finds the report clear, useful, and in agreement with his or her clinical impression. Results have been very favorable, but they obviously do not say anything about validity.

Eichman (1972) stated that "if the final recipient of the report is sophisticated in the use of psychological data . . . the services can be of considerable use." But what about the general practitioner or the psychiatrist or even the Ph.D. psychologist who knows nothing of psychometric theory and very little about the strengths and limitations of the MMPI? This individual receives a computerized report in the mail and, given the awe with which many people view computers, may believe that all the statements are accurate. Some systems try to protect the recipient of the report from this reaction by including a disclaimer, such as, "Although not a substitute for the clinician's professional judgment and skill, the MMPI can be a useful adjunct. . . ." How seriously this type of statement is taken is not known. Eichman (1972) concluded his review with the following warning: "Consequently I am as certain that the automated report will be misused as I am that it will be used. . . . Any marginally unethical or controversial use of these procedures is likely to damage the status of all mental health professionals."

By the time Butcher (1978) reviewed these systems for the *Eighth Mental Measurements Yearbook,* two other services—Automated Psychological Assessment and Psychological Assessment Service—were commercially available. The first of these is noteworthy in that the complete library of statements and the rules for selecting them are publicly available (Lachar, 1974). The second named service is a modification of the Roche program by Fowler for use with students, personnel, and law offenders. Butcher estimated that "several hundred individual patient reports are produced daily by electronic computer." He also pointed out several problems in addition to those we have already mentioned. One is that programs often fail to take into account age, sex, population, or other relevant demographic information. Hence, 68/86 code types generated by a black teenager in trouble with the law and a 30-year-old white female presenting with delusions of persecution may lead to the very same report. It can be frustrating and confusing for users to get interpretations that have no resemblance to the real, live client with whom they are dealing. The problem is accentuated, as Butcher points out, when the systems are used for screening in industry, police selection, and graduate school applications, which involve a low base rate of psychopathology.

Another feature of these systems is that, once programmed, they are unlikely to be changed or, as Butcher says, they become "chiseled in stone." In some cases the creators have good intentions, but in others one has to wonder if the originators ever gave a thought to updating the program. Butcher points out that when Pearson and Swenson gave their Mayo system to Psychological Corporation, they thought they would be kept as consultants to revise the program as needed. However, the call for help never came, and the Psychological Corproation reports are by now very outdated, while the actual Mayo program has been considerably revised. Other programs have not been changed for a decade or more, despite the fact that several important empirical studies of code type correlates have been published during that time period.

The most recent service, the Minnesota Interpretive Report for the MMPI, was brought forth by Butcher in 1981. It will be recalled that this author was one of the evaluators of the systems reviewed in the *Eighth Mental Measurements Yearbook* (Buros, 1978). His system attempts to meet his and others' criticisms of previous services. For example, reports are tailored according to demographic and ethnic factors, narratives are based on empirically derived scale and profile correlates to the degree that these are available, provisions are made for periodic updating of reports through an ongoing research and development program, and empirically derived critical items (Koss-Butcher and Lachar-Wrobel) are printed to provide the clinician with important themes.

A comparison of the earliest with the most recent commercial system for MMPI interpretation shows that many improvements and refinements have taken place over the past two decades. Creators of these systems still must rely on their experience for devising interpretations of relatively infrequent code types, however. It is hoped that empirical investigations will provide actuarial data to cover this final third of all profiles. Users must continue to recognize the dearth of validity studies and accept the reports with an "as if" philosophy. Some commercial systems are far better than others. In a "buyer beware" market, it behooves the consumer to obtain all the information available before selecting one for his or her clinic.

The Utility of Subtle versus Obvious Personality-Test Items

Tests constructed on a rational–theoretical or factor-analytic basis contain items whose scale membership is obvious, whereas tests constructed by the method of contrasted groups typically contain some items whose scale membership cannot be readily identified. Justification for the existence of such items was provided many years ago by Meehl (1945), who argued that the science of behavior was not sufficiently advanced to specify relations between verbal responses and behavior dynamics. Hence "nontest correlates . . . must be discovered by empirical means" (Meehl, p. 297).

These arguments seemed persuasive, but the more important issue was how useful or predictive subtle items are. This question is not satisfactorily answered by citing the intriguing bit of information that the criterion group of depressives for the MMPI responded "false" to "I sometimes tease animals" significantly more often than the normal control group. Wiener and Harmon (1946) developed subtle (S) and obvious (O) keys for MMPI Scales 2, 3, 4, 6, and 9. Their investigations showed that individuals of high ability have equal O and S scores, whereas those of lower ability have higher O than S scores; psychologically sophisticated individuals almost completely avoid significant O responses and have relatively high S scores; and unsuccessful students and on-the-job trainees have significantly more O than S scores compared to successful groups. In another early study Cofer, Chance, and Judson (1949) showed that subtle items were relatively unaffected by instructions to fake bad or fake good, whereas usage of obvious items varied as a function of instructions.

The above findings suggest that S–O usage varies with different personal attributes and that subtle items are relatively impervious to faking (see Holden & Jackson, 1981, for the opposite view). However, McCall (1958) found that Scale 2 items discriminated diagnosed depressives from nondepressed psychotics in proportion to their face validity. Also, Duff (1965) found that subtle items were much less effective than obvious items in differentiating a normal group from three hospitalized clinical groups.

Jackson (1971) challenged Meehl's presentation, arguing that empirical derivation of scales is justified only under circumstances of ignorance, which "hardly seems a suitable defense at the present time" (p. 232). Jackson contended that "a sample of item content most directly relevant to a particular trait will be the most efficient way of going about measuring it" (p. 234). Meehl (1972) did not attempt to refute Jackson's argument and, indeed, admitted that the "monolithically 'criterion-statistical' view on item analysis as that of my 1945 paper is too strong" (p. 150). He concluded that obvious items should be the best discriminators, but expressed the belief that subtle items may also have predictive power.

The question now becomes whether Jackson is correct in stating that subtle items do not belong on personality scales or Meehl is right in his less extreme view. If subtle items are retained, can we expect them to be equally useful with regard to prediction of different criterion behaviors?

To deal with these questions, Christian, Burkhart, and Gynther (1978) obtained mean subtle–obvious (with regard to psychopathology) ratings of all MMPI items answered true and false. Results of this comprehensive scaling showed that some MMPI clinical scales (1, 7, and 8) contain very few subtle items, whereas other MMPI scales (5 and 0) contain very few obvious items. The other five scales, however, contain sufficient subtle and obvious items to test Jackson's hypothesis.

A series of studies at Auburn University using college students as subjects has examined predictor-criterion relationships of the different scales. Gynther, Burkhart, and Hovanitz (1979) compared subtle and obvious Scale 4 scores to self-reported nonconforming behavior (Have you . . . written bad checks, driven a car while intoxicated, not paid parking tickets, etc.). Results showed that the obvious subscale is the most powerful predictor, but that the subtle subscale has a unique contribution to make. Burkhart, Gynther, and Fromuth (1980) examined relations between subtle and obvious components of Scale 2 and scores on the Profile of Mood States (POMS), the Beck Depression Inventory (BDI), and an abbreviated version of the Pleasant Events Schedule. Face-valid items were the best predictors of depression as measured by the three questionnaires used. Subtle Scale 2 items did not provide a unique contribution over and above obvious Scale 2 items. In fact, the correlations between the obvious subscale and the BDI and POMS were significantly greater than correlations between the total Scale 2 scores and scores on the other instruments. This finding suggests that the predictive power of this scale would be improved by removing the subtle items.

Hovanitz and Gynther (1980) investigated relations between subtle and obvious Scale 9 scores and performance on the Sensation Seeking Scale, an Activity-Level Biographic Data form, and the Porteus Maze. Examples of items on the biographic questionnaire are "How many different people have you dated?," "How many times have you run out of gas while driving your car?," and "How long do you spend eating breakfast?." Results of this study disclosed as many significant relationships associated with subtle items as there were with obvious items. The subtle items predicted Biographical Data and Thrill and Adventure Seeking scores, and the obvious items predicted Experience Seeking and errors and time taken on the Mazes. The subtle subscale was strongly associated with Harris and Lingoes's (1968) Imperturbability subscale, whereas the obvious subscale was associated with Psychomotor Acceleration, Ego Inflation, and Amorality. These results imply that the content of Scale 9 is more heterogeneous than that of Scale 4 or Scale 2.

Wilson (1980) studied the relationships between subtle and obvious Scale 3 items and scores on the Perley-Guze Hysteria Symptom Checklist, the Interpersonal Disposition Inventory, the Parent Behavior Form, and the Embedded Figures Test. The most significant correlations were between Scale 3 scores and the Symptom Checklist. The S–O results resemble those for Scale 4, on which obvious items were superior, but subtle items had a unique contribution to make. It is also worth noting that the obvious subscale is a much better predictor than the full scale. The final study was carried out by Hovanitz, Gynther, and Marks (in press), who examined relations between Scale 6 S–O subscores and Rotter's Interpersonal Trust Scale, the Einstellung test, Mehrabian's Stimulus Screening Questionnaire, and a paranoia questionnaire containing such items as "How many times have you had articles valued at $25 or more missing that you suspected had been stolen?." Results resembled those of the Scale 9 study in that the subtle items predicted some criteria (e.g., an unobtrusive measure of personalization) and the obvious items predicted other criteria (e.g., paranoia questionnaire).

Jackson's hypothesis about subtle items is confirmed only for Scales 2 and 3. Predictive power would be lost if the subtle items of Scale 4 were discarded. In the case of Scales 6 and 9, the obvious and subtle subscales provide complementary information not available from either scale alone. Yet it should be noted that our definitions of subtlety and obviousness are not shared by Jackson himself. To illustrate that alternative viewpoint, Holden and Jackson (1979) ask one to consider the item "I would enjoy the occupation of a butcher." Without a context, this item might be deemed subtle or not face valid. However, if one is instructed to think of it in connection with sadism, the substantive aspect of the item becomes obvious. From this perspective, our definitions may be too general. One should not ask (as we did) whether endorsement of an item implies the presence of a psychological problem, but instead whether endorsement of a Scale 4 or Scale 9 item indicates the presence of behaviors associated with psychopathy or hypomania. Thus, "When I get bored I like to stir up some excitement" may seem innocuous to raters sensitized to psychopathology in general, but quite meaningful to those alerted to various aspects of hyperactivity and impulsivity.

Future studies in this area should make use of clinical diagnostic groups. Relationships found for normals may not necessarily hold for people with problems. Patients diagnosed as having conversion reactions, for example, obtained high scores on both the admission and denial subscales of Scale 3, whereas this combination is rare for normals (Dahlstrom, 1969).

A number of years ago Cronbach (1970) said that separate keys for subtle and transparent items are "emphatically needed." He asserted that separately validated keys would be trustworthy where they confirm each other and a warning to the interpreter where they do not. The situation seems to be more complicated than he thought. In some cases removal of subtle items would result in better scales. In other cases the relative value of subtle or obvious keys is a function of the criterion to be predicted. These observations do not support Meehl's (1945) dustbowl empiricism, but are consistent with his more recent position (Meehl, 1972).

CONCLUDING REMARKS

It is our impression that there are more inventories being used for more assessments at present than ever before. There is no doubt that a large part of the increase in usage is due to the emergence of numerous computer scoring and interpretation services. Although we have restricted our comments in this chapter to the so-called objective personality inventories, a recent issue of the American Psychological Association *Monitor* advertises two different automated Rorschach interpretations, as well as computerized printouts for medical history, career assessment, and social history.

One might almost get the feeling that the millennium has been reached. But if one looks behind the report at the program and asks where the rules and branching statements come from, it becomes apparent that the advances in production of typed evaluations has not been accompanied by advances in validity studies, much less by relevant theory. The MMPI is in the best shape with respect to established external correlates of any of the inventories used to assess personality or psychopathology. Yet even in this case investigators have not followed up the basic empirical studies (e.g., Marks, Seeman, & Haller, 1974) with work to establish how applicable the findings are to people in places other than the original derivation setting.

The issues we discussed in the previous summary of this chapter, that is, the influence of the situation on behavior, the need to measure states as well as traits, the use of multiple criteria rather than single behaviors, and the basing of predictions on data collected from relevant reference groups continue to draw research attention. Although many articles might be cited, the papers of Cronbach (1975), Epstein (1979), and Mischel (1979) are especially noteworthy. Also, Meehl's (1978) depiction of the whys and wherefores of the slow progress in the area of personality is stimulating as well as sobering.

As to assessment considered more broadly, forms of evaluation that define the behavior of interest in concrete, observable terms and are concerned with the antecedents as well as consequences of that behavior are becoming used more often in clinical contexts. In addition, the predictive power of biographical data has been well established. Some researchers, such as Owens and Schoenfeldt (1979), believe that biodata are superior to the use of formal tests. We have also been intrigued by unobtrusive measures (Webb, Campbell, Schwartz, & Sechrest, 1966), with their circumvention of the reactivity problem, and wish that some ingenious person would develop methods for assessing personality and psychopathology by means of erosion and accretion measures. Highly structured interview schedules that technicians can use with incoming patients to determine whether the person has a psychiatric disorder and, if so, what kind, continue to be constructed (e.g., Othmer, Penick, & Powell, 1981).

To return from this brief excursion to self-report inventories, one might ask what the future holds. There are clear trends for intuitive–internal construction procedures to be favored over criterion keying in the development of new instruments and for inventories to include fewer items than in the past. One would anticipate future devices to follow this pattern. Potential test constructors may also wish to take note of the fact that individuals do not behave as consistently as they believe they do. Inventory developers who assume consistency across the dimensions being measured construct tests with built-in limitations. Better sampling of the trait domain might well entail developing very specific scales for specific purposes. These types of scales would enable the constructor to include items that range over a variety of situations. Users of such measures should be able to interpret the results directly as the self-perception that the individual is willing to make public to others.

Many theorists and practitioners have become thoroughly disenchanted with self-report inventories. However, encouraging findings have recently been reported (e.g., Hogan, DeSoto, & Solano, 1977; Jackson & Paunonen, 1980). Perhaps the new tests will surpass the old ones in forecasting criteria of clinical significance. However, to count on that would leave one open to probable disappointment. Whatever instrument is used should be part of a battery of indicators. Correct identification of the problem and selection of the most effective treatment modality are too important to be dependent on any single assessment device.

REFERENCES

Aaronson, B. S. Age and sex influence on MMPI profile peak distributions in an abnormal population. *Journal of Consulting Psychology*, 1958, **22**, 203–206.

Abbott, R. D. Improving the validity of affective self-report measures through constructing personality scales unconfounded with social desirability: A study of the Personality Research Form. *Educational and Psychological Measurement*, 1975, **35**, 371–377.

Acker, M. B. *The relation of achievement need, time perspective, and field articulation to academic performance*. Unpublished doctoral dissertation, University of California, 1967.

Allport, G. W. *Personality: A psychological interpretation*. New York: Holt, Rinehart & Winston, 1937.

Allport, G. W., & Vernon, P. E. *Study of Values*. Boston: Houghton-Mifflin, 1931.

Allport, G. W., Vernon, P. E., & Lindzey, G. *Study of Values* (Rev. manual). Boston: Houghton-Mifflin, 1970.

Barnes, D. F., & Berzins, J. I. A and B undergraduate interviewers of schizophrenic and neurotic inpatients: A test of the interaction hypothesis. *Journal of Consulting and Clinical Psychology*, 1978, **46**, 1368–1373.

Baucom, D. H. Independent CPI masculinity and femininity scales: Psychological correlates and sex role typology. *Journal of Personality Assessment*, 1980, **44**, 262–271.

Bayer, L. M., Whissell-Buechy, D., & Honzik, M. P. Adolescent health and personality: Significance for adult health. *Journal of Adolescent Health Care*, 1980, **1**, 101–107.

Bentler, P. M. *Response variability: Fact or artifact?* Unpublished doctoral dissertation, Stanford University, 1964.

Bernreuter, R. G. *The Personality Inventory*. Palo Alto, Calif.: Consulting Psychologists Press, 1931.

Berzins, J. I., Welling, M. A., & Welter, R. E. A new measure of androgyny based on the Personality Research Form. *Journal of Consulting and Clinical Psychology*, 1978, **46**, 126–138.

Betz, N. E., & Bander, R. S. Relationship of MMPI *Mf* and CPI *Fe* scales to fourfold sex role classifications. *Journal of Personality and Social Psychology*, 1980, **39**, 1245–1248.

Bither, S. W. *A study of the relationship among personalities in groups and group task performance*. Unpublished doctoral dissertation, University of Washington, 1969.

Black, J. D. The interpretation of MMPI profiles of college women. *Dissertation Abstracts*, 1953, **13**, 870–871.

Block, J. *The Q-sort method in personality assessment and psychiatric research*. Springfield, Ill.: C. C. Thomas, 1961.

Block, J. *The challenge of response sets: Unconfounding meaning, acquiescence, and social desirability in the MMPI*. New York: Appleton-Century-Crofts, 1965.

Bolton, B. Evidence for the 16 PF primary and secondary factors. *Multivariate Experimental Clinical Research*, 1977, **3**, 1–15.

Bolton, B. Personality (16 PF) correlates of WAIS scales: A replication. *Applied Psychological Measurement*, 1980, **4**, 399–401.

Braun, J. R., & Asta, P. Changes in Personality Research Form scores (PRF, Form A) produced by faking instructions. *Journal of Clinical Psychology*, 1969, **25**, 429–430.

Braun, J. R., & Costantini, A. Faking and faking detection on the Personality Research Form, AA. *Journal of Clinical Psychology*, 1970, **26**, 516–518.

Bridgwater, C. A. Construct validity of the Personality Research Form: Further evidence. *Educational and Psychological Measurement*, 1981, **41**, 533–535.

Brooks, J. B. Social maturity in middle age and its developmental antecedents. In D. H. Eichorn, J. A. Clausen, N. Haan, M. P. Honzik, & P. H. Mussen (Eds.), *Present and past in middle life*. New York: Academic Press, 1981.

Bull, R. W. *A tri-racial MMPI study*. Unpublished Master's thesis, University of North Carolina, 1976.

Burger, G. K. A short form of the California Psychological Inventory. *Psychological Reports*, 1975, **37**, 179–182.

Burger, G. K., & Cross, D. T. Personality types as measured by the California Psychological Inventory. *Journal of Consulting and Clinical Psychology*, 1979, **47**, 65–71.

Burger, G. K., & Kabacoff, R. I. Personality types as measured by the 16 PF. *Journal of Personality Assessment*, 1982, **46**, 175–181.

Burkhart, B. R., Gynther, M. D., & Fromuth, M. E. The relative predictive validity of subtle versus obvious items on the MMPI Depression scale. *Journal of Clinical Psychology*, 1980, **36**, 748–751.

Buros, O. K. (Ed.). *The eighth mental measurements yearbook*. Highland Park, N.J.: Gryphon Press, 1978.

Butcher, J. N. (Ed.). *Objective personality assessment: Changing perspectives*. New York: Academic Press, 1972.

Butcher, J. N. (Re: Minnesota Multiphasic Personality Inventory) Computerized scoring and interpreting services. In O. K. Buros (Ed.), *Eighth mental measurement yearbook* (Vol. 1). Highland Park, N.J.: Gryphon Press, 1978.

Butcher, J. N. (Ed.). *New developments in the use of the MMPI*. Minneapolis: University of Minnesota Press, 1979.

Butcher, J. N., Kendall, P. C., & Hoffman, N. MMPI short forms: Caution. *Journal of Consulting and Clinical Psychology*, 1980, **48**, 275–278.

Butcher, J. N., & Pancheri, P. *A handbook of cross-national MMPI research*. Minneapolis: University of Minnesota Press, 1976.

Campbell, D. P. *Manual for the Strong-Campbell Interest Inventory* (2nd ed.). Stanford, Calif.: Stanford University Press, 1977.

Campbell, D. T., & Fiske, D. W. Convergent and discriminant validation by the multitrait-multimethod matrix. *Psychological Bulletin*, 1959, **56**, 81–105.

Cardillo, J. P., & Sahd, D. *Personality profiles of different types of child abusing and neglecting parents*. Unpublished manuscript, Family Resource Center, Albuquerque, New Mexico, and University of New Mexico, 1977.

Carey, G., Goldsmith, H. H., Tellegen, A., & Gottesman, I. I. Genetics and personality inventories: The limits of replication with twin data. *Behavior Genetics*, 1978, **8**, 299–313.

Cattell, R. B. *The description and measurement of personality*. Yonkers-on-Hudson, N.Y.: World Book, 1946.

Cattell, R. B. *Manual for forms A and B: Sixteen Personality Factor Questionnaire*. Champaign, Ill.: Institute for Personality and Ability Testing, 1949.

Cattell, R. B. *Personality: A systematic theoretical and factual study*. New York: McGraw-Hill, 1950.

Cattell, R. B. *Personality and motivation, structure and measurement*. Yonkers-on-Hudson, N.Y.: World Book, 1957.

Cattell, R. B. Personality pinned down. *Psychology Today*, 1973, **7**, 40–46. (a)

Cattell, R. B. *Personality and mood by questionnaire*. San Francisco: Jossey-Bass, 1973. (b)

Cattell, R. B. *Personality and learning theory Vol. 1. The structure of personality in its environment*. New York: Springer, 1979.

Cattell, R. B. *Personality and learning theory Vol. 2. A systems theory of maturation and structured learning*. New York: Springer, 1980.

Cattell, R. B. *The inheritance of personality and ability*. New York: Academic Press, 1981.

Cattell, R. B. The development of attribution theory into spectrad theory, using the general perceptual model. *Multivariate Behavioral Research*, 1982, **17**, 169–192.

Cattell, R. B., Eber, H. W., & Tatsuoka, M. M. *Handbook for the Sixteen Personality Factor Questionnaire (16 PF)*. Champaign, Ill.: Institute for Personality and Ability Testing, 1970.

Cattell, R. B., & Nichols, K. E. An improved definition, from 10 researchers, of second-order personality factors in Q data (with cross-cultural checks). *Journal of Social Psychology*, 1972, **86**, 187–203.

Cattell, R. B., Price, P. L., & Patrick, S. V. Diagnosis of clinical depression on four source trait dimensions—V.I. 19, V.I. 20, V.I. 25, and V.I. 30—from the O-A Kit. *Journal of Clinical Psychology*, 1981, **37**, 4–11.

Cattell, R. B., & Scheier, I. H. *The IPAT Anxiety Scale Questionnaire: Manual* (2nd ed.). Champaign, Ill.: Institute for Personality and Ability Testing, 1963.

Cattell, R. B., Schmidt, L. R., & Bjerstedt, A. Clinical diagnosis by the Objective-Analytic Personality Batteries. *Journal of Clinical Psychology*, 1972, **28**, 239–312.

Cattell, R. B., & Warburton, F. W. *Objective personality and motivation tests: A theoretical introduction and practical compendium*. Urbana, Ill.: University of Illinois Press, 1967.

Christian, W. L., Burkhart, B. R., & Gynther, M. D. Subtle-obvious ratings of MMPI items: New interest in an old concept. *Journal of Consulting and Clinical Psychology*, 1978, **46**, 1178–1186.

Cline, V. B. Interpersonal perception. In B. A. Maher (Ed.), *Progress in experimental personality research* (Vol. 1). New York: Academic Press, 1964.

Cofer, C. N., Chance, J. E., & Judson, A. J. A study of malingering on the MMPI. *Journal of Psychology*, 1949, **27**, 491–499.

Cronbach, L. J. *Essentials of psychological testing* (3rd ed.). New York: Harper & Row, 1970.

Cronbach, L. J. Beyond the two disciplines of scientific psychology. *American Psychologist*, 1975, **30**, 116–127.

Cronbach, L. J., & Gleser, G. C. *Psychological tests and personnel decisions*. Urbana, Ill.: University of Illinois Press, 1957.

Cronbach, L. J., & Gleser, G. C. *Psychological tests and personnel decisions* (2nd ed.). Urbana, Ill.: University of Illinois Press, 1965.

Cross, D. T., Barclay, A., & Burger, G. K. Differential effects of ethnic membership, sex, and occupation on the California Psychological Inventory. *Journal of Personality Assessment*, 1978, **42**, 597–603.

Dahlstrom, W. G. Recurrent issues in the development of the MMPI. In J. N. Butcher (Ed.), *MMPI: Research developments and clinical applications*. New York: McGraw-Hill, 1969.

Dahlstrom, W. G., & Dahlstrom, L. (Eds.). *Basic readings on the MMPI: A new selection on personality measurement.* Minneapolis: University of Minnesota Press, 1980.

Dahlstrom, W. G., Welsh, G. S., & Dahlstrom, L. E. *An MMPI handbook: I. Clinical interpretation* (Rev. ed.). Minneapolis: University of Minnesota Press, 1972.

Dahlstrom, W. G., Welsh, G. S., & Dahlstrom, L. E. *An MMPI handbook: II. Research applications* (Rev. ed.). Minneapolis: University of Minnesota Press, 1975.

Dean, E. F. A lengthened Mini: The Midi-Mult. *Journal of Clinical Psychology,* 1972, **28,** 68–71.

Deathrage, E. *Schizophrenia, the opposite of actualization, as measured by the Personal Orientation Inventory.* Unpublished doctoral dissertation, U.S. International University, 1977.

Delhees, K. H., & Cattell, R. B. *Manual for the Clinical Analysis Questionnaire (CAQ).* Champaign, Ill.: Institute for Personality and Ability Testing, 1971.

Derogatis, L. R., Lipman, R. S., & Covi, L. The SCL-90: An outpatient psychiatric rating scale. *Psychopharmacology Bulletin,* 1973, **9,** 13–28.

Donovan, D. M., O'Leary, M. R., & Walker, R. D. Validation of a subjective helplessness measure. *Journal of Personality Assessment,* 1979, **43,** 461–467.

DuBois, P. H. *A history of psychological testing.* Boston: Allyn & Bacon, 1970.

Duff, F. L. Item subtlety in personality inventory scales. *Journal of Consulting Psychology,* 1965, **29,** 565–570.

Eber, H. W. *Some psychometric correlates of inmate behavior.* Unpublished manuscript, Georgia Department of Corrections, 1975.

Edwards, A. L. *Manual for the Edwards Personal Preference Schedule.* New York: Psychological Corporation, 1954.

Edwards, A. L. *Edwards Personal Preference Schedule.* New York: Psychological Corporation, 1959.

Edwards, A. L. *Edwards Personality Inventory: Manual.* Chicago: Science Research Associates, 1967.

Edwards, A. L., & Abbott, R. D. Relationships among the Edwards Personality Inventory scales, the Edwards Personal Preference Schedule, and the Personality Research Form scales. *Journal of Consulting and Clinical Psychology,* 1973, **40,** 27–32.

Eichman, W. J. (Re Minnesota Multiphasic Personality Inventory) Computerized scoring and interpreting services. In O. K. Buros (Ed.), *Seventh mental measurements yearbook.* Highland Park, N.J.: Gryphon Press, 1972.

Epstein, S. The stability of behavior: I. On predicting most of the people much of the time. *Journal of Personality and Social Psychology,* 1979, **37,** 1097–1126.

Eysenck, H. J. *Maudsley Personality Inventory.* London: University of London Press, 1959.

Eysenck, H. J., & Eysenck, S. B. G. *Eysenck Personality Inventory.* San Diego: Educational and Industrial Testing Service, 1963.

Eysenck, H. J., & Eysenck, S. B. G. *Eysenck Personality Inventory* (Rev. manual). San Diego: Educational and Industrial Testing Service, 1969.

Faschingbauer, T. R. A 166-item written short form of the group MMPI: The FAM. *Journal of Consulting and Clinical Psychology,* 1974, **42,** 645–655.

Faschingbauer, T. R., & Newmark, C. S. *Short forms of the MMPI.* Lexington, Mass.: Heath, 1978.

Fitts, W. H. *Tennessee Self Concept Scale Manual*. Nashville, Tenn.: Counselor Recordings and Tests, 1965.

Fowler, R. D., Jr. The automated MMPI. In C. S. Newmark (Ed.), *MMPI: Clinical and research trends*. New York: Praeger, 1979.

Fowler, R. D., Jr., & Athey, E. B. A cross-validation of Gilberstadt and Duker's 1-2-3-4 profile type. *Journal of Clinical Psychology*, 1971, **27**, 238–240.

Freud, S. *New introductory lectures on psychoanalysis*. New York: Norton, 1933.

Gilberstadt, H., & Duker, J. *A handbook for clinical and actuarial MMPI interpretation*. Philadelphia: W. B. Saunders, 1965.

Gilbride, T. V., & Hebert, J. Pathological characteristics of good and poor interpersonal problem-solvers among psychiatric patients. *Journal of Clinical Psychology*, 1980, **36**, 121–127.

Goldberg, L. R. The effectiveness of clinicians' judgments: The diagnosis of organic brain damage from the Bender-Gestalt Test. *Journal of Consulting Psychology*, 1959, **23**, 25–33.

Goldberg, L. R. Diagnosticians versus diagnostic signs: The diagnosis of psychosis versus neurosis from the MMPI. *Psychological Monographs*. 1965, **79** (9, Whole No. 602).

Goldberg, L. R. A historical survey of personality scales and inventories. In P. McReynolds (Ed.), *Advances in psychological assessment* (Vol. II). Palo Alto, Calif.: Science and Behavior Books, 1971.

Goldberg, L. R. Parameters of personality inventory construction and utilization: A comparison of prediction strategies and tactics. *Multivariate Behavioral Research Monographs*, 1972, **7**, No. 2.

Goldberg, L. R. Objective diagnostic tests and measures. *Annual Review of Psychology*, 1974, **25**, 343–366.

Goldberg, L. R. What if we administered the "wrong" inventory? The prediction of scores on Personality Research Form scales from those on the California Psychological Inventory, and vice versa. *Applied Psychological Measurement*, 1977, **1**, 339–354.

Goldberg, L. R., Norman, W. T., & Schwartz, E. The comparative validity of questionnaire data (16 PF scales) and objective test data (O-A battery) in predicting five peer-rating criteria. *Applied Psychological Measurement*, 1980, **4**, 183–194.

Goodstein, L. D., Crites, J. O., Heilbrun, A. B., Jr., & Rempel, P. P. The use of the California Psychological Inventory in a university counseling service. *Journal of Counseling Psychology*, 1961, **8**, 147–153.

Goodstein, L. D., & Lanyon, R. I. (Eds.). *Readings in personality assessment*. New York: Wiley, 1971.

Gough, H. G. *California Psychological Inventory manual*. Palo Alto, Calif.: Consulting Psychologists Press, 1957.

Gough, H. G. Conceptual analysis of psychological test scores and other diagnostic variables. *Journal of Abnormal Psychology*, 1965, **70**, 294–302.

Gough, H. G. An interpreter's syllabus for the California Psychological Inventory. In P. McReynolds (Ed.), *Advances in psychological assessment* (Vol. I). Palo Alto, Calif.: Science and Behavior Books, 1968.

Gough, H. G. *California Psychological Inventory* (Rev. manual). Palo Alto, Calif.: Consulting Psychologists Press, 1975.

Gough, H. G., & Heilbrun, A. B. *The Adjective Check List Manual*. Palo Alto, Calif.: Consulting Psychologists Press, 1965.

Graham, J. R. *The MMPI: A practical guide*. New York: Oxford University Press, 1977.

Grant, C., & Patton, M. A CPI comparison of engineers and managers. *Journal of Vocational Behavior*, 1981, **18**, 225–264.

Grayson, H. M. *A psychological admissions testing program and manual*. Los Angeles: Veterans Administration Center, Neuropsychological Hospital, 1951.

Green, S. B. Establishing behavioral correlates: The MMPI as a case study. *Applied Psychological Measurement*, 1982, **6**, 219–224.

Green, S. B., Burkhart, B. R., & Harrison, W. H. Personality correlates of self-report, role-playing, and in vivo measures of assertiveness. *Journal of Consulting and Clinical Psychology*, 1979, **47**, 16–24.

Greene, R. L. *The MMPI: An interpretive manual*. New York: Grune & Stratton, 1980.

Gregory, R. J., & Morris, L. M. Adjective correlates for women on the CPI scales: A replication. *Journal of Personality Assessment*, 1978, **42**, 258–264.

Guilford, J. P. *An inventory of factors STDCR*. Beverly Hills, Calif.: Sheridan Supply Co., 1940.

Guilford, J. P., & Martin, H. G. *The Guilford-Martin inventory of factors GAMIN: Manual of directions and norms*. Beverly Hills, Calif.: Sheridan Supply Co., 1943.

Guilford, J. P., & Zimmerman, W. S. *The Guilford Temperament Survey: Manual of instructions and interpretations*. Beverly Hills, Calif.: Sheridan Supply Co., 1949.

Guthrie, G. M. *A study of the personality characteristics associated with the disorders encountered by an internist*. Unpublished doctoral dissertation, University of Minnesota, 1949.

Gynther, M. D., Altman, H., & Sletten, I. W. Replicated correlates of MMPI two-point code types: The Missouri actuarial system. *Journal of Clinical Psychology*, 1973, **29**, 263–289.

Gynther, M. D., Altman, H., & Warbin, R. W. Behavioral correlates for the MMPI 4-9/9-4 code types: A case of the emperor's new clothes? *Journal of Consulting and Clinical Psychology*, 1973, **40**, 259–263. (a)

Gynther, M. D., Altman, H., & Warbin, R. W. The interpretation of uninterpretable MMPI profiles. *Journal of Consulting and Clinical Psychology*, 1973, **40**, 78–83. (b)

Gynther, M. D., Altman, H., Warbin, R. W., & Sletten, I. W. A new actuarial system for MMPI interpretation: Rationale and methodology. *Journal of Clinical Psychology*, 1972, **28**, 173–179.

Gynther, M. D., & Brilliant, P. J. The MMPI K+ profile: A reexamination. *Journal of Consulting and Clinical Psychology*, 1968, **32**, 616–617.

Gynther, M. D., Burkhart, B. R., & Hovanitz, C. Do face-valid items have more predictive validity than subtle items?: The case of the MMPI *Pd* scale. *Journal of Consulting and Clinical Psychology*, 1979, **47**, 295–300.

Gynther, M. D., & Mayer, A. D. The prediction of mental deficiency by means of the Kent-EGY. *American Journal of Mental Deficiency*, 1960, **64**, 988–990.

Hall, W. B., & MacKinnon, D. W. Personality inventory correlates of creativity among architects. *Journal of Applied Psychology*, 1969, **53**, 322–326.

Harris, J. G., Jr. Nomovalidation and idiovalidation: A quest for the true personality profile. *American Psychologist*, 1980, **35**, 729–744.

Harris, R. E., & Lingoes, J. C. *Subscales for the MMPI: An aid to profile interpretation.* Mimeographed materials, Department of Psychiatry, University of California, 1955. (Corrected version, 1968).

Hartshorne, H., & May, M. A. *Studies in deceit.* New York: Macmillan, 1928.

Hathaway, S. R. Personality inventories. In B. B. Wolman (Ed.), *Handbook of clinical psychology.* New York: McGraw-Hill, 1965.

Hathaway, S. R. Foreword to new edition. In W. G. Dahlstrom, G. S. Welsh, & L. E. Dahlstrom (Eds.), *An MMPI handbook Vol. I. Clinical interpretation* (Rev. ed.). Minneapolis: University of Minnesota Press, 1972.

Hathaway, S. R., & McKinley, J. C. A multiphasic personality schedule (Minnesota): I. Construction of the schedule. *Journal of Psychology.* 1940, **10**, 249–254.

Hathaway, S. R., & McKinley, J. C. *Manual for the Minnesota Multiphasic Personality Inventory.* New York: Psychological Corporation, 1943.

Hathaway, S. R., & McKinley, J. C. *Minnesota Multiphasic Personality Inventory: Manual* (Rev. ed.). New York: Psychological Corporation, 1951.

Hathaway, S. R., & McKinley, J. C. *Minnesota Multiphasic Personality Inventory* (Rev. manual). New York: Psychological Corporation, 1967.

Hathaway, S. R., & Meehl, P. E. *Adjective check list correlates of MMPI scores.* Unpublished materials, 1952.

Hedlund, J. L., Morgan, D. W., & Master, F. D. The Mayo Clinic automated MMPI program: Cross validation with psychiatric patients in an army hospital. *Journal of Clinical Psychology,* 1972, **28**, 505–510.

Heist, P., & Yonge, G. *Omnibus Personality Inventory manual.* New York: Psychological Corporation, 1968.

Helmes, E., & Jackson, D. N. The item factor structure of the Personality Research Form. *Applied Psychological Measurement,* 1977, **1**, 185–194.

Helmes, E., Reed, P. L., & Jackson, D. N. Desirability and frequency scale values and endorsement proportions for items of Personality Research Form E. *Psychological Reports,* 1977, **41**, 435–444.

Hoffman, H. Performance on the Personality Research Form under desirable and undesirable instructions: Personality disorders. *Psychology Reports,* 1968, **23**, 507–510.

Hoffman, H., Jackson, D. N., & Skinner, H. A. Dimensions of psychopathology among alcoholic patients. *Journal of Studies on Alcohol,* 1975, **36**, 825–837.

Hoffman, N. G., & Butcher, J. N. Clinical limitations of three Minnesota Multiphasic Personality Inventory short forms. *Journal of Consulting and Clinical Psychology,* 1975, **43**, 32–39.

Hogan, R. Personality Research Form. In O. K. Buros (Ed.), *Eighth mental measurements yearbook* (Vol. 1). Highland Park, N.J.: Gryphon Press, 1978.

Hogan, R., DeSoto, C. B., & Solano, C. Traits, tests, and personality research. *American Psychologist,* 1977, **32**, 255–264.

Holden, R. R., Helmes, E., Jackson, D. N., & Fekken, G. C. *Diagnostic efficiency of the Basic Personality Inventory.* Unpublished manuscript, University of Western Ontario, London, Canada, 1981.

Holden, R. R., & Jackson, D. N. Item subtlety and face validity in personality assessment. *Journal of Consulting and Clinical Psychology,* 1979, **47**, 459–468.

Holden, R. R., & Jackson, D. N. Subtlety, information, and faking effects in personality assessment. *Journal of Clinical Psychology*, 1981, **37**, 379–386.

Hovanitz, C., Gynther, M. D., & Marks, P. A. The prediction of paranoid behavior: Comparative validities of obvious versus subtle MMPI Paranoia (*Pa*) items. *Journal of Clinical Psychology*, in press.

Hovanitz C., Gynther, M. D., & Marks, P. A. The prediction of paranoid behavior: Comparative validities of obvious versus subtle MMPI Paranoia (*Pa*) items. *Journal of Clinical Psychology*, in press.

Howe, M. G., & Helmes, E. Validation of the 16 PF in a psychiatric setting. *Journal of Clinical Psychology*, 1980, **36**, 927–931.

Humm, D. G., & Wadsworth, G. W. The Humm-Wadsworth Temperament Scale. *American Journal of Psychiatry*, 1935, **92**, 163–200.

Jackson, D. N. *Personality Research Form manual*. Goshen, N.Y.: Research Psychologists Press, 1967.

Jackson, D. N. A sequential system for personality scale development. In C. D. Spielberger (Ed.), *Current topics in clinical and community psychology* (Vol. 2). New York: Academic Press, 1970.

Jackson, D. N. The dynamics of structured personality tests: 1971. *Psychological Review*, 1971, **78**, 229–248.

Jackson, D. N. *Orthogonal components of psychopathology: A fresh approach to measuring the constructs underlying MMPI clinical scales.* Paper presented at the annual meeting of the Society of Multivariate Experimental Psychology, Eugene, Oregon, November 1975.

Jackson, D. N., Chan, D. W., & Stricker, L. J. Implicit personality theory: Is it illusory? *Journal of Personality*, 1979, **47**, 1–10.

Jackson, D. N., & Guthrie, G. M. A multitrait-multimethod evaluation of the Personality Research Form. *Proceedings of the 76th Annual Convention, American Psychological Association*, 1968, **3**, 177–178.

Jackson, D. N. & Messick, S. *The Differential Personality Inventory.* Goshen, N.Y.: Research Psychologists Press, 1975.

Jackson, D. N., & Paunonen, S. V. Personality structure and assessment. *Annual Review of Psychology*, 1980, **31**, 503–551.

Johnston, R., & McNeal, B. F. Statistical versus clinical prediction: Length of neuropsychiatric hospital stay. *Journal of Abnormal Psychology*, 1967, **72**, 335–340.

Jones, E. E. Black-white personality differences: Another look. *Journal of Personality Assessment*, 1978, **42**, 244–252.

Karson, S., & O'Dell, J. W. *A guide to the clinical use of the 16 PF.* Champaign, Ill.: Institute for Personality and Ability Testing, 1976.

Kear-Colwell, J. J. The factor structure of the 16 PF and the Edwards Personal Preference Schedule in acute psychiatric patients. *Journal of Clinical Psychology*, 1973, **29**, 225–228.

Kelley, C. K., & King, G. D. Behavioral correlates for within-normal-limit MMPI profiles with and without elevated *K* in students at a university mental health center. *Journal of Clinical Psychology*, 1978, **34**, 695–699.

Kelley, C. K., & King, G. D. Behavioral correlates of the 2-7-8 MMPI profile type in students at a university mental health center. *Journal of Consulting and Clinical Psychology*, 1979, **47**, 679–685.

Kelly, G. A. The theory and technique of assessment. *Annual Review of Psychology*, 1958, **9**, 323–352.

Kendrick, D. C. The Kendrick battery of tests: Theoretical assumptions and clinical uses. *British Journal of Social and Clinical Psychology*, 1972. **11**, 373–386.

Kincannon, J. C. Prediction of the standard MMPI scale scores from 71 items: The Mini-Mult. *Journal of Consulting and Clinical Psychology*, 1968, **32**, 319–325.

Kleinmuntz, B. *Personality and psychological assessment*. New York: St. Martin's Press, 1982.

Klockars, A. J., & Walkup, H. R. The PRF and peer ratings. *Educational and Psychological Measurement*, 1980, **40**, 1099–1103.

Knapp, J. J. *Co-marital sex and marriage counseling: Sexually "open" marriage and related attitudes and practices of marriage counselors*. Unpublished doctoral dissertation, University of Florida, 1974.

Knudson, R. M. & Golding, S. L. Comparative validity of traditional versus S-R format inventories of interpersonal behavior. *Journal of Research in Personality*, 1974, **8**, 111–127.

Koss, M. P. Assessing psychological emergencies with the MMPI. In J. Butcher, G. Dahlstrom, M. Gynther, & W. Schofield (Eds.), *Clinical notes on the MMPI*, No. 4 Nutley, N.J.: Roche Psychiatric Service Institute, 1980.

Koss, M. P., & Butcher, J. N. A comparison of psychiatric patients' self-report with other sources of clinical information. *Journal of Research in Personality*, 1973, **7**, 225–236.

Koss, M. P., Butcher, J. N., & Hoffman, N. G. The MMPI critical items: How well do they work? *Journal of Consulting and Clinical Psychology*, 1976, **44**, 921–928.

Krug, S. E. The development of a validity scale for the Clinical Analysis Questionnaire. *Multivariate Experimental Clinical Research*, 1979, **4**, 125–131.

Krug, S. E. *Clinical Analysis Questionnaire manual*. Champaign, Ill.: Institute for Personality and Ability Testing, 1980.

Krug, S. E. *Interpreting 16 PF profile patterns*. Champaign, Ill.: Institute for Personality and Ability Testing, 1981.

Kusyszyn, I. Comparison of judgmental methods with endorsements in the assessment of personality traits. *Journal of Applied Psychology*, 1968, **52**, 227–233.

Kusyszyn, I., & Greenwood, D. E. Marlowe-Crowne defensiveness and personality scale faking. *Proceedings of the 78th Annual Convention, American Psychological Association*, 1970, **5**, 343–344.

Lachar, D. *The MMPI: Clinical assessment and automated interpretation*. Los Angeles: Western Psychological Services, 1974.

Lachar, D., Klinge, V., & Grisell, J. L. Relative accuracy of automated MMPI narratives generated from adult norm and adolescent norm profiles. *Journal of Consulting and Clinical Psychology*, 1976, **44**, 20–24.

Lachar, D., & Wrobel, T. A. Validating clinicians' hunches: Construction of a new MMPI critical item set. *Journal of Consulting and Clinical Psychology*, 1979, **47**, 277–284.

LaForge, R. A correlational study of two personality tests: The MMPI and Cattell 16 PF. *Journal of Consulting Psychology*, 1962, **26**, 402–411.

Lanyon, R. I. *Psychological screening inventory manual.* Goshen, N.Y.: Research Psychologists Press, 1973.

Lanyon, R.I., & Goodstein, L. D. *Personality assessment* (2nd ed.). New York: Wiley, 1982.

Laosa, L. M., Swartz, J. D., & Witzke, D. B. Cognitive and personality characteristics of high school students as predictors of the way they are rated by their teachers: A longitudinal study. *Journal of Educational Psychology,* 1975, **67,** 866–872.

Levin, J., & Karni, E. S. Cross-cultural structural stability of the California Psychological Inventory. *Journal of Cross-Cultural Psychology,* 1970, **1,** 253–260.

Levine, J., & Feirstein, A. Differences in test performance between brain-damaged, schizophrenic, and medical patients. *Journal of Consulting and Clinical Psychology,* 1972, **39,** 508–511.

Lewandowski, D., & Graham, J. R. Empirical correlates of frequently occurring two-point MMPI code types: A replicated study. *Journal of Consulting and Clinical Psychology,* 1972, **39,** 467–472.

Loehlin, J. C., & Nichols, R. C. *Heredity, environment, and personality: A study of 850 sets of twins.* Austin: University of Texas Press, 1976.

Lorr, M. Convergences in personality constructs measured by four inventories. *Journal of Clinical Psychology,* 1975, **31,** 182–189.

Lorr, M., & Klett, C. J. Life history differentia of five acute psychotic types. In M. Roff & D. F. Ricks (Eds.) *Life history research in psychopathology.* Minneapolis: University of Minnesota Press, 1970.

Lubin, B., Wallis, R. R., & Paine, C. Patterns of psychological test usage in the United States: 1935–1969. *Professional Psychology,* 1971, **2,** 70–74.

Marks, P. A., & Seeman, W. *The actuarial description of personality: An atlas for use with the MMPI.* Baltimore: Williams and Wilkins, 1963.

Marks, P. A., Seeman, W., & Haller, D. L. *The actuarial use of the MMPI with adolescents and adults.* Baltimore: Williams and Wilkins, 1974.

Martin, J. D., Blair, G. E., Dannenmaier, W. D., Jones, P. C., & Asako, M. Relationship of scores on the California Psychological Inventory to age. *Psychological Reports,* 1981, **49,** 151–154.

Maudal, G. R., Butcher, J. N., & Mauger, P. A. A multivariate study of personality and academic factors in college attrition. *Journal of Counseling Psychology,* 1974, **21,** 560–567.

McCall, R. J. Face validity in the *D* scale of the MMPI. *Journal of Clinical Psychology,* 1958, **14,** 77–80.

McNair, D. M. Clinical Analysis Questionnaire, Research Edition. In O. K. Buros (Ed.), *Eighth mental measurements yearbook* (Vol. 1). Highland Park, N.J.: Gryphon Press, 1978.

McReynolds, P. (Ed.). *Advances in psychological assessment* (Vol. IV). San Francisco: Jossey-Bass, 1978.

Meehl, P. E. The dynamics of "structured" personality tests. *Journal of Clinical Psychology,* 1945, **1,** 296–303.

Meehl, P. E. Wanted—a good cookbook. *American Psychologist,* 1956, **11,** 263–272.

Meehl, P. E. Reactions, reflections, projections. In J. N. Butcher (Ed.), *Objective personality assessment: Changing perspectives.* New York: Academic Press, 1972.

Meehl, P. E. Theoretical risks and tabular asterisks: Sir Karl, Sir Ronald, and the slow progress of soft psychology. *Journal of Consulting and Clinical Psychology,* 1978, **46,** 806–834.

Meehl, P. E., & Rosen, A. Antecedent probability and the efficiency of psychometric signs, patterns or cutting scores. *Psychological Bulletin,* 1955, **52,** 194–216.

Megargee, E. I. Undercontrolled and overcontrolled personality types in extreme anti-social aggression. *Psychological Monographs,* 1966, **80,** (3, Whole No. 611).

Megargee, E. I. *The California Psychological Inventory handbook.* San Francisco: Jossey-Bass, 1972.

Merrens, M. R. The relationship between personality inventory scores and self-ratings. *Journal of Social Psychology,* 1975, **97,** 139–140.

Miller, M. T. Unpublished materials. Roche Psychiatric Service Institute, Nutley, N.J., 1978.

Mills, C. J., & Bohannon, W. E. Personality characteristics of effective state police officers. *Journal of Applied Psychology,* 1980, **65,** 680–684.

Millon, T. *Modern psychopathology.* Philadelphia: Saunders, 1969.

Millon, T. *Millon Clinical Multiaxial Inventory manual.* Minneapolis: National Computer Systems, 1977.

Millon, T. *Disorders of personality: DSM III, Axis II.* New York: Wiley, 1981.

Millon, T. *Millon Clinical Multiaxial Inventory manual* (2nd ed.). Minneapolis: National Computer Systems, 1982.

Mischel, W. On the interface of cognition and personality: Beyond the person-situation debate. *American Psychologist,* 1979, **34,** 740–754.

Mitchell, J. V., Jr., & Pierce-Jones, J. A factor analysis of Gough's California Psychological Inventory. *Journal of Consulting Psychology,* 1960, **24,** 453–456.

Mungas, D. M., Trontel, E. H., Winegardner, J., Brown, D. S., Sweeney, T. M., & Walters, H. A. The Personality Research Form as a therapy outcome measure of social behavior. *Journal of Clinical Psychology,* 1979, **35,** 822–831.

Murray, H. A. *Explorations in personality.* New York: Oxford University Press, 1938.

Nerviano, V. J. Common personality patterns among alcoholic males: A multivariate study. *Journal of Consulting and Clinical Psychology,* 1976, **44,** 104–110.

Newmark, C. S., Ziff, D. R., Finch, A. J., & Kendall, P. C. Comparing the empirical validity of the standard form with two abbreviated MMPIs. *Journal of Consulting and Clinical Psychology,* 1978, **46,** 53–61.

Nichols, R. C., & Schnell, R. R. Factor scales for the California Psychological Inventory. *Journal of Consulting Psychology,* 1963, **27,** 228–235.

Norman, W. T. Psychometric considerations for a revision of the MMPI. In J. N. Butcher (Ed.), *Objective Personality assessment: Changing perspectives.* New York: Academic Press, 1972.

O'Dell, J. W. Method for detecting random answers on personality questionnaires. *Journal of Applied Psychology,* 1971, **55,** 380–383.

O'Dell, J. W., & Karson, S. Some relationships between the MMPI and 16 PF. *Journal of Clinical Psychology,* 1969, **25,** 279–283.

Othmer, E., Penick, E. C., & Powell, B. J. *Psychiatric diagnostic interview (PDI) manual.* Los Angeles: Western Psychological Services, 1981.

Overall, J. E. Associations between marital history and the nature of manifest psychopathology. *Journal of Abnormal Psychology,* 1971, **78,** 213–221.

Overall, J. E., & Gomez-Mont, F. The MMPI-168 for psychiatric screening. *Educational and Psychological Measurement,* 1974, **34,** 315–319.

Overall, J. E., & Gorham, D. R. The brief psychiatric rating scale. *Psychological Reports,* 1962, **10,** 799–812.

Overall, J. E., & Gorham, D. R. Organicity versus old age in objective and projective test performance. *Journal of Consulting and Clinical Psychology,* 1972, **39,** 98–105.

Owens, W. A., & Schoenfeldt, L. F. Toward a classification of persons. *Journal of Applied Psychology,* 1979, **65,** 569–607.

Palmer, W. H. *Actuarial MMPI interpretation: A replication and extension.* Unpublished doctoral dissertation, University of Alabama, 1970.

Pauker, J. D. Identification of MMPI profile types in a female, inpatient, psychiatric setting using the Marks and Seeman rules. *Journal of Consulting Psychology,* 1966, **30,** 90.

Penk, W. E., Robinowitz, R., Roberts, W. R., Dolan, M. P., & Atkins, H. G. MMPI differences of Hispanic-American, black, and white substance abusers. *Journal of Consulting and Clinical Psychology,* 1981, **49,** 488–490.

Pihl, R. O., & Spiers, P. Some personality differences among the multidisciplinary team. *Journal of Clinical Psychology,* 1977, **33,** 269–272.

Reitan, R. M., & Boll, T. J. Intellectual and cognitive functions in Parkinson's disease. *Journal of Consulting and Clinical Psychology,* 1971, **37,** 364–369.

Ritzema, R. J. *The effect of demographic variables on the behavioral correlates of MMPI two point code types.* Unpublished Master's thesis, Kent State University, 1974.

Rogers, M. S., & Shure, G. H. An empirical evaluation of the effect of item overlap on factorial stability. *Journal of Psychology,* 1965, **60,** 221–233.

Shostrom, E. L. *Manual for the Personal Orientation Inventory.* San Diego: Educational and Industrial Testing Service, 1966.

Shultz, T. D., Gibeau, P. J., & Barry, S. M. Utility of MMPI "cookbooks." *Journal of Clinical Psychology,* 1968, **24,** 430–433.

Simpson, R. H. The specific meanings of certain terms indicating different degrees of frequency. *Quarterly Journal of Speech,* 1944, **30,** 328–330.

Sines, J. O. Actuarial methods in personality assessment. In B. A. Maher (Ed.), *Progress in experimental personality research.* New York: Academic Press, 1966.

Skinner, H. A., & Jackson, D. N. The missing person in personnel classification: A tale of two models. *Canadian Journal of Behavioural Science,* 1977, **9,** 147–160.

Smith, C. P., & Graham, J. R. Behavioral correlates for the MMPI standard *F* scale and for a modified *F* scale for black and white psychiatric patients. *Journal of Consulting and Clinical Psychology,* 1981, **49,** 455–459.

Solomon, M. J. Dimensions of interpersonal behavior: A convergent validation within a cognitive interactionist framework. *Journal of Personality,* 1981, **49,** 15–26.

Spielberger, C. D., & Butcher, J. N. (Eds.). *Advances in personality assessment* (Vol 1). Hillsdale, N.J.: Lawrence Erlbaum, 1982.

Spitzer, R. L., & Endicott, J. DIAGNO II: Further developments in a computer program for psychiatric diagnosis. *American Journal of Psychiatry,* 1969, **125,** 12–21.

Spranger, R. *Types of Men* (Trans. by P. J. W. Pigors.) Halle: Niemeyer, 1928.

Star, B., Clark, C. G., Goetz, K. M., & O'Malia, L. *Psychosocial aspects of wife battering. Social Casework*, 1979, **60,** 479–487.

Stricker, L. J. Personality Research Form: Factor structure and response style involvement. *Journal of Consulting and Clinical Psychology*, 1974, **42,** 529–537.

Strong, E. K., Jr. A vocational interest test. *Educational Record*, 1927, **8,** 107–121.

Stroup, A. L., & Manderscheid, R. W. CPI and 16 PF second-order factor congruence. *Journal of Clinical Psychology*, 1977, **33,** 1023–1026.

Sue, S., & Sue, D. MMPI comparisons between Asian-American and non-Asian-American students utilizing a student health psychiatric clinic. *Journal of Counseling Psychology*, 1974, **21,** 423–427.

Sundberg, N. D. *Assessment of persons.* Englewood Cliffs, N.J.: Prentice-Hall, 1977.

Swenson, W. M., Pearson, J. S., & Osborne, D. *An MMPI sourcebook: Basic item, scale, and pattern data on 50,000 medical patients.* Minneapolis: University of Minnesota Press, 1973.

Taft, R. The ability to judge people. *Psychological Bulletin*, 1955, **52,** 1–23.

Thorndike, R. L. California Psychological Inventory. In O. K. Buros (Ed.), *The fifth mental measurements yearbook.* Highland Park, N.J.: Gryphon Press, 1959.

Trott, D. M., & Morf, M. E. A multimethod factor analysis of the Differential Personality Inventory, Personality Research Form, and Minnesota Multiphasic Personality Inventory. *Journal of Counseling Psychology*, 1972, **19,** 94–103.

Waid, W. M., Orne, M. T., & Wilson, S. K. Socialization, awareness, and electrodermal reponse to deception and self-disclosure. *Journal of Abnormal Psychology*, 1979, **88,** 663–666.

Walter, V. *Personal career development profile manual.* Champaign, Ill.: Institute for Personality and Ability Testing, 1979.

Ward, R. G., Cunningham, C. H., & Wakefield, J. A., Jr. Relationships between Holland's VPI and Cattell's 16 PF. *Journal of Vocational Behavior*, 1976, **8,** 307–312.

Webb, E. J., Campbell, D. T., Schwartz, R. D., & Sechrest, L. *Unobtrusive measures: Nonreactive research in the social sciences.* Chicago: Rand McNally, 1966.

Webb, J. T. *The relation of MMPI two-point codes to age, sex, and education level in a representative nationwide sample of psychiatric outpatients.* Paper presented at the Southeastern Psychological Association meetings, Louisville, Ky., April 1970.

Welsh, G. S. Factor dimensions *A* and *R.* In G. S. Welsh & W. G. Dahlstrom (Eds.), *Basic readings on the MMPI in psychology and medicine.* Minneapolis: University of Minnesota Press, 1956.

White, W. G. *A psychometric approach for adjusting selected MMPI scale scores obtained by blacks.* Unpublished doctoral dissertation, University of Missouri, 1974.

Wiener, D. N., & Harmon, L. R. *Subtle and obvious keys for the MMPI: Their development.* Advisement Bulletin No. 16, Regional Veterans Administration Office, Minneapolis, 1946.

Wiggins, J. S. Content dimensions in the MMPI. In J. N. Butcher (Ed.), *MMPI: Research developments and clinical applications.* New York: McGraw-Hill, 1969.

Wiggins, J. S. Personality Research Form. In O. K. Buros (Ed.), *Seventh mental measurements yearbook* (Vol. I). Highland Park, N.J.: Gryphon Press, 1972.

Wiggins, J. S. *Personality and prediction: Principles of personality assessment.* Reading, Mass.: Addison-Wesley, 1973.

Wilson, R. L. *A comparison of the predictive validities of subtle versus obvious MMPI Hy items: Predicting the elusive neurosis.* Unpublished Master's thesis, Auburn University, 1980.

Winder, P., O'Dell, J. W., & Karson, S. New motivational distortion scales for the 16 PF. *Journal of Personality Assessment,* 1975, **39**, 532–537.

Woodworth, R. S. *Personal Data Sheet.* Chicago: Stoelting, 1920.

Worell, J., & Worell, L. Support and opposition to the Women's Liberation Movement: Some personality and parental correlates. *Journal of Research in Personality,* 1977, **11**, 10–20.

Zuckerman, M., Tushup, R., & Finner, S. Sexual attitudes and experience: Attitude and personality correlates and changes produced by a course in sexuality. *Journal of Consulting and Clinical Psychology,* 1976, **44**, 7–19.

NOTES

1. Butcher, J. N. Personal communication, May, 1982.
2. Cattell, R. B. Personal communication, May, 1974.
3. Gough, H. G. Personal communication, February, 1982.
4. Jackson, D. N. Personal communication, May, 1982.
5. Lubin, B. Personal communication, March, 1983.
6. Millon, T. Personal communication, April, 1982.

CHAPTER 5

Behavioral Assessment

MARVIN R. GOLDFRIED

There is an instability that is inherent in any science and technology; to be successful, it must continually change and grow. This has characterized the field of personality assessment over the last 50 years, and it most certainly describes what has been going on in behavioral assessment in the past decade.

Shortly after the first edition of this volume appeared in 1976, there was a dramatic increase in the work done in the area of behavioral assessment. What was described in the earlier version of this chapter as an "emerging interest in behavioral assessment" (Goldfried, 1976, p. 281) has now become an unmistakable "body of knowledge." This growth is reflected by the numerous books on this topic (Barlow, 1981; Ciminero, Adams, & Calhoun, 1977; Cone & Hawkins, 1977; Haynes, 1978; Haynes & Wilson, 1979; Nay, 1979; Hersen & Bellack, 1976, 1981; Keefe, Kopel, & Gordon, 1978; Kendall & Hollon, 1981; Mash & Terdal, 1976, 1981; Merluzzi, Glass, & Genest, 1981), as well as by two journals devoted to behavioral assessment (*Behavioral Assessment* and *Journal of Behavioral Assessment*). Such increased interest is obviously associated with the ever-growing popularity of behavior therapy as an intervention procedure. It is generally accepted that effective clinical behavior therapy is only as good as its initial assessment, and that outcome research on behavior therapy cannot be conducted without measures of change. For reasons that will become increasingly apparent throughout the remainder of this chapter, most of the traditionally available personality assessments have relatively little utility to the behaviorally oriented clinician. Consequently, a different paradigm for assessment has had to be developed.

Exactly what is this "new" approach, and how is it different from what has traditionally been used? Which specific methods qualify as behavioral assessment procedures? How is behavioral assessment related to behavior therapy? And where does the field of behavioral assessment have to go in the future in order to establish itself firmly within the general scope of clinical psychology? The remainder of this chapter addresses these questions.

Preparation of this chapter was facilitated in part by Grant MH24327 from the National Institute of Mental Health.

THE DISTINCTION BETWEEN BEHAVIORAL
AND TRADITIONAL ASSESSMENT

The essential differences between the behavioral and traditional approaches to personality assessment are tied to the underlying assumptions that each approach adheres to in attempting to understand human functioning. Most nonbehavioral theories conceive of personality as consisting of certain relatively stable and interrelated motives, characteristics, and dynamics that underlie and are responsible for a person's overt actions. In order to understand fully why individuals behave the way they do, then, one needs to obtain a comprehensive understanding of the underlying dynamics. From this vantage point, simply to observe and tally overt behavior in various life situations is inadequate, in that the essence of personality is deeper and more inferential than what may be directly observed. Instead, the assessment frequently focuses on the structural or dynamic components assumed to make up personality structure. This may be done by means of paper-and-pencil questionnaires (see Chapter 4) or by projective tests (see Chapter 2) that presumably enhance the tendency of individuals to manifest underlying personality characteristics.

When behaviorally oriented clinicians and researchers talk about personality, they do so in a very different way. As Goldfried and Kent (1972) have observed, "personality may be construed as an intervening variable that is defined according to the likelihood of an individual manifesting certain behavioral tendencies in the variety of situations that comprise his day-to-day living" (p. 412). What this means is that personality is a more or less shorthand term summarizing how individuals interact with their social environment. An individual does not *have* a personality, but rather the concept *personality* is an abstraction one may make after assessing how a person interacts in a comprehensive sampling of situations.

In contrast to a more traditional conception of personality that focuses on such constructs as *drive, trait,* and *motive* as the basic unit of analysis to understanding personality functioning, Mischel has underscored that behavioral assessment is interested in "what a person *does* in situations rather than on inferences about what attributes he *has* more globally" (Mischel, 1968, p. 10). This viewpoint echoes the arguments made by Wendell Johnson (1946) for using operational terms in assessing and changing human behavior:

> To say that Henry is mean implies that he has some sort of inherent trait, but it tells us nothing about what Henry has done. Consequently, it fails to suggest any specific means of improving Henry. If, on the other hand, it is said that Henry snatched Billy's cap and threw it in the bonfire, the situation is rendered somewhat more clear and actually more helpful. You might never eliminate "meanness," but there are fairly definite steps to be taken in order to remove Henry's incentives or opportunities for throwing caps in bonfires. . . .
>
> What the psychiatrist has to do . . . is to get the person to tell him not what he *is* or what he *has*, but what he *does*, and the conditions under which he does it. When he stops talking about what *type* of person he *is*, what his outstanding *traits are*, and what

type of disorder he *has*—when he stops making these subject-predicate statements, and begins to use actional terms to describe his behavior and its circumstances—both he and the psychiatrist begin to see what specifically may be done in order to change both the behavior and the circumstances. [p. 220]

From within a behavioral framework, it is perhaps most useful to view an individual's personality as one would any other set of abilities or skills (see Wallace, 1967). Secretaries may show varying degrees of competence, depending on their ability to carry out various tasks, such as typing, shorthand, answering the telephone, making appointments, and so forth. Football players' abilities are determined by their effectiveness in the sum total of activities in which they are required to function. And a human being's interpersonal ability can similarly be described in reference to the various skills associated with functioning in various life situations.

In providing an abilities or skills conception of personality, it is obviously a most unwieldy task to make a statement about how an individual functions in "life situations." Rather than making generalizations about the sum total of such situations, behavioral assessors have looked for interpersonal competencies within certain classes of situations, such as those requiring assertiveness, interactions in social situations, and communication with a spouse. Considering the assessment of social skills, McFall (1982) has suggested that it would be fruitful to subclassify social situations according to their task requirements (e.g., initiating a conversation with an unfamiliar member of the opposite sex at a party), and then assess an individual's ability to handle such tasks effectively. Even after having delineated a certain class of situations, the behavioral assessor still needs to make some decision about the level of abstraction at which to evaluate an individual's skills. McFall has maintained that an appropriate level of analysis is somewhere between a global trait model (e.g., extrovert) and a molecular observation (e.g., duration of eye contact). Hence, the ability to deal with certain classes of social situations involves a number of subskills, including the accurate perception and interpretation of events, the ability to decide on what is socially appropriate in a given situation, and the capability of executing the appropriate response. By taking this more comprehensive, multisystem approach in the analysis of social skills, McFall maintains that the clinician is then in a better position to determine those faulty components of the entire system that ultimately should be the direct goal of therapeutic intervention. Many of the issues associated with the assessment and facilitation of social skills may be found in Curran and Monti (1982).

As one might expect, the different conceptions of personality associated with traditional and behavioral viewpoints have important implications for test construction. From within the more traditional framework, the nature of the situation in which the individual is functioning is of less interest in the assessment than are underlying motives, dynamics, or structural components. From within a behavioral orientation, the abilities conception of personality carries with it the implication that comprehensive and carefully sampled task requirements be reflected within one's personality measure. Thus the *content validity* of the test becomes particularly crucial, as one must obtain a representative sample of those situations in which a particular ability is likely to manifest itself. When the APA *Standards for Educational and Psychological Tests* (1974) spoke of content validity as a requirement for proficiency tests but not tests of personality, it clearly had not taken into account the behavioral approach to personality assessment.

The basic difference between traditional and behavioral assessment procedures is best reflected in a distinction originally made by Goodenough in 1949, when she drew the comparison between a *sample* and *sign* approach to the interpretation of tests. When test responses are viewed as a sample, one assumes that they parallel the way the individual is likely to behave in a nontest situation. Thus, if a person gives an aggressive response on a test, one assumes that this aggression occurs in other situations as well. When test responses are viewed as signs, an inference is made that the performance is an indirect or symbolic manifestation of some other characteristic. An example is the occurrence of Dimensionality responses on the Rorschach in which the percept is viewed as if it were being seen from a distance (e.g., "a far-off mountain"). In interpreting such responses, one typically does not conclude that the individual is in need of optometric care, but rather that the person is oriented toward critical self-examination, as if looking at himself or herself from a distance. For the most part, traditional assessment has employed a sign as opposed to a sample approach to test interpretation. In the case of behavioral assessment, only the sample approach makes sense.

Although the sample-sign distinction can help us to differentiate behavioral and traditional assessment procedures, it should be emphasized that there *are* instances in which sample approaches have been used within the context of more traditional assessment. Even in the case of the Rorschach, for example, it may be argued that the testing situation provides much the same function as a structured interview (Goldfried, Stricker, & Weiner, 1971), in that the subject's verbal and nonverbal responses to the test and the testing situation can be observed and interpreted as samples of the individual's behavior. This is clearly a legitimate interpretation, provided one's inferences regarding generalizability are made with caution. As far as the interpretation of the subject's response to the Rorschach itself is concerned, there are even scoring systems that make explicit use of the sample approach. One such system, developed by Friedman (1953), is used to assess the developmental level of perceptual organization. In the Friedman system the subject's percepts are interpreted as a sample of perceptual-cognitive behavior and are ordered along a scale of organization and integration. If one is interested in assessing where any given subject is with regard to level of perceptual organization, then a case can be made for the use of the Rorschach as one of the more direct assessment procedures. Not only does this approach make sense on an a priori basis, but it also has been found to be one of the most valid uses of the Rorschach (Goldfried et al., 1971). Exner elaborates in Chapter 2 of this volume on the approach to the Rorschach as a perceptual–cognitive, problem-solving task.

Despite the fact that some traditional assessment procedures might be interpreted along behavioral lines, behavioral assessors have preferred to develop new procedures that are more consistent with the assumptions underlying a behavioral view of personality. Goldfried and D'Zurilla (1969) have outlined certain general guidelines that may be followed for establishing the content validity of behavioral measures. In this *behavioral–analytic* model for assessing competence, an emphasis is placed not only on how an individual reacts to specific situations, but also on the way such responses are likely to be evaluated within the context of his or her particular environment. The behavioral–analytic approach to test construction involves a situational analysis, response enumeration, and response evaluation. Each of these steps is designed to produce as close a parallel as possible between what is being assessed and the ultimate criterion behaviors of interest.

In the *situational analysis*, what is required is some sort of empirical sampling of the various situations with which individuals must cope in the real-life setting. There are a number of ways in which this situational analysis may be accomplished, such as interviewing individuals who are familiar with the particular environment, self-observations of those who typically encounter these situations, and direct observations of what situations tend to occur in the setting in question.

During the *response enumeration* phase, a sampling of the possible responses to each of the frequently occurring situations derived from the situational analysis is determined. This response enumeration may be implemented by means of direct observation in naturalistic or contrived situations, via role playing, or by means of self-reports of how individuals have typically responded under such circumstances.

As with the two previous steps, the *response evaluation* phase involves an empirical rather than an a priori determination. Rather than having test constructors themselves make a decision as to how effective each response is in dealing with the situation at hand, these evaluations are obtained from significant others who typically make such effectiveness evaluations in real-life settings. These judgments may involve peers, supervisors, teachers, employers, relatives, or therapists, depending on the situations and responses of interest.

Taken as a whole, the behavioral–analytic model of assessment consists of a behaviorally oriented criterion analysis that ensures the content validity of the measure being developed. It provides both the items to be included in the measure and the criteria to be employed for scoring them. Each problematic situation or item may have associated with it an array of different responses, which can be grouped functionally according to their judged level of effectiveness. It should be emphasized that this procedure focuses primarily on the content validity of the measure, and does not specify the measurement format to be used in the ultimate sampling of the situation–response interactions. Depending upon the particular class of responses being assessed, as well as any realistic limitations imposed by the measurement setting, any one of a number of assessment methods may be used, including direct observation, role playing, self-reports, or physiological procedures. Each of these different assessment methods is described in greater detail in the section that follows.

The behavioral–analytic model was originally developed for the study of effectiveness of college freshmen (Goldfried & D'Zurilla, 1969), but has subsequently been applied to a wide variety of other content areas. These include the development of measures of social competence (Levenson & Gottman, 1978; Mullinix & Galassi, 1981); heterosocial skills (Bellack, Hersen, & Lamparski, 1979; Kulich & Conger, 1978; Perri & Richards, 1979); interpersonal skills among retarded adults (Bates, 1980); children's social skills (Edelson & Rose, 1978); skill deficits in delinquent boys (Freedman, Rosenthal, Donahoe, Schlundt, & McFall, 1978); social skills among delinquent girls (Gaffney & McFall, 1981); depression (Funabiki & Calhoun, 1979); guilt (Klass, 1982), assertiveness (MacDonald, 1974); guilt over assertion (Klass, 1980); methods of coping with chronic illness (Turk, 1979); occupational skills (Mathews, Lang, & Fawcett, 1980); and behavior management effectiveness (Bernstein, 1978).

Livingston (1977) has pointed out that in establishing the standard against which to compare any individual's performance on a behavioral measure, some of the work done in the area of educational assessment is particularly relevant. In the educational setting one is often interested in being able to determine how close any given person comes to some absolute criterion, not merely where this individual falls with regard to others. Under such circumstances the test is said to be *criterion referenced* rather than *norm referenced*. Inasmuch as behavioral assessment is often directed toward evaluating how close any given individual comes to effective functioning in a given situation, it would appear that the absolute standards associated with criterion-referenced tests would be most appropriate.

Livingston has also suggested that, unlike the traditional concept of reliability in which a test response is believed to comprise *true* score and *error* score components, generalizability theory (Cronbach, Gleser, Nada, & Rajaratnam, 1972) is particularly relevant for behavioral assessment. That is, the statement one makes about any given behavioral test score is the extent to which it can be generalized to other circumstances, be they different settings, different times, different scores, and so forth. According to Cone (1981), a behavioral conceptualization suggests the following: "Error is just a blanket way of referring to a host of 'don't knows,' none of which are random. Indeed, the term 'random' is really a pseudonym for 'haven't found out yet' from a behavioral perspective, since all behavior is lawful whether we know the precise controlling variables or not" (p. 61). This quotation reflects the microscopic approach taken by behavioral assessors in determining the variables within the individual as well as within the environment that may determine how people respond to particular situations.

One final point might be made before concluding this section. In comparing traditional and behavioral tests, the argument is not necessarily being made that behavioral assessment procedures have been found to be superior. Although indirect evidence does exist regarding the potentially greater predictive accuracy of behavioral tests (see Goldfried & Kent, 1972), few comparative prediction studies have been carried out as yet. What *is* being suggested is that the assumptions underlying behavioral assessment are fewer and more clearly delineated, and therefore more readily accessible to empirical confirmation. When the predictive efficiency of a test is less accurate than one might desire, one or more of the underlying assumptions associated with the prediction process are likely to be at fault. Not only do behavioral measures involve fewer assumptions, but also whatever assumptions do exist can more readily be tested empirically, and any necessary modifications made toward the goal of enhancing its predictive ability.

METHODS OF BEHAVIORAL ASSESSMENT

A variety of different approaches may be employed in sampling an individual's response to certain life situations. Behavioral assessment has made use of (a) direct observation in naturalistic settings, (b) the observation of responses to situations that have been contrived by the assessor, (c) responses that manifest themselves in role-playing situations, (d) the individual's own self-reports, (e) psychophysiological methods, and (f) the behavioral interview. These different approaches to assessment are discussed below, together with illustrations of actual assessment procedures that have used each methodology.

Observations in Naturalistic Settings

Consistent with the criterion-sampling orientation to behavioral assessment described in the previous section, behavioral assessors have made extensive use of direct observations in naturalistic settings. Such observations allow one to measure the various dimensions of an individual's response or an interaction (e.g., frequency, strength, pervasiveness), and they also provide a good opportunity to understand those external variables that may be currently maintaining the behavior.

Naturalistic observation is hardly an invention of behavior therapists. Psychologists, anthropologists, and sociologists have made ample use of such procedures long before the current behavioral orientation came into being. For example, Barker and Wright (1951) emphasized the importance of observing the "stream of behavior" in its appropriate ecological setting. They illustrated this approach to observation dramatically in their book *One Boy's Day*, in which they provide a detailed account of the activities of a 7-year-old boy whom observers literally followed around for an entire day. Any such attempt to observe the natural stream of behavior represents an admirable, if not staggering, undertaking, as is attested to by the fact that Barker and Wright's observational data for a single day fill an entire book.

Largely as a function of practical considerations, behaviorally oriented assessors have typically been more goal oriented in making their observations than were Barker and Wright. Thus, depending on the particular purpose of the assessment, behavioral codes are customarily devised that outline the categories of behavior to be attended to during the observation procedure. Different codes have been devised by investigators to observe behavior as it occurs in various settings, such as in schools, homes, and hospitals. These observations are typically carried out at specified periods of time and are tailored to the particular subject population being assessed. For detailed descriptions and evaluations of the current status of direct observations as used by behavioral assessors, the reader is referred to Haynes and Wilson (1979), Kazdin (1981), and Kent and Foster (1977).

One of the earliest attempts to employ behavioral observations within the school setting is described by O'Leary and Becker (1967). The main goal of their observation was to evaluate the effect of a token reinforcement program with a class consisting of disruptive children. Teams of trained observers recorded the incidence of various behavioral categories for specific time periods, typically lasting 1½ hours each. The observer sat toward the rear of the classroom and attempted to be as unobtrusive as possible. Included among the categories within the behavioral code were such actions as making disruptive noises, speaking without raising one's hand, and pushing. Based on extensive research and continual revisions, the code has been refined and updated (O'Leary & O'Leary, 1972).

An observation code has also been developed for the assessment of positively reinforcing behaviors (Bersoff & Moyer, 1973). Included among the 10 behavioral categories in this code are positive reactions (e.g., administration of concrete rewards, verbal or nonverbal praise, attention, physical contact), behaviors that presumably are neutral with respect to their reinforcement qualities (e.g., asking questions), and responses of an aversive nature (e.g., admonishment, nonverbal disapproval).

The use of behavioral observation codes involving frequency counts of various categories of behavior has provided researchers and clinicians with an invaluable approach for evaluating the effectiveness of various therapeutic intervention programs. Despite the obvious utility of such behavioral codes, one may nonetheless raise questions as to the relevance of data that they may ignore. Of particular importance is the likelihood that individuals behaving in a given way are probably reacting to some antecedent event in their environment, and that there also may be certain environmental consequences of the actions being observed.

Toward the goal of evaluating the antecedent and/or consequent occurrences that may maintain any particular behavior, Patterson, Ray, Shaw, and Cobb (1969) developed an observational code to evaluate the interaction between individuals and significant others in their environment. The observations specifically focus on predelinquent boys, particularly as they interact with members of their families within the home setting. The code essentially attempts to take the complex stream of behavior and break it down into categories focusing on various aspects of the child's behavior (e.g., yelling, talking, teasing, hitting, crying) and the way in which other members of the family react to him (e.g., positive physical contact, ignoring, disapproval). The behavioral code is utilized by trained observers who go directly to the home and record the family interactions on a time-sampling basis. Other codes have been constructed for similar evaluations of adult–child interactions in home, school, and institutional settings (e.g., Wahler, House, & Stambaugh, 1976).

A code for assessing interactions among adults has been developed by Lewinsohn and Shaffer (1971), who focused specifically on the observation of depressed individuals. Here too, observers go directly into the home and time-sample the interaction among family members at mealtime. Although the distinction at times may be difficult to make, Lewinsohn and Shaffer's code attempts to classify an individual's behavior as being either an *action* or a *reaction* to another family member's behavior. Among the class of actions are such categories as criticism, information request, statement of personal problem, and complaint. The reactions, which are presumed to have the potential of maintaining a given behavior, may be either positive or negative. Among the positive reactions are approval, laughter, and interest; the negative reactions comprise such responses as disagreement, criticism, punishment, and ignoring.

Within the context of observations in hospital settings, Paul and his associates (Mariotto & Paul, 1974; Paul & Lentz, 1977; Paul, Tobias, & Holly, 1972) developed a time-sample behavioral checklist for use with chronic psychiatric patients. Among the behaviors recorded by trained observers are such categories as verbalized delusions or hallucinations, repetitive and stereotypic movements, grimacing or frowning without apparent stimulus, physical assault, blank staring, and various other forms of inappropriate behavior. Interobserver reliability is high for this checklist, with coefficients typically in the .90s.

The use of naturalistic observation to develop *behavioral maps* has been described by Ittelson, Rivlin, and Proshansky (1970). This procedure, which was originally developed for use on a psychiatric ward, focuses both on behavior and on the physical location in which it occurs. The observer records the location, time of observation, and number and types of participants engaged in each category of behavior. The procedure offers a very valuable technique for examining the environmental influences on behavior in various kinds of settings.

Although it might appear at first blush that direct naturalistic observation is the best procedure for carrying out a behavioral assessment, there nonetheless are certain methodological problems associated with this approach. One such problem has to do with the extent to which the observers actually interfere with or influence the phenomena they are attempting to assess. This has been labeled the *reactivity* problem within behavioral observation methods. In studying this problem, Purcell and Brady (1966) attempted to determine the extent to which being monitored by a miniature wireless radio transmitter would alter the verbal behavior of a group of adolescents. The subjects were monitored one hour per day for a total of 10 successive days, and they seemed to behave more naturally after the first few days. However, the indications that their behavior became more natural were based on somewhat weak criteria, such as the decrease in the number of references made to the transmitter, the amount of talking done, and impressionistic reports of the subjects themselves.

The reactivity issue was investigated further by Moos (1968), who studied the effect of wearing a radio transmitter on a group of psychiatric patients observed both when they were and when they were not wearing the transmitter. His findings indicated that the effect of being monitored by the radio transmitter was small and occurred only among the more disturbed patients. One limitation to keep in mind in interpreting these data, however, is that what was really determined was patients' reactions to wearing a transmitter when they knew they were otherwise being observed. In other words, there was no "pure" measure of the patients' behavioral tendencies. The same interpretative limitation applies in a study by Johnson and Bolstad (1974), who found that tape-recorded family interactions were no different when observers were present than when they were absent.

The procedure of observing individuals without their knowledge is ethically questionable; in addition, the possibility of reactivity remains a methodological issue to which behavioral assessors must attend. Thus, observers are usually instructed to remain as unobtrusive as possible—to "become part of the furniture." One should also allow for a period of acclimation, to let subjects become accustomed to the presence of observers, and this initial period of observation should not be used as part of the actual baseline against which any behavior change is compared.

Another methodological problem in the use of direct observations involves potential biases due to the observer's expectations. The question here is whether any initial hypotheses or expectations regarding what is "supposed to be seen" can influence the observation process itself. Some data by Kent, O'Leary, Diament, and Dietz (1974) suggest that, to the extent to which one uses a behaviorally anchored observational code, biases resulting from differential expectancy can be kept to a minimum. They experimentally manipulated observers' expectations regarding the type of change likely to occur (i.e., a decrease versus no change in disruptive behavior). In reality, both groups of observers viewed the same videotapes, which in fact showed no change in the frequency of disruptive behavior from baseline to treatment phase. The study did not find any differences in the *use of the behavioral code* as a function of differential expectations; in contrast, the overall, more *impressionistic judgments* of change in the two conditions were significantly influenced by initial expectations. The influence on global impression is particularly striking, especially since these observers had just completed carrying out concrete and detailed observations providing information contrary to their overall impressions. A follow-up study by O'Leary, Kent, and Kanowitz (1975) found that it *was* possible to influence observers in the use of the concrete behavioral code, provided the experimenter gave them differential feedback in the "expected" direction each time they handed in their observations.

In dealing with the expectancy issue, then, every attempt should be made to have the behavioral categories be as concrete and operationally defined as possible. Observers should not be informed of the changes expected and, if possible, they should be kept "blind" as to experimental or therapeutic manipulations applied to the individuals being observed. Further, the observational data should not be inspected in any detail while the study is under way, so as to avoid any inadvertent reinforcement for what the observer has recorded.

A related methodological problem is the extent to which independent observers can reliably utilize a given behavioral code. Although it seems evident that potential sources of unreliability are reduced when one utilizes a coding system focusing on specific behaviors, it should also be pointed out that most behavioral codes nonetheless require a certain amount of interpretation. For example, if one is attempting to observe how often a child in a classroom is engaging in off-task behavior (e.g., not doing work), some problems of interpretation may arise. Such a category represents a class of behaviors into which a wide variety of specific behaviors may fall. Hence the observer needs to be familiar with potential specific behaviors that would be scored in this category, and to be able to differentiate them from on-task behaviors. There are times, however, when a judgment about a specific behavior may be very difficult to make (e.g., toying with a pencil during an arithmetic assignment). For each particular observational code, the specificity of guidelines for resolving such ambiguities can have substantial bearing on observer reliability.

A typical finding reported for behavioral observational codes has been that interobserver reliability is in fact very good. But what has emerged in looking at this issue more closely is that a kind of reactivity exists when observers realize that *their* behavior is being observed. This effect was dramatically demonstrated in a study by Reid (1970), who found that, in comparison to a reliability coefficient of .76 when observers thought their reliability was being evaluated, there was a sharp drop to a coefficient of .51 once the raters felt they were completely on their own. Romanczyk, Kent, Diament, and O'Leary (1973) confirmed Reid's results and additionally found that interobserver agreement could be increased further by providing the raters with information as to exactly who was going to be checking their reliability. In other words, it was possible for the observers to modify their interpretation of the code so as to be more consistent with the criteria employed by the specific person doing the reliability check.

Another potential source of unreliability that sometimes goes unnoticed is the *drift* problem (O'Leary & Kent, 1973). A typical procedure in the application of behavioral codes involves the use of teams of observers. Following the observation periods, the teams often have the opportunity to compare their observations more closely and discuss among themselves any potential sources of unreliability. As a result of the team members' collaboration, various ambiguities in the use of code are clarified. Although this at first does not seem to be an undesirable practice, the problem arises when each team begins to develop its own idiosyncratic interpretation of the code. This is not readily apparent, since the reliability checks made among pairs of observers lead one to conclude that interobserver agreement is good. However, even though teams of observers are in fact reliably applying the behavioral code, they may drift away from each other with regard to what they are actually observing. To the extent that such drift occurs, the different teams of observers are unwittingly utilizing somewhat different behavioral codes.

As in the case of the expectancy problem, unreliability among observers may be kept to a minimum by clarifying any ambiguities inherent in the behavioral code. Further, a more extensive training period can be utilized, the reliability of observers can be constantly monitored, and teams of observers can be continually rotated so as to avoid any potential drift.

Still another issue in the use of behavior observations in naturalistic settings is that of the representativeness of the behaviors sampled. In the case of the time-sample behavioral checklist developed by Paul and his colleagues for use with psychiatric patients (Paul & Lentz, 1977; Paul et al., 1972), this is not too much of a problem, since the observations are carried out for 2-second intervals during each of the patients' waking hours. The sampling issue does come into play, however, with codes in which the observations are made only during certain times and places. The question becomes the legitimacy of generalizing from what is observed to some larger class of behaviors or interactions. As yet, few research efforts have been directed toward this most important issue.

One final point might be made in this discussion of observations in naturalistic settings. From a practical point of view, it may not always be feasible to have trained observers readily available. In fact, much of what has been described thus far is more likely to be carried out within the context of a research program than in routine clinical work. The reason for this should be obvious: The systematic implementation of many of these observation procedures can be very costly. As a practical compromise, behavioral observations have been carried out by individuals typically present in the subject's naturalistic environment, such as friends, spouses, parents, teachers, nurses, and other significant individuals. Although their observations are not likely to be as detailed or precise as those of more highly trained observers, there is a definite advantage in obtaining information from individuals who have occasion to view the subject over relatively long periods of time, in a wide variety of situations, and with minimal likelihood of reactivity. An example of this procedure involves the Spouse Observation Checklist (Patterson, 1976; Weiss & Perry, 1979), which contains a long list of daily spouse behaviors that are likely to be either pleasing or displeasing. Other checklists that have been employed are those that utilize the observations of psychiatric nurses (Honigfeld, Gillis, & Klett, 1966), classmates (Wiggins & Winder, 1961), and teachers (Ross, Lacey, & Parton, 1965).

Situation Tests

A basic limitation associated with observations in naturalistic settings is that one typically has little control over the situation to which the subject or client must respond. Although every attempt is made to standardize the setting in which the observation is to take place—such as carrying out home observations during dinnertime—little can be done to control exactly what goes on during this time and place. Thus, depending on what may be said or done to individuals being observed, their behavior can vary greatly. As a way of circumventing these shortcomings, behavioral assessors have made use of various situation tests.

Situation tests have been used for assessment purposes in the past (e.g., OSS Assessment Staff, 1948), but their goal has typically been to draw conclusions about an individual's more general personality traits. By contrast, behavioral assessors present subjects with situations likely to elicit the type of behavior toward which the assessment is specifically directed. Not only is the individual's behavior objectively observed in such situations but, whenever relevant, subjective and physiological measures of anxiety are employed as well.

One frequently employed situation test was devised by Paul (1966) in conjunction with an outcome study on the effectiveness of systematic desensitization in treating speech anxiety. The situation test that was used as a measure of improvement required subjects to present a 4-minute speech before a live audience. Immediately before giving the talk, they were administered self-report and physiological measures of anxiety. During the speech itself, trained observers in the audience recorded various overt signs of anxiety, such as extraneous hand movements, hand tremors, pacing, and absence of eye contact. This type of situation test has proved useful in a variety of other clinical outcome studies (e.g., Goldfried & Trier, 1974; Meichenbaum, Gilmore, & Fedoravicius, 1971).

Situation tests have also been employed for the assessment of interpersonal anxiety (e.g., Borkovec, Fleischmann, & Caputo, 1973; Borkovec, Stone, O'Brien, & Kaloupek, 1974; Kanter & Goldfried, 1979). In these assessments the subject is required to maintain a brief conversation with one or two trained confederates, the interaction is videotaped, and the subject's performance is evaluated in terms of behavioral, subjective report, and physiological indices of anxiety. Research on this procedure has demonstrated that the interaction situation is capable of eliciting emotional arousal in individuals for whom interpersonal anxiety is a problem.

Numerous attempts have been made to assess assertive behavior by means of unobtrusive situation tests (Kazdin, 1974, McFall & Lillesand, 1971; McFall & Marston, 1970; McFall & Twentyman, 1973). Subjects are called on the telephone, and some unreasonable request is made of them. This request, which varies from study to study, entails either purchasing a subscription to several magazines or lending one's lecture notes immediately prior to a final examination. The subject's response is unobtrusively recorded and later evaluated by judges for its assertiveness. In most of these studies, however, the assessment procedure has failed to discriminate between individuals who were otherwise found to have changed as a function of assertion training.

Although it is certainly possible that the inability to obtain positive results is due to the failure to sample adequately from situations in which subjects actually achieved behavior change, positive results found by McFall and Twentyman (1973) suggest that the methodology may have been at fault. Instead of making a single unreasonable request during the telephone conversation, they presented subjects with a series of seven increasingly unreasonable requests. The telephone calls were made less than a week before a scheduled final examination, and the caller began by simply asking subjects to spend a few minutes discussing the lecture material. Subjects were then confronted with a series of more and more outlandish requests, which culminated in the request that they lend out their lecture notes for 2 full days prior to the examination. By extending the nature of the interaction in this manner. the assessment procedure was found to be more sensitive in detecting changes resulting from assertion training.

Linehan, Goldfried, and Goldfried (1979) successfully used an unobtrusive situation test to evaluate the results of an assertion training program. Participants were brought into a room to fill out a questionnaire and were informed that they were to complete it even though an individual in the room might interfere with their doing so. Because of ethical considerations that required participants to know the purpose of the assessment, the procedure was actually only quasi-obtrusive in nature. However, they were not told about the specific ways the other person would intrude, and every attempt was made to embed the interference within an ongoing social interaction. For example, the confederate told subjects that she had a friend who was participating in an assertion training program and found the whole topic to be very interesting. This led into a discussion of the questionnaire the subject was filling out, at which point the confederate asked, "Can I look at the questionnaire for a few minutes?" If the subject refused, the confederate came back with, "I'm really interested in having a look at it." If the subject again refused, the confederate persisted, for a total of five times. Six such interferences were embedded into the interaction, and the measure as a whole was found to be a sensitive indicator of the results of assertiveness training.

For the measurement of interpersonal skills, Goldsmith and McFall (1975) used an unobtrusive interaction to evaluate the results of a social skills training program. Participants were told that they were to interact with a stranger, who was actually a trained confederate. Although participants were instructed to initiate the conversation, ask this person to lunch, and end the conversation after 10 minutes, there were three unobtrusive *critical moments* built into the interaction. Specifically, the confederates did not catch the participants' name when introduced, gave ambiguous replies to the lunch invitation, and asked them to say something about themselves.

Another area in which situation tests have been used is the evaluation of marital interactions. As these tests are typically conducted, a couple is instructed to discuss uninterruptedly a conflict area in their marriage for approximately 10 minutes. Different coding systems have been developed to evaluate such problem-solving interactions. For example, Hops, Wills, Patterson, and Weiss (1972) developed a code that summarized six categories of interaction: problem solving, verbal positive, nonverbal positive, nonverbal negative, verbal negative, and neutral. A system has also been developed by Gottman (1974) that codes three aspects of each verbal message: the content (e.g., statements of opinion, problem-solving statements, feedback statements, commands, questions); the affective component (positive, negative or neutral); and the implications for the relationship (e.g., puts partner down, puts self down, puts partner up, puts self up). A later code developed by Gottman and his associates (Gottman, Notarius, Markman, Bank, Yoppi, & Rubin, (1976) for evaluating a couple's communication involves eight content codes (agreement, disagreement, communication talk, mind reading, proposing a solution, summarizing other, summarizing self, and problem information or feeling) and includes separate positive, negative, and neutral affect scorings. These codes have been developed specifically for use in ongoing research programs on marital counseling.

Situation tests have also been employed to observe how parents interact with their children. This is frequently done behind a one-way mirror, with the situation constructed in such a way as to sample the type of instances in which the child's problematic behaviors typically occur. For example, if the child's primary problem consists of having difficulty in working independently, one might set up a section of the room where he or she is asked to carry out various homework problems while the mother is involved in some other task in another section of the room. The behavior of both parent and child can then be observed to provide data useful for a functional analysis of the child's difficulties.

This observation procedure is nicely illustrated in a study by Wahler, Winkel, Peterson, and Morrison (1965), in which a mother and her son were observed in a playroom located behind a one-way mirror. The child's primary difficulty was that he was overly demanding, as manifested by such statements as "You go over there, and I'll stay here," "Now we'll play this," and "No, that's wrong! Do it this way!" Following a baseline period, the mother was told to reinforce cooperative statements positively and to ignore any demanding statements. Depending on the child's actual behavior, the observer would signal the mother by means of lights present in the playroom. As a result of such differential reinforcement, dramatic decreases were observed in the child's behavior. Not only does this approach demonstrate the way in which a situation test may be contrived so as to depict a typical parent–child interaction, but it also illustrates the very close interplay between behavioral assessment and behavior therapy.

An unobtrusive situation test for the assessment of alcohol consumption was independently developed by Marlatt, Demming, and Reid (1973) and Miller and Hersen (1972). The situation is presented to subjects in the form of a taste-rating task, and subjects are seated at a table on which there are a number of glasses containing either alcoholic or nonalcoholic beverages. The purpose of the task is presumably to have individuals rate each of the beverages on various dimensions (e.g., sweet–sour, strong–weak). Subjects are told that they may drink as much as they need in order to carry out the ratings. Unbeknownst to the subjects, their sip rate is being monitored, as is the total amount of alcoholic beverages consumed. This assessment procedure has been used to study the effect of different variables on alcohol consumption and also as an outcome measure following therapeutic intervention.

The final example of a situation test to be discussed represents one of the more frequently used behavioral assessment procedures. The assessment procedure is the Behavioral Avoidance Test (BAT), which is used as a means of evaluating the strength of fears and phobias. Although the exact procedures have varied somewhat from study to study (see Nietzel & Bernstein, 1981), the test basically requires that the individual enter a room in which the feared object is present (e.g., a snake in a cage), walk closer to the object, look at it, touch it, and if possible hold it. In addition to evaluating how close the subject is willing to come to the object, the procedure allows subjective, physiological, and overt behavioral indices of anxiety to be assessed. In addition to various small-animal phobias (e.g., snakes, rats, spiders, dogs), more clinically relevant fears have been assessed by means of the BAT, such as fears of enclosed places and heights.

Unlike the aims of situation tests that are unobtrusive in nature, the purpose of the BAT is readily apparent, and research has found that subjects' perception of the demand characteristics of the assessment can greatly influence the extent to which they will approach the feared object or stay in the phobic situation. A study by Miller and Bernstein (1972), for example, divided a group of claustrophobic subjects into two experimental conditions, after which they were individually put in a small dark chamber. Under a low-demand condition subjects were told that they could leave the room at any point by simply signaling, whereas under a high-demand condition they were encouraged to stay in the room regardless of how anxious they might be. Following this experimental procedure, the conditions were reversed, so that subjects who were initially in a low-demand group were now in a high-demand group, and vice versa. The findings clearly demonstrated the very powerful effect the demand characteristic instructions had on the subjects' behavior, in that subjects under low-demand instructions behaved more phobically than those under the high-demand condition. This was true when a comparison was made between groups of subjects and also when the instructions were changed for each subject individually. A second finding of some interest was that the experimental instructions, although they had a clear effect on the subjects' behavior, had no impact on their anxiety reactions as measured by either subjective report or physiological measures.

Further investigation of the effect of demand characteristics in using the BAT has similarly revealed that changing the subjects' perception of the task requirements can significantly influence their willingness to approach caged rats (Smith, Diener, & Beaman, 1974) and snakes (Bernstein & Neitzel, 1973). The Smith et al. study additionally confirmed the finding noted by Miller and Bernstein (1972) that, although the demand characteristics of the situation can significantly alter approach behavior, they have relatively little impact on subjective and physiological indices of anxiety.

In evaluating the BAT in light of the research findings on demand characteristics, as well as with the hindsight that the early users of this assessment procedure obviously did not have, it is not at all surprising to expect subjects to have their approach behavior influenced by factors unrelated to their actual phobia. All of us are aware of instances in which otherwise fearful individuals have been able to do things "on a dare," or in which people have displayed unusual acts of courage despite the high level of anxiety they might have been experiencing at the time.

The nature of the demand characteristics one chooses to convey in administering the BAT should probably vary as a function of the experimenter's or clinician's purpose for the assessment. If one wishes to screen out all but the most phobic of individuals, then the demand characteristics for approaching the feared objects should be set as high as possible. If, however, one wishes to predict how the individual is likely to respond in the more naturalistic context—such as when one is out in the woods and notices a snake climbing down a tree—then the BAT should be contrived so as to parallel more accurately the real-life situation. The exact way in which this parallel may be implemented and validated constitutes a challenge to the ingenuity of behavioral assessors.

One of the problems associated with the assessment of phobic behavior is that it comprises an operant as well as a respondent, which means that it can be influenced at times by external contingencies. The fact that demand characteristics are not necessarily an issue in all situation tests in which the purpose of the assessment is obvious, however, is illustrated in a study by Borkovec, Stone, O'Brien, and Kaloupek (1974). Borkovec et al. found that instructions to behave "in a relaxed, nonanxious manner" had no influence on subjects' performances in a situation test of heterosexual anxiety. In comparison with the assessment of phobic behavior, this situation test focused solely on anxiety, as measured by self-report, behavioral signs, and physiological indices. In all likelihood, the potential influence of demand characteristics on situation tests probably depends on the extent to which the behavior being measured is under the subject's voluntary control.

Role Playing

Whereas situation tests place individuals in real-life circumstances in which they must respond, role playing emphasizes that the subject react "as if" the event were really occurring. Although the line between the two at times may be a fine one, it is probably wise to maintain this distinction until it has been demonstrated empirically that the differences between the two procedures are nonfunctional.

The use of role playing for assessment purposes was described many years ago in a report by Rotter and Wickens (1948), whose stated rationale for the procedure is quite consistent with a behavioral orientation to assessment. They suggested that sampling behavioral interactions has considerable potential for providing the assessor with useful information, primarily because of the extent to which it parallels criterion behavior. Another early use of role playing as an assessment device is reported in a study by Stanton and Litwak (1955), who provided validity data of a most encouraging sort. Using foster parents and college students as their subject populations, they attempted to assess interpersonal competence. Highly significant correlations were found between competency ratings of the subjects' behavior during role-playing situations and evaluations of them obtained from individuals who knew them well. For the foster parents a correlation of .82 was found with social workers' ratings; in the case of students, friends' ratings correlated .93 with the scores obtained from the role-playing assessment. When the role playing was compared with an assessment based on 12 hours of intensive interviews, the role playing was found to fare considerably better in matching the ratings of well-acquainted individuals.

In more recent years role playing has gained in popularity among behavioral assessors as a means of evaluating the effectiveness of various therapeutic procedures. One of the initial uses of role playing in this context is described by Rehm and Marston (1968), who developed a procedure for assessing heterosexual anxiety in males. In an attempt to standardize the procedure and make it more feasible, a series of 10 social situations was presented orally on audiotape. Each situation begins with a description of the context (e.g., the narrator describes a scene in the college cafeteria in which the subject is walking out, and a female says, "I think you left this book"). For each of these situations subjects are asked to imagine that it is actually occurring to them at the moment and to respond as they would in real life. The response is recorded on a separate tape recorder and evaluated later for such characteristics as anxiety, adequacy of response, length of response, and delay before responding. In comparison to subjects not volunteering for a therapy program focusing on heterosexual anxiety, role-playing scores for those participating in the clinical research were found by Rehm and Marston to be significantly different. Performance on the role-playing assessment was furthermore found to change as a function of the therapeutic intervention. Performance on this measure has also been found to correlate well with peer ratings of heterosocial skills (Lavin & Kupke, 1980).

A role-playing assessment procedure similar to that used by Rehm and Marston was investigated by Arkowitz, Lichtenstein, McGovern, and Hines (1975), who compared the performance of high versus low socially competent males as determined independently on the basis of their frequency of dating and their subjective comfort, social skills, and general satisfaction in their heterosexual behaviors. Two role-playing situations were studied, one conducted *in vivo* with a female confederate and the other involving a role-played telephone conversation. In the face-to-face situation subjects were asked to imagine that they had just met this female and were attempting to get to know her better. In the telephone conversation the subject was instructed to ask the female confederate for a date. The primary finding was that the low socially competent individuals displayed a lower rate of verbal activity than the high socially competent subjects in each of these role-played situations.

In a comprehensive program designed to assess and facilitate interpersonal skills among psychiatric inpatients, Goldsmith and McFall (1975) employed the behavioral–analytic model (Goldfried & D'Zurilla, 1969) in developing a role-playing assessment procedure. Twenty-five separate situations were sampled from various aspects of the patients' typical day-to-day interactions, each of which was then presented to them on audiotape with instructions to respond as they would in a real-life situation. The subjects' responses to each situation were rated on the basis of certain predetermined and reliably applied criteria for interpersonal effectiveness. Goldsmith and McFall found that, as a result of a behavior training program designed to facilitate interpersonal skills, scores of these patients on the role-playing assessment procedures showed significant improvement. No change was found for control subjects who had been assigned to attention-placebo or no-contact conditions. Also using the format of a response to a tape-recorded situation and the behavioral–analytic model for sampling the situations in questions, role-playing procedures have been developed for the assessment of heterosocial skills in male college students (Perri & Richards, 1979), social skills to differentiate delinquent from nondelinquent adolescent boys (Freedman, et al., 1978), and social skills among delinquent and nondelinquent adolescent girls (Gaffney & McFall, 1981).

Another related problem area that has been assessed by means of role-playing procedures has involved assertive behavior. The initial work in this area was reported by McFall and Marston (1970), who sampled several situations representative of instances in which college students might be required to assert themselves. These included such situations as being interrupted by a friend while attempting to study, having one's laundry lost by the cleaners, and being asked to work by an employer at a time that would be inconvenient. Following the methodology originally devised by Rehm and Marston (1968), the situations were presented to subjects on audiotapes, and their responses were recorded on a second tape recorder. In this particular study the subjects' responses were not scored; instead, independent judges carried out a paired comparison between subjects' behavior before and after assertion training. These judges' ratings, which were completely blind as to which interaction was obtained before and which after therapy, revealed significant improvement in role-played assertive behavior.

A later report by McFall and Lillesand (1971) indicated that, when assertiveness was rated on the basis of a 5-point scale, interrater reliability was in the .90s. McFall and Lillesand also report some experimentation with a modification of the role-played assessment procedure. Rather than presenting the situation and asking subjects to give their typical response, they extended the interaction so as to parallel more closely what might occur in a real-life situation. Specifically, if subjects were successful in refusing the unreasonable request, the taped confederate would press them further for a total of five "pushes." This variation in the assessment procedure also revealed changes reflecting the effects of assertion training. Linehan et al. (1979) used this extended interaction format for evaluating the effects of an assertion training program for women in which a live rather than taped confederate was used. Galassi and Galassi (1976) compared various formats for assessing assertiveness and found that, although single-response and extended interaction procedures did not differ in the content of the response given, the latter method tended to yield shorter responses. They also found that subjects were more anxious when confronted with a live than with a taped confederate.

In commenting on the limitations of the extended interaction role-play test, McFall (1977) points out that although it is possible to write a confederate's script for all "pushes," this can be done only if the focus of the interaction remains with a given topic. Whatever potential advantage the extended interaction provides over the single-response format, it cannot evaluate how an individual will react in more complex interactions. In order to assess the individual's response in such naturalistic settings, and at the same time retain a certain amount of methodological standardization, McFall suggests the use of unobtrusive situation tests.

A series of studies on the role-playing assessment of assertive behavior within a population of psychiatric patients has been carried out by Eisler and his associates (Eisler, Hersen, & Agras, 1973a; Eisler, Hersen, & Agras, 1973b; Eisler, Hersen, & Miller, 1973; Eisler, Miller, & Hersen, 1973; Hersen, Eisler, Miller, Johnson, & Pinkston, 1973). The role-playing assessment procedure consisted of 14 situations in which a male psychiatric patient was required to interact with a female confederate in such situational impositions as having someone cut ahead in line, having one's reserved seat taken at a ball game, having a steak delivered overcooked at a restaurant, and having a service station carry out extensive repairs on one's car without previous approval. Unlike most role-playing measures of assertive training, the Eisler interaction is carried out in vivo, and the ratings of assertiveness are based on videotape recordings of the interaction. The reliability is generally high for both an overall rating of assertiveness and ratings of several behavioral components. Among those components that have been found to improve as a result of assertion training are duration of reply, affective quality of response, loudness of response, and content of assertive reply (Eisler, Hersen, & Miller, 1973).

The question of demand characteristics is an issue in the use of role-playing assessment. Are subjects truly "in role" during the assessment procedure, or are they somehow responding to some unique aspects of the demand characteristics

within the assessment setting? In a methodological study of the effects of instructions on a role-playing measure of assertiveness, Westefield, Galassi, and Galassi
(1980) found that they could influence subjects' performance by noting that the
situations required an assertive response, specifying the characteristics of assertive
behavior, and urging subjects to respond as assertively as they could. Inasmuch as
role-play assessment procedures are not standardized among those who use them, it
is possible that these and perhaps even other potentially important variables may
make it difficult to interpret findings from study to study.

The validity of role-playing assessment procedures has recently received more
attention. Although successful in distinguishing among different groups, being consistent with ratings of others who know the subjects well, and being sensitive to
changes as a result of intervention, correlations between role-play tests and external
criteria are not always as high as one would like (Bellack, Hersen, & Lamparski,
1979; Bellack, Hersen, & Turner, 1978; van Hasselt, Hersen, & Bellack, 1981).
Individual differences have also been found in using role playing to assess social
skills, in that validity has been obtained more for females than for males (Bellack et
al., 1979). In each of these studies the external criterion was obtained after the role-
playing assessment, thereby indicating that it is the predictive ability of role-playing
procedures that leaves something to be desired. However, in instances in which
individuals are asked to role-play how they have actually behaved in certain kinds of
situations—information that is useful within an actual clinical setting—validity coefficients with external, unobtrusive measures of interpersonal skills have been
found to be favorable (Kern, 1982).

Self-Report

In using self-report procedures, behavioral assessors have focused on the report of
specific behavioral interactions, on subjective reports of emotions, perceptions of
environmental settings, and self-reports of cognitions. Each of these areas of assessment is dealt with below, as is the general procedure of self-monitoring.

Self-Report of Overt Behavior.   A behavioral characteristic that has been the focus
of several self-report measures of overt behavior is assertiveness. For example,
Wolpe and Lazarus (1966) describe a series of 30 questions that they recommend be
asked of clients in assessing the extent to which they may be inhibited in expressing
their opinion in interpersonal situations. More recent questionnaires have been
reported by Rathus (1973), Gallassi, DeLo, Galassi, and Bastien (1974), Gay,
Hollandsworth, and Galassi (1975), and Gambrill and Richey (1975). These questionnaires either drew from the items outlined by Wolpe and Lazarus, obtained
items on a somewhat unsystematic basis from clients or college students, or constructed items on an a priori basis. They are consequently limited in failing to deal
with the content validity issue that is essential in the development of behavioral
assessment procedures. These inventories assume the general trait of assertiveness,
and no subscales reflecting different aspects of one's interactions (e.g., with
friends, strangers, authority figures) are available.

A more sophisticated approach to the development of a measure of assertiveness appears in the work of McFall and Lillesand (1971), who focused specifically on the ability of college students to refuse unreasonable requests. Their Conflict Resolution Inventory consists of 35 items, each of which is specific to a particular situation involving some unreasonable request (e.g., "You are in the thick of studying for exams when a person whom you know only slightly comes into your room and says, 'I'm tired of studying. Mind if I come in and take a break for awhile?' "). For each item subjects are to indicate how likely they would be to refuse the request and how comfortable they would feel about either refusing or giving in. Unlike the developers of the other assertiveness questionnaires described above, McFall and Lillesand derived their items empirically on the basis of extensive pilot work, in which the sample of college students used in generating the initial item pool was similar to the subject population to which the assessment measure was later to be applied. The Conflict Resolution Inventory has proved useful as a dependent variable in clinical outcome studies (McFall & Lillesand, 1971; McFall & Twentyman, 1973), in which change has been found to occur as a function of assertion training.

A self-report measure of interpersonal skills for use with a general adult population described by Trower, Bryant, and Argyle (1978) entails self-ratings of both the difficulty and frequency of occurrence of various social situations. Using the behavioral–analytic model to ensure content validity (Goldfried & D'Zurilla, 1969), Goldsmith and McFall (1975) developed a 55-item multiple-choice questionnaire to determine how effectively psychiatric patients could deal with certain social situations. Questionnaires have also been developed to measure initiation in versus avoidance of situations related to dating, applicable to both a male (Twentyman & McFall, 1975) and female college population (Williams & Ciminero, 1978). Levenson and Gottman (1978) report on the successful use of a self-report measure of college student social competence that comprises dating and assertion subscales.

A paper-and-pencil measure for assessing academic behavior is the Survey of Study Habits and Attitudes (Brown & Holtzman, 1966). As this title suggests, two subscales are available: Study Habits which reflects behavioral tendencies associated with effective academic work, and Study Attitudes, which reflects opinions and beliefs about academic matters. Validity data on this measure are encouraging and include demonstrated ability of the Study Habits score to predict peer ratings of college freshmen effectiveness in dealing with academic work (Goldfried & D'Zurilla, 1973).

Self-Report of Emotion.   Although the assessment of overt behavior—whether via self-reports of behavior, naturalistic observation, situation tests, or role playing—holds considerable promise, there is more to human functioning than a person's outward behavior can reveal. In fact, several reports indicate that even when demand characteristics influence an individual's performance on a behavioral avoidance test, subjective reports of anxiety remain unaffected (Miller & Bernstein, 1972; Smith et al., 1974). Furthermore, there are instances, as in an outcome study on acrophobia reported by Jacks (1972), in which subjective reports of anxiety may be more sensitive to differential change than is approach behavior.

A measure frequently used by behavioral assessors in the self-report of anxiety is the Fear Survey Schedule (Geer, 1965). The schedule consists of a series of 51 potentially anxiety-arousing situations and objects (e.g., snakes, being alone, looking foolish), which subjects are asked to rate for the degree of fear typically elicited by them. The schedule is at best a gross screening device and should probably be viewed as nothing more than that. Although some researchers have attempted to carry out extensive factor analyses of the schedule to determine the potential dimensions of fear, such research activities are of dubious value, especially as no attempt had originally been made to sample representatively the full range of fears and phobias typically present in most individuals' lives.

Although several attempts have been made to use the Fear Survey Schedule to predict subjects' reactions to a behavioral avoidance task, the data on its predictive efficiency have been mixed. In viewing these conflicting findings, Goldfried and Sprafkin (1974) have pointed out that it is important to keep in mind that these two measures of fear are of very different forms; one is primarily verbal and the other more behaviorally observable. Moreover, these two measures appear to be focusing on different aspects of anxiety. The Fear Survey Schedule asks subjects to state how afraid they would feel when in the presence of certain situations or objects. When subjects are placed in the behavioral avoidance task, the primary measure consists of the extent to which they will approach the fearful object. As noted earlier, there are often situations in which the demand characteristics or task requirements are such that individuals, despite their feelings of fear and trepidation, will approach a fearful object or remain in anxiety-producing circumstances.

Whatever assets the Fear Survey Schedule may have as a relatively quick and easily administered screening device, there are nonetheless certain limitations that severely restrict its utility. Perhaps the most telling of these is the fact that subjects are required to indicate their degree of fear about situations or objects that are described in only general and very vague terms (e.g., being criticized). The specific nature of the situation (e.g., who is doing the criticizing, what the criticism is about) is left unspecified. Furthermore, the nature of the person's anxiety response (e.g., sweaty palms, increased heart rate, desire to run away) is not assessed by the questionnaire.

A commonly used self-report measure of anxiety that takes into account the nature of the situation, as well as each of the possible components of the anxiety response, is described by Endler, Hunt, and Rosenstein (1962). Their assessment procedure, called the S-R Inventory of Anxiousness, consists of a series of potentially anxiety-arousing situations that are briefly described in writing, after which there is a series of rating scales reflecting varying ways in which a person might become anxious. For example, one such situation is "You are about to take an important final examination," for which subjects are asked to indicate the extent to which their "heart beats faster," they "get an uneasy feeling," and their "emotions disrupt action," and several other reactions indicative of anxiety. The S-R Inventory is important as a dependent measure and also as a vehicle for studying the question of cross-situational behavioral consistency. In keeping with the behavioral assessment emphasis on the importance of the situation, research with the S-R Inventory is useful in learning more about the extent to which individual differences and consistencies may manifest themselves in various types of situations.

Both the Fear Survey Schedule and the S-R Inventory ask subjects to indicate their typical reaction. In a sense these self-reports are hypothetical, since they are based on subjects' *recollections* of how they reacted in the past to certain types of situations. Consistent with the overall philosophy that behavioral assessment should focus directly on criterion behavior, it seems only reasonable that behavioral assessors have also made attempts to elicit self-reports of emotional reactivity when individuals are actually *in* certain situations, rather than when they are recollecting them. Among the several available subjective measures of situational state anxiety are Spielberger, Gorsuch, and Lushene's (1970) State-Trait Anxiety Inventory and Zuckerman and Lubin's (1965) Multiple Affect Adjective Checklist. The former measures involve a series of descriptive statements, such as "I am tense," "I am jittery," and "I feel calm," which the subject is asked to rate on a 4-point scale for its accuracy as a self-descriptive statement. In the case of the Multiple Affect Adjective Checklist, feelings of depression and hostility are assessed along with anxiety. For both of these measures appropriate changes are frequently found in response to various kinds of experimental manipulations, such as those intended to elicit or reduce stress.

In assessing emotional reactions, behavioral assessors have also made use of questionnaires that focus on specific problem areas. For example, the Social Avoidance and Distress scale (Watson & Friend, 1969) assesses the anxiety that individuals experience in social situations. A more specific class of social situations is evaluated by the Situation Questionnaire, which was developed by Rehm and Marston (1968) to evaluate the anxiety college males experience in heterosocial situations. Another frequently used measure is the Beck Depression Inventory (Beck, 1972), which is a 21-item questionnaire in which subjects report on such symptoms associated with depression as somatic problems, sleep difficulties, diminished interest in sex, and irritability.

In addition to focusing on various negative emotional states, behavioral assessors have developed self-report measures to assess positive feelings. For example, Cautela and Kastenbaum (1967) developed a Reinforcement Survey Schedule that in part parallels the Fear Survey Schedule. Various objects and situations are presented in questionnaire form, and subjects are asked to indicate the extent to which they hold a personal preference for each of them. This measure suffers from numerous problems, not the least of which is the fact that the items themselves were not empirically derived from a pool of potentially reinforcing events of objects.

In contrast, the Pleasant Events Schedule constructed by MacPhillmay and Lewinsohn (1982) includes items generated from an actual situational analysis. College students were asked to specify "events, experiences, or activities which you find pleasant, rewarding, or fun," and the net result of this sampling was a series of 320 items of both a social and nonsocial type. In responding to the Pleasant Events Schedule, subjects are asked to indicate not only how often each of these various events might have occurred within the past month, but also how pleasant and enjoyable each was. If for some reason subjects have not experienced any particular event, they are simply asked to estimate how enjoyable it might have been if it had occurred. On the basis of a factor analysis, a number of subscales are available. This more sophisticated approach to the assessment of potential reinforcers has been found to be useful in research in the area of depression (Harmon, Nelson, & Hayes, 1980; Lewinsohn & Graf, 1973; Lewinsohn & Libet, 1972; Rehm, Fuchs, Roth, Kornblith, & Romano, 1979).

Self-Report of Environment.   Consistent with the behavioral assessor's interest in the nature of the social environment with which individuals must interact, there is a growing interest in what has been referred to as *social ecology* (Insel & Moos, 1974; Moos, 1973). Moos and his colleagues have been actively involved in developing questionnaires for assessing the social psychological impact made by various environments, including psychiatric wards, community-oriented psychiatric treatment programs, correctional institutions, military basic training companies, university student residences, junior and senior high school classrooms, work environments, and social, therapeutic, and decision-making groups. The questionnaires focus on the individual's perception of various aspects of his or her social environment and include items such as "On this ward everyone knows who's in charge," "Members are expected to take leadership here," and "Members here follow a regular schedule every day."

In assessments of the impact made by varying environmental settings, three dimensions appear to be common across several diverse environmental contexts: the nature and intensity of interpersonal relationships (e.g., peer cohesion, spontaneity); personal development opportunities (e.g., competition, intellectuality); and the stability and responsivity of the social system to change (e.g., order and organization, innovation). In much the same way as the assessment of behavioral characteristics within an individual has relevance for behavioral change, the various environmental assessment questionnaires have implications for the modification of social environments (Moos, 1974).

Self-Report of Cognitions.   Whatever promise the self-report of behavioral, emotional, or environmental factors may have, any comprehensive assessment must also take account of cognitive variables. This need for a more complete assessment model is nicely illustrated with a classic story of a boy playing with a worm. During the course of play, he takes out a knife, cuts the worm in half, and smiles in a self-congratulatory way. This sequence has been observed by an onlooker, who disapprovingly interprets the child's behavior as a cruel and sadistic act. What the observer could not see, however, was that the boy—who happened to have few friends— thought to himself as he cut the worm in half: "There! Now you'll have someone to play with." Without the assessment of cognitions, we often do not have all the information required to understand human behavior fully.

Accompanying a growing interest in cognitive behavior therapy, the past several years have witnessed a fair amount of work in the area of cognitive assessment. In addition to articles and chapters written on cognitive assessment (e.g., Hollon & Bemis, 1981; Kendall & Korgeski, 1979), two recent books have been devoted specifically to this topic (Kendall & Hollon, 1981; Merluzzi, Glass, & Genest,

1981). Providing an overview of this rapidly developing field, workers in the area of cognitive assessment (Hollon & Bemis, 1981; Kendall & Korgeski, 1979) have specified the purposes of self-report measures of cognitions. Included among these are the inherent interest in cognitive processes and contents, the role that may be played by cognitions in the cause and maintenance of various behavior problems, and the wish to determine the extent to which cognitive changes result from therapeutic intervention.

There has been considerable variation in the form with which behavioral assessors have obtained self-reports of cognitions. Assessment procedures have been verbal and written, have involved the endorsement of items or the actual production of responses, have been appropriate to the population at large or to some specific clinical groups, and have been applied to specific instances or to thoughts occurring in a variety of different situations. As it would be well beyond the scope of this chapter to cover all the work that has been done in this area, a sampling of but a few of the more popular measures and procedures will have to suffice.

A paper-and-pencil measure used in conjunction with the investigation of social anxiety is the Fear of Negative Evaluation scale (Watson & Friend, 1969). As described by its title, this true–false questionnaire is designed to assess subjects' worrisome thoughts regarding the impact they are likely to have on others (e.g., "I am usually worried about the kind of impression I make"). A cognitive assessment measure of social anxiety more recently developed by Glass, Merluzzi, Biever, and Larsen (1982) obtained its items by having individuals actually list the thoughts that occurred to them when imagining themselves in various social situations. The measure involves having subjects rate the frequency of various positive ("This will be a good opportunity") and negative self-statements ("I hope I don't make a fool of myself"). In the assessment of cognitions associated with depression, Weissman and Beck (1978) developed a Dysfunctional Attitude Scale, which focuses on the more general attitudes or philosophies that individuals may hold ("If you cannot do something well, there is little point in doing it at all."). Also addressing cognitions associated with depression, but dealing with more specific thoughts that have been found frequently to occur with depression, Hollon and Kendall's (1980) Automatic Thoughts Questionnaire asks subjects to indicate the frequency of occurrence and degree to which they believe certain specific self-statements (e.g., "Why can't I ever succeed?"). In their Relationship Belief Inventory, Epstein and Eidelson (1981) assess a number of unrealistic beliefs that couples in therapy may have about their marital relationship, such as the inability of partners to change and the destructiveness of disagreeing with each other on anything. A measure of attributional style has been developed (Peterson, Semmel, von Baeyer, Abramson, Metalsky, & Seligman, 1982; Seligman, Abramson, Semmel, & von Baeyer, 1979) in which 12 hypothetical situations with both positive and negative outcomes are presented to subjects who provide a likely reason for each and then rate the extent to which the cause is external versus internal, stable versus unstable, and general versus specific to the situation at hand.

In addition to paper-and-pencil self-report measures, procedures have been developed to obtain self-reports of cognitions that occur within a context of specific situations. Spontaneous verbal or written accounts of individuals' thoughts have been assessed immediately before a specific event or interaction (Glass & Merluzzi, 1981), during an event itself (Cacioppo & Petty, 1981; Davison, Robins, & Johnson, 1983; Genest & Turk, 1981), shortly after an event (Cacioppo & Petty, 1981), or at randomly sampled intervals (Hulbert & Sipprelle, 1978). Depending upon the nature and the purpose of the assessment, different procedures for categorizing the thoughts have been used.

As behavioral assessors have moved into the area of measuring cognitions, certain important and intriguing issues have arisen. One such issue involves the accessibility of cognitions to direct verbal report. Recognizing that individuals may not necessarily be aware of all the cognitive processes that serve to direct their behavior and feelings, behavioral assessors have begun to grapple with topics that have been of concern to those who have been involved with more traditional approaches to assessment. We shall return to this issue toward the end of the chapter.

Self-Monitoring. A relatively inexpensive and versatile method for obtaining self-reports has consisted of self-monitoring. Using either simple self-administered checklists or other devices (e.g., golf counters) for counting the frequency or intensity of certain kinds of events, self-monitoring procedures have the advantage of tailor-making the assessment to the individual needs of the client or research project in question.

Although self-monitoring enables individuals to be highly specific in their self-report assessments, it frequently does something else as well; it changes the frequency or magnitude of what is being monitored, even though this change may be only temporary. This is the issue of *reactivity* we discussed earlier in conjunction with the potential effects of being observed by others. As a result of these findings, self-monitoring has been recognized as constituting an essential ingredient of many intervention procedures. This reactivity effect should really not be very surprising, as clinical observations have suggested that objective feedback may be a common denominator underlying all approaches to therapy (Goldfried, 1980).

The direction, extent, and duration of change associated with self-monitoring depend on what is being monitored. Behavior that is under voluntary control (e.g., studying) is more likely to change as a function of self-monitoring than are more involuntary reactions (e.g., anxiety). Moreover, the direction of change can vary as a function of whether the individual perceives the phenomenon as having positive or negative consequences (e.g., number of hours studied versus number of cigarettes smoked). Ciminero, Nelson, and Lipinski (1977) review some of the variables associated with such reactivity and make numerous suggestions for the assessor who wishes to use self-monitoring for assessment rather than therapeutic purposes. Their general conclusion is that in order for self-monitoring to provide one with accurate assessment data, actual training in the self-monitoring process may be needed.

Psychophysiological Methods

The ever-increasing use of psychophysiological measurement procedures by behavioral assessors may be traced to a number of different factors, including the rapidly emerging field of behavioral medicine, the popularity of various programs for the treatment of sexual dysfunctions, and technical advances that have been made in the field of electronics (e.g., computers, portable monitoring devices). For a detailed description of the diverse uses to which psychophysiological methods have been put by behavioral assessors, the reader is referred to a number of excellent chapters and books on this topic (e.g., Geer, 1977; Haynes, 1978; Haynes & Wilson, 1979; Heiman, 1978; Hoon, 1979; Kallman & Feuerstein, 1977; Karacan, 1978). This section focuses on the psychophysiological assessment of two of the most thoroughly developed areas: anxiety and sexual arousal.

Behavioral assessors have long acknowledged that the construct of anxiety may be manifested by three modes of expression: self-report, behavioral, and physiological (Lang, 1971). With regard to this last sphere, extensive research on the effect of anxiety-provoking events on autonomic arousal has generally found that blood pressure, heart rate, electrodermal activity, and adrenal gland secretion typically manifest increases. Different assessment procedures have been developed to monitor the different psychophysiological signs of anxiety. As a measure of heart rate, the electrocardiograph has been used to monitor the electrical activity of the heart itself. A strain gauge placed around a finger is used to measure finger pulse volume. The sphygmomanometer is a device used to measure blood pressure. Electrodermal activity is measured by passing a small electric current between two electrodes attached to the skin surface. Muscle tension can be measured by using surface electrodes to monitor muscle activity. Finally, hormonal secretions can be assessed through the use of blood tests.

In assessing anxiety level that is anything less than very extreme, the responses from any one particular psychophysiological system cannot necessarily be predicted from monitoring the reactions of another system. In some of the pioneering work in this area, Lacy, Bateman, and Van Lehn (1952) reached the conclusion that this lack of correlation among various response systems might actually be a manifestation of individual differences in psychophysiological response to stress. Different patterns of autonomic responsivity were found to occur, such that one person might show changes in electrodermal activity and another might react by increases in heart rate. What is required, then, is a more comprehensive sampling of all psychophysiological responses of an individual by means of a polygraph, so as to determine his or her unique pattern of autonomic reactivity.

In a review of the current status of psychophysiological assessment, Ray and Raczynski (1981) indicate how the issue of unique response patterning has been examined in even greater detail, particularly with regard to effects due to lateralization. Thus, one needs to take into account not only the particular response system (e.g., electrodermal activity), but also the location of the body at which such measurements are taken (e.g., which hand).

Extending the well-known studies of Masters and Johnson (1966), a considerable amount of research has been conducted on the psychophysiological measurement of sexual arousal. Specific physiological changes in heart rate, blood pressure, respiratory rate, and muscle tension have been found to accompany the excitement, plateau, orgasmic, and resolution phases of the sexual response. Genital changes accompanying sexual arousal in the male include penile erection, tensing of the scrotum, and at times color changes in the glans. In the case of the female, genital changes during arousal reflect an increase in blood flow, change in the vaginal wall color, distention and lengthening of the vagina, and increased lubrication.

Most of the work on the psychophysiological assessment of sexual arousal has tended to focus on the accompanying genital changes. In measuring arousal in the male, the penile plethysmograph has most frequently been used (Freund, 1963). The device consists of a glass cylinder into which the penis is inserted, and penile volume is measured by the amount of air that becomes displaced in the cylinder as the penis becomes more erect. Another device for measuring degree of erection has been developed by Barlow, Becker, Leitenberg, and Agras (1970), which consists of a semicircular ring placed around the penis and attached to a strain gauge. Unlike the plethysmograph, this device measures penile circumference. As yet, there is insufficient evidence to indicate the superiority of one of these procedures over the other. These procedures have been used extensively as a measure of sexual arousal among men, both to advance basic research and to provide an important index of therapeutic change.

For the genital measurement of female sexual arousal Cohen and Shapiro (1970) developed a thermal flow meter, which consists of a device inserted within a diaphragm and placed into the vagina to measure blood flow. A procedure developed by Geer and his associates (Geer, Morokoff, & Greenwood, 1974; Sintchak & Geer, 1975) for measuring the vasocongestion associated with sexual arousal that has received a good deal of use by sex researchers consists of an insertion probe with a photocell detector to measure the amount of light that is reflected from the vaginal wall. Further work on the refinement of this procedure has been conducted by others (Hoon, Wincz, & Hoon, 1976). As is the case with the genital measure of arousal in males, these procedures for monitoring female arousal have been used extensively in basic research as well as therapy studies.

The Behavioral Interview

The very frequent use of interview procedures by behavior therapists in clinical practice is based largely on practical considerations. Direct observations by trained assistants, recourse to simulated and role-playing assessment, and/or use of psychophysiological methods may not always be feasible. Moreover, in order even to apply many of the focal measures used by behavioral assessors, one must first have made the decision that these are relevant areas for evaluation.

In considering the issue of how general or specific an assessment should be, Cronbach and Gleser (1965) have referred to the *bandwidth–fidelity dilemma*. Based on concepts from information theory that are used to study electronic communication systems, this dilemma has to do with decisions to be made when attempting to convey information within an allotted amount of space. The term *bandwidth* refers to the amount of space available for communicating information, and *fidelity* refers to the accuracy or clarity of this information. A tradeoff exists in that the more information that is communicated, the lower its level of fidelity. In conducting a behavioral assessment, the clinical interview can provide a good deal of information about many areas of a client's life, but not necessarily with the degree of accuracy or clarity that would be achieved if the entire amount of time were spent on assessing one area. As a compromise, the behavioral interview is often used initially as a strategy for obtaining information with lower fidelity, so that relevant areas may eventually be followed up with more precise assessment procedures.

Many of the interview techniques used by behavioral assessors closely resemble those employed by clinicians of other orientations. Thus, Sullivan's (1954) *The Psychiatric Interview* can offer behavioral assessors numerous suggestions for conducting an effective interview. Guidelines that are specifically relevant to the behavioral interview may be found in Gelfand and Hartman (1975), Linehan (1977), Meyer, Liddell, and Lyons (1977), Morganstern and Tevlin (1981), Peterson (1968), and Storrow (1967). In contrast to clinicians of other orientations, behavioral assessors tend to focus more on the individual's response to specific situations and to the resulting consequences than on the use of the interview procedure. The kinds of questions used in the behavioral interview with adult and child clients are illustrated in Figures 5.1 and 5.2, respectively. As both of these tables show, the behavioral interview is used to focus on the details of the individual's interaction with the environment. The relevance of this information for purposes of therapeutic intervention is considered next.

BEHAVIORAL ASSESSMENT AND BEHAVIOR THERAPY

If one interprets behavior therapy in its broadest sense as involving the application of what we know about psychology in general to problems that may manifest themselves within the clinical setting (Goldfried & Davison, 1976), it follows that the number and variety of behavior therapy procedures available to the clinician will be large and forever changing. This is clearly a double-edged sword, since clinicians are provided with several potentially effective treatment methods together with the dilemma of which to use in any given case. Consequently, the assessment phase represents a crucial and difficult component of clinical behavior therapy.

Exactly what should the behavioral assessor look for, and how does the information obtained become organized so as to have implications for the treatment plan? These issues are touched on below.

A Behavioral Analysis of the Problem

One of the initial tasks of behavioral assessors in the clinical setting is to take what the client may have presented as a very general problem or set of problems and define it in concrete and operational terms. Individuals seeking professional help sometimes talk in abstractions, frequently complaining, "Things are not right," or "I don't seem to have any direction," or "The joy of life is just not there." The task for the behavioral assessor, then, is to find out more precisely what the person may or not be doing or thinking that is resulting in such vaguely described feeling states.

A. Definition of problem behavior
   1. Nature of the problem as defined by client
      As I understand it, you came here because . . . (discuss reasons for contact as stated by referral agency or other source of information).
      I would like you to tell me more about this. What is the problem as you see it? (Probe as needed to determine client's view of his own problem behavior, i.e., what he is doing, or failing to do, which he or somebody else defines as a problem.)
   2. Severity of the problem
      a. *How serious a problem is this as far as you are concerned?* (Probe to determine perceived severity of problem.)
      b. *How often do you* . . . (exhibit problem behavior if a disorder of commission, or have occasion to exhibit desired behavior if a problem of omission. The goal is to obtain information regarding frequency of response).
   3. Generality of the problem
      a. Duration
         How long has this been going on?
      b. Extent
         Where does the problem usually come up? (Probe to determine situations in which problem behavior occurs, e.g., Do you feel that way at work? How about at home?)
B. Determinants of problem behavior
   1. Conditions which intensify problem behavior
      Now I want you to think about the times when . . . (the problem) *is worst. What sort of things are going on then?*
   2. Conditions which alleviate problem behavior
      What about the times when . . . (the problem) *gets better? What sorts of things are going on then?*
   3. Perceived origins
      What do you think is causing . . . (the problem)?
   4. Specific antecedents
      Think back to the last time . . . (the problem occurred). *What was going on at that time?*
      As needed:
      a. Social influences
         Were any other people around? Who? What were they doing?
      b. Personal influences
         What were you thinking about at the time? How did you feel?
   5. Specific consequences
      What happened after . . . (the problem behavior occurred)?
      As needed:
      a. Social consequences
         What did . . . (significant others identified above) *do?*
      b. Personal consequences
         How did that make you feel?
   6. Suggested changes
      You have thought a lot about . . . (the problem). *What do you think might be done to* . . . (improve the situation)?
   7. Suggested leads for further inquiry
      What else do you think I should find out about to help you with this problem?

Figure 5.1. A guideline for questions used in behavioral interviews with adult clients. From D.R. Peterson, *The Clinical Study of Social Behavior*. New York: Appleton-Century-Crofts, 1968, p. 121. Reprinted by permission.

1. *Specific description.* Can you tell me what (child's name)'s problem seems to be?
   (If caretaker responds in generalities such as, "He is always grouchy," or that the child is rebellious, uncooperative, overly shy, then ask him to describe the behavior more explicitly.)
   What, exactly, does (he or she) do when (he or she) is acting this way?
   What kinds of things will (he or she) say?
2. *Last incident.* Could you tell me just what happened the last time you saw (the child) acting like this?
   What did you do?
3. *Rate.* How often does this behavior occur?
   About how many times a day (or hour or week) does it occur?
4. *Changes in rate.* Would you say this behavior is starting to happen more often, less often, or staying about the same?
5. *Setting.* In what situation does it occur?
   At home?
   At school?
   In public places or when (the child) is alone?
   (If in public places) Who is usually with him? How do they respond?
   At what time of day does this happen?
   What else is (the child) likely to be doing at the time?
6. *Antecedents.* What usually has happened right before (he or she) does this? Does anything in particular seem to start this behavior?
7. *Consequent events.* What usually happens right afterward?
8. *Modification attempts.* What things have you tried to stop (him or her) from behaving this way?
   How long did you try that?
   How well did it work?
   Have you ever tried anything else?

Figure 5.2. A guideline for questions used in behavioral interviews associated with child clients. From D.M. Gelfland and D.P. Hartman, *Child Behavior Analysis and Therapy.* Elmsford, N.Y.: Pergamon Press, 1975, p. 295. Reprinted by permission.

What one is confronted with in the clinical interaction may be understood by conceptualizing the client's current status as entailing numerous dependent and independent variables. In the most general sense, when a person comes in with a problem, the behavioral assessor assumes that this presenting problem represents a dependent variable. The behavioral assessor's task is to look for the independent variable or variables that may be maintaining this problem behavior, which then become the focus of the therapeutic intervention.

Behavior therapists have frequently been faulted for dealing with symptoms and failing to acknowledge the potential operation of underlying causes. However, the attempt to obtain a parsimonious understanding of behavior in no way implies that behavioral assessment needs to be superficial. For example, take the case of a man whose presenting problem is that he and his wife have frequent fights. Although there might be an initial temptation to instigate and reinforce directly cooperative or affectionate behavior between the couple, such a procedure might be clinically naive under certain circumstances. A possible reason may be that the man drinks heavily and his drinking makes him aggressive. And the reason he drinks so much may be that he is very anxious. And the reason he is so anxious may be that he finds himself under continual pressure at work. And the reason he is under such pressure may be that he expects too much of himself and others. The question here becomes: What variable should one focus on in order to decrease the fighting behavior? A related question is where to stop in this search for underlying causes.

From within the behavioral orientation, the guideline employed is that one stops looking when it seems likely that the variable being explored is no longer operating. Take the above example of an individual with unrealistic standards of perfection for himself and others. Why is he that way? In all likelihood he has modeled such standards from significant figures during his early social learning experiences. However, one cannot go back and change past interactions, but must instead work with what exists at present. Thus, in this example one would probably want to focus on the person's unrealistically high standards as they are currently manifested, with the assumption that the other problematic behaviors in his life are maladaptive consequences of his distorted expectations and attitudes.

In focusing on the types of variables one attends to in a behavioral assessment, the acronym SORC has frequently been employed (Goldfried & Sprafkin, 1974). This indicates the focus on *s*ituational antecedents, *o*rganismic variables, *r*esponse dimensions, and *c*onsequences.

In evaluating the *situational antecedents* of behavior, behavioral assessors differ most radically from those who use a more traditional approach to assessment. For example, focus is placed on obtaining a detailed account of the specific situations likely to make an individual anxious. This information is useful not only for assessment purposes, but also for its implications for therapeutic intervention, such as in the case of systematic desensitization. In addition to identifying the situations that elicit various forms of emotional response, the situational antecedents that are assessed can be discriminative, in that they serve as cues for the person to behave in different ways. Here the distinction being made is between respondents and operants. In the case of operants, knowledge of the specific nature of the discriminative stimuli as well as of the problematic responses can have implications for treatment. For example, with a child showing certain behavior problems, simple knowledge that he or she behaves appropriately in school but is a problem at home requires further clarification, with the assessment focusing on exactly what events at home and at school serve as cues for appropriate and inappropriate behaviors.

Among those *organismic* variables involved in a behavioral assessment are such aspects of an individual's physiological makeup as general energy or activity level, hormonal and chemical imbalance, and any psychoactive drugs present within one's system, all of which can serve as important determinants of behavior. Also included among relevant organismic variables are cognitive factors. Except when one is working with young children, mental retardates, or back-ward schizophrenics, the failure to attend to mediating cognitive processes can easily lead one to overlook what may be an essential determinant of maladaptive functioning. Based on early learning experiences, individuals develop various *schemas* about the world around them, some of which may be distorted and serve to mediate various maladaptive responses and emotional reactions. Thus, if an individual walks around with the expectation that large classes of situations are potentially dangerous, the emotional reaction that creates the problem may be a direct and appropriate reaction to what essentially is a distorted perception. In such instances the important maintaining variable may be the distortion, which should eventually be the direct target of the therapeutic intervention (Beck, 1976; Ellis, 1962; Goldfried & Davison, 1976).

In focusing on *response* variables, we are referring to what is often synonymous with behavioral assessment, namely, the sampling of various behaviors. The dimensions one focuses on in looking directly at behavioral tendencies include frequency, strength, duration, and latency of response. As already noted, one frequently makes the distinction between respondents and operants, the former referring to some emotional reaction and the latter to some voluntary behavior. In some cases this distinction may not be clear-cut, as in the case of an individual who shows some reluctance to go out and find a job. Although he or she may be truly fearful of seeking employment, the reluctance may be reinforced by various other consequences, such as unemployment checks and the attention and sympathy of others.

The fourth class of variables is the *consequences* of certain behaviors, which are important because of the well-established principles that so much of what we do— whether it be deviant or adaptive—is maintained by its consequences. Even when a given course of action has a mixed payoff (both positive and negative outcomes), the fact that the behavior continues to persist is frequently explained by the immediate positive as opposed to long-range negative consequences that ensue. Thus drug users have obvious pleasurable sensations after a fix, but experience numerous long-term consequences because of their involvement with drugs. In focusing on the larger social system, we sometimes come across a setting that inadvertently reinforces behaviors it also labels as maladaptive. As Goffman (1961) and Rosenhan (1973) have vividly described, there are numerous instances in which psychiatric hospitals force dependence on patients and then interpret this dependence as being indicative of their disturbance. Wherever maladaptive behavior exists by virtue of conflicting incentives in the environment, the appropriate direction to take therapeutically is toward environmental and not individual modification.

In focusing on each of the SORC variables, it should be apparent that the analysis of problem behaviors in such terms has clear implications for therapeutic intervention. As has been argued by Kanfer and Saslow (1965), this is in sharp contrast to the more traditional, Kraepelinian nosological system. An alternate classification system has been suggested by Staats (1963) and elaborated by Bandura (1968) and Goldfried and Sprafkin (1974). This alternate approach to classification, which categorizes behavior according to the variables likely to be maintaining it, is outlined in Figure 5.3. It should be noted that these categories are not mutually exclusive, and a given problem may be classified under more than one heading. The primary purpose of the system is to alert clinicians to those variables that need to be dealt with in therapy.

In addition to conducting an evaluation of those variables required for a behavioral analysis of the presenting problem, the behaviorally oriented clinician focuses on several variables that have similar implications for the implementation of appro-

I.   Difficulties in stimulus control of behavior
        A. Defective stimulus control
        The individual is capable of adequate functioning, but is not discriminating those situations in which certain behaviors may be appropriate. For example, there are children who may be capable of solitary play, but may fail to do so at certain times when it may be desirable (e.g., when mother is speaking on the telephone).
        B. Inappropriate stimulus control
        This category refers to instances when a realistically nonthreatening situation elicits an intense negative emotional reaction. Such emotional reactions presumably have been conditioned to certain kinds of cues, either from direct experience or through social modeling. The most typical example of this consists of simple phobias.
II.   Deficient behavioral repertoires
        This category refers to those instances in which individuals lack the actual ability or the skills needed in order to deal with certain situations effectively. Hence, an individual may never have learned appropriate ways for interacting with members of the opposite sex. Such difficulties are also complicated by the fact that negative thoughts and emotions often accompany such skill deficits.
III.   Aversive behavioral repertoires
        The aversiveness associated with problems falling in this category has to do with the negative impact that individuals may have on others. Some behavioral assessors have categorized such individuals as manifesting a "behavioral excess." Examples of this would be excessive aggressiveness or other forms of behavior that involve lack of consideration for others.
IV.   Difficulties with incentive systems (reinforcers)
        A. Defective incentive system in individual
        This category includes those instances where those social stimuli that typically are reinforcing for most individuals are not for the person in question. Examples of this would be autistic children, who do not respond to social reinforcement, or delinquents, who do not respond to many of the social reinforcers associated with the larger society.
        B. Inappropriate incentive system in individual
        Here we have individuals whose incentive systems are maladaptive, in that what is reinforcing for them may be harmful (e.g., drugs) and/or culturally disapproved (e.g., pedophilia).
        C. Absence of incentives in environment
        Because of a personal loss, or an impoverished life situation, individuals may have few reinforcers. The clinical symptoms frequently associated with this category are depression, apathy, and boredom.
        D. Conflicting incentives in environment
        In social situations that are multifaceted or in the process of change, individuals may experience both reinforcement and punishment for the same set of behaviors. Thus, the class clown gets punished by those in authority, but receives attention from peers. Women who pursue more achievement-oriented goals in their lives experience both positive and negative feedback from those around them.
V.   Aversive self-reinforcing system
        This category focuses on the cognitive processes of the individual, particularly the standards used for self-reinforcement. Hence, there are individuals who may be functioning quite adequately and obtaining what presumably should be clear and unequivocal positive reinforcement from the environment, but may nonetheless possess such unrealistically high standards that they can never please themselves. Such absence of self-reinforcement may result in depression and subjective feelings of inadequacy.

Figure 5.3.   System for classifying behavior disorders.

priate treatment procedures. Before actually initiating any therapeutic intervention program, behavior therapists frequently focus on their clients' expectations for improvement. As suggested by Goldstein (1962), positive expectations of at least a moderate nature are required in order to ensure therapeutic success. Clients' expectancies about the nature of the therapeutic relationship should also be assessed. Individuals vary considerably with regard to the amount of control and guidance they wish from the therapist, ranging from some who feel they must be in complete control of the change process to others who figuratively throw themselves at the therapist's feet. There are other types of behavioral tendencies that may hinder treatment. For example, individuals who tend to procrastinate or give up easily may be reluctant to initiate and follow through on various between-session homework assignments (e.g., relaxation training, self-monitoring). For a discussion of how such issues may be handled therapeutically, the reader is referred to Goldfried (1982a), Goldfried and Davison (1976), Lazarus and Fay (1982), Meichenbaum and Gilmore (1982), and Turkat and Meyer (1982).

The Intake Evaluation

During the initial assessment, the task of the behavioral assessor becomes one of collating the information that has been obtained—whether by means of interview procedures or by means of any other behavioral assessment method available—and organizing it in such a way as to arrive at a preliminary behavioral analysis of the presenting problems and at some decision regarding appropriate treatment procedures. In order to help focus behavioral assessment reports on information likely to be relevant to subsequent treatment procedures, Pomeranz and Goldfried (1970) have suggested an intake report format. Depending on the case at hand, some aspects of the format may be more relevant than others. An outline of the intake report format is supplied in Figure 5.4, and an illustrative report appears in Figure 5.5.

FUTURE DIRECTIONS

In an overview of the current status and future directions in clinical assessment, Korchin and Schuldberg (1981) have observed that although the field is alive and only moderately well, it appears to be experiencing a renewed sense of vitality. They note that some of the indications of this upward swing have been the development of more focal assessment procedures, fewer inferential steps in the interpretation of test responses, a greater recognition of situational determinants of behavior, and more attention to the evaluation of individuals' own views of themselves and life circumstances. It is probably safe to say that the work done in behavioral assessment over the past several years has served to influence these trends.

Despite the advances in behavioral assessment that have been made to date, the need for measures continues to outstrip what is currently available. As a result, there is a danger that poorly conceived procedures may proliferate and, because they fill a need at the time, establish themselves within the scope of behavioral assessment. This is reminiscent of what happened in the development of both projective techniques and measures of intelligence: Tests that were developed on idiosyncratic hunches became established and sometimes firmly entrenched within the clinician's test battery. As also noted in Chapters 2 and 4 of this book, tests once reported in the literature seem to develop a momentum of their own, regardless of what sophisticated methodological analyses of their procedures may reveal, to say nothing of disappointing validity data.

I. *Behavior during interview and physical description.* The behavioral assessor includes here any observations construed as providing relevant samples of the client's behavior, whether they are specific to the therapeutic interaction or indicative of a more general behavioral tendency. To the extent that the person's physical appearance may be typical or atypical of those in his or her social milieu, one may raise hypotheses (i.e., leads for further assessment) regarding the likelihood of the client's having a positive or negative impact on others.

II. *Presenting problem*

A. *Nature of problem(s).* Included here is a statement of the problem as described by the client. This may involve one or more possible difficulties, and they may need to be reconstrued by the behavioral assessor in conceptual terms different from those used by the client.

B. *Historical setting events.* Although behavior therapists make few attempts to deal with historical material, this in no way implies that such information is always irrelevant (Kanfer & Saslow, 1969; Wolpe & Lazarus, 1966). The need for such data is particularly important when the client's presenting problems are vague or difficult to conceptualize in functional terms. Thus, by learning more about the person's past (e.g., overly perfectionistic parent), one may make inferences as to the likely consequences of early social learning experiences. Such added information can often help to clarify the nature of the presenting complaints and alert the clinician to potential problematic behavior patterns.

C. *Current situational determinants.* Inasmuch as the report is often written after just a few assessment sessions, sufficient information may not yet be available regarding the specific nature of those situations that either elicit respondents or serve as discriminative stimuli for operants. Consequently, the information included here might entail general classes of situations, each of which has to be followed up as the treatment progresses.

D. *Relevant organismic variables.* In addition to any physiological states that may account for the client's problem, information bearing on the client's cognitive processes should be included here. Such covert self-statements may serve as an actual determinant of the problem (e.g., "I must be perfect in everything I do."), or they may consist of a more secondary attribution that is applied to the problem behavior itself (e.g., "My heart beating faster means that I am about to have a heart attack.").

E. *Dimensions of problem(s).* The problematic response is analyzed here in terms of duration, pervasiveness, magnitude, and frequency of occurrence.

F. *Consequences of problem(s).* The information included here can refer either to potentially reinforcing consequences in the individual's environment (e.g., the reaction of others) or to the impact the problem has on various aspects of the person's current functioning (e.g., ability to maintain friendships, job status).

III. *Other problems.* Included here are any problems that emerged during the assessment, but were not stated as the original reason for the therapeutic contact. Whether or not such problems constitute a therapeutic goal depends on the client's and therapist's discussions about treatment priorities.

IV. *Personal assets.* The information included in this category involves not only the individual's positive attributes (e.g., intelligence, attractive physical appearance), but also any interests or personal preferences that may serve as potential reinforcers in his or her life. Any aspect of the environment that has a potential for being therapeutically useful (e.g., a cooperative spouse) can also be included here as well.

V. *Target(s) for modification.* In many respects this section provides a culmination of the behavioral assessment procedures, in that it specifies exactly what variables are in need of therapeutic attention, whether situational antecedents, organismic variables, components of the problem behavior itself, and/or consequent reinforcers. If possible, some ordering of priorities should be indicated.

VI. *Recommended treatment(s).* The therapeutic intervention procedures for intervening with each of the targets indicated above are described here.

VII. *Motivation for treatment.* Based on the client's perception of the severity of the problem, his or her verbal commitment, past attempts at change, and any other relevant indices, some general classification of motivation (e.g., high, medium, or low) should be indicated.

VIII. *Prognosis.* An indication of the likelihood of change (e.g., very poor, fair, good, or very good) may be based on such information as the duration of the problem, past success with similar kinds of problems, relevant client variables, and the individual's life circumstances.

IX. *Priority of treatment.* This category is particularly useful in a clinic setting, where requests for treatment typically outweigh the available therapeutic time. A simple low-, medium-, or high-priority rating may be given, based on an evaluation of the possible consequences of *not* treating a given client.

X. *Expectancies.* Expectancies regarding the client's perception of the likelihood of change, as well as his or her view of the nature of the therapeutic relationship, should be included here.

XI. *Other comments.* In this category can be placed any information not readily included above, such as any leads, hunches, or areas to follow up in subsequent interviews.

Figure 5.4. Outline of intake report format.

Name: BRIAN, James (fictitious name) *Age:* 22 *Sex:* Male
Class: Senior *Date of interview:* March 25, 1974
Therapist: John Doe

I. *Behavior during interview and physical description*

James is a clean-shaven, long-haired young man who appeared for the intake interview in well-coordinated college garb: jeans, wide belt, open shirt, and sandals. He came across as shy and soft-spoken, with occasional minor speech blocks. Although uneasy during most of the session, he nonetheless spoke freely and candidly.

II. *Presenting problem*

A. *Nature of problem.* Anxiety in public speaking situations, and other situations in which he is being evaluated by others.

B. *Historical setting events.* James was born in France, and arrived in this country 7 years ago, at which time he experienced both a social and language problem. His social contacts had been minimal until the time he entered college, at which time a socially aggressive friend of his helped him to break out of his shell. James describes his father as being an overly critical and perfectionistic person who would, on occasion, rip up his homework if it fell short of the mark. The client's mother is pictured as a controlling, overly affectionate person who was always showing concern about his welfare. His younger brother, who has always been a good student, was continually thrown up to James by his parents as being far better than he.

C. *Current situational determinants.* Interaction with his parents, examinations, family gatherings, participation in classes, initial social contacts.

D. *Relevant organismic variables.* The client appears to be approaching a number of situations with certain irrational expectations, primarily unrealistic strivings for perfection and an overwhelming desire to receive approval from others. He is not taking any medication at this time except as indicated under *X* below.

E. *Dimensions of problem.* The client's social and evaluative anxiety are long-standing and occur in a wide variety of day-to-day situations.

F. *Consequences of problem.* His chronic level of anxiety resulted in an ulcer operation at the age of 15. In addition, he has developed a skin rash on his hands and arms, apparently from excessive perspiration. He reports that his nervousness at one time caused him to stutter, but this appears to be less a problem in more recent years. His anxiety in examination situations has typically interfered with his ability to perform well.

III. *Other problems*

A. *Assertiveness.* Although obviously a shy and timid individual, James said that lack of assertiveness is no longer a problem with him. At one time in the past, his friends would take advantage of him, but he claims that this is no longer the case. This should be followed up further, as it is unclear what he means by assertiveness.

B. *Forgetfulness.* The client reports that he frequently misses appointments, misplaces items, locks himself out of his room, and generally is absent-minded.

IV. *Personal assets*

The client is fairly bright and comes across as a warm, friendly, and sensitive individual.

V. *Targets for modification*

Unrealistic self-statements in social-evaluative situations; possibly behavioral deficits associated with unassertiveness; and forgetfulness.

VI. *Recommended treatment*

It appears that relaxation training would be a good way to begin, especially in light of the client's high level of anxiety. Following this, the treatment should move along the lines of rational restructuring, and possibly behavioral rehearsal. It is unclear as yet what would be the best strategy for dealing with forgetfulness.

VII. *Motivation for treatment*

High

Figure 5.5. Sample behavioral intake report. From M.R. Goldfried and G.C. Davison, *Clinical Behavior Therapy.* New York: Holt, Rinehart & Winston, 1976, pp. 52–53. Reprinted by permission.

VIII. *Prognosis*
   Very good.
IX. *Priority for treatment*
   High.
X. *Expectancies*
   On occasion, especially when going out on a date with a female, James would take half a sleeping pill to calm himself down. He wants to get away from this, and feels what he needs is to learn to cope with his anxieties by himself. It would appear that he will be very receptive to whatever treatment plan we finally decide on, especially if the emphasis is on self-control of anxiety.
XI. *Other comments*
   Considering the brief time available between now and the end of the semester, between-session homework assignments should be emphasized as playing a particularly important role in the behavior change process.

Figure 5.5. (*Continued*)

This is not to say that research on the development of new assessment procedures is not called for. Quite the contrary. Perhaps one of the greatest needs that exists at present is for behavioral assessment procedures of a more standardized nature (Kanfer, 1972). Although various methods of behavioral assessment are used in clinical practice, they tend to vary from therapist to therapist. Even when the same methods are used by researchers to assess a given target behavior from one study to the next, there exist procedural variations that make interpretations difficult (see Bernstein & Nietzel, 1973; Jeger & Goldfried, 1976). In what we hope may represent a new research phase in behavioral assessment, Curran and his colleagues have begun to investigate the comparability of standards for assessing social adequacy across different laboratory settings (Curran, Wessberg, Farrell, Monti, Corriveau, & Coyne, 1982).

With the recent availability of low-cost computer facilities, it is very likely that this technology will be used in the future for purposes of behavioral assessment. Some work along these lines has already begun (e.g., Angle, Hay, Hay, & Ellinwood, 1977; McCullough, 1981), making possible the collection and collation of numerous sources of relevant information. Such information can be used not only for purposes of individual clinical assessment, but also for the creation of data banks that will allow us to gain a better understanding of the functional relationships among different variables, especially in relation to the maintenance and amelioration of various clinical problems.

Most of the work that has been done in the area of behavioral assessment has focused primarily on the development of procedures to be used in a research context. By contrast, relatively little attention has been paid to the investigation of how assessment information is used clinically to individualize any given treatment program. To be sure, in order to do this one needs valid assessment procedures. However, clearly delineated rules for the clinical decision-making process are also needed. As observed by Nelson and Hayes (1981), behavior therapy has been slow to develop such rules. With the increasing popularity of behavior therapy in clinical settings, one may expect to see work done in this area in the future.

As a result of the increased interest given to the role that cognitive variables play in the maintenance and alteration of clinical problems, behavior therapists have found themselves confronted with a number of important issues. For example, Arnkoff and Glass (1982) have suggested that for behavior therapists to incorporate cognitive concepts into their clinical work, they need to gain more information about the function as well as the content of certain cognitions; the interrelationship between cognitive variables and both overt behavior and emotion; the parameters associated with changes in cognitions; and those specific therapeutic activities that will ultimately lead to cognitive change.

In an extensive conceptual and methodological discussion of the assessment of social skills, McFall (1982) has pointed out that we need to be able to evaluate not only the overt skills that an individual may possess, but also the availability of the individual's knowledge of those rules or scripts that are necessary for appropriate social interaction. As behavior therapists have immersed themselves in this general area of cognitive assessment, there has been an increasing acknowledgment that not all cognitive processes may be readily accessible to individuals (Arnkoff, 1980; Beck, 1976; Goldfried, 1979; Kendall & Korgeski, 1979; Landau & Goldfried, 1981; Mahoney, 1980; Meichenbaum & Cameron, 1981). Behavior therapists do not refer to such phenomena as reflecting "unconscious" processes—which carries with it other theoretical connotations—but instead view them as involving certain implicit meaning structures having affective associations. Many concepts from information processing have started to appear in the behavioral literature (e.g., *schema*), and they may ultimately provide us with a language system that is capable of transcending different theoretical orientations (see Goldfried, 1982b).

REFERENCES

Angle, H. V., Hay, L. R., hay, W. M., & Ellinwood, E. H. Computer assisted behavioral assessment. In J. D. Cone & R. P. Hawkins (Eds.), *Behavioral assessment: New directions in clinical psychology.* New York: Brunner/Mazel, 1977.

American Psychological Association. *Standards for educational and psychological tests.* Washington, D.C.: American Psychological Association, 1974.

Arkowitz, H., Lichtenstein, E., McGovern, K., & Hines, P. The behavioral assessment of social competence in males. *Behavior Therapy,* 1975, **6,** 3–13.

Arnkoff, D. B. *Future directions for research on cognitive counseling and therapy.* Paper presented at the meeting of the American Psychological Association, Montreal, 1980.

Arnkoff, D. B., & Glass, C. R. Clinical cognitive constructs: Examination, evaluation, and elaboration. In P. C. Kendall (Ed.), *Advances in cognitive-behavioral research and therapy* (Vol. 1), New York: Academic Press, 1982.

Bandura, A. A social learning interpretation of psychological dysfunctions. In P. London & D. Rosenhan (Eds.), *Foundations of abnormal psychology.* New York: Holt, Rinehart, & Winston, 1968.

Barker, R. G., & Wright, H. F. *One boy's day.* New York: Harper & Row, 1951.

Barlow, D. H. (Ed.). *Behavioral assessment of adult disorders.* New York: Guilford Press, 1981.

Barlow, D. H., Becker, R., Leitenberg, H., & Agras, W. S. A mechanical strain gauge for recording penile circumference change. *Journal of Applied Behavior Analysis,* 1970, **3,** 73–76.

Bates, P. The effectiveness of interpersonal skills training on the social skill acquisition of moderately and mildly retarded adults. *Journal of Applied Behavioral Analysis,* 1980, **13,** 237–248.

Beck, A. T. *Depression: Causes and treatment.* Philadelphia: University of Pennsylvania Press, 1972.

Beck, A. T. *Cognitive therapy and the emotional disorders.* New York: International Universities Press, 1976.

Bellack, A. S., Hersen, & Lamparski, D. Role-play tests for assessing social skills: Are they valid? Are they useful? *Journal of Consulting and Clinical Psychology,* 1979, **47,** 335–342.

Bellack, A. S., Hersen, M., & Turner, S. M. Role-play tests for assessing social skills: Are they valid? *Behavior Therapy,* 1978, **9,** 448–461.

Bernstein, G. S. *Behavior manager effectiveness inventory.* Unpublished manuscript, 1978.

Bernstein, D. A., & Nietzel, M. T. Procedural variation in behavioral avoidance tests. *Journal of Consulting and Clinical Psychology,* 1973, **41,** 165–174.

Bersoff, D. N., & Moyer, D. *Positive Reinforcement Observation Schedule (PROS): Development and use.* Paper presented at the annual meeting of the American Psychological Association, Montreal, August, 1973.

Borkovec, T. D., Fleischmann, D. J., & Caputo, J. A. The measurement of anxiety in an analogue social situation. *Journal of Consulting and Clinical Psychology,* 1973, **41,** 157–161.

Borkovec, T. D., Stone, N. M., O'Brien, G. T., & Kaloupek, D. G. Evaluation of a clinically relevant target behavior for analog outcome research. *Behavior Therapy,* 1974, **5,** 503–513.

Brown, W. F., & Holzman, W. H. *Survey of study habits and attitudes.* New York: The Psychological Corporation, 1966.

Cacioppo, J. T., & Petty, R. E. Social psychological procedures for cognitive response assessment: The thought-listing technique. In T. V. Merluzzi, C. R. Glass, & M. Genest (Eds.), *Cognitive assessment.* New York: Guilford Press, 1981.

Cautela, J. R., & Kastenbaum, R. A. A reinforcement survey schedule for use in therapy, training, and research. *Psychological Report,* 1967, **20,** 1115–1130.

Ciminero, A. R., Adams, H. E., & Calhoun, K. S. *Handbook of behavioral assessment.* New York: Wiley, 1977.

Ciminero, A. R., Nelson, R. O., & Lipinski, D. P. Self-monitoring procedures. In A. R. Ciminero, H. E. Adams, & K. S. Calhoun (Eds.), *Handbook of behavioral assessment.* New York: Wiley, 1977.

Cohen, H. D., & Shapiro, A. A method for measuring sexual arousal in the female. *Psychophysiology,* 1970, **8,** 251.

Cone, J. D. Psychometric considerations. In M. Hersen & A. S. Bellack (Eds.), *Behavioral assessment: A practical handbook* (2nd ed.). Elmsford, N.Y.: Pergamon Press, 1981.

Cone, J. D., & Hawkins, R. P. (Eds.). *Behavioral assessment: New directions in clinical psychology.* New York: Brunner/Mazel, 1977.

Cronbach, L. J., & Gleser, G. C. *Psychological tests and personnel decisions* (2nd ed.). Urbana: University of Illinois Press, 1965.

Cronbach, L. J., Gleser, G. C., Nada, H., & Rajaratnam, N. *The dependability of behavioral measures.* New York: Wiley, 1972.

Curran, J. P., & Monti, P. M. (Eds.). *Social skills training: A practical handbook for assessment and treatment.* New York: Guilford Press, 1982.

Curran, J. P., Wessberg, H. W., Farrell, A. D., Monti, T. M., Corriveau, D. P., & Coyne, N. A. Social skills and social anxiety: Are different laboratories measuring the same constructs? *Journal of Consulting and Clinical Psychology,* 1982, **50,** 396–406.

Davison, G. C., Robins, C., & Johnson, M. K. Articulative thoughts during simulated situations: A paradigm for studying cognition in emotion and behavior. *Cognitive Therapy and Research,* 1983, **7,** 17–39.

Edelson, J. L., & Rose, S. D. *A behavioral roleplay test for assessing children's social skills.* Paper presented at the 12th Annual Convention of the Association for the Advancement of Behavior Therapy. Chicago, 1978.

Eisler, R. M., Hersen, M., & Agras, W. S. Videotape: A method for the controlled observation of non-verbal interpersonal behavior. *Behavior Therapy,* 1973, **4,** 420–425. (a)

Eisler, R. M., Hersen, M., & Agras, W. S. Effects of videotape and instructional feedback on non-verbal marital interactions: An analogue study. *Behavior Therapy,* 1973, **3,** 551–558. (b)

Eisler, R. M., Hersen, M., & Miller, P. M. Effects of modeling on components of assertive behavior. *Journal of Behavior Therapy and Experimental Psychiatry,* 1973, **4,** 1–6.

Eisler, R. M., Miller, P. M., & Hersen, M. Components of assertive behavior. *Journal of Clinical Psychology,* 1973, **24,** 295–299.

Ellis, A. *Reason and emotion in psychotherapy.* New York: Lyle Stuart, 1962.

Endler, N. S., Hunt, J. McV., & Rosenstein, A. J. An S-R inventory of anxiousness. *Psychological Monographs,* 1962, **76,** 1–33.

Epstein, N., & Eidelson, R. J., Unrealistic beliefs of clinical couples: Their relationship to expectations, goals, and satisfaction. *The American Journal of Family Therapy,* 1981, **9,** 13–22.

Freedman, B. J., Rosenthal, L., Donahoe, C. P., Jr., Schlundt, D. J., & McFall, R. M. A social-behavioral analysis of skill deficits in delinquent and nondelinquent adolescent boys. *Journal of Consulting and Clinical Psychology,* 1978, **46,** 1448–1462.

Freund, K. A laboratory method for diagnosing predominance of homo- or hetero-erotic interest in the male. *Behavior Research and Therapy,* 1963, **1,** 85–93.

Friedman, H. Perceptual regression in schizophrenia: An hypothesis suggested by use of the Rorschach test. *Journal of Projective Techniques,* 1953, **17,** 171–185.

Funabiki, D., & Calhoun, J. F. Use of a behavioral-analytic procedure in evaluating two models of depression. *Journal of Consulting and Clinical Psychology,* 1979, **47,** 183–185.

Gaffney, L. R., & McFall, R. M. A comparison of social skills in delinquent and nondelinquent adolescent girls using a behavioral role-playing inventory. *Journal of Consulting and Clinical Psychology,* 1981, **49,** 959–967.

Galassi, J. P., DeLo, J. S., Galassi, M. D., & Bastien, S. The college self-expression scale: A measure of assertiveness. *Behavior therapy,* 1974, **5,** 165–171.

Galassi, M. D., & Galassi, J. P. The effects of role playing variations on the assessment of assertive behavior. *Behavior Therapy,* 1976, **7,** 343–347.

Gambrill, E. D., & Richey, C. A. An assertion inventory for use in assessment and research. *Behavior Therapy,* 1975, **6,** 550–561.

Gay, M. L., Hollandsworth, J. G., & Galassi, J. P. An assertiveness inventory for adults. *Journal of Counseling Psychology, 1975, **4**, 340–344.*

Geer, J. H. The development of a scale to measure fear. *Behaviour Research and Therapy, 1965, **3**, 45–53.*

Geer, J. H. Sexual functioning: Some data and speculations on psychophysiological assessment. In J. D. Cone & R. T. Hawkins (Eds.), *Behavioral assessment: New directions in clinical psychology.* New York: Brunner/Mazel, 1977.

Geer, J. H., Morokoff, P., & Greenwood, P. Sexual arousal in women: The development of a measurement device for vaginal blood volume. *Archives of Sexual Behavior, 1974, **3**, 559–564.*

Gelfand, D. M., & Hartmann, D. P. *Child behavior: Analysis and therapy.* New York: Pergamon Press, 1975.

Genest, M., & Turk, D. C. Think-aloud approaches to cognitive assessment. In T. V. Merluzzi, C. R. Glass, & M. Genest (Eds.), *Cognitive assessment.* New York: Guilford Press, 1981.

Glass, C. R., & Merluzzi, T. V. Cognitive assessment of social-evaluative anxiety. In T. V. Merluzzi, C. R. Glass, & M. Genest (Eds.), *Cognitive assessment.* New York: Guilford Press, 1981.

Glass, C. R., Merluzzi, T. V., Biever, J. L., & Larsen, K. H. Cognitive assessment of social anxiety: Development and validation of a self-statement questionnaire. *Cognitive Therapy and Research, 1982, **6**, 37–55.*

Goffman, E. *Asylums.* Garden City, N. Y.: Doubleday, 1961.

Goldfried, M. R. Behavioral assessment. In I. B. Weiner (Ed.), *Clinical methods in psychology.* New York: Wiley-Interscience, 1976.

Goldfried, M. R. Behavioral assessment: Where do we go from here? *Behavioral Assessment, 1979, **1**, 19–22.*

Goldfried, M. R. Toward the delineation of therapeutic change principles. *American Psychologist, 1980, **35**, 991–999.*

Goldfried, M. R. Resistance and clinical behavior therapy. In P. L. Wachtel (Ed.). *Resistance: Psychodynamic and behavioral approaches.* New York: Plenum, 1982. (a)

Goldfried, M. R. (Ed.). *Converging themes in psychotherapy: Trends in psychodynamic, humanistic, and behavioral practice.* New York: Springer, 1982. (b)

Goldfried, M. R., & Davison, G. C. *Clinical behavior therapy.* New York: Holt, Rinehart, & Winston, 1976.

Goldfried, M. R., & D'Zurilla, T. J. A behavioral-analytic model for assessing competence. In C. D. Spielberger (Ed.), *Current topics in clinical and community psychology* (Vol. 1). New York: Academic Press, 1969.

Goldfried, M. R., & D'Zurilla, T. J. Prediction of academic competence by means of the Survey of Study Habits and Attitudes. *Journal of Educational Psychology, 1973, **64**, 116–122.*

Goldfried, M. R., & Kent, R. N. Traditional vs. behavioral assessment: A comparison of methodological and theoretical assumptions. *Psychological Bulletin, 1972, **77**, 409–420.*

Goldfried, M. R., & Sprafkin, J. N. *Behavioral personality assessment.* Morristown, N.J.: General Learning Press, 1974.

Goldfried, M. R., Stricker, G., & Weiner, I. B. *Rorschach handbook of clinical and research applications*. Englewood Cliffs, N. J.: Prentice-Hall, 1971.

Goldfried, M. R., & Trier, C. S. Effectiveness of relaxation as an active coping skill. *Journal of Abnormal Psychology*, 1974, **83**, 348–355.

Goldsmith, J. B., & McFall, R. M. Development and evaluation of interpersonal skill-training program for psychiatric in-patients. *Journal of Abnormal Psychology*, 1975, **84**, 51–58.

Goldstein, A. P. *Therapist-patient expectancies in psychotherapy*. New York: Pergamon Press 1962.

Gottman, J. *Couples Interaction Scoring System (CISS): Instructions for use of CISS*. Unpublished manuscript, Indiana University, 1974.

Gottman, J., Notarius, C., Markman, A., Bank, S., Yoppi, B., & Rubin, M. E. Behavior exchange theory and marital decision-making. *Journal of Personality and Social Psychology*, 1976, **34**, 14–23.

Harmon, T. M., Nelson, R. O., & Hayes, S. L. Self-monitoring of mood vs. activity by depressed clients. *Journal of Consulting and Clinical Psychology*, 1980, **48**, 30–38.

Haynes, S. N. *Principles of behavioral assessment*. New York: Gardner, 1978.

Haynes, S. N., & Wilson, C. C. *Behavioral assessment: Recent advances in methods, concepts, and applications*. San Francisco: Jossey-Bass, 1979.

Heiman, J. R. Uses of psychophysiology in the assessment and treatment of sexual dysfunction. In J. LoPiccolo & L. LoPiccolo (Eds.), *Handbook of sex therapy*. New York: Plenum, 1978.

Hersen, M., & Bellack, A. (Eds.), *Behavioral assessment: A practical handbook*. Elmsford, N.Y.: Pergamon Press, 1976.

Hersen, M. & Belleck, A. (Eds.) *Behavioral assessment: A practical handbook* (2nd ed.). Elmsford, N.Y.: Pergamon Press, 1981.

Hersen, M., Eisler, R. M., Miller, P. M., Johnson, M. B., & Pinkston, S. G. Effects of practice instructions and modeling on components of assertive behavior. *Behaviour Research and Therapy*, 1973, **11**, 443–451.

Hollon, S. D., & Bemis, K. M. Self-reports and assessment of cognitive functions. In M. Hersen & A. S. Bellack (Eds.), *Behavioral assessment: A practical handbook* (2nd ed.). Elmsford, N.Y.: Pergamon Press, 1981.

Hollon, S. D., & Kendall, P. C. Cognitive self-statements in depression: Development of an automatic thoughts questionnaire. *Cognitive Therapy and Research*, 1980, **4**, 383–395.

Honigfeld, G., Gillis, R. D., & Klett, C. J. Nosie-30: A treatment-sensitive ward behavior scale. *Psychological Reports*, 1966, **19**, 180–182.

Hoon, P. W. The assessment of sexual arousal in women. In M. Hersen, R. M. Eisler, & P. M. Miller (Eds.), *Progress in behavior modification* (Vol. 7). New York: Academic Press, 1979.

Hoon, E. F., Wincz, J. P., & Hoon, E. Physiological assessment of sexual arousal in women. *Psychophysiology*, 1976, **13**, 196–204.

Hops, H., Wills, T. A., Patterson, G. R., & Weiss, R. L. *Marital interaction coding system*. Eugene, Ore.: University of Oregon and Oregon Research Institute, 1972.

Hulbert, R. T., & Sipperelle, C. M. Random sampling of cognitions in alleviating anxiety attacks. *Cognitive Therapy and Research*, 1978, **2**, 165–169.

Insel, P. M., & Moos, R. H. Psychological environments: Expanding the scope of human ecology. *American Psychologist*, 1974, **29**, 179–188.

Ittelson, W. H., Rivlin, G., & Proshansky, H. M. The use of behavioral maps in environmental psychology. In H. M. Proshansky, W. H. Ittelson, & L. G. Rivlin (Eds.), *Environmental psychology*. New York: Holt, Rinehart, & Winston, 1970.

Jacks, R. N; *Systematic desensitization versus a self-control technique for the reduction of acrophobia*. Unpublished doctoral dissertation. Stanford University, 1972.

Jeger, A. M., & Goldfried, M. R. A comparison of situation tests of speech anxiety. *Behavior Therapy*, 1976, **7**, 252–255.

Johnson, W. *People in quandaries*. New York: Harper & Row, 1946.

Johnson, S. M., & Bolstad, O. D. *Reactivity to home observation: A comparison of audio recorded behavior with observers present or absent*. Unpublished manuscript, University of Oregon, 1974.

Kallman, W. M., & Feuerstein, M. Psychophysiological procedures. In A. R. Ciminero, K. S. Calhoun, & H. E. Adams (Eds.), *Handbook of behavioral assessment*. New York: Wiley, 1977.

Kanfer, F. H. Assessment for behavior modification. *Journal of Personality Assessment*, 1972, **36**, 418–423.

Kanfer, F. H., & Saslow, G. Behavioral analysis: An alternative to diagnostic classification. *Archives of General Psychiatry*, 1965, **12**, 529–538.

Kanfer, F. H., & Saslow, G. Behavioral diagnosis. In C. M. Franks (Ed.), *Behavior therapy: Appraisal and status*. New York: McGraw-Hill, 1969.

Kanter, N. J., & Goldfried, M. R. Relative effectiveness of rational restructuring and self-control desensitization in the reduction of interpersonal anxiety. *Behavior Therapy*, 1979, **10**, 472–490.

Karacan, I. Advances in the psychophysiological evaluation of male erectile impotence. In J. LoPiccolo & L. LoPiccolo (Eds.), *Handbook of sex therapy*. New York: Plenum, 1978.

Kazdin, A. E. Effects of covert modeling and model reinforcement on assertive behavior. *Journal of Abnormal Psychology*, 1974, **83**, 240–252.

Kazdin, A. E. Behavioral observation. In M. Hersen & A. S. Bellack (Eds.), *Behavioral assessment: A practical handbook* (2nd ed.).Elmsford, N. Y.: Pergamon Press, 1981.

Keefe, F. J., Kopel, S. A., & Gordon, S. B. *A practical guide to behavioral assessment*. New York: Springer, 1978.

Kendall, P. C., & Hollon, S. D. (Eds.). *Assessment strategies for cognitive-behavioral interventions*. New York: Academic Press, 1981.

Kendall, P. C., & Korgeski, G. P. Assessment and cognitive-behavioral interventions. *Cognitive Therapy and Research*, 1979, **3**, 1–21.

Kent, R. N., & Foster, S. L. Direct observational procedures: Methodological issues in naturalistic settings. In A. R. Ciminero, K. S. Calhoun, & H. E. Adams (Eds.), *Handbook of behavioral assessment*. New York: Wiley, 1977.

Kent, R. N., O'Leary, K. D., Diament, C., & Dietz, A. Expectation biases in observational evaluation of therapy change. *Journal of Consulting and Clinical Psychology*, 1974, **42**, 774–780.

Kern, J. M. *The comparative external and concurrent validity of three role-plays for assessing heterosocial performance*. Unpublished manuscript, Texas A & M University, 1982.

Klass, E. T. *A cognitive-behavioral approach to research on guilt.* Paper presented at 25th Anniversary Conference on Rational-Emotive Therapy, June 1980, New York City.

Klass, E. T., *Situational assessment of guilt: Development of a self-report measure.* Unpublished manuscript, C.U.N.Y., 1982.

Korchin, S. J., & Schuldberg, D. The future of clinical assessment. *American Psychologist,* 1981, **36,** 1147–1158.

Kulich, R. J., & Conger, J. *A step towards a behavior analytic assessment of heterosocial skills.* Paper presented at Association for Advancement of Behavior Therapy, Chicago, 1978.

Lacy, J. I., Bateman, D. E., & Van Lehn, R. Autonomic response specificity: An experimental study. *Psychosomatic Medicine,* 1952, **14,** 256–260.

Landau, R. J., & Goldfried, M. R. The assessment of semantic structure: A unifying focus in cognitive, traditional, and behavioral assessment. In S. D. Hollon & P. C. Kendall (Eds.), *Assessment strategies for cognitive-behavioral interventions.* New York: Academic Press, 1981.

Lang, P. Autonomic control or learning to play the internal organs. In T. Barber, L. DiCara, J. Kamiya, N. Miller, D. Shapiro, & J. Stoyva (Eds.), *Biofeedback and self-control—1970.* Chicago: Aldine-Atherton, 1971.

Lavin, P. F., & Kupke, T. E. Psychometric evaluation of the situation test of heterosocial skill. *Journal of Behavioral Assessment,* 1980, **2,** 111–121.

Lazarus, A. A., & Fay, A. Resistance or rationalization? A cognitive-behavioral perspective. In P. Wachtel (Ed.), *Resistance: Psychodynamic and behavioral approaches.* New York: Plenum, 1982.

Levenson, R. W., & Gottman, J. M. toward the assessment of social competence. *Journal of Consulting and Clinical Psychology,* 1978, **46,** 453–462.

Lewinsohn, P. M., & Graf, M. Pleasant activities and depression. *Journal of Consulting and Clinical Psychology,* 1973, **41,** 261–268.

Lewinsohn, P. M., & Libet, J. Pleasant events, activity schedules, and depressions. *Journal of Abnormal Psychology,* 1972, **79,** 291–295.

Lewinsohn, P. M., & Shaffer, M. Use of home observations as an integral part of the treatment of depression: Preliminary report and case studies. *Journal of Consulting and Clinical Psychology,* 1971, **37,** 87–94.

Linehan, M. M. Issues in behavioral interviewing. In J. D.. Cone & R. P. Hawkins (Eds.), *Behavioral assessment: New directions in clinical psychology.* New York: Brunner/Mazel, 1977.

Linehan, M. M., Goldfried, M. R., & Goldfried, A. P. Assertion training: Skill acquisition or cognitive restructuring. *Behavior Therapy,* 1979, **10,** 372–388.

Livingston, S. A. Psychometric techniques for criterion-references testing and behavioral assessment. In J. D. Cone & R. P. Hawkins (Eds.), *Behavioral assessment: New directions in clinical psychology.* New York: Brunner/Mazel, 1977.

MacDonald, M. L. *A behavioral assessment methodology applied to the measurement of assertion.* Unpublished doctoral dissertation. University of Illinois, 1974.

MacPhillamy, D. J., & Lewinsohn, P. M. The Pleasant Event Schedule: Studies on reliability, validity, and scale intercorrelation. *Journal of Consulting and Clinical Psychology,* 1982, **50,** 363–380.

Mahoney, M. J. Psychotherapy and the structure of personal revolution. In M. J. Mahoney (Ed.), *Cognition and clinical science.* New York: Plenum, 1980.

Mariotto, M. J., & Paul, G. L. A multimethod validation of the inpatient multidimensional psychiatric scale with chronically institutionalized patients. *Journal of Consulting and Clinical Psychology,* 1974, **42,** 497–508.

Marlatt, G. A., Demming, B., & Reid, J. B. Loss of control drinking and alcoholics: An experimental analogue. *Journal of Abnormal Psychology,* 1973, **81,** 214–233.

Mash, E. J., & Terdal, L. G. (Eds.). *Behavioral therapy assessment.* New York: Springer, 1976.

Mash, E. J., & Terdal, L. G. (Eds.). *Behavioral assessment of childhood disorders.* New York: Guilford Press, 1981.

Masters, W., & Johnson, V. *Human sexual response.* Boston: Little, Brown, 1966.

Mathews, R. M., Whang, P. L., & Fawcett, S. B. Development and validation of an occupational skills assessment instrument. *Behavioral Assessment,* 1980, **2,** 71–85.

McCullough L. *Systematic evaluation of the impact of computer-acquired data on psychiatric care.* Paper presented at the Fifth Annual Symposium on Computer Applications in Medical Care, November, 1981.

McFall, R. M. Analogue methods in behavioral assessment: Issues and prospects. In J. D. Cone & R. P. Hawkins (Eds.), *Behavioral assessment: New directions in clinical psychology.* New York: Brunner/Mazel, 1977.

McFall, R. M. A review and reformulation of the concept of social skills. *Behavioral Assessment,* 1982, **4,** 1–33.

McFall, R. M., & Lillesand, D. V. Behavior rehearsal with modeling and coaching in assertive training. *Journal of Abnormal Psychology,* 1971, **77,** 313–323.

McFall, R. M., & Marston, A. An experimental investigation of behavior rehearsal in assertive training. *Journal of Abnormal Psychology,* 1970, **76,** 295–303.

McFall, R. M., & Twentyman, C. T. Four experiments on the relative contributions of rehearsal modeling, and coaching on assertion training. *Journal of Abnormal Psychology,* 1973, **81,** 199–218.

Meichenbaum, D., & Cameron, R. Issues in cognitive assessment: An overview. In T. V. Merluzzi, C. R. Glass, & M. Genest (Eds.), *Cognitive assessment.* New York: Guilford Press, 1981.

Meichenbaum, D., & Gilmore, J. B. Resistance from a cognitive-behavioral perspective. In P. L. Wachtel (Ed.), *Resistance: Psychodynamic and behavioral approaches.* New York: Plenum, 1982.

Meichenbaum, D. H., Gilmore, J. B., & Fedoravicious, A. Group insight versus group desensitization in treating speech anxiety. *Journal of Consulting and Clinical Psychology,* 1971, **36,** 410–421.

Merluzzi, T. V., Glass, C. R., & Genest, M. *Cognitive assessment.* New York: Guilford Press, 1981.

Meyer, V., Liddell, A., & Lyons, M. Behavioral interviews. In A. R. Ciminero, K. S. Calhoun, & H. E. Adams (Eds.), *Handbook of behavioral assessment.* New York: Wiley, 1977.

Miller, B., & Bernstein, D. Instructional demand in a behavioral avoidance test for claustrophobic fears. *Journal of Abnormal Psychology,* 1972, **80,** 206–210.

Miller, P. M., & Hersen, M. Quantitative changes in alcohol consumption as a function of electrical aversive conditioning. *Journal of Clinical Psychology,* 1972, **28,** 590–593.

Mischel, W. *Personality and assessment.* New York: Wiley, 1968.

Moos, R. H. Behavioral effects of being observed. Reactions to wireless radio transmitter. *Journal of Consulting and Clinical Psychology,* 1968, **32,** 383–388

Moos, R. H. Conceptualizations of human environments. *American Psychologist,* 1973, **28,** 652–665.

Moos, R. H. *Evaluating treatment environments: A social ecological approach.* New York: Wiley, 1974.

Morganstern, K. P., & Tevlin, H. E. Behavioral interviewing. In M. Hersen & A. S. Bellack (Eds.), *Behavioral assessment: A practical handbook* (2nd ed.). Elmsford, N.Y.: Pergamon Press, 1981.

Mullinix, S. D., & Galassi, J. P. Deriving the content of social skills training with a verbal response components approach. *Behavioral Assessment,* 1981, **3,** 55–66.

Nay, W. R. *Multimethod clinical assessment.* New York: Gardner, 1979.

Nelson. R. O., & Hayes, S. C. Nature of behavioral assessment. In M. Hersen & A. S. Bellack (Eds.), *Behavioral assessment: A practical handbook.* Elmsford, N.Y.: Pergamon Press, 1981.

Nietzel, M. T., & Bernstein, D. A. Assessment of anxiety and fear. In M. Hersen & A. S. Bellack (Eds.), *Behavioral assessment: A practical handbook* (2nd ed). Elmsford, N.Y.: Pergamon Press, 1981.

Office of Strategic Services Assessment Staff. *Assessment of men.* New York: Rinehart, 1948.

O'Leary, K. D., & Becker, W. C. Behavior modification of an adjustment class: A token reinforcement program. Exceptional Children, 1967, **33,** 637–642.

O'Leary, K. D., & Kent, R. Behavior modification for social action: Research tactics and problems. In L. A. Hamerlynch, L. C. Handy, & E. J. Mash (Eds.), *Critical issues in research and practice.* Champaign, Ill.: Research Press, 1973.

O'Leary, K. D., Kent, R. N., & Kanowitz, J. Shaping data collection congruent with experimental hypothesis. *Journal of Applied Behavior Analysis,* 1975, **8,** 43–51.

O'Leary, K. D., & O'Leary, S. G. (Eds.). *Classroom management.* Elmsford, N.Y.: Pergamon Press, 1972.

Patterson, G. R. Some procedures for assessing changes in marital interaction patterns. *Oregon Research Institute Bulletin,* 1976, whole No. 16.

Patterson, G. R., Ray, R. S., Shaw, D. A., & Cobb, J. *Manual for coding of family interactions, 1969.* Available from ASIS/NAPS, c/o Microfiche Publications, 305 E. 46th Street, New York NY 10017, Document #01234.

Paul, G. L. *Insight vs. densensitization in psychotherapy.* Stanford, Calif.: Stanford University Press, 1966

Paul, G. L., & Lentz, R. J. *Psychosocial treatment of mental patients.* Cambridge, Mass.: Harvard University Press, 1977.

Paul, G. L., Tobias, L. L., & Holly, B. L. Maintenance psychotropic drugs in the presence of active treatment programs: A"triple-blind" withdrawal study with long-term mental patients. *Archives of General Psychiatry,* 1972, **27,** 106–115.

Perri, M. G., & Richards, C. S. Assessment of heterosocial skills in male college students:

Empirical development of a behavioral role-playing test. *Behavior Modification,* 1979, **3,** 337–354.

Peterson, C., Semmel, A., von Baeyer, C., Abramson, L. Y., Metalsky, G. I., & Seligman, M. E. P. The attributional style questionnaire. *Cognitive Therapy and Research,* 1982, **6,** 287–300.

Peterson, D. R. *The clinical study of social behavior.* New York: Appleton-Century-Crofts, 1968.

Pomeranz, D. M., & Goldfried, M. R. An intake report outline for behavior modification. *Psychological Reports,* 1970, **26,** 447–450.

Purcell, K., & Brady, K. Adaptation to the invasion of privacy: Monitoring behavior with a miniature radio transmitter. *Merrill-Palmer Quarterly of Behavior and Development,* 1966, **12,** 242–254.

Rathus, S. A. A 30-item schedule for assessing assertive behavior. *Behavior Therapy,* 1973, **4,** 398–406.

Ray, W. J., & Raczynski, J. M. Psychophysiological assessment. In M. Hersen & A. S. Bellack (Eds.), *Behavioral assessment: A practical handbook* (2nd ed.). Elmsford, N.Y.: Pergamon Press, 1981.

Rehm, L. P., Fuchs, C. Z., Roth, D. M., Kornblith, S. J., & Romano, J. M. A comparison of self-control and social skills treatments of depression. *Behavior Therapy,* 1979, **10,** 429–442.

Rehm, L. P., & Marston, A. R. Reduction of social anxiety through modification of self-reinforcement: An instigation therapy technique. *Journal of Consulting and Clinical Psychology,* 1968, **32,** 565–574.

Reid, J. B. Reliability assessment of observation data: A possible methodological problem. *Child Development,* 1970, **41,** 1143–1150.

Romanczyk, R. G., Kent, R. N., Diament, C., & O'Leary, K. D. Measuring the reliability of observational data: A reactive process. *Journal of Applied Behavior Analysis,* 1973, **6,** 175–184.

Rosenhan, D. L. On being sane in insane places. *Science,* 1973, **179,** 250–258.

Ross, A. O., Lacey, H. M., & Parton, D. A. The development of a behavior checklist for boys. *Child Development,* 1965, **36,** 1013–1027.

Rotter, J. B., & Wickens, D. D. The consistency and generality of ratings of "social aggressiveness" made from observations of role playing situations. *Journal of Consulting Psychology,* 1948, **12,** 234–239.

Seligman, M. E. P., Abramson, L. Y., Semmel, A., & von Baeyer, C. Depressive attributional style. *Journal of Abnormal Psychology,* 1979, **88,** 242–247.

Sintchak, G., & Geer, J. A vaginal plethysmograph system. *Psychophysiology,* 1975, **12,** 113–115.

Smith, R. E., Diener, E., & Beaman, A. L. Demand characteristics and the behavioral avoidance measure of fear in behavior therapy analogue research. *Behavior Therapy,* 1974, **5,** 172–182.

Spielberger, C. D., Gorsuch, R. L., & Lushene, R. E. *The state-trait anxiety inventory (STAI) test manual for form X.* Palo Alto, Calif.: Consulting Psychologists Press, 1970.

Staats, A. W. (with contributions by C. K. Staats). *Complex human behavior.* New York: Holt, Rinehart, & Winston, 1963.

Stanton, H. R., & Litwak, E. Toward the development of a short form test of interpersonal competence. *American Sociological Review,* 1955, **20,** 668–674.

Storrow, H. A. *Introduction to scientific psychiatry.* New York: Appleton-Century-Crofts, 1967.

Sullivan, H. S. *The psychiatric interview.* New York: Norton, 1954.

Trower, P., Bryant, B., & Argyle, N. *Social skills and mental health.* London: Methuen, 1978.

Turk, D. C. Factors influencing the adaptive process with chronic illness: Implications for intervention. In I. Sarason & C. Spielberger (Eds.), *Stress and anxiety* (Vol. 6). Washington, D. C.: Hemisphere, 1979.

Turkat, I. D., & Meyer, V. The behavior-analytic approach. In P. L. Wachtel (Ed.), *Resistance: Psychodynamic and behavioral approaches.* New York: Plenum, 1982.

Twentyman, G.T., & McFall, R.M. Behavioral training of social skills in shy males. *Journal of Consulting and Clinical Psychology,* 1975, **43,** 384–395.

van Hasselt, V. B., Hersen, M., & Bellack, A. S. The validity of role play tests for assessing social skills in children. *Behavior Therapy,* 1981, **12,** 202–216.

Wahler, R. G., House, A. E., & Stambaugh, E. E. *Ecological assessment of child problem behavior: A clinical package for home, school, and institutional settings.* Elmsford, N.Y.: Pergamon Press, 1976.

Wahler, R. G., Winkel, G. H., Peterson, R. F., & Morrison, C. C. Mothers as behavior therapists for their own children. *Behavior Research and Therapy,* 1965, **3,** 113–124.

Wallace, J. What units shall we employ? Allport's question revisited. *Journal of Consulting Psychology,* 1967, **31,** 56–64.

Watson, D., & Friend, R. Measurement of social-evaluative anxiety. *Journal of Consulting and Clinical Psychology,* 1969, **33,** 448–457.

Weiss, R. L., & Perry, B. A. *Assessment and treatment of marital dysfunction.* Eugene, Oregon: Oregon Marital Studies Program, 1979.

Weissman, A. N., & Beck, A. T. *Development and validation of the Dysfunctional Attitude Scale: A preliminary investigation.* Paper presented at the meeting of the American Educational Research Association, Toronto, 1978.

Westefield, J. S., Galassi, J. P., & Galassi, M. D. Effects of role-playing instructions on assertive behavior: A methodological study. *Behavior Therapy,* 1980, **11,** 271–277.

Wiggins, J. S., & Winder, C. L. The peer nomination inventory: An empirical derived sociometric measure of adjustment in preadolescent boys. *Psychological Reports,* 1961, **9,** 643–677.

Williams, C. L., & Ciminero, A.R. Development and validation of a hctcrosocial skills inventory: The Survey of Heterosexual Interactions for Females. *Journal of Consulting and Clinical Psychology,* 1978, **46,** 1547–1548.

Wolpe, J., & Lazarus, A. A. *Behavior therapy techniques.* New York: Pergamon Press, 1966.

Zuckerman, M., & Lubin, B. *Manual for the multiple affect adjective checklist.* San Diego, Calif.: Educational and Industrial Testing Service, 1965.

CHAPTER 6

Neuropsychological Assessment

THOMAS J. BOLL

Neuropsychology is both a discipline and an area of professional practice. As a discipline neuropsychology encompasses a study of the relationship between brain functions and behavior. As a profession neuropsychology is most frequently characterized by the use of a wide array of evaluative and assessment procedures and techniques to appreciate the full range of human behaviors as these behaviors are influenced by the development, maintenance, and deterioration of brain and brain function.

The underlying premise of neuropsychology is that the brain is the organ of simple and complex behavior in all species, and in humans is the organ of the mind. Interest in neuropsychological issues is at once as old as recorded medical history and as fledgling as the developments in applied psychology upon which these issues, in large part, rely.

Neuropsychology, however, is not limited to an assessment function. The frontier of neuropsychology is identified with developments in the science and technologies of behavior change, cognitive functioning, and physical, mental, and social rehabilitation as these are applied to patients whose psychoneurological capacity has been compromised. Despite considerable interest in retraining, rehabilitating fixing, and even improving coping strategies, the literature in the area of rehabilitation most broadly considered is far less reflective of clinically applicable advances subject to widespread utilization than has been the case for the same technologies when applied to more traditionally understood psychiatric behavioral deviations, such as anxiety-based disorders and depression (Diller & Gordon, 1981; Barth & Boll, 1980; Cleeland, 1981). Major efforts to advance the efficacy of intervention strategies for aiding patients suffering a variety of neurobehavioral disorders will undoubtedly characterize the single greatest research activity of neuropsychologists for the remainder of the twentieth century. Despite the recognition of the importance of this activity over the last three decades, and despite some significant efforts to remediate the deficiency already undertaken, a scientifically validated intervention strategy with applicability to behavioral deficits of any sizable number of patients whose difficulties stem from neurological disorder has yet to be established. Neuropsychology then continues to be best understood and most commonly practiced as an applied evaluation discipline oriented toward assessment and understanding of changes in human capacity known or thought to be due to alterations or abnormalities in brain development or function.

Interest in the relationship between human behavior and biological function and dispute over the localization of that function are at least 2500 years old. Alcmaeon of Croton correctly located mental processes in the brain, whereas Empedocles felt the same processes resided in the heart. Plato opined that, due to its placement in the body closest to the heavens (the head), the brain must be responsible for human-kind's highest rational nature. Aristotle, on the other hand, despite his knowledge of brain structure, believed that the warmth of the heart reflected its primary role in mental processes. While philosophers argued and speculated, physicians such as Hippocrates and Galen, who were familiar with the disorders of behavior experienced by their patients following brain afflictions, were convinced on this clinical basis that the brain was primary in the regulation of human behavior.

Establishment of the brain and not the heart as the organ primarily involved in the regulation of human behavior by no means reduced the role of the philosopher in consideration of mind-brain-behavior issues, nor did it signal the establishment of medical-psychologic-scientific method as the means for advancing understanding in these areas. In fact, to this day the role of the mind in, or possibly separate from, the bra'n is by no means settled in the opinion of all.

Descartes is most closely identified with the division between mind and body. To Descartes, the body was a material structure whose machine-like behaviors could well be accounted for by a variety of brain functions. Nevertheless, explanations of purely human behaviors required an understanding not only of body mechanics but also of the nonmaterial mind that existed quite separate from, yet in close interaction with, the body. The fact that the mind was nonmaterial removed any possibility for compartmentalizing and thus brought about a more holistic view of mental processes that reflected not only seventeenth century philosophizing but also nineteenth and twentieth century neurological theorizing. It also characterized twentieth century clinical psychological practice, at least prior to the establishment or more formal recognition of specifically neuropsychological practices and procedures.

While philosophers argued about the nature of mind and its relationship to biological structure, anatomists continued to explore the function of various portions of the brain itself. Arguments were presented that it was in fact the fluid within the cavities of the brain, called the ventricles, that controlled human behavior. Nerves were understood as hollow tubes through which fluid flowed, exerting control in a hydraulic fashion. Descartes, on the other hand, proceeding more on a rational than a scientific basis, determined that the mind would be located within brain tissue in its most central place. He thus identified the pineal gland as that most nondivisible and centrally located portion (well protected by the inert outer bark or cortex) of the brain that must serve as the mind's home. Thus both philosophically, by declaring the mind essentially nonmaterial, and neuroanatomically, by locating the center for the mind in a centrally placed and nonsymmetrical body, Descartes staked out the ultimate in nonlocalizationist positions.

The true beginning of neuropsychological understanding can be traced to individuals far more associated with the discredited phrenology than with brilliant anatomical-behavioral insights. Josef Gall (1758–1828) and Johann Spurzheim (1776–1832) believed on the basis of their anatomical investigations that it was possible to identify several areas of the brain, each responsible for an identifiable human psychological characteristic. Their localizationist views were overly precise and lacked knowledge of the integration of brain functions, and their categorizing of human behaviors subdivided human personality in idiosyncratic fashion; however, it was not these technical errors that undermined their credibility. Gall observed that certain individuals with predominant psychological characteristics had correspondingly predominant characteristics of their cranial vaults. This unfortunately led to an applied activity of personality analysis, referred to as *cranioscopy,* that has been a subject of ridicule from that time to this. Flourens (1794–1867) not only specifically attacked Gall and Spurzheim but also concluded from his animal experiments that the cerebrum, which was the site of intellectual functioning, suffered damage to its functions in direct proportion to the quantity of structural damage, however situated, that was exacted upon the brain as a whole.

In 1836 Marc Dax presented his finding that loss of speech capacity was associated with damage to the left cerebral hemisphere. Although his contribution was not formally identified until read by his son in 1863 and published 2 years later, his findings were recognized in a report by Broca, who has received the lion's share of credit for the finding that language is a function of the left cerebral hemisphere.

Broca initially saw two and eventually eight patients whose clinical presentations were most notable for their inability to carry on a conversation. Of the first two, one was unable to speak and the other could only utter the word "tan." In both instances it was claimed that the patient could understand speech and provided other evidence of intelligent functioning. Upon the death of each, Broca examined the brain and determined the presence of damage in the posterior inferior portion of the left frontal lobe to be the primary cause of difficulty. Broca referred to the behavioral difficulties that these patients experienced as *aphemia;* a term that was later rejected in favor of *aphasia,* suggested by Trousseau. Carl Wernicke (1848–1904) determined that more than one language area must exist and that, even when identified language areas had been spared, language could be impaired, very possibly by disruption of fibers connecting those areas.

Marie (1906) criticized these and other clinical impressions of the day and indicated (a) that the anatomical data on which the correlations for location of language had been developed were inadequate and (b) that the clinical examination on which the behavioral description was based was also insufficient. In the case of Broca's research Marie pointed out that, while his original two patients indeed had deficiencies in speech production, they also could not write and were apparently limited in understanding to a degree sufficient to characterize them as demented, and furthermore that no evidence as to these patients' capacity to read was ever presented.

The position that various types of human activity could be associated with specific areas within the brain was significantly advanced by the work of Fritsch and Hitzig, who conducted experiments with electrical stimulation of the cerebrum. In 1870 they reported,"Furthermore, it may be concluded from the sum of all of our experiments that, contrary to the opinion of Flourens and most investigators who followed him, the soul in no case represents a sort of total function of the whole cerebrum, the expression of which might be destroyed by mechanical means in toto, but not in its individual parts. Individual psychological functions, and probably all of them, depend for their entrance into matter or for their formation from it, upon circumscribed centers of the cerebral cortex."

Electrical stimulation of an individual clinical patient was first reported by Bartholow in 1874, from which work he reported as follows:

> To test faradic reaction of the posterior lobes. Passed an insulated needle into the left posterior lobe so that the non-insulated portion rested entirely in the substance of the brain. The other insulated needle was placed in contact with the dura matter, within one-fourth of an inch of the first. When the circuit was closed, muscular contraction in the right upper and lower extremities ensued, as in the preceding observations. Faint but visible contraction of the left obicularis palpebrarum, and dilation of the pupils, also ensued. Mary complained of a very strong and unpleasant feeling of tingling in both right extremities, especially in the right arm, which she seized with the opposite hand and rubbed vigorously. Notwithstanding the very evident pain from which she suffered, she smiled as if much amused. [Bartholow, 1874]

Far from being universally accepted, the localizationist position was greeted with significant resistance from such notables as Henry Head. Head claimed that the localizationist position was simply an argument of convenience identifying areas of brain with behaviors for which we had previous notions of importance, such as speech. In so doing he claimed localizationists were imposing upon the brain arbitrarily created organization, which they then set out to discover. Goltz, in work with animals, demonstrated that, although removal of portions of the cortex resulted in a lowering of intellectual and volitional capacity, this was accomplished in proportion to the amount of cortex removed independent of its localization. Following World War I, in fact, localizationist neurology and compartmentalist theories of psychology fell simultaneously out of favor, with preference going to a more holistic approach to mental apparatus and its biological structure. Lashley, relying on specific experiments rather than information derived from clinical examples of patients, proposed a theory of mass action of the brain. He suggested that the effects of damage to brain structure on human behavior were entirely dependent on the amount of brain removed and not on the location of the lesion itself. Henry Head (1926) dismissed the case report data and conclusions of Wernicke by stating,"No better example could be chosen of the manner in which the writers of this period were compelled to lop and twist their cases to fit the Procrustean bed of their hypothetical conceptions."

It is striking to note the contributions of John Hughlings Jackson (1835–1911), who thought of the nervous system as being organized in hierarchical fashion. He perceived the central nervous system as consisting of a number of layers, with each level representing higher levels of complexity of human behavior than the preceding one. He conceived of these levels as interactive and mutually dependent. Jackson identified the three basic components of the nervous system as (a) the spinal cord column, (b) the basal ganglia and the motor cortex, and (c) the frontal cortex. His underlying theory was one of evolutionary development, with each evolutionary step providing increases in capacity for more complex behaviors.

Just as he viewed increase in complexity as the result of evolution, so Hughlings Jackson viewed brain damage as a process of *dissolution*. In 1898 he stated:

> There are other ways of studying nervous maladies, for example, they are dissolutions, that is as they are reversals of Evolution of this or that part of the nervous system, that is, as they are departures from normal states. In these investigations we do not abandon clinical work: we must study nervous maladies by type first of all. One advantage of considering nervous maladies as dissolutions, is, that in so doing we are obliged in each case to deal with the diseased part as a flaw in the whole nervous system; we thus have to take into account the undamaged remainder and the evolution still going on in it. Apart from these applications of the doctrines of evolution and dissolution, I would urge as I have often done, that a great part of symptomatologies in nervous maladies with negative lesions is the outcome of activities of undamaged, healthy structures— that that part is a problem, not in pathology, but in physiology. Jackson, 1898, [p. 422].

The currency of this viewpoint is reflected in a review of modern surgical treatments of epilepsy by Wilson (1973), who states, "But the vagaries, surprises and disappointments of medical and surgical neurological practice constantly remind us that the signs and symptoms we discern in our patients depend less upon the lesion than upon the altered function of the whole brain in which that lesion is situated."

The work of Hughlings Jackson enjoyed only modest currency in his own time but is now considered of major significance, and in important ways it presaged the work of Luria, which represents a current major neurological theory. Luria, in describing the rationale for his behavioral–neurological evaluation, provides information not available through routine or even extraordinary neurological, neuroradiological, and neurosurgical procedures, and he states as follows:

> The restricted limits of regular, neurological symptoms is a result of some very important facts: lesions of the highest (secondary or tertiary) zones of the cortex—which are considered as specifically human parts of hemispheres—do not result, as a rule in any elementary sensory or motor defects and remain inaccessible for classical neurological examination. They are associated with alterations of very complex behavioral processes (cognitive processes, elaboration of complex programs of behavior and their control), and that is why one has to establish new complex methods that could be used to study dysfunctional disorders evoked by their injuries. It is thus necessary to apply methods of Neuropsychology for local diagnosis of lesions of those complex cortical zones. [Luria, 1973]

Donald Hebb (1949) is generally credited with the first formal use of the term *neuropsychology*, which appeared as a subtitle to his book, *The Organization of Behavior: A Neuropsychological Theory*. Despite the fact that Hebb did not use this term again after the title page, the following two decades saw sufficient formal development of the field that in 1970 Parsons was able to document its formal existence as follows:

> The selected papers of one of the most influential psychologists of our century, Karl Lashley, were edited almost a decade ago under the title of "The Neuropsychology of Lashley" (Beach, Hebb, Morgan, & Nissen, 1960). New journals such as *Neuropsychologia* and *Cortex* are devoted to studies explicitly neuropsychological in nature. During the mid sixties the International Neuropsychology Society was formed, primarily composed of psychologists of whom many identified themselves as specialists in neuropsychology. Professorships in neuropsychology have been created at several universities and at least one university Ph.D. program offers an area of specialization in neuropsychology. [Parsons, 1970]

Only one decade later, training of at least an introductory nature was claimed by over half of all doctoral programs in clinical psychology and clinical internship settings as part of their curricular offerings (Golden & Kuperman, 1980).

Recognition of the brain as the organ of the mind forces consideration of neuropsychological issues that go considerably beyond the identification of brain damage. The organization of mental functions determines, along with all other factors thought or known to be relevant, how we succeed and fail, develop or regress, learn and appreciate, and are perceived by ourselves and others. If the brain is recognized as the biological organ of our mental organization, it must be seen as playing a central role in any attempt at understanding individual differences. Available data demonstrate that organization and/or impairment to brain functions has been found to have relevance for general emotional adjustment (Rutter, 1977), academic competence (Rourke, 1981), intellectual development (Boll, 1981), occupational capacity (Newman, Heaton, & Lehman, 1978), emotional reactions (Galin, 1977), sex differences (Restak, 1979), and even certain behavioral differences among individuals of varying ethnic and cultural backgrounds (Martindale, 1978).

The time has long since passed when the state of the art in neuropsychology can be adequately represented by listing tests for brain damage, tests of organicity, or tests that have been found, utilizing group data, to separate brain-damaged from non-brain-damaged individuals. It is no longer appropriate to hold out members of these lists, taken individually, as competent examples of technology in this field. It is neither competent or responsible to do this for several reasons. It is well understood, as has been pointed out in this chapter already, that any unitary concept of brain damagedness or "organicity" that views all brain damage as pretty much similar in a neurobiological sense and that ignores all of the variables known to influence it flies in the face of at least 100 years of vigorous scientific debate and advance. It is well understood that variables such as type of damage, be it traumatic, vascular, neoplastic, degenerative, demyelinating, infectious, metabolic, or other, play a significant role in the *neuropathological correlates* of that damage. These types of damage play an equally significant role in the *neurobehavioral correlates* of that damage. Location of brain damage, be it anterior or posterior in the brain, involving primarily the right or the left side of the brain, focal or diffuse, involving cortical, subcortical, or a combination of such tissues, plays at least an equally important role in all types of determinations of brain behavior relationships. The age at which brain damage has been sustained, particularly in relationship to all of our knowledge about psychological development; the length of time that the condition of brain damage has been endured; the rate at which brain damage occurred and its current state of progress, restitution, or stability; and of course the size or amount of actual brain tissue that has been damaged—all play undeniable and unignorable roles in any effort to understand brain behavior relationships.

Just as no single type of brain damage or organicity exists, neither does a single characteristic human behavior emerge from the neuropsychological literature as most likely to be impaired following brain damage. Just the opposite is true. The more we learn of the relationship between human behavior on the one hand and brain function and brain impairment on the other hand, the clearer it becomes that the variety of brain-behavior relationships and the *inconsistency of behavioral function following neurological impairment are most outstanding,* and not the uniformity or consistency of behavioral impairment following brain damage that emerges from such investigations. It is not possible to specify that damage to any particular part of the brain will always produce any single type of behavioral abnormality, nor is it possible to specify that any single behavioral abnormality always results from damage to the brain in any specific area. Whereas general rules certainly have been established and some relationships can be characterized as reasonably dependable, it is nevertheless only through careful experimental investigation and competent and thorough clinical evaluation that reasonable knowledge reflecting the state of the art can emerge with respect to an assessment of a person's behavioral repertoire as it relates to the functional integrity of his or her central nervous system.

Any unitary test that would purport to be usable as an index of presence or absence of brain damage not only denies the complex relationship that is now known to exist between behavior and brain function but also encourages or at least perpetuates the trivialization of neuropsychological activity. It represents, in part, an espousal of diagnosis for its own sake at a time when information to enhance the understanding and management of an individual patient, whether or not this includes arriving at a diagnostic formulation, is the only responsible goal and one that sets off neuropsychology in the last quarter of the twentieth century from various forms of preneuropsychological thought and practice and in many instances from preclinical psychological thought and practice most characteristic of the first half of the twentieth century.

BRAIN FUNCTION AND BRAIN DISORDER

Even the most rudimentary description of the brain belies the simple or unitary nature of its organization and function. A description of those things that go wrong with the brain further suggests that the complex nature of neuropathology is far more likely than unlikely to have complex effects on those aspects of humanity for which the brain is responsible. Detailed descriptions of brain anatomy and brain pathology are available in any clinical neurology text, and a good overview of neuropsychological function in considerable detail is available from a book entitled *Fundamentals of Human Neuropsychology* (Kolb & Whitshaw, 1980).

The human brain weighs about 3 pounds and consistently conforms to a ratio of about 1 pound of brain to 50 pounds of body weight. This is proportionally larger in the human than in any other species. The brain consists of 10 billion neurons and 100 billion glial cells, each of which has multiple connections that, in sum, represent an incomprehensibly complex network of neurological organization. The most complex and distinctively human portions of the brain, the cerebral hemispheres, are upon superficial inspection seen to consist of right and left sides of about equal size, which are referred to as the right and left cerebral hemispheres. Within each hemisphere four lobes have been identified. These lobes are not functional demarcations, either neurologically or neuropsychologically, but rather are neuroanatomic/geographic areas of convenience to further communication. Their name originally came from overlying skull bones rather than from any specific characteristics of brain itself. Within the brain are four cavities referred to as ventricles. These provide a route for circulation of cerebral spinal fluid within and around the brain, inside the skull as well as to and from the spinal column.

The brain's blood supply is provided by four major arteries: the left and right internal carotid arteries and the left and right vertebral arteries. The vertebral arteries form a single basilar artery at the base of the brain and with the two internal carotid arteries join a complex network of communicating arteries to form the Circle of Willis. From this circle of arteries arises the cerebral circulation system. The lateral or outside surface of the cerebral hemispheres is supplied primarily by the middle cerebral artery on either side. The forward inside portion of the cerebral hemispheres is supplied by the anterior cerebral artery, and the rear-most or posterior portion of the inner side of the cerebral hemispheres is supplied by the posterior cerebral artery.

The four lobar divisions within each cerebral hemisphere are identified as follows: the *frontal lobes,* which represent the largest single division of the brain, taking up approximately the anterior one-third of the cerebral hemispheres; the *parietal lobes,* which lie immediately behind the frontal lobes; the *temporal lobes,* which lie behind the frontal lobes and below the parietal; and the *occipital lobes,* which represent that portion of the brain covered by the occiput or rear of the skull.

There has been considerable fuss, particularly in pop psychological circles, about the right and the left cerebral hemispheres as specific representations of particular human functions. Much of this is based on exaggerations of known scientific data. It is true that damage to particular areas of the brain may, in many instances, produce human behavioral changes identifiably different from those produced by damage to other areas. Nevertheless, no simple one-to-one relationship between brain area and higher-level mental functions has been identified. Only in the area of simple motor and certain specific sensory functions have any one-to-one brain-to-behavior relationships been identified. Even here alternative sites of damage can produce similar deficits. Arguments with regard to ipsalateral versus contralateral representation and complex versus simple organization of these superficially basic human behaviors continue to be heard.

In broadest terms the frontal lobes, which previously had been thought of as the primary site for human intelligence, are no longer regarded in this manner. It is quite clear that what we typically consider intellectual or higher cognitive functions are not primarily the province of the frontal lobes. Therefore, damage to these areas very commonly does not produce specific changes in formal psychometric IQ levels or in other performances that might well be associated with the content of intelligent functioning. This is not to say that the frontal lobes do not play a role in the process of these kinds of activities. Nevertheless, the suggestion that the frontal lobes are the site of human intelligence represents a historical view that has not withstood scientific verification.

The frontal lobes appear to play two at least equally important roles in human mental capacity and function that can be seen as integral to the process of intelligent behavior. The first is a *comparator* function. The frontal lobes allow us to observe and compare our behavior and the reactions of others to the behavior in order to obtain the necessary feedback to alter our behavior in the required ways to achieve the desired goals. It also provides us the ability to determine appropriately our desired goals and to make those judgments necessary to set a course to include the required activities necessary for goal accomplishment. The second is an *inertia-overcoming* function. Being able to accomplish something under close direction is very different from being able to initiate, accomplish, and conclude a task in an appropriate and timely fashion. Overcoming inertia means not only initiating a task when such is appropriate but also ceasing a particular behavior when the proper time has arrived. Individuals with marked deficiency in frontal lobe functions are frequently seen as evidencing serious failures in social judgment. Careful evaluation frequently reveals that these failures include inappropriate approach behaviors and difficulty or inability in ceasing social approach or other behaviors when they are no longer desired, appropriate, or productive. The behaviors themselves may, taken in isolation, not be bizarre; but the context and the manner in which they are managed give them their peculiar flavor. This would appear to be due to the inability of people, without the benefit of adequate frontal lobe monitoring, both to benefit from the feedback they are receiving and to alter or overcome significantly the inertia of their behaviors in order to bring them into conformity with social requirements.

The parietal lobes play a particular role in tactile and kinesthetic perception and understanding, spatial perceptual capacity, and certain aspects of language understanding and processing as well. The parietal lobes also play a special role in body awareness, so that damage to these areas can produce significant deficits in recognition of one's own and others' bodily characteristics, including recognition of familiar faces, difficulties in voluntary complex movements such as dressing, disorientation of right from left, and in some instances, even denial of body parts as belonging to oneself.

The temporal lobes are intimately involved in linguistic expression, reception, and analysis. They also play an important role in nonlanguage auditory processing of tones, meanings, sounds, and rhythms. This allows us to comprehend not only the content of what is being presented but also the process most commonly reflected by such variables as tone of voice, pitch, and speed that are used in most language systems as an integral part of communication. The occipital lobes are concerned primarily with visual processing, including some aspects of visually medicated memory.

Neuropathological categories, obviously an appropriate topic for an entire set of texts, can nevertheless be divided for purposes of the present discussion into six major categories of acquired disorder: vascular, neoplastic, degenerative, traumatic, infectious, and metabolic.

Cerebral Vascular Disease

This kind of disorder, which is commonly referred to in its extreme form as stroke, is most correctly understood as any type of cerebral vascular accident that involves blockage or rupture of cerebral vessels. This continues to be a common cause of morbidity and mortality, particularly among adults. The most common type of cerebral vascular difficulty results from occlusion of cerebral vessels. The two most common causes of occlusion are thrombus and embolus. A thrombus is a bolus or ball of fatty material building up on the side of a cerebral wall that gradually reduces the amount of blood flowing past it until the blood flow is completely stopped. Such occlusion may be sufficiently gradual that the development of a complete stoppage goes unnoticed in terms of observable symptoms, and it may be so gradual, in fact, that collateral circulation around the site of the occlusion develops to a sufficient degree that little impairment is noticed even on careful evaluation. Embolus, on the other hand, is a ball of substance that could be fat, clotted blood, or even air, floating within the vascular tree until it reaches a branch through which it can no longer pass. At that point it constitutes a blockade that suddenly stops further vascular flow and causes a rather suddenly occurring, acute cerebral vascular incident whose symptoms often include headache, motor difficulties such as weakness, paralysis, or numbness, and mental difficulties including speech problems, confusion, memory impairment, and not uncommonly unconsciousness.

Cerebral hemorrhage, most commonly seen in elderly patients, results from a combination of weakness in the cerebral wall and increase in vascular pressure against that weak area. This may result not only from primary cerebral vascular disease but also from other disorders, such as impairments of kidney function which are associated with increases in blood pressure. Also causes of cerebral hemorrhage are the varieties of congenital abnormalities of the vascular system. Due to their congenital nature they obviously represent disorders appearing in childhood as well as during adult years. Aneurysmal outpouching along the vascular wall, when subject to increases in blood pressure, may well leak, producing a spillage of blood into the cranial cavity and actually, on occasion, into the substance of the brain itself. Arterial and venous malformations are characterized by irregular and disorganized distributions of the vascular system. As a result, certain areas of the brain appear heavily covered while others appear barren with respect to vascular irrigation. Such structures are inefficient in their function and represent a site of risk for hemorrhage. Such congenital abnormalities have been found in up to 2% of autopsied adults who have died from other causes. The area of connection of the basilar and internal carotid arteries at the Circle of Willis is the site for the greatest number of vascular anomalies, whereas the internal carotid and middle cerebral artery systems are the sites for the preponderance of occlusive vascular accidents.

Strokes are cerebral vascular accidents of all types and most commonly produce significant physical difficulties, including unconsciousness and noticeable motor and sensory difficulties. Higher mental function deficits such as significant impairment in language processing and spatial organizational capacity are also frequently seen. On the other hand, many patients show no impairments in these areas, have excellent conversational ability, and can perform very well on many traditional psychometric instruments. At the same time, and to more sensitive and sophisticated examinations, however, they frequently demonstrate significant losses of judgment, memory, abstractive capacity, mental efficiency, learning ability, and general mental stamina not addressed in traditional IQ and mental status exams (Meier, 1970; Benton, 1970; Smith, 1975).

Neoplastic Disease

Neoplastic disease (brain tumors) falls into three major categories: intracerebral, extracerebral, and metastatic. Intracerebral neoplasms are more common among adults, whereas extracerebral neoplasms are more common among children. Metastatic neoplasms are tumors originating not primarily within the brain but in other sites, typically due to cancer of such areas as breast or lung, and infiltrating usually through transportation through the vascular system to a secondary site in the brain.

Brain tumors exert their initial symptomatic influence through the mechanism of the production by the increased mass in the brain of signs of increased intracranial pressure. These symptoms, regardless of etiology, include headache, nausea, dizziness, vomiting, seizures, and eventual unconsciousness.

Extracerebral neoplasms, most commonly represented by tumors of the meninges and referred to as meningiomas, comprise 25% of all tumors in the cranial vault (skull). They are referred to as extracerebral because they do not infiltrate brain tissue, but rather grow on support tissue outside, exerting their influence through pressure and increases in mass within the skull.

Intracerebral tumors, on the other hand, exert their influence in three specific ways. First, the tumor destroys normal brain tissue during the process of its growth. Second, the tumor replaces the normal brain tissue with abnormal tissue of the tumor itself. Third, the abnormal replacement tumor tissue grows to an extent that its amount exceeds that of the normal tissue destroyed, thus producing the effects of increased mass within the brain in addition to the effects of the abnormal tissue itself and the effects of the destruction of normal brain tissue. As intracerebral tumors are able to invade brain tissue in a very complex and insidious fashion, it is frequently impossible to determine, until laboratory studies have been performed, the actual extent of the tumor itself, which makes complete surgical removal essentially impossible in many instances.

Degenerative Disease

Conditions involving primary neuronal degeneration include two with a venerable and well-known history and one that is undoubtedly the most common but has only recently achieved recognition as a major cause of mental difficulties. These three conditions are Parkinson's disease, Huntington's chorea, and Alzheimer's disease.

Parkinson's disease, which produces lesions of the basal ganglia and cerebral cortex, is most commonly found with onset between ages 40 and 60. Motor signs include stooped posture, muscular rigidity, shuffling, small-stepped gait, reduced associated movements such as swinging of the arms when walking, and marked tremor. Parkinson's disease patients were once believed to be of normal intellectual function, and most if not all of their mental difficulties were attributed to depression in reaction to their motor symptoms. However, carefully controlled research (Reitan & Boll, 1971) has demonstrated that, although such patients may perform within the average range on a variety of IQ tests, they have nevertheless sustained significant declines in a variety of cognitive capacities that careful control comparisons reveal actually to include the IQs themselves. These psychological difficulties involve not only motor and sensory dysfunction but also marked impairments in memory and abstractive capacity and learning difficulties.

Huntington's chorea is a hereditary disease that, like Parkinson's disease, involves cortical and subcortical tissues with onset typically between ages 30 and 50. Here too the primary features involve disorders of movement including abrupt, jerky movements of the arm and an overall restless and jittery motor style. Such difficulties are increased by emotional tension and stress, which led initially to associating Huntington's chorea with early emotional deterioration. Little specific attention was paid to cognitive decline until recently. Current investigative efforts reveal, however, that no specific psychiatric syndrome is associated with Huntington's chorea, but that instead a general decline in cognitive and associated emotional capacity of an increasing and eventually severe nature characterizes a significant population of these patients (Boll, Heaton, & Reitan, 1974).

Alzheimer's disease is a progressive cerebral degeneration with pathological and behavioral characteristics of senility during late middle age. Alzheimer's disease usually develops between the ages of 40 and 60, with behavioral symptoms of progressive mental deterioration, difficulties in voluntary motor actions, and initially mild and eventually severe speech and language disturbances along with memory and judgment disorders. Neuropathological changes include a granulovacuolar degeneration in nerve cells, intraneural fibrillary tangles, and senile plaques in the cortex. Although most if not all of these changes can be found in the brains of apparently nondemented elderly patients, there is a quantitative relationship between the severity of the dementia and the severity and widespread presence of the pathological changes described.

Head Injury

Accidents involving injury to the head occur to over 9,000,000 persons each year (Cavaness, 1977), with the majority of these being sufficiently mild as to be (probably incorrectly) considered to have little psychological-behavioral short-term or long-term significance. A majority of patients with head injuries are not hospitalized, and, among those who are, the majority spend less than 48 hours in the hospital and are discharged with normal findings on physical, neurological, and electroencephalographic examination. They are reassured by their physician that, as these examinations and the nature of their injury point to little significant damage, nothing of a permanent nature is likely to have occurred. Unfortunately, in a large proportion of patients this is simply not the case. Even with cerebral concussion involving very brief or even no unconsciousness and no physical or electroencephalographic abnormalities, several investigators (e.g., Gronwall & Wrightson, 1975; Rimel et al., 1981; Boll, 1982) have demonstrated what Sir Charles Symonds reported fully two decades previously. His findings suggested that diffuse loss of neurons may be present after concussion without any symptoms being apparent either to the subject or to experienced observers. He went on to point out that head injuries were very probably cumulative events and that it was unlikely that anyone actually fully recovered from even the mildest of traumatic injury.

Further investigations of a far more systematic and neuropsychological nature by individuals such as Gronwall and Wrightson (1975) have pointed out that careful neuropsychological evaluation can reveal striking deficits in a variety of complex higher-level mental functions, even in patients who appear to all superficial estimates to be functioning not only normally but even at a high level of intellectual competence. Although this does not mean that every patient who has had a head injury is going to experience difficulties of a neuropsychological nature, or even that every one should have a neuropsychological examination, it certainly does suggest that our threshold for suspicion in this regard should be lower and that our awareness that unusual symptoms may well be associated with unreported neurologic disorders, including trauma, should be significantly greater than it currently is.

Infections of the Central Nervous System

Infectious processes include those borne by ticks and mosquitos, those transmitted in other fashions as in the case of mumps or infectious mononucleosis and those transmitted by ingestion of infected material (e.g., Kuru, a degenerative disease found in the eastern islands of New Guinea). Involvement of brain and surrounding brain tissue not uncommonly produces motor and sensory disorders or language and higher mental processing disorders that go significantly beyond the obvious and superficial confusion during the acute stages of the illness. These illnesses can attack both children and adults and may result in permanent long-term sequelae, including deficits in mental process of a wide variety of types and severity.

Metabolic and Deficiency Disorders

These disorders represent a broad spectrum of medical difficulties, many of which are only now being encountered and/or recognized with regard to their central nervous system and neurobehavioral deficits. Study of these disorders is creating broader recognition that illnesses not identifiably or immediately influencing central nervous system processes may well do so secondarily or even primarily and in ways that have escaped attention. They have not been seen until recently largely because they have not been looked for. The functions of vitamins and minerals the absence of which can produce selective starvation have in some instances been subject to clear delineation. A prominent example of this is the identification of a thiamine deficiency in severe alcoholism that produces a lesion in the dorsal medial nucleus of the thalamus and results in Korsakoff's syndrome (Victor, Adams, & Collins, 1971).

Additional causes of central nervous system deficit and neurobehavioral deficiency include a variety of environmental poisonings such as those that occur from lead, mercury, arsenic, and carbon monoxide and from disorders occurring internally, such as hepatic failure and amino acid disorders most prominent among which is phenylketonuria. As nutritional disorders become more clearly understood and more the focus of specific neurobehavioral investigation, it is clear that the role of subtle disorders, such as toxic shock syndrome (Rosene, Copass, Kastner, Nolan, & Eschenbach, 1982), and not so subtle disorders, such as renal disease (Ryan, Souheaver & DeWolfe, 1981) in body chemistry balance in the maintenance of a normal mental state will be appreciated not only in a general conversational sense but also in the more specific scientific sense necessary for the development of adequate intervention programs and documentation of specific preventive requirements.

TEST SELECTION IN NEUROPSYCHOLOGICAL EVALUATION

It is becoming widely recognized that the primary role of neuropsychology is not neurodiagnosis, much less playing the game of "guess my lesion." Neuropsychological procedures have been demonstrated to possess the necessary validity to describe the behavioral correlates of a variety of neurological disorders. Thus it is possible to describe the neurological disorders underlying those behavioral deficits. This type of validity serves as the underpinning for the psychological science of neuropsychology, not as the underpinning for the development of simply another branch of neurodiagnostic technology in behavioral neurology. Binary decisions with respect to presence or absence of organic disorder, when appropriate at all, must be ultilized to make some valid decision or to implement some form of intervention that would not have been possible or that would have been accomplished in an identifiably different fashion had that diagnosis not been made. Even when such is the case, however, it can be seen as only a waste of the psychology profession to limit one's activities to that most circumscribed of activities most adequately performed by others. Rather it falls to neuropsychologists to utilize his or her unique capacity for human evaluation of a patient who most undoubtedly can be characterized in a richer fashion by psychological procedures than would be possible through use of simple dichotomous classification techniques.

If one can recognize that the use of psychological tests to arrive at binary decisions such as presence or absence of brain damage is far from the best use of neuropsychological procedures, what then is the role of neuropsychological assessment and diagnosis in patients with known neurological disorders? And what is its role with patients whose behaviors raise the suspicion of underlying neurological disruption? The approach to neuropsychological or brain behavior relationships investigations most commonly (and I feel most appropriately) used is developmental or normative rather than dichotomous in nature. Its goal is descriptive and inclusive rather than diagnostic or selective. The neuropsychological model goes beyond a search for or focus on pathology no matter how exactly identified. The inclusion of tasks subject to normative rather than simply dichotomous evaluation allows for comments about degrees of health or excellence of behavior as well as comments about impairments or deficiencies. It is the interaction of human ability strengths and weaknesses, as influenced by the organization, development, and deterioration of brain and brain function as assessed through neuropsychological procedures, that represents the uniqueness of neuropsychology in the context of the overall neuroevaluative or psychoevaluative undertaking.

As Reitan (1974) stated, "It seems entirely conceivable that the principal correlates of brain lesions may be reflected in alterations of relationships among the behavioral variables and if this does turn out to be the case, it obviously will have been necessary to have used a sufficient number of variables to study their interrelationships and configurations" (p. 22).

The areas of human functioning to be assessed through neuropsychological procedures have no conceptual limits. Even before formal neuropsychological procedures emerged, individual areas of human fuction recognized as important for assessment in the context of questions in brain integrity included intelligence (Fulton, 1933); attention (Franz, 1907); highest integrative functions (Chapman & Wolff, 1959); reasoning (Rylander, 1939); and imagination (Fremann & Watt, 1942). Additional nominations in recent reviews by Boll (1978, 1981), Lezak (1976), Smith (1975), and Davison (1974) include learning; abstraction; sensory functions; information processing; memory, language, motor, and sensory activities; tactile, auditory, and visual perceptual competencies; and a variety of specific cognitive processes and strategies currently the subject of many experimental investigations. Affective processes ranging from depression and irritability to euphoria and psychological disorders from pathological denial to psychoses are equally grist for the neuropsychologist evaluative mill.

Factors involved in test choice range from those determined by the use to which the tests will be put to a variety of technical decisions regarding the adequacy, availability, and specific physical characteristics of the tasks themselves. A list of specific test factors that might be identified as desirable or at least worthy of attention include: (a) the test's availability in alternate forms; (b) its adequacy of standardization; (c) its objective scorability; (d) its portability; (e) its cost; (f) its ability to evaluate simultaneously a variety of integrated human abilities; (g) its ability to tap a single human ability uncontaminated by requirements for other skills; (h) its appropriateness to a specific or broad age range; (i) its ability to assess both multiple materials and multiple modalities of psychological function; (j) its demonstrated validity and/or reliability; and (k) its appropriateness to the physical and emotional limitations of the patient (paralysis, blindness, depression, anxiety, receptive language disorder, etc.). Although such a list could be expanded almost indefinitely, these considerations must be dealt with explicitly in any development of a neuropsychological battery. In addition, it has become common to consider the availability of these procedures for evaluation through multiple inferential processes rather than to choose tasks limited to interpretation by a single method of inference alone.

Two types of patients are most commonly referred for neuropsychological evaluation, the first being those with known neurological damage or disorder. In such patients the question very appropriately asked by a variety of referring sources, from rehabilitation counselors to neurological physicians to the families and patients themselves, is that of consequence. The fact that a patient has had neurological damage may or may not result in specific and identifiable physical or mental symptom development. Those symptoms that do develop may or may not persist. Nevertheless, the patient may well experience difficulties in a broad range of functions without obvious signs of neurological deficits to underlie their explanation. Patients who have had any form of central nervous system disease, disorder, or damage are clearly at high risk for behavioral sequelae. Such patients need and deserve a neuropsychological evaluation to aid them in dealing with all that they will encounter and to aid their families in similar regard.

Almost nothing more disorganizing and disabling can be done to a patient following a stroke, head injury, or other neurological disease or disorder than to turn him or her out of the hospital with the indication that all is well or stable and with no suggestion at all that mental changes may well have occurred. Such changes may alter patients' ability to work, relate, solve problems, and even care for himself or herself adequately or at least as well as was managed prior to the medical event. Vague reassurances, far from doing a little good, are positively harmful. On the other hand, a commonly voiced concern that indications of risk may well become self-fulfilling prophecies is simply not found to be the case. It is found instead that patients who are forewarned are forearmed. Such patients cope and maintain themselves and their families far better than those who are left to encounter the untoward consequences of their neurological events alone and unaided and who are left as well to conjure up reasons for the difficulties they are experiencing, having been provided none by their physicians. Rehabilitation counselors and families frequently have little or no training in understanding the behavioral correlates of neurological disease. They too are left to provide for the patients in their various ways without any basic understanding of the nature of the difficulty the patients are in fact experiencing.

The second group of patients for whom neuropsychological disorder is not only appropriate but common comprises those in whom behavioral difficulties are noted that may well be explained on the basis of neurobehavioral deficits. In those instances it is anticipated that the neurobehavioral explanation, far from simply documenting an abstract etiological basis, will aid in altering the remedial intervention strategies and in understanding the actual nature of the behavior being encountered and thus the reactions of individuals specifically as well as informally in the environment to those behaviors. Such individuals range from the child performing poorly in school, in whose case a decision as to whether his or her deficits are neurodevelopmental in nature or psychosituational will be critical in the intervention process, all the way to the patient who has transgressed the criminal code but whose intellectual process is compromised in such a way as to alter his or her ability to understand the nature of the act, to participate in his or her own defense, or even to be seen as having been meaningfully involved in the commission of an actual crime at all.

Smith (1975) described the utility of neuropsychological examination on patients with suspected or confirmed central nervous system disorders and indicated that there were three areas to which neuropsychological evaluation contributed:

> 1) In cases with verified cerebral pathology, initial neuropsychological studies contribute objective quantitative and qualitative measures of sensory, motor, language and mental functions in practical behavioral terms. Thus in patients with aphasia, hemiplegia, or other readily apparent and neurological deficits, specialized neuropsychological tests provide objective measures of mental capacity at different stages in the course of the underlying disorder that are often essential in considering rehabilitation or special therapy programs. In others they may reveal covert disorders in language, memory, and verbal and nonverbal reasoning that are not revealed in routine clinical evaluations of mental status. Repeated studies afford opportunities for defining the rate and degree of functional recovery and persisting deficits that may not be readily apparent. 2) In a smaller but significant proportion of cases in which neurological diagnostic studies are uniformly negative and fail to indicate an organic basis for the presenting symptoms, or in those in which such studies yield equivocal or inconsistent findings, neuropsychological testing affords a safe and relatively economic method that can contribute to the accuracy of the neurologist's conclusion. 3) In addition to their immediate practical value as an integral part of a neurological examination in individual cases, the systematic accumulation of objective data derived in routine neuropsychological testing has contributed to the increasing definition of human brain structure–function relationships and the development of more refined diagnostic techniques. With the accumulating elucidation of specific patterns of deficits in higher and lower levels of cerebral functions characteristic of lesions and different parts of either or both hemispheres, the accuracy of neuropsychological diagnostic tests may be increasingly refined, and depending upon their economy and efficacy selected brief tests may be usefully incorporated as part of the standard clinical neurological examination. [p. 73]

The maximization of multiple inferential methods involves first recognizing the possibilities in this area. Among the most commonly used methods of inference are level of performance, pattern of performance, specific sign of deficit, compared efficiency of the two sides of the body, pre- and postdisorder evaluation, and progress over time with regard to improvement or deterioration of behavioral functions. The last two methods provide little information or impose few requirements with respect to test selection or choice, whereas the first four clearly provide clues with regard to the kinds of procedures that one might employ and the interactive way in which one might utilize interpretive strategies depending on these multiple inferential approaches.

Level of performance suggests a quantitative and standardized use of data derived from procedures that allow comparisons among subjects or patients as to the relative degree of adequacy of their performance. Such commonly used tests as measures of IQ fit well into this model, as do those of academic achievement and even measures of simple motor performance such as speed and coordination. It is important to understand the level at which the patient is currently performing. Understanding of the particular types of abilities possessed by the patient, as these abilities are affected by the condition in question, may well change significantly depending on the validity and sensitivity of the tasks on which the patient achieved those levels. Nevertheless, even assuming the levels to be valid on their face (which is frequently not the case), *level* does not provide considerable information of importance with regard to the *process* of a patient's mental performance. No information is provided as to whether patients have ever been any better, whether they may well be improving or whether their condition may in fact be worsening. Nevertheless, such information does by itself give an excellent base for comparison of a patient with other known groups, and it provides an important point of reference with regard to interpretation of other measures.

Pattern of performance refers to characterizing the comparative ability strengths and weaknesses of a patient, even within a test that is initially looked upon as a measure of level of performance. Such measures as the Wechsler scales, that which provide data on level of performance, also provide a large number of scores (Verbal and Performance subtests as well as Verbal and Performance and Full Scale IQ scores) that, as elaborated by Kaufman and Reynolds in Chapter 3 of this book, are subject to a variety of pattern analysis strategies and factor-analytic breakdowns. As tests are added to one's evaluation procedure, the relative number of comparisons goes up multiplicatively rather than additively. In this way utilization of the maximum number of patterns greatly enhances the actual number of data points available in relation to the number of tests given to obtain those numbers of data points.

Specific sign of damage to mental process appears to be qualitative evaluative approach, although it is fully subject to quantification and requirements for scientific rigor. Certain behaviors and disorders (e.g., paralysis, aphasia) essentially never occur in a normally functioning individual, and no normative network is required in order to understand their negative implications for normal human functioning. Patients who are incapable of performing a variety of tasks such as recognizing familiar faces, reproducing the spatial aspects of simple geometric forms, copying, reading, repeating or pronouncing words, or carrying out other routine activities are giving an indication of deficit. Such deficits, when undeniably present, will have special significance that may well not be appreciated through evaluation of more standard kinds of procedures such as the Wechsler scales. It comes as no surprise to any experienced neuropsychologist that it is quite possible for a patient to have a Verbal IQ in the bright normal or even superior range and still be identifiably aphasic. If one is an expert in aphasiology, it may be possible to tease out those subtle deficits through qualitative analysis of verbalizations on the Wechsler scales, although the Wechsler is clearly not designed for such a purpose. A more direct and appropriate (not to mention scientifically more rigorous) method is to give an examination designed to evaluate language functions specifically in the confrontational format most likely to produce the required results.

Right–left comparisons of the efficiency of the two sides of the body also provide information not typically obtained in the traditional psychological evaluation produced by nonneuropsychological clinicians. At the same time they provide direct information about the types of psychological tests that might well be most useful in multiplying data-point comparisons. Although it is informative to know whether or not a patient is coordinated, quick, or strong, additional information is immediately provided. Comparisons of intellectual performance with motor performance and comparisons of the right and left sides of the body provide three looks at the same piece of data, and all of these are obtained at the price of a 2- or 3-minute motor examination. It is obvious that a variety of etiologies, although possibly negatively influencing level of performance, are unlikely to have systematic impact on right–left comparison information. No one has yet suggested that patients are likely to be more schizophrenic on one side of the body than they are on the other, for example.

When one composes a battery designed to maximize the complementary use of multiple inferential methods, it is quite possible to identify a number of tests used in conjunction with one another that can be arrayed in such a way as to provide a significant number of data points in a very manageable time period. It is also possible for this selection of tests to cover a broad range of higher and lower psychological functions. In so doing this test "battery" provides a reasonable screening of brain behavior relationships when utilized by a knowledgeable and trained clinical neuropsychologist. Obviously, the corollary to this is that the most comprehensive and well-conceived battery in the world, when used by an individual not trained in this professional area, is as useful as any other set of professional procedures, be it computerized axial tomography or a surgical laser, when wielded by an individual who is not appropriately trained. No technology by itself, no matter how well standardized or widely described, can be employed simply because it is available. Rather (and this should go without saying but nevertheless will not), neuropsychological technology is totally dependent on the professional training and competence of available neuropsychological personnel for its clinically useful, not to say ethically appropriate, employment.

THE HALSTEAD-REITAN NEUROPSYCHOLOGICAL TEST BATTERY AND ALLIED PROCEDURES

This battery includes several widely used general clinical procedures in addition to a series of experimental procedures adapted to particular measurement goals and requirements and modified for differing age ranges. These psychologically and psychometrically based tasks continue to be the most widely utilized general set of neuropsychological examination procedures in clinical practice and therefore will be described in some detail, as the present author has done in an earlier article (Boll, 1981).

The tests that make up the complete set of neuropsychological examination procedures vary somewhat according to the patient's age. The adult battery for persons 15 years of age and older is called the Halstead Neuropsychological Test Battery and Allied Procedures. The procedure for children ages 9 to 15 is the Halstead Neuropsychological Test Battery for Children and Allied Procedures. The battery for children ages 5 to 9 is the Reitan Indiana Neuropsychological Test Battery for Children. The Wechsler Intelligence Scales, the Wide Range Achievement Test, and the MMPI for adults are generally familiar to clinicians and will not be described in this chapter. The last three well-known procedures are frequently utilized alone or as independent contributors to many evaluation batteries. They are included with the neuropsychological batteries of Halstead and Reitan because of their considerable clinical utility in understanding patient abilities. Their validity alone and in the context of broader batteries of tests has been recently reviewed (Boll, 1978; Matarazzo, 1972).

The neuropsychological battery for adults (The Halstead Neuropsychological Test Battery) has been modified considerably from its original form, which comprised seven tests measuring 10 variables. Two tests measuring 3 variables have been eliminated. The Critical Flicker Fusion Test was eliminated because of inadequate statistical validation (Reitan, 1955). The Time Sense Test, although found consistently to separate groups of brain-damaged from non-brain-damaged persons with acceptable statistical confidence, has not proved helpful in evaluating the performance of patients considered individually, and therefore it also has been eliminated from the neuropsychological examination (Boll, 1974). This leaves five tests and 7 variables in the Halstead battery, from which an Impairment Index is computed.

The Impairment Index is a summary value computed from the seven scores derived from the five tests in the Halstead battery (Category Test, Tactual Perceptual Test (time, memory, and localization), Speech Sounds, Perception Test, Seashore Rhythm, and Finger Oscillation). The total number of scores falling in the impaired range is divided by seven and rounded off as shown in Table 6.1. The scores on each test referred to as impaired are those found in Halstead's original studies to be most characteristic of patients with impaired rather than normal brain function. These values, presented in Table 6.2, were established on adult males.

Other investigators have attempted to broaden this index to include other tests or to consider age and other factors that influence patient performance (Matthews, 1977). These efforts, although meritorious, have not achieved wide acceptance because of the reduced reliance among neuropsychologists on best test, summary values, and level of performance as the sole inferential method on which interpretation is based. These factors and the emphasis on neuropsychological examination as a valid descriptor of brain–behavior relationships, rather than as solely or even primarily a diagnostic tool, have led neuropsychological research into areas of inves-

Table 6.1. Halstead Impairment Index for Adults

Number of Tests in Impaired Range	Impairment Index
0	0.0
1	0.1
2	0.3
3	0.4
4	0.6
5	0.7
6	0.9
7	1.0

Table 6.2. Normal Range and Cutoff Scores for Six Scores Contributing to Impairment Index for Adult Neuropsychology Battery

Test	Normal Range (0 to 50 Errors)	Impaired Range (51 or More Errors)
Tactual Performance Test		
Total Time	15.6 minutes or less	15.7 or more minutes
Memory	6 or more	5 or fewer
Localization	5 or more	4 or fewer
Seashore Rhythm Test (Rank Score)	5 or below	6 or above
Speech Sounds Perception Test	7 or fewer	8 or more
Finger Oscillation Test (Dominant Hand)	51 or more	40 or fewer

tigation not mainly focused on perfecting an impairment index. Its usefulness then is as a summary score, not as an indicator of brain damage, and even then only in the context of other data understood through application of multiple inferential methods. Impairment indices are computed only for the adult battery, and no similar cutoff scores are available for the intermediate or young children's batteries.

The nature of the five Halstead tests that are included in the neuropsychological examination procedures for adults is elaborated next.

Halstead Category Test

The Category Test consists of 208 items divided into seven subsets. The items, on slides, are presented one at a time by a self-contained projection apparatus on a screen placed in front of the patient. At the front of this projection-screen apparatus (category box) is a panel with four lights numbered 1 to 4, and beneath each light is a lever. The patient is told that something about the stimulus on the screen will suggest a number between 1 and 4. The patient must pull the lever under the number thought to be correct. Only one response is allowed for each item. If the patient pulls the correct lever, a pleasant doorbell will sound. An incorrect response produces a buzzer. The patient is told that each subtest contains only a single principle. Correct responses to the first few items in each subtest are partly a matter of luck. The patient should soon learn from the pattern of bells and buzzers to modify responses by developing and testing new hypotheses until the correct principle is grasped. The patient is never told the principle, either during or after the test. The patient is told at the end of each subtest that a new subtest is about to begin in which the principle may be the same or may be different from that of the last subtest.

The first subtest of 8 items requires identification of Roman numerals. The second subtest of 20 items requires that the patient respond to the number of items on the screen. Subtests three, four, five, and six have 40 items each. Subtest three requires the patient to identify the position of the figure that is different from the others. Subtest four requires that the patient identify one of the four quadrants of the stimulus figure that either has something missing or is missing itself. Subtests five and six utilize the same principle, in which the characteristic of the stimulus to be noted is the proportion of the figure drawn with solid versus dotted lines. If two quarters of the figure have solid lines the answer is *two,* and if three quarters have solid lines the answer is *three,* and so forth. The patient is told that subtest seven is made up of items from subtests one through six and that it is necessary to remember and use the principles previously learned to get the correct response. These instructions are not strictly correct. Several of the 20 items in subtest seven do not appear elsewhere, and the patient must determine the correct response in ways not totally dependent on recall of previous subtest items.

There is no time limit for the Category Test, and, although the patient is instructed to respond carefully, encouragement for prompt response is also provided. The score is the total number of errors on the seven subtests. The great majority of patients make no errors on subtests one and two, as these are purposely designed to be relatively simple, to allow time to be certain that the patient comprehends and is responding to the task at hand and is not so grossly impaired or negatively motivated as to render the final score reflective of a problem not at all specific to the special requirements of this test. Verbal response by the patient is not required, and instructions can be delivered through pantomime. The Category Test is really a learning experiment and taps current learning skill, abstract concept formation, and mental efficiency. Patients who do poorly here are often characterized as having poor judgment and memory problems, and as behaving in self-defeating ways without being aware of the reactions their behaviors will cause.

Tactual Performance Test (Time, Memory, and Localization)

The Tactual Performance Test (TPT) uses a modification of the Seguin-Goddard Form Board. The board, containing spaces for 10 blocks, is held vertically in a stand placed in front of the patient. The blocks are placed between the board and the patient.The patient is blindfolded before and is not allowed to see them before, during, or after the test. The task is to place the variously shaped blocks into their proper holes on the board as rapidly as possible. The patient is instructed to use only the preferred hand for the first trial. At the end of that trial the blocks are removed from the board and placed on the table in front of the patient, who is then told to perform the task again, this time with the nonpreferred hand. Finally, a third trial is announced, this time allowing the use of both hands. Because of the learning involved from one trial to another, normal expectation is for approximately 30% to

40% improvement in time to completion from trial to trial. The total time for all three trials is the score that contributes to the impairment index. Time for each trial separately is also noted. The time score allows for evaluation of the data as to level of performance and compararive efficiency of the two sides of the body, working alone and together.

After the board and blocks have been placed out of sight, the blindfold is removed and the patient is asked to draw the board on a piece of paper. The patient is then asked to draw in all of the blocks that can be remembered, with each block drawn in its proper place. If the patient can remember a block but not its position on the board, it may be drawn in anywhere. A score for memory—number of blocks remembered and localization—number of correctly placed blocks is obtained. If a shape is drawn that does not look like any of the blocks but is identified by the patient verbally as one of the shapes on the board, credit is given. *Juxtaposition* might be a better choice of words than *localization,* because the critical compenent is the relative position of the blocks to each other and not their absolute position in the drawing of the board. The Tactual Performance Test assesses several abilities, including motor speed, utilization of tactile and kinesthetic cues to enhance psychomotor coordination, learning, response to the unfamiliar, and ability to remember things when not explicitly directed to do so (incidental memory).

Rhythm Test

This is a subtest of Seashore's Test of Musical Talent. Thirty pairs of rhythmic beats are presented by a tape recorder. The patient's task is to identify the pairs as either the same or different. The score is a scaled score based on the number of correct identifications, with 1 being the best and 10 the worst possible scaled score. This task measures nonverbal auditory perception, attention, and sustained concentration.

Speech Sounds Perception Test

Sixty nonsense words are presented by tape recorder. The patient is presented with a paper containing six subtests with 10 rows of four words in each subtest. After a word is spoken, the patient must identify, from four words on the appropriate line, the one which has been said. The score is the number of misidentifications. This task taps auditory verbal perception, auditory visual coordination of language processing, and sustained attention and concentration throughout a relatively complex and rapid task.

Finger Oscillation Test

This is a test of motor speed in which the patient must use the index finger to depress a lever connected to a manual counter. Each trial lasts 10 seconds, and the patient is encouraged to tap as rapidly as possible. The patient is given several consecutive trials with each hand (traditionally five, although this varies across labs). The score for each hand is the average of five trials within a 5-point range of each other. Here too, level of performance is combined with right–left comparisons in analyzing these motor speed results. Expectation is for the preferred hand to exceed the non-preferred hand by 10%.

Neuropsychological examinations routinely include procedures that were not part of the original Halstead battery. These tests, which are not integral to neuropsychological examination and are often referred to as Allied Procedures, include the following:

Trail Making Test

This test consists of two parts, A and B. Part A consists of 25 circles distributed over an 8½-by-11-inch sheet of white paper. The circles have numbers within them from 1 to 25. Instructions are given and practice provided on a separate brief example. The patient is instructed to connect the circles with a pencil in numerical order from 1 to 25 as rapidly as possible. If a circle is connected out of order the patient is stopped, corrected, and begun again from that point. The score is the total time, including that spent due to errors. Part B also consists of 25 circles distributed over plain paper. The circles are either numbered 1 to 13 or lettered A to L. The patient's task is to connect the circles in order alternating between numbers and letters, that is, *1-A-2-B-3-C,* and so on. The score is time to completion. Part B is roughly two and one-half times more difficult than Part A. Both parts require speed, visual scanning, and ability to progress in sequence. Part B requires in addition use of numeric and alphabetic symbols and ability to maintain and integrate two simultaneous series while alternating between them.

Strength of Grip Test (Hand Dynamometer)

A plunger-type dynamometer with grip adjustable for hand size is used to measure strength. Two trials alternating between preferred and nonpreferred hand are given. An average of the two trials provides the score for each, recorded in kilograms or pounds. This test measures grip strength in the upper extremities and provides another right–left comparison.

Sensory Perceptual Examination—Tactile, Auditory, and Visual

This procedure requires determination of whether the patient can perceive unilaterally presented stimuli on each side of the body. Following this determination, stimuli are presented in a bilaterally equal and simultaneous manner to determine whether the patient perceives both stimuli or whether stimuli to one side of the body that were perceived when presented alone are not noted when presented in competition with stimuli to opposite side.

Tactile Stimulation.   The back of each hand is touched lightly when the patient's eyes are closed. The patient's task is to identify which hand is touched. Unilateral stimuli are also presented to the right and left sides of the face. Patients who can perceive unilaterally are then presented with double simultaneous stimulation (hand–hand or hand–contralateral–face) interspersed among unilateral stimulation. The score is the number of times only one side is reported on bilateral simultaneous trails. The number of "errors" or suppressions and the side on which stimulation was not noted are recorded. This provides an overall index of difficulty and side of body impaired. The patient is never told that stimuli will be applied to both sides simultaneously.

Visual Stimulation.   The patient looks at the examiner's nose as the patient and examiner sit facing each other knee to knee. The examiner's hands are held equidistant from the examiner and the patient and extended to the side at eye level (peripheral vision). The patient must indicate whether the fingers on the right or on the left or both are moving. This procedure is repeated at two other levels of peripheral vision, above and below eye level. Here again, the patient is never told there will be double simultaneous stimulation.

Auditory Stimulation.   The examiner stands behind the patient and makes a slight noise (pressing fingers together and separating) in each ear, unilaterally. If the patient accurately identifies unilateral stimulation to each ear, bilateral simultaneous and unilateral stimuli are interspersed, with the final score being the number of suppressions on bilateral simultaneous trials. The patient is not informed of the bilateral simultaneous stimulation.

Tactile Finger Localization

Light tactile stimuli (finger touch) are presented to each finger beginning with the preferred hand. The order of finger touch is predetermined and stimuli are presented with the patient's eyes closed. A system allowing the patient to identify which finger is touched is established before the test begins. Most patients prefer to number the fingers from 1 to 5 starting with the thumb. Each finger on each hand is touched four times. The score is the number of errors out of 20 trials for each hand.

Fingertip Number Writing Perception

Numbers are written with an empty ball point pen or stylus (preferable to pencil for stimulus consistency) on the balls of the patient's fingertips. The numbers *3, 4, 5,* and *6* are written four times on each finger in predetermined order. Prior to writing on fingertips, the numbers are written larger on the patient's palm to identify the way the numbers are formed, and the patient is told which four numbers will be written. The test is performed with the patient's eyes closed, and the score is the number of errors out of 20 trials for each hand.

Tactile Form Recognition

The patient places one hand through a hole in a board. Into the fingers of that hand is placed a plastic chip in one of four forms (square, cross, circle, or triangle). The patient's task is to point with the other hand to the corresponding chip displayed on the side of the board facing the patient. The patient need not name the chip or make any verbal response. Each of the four chips is presented twice to each hand. The score is the number of errors for each hand and the total response time for each hand, from the time the chip is placed on the fingers until identification is made with the other hand.

Modified Halstead-Wepman Aphasia Screening Test

This procedure provides information about several aspects of language ability and usage, including the ability to name objects, spell, read, identify numbers and letters, write, do arithmetic calculations, enunciate, identify body parts, pantomime simple actions, understand the meaning of spoken language, follow directions, and differentiate right from left. It also provides several samples of a patient's ability to reproduce the spatial configuration of simple geometric forms. Figures 6.1 and 6.2 present the tasks required and the organization of the items. No scoring system is used, since high interjudge reliability is relatively quickly achieved with training in response evaluation. The impressive validity of this procedure is described in a later section.

PATIENT'S TASK	EXAMINER'S INSTRUCTIONS TO THE PATIENT
1. Copy SQUARE (A).	FIRST, DRAW THIS ON YOUR PAPER (Point to square, item A). I WANT YOU TO DO IT WITHOUT LIFTING YOUR PENCIL FROM THE PAPER. MAKE IT ABOUT THE SAME SIZE (Point to square.) Elaborate on the requirement for a continuous line if necessary. If the patient is concerned about making a heavy or double line, point out that only a reproduction of the shape is required. If the patient has obvious difficulty in drawing any of the figures, encourage him to proceed until it is clear that he can make no further progress. If he does not accomplish the task reasonably well on his first try, ask him to try again, and instruct him to be particularly careful to do it as well as he can.
2. Name SQUARE	WHAT IS THAT SHAPE CALLED?
3. Spell SQUARE	WOULD YOU SPELL THAT WORD FOR ME?
4. Copy CROSS (B)	DRAW THIS ON YOUR PAPER. (Point to cross.) GO AROUND THE OUTSIDE LIKE THIS UNTIL YOU GET BACK TO WHERE YOU STARTED. (Examiner draws a finger-line around the edge of the stimulus figure.) MAKE IT ABOUT THIS SAME SIZE. (Point to cross.) Additional instructions, if necessary, should be similar to those used with the square.

Figure 6.1.   Modified Halstead-Wepman Aphasia Screening Test.

5. Name CROSS	WHAT IS THAT SHAPE CALLED?
6. Spell CROSS	WOULD YOU SPELL THAT FOR ME?
7. Copy TRIANGLE (C)	Similar to 1 and 4 above.
8. Name TRIANGLE	WHAT IS THAT SHAPE CALLED?
9. Spell TRIANGLE	WOULD YOU SPELL THAT WORD FOR ME?
10. Name BABY (D)	WHAT IS THIS? (Show baby, item D.)
11. Write CLOCK (E)	NOW I AM GOING TO SHOW YOU ANOTHER PICTURE BUT DO *NOT* TELL ME THE NAME OF IT. I DON'T WANT YOU TO SAY ANYTHING OUT LOUD. JUST WRITE THE NAME OF THE PICTURE ON YOUR PAPER. (Show clock, item E.)
12. Name FORK (F)	WHAT IS THIS? (Show fork, item F.)
13. Read 7 SIX 2 (G)	I WANT YOU TO READ THIS. (Show item G.) If the subject has difficulty, attempt to determine whether he can read any part of the stimulus figure.
14. Read M G W (H)	READ THIS. (Show item H.)
15. Reading I (I)	NOW I WANT YOU TO READ THIS. (Show item I.)
16. Reading II (J)	CAN YOU READ THIS? (Show item J.)
17. Repeat TRIANGLE	NOW I AM GOING TO SAY SOME WORDS. I WANT YOU TO LISTEN CAREFULLY AND SAY THEM AFTER ME AS CAREFULLY AS YOU CAN. SAY THIS WORD: TRIANGLE.
18. Repeat MASSACHUSETTS	THE NEXT ONE IS A LITTLE HARDER BUT DO YOUR BEST. SAY THIS WORD: MASSACHUSETTS.
19. Repeat METHODIST EPISCOPAL	NOW REPEAT THIS ONE: METHODIST EPISCOPAL.
20. Write SQUARE (K)	DON'T SAY THIS WORD OUT LOUD. (Point to stimulus word "square," item K.) JUST WRITE IT ON YOUR PAPER. If the patient prints the word, ask him to write it.
21. Read SEVEN (L)	CAN YOU READ THIS WORD OUT LOUD. (Show item L.)
22. Repeat SEVEN	NOW, I WANT YOU TO SAY THIS AFTER ME: SEVEN.
23. Repeat-explain, HE SHOUTED THE WARNING	I AM GOING TO SAY SOMETHING THAT I WANT YOU TO SAY AFTER ME, SO LISTEN CAREFULLY: HE SHOUTED THE WARNING. NOW YOU SAY IT. WOULD YOU EXPLAIN WHAT THAT MEANS? Sometimes it is necessary to amplify by asking the kind of situation to which the sentence would refer. The patient's understanding is adequately demonstrated when he brings the concept of impending danger into his explanation.
24. Write: HE SHOUTED THE WARNING	NOW I WANT YOU TO WRITE THAT SENTENCE ON THE PAPER. Sometimes it is nec-

Figure 6.1 (*Continued*)

	essary to repeat the sentence so that the patient understands clearly what he is to write.
25. Compute $85 - 27 = (M)$	HERE IS AN ARITHMETIC PROBLEM. COPY IT DOWN ON YOUR PAPER ANY WAY YOU LIKE AND TRY TO WORK IT OUT. (Show item M.)
26. Compute $17 \times 3 =$	NOW DO THIS ONE IN YOUR HEAD: 17×3
27. Name KEY (N)	WHAT IS THIS: (Show item N.)
28. Demonstrate use of KEY (N)	IF YOU HAD ONE OF THESE IN YOUR HAND, SHOW ME HOW YOU WOULD USE IT. (Show item N.)
29. Draw KEY (N)	NOW I WANT YOU TO DRAW A PICTURE THAT LOOKS JUST LIKE THIS. TRY TO MAKE YOUR KEY LOOK ENOUGH LIKE THIS ONE SO THAT I WOULD KNOW IT WAS THE SAME KEY FROM YOUR DRAWING. (Point to key, item N.)
30. Read (O)	WOULD YOU READ THIS? (Show item O.)
31. Place LEFT HAND TO RIGHT EAR	NOW, WOULD YOU DO WHAT IT SAID?
32. Place LEFT HAND TO LEFT ELBOW	NOW I WANT YOU TO PUT YOUR LEFT HAND TO YOUR LEFT ELBOW. The patient should quickly realize that it is impossible.

Figure 6.1   (*Continued*)

THE HALSTEAD NEUROPSYCHOLOGICAL TEST BATTERY FOR CHILDREN AND ALLIED PROCEDURES

The extension of the neuropsychological examination to persons below age 15 was accomplished by Reitan and his colleagues at the Indiana University Medical Center starting in 1951. The first extension, which resulted in a battery highly similar to that used with adults, is referred to most commonly as the intermediate or "old kids" battery and is appropriate for children ages 9 to 15 (through 14). The instructions from the adult battery have been retained, and the modifications in individual tests are presented below.

Category Test

The intermediate version has 168 items distributed into six tests. Some items from the adult test were reordered to attain a more consistent increase in difficulty, and all of the colored items were omitted. The 40-item fourth subtest of the adult version was also eliminated. Finally, the summary sixth subtest consists only of those items that actually have appeared before as claimed in the instructions.

Tactual Performance Test

Initial modifications of this test utilized an eight-block board before finally settling on a six-block board held vertically in its stand. Four blocks (triangle, star, circle,

Figure 6.2. Stimulus figures for testing cerebral functions. This test is the Halstead-Wepman screening test, as modified by Ralph Reitan and currently used in the Neuropsychology Laboratory at The University of Alabama in Birmingham and many other testing centers.

and long six-sided figure) were omitted. The stand and remaining six blocks are the same as those used in the adult form.

Speech Sounds Perception Test

The stimuli are still presented by a tape recorder, and the number of items remains unchanged. The number of nonsense words on each line of the answer sheet was reduced from four to three.

Trail Making Test

The number of items involved in Part A and Part B is reduced from 25 to 15. The overall organization and procedure remain unchanged. Part A now includes circles from 1 to 15. Part B has circles from A through G and numbers from 1 through 8.

Impairment Index

An impairment or other summary score is not computed for the intermediate battery.

All other tests in the intermediate battery are identical to those administered to adults.

THE REITAN INDIANA NEUROPSYCHOLOGICAL TEST BATTERY FOR CHILDREN

A further downward extension in age of children able to participate in neuropsychological examination procedures was begun by Reitan in 1955. The modifications found necessary for children from ages 5 to 9 (through 8) proved to be considerably more extensive than those required for children 9 to 15. Some tests were further modified and some were eliminated entirely, and several new procedures were developed. The battery for young children, although very different from the other two batteries, retains many of the same principles and characteristics. Test procedures were sought that tapped a wide array of human abilities through several modalities. Tests characterized as both narrow band and wide band in nature were included. The tests were chosen to maximize the complementary use of multiple and inferential methods. Changes both in task and instruction complexity and in the assumptions about baseline knowledge and experience were necessary.

Category Test

It would be incorrect to assume that children of this age are all familiar with numbers. For this reason the lights over the response levers were changed to red, blue, yellow, and green. The stimulus characteristics of the colors were designed to minimize, if not eliminate, disadvantages due to colorblindness. The test was shortened to 80 items across five subtests. Color knowledge or naming is not required. Instead, some aspect of the stimulus suggests a particular color, and, if the lever under that color is pulled, the patient is positively reinforced by the bell. The first subtest of 10 items requires the patient to choose the response lever under the color that appears on the screen. Subtests two, three, and four have 20 items each. Subtest two requires response to the color present in the greatest quantity on each slide. Subtest three utilizes an oddity principle. Some characteristic of the stimulus other than color (size, shape) determines the response. Subtest four requires response to the color least predominatly present or totally absent. The fifth subtest is made up of 10 items drawn from the other subtests.

Tactual Performance Test

The same six-block board used for the intermediate version is retained but it is turned 90° and presented horizontally instead of vertically to accommodate the shorter reach of younger children.

The Strength of Grip and Finger Oscillation Tests

These tests are included without modification. An electric finger-tapping apparatus was introduced to present a task easier for patients with shorter fingers. The technical disadvantages of this procedure were found to outweigh its advantages. Younger children are able to manage well with the manual tapper, and use of the electric apparatus is neither necessary nor recommended.

Aphasia and Sensory Perceptual Examination

The aphasia test is reduced to 22 items and, as can be seen from Figure 6.3, the items have been simplified to take into account normal expectations for children ages 5 to 9. The Fingertip Symbol Writing Test (x's and o's) is substituted for Fingertip Number Writing Test. The Tactile Finger Localization and Tactile Form Recognition procedures and the bilateral simultaneous tactile, visual, and auditory procedures are included without modification. The Rhythm, Speech Sounds Perception, and Trail Making Tests are not administered to children under age 9.

Marching Test

This test was designed to assess gross skeletal muscular function and coordination. The test has two parts. In the first part the patient is to move from the bottom to the top of a legal-sized sheet tapping a crayon in each of a series of circles. On each of the five pages the alignment of the circles deviates by increasing amounts from the perfectly vertical arrangement of the first sheet. The patient must simply "march" up the page one hand at a time hitting each circle with a crayon. The second part requires the use of both arms. The examiner "marches" up the page alternating movements from one hand to the other at a rate of one circle per second. The patient is required to follow the examiner simultaneously up the page. The score is the number of circles completed.

(Ages 5 through 8 years)

Name_____Date_____Examiner_____

Write NAME	COUNT fingers
Copy SQUARE	COMPUTE 2 + 2 (Verbal)
Copy CROSS	COMPUTE 2 + 1 (Written)
Copy TRIANGLE	COMPUTE 4 + 3 (Verbal)
Name BABY	Name KEY
Name CLOCK	Put FINGER on NOSE
Name FORK	Show TONGUE
Read 7 SIX 2	Where is EYEBROW?
Read MGW	Point to ELBOW
Read SEE THE BLACK DOG	Put RIGHT HAND on NOSE
Print SQUARE	Put LEFT HAND on HEAD

Sensory-Perceptual Examination

Indicate instance in which stimulus is not perceived or is incorrectly perceived:

Tactile: RH ▢ LH ▢ BH: RH ▢ LH ▢
RH ▢ LF ▢ B: RH ▢ LF ▢
LH ▢ RF ▢ B: LH ▢ RF ▢

Auditory: RE ▢ LE ▢ B: RE ▢ LE ▢

Visual: RV ▢ LV ▢ B: RV ▢ LV ▢

Tactile Finger Right: 1 2 3 4 5
Recognition: Left: 1 2 3 4 5

Finger-tip Symbol Writing Recognition: Right: 1 [0 0 X X] 2 [X X 0 0] 3 [X C X 0] 4 [X 0 0 X] 5 [0 X X 0]
Left: 1 2 3 4 5

Tactile Form Recognition Test: RH: [○ □ △ ✚] LH: [△ ✚ ○ □] RH: [✚ ○ □ △] LH: [□ △ ✚ ○]

LATERAL DOMINANCE EXAMINATION

Name_____Date_____Examiner_____

1. Show me your right hand_____; left ear_____; right eye_____

2. Show me how you   throw a ball _____
                      hammer a nail _____
                      cut with a knife _____
                      turn a door knob _____

Figure 6.3. Aphasic and perceptual disorders (ages 5 through 8 years).

use scissors _____
use an eraser _____
write your name _____

3. Write your full name

preferred hand (_____) _____seconds
nonpreferred hand (_____) _____seconds

4. Show me how you look through a telescope. _____eye.
   Aim this gun at the top of my nose. _____shoulder. _____eye.

5. Show me how you kick a football. _____foot
                 step on a bug. _____foot

6. Strength of grip. (Hold dynamometer at arm's length, point to the floor, and squeeze as hard as you can.)

   1. preferred (_____) _____kgs.   2. nonpreferred (_____) _____kgs.

   3. preferred   _____kgs.   4. nonpreferred   _____kgs.

                 Total: _____kgs.   Total: _____kgs.

            Hand Mean: _____kgs.   Hand Mean: _____kgs.

7. ABC Test for Ocular Dominance

   (1)_____   (6)_____
   (2)_____   (7)_____
   (3)_____   (8)_____   Right: _____
   (4)_____   (9)_____
   (5)_____   (10)_____   Left: _____

Figure 6.3. (*Continued*)

Color Form Test

This test presents geometric shapes of several colors on an 8½- by -11-inch board. The patient is required to move his or her finger from one figure to another following an alternating sequence of color–shape–color–shape. The score is the time to completion. The patient must be able to attend to one characteristic (color or shape) of a figure while ignoring the other and progress by alternation from one to the other.

Progressive Figures Test

This test presents a series of geometric figures with smaller and different shapes inside. The figures are distributed on an 8½-by-11-inch sheet. The patient uses the inside figure as a guide and progresses to an outside figure of that shape until each figure has been connected. The score is the time to completion. The Color Form and

Progressive Figures Tests tap capabilities such as attention, concentration, visual scanning, flexibility, and speed as does the Trail Making Test, which is organized in a similar fashion.

Matching Pictures Test

This task requires matching two sets of pictures of increasing degrees of physical dissimilarity. Matching progresses from physical resemblance to categorical similarity. The score is the number correct.

Target Test

An 18-by-18-inch card with nine black dots in a 3-by-3 square on it is placed on a wall in front of the patient. The patient is given an 8½-by-11-inch sheet with 20 similar 3-by-3 dot squares. The examiner taps out a design by striking various dots on the large card. Following a 3-second delay, the patient is to draw a line on one of the figures on the answer sheet, connecting dots that were tapped by the examiner. The score is the number of correct designs.

Matching V's and Matching Figures Tests

A card with seven figures is placed in front of the patient. Seven small squares, each containing one of the figures on the card, are laid out in mixed order. The patient must place the small squares under the identical figures. The V's vary as to width of the angle, and the figures vary as to degree of complexity of the internal design. The score is the time to completion for each and number of errors committed.

VALIDITY OF PSYCHOLOGICAL–NEUROPSYCHOLOGICAL PROCEDURES

The work of validation of the original Halstead procedures and the now more familiar procedures reflecting Reitan's modifications and additions has taken a step-by-step approach. The earlier studies by Halstead (1947), Reitan (1955), and Vega and Parsons (1967) focused on a simple differentiation of groups of patients with or without brain damage, without further specification. The work to be discussed in more detail below then progressed to greater degrees of sophistication and included issues such as lateralization, location and type of pathology, and chronicity.

The initial validation of the full set of neuropsychological procedures including the Halstead battery was reported by Reitan in 1955. This study also presented a cross-validation of Halstead's work accomplished at different locations with different examiners, patients, and investigators. Expectation is for some reduction in significance from the initial finding. In this study 50 patients with a heterogeneous selection of documented brain damage were compared with 38 non-brain-damaged hospitalized patients and 12 nonpatients. With the exception of Critical Flicker Fusion, all of the tests in this battery produced statistically significant separations between those two groups at levels that met or exceeded those obtained in Halstead's original study. Reitan also reported that the Trail Making Test separated brain-damaged from non-brain-damaged patients at the .001 level for both Part A and Part B. He then compared 200 brain-damaged and 84 non-brain-damaged patients and again found that Part A and Part B produced group separations beyond the .001 level (Reitan, 1958). The clinical criteria or levels of expectation for non-brain-damaged patients derived from this study were completion of Part A in 38 seconds or less and Part B in 88 seconds or less. Using these scores, Part A was found to classify 70% of non-brain-damaged and 78.5% of brain-damaged patients correctly. Part B classified 81% of non-brain-damaged and 88.5% of brain-damaged patients correctly. Use of these two scores as a weighted sum failed to improve the percentage of correct classification for either group.

Vega and Parsons (1967) reported the first major cross-validation of this battery of procedures by investigators other than Halstead or Reitan and their immediate associates. This investigation compared hospitalized and nonhospitalized brain-damanged and non-brain-damaged patients. Their results for brain-damaged and non-brain-damaged patients alike reflected significantly poorer levels of performance than those reported by Halstead and Reitan. Several factors, such as differences in geographic and cultural background and the vigor with which the examinations were administered, present possible explanations for these differences. Nevertheless, the ability of these procedures to achieve highly significant separations between brain-damaged and non-brain-damaged patients despite the poor performance of both groups was a gain demonstrated.

More recently, studies in independent neuropsychological laboratories in Wisconsin (Matthews, Shaw, & Klove, 1966), British Columbia (Klonoff, Fibiger, & Hutton, 1970), Oregon (Goldstein, Deysach, & Kleinkecht, 1973), and St. Louis (Schreiber, Goldman, Kleinman, Goldfader, & Snow, 1976) have confirmed the statistical and clinical validity and the utility of these procedures in the hands of well-trained neuropsychologists.

The studies by Filskov and Goldstein (1974) and by Matthews, Shaw, and Klove (1966) are of particular clinical relevance and will be discussed in more detail. The Filskov and Goldstein study makes it clear that the usual neurodiagnostic process includes a step-by-step approach and is not at all characterized by reliance on any single indicator of brain damage versus absence of brain damage. As questions arise and information is obtained, examination procedures are utilized that are specifically designed to assess areas in question or to provide more detailed and confirming data prior to arrival at a final and complete diagnosis. It should be noted that many purely neurological medical procedures such as computerized axial tomography (CAT Scan) and electroencephalography (EEG) are designed to provide information about the entire area of the brain or skull as well as about the particular region in question. It is well understood that any purely selective pursuit of the apparent area of deficit may overlook two important aspects of brain disorder in order to learn about one. First, other areas of the brain may be impaired without obvious contribution to the presenting complaint, the initial symptoms, or the diagnostic findings.

Only a more careful and complete evaluation can hope to provide the necessary information about the patient's total situation instead of providing a selective focus on that aspect initially assumed to be most critical. Second, knowledge of areas of health and normality of structure and function not only aid in limiting the area of impairment but also provide the major source for understanding and predicting recovery and response to treatment. It can also be noted that the several steps in the neurodiagnostic process provide information that is not totally redundant but rather comes from differing *kinds* of examinations, such as the brain's external structure, skull integrity, electrical activity, and internal structure and, to a very limited extent, its behavioral repertoire.

A series of studies has focused on the relationship of neuropsychological functions and individual neurodiagnostic procedures such as the physical neurological examination, electroencephalogram, and pneumoencephalogram. Klove (1963) compared two groups of brain-damaged patients and a group of normals. One brain-damaged group had abnormal physical neurological examination results, while the other was rated normal on this procedure, which examines reflexes, coordination, locomotion, strength, and sensation and includes ophthalmoscopy, oscultation of the head, and examination of the cranial nerves. Brain-damaged patients were correctly identified through neuropsychological examination independent of the results of physical examinations. Results on physical examination represent scant basis on which to determine presence or absence of brain damage or likelihood of finding useful information following more comprehensive behavioral evaluation. Klove (1959), in a similarly designed study, demonstrated that neuropsychological procedures were sensitive to behavioral deficits related to impaired brain functions independent of whether the brain-damaged patients had normal or abnormal electroencephalograms. Klove and White (1963) found more severe neuropsychological impairment in brain-damaged patients with severely abnormal EEGs than in brain-damaged patients with normal EEGs. Matthews and Booker (1972) compared degree of neuropsychological impairment to degree of deficit reflected on pneumoencephalogram as determined by amount of dilatation of the lateral ventricles. They found that those patients with greatest dilatation showed consistently poorer neuropsychological functions than did those with least ventricular enlargement. Neurological examination of any patient is enhanced by inclusion of a neuropsychological assessment of the patient's behavioral repertoire that is designed to contribute to the stepwise information-gathering and decision-making process. This process does not end with diagnosis. Benefit also occurs through contribution to an understanding of those characteristics most descriptive of the patient's ability to comprehend and comply with medical regimes, to experience recovery, and to participate in and benefit from the available variety of remediation and rehabilitation procedures. Filskov and Goldstein (1974) demonstrated that neuropsychological examination can, without risk of death or injury, provide clinical information whose validity compares favorably with the other equally necessary procedures and allows clinicians to get a complete picture of the patient's situation and to make recommendations for the patient's optimum treatment and management.

A particularly troublesome group of patients for many clinicians comprises those who present with peculiar physical symptoms or a conglomeration of physical and emotional difficulties. It often falls to neuropsychological examination to attempt to sort out several aspects of such a situation utilizing procedures whose primary validity was established on patients with disorders that are far more readily identifiable. Matthews et al. (1966) demonstrated the clinical utility in such situations of a neuropsychological battery, while cautioning that attempts to reduce the number of tests employed resulted in rapid and significant reductions in statistical and clinical confidence in attaining the required information. These investigators examined patients admitted to the neurology inpatient service for complaints and symptoms that included nausea, headache, dizziness, motor weakness, visual difficulties, and ictal episodes simulating epilepsy. Within this group some patients were eventually determined to suffer from identifiable neurological disorders. Others, however, were found following complete evaluation not to have identifiable neurological disorders, and of these many were eventually found to require treatment for a variety of emotional–adjustmental difficulties. The complete neuropsychological evaluation, although not lasting as long as often anticipated, provides in the hands of a trained neuropsychologist information of sufficient accuracy, completeness, and clinical utility to earn for itself wide acceptance as an undertaking of high cost- and time-effectiveness.

Flexible Approach with Core Battery

Most neuropsychologists in clinical practice (whether they claim to be from the school of thought that recommends the utilization of a standardized battery of tests or from the school of thought that suggests that individual procedures should be selected on an individual patient basis with no more rationale than that provided by the psychologist at the moment) wind up selecting a set of baseline procedures from which they may choose to deviate once that irreducible minimum amount of behavior has been obtained and interpreted. Certainly no one would disagree that individual choices and clinical flexibility must be maintained in order to respond to clinical questions, the needs of the patients, and particular requirements of a clinical as well as a research nature. Certainly too, in some instances, information may well not be required because it is redundant or irrelevant to the clinical questions at hand. Muriel Lezak, a proponent of a flexible approach to test selection, begins with a battery of procedures from which she deviates as individual clinical requirements suggest. Such deviations and individual choices of course represent responsible practice. In the hands of a highly trained and skilled neuropsychologist, the utilization of flexible procedures represents less of a risk than does the utilization of standardized procedures in the hands of an individual who is not trained. Lezak (1976) makes this recommendation:

> The following tests comprised the individually administered part of my battery:
>   1. The Wechsler Adult Intelligence Scale (WAIS): information, comprehension, arithmetic, similarities, digit span, picture completion, block design, picture arrangement and object assembly subtests.

2. The Symbol Digit Modalities Tests (SOMT) (instead of the WAIS digit symbol subtest since the SDMT provides an opportunity to compare spoken and written responses to a symbol substitution test and allows patients with motor slowing or motor handicaps to be tested by this technique).
3. The Ray Auditory–Verbal Learning Test.
4. Subtracting Serial Sevens (SSS) Test.
5. Draw a Bicycle.
6. The Benton Visual Retention Test (BVRT) Administrations A and D.
7. The Purdue Peg Board Test.
8. The Trail Making Test (TMT).
9. The Rorschach Ink Blot Technique.
10. The Bender Gestalt Test.

Lezak adds that a series of paper-and-pencil tests, frequently taken by patients either in their hospital rooms or at home to be mailed back later, are also included:

My Paper and Pencil Neuropsychological Test Packet includes:
1. Self-Administered Battery (SAB), a collection of intellectual and personality tests and test samples suitable for adult patients generally. The SAB we currently use contains a set of 24 Wechsler-Type Information questions, ten Wechsler-Type Arithmetic Story Problems, 25 multiple-choice vocabulary items, three Bender-Gestalt Cards to be copied, the Draw-a-Person Test (DAP), a set of 20 sentence completion stems, one card from the Thematic Apperception Task (TAT) with instructions to write a story, one Rorschach Card with instructions to write three associations, three proverbs with instructions to "write what each of these sayings mean," two simple geometric forms to copy and two to draw from memory, Sentence Building I or II of the Stanford-Binet (Form M) depending on the patient's apparent verbal skill level.
2. The Arithmetic section of the Wide Range Achievement Test (WRAT).
3. The Raven Progressive Matrices (RPM), standard or colored form on the patient's apparent capabilities.
4. The Cooper Visual Organization Test (VOT).
5. Vocabulary and Comprehension Subtests of the Gates-MacGinitie Reading Tests (usually Form F but lower level forms can be substituted as needed).
6. The Personal History Inventory, a multiple-choice and statement-completion biographical questionnaire.

Lezak indicates that patients generally take from 3 to 6 hours to complete the paper-and-pencil tests alone. Unfortunately, no reports on the validity of these tests, in battery form when used together for neuropsychological purposes, have appeared, and one is therefore left to recognize that at this point this must be considered a battery with perhaps some heuristic experimental interest. It is not one that can be scientifically recommended for individual use in a clinical setting, lest one make the error of assuming that test and subtest individual reliability, established in one context such as the Wechsler Adult Intelligence Scale as a whole, can be transferred to a totally different context on a pick-and-choose basis and carry its validity and reliability with it to that totally different context. This kind of psychometric error, although committed all too frequently in all forms of assessment practice, is certainly not one that Lezak would espouse or condone, and therefore initial developmental work on this very interesting set of clinical procedures represents an opportunity yet to be fully realized.

Luria-Nebraska: Behavioral Neurology Standardized

A third battery in addition to the above two recommended by Lezak, and one which has gained increasing popularity and widespread familiarity in the last 5 years, is the Luria-Nebraska Neuropsychological Battery developed by Charles Golden and his colleagues. Golden (1981) states as follows:

> The development of the battery began with the published work of A. R. Luria [1973] and that of Anne-Lise Christensen. Luria presents his approaches in his books, including sample ideas and a general approach to his tests, especially in *Higher Cortical Functions in Man*. Christensen presented a variety of specific items with general instructions and cards that can be used as stimuli for various items. Christensen's format was adopted to develop several hundred items in ten major areas.

> These initial items were tested on normal controls, and some were discarded because they were repetitious, some because they could not be performed by the normal controls, and others because of an inability to develop a reliable scoring system. Eventually, a two hundred and eighty two item version was developed that was administered to two hundred control (both psychiatric and normal) and neurological patients. From this initial testing . . . thirteen more items were discarded that failed to discriminate between normal and brain-damaged patients, leaving a battery of two hundred and sixty nine items that could be administered in about two to two and a half hours. The items of this final version were divided into eleven sections, including sections for motor skills, rhythmic and pitch skills, tactile skills, expressive language skills, receptive language skills, reading, writing, arithmetic, memory, visual-spatial skills, and intellectual skills.

Golden makes it clear that these procedures can be given by technicians and scored quantitatively, and from these scores an MMPI-like profile is derived. The profile includes not only the above-mentioned scales, but also scales of both presence and absence of impairment (Pathognomonic Scale) and a right hemisphere and left hemisphere lateralizing scale. The last two scales are based primarily on the motor and sensory scale items. Golden is equally strong, however, in indicating the need for qualitative analysis, and for in-depth interpretation of individual performances within the scales. He too rejects the utilization of neuropsychological procedures for purely diagnostic classificatory purposes. His goals were to achieve a set of procedures that represented a comprehensive assessment of impaired neuropsychological functions broken down into their most basic components. Procedures were designed to take 2 to 2½ hours, even when administered to neuropsychologically impaired patients. Such a battery should allow advantage to be taken of the strengths of Luria's qualitative approach while still being subject to experimental evaluation and quantitative analysis through objective scoring procedures. Finally, Golden feels that tests must not be oriented simply toward diagnostic decisions, "but toward the development of rehabilitation programs. In allowing for a detailed examination of the deficits underlying any injury, the tests allow the examiner to design rehabilitation programs aimed at the individual deficits in the most efficient manner possible. This allows rehabilitation efforts to be directed toward those areas and to involve those techniques that optimize recovery and minimize staff time" (Golden, 1981).

The 12 scales of the Luria-Nebraska Battery can be described as follows:

Motor Functions.   This section has 51 items covering such motor areas as fine motor skill, motor persistence, speed, pantomime, and competence of right and left upper extremities as well as movements of tongue, lips, and motor reactions to spoken instructions.

Rhythm (Acoustico-Motor) Section.   This section involves 12 items including assessment of patient's ability to perceive differences in pitch, tonal sequence, rhythm, and loudness.

Tactile (Higher Cutaneous and Kinesthetic Functions).   This section contains 20 items primarily assessing bodily awareness through the tactile modality and asteriognostic skills through tracing of shapes on the patient's right or left wrist.

Visual (Spatial) Functions.   This scale with 14 items requires the subject to recognize a variety of pictures presented with varying degrees of obscurity and to identify the number of blocks presented pictorially in a three-dimensional array. Mental rotation of geometric figures is also required.

Receptive Speech.   This section with 33 items evaluates the patient's capacity for understanding spoken speech. It begins with the identification of simple phonemes through both repetition and written responses and extends to following a command, providing word definitions, and grasping complex logical relationships when presented in the form of verbal instructions.

Expressive Speech.   This scale involving 42 items requires patients to express speech orally. Patients must repeat phonemes and words, read aloud, count, say the days of the week, and organize a jumble of words into a logical verbally expressed statement.

Writing.   This scale involving 13 items requires the copying of letters and words from cards and from memory and spontaneous writing on a designated topic.

Reading Skills.   This scale with 13 items requires the reading of syllables, words, sentences, and a small story.

Arithmetical Skills.   This scale with 22 items taps skills ranging from simple number identification to algebraic manipulations.

Memory.   This scale with 13 items involves both verbal and nonverbal mnemonic capacity. Patients must not only learn words but also predict their own learning rate. Patients are also required to learn under various sources of memory interference, to draw from memory, to memorize nonlinguistic rhythmic patterns, recall body positions and a logical story, and engage in associative learning as well.

Intellectual Process. This scale with 34 items includes several items common to many standard psychometric measures of intelligence including picture sequencing, proverb explanation, word definition, verbal abstraction, identification of opposites and analogous relationships, and arithmetic reasoning.

The Pathognomonic Scale. This scale consists of 32 items found to be the most discriminating in the initial study on the battery presented by Golden, Hammeke, and Purisch (1978). Two additional scales designed to be particularly sensitive to the effects of right hemisphere and left hemisphere disorders are also presented. These consist of all items from the Motor and Tactile sections that are performed by the right and left hand independently. They offer a comparison of the right and left sides of the body on basic tactile and motor skills with the right cerebral hemisphere scale being made up of tasks performed by the left side of the body while the left cerebral hemisphere scale represents tasks on the right side of the body. The difference between these two scales is presented as an index for discriminating laterality of brain dysfunction.

At the current time the Luria-Nebraska scales are standardized and validated only for adult populations, although a children's version is currently under construction and initial investigation.

A series of studies comparing performance on the Luria-Nebraska battery of patients with and without neurological impairment has demonstrated the success of this set of procedures in separating these two groups. Hammeke, Golden, and Purisch (1978) obtained a 100% discrimination between 50 brain-damaged and 50 normal patients on 30 of the 269 items, and 252 were found to discriminate significantly at or beyond the .05 level. A cross-validation by Moses and Golden (1979) produced hit rates ranging from 62% to 80% for the brain-injured group and 72% to 98% for the control group, a percentage consistent with that which has been found for the last two decades as characteristic of the separation capacity of single tests and batteries of tests when evaluating the performance of groups of brain-damaged and nonneurological control patients (Spreen & Benton, 1965). Osmon, Golden, Purisch, Hammeke, and Blume (1979) examined the ability of the battery to discriminate between lateralized and diffusely injured subjects. Using discriminate analysis techniques based on 14 summary indices of the Luria-Nebraska battery, 59 of the 60 patients were correctly classified, with the left and right hemisphere scales achieving hit rates of 75%. The battery gave its worst performance in dealing with individuals with specific left hemisphere damage and its best performance in individuals with right cerebral hemisphere damage.

Finally, Golden attempted to classify clinically 78 cases on the basis of 14 clinical scales alone. Forty patients were brain-damaged, 20 were psychiatric patients, and 18 were normal controls. Seventy of 78 correct classifications were achieved in terms of a brain-damage versus non-brain-damage dichotomy. Within the brain-damage group, 34 of 40 cases were correctly classified as to right, left, or diffuse neurological involvement. For the 24 that were categorized on the basis of neurological criteria as having lateralized damage into one of four quadrants of the brain, accurate classification according to that schema was accomplished in 22 out of 24 cases.

Golden concludes, "Overall, the validity studies to date suggest that the Luria can be a strong and useful instrument in the diagnosis and localization of brain damage. Although its effectiveness will vary in different populations, depending on such factors as severity and number of significant cognitive deficits, as will the effectiveness of any psychological tests, the studies support the efficacy of the Luria as a clinical instrument."

A discussion of neuropsychological procedures could go on almost indefinitely if one were to include and describe every test that has ever been associated with separating groups of brain-damaged from non-brain-damaged individuals or that has been included in one or another grouping of tests under the rubric of a battery of neuropsychological procedures. Lezak (1976) very courageously takes on the task by devoting no fewer than 11 chapters of her book to discussion of individual tests of such content areas as cognitive functions, orientation, attention and self-regulation, personal and social adjustment, memory, visuo-practic functions and manual dexterity, perceptual functions, verbal functions, and intellectual functions.

Two other sources of test lists can be recommended. The first is the previously mentioned article by Smith (1975) on the purposes and validities of neuropsychological testing in neurological disorder which ends with a discussion of a number of tasks that might well be employed in combination for clinical purposes or individually for experimental purposes that have already enjoyed such usage. Reitan and Davison (1974) devote the last 20 pages of their book to listing various tests found within and outside of recognized neuropsychological batteries. It is not the purpose of this chapter to deal with individual tests. The use of psychological tests individually has been thoroughly discredited. It is impossible to indicate in any exhaustive fashion which groupings of tests have and which have not enjoyed the establishment of independent validity. Therefore, the sample presented here must stand as representative of the kind of procedures that could be developed and, in the instances of the Halstead Reitan and Luria-Nebraska batteries, as examples of those procedures on which considerable validity research has already been accomplished with positive results.

The Wechsler Scales

This author's position on the utilization of any single test, no matter how complex or impressive its nature, as an adequate behavioral representation of the results of impairment of brain function has been stated above and elsewhere (Boll, 1974, 1978, 1981). Notwithstanding the documented need for a neuropsychological evaluation, rather than merely for tests of brain damage, any commentary on the current state of clinical practice requires discussion of one test, the Wechsler, because of its clinical ubiquity. As amplified by Kaufman and Reynolds in Chapter 3, this test is characterized by considerable internal complexity and is the single most widely used psychological assessment device of higher mental functions. For that reason, it deserves discussion as to its role as a neuropsychological technique. This is true not only because of its breadth of application but also because of the amount of misinformation that has been provided that may tend to compromise its appropriate use.

The early history of the use of Wechsler-Bellevue scales and the ratios of various subtests derived therefrom as indices of impaired or nonimpaired brain function have been outlined previously and need not be recounted in detail here (Matarazzo, 1972; Boll, 1978). Many attempts have been made to develop techniques for utilizing Wechsler scales to assess the condition of the brain. The one internal characteristic that has continually enjoyed validation with regard to its sensitivity to impairment and to differential location and type of impairment of brain function is the relationship between scores on the verbal and scores on the nonverbal scales, often referred to as the Verbal–Performance split or lack thereof.

The initial reports of the phenomena were presented by Andersen (1950, 1951), who found that damage to the left cerebral hemisphere selectively lowered the Verbal IQ, whereas damage to right cerebral hemisphere had the opposite effect, selectively lowering Performance IQ. Additional studies confirming these findings were reported over the next 20 years (Klove 1959; Satz, 1966; Satz, Richard, & Daniels, 1967; Parsons, Vega, & Burn, 1969; Simpson & Vega, 1971). A Verbal–Performance difference of 10 points occurs in 30% of normals and a difference of 15 points occurs 18% of the time among normals (Matarazzo, 1972). Obviously then, a certain percentage of brain-damaged patients may well have 10- to 15-point Verbal–Performance discrepancies on the basis of factors not related to the brain damage ostensibly being investigated. As has also been pointed out, several additional neurological variables, such as acuteness of lesion and neuropathological type, must be understood when evaluating the behavioral significance of lateralization of brain damage as it is expressed in any behavioral index, such as the Verbal–bal–Performance discrepancy (Boll, 1978). With regard to these latter two neurological variables, Fitzhugh, Fitzhugh, and Reitan (1961) reported that Verbal–Performance splits were found in patients with lateralized *acute* neurological damage. Patients with *chronic* lateralized neurological impairment, however, did not perform in a matter productive of Verbal–Performance discrepancies on the Wechsler scales. Russell (1972) confirmed these earlier findings when he studied 34 patients with static lateralized brain damage and reported an absence of Verbal–Performance IQ discrepancies.

Reed (1962) reported an interaction between type of lesion and effect of lateralization on Verbal–Performance IQ discrepancy. Reed examined patients with four types of brain damage including head injury, cerebral vascular disease, extracerebral neoplasm, and intracerebral neoplasm. Reed found that the patients with lateralized brain damage of an acute nature whose brain damage was characterized by tissue destructive and/or invasive effect were characterized as having Verbal–Performance splits. The differences between verbal and performance capacity were in the expected direction. Patients with left cerebral hemisphere cerebral vascular accidents and intracerebral tumors had lower Verbal without lower Performance IQs, whereas patients with right cerebral hemisphere intracerebral neoplasms and strokes had reduced Performance IQ functions. Patients with equally acute but noncortically invasive brain impairments such as extracerebral neoplasms and head injuries did not demonstrate Verbal–Performance discrepancies. This is true despite the fact that extracerebral neoplasms represent the most purely lateralized type of neurological pathology of the groups studied. Whether it was, as postulated, the fact of tissue-destructive versus non-tissue-destructive damage that represented the area of difference in determining which types of acute lateralized brain damage did and which types of acute lateralized brain damage did not produce Verbal–Performance splits is not the critical issue. The critical issue is one of the sensitivity of the Wechsler scales.

Far from being insensitive to various types of brain damage and even further from providing inaccurate information, the fact is that the Wechsler scales provide so much information of such a high degree of accuracy as to render them essentially uninterpretable by themselves. In other words, the Wechsler scales with a limited number of data points such as Verbal and Performance IQs are unable to communicate, in systematic and quantitative fashion, decisions about presence or absence, right versus left, acute versus static, and tumor versus trauma versus stroke simply because the type of information sought outnumbers the available choices provided by the Wechsler scales themselves. One could, with tongue planted firmly in cheek, suggest that the *absence* of a Verbal–Performance split is diagnostic of a chronic lateralized or acute lateralized brain lesion (depending on type), whereas the presence of a Verbal–Performance split is diagnostic of an acute lateralized brain disorder. In either case, of course, both presence of absence of Verbal–Performance splits can also be diagnostic of normality. This suggests that the information from Wechsler scales simply cannot be used alone in a responsible fashion to make these kinds of decisions.

In fact, the Wechsler scales are not best used for determination of presence or absence of brain damage. If, however, independent evidence exists that the patient is in fact neurologically impaired, then the Wechsler data may well be exceptionally useful in providing additional information about various aspects of the independently documented neurological impairment. This is especially true when this information is utilized in the context of a complete neuropsychological evaluation. Such evaluation includes tests of lower-level psychological functions, such as motor and sensory capacity, as well as other higher-level psychological capacities not adequately represented on the Wechsler scales, such as memory, concept formation, learning capacity, and information processing skills. Only when it is misused is the Wechsler likely to produce inaccurate information, and no test in the world is immune to this type of circumstance.

CONCLUSION

Neuropsychology is a professional applied specialty with its roots embedded equally firmly in neurological science, basic psychological science, and clinical psychology. Without training in all three areas, adequate preparation for responsible clinical practice cannot be demonstrated. The danger then obviously exists that individuals without sufficient clinical training will provide, on a rote and technical basis, a variety of neurobehavioral procedures, with little understanding of the overall requirements of the psychologist–patient relationship. On the other hand, clinical psychologists, failing to understand the complexity of neurobehavioral theory and science, have been known to employ, cookbook style, a set of quantitative prescriptions or qualitative judgments to which adequate training has not been brought for their valid development.

Neuropsychology is not simply another type of psychological test within the overall clinical armamentarium. It instead represents a discipline or subdiscipline on the one hand, and a specialty or subspecialty on the other. Each requires identifiable training and practice supervision. Neuropsychology and neuropsychological procedures cannot be understood well enough to be applied routinely by nontrained clinicians as yet another aspect of their general psychological practice. Rather, neuropsychology, whether practiced alone or in conjunction with other more traditional procedures, is a professional speciality in its own right. It may utilize many procedures in common with other clinical specialties, but it constitutes a distinct sphere of practice.

Neuropsychology then represents not only an interesting area of knowledge and clinical practice, but also a prototype for the emerging role of professional psychology as issues of specialty and subspecialty emerge. Differences in preparation for these have become identified (Meier, 1981) and will be subject to continuing argument and discussion at least through the 1980s.

Neuropsychology as an evaluation activity requires the broad assessment of the human behavioral repertoire by procedures validated with regard to their relationship to normal and impaired brain functions. It is performed, in the context of that evaluation, not simply for the purpose of neurological diagnostic verification or identification, but for the broader purpose of understanding of the role played by the development, maintenance, and impairment of brain functions in the broad expression of human behavior.

With regard to intervention strategies, which represent a frontier area, neuropsychologists even at this early stage have much to offer, for the simple reason that knowledge may be the single most powerful therapeutic tool available to clinicians generally. Imparting information to patients with regard to the behavioral sequelae of their neurologic disorder or with regard to the neurological base of their behavioral disorder or with regard to the neurological base of their behavioral disorder frequently changes the perspective not only of the patient, but also of the individuals in the patient's environment, ranging from family to employer. This allows a more realistic approach, not only to the problem, but also to the patient. From this realistic understanding can come specific attempts at intervention and their eventual validation in a way not possible until those understandings are routinely achieved.

REFERENCES

Andersen, A. P. L. The effects of laterality localization of brain damage on Wechsler-Bellevue indices of deterioration. *Journal of Clinical Psychology,* 1950, **6,** 191–194.

Andersen, A. P. L. The effect of laterality localization of focal brain lesions on Wechsler-Bellevue subtests. *Journal of Clinical Psychology,* 1951, **7,** 149–153.

Barth, J., & Boll, T. J. Rehabilitation and treatment of central nervous system dysfunction: A behavioral medicine perspective. In L. A. Bradley & C. Prokov (Eds.), *Medical psychology: A new perspective.* New York: Academic Press, 1980.

Bartholow, R. Experimental investigation into the functions of the human brain. *American Journal of Medical Sciences,* 1874, **67,** 305–313.

Beach, F., Hebb, D. O., Morgan, C. T., & Nissen, H. W. Neuropsychology of Lashley. New York: McGraw-Hill, 1960.

Benton, A. L. Behavioral changes in cerebral vascular disease. In R. P. Siekert (Ed.), *Cerebral vascular survey report.* Washington D.C.: Joint Councils Subcommittee on Cerebral Vascular Disease, 1970.

Boll, T. J. Behavioral correlates of cerebral damage in children aged 9–14. In R. M. Reitan & L. A. Davison (Eds.), *Clinical neuropsychology: Current status and applications.* Washington, D.C.: Winston, 1974.

Boll, T. J. Diagnosing brain impairment. In B. B. Wolman (Ed.) *Clinical diagnosis of mental disorders.* New York: Plenum, 1978.

Boll, T. J. The Halstead-Reitan Neuropsychology Battery. In S. Filskov & T. J. Boll (Eds.), *Handbook of clinical neuropsychology.* New York: Wiley, 1981.

Boll, T. J. Behavioral sequelae of head injury. In P. R. Cooper (Eds.), *Management of head injuries.* Baltimore: Williams and Wilkins, 1982.

Boll, T. J., Heaton, R., & Reitan, R. M. Neuropsychological and emotional correlates of Huntington's chorea. *Journal of Nervous and Mental Disease,* 1974, **158,** 61–69.

Caveness, W. Incidence of cranial cerebral trauma in the United States. *Transamerican Neurological Association,* 1977, **102,** 136–138.

Chapman, L. & Wolff, H. G. The cerebral hemispheres and the highest integrated functions of man. *American Medical Association Archives of Neurology,* 1959, **1,** 357.

Cleeland, C. Biofeedback as a clinical tool: Its use with the neurologically impaired patient. In S. Filskov & T. J. Boll (Eds.), *Handbook of clinical neuropsychology.* New York: Wiley, 1981.

Davison, L. A. Current status of clinical neuropsychology. In R. M. Reitan & L. A. Davison (Eds.), *Clinical neuropsychology: Current status in applications.* Washington, D.C.: Winston, 1974.

DeJong, R. N. *The neurologic examination.* Houke, N. Y.: Hober, 1967.

Diller, L., & Gorden, W. Rehabilitation and clinical neuropsychology. In S. Filskov & T. J. Boll (Eds.), *Handbook of clinical neuropsychology.* New York: Wiley, 1981.

Eson, M. & Bourke, R. *Assessment of information processing deficits after serious head injury.* Paper presented at the Eighth Annual Meeting of the International Neuropsychology Society, 1980.

Ewing, R., McCarthy, D., Gronwall, D., & Wrightson, P. Persisting effects of minor head injury observable during hypoxic stress. *Journal of Clinical Neuropsychology,* 1980, **2,** 147–155.

Filskov, S. B., & Goldstein, S. G. Diagnostic validity of the Halstead-Reitan Neuropsychological Battery. *Journal of Consulting and Clinical Psychology,* 1974, **42,** 383–388.

Fitzhugh, K. B., Fitzhugh, L. T., & Reitan, R. M. Psychological deficits in relation to acuteness of brain dysfunction. *Journal of Consulting and Clinical Psychology,* 1961, **25**, 61–66.

Fitzhugh, K. B., Fitzhugh, L. T., & Reitan, R. M. Wechsler-Bellevue comparisons in groups of "chronic" and "current" lateralized and diffuse brain lesions. *Journal of Consulting Psychology,* 1962, **26**, 306–310.

Franz, S. I. On the functions of the cerebral: The frontal lobes. *Archives of Psychology,* 1907, **2**, 1.

Freeman, W. P., & Watt, J. Psychosurgery. Springfield, Ill.: Thomas, 1942.

Fulton, J. F. *Functional localization in the frontal lobes and cerebellum.* Oxford: Clarendon Press, 1933.

Galin, D. Lateral specialization and psychiatric issues: Speculations on development and the evolution of consciousness. *Annals of the New York Academy of Science,* 1977, **299**, 397–411.

Golden, C. J. A standardized version of Luria's neuropsychological tests: a quantitative and qualitative approach to neuropsychological evaluation. In S. Filskov & T. J. Boll (Eds.), *Handbook of clinical neuropsychology.* New York: Wiley, 1981.

Golden, C. J., Hammeke, T., & Purish, A. Diagnostic validity of the Luria neuropsychological battery. *Journal of Consulting and Clinical Psychology,* 1978, **46**, 1258–1265.

Golden, C. J., & Kupperman, S. Graduate training in clinical neuropsychology. *Professional Psychology,* 1980, **11**, 55–63.

Goldstein, S. G., Deysach, R. E., & Kleinknecht, R. A. Effect of experience and amount of information on identification of cerebral impairment. *Journal of Consulting and Clinical Psychology,* 1973, **41**, 30–34.

Gronwall, D. & Wrightson, P. Cumulative effects of concussion. *Lancet,* 1975, II, 995–997.

Halstead, W. C. *Brain and intelligence: A quantative study of the frontal lobes.* Chicago: University of Chicago Press, 1947.

Hammeke, T., Golden, C. J., & Purish, A. A short comprehensive and standardized version of Luria's Neuropsychological Tests. *International Journal of Neuroscience,* 1978, **8**, 135–141.

Head, H. *Aphasia and kindred disorders of speech.* London: Cambridge University Press, 1926.

Hebb, D. O. *The organization of behavior: A neuropsychological theory.* New York: Wiley, 1949.

Klonoff, H., Fibiger, C. H., & Hutton, G. H. Neuropsychological patterns in chronic schizophrenia. *Journal of Nervous and Mental Disease, 1970,* **150**, 291–300.

Klove, H. Relationship of differential electroencephalographic patterns to distribution of Wechsler-Bellevue scores. *Neurology,* 1959, **9**, 871–876.

Klove, H. *Relationship between neuropsychologic test performance and neurologic status.* Paper presented at the American Academy of Neurology, Minneapolis, 1963.

Klove, H., & White, P. T. The relationship of degree of electroencephalographic abnormalities to the distribution of Wechsler-Bellevue scores. *Neurology,* 1963, **13**, 423–430.

Kolb, B., & Whishaw, I. Q.: *Fundamentals of human neuropsychology.* San Francisco: W. H. Freeman, 1980.

Lezak, M. D. *Neuropsychological assessment.* New York: Oxford University Press, 1976.

Luria, A. R. *The working brain.* New York: Penguin Books, 1973.

Martindale, C. Hemisphere asymmetry and Jewish intelligence patterns. *Journal of Consulting and Clinical Psychology,* 1978, **46,** 1299–1301.

Matarazzo, J. D. *Wechsler's measurement and appraisal of adult intelligence* (5th ed.). Baltimore: Williams and Wilkins, 1972.

Matthews, C. G. Adult (C.A.) 15 and Older: Neuropsychological Test Battery. Madison, Wisc., 1977, 1–32.

Matthews, C. G., & Booker, H. E. Pneumoencephalographic measurements and neuropsychological test performance in human adults. *Cortex,* 1972, **8,** 69–92.

Matthews, C. G., Shaw, D. J., & Klove, H. Psychological test performances in "pseudo neurologic" subjects. *Cortex,* 1966, **11,** 244–253.

Meier, M. J. Objective behavioral assessment in diagnosis and prediction. In A. L. Benton (Eds.), *Behavioral change in cerebral vascular disease.* New York: Hoeber, 1970.

Meier, M. J. Education for competency assurance in human neuropsychology: Antecedents, models, and directions. In S. Filskov and T.J. Boll (Eds.), *Handbook of clinical neuropsychology.* New York: Wiley, 1981.

Moses, J. A., & Golden, C. J. Cross-validation of the discriminative effectiveness of the standardized Luria-Nebraska Neuropsychological Test Battery. *International Journal of Neuroscience,* 1979, **9,** 149–155.

Newman, O. S., Heaton, R. P. K., & Lehman, R. A. Neuropsychological and MMPI correlates of patient's future employment characteristics. *Perceptual and Motor Skills,* 1978, **46,** 635–642.

Osmon, D. C., Golden, C. J., Purish, A. D., Hammeke, T. A., & Blume, H. G. The use of a standardized battery of Luria's test in the diagnosis of lateralized cerebral dysfunction. *International Journal of Neuroscience,* 1979, **9,** 1–9.

Parsons, O. A. *Neuropsychology. Current topics in clinical and community psychology.* New York: Academic Press, 1970.

Parsons, O. A., Vega, A., & Burn, J. Different psychological effects of lateralized brain damage. *Journal of Clinical and Consulting Psychology,* 1969, **33,** 551–557.

Reed, H. B. C. *Differentiated impairment on the Wechsler-Bellevue scale as a function of type and laterality of cerebral pathology.* Paper presented at the Midwestern Psychological Association, Chicago, 1962.

Reitan, R. M. An investigation of the validity of Halstead's measures of biological intelligence. *Archives of Neurology and Psychiatry,* 1955, **73,** 28–35.

Reitan, R. M. Validity of the Trail Making Test as an indicator of brain damage. *Perceptual and Motor Skills,* 1958, **8,** 271–276.

Reitan, R. M. Methodological problems in clinical neuropsychology. In R. M. Reitan & L. Davison (Eds.), *Clinical neuropsychology: Current status and applications.* Washington, D.C.: Winston, 1974.

Reitan, R. M., & Boll, T. J. Intellectual and cognitive functions in Parkinson's disease. *Journal of Consulting and Clinical Psychology,* 1971, **37,** 364–369.

Reitan, R. M., & Davison, L. *Clinical neuropsychology: Current status in applications.* Washington, D. C.: Winston, 1974.

Restak, R. *The brain: The last frontier.* New York: Doubleday, 1979.

Rimel, R. W., Giordani, B., Barth, J. T., Boll, T. J., & Jane, J. A. Disability caused by minor head injury. *Neurosurgery*, 1981, **9**, 221–228.

Rosene, K., Copass, M., Kastner, L., Nolan, C., & Eschenbach, D. Persistent neuropsychological sequelae of toxic shock syndrome. *Annals of Internal Medicine*. 1982, **96**, 865–870.

Rourke, B. P. Neuropsychological assessment of children with learning disabilities. In S. Filskov & T. J. Boll (Eds.), *Handbook of clinical neuropsychology*. New York: Wiley, 1981.

Russell, E. W. WAIS factor analysis with brain-damaged subjects using criterion measures. *Journal of Consulting and Clinical Psychology*, 1972, **39**, 113–319.

Rutter, M. Brain damage syndromes in childhood: Concepts and findings. *Journal of Child Psychology and Psychiatry*, 1977, **18**, 1–21.

Ryan, J., Souheaver, G., & DeWolfe, A. Halstead-Reitan test results in chronic hemodialysis. *Journal of Nervous and Mental Disease*, 1981, **169**,311–314.

Rylander, G. *Personality changes after operation on the frontal lobes: A clinical study of 32 cases*. Copenhagen: Munksgaard, 1939.

Satz, P. Specific and non-specific effects of brain lesions in man. *Journal of Abnormal Psychology*, 1966, **71**, 65–70.

Satz, P., Richard, W., & Daniels, A. The alteration of intellectual performance after lateralized brain injury in man. *Psychonomic Science*, 1967, **7**, 369–370.

Schreiber, D. J., Goldman, H., Kleinman, K. M., Goldfader, P. R., & Snow, M. Y. The relationship between independent neuropsychological and neurological detection and localization of cerebral impairment. *Journal of Nervous and Mental Disease*, 1976, **162**, 360–365.

Simpson, C. D., & Vega, A. Unilateral brain damage and patterns of age-corrected WAIS subtest scores. *Journal of Clinical Psychology*, 1971, **27**, 204–208.

Smith, A. Neuropsychological testing in neurological disorders. *Advances in Neurology*, 1975, **7**, 49–110.

Spreen, O., & Benton A. L. Comparative studies of some psychological tests for cerebral damage. *Journal of Nervous and Mental Disease*. 1965, **140**, 323–333.

Symonds, C. P. Concussion and its sequelae. *Lancet*, 1962, I, 1–5.

Tsushima, W. T., & Towne, W. S. Neuropsychological abilities of young children with questionable brain disorders. *Journal of Consulting and Clinical Psychology*, 1977, 45, **7**, 757–762.

Vega, A., & Parsons, O. Cross-validation of the Halstead-Reitan test for brain damage. *Journal of Consulting Psychology*, 1967, **31**, 619–625.

Victor, M., Adams, R. E., & Collins, G. H. *The Wernike-Korsakoff syndrome*, Philadelphia: F. A. Davis, 1971.

Wechsler, I. S.: *Clinical neuropsychology*. Philadelphia: Strauss, 1963.

Wilson, P. J.: The surgical treatment of epilepsy. *British Journal of Hospital Medicine*, 1973, **February**, 161–168.

PART TWO

Methods of Intervention

CHAPTER 7

Individual Psychotherapy

IRVING B. WEINER AND EDWARD S. BORDIN

The second half of this handbook is devoted to six methods of intervention by which clinicians attempt to meet the psychological needs of people who seek their help: individual psychotherapy, group therapy, family therapy, behavior modification, crisis intervention, and community intervention. This chapter, while addressed primarily to individual psychotherapy, introduces the reader to the broad area of psychotherapy theory, research, and practice by (a) defining the nature of psychotherapy; (b) describing the major theories of psychotherapy; (c) identifying the general and specific factors that promote behavior change in psychotherapy; (d) outlining the course of psychotherapy in the initial, middle, and final phases of treatment; and (e) commenting briefly on trends in psychotherapy research, particularly with respect to treatment outcome.

THE NATURE OF PSYCHOTHERAPY

Like putting styles among golfers, definitions of psychotherapy sometimes appear as numerous as people who propose them. Reisman (1971), in a detailed analysis of the implications and shortcomings of various ways of describing psychotherapy, listed 31 different definitions offered by influential clinicians. To grasp the essential nature of psychotherapy, it is helpful to begin with a workable definition and then to consider the appropriate *goals* of psychotherapy, the distinction between *uncovering* and *supportive approaches* in psychotherapy, and the complementary role of *strategy* and *tactics* in working toward the treatment goals.

Defining Psychotherapy

Despite differences in emphasis and perspective, the myriad attempts to define psychotherapy share four common characteristics: (a) the use of psychological measures to assist people who are experiencing emotional problems in living; (b) the wish of the therapist to be of help to his or her client; (c) an attude of respect by the therapist for the personal integrity of the client; and (d) reliance on an understanding of the client to guide the conduct of the treatment.

With these core characteristics in mind, Weiner (1975, p. 3) defines psychotherapy as "an interpersonal process in which one person communicates to another that he understands him, respects him, and wants to be of help to him." Garfield (1980, p. 9) offers the following similar integration of the defining characteristics of psychotherapy: "Psychotherapy thus appears to be largely a verbal interaction between two people, a therapist and a client, by means of which the former somehow attempts to help the latter overcome his difficulties."

As an important supplement to this emphasis on the message and the relationship, Bordin (1979, 1980a) stipulates that psychotherapy also includes the choice by the therapist of collaborative tasks that are anticipated to achieve whatever treatment goals the client and therapist have agreed upon. The relationship aspect of psychotherapy is relatively heavily laden with the personality of the therapist, as it has evolved from development, personal therapy, and, to some extent, training; the choice of tasks, on the other hand, reflects mainly the therapist's training, theoretical orientation, and application of research findings.

This way of defining psychotherapy serves clinicians well in identifying what they have to learn and do in order to become effective therapists and in distinguishing psychotherapy from other kinds of interpersonal interactions, whether for clinical or for research purposes. The fact that psychotherapy comprises both a relationship and a technical discipline will be elaborated in the discussion of general and specific factors that promote behavior change. Two other implications of this definition of psychotherapy that can be clarified at this point are (a) the distinction between *psychotherapy* and what may be psychotherapeutic, and (b) the bearing of a professional relationship on the likelihood the psychotherapy will occur.

Distinguishing Psychotherapy from What May Be Psychotherapeutic. As just defined, psychotherapy is a treatment approach in which therapists seek to enhance their clients' understanding of themselves and to help them think, feel, and act in more self-fulfilling and less self-defeating ways. Psychotherapy includes work with groups and families as well as individuals (see Chapters 8 and 9), but, regardless of who is being helped, it should be distinguished from nonpsychological approaches to promoting behavior change. Purely physiological treatments, for example, such as psychoactive drugs or electric shock, may be psychotherapeutic, in that they relieve a person's emotional distress, but they do not constitute psychotherapy.

Other kinds of prescriptive approaches—such as directing certain activities, manipulating the environment, or offering concrete advice—involve more subtle distinctions between psychotherapy and what may be psychotherapeutic. In these instances it is necessary to distinguish between prescriptions that are designed to bring behavior and experience within an individual's control and those that are aimed at placing the individual in a more benign situation or making him or her feel more comfortable. When therapists prescribe activities that promote client involvement and self-regulation, including many of the behavioral interventions described in Chapter 10, they are practicing psychotherapy. When they are telling clients what to do or altering their environment, without the clients' active participation in deciding and implementing what seems best to do, they are not practicing psychotherapy—even though the outcome may be psychotherapeutic.

Limiting the term *psychotherapy* in this way helps to avoid unnecessary confusion and to establish useful boundaries for clinical practice and research. To learn and apply principles for the effective conduct of psychotherapy, therapists must be able to distinguish when they are providing psychotherapy from when they are employing other procedures that should be guided by other or more general clinical considerations. To design and conduct useful research on psychotherapy, researchers must be able to define in a precise and replicable fashion the kinds of clinical interaction that should be the subject of their investigations. Unless such distinctions are made, neither clinical nor experimental findings can systematically shape knowledge about psychotherapy.

The Bearing of a Professional Relationship on the Likelihood That Psychotherapy Will Occur. When psychotherapy is regarded as the communication of understanding, respect, and a wish to be of help, it is possible to conceive of its occurring in many kinds of interpersonal relationships, and even occurring inadvertently. For several reasons, however, the behaviors that constitute psychotherapy are more likely to occur in the context of a professional relationship designed to provide psychotherapy than in any other kind of relationship.

First, the likelihood that understanding, respect, and a wish to be of help will be communicated in a relationship between two people is enhanced if one of them is a professional trained in the understanding of human behavior and consciously intent on applying this training for the benefit of the other. Although naturally intuitive people may be keenly sensitive to the thoughts and feelings of others, they cannot be expected to translate their sensitivity into the communication of understanding as frequently and consistently as people trained in and dedicated to doing so. Whereas professional therapists focus their sessions on significant treatment issues, for example, inherently helpful but untrained people from whom others seek counsel are found to engage primarily in informal conversation and advice giving (Gomes-Schwartz & Schwartz, 1978).

Second, a professional psychotherapy relationship is designed primarily for the benefit of the client and does not depend on the therapist's receiving any equal share of understanding, respect, and help. Whereas most other kinds of interpersonal relationships must be sustained by mutual need gratification, a professional psychotherapy relationship is based on one person's (the therapist) single-mindedly serving the psychological needs of another person (the client), without seeking to gratify any needs of his or her own other than to be an effective psychotherapist. Research findings confirm in this regard that friends trying to help each other discuss personal problems are much more likely than professional therapists to talk about their own ideas and experiences, and much less likely to express statements of empathic understanding (Reisman & Yamokoski, 1974).

Third, a professional psychotherapy relationship involves arrangements and commitments that increase the prospects for understanding to be communicated in a systematic fashion. The participants meet on a regularly scheduled basis for a specified length of time, and neither their intercurrent personal affairs nor their feelings about each other are ordinarily allowed to disrupt their work together. Moreover, the psychotherapy relationship continues as long as it serves the needs of the client, and, unlike other kinds of interpersonal relationships, it is not broken off during transient periods of waning enthusiasm. Indeed, as we shall see, a number of conceptions of psychotherapy, especially those stressing the relationship as the medium of change, anticipate disruptions in the relationship and variations in enthusiasm for the change enterprise as unavoidable events intimately related to the kinds of difficulties and pains that prompted the search for therapy. These disruptions and losses of motivation, according to such conceptions, provide opportunities for concrete change experiences that it is hoped will generalize to other areas of the client's life.

Goals of Psychotherapy

People seek psychotherapy for three primary reasons. Some are troubled by distressing symptoms, such as anxiety, depression, phobias, or difficulty in thinking clearly. Some experience certain problems in living, such as work inhibition, school failure, marital discord, or social withdrawal. And some are generally dissatisfied with themselves for failing to become the kinds of people they would like to be. These reasons identify what the goals of the treatment should be, that is, to relieve emotional distress, to promote solutions to problems in living, and to minimize conflicts and concerns that limit a person's realization of his or her potential for productive work and rewarding interpersonal relationships.

Because psychotherapy is defined in part by the explicit communication of understanding, it is sometimes assumed that the goal of the treatment is insight, which consists of clients' being able to understand their thoughts, feelings, and actions. However, any such assumption incorrectly equates the methods of psychotherapy with its goals. Effective communication by the therapist should increase clients' understanding of themselves, but this increased insight is not an end in itself. Insight in psychotherapy is only a means to the end of achieving the behavior changes sought by the client. Psychotherapy without behavior change, whether in the form of symptom relief, problem resolution, or progress toward a more rewarding life style, has not achieved its goals. Whenever clients remain unwilling or unable to translate increased self-understanding into desired behavior change, further or more incisive treatment is required.

However, even with desired behavior change as a guide, it is easier to enumerate the goals of psychotherapy than it is to identify when they have been achieved. How fully should psychotherapy relieve emotional distress, for example? How thoroughly should it resolve conflicts and concerns? How perfectly should it promote solutions to problems? How extensively should it enhance life satisfaction? The constraints of reality recommend modest rather than ambitious answers to these questions. Biogenetic and sociocultural factors limit the degree to which people can alter their personalities or redirect their ways of living. Moreover, behavior patterns that are ideal at one point in the life cycle can become less adaptive and less self-fulfilling as a person's capacities and circumstances change. As a further consideration, certain stresses and strains are natural accompaniments of living. For example, seeking to avoid the emotional stresses of grief may lead to more enduring emotional behavioral difficulties than a direct encounter with the grief experience, which provides opportunities for mastery of the loss.

Hence psychotherapy cannot be expected to achieve complete cures or perfect resolutions, nor can increments in self-understanding be expected to provide indefinite insulation against psychological difficulties. Working toward such utopian goals runs the risk of what Freud (1937) aptly labeled "analysis interminable." To avoid interminable treatment, psychotherapy should be regarded as a helping procedure, not a curative one, and as a means of facilitating progress toward desired behavior change, not a route to total and permanent change. Thus psychotherapy should end when clients have made substantial progress toward achieving the goals with which they entered treatment, and when they appear unlikely to make sufficient further progress to justify the time, effort, and expense that such progress would require.

Uncovering and Supportive Approaches in Psychotherapy

Originally, within the framework of psychoanalytic theory, *uncovering* approaches in psychotherapy referred to efforts to achieve fundamental changes in a client's personality by exploring the origins of his or her characteristic ways of thinking, feeling, and acting. By contrast, *supportive* approaches referred to efforts to carry a person over some distressing or crisis-dominated period of life and return him or her to a previous level of functioning. Whereas uncovering psychotherapy thus consisted of personality reconstruction through insight, supportive psychotherapy involved using limited insight or educative procedures to help people bring their existing personality characteristics and current personal resources more effectively to bear in overcoming their psychological difficulties.

Over time this categorical distinction between seeking change and restoring the equilibrium has evolved into an important basis for distinguishing between *psychotherapy proper* and *crisis intervention* (see Chapter 11). In addition, the differences between relatively uncovering and relatively supportive psychotherapy remain helpful in identifying the type and breadth of change being sought in a treatment relationship.

To illustrate this difference between uncovering and supportive approaches, suppose that a male client has been performing poorly in his work, and suppose further that a characterological preoccupation with details appears responsible in part for this problem. Uncovering psychotherapy for this man would focus on the origins and manifestations of his apparently obsessive–compulsive personality style. By becoming more fully aware of this feature of his personality, especially in relation to his inefficient functioning on the job, the client would gain increased capacity to modify it. The resulting reduction in his compulsivity would alleviate both the work problem for which he sought help and any other problems caused by his preoccupation with detail.

Supportive psychotherapy for this same man would focus on the nature of his work, on the ways in which his organization and execution of tasks assigned to him had proved inefficient, and on alternative means of planning and carrying out his assignments so as to reduce or eliminate his inefficiency. In this approach the same amount and kind of attention would be paid as in an uncovering approach to helping him understand the interworkings of his personality style, his preoccupation with details, and his poor work performance. However, instead of exploring and seeking to modify the personality style underlying his preoccupation, as would be done in uncovering psychotherapy, a supportive approach would avoid probing the client's personality style and would instead work toward more effective functioning within it. Thus this client could be helped to weigh the component parts of a task assigned to him, in an obsessive-compulsive fashion, and then to use judgment about their relative importance to guide him in concentrating on the more important parts of the task and minimizing distraction by less important details.

As this illustration should make clear, supportive psychotherapy keeps its focus on the concrete immediate problem, whereas uncovering psychotherapy instigates a broad self-examination from the perspectives of past and present as well as future expectations. Later we will describe forms of brief therapy in which the use of focus has been refined to achieve changes that, although not as encompassing as those sought in uncovering psychotherapy, can draw a very fine line between support and uncovering. On the other hand, supportive psychotherapy still remains clearly distinct from and should not be confused with the general meaning of being supportive, which may include giving advice, reassurance, and sympathy, or even lending a client money. However supportive or psychotherapeutic such actions may be, they do not constitute psychotherapy, since they involve neither the relationship nor the task elements that define this treatment method.

Because uncovering and supportive approaches in psychotherapy differ mainly in the kinds and extent of understanding they seek to communicate, they represent degrees of emphasis rather than mutually exclusive types of treatment. Psychotherapy addressed to modifying personality characteristics inevitably gives some consideration to how certain problems can be resolved within the framework of existing personality characteristics. Likewise, psychotherapy focused on bringing existing personality characteristics more effectively to bear on current problems almost always devotes some attention to understanding the origin of these personality characteristics. In actual practice, then, psychotherapy for the individual client tends to be primarily uncovering or primarily supportive in nature, and not exclusively one or the other.

Finally, in this regard, it is important to dispel the lingering myth that uncovering psychotherapy, because it aims at personality modification, is generally preferable to and better than supportive psychotherapy. What is preferable in psychotherapy is what best meets clients' needs and most fully helps them achieve desired behavior change. Depending on the nature of clients' problems, the extent and kind of changes they seek, the flexibility of their personality styles, and the amount of effort they are able and willing to devote to psychotherapy, either a primarily uncovering or a primarily supportive approach may best serve their needs (see Dewald, 1971, Chapter 8; Wolberg, 1977, Chapter 13).

Strategy and Tactics in Psychotherapy

To conduct psychotherapy in a manner that consistently meets the needs of their clients, psychotherapists must operate with a keen sense of strategy and tactics.

Strategy refers to what therapists are trying to accomplish at a given point, whereas *tactics* refers to the particular means by which they are attempting to accomplish it. For example, a therapist whose strategy is to learn more about a client's mother without asking any direct or specific questions that would curb the client's spontaneity may select the tactics of an indirect observation ("You haven't said much about what your mother is like") or a general request for information ("Tell me about your mother"). The timing of such questions to blend into the flow of a client's communications will be as important a feature of the tactic as the question's content; for example, the psychotherapist might ask about the client's mother at a point when the client is speaking of mother-like persons or about someone else's mother. As another example, a therapist may feel inclined at a particular point to help a client recognize an obvious avoidance of sexual matters (the strategy), but to approach this topic gradually (the tactics), beginning with "I get the feeling there are some things you are finding it hard to talk about today."

Like uncovering and supportive approaches, strategy and tactics play complementary roles in effective psychotherapy. The most perceptive strategies go for naught unless they are joined with tactics for implementing them; the most brilliant tactics serve little purpose unless they are guided by strategies for where and when they should be employed. The good strategist who lacks tactical sense often knows what should be done but not how to do it; the good tactician who lacks a grasp of strategy is prone to doing the right things but at the wrong times. The strategist may be acutely aware of how psychotherapy is proceeding and what directions it ought to take, but be unable to do or say what is necessary to move it in these directions; the tactician may respond brilliantly to clients on an occasional basis, but be unable to help them progress in any systematic fashion toward the goals of the treatment.

The distinction between strategy and tactics in psychotherapy has important implications for theory and research as well as for practice. As discussed next, several different theories of psychotherapy have emerged out of alternative ways of conceptualizing personality functioning and behavior change. The practical differences among these theories reside primarily in the distinctive tactics they recommend, and, as we shall see, psychotherapists of all persuasions endorse many of the same treatment strategies, such as providing a warm and accepting atmosphere and having their clients engage in new, corrective experiences.

THEORIES OF PSYCHOTHERAPY

Clinicians with different views on the origins of psychological disturbance and on the therapist's role in helping to alleviate it have developed many different theories or schools of psychotherapy. As among the classical philosophers, there has been some historical tendency among psychotherapists for each "new" view to be promulgated as if it constituted a radical departure from all previous views and provided a necessary corrective to errors of the past. In reality, however, even the most seemingly divergent schools of psychotherapy share many common threads in the goals they pursue and the methods they employ.

The following discussion summarizes several prominent theories of psychotherapy and comments on their historical significance. For a more extensive and detailed analysis of systems of psychotherapy than is possible in this brief overview, the reader is referred to contributions by Corsini (1979), Ford and Urban (1963), Heine (1971), Prochaska (1979), and Wolberg (1977, Chapters 9–11).

Classical Psychoanalysis: Freud

Classical psychoanalysis, which was the first formal theory of psychotherapy to be elucidated, emerged from Sigmund Freud's efforts to treat patients troubled by anxiety, conversion, and phobic symptoms. Freud's collaboration with Josef Breuer led to the publication of *Studies on Hysteria* (Breuer & Freud, 1893–1895). Freud's chapter on psychotherapy in this volume is generally regarded as marking the inception of the psychoanalytic method. Here Freud explicated the two key features of his treatment approach: *free association,* which consisted of having patients express whatever thoughts and feelings came into their minds, without exercising any censorship or making any prior judgments as to their relevance, importance, logicality, or propriety; and *interpretation,* a process of pointing out to patients aspects of their personality and previous experience that influence their behavior without their being aware of them.

Whereas these basic elements of the psychoanalytic method were derived from clinical experience, Freud subsequently elaborated them in terms of his theories of personality development, neurotic symptom formation, and the topography and structure of the mental apparatus. Because he believed that personality was shaped for better or worse by conflicts arising during the early years of life, Freud stressed that the way to resolution of adult problems lay through genetic reconstruction and resolution of the *infantile neurosis.* In the treatment these conflicts from the early formative years are reactivated in the patient's relationship to the therapist. Specifically, the intrusion of infantile conflicts into the patient's feelings and attitudes toward the therapist *(transference)* becomes a source of interference in the therapeutic collaboration *(resistance)* that parallels the ways in which the neurosis interferes with everyday functioning.

The work of interpretation in psychoanalysis aims at increasing patient awareness of the self-defeating consequences of response patterns rooted in unresolved early life conflicts. This paves the way for confronting one's impulses more directly and giving up maladaptive defenses, which in turn increases possibilities for a more realistic, self-fulfilling mode of response. In classical analysis the patient becomes so concentrated on the therapist that a *transference neurosis* is developed, by which is meant that virtually all features of the patient's difficulties are now vested in the relationship to the therapist. A successful resolution of the transference neurosis will thus free the patient from his or her emotional problems.

With regard to symptom formation, Freud attributed neurosis to repressed or warded-off impulses that press for discharge through numerous *derivatives,* including neurotic symptoms, dreams, and such "every-day psychopathology" as slips of the tongue and convenient forgetting. In Freud's topographic terms, the psychoanalytic method seeks to bring these unconscious impulses into conscious awareness; in the language of his later structural theory, "Where id was, there shall ego be" (Freud, 1933, p. 80). To this end derivatives, along with transference phenomena and childhood recollections, are utilized to uncover the early origins of patients' psychological difficulties and to bring them into their awareness. In this process current situations and reality factors are prevented as much as possible from intruding on the recognition and analysis of derivatives.

Unfortunately, matters of psychoanalytic technique never received Freud's concentrated attention following the *Studies on Hysteria*. Of considerable value, however, are several papers in which he made specific recommendations for conducting various aspects of the treatment (Freud, 1904, 1910, 1912, 1913, 1915). For additional reading on classical psychoanalysis, comprehensive texts by Brenner (1973), Glover (1955), Kubie (1950), Lorand (1946), Menninger and Holzman (1973), and Nunberg (1932) are recommended.

The Early Dissenters: Jung, Adler, and Rank

Freud's early circle of followers included three who came to disagree with him about the origins of neurosis. Their dissenting views have exerted broad influence on current concepts of psychotherapy, sometimes with and sometimes without adequate appreciation of where these concepts originated.

Jung's Analytic Psychology.   Gustav Jung (1911, 1923, 1933) became less interested in early childhood conflicts as the source of neurotic problems than in the challenges to individual personality growth posed by the primordial experience of the human race. In a highly abstract and somewhat mystical fashion Jung postulated that each person has both a *personal unconscious,* which is similar to the unconscious as described by Freud, and a *collective unconscious,* which consists of various inborn images or *archetypes* based on the shared expreience of the human race. Neurosis, according to Jung, represents the struggle of people to free themselves from the interference of these archetypes with their progress toward personality integration and fulfillment of their human potential. In this sense neurosis signified for Jung not so much illness as a striving toward psychological maturity.

The task of the Jungian analyst, as in classical psychoanalysis, is to utilize interpretation to help the patient become aware of his or her unconscious, but in both its personal and its collective aspects. Because of the nature of the collective unconscious, there is a particular focus on the symbolic meanings of dreams, myths, and folklore as a means of bringing individuals into contact with the deposit of the racial past. The therapist's role is conceived of as an active effort to guide the patient into a productive relationship with elements of his or her unconscious and thereby to liberate the creative, growth-promoting forces within his or her personality. To this end, directed focusing of the interviews rather than free association and an exchange of ideas at the level of a real relationship between patient and therapist rather than the development of a transference neurosis characterize the treatment method.

Jung's voluminous writings pay relatively little attention to psychotherapy, and current literature written outside a specific Jungian framework rarely alludes to his contributions in this area. As the preceding capsule of his views should make clear, however, Jung anticipated several central features in subsequent theories of psychotherapy, including the individual's innate potential for positive personality growth and the utility of an active, focused, and realistic patient–therapist relationship. For the interested reader, Fordham (1978) provides an overview of Jungian psychotherapy, and summaries of Jung's psychology have been published by Ellenberger (1970, Chapter 9), Jacobi (1963), and Progoff (1969).

Adler's Individual Psychology.   Alfred Adler (1907, 1924, 1933) believed that the primary source of neurosis lay not in repressed impulses pressing for discharge, but in maladaptive efforts to compensate for feelings of inferiority. Feelings of inferiority develop in all people, said Adler, either in relation to some real or perceived organ inferiority or as a result of the early life experience of being relatively small, weak, and helpless. People strive in their individual ways to overcome their feelings of inferiority and achieve power, and the various attitudes, aspirations, and behavior patterns they employ toward this end, including such *guiding fictions* as a sense of superiority, constitute their *life-styles.* The more individuals' life-styles are bound up with struggles for power, at the expense of *social feelings,* the more likely they are to engage in neurotic and maladaptive patterns of behavior.

The focus of Adlerian psychotherapy is on exploring the nature of the patients' life-styles and guiding them into more effective ways of functioning, with particular attention to replacing their struggles for power with social interests. Although interpretation is the main tool for this purpose, the topics selected for interpretation differ markedly from those selected in a Freudian genetic reconstruction or a Jungian elaboration of symbolic meaning. Adler stressed analysis of patients' current concerns and future goals rather than their past conflicts, and he recommended a pragmatic, problem-solving approach addressed to actual daily behavior rather than to any highly inferential significance of this behavior. Adlerian therapy can best be characterized as an educational process in which the therapist tries to influence patients to surrender their neurotic strivings, to form more positive attitudes toward themselves and others, and to adopt more effective and socially acceptable patterns of living.

Even more so than Jung, Adler anticipated numerous subsequent developments in psychotherapy for which he rarely receives credit. His emphasis on characterological style as expressed in current adjustment difficulties became a central feature of the later neo-Freudian and ego-analytic approaches to psychotherapy, and his preference for an active, problem-solving therapist role is reflected in most directive and counseling approaches to psychotherapy. For an integrated summary of Adler's views on personality development and psychotherapy the reader is referred to Ellenberger (1970, Chapter 8) and to books by Ansbacher (1980), Ansbacher and Ansbacher (1956), and Dinkmeyer, Pew, and Dinkmeyer (1979).

Rank's Will Therapy.   Otto Rank (1929, 1945) concluded from his clinical work that the stressful experience of birth is paradigmatic of a series of separations on which personality development rests. According to Rank, the traumatic experience of being born initiates a lifelong sequence of events, leading to the ultimate separation of death, in which people seek to reconcile wishes for intimacy or oneness with others, on the one hand, and an equally strong push on the other hand toward individuality or separation from others. A positive resolution of this conflict consists of accepting each new growth (separation) experience for both its enhancement of individuality and its introduction of new kinds of intimacy.

Neurotic individuals for Rank are people who cannot escape fearing either their desire for oneness, as a loss of individuality *(death fear)*, or their desire for separation, as a loss of protection *(life fear)*. Such fears culminate in insufficient *will* to establish a comfortable independent existence. The Rankian approach, which he called *relationship therapy*, is thus directed toward an individual's struggles with self-differentiation and pointed toward the successful separation (birth) from the therapist at a stipulated end date.

Instead of being led through a content-oriented review of their past traumatic experiences, then, patients in Rankian therapy are encouraged to focus on their current reaction patterns, to strengthen and assert their will in relation to the therapist, and to determine for themselves how their strengthened will can best be exercised in the future. As an important aspect of promoting movement toward separation and individuation, the treatment relationship itself is defined as finite, and a specific time limit is set for its duration.

These recommendations for the conduct of psychotherapy have had a far more significant and lasting impact than the theoretical notions from which Rank derived them. His focus on an essentially nondirective approach in which patients work toward self-determination has become a central feature of client-centered and humanistic psychotherapy, and his use of a finite treatment relationship to foster individuation is reflected in considerable current interest in short-term psychotherapy (see Budman, 1981; Davanloo, 1978; Malan, 1976; Sifneos, 1972; Small, 1979; Wolberg, 1980) and in the effective utilization of time-limited psychotherapy (see Goldring, 1980; Mann, 1973; Mann & Goldman, 1981). Also of note is the subsequent influence of Rank's approach on the development of the *functional* school of social work, through the writings of Jessie Taft (1933, 1948), and on psychotherapeutic work with children, through the work of Frederick Allen (1942). For further perspectives on the legacy of Rank's approach the reader is referred to a recent book by Menaker (1982).

The Neo-Freudians: Horney, Fromm, and Sullivan

Subsequent to the major contributions of Freud and the early dissenters, a distinguished group of clinicians often referred to as *neo-Freudians* took issue with the view that personality evolves from balances struck between basic drives and adaptive strivings within the individual. The neo-Freudians argued instead that men and women are social beings shaped primarily by their cultural and interpersonal environment, and that personality accordingly evolves from the manner in which each individual learns to adapt to his or her sociocultural context. In this frame of reference psychological disturbance results from faulty learning and consists of a characterologically maladaptive style of interacting with the environment.

Neo-Freudian psychotherapy employs a free-associational, insight-oriented approach that differs from classical psychoanalysis mainly in the kinds of insights that are emphasized. Although unconscious conflicts are elicited and explored, the focus is less on conflicts between impulses pressing for discharge and efforts to repress these impulses than it is on conflicts among inconsistent ways of attempting to relate to the environment in an anxiety-free and productive manner. Likewise, although the patient–therapist interaction is analyzed extensively, the treatment relationship is used not to foster a transference neurosis from which early experiences can be reconstructed, but to identify and modify maladaptive ways in which patients are currently dealing with the people in their lives.

Among the neo-Freudians Karen Horney (1937, 1939, 1945) and Erich Fromm (1941, 1947, 1955) stand out for their rich discussions of character types. Horney postulated that childhood experiences of rejection and disapproval produce a *basic anxiety* that motivates efforts to escape from it. These escape efforts lead to the emergence of three kinds of neurotic character types: the *complaint* type, who moves excessively toward others; the *aggressive* type, who moves excessively against others; and the *detached* type, who moves excessively away from others. According to Horney, psychotherapy should concentrate on helping patients to recognize the ineffectiveness of their characterological styles of interacting with people and to alter their patterns of "thinking, feeling, valuing, and acting," so that they can achieve greater "responsibility, inner dependence, spontaneity of feeling, and wholeheartedness."

Fromm stressed in his basic writings the manner in which environmental restrictions, primarily in the form of institutional authority, can suppress and eventually eliminate creative aspects of the self. Not only to retain the security of infantile emotional ties, in the sense emphasized by Rank and Horney, but also to fit themselves to the demands of their social, political, and economic environments, individuals may become motivated to escape the dangerous freedom of being themselves. Instead of developing into independent and productive persons, then, individuals will cling to irrational authority and relate to their social groups through such nonactualizing character styles as the *receptive* orientation, the *exploitative* orientation, the *hoarding* orientation, and the *marketing* orientation. Psychotherapy in Fromm's opinion should therefore focus on helping the patient to distinguish between rational and irrational authority and to replace all other characterological orientations with a *productive* orientation, which allows a person "to ultilize his powers and to realize the potentialities inherent in him."

Harry Stack Sullivan (1953, 1954, 1956), the founder of the *interpersonal* school of psychiatry, is the best known and most influential of the neo-Freudians. His impact derives from the sensitivity reflected in his writings, the systematic detail with which he elaborated his theories of personality structure and development, and the wide range of his attention to clinical problems. Central to Sullivan's approach are the postulates (a) that interpersonal relationships during the developmental years pose a successive series of threats to an individual's security and (b) that people learn from their experience various *security operations* for coping comfortably with the *significant others* in their lives.

Since in Sullivan's view the interpersonal context is the essence of the human condition, the nature of the security operations people use defines their character style, and the effectiveness of these operations determines whether they encounter psychological problems in living. Psychotherapy then becomes an interpersonal experience in which therapists, acting as *participant observers,* engage patients in examining their difficulties in relating to people. The treatment relationhip is used to facilitate identifying and correcting patients' tendencies to misperceive or misinterpret the behavior of others *(parataxic distortions).*

In addition to his contributions to theories of personality and psychotherapy, Sullivan innovated the application of psychodynamic concepts to the treatment of schizophrenic patients. A significant body of literature concerning the practice of psychotherapy with schizophrenics, including the work of Frieda Fromm-Reichmann (1950, 1969) and Harold Searles (1965), has emerged within the Sullivanian framework. Also of note was Sullivan's flexibility in such respects as having the patient sit face to face with the therapist, instead of reclining on a couch in the classical psychoanalytic fashion, which anticipated the prevailing mode in most current psychotherapies.

Current Psychoanalytic Trends

Out of the variety of crosscurrents within the mainstream of ideas emanating from Freud's seminal contributions, three trends evolved that bear heavily on the nature of psychoanalytically oriented psychotherapy as currently practiced. These are presented roughly in their historical order.

Ego-Analytic Approaches.   Ego-analytic approaches to psychotherapy evolved gradually within the mainstream of psychoanalysis, independent of any spirit of dissent or intent to establish a new school of thought. From the writings of such theorists as Anna Freud (1936), Heinz Hartmann (1939), Ernst Kris (1950), Rudolph Loewenstein (1953), David Rapaport (1950, 1951, 1953), and Erik Erikson (1950, 1956) emerged a psychoanalytic ego psychology generally considered the most important single development in psychoanalysis from Freud's basic contributions to the present time (see Hofling & Meyers, 1972). Psychoanalytic ego psychology differs from classical psychoanalysis primarily in the emphasis it places on adaptive rather than instinctual strivings in people, in the importance it assigns to environmental influences as well as inner impulses in molding and modifying behavior, and in the attention it devotes to the lifelong cycle of personality development rather than to any crystallization of personality determined by early life experiences.

Ego-analytic psychotherapy, which is also commonly referred to as *psychoanalytically oriented* or *dynamic* psychotherapy, employs the exploratory and interpretive procedures of classical psychoanalysis but attempts neither a reconstruction of infantile experiences nor the fostering of a regressive transference neurosis. Instead, the treatment seeks to expand the patients' awareness of and conscious control over whatever intrapsychic, interpersonal, or environmental events are currently creating psychological difficulties for them. In many respects psychodynamic psychotherapy differs from psychoanalysis more in degree—that is, in how intensive and uncovering the process is—than in kind, and it also has many features in common with the neo-Freudian focus on characterological coping styles.

Because the ego-analytic approach incorporates the thinking of many able clinicians, without being tied to the theoretical eccentricities or idiosyncratic terminology of any one systematizer, and because it relates closely to widely employed psychodynamic conceptualizations of pyschopathology and personality development, it is among the most commonly applied psychotherapies in current clinical practice. From a long list of books concerned with the theory and methods of dynamic psychotherapy, those by Chessick (1973), Dewald (1971), Langs (1973, 1974), Paolino (1981), Reid (1980), and Weiner (1975) are especially recommended for further reading.

Working Alliance Theory. Freud (1913) recognized early that the successful analysis of transference and resistances requires a good rapport in the treatment situation. Hence a first aim of treatment is attaching the patient to it and to the person of the therapist. Sterba (1934) spoke in this regard of the client's identifying with the therapist's rational or observing ego. It was not until many years later, however, that Ralph Greenson (1967) provided a full theoretical devlopment of the role of what he termed the *real relationship*.

As Greenson formulated this addition to psychoanalytic theory, the therapist, through explicit attention to the pain and trauma in the patients' life and careful explanation of his or her procedures, builds a nonneurotic, rational alliance that makes it possible for the patient to work purposefully in the treatment. A compassionate and empathic tone and consistent emphasis on insight rather than moral judgment contribute to the development of this alliance. Some classical psychoanalysts have expressed reservations about this approach, because they find it incompatible with their conviction that the methods of free association and interpretation work best when the therapist remains a nonreal, noncommittal figure—a *blank screen*. According to Stone (1961), however, it is not possible for an analyst to remain a totally blank screen, even if he or she wishes to, and Greenson (1967, pp. 216–224) argues further that dogmatic adherence to the blank-screen stance can lead to destructive lapses of empathy. From his perspective a delicately managed treatment relationship can preserve elements of transference.

Greenson's contributions have resulted in the working alliances taking its place beside free association and interpretation as major facets of the psychoanalytic view of the change process. More recently Bordin (1979, 1980b) has proposed a broadened conception of the therapeutic working alliance in terms that fit any relationship between a person who seeks changes in thoughts, feelings, or behavior and a person who offers to act as a change agent. In his view the amount of change achieved is a function of the strength of the working alliance, which derives from how clear the mutual understanding and agreement are about the goals and tasks of the treatment and about the bonds established between the partners.

Bordin suggests further that distinctive approaches to psychotherapy will differ in the change goals selected, the tasks assigned to each partner, the bonds required between them, or some combination of the three. Thus the psychoanalytic working alliance will differ in kind from the client-centered and the behavioral working alliances, and the last two will differ from each other. Working alliances may also differ in strength from one approach to the next or within a single approach. Eclectic therapists, by drawing on various approaches, are able to work toward varied change goals, adapting the tasks introduced to the goals and the nature of the person seeking change.

Finally, Bordin observes that the power of the task assigned to a patient resides in its relationship to the difficulties in thinking, feeling, and acting that brought the person to seek change. To the extent that the patient's tasks in therapy tap into these difficulties, the problems encountered in carrying out his or her part of the therapeutic collaboration and overcoming them become intrinsic to the treatment. Repairing breaks in the therapeutic alliance is thus no longer seen as restoring rapport so that treatment can proceed, but instead is seen as being the treatment, at least insofar as the first step in reducing self-defeating behavior is modifying it within the therapeutic collaboration.

Object–Relations Approaches.   Object–relations approaches represent another mainstream development within psychoanalysis in which clinicians with an ego-analytic orientation have focused on early life events that shape capacities for interpersonal relatedness. Object–relations theorists are concerned primarily with the processes and adequacy with which infants and young children form internalized concepts of themselves and others *(object representations)* that are differentiated and stable *(object constancy)*. From this perspective varying types of psychopathology result when abnormal developments in the internalization of object relations disrupt the integrity of a person's ego functioning.

This contemporary branch of psychoanalytic ego psychology traces its origins to the work of William Fairbairn (1952), Edith Jacobson (1964), Melanie Klein (1948), and Margaret Mahler (1968), who elaborated theoretical propositions on the early development of internalized objected representations (see also Blanck & Blanck, 1974; Mendez & Fine, 1976). More recently these theories have been translated into specific explanations of why people become disturbed in certain ways and how best to treat them. A prominent example in psychopathology is the elaboration by Kernberg (1967, 1976) of the concept of *object splitting*, which consists of a tendency to view people as "all good" or "all bad" and is hypothesized to result from developmental arrest between 6 and 18 months of age, when capacities for integrated object representations are presumably being formed. Kernberg postulates that object splitting underlies the kinds of strained and unstable interpersonal relationships characteristic of the condition known as *borderline personality organization*.

Psychotherapy in the object-relations framework pays special attention to helping patients differentiate a clear sense of themselves and form balanced, realistic attitudes toward others. The treatment relationship, with the therapist playing an active role and avoiding any blank-screen invisibility, provides the primary tool for promoting such improvements. As stated by two leading proponents of this approach, "First and foremost the therapist must be a *real person,* who maintains a consistent, positive supportive attitude" (Masterson, 1976, p. 90), and "The pretense of being an inhuman computer-like machine [does not] supply the psychological milieu for the most undistorted delineation of the normal and abnormal features of a person's psychological makeup" (Kohut, 1977, p. 253).

Client-Centered Therapy

Client-centered therapy, as formulated by Carl Rogers (1942, 1951, 1961), rests on the premise that all people have inborn capacities for purposive, goal-directed behavior and, if free from disadvantageous learning conditions, will develop into kind, friendly, self-accepting, and socialized human beings. In an atmosphere antithetical to personal growth, however, faulty learning can cause people to become hateful, self-centered, ineffective, and antagonistic to others. Therapy should aim to correct such faulty learning by providing clients an opportunity to expand their awareness of and liking for themselves.

Central to Rogers' approach was the conviction that a person's behavior can be understod only from that person's own subjective point of view and can be changed only through his or her own determination to change. Hence the task of the client-centered therapist is not to offer direction or make interpretations, but to create an accepting, nonthreatening atmosphere in which clients can examine and reconsider their ways of thinking and feeling. By listening in a friendly and empathic manner, reflecting the feeling tone of their clients' remarks, and encouraging clients to manage their own affairs, the therapist makes it possible for them to grow through the relationship, to form a more positive view of themselves, and to direct themselves toward more rewarding and self-actualizing patterns of behavior.

The client-centered approach has had an enormous impact on the field of psychotherapy, far beyond the number of clinicians who specifically employ it. Perhaps most importantly, Rogers' vision of the therapist as someone who creates an atmosphere in which clients can seek their own solutions, instead of someone who suggests solutions through interpretation, directed increased attention to the role of therapist dimensions in psychotherapy. Whereas much had been said previously about *what therapists should do,* before Rogers little consideration had been given to *how they should be.* There is reason to believe that success in psychotherapy depends in part on therapists' being able to display certain personal qualities in the treatment relationship, and this advance in knowledge can be directly credited to Rogers' influence.

Rogers also contributed to advancing knowledge in the field by encouraging his colleagues to formulate testable hypotheses about psychotherapy and to conduct research on the validity of these hypotheses. Empirical studies of client-centered therapy constituted the first systematic effort to bring the methods of behavioral science to bear on understanding psychotherapy, and investigations conducted within the client-centered framework account for a large portion of the psychotherapy research literature. Additionally, the example set by client-centered researchers has had a salutary effect on the entire field, stimulating empirical studies within and across many theoretical contexts.

Like psychoanalytic psychotherapy, client-centered therapy has evolved into varying degrees of classicism and revisionism. Rogers himself has modified many of this views over the course of a long and prolific career. Furthermore, just as Freud was followed by a neo-Freudian generation, important contributions to theory and practice in psychotherapy have been made by clinicians who would appropriately be called neo-Rogerians. For overviews of these developments in the client-centered approach, the reader is referred to edited volumes by Hart and Tomlinson (1970) and Wexler and Rice (1974).

Humanistic Psychotherapy

Humanistic psychotherapy is in many respects an outgrowth of the client-centered method, although it reflects a humanistic psychology that has in its own right entered the mainstream of approaches to conceptualizing human behavior. As expressed in the writings of Bugental (1965), Buhler and Allen (1971), Jourard (1964), and Maslow (1962), humanistic psychology is concerned above all with the uniqueness and wholeness of each person. Humanism is an idiographic psychology, and as such it rejects efforts to group people according to shared personality traits or diagnostic labels. Instead, humanism attends to the process by which an individual comes to experience and enjoy himself or herself "as the sole member of his or her class." Difficulties in experiencing oneself, inability to find pleasure and fulfillment in one's activities, and failure to make meaningful contact with others are viewed as the basic problems in living for which psychotherapy may be indicated.

Treatment within the humanistic framework is essentially an experiential process in which clients, through an open relationship with the therapist, increase their awareness of themselves and their capacity to relate both to other people and to their own needs, talents, and future prospects. As in client-centered therapy, the solutions to clients' difficulties remain entirely in their hands, and their destiny remains theirs alone to determine. In addition, however, humanistic therapists may employ various active techniques intended to promote openness to experience and the ability to share intimate experiences with others. Of particular note in this regard is having therapists disclose their own feelings and experiences as a means of encouraging clients to do likewise (see Bugental, 1978; Jourard, 1971; Mahrer, 1978).

Existential Therapy

As exemplified in the writings of Rollo May (1958, 1969), Medard Boss (1963), and Victor Frankl (1965, 1966), existential psychotherapy is rooted less in theories of personality development than in the philosophy of Kierkegaard, Husserl, and Heidegger. Existentially oriented clinicians are concerned not so much with psychological disturbance and its amelioration as with the conditions of human existence, or being in the world. Because of the nature of the world, especially in modern times when existence seems so precarious, anxiety about survival interferes with finding purpose and meaning in life and discourages people from committing themselves to each other and to productive pursuits. The challenge people face is to exercise their freedom to choose a rewarding way of being and thereby undertake commitments both to intimate interpersonal relationships and to creative endeavors.

The role of the therapist in the existential approach is to provide clients an encounter in which they can first come into closer contact with what they are experiencing and then create for themselves some positive values and aspirations that will give purpose and meaning to their existence. As in humanistic psychotherapy, the therapist's wish to have clients find their own solutions to life's problems does not restrict him or her to a passive role in the treatment. Rather, the therapist employs various procedures, including mutual self-revelations, to expand clients' experiencing of themselves. Current elaborations of the existential approach in psychotherapy are provided by Edwards (1981) and Yalom (1980).

Gestalt Therapy

Gestalt therapy is a relatively recent treatment approach to have exerted a significant impact on the field of psychotherapy and attracted substantial number of adherents. Introduced by Fritz Perls in 1951 (Perls, Hefferline, & Goodman, 1951), it received little attention in the literature until the appearance of books by Perls (1969), Fagan and Shepherd (1970), and Polster and Polster (1973). The basic tenets of gestalt theory are that people structure their experience as whole, integrated organisms, not in cognitive or affective fragments; that individual experience consists of *gestalts,* which are configurations of *figures* (what is being attended to) and *grounds* (what is being ignored or overlooked); and that individuals must have sufficient initiative to close some gestalts and break others up, in order to maintain flexible and adaptive contact with their own needs and with their environment. Inability to close or to shift gestalts produces personality fragmentation, limited awareness of one's experience, and deficiencies in responsibility, authenticity, and self-regulation.

The gestalt therapist seeks to redress such personality limitations by enhancing individuals' capacity to communicate with themselves and others. The treatment approach is very active and, in common with Rogerian, humanistic, and existential approaches, it focuses more on experiencing and affective expression than on a cognitive analysis of behavior. More so than in these other approaches, however, the gestalt method utilizes a variety of specific and graded exercises in experiencing and self-expression, prescribed by the therapist in a hierarchical fashion, to promote progress toward the goals of the treatment. For recent discussions of methods used in the gestalt approach, the reader is referred to contributions by Hatcher and Himelstein (1976) and by Zinker (1977).

Comment

This brief summary of approaches to psychotherapy identifies two basic respects in which they apparently differ. First, some approaches advocate a relatively passive role for therapists, in which their main task is to interpret or reflect the client's remarks, whereas other approaches encourage a more active role in which therapists direct associations, disclose aspects of their own experience, or employ specific training exercises. Second, some approaches regard the therapist's technical procedures as the primary agent of change in psychotherapy, whereas other approaches stress the atmosphere and the interpersonal relationship provided by the therapist as the major impetus to change.

Both of these dimensions of psychotherapy can be objectively measured and are therefore suitable for attempting to categorize treatment approaches. However, any effort in this direction quickly turns up as many exceptions as neat categories. For example, it is not uncommon for psychoanalytic and psychodynamic approaches to be classified as relatively therapist-passive and technique-oriented methods, and for client-centered and experiential approaches (humanistic, existential, and gestalt) to be classified as relatively therapist-active and relationship-oriented methods. Yet included in the psychoanalytic and psychodynamic framework are Adler's active problem-solving approach, Rank's explicit utilization of the treatment relationship, and Sullivan's emphasis on therapists' being participant observers. Included in the client-centered and experiential framework are Rogers' recommendation for relatively passive, nondirective therapist behavior and the gestalt therapist's use of prescribed exercises that constitute a highly specific technical procedure.

Moreover, the active–passive and technique–relationship dimensions themselves generate much ambiguity. In a presumably passive approach such as psychoanalysis, for example, the therapist's interpretations intrude very actively and with considerable impact on the patient's consciousness; by contrast, the unstructured opportunities for personal growth provided in the presumably active experiential approaches constitute a passive, nonintrusive therapist stance. Furthermore, technique-oriented therapists regularly acknowledge that the effectiveness of their procedures depends on the support of an open and trusting patient–therapist relationship, and relationship–oriented therapists devote much attention to the techniques for establishing and sustaining a treatment relationship from which clients can derive benefit.

In short, then, approaches to psychotherapy begin to converge when attention shifts from their terminology and personality theories to their aims and methods in the treatment. First, all of them are actively concerned with exerting a beneficial influence on the client's lives, whether through interpretations or through providing a growth experience, and all of them rely on both technical procedures and relationship variables to promote progress toward their aims. Second, although interpretive approaches are sometimes viewed as being primarily cognitive in their orientation and experiential approaches as being primarily affective, all approaches seek to bring clients into more effective contact with both their thoughts and their feelings. Finally, it should be apparent from the previous summary that all approaches, regardless of the language in which they express their goals, seek through psychotherapy to expand clients' self-awareness, to increase their capacity to understand their behavior, and to promote their finding for themselves rewarding and self-fulfilling ways of life.

Consistent with these convergences, research confirms the point made earlier that therapists of different theoretical persuasions display many commonalities in their treatment strategies. Furthermore, even though psychotherapists with different orientations may conduct treatment sessions in distinctive ways and employ some mutually exclusive tactics—such as the use of a couch by a psychoanalyst and of systematic self-disclosure by a humanistic psychotherapist—the verbal messages they use to communicate understanding, respect, and a wish to be of help bear many similarities (Bruinink & Schroeder, 1979; Fiedler, 1950; Gomes-Schwartz, 1978; Marmor, 1976; Strupp, 1976).

Finally, despite occasional partisan claims to the contrary, outcome research to date provides no evidence that any one type of psychotherapy is more effective than any other when a broad spectrum of clients is considered. Similarly, although some kinds of disorder may be especially responsive to particular treatment techniques, there is no evidence that types of psychotherapy differ generally in the kinds of personality change they produce (see Frank, Hoehn-Saric, Imber, Liberman, & Stone, 1978; Lazarus, 1980; Luborsky & Spence, 1978; Luborsky, Singer, & Luborsky, 1975; Smith, Glass, & Miller, 1980). Hence there is no justification for propounding one method of psychotherapy as pure truth and deprecating other methods as ill-conceived. Some early words of Freud (1904) remain apt in this respect: "There are many ways and means of practicing psychotherapy. All that lead to recovery are good" (p. 259).

GENERAL AND SPECIFIC FACTORS PROMOTING CHANGE IN PSYCHOTHERAPY

As the preceding discussion implies, it is generally recognized that behavior change in psychotherapy is promoted by both general and specific factors in the treatment situation (see Bordin, 1980; Kazdin, 1979a; Strupp, 1970, 1973; Strupp & Hadley, 1979). The term *general factors* refers to aspects of the psychotherapy relationship, whereas the term *specific factors* refers to technical procedures employed within this relationship. In the actual conduct of psychotherapy these general (relationship) and specific (technique) factors are intertwined rather than discrete. A helpful psychotherapy relationship comes into being only when the therapist employs adequate procedures for establishing it, and technical procedures promote progress only when they are employed in the context of a good treatment relationship. Nevertheless, distinguishing between the general and specfic factors that promote change in psychotherapy provides a useful perspective on divergent lines of psychotherapy research and helps to identify the kinds of activity in which therapists must learn to engage.

General Factors Promoting Change

The general factors that promote behavior change in psychotherapy comprise five aspects of the treatment relationship, each of which has important implications for effective conduct of the treatment: (a) opportunity for catharsis, (b) expectations of change, (c) attention from the therapist, (d) reinforcement effects, and (e) the strength of the therapeutic alliance.

Opportunities for Catharis. It is a common experience for people to feel better on getting worrisome concerns off their chests, and for clearer perspectives on a vexing problem to emerge from talking it out. Psychotherapy, by encouraging clients to express themselves, provides such a cathartic opportunity to find relief from distress and routes to improved problem solving. Prior to formulating his psychoanalytic method, Freud emphasized catharsis as the primary means of alleviating his patients' symptoms. To this end he employed exhortation, insistence, hypnosis, and even pressing with his hand on the patient's forehead as techniques for inducing people to unburden themselves and thereby find relief: "The patient only gets free from the hysterical symptom by reproducing the pathogenic impressions that caused it and by giving utterance to them with an expression of affect, and thus the therapeutic task consists solely in inducing him to do so" (Breuer & Freud, 1893–1895, p. 283).

Freud soon abandoned the cathartic method in favor of the free-associative and interpretive methods of psychoanalysis, because he found people limited in how extensively they could report their difficulties and benefit just from doing so. Nevertheless, the limitations of catharsis as a total treatment procedure do not negate its potential for contributing to the helping process in psychotherapy. As testimony to the value of catharsis, Stollak and Guerney (1964) found beneficial introspection to occur in a sample of clients who came regularly for sessions in which they simply talked into a tape recorder, without a therapist's even being in the room. Although these clients would presumably have derived even more benefit from a traditional psychotherapy relationship, in which other aspects of the treatment situation that promote change could have been combined with the opportunity for catharsis, these and other data indicate that catharsis alone can account for some of the effects of psychotherapy (Marmor, 1975; Nichols & Zax, 1977).

Expectation of Change. It is a well-established fact that what people experience as happening can be influenced by what they expect to happen. This phenomenon has had a long history of application in medical practice in the form of *placebo* treatment, which involves the judicious use of nonactive substances or benign procedures accompanied by firm assurances that symptom relief will ensue (see Shapiro & Morris, 1978). The potency of placebo treatment is sufficiently well documented for it to have become a standard feature of studies on the effectiveness of psychoactive drugs. In these studies a control group is administered placebos in the same number as the experimental group is administered the drug being assessed, since only in this way can it be determined whether changes induced by the drug relate to its psychopharmacological properties or merely to expectations of change induced by receiving medication.

In psychotherapy expectation of change comes from several sources, including (a) preconceived notions clients bring to therapy about the benefits they will derive from it, (b) the professional status of the therapist and his or her reputation for helping people, (c) information the therapist may provide about the potential of psychotherapy to promote behavior change, (d) the promise of good results implicit in the therapist's recommending a course of treatment and arranging to provide it, and (e) the anticipation of future gains that is fostered by initial gains in the treatment. Regardless of whatever else about psychotherapy proves helpful to them, clients who benefit from psychotherapy probably owe some part of their improvement to their own hopeful expectations.

Experiemental studies of expectancy effects in psychotherapy, which were stimulated primarily by the work of Jerome Frank (1961; Rosenthal & Frank, 1956) and Arnold Goldstein (1960, 1962) appear to document that clients who receive instructions intended to instill high expectancy of gain from psychotherapy are more likely to continue in and benefit from treatment than clients who receive low-expectancy instructions. There has been some question as to whether such instructions need to include specific assurances that the client will soon begin to feel and function better. However, considerable research suggests that simply preparing clients with explanations of how psychotherapy works, what their role in it will be, and what they can expect from the therapist contributes as much to subsequent improvement as does combining such explanations with specific assurances (Childress & Gillis, 1977; Hoehn-Saric et al., 1964; LaTorre, 1977; Sloane et al., 1970).

Some writers have criticized the methods used in studies of expectancy effects and concluded that the evidence is insufficient to support this notion (see Lick & Bootzin, 1975; Wilkins, 1973). By and large, however, their criticisms are not applicable to the research specifically addressed to effects of preparing clients for their role in psychotherapeutic collaboration. Although the evidence on role preparation is somewhat mixed with respect to outcome measured at the end of therapy, available data clearly indicate that such preparation reduces the frequency of premature termination and other signs of inadequate collaboration, especially among economically and socially disadvantaged clients (Garfield, 1978; Heitler, 1973, 1976; Lorion, 1973; Parloff, Waskow, & Wolfe, 1978).

Thus clients can be helped to avoid becoming prematurely discouraged or alienated in the early stages of therapy if care is taken to foster hope founded in a realistic understanding of the process in which they are to participate. Included in effective modes for this socialization process are explanation, exposure to models, and opportunities to practice.

Attention from the Therapist.   Psychotherapy provides clients an opportunity to meet regularly with another person who listens to what they say, respects their dignity, and conscientiously attempts to understand and be helpful. To be accepted as a person worthy of respect and to receive the undivided attention of a trained professional who is bringing his or her every skill to bear in one's behalf inevitably contribute to clients' feeling better about themselves and about what the future holds for them. Accordingly, attention from the therapist promotes change in psychotherapy partly by enhancing client expectations of change. In addition, the experience of being accorded dignity, respect, and an unswerving professional effort serves to increase a person's feelings of self-worth and self-confidence and thereby to facilitate his or her achievement of positive behavior change.

The significant role of therapist attention in promoting behavior change was first elaborated by Rogers (1951) in his previously described formulations of client-centered therapy. Rogers (1974) later restated the basic tenets of his approach with a clear emphasis on the importance of the climate that therapists create: "It was the gradually formed and tested hypothesis that the individual has within himself vast resources for self-understanding, for altering his self-concept, his attitudes, and his self-directed behavior—and that these resources can be tapped if only a definable climate of facilitative psychological attitudes can be provided" (p. 116).

In research stimulated by Rogers' views on the treatment relationship, therapist attention to the client has frequently been translated into measures of *empathy, warmth,* and *genuineness. Empathy* is the means by which therapists convey to clients that they are being listened to and understood. It consists of demonstrating sensitivity to clients' needs, appreciation for the distress they feel, and comprehension of the difficulties that brought them for help. Empathy does not mean being curious or intrusive, nor does it mean being generally intuitive about the motives that influence human behavior. Rather, empathy means commenting accurately on the specific hopes, fears, conflicts, and concerns influencing the client as a unique individual.

Warmth is the means by which therapists create an atmosphere in which their clients can feel safe, secure, and respected as people. It consists of valuing clients as individuals in their own right; accepting whatever they say or do as worthy of being understood; refraining from passing judgment on their actions or assuming responsibility for their decisions; maintaining a consistently friendly, receptive, and non-dominating attitude; and conveying a strong sense of caring and commitment. Being warm does not mean sparing clients' feelings by avoiding critical examination of features of their behavior that appear self-defeating or incongruent with their talents or aspirations. It means that, in conducting such potentially painful aspects of the treatment, therapists take care not to denigrate their clients' worth as people or their right to lead whatever kinds of lives they choose for themselves.

Genuineness is the means by which therapists facilitate clients' talking in an open, truthful, and nondefensive manner. It consists of engaging clients in a direct personal encounter in which therapists are truthful and authentic people who say only what they believe and do only what is comfortable and natural for them to do. Genuineness does not mean participating with clients in a mutual sharing of opinions, recollections, and concerns, except insofar as there are specific reasons for doing so. Rather, genuineness means that whatever therapists choose to disclose represents a real aspect of themselves, and however they choose to express themselves is congruent with their personality style.

Earlier research pointed to a positive relationship between successful outcome in psychotherapy and ratings of the extent to which therapist empathy, warmth, and genuineness characterized a treatment relationship (see Truax & Carkhuff, 1967; Truax & Mitchell, 1971). However, the rating scales developed to measure these therapist behaviors appear to have serious shortcomings (see Bordin, 1974, pp. 128–131; Chinsky & Rappaport, 1970), and recent reviews note persistent methodological inadequacies in this area of research as well as an accumulation of negative or nonsupportive findings (Lambert, DeJulio, & Stein, 1978; Mitchell, Bozarth, & Krauft, 1977; Parloff, Waskow, & Wolfe, 1978). Yet few practicing clinicians doubt that a treatment climate of caring, commitment, trust, respect, and understanding contributes to behavior change. This remains an area where considerable work must be done to close the gap between cumulative clinical wisdom and replicated empirical findings.

Reinforcement Effects.　Psychotherapists are constantly engaged in responding to their clients' statements or actions. They may respond by sitting silently and without facial expression. They may respond with some bodily communication, such as smiling and frowning, nodding their heads or shaking them from side to side, and leaning forward in their chairs toward clients or sitting back away from them. They may respond with brief utterances intended to help a client continue talking, such as "mm-hmm," "uh-huh," "I see," "go on," or "and then?" Or they may respond with substantive comments or questions addressed to what a client has been saying or doing. All of these responses, by virtue of their timing and the feeling tone they convey, influence client behavior through reinforcement effects.

With respect to timing, first of all, active responsiveness of any kind suggests that what the client is saying at the moment is of interest to the therapist and of some importance, whereas passive responsiveness, that is, not saying or doing anything, conveys the therapist's lack of interest and unimportance of what the client is saying. Accordingly, what therapists respond to actively tends to be discussed and thought about further by clients, thereby increasing the likelihood of related behavior change, whereas what they ignore tends to receive reduced attention from clients and not to become involved in behavior change.

Regarding feeling tone, second, therapists cannot avoid having their responses convey positive or negative attitudes, no matter how noncommittal they intend them to be, and thereby positively or negatively reinforce aspects of their clients' behavior. In positive terms, for example, "I see" can communicate "you're absolutely right"; "mm-hmm" can mean "I approve"; and "go on" may say "I really care." By virtue of the reinforcement effects they create, such messages participate in behavior change by influencing what clients choose to talk about and which aspects of themselves they consider modifying.

Research on the reinforcing effects of therapist behavior developed from some innovative work by Greenspoon (1955) on verbal conditioning. In Greenspoon's initial study subjects were asked to say all the words they could think of, and the experimenter responded with "mm-hmm" whenever a plural noun was verbalized. Over time subjects were found gradually to increase the frequency with which they gave plural nouns. Subsequent studies have demonstrated that many features of what people say and how they say it can similarly be influenced by verbal reinforcers.

In an actual interview situation, for example, Williams and Blanton (1968) found that subjects who received verbal reinforcement for statements expressing feeling made an increasing percentage of feeling statements in later interviews, whereas subjects who received reinforcement for statements without feeling content expressed feelings with decreasing frequency. Additional basic research on verbal conditioning is reviewed by Greenspoon (1962), Kanfer (1968), and Williams (1964), and studies relating such reinforcement effects to behavior in clinical interviews are summarized by Wiens in Chapter 1 of this volume and by Garfield (1980, pp. 106–113), Krasner (1965), Matarazzo and Wiens (1972), and Pope (1979, Chapter 3).

The Strength of the Therapeutic Alliance.   In recent years research interest has turned to integrating the above four general factors into an index of the strength of the partnership established between therapist and client, called the *therapeutic* or *working alliance.* These terms refer to "the complex of understandings and attachments that are formed when a person in a state of personal crisis . . . turns to another for his or her expert help and a contract is made. This contract or alliance represents a subtle mixture of explicit and implicit understandings and acknowledged and unacknowledged attachments" (Bordin, 1976, p. 2).

Investigators have devised a variety of methods for obtaining indices of the strength of this collaboration, how clear and mutually accepted are the understandings, how strong are the attachments, and how well adapted to their respective tasks are the participants (Horvath, 1981; Hartley, 1978; Ryan, 1973; Luborsky, 1976; Marziali, Marmar, & Krupnick, 1981). Although not universally positive or methodologically pure, the results have been sufficiently encouraging to interest an increasing number of investigators. Positive results have included evidence that a weak therapeutic alliance forecasts premature termination (Sarnat, 1975) and that measures based on both therapist and client reports can forecast outcome in a diverse sample of therapies, including psychodynamic, humanistic, and behavioral approaches (Horvath, 1981).

The Complementarity of General and Specific Factors Promoting Change

The preceding discussion of factors in the psychotherapy relationship that can promote behavior change identifies the kind of atmosphere therapists should seek to create: an atmosphere in which clients feel safe and secure, express themselves freely and openly, believe they are respected and understood, and anticipate deriving some benefit from the treatment procedures. As noted earlier, however, the beneficial properties of such an atmosphere depend for their existence on the therapist's skill in blending the ingredients of a good treatment relationship. Once established, an atmosphere conducive to change also supports various technical procedures that promote faster and fuller progress than reliance on the relationship alone.

Thus the general and specific factors promoting change in psychotherapy are without question complementary. Relationship factors in psychotherapy owe their effectiveness to the skill of the therapist in establishing and sustaining them, and only when a sound treatment relationship is augmented by techniques for promoting clients' understanding and control of their behavior does psychotherapy progress maximally toward its goals.

The complementarity of general and specific factors promoting change contradicts two notions about the treatment relationship in psychotherapy that occasionally appear in the literature. First, it is sometimes maintained that, since a human relationship is the essence of psychotherapy, anyone with mature interpersonal skills who wants to help someone else can do so as effectively as a trained professional. Second, it is sometimes argued that effective use of catharsis, expectancy, therapist attention, and reinforcement is sufficient to accomplish all the possible ends of psychotherapy, independently of what the client talks about or the therapist says in response.

Regarding the human relationship, it is tempting to conclude that, if behavior change can be promoted just by listening to people talk, encouraging them to expect change, paying special kinds of attention to them, and reinforcing the positive things they say and do, then anyone who is a decent, caring, sensitive person can function well as a psychotherapist without professional education and training. But what are the best means of helping people talk freely about themselves? How should the therapist act so as to foster expectation of change? When should therapists make some special effort to display empathy, when should they attempt to convey warmth, and when should they emphasize their genuineness? How can these kinds of therapist attention be most clearly expressed? What items in the clients' comments or actions should be reinforced, and what are the most effective means of reinforcing them?

The training and experience of professional clinicians provide answers to these questions; they teach them how to translate their interpersonal skills into specific words and deeds that are timed, phrased, and modulated so as to foster a helpful treatment relationship. Research findings in this regard confirm that the amount of empathy, warmth, and genuineness therapists are capable of expressing to their clients is directly related to the amount of training and experience they have had, and that with increasing experience novice therapists become more adept at grasping the messages their clients are trying to convey and in formulating and timing their interventions (Beery, 1970; Cicchetti & Ornston, 1976; Hayden, 1975; Hill, Charles, & Reed, 1981; Perlman, 1973).

Nevertheless, even though most clinicians would agree with Strupp and Hadley (1979) that "the 'techniques' of professional therapists . . . potentiate the healing processes inherent in a 'good human relationship' " (p. 1136), there has been a disconcerting lack of clear research evidence relating therapist experience level to treatment outcome. Generally speaking, outcome studies involving experienced therapists have been much more likely to report positive results than studies in which the therapists were relatively inexperienced (Bergin, 1971). Within individual studies, however, the findings have been inconsistent concerning whether differences in therapist level of experience have any bearing on the results achieved. The most that can be said on the basis of reviews of this research is that there appears to be a modest relationship between therapist experience level and outcome, but that this relationship has not yet been demonstrated to account for very much of the variance (Auerbach & Johnson, 1977).

Note should also be taken of the fact that numerous studies have failed to find any difference in the outcomes achieved by professional psychotherapists and paraprofessional helpers (see Durlak, 1979). With few exceptions, however, these studies have involved carefully selected "helpers" who worked only with mildly disturbed clients in a brief treatment relationship addressed to some narrowly defined problem, and who received some training in how to carry out their clinical role. Hence this research provides useful information on successful utilization of paraprofessional mental health workers, but it does not contradict the value of training clinicians in specific skills necessary for promoting maximum behavior change in ongoing psychotherapy with a broad range of unselected clients.

Turning to the effects of the treatment relationship, the documented potential of catharsis, expectancy, therapist attention, reinforcement, and a therapeutic alliance to foster behavior change has tempted some clinicians to conclude that these relationship factors can produce all of the possible and necessary changes in psychotherapy. However, even though a good working relationship is essential to progress in psychotherapy, the extent and durability of any improvement clients make will be limited unless they have acquired some understanding of the problems that brought them for help and of the basis on which they may have resolved them.

The importance of giving clients an opportunity to profit not only from generally beneficial aspects of the treatment relationship but also from specific information provided to them by the therapist about their problems is endorsed by most clinicians, including many who have been influential primarily for their attention to relationship factors. Rogers (1974), for example, notes, "I had learned through hard and frustrating experiences that simply to listen understandingly to a client and *to attempt to convey that understanding* were potent forces for individual therapeutic change" (p. 116; italics added). Frank (1971) includes among the features of the psychotherapy situation that contribute to its success the "provision of new information concerning the nature and sources of the patient's problems and possible alternative ways of dealing with them" (p. 356).

Schofield (1964, 1970), who argues that some people with psychological concerns can benefit merely from the opportunity for a sympathetic friendship, nevertheless urges trained psychotherapists not to devote their professional time to providing such friendships, because of "the large number of persons with emotional or psychological disorders who require specific treatment over and above the meliorating effects of a relationship" (Schofield, 1970, p. 218). Current trends in behavioral approaches, which have traditionally emphasized reinforcement procedures for effecting behavior change, stress that cognitive mediation of these changes increases a client's future capacity to think through and regulate his or her own behavior (see Goldfried & Merbaum, 1973; Kazdin, 1979b; Mahoney & Arnkoff, 1978).

Thus, despite the lack of clear supporting evidence, there is broad consensus that effective psychotherapy requires therapists to be technically skilled both in nurturing a helpful treatment relationship and in communicating useful information to clients about themselves. If it is assumed that therapists comprehend the meaning of their clients' behavior and have a treatment strategy in mind, every tactical decision they make about precisely when to share their understanding and how to implement their strategy will call on their technical skill. Although it is conceivable that therapists with limited skill might by hunch or happenstance say or do just the right thing at the right time to sustain a treatment relationship and expand their clients' self-awareness, there is little likelihood of their doing so on any but an occasional or irregular basis. On the other hand, the greater the technical skill therapists have acquired from their training and experience, the more frequently and systematically they are likely to respond to their clients in ways that expand self-knowledge and sustain the treatment relationship.

Specific Factors Promoting Change

The specific factors promoting change in psychotherapy comprise technical procedures employed by therapists to engage and sustain clients' involved participation in the treatment and to increase their ability to understand and control their behavior. The technical procedures used in all forms of psychotherapy derive mainly from the two cornerstones of Freud's psychoanalytic method, free association and interpretation.

With respect to free association, psychotherapy can promote behavior change only if therapists can induce their clients to express themselves. Unless clients reveal their thoughts and feelings, there is little basis from which therapists can gain an understanding of the problems they are trying to help resolve. To generate adequate information with which to work, therapists must command a repertoire of procedures for motivating clients to talk, for aiding them to recall and report experiences both close to and remote from prior awareness, and for helping them continue to express themselves even when it becomes painful or embarrassing to do so. The more skillful the therapists' techniques in this regard, the more information will become available for pursuing the goals of the treatment. Therapists vary in how explicit their techniques are for inducing client expressiveness, usually in relation to their theoretical orientation. Silence, the direction of attention to the client, and responsiveness by acknowledgment and understanding are among the common tactics for fostering self-expression and communication, and some therapists, especially in the gestalt approach, are likely to suggest specific tasks for this purpose, such as repeating or exaggerating certain gestures and oral expressions.

With respect to interpretation, the effectiveness of psychotherapy depends on how well therapists can combine their skills in eliciting information from their clients with skills in formulating useful responses to this information, especially responses that expand client self-awareness. This is not to suggest that every response of the therapist constitutes an interpretation, even though such a view is occasionally advanced in the literature. Although every therapist response has the potential for influencing how a client thinks and feels, interpretations differ from four other kinds of intervention in the nature of the impact they are likely to have. Hence it is helpful to distinguish among the following kinds of therapist intervention:

1. *Questions.* Direct questioning ("What kind of person is your father?" "How do you feel about that?" "What happened next?") serves to elicit information and to help clients continue talking. Although questions focus clients' attention on certain subjects, they communicate little new information to them and thus have minimal impact on their progress in the treatment.

2. *Clarifications.* Clarifications convey the possible significance of certain subjects by directing clients' further attention to them ("Perhaps you could go over that experience again and fill in some more of the details") or by recapitulating their remarks ("If I follow you correctly, you think that your feeling uncomfortable around women has to do with sexual fantasies you have"). Although helpful by virtue of the emphasis they create, clarifications go little further than questions in presenting clients with new ideas or possibilities about themselves.

3. *Exclamations.* Exclamations include various noncommittal therapist utterances intended to facilitate the clients' talking, such as "mm-hmm" or "I see." As noted previously, such exclamations can exert potent reinforcement effects on what clients choose to think or talk about, and hence on the areas in which their attitudes and behavior are likely to undergo change. Like questions and clarifications, however, they do not provide clients substantive information or specifically influence the content of their self-reflections.

4. *Confrontations.* Confrontations are statements that call clients' attention to factual aspects of their behavior that have escaped their notice but can readily be made apparent to them. Confrontations may be addressed to what clients are saying ("You've described your husband physically, but you haven't said anything about what he's like as a person"); to what they are doing ("You've been drumming your fingers on the desk for the last 5 minutes or so, since you began talking about your boss"); or to their recollections ("The feelings you just described as having toward your father are the same kind of feelings you've been having about me"). In contrast to questions, clarifications, and exclamations, confrontations *do* present clients with information beyond that which they are already fully aware of. Unlike interpretations, however, they refer to obvious facts rather than to hypotheses or alternatives, and their accuracy requires no documentation.

5. *Interpretations.* Interpretations suggest some previously unrecognized meaning of or connection among a client's thoughts, feelings and actions. Although interpretations may prove congruent with how clients are experiencing themselves, and it is hoped that they do, they are never obvious facts requiring no further documentation. Instead, they constitute possibilities or alternative hypotheses for exploration, and they should accordingly be phrased in the language of conjecture and probability ("Could it be that your lack of interest in studying relates to some reluctance you have to graduate and complete your career as a student?" "From what we've learned, it seems likely that your dissatisfaction with yourself has little to do

with what you're like as a person, but has to do with an image you've carried around since childhood of being bad and unworthy").

What is unique about interpretations, then, is that they communicate new self-knowledge to clients that they can use to restructure their ways of looking at and feeling about themselves, and from which they can identify more rewarding and self-fulfilling ways of behaving. Questions, clarifications, exclamations, and confrontations contribute to the interpretive process by helping clients talk and by preparing them in gradual stages to understand and consider interpretations when they are finally offered. As just noted, however, these other interventions lack the impact of interpretations because they do not provide clients new information about themselves.

Research by Garduk and Haggard (1972) lends empirical support to this distinction between interpretations and other interventions. Analyzing the content of psychotherapy interviews, Garduk and Haggard found that clients spend more time thinking about interpretive than noninterpretive statements, apparently as a function of the greater impact they have, and give more indications of understanding and insight ("I see what you mean"; "I never realized that about myself before, but it's clear to me now") in response to interpretations than in response to other kinds of therapeutic response.

THE COURSE OF PSYCHOTHERAPY

Psychotherapy proceeds through three continuous but nevertheless distinct phases. The *initial* phase of the treatment consists of evaluating the client who has come for help, assessing the appropriateness of psychotherapy to meet his or her needs, and arranging an appropriate contract for the conduct of the treatment. The *middle* phase, which is usually by far the longest, involves the communication of understanding through interpretation and the resolution of such phenomena of the psychotherapy process as resistance, transference, and countertransference. The *final* phase of psychotherapy is devoted to consolidating the client's gains in the treatment and arranging for termination of the treatment contract. The following overview of these three phases of psychotherapy summarizes the typical course of the treatment and provides some basic guidelines for the therapist's activity in conducting it. The presentation draws mainly on psychodynamic formulations of the treatment process and is elaborated in detail in Weiner's (1975) *Principles of Psychotherapy*.

The Initial Phase: Evaluation, Assessment, and the Treatment Contract

Psychotherapy begins with a series of interviews in which the therapist accomplishes three tasks. First, he or she evaluates the client's personality functioning and the nature of the problems for which the client has sought help. Second, the therapist assesses the client's capability for participating in and benefiting from psychotherapy. Third, the therapist draws up a treatment contract in which client and therapist agree to the means and objectives of their ensuing work together. Although evaluation, assessment, and the formation of a treatment contract involve many of the same kinds of information about the client, they direct the therapist's attention to separate sets of issues.

Evaluating the Client.   Adequate evaluation consists of ascertaining the nature and background of clients' presenting problems and arriving at some understanding of them as people, including their characterological styles of coping with experience, their attitudes toward the important people in their lives, and the developmental events that have most significantly influenced them. This evaluation should yield both a *clinical* and a *dynamic* working formulation. The clinical formulation will specify clients' primary symptoms (e.g., anxiety reaction), their characterological style (e.g., passive–aggressive personality), and the extent of their personality resources and limitations. The dynamic formulation will identify the major sources of conflict and concern that appear to be causing clients problems in living or dissatisfaction with themselves.

Methods of obtaining such information from a person who seeks psychotherapy are elaborated in the previous six chapters of this book and need not be considered further here. However, it should be stressed that preliminary diagnostic information is essential to responsible planning in psychotherapy. Psychotherapy is but one among many potentially psychotherapeutic treatment methods. It embraces various different approaches, and each of these approaches can be tailored to the particular problems and concerns of the client.

Hence there is no justiication for assuming equipotentiality among people seeking help for psychological difficulties. Some are served best by treatment approaches other than psychotherapy, some are suitable for primarily uncovering and others for primarily supportive psychotherapy, and, whatever approach is employed, individual clients benefit most if the treatment they receive is focused on the particular issues underlying their need for help. Proper selection from among these alternatives is possible only in the presence of sufficient diagnostic information to guide treatment planning.

The necessity of a working formulation to guide differential treatment planning does not mean that a detailed diagnostic case study must be made prior to establishing a treatment contract. Indeed, there may be some disadvantage in pursuing an extensive case history in the initial phase of treatment. Acting as a diagnostician can cast the therapist in the role of someone who is more interested in obtaining information than in understanding it, and pressing for detailed information may limit the spontaneity with which the information can emerge in subsequent psychotherapy. What is needed initially is just enough information to support tentative formulations from which the appropriateness of psychotherapy can be adequately assessed (see Shectman, de la Torre, & Garza, 1979; Weiner, 1975, Chapter 5).

Assessing the Appropriateness of Psychotherapy.   Assessing the appropriateness of psychotherapy involves determining whether a person who appears in need of psychological help is capable of participating in and benefiting from this form of treatment. Considerable attention has been devoted in the literature to identifying characteristics of the "good candidate" for psychotherapy. However, research findings indicate that successful outcomes in psychotherapy may depend less on the characteristics of the client than on how the therapist conducts the treatment, with respect to creating a positive atmosphere, building a strong working alliance, and employing effective techniques. Hence responsible clinicians should avoid selecting clients to fit a particular treatment approach and should concentrate instead on selecting a treatment approach geared to the needs of the particular client.

Nevertheless, as elaborated by Weiner (1975, Chapter 2) and Garfield (1980, Chapter 3), there is reason to believe that at least three characteristics generally increase the likelihood of the prospective client's being able to participate in and benefit from psychotherapy. First, clients should be motivated to receive psychotherapy and have some expectation that it will be helpful to them. Motivation for psychotherapy consists of sufficient felt distress about their problems to induce clients to persevere in the treatment even when the work of the therapy becomes difficult or distressing. Regarding expectation, it has already been noted that a belief in the potential of the treatment to be helpful promotes a favorable outcome in psychotherapy.

Second, despite the level of their felt distress, clients should demonstrate reasonably well-integrated personality functioning. Generally speaking, the more consistently people have been able to engage in goal-directed behavior and the more successfully they have met previous life challenges, the better their prospects are for continuing and progressing in psychotherapy.

Third, clients should have some capacity to express and reflect on their experiences. As a verbal treatment method that revolves around what the client says, psychotherapy has little potential for benefiting people who are unwilling or unable to talk about themselves. In this regard, it is sometimes suggested that working-class, disadvantaged, and minority-group persons are poor candidates for psychotherapy because they are not oriented toward verbal self-expression. However, there is good reason to wonder whether negative outcomes with such clients are due to incapacity or reluctance on their part to participate in verbal psychotherapy, or reflect instead the inability of many advantaged, middle-class therapists to communicate effectively with them. Accumulating research points toward the second of these alternatives. Specifically, these studies suggest that verbal psychotherapy can be highly successful with working-class and minority-group clients if the therapist is able to grasp the sociocultural context of their problems and convey understanding and respect to them (see Karon & Vandenbos, 1977; Lerner, 1972; Lorion, 1973, 1978; Shen & Murray, 1981; Siassi & Messer, 1976).

Arranging the Treatment Contract. When therapists have concluded from their evaluation and assessment that psychotherapy is indicated and appropriate, their next task is to arrange an explicit treatment contract with the client. The first step in arranging this contract is obtaining the client's agreement to undertake psychotherapy. To provide a basis for such an agreement, therapists need to summarize their impressions of the client's difficulties, specifically recommend psychotherapy as a means of attempting to ameliorate these difficulties, and explain briefly how psychotherapy works to accomplish its aims.

No assumptions should be made about what clients already want or know in these respects. To begin psychotherapy without inviting clients to accept or reject a specific recommendation for treatment is an affront to their dignity, no matter how obvious their wishes in the matter seem to be. To ask them to decide about undertaking psychotherapy without first providing them some explanation of the treatment process may deny them the opportunity to give their informed consent, even if they have appeared to be psychologically sophisticated. In either case the therapist risks conveying a lack of respect that may detract from the effectiveness of the treatment relationship (see Weiner, 1975, Chapter 6).

Following agreement to undertake psychotherapy, the second step in formulating a treatment contract is to discuss the goals of the therapy and the procedures that will be employed in pursuing them. Although the treatment goals usually have become apparent during the evaluation of a client's reasons for seeking help, the treatment contract should include an explicit review of the objectives of the treatment. Such an explicit listing of objectives, whether they consist of symptom relief, resolution of life problems, or modification of personality characteristics, serves better than any presumed goals to guide the focus of the treatment and help monitor its progress.

The increasing interest noted earlier in brief and time-limited therapy has put a special spotlight on the form and statement of the goal as presented in arranging the treatment contract. Proponents of brief therapy are generally agreed on the central importance of having a focus clearly addressed to a nuclear conflict or one of its derivatives. Thus Mann's (1973) time-limited approach calls for an explicit statement of focus that stresses the particular nature of the client's enduring psychological pain: "You seem to be a decent sort of man and you have tried to please others, yet you feel and have always felt that you are not wanted"—to a 25-year-old man depressed and given to unpredictable and impulsive fights with his wife (Mann & Goldman, 1981, p. 36). Similarly, Sifneos (1972), in beginning work with a 23-year-old woman presenting anxiety and heterosexual difficulties, proposed a focus on her difficulty with men which could be traced to her relationship with her father.

Malan's approach does not require an explicit statement of the focus as part of the treatment contract, but his initial formulations construct one: "The evidence suggests that she feels guilty about aggressive feelings toward both her parents: toward her father for not being close to her, and toward her mother for standing between her and her father. These feelings have interfered with the development of mature sexuality. She defends against it by idealizing her parents and herself behaving in a very proper and conventional manner"—about a 22-year-old woman with a pattern of having to keep everything "nice," complaining of mild depressive symptoms (Malan, 1976, p. 94). These and other writers concur that the power of brief therapy rests in therapists' being able to keep both their own and their clients' attention on the focus. This does not mean that clients should be constrained from talking about matters that are not directly related to the focus, but only that therapists should react to all communications in terms of their possible connections to the agreed-upon focus.

As for the procedures to be employed, clients should be informed about what their role and the role of the therapist will be in the treatment sessions. Although the kinds of information given in this regard may vary with the particular treatment approach to be used, by and large some relatively brief indication that clients will be responsible primarily for expressing themselves and the therapist primarily for communicating understanding should suffice: "Your job will be to talk about yourself as freely as you can, and my job will be to listen, to help you talk, and to help you learn more about yourself from what you're able to say."

The third step in formulating a treatment contract consists of making specific arrangements for the time, place, and fee for sessions and the frequency with which they will be held. The elements of advantageous planning in these respects are beyond the scope of this discussion and are elaborated in the psychotherapy textbooks recommended elsewhere in the chapter. However, given the importance noted above of avoiding assumptions in the treatment contract, it can be emphasized that no feature of the specific arrangements for psychotherapy should be legislated or left to chance. Instead, therapists should complete arrangements for the treatment through a series of recommendations that their clients fully understand and can accept, reject, or counter with an alternative suggestion ("Could I come at one o'clock rather than two, so I could make it part of my lunch hour?").

The Middle Phase: Interpretation, Resistance, Transference, and Countertransference

The middle phase of psychotherapy involves the major work of the treatment, that is, the effort to expand clients' ability to understand and control their behavior. During the evaluation interviews the general factors promoting change in psychotherapy, especially those deriving from the treatment relationship, may already have increased clients' sense of well-being and perhaps even relieved some of their symptoms. However, it is not until a client has formally agreed to a treatment contract that the therapist has the right to proceed with various technical procedures for the communication of understanding, and it is at this point that the middle phase of treatment begins.

As indicated in the preceding section, the major technique for the communication of understanding in psychotherapy is *interpretation*. Difficulties associated with clients' responsibility for expressing themselves inevitably lead to *resistances,* which comprise various forms of interference with their therapeutic collaboration. Often these interferences incorporate irrational feelings and attitudes toward the therapist, called *transference,* and therapists are subject to irrational feelings and attitudes toward their clients, called *countertransference.* Such interferences must be relieved or circumvented and such irrationalities must be resolved in order for therapy to progress toward a successful conclusion. As we noted earlier, there is good reason to concentrate on helping clients recognize how interferences in the treatment mirror the difficulties in living that led them to seek therapy. Through being helped to overcome these obstacles to effective collaboration in the treatment, clients take a critical step toward learning to master their real-life difficulties.

Interpretation. As already defined, interpretations are statements that bring to clients' attention aspects of themselves and their behavior that they have not previously recognized. To make effective use of interpretation, therapists need to decide *what* to interpret, *when* to interpret it, and *how* best to construct the interpretive sequence.

Regarding decisions about what to interpret, interpretations should be selectively addressed to features of clients' thoughts, feelings, or actions that seem distressing to them or that reflect distorted, unrealistic, inconsistent, or ineffective means of coping with experience. Rather than being spread in shotgun fashion over every facet of clients' behavior, in other words, interpretations should be reserved for what appears to be causing trouble in their lives.

In addition to being selectively focused on content related to clients' difficulties, interpretations should suggest connections or relationships close to their awareness, so that they can sense their plausibility. Interpretations addressed to thoughts and feelings of which clients are not even remotely aware are more likely to create dissonance than to provide a logical next step in the self-exploratory process. Accordingly, a sound general principle of psychotherapy is to interpret near the surface of the client's awareness. As a corollary principle, deeply unconscious concerns should not be interpreted until the uncovering effects of the treatment have brought them close to conscious awareness.

Knowing when to offer interpretations is a matter of good *timing* and proper *dosage*. The best time for clients to receive an interpretation is when they are approaching awareness of the particular connection or explanation it suggests and when they seem both open to new ideas and enthusiastic about the treatment process. If a client does not appear to be in a receptive frame of mind, then interpretations should be reserved for another time, unless they are addressed specifically to his or her inability or unwillingness to come to grips with new information. Additionally, therapists should offer interpretations only when they are reasonably sure that they are accurate and can be documented in reference to matters previously discussed in the therapy. Interpretations that lack congruence with clients' experiencing of themselves and cannot be supported with evidence from prior interviews add little to clients' self-knowledge and give them cause to question the therapist's empathic capacity (see Spence, 1982).

Proper dosage consists of offering interpretations only as frequently as the client is able to think them through. Because they provide new information, interpretations require some reflection, and bombarding people with interpretations more rapidly than they can integrate them can create an information overload. It is important in this regard not to "save" interpretations for the end of a session, as a culmination of the interview, since clients are then deprived of an adequate opportunity to explore with the therapist either the basis of the interpretation or its implications for their behavior.

Constructing an interpretive sequence involves using a graded series of interventions to pave the way for each interpretation. For example, the therapist might begin an interpretative sequence with a clarification ("As I hear you, then, you found yourself saying something insulting when you really wanted to become more friendly"); continue with a confrontation ("We've seen several times now when you were on the verge of getting closer to someone and then spoiled things for yourself by saying or doing something offensive"); and conclude with an interpretation ("It's as if you have some underlying fear of getting close to others, so that you have to prevent it from happening").

This example illustrates several characteristic features of the interpretive process. The sequence moves with deliberation, sticking close to the data and allowing the client opportunities along the way to demur or ask about the nature of the evidence. The conclusion of the sequence is expressed conjecturally ("It's as if . . ."), which is appropriate to the fact that interpretations are no more than alternative hypotheses until the client confirms them. And the interpretation itself, if accepted, can be used as a confrontation ("We've learned that you have some underlying fears of getting close to people.") in a subsequent interpretive sequence that takes the exploratory process one step further, as to an interpretation concerning the origin of the client's fears of personal intimacy. Dramatic revelations that cut immediately to the nub of clients' problems, eliminate their neurosis, and earn their undying gratitude exist only in fictionalized versions of uncovering psychotherapy. In reality, this treatment method is a painstaking process in which learning derives from the gradual accrual of new information and progress is measured in hard-won increments of self-understanding (see Weiner, 1975, Chapter 8).

Resistance.   Resistance consists of a temporary inability or unwillingness on the part of the client to adhere to the terms of the treatment contract. As such, resistance originates in four kinds of motivation that run counter to the client's conscious wish to participate in and benefit from psychotherapy.

First, clients may be reluctant to give up their present life patterns, no matter how much difficulty they are causing, or they may become uneasy about accommodating to the new life patterns that are emerging out of the therapy, no matter how potentially rewarding they promise to be. In these circumstances *resistance to change* is likely to develop.

Second, clients may have preferred styles of coping with cognitive and affective experience that oppose the demands of psychotherapy for integrated coping with both kinds of experience. In this situation a *characterological resistance* to the treatment process may become manifest.

Third, because psychotherapy inevitably confronts people with aspects of themselves and their experiences that may be painful, depressing, or embarrassing for them to think or talk about, it produces in all clients periods of *resistance to content*.

Fourth, virtually all clients develop thoughts and feelings about their therapist that at times command more of their attention in the treatment sessions than the problems for which they are seeking help. At these times *transference resistance* is being expressed.

Whatever its origins, resistance leads to certain characteristic treatment behaviors from which therapists can identify its presence. Resisting clients may reduce the amount of time they spend in psychotherapy by skipping, canceling, or coming late for sessions. They may limit the amount and range of their conversation in the sessions by falling silent, by concentrating on certain aspects of their experience (such as past events) and ignoring others (such as what is happening currently), or by engaging in superficial and mundane conversations that have little to do with their problems. At other times, resistance may be expressed through efforts to ward off the impact of psychotherapy. In these instances clients may seek to make the therapist more of a personal friend than a helping professional, or they may take certain actions precipitously instead of discussing alternative possibilities with the therapist, or they may develop a "flight into health," which consists of a sudden and unjustified feeling that all is well and psychotherapy is no longer needed.

Although these patterns of resistance interfere with communication in psychotherapy and may lead to premature termination of the treatment relationship, resistance behavior can also yield valuable information about clients' personality styles and the sources of their anxiety. By addressing timely interpretations to the circumstances that elicit resistance and the manner in which it is expressed, therapists can both minimize the interference it causes and help clients learn more about themselves (see Langs, 1981; Wachtel, 1981; Weiner, 1975, Chapter 9).

Transference.   The psychotherapy relationship includes three concurrent levels of interaction between client and therapist. First, there is a *real* relationship between them. This consists of the client's factual knowledge about his or her therapist, including such matters as sex, approximate age, overt physical characteristics, and manner of dress. It also consists of practical discussions concerning such matters as a necessary change in appointment time and of such social exchanges as "hello," "goodbye," and "merry Christmas."

Second, there is the previously mentioned *working alliance* between them, which consists of their commitments to the treatment contract and to the roles prescribed by it. Because the working alliance is conceived of and implemented on a realistic basis, it may appear to constitute part of the real relationship between client and therapist. However, by virtue of the asymmetric interpretive relationship it creates, in which clients are to express themselves without restraint and therapists are to listen and comment, the working alliance differs sharply from the kinds of interpersonal relationships people usually establish in real life.

Third, clients in psychotherapy develop a *transference relationship* to their therapist, which consists of positive or negative feelings and attitudes originally held toward other people in their lives and now transferred without justification in reality to the person of the therapist. When transference feelings and attitudes arise, they may be expressed either in veiled or direct form. In its most veiled form, transference is expressed in thoughts, fantasies, and dreams in which the therapist is not identified but appears to play a role. In somewhat less veiled form, transference may appear in such behavior as a client's sitting closer to or farther away from the therapist during sessions, asking for more frequent and longer interviews or less frequent and shorter ones, or trying to impress the therapist with his or her personal attributes or to convey disdain for what the therapist may think of him or her.

Expressed more directly, transference may take the form of favorable or unfavorable comments about the therapist's profession ("Some of my friends have been telling me that psychotherapy didn't help them a bit"), about his or her trappings ("I wish your office wasn't so hard to get to"), or about his or her person ("That's a handsome tie you're wearing"). Even more directly, the client may specifically express such feelings toward the therapist as love, hate, admiration, anger, envy, or sexual attraction. Although these feelings may have some elements of reality in them, as transference they have more to do with how the client has felt or feels about others than with any cause the therapist has given the client to feel that way about him or her.

Whenever clients are experiencing or expressing transference feelings, their attention is being diverted from the problems for which they have sought help. Hence transference always constitutes a resistance to the treatment process. Like resistance, then, transference both interferes with communication in psychotherapy and provides a source of important information about clients, particularly with respect to their interpersonal attitudes and their characteristic styles of expressing these attitudes. Whether transference phenomena are used to reconstruct earlier experiences or to identify maladaptive patterns of coping with current experience, they facilitate progress toward increased self-understanding when they are correctly identified and interpreted.

The interpretation of transference begins with helping clients recognize that many of the feelings and attitudes they experience toward the therapist are not justified in reality and must reflect interpersonal dispositions they have brought with them into the treatment situation. Clients can then draw on their transference experiences to trace these feelings and attitudes to their true origins, whether they stem from anger toward a rejecting mother, generalized resentment of authority figures, or whatever. In this way they can gain increased understanding and control over the extent to which their previous experiences exert a maladaptive influence on their current interpersonal behavior (see Greenson, 1967, Chapter 3; Langs, 1980; Weiner, 1975, Chapter 10).

Countertransference.   Therapists are also subject to inappropriate personal reactions in the treatment relationship, known as countertransference. Countertransference can result from generalized attitudes therapists have toward certain kinds of people (e.g., enormous admiration for creative artists or limited patience with passive-aggressive individuals) or from discussions in the treatment that touch on areas in which they themselves have unresolved conflicts. However they originate, inappropriate reactions of therapists to their clients can undermine the working alliance if their manifestations are not promptly recognized and controlled.

The manifestations of countertransference, like those of transference, may be more or less direct. In overt countertransference therapists openly experience positive or negative feelings toward a client that cannot be justified in light of the treatment contract. The treatment contract calls on therapists to respect clients, not to judge them, and to understand their behavior, not react to it. This means, for example, that distaste for clients who brutalize their children, or anger in response to clients who are being insulting, although justifiable in a real interpersonal context, is inappropriate to the treatment situation and constitutes countertransference. The therapist's task is to explore with the client the origins and self-defeating consequences of such brutal or insulting behavior, not to respond in terms of his or her personal feelings about it.

Therapists' personal feelings may at times sensitize them to implications of a client's behavior and even prove useful to mention ("You're making me angry, and we have to wonder why you're apparently trying to provoke me"). However, personal values and sensitivities cannot be allowed to direct therapists away from their primary responsibility, which is meeting their client's needs, not seeing to their own.

In its less overt forms countertransference reactions can subtly influence therapists' behavior without their immediately being aware of this. Therapists may find themselves looking forward eagerly to a client's next visit or "forget" to inform the client of a necessary cancelation. They may become inattentive or drowsy in sessions with a client, or allow the sessions to run overtime. They may attack the client with an overzealous series of anxiety-provoking interpretations or spare his or her feelings by withholding appropriate interpretations. They may encounter a client in their own dreams and fantasies, in either a pleasant or unpleasant context. These and similar phenomena identify countertransference reactions, positive or negative as their content suggests. When present, they should alert therapists to the possibility that their conduct of the treatment is being inappropriately influenced by their personal needs and should be modified accordingly. The only appropriate use of countertransference is as a clue to a better understanding of a client and of his or her impact on others (see Epstein & Feiner, 1979; Tauber, 1978; Weiner, 1975, Chapter 11).

The Final Phase: Termination

As the interpretive process continues, clients in psychotherapy gradually increase their knowledge of themselves and their behavior. However, as implied early in this chapter, the insight produced by interpretation does not automatically unlock an individual's self-actualizing potential and effect positive behavior change. The initial comprehension of previously unrecognized aspects of oneself is only a first step in the process of behavior change. To be effective, interpretations must be thoroughly worked through, which means that they must be reassessed in a variety of contexts for the consistency with which they can account for perplexing or maladaptive thoughts, feelings, and actions (see Mendel, 1975).

Not until an interpretation has been extensively cross-validated in recurrent experiences are clients ready to begin modifying their behavior in light of it. "If my feeling that other people are better than I am is really something I've been carrying around from childhood and has no basis in what I'm like as an adult," a client may come to think, "it should be safe for me at least to experiment with being more assertive." When such a point is reached, behavior change starts to follow in the wake of enhanced self-understanding, tentatively at first but with gradually increasing regularity and decreasing self-consciousness, until the desired behavior change becomes a natural and integrated feature of the person's life style.

When a client has made substantial progress toward integrating desired behavior change, psychotherapy enters its final phase. As also mentioned earlier, "substantial progress" does not necessarily mean that all of the objectives with which the treatment began have been fully and permanently realized. Rather, termination can appropriately be considered when it seems to both client and therapist that a satisfactory amount of progress has been made, and that a point of diminishing returns has been reached that would make further gains more costly in time and effort than appears justified.

Once a client has made substantial progress toward the goals of the treatment and reached a point of diminishing returns, two other considerations help determine when psychotherapy should be terminated. First, any lingering transference elements in the treatment relationship must be resolved, so that client and therapist can complete their work together primarily on the level of the real relationship. Clients who leave psychotherapy harboring unexpressed feelings toward their therapists may continue to be troubled by them, just as they were troubled by other unfinished psychological business when they entered the treatment. To avoid merely exchanging one set of problems for another, the therapist should work through all aspects of the transference relationship before the treatment is stopped.

Second, clients should appear capable of continuing on their own to engage in the kinds of self-observation that they have profited from in the treatment. Successful completion of therapy does not inoculate the client against future psychological distress when new or recurrent difficulties arise. However, psychotherapy should provide the successfully treated person with a reservoir of techniques to draw on for evaluating and dealing constructively with new problems as they arise. Hence when improved clients whose transference reactions have been worked through begin to use their sessions less for discussing unsolved problems than for recounting problem situations that they have already brought to a satisfactory resolution by themselves, the time has come to consider terminating the treatment contract.

Therapists must be wary of underestimating the importance and difficulty of working through this termination phase. The longer and more involving the therapy has been, the more time and attention will usually be necessary to manage the work of termination adequately. It is the therapist's responsibility to initiate the final phase of treatment by calling attention to indications that termination is imminent and negotiating an ending date. Beside the existential process of saying goodbye and of extricating oneself from such an important relationship, the act of parting often provides one last opportunity to identify and resolve lingering aspects of the client's problems. For these reasons the termination phase requires every bit as much sensitivity and skill on the part of the therapist as do getting the treatment underway and carrying it through its middle phase (see Firestein, 1974, 1978; Maholick & Turner, 1979; Weiner, 1975, Chapter 12).

TRENDS IN PSYCHOTHERAPY RESEARCH

It is the ethical responsibility of clinicians who practice psychotherapy to keep abreast of progress in psychotherapy research. This chapter accordingly concludes with some comments on trends in psychotherapy research and some recommendations for further reading in this area.

Psychotherapy research literature is about evenly divided between attention to *method* and attention to *substance*. Attention to method focuses on the manner in which psychotherapy research should be done, whereas attention to substance concerns the findings that emerge from such research. Psychotherapy research can be categorized further according to whether it addresses *outcome* or *process* aspects of the treatment situation. Outcome research is concerned with the effectiveness of psychotherapy and with identifying variables related to the amount and kinds of personality change that take place as a result of the treatment. Process research is concerned with events occurring within the treatment situation, that is, with the influence of one set of client–therapist behaviors (e.g., therapist warmth) on another set of client–therapist behaviors (e.g., client openness). In the end, of course, process research is also concerned with outcome, since its purpose in identifying influences within the treatment is to find ways of making psychotherapy more effective and more efficient (see Orlinsky & Howard, 1978; Sargent, 1961).

With this distinction in mind, it is possible to catalog the relatively short history of psychothcrapy research by its shifting emphasis from outcome to process studies and back again. Empirical work in the field emerged out of the natural interest of clinicians in whether their efforts to help people were achieving this desired end, and research accordingly began with efforts simply to tabulate numbers of successful and unsuccessful outcomes. When early studies of this kind came under the scrutiny of sophisticated investigators, however, they were found to suffer numerous methodological limitations.

Particularly important in this regard were shortcomings in the criteria of success and failure used in the early outcome work. Many of the studies relied entirely on *phenomenological* criteria consisting of clients' reports of whether they considered their therapy to have benefited them; such self-reports were appropriately criticized as being open to many sources of bias and distortion and hence unreliable. Other studies used *intratherapy* criteria consisting of measures or ratings of behavior change within the therapy interviews; these measures and ratings were justly criticized as being unvalidated with respect to behavior change occurring outside the therapy. In a then-very-influential summary of these criticisms, Zax and Klein (1960) concluded that the only adequate basis for evaluating treatment outcome would be external measures of client behavior or, more specifically, systematic assessment of clients' pretherapy and posttherapy behavior in their real-life activities. The difficulty of mounting studies that could sample clients' behavior at home, at work, and in social situations both before and after psychotherapy cast a pall on outcome research for several years to come.

Concurrently with discouragement about the obstacles to doing adequate outcome research, some creative advances in methodology stimulated considerable interest in process studies of psychotherapy. The publication by Rogers and Dymond of *Psychotherapy and Personality Change* (1954) and preliminary reports from the University of Michigan Psychotherapy Research Project (Bordin et al., 1954; Harway et al., 1955; Speisman, 1959) presented researchers with intriguing illustrations of how tape-recorded interviews could be used in combination with other kinds of patient and therapist data to study not only change in client status over time, but also such complex dimensions of psychotherapy as resistance and depth of interpretation.

Process research tapping many different features of the client–therapist interaction continues to the present time to figure prominently in the psychotherapy literature. However, following papers by Bergin (1963) and Strupp (1963), which "revisited" problems in psychotherapy outcome research, outcome studies experienced a renaissance that brought them back into equal prominence with studies of process. Two factors in particular accounted for this renewed interest in outcome research. First, process studies were found to pose their own share of methodological difficulties, particularly with respect to developing adequate measures of client and therapist interview behaviors (see Kiesler, 1966, 1973). These methodological difficulties led many researchers to redirect their interest toward extratherapy criteria of behavior change, especially criteria that can be objectively measured, and thus to seek better ways of conducting outcome research instead of abandoning it as a hopeless pursuit.

Second, advances in personality and behavior assessment answered many of the criticisms reviewed by Zax and Klein. New assessment techniques were developed that are more suitable for evaluating psychotherapy outcome than the phenomenological methods previously found unreliable, and subsequent research demonstrated reasonable validity for numerous intratherapy measures in representing extratherapy behavior. Several kinds of outcome criteria, some simple and some complex, involving observational, behavioral, and psychodiagnostic measures of symptom relief, goal attainment, and improved psychological functioning have proved useful for measuring the effects of therapeutic interventions (see Bergin & Lambert, 1978; Kazdin & Wilson, 1978; Kendall & Norton-Ford, 1982; Mahoney, 1978; Mintz, 1981; Mintz & Kiesler, 1982).

For further reading on the methodological challenges of designing adequate outcome and process studies in psychotherapy, the reader is referred to valuable contributions by Bordin (1965, 1974), Fiske (1977), Garfield (1980, Chapter 11), Gottman and Markman (1978), Gottschalk and Auerbach (1966), Kiesler (1978), and Strupp and Bergin (1969). Regarding the significant new substantive trends in psychotherapy research, it is relevant to close this chapter with a brief review of the history of outcome studies, their current status, and their future directions.

Outcome Research in Psychotherapy

Outcome research may be said to have come to the end of an era introduced by Eysenck's publication in 1952 of "The Effects of Psychotherapy" (see also Eysenk,

1961), in which he concluded from an exhaustive search of the literature that the effects of psychotherapy were "small or nonexistent." Furthermore, said Eysenck, psychotherapy at best produces no advantage over everyday events in a person's life ("spontaneous remission") in alleviating neurotic disturbance. Eysenck's devastating critique stimulated numerous rejoinders and a spate of outcome studies that incorporated increasingly sophisticated research designs. This burgeoning research led to new reviews of the question, "Is psychotherapy effective?" As we shall see, this general, oversimplified question pretty much lies behind us now, and much more specific outcome questions are being addressed in psychotherapy research.

Three of the criticisms leveled at Eysenck's survey merit special mention, mainly because of their implications for research design. First, Eysenck lumped the work of experienced and inexperienced therapists used in outcome studies. Most clinicians would agree that the true test of a method of intervention is the results it achieves in the hands of practitioners skilled and experienced in employing it. This is not just an abstract proposition. In a detailed critique of Eysenck's position and a reanalysis of his data, Bergin (1971) concluded that the demonstrated benefits of psychotherapy, although modest, were far from "nonexistent." In updating this analysis 7 years later, Bergin concluded that recent outcome data look even more favorable and "yield clearly positive results," largely because "more experienced and competent therapists have been used in recent studies" (Bergin & Lambert, 1978, p. 180).

Second, Eysenck's comparisons of treatment results with spontaneous remission rates have been found wanting. He asserted that two-thirds of neurotically disturbed adults recover within 2 years without treatment and hence that only treatments showing a recovery rate of better than two-thirds could be considered effective. However, careful reviews of the evidence have demonstrated (a) that average rates of spontaneous remission fall far below two-thirds of neurotically disturbed persons and (b) that variability in these rates across different populations makes them unreliable as a sutstitute for a no-treatment control group in comparative studies (Bergin & Lambert, 1978; Lambert, 1976).

Moreover, in many earlier studies of spontaneous remission "untreated" comparison groups were drawn from clients on clinic waiting lists. Such a research design overlooks the hopeful expectations that can flow from being placed on a waiting list to receive psychotherapy, and it also ignores the beneficial impact of whatever evaluation procedures precede being wait-listed. Hence question can be raised as to whether clients on waiting lists can be considered untreated for purposes of serving as a comparison group in studies of the effects of psychotherapy (see Goldstein, 1960; Malan, Heath, Bacal, & Balfour, 1975; O'Leary & Borkovec, 1978).

Third, Eysenck's analysis placed in the same pot a broad range of outcome criteria, from discharge from inpatient status to complete personality change, and some were of doubtful appropriateness. For example, in assessing results reported from the Berlin Psychoanalytic Institute, Eysenck counted premature terminations as treatment failures. Bergin and Lambert (1978) observe that if the effectiveness of the psychoanalytic treatment offered in the institute is measured only on people who actually participated in it—and the premature dropouts are eliminated from the sample—the improvement rate rises dramatically from 39% reported by Eysenck to 91% of people treated.

Over the years accumulating data from outcome studies have led almost all reviewers to conclude, in disagreement with Eysenck, that psychotherapy is at least modestly effective in promoting positive behavior change (Bergin & Lambert, 1978; Frank, 1979; Garfield, 1980, Chapter 12; Luborsky et al., 1975; Meltzoff & Kornreich, 1970). Most recently Smith, Glass, and Miller (1980; see also Smith & Glass, 1977) have compiled some impressive data using a quantitative method called *meta-analysis,* which provides for statistical averaging of the standardized results of a large number of studies. From their meta-analysis of 475 controlled studies involving tens of thousands of persons, they conclude that "the results show unequivocally that psychotherapy is effective" and that the average client at the end of treatment "is better off than 80 percent of those who need therapy but remain untreated" (Smith et al., 1980, p. 124). Although some researchers have expressed reservations about the meta-analysis method, strong confirmation that it justifies positive conclusions about the efficacy of psychotherapy has begun to appear in the literature (see Landman & Dawes, 1982).

Thus the vital doubt as to whether psychotherapy should be taken seriously as a method of treating psychological problems seems to have been laid to rest, and researchers are readier than before to turn to some of the more complex questions that remain unanswered. One of these concerns the potential of psychotherapy for harmful as well as beneficial effects. In one of his early discussions of outcome research, Bergin (1963) suggested that average results in a sample of treated clients may not tell the whole story about how helpful psychotherapy can be when it is helpful at all. His point was that psychotherapy is not a benign intervention with an impact ranging from zero to some degree of benefit; instead, it is a potent treatment that in some cases, for some reasons, can make people worse off than they were before.

This potential potency for harm, which has come to be referred to as *deterioration* or *negative effects* in psychotherapy, has attracted considerable interest in recent years (see Bergin, 1980; Lambert, Bergin, & Collins, 1977; Strupp, Hadley, & Gomes-Schwartz, 1977). Still unknown, however, are the magnitude and frequency of these effects, the nature of the cases in which they are likely to occur, and the reasons for their development.

A second topic for future research involves the relative contribution of client and therapist variables to psychotherapy outcome. In earlier parts of this chapter we summarized compelling reasons to believe that what clients and therapists bring to the treatment situation (motivation, expectation, personality integration, and expressive capacity for the former; interpersonal skills and professionally honed techniques for the latter) has considerable bearing on a successful outcome—only to add that available research data fall far short of documenting such cumulative clinical wisdom. Much remains to be done to determine the precise significance of these variables and to resolve controversies over whether the client or the therapist has more to do with whether psychotherapy proves beneficial.

There is also considerable need for further research on so-called *dyadic* variables in psychotherapy. Many clinicians have argued convincingly that successful therapy derives not from characteristics of clients or therapists taken separately, but instead from felicitous matchups between the treatment partners—that is, the right therapist for the right client. Once again, as good as this may sound, empirical data have not yet been mustered to support such a belief.

A prominent example is the concept of *A-type* and *B-type* therapists introduced by Whitehorn and Betz in 1954. "A-type" therapists are oriented primarily toward establishing a meaningful treatment relationship and are expected to work relatively effectively with schizophrenic persons; "B-type" therapists are oriented primarily toward helping their clients achieve insight into their difficulties and are expected to work relatively effectively with neurotically disturbed people. Unfortunately, subsequent research has produced few consistent results to validate this dyadic variable, although numerous writers continue to feel that this and other client–therapist matching effects exist and have simply not yet been adequately measured (see Berzins, 1977; Daugherty, 1976; Heaton, Carr, & Hampson, 1975; Razin, 1977; Stephens, Shaffer, & Zlotowitz, 1975).

Finally, within the frame of reference that none of the widely used psychotherapies has been found more beneficial than any other for clients in general, adequate efforts have only recently begun to identify specific procedures that will work best in treating specific conditions. As a leading example of current efforts to develop treatment packages aimed at particular kinds of clients, the National Institute of Mental Health is funding and coordinating a massive multi-institutional clinical study comparing cognitive (Beck et al., 1979), interpersonal (Klerman et al., 1979), and drug treatments for depression (Kolata, 1981). Originally the plans called for simply pitting these three modes of treatment against each other along with a placebo control group. Subsequently in line with recommendations by Bordin (1981) and Strupp (1981), the research plan was amended to include the investigation of process factors in the outcome as well (Bordin, 1981).

So the search for therapeutic knowledge and power continues to move in the direction of greater specificity of procedure and target. Whether the future holds increasing formation of treatment packages, greater emphasis on the working alliance and the power of specific tasks, or some combination of both remains to be seen.

REFERENCES

Adler, A. (1907) *Study of organic inferiority and its psychical compensation.* New York: Nervous and Mental Diseases Publishing Company, 1917.

Adler, A. (1924) *The practice and theory of individual psychology.* New York: Harcourt, Brace & World, 1927.

Adler, A. (1933) *Social interest: A challenge of mankind.* London: Faber and Faber, 1938.

Allen, F. H. *Psychotherapy with children.* New York: Norton, 1942.

Ansbacher, H. L. *Alfred Adler revisited.* New York: Praeger, 1980.

Ansbacher, H. L., & Ansbacher, R. R. *The individual psychology of Alfred Adler.* New York: Basic Books, 1956.

Auerbach, A. H., & Johnson, M. Research on the therapist's level of experience. In A. S. Gurman & A. M. Razin (Eds.), *Effective psychotherapy.* New York: Pergamon Press, 1977.

Beck, A. T., Rush, A. J., Shaw, B. F., & Emery G. *Cognitive therapy of depression.* New York: Guilford, 1979.

Berry, J. W. Therapists' responses as a function of level of therapist experience and attitude of the patient. *Journal of Consulting and Clinical Psychology,* 1970, **34,** 239–243.

Bergin, A. E. The effects of psychotherapy: Negative results revisited. *Journal of Counseling Psychology,* 1963, **10,** 244–250.

Bergin, A. E. The evaluation of therapeutic outcomes. In A. E. Bergin & S. L. Garfield (Eds.), *Handbook of psychotherapy and behavior change.* New York: Wiley, 1971.

Bergin, A. E. Negative effects revisited: A reply. *Professional Psychology,* 1980, **11,** 93–100.

Bergin, A. E., & Lambert, M. J. The evaluation of therapeutic outcomes. In S. L. Garfield & A. E. Bergin (Eds.), *Handbook of psychotherapy and behavior change* (2nd ed.). New York: Wiley, 1978.

Berzins, J. I. Therapist-patient matching. In A. S. Gurman & A. M. Razin (Eds.) *Effective psychotherapy.* New York: Pergamon Press, 1977.

Blanck, G., & Blanck, R. *Ego psychology: Theory and practice.* New York: Columbia University Press, 1974.

Bordin, E. S. Simplification as a strategy for research. *Journal of Consulting Psychology,* 1965, **29,** 493–503.

Bordin, E. S. *Strategies in psychotherapy research.* New York: Wiley, 1974.

Bordin, E. S. *The working alliance: Basis for a general theory of psychotherapy.* Paper presented at the meeting of the American Psychological Association, Washington, D.C., 1976.

Bordin, E. S. The generalizability of the psychoanalytic concept of the working alliance. *Psychotherapy: Theory, Research and Practice,* 1979, **16,** 252–259.

Bordin, E. S. A psychodynamic view of counseling psychology. *Counseling Psychologist,* 1980, **9,** 62–70. (a)

Bordin, E. S. *Of human ties that bind or free.* Paper presented at the meeting of the Society for Research in Psychotherapy, Pacific Grove, California, 1980. (b)

Bordin, E. E. Effectiveness of psychotherapy. *Science,* 1981, **213,** 394–395.

Bordin, E. S., Cutler, R. L., Dittman, A. T., Harway, N. I., Raush, H. L., & Rigler, D. Measurement problems in process research on psychotherapy. *Journal of Consulting Psychology,* 1954, **8,** 79–82.

Boss, M. *Psychoanalysis and daseinalysis.* New York: Basic Books, 1963.

Brenner, C. *An elementary textbook of psychoanalysis.* New York: International Universities Press, 1973.

Breuer, J., & Freud, S. (1893–1895) Studies on hysteria. *Standard Edition.* Vol. II. London: Hogarth, 1955.

Bruinink, S. A., & Schroeder, H. E. Verbal therapeutic behavior of expert psychoanalytically oriented, Gestalt, and behavior therapists. *Journal of Consulting and Clinical Psychology*, 1979, **47**, 567–574.

Budman, S. H. (Ed.). *Forms of brief therapy*. New York: Guilford, 1981.

Bugental, J. F. T. *The search for authenticity*. New York: Holt, Rinehart & Winston, 1965.

Bugental, J. F. T. *Psychotherapy and process: The fundamentals of an existential-humanistic approach*. Reading, Mass.: Addison-Wesley, 1978.

Buhler, C. & Allen, M. *Introduction into humanistic psychology*. Belmont, Calif.: Brooks/Cole, 1971.

Chessick, R. D. *Technique and practice of intensive psychotherapy*. New York: Aronson, 1973.

Childress, R., & Gillis, J. S. A study of pretherapy role induction as an influence process. *Journal of Clincial Psychology*, 1977, **33**, 540–544.

Chinsky, J. M., & Rappaport, J. Brief critique of the meaning and reliability of "accurate empathy" ratings. *Psychological Bulletin*, 1970, **73**, 379–382.

Cicchetti, D. V., & Ornston, P. S. The initial psychotherapy interview: A content analysis of the verbal responses of novice and experienced therapists. *Journal of Psychology*, 1976, **93**, 167–174.

Corsini, R. J. *Current psychotherapies* (2nd ed.). Itasca, Ill.: Peacock, 1979.

Daugherty, F. E. Patient therapist matching for prediction of optimal and minimal therapeutic outcome. *Journal of Consulting and Clinical Psychology*, 1976, **44**, 889–897.

Davanloo, H. (Ed.) *Basic principles and techniques in short-term dynamic psychotherapy*. New York: Spectrum, 1978.

Dewald, P. A. *Psychotherapy: A dynamic approach* (2nd ed.). New York: Basic Books, 1971.

Dinkmeyer, D. C., Pew, W. C., & Dinkmeyer, D. C., Jr. *Adlerian counseling and psychotherapy*. Monterey, Calif. Brooks/Cole, 1979.

Durlak, J. A. Comparative effectiveness of paraprofessional and professional helpers. *Psychological Bulletin*, 1979, **86**, 80–92.

Edwards, D. G. *Existential psychotherapy: The process of caring*. New York: Gardner Press, 1981.

Ellenberger, H. F. *The discovery of the unconscious: The history and evolution of dynamic psychiatry*. New York: Basic Books, 1970.

Epstein, L., & Feiner, A. (Eds.). *Countertransference*. New York: Aronson, 1979.

Erikson, E. H. *Childhood and society*. New York: Norton, 1950.

Erikson, E. H. The problem of ego identity. *Journal of the American Psychoanalytic Association*, 1956, **4**, 56–121.

Eysenck, H. J. The effects of psychotherapy: An evaluation. *Journal of Consulting Psychology*, 1952, **16**, 319–324.

Eysenck, H. J. The effects of psychotherapy. In H. J. Eysenck (Ed.), *Handbook of abnormal psychology*. New York: Basic Books, 1961.

Fagan, J., & Shepherd, I. L. (Eds.). *Gestalt therapy now*. Palo Alto, Calif.: Science and Behavior Books, 1970.

Fairbairn, W. R. D. *An object-relations theory of personality*. New York: Busic Books, 1952.

Fiedler, F. E. A comparison of therapeutic relationship in psychoanalytic nondirective and Adlerian therapy. *Journal of Consulting Psychology*, 1950, **14**, 436–445.

Firestein, S. K. Termination of psychoanalysis of adults: A review of the literature. *Journal of the American Psychoanalytic Association*, 1974, **22**, 873–894.

Firestein, S. K. *Termination in psychoanalysis*. New York: International Universities Press, 1978.

Fiske, D. W. Methodological issues in research on the psychotherapist. In A. S. Gurman & A. M. Razin (Eds.), *Effective psychotherapy*. Oxford: Pergamon Press, 1977.

Ford, D. H., & Urban, H. B. *Systems of psychotherapy: A comparative study*. New York: Wiley, 1963.

Fordham, M. *Jungian psychotherapy*. New York: Wiley, 1978.

Frank, J. D. *Persuasion and healing*. Baltimore: Johns Hopkins University Press, 1961.

Frank, J. D. Therapeutic factors in psychotherapy. *American Journal of Psychotherapy*, 1971, **25**, 350–361.

Frank, J. D. The present status of outcome studies. *Journal of Consulting and Clinical Psychology*, 1979, **47**, 310–316.

Frank, J. D., Hoehn-Saric, R., Imber, S. D., Liberman, B. L., & Stone, A. R. *Effective ingredients of successful psychotherapy*. New York: Brunner/Mazel, 1978.

Frankl, V. E. *The doctor and the soul: From psychotherapy to logotherapy*. New York: Knopf, 1965.

Frankl, V. E. Logotherapy and existential analysis: A review. *American Journal of Psychotherapy*, 1966, **20**, 252–260.

Freud, A. (1936) *The ego and the mechanisms of defense*. New York: International Universities Press, 1946.

Freud, S. (1904) On psychotherapy. *Standard Edition* (Vol. XI). London: Hogarth, 1953.

Freud, S. (1910) "Wild" psycho-analysis. *Standard Edition* (Vol. XI). London: Hogarth, 1957.

Freud, S. (1912) Recommendations to physicians practising psycho-analysis. *Standard Edition* (Vol. XII). London: Hogarth, 1958.

Freud, S. (1913) On beginning the treatment (further recommendations on the technique of psycho-analysis I). *Standard Edition* (Vol. XII). London: Hogarth, 1958.

Freud, S. (1915) Observations on transference-love (further recommendations on the technique of psycho-analysis III). *Standard Edition* (Vol. XII). London: Hogarth, 1958.

Freud, S. (1933) New introductory lectures on psycho-analysis. *Standard Edition* (Vol. XXII). London: Hogarth, 1964.

Freud, S. (1937) Analysis terminable and interminable. *Standard Edition* (Vol. XXIII). London: Hogarth, 1964.

Fromm, E. *Escape from freedom*. New York: Farrar & Rinehart, 1941.

Fromm, E. *Man for himself*. New York: Rinehart, 1947.

Fromm, E. *The sane society*. New York: Rinehart, 1955.

Fromm-Reichmann, F. *Principles of intensive psychotherapy*. Chicago: University of Chicago Press, 1950.

Fromm-Reichmann, F. *Psychoanalysis and psychotherapy*. Selected papers edited by D. M. Bullard. Chicago: University of Chicago Press, 1959.

Garduk, E. C., & Haggard, E. A. Immediate effects on patients of psychoanalytic interpretations. *Psychological Issues,* 1972, 7, No. 4.

Garfield, S. L. Research on client variables in psychotherapy. In S. L. Garfield & A. E. Bergin (Eds.), *Handbook of psychotherapy and behavior change* (2nd ed.). New York: Wiley, 1978.

Garfield, S. L. *Psychotherapy: An eclectic approach.* New York: Wiley, 1980.

Glover, E. *The technique of psycho-analysis.* New York: International Universities Press, 1955.

Goldfried, M. R. & Merbaum, M. A perspective on self-control. In M. R. Goldfried & M. Merbaum (Eds.), *Behavior change through self-control.* New York: Holt, Rinehart & Winston, 1973.

Goldring, J. *Quick response therapy: A time-limited approach.* New York: Human Sciences Press, 1980.

Goldstein, A. P. Patient's expectancies and non-specific therapy as a basis for (un)-spontancous remission. *Journal of Clinical Psychology,* 1960, **16,** 399–403.

Goldstein, A. P. *Therapist-patient expectancies in psychotherapy.* New York: Pergamon Press, 1962.

Gomes-Schwartz, B. Effective Ingredients in psychotherapy: Prediction of outcome from process variables. *Journal of Consulting and Clinical Psychology,* 1978, **46,** 1023–1035.

Gomes-Schwartz, B., & Schwartz, J. M. Psychotherapy process variables distinguishing the "inherently helpful" person from the professional psychotherapist. *Journal of Consulting and Clinical Psychology,* 1978, **46,** 196–197.

Gottman, J. M., & Markman, H. J. Experimental designs in psychotherapy research. In S. L. Garfield & A. E. Bergin (Eds.), *Handbook of psychotherapy and behavior change* (2nd ed.). New York: Wiley, 1978.

Gottschalk, L. A., & Auerbach, A. H. *Methods of research in psychotherapy.* New York: Appleton-Century-Crofts, 1966.

Greenson, R. R. *The technique and practice of psychoanalysis* (Vol. I). New York: International Universities Press, 1967.

Greenspoon, J. The reinforcing effect of two spoken sounds on the frequency of two responses. *American Journal of Psychology,* 1955, 68, 409–416.

Greenspoon, J. Verbal conditioning and clinical psychology. In A. J. Bachrach (Ed.), *Experimental foundations of clinical psychology.* New York: Basic Books, 1962.

Hart, J. T., & Tomlinson, T. M. (Eds.). *New directions in client-centered therapy.* Boston: Houghton-Mifflin, 1970.

Hartley, D. E. Therapeutic alliance and success of brief individual therapy. Unpublished doctoral dissertation, University of Michigan, 1978.

Hatcher, C., & Himelstein, P. (Eds.). *Handbook of gestalt therapy.* New York: Aronson, 1976.

Hartmann, H. (1939) *Ego psychology and the problem of adaptation.* New York: International Universities Press, 1958.

Harway, N. I., Dittmann, A. T., Raush, H. L., Bordin, E. S., & Rigler D. The measurement of the depth of interpretation. *Journal of Consulting Psychology,* 1955, **23,** 379–386.

Hayden, B. Verbal and therapeutic styles of experienced therapists who differ in peer-rated therapist effectiveness. *Journal of Counseling Psychology,* 1975, **22,** 384–389.

Heaton, R. K., Carr, J. E., & Hampson, J. L. A-B therapist characteristics vs. psychotherapy outcome: Current status and prospects. *Journal of Nervous and Mental Disease,* 1975, **160,** 299–309.

Heine, R. W. *Psychotherapy.* Englewood Cliffs, N.J. Prentice-Hall, 1971.

Heitler, J. B. Preparation of lower class patients for expressive group therapy. *Journal of Consulting and Clinical Psychology,* 1973, **41,** 251–260.

Heitler, J. B. Preparatory techniques in initiating expressive psychotherapy with lower class unsophisticated patients. *Psychological Bulletin,* 1976, **83,** 339–352.

Hill, C. E., Charles, C., & Reed, K. G. A longitudinal analysis of changes in counseling skills during doctoral training in counseling psychology. *Journal of Counseling Psychology,* 1981, **28,** 428–436.

Hoehn-Saric, R., Frank, J. D., Imber, S. D., Mansh, E. H., Stone, A. R., & Battle, C. C. Systematic preparation of patients for psychotherapy. I. Effects on therapy behavior and outcome. *Journal of Psychiatric Research,* 1964, **2,** 267–281.

Hofling, C. K., & Meyers, R. W. Recent discoveries in psychoanalysis. *Archives of General Psychiatry,* 1972, **26,** 518–523.

Horney, K. *The neurotic personality of our time.* New York: Norton, 1937.

Horney, K. *New ways in psychoanalysis.* New York: Norton, 1939.

Horney, K. *Our inner conflicts.* New York: Norton, 1945.

Horvath, A. O. *An exploratory study of the working alliance: Its measurement and relationship to therapy outcome.* Doctoral thesis, University of British Columbia, 1981.

Jacobi, J. *Psychology of C. G. Jung.* New Haven: Yale University Press, 1963.

Jacobson, E. *The self and the object world.* New York: International Universities Press, 1964.

Jourard, S. M. *The transparent self: Self-disclosure and well-being.* Princeton, N.J.: Van Nostrand, 1964.

Jourard, S. M. *Self-disclosure: An experimental analysis of the transparent self.* New York: Wiley, 1971.

Jung, C. G. (1911) *Psychology of the unconscious.* New York: Moffat, Yard, 1916.

Jung, C. G. *Psychological types or the psychology of individuation.* New York: Harcourt, Bracè, 1923.

Jung, C. G. Modern man in search of a soul. New York: Harcourt, Brace, 1933.

Kanfer, F. H. Verbal conditioning: A review of its current status. In T. R. Dixon & D. L. Horton (Eds.), *Verbal behavior and general behavior theory.* Englewood Cliffs, N.J.: Prentice-Hall, 1968.

Karon, B. P., & Vandenbos, G. R. Psychotherapeutic technique and the economically poor patient. *Psychotherapy: Theory, Research and Practice,* 1977, **14,** 169–180.

Kazdin, A. E. Nonspecific treatment factors in psychotherapy outcome research. *Journal of Consulting and Clinical Psychology,* 1979, **47,** 846–851. (a)

Kazdin, A. E. Fictions, factions, and functions of behavior therapy. *Behavior Therapy,* 1979, **10,** 629–654. (b)

Kazdin, A. E., & Wilson, G. T. Criteria for evaluating psychotherapy. *Archives of General Psychiatry,* 1978, **35,** 407–416.

Kendall, P. C., & Norton-Ford, J. D. Therapy outcome research methods. In P. C. Kendall

& J. N. Butcher (Eds.), *Handbook of research methods in clinical psychology*. New York: Wiley, 1982.

Kernberg, O. Borderline personality organization. *Journal of the American Psychoanalytic Association*, 1967, **15,** 641–685.

Kernberg, O. Technical considerations in the treatment of borderline personality organization. *Journal of the American Psychoanalytic Association*, 1976, **24,** 795–829.

Kiesler, D. J. Basic methodologic issues implicit in psychotherapy process research. *American Journal of Psychotherapy*, 1966, **20,** 135–155.

Kiesler, D. J. Experimental designs in psychotherapy research. In A. E. Bergin & S. L. Garfield (Eds.), *Handbook of psychotherapy and behavior change*. New York: Wiley, 1971.

Kiesler, D. J. *The process of psychotherapy: Empirical foundations and systems of analysis*. Chicago: Aldine, 1973.

Klein, M. *Contributions to psychoanalysis 1921–1945*. London: Hogarth, 1948.

Klerman, G. L., Rounsaville, B. J., Chevron, E., New, C., & Weissman, M. *A manual for short-term interpersonal psychotherapy of depression*. New Haven: Yale University, School of Medicine, 1979.

Kohut, H. *The restoration of the self*. New York: International Universities Press, 1977.

Kolata, G. B. Clinical trial of psychotherapies is under way. *Science*, 1981, **212,** 432–433.

Krasner, L. Verbal conditioning and psychotherapy. In L. Krasner & L. P. Ullmann (Eds.), *Research in behavior modification*. New York: Holt, Rinehart & Winston, 1965.

Kris, E. On preconscious mental processes. *Psychoanalytic Quarterly*, 1940, **19,** 540–560.

Kubie. L. S. *Practical and theoretical aspects of psychoanalysis*. New York: International Universities Press, 1950.

Lambert, M. J. Spontaneous remission in adult neurotic disorders: A revision and summary. *Psychological Bulletin*, 1976, **83,** 107–119.

Lambert, M. J., Bergin, A. & Collins, J. Therapist-induced deterioration in psychotherapy. In A. Gurman & A. Razin (Eds.), *Effective psychotherapy*. New York: Pergamon Press, 1977.

Lambert, M. J., DeJulio, S. S., & Stein, D. M. Therapist interpersonal skills: Process, outcome, methodological considerations, and recommendations for future research. *Psychological Bulletin*, 1978, **85,** 467–489.

Landman, T. J., & Dawes, R. M. Psychotherapy outcome: Smith and Glass' conclusions stand up under scrutiny. *American Psychologist*, 1982, **37,** 504–516.

Langs, R. *The technique of psychoanalytic psychotherapy* (Vol. 1). New York: Aronson, 1973.

Langs, R. *The technique of psychoanalytic psychotherapy* (Vol. 2). New York: Aronson, 1974.

Langs, R. *Interactions: The realm of transference and countertransference*. New York: Aronson, 1980.

Langs, R. *Resistances and interventions: The nature of therapeutic work*. New York: Aronson, 1981.

LaTorre, R. A. Pretherapy role induction procedures. *Canadian Psychological Review*, 1977, **18,** 308–32.

Lazarus, A. A. Toward delineating some causes of change in psychotherapy. *Professional Psychology*, 1980, **11**, 863–870.

Lerner, B. *Therapy in the ghetto*. Baltimore, Md.: Johns Hopkins University Press, 1972.

Lick, J., & Bootzin, R. Expectancy factors in the treatment of fear: Methodological and theoretical issues. *Psychological Bulletin*, 1975, **82**, 917–931.

Lowenstein, R. M. *Drives, affects and behavior*. New York: International Universities Press, 1953.

Lorand, S. *Techniques of psychoanalytic therapy*. New York: International Universities Press, 1946.

Lorion, R. P. Socioeconomic status and traditional treatment approaches reconsidered. *Psychological Bulletin*, 1973, **79**, 263–270.

Lorion, R. P. Research on psychotherapy and behavior change with the disadvantaged. In S. L. Garfield & A. E. Bergin (Eds.), *Handbook of psychotherapy and behavior change* (2nd. ed.). New York: Wiley, 1978.

Luborsky, L., Singer, B., & Luborsky, L. Comparative studies of psychotherapies. *Archives of General Psychology*, 1975, **32**, 995–1008.

Luborsky, L. & Spence, P. B. Quantitative research on psychoanalytic therapy. In S. L. Garfield & A. E. Bergin (Eds.), *Handbook of psychotherapy and behavior change* (2nd ed.). New York: Wiley, 1978.

Mahler, M. S. *On human symbiosis and the viscissitudes of individuation. (Vol. 1.) Infantile psychosis*. New York: International Universities Press, 1968.

Maholick, L. T., & Turner, D. W. Termination: That difficult farewell. *American Journal of Psychotherapy*, 1979, **33**, 583–591.

Mahoney, M. J. Experimental methods and outcome evaluation. *Journal of Consulting and Clinical Psychology*, 1978, **46**, 660–672.

Mahoney, M. J. & Arnkoff, D. Cognitive and self-control therapies. In S. L. Garfield & A. E. Bergin (Eds.), *Handbook of psychotherapy and behavior change* (2nd ed.). New York: Wiley, 1978.

Mahrer, A. R. *Experiencing: A humanistic theory of psychology and psychiatry*. New York: Brunner/Mazel, 1978.

Malan, D. H. *The frontier of brief psychotherapy*. New York: Plenum, 1976.

Malan, D. H., Heath, E. S., Bacal, H. A., & Balfour, F. H. Psychodynamic changes in untreated neurotic patients. II. Apparently genuine improvements. *Archives of General Psychiatry*, 1975, **32**, 110–126.

Mann, J. *Time-limited psychotherapy*. Cambridge, Mass.: Harvard University Press, 1973.

Mann, J., & Goldman, R. *A casebook in time-limited psychotherapy*. New York: McGraw-Hill, 1982.

Marmor, J. The nature of the psychotherapeutic process revisited. *Canadian Psychiatric Association Journal*, 1975, **20**, 557–565.

Marmor, J. Common operational factors in diverse approaches to behavior change. In A. Burton (Ed.), *What makes behavior change possible?* New York: Brunner/Mazel, 1976.

Marziali, E., Marmar, C., & Krupnick, J. Therapeutic alliance scales: Development and relationship to psychotherapy outcome. *American Journal of Psychiatry*, 1981, **138**, 361–364.

Maslow, A. H. *Toward a psychology of being.* Princeton, N.J.: Van Nostrand, 1962.

Masterson, J. F. *Psychotherapy of the borderline adult.* New York: Brunner/Mazel, 1976.

Matarazzo, J. D., & Wiens, A. N. *The interview: Research on its anatomy and structure.* Chicago: Aldine-Atherton, 1972.

May, R. *Love and will.* New York: Norton, 1969.

May, R. Angel, E., & Ellenberger, H. F. (Eds.). *Existence: A new dimension in psychiatry and psychology.* New York: Basic Books, 1958.

Meltzoff, J., & Kornreich, M. *Research in psychotherapy.* New York: Atherton, 1970.

Menaker, E. *Otto Rank: A rediscovered legacy.* New York: Columbia University Press, 1982.

Mendel, W. M. Interpretation and working through. *American Journal of Psychotherapy,* 1975, **29,** 409–414.

Mendez, A. M., & Fine, H. J. A short history of the British school of object relations and ego psychology. *Bulletin of the Menninger Clinic,* 1976, **40,** 357–382.

Menninger, K. A., & Holzman, P. S. *Theory of psychoanalytic technique* (2nd ed.). New York: Basic Books, 1973.

Mintz, J. Measuring outcome in psychodynamic psychotherapy. *Archives of General Psychiatry,* 1981, **38,** 503–506.

Mintz, J., & Kiesler, D. J. Individualized measures of psychotherapy outcome. In P. C. Kendall & J. N. Butcher (Eds.), *Handbook of research methods in clinical psychology.* New York: Wiley, 1982.

Mitchell, K. M., Bozarth, J. D., & Krauft, C. C. A reappraisal of the therapeutic effectiveness of accurate empathy, nonpossessive warmth, and genuineness. In A. S. Gurman & A. M. Razin (Eds.), *Effective psychotherapy: A handbook of research.* New York: Pergamon Press, 1977.

Nichols, M. P., & Zax, M. *Catharsis in psychotherapy.* New York: Gardner Press, 1977.

Nunberg, H. (1932) *Principles of psychoanalysis.* New York: International Universities Press, 1955.

O'Leary, K. D., & Borkovec, T. D. Conceptual, methodological, and ethical problems of placebo groups in psychotherapy research. *American Psychologist,* 1978, **33,** 821–830.

Orlinsky, D. E., & Howard, K. I. The relation of process to outcome in psychotherapy. In S. L. Garfield & A. E. Bergin (Eds.). *Handbook of psychotherapy and behavior change* (2nd ed.). New York: Wiley, 1978.

Paolino, T. J. *Psychoanalytic psychotherapy.* New York: Brunner/Mazel, 1981.

Parloff, M. B., Waskow, I. E., & Wolfe, B. E. Research on therapist variables in relation to process and outcome. In S. L. Garfield & A. E. Bergin (Eds.), *Handbook of psychotherapy and behavior change* (2nd ed.). New York: Wiley, 1978.

Perlman, G. Change in "central therapeutic ingredients" of beginning psychotherapists. *Psychotherapy: Theory, Research and Practice,* 1973, **10,** 48–51.

Perls, F. *Gestalt therapy verbatim.* Lafayette, Calif.: Real People Press, 1969.

Perls, F., Hefferline, R., & Goodman, P. *Gestalt therapy.* New York: Julian Press, 1951.

Polster, E., & Polster, M. *Gestalt therapy integrated.* New York: Brunner/Mazel, 1973.

Pope, B. *The mental health interview.* New York: Pergamon Press, 1979.

Prochaska, J. O. *Systems of psychotherapy: A transtheoretical analysis.* Homewood, Ill.: Dorsey Press, 1979.

Progoff, I. *Jung's psychology and its social meaning* (Rev. ed.). New York: Julian Press, 1969.

Rank, O. *The trauma of birth.* New York: Harcourt, Brace, 1929.

Rank, O. *Will therapy and reality.* New York: Knopf, 1945.

Rapaport, D. On the psychoanalytic theory of thinking. *International Journal of Psychoanalysis,* 1950, **31,** 161–170.

Rapaport, D. The autonomy of the ego. *Bulletin of the Menninger Clinic,* 1951, **15,** 113–123.

Rapaport, D. On the psychoanalytic theory of affects. *International Journal of Psycho-Analysis,* 1953, **34,** 177–197.

Razin, A. M. The A-B variable: still promising after twenty years? In A. S. Gurman & A. M. Razin (Eds.), *Effective Psychotherapy.* New York: Pergamon Press, 1977.

Reid, W. H. *Basic intensive psychotherapy.* New York: Brunner/Mazel, 1980.

Reisman, J. M. *Toward the integration of psychotherapy.* New York: Wiley, 1971.

Reisman, J. M., & Yamokoski, T. Psychotherapy and friendship: An analysis of the communications of friends. *Journal of Counseling Psychology,* 1974, **21,** 269–273.

Rogers, C. R. *Counseling and psychotherapy.* Boston: Houghton, Mifflin, 1942.

Rogers, C. R. *Client-centered therapy.* Boston: Houghton-Mifflin, 1951.

Rogers, C. R. *On becoming a person: A therapist's view of psychotherapy.* Boston: Houghton-Mifflin, 1961.

Rogers, C. R. In retrospect: Forty-six years. *American Psychologist,* 1974, **29,** 115–123.

Rogers, C. R., & Dymond, R. R. (Eds.). *Psychotherapy and personality change.* Chicago: University of Chicago Press, 1954.

Rosenthal, D., & Frank, J. D. Psychotherapy and the placebo effect. *Psychological Bulletin,* 1956, **53,** 294–302.

Ryan, E. R. *The capacity of the patient to enter an elementary therapeutic relationship in the initial psychotherapy interview.* Unpublished doctoral dissertation, University of Michigan, 1973.

Sargent, H. D. Intrapsychic change: Methodological problems in psychotherapy research. *Psychiatry,* 1961, **24,** 93–101.

Sarnat, J. E. *A comparison of psychoanalytic and client centered measures of initial in-therapy patient participation.* Unpublished doctoral dissertation, University of Michigan, 1975.

Schofield, W. *Psychotherapy: The purchase of friendship.* Englewood Cliffs, N.J.: Prentice-Hall, 1964.

Schofield, W. The psychotherapist as friend. *Humanitas,* 1970, **6,** 221–223.

Searles, H. *Collected papers on schizophrenia and related subjects.* New York: International Universities Press, 1965.

Shapiro, A. K., & West, L. A. Placebo effects in medical and psychological therapies. In S. L. Garfield & A. E. Bergin (Eds.), *Handbook of psychotherapy and behavior change* (2nd ed.). New York: Wiley, 1978.

Shectman, F., de la Torre, J., & Garza, A. C. Diagnosis separate from psychotherapy: Pros and cons. *American Journal of Psychotherapy,* 1979, **33,** 291–302.

Shen, J., & Murray, J. Psychotherapy with the disadvantaged. *American Journal of Psychotherapy,* 1981, **35,** 268–275.

Siassi, I., & Messer, S. B. Psychotherapy with patients from lower socioeconomic group. *American Journal of Psychotherapy,* 1976, **30,** 29–40.

Sifneos, P. E. *Short-term psychotherapy and emotional crisis.* Cambridge, Mass.: Harvard University Press, 1972.

Sloane, R. B., Cristol, A. H., Pepernik, M. C., & Staples, F. R. Role preparation and expectation of improvement in psychotherapy. *Journal of Nervous and Mental Disease,* 1970, **150,** 18–26.

Small, L. *The briefer psychotherapies* (Rev. ed.). New York: Brunner/Mazel, 1979.

Smith, M. L., & Glass, G. V. Meta-analysis of psychotherapy outcome studies. *American Psychologist,* 1977, **32,** 752–760.

Smith, M. L., Glass, G. V., & Miller, T. I. *The benefits of psychotherapy.* Baltimore: Johns Hopkins University Press, 1980.

Speisman, J. C. Depth of interpretation and verbal resistance in psychotherapy. *Journal of Consulting Psychology,* 1959, **23,** 93–99.

Spence, D. P. *Narrative truth and historical truth: Meaning and interpretation in psychoanalysis.* New York: Norton, 1982.

Stephens, J. H., Shaffer, J. W., & Zlotowitz, H. I. An optimun A-B scale of psychotherapy effectiveness. *Journal of Nervous and Mental Disease,* 1975, **160,** 267–281.

Sterba, R. F. The fate of the ego in analytic therapy. *International Journal of Psychoanalysis,* 1934, **15,** 117–126.

Stollak, G. E., & Guerney, B., Jr. Exploration of personal problems by juvenile delinquents under conditions of minimal reinforcement. *Journal of Clinical Psychology,* 1964, **20,** 279–283.

Stone, L. *The psychoanalytic situation.* New York: International Universities Press, 1961.

Strupp. H. H. The outcome problem in psychotherapy revisited. *Psychotherapy: Theory, Research and Practice,* 1963, **1,** 1–13.

Strupp, H. H. Specific vs nonspecific factors in psychotherapy and the problem of control. *Archives of General Psychiatry,* 1970, **23,** 393–401.

Strupp, H. H. On the basic ingredients of psychotherapy. *Journal of Consulting and Clinical Psychology,* 1973, **41,** 1–8.

Strupp, H. H. The nature of the therapeutic influence and its basic ingredients. In A. Burton (Ed.), *What makes behavior change possible?* New York: Brunner/Mazel, 1976.

Strupp, H. H. Toward the refinement of time-limited dynamic psychotherapy. In S. H. Budman (Ed.), *Forms of brief therapy.* New York: Guilford, 1981.

Strupp, H. H., & Bergin, A. E. Some empirical and conceptual bases for coordinated research in psychotherapy: A critical review of issues, trends, and evidence. *International Journal of Psychiatry,* 1969, **7,** 18–90.

Strupp, H. H., & Hadley, S. W. Specific vs nonspecific factors in psychotherapy. *Archives of General Psychiatry,* 1979, **36,** 1125–1136.

Strupp, H. H., Hadley, S. W., & Gomes-Schwartz, B. *Psychotherapy for better or worse: The problem of negative effects.* New York: Aronson, 1977.

Sullivan, H. S. *The interpersonal theory of psychiatry.* New York: Norton, 1953.

Sullivan, H. S. *The psychiatric interviews.* New York: Norton, 1954.

Sullivan, H. S. *Clinical studies in psychiatry.* New York: Norton, 1956.

Swenson, C. H. Commitment and the personality of the successful therapist. *Psychotherapy: Theory, Research and Practice,* 1971, **8**, 31–36.

Taft, J. *The dynamics of therapy in a controlled relationship.* New York: Macmillan, 1933.

Taft, J. *Family casework and counseling. A functional approach.* Philadelphia: University of Pennsylvania Press, 1948.

Tauber, E. S. Countertransference re-examined. *Contemporary Psychoanalysis,* 1978, **14**, 38–47.

Truax, C. B., & Carkhuff, R. R. *Toward effective counseling and psychotherapy.* Chicago: Aldine, 1967.

Truax, C. B., & Mitchell, K. M. Research on certain therapist interpersonal skills in relation to process and outcome. In A. E. Bergin & S. L. Garfield (Eds.), *Handbook of psychotherapy and behavior change.* New York: Wiley, 1971.

Wachtel, P. L. (Ed.). *Resistance: Psychodynamic and behavioral approaches.* New York: Plenum, 1981.

Weiner, I. B. *Principles of psychotherapy.* New York: Wiley, 1975.

Wexler, D. A., & Rice, L. N. (Eds.). *Innovations in client-centered therapy.* New York: Wiley, 1974.

Whitehorn, J. C., & Betz, B. J. A study of psychotherapeutic relationships between physicians and schizophrenic patients. *American Journal of Psychiatry,* 1954, **111**, 321–331.

Wilkins, W. Expectancy of therapeutic gain: An empirical and conceptual critique. *Journal of Consulting and Clinical Psychology,* 1973, **40**, 69–77.

Williams, J. H. Conditioning of verbalization: A review. *Psychological Bulletin,* 1964, **62**, 383–393.

Williams, R. I., & Blanton, R. L. Verbal conditioning in a psychotherapeutic situation. *Behavior Research and Therapy,* 1968, **6**, 97–103.

Wolberg, L. R. *The technique of psychotherapy* (3rd ed.). New York: Grune & Stratton, 1977.

Wolberg, L. R. *Handbook of short-term psychotherapy.* New York: Thieme-Stratton, 1980.

Yalom, I. D. *Existential psychotherapy.* New York: Basic Books, 1980.

Zax, M., & Klein, A. Measurement of personality and behavior changes following psychotherapy. *Psychological Bulletin,* 1960, **57**, 435–448.

Zinker, J. *Creative process in gestalt therapy.* New York: Brunner/Mazel, 1977.

CHAPTER 8

Group Therapy

BERNARD LUBIN

This chapter presents an orientation to the field of group psychotherapy, a field in which there are exciting developments and rapid growth. Increases in the use of the group method for treatment purposes, in publications on group therapy, in training opportunities, and in research output have led to the questioning of many previously stated "self-evident" truths concerning group methods of intervention, and to the relaxation of previously narrowly drawn and fiercely held boundaries.

The history and development of group therapy are presented in the first section of the chapter, and the sections that follow discuss types of group therapy, intensive small-group experiences, research and training in group therapy, group therapy with specialized populations, and issues (trends and needs) in the area of group therapy. An attempt is made to indicate where the cutting edge of the group therapy field lies and the kinds of areas that invite eventual contributions from newcomers.

It had been suggested at times that the term *group psychotherapy* should be restricted to those forms of group work based primarily on a psychoanalytic approach involving the analysis of resistance and transference, and that it should be distinguished from *group therapy* or *group counseling* approaches, which deal less with historical–genetic material, are briefer in length, and are not concerned with "reconstructing personality" (see Slavson, 1964). However, in keeping with clear-cut trends in general practice, these various terms are used interchangeably here.

Three separate streams—group therapy, laboratory training, and encounter groups—each with a separate origin and development, are finding more and more points of convergence as group therapists explore the other two areas and adapt concepts and techniques from them into their practice of group therapy. Which ones are tributaries and which the main flow may be debatable, but group therapy has unquestionably been affected by engagement with laboratory training and encounter groups. For many contemporary group therapists goals of practice include growth as well as psychological repair, and many therapists, regardless of their primary orientation, are showing an increased appreciation for the contributions of the group to the therapy process. Hence the following brief history of the development of group therapy is amplified in the later discussion of intensive small-group experiences.

THE HISTORY AND DEVELOPMENT OF GROUP PSYCHOTHERAPY

Group psychotherapy can be traced back to classes for tubercular patients held by Joseph H. Pratt, a Boston internist, in 1905. Between then and World War II a literature large enough to justify a bibliographic summary (Corsini & Putzey, 1957) was produced. Only since World War II, however, have the use of group methods for therapeutic purposes and the published work in this area increased sharply.

Some indication of the growth in the use of group methods can be seen in the increase in the membership of the American Group Psychotherapy Association over the past 30 years, from fewer than 20 members in 1943 (Mullan & Rosenbaum, 1962) to approximately 3000 in 1982. Publication trends show the same picture. The first year in which the total number of published writings in group therapy (books and articles) exceeded 100 items was 1947 (Corsini & Putzey, 1957). The total output reached 200 items in 1957, and over 700 publications on group therapy appeared in 1981. Comprehensive bibliographies of the group therapy literature from 1956 to the present are provided chronologically by Lubin and Lubin (1966), MacLennan and Levy (1966, 1967, 1968, 1969, 1970, 1971), Lubin, Sargent, and Lubin (1972), Lubin and Lubin (1973), Reddy and Lansky (1974), Reddy, Colson, and Keys (1975), Lubin, Reddy, Stansberry, and Lubin (1977), Lubin, Reddy, Taylor, and Lubin (1978), Lubin, Lubin, and Taylor (1979), Silver, Lubin, Silver, and Dobson (1980), Silver, Lubin, Miller, and Dobson (1981), and Silver, Miller, Lubin, and Dobson (1982). A 74-year comprehensive bibliography of the group psychotherapy literature contains more than 14,000 items (Lubin & Lubin, in press).

Economics was prominent among the early reasons given for the growth in the use of groups for treatment and therapy; that is, more patients could receive professional assistance at less cost. More recently, on the basis of accumulating experience, group therapy has become accepted as the treatment of choice for certain psychological–behavioral conditions, independently of economic considerations, and as a suitable adjunct to other treatment programs for many other conditions (Anthony, 1972).

Dating the exact beginning of a historical movement such as group therapy is difficult and at best arbitrary. As one approach, it is possible to list those persons and events generally thought to have been influential in the development of group therapy. Some of the following early historical material is drawn from Rosenbaum and Berger (1963).

Joseph H. Pratt, as already noted, is generally credited with being the first person to practice a rudimentary form of group therapy. In his earlier writings Pratt was primarily concerned with describing his *class method* of instructing tuberculosis patients in methods of physical hygiene. By means of an inspirational approach involving lectures and group discussions he counteracted patients' depression about their condition and motivated them to provide better self-care. Through observations of their own work, some contact with psychiatrists, and their readings of the literature, Pratt and his co-workers became impressed with the important role that emotions played in their treatment program. They subsequently extended their *thought control class method* to diabetic and cardiac patients, and other physicians used the method with undernourished children, hypertensive adults, and patients with peptic ulcers (AGPA, 1971).

Lazell adapted the Pratt method (inspirational approach, exhortation, and supportive techniques) for use with psychiatric patients at St. Elizabeth's Hospital in 1921. Pratt's authoritarian–inspirational approach was also practiced in an extreme form by Cody Marsh, a minister who became a psychiatrist. Whereas Lazell used a lecture method, Marsh's approach to group work with psychotic patients was very active and included art classes and dance classes as well as talking.

During this early period neither psychology nor psychiatry showed much interest in the use of group methods of treatment. There were a few prominent exceptions, however. A form of *collective counseling* for neurotic patients, alcoholics, stammerers, and patients with sexual disturbances was practiced by several German and Austrian psychotherapists between 1900 and 1930. During this same period, Paul Schilder used a psychoanalytic frame of reference in working with outpatient groups at Bellevue Hospital.

From 1910 to 1914 Jacob L. Moreno experimented with group methods in Vienna, and in 1925 he introduced psychodrama to the United States. In addition to psychodrama and sociodrama, Moreno's contributions to the field of group work include role playing and sociometry, a method for mapping the positive and negative affective ties that exist within a group. Moreno in 1932 was among the first to use the term *group therapy* in print. Another early group psychotherapist was Louis Wender, a psychoanalytically oriented clinician who began treating groups of hospitalized mental patients in 1929.

As noted by Rosenbaum (1965), important early contributions of Trigant Burrow to group therapy have been relatively ignored. Burrow, one of the first psychoanalysts to practice in the United States, employed the term *group analysis* in 1925. He argued against the tendency of psychoanalysis to deal primarily with the individual to the exclusion of social factors. His work took place in residential settings where therapists and patients lived together. Burrow is also credited with introducing the concepts *here and now* and *analysis of group tensions* (AGPA, 1971).

During the 1930s Slavson developed and conducted a program of activity group therapy for emotionally disturbed adolescents at the Jewish Board of Guardians. Patients were encouraged to work through their problems within a permissive but controlled play setting, and, although psychoanalytic concepts were used to study the patients' problems, interpretations were not made directly to them. The average activity group consisted of eight children of the same age and sex selected carefully in order to construct groups with a certain degree of sociopsychological balance. During this same period, in 1938, Alexander Wolf began a group of analysands and referred to his method as the *psychoanalysis of groups*. Wolf is credited with innovating the method of "going around," in which each patient in turn is asked to talk about his or her problems.

The American Group Psychotherapy Association

Slavson is a particularly central figure in group therapy for his contributions to the development of the American Group Therapy Association and to the increase in the number of people using group treatment methods. He convened an interest group at the New York meetings of the American Orthopsychiatric Association in 1943, and it was this group that decided to form the American Group Therapy Association with Slavson as its first president. Slavson also served as the first editor of the association's journal, and the association operated from his office at the Jewish Board of Guardians between 1943 and 1956. Because so few people were doing group therapy during that period, much effort was expended to promote the method through conferences, discussions, and publications.

The name of the organization was changed in 1952 from the American Group Therapy Association to the American Group Psychotherapy Association, "thus definitively acknowledging the Association's commitment to psychotherapy as contrasted to other uses of groups for helping people, which the previous title may have suggested, though not intended." (AGPA, 1971, p. 432). This represented a victory at that time for those who favored exclusion rather than inclusion. In more recent years the association seems to be developing a broader base, and the *International Journal of Group Psychotherapy,* the journal of the organization, reflects a more inclusive intellectual base than formerly. The association passed another milestone in 1968 when a previously unresolved question concerning its nature and purpose was settled by its assuming responsbility for certifying the competence of group therapy practitioners.

The Impact of World War II and Subsequent Growth

During and immediately after World War II the number of patients who needed psychological treatment or counseling, particularly in the armed forces, sharply increased. Necessity led to great expansion in training and treatment programs utilizing group methods. The Veterans Administration was an acknowledged leader in this upsurge, as the niceties of intellectual debate and interprofessional territorial struggles gave way to a pragmatic orientation which asked only; "How can we provide services to all those in need?" Group methods flourished; just about every school of psychotherapy began to practice its form of treatment in group settings, even though its theory and techniques had been developed for use in the dyadic situation. In most cases no attempt was made to articulate a more elaborate rationale for the use of these techniques in group settings.

The post–World War II years have seen additional professional organizational development, development of accreditation criteria, and professional development programs. There has also been an emergence of many types of group therapy and a number of categorization schemes attempting to classify these various types. Spotnitz (1972b) provides a useful history of group therapy as seen through successive attempts to classify the types of group therapy influential in each period. It is obvious from the successive schemas that some types of group therapy have not survived and that the classifications have shifted over the 15-year period from method-oriented to goal-oriented classifications. During this period there seems to have been some tendency toward greater specificity in the statement of goals and methods and also, somewhat paradoxically, greater flexibility in attempting innovative methods in a greater variety of settings.

TYPES OF GROUP THERAPY

A brief description of some of the types of group therapy that have developed during the period following World War II is presented under two categories: (a) group psychotherapy with the focus on individuals; and (b) group psychotherapy with a group focus. These categories are analogous to an attempt by Astrachan (1970) to apply a social systems model to therapeutic groups by noting who communicates with whom, whether member with therapist, group with therapist, or member with member.

Group Psychotherapy with the Focus on Individuals

As is true in the field of individual psychodynamic psychotherapy, considerable variability in practice obtains among analytically oriented group therapists. A major source of this variation involves the degree to which the group therapist incorporates group processes into his or her theory and interventions. Practice ranges from the literal translation of techniques developed for individual psychoanalysis into a group setting to experimentation with methods uniquely suited to working effectively with individuals being seen in groups rather than singly.

The previously mentioned work of Trigant Burrow, for example, was based on his familiarity with psychoanalysis, but involved methods bearing little resemblance to individual psychoanalytic therapy. To avoid confusion, he later changed the name of his method from *group analysis* to *phyloanalysis,* by which he intended to indicate his interest in studying man's evolutionary status. The other major types of group therapy focused on individuals derive from the approaches of Slavson, Wolf, and Foulkes, from transactional analysis, and from behavior therapy.

Slavson's Analytic Group Psychotherapy.   Although Slavson was certainly aware of group processes, he emphasized in developing his approach to group therapy the analysis of the individual in the group setting. Accordingly, his analytic group therapy involves aspects of free association, interpreting resistance and transference, and working through, as described in the previous chapter. At the same time, Slavson introduced new notions concerning the variety of intermember effects and the influence of multiple transferences in group therapy, and he also acknowledged that the member–therapist transference is modified in the group setting (Slavson, 1964).

Wolf's Psychoanalysis in Groups.   Wolf took issue with the lingering antigroup bias of psychoanalysis by stating his belief that psychoanalysis could take place in groups as well as in the individual therapy situations (Wolf, 1968). Contrary to statements by many other psychoanalysts, Wolf maintained further that each member's identification with the group ego increases his or her anxiety tolerance and thereby enables deeper analytic exploration in many cases than is possible in individual psychoanalysis.

Specifically, Wolf believed that the following six parameters of a well-structured group make the therapeutic conditions more readily available to the patients than is the case in individual psychoanalysis: (a) the dimension of *multiple reactivity* among group members and between members and the therapist; (b) *hierarchical* and *peer vectors,* which refer to authority and intimacy relationships among group members; (c) the opportunity to observe each patient's intercommunication patterns; (d) the *principle of shifting attention,* which refers to the nonexclusive attention of the therapist to each patient and the patient's relief from sustained scrutiny; (e) the *principle of alternating roles,* in that each patient is a *help giver* as well as a *help receiver;* and (f) *forced interaction,* or the pressure toward and expectation of maximal interaction.

Wolf also pioneered in proposing the *alternate meeting,* a weekly meeting held in addition to the regular session but with the therapist absent. He saw the alternate meeting as important in precipitating early transference attitudes toward the therapist and thereby shortening the duration of therapy, in facilitating participation by reserved and shy patients, and in making it easier for patients to criticize the therapist. Further, since his method calls for discussing the alternate session in the regular session, discrepancies in behavior in the two settings can be highlighted.

Although Slavson and Wolf differ in several respects in the ways in which they see the possibilities for conducting psychoanalysis in groups, they agree that the emphasis should be on individual analysis enhanced by the group setting, and not on the group and its dynamics. Both of them emphasize further that it is the therapist rather than the group, or the leader–member relationship rather than the peer relationships, that is the all-important treatment factor (Slavson, 1964; Wolf, 1968).

Foulkes.   Although trained in psychoanalysis, the British psychiatrist Foulkes developed a system of group psychotherapy that is very different from those of Slavson and Wolf. The therapist (called the conductor) meets for 1½ hours with seven or eight patients, which is a format similar to Wolf's. While Wolf's groups are led by therapists, however, Foulkes' groups proceed without directions from the therapist, and spontaneous contributions of the members are treated by the group as free associations. The therapist functions as a participant–observer, interprets transferences and resistances, and notes the various relationships in the total group field. He is primarily responsible for developing and maintaining an analytic attitude and a therapeutic atmosphere in the group. Foulkes acknowledges that his conceptualization was influenced by Kurt Lewin's field theory and by gestalt psychology via Kurt Goldstein. Anthony (1972) characterizes Foulkes' emphasis as falling "on the interpersonal rather than on the group as a whole."

Transactional Analysis.   Much of the early development of transactional analysis (TA) as a theory of personality and therapy took place at the San Francisco Social Psychiatry Seminars held in Eric Berne's office beginning in 1958. The title of the seminars was later changed to the San Francisco Transactional Analysis Seminars, and they are now known as the Eric Berne Seminars of San Francisco. TA has grown considerably in its organizational membership and general influence during the past 10 years. In 1964, the year of formation, membership in the International Analysis Association was 168; by 1974 membership had grown to 6500 (Calahan, 1974). Although influence is difficult to measure, there are also informal indications that some group therapists who do not practice TA have modified their techniques in response to considerations highlighted by the exposition of TA.

The structural analysis model of TA has become well known (Berne, 1961) and consists of three ego states: Parent, Adult, and Child. These ego states are not to be confused with the structural model of psychoanalysis, which comprises id, ego, and superego. The ego states with which TA is concerned can usually be directly inferred from such observable behavior as gestures, mannerisms, voice tone and quality, and the use of specific words.

The Parent ego state is divided into the Nurturant Parent and the Critical Parent. Cues diagnostic of the latter include pointing the finger and making moralizing ("You should . . .") or prejudicial ("They are all the same") statements. The Child ego state is observable in labile displays of feelings, as in laughing or crying, expansive behavior such as jumping and clapping, and use of such expressions as *golly* and *gee*. The Child ego state can be further subdivided into the Adapted Child (fashioned to parental demands), the Professor (a bright, inquisitive stance), and the Natural Child (the free emotive aspect of the personality, which gathers data about the world through the senses and processes these data in a logical manner for the purpose of making predictions).

The analysis of *transactions,* which are defined as consisting of the stimuli and responses between specific ego states in two or more people, is a fundamental activity in TA, as the title of this form of therapy indicates. Transactions are classified as being *simple* (parallel or complementary), *crosses,* or *ulterior.* Communication continues as long as transactions are parallel or complementary, but is interrupted when transactions are crossed. Ulterior transactions are those that contain a psychological level different from the social level, and transactions of this kind produce a *game,* which is a frequently used method of structuring time between individuals.

Berne also introduced the concept of *stroke economy,* the intricacies of which have been developed further by other writers (Dusay & Steiner, 1971). According to this concept, all higher organisms have a need for stimulation, and this need is satisfied in the young organism by physical stroking. Later, praise and recognition become substitutes for physical stroking, so that much of interpersonal activity involves the psychological exchange of strokes. Other recurring concepts in the TA literature analysis are *positions* (postures toward self and others, e.g., "I'm okay—you're okay," "I'm not okay—you're okay," "I'm not okay—you're not okay"); *games* (an orderly series of transactions containing ulterior motives which serve as a mechanism for obtaining strokes and avoiding intimacy); and *scripts* (those life blueprints developed out of childhood decisions which control the major moves in a person's life).

The positive, action-oriented climate of transactional analysis theory and practice makes it attractive to group therapists who are frustrated with the slowness and long-term aspects of group treatment by other means. Both the therapist and the patient seem to have greater control over moment-to-moment interpersonal events. The heavy emphasis placed on studying the options available to the person and considering consequences of behavior reinforces the notion of patient responsibility for his or her actions and feelings and provides a hopeful climate for change in patient behavior. Since both the patient and the therapist conceptualize events within the same theoretical system, any elitist status of the therapist is eliminated and patients can continue to work on ongoing problems and situations between therapy sessions. The instructional aspect of the therapist's role is clearly legitimized, thus ensuring that patient and therapist are using the same language. Some TA therapists who were trained initally with a psychoanalytic orientation appreciate TA's seeming conceptual simplicity and pragmatism. Even when concepts appear to be translations or paraphrases from other theoretical systems, they seem to take on more of a utilitarian ring in TA.

Transactional analysis has also drawn sharp criticism, however. It has been accused among other things of "trivializing" human experience by denying the tragic nature of man and by implying that complex, overlearned self-destructive tendencies can be unlearned with relative ease (Todd, 1973). Other writers have objected to the popularization of TA theory, to the entrepreneurial zest of some of its practitioners, and to the strong use of suggestion made by the method.

The fact that TA has not produced a body of research makes it difficult to evaluate the theory and method in objective terms. Indeed, a straightforward comparative analysis of TA versus other types of group therapy with suitable control groups would be difficult to design, for some bias in favor of positive outcomes for TA would seem to be assured by the emphasis in TA on the contract, that is, on working with patients who have made a strong therapeutic work commitment. It would be necessary, therefore, to provide a means to insure a comparable level of patient commitment to the process in each of the other groups in a comparative study of treatment effectiveness.

Behavior Therapy in Groups.   Behavior therapy attempts to apply the methods and findings of experimental psychology to behavior problems, specifically by drawing as appropriate on such learning procedures as extinction, generalization, and counterconditioning (see Chapter 9). Behavior therapy in groups follows the same general principles as behavior therapy in individual cases, but with added possibilities for the potentiating, intensifying, and clarifying influence of the group situation (Harris, 1979). Some behavior therapists such as Lazarus (1968) have specifically welcomed the additional nonspecific effects available in the group setting: "Group discussions provide a fertile terrain for discrimination learning. Individual therapy obviously imposes limitations upon the person to person exploration of certain specific behaviors (which include attitudes and belief)" (Lazarus, 1968, p. 150).

Lazarus (1968) also provides a broad statement of the goals of behavior therapy, namely, "to eliminate suffering by changing habits judged undesirable" (p. 152). Beyond this, the goals of the behavior therapist are compatible with those of therapists of almost all other theoretical orientations: to increase the individual's capacity for productive work, to increase his or her enjoyment of interpersonal relationships, to increase his or her enjoyment of sex, and to improve his or her ability to cope with the more usual of life's stresses.

Specificity in diagnosis and in treatment are obvious advantages of a method derived from experimental psychology. Lazarus, however, is quick to acknowledge the importance of nonspecific benefits patients derive from being members of a therapy group. Moreover, although he does not believe insight to be an effective agent of behavioral change, he states, "There is nothing in modern learning theory to justify withholding the combined advantages of interpretation and desensitization, or any other method or technique which seeems to have beneficial effect" (Lazarus, 1968, p. 155). In a more recent work Lazarus (1971) presents an array of group procedures and suggestions which could as easily have been put forward by a humanistic encounter group leader as by a behavior therapist.

Goldstein and Wolpe (1972) list several advantages of the group over the individual situation in behavioral work. For behavioral analysis there is greater thoroughness in the group situation; that is, observations of the patient's behavior in relation to each group member are available in addition to those in relation to the therapist. In the realm of therapeutic interventions, there are several options that either do not exist in the individual situation or exist in attenuated form, such as feedback by therapist and group members, modeling by therapist and group members, behavioral rehearsal including role reversal, and group motivational factors and social reinforcement.

In some kinds of group behavior therapy, especially in the assertiveness training form of group desensitization, there is considerable contamination of learning with nonspecific effects. An anecdotal account of an assertive training group provided by Lazarus (1968) in fact resembles accounts of sessions from several other theoretically varied intensive small-group experiences in the diversity of procedures used. Needless to say, this loss in specificity among treatment approaches complicates the task of objectively evaluating their differential effectiveness.

Originally excluded from the concern of behaviorists because the phenomena seemed to be beyond objective study, cognitive theory and constructs gradually gained acceptance as an important domain of explanatory concepts and treatment stratagems (Giles, 1981; Meichenbaum, 1977). Meichenbaum (1977) summarizes the differences between the two areas and the ways that they complement each other as follows:

> [Cognitive-behaviorism] focus[es] on altering clients' inner speech, which encourages the production of new behaviors and an examination of the resultant behavioral outcomes which permitted an exploration of the client's cognitive structures. The behavior therapy approaches usually limit their focus to the acquisition of new behaviors and ensure that the resultant behavioral outcomes will be favorable by means of manipulating graded task assignments and environmental consequences [reinforcements]. [p. 226]

Group Psychotherapy with the Focus on the Group

The theoretical positions mentioned thus far, despite differences in concepts and methods, are similar in that their major focus is on individual therapy in a group setting. Each of them originated as a theory or method for use with individuals and was later adopted for use in a group context. Indeed this has been and continues to be the pattern of development; almost every form of individual therapy has at some time been tried in a group setting. The key therapeutic agent is believed to be the therapist, who initiates or guides patient change by means of his or her interventions or the reinforcement contingencies he or she arranges. The group setting functions as a catalyzing, potentiating, reinforcing medium in which the individual therapy takes place. Although a patient's relationships with other group members are brought into the discussion, this is done mainly to cast light on the patient's problems and his or her attempts to cope with them. Allowing for some variation in the behavior of group therapists who practice individual therapy in a group, it still seems accurate to state that the group as a group receives little or no direct attention from them. In contrast, the next three theorists to be presented—Bion, Ezriel, and Whitaker and Lieberman—attempt to make direct use of the group process at the molar level as a means of treating patients' problems.

Bion.   Interestingly, it is not clear that Bion ever claimed to do group psychotherapy; although trained in psychoanalysis, Bion (1961) refers in his writings only to his "experiences in groups" with neurotic patients.

One of Bion's major contributions was to delineate the two levels of functioning in which all groups engage: the level of the *work group* and the level of the *basic assumption group.* The work group has to do with those aspects of group functioning that are in operation as the group realistically attempts to work on its task. It is observable in the rational problem-solving, planning, and decision-making aspects of the group's work. According to Bion, groups also frequently function on another level, the basic assumptions level, which can be inferred from observable behavior. The basic assumptions are the tacit assumptions that are operative usually outside the awareness of group members and that are brought to awareness, as appropriate, by the group leaders.

Dependency, fight–flight, and *pairing* are the three basic assumptions about the group that can be deduced from the group members' behavior. The basic assumption *dependency group* assumes that the group has met for the purpose of achieving security through the protection of an omnipotent, omniscient leader. The leader's refusal to serve in this role leads to resentment and feelings of abandonment. The group sometimes attempts to manipulate the leader into this role by pushing one of its members forward in the sick role (Rioch, 1972). When frustrated by the leader's consistent refusal to gratify these group needs, the group usually finds a substitute leader among its members who serves briefly in this role and then is discarded.

The hypothesis involved in the basic assumption *fight–flight group* is that the survival of the group is at stake and that fighting or running away is the only means for insuring the group's survival. Individual survival definitely is a secondary consideration. The orientation is toward action, and the prized leader is one who will energize and guide the group for aggression or flight. The group mood is strongly hostile to the goal of self-study.

In the *pairing group* basic assumption it is as if the group believes that a pair of members will produce a creative act (a thought, a leader, a solution, etc.), which will deliver them from their problems. The group's mood is a hopeful one.

Bion's concepts are interesting as ways of understanding seemingly irrational aspects of group behavior. His concept of *valency* is the vehicle through which the contribution of individual behavior to group behavior can be understood. Valencies refer to the inclination of individuals to enter into various of the group's basic assumptions. Although each person has the capacity to enter into all three of the basic assumption groups, all people have a tendency to engage more in some of the three. Even though these valencies are thought to be fundamental personal tendencies and not greatly alterable, it is of use to individuals to learn from the group experience about the nature of their own valencies.

Ezriel.   Whereas Bion described the emotional climate of a group in terms of the three basic assumption groups mentioned above, Ezriel attempted to understand group interaction as a manifestation of an unconscious, common group tension, which is the common denominator of the dominant unconscious fantasies of the group. The common group tension is related to by each group member in terms of his or her individual defensive style.

Therapist interpretations in Ezriel's approach are limited to the here and now. It is believed that, if the interpretation is accurate, the patient will link up the interpretation with relevant historical material. When suitable clarity as to the nature of the common group tension has emerged, the group therapist characteristically makes an interpretation in terms of three levels: (a) the *required relationship* (the relationship sought with the therapist); (b) the *avoided relationship* (expression of feelings of anger, dependence, helplessness, and the like); and (c) the *calamitous relationship* (fear of embarrassment and/or rejection by the therapist). The patient seeks to develop an optimal relationship with the therapist (required relationship) and attempts to control those feelings (avoided relationship) that might create a calamitous relationship. The latter would prevent development of the required relationship. The therapist then describes each group member's contribution to the common group tension (Heath & Bacal, 1972).

Whitaker and Lieberman.   Although more psychologically sophisticated, *Psychotherapy through the Group Process* (Whitaker & Lieberman, 1964) shows structural similarities to the formulations of Bion, and particularly Ezriel. The *group focal conflict* supplants the common group tension as the organizing principle for a variety of subsurface group forces both seeking and avoiding expression at any moment. An equilibrium exists between the relatively equal forces of the *disturbing motive* (e.g., resentment toward the therapist, wish to be the "favorite child") and the *reactive motive* (e.g., fear of appearing foolish).

The *group solution* represents a compromise between opposing motives and attempts in particular to reduce the reactive motives or fears. A secondary objective of a group solution is to satisfy as much as possible the disturbing motive or impulse. Group solutions are identified as *enabling* or *restrictive*. Enabling solutions are those that alleviate anxiety but at the same time allow for some satisfaction, expression, or exploration of the disturbing motive. Restrictive solutions are also directed toward alleviating anxiety, but do so at the expense of satisfying, expressing, or exploring the disturbing motive. The equilibrium between the disturbing motive and the reactive motive constantly shifts, thus stimulating new group behavior and group solutions. A group's *culture* is defined by the nature of the aggregate of its solutions. Initially the group's culture is restrictive, but over time it tends to become more enabling and to permit the group to explore disturbing motives that earlier were defended against.

Therapy for the individual group member takes place as his or her *nuclear conflicts* (derivatives of earlier experiences) are activated by group focal conflicts. The adequacy of the individual's habitual solutions is tested as he or she attempts to cope with the anxiety that is aroused. If the habitual solution is not successful, he or she usually will attempt to influence the group solution or will insulate himself or herself psychologically from the group focal conflict. If a group's culture is dominated by enabling solutions, a group member is more likely to feel free to question his or her own solutions and to experiment with other solutions. Conditions for change include (a) the patient's experience of personal focal conflicts relevant to core nuclear conflicts, (b) the failure of the patient's maladaptive solutions to cope with anxiety generated in the group situation, and (c) the patient's experience that giving up his or her maladaptive solutions is potentially beneficial rather than catastrophic (Glassman, 1967).

Although this group-as-a-whole approach seems to have a useful perspective on the unique possibility for development of a group therapy, it should be said that most of the practice of group therapy today is in the "group therapy with the focus on individuals" genre. Also, the focus-on-the-group approach as developed by Bion and Ezriel is seen as fostering a counterproductive, overly strong dependence on the leader at the expense of interactional learning (Kibel & Stein, 1981).

Publication on group therapy in the past two decades has been dominated by those writing on variants of group therapy with the focus on individuals. To some extent a group-focused perspective has been provided by the T-group movement and the continuing education opportunities in which group therapists have engaged. These are discussed in a later section.

Additional Categories

As mentioned earlier, the foregoing was not intended as an exhaustive listing of forms of group therapy. Two major omissions are gestalt group therapy and psychodrama, which were omitted because they did not fit neatly into the previously employed categories. Both are important, however, if one wishes to become familiar with the history and current practice of group psychotherapy.

Gestalt Group Therapy.   Gestalt group therapy, perhaps more than any other method, focuses with sustained intensity on the experience of individuals. The concept of the *hot seat,* seemingly the ultimate in individual focus, was devised by the founder of gestalt therapy, Fritz Perls (1973). Gestalt therapy deals with experiences of the here and now in a fundamental sensory manner. In this sense gestalt therapy focuses keenly on the individual, and it has made a major contribution to general therapeutic practice by explicating the concept of responsibility in interpersonal relationships (Levitsky & Perls, 1969; Harman, 1974; Healy, 1980; Korb & Themus, 1980). The influence of gestalt therapy has gone far beyond the number of people who practice it, primarily as a result of its impact on group therapists of various persuasions who have attended gestalt group therapy workshops and seminars. It is generally the case that group therapists' attempts to achieve genuineness, to be more in touch with their experience, and to work toward a meaningful sense of responsibility have influenced their therapeutic work in important ways regardless of their fundamental orientation.

Psychodrama.   Psychodrama is another method that has influenced the development and practice of group therapy out of proportion to the actual number of individuals who claim to practice it. Many group therapists have come to use such psychodramatic techniques as the alter ego, the double, and role reversal (see Moreno, 1946; Wood et al., 1981) when they deem them appropriate. Psychodrama's message about how important spontaneity and empathy training are for effective living, and therefore for progress in treatment groups, has permeated general group therapy practice. Psychodrama remains difficult to categorize, however; although much attention is given in each session to individuals, processes occurring within the group also play a prominent role in the method.

Therapeutic Factors

In the absence of definitive comparative data, a summary of alleged "therapeutic factors" is helpful in indicating a final respect in which the various types of group therapy appear to differ. Among types of group therapies focused on the individual, first of all, those with a psychoanalytic orientation emphasize the importance of successful outcome of the twin factors of (a) patient motivation and (b) therapist skill in the interpretation of transferences and resistances. Three very important *curative factors* said to reside in the behavior of the TA group therapist are *potency, permission,* and *protection* (Dusay & Steiner, 1971). In the behavioral group therapies the leader's arrangement of suitable reinforcement contingencies is seen to be the crucial change agent.

   In those forms of group therapy that focus more upon the group, it is the group leader's skill in keeping the group at work while at the same time preventing its members from grasping at quick, anxiety-reducing solutions that appears to be considered most important for achieving the treatment goals. The leader's skill in these two respects increases the likelihood of the activation and exploration of individual patient problems.

   Yalom (1975), writing from an eclectic orientation to group therapy, delineates the following 12 categories of curative factors: altruism, group cohesiveness, universality, interpersonal learning (input), interpersonal learning (output), guidance, catharsis, identification, family reenactment, insight, instillation of hope, and existential factors, for instance, "recognizing that ultimately there is no escape from some of life's pain and death" (pp. 66–69). Yalom's list has generated some research (Corder et al., 1981; Freedman & Hurley, 1980). Freedman and Hurley

(1980), for example, found that college upperclassmen viewed the following as most important in increasing each individual's awareness and sensitivity to his or her own behavior in interaction with others: improving social skills, learning how to relate to others, learning to express emotions, and discovering and accepting unacceptable facets of oneself.

Bloch et al. (1982) provide a useful review of the attempts to elucidate curative or therapeutic factors in group psychotherapy. They conclude with some questions whose answers would seem to move theory building, research, and practice forward. They ask;

> What is the relationship between TFs (therapeutic factors) and group differences (e.g., long- vs. short-term, inpatient vs outpatient, homogeneous vs. heterogeneous)? Are TFs related to individual differences (e.g., age, diagnosis, psychological-mindedness, intelligence)? What is the association between particular TFs and outcome? . . . Is there an association between TFs and group development (i.e., are some factors more relevant than others at particular phases of the group?)? What is the relationship between TFs, conditions for change, and techniques? What is the optimal method for measuring TFs? [p. 525]

Although it may be too early to know which if any of these are necessary and sufficient conditions for patient improvement in group psychotherapy, an impressive amount of evidence is accumulating regarding the importance of the group therapist's accurate empathy, nonpossessive warmth, and genuineness (Truax, 1971).

Some of the therapeutic factors listed above can be understood as mechanisms through which behavior and attitude change are thought to take place. In connection with these mechanisms, the potential of intermember and leader–member mutual influences to foster behavior and attitude change in the group situation has been recognized for some time (Scheidlinger, 1955; Frank, 1961). Formulations by Kelman (1963) provide a particularly useful way of conceptualizing the influence process that takes place in groups, regardless of the type of group. He posits three processes that underlie the acceptance of influence: *compliance, identification,* and *internalization.* Each process has its own antecedent conditions and its own consequents. This formulation cuts across various types of groups, including both therapy groups and the intensive small-group experiences to be discussed next, and enables one to identify key factors in the social influence process.

INTENSIVE SMALL-GROUP EXPERIENCES

The current group therapy scene overlaps at several points between traditional group therapy and intensive small-group experiences. The latter has taken a different evolutionary route, however, which merits a brief review. As with the history of group therapy, the listing of starting points and contributors to the development of the intensive small-group experience is somewhat arbitrary. Rosenbaum and Berger (1963) present what seems to be a logical line of development, from Charles H. Cooley in the early 1900s through Mead, LeBon, Durkheim, Park, Zorbaugh and Trasher, White, Mayo, and Sapir, and their contribution is recommended for further reading on these historical matters.

A man whose name is closely linked to the development of laboratory education, which is the generic form of the intensive small-group experience (Lubin & Eddy, 1970), is Kurt Lewin, a German gestalt psychologist whose research interests ranged over a wide spectrum. Together with two of his students, Ronald Lippitt and Ralph K. White, Lewin conducted classical experiments on the effects of leadership style (authoritarian, laissez faire, and democratic) on group structure, functioning, and climate (Lippitt & White, 1958). One of his abiding interests was the study of attitude and behavior change of individuals as a result of their participation in group discussions. His success in using group discussion and public commitment to change the food-purchasing habits of American housewives during World World War II in the direction of less preferred meats is well known (Lewin, 1943).

These interests of Lewin, as well as his general dedication to action research and to developing effective means for resolving social tensions, led Frank Simpson, executive director of the Connecticut Interracial Commission, to ask him to assist in training group leaders (school teachers, businesspersons, other community leaders) who it was hoped would be instrumental in changing racial attitudes and working effectively with interracial tensions. The specific need was for a training conference to implement the newly enacted Connecticut Fair Employment Practices Act. In response to this request, Lewin in June of 1946 organized and conducted a workshop at New Britain, Connecticut. The workshop comprised three 10-person groups of participants led by Leland Bradford, Kenneth Benne, and Ronald Lippitt. The small discussion groups, which looked at "back-home" problems of participants, were to be studied by Lewin and a small research staff, and each of the small groups accordingly contained a research observer. These observers—Morton Deutsch, Murray Horwitz, and Melvin Seeman—used pretested schedules, coded interactions, and behavioral sequences to record and report their groups' processes to the evening meeting of the trained staff.

Participants who received permission to attend the evening staff meeting showed keen interest in the reports of individual, group, and leader interactions. Within a few days all the participants were attending the evening meeting on a voluntary basis and were permitted to interact around the observations. It was apparent to participants and staff that there was a high level of interest in acquiring objective observations of one's behavior and its effects on others and in learning about the formation and development of small groups.

The next year, 1947, Leland Bradford (National Education Association), Ronald Lippitt (Research Center for Group Dynamics), and Kenneth D. Benne (Columbia University) organized a 3-week summer session in Human Relations Training at Gould Academy in Bethel, Maine. This isolated "cultural island" was chosen for the training session in order to capitalize on Lewin's conviction that reducing or eliminating the usual situational forces that tend to resist change would increase the likelihood that change would take place. From these beginnings emerged significant current directions in the use of T groups and laboratory training.

The T Group

A major component of the 3-week session held in Bethel in 1947 was a *basic skills training group,* which in 1949 came to be referred to more briefly as a *T group.* This was a small discussion group which included a *trainer* who helped the group to evaluate and generalize from what it was learning from the observer's comments and the data supplied by participants.

It was an ebullient era. Creativity, drive, optimism, and energy led to the setting of an impossibly large and diverse range of objectives for the basic skills training group. Here are the objectives, as reported by Benne (1964): (a) group members were to learn in a meaningful way sets of concepts, including concepts of planned change and associated skills, indices, and criteria of group development; (b) the group was to provide an opportunity for members to practice diagnostic action skills of the change agent, group leader, and member via skill practice and role playing; (c) the behavioral perspective was to shift from the interpersonal to the group to the intergroup and organizational levels; (d) opportunities were to be provided for generalization and plans for application to the back-home situation; (e) members were to receive feedback about their relationship and communication style and its impact on other members and on the development of the group; (f) members were to develop a greater appreciation for democratic values; and (g) members were also to acquire trainer skills with which to help others function as change agents and group members.

It is important to notice that "personal growth" in a quasi-therapeutic sense is absent from this list of objectives, or present in embryonic form only. The emphasis was on experimental education, skill development, value exploration, and a posture of inquiry, with high value placed on the collection and evaluation of objective as well as subjective (feelings, perceptions, reactions) data.

The National Training Laboratories, now the NTL Institute for Applied Behavioral Science, was established as a branch of the National Education Association and was led from its inception in 1949 to 1970 by its director, Leland P. Bradford. In 1971 the NTL Institute became an independent nonprofit organization which provides training, consultation, and research in the applied behavioral sciences. The NTL Institute is recognized as the parent organization that has made major contributions to and has overseen the development of laboratory training, particularly but not exclusively in the United States.

Benne (1964) delineates two phases in the evolution of the method. From 1949 through 1955 there were many attempts to experiment with training formats and technologies with which to implement learning objectives that did not seem to be squarely within the purview of the T group. The latter had emerged as a unique educational vehicle which was emotionally intense, somewhat anti-intellectual in philosophy, and rejecting of discussions not concerned with immediate data (the here and now). As various kinds of special groups were formed in order to concentrate on these additional objectives, the T group was experienced at times as not sufficiently integrated into the rest of the design for conferences at the NTL. In the second phase, from 1956 to the present, attempts were made to reintegrate the T group and T-group-type experiences into laboratory designs for residential setting conferences.

Until 1962, the evolutionary routes of group psychotherapy and laboratory training clearly were traced from different points of origin, followed different courses, and sought to arrive at different destinations (objectives). The objectives of group psychotherapy were healing, repair, restoration of function, and alleviation of distress; the objectives of laboratory training were to provide a vehicle for experiential learning of group leadership and membership skills, and for greater understanding and effective ways of intervening in the field of forces at work in the formation, development, and functioning of small groups. Although it was noted even in the conference that preceded the first Human Relations Laboratory that participants seemed fascinated with the opportunity to receive direct feedback about the effects of their behavior and style, and even though intimacy was a definite phase of the development of each T group (Benne, 1964), this aspect of laboratory training received secondary billing for several years.

The Personal Development T Group

In 1962 three members of the NTL Institute's Western Training Laboratory, Irving R. Weschler, Fred Massarick, and Robert Tannenbaum, published what became the conceptual basis for a shift in emphasis from the group-process T group to the T group with a personal–interpersonal focus. Weschler et al. (1962) referred to their method as "group therapy for normals."

The need for such an approach is detailed by these authors in terms of the *cultural neurosis* that afflicts everyone. For the *pseudohealthy* person, "tensions below the surface debilitate realization of potential capacities, stunt creativity, infuse hostility into a vast range of human contact, and frequently generate hampering psychosomatic problems" (Weschler et al., 1962, p. 34). A person who lives under conditions that alienate him or her so profoundly from others and from himself or herself needs intensive small-group experiences that deal "with his tendency to control or be controlled by others, with his management of anger, with his ability to express and receive love or affection, with his feelings of loneliness, with his search for personal identity, [and] with his testing of his own adequacy" (p. 35).

These views represented a definite shift away from group process to a focus on the enhancement of individual development. Shortly after the development of the self-in-process model of the T group, residential laboratories conducted by the NTL Institute began to show greater differentiation than previously. The name of the Human Relations Laboratory was changed to the Human Interaction Laboratory, thus indicating a change in emphasis to include the interpersonal realm as well as group process. New offerings included a Personal Growth Laboratory and an Advanced Personal Growth Laboratory.

It is important to recognize that professionals as well as the public subsequently contributed to considerable terminological confusion by using such terms as *group therapy, sensitivity training, marathon group, growth group, T group, laboratory training,* and *integrity group* interchangeably (Lubin & Eddy, 1970). To achieve clarity of exposition and delineate the unique contribution of laboratory training, the term should be reserved for referring "to a range of experience-based learning activities in which participants are centrally involved in goal setting, observing, feeding back, analyzing data, planning action or change steps, evaluating, etc. Data which are within the learning situation itself provide the material for learning. The format may take a number of forms; the best known form, the 'laboratory,' has the character of a conference" (Lubin & Eddy, 1970, p. 306).

Another description that clarifies the nature of the laboratory further states that it consists of

> different groupings of participants with differing technologies of training in the service of various learning objectives. Staff members are in continuous communication in order to establish and maintain relationships among the parts of the laboratory experience. As the laboratory proceeds in time, participants are brought together in integrating sessions designed to help them relate the parts of their overall laboratory experience. Integration of learnings becomes a central concern for participants in work on problems of application of laboratory learnings in their home situations. [Benne, 1964, pp. 108–109]

The notions of "conference" and "range of experience-based learning activities" imply various kinds of groupings (T group, general sessions for conceptual input, total conference exercises and simulations, intergroup sessions) arranged in such a manner as to potentiate and assist in the integration of different kinds of learning. Unfortunately, it is to just one of the components of the laboratory, albeit an important component—the T group—that many writers refer in discussing laboratory training, while ignoring the rest of the design. The situation is much like that of the symphony orchestra. The string section is important and colorful and can function independently of the rest of the orchestra; by separating this section from the rest, however, one loses depth and range, counterpoint, variety and contrast, a sense of shifting focus, blend and resolution, and so forth.

Laboratory Training and Stress

It has been said that small-group experiences produce excessively high levels of stress for the participants *(Business Week,* 1963; Kutash, 1971; Winthrop, 1971). As mentioned above, in these allegations laboratory training frequently is included under the general rubric of sensitivity training or small groups. In point of fact, two types of data indicate that the probability of laboratory training's producing psychological casualty is very small. The records of the NTL Institute for Applied Behavioral Science indicate that "of 14,200 participants in its summer and industrial programs between 1947 and 1968, for 33 (0.2%) the experience was stressful enough to require them to leave the program prior to its completion" *(NTL Institute News and Reports,* 1969). These findings are supported by the outcome of a long-term study of an intensive program of laboratory training in the YMCA. Data collected in interviews from participants, their work supervisors, their trainers, and other group members indicate that in only 0.3% of the cases did a severe negative experience occur (Batchelder & Hardy, 1968, pp. 83–84).

Another line of investigation has produced the sobering finding that T groups, at their most stressful points, arouse significantly less anxiety, depression, and hostility (all of which are subjective indicators of stress) than do regularly scheduled college examinations (Lubin & Lubin, 1971).

Using the Lieberman, Yalom, and Miles definition of a casualty, Bramlette and Tucker (1981) also found that 8% to 10% of the participants had "negative experiences." However, upon inquiring further to identify those who had negative experiences without any offsetting positive experiences, they found the casualties reduced to 3%. The ethical and professional concerns regarding potential negative outcomes, however, continue to be important (Bramlette & Tucker, 1981; Howes, 1981).

Encounter Groups

In the same period during which the Personal Development T Group developed, another form of intensive small-group experience appeared initially at the Esalen Institute in Big Sur, California (Murphy, 1967), and then spread to various "growth centers" around the country. The *encounter group,* as many of these offerings were called, varied in format, duration, and emphasis from leader to leader and from one growth center to the next. Emphases on the nonverbal, on feelings, on physical contact, and on the use of fantasy techniques and movement are some of the parameters encounter groups have in common (Lubin & Eddy, 1970). Inasmuch as Fritz Perls was the psychiatrist in residence at Big Sur, his orientation and philosophy had a strong influence on the development of encounter groups. Thus, despite considerable diversity in form and method, most encounter groups espouse concerns for genuineness, contact, personal growth, and game-free interaction. The absence of a parent organization to guide and supervise the overall development of the encounter group movement appears to have resulted in some excesses in its use, but it has also permitted a kind of freedom that has encouraged innovations in many dimensions of the encounter group experience (Stoller, 1972).

Participants in encounter groups report being captivated by the immediacy, vividness, sense of release, and experience of intimacy created by these experiences. Some writers speculate that the popularity of these short-lived groups stems mainly from the rare and welcome contrast they provide to the widespread alienation and mechanization of Western culture (Rogers, 1968; Yalom, 1975).

As suggested above, frequent concern has been expressed about the relative absence of standards for the practice of encounter group work and the qualifications of its practitioners (Lakin, 1969; Lubin & Eddy, 1970 *; Strassburger, 1971; Wysor, 1971). Much of this concern has arisen from the alleged psychonoxious aspects of the intensive encounter group experience. Lieberman, Yalom, and Miles (1973), in one of the more important contributions in this area, added weight to such concern by reporting a relationship between encounter group leader style and casualty rate in encounter groups. Evidence in this regard is still very meager, however, and the Lieberman et al. study has been questioned on methodological grounds (Schutz, 1974). Generally speaking, the encounter group movement has produced very little research to date. However, a considerable volume of research has been associated with the laboratory training area (Lubin & Eddy, 1970), and Gibb (1974) summarizes the research in this field that appeared between 1947 and 1972.

RESEARCH IN GROUP THERAPY

Some therapists find the group situation with its multiple interactions so complex and tension producing that they avoid it and do only individual therapy (Bach, 1956). This complexity also confronts anyone who proposes to conduct meaningful research on group therapy. Conceptualization and design problems are more complex in group than in individual therapy research, because there is an additional class of variables that needs to be considered (group variables) and because an increased number of interactions among variables (patient variables, therapist variables, situational variables, and outcome variables) is possible. Consequently, it is not surprising that, despite an increase in the volume of group therapy research, it is difficult to compare the findings of various studies with each other or to see systematic progress in the accumulation of knowledge in this area.

Several reviewers have commented thoughtfully on the need to improve research efforts in group therapy (Goldstein, Heller, & Sechrest, 1966; Gundlach, 1967; Lewis & McCants, 1973; Psathas, 1967; Stollak, et al., 1966; Yalom, 1975; Bednar & Kaul, 1979; Bednar & Moeschl, 1981; Parloff & Dies, 1977). In the past, wasted effort and conceptual confusion have resulted from what has been called the *uniformity myths*. These myths refer to the tendency of earlier researchers to proceed as if they were attempting to evaluate "the effect of something called 'group psychotherapy' on somebody called 'patients,' 'outpatients,' or 'schizophrenics.' Group psychotherapy is not a homogenous treatment condition; group psychotherapists differ from one another in a multitude of ways, and so do group therapy patients" (Lewis & McCants, 1973, p. 271). Uniformity myths are growing less apparent in the research literature, but by no means have they been demolished. There remains a pressing need for much greater specification of variables in future research (MacKenzie & Dies, 1982; Parloff & Dies, 1978).

---

* This concern refers to the specific field of encounter groups. A note regarding accreditation for practitioners of various forms of laboratory training appears later in this chapter.

Outcome of therapy is another concept that has been a candidate for the uniformity myth category. Outcome has been treated in the past as if everyone agreed as to what form of outcome was conceptualized as long as posttreatment measurements were made. To the contrary, the evidence suggests that improvement is not a unitary process and that changes in different outcome measures and criteria do not necessarily occur together (Kelman & Parloff, 1957). Kurtz & Grummon (1972) have shown that six different measures of the same construct (therapist empathy) have different relationships to a process measure (depth of self-exploration) and to four different outcome measures.*

In this same vein, the importance of individualizing the goals of therapy, and, accordingly, the assessment of outcome for each patient, has been mentioned by several reviewers (Lewis & McCants, 1973; Parloff, 1973; Yalom, 1970). Such an idiographic orientation to the measurement of outcome would be consistent with clinical practice, in which, for example, achieving a lower level of anxiety is the treatment goal for one patient, whereas achieving a higher level of anxiety is a treatment goal for another patient.

Two suggested solutions to the problems of conducting research in group therapy in the clinical setting are (a) designing laboratory analogs to group therapy and (b) extrapolating the findings of appropriate small-group research to group therapy. Heller (Goldstein et al., 1966) is a proponent of the analog approach, which is a method that has worked well in engineering and experimental medicine. Given adequate ingenuity of the research, knowledge of the processes and mechanisms of group therapy can potentially be advanced by this method. The important point in evaluating the adequacy of this approach of course is to determine that the major points in the analog are truly analogous to the clinical practice of group therapy.

Goldstein et al. (1966) strongly urge the group therapy researcher to look to the field of small-group research as a source of group-relevant variables. They review several studies, make extrapolations from the field of small-group research, and state hypotheses for testing in the following areas: group composition and initial structure, group size, initiation into the therapy group, group therapist orientation, and group cohesiveness. The small-group approach also seems promising, although confidence in it must await more demonstrations that important small-group research findings can be replicated in the group therapy situation.

Additional worthwhile overviews of research in group therapy can be found in Dies (1979), Parloff and Dies (1977, 1978), Reddy and Lippert (1980), Wolfgang and Pierson (1977), and Colson and Horwitz (1981). Reviews of research in selected areas are available for schizophrenia (Mosher & Keith, 1979), juvenile delinquency (Julian & Kilman, 1979), the elderly (Lieberman & Gourash, 1979), and homosexuality (Rogers, et al., 1976). In turning from issues to substantive findings, self-disclosure and group composition are two areas in which several interesting studies on group therapy have been reported.

---

* The nature of outcome and process research in psychotherapy is elaborated in Chapter 7.

Self-Disclosure

Current concern about the issue of group therapist transparency has no doubt fueled the large number of articles that are appearing on self-disclosure (SD), although the obvious importance of SD as a patient variable has been known for many years. It is through SD that much of the interpersonal learning in group therapy takes place; that is, the "universality" of one's problems is established, and important data for the feedback process are made available (Harris, 1980; Mitchell, 1980; Spaulding, 1980).

The literature on SD is reviewed by Allen (1973), who draws from it some implications for group therapy practice. The relevance to group therapy of earlier findings on SD is not clear, as many of the studies are based on high school and college students who are unrepresentative of the population of group therapy patients in terms of psychopathology. Moreover, the findings derive from dyadic interactions rather than group situations, and most of them have been concerned with nonthreatening, nonintimate disclosures. A comprehensive critique of the SD construct has been presented by Goodstein and Reinecker (1974), who discuss the philosophical background of the concept of SD, the content of what is disclosed, characteristics of the target of the disclosures, characteristics of the discloser, situational determinants of SD, and problems in the measurement of SD.

Block and Goodstein (1971), in an earlier critique of work by Jourard and Jaffe (1970) on SD, called particular attention to the potential complexity of the construct, and this complexity of SD has been further delineated by three recent studies. In the first of these studies, Simonson and Bahr (1974) examined relationships among three patterns of disclosure (no disclosure, disclosure of demographic information, and personal disclosure) and two levels of therapist affiliation (professional and paraprofessional). Professional therapist disclosure of personal information resulted in less attraction and disclosure of demographic information. However, subjects displayed greater attraction and disclosure when exposed to personal disclosure by the paraprofessional therapist than when exposed to demographic disclosure by him.

In addition to suggesting the complexity of SD, the second study also has implications for its manipulability. In an investigation of the effect of an explicit group contract on self-disclosure and group cohesiveness, Ribner (1974) found that "the contract [to disclose] served to increase significantly both the frequency and depth of self-disclosure but did not affect the level of intimacy of the topics discussed." He also concluded that "the contract [to disclose] significantly enhanced the cohesiveness of the groups [i.e., attraction to the group] but had the opposite effect on members' mutual liking" (p. 116). The third study, by Coche, Plikoff, and Cooper (1980), refers again to the bimodal relationship between amount of self-disclosure and beneficial outcome of group therapy. In severely disturbed inpatients it was found that the higher the self-disclosure, the lower the chances for successful therapy outcome.

Some findings on SD, if treated with caution, do seem to have implications for group therapy. The facts that SD is manipulable (Jourard & Friedman, 1970;

Ribner, 1974) and that it tends to be reciprocal (Culbert, 1970) are cases in point. Also instructive is an apparent curvilinear relationship between SD and adjustment (Culbert, 1970; Jourard, 1964); that is, very high and very low SD seem to be associated with maladjustment. In selecting patients and composing groups, therefore, the principle of balance in SD tendency among patients seems to be worth considering.

Although the therapist variable has received relatively little study in the group therapy literature, it seems to be a potentially fruitful domain. SD tendency of the group therapist seems likely to be observable in his or her SD behavior, in the group therapy philosophy he or she espouses, in the way in which he or she structures the group, and in his or her style of interacting with patients. Continued study of consequences of various combinations of therapist–group SD should prove worthwhile.

Group Composition

Group composition is another area that has attracted a large volume of research interest. Reddy (1975), in a very useful review of the literature of group composition research, indicates that studies can be grouped into those concerned with the dimension of homogeneity–heterogeneity and those in the area of compatibility–incompatibility of needs. These two dimensions have frequently been confused. In summarizing the findings of several studies, Reddy (1975) states that "composition based upon the homogeneous–heterogeneous dimension influences the change process in groups (and) . . . heterogeneous composition leads . . . to a wider range of alternative behaviors and change" (p. 8).

The Fundamental Interpersonal Relationship Orientation (FIRO-B) inventory developed by Schutz (1958) is the major instrument used to study the effects of need compatibility–incompatibility. The basic social needs addressed by this instrument are inclusion, control, and affection. According to Schutz, these three needs are sufficient for prediction of interpersonal and group behavior. The self-report instrument (FIRO-B) measures two aspects of each of these three needs, the amount of the need the person desires, and the amount he expresses. The "fit" between the degree of a need one person wants and that which another person expresses defines the interchange compatibility score, which has been found to be positively related to group goal achievement and satisfaction (Schutz, 1958). Focusing on the affection dimension, Reddy developed a model of interaction within the FIRO-B structure which, although developed for the T-group setting, might be usefully tested in the group therapy situation (Reddy, 1975).

Homogeneity–heterogeneity, as mentioned earlier, is a special aspect of the group composition issue. Earlier discussions of this dimension led to many overgeneralizations concerning it (Frust, 1963), but subsequent research findings have fortunately been more specific and limited. Thus there is evidence that homogeneity tends in some cases to promote a feeling of security among group members, whereas heterogeneity seems to result in less security but more learning in the group (Harrison & Lubin, 1965).

Experience in therapy with special groups of people all having similar problems, such as alcoholics, drug addicts, and parents of children with problems, suggests that homogeneity of type of problem heightens the visibility of the problem as well as the characteristic defenses and life styles of the patients. However, homogeneity seems to foster superficial, problem-focused discussions (Mullan & Rosenbaum, 1962; Powdermaker & Frank, 1953). Yalom's (1975) discussion of this issue is helpful. He asks, "Homogeneous for what? Heterogeneous for what?" (p. 193). He then supports Whitaker and Lieberman (1964) in indicating that the therapist might want to consider *both* homogeneity and heterogeneity in composing therapy groups, for example, heterogeneity in patients' areas of conflict and styles of coping, but homogeneity in patients' tolerance for anxiety.

Elsewhere it has been suggested that the complexity of the group therapy situation requires study by means of multivariate designs. Thus the interactions of therapist style, group composition, and stage of group development are likely to be rich exploratory domains for advancing knowledge of group therapy as a clinical and social psychological phenomenon, and also for improving the applied aspects of the method (Budge, 1981). As to the former, it might well be that absolute differences among patients on a variety of dimensions are less important than the therapist's manner of relating to these differences, for example, *leveling–sharpening* (Byrne, 1964). Effects of treatment on patients' moods and response tendencies, for example, have been shown to be a function of type of group therapy orientation and patients' pretreatment interpersonal styles (Glad & Glad, 1963; Glad, Ferguson, Hayne, & Glad, 1963; Glad, Glad, & Barnes, 1959). In regard to the applied considerations, lack of readiness seems to be a factor in some cases of individuals who drop out of group therapy during the early phases. Conceptualizing this problem as arising out of the interaction of several factors might alert the therapist to the need to provide protection and encouragement for those patients whose anxiety tolerance and self-disclosure tendencies are lower than those of the rest of the group.

Despite the large number of research studies in group therapy reported during the past 2 decades, many practicing group therapists perceive this research as irrelevant to their work (Coche & Dies, 1981; Dies, 1979; Wolfgang & Pierson, 1977). Is it the case that much of the research is not relevant, or have training programs failed to convince practitioners of the relevancy of the research and failed to urge them to continue to read the research literature?

TRAINING IN GROUP THERAPY

Discussions of training in group psychotherapy have centered around conceptual, skill, and personal considerations (Dies, 1980). Several writers agree on the importance of a strong didactic phase in group therapy training programs (Konopka, 1949; Schwartz, 1981; Slavson, 1974), although they differ somewhat in the material they recommend covering in didactic exercises. There are furthermore considerable differences in the suggested items included in various published reading lists for learning about group therapy, and several of these lists contain more books and articles drawn from the field of individual therapy than from the group therapy field. The key elements to consider in reviewing training methods in group therapy are *cotherapy, training aids, experience as a patient,* and *continuing education.*

Cotherapy

In many training settings the actual learning and practice of the skills of the group therapist take place by means of a tutorial model in which the student either serves as cotherapist with an experienced group therapist or conducts group therapy under the observation of an experienced group therapist who sits with the group or views the session through a one-way mirror. The discussion that follows the sessions may be used for the training of students other than the therapist, if they too have observed the session.

Most students serve at some time during their training in a cotherapy relationship (Bergman, Messersmith, & Mullens, 1972; Gonzales et al., 1982; McGee & Shuman, 1970; Silverstein, 1981), and this technique appears to be a helpful vehicle for learning group therapy. The cotherapist role allows beginners initially to function mainly as observers with little responsibility for active participation. Later, as their learning progresses, they gradually increase their level of activity in the sessions. As developing but still inexperienced cotherapists become increasingly active, however, it is necessary to guard against their assuming roles that, although comfortable, might not be responsive to the changing needs of the patients, the group, or the cotherapy team.

Training Aids

Group therapists learn by means of the same mechanisms that group therapy patients learn, namely, by receiving feedback on the effects of their behavior and by practicing alternative behaviors. Given this premise, recordings, diaries, and rating scales are useful aids in the growth of the group therapist.

Recordings.   The past few years have seen a growing use of audiovisual equipment as an adjunct to training in group therapy (Bodin, 1969; Sadock & Kaplan, 1971). An accurate account of patient and therapist behavior and their verbal and nonverbal communication, as captured on videotape, is becoming an important part of supervisory training sessions (Berger, 1971). The learning potential of seeing one's behavior on videotape is considerable, and the use of this training aid is recommended whenever feasible. In the absence of videotape equipment, audiotaping provides a less rich but still instructive replacement.

Diaries.   A systematically kept diary as an adjunct to postsession group notes can document the self in process of the group therapist in the same manner in which the group notes document the group in process. To be most useful as a training aid, the student group therapist's diary should contain technical questions about the tactics he or she is employing, thoughts and feelings in regard to his or her role and personal development, and goals and plans he or she has for modifying his or her own behavior.

Rating Scales.   Rating scales are a third means, along with recordings and diaries, of providing feedback regarding the behavior of the group therapist. Rating scales can aid both self-assessment and supervisor assessment processes, especially if at least some of them are constructed so as to be bipolar, for example, confronting–supportive, and descriptive rather than judgmental and evaluative. An additional suggestion is that some of the scales be constructed by the trainee in consultation with his or her supervisor, so as to indicate those dimensions on which the trainee believes feedback would be helpful.

Experience as a Patient

A survey of senior members of the American Group Psychotherapy Association who were involved in training group therapists revealed some differences in attitude concerning whether a group therapist in training should have an experience as a patient in a group (Stein, 1963). Favorable respondents indicated that participation of the traineee in a group gives him or her some appreciation for how the patient feels in group therapy, helps the trainee to discern the differences between individual and group therapy, and enables him or her to work through problems in relating to groups, authority figures, and peers.

Regardless of individual differences in viewpoint, however, centers that train group therapists seem to agree that an experiential dimension to the training program is essential: "Neither the seminar method nor individual supervision seems able to convey to the therapist more than an intellectual awareness of his patterns of operation in the group, especially since these patterns often are ego-syntonic in nature and, therefore, most difficult for the therapist to grasp fully" (Leichter, 1963, p. 74). Wanting the trainee to experience how the patient feels in group therapy is a salutary reason for expecting him or her to have a group experience, but more important as a reason for the requirement is the fact that it is useful for the group therapist to have an accurate picture of the effects of his or her behavior on individual group members and on the group—effects of personal leadership style and style of communicating, relating, managing conflict, dealing with feelings, working with negative affect and resistances, handling criticism and attack, dealing with depression and hope, and so on. The best opportunity for obtaining accurate information of this nature is participation in a small, agenda-less group conducted by a leader who is trained in both clinical psychology and group dynamics.

An even more ideal training program envisions each student group therapist as being a member of two different experiential groups, one an encounter group and the other a T group, in addition to attending other didactic and experimental sessions. The encounter group experience would enable the student to deal directly and at some depth with such issues as dependency–autonomy, dominance–submission, and feelings about himself or herself and his or her body. Some of these same issues would surface in varied forms in the T group, but there the student could explore in addition the self in relation to a range of group-level phenomena: leadership, cohesion, norms, procedures, decision making, inclusion, and so forth. The two types of experiences would be designed to supplement each other; thus to the impactful personal perspective a frame of reference would be added which alerts the student to alterable group properties that influence the quality and nature of the group experience. Each type of group experience then would become both a corrective and an extension for the other.

The similarities and differences between these two types of group experiences and their relevance for learning about group therapy merit further attention from group therapists concerned with training. Individual students tend to be attracted to one type of experience or the other, depending on its fit with their personal needs and the personal benefit they perceive in it. A balanced approach, however, should recognize that leadership styles and procedures appropriate for the group therapist may at times resemble those used by the leader of the encounter group or the T group, but may also vary with respect to the objectives of the treatment, the nature of the patient population being seen, the setting in which the group therapy is taking place, and the phase the therapy is in (Schein & Bennis, 1965; Yalom, 1975). For additional discussions of the roles of supervision and experiential learning in training for group therapy, the reader is referred to contributions by Abels (1970), Gladfelter (1970), Glatzer (1971), Goldberg (1982), Grossman and Karmiol (1973), Grotjahn (1970), Kadis (1971), Lanning (1971), MacLennan (1971), Rockwell (1971), and Schwartz (1981).

Continuing Education

More than ever before, professionals are experiencing the need and finding opportunities to participate in additional group therapy training at training institutes and seminars. Training institutes with offerings in group therapy are held in connection with the annual meetings of the American Psychological Association. In addition, periodic, brief, specialized sessions in group therapy are offered by various centers during the year. Information about these training sessions can be obtained by writing to the appropriate organization.* It may be that the intangible aspects of hope are most meaningfully communicated to patients when they sense that the group therapist has developmental expectations for himself or herself as well as for his or her patients.

---

* American Group Psychotherapy Association, Inc., P.O. Box 230, 150 Christopher Street, New York, New York 10014; American Society of Group Psychotherapy and Psychodrama, Inc., Beacon House, Inc., 259 Wolcott Avenue, Beacon, New York, 12508; Gestalt Institute of Cleveland, Inc., 1291 Euclid Avenue, Cleveland, Ohio 44112; International Transactional Analysis Association, Inc., 3155 College Avenue, Berkeley, California 94705; International Association of Applied Social Scientists, Inc., Suite 300, 1755 Massachusetts Avenue, N.W., Washington, D.C. 20036.

GROUP THERAPY WITH SPECIALIZED POPULATIONS

In this section the use of the group therapy method with the following specialized populations is surveyed: inpatients, outpatients, children and their parents, adolescents, the aged, medical patients, drug abusers, and alcoholics.

Inpatients

In addition to regularly scheduled group therapy sessions for hospitalized psychiatric patients (Erickson, 1981), some inpatient settings provide a unique form of group experience known as *the therapeutic community* or *milieu therapy*. This form of therapy involves attempts to restructure the hospital environment to make it more beneficial and therapeutic. An important feature of a therapeutic community is an underlying democratic philosophy. Through ward groups, patients participate in decisions that affect them and in the general governance of their setting (Gustafson, 1979).

Outpatients

Patients with different kinds of psychiatric histories are referred to outpatient therapy groups. These include some who have no previous psychiatric history, some for whom the group experience represents an opportunity to explore psychological problems in depth after hospitalization, and some for whom a posthospitalization group primarily serves a supportive function while they are being maintained on medication (Linn, 1979; Mosher & Keith, 1979).

Children and Their Parents

Several considerations influence the form and orientation of group therapy conducted with children, mostly in relation to their immaturity. In particular, the short attention span of children, their incompletely developed capacity for dealing with verbal abstractions, and their natural proclivity to learn and develop through the various modalities involved in play have led to widespread use of group play-therapy methods. These methods differ from other group therapy methods in the extent to which the child's behavior, interactions, verbalizations, and productions are actively interpreted (Dana & Dana, 1969; Dietrich, 1982; Rhodes, 1973; Rose, 1972; Witenberg & Bruseloff, 1972). Children in play groups are encouraged to describe their phenomenological world, and in the process can be helped to explicate their difficulties by projecting their feelings and attitudes on a fantasy level onto toys and other materials. As the group therapy situation is analogous in some ways to the family, opportunities arise for the group therapist to provide interpretations and sometimes reassurance regarding feelings of jealousy, abandonment, affectional hunger, and the like (Witenberg & Bruseloff, 1972; Lockwood, 1981).

The child's real dependency situation also places constraints on the group therapy approach and requires that the group therapist have insight into the effects of his or her own parenting needs and tendencies. Typically, it is necessary for the group therapist to be nurturant at one time and to set firm limits at another time with the same child or with different children (Harper, 1973; Ginott, 1961; Gratton & Rizzo, 1969).

It is logical to involve parents in a therapeutic alliance wherever possible in the treatment of children. In some cases the behavior of parents is directly implicated in the difficulty the child is having, and individual therapy for one or both parents may be indicated. If the child's difficulties are thought to reflect complex interactions among parents and siblings, then the child's group therapy might be supplemented with family therapy (Westman et al., 1963; Woods, 1974; Leone & Gumaer, 1979; Merkin & Bruseloff, 1981).

Parent guidance groups, using a somewhat conventional educational format to present general principles of parenting, may also be useful. Parents in these groups are helped to personalize the concepts discussed and to achieve at least a beginning grasp of the consequences of their parenting styles. Sometimes parents are encouraged to mention specific problems they are having with their children; as they share in the group problems and attempts to handle the problems, their anxiety and frustration frequently diminish.

Because of the importance of school in the social and educational development of children, it is not surprising that various attempts to assist children with behavioral–emotional problems take place in group situation in the school. The formats for these groups range from those that utilize conventional educational methods primarily to those that emphasize more clinical or psychotherapeutic approaches (Rhodes, 1973). Life-adjustment classes for children who have been referred by teachers because of disruptive behavior are an example of the former, whereas group therapy conducted by specially trained clinical personnel is an example of the latter. It should also be noted that behavior analysis and behavior modification methods employed in groups seem to be increasing in use, and that many of the same behavioral principles and methods utilized with adults seem to apply with children also (Goldstein & Wolpe, 1972; Lazarus, 1971).

Children's hospital provide another important setting for the use of group psychotherapy, particularly to alleviate psychological and behavioral problems associated with surgery and its sequelae, asthma, phobias, homesickness, and other similar difficulties (Wohl, 1967). Clinicians working in day hospitals and day-care centers, aware of children's educational as well as psychological needs, have contributed to the development of a variety of group activities having psychoeducational goals. Psychoeducational approaches have been used appropriately to address problems that are sometimes seen as psychopathology and sometimes as learning disabilities, but appear to embrace both kinds of causation (Kraft, 1971).

Adolescents

Much as was the case with children, particular aspects of adolescents' developmental state have influenced the format, methods, and nuances of group therapy with patients of this age (Chasonoff & Schrader, 1979; Raubolt, 1981). The adolescent has often been characterized as being no longer a child but not yet an adult (Kraft, 1971; Spotniz, 1972a). The existential task of the adolescent, as described by Rachman (1972), has much to do with a need to understand, modulate the effects of, and grow with the emergence of new biological, hormonally related, and culturally shaped impulses. Effective group work with adolescents requires the therapist to be familiar with these sources of developmental confusion and turmoil during the teenage years and to be able to distinguish them from serious psychopathology (Meeks, 1973; Spotnitz, 1972a; Raubolt, 1981).

As with therapy groups for younger children, adolescent therapy groups are capable of evoking sibling rivalry and parent–child conflict situations which need to be worked through. Success in this regard seems to be related to the ability of the group therapist to maintain a nurturant motivational posture toward the adolescents and toward the group, while at the same time setting appropriate limits on both. Given the intermediate emotional developmental state of the adolescent, the group therapist must avoid either overindulging the child in him or expecting too much from the adult in him (Lichtenstein & Kozberg, 1981).

The proclivity of adolescents to redirect their emotional dependence away from adults and toward peers creates an important dynamic for the beneficial effects of group therapy with these clients (Akister & Canever, 1980; Berkovitz, 1972; Greene & Crowder, 1972; MacLennan & Felsenfeld, 1970). Group therapists who are trained in and who make consistent use of group processes in their work thus have a particularly effective set of skills for utilizing adolescents' peer-group orientation to enhance their participation in and benefit from group therapy (Gaines, 1981).

Because sexual and aggressive concerns and activity increase generally during adolescence, circumstances sometimes require special groupings that accentuate these issues of discussion. For example, groups of pregnant adolescent girls may work meaningfully together on such topics as sex, boy–girl relationships, and personal hygiene, in addition to exploring their shared concerns about pregnancy, delivery, relationships with parents, plans for the child, and so on. There are differences of opinion, however, concerning whether male and female adolescents can be treated better in separate or in combined groups. Having groups of just one sex helps to minimize sexual acting out. Having both sexes in the same group, however, although potentially more tumultuous, is more reality based and probably more growth facilitating (Kraft, 1971).

As for general considerations in the treatment of adolescents, Spotnitz (1972a) believes that patients can be divided into two different diagnostic groups having different treatment implications: (a) patients who are "emotionally overcharged" and vulnerable to developing high states of tension, and (b) those who exhibit high levels of "emotional hunger" and tendencies to relate to authority in childlike, dependent ways. The first group of patients requires a minimum of intervention on the part of the group therapist and a calm, constructive environment; the second group needs a high level of communication with the therapist and seems to profit from a nurturant family situation. Based on this formulation, Spotniz describes a novel method of treatment he has been using with emotionally hungry patients, which he calls *constructive emotional interchange*. In this method, the usual attempt to enlist the cooperation of the parents to assist in the treatment of the adolescent is reversed; the adolescent is involved as the "therapist's assistant" in training his or her parents regarding his or her needs and in assisting them to develop more effective coping mechanisms for their own feelings.

The Aged

Group therapy with the aged has taken various forms as a reflection of the multiple service needs of these patients. As a result, the term *group therapy* has been used broadly to refer to such intervention modalities as group counseling, activity therapy, and social group work.

According to Linden (1956), "The complete series of steps in the development of the severe emotional disturbances which lead to physiological breakdown if unimpeded are as follows: (1) disillusionment, (2) partial neurotic surrender, (3) senescent melancholy, (4) attempted reorganization, (5) secondary surrender, (6) senescent decline, (7) emotional regression, and (8) combined physiological and psychological recession" (pp. 131–132). Hence, Linden continues, a treatment program for the aged should include the following components as a minimum: (a) environmental manipulation (surroundings that provide acceptance for the elderly); (2) activity (movement and moderate excitement); (3) resocialization opportunities (reversal of withdrawal tendencies); and (4) psychotherapy. Group therapy for these elderly patients can prove particularly useful, Linden concludes, in alleviating depressive moods, increasing alertness, reducing confusion, improving orientation, and promoting the exchange of concern and affection.

Families of the aged are also likely to benefit from the improved functioning these patients are able to realize through group therapy. Family members of elderly patients are frequently burdened with feelings of guilt related to self-accusations of abandonment or neglect of the patient. These painful feelings are usually reduced following apparent improvement in the mood of the aged patients, in the enjoyment they are finding in their relationships, and in their mental efficiency. As the complaints of the patients lessen, family members experience some release from a sense of futility and feelings of frustration.

Group therapy for the aged is being provided both in outpatient and in inpatient settings (Berger & Berger, 1971; Euster, 1971; Liederman, Green, & Liederman, 1967; Wolff, 1962; Berland & Poggi, 1979; Britnell & Mitchell, 1981). Older people who are ambulatory and in relatively good physical and psychological condition receive outpatient group therapy conducted in such settings as community centers, day centers, social agencies, and senior citizens' clubs (Liederman et al., 1967), as well as in outpatient departments of general hospitals. In all these settings group therapy programs frequently include an educational as well as a treatment component (consumer purchasing information, self-protection strategies, social skills, etc.) (Conrad, 1974; Goldfarb, 1972).

The aged population in inpatient settings, especially state hospitals, includes many patients who have been in the hospital for many years with a diagnosis of schizophrenia or who entered the hospital with diagnosis of organic brain syndrome when they were already old. Thus group therapy with elderly patients in state hospitals needs to include among its objectives attempts to reverse or arrest the process of "institutionalitis" and consequent dependency and social withdrawal (Burnside, 1970, 1971; Mansaster, 1972; McNiel & Verwoerdt, 1973). There has been a recent movement to shift elderly patients where possible from state hospitals to community agencies such as nursing and boarding homes, and group-therapy programs are now developing in these newer settings also (Saul & Saul, 1974). The reflections of Lieberman and Gourash (1979) would seem to be useful for those planning programs for or doing research with the elderly.

The student of group therapy should not overlook the potential opportunity for continued personal and professional growth provided by therapeutic work with the elderly. Many young group therapists have been reared in surroundings from which grandparents and elderly aunts and uncles were removed years earlier by reason of death or institutionalization. Children reared in such environments missed an opportunity to live through and work through important relationships and their feelings about physical and psychological decline and death (Kubler-Ross, 1969). Opportunities available to the therapist to deepen his or her appreciation for the full cycle are to be valued.

Medical Patients

It was mentioned earlier in the chapter that group therapy in the United States originated with the work of Pratt with tuberculosis patients in the early 1900s. Pratt's *class method* attempted to assist patients with attitudinal, emotional, and behavioral aspects of their illness. The field of psychosomatics has grown over the past few decades in both scope and conceptual sophistication. Earlier psychoanalytic contributions in this area promoted the concept of psychogenicity, which focused usefully on needs for psychological treatment of psychosomatic disorders but limited development in the field by suggesting greater specificity in the relationship between certain psychological concerns and certain physical illnesses than could be justified. Lipowski (1968) provides a well-reasoned review and critique of changes in psychosomatic concepts, and two of his concluding remarks indicate the degree to which the field has moved from overspecificity to a general and comprehensive position:

> Human health and disease are viewed as states without a sharp dividing line between them; they are determined by multiple factors: biological, psychological, social; any event at any level of organization of the human organism—from the symbolic to the molecular—may have repercussions at all other levels. . . . Psychotherapy may be of value whenever psychological factors are recognized as significantly contributing to the precipitation, maintenance, or exacerbation of any illness in a given person. [p. 414]

Group therapy has been employed in treating a wide range of physical illness to reduce precipitating, concomitant, exacerbating, or subsequent anxiety and depression. Among the groups with whom the methods have been used are asthmatics (Groen & Pelser, 1960; Mascia & Teiter, 1971; Reckless, 1971; Reed, 1962, Wohl, 1963), parents of asthmatic children (Abramson & Peshkin, 1960), peptic ulcer patients (Fortin & Abse, 1956), diabetics (Frizzell, 1968), parents of diabetics (Hefferman, 1959), and cardiac and hypertensive illness patients (Adsett & Bruhn, 1968; Bilodeau & Hackett, 1971; Goldner & Kyle, 1960; Mone, 1970; Oradei & Waite, 1974; Titchener, Sheldon, & Ross, 1959). Helpful applications of group therapy have also been reported with brain-injured patients (Edwards, 1967), patients with multiple sclerosis (Whally & Strehl, 1969), cystic fibrosis patients (Farkas & Shwachman, 1973), adult male patients with cerebral palsy (Lubin & Slominski, 1960), patients with Parkinson's disease (Szekely, Kosanovich, & Sheppard, 1982), and parents of cerebral-palsied children (Heisler, 1974). Patients on hemodialysis (Hollon, 1973), those with irritable bowel syndrome (Wise, Cooper, & Ahmed, 1982), the deaf (Landau, 1968; Sarlin & Altshuler, 1968; Stinson, 1971), and obese patients (Holt & Winick, 1961; Lassiter & Willett, 1973; Penick, 1970; Slawson, 1965; Snow & Held, 1973; Battegay, Lipp, Miest, Glauser, & Rauchfleisch, 1981) also have been treated with group methods. Finally, of note are pregnancy, delivery, and abortion, all of which are experiences that at some time have been associated with anxiety, fear, guilt, and depression (Lubin, Gardiner, & Roth, 1975). Group therapy has been used with each of these conditions (Bernstein & Tinkham, 1971; Black, 1972; Coleman, 1971).

Drug Abuse

Comprehensive drug-abuse treatment programs have tended to be of two kinds: total abstention programs have employed group psychotherapy to assist in reducing the addict's anxiety and thus the need for the narcotic, to help the addict to confront and change his or her stress-avoidant strategies, and to reduce his or her sense of alienation and loneliness (Kaufman, 1972; Ketai, 1973; Ross, McReynolds, & Berzins, 1974; Skolnick, 1979). Provision of emotional support during the period of abstinence is another important use for group therapy (Kaufman, 1972), which in abstinence-oriented programs has varied from brief, supportive meetings to intensive, time-extended sessions in total-control environments (Ross et al., 1974). Many of these groups are led by trained former addicts who are thoroughly familiar with the nuances of the addict's life style and defenses. Confrontive techniques originally developed at Synanon are used in many of these programs (Casriel, 1964).

The success of abstinence-oriented programs, as measured by the proportion of patients who remain in the program and abstain from the use of narcotics, has been less than hoped for (Binot, 1973; Ross et al., 1974). This has led to the search for and discovery of a substitute drug (methadone) that could block the addict's craving for heroin and thus bring his or her overall behavior under therapeutic guidance. Dole, Nyswander, and Warner (1968), originators of the methadone maintenance program, reasoned that much of the heroin addict's difficulties were circular and stimulated by the buildup of a craving for the drug. The methadone program is controversial, as some claim that the addiction itself remains unchanged even though the addict's drug-associated behavior has been brought under control. Of note in the present context is that group therapy has played a role in the design of methadone maintenance programs for heroin addicts (La Rosa, Lipsius, & La Rosa, 1974; Willet, 1973; Benyehuda, 1980).

Alcoholism

Alcoholism is a complex behavioral–emotional–physiological problem which in the recent past was viewed as an example of failure of will, slothfulness, and general moral inferiority. It is now seen as a debilitating condition causing widespread social and economic problems, and as a condition that can afflict people of any socioeconomic level and of any ethnic, racial, or religious group.

A variety of group and group-related treatment programs has been reported in which group therapy for alcoholics has been used in conjunction with Psychodrama (Cabrera, 1961; Weiner, 1966), individual psychotherapy (Preston, 1960), hypnotherapy (Paley, 1952), aversive drug therapy (Greenbaum, 1954), and crisis intervention (Chafetz & Blane, 1963). Anecdotal and quasi-evaluative studies report successful outcomes in the use of such group methods with alchoholic patients (Hartocollis & Sheafor, 1968; Pittman & Tate, 1969; Westfield, 1972).

The importance of relationship and communication factors in the continuance and exacerbation of the alcoholic's problems has led to the development of several concurrent group treatment programs for the spouses of alcoholics (Arielli, 1981; Cadogan, 1973; Kotis, 1968; Smith, 1969). Wives and husbands of alcoholics have been found to need therapy for their own problems, not only because they may themselves have a drinking problem but also because they may have such characterological problems as oversubmissiveness or overdominance with attendant manifestations of anxiety and depression. In addition, the wife or husband of the alcoholic often needs support and other assistance in dealing with the vicissitudes of the spouse's condition. In those cases in which the stability of the marital relationship depends heavily on rather rigidly defined personality and/or role complementarity, change in the patient's behavior that implies change in the tenuously balanced marital relationship can stimulate the spouse to attempt to reestablish the prior relationship. Group therapy for the spouse in such a case would reduce the need for this countertherapeutic response and would involve the spouse as a therapeutic agent for the patient.

Inasmuch as an alcoholic's treatment needs vary at different times, group treatment has been offered in general hospitals and state hospitals, in partial hospitalization contexts, in halfway houses, and in clinics and community mental health centers (Kanas & Barr, 1982). More and more business organizations are providing company facilities and resources for various treatment programs for employees with alcohol-related problems.

The complexity of the alcoholic's problems has resulted in the employment of group treatment methods varying considerably in format, intensity, and duration (Flores, 1982). As one example, the *orientation group* was devised to help alcoholics overcome their resistances to treatment, provide instruction on the objectives and procedures of group therapy, and ease them into a treatment situation by making their entry less threatening. Institutions sometimes use the orientation group as a "holding" mechanism in order to initiate patients into the treatment environment before decisions about more definite treatment assignments are made (Lubin et al., 1973). As other examples, the *activity group* stresses pleasant group-centered projects (dance, music, recreational therapy, occupational therapy, work projects), whereas the *therapeutic group* represents an opportunity in addition to the activity group for patients to improve their socialization skills (Oei & Jackson, 1980; Vannicelli, 1982).

Alcoholics Anonymous is the best known of the peer-led self-help groups for alcoholics. The aspects of mutual support, avowal of the alcohol problem, and denial of psychological illness fostered by A.A. are well known, and many patients who have been helped by A.A. had previously failed to profit from more professional psychological methods. In general, the methods used in group therapy for alcoholics are similar to those used with other types of psychological problems. Steiner (1971), however, has classified different types of alcoholics in TA terms, explicated the games employed by alcoholics, and accordingly devised differential strategies for use in treatment.

Self-Help Groups

A recent upsurge of the self-help group phenomenon seems to have been produced in part by the general antiauthoritarian attitude of the 1960s and 1970s and by the concomitant increase in consumer awareness and assertiveness (Gartner & Riessman, 1977; Tracy & Gussow, 1976). Many members of self-help groups believe that existing social institutions are not adequate to meet their needs (Katz & Bender, 1976), and the absence of direct professional involvement in these groups is a common factor (Lieberman & Bond, 1979). Professionals are either not involved at all or used mainly to train indigenous leaders (Rodolfa & Hungersford, 1982). A review of such groups shows that they tend to fall into two types: (a) those that offer conditions for change, information, or support for members, and (b) those whose primary purpose is political activity toward the end of improving the situation of a group of people (Lieberman & Borman, 1979).

Rodolfa and Hungerford (1982) list the important elements of self-help groups as:

1. *Involvement.*   Identification with the new group facilitates acquisition of new behavior patterns.
2. *Interaction.*   Coping with difficulties is facilitated by establishing mutual resources.
3. *Acknowledgement.*   "Prior to self-forgiveness, one must accept responsibility for the action" (p. 348).
4. *Helper therapy.*   Giving help to others is associated with one's own improvement partly because of the high status role of the helper.
5. *Modeling.*   More successful group members provide examples of valued behavior and instill hope.

On the positive side, self-help groups provide training for patients to become active participants in their own treatment/care situations instead of offering the passivity training required all too often by the traditional patient role. Also, participants report achieving a sense of belonging rarely mentioned by members of therapy groups. On the negative side, the freedom from professional control can bring with it vulnerability to exploitation by those who are unscrupulous or who have hidden agendas. Additionally, these groups sometimes enshrine cohesion at the expense of meaningful member change. On the whole, however, many professionals view self-help groups positively, whereas they initially tended to distrust this movement (Levy, 1979).

More information about the participants and about these groups may suggest (a) ways in which conventional group treatment is perceived by those who are dissatisfied with it, (b) the need for changes in public information programs, and possibly (c) new group treatment methods to be included in the conventional armamentarium. As more people enter conventional group therapy with prior or concomitant experience in self-help groups, pressure to alter group norms and procedures will occur. Group leaders need to be prepared for this occurrence and to be able to use the situation to therapeutic advantage by restructuring and sharpening the differences between therapy and self-help groups while at the same time acknowledging the positive aspects of self-help groups.

Earlier we recommended experience in intensive small groups and encounter groups as important to psychotherapy training. For the same reasons we would recommend that students should be exposed to both didactic and observational experiences of self-help groups. They need to know how to evaluate such groups, particularly with respect to their success potential and their leadership style, in order to make responsible referrals (Rodolfa & Hungerford, 1982).

Consultation

Partly because of the potential transfer of clinical skills from the group therapy situation and partly because of the increasing need for general mental health program support and development, more and more psychologists in clinical settings are being asked to engage in the indirect service called *consultation*.

The mental health consultant provides problem-solving, educational, and clinical expertise to individuals and groups within organizations regarding the management or treatment of different cases, review of programs and plans, and program evaluation (Bloom, 1977). Here we can see the potential for considerable benefit and/or confusion. Group therapy training and experience should equip the psychologist with the knowledge and skills to conduct group sessions and the ability and sensitivity to problem-solve interpersonal problems. On the liability side, a naive extension of the "clinical" orientation to the consultation situation can result in difficulties of several kinds. The group therapist is a trained professional who provides insight, behavior change, and emotional reeducation within a group context to individuals who are self-defined as needing psychological assistance or being psychologically uncomfortable. Mental health consultants provide their expertise to people who are psychologically healthy or at least have not defined themselves as psychologically ill. Thus the latter is not a clinical situation, and the client in it has not contracted for "therapy." Consultants should accordingly be careful to avoid intervening on the level of the client's motivations and feelings (Heller & Monohan, 1977). Clearly, special training is necessary to function adequately in this role (Stum, 1982).

In the field of mental health, consultation is referred to as an indirect service; the consultant shares knowledge and skills with programs, agencies, and organizations rather than providing direct service to an individual or a few individuals. Consultation has become a highly valued function in the mental health field (Bloom, 1977), which Caplan (1970) differentiates into the following categories:

1. *Client-centered case consultation.* The consultant is asked to make an expert assessment of the client's problem (treatment or management of a difficult case or cases) and suggest ways to handle the case.

2. *Consultee-centered case consultation.* The consultant involves himself or herself with the difficulties that the consultee is having in working with a patient or patients.

3. *Program-centered administrative consultation.* It is the program itself that is the focus of interest–not the consultee's difficulties with the program.

4. *Consultee-centered administrative consultation.* This type of consultation focuses on the consultee's program-related work—his or her knowledge, attitudes, and so forth.

The activity in which the transfer of group skills is most likely to take place is that of group consultation. In this type of consultation there are meetings of a consultant with a group of consultees. Group consultation has been found in at least one study to be as effective as individual consultation in general and more effective in the area of providing general information and eliciting useful interactions (Tobiessen & Shai, 1971).

The range of care givers and human service provers to whom mental health consultation has been given is broad and includes the police, nurses, school personnel, bartenders, and hairdressers, among others (Mannino & Shore, 1972). Considering the prospects for diminished funding of mental health services during the next several years, it would seem that consultation services to primary care givers, a less costly method of improving mental health services, should increase (Alpert et al., 1981; Medway, 1982). These considerations are elaborated by Cowen in Chapter 12 of the volume.

Additional Special Groups

Therapy has been conducted with numerous other homogeneously composed groups of patients. Of particular interest for further reading are descriptions of group therapy with predelinquents, delinquents, and prison inmates provided in reports by

Arnold and Stiles (1972), Baumgold (1970), Federn (1962), Hersko (1962), Kassoff (1958), McCarty (1972), O'Donnell (1973), Rappaport (1971), and Slaikeu 1973). Also of note are reports of group therapy with marital couples by Cochrane (1973), Gurman 1973), Leichter (1973), Burns (1972), Nadeau (1972), Glendening and Wilson (1972), Hardcastle (1972), Wadeson (1972), Kohn (1971), Lindenauer (1971), and McClellan and Stieper (1971).

In addition, group therapy has been described with the visually impaired elderly (Evans & Jaureguy, 1981; Galler, 1981), gay men (Conlin & Smith, 1982), gender-identity patients (Keller, Althof, & Lothstein, 1982), sexually abused adolescents (Lubell & Soong, 1982), borderline patients (Greenblum & Pinney, 1982), learning-disabled adolescents (Berg & Wages, 1982), anorgasmic patients (Kuriansky, Sharpe, & O'Connor, 1982), mothers who physically abuse and/or seriously neglect their children (Sinclairbrown, 1982), Hispanic female patients (Hardy-Fanta & Montana 1982), parents of adult chronic schizophrenics (Fink, 1981), cases of staff burnout (Forsyth & Cannady, 1981), adult children of alcoholics (Cermak & Brown, 1982), rape victims (Gallese & Treuting, 1981), suicide attempters (Hackel & Asimos, 1981), Vietnam veterans (Walker & Nash, 1981), and drunk drivers (Lane, 1981).

In the use of group therapy with groups of people who have similar special problems of the kinds mentioned in this section, it is well to remember that the act of composing homogeneous groups may influence the group therapist to spotlight the common problem and not attend sufficiently to the patients' individual growth and learning needs. As mentioned earlier, however, emphasizing the shared problems increases the sense of universality (Yalom, 1975), increases group cohesion, and makes the problems more visible. A challenge to the group therapist, then, is to remain aware of and to relate to the full range of intragroup differences while working with the general and unique properties and developments in the homogeneous group.

ISSUES, TRENDS, AND NEEDS

Several issues currently being discussed and debated among group therapists are either explicitly stated or implied in the earlier discussions in the sections on types of group therapy and intensive small-group experiences. Salient among these issues are genetic–historical insight versus learning from interactional feedback, leader centrality, high versus low structure, the therapist's social role, group leader accreditation, and the extension of group therapy services to underinvolved populations.

Genetic–Historical Insight versus Learning from Interactional Feedback

The strong psychoanalytic influence on psychotherapy practice until a decade ago and the relative paucity of empirical studies of what is therapeutic and how learning takes place during group therapy prolonged an overreliance on the importance of genetic–historical insight as a *curative factor* (Winer, 1974). The success of the application of learning theory principles (Lazarus, 1968) and the widespread enthusiasm for the small-group movement (Bradford et al., 1964) during the past decade have reduced the reliance placed on genetic–historical insight in bringing about behavior change. The nature of this issue certainly lends itself to empirical study, however, rather than to conclusions based on belief or enthusiasm, and much group therapy investigative work remains to be done in this regard.

Change toward a more interactive focus in group psychotherapy on what is therapeutic seems to have been influenced primarily by the factors: movement away from a structural and toward an interpersonal emphasis in psychotherapy by such influential neo-Freudian analysts as Horney (1950) and Sullivan (1955), and the growing number of group therapists who have acquired experience as participants in and leaders of brief intensive small groups. These group therapists have been impressed by the apparent impact of behaviorally based feedback on behavior change. Major advantages of interpersonal feedback in a supportive climate as a precursor of change are its immediacy and the fact that the protagonist is given specific behavioral change cues.

In actual practice, most group therapists seem to work in their sessions with both aspects of the patient's past life as it seems relevant in the present and aspects of his or her current interpersonal behavior. They differ of course in the relative emphasis, timing, and prominence they give to these two factors.

Leader Centrality

The theoretical positions of some of the previously presented schools of group therapy have relevance for the degree of centrality of the group therapist's position and for the rate and nature of his or her activity. The psychoanalytic and TA positions are quite clear in emphasizing that the group therapist is one of the central agents in the change process. Those theorists who rely more on "psychotherapy through the group process," however, such as Whitaker and Lieberman (1964), see the therapist as more of a facilitator than a teacher or purveyor of psychological insights.

These considerations are related to the issue of leader structuring versus working with the common group tension (Bion, 1961; Ezriel, 1950; Foulkes, 1965). Obviously, if a therapist seeks to discover common group themes and concerns, he or she is likely to regulate his or her own activity so as to facilitate the emergence of this material. In some cases, this might mean relatively little verbal participation by the group therapist. In other words, then, the degree and type of activity engaged in by the group therapist are likely to be related to his or her theory of *change*, that is, the way in which he or she believes change to occur and what he or she believes the primary agents of change to be.

Those theorists who hold an eclectic view of the nature of the curative factors in group therapy and are willing to acknowledge and work with *nonspecific effects* (Fish, 1973) vary their behavior in terms of their judgment of the needs of individual patients and/or group conditions. A therapist who subscribes to Yalom's (1975, pp. 66–69) previously mentioned list of curative factors, for example, shows considerable variation in his or her behavior both within and across sessions.

The therapist's personality and needs certainly influence his or her choice of style and theory of group therapy (Bach, 1956). The activity–passivity dimension of the group therapist's personality can affect his or her behavior in at least two ways: the general rate of activity and, insofar as there is likely to be correlation between the general trait of activity–passivity and an activity orientation to change situations, the selection of techniques.

In addition to experimentation with the variables of therapist personality and attitude, therapist participation in small, intensive, group experiences has stimulated a great deal of experimentation with format and activities. Cases in point are extending the length of the session (Mintz, 1969), physically touching patients (O'Hearne & Glad, 1968), and using structured experiences (Pfeiffer & Jones, 1969), which are innovations intended to intensify the group experience and shorten the length of the treatment.

High versus Low Structure

How much structure and patient preparation should be provided prior to the beginning of group psychotherapy? Group therapists differ on this issue. Those with a more psychoanalytic orientation seem to believe that patient selection, the admonition to "speak spontaneously," and the obvious role differential of therapist and patient are sufficient to launch and maintain the treatment process. Group therapists with a more active orientation and those who work more in the ego-psychology domain tend to face the therapeutic task as an educational procedure which includes thorough initial orientation (Rabin, 1970), perhaps including viewing a film for induction into the role of a group therapy patient (Logue, Peterson & Miller, 1969; Strupp & Bloxom, 1973), setting of a therapeutic contract (Mallucio & Marlow, 1974), assigning homework and extragroup tasks, periodic review of progress toward patients' personal goals, and so on. The philosophy is more in keeping with a consumer model in which the patient's wishes regarding treatment are given credence (Berne, 1961; Hornstra et al., 1972).

Therapist's Social Role

Another issue on which group therapists differ is one that has current sociopolitical significance—the issue of the adjustment of the individual to society's norms versus the facilitation of individual development even if it means a challenge to social norms. Should the group therapist facilitate the raising to awareness and discussion of racist–sexist–ageist issues or should she or he view these as individual and group resistances when they occur? Or should the group therapist be an advocate of the individual even though the client's behavior challenges social norms? (Fried, 1974; Franks & Vasanti, 1974; Steiner, 1971)

Group Leader Accreditation

As noted previously, professional organizations have been devoting attention to the task of devising standards of practice and standards for the training of practitioners. Specifically, criteria and procedures for accreditation within their own fields have been developed by the American Group Psychotherapy Association (AGPA, 1978), the American Society of Group Psychotherapy and Psychodrama, the Gestalt Institute of Cleveland, and the International Transactional Analysis Association. Certified Consultants International, Inc. was formed in 1971 as a nonprofit professional organization in order to accredit practitioners of group methods deriving from the laboratory training model. Accreditation is based on demonstrated conceptual and behavioral competence and is evaluated by regional peer review panels. Currently, accreditation is available for the following positions: laboratory educator, organization development consultant, and personal growth group consultant (APA Monitor, 1971).

Extension of Group Therapy Services to Underinvolved Populations

In addition to the substantive research needs mentioned earlier, there is an urgent need to develop effective methods for providing group therapy–type services to populations who have been relatively neglected up to now (e.g., children and the aged; see Lubin & Lubin, 1973), who typically are late to apply for such services (Lubin et al., 1973), or who do not continue in programs once they have begun them. The experience of public mental health facilities, including comprehensive community mental health centers, with the dropout problem among patients of lower socioeconomic classes has been distressing (Reissman, Cohen, & Pearl, 1964), and Cobb's (1971) survey of the literature on outpatient services for lower socioeconomic patients at community mental health centers found very few attempts to develop and evaluate novel programs. Exploration of adaptations and modifications to existing programs to make them more suitable for those who typically do not regularly attend therapy programs should receive some impetus from the work of Warren and Rice (1972), who demonstrated that by careful planning and slight modification of the general routine, the therapy attrition of low-prognosis patients can be reduced, their total therapy involvement lengthened, and their general improvement enhanced.

SUMMARY AND CONCLUSIONS

In this concluding section, major points from the preceding pages are presented together with some summary statements. Group therapy is going through an exciting period in its history. A variety of approaches and techniques from parallel-developing intensive small-group field (laboratory training and encounter groups) are being employed by group therapists of various theoretical persuasions. Professional organizations are beginning to turn their attention to such important issues as certifying practitioners and educating the public regarding the effectiveness and limitations of the various group methods. Publication, another index of a field's vitality, shows a consistent increase in the area of group therapy.

What are the curative factors in group therapy? Various ones have been put forward and, not unexpectedly, the factors mentioned are consistent with the individual or group focus of the proponent's theory. Psychoanalytically oriented theories posit patient motivation and therapist analysis of transference and resistance as all-important. For the practitioner of transactional analysis, patient–therapist change contracts and therapist potency, protection, and permission are the crucial factors. The behavior group therapist attempts to diagnose and manage suitable reinforcement contingencies for individual behavior within the group setting. Those theorists who focus on the group see one of the major functions of the group therapist to be guiding the group away from premature anxiety-reducing solutions produced by immediate authority and peer-relationship problems.

The recent research literature indicates an attempt to come to grips with the complexity of the group therapy situation by achieving greater specificity in the manipulation of patient, therapist, group, situational, and outcome variables, and by using multivariate designs. Extrapolating the findings of suitable small-group research to the group therapy field and studying group therapy by means of analog research are two additional methods that have been suggested, and SD and group composition are two substantive areas that have received recent research interest.

The components of many group therapy training programs include a didactic phase plus readings and an apprenticeship arrangement (cotherapy). There is an increasing tendency for training centers also to include an experiental phase for the student group therapist.The use of recordings (videotape and audiotape), diaries kept by trainees, and rating scales to be used for feedback regarding the performance of student group therapists is recommended. In addition, considering the need for group therapists to be knowledgeable about and skilled in influencing group forces, and also to continue their own growth in such areas as authority relationships, feelings of affection, hostile feelings, and the like, it is suggested that the training program include experience in a group process seminar and in an encounter group. In order to supplement a possible pendulum swing in the direction of too much influence from brief intensive group experiences, group therapists should be aware of the need to acquire experience with people who are under considerable stress and the need for experience in working with the same groups over a period of a year or more.

The continued development of group therapy requires freedom for group therapists to try new methods. However, ethical considerations and the continued development of group therapy also require that the *safety* as well as the effectiveness of these newer methods be determined. Despite the exploratory use of various methods by some group therapists, most group therapy is still conducted in a small, circular group within a discussion format. As an education or reeducative technique, patients in group therapy might benefit from experimentation with a wide range of educational formats and electronic aids.

REFERENCES

Abels, P. A. On the nature of supervision: The medium is the group. *Child Welfare*, 1970, **4**, 304–311.

Abramson, H., & Peshkin, M. Psychosomatic group therapy with parents of children with intractable asthma. *Annals of Allergies*, 1960, **19**, 87–91.

Adsett, C. C., & Bruhn, J. G. Short-term group psychotherapy for postmyocardial infarction patients and their wives. *Canadian Medical Association Journal*, 1968, **99**, 577–584.

Akister, J., & Canever, N. A year in the life of an adolescent group. *Journal of Adolescence*, 1980, **3**, 155–163.

Allen, J. G. Implications of research in self-disclosure for group psychotherapy. *International Journal of Group Psychotherapy*, 1973, **23**, 306–321.

Alpert, J. L., Ballantyne, D., & Griffiths, D. Characteristics of consultants and consultees and success in mental health consultation. *Journal of School Psychology*, **19**, 312–322.

American Group Psychotherapy Association. Committee on History. A brief history of the American Group Psychotherapy Association 1943–1968. *International Journal of Group Psychotherapy*, 1971, **21**, 406–435.

American Psychological Association. New professional association formed; Focus: certification and public education. *APA Monitor*, 1971, **2**(11), 7.

Anthony, E. J. Comparison between individual and group psychotherapy. In H. I. Kaplan & B. J. Sadock (Eds.), *The evolution of group therapy*. New York: Aronson, 1972.

Arielli, A. Multicouple group therapy for alcoholics. *International Journal of the Addictions*, 1981, **16**, 737–782.

Arnold, W. R., & Stiles, B. A summary of increasing use of group methods in correctional institutions. *International Journal of Group Psychotherapy*, 1972, **22**, 77–92.

Astrachan, B. M. Towards a social systems model of therapeutic groups. *Archives of General Psychiatry*, 1970, **5**, 110–119.

Bach, G. R. Current trends in group psychotherapy. In D. Brower & L. E. Abt (Eds.), *Progress in clinical psychology* (Vol. II). New York: Grune & Stratton, 1956.

Batchelder, R. L., & Hardy, J. M. *Using sensitivity training and the laboratory method: An organizational case study in the development of human resources*. New York: Association Press, 1968.

Battegay, R., Lipp, H., Miest, V., Glauser, C., & Rauchfleisch, V. Group psychotherapy with obese patients. *Gruppenpsychotherapie & Gruppendynamik*, 1981, **17**, 163–172.

Baumgold, J. Prison notes. *Voices: Art and Science of Psychotherapy*, 1970, **6**, 37–41.

Bednar, R. L., & Kaul, T. J. Experiential group research: Current perspectives. In S. Garfield & A. Berzin (Eds.), *Handbook of psychotherapy and behavior change*. New York: Wiley, 1978.

Bednar, R. L., & Kaul, T. J. Experiential group research: What never happened! *Journal of Applied Behavioral Science*, 1979, **15**, 311–319.

Bednar, R. L., & Moeschl, M. J. Conceptual and methodological considerations in the evaluation of group psychotherapies. In R. McReynolds (Ed.), *Advances in psychological assessment* (Vol. 5). San Francisco, Calif. Jossey-Bass, 1981.

Benne, K. D. History of the T-Group in the laboratory setting. In L. P. Bradford, J. R. Gibb,

& K. D. Benne (Eds.), *T-Group theory and laboratory method: Innovation in re-education*. New York: Wiley, 1964.

Benyehuda, N. Group therapy with methadone-maintenance patients: Structural problems and solutions. *International Journal of Group Psychotherapy*, 1980, **39**, 331–346.

Berger, M. *Videotape techniques in psychiatric training and treatment*. New York: Brunner/Mazel, 1971.

Berger, M. M., & Berger, L. F. Psychogeriatric group approaches. In H. I. Kaplan & B. J. Sadock (Eds.), *Comprehensive group psychotherapy*. Baltimore: Williams & Wilkins, 1971.

Berg, R. C., & Wages, L. Group counseling with the adolescent learning disabled. *Journal of Learning Disabilities*, 1982, **15**, 276–277.

Bergman, A. L., Messersmith, C. E., & Mullens, B. N. Profile of group-therapy practice in university counseling centers. *Journal of Counseling Psychology*, 1972, **19**, 353–354.

Berkovitz, I. H. (Ed.). *Adolescents grow in groups: Clinical experiences in adolescent group psychotherapy*. New York: Brunner/Mazel, 1972.

Berland, D. I., & Poggi, R. Expressive group psychotherapy with the aging. *International Journal of Group Psychotherapy*, 1979, **29**, 87–108.

Berne, E. *Transactional analysis in psychotherapy*. New York: Grove Press, 1961.

Bernstein, N. R., & Tinkham, C. B. Group therapy following abortion. *Journal of Nervous and Mental Disease*, 1971, **152**, 303–314.

Bilodeau, C. B., & Hackett, T. P. Issues raised in a group setting by patients recovering from myocardial infarction. *American Journal of Psychiatry*, 1971, **128**, 105–110.

Binot, E. Group therapy for hospitalized drug addicts: Review of four years of experience. *Toxicomanies*, 1973, **5**, 31–45.

Bion, W. R. *Experiences in groups*. London: Tavistock, 1961.

Black, S. Group therapy for pregnant and nonpregnant adolescents. *Child Welfare*, 1972, **51**, 514–518.

Bloch, S., Crouch, E., & Reibstein, J. Therapeutic factors in group psychotherapy: A review. *Archives of General Psychiatry*, 1982, **27**, 316–324.

Block, E. L., & Goodstein, L. D. Comment on "Influence of an interviewer's disclosure on the self-disclosing behavior of interviewees." *Journal of Counseling Psychology*, 1971, **18**, 595–597.

Bloom, B. L. *Community mental health: A general introduction*. Belmont, Calif. Wadsworth, 1977.

Bodin, A. M. Videotape applications in training family therapists. *Journal of Nervous and Mental Disease*, 1969, **148**, 251–261.

Bramlette, C. A., & Tucker, J. H. Encounter groups: Positive change or deterioration—More data and a partial replication. *Human Relations*, 1981, **34**, 303–314.

Britnell, J. C. & Mitchell, K. E. Inpatient group psychotherapy for the elderly. *Journal of Psychiatric Nursing*, 1981, **19**, 19–24.

Budge, S. Group cohesiveness reexamined. *Group*, 1981, **5**, 10–18.

Burns, C. W. Effectiveness of the basic encounter group in marriage counseling. *Dissertation Abstracts International*, 1972, 1281B.

Burnside, I. M. Loss: A constant theme in group with the aged. *Hospital and Community Psychiatry*, 1970, **21**, 175–177.

Burnside, I. M. Long-term group work with hospitalized aged. *Gerontologist*, 1971, **11**, 213–218.

Byrne, D. Repression-sensitization as a dimension of personality. In B. A. Maher (Ed.), *Progress in experimental personality research*. New York: Academic Press, 1964.

Cabrera, F. J. Group psychotherapy and psychodrama for alcoholic patients in a state hospital rehabilitation program. *Group Psychotherapy*, 1961, **14**, 151–159.

Cadogan, D. A. Marital group therapy in the treatment of alcoholism. *Quarterly Journal of Studies in Alcohol*, 1973, **34**, 1187–1194.

Calahan, S. Personal communication, 1974.

Caplan, G. *The theory and practice of mental health consultation*. New York: Basic Books, 1970.

Casriel, D. *So fair a house: The story of Synanon*. Englewood Cliffs, N.J.: Prentice-Hall, 1964.

Cermak, T. L., & Brown, S. Interactional group therapy with the adult children of alcoholics. *International Journal of Group Psychotherapy*, 1982, **32**, 375–390.

Chafetz, M., & Blane, H. T. Alcohol-crisis treatment approach and establishment of treatment relations with alcoholics. *Psychological Reports*, 1963, **12**, 862.

Chasonoff, E., & Schrader, C. Behaviorally oriented activities therapy program for adolescents. *Adolescence*, 1979, **14**, 567–578.

Cobb, C. W. Community mental health services and the lower socio-economic classes: A summary of research literature on outpatient treatment (1963–1969). *American Journal of Orthopsychiatry*, 1971, **43**, 404–414.

Coche, E., Plikoff, B., & Cooper, J. Participant self-disclosure in group therapy. *Group*, 1980, **4**, 28–35.

Cochrane, N. Some reflections on the unsuccessful treatment of a group of married couples. *British Journal of Psychiatry*, 1973, **123**, 395–401.

Coleman, A. Psychology of a first baby group. *International Journal of Group Psychotherapy*, 1971, **21**, 74–83.

Colson, D. B., & Horwitz, L. Overview of research in group psychotherapy: A clinical perspective. In H. I. Kaplan & B. J. Sadock (Eds.), *Comprehensive overview of group psychotherapy*, Baltimore: Williams & Wilkins, 1982.

Conlin, D., & Smith, J. Group psychotherapy for gay men. *Journal of Homosexuality*, 1982, **7**, 105–112.

Conrad, W. K. A group therapy program with older adults in a high-risk neighborhood setting. *International Journal of Group Psychotherapy*, 1974, **24**, 358.

Corder, B. F., Whiteside, L., & Haizlip, T. M. A study of curative factors in group psychotherapy with adolescents. *International Journal of Group Psychotherapy*, 1981, **31**, 345–354.

Corsini, R. J., & Putzey, L. J. *Bibliography of group psychotherapy 1906–1956*. Psychodrama and Group Psychotherapy Monographs, No. 29. New York: Beacon House, 1957.

Culbert, S. A. The interpersonal process of self-disclosure: It takes two to see one. In R. T. Golembewski & A. Blumberg (Eds.), *Sensitivity training and the laboratory approach*. Itasca, Ill.: Peacock, 1970.

Dana, R. H., & Dana, J. M. Systematic observation of children's behavior in group therapy. *Psychological Reports*, 1969, **24**, 134.

Dies, R. R. Group psychotherapy: Reflections on three decades of research. *Journal of Applied Behavioral Science*, 1979, **15**, 361–373.

Dies, R. R. Current practice in the training of group therapists. *International Journal of Group Psychotherapy*, 1980, **30**, 169–185.

Dietrich, H. Group therapy with children. *Praxis der Kinderpsychologie und Kinderpsychiatrie*, 1982, **31**, 9–14.

Dole, V. P., Nyswander, M., & Warner, A. Successful treatment of 750 criminal addicts. *Journal of the American Medical Association*, 1968, **206**, 2708.

Dusay, J. M., & Steiner, C. Transactional analysis in groups. In H. I. Kaplan & B. J. Sadock (Eds.), *Comprehensive group psychotherapy*. Baltimore: Williams & Wilkins, 1971.

Edwards, S. L. Group work with brain damaged patients. *Hospital and Community Psychiatry*, 1967, **18**, 267–270.

Erickson, R. C. Small group psychotherapy with patients on a short stay ward: An opportunity for innovation. *Hospital and Community Psychiatry*, 1981, **32**, 269–272.

Euster, G. L. A system of groups in institutions for the aged. *Social Casework*, 1971, **52**, 523–529.

Evans, R. L., & Jaureguy, B. M. Group therapy by phone: A cognitive behavioral program for visually impaired elderly. *Social Work in Health Care*, 1981, **7**, 79–90.

Ezriel, H. A psycho-analytic approach to group treatment. *British Journal of Medical Psychology*, 1950, **23**, 59–74.

Farkas, A., & Shwachman, H. Psychological adaptation to chronic illness: A group discussion with cystic fibrosis patients. *American Journal of Orthopsychiatry*, 1973, **43**, 259–260.

Fink, P. The relatives group: Treatment for parents of adult chronic schizophrenics. *International Journal of Group Psychotherapy*, 1981, **31**, 453–468.

Fish, J. M. *Placebo therapy*. San Francisco: Jossey-Bass, 1973.

Flores, P. J. Modification of Yalom's interactional group therapy model as a mode of treatment for alcoholism. *Group*, 1982, **6**, 3–16.

Forsyth, D. M., & Canady, N. J. Preventing and alleviating staff burnout through a group. *Journal of Psychosocial Nursing and Mental Health Services*, 1981, **75**, 35–38.

Fortin, J., & Abse, D. Group psychotherapy with peptic ulcer: A preliminary report. *International Journal of Group Psychotherapy*, 1956, **6**, 383–391.

Foulkes, S. H. *Therapeutic group analysis*. New York: International Universities Press, 1965.

Frank, J. D. *Persuasion and healing: A comparative study of psychotherapy*. Johns Hopkins University Press, 1961.

Franks, V., & Vasanti, B. *Women in therapy: New psychotherapies for changing society*. New York: Brunnel/Mazel, 1974.

Freedman, S. M., & Hurley, J. R. Perceptions of helpfulness and behavior in groups. *Group*, 1980, **4**, 51–58.

Fried, E. Does woman's new self-concept call for new approaches in psychotherapy? *International Journal of Group psychotherapy*, 1974, **24**, 265–272.

Frizzell, M. K. Group therapy for diabetic mental patients. *Hospital and Community Psychiatry*, 1968, **19**, 287–298.

Frust, W. Homogeneous versus heterogeneous groups. In M. Rosenberg & M. Berger (Eds.), *Group psychotherapy and group function*. New York: Basic Books, 1963.

Gaines, T., Jr. Structured activity-discussion group psychotherapy for latency-aged children. *Psychotherapy: Theory, Research & Practice*, 1981, **18**, 537–541.

Galler, E. H. A long-term support group for elderly people with low vision. *Journal of Visual Impairment and Blindness*, 1981, **75**, 173–175.

Gallese, L. E., & Treuting, E. G. Help for rape victims through group therapy. *Journal of Psychosocial Nursing and Mental Health Services*, 1981, **19**, 20–21.

Gartner, A. J., & Riessman, F. *Self-help in the human services*. San Francisco: Jossey-Bass, 1977.

Gibb, J. R. The message from research. In J. W. Pfeiffer & J. E. Jones (Eds.), *The 1974 annual handbook for group facilitators*. La Jolla, Calif.: University Associates, 1974.

Giles, T. R., & McMullin, R. E. *Cognitive-behavior therapy: A restructuring approach*. New York: Grune & Stratton, 1981.

Ginott, H. *Group psychotherapy with children*. New York: McGraw-Hill, 1961.

Glad, D. D., Ferguson, R., Hayne, M., & Glad, V. B. Schizophrenic factor reactions to four group psychotherapy methods. *International Journal of Group Psychotherapy*, 1963, **13**, 196–210.

Glad, D. D., & Glad, V. B. *Interpersonality synopsis*. New York: Libra, 1963.

Glad, D. D., Glad, V. B., & Barnes, R. H. *Operational values in psychotherapy*. New York: Oxford University Press, 1959.

Gladfelter, J. H. Videotape supervision of co-therapists. *Journal of Group Psychoanalysis and Process*, 1970, **2**, 45–46.

Glassman, S. *Group psychotherapy*. Unpublished manuscript, Ft. Logan Mental Health Center, Denver, 1967.

Glatzer, H. T. Analytic supervision in group psychotherapy. *International Journal of Group Psychotherapy*, 1971, **21**, 436–443.

Glendening, S. E., & Wilson, A. J., III. Experiments in group premarital counseling. *Social Casework*, 1972, **53**, 551–562.

Goldberg, C. Simulated situations in group psychotherapy training revisited. *Group*, 1982, **6**, 35–40.

Goldfarb, A. L. Group therapy with the old and aged. In H. I. Kaplan & B. J. Sadock (Eds.) *Group treatment of mental illness*. New York: Dutton, 1972.

Goldner, R., & Kyle, E. A group approach to the cardiac patient. *Social Casework*, 1960, **41**, 346.

Goldstein, A. P., Heller, K., & Sechrest, L. B. *Psychotherapy and the psychology of behavior change*. New York: Wiley, 1966.

Goldstein, A., & Wolpe, J. Behavior therapy in groups. In H. I. Kaplan & B. J. Sadock (Eds.), *New models for group therapy*. New York: Dutton, 1972.

Gonzales, J. L., In Mathmann, C. D., & Doring, R. Co-therapy in a group of lower class psychosomatic patients. *Dynamic Psychiatry*, 1982, **72/73**, 21–33.

Goodstein, L. D., & Reinecker, V. M. Factors affecting self-disclosure: A review of the literature. In B. Maher (Ed.), *Progress in experimental personality research* (Vol. 7). New York: Academic Press, 1974.

Gratton, L., & Rizzo, A. E. Group therapy with young psychotic children. *International Journal of Group Psychotherapy*, 1969, **19**, 63–71.

Greenbaum, H. Group psychotherapy with alcoholics in conjunction with antiabuse treatment. *International Journal of Group Psychotherapy*, 1954, **4**, 30.

Greenblum, D. N., & Pinney, E. L. Some comments on the role of cotherapists in group psychotherapy with borderline patients. *Group*, 1982, **6**, 41–47.

Greene, R. J., & Crowder, D. L. Group therapy with adolescents. *Journal of Contemporary Psychotherapy*, 1972, **5**, 55–61.

Groen, J., & Pelser, H. Experiences with and results of group psychotherapy in patients with bronchial asthma. *Journal of Psychosomatic Research*, 1960, **4**, 191–205.

Grossman, W. K., & Karmiol, E. Group psychotherapy supervision and its effects on resident training. *American Journal of Psychiatry*, 1973, **130**, 920–921.

Grotjahn, M. The analytic group experience in the training of therapists. *Voices: Art and Science of Psychotherapy*, 1970, **5**, 108–109.

Gundlach, R. H. Overview of outcome studies in group psychotherapy. *International Journal of Group Psychotherapy*, 1967, **177**, 196–210.

Gurman, A. S. The effects and effectiveness of marital therapy: A review of outcome research. *Family Process*, 1973, **12**, 145–170.

Gustafson, J. P. The large group meeting in a brief-stay inpatient psychiatry service: Toward the definition of a working model. In L. Wolberg & M. Aronson (Eds.), *Group therapy 1979: An overview*. New York: Stratton Intercontinental Medical Book Co., 1979.

Hackel, J., & Asimos, C. T. Resistances encountered in starting a group therapy program for suicide attempters in varied administrative settings. *Suicide and Life Threatening Behavior*, 1980, **10**, 100–105.

Hardcastle, D. R. Measuring effectiveness in group marital counseling. *Family Coordinator*, 1972, **21**, 213–218.

Hardy–Fanta, C., & Montana, P. The Hispanic female adolescent: A group therapy model. *International Journal of Group Psychotherapy*, 1982, **32**, 351–367.

Harman, R. L. Goals of Gestalt therapy. *Professional Psychology*, 1974, **5**, 178–184.

Harper, J. Embracement and enticement: A therapeutic nursery group for autistic children. *Slow Learning Child*, 1973, **20**, 173–176.

Harris, F. C. The behavioral approach to group therapy. *International Journal of Group Psychotherapy*, 1979, **29**(4), 453–469.

Harris, T. L. Relationship of self-disclosure to several aspects of trust in a group. *Journal of Specialists in Group Work*, 1980, **5**, 24–28.

Harrison, R. L., & Lubin, B. Interpersonal perception and interpersonal behavior in training groups: A study in group composition. *Journal of Applied Behavioral Sciences*, 1965, **1**, 13–16.

Hartocollis, P., & Sheafor, D. Group psychotherapy with alcoholics: A critical review. *Psychiatric Digest*, 1968, **29**, 15–22.

Healy, J. M. *Predicting benefit from a Gestalt therapy marathon workshop*. Unpublished doctoral dissertation, United States International University 1979. *Dissertation Abstracts International*, 1989, **40**, 3782-A.

Heath, E. S., & Bacal, H. A. A method of group psychotherapy at the Tavistock Clinic. In

C. J. Sager & H. S. Kaplan (Eds.), *Progress in group and family therapy.* New York: Brunner/Mazel, 1972.

Hefferman, A. An experiment in group therapy with mothers of diabetic children. *Acta Psychotherapy,* 1959, **7**(Suppl.), 155.

Heisler, V. Dynamic group psychotherapy with parents of cerebral palsied children. *Rehabilitation Literature,* 1972, **35**, 329–330.

Heller, K., & Monohan, J. *Psychology and community change.* Homewood, Ill.; Dorsey, 1977.

Hersko, M. Group therapy with delinquent adolescent girls. *American Journal of Orthopsychiatry,* 1962, **32**, 169–175.

Hollon, T. H. Modified group therapy in the treatment of patients on chronic hemodialysis. *American Journal of Psychotherapy,* 1973, **26**, 501–510.

Holt, H., & Winick, C. Group psychotherapy with obese women. *Archives of General Psychiatry,* 1961, **5**, 156.

Horney, K. *Neurosis and human growth.* New York: Norton, 1950.

Hornstra, R. K., Lubin, B., Lewis, R. V., & Willis, B. S. Worlds apart: Patients and professionals. *Archives of General Psychiatry,* 1972, **27**, 553–557.

Howes, R. J. Encounter groups: Comparisons and ethical considerations. *Psychotherapy, Theory, Research and Practice,* 1981, **18**, 229–239.

Jourard, S. M. *The transparent self: Self-disclosure and well-being.* Princeton, N.J.: Van Nostrand, 1964.

Jourard, S. M., & Friedman, R. Experimenter-subject "distance" and self-disclosure. *Journal of personality and Social Psychology,* 1970, **15**, 278–282.

Jourard, S. M., & Jaffe, P. E. Influence of an interviewer's disclosure on the self-disclosing behavior of interviewees. *Journal of Counseling Psychology,* 1970, **17**, 252–257.

Julian, A., & Kilman, P. R. Group treatment of juvenile delinquents: A review of the outcome literature. *International Journal of Group Psychotherapy,* 1979, **27**, 3–37.

Kadis, A. L. A new group supervisory technique for group therapists. *Voices: The Art and Science of Psychotherapy,* 1971, **7**, 31–32.

Kanas, N., & Barr, M. A. Outpatient alcoholics view group therapy. *Group,* 1982, **6**, 17–20.

Kassoff, A. L. Advantage of multiple therapists in a group of severely acting-out adolescent boys. *International Journal of Group Psychotherapy,* 1958, **8**, 70–75.

Katz, A. H., & Bender, E. I. Self-help groups in western society: History and prospects. *Journal of Applied Behavioral Science,* 1976, **12**, 265–282.

Kaufman, E. A psychiatrist views an addict self-help program. *American Journal of Psychiatry,* 1972, **128**, 846–852.

Keller, A. C. Althof, S. E., & Lothstein, L. M. Group therapy with gender-identity patients—a 4-year study. *American Journal of Psychotherapy,* 1982, **36**, 223–228.

Kelman, H. C. The role of the group in the induction of therapeutic change. *International Journal of Group Psychotherapy,* 1963, **13**, 399–432.

Kelman, H. D., & Parloff, M. B. Interrelations among three criteria of improvement in group therapy: Comfort, effectiveness, and self-awareness. *Journal of Abnormal and Social Psychology,* 1957, **54**, 281–288.

Ketai, R. Peer-observed psychotherapy with institutionalized narcotic addicts. *Archives of General Psychiatry*, 1973, **29**, 51–53.

Kibel, H. D., & Stein, A. The group-as-a-whole approach: An appraisal. *International Journal of Group Psychotherapy*, 1981, **31**, 409–427.

Konopka, G. Knowledge and skill in the group therapist. *American Journal of Orthopsychiatry*, 1949, **19**, 56–60.

Kohn, R. Treatment of married couples in a group. *Group Process*, 1971, **4**, 96–105.

Korb, M. P., & Themus, S. The importance of group process in gestalt therapy. *Journal of Specialists in Group Work*, 1989, **5**, 36–40.

Kotis, J. P. Initial sessions of group counseling with alcoholics and their spouses. *Social Casework*, 1968, **49**, 228–232.

Kraft, I. A. Child and adolescent group psychotherapy. In H. I. Kaplan & B. J. Sadock (Eds.), *Comprehensive group psychotherapy*, Baltimore: Williams & Wilkins, 1971.

Kubler-Ross, E. *On death and dying*. New York: Macmillan, 1969.

Kuriansky, J. B., Sharpe, L., & O'Connor, D. The treatment of anorgasmia: Long-term effectiveness of a short-term behavioral group therapy. *Journal of Sex & Marital Therapy*, 1982, **8**, 29–43.

Kurtz, R. R., & Grummon, D. L. Different approaches to the measurement of therapist empathy and their relationship to therapy outcomes. *Journal of Consulting and Clinical Psychology*, 1972, **39**, 106–115.

Kutash, S. B. Values and dangers in group process experiences. *Group Process*, 1971, **3**, 7–11.

Lakin, M. Some ethical issues in sensitivity training. *American Psychologist*, 1969, **24**, 923–928.

Landau, M. E. Group psychotherapy with deaf retardates. *International Journal of Group Psychotherapy*, 1968, **18**, 345–351.

Lane, J. *Group counseling effectiveness with persons arrested for driving while intoxicated.* Doctoral dissertation, Arizona State University, 1981. *Dissertation Abstracts International*, 1981, 42, 614-A. (University Microfilms No. 8117174)

Lanning, W. L. A study of the relation between group and individual supervision and three relationship measures. *Journal of Counseling Psychology*, 1971, **18**, 401–416.

La Rosa, J. C., Lipsius, S. H., & La Rosa, J. H. Experiences with a combination of group therapy and methadone maintenance in the treatment of heroin addiction. *International Journal of the Addictions*, 1974, **9**, 605.

Lassiter, R. E., & Willett, A. B. Interaction of group therapists in the multidisciplinary team treatment of obesity. *International Journal of Group Psychotherapy*, 1973, **23**, 82–92.

Lazarus, A. A. Behavior therapy in groups. In G. M. Gazda (Ed.), *Basic approaches to group psychotherapy and group counseling*. Springfield, Ill.: Thomas, 1968.

Lazarus, A. A. *Behavior therapy and beyond*. New York: McGraw-Hill, 1971

Leichter, E. Use of group dynamics in the training and supervision of group therapists in a social agency. *International Journal of Group Psychotherapy*, 1963, **13**, 74–79.

Leichter, E. Treatment of married couples groups. *Family Coordinator*, 1973, **22**, 31–42.

Leone, S. D., & Gumaer, J. Group assertiveness training of shy children. *School Counselor*, 1979, **2**, 134–141.

Levitsky, A., & Perls, F. The rules and games of Gestalt therapy. In H. M. Ruitenbeek (Ed.), *Group therapy today: Styles, methods, and techniques.* New York: Atherton Press, 1969.

Levy, L. H. Self-help groups: Types and psychological processes. *Journal of Applied Behavioral Sciences,* 1976, **12,** 310–322.

Lewin, K. Forces behind food habits and methods of change. *Bulletin of the National Research Council,* 1943, **108,** 35–65.

Lewis, P., & McCants, J. Some current issues in group psychotherapy research. *International Journal of Group Psychotherapy,* 1973, **23,** 268–291.

Lichtenstein, L., & Kozberg, S. The development of an outpatient therapy group for severely disturbed adolescents. In P. Olsen (Ed.), *Comprehensive Psychiatry* (Vol. 2). New York: Gordon & Breach, 1981.

Lieberman, M. A., & Bond, G. R. Women's consciousness raising as an alternative to psychotherapy. In M. A. Lieberman & L. D. Borman (Eds.), *Self-help groups for coping with crisis: Origins, members, processes, and impact.* San Francisco: Jossey-Bass, 1979.

Lieberman, M. A., & Borman, L. D. (Eds.). *Self-help groups for coping with crisis: Origins, members, processes, and impact.* San Francisco: Jossey-Bass, 1979.

Lieberman, M. A., & Gourash, N. Evaluating the effects of change groups on the elderly. *International Journal of Group Psychotherapy,* 1979, **29,** 283–304.

Lieberman, M. A., Yalom, I. D., & Miles, M. B. *Encounter groups: First facts.* New York: Basic Books, 1973.

Liederman, P. C., Green, R., & Liederman, B. R. Outpatient group therapy with geriatric patients. *Geriatrics,* 1967, **22,** 148–153.

Linden, M. E. *Geriatrics in the field of group psychotherapy.* New York: International Universities Press, 1956.

Lindenauer, G. G. Marriage education in a group therapy setting. *Journal of Emotional Education,* 1971, **11,** 165–177.

Linn, M. W. Day treatment and psychotropic drugs in the after-care of schizophrenic patients: A veterans administration cooperative study. *Archives of General Psychiatry,* 1979, **36,** 1055–1066.

Lipowski, Z. J. Review of consultation in psychiatry and psychosomatic medicine. III. Theoretical issues. *Psychosomatic Medicine,* 1968, **30,** 395–422.

Lippitt, R., & White, R. K. An experimental study of leadership and group life. In E. E. Maccoby, T. M. Newcomb, & E. E. Hartley (Eds.), *Readings in social psychology.* New York: Holt, 1958.

Lockwood, J. L. Treatment of disturbed children in verbal and experiental group psychotherapy. *International Journal of Group Psychotherapy,* 1981, **31,** 355–366.

Logue, P. E., Peterson, L., & Miller, C. An orientation video tape for psychiatric patients. *Mental Hygiene,* 1969, **53,** 301–302.

Lubell, D., & Soong, W. T. Group therapy wiih sexually abused adolescents. *Canadian Journal of Psychiatry,* 1982, **27,** 311–315.

Lubin, B., & Eddy, W. B. The laboratory training model: Rationale, method, and some thoughts for the future. *International Journal of Group Psychotherapy,* 1970, **20,** 305–339.

Lubin, B., Gardiner, S., & Roth, A. Mood and symptoms during pregnancy. *Psychosomatic Medicine,* 1975, **37,** 136–146.

Lubin, B., Hornstra, R. K., Lewis, R. V., & Bechtel, B. S. Correlates of initial treatment assignment in a community mental health center. *Archives of General Psychiatry,* 1973, **29,** 497–500.

Lubin, B., & Lubin, A. W. *Group psychotherapy: A bibliography of the literature from 1956 through 1964.* East Lansing: Michigan State University Press, 1966.

Lubin, B., & Lubin, A. W. Laboratory training stress compared to college examination stress. *Journal of Applied Behavioral Science,* 1971, **7,** 502–597.

Lubin, B., & Lubin, A. W. The group psychotherapy literature: 1972. *International Journal of Group Psychotherapy,* 1973, **23,** 474–513.

Lubin, B., & Lubin, A. W. *A comprehensive bibliography of the group therapy literature from 1906 through 1980.* New York: International Universities Press. In press.

Lubin, B., Lubin, A. W. & Taylor, A. The group psychotherapy literature: 1978. *International Journal of Group Psychotherapy,* 1979, **29,** 523–576.

Lubin, B., Reddy, W. B., Stansberry, C., & Lubin, A. W. The group psychotherapy literature: 1976. *International Journal of Group Psychotherapy,* 1977, **27,** 521–552.

Lubin, B., Reddy, W. B., Taylor, A., & Lubin, A. W. The group psychotherapy literature: 1977. *International Journal of Group Psychotherapy,* 1978, **28,** 509–555.

Lubin, B., Sargent, C. W., & Lubin, A. W. The group psychotherapy literature: 1971. *International Journal of Group Psychotherapy.* 1972, **22,** 492–529.

Lubin, B., & Slominski, A. A counseling program with adult male cerebral palsied patients. *Cerebral Palsy Review,* 1960, **21,** 3–5.

MacKenzie, K. R., & Dies, R. R. CORE Battery. New York: American Group Psychotherapy Association, 1982.

MacLennan, B. W. Simulated situations in group psychotherapy training. *International Journal of Group Psychotherapy,* 1971, **21,** 330–332.

MacLennan, B. W., & Felsenfeld, N. *Group counseling and psychotherapy with adolescents.* New York: Columbia University Press, 1970.

MacLennan, B. W., & Levy, N. The group psychotherapy literature: 1965. *International Journal of Group Psychotherapy,* 1966, **16,** 233–241.

MacLennan, B. W., & Levy, N. The group psychotherapy literature: 1966. *International Journal of Group Psychotherapy,* 1967, **17,** 387–398.

MacLennan, B. W., & Levy, N. The group psychotherapy literature: 1967. *International Journal of Group Psychotherapy,* 1968, **18,** 393–408.

MacLennan, B. W., & Levy, N. The group psychotherapy literature: 1968. *International Journal of Group Psychotherapy,* 1969, **19,** 382–408.

MacLennan, B. W., & Levy, N. The group psychotherapy literature: 1969. *International Journal of Group Psychotherapy,* 1970, **20,** 280–411.

MacLennan, B. W., & Levy, N. The group psychotherapy literature: 1970. *International Journal of Group Psychotherapy,* 1971, **21,** 345–380.

McCarty, P. T. Effects of sub-professional group counseling with probationers and parolees. *Dissertation Abstracts International,* 1972, 5550A.

McClellan, T. A., & Stieper, D. R. A structured approach to group marriage counseling. *Mental Hygiene,* 1971, **55,** 77–84.

McGee, T. F., & Schuman, B. N. The nature of the co-therapy relationship. *International Journal of Group Psychotherapy,* 1970, **21,** 25–36.

McNiel, J. N., & Verwoerdt, A. Group treatment program combines with work project on geriatric unit of state hospital. *Psychiatric Digest,* 1973, **34,** 11–17.

Mallucio, A. N., & Marlow, W. D. The case for the contract. *Social Work,* 1974, **19,** 28–36.

Manaster, A. Therapy with the "senile" geriatric patient. *International Journal of Group Psychotherapy,* 1972, **22,** 250–257.

Mannino, F. V., & Shore, M. F. Research in mental health consultation. In S. E. Golann & C. Eisdorfer (Ed.), *Handbook of community mental health.* New York: Appleton-Century-Crofts, 1972.

Mascia, A. V., & Teiter, S. R. Group therapy in rehabilitation of severe chronic asthmatic children. *Annals of Children,* 1971, **29,** 223.

Medway, F. J. School consultation research; Past trends and future directions. *Professional Psychology,* 1982, **13,** 422–430.

Meeks, J. E. Structuring the early phase of group psychotherapy with adolescents. *International Journal of Child Psychotherapy,* 1973, **2,** 391–405.

Meichenbaum, D. *Cognitive-behavior modification: An integrative approach.* New York: Plenum, 1977.

Merkin, M. N., & Brusiloff, P. Group therapy with pre-school children. *Family and Child Mental Health Journal,* 1981, **7,** 55–65.

Mintz, E. E. Time-extended marathon groups. In H. M. Ruitenbeek (Ed.), Group therapy today: Styles, methods, and techniques. New York: Atherton Press, 1969.

Mitchell, B. A. An investigation of therapist and patient self-disclosure in an outpatient therapy group. Unpublished doctoral disseratation, Rutgers University, State University of New Jersey, 1980. *Dissertation Abstracts International,* 1980, **41,** 1119-B.

Mone, L. C. *Short-term group psychotherapy with the post-cardiac patients.* Paper presented at the 27th Annual Conference of the American Group Psychotherapy Association, New Orleans, January 1970.

Moreno, L. *Psychodrama: Foundations of psychotherapy* (Vol. II). New York: Beacon House, 1946.

Mosher, L. R., & Keith, S. J. Research on the psychosocial treatment of schizophrenia: A summary report. *American Journal of Psychiatry,* 1979, **136,** 623–631.

Mullan, H., & Rosenbaum, M. *Group psychotherapy.* New York: Free Press, 1962.

Murphy, M. Esalen's where it's at. *Psychology Today,* 1967, **1,** 34–39.

Nadeau, H. G. An examination of some effects of the marital enrichment group. *Dissertation Abstracts International,* 1972, 5453B.

National Training Laboratories Institute. *News and Reports,* 1969, **3**(4), 1.

Nurco, D. N., & Makofsky, A. The self-help movement and narcotic addicts. *American Journal of Drug and Alcohol Abuse,* 1981, **8,** 139–152.

O'Donnell, C. R. Predicting success in a group treatment for delinquent males. *Proceedings of the 81st Annual Convention of the American Psychological Association,* Montreal, 1973, **8,** 951–952.

Oei, P., & Jackson, P. Long-term effects of group and individual social skills training with alcoholics. *Addictive Behavior,* 1980, **5,** 129–136.

O'Hearne, J. J., & Glad, D. D. *The case for interaction.* Paper presented at meetings of the American Group Psychotherapy Association, Chicago, January 1968.

Oradei, D. M., & Waite, N. S. Group psychotherapy with stroke-patients during the immediate recovery phase. *American Journal of Orthopsychiatry,* 1974, **44**, 386–395.

Paley, A. Hypnotherapy in the treatment of alcoholism. *Bulletin of the Menninger Clinic,* 1952, **16**, 14.

Parloff, M. B. Some current issues in group psychotherapy research: Discussion. *International Journal of Group Psychotherapy,* 1973, **23**, 282–288.

Parloff, M. B., & Dies, R. R. Group psychotherapy outcome research 1966–1975. *International Journal of Group Psychotherapy,* 1977, **27**, 281–319.

Parloff, M. B., & Dies, R. R. Group therapy outcome instrument: Guidelines for conducting research. *Small Group Behavior,* 1978, **9**, 243–285.

Penick, S. B. *Group treatment of obesity in a day hospital.* Paper presented at the 27th Annual Conference of the American Group Psychotherapy Association, New Orleans, January 1970.

Perls, F. *The gestalt approach and eye witness to therapy.* Palo Alto, Calif.: Science and Behavior Books, 1973.

Pfeiffer, J. W., & Jones, J. E. (Eds.). *Handbook of structure experiences for human relations training* (Vol. I). La Jolla, Calif.: University Associates, 1969.

Pittman, D. J., & Tate, R. L. A comparison of two treatment programs for alcoholics. *Quarterly Journal of Studies of Alcohol,* 1969, **30**, 388–389.

Powdermaker, F. B., & Frank, J. D. *Group psychotherapy: Studies in methodology of research and therapy.* Cambridge, Mass.: Harvard University Press, 1953.

Preston, F. B. Combines individual joint and group therapy in the treatment of alcoholism. *Mental Hygiene,* 1960, **44**, 522.

Psathas, G. Overview of process studies in group psychotherapy. *International Journal of Group Psychotherapy,* 1967, **17**, 225–235.

Rabin, H. N. Preparing patients for group therapy. *International Journal of Group Psychotherapy,* 1970, **20**, 135–145.

Rachman, A. W. Group psychotherapy in treating the adolescent identity crisis. *International Journal of Child Psychotherapy,* 1972, **1**, 97–119.

Rappaport, R. G. Group therapy in prison. *International Journal of Group Psychotherapy,* 1971, **21**, 489–496.

Raubolt, R. The history and development of adolescent group psychotherapy. Doctoral Dissertation, The Fielding Institute, 1979. *Dissertation Abstracts International,* 1981, **41**, 4275-B.

Reckless, J. B. A behavioral treatment of bronchial asthma in modified group therapy, *Psychosomatics,* 1971, **12**, 168–173.

Reddy, W. B. Interpersonal affection and change in sensitivity training: A composition model. In C. Cooper (Ed.), *Theories of group processes.* New York: Wiley, 1975.

Reddy, W. B., Colson, D. B., & Keys, C. B. The group psychotherapy literature: 1974. *International Journal of Group Psychotherapy,* 1975, **25**, 429–479.

Reddy, W. B., & Lansky, L. M. The group psychotherapy literature: 1973. *International Journal of Group Psychotherapy,* 1974, **24**, 477–517.

Reddy, W. B., & Lippert, K. M. Studies of the processes and dynamics within experiental groups. In P. B. Smith, *Small groups and personal change*. London: Methuen, 1980.

Reed, J. Group therapy with asthmatic patients. *Geriatrics*, 1962, **17**, 823.

Reissman, F., Cohen, J., & Pearl, A. (Eds.), *Mental health of the poor*. New York: Free Press, 1964.

Rhodes, S. L. Short-term groups of latency-age children in a school setting. *International Journal of Group Psychotherapy*, 1973, **23**, 204–216.

Ribner, N. G. Effects of explicit group contract on self-disclosure and group cohesiveness. *Journal of Counseling Psychology*, 1974, **21**, 116–120.

Rioch, M. J. The work of Wilfred Bion on groups. In C. J. Sager & H. S. Kaplan (Eds.), *Progress in group and family therapy*. New York: Brunner/Mazel, 1972.

Rockwell, D. Some observations on "living in." *Psychiatry*, 1971, **34**, 214–233.

Rodolfa, E. R., & Hungerford, L. Self-help groups a referral resource for professional therapists. *Professional Psychology*, 1983, **13**, 345–353.

Rogers, C. R. Interpersonal relations: Year 2000. *Journal of Applied Behavioral Science*, 1968, **4**, 265–280.

Rogers, C., Roback, H., McKee, E., & Calhoun, D. Group psychotherapy with homosexuals: A review. *International Journal of Group Psychotherapy*, 1976, **26**, 3–27.

Rose, S. D. *Treating children in groups*. San Francisco: Jossey-Bass, 1972.

Rosenbaum, M. Group psychotherapy and psychodrama. In B. B. Wolman (Ed.), *Handbook of clinical psychology*. New York: McGraw-Hill, 1965.

Rosenbaum, M., & Berger, M. (Eds.). *Group psychotherapy and group function*. New York: Basic Books, 1963.

Ross, W. F., McReynolds, W. T., & Berzins, J. I. Effectiveness of marathon group psychotherapy with hospitalized female narcotic addicts. *Psychological Reports*, 1974, **34**, 611–616.

Sadock, B. J., & Kaplan, H. I. Training and standards in group psychotherapy. In B. J. Sadock & H. I. Kaplan (Eds.), *Comprehensive group psychotherapy*. Baltimore: Williams & Wilkins, 1971.

Sarlin, M. B., & Altshuler, K. Z. Group psychotherapy with deaf adolescents in a school setting. *International Journal of Group Psychotherapy*, 1968, **18**, 337–344.

Saul, S. R., & Saul, S. Group psychotherapy in a propietary nursing home. *Gerontologist*, 1974, **14**, 446–450.

Scheidlinger, S. The relationship of group therapy to other group influence attempts. *Mental Hygiene*, 1955, **39**, 367–390.

Schein, E. H., & Bennis, W. G. *Personal and organizational change through group methods: The laboratory approach*. New York: Wiley, 1965.

Schutz, W. C. *FIRO-B: A three dimensional theory of interpersonal behavior*. New York: Holt, Rinehart & Winston, 1958.

Schutz, W. C. Not encounter and certainly not facts: A review of "Encounter groups: First facts" by Lieberman, M. A., Yalom, I. D., & Miles, M. B. in J. W. Pfeiffer & J. E. Jones (Eds.), *The 1974 annual handbook for group facilitators*, San Diego, Calif.: University Associates, 1974.

Schwartz, B. D. An eclectic group therapy course for graduate students in professional psychology. *Psychotherapy: Theory, Research and Practice*, 1981, **18**, 417–423.

Silver, R. J., Lubin, B., Miller, D. R., & Dobson, N. H. The group psychotherapy literature: 1980. *International Journal of Group Psychotherapy,* 1981, **31,** 469–526.

Silver, R. J., Lubin, B., Silver, D. S., & Dobson, N. H. The group psychotherapy literature: 1979. *International Journal of Group Psychotherapy,* 1980, **30,** 491–538.

Silver, R. J., Miller, D. R., Lubin, B., & Dobson, N. H. The group psychotherapy literature: 1981. *International Journal of Group Psychotherapy,* 1982, **32,** 481–554.

Silverstein, H. Group therapists' attitudes toward cotherapy and intimacy. Unpublished doctoral dissertation, Temple University, 1981. *Dissertation Abstracts International,* 1981, **42,** 1966-A. (University Microfilms No. 8124586.)

Sinclair-Brown, W. A TA redecision group therapy treatment program for mothers who physically abuse and/or seriously neglect their children. *Transactional Analysis Journal,* 1982, **12,** 39–45.

Skolnick, N. J. Personality change in drug abusers: A comparison of therapeutic community and prison groups. *Journal of Consulting and Clinical Psychology,* 1979, **47,** 768–770.

Simonson, N. R., & Bahr, S. Self-disclosure by the professional and paraprofessional therapist. *Journal of Consulting and Clinical Psychology,* 1974, **42,** 359–363.

Slaikeu, K. A. Evaluation studies on group treatment of juvenile and group offenders in correctional institutions. A review of the literature. *Journal of Research in Crime and Delinquency,* 1973, **10,** 87–100.

Slavson, S. R. Qualification and training of group therapists. *Mental Hygiene,* 1947, **31,** 386–396.

Slavson, S. R. *A textbook in analytic group psychotherapy.* New York: International Universities Press, 1964.

Slawson, P. F. Group psychotherapy with obese women. *Psychosomatics,* 1965, **6,** 206–209.

Smith, C. G. Alcoholics: Their treatment and their wives. *British Journal of Psychiatry,* 1969, **115,** 1039–1042.

Snow, D. L., & Held, M. L. Group psychotherapy with obese adolescent females. *Adolescence,* 1973, **8,** 407–414.

Spaulding, D. L., Jr. Empathy, degree of client's verbal participation, and client self-disclosure in group therapy. Unpublished doctoral dissertation, 1980. *Dissertation Abstracts International,* 1980, **40,** 3425-B.

Spotnitz, H. Constructive emotional interchange in adolescence. In C. J. Sager & H. S. Kaplan (Eds.), *Progress in group and family therapy.* New York: Brunner/Mazel, 1972. (a)

Spotnitz, H. Comparison of different types of group psychotherapy. In H. I. Kaplan & B. J. Sadock (Eds.), *The evaluation of group therapy.* New York: Aronson, 1972. (b)

Stein, A. The training of the group psychotherapist. In N. Rosenbaum & M. Berger (Eds.), *Group psychotherapy and group function.* New York: Basic Books, 1963.

Steiner, C. *Games alcoholics play.* New York: Grove, 1971.

Stinson, M. Group communication for the deaf. *Journal of Rehabilitation,* 1971, **37,** 42–44.

Stollak, G. E., Guerney, B. G., Jr., & Rothberg, M. *Psychotherapy research: Selected readings.* Chicago: Rand-McNally, 1966.

Stoller, F. H. Marathon groups: Toward a conceptual model. In L. N. Solomon & B. Berson (Eds.), *New perspectives on encounter groups.* San Francisco, Jossey-Bass, 1972.

Strassburger, F. Ethical guidelines for encounter groups. *APA Monitor,* 1971, **2**(7), 3, 32.

Strupp, H. H., & Bloxom, A. L. Preparing lower-class patients for group psychotherapy: Development and evaluation of a role-induction film. *Journal of Consulting and Clinical Psychology,* 1973, **41**, 373–384.

Stum, D. L. DIRECT: A consultation skills training model. *Personnel and Guidance Journal,* 1982, **60**, 296–301.

Sullivan, H. S. *Conceptions of modern psychiatry.* London: Tavistock, 1955.

Szafranski, L. M. Using patient co-leaders in group sessions. *Aging,* 1981, Nos. 321–322, 21–24.

Szekely, B. C., Kosanovich, N. N., & Sheppard, W. Adjunctive treatment in Parkinson's disease: Physical therapy and comprehensive group therapy. *Rehabilitation Literature,* 1982, **43**, 72–76.

Titchener, J. L., Sheldon, M. B., & Ross, W. D. Changes in blood pressure of hypertensive patients with and without group psychotherapy. *Journal of Psychosomatic Research,* 1959, **4**, 10–12.

Tobiessen, J., & Shai, A. A comparison of individual and group mental health consultation with teachers. *Community Mental Health Journal,* 1971, **7**, 218–226.

Todd, R. I am nobody—Who are you? *The Atlantic Monthly,* 1973, **232**, No. 5, 108–114.

Tracy, G. S., & Gussow, Z. Self-help groups: A grass-roots response to a need for services. *Journal of Applied Behavioral Science,* 1976, **12**, 381–396.

Truax, C. B. Perceived therapeutic conditions and client outcome. *Comparative Group Studies,* 1971, **2**, 301–310.

Vannicelli, M. Group psychotherapy with alcoholics: Special techniques. *Journal of Studies on Alcohol,* 1982, **43**, 17–37.

Wadeson, H. Conjoint marital art therapy techniques. *Psychiatry,* 1972, **35**, 89–98.

Walker, J. I., & Nash, J. L. Group therapy in the treatment of Vietnam combat veterans. *International Journal of Group Psychotherapy,* 1981, **31**, 379–389.

Warren, N. C., & Rice, L. N. Structuring and stabilizing of psychotherapy for low-prognosis clients. *Journal of Consulting and Clinical Psychology,* 1972, **39**, 173–181.

Weiner, H. B. An overview of the use of psychodrama and group psychotherapy in the treatment of alcoholism in the United States and abroad. *Group Psychotherapy,* 1966, **19**, 159–165.

Weschler, I., Massarik, F., & Tannenbaum, R. The self in process: A sensitivity training emphasis. In I. Weschler & E. Schein (Eds.), *Issues in human relations training* (Selected Readings Series, No. 5). Washington, D.C.: National Training Laboratories, 1962.

Westfield, D. R. Two year's experience of group methods in the treatment of male alcoholics in a Scottish mental hospital. *British Journal of Addiction,* 1972, **67**, 267–276.

Westman, J. C., Kansky, E. W., Erikson, M. E., Arthur, B., & Vroom, A. L. Parallel group psychotherapy with the parents of emotionally disturbed children. *International Journal of Group Psychotherapy,* 1963, **13**, 52.

Whally, M., & Strehl, C. Evaluation of the three year group therapy program for multiple sclerosis patients. *International Journal of Group Psychotherapy,* 1969, **13**, 328–353.

Whitaker, D. S., & Lieberman, M. A. *Psychotherapy through the group process.* New York: Atherton Press, 1964.

Willett, E. A. Group therapy in a methadone treatment program: An evaluation of changes in interpersonal behavior. *International Journal of Addiction,* 1973, **8,** 33–39.

Winer, M. F. Genetic versus interpersonal insight. *International Journal of Group Psychotherapy,* 1974, **24,** 230–237.

Winthrop, H. Abuses of sensitivity training on the American campus. *Bulletin of the Menninger Clinic,* 1971, **35,** 28–41.

Wise, T. N., Cooper, J. N., & Ahmed, S. The efficacy of group therapy for patients with irritable bowel syndrome. *Psychosomatics,* 1982, **23,** 465–474.

Witenberg, M. J., & Bruseloff, P. A therapeutic nursery group in a day care center. *International Journal of Child Psychiatry,* 1972, **1,** 7–16.

Wohl, T. H. The role of group psychotherapy for mothers in a rehabilitative approach to juvenile interactable asthma. *Mental Hygiene,* 1963, **47,** 151.

Wohl, T. H. The group approach to the asthmatic child and family. *Journal of Asthma Research,* 1967, **4,** 237.

Wolf, A. Psychoanalysis in groups. In G. M. Gazda (Ed.), *Basic approaches to group psychotherapy and group counseling.* Springfield, Ill.: Thomas, 1968.

Wolff, K. Group psychotherapy with geriatric patients in a psychiatric hospital: Six year study. *Journal of the American Geriatric Society,* 1962, **10,** 1077–1080.

Wolfgang, A., & Pierson, D. The relationship of group research and current practices in group counseling and therapy in metro Toronto. *Canadian Counselor,* 1977, **11,** 185–191.

Wood, D., Del Nuovo, A., Bucky, S. F., Schein, S. F., & Michalik, M. Psychodrama with an alcohol abuser population. *U.S. Navy Medicine,* 1981, **72,** 22–30.

Woods. T. L. A group method of engaging parents at a child psychiatry clinic. *Child Welfare,* 1974, **53,** 394–401.

Wysor, B. Encounter games: A dangerous new trend. *Harpers Bazaar,* 1971, **104,** 60–61.

Yalom, I. D. *The theory and practice of group psychotherapy.* New York: Basic Books, 1970.

Yourself as others see you. *Business Week,* March 16, 1963, p. 160.

CHAPTER 9

Family Therapy

RONALD E. FOX

Family therapy is a method of psychological treatment aimed at improving the functioning of the family as a system through appraisal of the family unit and through intervention calculated to bring about changes in the family's interpersonal relationships. This chapter traces the development of family therapy, discusses family assessment methods, and reviews selected current theories and techniques of family intervention. The chapter concludes with consideration of family therapy outcome studies, ethical issues peculiar to this treatment method, and approaches to training.

THE DEVELOPMENT OF FAMILY THERAPY

The development of family therapy, both as a method for alleviating emotional distress and as a conceptual tool for understanding emotional disturbances, is a relatively recent phenomenon, dating only to the 1950s. In less than three decades, the field has experienced remarkable growth. Currently there are almost two dozen English and foreign-language journals devoted primarily to family therapy. Membership in the American Association for Marriage and Family Therapy (one of two major national family therapy associations) grew from 1973 members in 1970 to 7565 in 1979. There are now over 300 free-standing family institutes in the United States (Gurman and Kniskern, 1981).

Of the multiple historical and social forces that gave rise to the idea of studying and treating families instead of individuals, only a few general trends can be mentioned: increasing sophistication in the conceptualization of individual psychotherapy, the child guidance movement of the 1930s and 1940s, the emergence of group therapy, the emergence of marriage counseling as a profession, intensified research efforts to understand intractable clinical problems such as schizophrenia, and serendipitous influences. Several of these factors also have been mentioned in excellent reviews by Haley (1971), Broderick and Schrader (1981), and Brodkin (1980).

To elaborate, *individual psychotherapy* in the early 1950s was heavily dominated by psychoanalytic theories and techniques. The primary emphasis was on the individual patient's symptoms, and therapeutic efforts were directed primarily at helping the patient achieve insight into unconscious defenses and motivations. In achieving such insight, much time was spent in helping the patient to understand that many current methods of relating to others (including the therapist) are repetitions of patterns that had been established in the patient's family of origin. What was important was not so much what the patient's family had actually been like, but rather, how the patient had perceived them. The basic idea was that the patient as a child had been involved in an interpersonal field (family) that had led to the development of a mental disturbance. Actual therapeutic contact with the patient's family was discouraged out of fear that the patient–therapist transference relationship would be disrupted.

Over time, however, it became increasingly evident that the patient's current family, as well as the family of origin, was an important mediating factor in the success of the analytic undertaking. Family members seemed able to potentiate or to prevent efforts of the patient to change even after very thorough analysis. It was also commonly observed that individual patients often made dramatic changes following major shifts in the structure of the family, and these changes frequently could not be linked to the results of individual psychotherapy. The need for rapid treatment of psychiatric casualties during World War II had also helped clinicians to see that an understanding of each person's milieu, as well as internal conflicts, was essential in quickly restoring individuals to optimal functioning. It was considerations such as these, as well as the desire to prevent the occurrence of later problems in the children of identified patients, that led one psychoanalyst, Nathan Ackerman (1958), to establish the first Family Mental Health Clinic in the United States and thus extend the scope of therapeutic interventions.

Other psychotherapists were heavily influenced by clinicians such as Sullivan, Fromm, Erikson, and Horney who emphasized the interpersonal nature of neurotic behaviors. Sullivan regarded interpersonal pressures and the need to respond to, control, and mediate their effects, rather than intrapsychic conflict, as being the most crucial for an understanding of emotional disturbances. From this viewpoint it was but a short conceptual step to the study and treatment of the family unit. Neurosis was no longer something that resided within the individual like a germ or infection; it was also a part of an interpersonal process and therefore involved forces outside of the patient as well. Several of the early innovators in family therapy were heavily influenced by Sullivan, Don Jackson being a prominent example.

The *child guidance movement* in this country was a major phenomenon in the mental health field in the 1930s and 1940s. As increasing attention was paid to the emotional problems of children, the influence of parents in the etiology and amelioration of these problems became evident. At first it was primarily the mother who was the focus of attention, partly because of her greater availability and partly because of the assumed importance of the early mother–child relationship in a child's subsequent emotional development. Gradually it was discovered that the father also had a significant effect on the child's development. When it was observed repeatedly that parents often seemed to involve their children in their own emotional problems, that they often resisted what clinicians felt were normal growth changes in the child, and that they frequently removed the child from treatment just when the therapist felt that real progress was underway, clinics began to involve the parents in the treatment process. Although this step initially was taken more to help the parents understand their child (and not interfere with the treatment) than to help the parents themselves, it was no longer being denied that patients have families. The typical treatment format was for a therapist to work with the child (the primary patient) and for a social worker to interview the parent(s). As information and experience accumulated, it became obvious that each person in the system contributed to the problem. To assign each of these people an individual therapist proved so costly that sooner or later the idea that one therapist could work with the whole family together was bound to come up.

The emergence of *marriage counseling* as a profession in some ways parallels the development of the family therapy movement and is an offshoot of it. In other ways it is an independent field of endeavor with its own historical roots. In any event, the cross-fertilization between family therapy and marriage counseling has been evident. A prominent example, to cite just one of many, involves the role of sexuality in family and marital life. Marriage counselors were among the first to point out the damaging effects on marriages of misconceptions about sex and to cite the need for better understanding of normal sexual behavior patterns. Some of the techniques they developed for treating sexual difficulties later were utilized by family therapists. Conversely, family therapists' findings concerning the importance of family interaction styles in understanding how individual problems were developed and maintained were taken over by marriage counselors. Masters and Johnson (1970), Kaplan (1974), and Vincent (1973) provide excellent examples of the blending of sexual counseling and family therapy techniques. As marriage counselors accumulated experience with couples, the contribution of marital problems to the development of individual symptoms and vice versa became obvious. Thus an understanding of the entire family unit became increasingly important. Broderick and Schrader (1981) should be consulted for a detailed history of the marriage counseling profession.

Group therapy as a method of intervention gained in popularity during and after World War II as the demand for mental health services rapidly outstripped society's ability to produce practitioners. By its emphasis on the significance of the peer group and the interpersonal milieu, this movement helped create the *Zeitgeist* that gave rise to family therapy. In the 1940s and 1950s there were several reports of group therapy with schizophrenic patients and their parents (see Ross, 1948, for an early example). The superficial similarities between group and family therapy seem to be obvious. Yet there are also important differences between the two approaches, as noted by Handlon and Perloff (1962).

Although group therapy may not be a generic form of treatment of which family therapy is a specific class, the willingness to look at the phenomena of groups in clinical settings helped create an atmosphere in which the idea of family treatment was likely to emerge. In addition, as clinicians became more familiar with the idea of meeting with several patients simultaneously, reluctance about meeting with the whole family was easier to overcome. This latter point should not be underemphasized, as anyone familiar with the fervor with which the sanctity, inviolability, and absolute necessity of an exclusive therapist–patient relationship were once defended can attest. Brodey (1963) poetically described another source of such reluctance: "Why has family therapy been/avoided/in the past?/Remember it's man's first institution/ . . . It's too damn close/to home!"

Efforts to understand and resolve perplexing clinical problems such as schizophrenia also led many investigators to the utilization of family assessment and treatment techniques. The most influential studies in this area were conducted by several investigators who worked with limited knowledge of each other but who came to similar conclusions regarding the importance of understanding the schizophrenic's family in order fully to understand the schizophrenic process. Each of these efforts had its own historical antecedents, which have been adequately summarized elsewhere (Zuk & Rubinstein, 1965). Their historical progression is described by Haley (1959b): "A transition would seem to have taken place in the study of schizophrenia; from the early idea that the difficulty in these families was caused by a schizophrenic member, to the idea that they contained a pathogenic mother, to the discovery that the father was inadequate, to the current emphasis upon all three family members involved in a pathological system of interaction."

One of the research teams whose conceptualizations, theories, and treatment techniques have enjoyed widespread popularity comprises the Palo Alto Group: Gregory Bateson, Don Jackson, Jay Haley, and, later, Virginia Satir, and others. Since this group began their investigations with an interest in communication, it is perhaps not too surprising that the theory of schizophrenia they developed placed primary emphasis on the causal nature of family patterns of communication. Despite its possibly limited focus, their *double-bind* theory of schizophrenia (Bateson et al., 1956) has proved highly useful in stimulating subsequent research, theoretical developments, and treatment approaches.

Another research team, headed by Theodore Lidz, began by studying the intrafamilial environment of 14 families with a schizophrenic member. They came to view the primary etiological factor as a pathological marital relationship. In such families the marriage partners fail to meet each other's emotional needs, which paves the way for one parent or the other to form a pathological alliance with the child (Lidz et al., 1957a, 1957b).

Murray Bowen (1959, 1960) began some other studies of schizophrenia by focusing on female patients and their mothers. After failing in his efforts to affect the schizophrenic process significantly by working with such dyads, he arranged for several schizophrenic patients and their parents to live in a hospital ward for periods of up to 2½ years. The direct observations of these whole families led to the clearcut finding that the entire unit was in serious turmoil. Like Lidz, Bowen came to view a pathological marital relationship in parents of schizophrenics as an important etiological factor, but he used different terms to characterize the observed types of marital disharmonies.

Lyman Wynne and his colleagues (Wynne et al., 1958; studied the families of hospitalized schizophrenics through the use of concurrent interviews. They concluded that pathological relationships in the family unit were the major causative factors in schizophrenia. Unlike the Bateson group, which focused primarily on disturbed communication patterns, Wynne's emphasis was more "broad-gauged" and made use of psychoanalytic concepts such as identification and internalization: "The fragmentation of experience, the identity diffusion, the disturbed modes of perception and communication, and certain other characteristics of the acute reactive schizophrenic's structure are to a significant extent derived, by process of internalization, from characteristics of the family social organization".

The theories of these investigators have been the subject of several critical reviews (Zuk & Rubenstein 1965; Mishler & Waxler, 1966; Beels & Ferber, 1969). It is clear that, as in the story of the blind men describing an elephant from what each can discern by touching, each theorist seems to be holding a different animal. But, in spite of differences in descriptive terms, in assumptions about schizophrenia, in relative emphasis on communication or affective tone, and in the importance attached to social roles or to personality dynamics, there are common themes in this work: (a) The parents of schizophrenics are seen as immature people, anxious and conflicted, who tend to use primitive mechanisms of defense; (b) marital relationships are unsatisfactory; (c) family roles are rigid; (d) ways of meeting each other's needs are disturbed; (e) there is chronic family disequilibrium; (f) the child who became schizophrenic was typically weak, sick, or in need of special care to begin with; and (g) the process is transactional in nature. That is, the pathological influence is no longer viewed as a unidirectional one with the schizophrenic as an innocent victim. Instead, the child and the parents are seen as engaging in a reciprocal process in which each is both acting on and being acted on by others (Mishler & Waxler, 1966).

The implications of the above observations went beyond the original aim of understanding schizophrenia. First, schizophrenic pathology (and, by implication, other pathological states) was found to occur in a context of intense family relationships that enhanced, maintained, and gave rise to symptomatic behavior in one or more members and subclinical symptoms in others. Improvement in one often led to disruption of equilibrium in another, which led to resistance by the entire unit. Second, the unit of study and intervention in schizophrenia (and probably other syndromes) had to be extended beyond the identified patient. Third, in families, as in chemistry, the whole is greater than the sum of the parts. Pathology in interaction can be discovered (or changed) only by observing interaction directly. Transactions cannot be reconstructed on the basis of the individual dynamics of the several family members. Fourth, more complex models of causation are called for than was previously believed. Schizophrenia is not caused by a schizophrenogenic mother or a passive father, but by the nature of the parents' relationship with each other, which in turn is a result of the relationship each had with his or her parents. This leads to a three-generation model of schizophrenia that may apply to other syndromes as well. Fifth, the concept of the schizophrenic as a passive victim was altered. Far from being helpless, schizophrenic persons when observed with their families were seen to be enormously powerful in controlling their destinies. There appeared to be some compliance on the patient's part to fit into a particular family role and thus obtain certain rewards. "The patient may believe, consciously or unconsciously, that no other role in life could give him equal satisfaction" (Zuk & Rubinsteiin, 1965).

Serendipity also played a prominent role in the development of family therapy.

Bateson, Bowen, Lidz, and others began their studies in an effort to learn more about schizophrenia. In the process they learned a great deal about families, saw new possibilities for the understanding of psychopathology, and developed new treatment approaches. Bell (1961) gives an amusing account of how he "accidentally" began doing family therapy. During a visit to the Tavistock Clinic in London, Bell was told that one of the psychiatrists at the clinic was having the whole family of the patient come in for treatment. The conversation was interrupted before Bell could pursue the matter further. When he returned to the United States he was sufficiently intrigued by what he had heard to begin treating some family units in his own practice. He became an influential figure in supporting and encouraging other early family therapists in the United States. It was not until several years after the visit to England mentioned above that Bell discovered that he had misunderstood what his British colleague had meant by having the whole family of the patient come in. What had been meant was that collateral sessions would be held with other family members while the primary patient was in individual psychotherapy, supplemented by an occasional session with the entire family. This was an old model of treatment in the United States, particularly in child guidance clinics; Bell had incorrectly assumed that his English colleague was talking about something different. Perhaps it is not too speculative to say that Bell was operating in a social–professional–intellectual climate in which a different way of thinking could take root and flourish. In the 1950s family therapy was an idea whose time had come, and widely scattered clinicians suddenly "discovered" that patients had fathers, siblings, and grandparents, as well as mothers!

Since the family approach developed from the work of several investigators with different backgrounds and different intellectual predecessors, the field has always shown a healthy diversity. In family therapy there is little in the way of orthodoxy either to provide security for the neophyte or to limit experimentation. Even in what to call this approach there is diversity. The terms used may be descriptive of a specialized form of family therapy, for instance, *multiple-impact family therapy* (Macgregor et al., 1964), but this is not always the case. *Conjoint family therapy* (a term first used by Jackson, 1959) refers to joint interviews of members of the family and the identified patient. *Family group therapy* sometimes refers to joint interviews with several families together (also called *multiple family therapy* by Laquer et al., 1964), while at other times it is simply another name for what Jackson calls *conjoint family therapy* (Grosser & Paul, 1964). *Experimental family therapy* is used by Kempler (1965) to emphasize the here-and-now nature of his approach, whereas *psychoanalytic family therapy* refers to the theoretical orientation of the therapist (Grotjahn, 1965).

Diversity also exists in deciding which members of a family should be seen in order to call the effort *family therapy*. Satir (1965) states flatly that "treating the family as a unit means having all family members present at the same time in the same place with a single therapist or with male and female cotherapists." Wynne (1971) draws the distinction between family therapy as an orientation and family therapy as a method of treatment. In the former a therapist may see only one member of a family at a time while giving special attention to the family system and thus treating the system indirectly. Wynne prefers to reserve the term *family therapy* for "the special circumstance when two or more family members actually meet together (conjointly) with the therapist." Others are more flexible on this point. According to Jackson (1961), "Any combination of the basic group's members may be seen as outside necessity . . . dictates, or if the therapist feels it technically wise. We used to be fairly rigid about meeting only if all members could be present. Now, although the general emphasis remains on the whole group, there is variation on this among our several therapists."

Bowen (1966) goes even further. After assessing the family system, he may work exclusively with one family member who is helped to make changes that will then force complementary changes in other members of the family group. From his orientation "a theoretical system that 'thinks' in terms of family and works toward improving the family system *is* family psychotherapy."

My own viewpoint is closer to Bowen's than Satir's. If the family is functioning as an integrated transactional system, and if the therapist understands that system, then changes may be effected in the system by facilitating change in any of its component parts. Practically speaking, some persons are more capable of change than others. In my own work, I try to determine which person(s) is capable of change and which of the possible changes if likely to be most beneficial and least harmful to the family as a whole. Once this is determined, I proceed. With Bowen, I agree that the more family members there are who are willing and able to change, the greater the likelihood of a positive outcome and the shorter the treatment is likely to be. Beels and Ferber (1969) summarized current opinions on this topic as follows: "Family therapy's attention is devoted towards a family group, but the whole group does not need to be present at any one time. The *interest* and *allegiance* of the therapist is towards the whole family, and this interest and allegiance defines family therapy, not the number of people in the room."

Besides differences on the choice of preferred labels for family therapy and degrees of flexibility with respect to which members are seen when, experts also differ on several other variables, including (a) the extent of their reliance on psychoanalytic concepts, (b) their conceptualization of pathology (e.g., disturbed communication vs. shared unconscious fantasies), (c) their goals (e.g., changing how people communicate vs. increasing insight), and (d) the implications they assign to the family therapy approach (e.g., simply another therapeutic technique vs. "a new orientation to the human condition" (Framo, 1973). As Nathan Ackerman (1972), one of the founding fathers of the family therapy movement, once observed, there are "almost as many forms of family treatment as there are therapists."

In spite of differences among themselves, family therapists have succeeded in calling attention to the functioning of the family as a biosocial unit in relation to mental health. The impact and full implications of these efforts have only begun to be appreciated. Many would agree with Framo's (1973) assertion that "the view that craziness or odd behavior is an adaptive and socially intelligible response to a disordered or crazy context has a significance as momentous as the shift from demonological thinking several centuries ago." For a fascinating review of the growth and development of the family therapy movement from a sociological perspective, the interested reader should consult Brodsky (1980).

In subsequent sections the discussion turns to methods of evaluating families, to techniques for corrective intervention, and then to the assessment of results. The final two sections are devoted to training and ethical issues.

ASSESSMENT OF FAMILIES

In this section major trends in family assessment, illustrative examples of promising approaches, and difficulties inherent in the family approach to assessment are covered. For a more complete cataloging and evaluation of family assessment techniques, the reader is referred to excellent reviews by Bodin (1968) and Straus and Brown (1978).

In determining the utility of the various family assessment techniques, it is important to bear in mind the associated conceptual and procedural problems. Bodin (1968) points out, "The majority of our present techniques focus, either explicitly or implicitly, on *traits* as inherent characteristics of and in individuals. A new view is emerging, however, that gives increased emphasis to the social learning context in which maladaptive behaviors are instigated and maintained as inappropriate response patterns."

This "new view" requires not only different assessment instruments, but new conceptualizations as well. In traditional assessment the focus is on the individual, whereas in family assessment the focus is on the interaction patterns of family systems. Observed intellectual and personality characteristics may change dramatically from individual to family settings when members are tested (Wechsler, Rorschach, TAT) both individually and jointly (Roman & Bauman, 1960). Since the family group is a unique entity, group methods of assessment are needed to understand it.

One difficulty in devising appropriate assessment techniques can be traced to the number of competing theories of family pathology. Each theory demands different techniques to assess different variables that are presumed to be important. Bodin's (1968) observation of the situation is as accurate today as it was 15 years ago:

> Enthusiasts for both intra- and inter-personal points of view sometimes abandon their scientific objectivity and engage in polemics about which of their special vocabularies is the "right" one to reflect "reality" accurately. Those who prefer to focus on the family are still handicapped in such disputes by the fact that there are not yet very many terms that are specifically suited to describing what goes on between individuals in a social system.

In this context, it is impossible to conceive of a single assessment technique, or even a manageable battery, that could hope to achieve widespread acceptance among adherents to diverse theoretical persuasions.

Another major difficulty lies in the fact that the very act of assessment can change the object of assessment. Family members interacting under the watchful eye of an expert or via contrived communication modalities or in an unfamiliar setting may not interact at all as they do with only each other to observe and with no restrictions on modes of communicating. Whether the differences are significant remains to be determined, but in the meantime they cannot be ignored. Naturalistic observation of the family introduces the least bias, but provides the least amount of precision and allows for maximum distortion via observer reports; highly structured tasks, on the other hand, may offer precision at the cost of introducing bias (e.g., a family's customary use of withdrawal and other physical means to resolve conflict may not be sampled by an experimental situation requiring a verbal resolution). In this latter regard, O'Rourke (1963) studied the decision-making behavior of family groups in both laboratory and home settings. When seen at home, families showed less disagreement and less activity, but more efficiency in decision making and more emotionality, than when seen in the laboratory. Bodin (1968) has correctly pointed out that lack of a counterbalanced order in O'Rourke's research design may seriously compromise the validity of his conclusions. Nevertheless, the study does raise the issue of contextual effects on family performance, and this issue has not been put to rest.

A third difficulty in assessing families is the problem of defining features that are characteristic of normal families as opposed to "artificial" families composed of unrelated individuals. Compared to the amount of knowledge we possess about the natural development of individuals, what we know about the developmental stages of families and about normative family interaction is extremely limited. Our knowledge of what normal families are like must be vastly increased if progress in the assessment of families is to continue. In turn, normal families cannot be understood simply in terms of how they differ from abnormal or unusual or atypical ones. We must understand some of the essence of what it means to be "in a family." Being a member of a family is obviously different from being in an artificial family of strangers, even though certain instrumental behaviors may be found in each. The crucial differences, in terms of transactional behaviors, between "real" and "artificial" families have not been adequately delineated, and this in turn hampers the development of techniques designed to test for differences among families.

Additional problems are encountered when it is noted that a normal family asked to interact together for purposes of study is in a situation with different demand characteristics than a family that comes for help because of problems. The test situation for the former implies approval, whereas for the latter there is a covert accusation, usually about the parents. This cannot help but influence the candor and openness of the respective groups.

A final problem in assessment is the very richness and wealth of the data generated in even a small sample of behavior. Consider a single, simple example. A father says to his wife: "Women who wear lipstick are all tramps." His wife nods her head in agreement and replies, "I don't wear lipstick." The daughter, who is wearing lipstick, is silent. At one level this can be taken as a simple statement of belief by the husband with which the wife agrees. However, if it is noted that these comments are made in the presence of their daughter who is wearing lipstick, the matter becomes complicated. Although the father appears to be addressing the mother, indirectly he may be addressing the daughter. Commenting to the mother on something he does not like about the daughter may be a reflection of father's inability to deal with the daughter directly. Moreover, he may be blaming the mother for condoning or allowing some behavior of the daughter of which he disapproves. His comment, then, becomes a rebuke rather than a simple statement of fact—and the rebuke may be directed at either or both of the other two persons.

Or, as another possibility, this may be a father who is prone to provoking "friendly" arguments between others. By calling attention to a source of disagreement between them, he can start the argument he wants and thereby divert attention from himself, or set up a conflict that allows him to be the wise arbiter, or whatever. Conversely, the mother may be agreeing in order to avoid a fight. Or she may be waiting to see what daughter's response will be. Or she may be trying to establish a coalition with her husband against the daughter. The possibilities are almost limitless, even without attending to such variables as the complex of nonverbal behaviors that can significantly alter the meaning of any verbal message. A simple measure of who is talking to whom in the family is not always simple, as can be seen from the above example. Given the complexity of the data and the multifaceted nature of human interaction, it is little wonder that the assessment of family interaction patterns is in a primitive state.

Individual, conjoint, and combined methods are the principal approaches that have been used by family diagnosticians. Since individual assessment techniques are covered elsewhere in this volume (see Chapters 1 through 6), the present discussion will be limited to conjoint and combined approaches. The techniques most widely used in these approaches are interviews (structured and unstructured), projective and objective tests, and self-report inventories.

Interview and Natural Observation Techniques

Unstructured family interviews are widely used by clinicians to determine the suitability of the family for therapy, to assess the family's interaction style, and to identify family strengths and weaknesses. As in unstructured individual diagnostic interviews, each clinician has a unique style, with favorite questions, and preferred areas of functioning about which information is desired. Diversity abounds and comparability of findings is thereby rendered elusive. Nevertheless, such interviews have high utility for the practicing clinician in making practical decisions about whom to see and what to do. Fitzgerald (1973) uses a combined method of individual and conjoint interviews. Individual sessions are utilized to obtain a traditional history, formulate dynamics, and gather each person's view of the family problems. Joint interviews are then begun, with each person in the family feeling that there has been ample opportunity to present his or her own viewpoint. Joint diagnostic sessions are designed to relate individual dynamics to family transactions and to formulate treatment goals in conjunction with the family unit.

A similar use of both individual and conjoint interviews in assessment is employed by a team of clinicians in the multiple-impact family-therapy approach reported by Macgregor ct al., (1964). Families spend up to 2½ days with the clinic team, during which the family members meet with all clinic team members conjointly and in various combinations with one or more clinicians. The power of this technique lies in the opportunity it presents for the family to be seen by different therapists in different combinations, while information gathered from any component group is constantly shared with the others for corrective information or reaction. In such a context stylized interaction patterns quickly become apparent, and the sheer pressure of events forces the family to test alternative methods of relating and challenges it to discover new resources. This approach is expensive in professional time, and the nature of the information gathered may vary considerably from one family to another, since there are no formal guidelines for conducting the interviews. Emphasis is placed on flexibility in order to gear the diagnostic study and the treatment as much as possible to the specific needs of each family.

One difficulty of the two approaches described above is summarizing adequately the abundance of data that is generated. In order to address this difficulty, some investigators have developed observational coding systems that appear promising. For example, Robinson and Eyberg (1981) utilized 5-minute segments of parent–child interactions as the data base for a coding system that is both relatively easy to learn and practical for clinical use. This coding system successfully differentiated conduct-problem families from normal families, and scores on it were significantly related to parental reports of behavior problems at home.

The Home Observation Assessment Method developed by Steinglass (1980) provides another method for systematizing and integrating observational data. Since this method requires two observers who make several home visits over a several-month time period, it is too time-consuming and cumbersome for use in most clinical settings. The approach seems worth pursuing as a research device, however, since some dimensions of home behavior were found to be highly correlated with traditional clinical measures of psychiatric symptomatology, severity of alcoholism, and family boundaries. If more efficient observational methods can be developed, investigators can more easily look for relationships between a family's regulation of its internal environment and its style of dealing with commonly encountered clinical problems.

The line between unstructured diagnostic interviews and therapy is a thin one. In many respects it appears that many family therapists have simply adapted the typical language of individual therapy to work with families; that is, they arbitrarily refer to the initial interview or interviews as *diagnosis* and subsequent sessions as *therapy* even though the demonstrable difference between the two is often more apparent than real. Insofar as I am aware, there exists not a single study that compares the utility of the unstructured family diagnostic interview with other methods of assessment, in spite of the fact that it is without doubt the most widely used diagnostic approach. For most clinics advantages such as flexibility and relatively low cost compared to other techniques apparently are sufficient to offset such disadvantages as the risk of subjective bias in the interpretation of the findings.

Structured or focused interviews have also received wide attention in family evaluation efforts. The structure is provided by either a standardized set of questions or focus on a particular event or laboratory situation. The disadvantages of structured interviews are similar to those of the questionnaire, especially in restriction of coverage to the questions asked, which may not be appropriate to a particular family situation. A further problem may occur in quantifying results when answers are not restricted to a simple "yes" or "no." However, the structure does provide common experiences across subjects and thus make comparisons easier. Also, respondents can be subjected to a particular experience and then interviewed concerning their feelings and reactions. The combination of (a) common tasks or questions and (b) open-ended (nonrestricted) responses has proved particularly popular. Two examples will be considered here: the Wiltwyck Family Task and the MRI Structured Family Interview.

The Wiltwyck Family Task.   This interview (Elbert, et al., 1964) consists of eight tasks for the whole family. The first six tasks are presented via a tape recorder with the examiner watching through a one-way screen. As one feature of the evaluation process, the nonparticipant observer model is useful in that it is possible to observe the family interact without the distortion inevitably introduced by an outsider. The tasks prescribed via audiotapes include (a) agreeing on a meal everyone would enjoy; (b) discussing "who's the most bossy," "the biggest troublemaker," "the one who gets away with most," and "the biggest crybaby in the family"; (c) discussing a remembered argument at home, including how it started, how it developed, and what the outcome was; (d) agreeing on a way to spend a hypothetical $10 gift that would be satisfying to all; (e) asking members to tell what things every other member does that please them most and make them feel good, and what things each one does that displease them most and make them feel unhappy or mad; (f) reassembling an asymmetric construction, each member starting with an equal number of pieces.

The remaining two tasks are presented by the observer, who leaves the room after offering gifts about which the family must make decisions: (a) The family is offered its choice of a single gift, valued at $1.00 to $1.50, from a group of three, a group game, an individual game, and an age- or sex-specific game; and (b) the family is offered refreshments but provided one cupcake, one soda, and one cup less than the number of members present. The family is left to decide how to dispense the food and, as in the previous task, must live with the decision made.

Steidl et al. (1980) used the Wiltwyck Family Task to study families of patients receiving long-term dialysis treatment. Videotapes of the families then were rated on selected aspects of family structure and interaction. It was possible to identify early patients at risk for poor adherence to the treatment regime who consequently had a poor prognosis.

The Structured Family Interview.   Developed by Bateson, Haley, and Weakland at the Mental Research Institute (MRI) in Palo Alto, this interview has been the subject of much attention (see Watzlawick, 1966, and Bodin, 1981, for the most complete discussion and present development. Designed to give observers valuable clinical impressions in the space of an hour, the interview is conducted by an interviewer and observed by the therapist. After the completion of the interview, the therapist is introduced to a family already keyed to looking at themselves as an interacting unit. The procedure was created as a clinical tool to provide a catalyst in the initial stage of therapy and to provide the therapist with early information that might be more difficult to obtain through direct questioning.

The five tasks in the interview utilize individual, dyadic, and whole-family observations. First, each member is asked, "What do *you* think are the main problems in your family?" Then the group is assembled, told that several discrepancies arose in the individual responses (whether they did or not), and asked to discuss the question together. The interviewer observes the discussion through a one-way screen. As their second task, the family group is asked to plan something together, such as an outing. Third, with the children excused, the parents are asked to describe how they met each other. Fourth, the parents are asked to discuss the meaning of a proverb and then to bring the children into the room and teach them the meaning of the proverb. Fifth, the interviewer gives each person an index card and a pencil. Each member is asked to write down the main fault of the person on his or her left. The interviewer collects the cards and announces that he or she is adding two statements to the group. These statements are always "too good" and "too weak," but this fact is not revealed. After shuffling the cards, the interviewer reads each one to every member in turn, beginning with the father, and asks, "To whom do you think this applies?" Several variations on the basic structured interview have been reported and are summarized by Bodin (1981).

L'Abate (1974) has noted several values of the MRI Structured Interview for research purposes. These include having a set form of administration for comparing results, obtaining input from all members, allowing a view of family as process, having an empirical basis of portions of the interview and some objective scoring procedures, providing guidelines for administration (which helps standardization), and offering suggestions for how to evaluate the interaction patterns elicited. However, the objective measures rely on judges' ratings, which are a particular problem in family assessment. All outside observers are severely limited in their capacity to judge a system that has a shared history, traditions, and way of communicating.

Projective Tests

Projective tests utilized in family assessment run the gamut from drawings (Kwiatkowska, 1967) and a marbles test (Usandivaras et al., 1963) to traditional materials such as the TAT and Rorschach. The last two are the most frequently used, perhaps due to their greater familiarity as popular individual-assessment techniques.

Family projective tests are more time-consuming to administer and more difficult to score than objective tests. In addition, they are subject to the same criticisms concerning subjectivity and validity that have been raised about their use as individually administered instruments.

Initially, projectives were given to individual family members and subjected to the same kind of content analysis used in the usual scoring of Rorschachs or TATs. Interpretations were focused on individual dynamics and on attempts to reconstruct relationships within the family. (See Fisher & Mendell, 1956; Singer & Wynne,

1965, for examples of this approach at its best.) Later observers adapted the tests for group administration so that interaction could be observed more directly in the production of fantasy material. Some examples of the latter approach are given below.

Winter, Ferreira, and Olson (1965) asked family triads to produce three TAT stories based on nine cards. Using standardized scoring methods developed by others, these investigators were able to differentiate between normal and abnormal families on the basis of their stories. In a subsequent study Winter and Ferreira (1969) factor-analyzed TAT stories given by 33 abnormal family triads and 22 normal control triads. Seven factors were identified that differentiated the two groups: (a) middle-class good adjustment; (b) task orientation; (c) silence; (d) emotionality; (e) inefficiency; (f) pathological productivity; and (g) dependency.

There have been just a few attempts to develop stimulus cards specifically designed for conjoint family use. A notable exception is the Family Interaction Apperception Test (FIAT) developed by Elbert, Rosman, Minuchin, and Guerney (1964) for use with the Wiltwyck Family Task discussed earlier. The FIAT consists of 10 cards depicting familiar, recognizable family scenes that are sufficiently concrete to be usable with less educated, nonverbal subjects as well as typical middle-class families. Another excellent feature of the FIAT is that the people depicted are drawn with ambiguous racial characteristics so as to permit identification with the figures by a wide range of ethnic groups. Despite its promise as a family projective test, interest in the FIAT has not been forthcoming.

The Rorschach has enjoyed even wider use than the TAT, in keeping with its greater popularity in clinical use. Levy and Epstein (1964), in a typical example of the conjoint use of the test, administered the test to each family member individually, following which the whole family was asked to discuss each card and decide upon consensus responses. In addition to the responses, the discussions were recorded so that family interactions and communication patterns could be studied. A less time-consuming approach has been reported by Behrens, Rosenthal, and Chodoff (1968). Using only Cards I, II, and III, the authors dispensed with the individual administration. Clinicians' analysis of the protocols differentiated white families from black families and "schizophrenic families" from "normal families" at a statistically significant level. Statistically reliable ratings of communication and pathological interaction were also achieved. For a more thorough discussion of family Rorschach procedures and issues the reader is referred to a report of a Consensus Rorschach Symposium in the 1968 volume of the *Journal of Projective Techniques and Personality Assessment*.

The advantages of the family Rorschach include the fact that it is a standard procedure, the noninvolvement of the experimenter, the opportunity it offers to observe interaction and communication patterns, and a data yield that taps both conscious and unconscious processes. Its disadvantages, as previously mentioned, include subjectivity of interpretation, overwhelming richness of data, and inordinate expense in terms of professional time. Loveland, Wynne, and Singer (1963) provide a thorough discussion of the advantages and disadvantages of the family Rorschach.

Projective techniques have been widely criticized but continue to be utilized by many clinicians. With specific respect to families, Dorr (1981) reports on the routine use of a battery consisting of the Rorschach, TAT, MMPI, and the Edwards Personal Preference Schedule for marital assessments. Typically 1½ days are consumed by the testing procedures, followed by 3 to 6 hours devoted to face-to-face interpretation and feedback with the couple.

Objective Tests

Objective tests have not been used to a significant extent in conjoint family assessment. The clear trend has been to use objective tests in what Bodin (1968) called *individual approaches* to family assessment and to use projective or task intervention devices in the conjoint sessions. A notable exception to this trend is the ingenious work of Bauman and Roman (1966), who developed interaction scores based on the Wechsler-Bellevue Intelligence Scale. The procedure consists simply of administering the Wechsler to each member of the family in the typical fashion and then readministering it to the family together. Only the Comprehension and Similarities subtests are used, but Forms I and II of the W-B are combined to increase the number of items. Several interesting comparisons are possible, For example, prorated IQ scores can be computed for each individual and for the family as a whole. Also, by taking the best answer given by any individual to each item, it is possible to compute a "potential IQ" score for the family. Theoretically, a family that is efficient at recognizing and utilizing information known to be available in the system should achieve an actual conjoint score close to the potential IQ score. In fact, many families do not. Some families score more poorly together than any member scores alone! It is also common to encounter couples whose conjoint score is lower than the score of one of the spouses.

Self-Report Inventories

In the past decade there has been a virtual explosion in the development of a variety of self-report instruments, questionnaires, inventories, and checklists, all of which are aimed at a more precise delineation of family problem areas. Only a sample of the studies available is reported here to give the reader the flavor of these newer directions in family assessment.

Several investigators have utilized family members' ratings of themselves and others in the family on dimensions that the investigator believes to be important. The responses of different types of family groups are then compared to see whether their responses separate one type from another. Frank et al. (1980) compared couples' self-ratings regarding which spouse should and which spouse does assume responsibility in eight marital role areas, for 80 nonpatient couples, 50 couples seeking sex therapy, and 50 couples seeking marital therapy. Couples in marital therapy reported the greatest discrepancy between actual role performance and ideal role performance (the greatest marital strain). Sex therapy couples reported the next most marital strain, and the nonpatient couples reported the lowest discrepancies.

A promising development is the Inventory of Family Feelings (IFF), a self-administered measure of interpersonal affect. IFF scores appear to be both reliable and valid (Lowman, 1980). Couples in marital therapy and families with an identified patient (IP) show less positive affect than control families. In families with an IP, most of the negative affect centers on and arises from the IP. IFF scores correlate with independent ratings of affect based on audiorecordings, with scores on a standard marital adjustment inventory (Locke, Wallace Short Marital Adjustment Test), and negatively with MMPI measure of pathology. Although the affective component of family life is the sole focus of the IFF, it is a central dimension in a variety of theoretical approaches to family therapy.

Behavioral therapists have been especially prolific in developing family assessment devices, as recently summarized by Jacobson (1981). Three noteworthy assessment questionnaires developed by these investigators are the Marital Adjustment Test (MAT), the Areas of Change Questionnaire (A-C) and the Marital Status Inventory (MSI). The MAT (Locke & Wallace, 1959) yields a global rating of marital satisfaction. The MSI (Weiss & Cerreto, 1975) is a set of true and false questions regarding the steps already taken by both spouses toward separation and divorce. The A-C (Weiss, Hops & Patterson, 1973) asks couples to indicate which of 34 behaviors they would like their partner to change and how much change is desired.

The MAT provides a well-validated index of marital satisfaction. It is somewhat limited in planning for behavioral therapy, however, in that it does not provide specific information regarding problem areas that should be the focus of therapeutic efforts. The A-C, on the other hand, does provide useful information regarding specific problem areas, and it correlates highly with the MAT. The MSI is useful in providing a way for couples to indicate the steps they have taken toward separation that they sometimes are reluctant to admit in the therapy situation. Its 280 items comprise a validity scale, a global affective scale, and nine scales assessing specific dimensions of marital interaction. Snyder, Wills, and Keiser (1981) have reported promising efforts to identify scale correlates and thus establish the actuarial validity of the MSI.

One of the main difficulties encountered by the interested investigator is the lack of studies that attempt to compare the various assessment devices with each other. Each investigator invents a new questionnaire without attempting to determine how similar or dissimilar it may be from existing instruments. In part this state of affairs stems from the fact that different theorists proceed from different premises regarding the important dimensions to be measured. However, Birchler and Spinks (1980) have demonstrated that behavioral approaches and systems approaches to therapy can be integrated both conceptually and in clinical work, and that the differing approaches to assessment taken by these two theories can be mutually enriching. More such efforts are needed.

The problems with all of the assessment techniques thus far developed are numerous and glaring: Differing classification schemes are used, the mode of communication studied varies from one approach to another, the unit of analysis varies, and differing definitions of *abnormal* are applied. Fisher (1976) identified 175 criteria that have been used for the assessment of families by various investigators.

An additional problem is that the effect of cultural influences on family behavior is one of the most frequently mentioned but the most poorly articulated dimension of family assessment reports (Fisher, 1976). A rare exception to this state of affairs is provided by Henggeler and Tavormina (1980). In a carefully controlled and well-designed experiment the authors failed to find the race and social-class differences that have been reported previously. Lower-class families have been described as less warm (Bayley & Schaefer, 1960; Radin 1972) and more conflictual than middle-class families (Jacob, 1974). Similar findings have been reported for black families (Blood & Wolfe, 1969; Davis & Havinghurst, 1946). Pointing to several procedural and design errors in previous studies, Henggeler and Tavormina warned that "clinicians must take care not to infer 'deficits' when they have observed 'differences.' "

All of the above problems seriously hamper the generalizability and practical utility of the several family assessment methods currently in use. In addition, reliability tends to be defined differently from one method to the next, validity is often ignored, and replications are scarce. In view of these problems one can conclude that as of the present, family assessment is more a goal than an accomplished fact, more an artistic tool than a scientific technique.

THEORIES OF FAMILY INTERVENTION

This section describes and summarizes the major concepts of three broad schools of thought: structural, dynamic, and behavioral.

Structural/Process Approaches

The approaches somewhat arbitrarily assigned to this group include the *communication systems* or *interactional approach* of Jackson (1957), the *problem-solving approach* of Haley (1976), the *brief problem focused approach* of Watzlawick, Weakland, and Fisch (1974), the *process approach* of Satir (1964), and the *structural approach* of Minuchin and Fishman (1981). Among the many major concepts developed by some of those adhering to this approach are the *double-bind hypothesis* and the notion of *family homeostasis*.

The basic ingredients of the double bind as originally formulated by Bateson, Jackson, Haley, and Weakland (1956) are: (a) two or more persons; (b) repeated experiences; (c) issuance of a primary injunction taking one of two forms ("Do not do this or I will punish you" or "If you don't do this, I will punish you"); (d) a secondary injunction conflicting with the first at a more abstract level and also enforced by punishment (this secondary injunction is generally nonverbal and disqualifies some important aspect of the first injunction, for example, "Do not see this as a punishment. Do not think of what you must not do"); and (e) a tertiary negative injunction prohibiting the "victim" from escaping from the field. When the victim has learned to perceive the universe in double-bind patterns, the complete set of ingredients is no longer necessary to elicit and maintain the behavior.

In order to understand this concept fully, it must be realized that it is grounded in "our most basic conception about communication as the chief means of human interaction and influence: that in actual human communication, a single and simple message never occurs, but that communication always and necessarily involves a multiplicity of messages, of different levels, at once" (Jackson & Weakland, 1961).

The different messages may be conveyed verbally, by gestures, by facial expression or by body posture, by tone and inflection of voice, by the context in which the message occurs, and so forth. Incongruity among messages sent at different levels seems part and parcel of the rich fabric of human communication and is sometimes used deliberately in order to achieve a desired reaction, as in irony and humor. But incongruities have also been seen as fundamental to the character of certain symptoms such as inappropriate affect. The essence of the double bind is not the fact that contradictory messages are issued; rather, it is the fact that other messages are also sent that conceal, deny, and otherwise prevent the recipient from noticing the incongruence and handling it effectively, for instance, by commenting on it. Within important relationships, such as the family, where messages cannot simply be ignored or avoided, people learn to respond in adaptive ways to the system, although their behavior might appear bizzare to the outside observer.

It was originally thought that the schizophrenic or "identified patient" was the victim of the family interaction style. Later this view was modified (Bateson, Jackson, Haley, & Weakland, 1963; Watzlawick, 1963), as it was seen that the double bind always binds both parties, so that there are at least two victims, rather than a single one: "The most useful way to phrase double-bind description is not in terms of a binder and victim, but in terms of people caught up in an ongoing system which produces conflicting definitions of the relationship and consequent subjective distress" (Watzlawick, 1963). Additionally, the double bind is no longer seen as both a necessary and sufficient cause of schizophrenia. What can be said is that where the double bind is the prevailing communication mode in a family and attention is limited to the ostensibly most disturbed individual, then the behavior of this individual satisfies the usual criteria of schizophrenia. Watzlawick (1963) describes three possible reactions of such individuals and points out their similarity to familiar symptomatic behaviors: (a) They can conclude that they are overlooking vital clues seen by others or that others are withholding and thus become obsessed with searching out the obscure or concealed information; (b) they can comply literally with all injunctions; or (c) they can withdraw from all human involvement.

An example of a double bind should help to clarify. Bateson et al. (1956) describe a brief interaction sequence that occurred between a hospitalized male schizophrenic patient and his mother. When visited by his mother, the young patient impulsively put his arm around her shoulders only to feel her stiffen. When he quickly withdrew his arm, she asked, "Don't you love me any more?" When the patient then blushed, the mother admonished him: "Dear, you must not be so easily embarrassed and afraid of your feelings." Thus the son is in an impossible dilemma: If he shows his love, he is wrong; if he withholds his love, he is wrong; if he comments on the paradox (by blushing), he is wrong. In such a context so-called schizophrenic behavior such as withdrawal, irrelevant comments, non sequiturs, and the like are adaptive in terms of maintaining the relationship while avoiding the trap of responding to either of the conflicting messages ("love me," but "do not show that you love me") and not commenting on the conflict in which the person has been placed. It is believed that schizophrenic communication is learned as a result of continual experiences of the kind shown in this example.

Whereas incongruity of messages is basic to the theory and emphasis is thereby placed on what is overt and directly observable, fantasies and individual nonperceptions are implied. The basic dynamic in this theory is presumed to be a mother who is afraid of closeness but unwilling to admit it or the consequent hostility generated, and who masks it by assuming a too-loving attitude toward the child. Further, there is an absence of a strong, insightful person (e.g., the father) who could support the child. In order to control her anxiety with the child, the mother manipulates the communication to produce a degree of tolerable emotional closeness, and the father collaborates in the deception. The child may become aware of the fact that mother's zealous concern masks a basic hostility, but he or she cannot communicate the awareness out of fear of losing the small amount of love that is provided. Thus he or she recognizes that it is incorrect to respond to her too-loving attitude, but it is also incorrect to respond to her underlying hostility. The child is damned either way, or caught in a double bind. The whole basis for the double bind, however, is embedded in hypothesized rather than directly observable behavior, and in this sense there is more overlap between this theory and psychoanalytic theory than the structural/process theorists are willing to admit. In terms of relative emphasis, it is true that this group has been instrumental in calling attention to the powerfulness of the current ongoing transactions in families in maintaining symptomatic behavior in one or more of their members.

The double-bind theory was initially formulated as a process believed to be important in the etiology of schizophrenia. Gradually, it was seen that the concept could be applied to much of our current thinking about psychopathology in general. Ferreira (1960) suggested that a double bind of a different variety was operative in a delinquent's family. Instead of the incongruent messages emanating from a single person or a single coalition, the incongruency is split and "the victim is caught in a sort of bipolar message in which A emanates from father, for instance, and B (a message about message A) from mother. The consideration of this different kind of double bind" seemingly illuminates some important aspects in the communicational process that leads to delinquent behavior (Ferreira, 1960). Thus schizophrenia appeared to result from a special type of double-bind situation rather than from the fact of double finding per se.

Haley (1963) and Watzlawick et al. (1967) have significantly extended the communicational approach to other types of families. In looking at double binds more broadly, Haley points out that conflicting messages can easily be viewed as attempts to define the relationship in terms of what type of communicative behavior is to take place on one level, while denying or qualifying the definition on another level. When the messages are incongruent, interpersonal difficulties are considered inevitable. He suggests that a primary issue in all human relationships has to do with who is going to set the rules for the relationship and, on a more abstract level, who is to decide who sets the rules. With this concept it is possible to see how the passive victim of an interpersonal exchange may in fact be very powerful; by defining the relationship as one in which he/she is to be passive, the "victim," at a meta-communication level, is also saying, "I am in charge of saying who is in charge here and I decide that you must be in charge." In this way the "passive victim" may wield much control while appearing to be helpless. While controlling the relationship, the "victim" denies that this is so by attributing it to an illness rather than to a volitional choice. Haley (1963) listed several ways a person can define or avoid defining a relationship by pointing out that any message can be broken down into the following elements:

1. I
2. am saying something
3. to you
4. in this situation.

By negating or disqualifying any of these elements, a person can achieve control of a relationship while not appearing to do so. For example, the wife who refuses sexual advances with the excuse of a headache is indicating that she is not defining the relationship as one in which she refuses the husband; after all, it is the headache that prevents cooperation, not she. The extreme methods that can be used to disqualify the defining (i.e., controlling) of relationships constitute a list of schizophrenic symptoms (Haley, 1959): (a) People may deny that they are *communicating* by claiming to be someone else; (b) they may deny that they are *saying something* by using meaningless language; (c) they may deny that they are *addressing another person* by claiming that they are talking to themselves or that the other is really a secret agent; or (d) they may deny that they are saying something *in this situation* by claiming to be in some other place, such as Mt. Olympus. Haley also points out how other interesting interpersonal events such as hypnosis can be understood via this process; the hypnotist denies that he or she is controlling by claiming that the subject is doing it, and the subject complies by becoming "hypnotized" and claiming that the behavior is not under voluntary control. That is, subjects "accept" the hypnotist's definition of the relationship as one in which they will comply with the given instructions and not hold themselves responsible. In effect, different ways of denying elements of a message appear to be varieties of double binds. In schizophrenia the pattern is simply more pervasive, the range of behaviors more restricted, and the denial more absolute than in other types of pathological families.

Jackson's (1957) concept of *family homeostasis* emerged as a result of noting the rigidity and resistance to change that families evidence when attempts are made to point out, change, or interrupt the double-bind sequences. One example he gave was that of a husband who called his wife's therapist to express concern over her suicidal impulses. The therapist reassured him that his wife's depression was actually considerably improved. The next day the husband committed suicide by shooting himself. Jackson (1957) goes on to say that these observations "suggested that a family forms a dynamic steady-state system; the characteristics of the members and the nature of their interaction—including any identified patient and his sick behavior—are such as to maintain a status quo of the family, and to react toward the restoration of the status quo in the event of any change, such as is proposed by the treatment of any member."

Similarly, Haley (1962) talks of an error-activated system for describing families. Noting that families often restrict themselves to repetitive patterns of behavior within a wider range of possibilities, as if confined to that pattern by a kind of governing process, he states, "No outside governor requires the family to behave in their habitual patterns, so this governing must exist within the family." When people interact, they establish rules for their joint behavior and thereby establish a system that appears to be error activated. When one member "breaks the rules" of the family by exceeding the range of permitted behavior, the others are activated to pressure that member into conforming to the rule. If the person succeeds in establishing a new range of permitted behaviors, new rules are established and a new homeostasis achieved. Bateson (1960) used the homeostasis concept to explain how only one person may be symptomatic when the entire family is seen as schizophrenogenic. He hypothesizes that homeostasis in such families is achieved by only one member's being overtly psychotic. Some evidence for this theory can be found in the frequently observed instance of an identified patient's improvement being followed by the emergence of psychological distress in another family member. Perhaps the homeostasis was upset by improvement in the identified patient, resulting in the creation of another "sick" person to restore the balance.

The development of family myths may also serve to maintain family homeostasis. Claiming that the family myth "is to the relationship what the defense is to the individual," Ferreira (1963) defines such myths as "a series of fairly well-integrated beliefs shared by all family members, concerning each other and the mutual position in the family, beliefs that go unchallenged by everyone involved in spite of the reality distortions which they may conspicuously imply."

These shared beliefs and the struggle to maintain them are seen as part of the struggle to maintain the relationship. To expose the myth one must break certain implied rules concerning shared beliefs about the family, which threatens the homeostatic balance and is resented by other family members. An example of a powerful three-generation family myth has been reported by Ewing and Fox (1968). A teenage boy who was referred for treatment explained his behavior as the result of having a highly neurotic mother. Her problems were attributed to her having been raised in a family containing an alcoholic father. The boy's mother confirmed her son's story.

When the grandparents were subsequently interviewed, their version of the family history was the same as their daughter's and grandson's. It emerged, however, that the grandfather was a successful member of his community (having been once elected mayor by write-in ballot) and did not have a drinking problem. What he did have was an immature, demanding wife, and he occasionally removed himself from her tirades to go for a drink. The wife would then complain to the children that, in addition to her other trials, she had a husband who drank. The entire family (including her husband) collaborated in supporting mother by accepting her distorted version of reality, and the myth was being used to explain the behavior of a boy two generations later. It was as if there were a family rule against criticizing mother; a balance in relationships was achieved thereby, and a myth created to lend credence to the entire construction. Family homeostasis has proved to be such a highly useful construct that Carson (1969) has labeled it "the central concept that, in my view, ties together all of this research."

The major problems that some clinicians find with the double-bind theory have been summarized by Mishler and Waxler (1966). First, there is a lack of precision and clarity with respect to the types of interaction sequences that do and do not fall within the definition of the double bind. "From the way the concept is used, it sometimes appears that all communication sequences may be interpretable, at some level of analysis, as double binds, and, if this is so, the concept loses all usefulness" (Mishler & Waxler, 1966). Second, by ignoring content and emphasizing the style of interaction that occurs irrespective of the topic being discussed, the theory has ignored the possibility that double binds centering around significant family norms may have more significance than ones involving trivial matters. However, Jackson for one is not impressed by this criticism, stating that in his view, "the act itself alerts the participants that there is a conflict and in itself constitutes a kind of psychological trauma, whatever the substantive issue" (personal communication quoted in Mishler & Waxler, 1966). Third, the criteria for deciding whose perspective is to be used in determining the presence of incongruency are not specified. What appears contradictory to an observer may not appear so to an individual who shares a common communicative history with the rest of his or her family. Whose perspective is to be used, and who decides which perspective is correct?

In reply to these criticisms Bateson (1966) admits, "Personally, I do not believe that the theory is at present subject to rigorous empirical testing." He also points out that this theory and many of the other currently popular ones are "really not theories in the ordinary sense, but are more like new languages or perhaps new epistemologies. A language can be confusing or enlightening . . . convenient or clumsy . . . but it cannot, in itself, be true or false."

The similarities and differences among theorists utilizing the structural or process paradigm of family intervention have been summarized by Levant (1980). All of these theorists are concerned primarily with the family's current patterns of interaction and how these patterns relate to the presenting problems or symptoms of the identified patient. They differ with respect to whether the interaction patterns should be viewed from a structural (Minuchin, 1974) or a process perspective (Satir, 1964); and whether or not the primary goal of therapy is to change the structure (i.e., the boundaries and coalition between generations) (Minuchin, 1974) or remove the symptom (Haley, 1976). The structuralists dismiss the history taking, careful uncovering, insight, and interpretation that are central to dynamic approaches, and they are not impressed by the importance of affect in the treatment process. Their aim is to rearrange the family system in such a manner that dysfunctional elements that produce or maintain the system are removed. In achieving this goal, the structural therapist assumes the role of an expert whose task is to diagnose dysfunctional elements in the family system and develop interventions to correct them. Directive instructions (often paradoxical in nature) may be used to force or trick the family into new interactional patterns or sequences.

Critics of the structural approach point out that it ignores important resistances to change by family members. These include the tendency of each individual to ward off the anxiety generated by growing awareness of split-off aspects of oneself that had been denied and attributed to another, and the tendency of family members to reinforce each other's efforts to avoid or escape such reintegration (Gurman, 1980). Since the structural approach primarily was developed out of experiences with schizophrenic families that are highly resistant to change, it is ironic that such a criticism should be directed at these theorists.

Dynamic and Historical Approaches

This paradigm includes such psychodynamic approaches as Wynne (Wynne, Ryckoff, Day, & Hirsch, 1958) and Lidz (1963) and the multigenerational approach of Bowen (1960). The previously noted review by Levant (1980) summarizes the similarities among the therapists in this group. All are concerned with the person within the family system, in contrast to the structuralists' sole concern with the system. The dynamic theorists pay particular attention to attachments to past figures that are represented in the individual's current functioning and are likely to be transmitted to future generations. Although all of the dynamicists have some commitments to psychoanalytic theory, their perspectives encompass a broader range of interactional patterns than is typical for psychoanalysis, as well as the transmission of interactional patterns across generations. In general, dynamic family therapists try to free the individual from excessive attachments to earlier generations by uncovering their existence, demonstrating their inappropriateness, and helping the individual gradually to abandon them. The therapist plays a facilitative role in this process through interpretation or what Bowen calls *coaching*.

Lidz.   In many respects Lidz's formulations are psychoanalytic concepts applied to the family triad; as a result they have the virtue of being easily understood by professionals accustomed to thinking in these terms. Role differentiation with respect to age and sex appropriateness plays a central role in the Lidz group's analysis of family pathology. The basic problem in all family difficulties is seen as a distortion of normal parent–child relationships: "What appears to be essential can be stated simply. . . . The spouses need to form a coalition as members of the parental generation maintaining their respective gender-linked roles, and be capable of transmitting instrumentally useful ways of adaptation suited to the society in which they live" (Lidz, 1963).

Two deviant types of marital relationships have been identified, each of which leads to impaired parenting and disrupted sex-role learning in the child: marital schism and marital skew.

Marital schism is used to describe relationships in which there is a state of severe, chronic discord and disequilibrium. Threats of separation are common and recurrent. Communication centers around power struggles, resistance, and fighting and/or efforts to conceal or avoid facing the deep schism between the spouses. Having little to gain from each other, the parents tend to seek support from their children. In competition for their loyalty, each attempts to diminish the worth of the other to the children. Schizophrenia in females is believed to be particularly common in families marked by a schismatic marriage.

In *marital skew* the relationship is not threatened by separation, but is distorted or skewed toward meeting the needs of one member at the expense of the needs of others. Typically there is a domineering mother who forms an overly close relationship with one child at the expense of the other children and a husband who passively accedes to his wife's wishes. Schizophrenic males are believed relatively likely to come from such families.

In both types of marital relationship there is a failure to develop a reciprocally rewarding parental coalition. Age- and sex-appropriate role behaviors are impaired and poorly modeled for the children. Role reciprocity, which Lidz et al. (1957b) define as a "common understanding and acceptance of each other's roles, goals, and motivation, and a reasonable sharing of cultural value orientations," is missing.

The theoretical constructs developed by Lidz and his colleagues have broad application in the understanding of many symptomatic behaviors, even though they were originally developed to help explain the phenomenon of schizophrenia. For example, school phobic behavior can be seen as a situation in which children somehow take for themselves a decision that in most families is reserved for adults: whether or not the child is to attend school.

The major criticism of this theory is that its concepts are not integrated into a unified system. Concepts from several disciplines are used without being systematically related to each other. A second criticism is that it is oriented to the individual rather than the family. Although frequent references are made to the family social system and social roles, the fact is that children develop problems because of poor marriages, which in turn result from psychological problems brought to the marriage by the individual spouses. In order to understand the family, we have to understand the dynamics of the individuals. As Mishler and Waxler (1966) summarize the matter, "It appears that we have to depend on an understanding of the psychodynamics of the parents; to the extent that this is necessary, the analysis of the family as a social system is superfluous." However, the appeal of Lidz's approach lies in calling attention to the concrete but powerful parameters of age- and sex-role behaviors, their development, and their vicissitudes.

Wynne.   Wynne and his colleagues are interested in the impact of the family system as a unit on the quality and structure of the role relationships within that unit. They have identified four features of schizophrenic families that seem to differentiate them from families in general (Wynne & Singer, 1964):

1.   Patterns of handling attention and meaning that interfere with the capacity for purposive behavior and selective attention

2.   Erratic and inappropriate styles of relating leading to unpredictable closeness and distance

3. Underlying feelings of meaninglessness, pointlessness, and emptiness that pervade all interpersonal relationships

4. A collusive family structure that scrvcs to deny or reinterpret the reality of anxiety-producing feelings or events

Although some of these features have been found in less seriously disturbed families as well, this discussion will be limited to schizophrenic families for illustrative purposes. With respect first to describing patterns of handling attention and meaning (transactional thought disorders) in schizophrenic families, Wynne and Singer (1964) classify them along a continuum from *amorphous* to *fragmented*. Amorphous patterns are characterized by vague drifting and blurring of attention and meaning, so that attention and meaning are neither object oriented nor specific. Fragmented patterns are poorly integrated messages resulting from the intrusion of unconscious thought processes, from using odd vantage points for communication, and from crypticness. The authors cite as an example of such fragmentation one parent's complete response to a Rorschach card: "If you read stories of Cossacks, that's self-explanatory." Amorphous or fragmented patterns are not seen as characteristics of a single parent, but are thought to be prominent features of the entire family system.

The second characteristic of disturbed families is an erratic and inappropriate style of relating that leads to unpredictable distance and closeness. Wynne and Singer are not talking here simply about interpersonal distance and affective functions; cognitive functions and distance from ideas are also included. The distance taken both from people and from ideas varies unpredictably and often inappropriately, from being too distant to being too close.

Wynne and his colleagues believe that the disturbed family's patterns of handling meaning and attention and their erratic modes of relating function as defenses that help the family deny or mitigate underlying feelings of helplessness and meaninglessness. Such feelings are thought to be pervasive in the family but not consciously experienced. Rather, it is when they threaten to come into awareness that the behaviors listed above are most likely to be brought into use.

Finally, the collusive family structure adopted serves to deny and reinterpret disturbing experiences and also to bolster the defensive patterns listed previously. Two structural patterns of this process that have been identified are *pseudomutuality* and *pseudohostility*. The difference between these two patterns is less important than their similarity: Both are *pseudo* states that are fixed and rigid. Pseudomutuality implies the opposite of mutuality and complementarity in interpersonal relationships. Energy is directed more toward maintaining a sense of reciprocity than toward the actual development of mutually acknowledged and supported individuation. Pseudohostility is defined as a fixed and rigid state of hostility that protects the family both from the threat of too much closeness and from any real anger and disillusionment that may emerge. Deviations from the family's rigid role structure are not permitted, but it is not obvious that they are not permitted. Rather, deviations from the family norm are either excluded from awareness or reinterpreted so that an illusion of harmony and closeness or an illusion of hostility is maintained. Family myths or legends may be used to communicate and teach the negative consequences attendant on divergence from the rigidly defined roles. Such efforts tend to cut off or sharply delimit separation from the family and involvement in the broader society. As a result, the possible corrective effects of extrafamilial influences are minimized, while the corrosive effects of the intrafamilial environment are maximized.

Summarizing Wynne's work, Mishler and Waxler (1966) point out that he tends to use concepts at several levels of analysis without specifying their relationships. Consequently, the theory is neither systematic nor complete. However, this group perhaps more than any other is empirically oriented—that is, they have attempted to accumulate data concerning which family patterns are found together rather than defining connections theoretically and then attempting to verify the hypothesized connections via observations.

Bowen.   The Bowen group, who began studying hospitalized families at NIMH in the mid-1950s, came to the view that families function as a single organism and the identified patient is that part of the organism through which overt symptoms are expressed (Bowen, 1960). Bowen regards schizophrenia as the result of a family process that takes place over at least three generations, as follows: Grandparents may be relatively mature, but their combined immaturities are somehow acquired by one child (typically the one who is most attached to the mother); this child then marries a spouse of equal immaturity and their combined immaturities are also focused on a single child (again, the one most attached to the mother); it is this child, carrying the collective immaturities of two prior generations, who is the most immature and the most likely candidate for the development of severe psychological symptoms.

Bowen's central theoretical concept is the *undifferentiated family ego mass*, which refers to the conglomerate emotional oneness that exists at various levels of intensity and shifts about within the family in definite patterns of emotional responsiveness. A mother–child symbiotic relationship is one example of a part or fragment of such a pattern. The point of the concept is that individual members do not act or react as autonomous, mature, differentiated individuals, but instead as subunits of a larger system. It is the system that reacts and thereby dictates and controls the reactions of individuals or subunits.

A prime example of how persons operate as part of an undifferentiated system is a relationship between the spouses in which there may be an *emotional divorce*. Although both partners are immature, only one acts immaturely. The other denies the immaturity and functions with a facade of overadequacy. One appears more immature and the other more mature than is realistic. As part of the same ego mass, however, both components are expressed. The wife shows adequacy as well as immaturity, and the husband is inadequate at times and adequate at others. In an undifferentiated ego mass each spouse takes on a role that expresses only one half of the equation, and their roles are rigidly maintained. Between them they make a whole person. The emotional divorce allows them to maintain a relationship without meaningful interaction, which would threaten their respective roles, while appearing to be happily married.

In the families studied it was noted that the mother often had related well to the identified patient when the patient was an infant. It was as if the child's helplessness aided the mother in denying similar states in herself by projecting them onto the child. As an infant a child is realistically helpless, but with more maturity and the development of greater independence the formerly fixed relationship is threatened, and the child is pressured by the system to remain helpless and immature in order to preserve the relationship and protect the mother.

Bowen feels that the mother in such a family makes two main demands on her child: (a) be helpless (usually communicated at an emotional level); and (b) be gifted, special, and mature (usually communicated at an overt, verbal level). Since the verbal message contradicts the emotional message, the child is placed in a situation in which he or she must talk one way while feeling another. The system closely resembles those described by Bateson (*double bind*) and Wynne (*pseudo*).

A prominent feature of the mother–child relationship is projection whereby the mother focuses concerns about her own safety, competence, and helplessness on the child, and the child accepts this ascribed role. Further, the father complies with both the projection and the acceptance in order to preserve the family system. This paternal collusion is vital to the system, since the mother–child closeness could never develop with the father's functional approval. The mother ascribes her helplessness to the child and then "mothers" the helplessness in the child with her adequate self; what began as a feeling in the mother thus becomes a fact in the child. Sometimes anxiety in one person results in physical symptoms in the other. Bowen described seesaw movements in several families in which improvement in one person led to physical illness in the other, and vice versa.

The theory leans heavily on psychoanalytic concepts such as projection, unconscious fears, and the like, but it lacks precision. Although Bowen has developed a "scale" of ego differentiation to help define various levels of functioning (Bowen, 1966), the ratings are purely subjective. A major virtue of Bowen's theory is his delineation of the family ego mass concept. This concept helps therapists to see how changes in one individual's differentiation might force the family into a new equilibrium around a new level of separateness–connectedness. If the family for some reason cannot be treated as a unit, it still may be possible to effect needed changes in the system.

Behavioral or Social Learning Approaches

Since adherents to this approach rely heavily on the general behavior therapy theory that is described elsewhere in this volume (see Chapter 10), little attention will be given to theoretical matters in this section. Suffice it to say that the behaviorists utilize principles of learning derived from experimental psychology and, to a lesser extent, from social, developmental, and cognitive psychology to understand and correct family problems. The social learning theory approach has become increasingly popular among family therapists (particularly marital therapists) over the past decade, as evidenced by numerous major reviews summarizing recent developments and research (Greer & D'Zurilla, 1975; Jacobson & Martin, 1976; Jacobson, 1979; Weiss, 1978; Weiss & Margolin, 1977).

Social learning theorists share a belief in three general principles concerning successful and unsuccessful marital relationships that in turn dictate a particular approach to assessment and intervention:

1. A principle of reciprocity is recognized in all relationships that exist over time. According to this principle, the degree of satisfaction derived from a relationship and the rate of rewards directed toward the spouse are a direct function of the rate of reinforcers received from the spouse (Robinson & Price, 1980).

2. Since conflict seems inevitable in any relationship, a successful marriage is ultimately dependent upon the couple's skills in conflict resolution (Jacobson & Margolin, 1979).

3. Since the value of specific reinforcing behaviors is likely to change as the relationship matures, successfully married couples must be able to expand their mutual reinforcement power by change and growth to acquire new domains for positive exchange.

It should be obvious from these principles that the success of a relationship ultimately depends on the nature and characteristics of the social exchanges between spouses and the environmental forces to which they are subjected. Historically shaped personality characteristics and even individual learning histories are important primarily in providing the initial attraction that brings people together, not in predicting what happens once the relationship is formed.

In social learning theory there are several predictable distinctions between distressed and nondistressed couples that generally are evident: (a) Distressed couples participate in more punishing and fewer positive exchanges than nondistressed couples; (b) distressed couples are more likely to respond in kind to their partners' use of punishment; (c) distressed couples appear more likely to notice selectively and respond immediately to negative behaviors; and (d) distressed couples are more likely to seek change in each other through punishment and reward withholding.

Compared to other approaches, behavioral therapists place more emphasis on the assessment phase of therapeutic undertaking. They are primarily concerned with specifying those behaviors that produced the dissatisfaction and those that tend to elicit them. In order to achieve the desired specificity, behaviorists emphasize the direct measurement and quantification of behavior. As elaborated by Goldfried in Chapter 5 of this book, the treatment plan that ultimately is developed is related to the results of the assessment more directly than appears to be the case in other approaches.

The assessments utilized consist of a variety of assessment questionnaires and self-report measures that were summarized in a previous section of this chapter. These measures are useful in pinpointing levels of satisfaction and the behaviors that trouble or please each partner. In addition, emphasis is placed on home observations by the couple in order to establish baselines for the occurrence of selected behaviors and to measure progress as therapy proceeds. Some therapists utilize ad hoc methods of observational data collection in which spouses are asked to observe and record frequencies of certain behaviors. Other therapists prefer to use instruments that aid couples in the collection of data at home. The Spouse Observation Checklist (SOC) developed by Weiss, Hops, and Patterson (1973) is a good example of the latter. The SOC consists of 400 spouse behaviors grouped into 12 categories such as companionship, affection, work activities, and so forth. Each spouse is instructed either to check each item that occurs in a 24-hour period or to limit recordings to those behaviors that are pleasing or displeasing to him or her. In addition spouses rate their overall satisfaction with the marital relationship on a 7-point scale. With this information the therapist can observe the frequency of given behaviors, determine those behaviors that are most important to spouse satisfaction, and monitor progress.

In addition to self-report and organized spouse observation measures, behavioral therapists utilize direct observations of the couple's communication and problem-solving skills to refine and test hypotheses developed from the more objective instruments. Although the interview is an important source of data, behaviorists generally place far less emphasis on the therapist–client interaction as an assessment device than do therapists favoring other theoretical approaches (Jacobson & Margolin, 1979). Once the assessment is completed and the results have been discussed with the couple, a treatment program designed to alleviate the problem is outlined and therapy begins.

The details of the treatment phase will vary from couple to couple, but in general the process follows a logical progression (Jacobson, 1981). The first phase typically consists of·asking couples to identify and increase behaviors that are pleasing to the other utilizing any one of several behavior-exchange procedures. A common example involves having both people list three spouse behaviors that they would like increased in frequency. The couple then is instructed to increase systematically the rate of beneficial exchange, thereby immediately enhancing each spouse's satisfaction at minimal cost to the other. Certain constraints govern the behavioral exchanges at this early stage of therapy: (a) The exchange must not involve behaviors or behavioral sequences that are matters of fundamental disagreement; (b) since one aim of treatment is gradually to prepare the couple for subsequent collaboration, the initial behavioral exchange should not depend on collaboration; and (c) the focus of the exchange should be on increasing the frequency of positive behaviors, not on decreasing the frequency of negative ones.

A variant on the usual behavioral exchange techniques that avoids such constraints is described by Jacobson and Margolin (1971). Utilizing study of each other's observations of various behaviors on the SOC as well as their daily ratings of relationship satisfaction, each person is instructed to try to identify the behaviors that seem most important to satisfaction in the other and then to test his or her "hypothesis" by increasing those behaviors and observing changes in the satisfaction ratings. The goal for each person is to increase the daily satisfaction rating of the partner. If presented properly as a challenge to determine whether or not each partner is capable of pleasing the other, the technique can be a powerful method for demonstrating the influence that each person retains to improve a soured relationship.

The second general phase of behavioral therapy is devoted to a more specific focus on exchanging particular behaviors. Couples may be instructed to alternate "caring days" in which each spouse devotes the day to demonstrating caring for the other in as many ways as possible (Stuart, 1976). In addition, efforts are made to help the partners ask directly and simply for what they want from each other with the decision left to the receiver as to whether or not he or she will comply with the request. In order to make these exchanges profitable, partners may be taught to weigh the costs and benefits for each of them in meeting the differing requests. The behavior changes may be part of a contingency contract whereby each person's desired behaviors are contingent upon the other person's sharing desired behaviors. Jacobson (1981) describes several features of the successful contingency contract: (a) The perceived cost and benefit of the exchange should be equal for both spouses; (b) the exact parameters of the contingency must be specified (i.e., how much of the desired behavior is required in order to produce the partner's reinforcer); and (c) there should be specification of the means for reinstating an exchange should either partner default.

In the final phase of therapy the couple learns specific communication and problem-solving skills for dealing with major problem areas. (The last phase of therapy may be unnecessary for couples who already have achieved the desired changes.) The specific training that the couple is given relies on systematic modeling of desired behaviors by the therapist, a rehearsal by the couple during the therapy hour, and careful feedback by the therapist. Problem-solving training is utilized for those relationship problems that are not easily amenable to behavior-exchange procedures, either because the recipient of the complaint will not agree to the requested change or because the problem does not lend itself to a readily discernible behavioral solution.

Problem-solving programs may vary somewhat from one therapist to another, but the general procedure is for the couple to learn simple techniques such as agreeing to discuss only one problem at a time, avoiding aversive exchanges during problem-solving activity, avoiding making inferences about each other's motives or attitudes, and learning to paraphrase each other's remarks until the speaker agrees that the summary is accurate. To these general techniques are added several guidelines for problem definition, including beginning with a positive statement when delineating a problem, stating the problem in precise behavioral terms, incorporating feeling expressions into the statement of the problem, and acknowledging mutuality in perpetuating the problem. Once the problem is defined, the couple is taught to proceed then with a discussion of solutions. The solution phase of the process emphasizes the use of brainstorming, mutuality and compromise, and committing final agreements to writing in highly specific and concrete behavioral terms.

Problem-solving training appears to be a powerful treatment strategy for a wide variety of marital problems. Furthermore, if therapists are instrumental in helping couples learn skills that can be applied independently of the therapist to new situations, the technique can serve an important preventive function (Jacobson & Margolin, 1979).

Behavioral approaches to family therapy have much in common with the structural/systems approaches (Birchler & Spinks, 1980). Both approaches focus on present behaviors rather than past history, on interactional instead of intraindividual events, on observable and not unobservable behaviors, on interactional influences on current behavior, and on increasing members' cooperative problem-solving abilities. Both approaches assign primary importance to communication variables in the formulation of problems and in the development of ameliorative techniques. Behaviorists and systems therapists emphasize strategies for brief therapy and advocate the use of directive techniques (such as the assignment of homework) by the therapist. The differences between the two approaches include: (a) a greater emphasis on assessment procedures by behaviorists; (b) more explicit therapist modeling of desired behaviors by behaviorists; (c) less reliance on explicit therapeutic prescriptions based on principles of social learning by systems theorists; and (d) a greater tendency by behaviorists to account for reluctance to change in terms of case management variables instead of viewing it as an almost unavoidable aspect of the treatment solution.

A few years ago there appeared in the literature an elaborate and heated debate over the adequacy of the behavioral approach to marital and family therapy (Gurman & Kniskern, 1978; Gurman & Knudson, 1978; Gurman, Knudson, & Kniskern, 1978; Jacobson & Weiss, 1978; Jacobson, 1981) that will not be reviewed in detail here. Most of the criticisms focused on the behaviorists' assumption that clients are capable of collaborating in a programmed reciprocal effort to improve their relationship, on their tendency to focus exclusively on changing the frequency of overt behavior, on their generalizations concerning what is and what is not good communication, on their lack of attention to marital anger and hostility, and on their relative lack of emphasis on the importance of the therapist's interpersonal relationship skills. Each of these criticisms can be substantiated on various grounds, and each can be rebutted on certain other grounds. At this point in time concerned clinicians must determine for themselves which body of evidence is most convincing.

There do appear to be some shortcomings of the behavioral approach that are not easily answered, however. As Gurman (1980) has correctly noted, behaviorists have largely ignored what many others see as the principal source of resistance to change in marital and family therapy, namely the strong tendency of each individual to maintain his or her self-esteem and sense of identity. The resistance of the family qua family to change relates directly to this tendency as a function of (a) the amount of anxiety aroused in each person in the family as he or she confronts denied aspects of the self and (b) the extent to which family members participate in each other's efforts to avoid or escape from reintegration. Gurman (1980) states, "I believe that in the next decade, BMT (Behavioral Marital Therapy) will fall short of the mark in its efforts to become integrated with other methods of family therapy if it fails to acknowledge that family members themselves require reintegration as individuals in order for the family as a system to function effectively."

Another major shortcoming of the behavioral approach lies in the steadfast refusal to challenge the legitimacy of *any* problem as long as one member of the family is bothered or upset by a deficit or excess in the other's behavior. As Jacobson (1981) observes, from a behavioral perspective the issue of legitimacy of a complaint is "irrelevant to a problem-definition, since, when a behavior is upsetting to one spouse, it is *a priori* valid." But from a broader perspective the unilateral granting by the therapist of the right of each member of the family to set his or her own goals can lead to serious problems. As Gurman and Klein (1980) have pointed out, unquestioning acceptance of patient behavior-change goals can lead to the reinforcement of social stereotypes regarding social role behaviors that may be in themselves harmful to one or both participants.

Despite such criticism, behavioral therapy remains a powerful approach with well-developed and documented techniques for producing behavioral change. Most of the criticisms are aimed at theoretical and clinical differences regarding the practice of behavior therapy in its pure form and the exclusive reliance on social learning theory to explain all family interactions. Even the sharpest critics concede that behavioral approaches often are extremely useful and efficient in helping families to live together more productively (Gurman, 1980).

OBJECTIVES IN FAMILY INTERVENTION

In discussing the objectives of family intervention, some attention must be given first to the types of family problems that are most responsive to family intervention techniques. There is no universal agreement on this matter. At one extreme Williams (1967) essentially proposes using family therapy only as an adjunct or aid to individual therapy efforts, particularly when the identified patient is a child. Jackson and Weakland (1961), however, seem to imply that family intervention may be suitable for treating virtually any problem or type of family.

Among more denotative approaches to the question, Rabiner, Molinski, and Gralnick (1962) list several criteria for the selection of family cases on an inpatient unit. First, family intervention can be considered when current or anticipated family problems seem to be substantially affecting the inpatient's current and/or potential adjustment. Second, the involved family members must be able to attend sessions at least once a week. Third, the staff must have sufficient knowledge about the family to judge that (a) serious decompensation will be unlikely to result in any member as a result of conjoint sessions, (b) unfulfilled but potentially mutually gratifying needs are present, (c) the stress generated by conjoint sessions will be therapeutically manageable, and (d) the primary patient's relationship with the therapist is sufficiently strong that it is unlikely to be jeopardized by family sessions.

Jacobson (1981) lists and discusses several contraindications for behavioral marital therapy. First, marital therapy is not the treatment of choice as the sole intervention when the marital problems are due primarily to a medical problem or severe psychological disturbance of one spouse. Schizophrenia is listed as a prominent example of a severe disturbance that requires individual rather than marital treatment. Other family therapists, especially the systems theorists such as Jackson and Haley, believe that schizophrenic symptoms are the result of faulty family interactions and that family therapy, not individual therapy, is the treatment of choice in such instances. Second, Jacobson believes that marital therapy is futile when the principal source of distress is one spouse's involvement in an extramarital sexual relationship. Third, marital therapy is contraindicated when one or both spouses prefer to end the relationship. Divorce counseling may be helpful in such situations, but it involves different goals and tactics from those of marital therapy. As Jacobson observes, "The mandate of a marital therapist is to serve the interests of the clients, not to protect or foster the institution of marriage." Fourth, Jacobson does not believe that the usual behavioral therapy approach, with its extended assessment process, is appropriate for families in crisis situations. Finally, behavioral marital therapy may be contraindicated simply because it impresses some couples as excessively contrived or mechanical.

Wynne (1971) has written cogently about indications for deciding to initiate exploratory family therapy. He recommends its consideration with the following types of family problems: (a) adolescent separation problems, which can also include older patients who have never effected a real separation from their parents; (b) families characterized by a trading of dissociations such that members locate the totality of a trait or feeling in another family member while being blind to similar traits in themselves; (c) families characterized by collective cognitive chaos and erratic distancing; and (d) families marked by fixed interpersonal and cognitive distancing with eruptive threats and episodes.

Wynne (1971) also speaks of conditions that, if not met, limit the advisability or practicality of family therapy. First, there must be a family constellation available in which the members are emotionally invested and entangled and not simply intellectually interested in going along with the therapist. Wynne does not rigidly define which members are to be included, but only specifies that it should be "those who are functionally linked together, within discernible psychological boundaries." Second, the initiation of family therapy must fit constructively with the overall therapeutic process in which the identified patient is engaged. For example, in instances in which the family is very entangled, family sessions may precede any other therapeutic efforts. At other times individual therapy may best be interrupted to treat emerging family problems and resumed after the family therapy is completed. Such shifts must be carried out in a therapeutically strategic rather than haphazard manner if therapeutic trust is to be maintained. The author has provided elsewhere an example of a case that required several shifts from individual to family therapy and back again (Fox, 1974).

Third, the right kind of therapist must be available for conducting family therapy. Wynne (1971) lists as desirable qualities of the family therapist self-awareness, capacity for restraint, capacity for active limit-setting behavior, and capacity for sustained interest. To Wynne's list, I add only a few considerations. A cotherapist is often highly useful with severely disturbed families and families lacking an adequate opposite-sex role model. Also, I like to structure therapy so that the form of treatment parallels the goals that are set. For example, in treating adolescent separation problems, I commonly obtain a different individual therapist for the adolescent. This treatment is in addition to the family therapy sessions. The adolescent is under no requirement to divulge the details of the individual therapy to either the rest of the family or to me. This treatment format emphasizes the adolescent's separateness, while at the same time recognizing his other continuing ties to the family. Thus, the treatment process, which aims at the achievement of separateness, proceeds by treating the adolescent separately.

It can be advanced as a general principle that family therapists' techniques should be closely tied to their objectives, which in turn flow from some idea or theory about what families should be like and what is "wrong" with the unit at hand. In the face of considerable diversity, some broadly endorsed objectives of family therapy can be noted. Hess and Handel (1967), for example, have identified five objectives related to concerns common to all family units:

1. Establishing patterns of separateness and connectedness
2. Establishing a satisfactory congruence of images through the exchange of suitable testimony, for example, of self, of others, of the family
3. Evolving modes of interaction in central family concerns or themes
4. Establishing the boundaries of the family's world of experience
5. Dealing with significant biosocial issues of family life, as in defining *male* and *female* and *old* and *young*

Sprankle and Fisher (1980) surveyed 600 clinical members of the American Association of Family Therapists regarding their goals as family therapists. A list of 34 goals was compiled by the authors from the literature and grouped into three clusters or dimensions that had been delineated by Olson, Sprenkle, and Russell (1979): adaptability, communication, and cohesion. Respondents were asked to rate each goal on a Likert-type scale and rank their top seven choices from among the 34 goals. Their final sample consisted of 310 respondents from a broad spectrum of theoretical orientations. In terms of adaptability (the ability of the system to change its roles, rules, and power structure in response to stress), these family therapists favored helping clients to negotiate differences successfully, to change interaction patterns, or to generate new ideas in the face of new information. On the communication dimension they emphasized helping members listen attentively to each other, value the input of others and of themselves, speak for themselves rather than others, and share their feelings. Under the cohension dimension (the emotional bonding that family members feel toward each other) the respondents rated most highly the goals of helping family members be autonomous and self-responsible and helping them validate and nurture one another with regard to emotional needs.

All of the theorists discussed in the preceding section point to the need to help troubled families meet one or more of the above goals. Three broad related goals or objectives that most theorists share are (a) strengthening the family as a system, (b) increasing separation–individuation, and (c) strengthening the marital relationship.

Strengthening the Family System

The objective of strengthening the family system has several implications for the kinds of techniques employed in family therapy. First and foremost, the therapist attempts to help the system function better by helping the flow of communications. The techniques for doing this include modeling clear, direct, and open communication for the family, reinterpreting messages, checking out what message was sent and how it compared with the message received, forcing members to talk *to* each other rather than *about* each other through the therapist, directing members to rephrase questions as demands, and identifying and making overt emerging feeling tones (Satir, 1964). It is important to note here a common misconception of beginners that family therapy does not take place unless the family members constantly talk to each other. If excessive, this concern may lead the therapist to deprive the family of significant corrective experiences and allow them simply to repeat past interactive patterns. Even while not engaged in conversation directly, other members may gain a great deal from hearing one member describe feelings or interact intensely with the therapist in a manner different from anything they have seen before. In this sense it is proper to say that individual therapy conducted in the presence of the family has an impact far different from that of individual therapy conducted in isolation. The impact is different for the individual and for the others who witness his or her struggle. Some writers have speculated that the whole key to change in family therapy is communication in each other's presence and not necessarily communication *with* each other (Beels & Ferber, 1969).

Naturally, therapists cannot help the family system unless they first succeed in getting them to view themselves as a system rather than as a family with a member who has a problem (identified patient). One of the basic methods for doing this is to see all the family together, at least in the initial treatment phase. Joint sessions help bring to light other family issues that may be important, and they dramatically illustrate the premise that the identified patient became disturbed in a social context and can best be understood and helped in that context. Another common misunderstanding of beginning therapists occurs at this point. In an effort to broaden the treatment context from an individual to a family one, the neophyte often ignores the identified patient. This is a mistake. Although therapists want to "get to the family," they cannot afford to ignore the pain in any of its members. Their task is to keep both individual reactions and family processes in mind without allowing the family to exclude either one from attention. In this connection, Bell's (1963) admonition is appropriate: "Let it be recognized . . . that although family group treatment seeks the well-being of the family, secondarily it has important consequences for the states of individuals who make up the family."

As a rule, family therapists tend to place more emphasis on changing patterns of interaction than on increasing understanding. Thus for Zuk (1967) the goal is to "shift the balance of pathogenic relating among family members so that new forms of relating become possible." This is accomplished by the therapist's taking sides in order to intensify and then reduce conflicts (Zuk, 1971). Similarly, Jackson and Weakland (1961) believe that pointing out repetitive, self-defeating patterns does little good, and they accordingly counsel therapists to pay less attention to noting and describing the content of patterns and more to influencing or changing the patterns. Not all therapists denigrate increased understanding to the extent that Jackson does, however. Laquer et al. (1964) list as a primary objective the development of better understanding of the reasons for the family members' disturbing behavior toward each other. Schaffer et al. (1962) also attach importance to increasing the family's understanding of maladaptive behavior patterns. The point is that all therapists emphasize the necessity of activity changing patterns rather than simply pointing them out. As Framo (1969) says, "Any therapist worth his salt knows that just pointing out, confronting, or interpreting things to people cannot work by itself." Some therapists feel that increased understanding helps bring about this change; others do not: "The goal of changing the family system of interaction is family therapy's most distinctive feature, its greatest advantage and, especially to those who come to it from other disciplines, its greatest stumbling block" (Beels & Ferber, 1969).

The deemphasis on increasing understanding is part of a general trend, both in individual and in family therapy, to emphasize action and change rather than insight. Bell (1963) has best summarized the changing viewpoint: "Whereas formerly we assumed that insight ultimately led to action by some unknown process, we now concluded that action may be seen more fruitfully as coming before insight. Action has the primacy rather than insight." Accordingly, a family therapist may actively encourage the formation of a father–son coalition before anyone in the family "understands" that mother and son have been "too close," that father has assented by withdrawing, and that these actions protect each of them from acknowledging painful affects. Sometimes the understanding follows, but commonly it does not. This is different from a model that helps the family attain "insight" and then waits for them to put the understanding into practice, and it is a cardinal feature of the attitude of many family therapists.

Wynne (1969) suggests that the concept of insight is dead and should be left to die in peace, since it is no longer seen as the primary agent of change even by many classical psychoanalysts. Wynne feels that "if the term is to be used at all, the gaining of 'insight' about the family may be useful to the therapist, rarely to the family." The changing ideas about the value of insight are not restricted to family therapists, who in this respect seem to be part of the current therapeutic *Zeitgeist*. Strupp (1973), a leading psychoanalytic scholar, labeled the idea that insight leads to therapeutic change a "convenient fiction" with no adequate empirical evidence to support it. Although admitting that some patients during the course of therapy do gain understanding of motivations (particularly those that lead to neurotic entanglements), Strupp (1973) maintains that "such understanding may be intellectually satisfying and have an aesthetic appeal to certain patients. However, as far as behavior and personality change is concerned, I feel that, by and large, it is not a highly potent force in producing change."

Strengthening the family system as a system also has implications for the therapist. Once a system's approach is adopted, it then becomes as impossible to view therapy as something that involves only the family as it is to view pathology as something that involves only the identified patient. The therapist becomes involved in a system of interactions with the family as a participant rather than as a distant "healer." Such involvements make it difficult to blame failures glibly on the family because they are "too defensive." Rather, the explanation has to be more along the following lines: Therapy failed because the therapist collaborated in establishing a relationship in which several members were allowed to be less than candid and to continue to use rigid modes of interacting. Shapiro and Budman (1973), in a study of individual and family cases who continued treatment as opposed to those who terminated, found that the therapist's behavior was pivotal. A majority of terminators, both individual and family, cited the therapist's behavior as an important factor in termination. Among continuers there was an important difference between individual and family cases. Family continuers lauded high levels of therapist activity, whereas terminators deplored therapist inactivity. Individual continuers, however, emphasized the therapist's empathy and concern.

Increasing Separation–Individuation

A second broad objective of family treatment is to help each of the members achieve increased separation–individuation. In a sense, this is a general objective of all psychotherapies. An increased sense of autonomy, of personal responsibility, and of being responsive to but not overly dependent on others is a primary goal of psychoanalysis, gestalt therapy, and a host of other approaches. In adopting this objective, therapists are reflecting an ideal of human behavior that has been seen as the key to happiness by widely varying cultures across several centuries. It has been knitted into the fabric of religions as diverse as Zen and Christianity (e.g., Buber, 1958), into sociological theories such as Riesman's (1950) ideal of the autonomous man, and into various other systems of thought such as that described in Castaneda's (1972) anthropological studies. The ancient Zen writers captured the essence of the idea as well as any (Kapleau, 1965). For them, man should strive to be as a stick in a river. The stick flows fast or slowly as the water dictates, always responsive to its varying shifts. Yet the stick is always stick, it never becomes water. This is very similar to Riesman's idea of *autonomous* people who are keenly responsive and attuned to their interpersonal climate without ever sacrificing their own identity and separateness. It is this ideal that has been incorporated into many theories of psychotherapy, including most of the family approaches.

Bowen (1966) probably has placed more emphasis on this goal than any other writer in the family therapy literature. Ideally, he believes, the best results are obtained when family members can work together mutually to encourage and affirm higher levels of autonomy in each other. When this is impossible, the therapist can start the differentiation in one member, support his or her independence through the period of counter-pressures from the family, and then help the family unit to develop a new homeostasis on a new level of differentiation. Bell (1963) states the objective here: "The therapist does not simply try to make the family more 'groupy,' more cohesive, but on the contrary, tries to promote its growth and differentiation." As differentiation is achieved, pressures to constrict behavior in order to protect or help some other member of the family are lessened and greater flexibility in the system is manifest. Szasz (1959) has reacted to the tendency of family members to hold each other responsible for their individual happiness: "Given a certain (considerable) measure of autonomy, and therefore of separateness between people, it becomes quite impossible for anyone to 'make someone (else) happy.' The only person toward whose happiness we can contribute directly is our own. To the happiness of others, as I see it, we can contribute at most indirectly."

Strengthening the Marriage

The third broad objective of family therapy, strengthening the marital relationship, is not independent of the two previously mentioned objectives but is separated here for purposes of discussion. As Bowen (1966) has observed, intense marital conflict does not always cause emotional problems in the offspring, and, conversely, children can develop serious impairment when the marital relationship of the parents is not disrupted. However, it is the general rule that in dysfunctional families impaired marital relationships are probable. Many family therapists see the marital relationship as the basic relationship on which all others in the family depend. Change in this relationship can thus lead to rapid and widespread changes throughout the family system. "If the illness is in the family group, one should start with the group's leadership, and the parents are, in Satir's phrase, the architects of the family, the place where the main authority ought to be and where lasting sexual and contractual bonds should be cemented" (Beels and Farber, 1969).

Although strengthening the family system is a goal of most family therapists, it is not the case that the therapy has failed if the marital pair decides to separate. Any experienced therapist has encountered the couple who comes to treatment for permission to separate. It is frequently the case that such couples already have decided that divorce is the best option available to them but then become so frightened or overwhelmed by the implications and the problems generated by a divorce that they shrink from facing the difficulties and make inadequate attempts to improve the marriage. This approach–avoidance behavior on the part of one or both spouses is particularly evident in guilt-prone individuals. In such instances it becomes the task of the therapist to help the immobilized pair to verbalize and deal directly with an explicit or implicit decision that already has been made. Observing that the decision-making process is not easier or shorter than other forms of family therapy, Birchler and Spinks (1980) conclude that "it is important to realize that treating the terminating marriage is an essential part of relationship therapy which requires as much skill as endeavors to keep the spouses together." Family therapists should never fail to recognize or accept dissolution or divorce as a reasonable option for many couples.

In my experience, the families that make the most rapid and lasting changes are those in which there is an early identification of marital problems that the parents are willing to work at alleviating. At this point in the treatment children are typically excused, even when they are a part of the presenting problem. One reason for excusing the children is to emphasize thereby the separation of differing roles in the two generations. Parents handle adult problems without the unnecessary involvement of the children. If therapists are successful in "getting to the marriage," they often have the battle more than half won. Dramatic changes in children almost regularly follow real changes in the parental relationship. Some families appear to contain a disruptive marital relationship to which everyone in the family resists attending. In such cases it is sometimes possible to help the family alter some interactions resulting in a particularly painful role for one of its members without changing the marital relationship. In this case the therapist helps the family "accommodate to the symptom" rather than change it.

FAMILY INTERVENTION TECHNIQUES

Jackson and Weakland (1961) list several aspects of the family therapist's attitude and behavior that are different from those of the individual therapist. The family therapist typically finds it necessary to be more active, assertive, and directive than the individual therapist. If he or she is merely a passive listener, then the therapist will typically find that the family either ignores his or her comments and reflections or incorporates them into the ongoing interaction pattern with no apparent change in behavior. Similarly, the therapist may find it necessary to intervene forcefully by directing one member to be silent or by encouraging another to rephrase a comment, or by asking for a change in the seating arrangement to facilitate or discourage certain interactions.

A family's destructive interaction patterns are typically noticed very early, and the therapist becomes more interested in identifying and changing such patterns than in understanding individual dynamics. This means that the therapist's behavior is directed less toward individual motives or fantasies and more toward interpersonal perceptions and transactional sequences. This leads to a corresponding decrease in emphasis on asking the kinds of questions that are considered useful in establishing individual diagnoses. Thus, when confronted with profound sadness in one member, the therapist is less inclined to ask about such factors as changes in sleep patterns, loss of appetite, changes in memory, and the like and more inclined to look for the function of the sadness in the family system. A family seen by the author was referred because of a 13-year-old son who was expressing suicidal thoughts. It was subsequently learned that the behavior emerged following the loss of his maternal grandmother, to whom he had not been particularly close. However, his mother had been very close to the grandmother, and, as his mother began to experience and work through her own profound sadness and loss, the boy's depression lifted. In terms of the system, concern over the son's depression made it possible for the family to ignore a more serious depression in the mother.

A technique sometimes used involves working with one member alone to help the individual make essential changes that force changes in crucial family interaction. Bowen (1966) describes this process as one in which one member is helped to become an expert on how the family system operates and thus is in a position to effect important changes in times of family disequilibrium. Ewing and Fox (1968) report in this regard working with wives of alchoholics to help them change their pattern of rescue, protection, and belittling behavior vis-à-vis their husbands. As these wives' behavior changed, there were often changes in their husbands' drinking behavior, even though they had not been in therapy themselves.

This technique can be especially useful in circumventing therapeutic impasses. A couple consulted me who were on the verge of divorce because of the husband's infidelity, his confusion over whether or not he still wanted to be married, and his inability to escape from a domineering father who owned the business in which the husband worked. The husband felt pressured from all sides to make important decisions concerning marriage, work, and the future of his relationship with his paramour. In this context therapy was seen by him as further pressure to explain himself and take responsibility. His response to the various pressures was to withdraw into a very schizoid-like state, which served to stimulate the wife into more desperate requests for reassurance concerning the viability of the marriage. In conjoint sessions he became progressively more silent as his wife's attempts to make him discuss his feelings steadily escalated. When initial attempts to break through the husband's resistance to therapy failed, I excused him and worked with the wife. The aim was to help the wife moderate her desperate attempt to secure some sign of love from her husband. After three sessions she was highly successful in altering her interactions with her husband, and he changed dramatically for the better. Friends who knew the couple were in therapy but who were unaware of the approach being used commented on the obvious changes that had taken place in them. These comments helped to reinforce the new pattern and encouraged the husband to reenter therapy. He requested joint sessions in order to further the marital relationship and a major resistance to treatment was avoided.

Still another method of altering pathological family alliances is through the encouragement of new coalitions that make maintenance of the original, pathological one more difficult. Hoffman (1971) cites example of changing the role of a family scapegoat by creating a new scapegoat, that is, by emphasizing problems and/or disruptive behaviors present in another member that have been ignored by the family. Minuchin (1974) presents a comprehensive and lucid description of how to understand family coalitions and then use this understanding to effect more functional patterns of interaction.

Some family therapists, especially those following a systems approach, utilize paradoxical directives or prescriptions to circumvent impasses created by family resistances or homeostatic efforts (Palazzoli-Selvini et al., 1978; Andolfi, 1980). Faced with a family that paradoxically seeks family therapy but rejects all efforts by the therapist to effect change, the therapist may direct the family members to continue or intensify the problem behaviors (prescribing the symptom). The prescription is paradoxical in that the therapist is attempting to change the system by advising the family not to change. When used skillfully, the technique can be extremely effective in breaking through seemingly impenetrable barriers.

Family therapists also use teaching methods oriented toward improving communication skills as a method of effecting changes in the family, as was mentioned in the section of this chapter dealing with behavioral therapy approaches. Ely, Guerney, and Stover (1973) describe a training program that involves 8 to 10 2-hour sessions focusing on communication skills (such as listening for and reflecting feeling tones). This is supplemented by scheduled practice sessions at home ½ hour a week and working through a programmed text, 1 hour a week for 6 weeks. Weissman and Montgomery (1980) report the use of a group educational process using coaching and videotape feedback to teach families communication and problem-solving skills. Some families are able to resolve difficulties of family members following this educational process. In these approaches the therapist is clearly in the role of a teacher helping each person be an effective, empathic listener. This approach prevents family members from seeing the therapist as the only one who can truly understand them and thereby becoming increasingly resentful toward each other. Such training has been found to be highly effective in bringing about communication-pattern changes highly correlated with better marital adjustment.

In a similar vein, I have had some success in teaching family members to listen for the statement about self that is implicit in practically every interpersonal statement and in all accusations. For example, when a wife angrily says to her husband, "You think more of your job than you do of me," she is making a statement both about the husband and about herself. Besides accusing the husband of neglect, she is also expressing hurt over not being more important to him. If the husband can be helped to listen for and respond to his wife's hurt and desire for affection rather than to the accusation, a meaningful discussion rather than a fight is likely to ensure. If he responds only to the statement about himself, a cycle of defense, charge, and countercharge is likely. By responding to the part of the message that reflects something about the sender's feelings, the receiver can avoid cyclical, self-defeating patterns of interaction. Fitzgerald (1973) has pointed out the positive benefits of increased willingness to listen in highly conflicted couples. As mentioned previously, this may help account for the fact that having a spouse present and listening while the therapist works with the partner can be highly beneficial to the relationship.

The ability to listen effectively depends very much on the ability to disengage oneself sufficiently from the interaction process to be able to observe its pattern and effects. If one is only an observer or only a participant, the ability to be participant–observer is lost. Bowen, as described by Beels and Farber (1969), seems to help patients achieve this role by instructing them to visit their parents and take an extensive family history from them. Beels and Farber (1969) note that this process often has a "surprisingly powerful effect on the mutual understanding of both parties; it must be tried to be appreciated." It may be that the technique gains some of its effectiveness from emphasizing the patient's role as observer rather than merely as an unwitting participant.

Another method of helping a person be more observant and not simply a participant has been described by Minuchin and Montalvo (1967). These authors sometimes ask a family member to observe from behind a one-way screen while others in the family interact. Minuchin (1974) asks members of a family coalition to interact in the middle of the room while other members observe from an outer circle. Perlmutter et al. (1967) use videotape playbacks of portions of family sessions as material in subsequent family sessions. All are methods for creating distance in order to increase the ability to observe, to understand, and, it is hoped, to change.

The use of multiple therapists has been reported by several clinicians. This technique seems especially useful in time-limited approaches in which intensive interaction over brief periods is indicated. The multiple-impact approach employed by McGregor et al. (1964) necessitates intense interaction of various combinations of family members with different therapists. Similarly, the highly successful crisis model developed at the University of Colorado Medical Center (Langsley et al., 1968) employs several therapists in flexible combinations with various family groupings to prevent hospitalization of the identified patient. Using this approach, the team prevented hospitalization in over 90% of the acute crises in which an independent expert had already deemed hospitalization necessary.

Many clinicians prefer to work with a cotherapist when treating families, although there is no empirical evidence that two therapists obtain better results than one therapist (Gurman, 1973). There are numerous advantages to this technique, however:

1. The family is provided with multiple models of interaction styles.
2. If the cotherapists are male and female, the family has a model of a healthy adult heterosexual relationship, which enriches potential transference effects.
3. General clinical expertise and therapeutic power are enhanced.
4. Differing vantage points allow for cross-validation of hypotheses and observation.
5. The therapists' willingness to expose and deal openly with their differing perceptions is an effective modeling technique.

Woody and Woody (1973) list three essential prerequisites if cotherapists are to work together effectively. First, each must have a full understanding of the other's style of functioning, so that he or she can almost predict how the cotherapist will respond in a given interaction. Second, there must be professional respect and an appreciation of why the other functions as he or she does and how this is justified theoretically. Third, and most important, there must be a relationship characterized by "honest, personalized intimacy." Mutual knowledge, professional acceptance, and shared respect are not sufficient; there also must be an open, frank, and genuinely positive relationship.

Behavior modification techniques have been used extensively by some therapists. Many of the techniques developed by behavior therapists were covered in an earlier section of this chapter. Birchler and Spinks (1980) summarize a number of behavioral intervention techniques in attempting to demontrate how a behavioral approach can be integrated with a systems approach in clinical work. Haley (1971), perhaps reacting to the fact that marital therapists have been particularly fascinated by behavioral approaches, believes that behavior therapists think only in terms of dyads and not in terms of larger units. Thus, he comments, they speak of the manner in which one parent or the other reinforces the child and not in terms of conflicts between parents about the child. This is not completely true, even in the relatively simple instances of increasing the frequency of desired behavior through reinforcement. Liberman (1970), for example,observes that family behavior therapy progresses best when all of the members of an interlocking, rigid family system learn to change their behavior (response) toward other members: "Instead of rewarding maladaptive behavior with attention and concern, the family members learn to give each other recognition and approval for desired behavior." Liberman is clearly talking about the whole family system rather than specific dyads.

Desensitization has been employed to change behaviors such as sexual inhibitions. Some techniques utilized by Masters and Johnson (1970) and Kaplan (1974) can easily be conceptualized as desensitization, for example, when couples are instructed to work on sexual inhibitions via a programmed sequence of exercises involving increasing intimacy. Other types of hierarchies can be developed for several members of the family and worked through (deconditioned) in the actual family setting. This is superior to the usual practice of asking an individual patient to fantasize increasingly fearful scenes while in a relaxed state. Used in a family context, the technique can be particularly powerful in that the interpersonal milieu in which one undergoes change is the very one in which each individual must operate daily on a face-to-face basis.

Role playing is a further behavioral technique that has enjoyed widespread use in work with families. Family members can be assigned roles designed to help them deal directly with alternative interaction styles. Another variation is to ask members to switch roles so as to increase their appreciation of how the others are behaving. Role playing has proved particularly effective in reinforcing desired assertive behaviors for a particular family member (Lazarus, 1971). Again, it is worth emphasizing that practicing such behavior with one's family in a context of mutual understanding and support often has far greater impact than similar practice with the therapist alone.

A misconception commonly found in criticisms of behavior modification approaches is that the therapist relies on prescribed formulas for particular symptoms, which are then applied more or less blindly. In fact, however, behavior therapists rely as much on what others would call "clinical skills" (e.g., intuitive judgment) as do other types of therapists. After observing behavior therapy as practiced at one leading center, Klein, Dittman, Parloff, and Gill (1969) reported: "The selection of problems to be worked on seemed quite arbitrary and inferential. We were frankly surprised to find the presenting symptomatic complaint was often sidestepped for what the therapist intuitively considered to be more basic issues. Most surprising to us, the basis for this selection seemed often to be what others would call dynamic considerations" (p. 261).

For a thorough discussion of behavioral approaches in family treatment, the interested reader should consult Jacobson (1981). For our purposes it is sufficient to say that behavior modification has contributed numerous techniques whose applications to family difficulties seem limited only by the ingenuity of the therapist. Typically, family therapists as a group demonstrate a pragmatic willingness to draw techniques from any theory if that technique promises to be of help. Behavior modification has proved to be a rich source of techniques and of theoretical insights.

Before concluding the discussion of techniques, a word of caution concerning their use is in order. Many techniques from widely divergent theoretical systems seem to produce results. All family therapists who are willing to make the effort to learn and use different methods of dealing with the same problem can easily demonstrate this to their own satisfaction. An example may be helpful:

A 26-year-old woman, married for 2 years, was referred to an outpatient clinic because of a paralysis of the lower right arm and hand. Neurological and physical examinations were negative. Psychological testing and diagnostic interviews revealed "sexual conflict, guilt over masturbatory practices, and strong but poorly recognized dependency needs." The paralysis was believed to be a result of her conflicts, and intensive depth-oriented psychotherapy was recommended. Since no individual therapist was available, the social worker in charge of the case decided to interview the patient's husband for further study and clarification. New material was discovered that made it possible to conceptualize the problem in a completely different manner. The patient's husband was a dependent person who was still very attached to his mother. Shortly after his marriage he was discharged from military service and returned with his wife to live with his mother. He was unable to decide whether to return to college or go to work and had delayed a decision for almost 2 years. As the living pattern of the triad eventually developed, the husband and his mother did the household shopping, took short trips together, and the like, while the wife worked to support them. The wife resented her husband's lack of direction and closeness with his mother, but never refused to provide financial support. After 2 years the sudden arm paralysis prevented her continued work as a typist. Family therapy was initiated with the aim of helping the couple to establish more independence from the husband's mother. This was accomplished rather quickly and was followed a few weeks later by the husband's decision about a career goal and a disappearance of the wife's paralysis.

The point here is not that family therapy is superior to individual therapy. Hysterical conversion symptoms are frequently treated in dynamic psychotherapy with good results. The point is that the explanations for the cause of the symptom are quite different from different theoretical vantage points, and thus different approaches (techniques) are indicated. Psychoanalysis would explain the symptom as a sexual conflict (which was certainly present in this instance) and propose individual psychotherapy. A family systems theorist would explain the symptom in interpersonal–interactional terms and propose the treatment that was in fact used. I have little doubt that either approach would have worked. But, in view of the fact that different approaches based on divergent explanations often yield similar results, the neophyte would do well to avoid dogmatic adherence to any particular system or set of techniques. Strupp (1973) has summarized this point very well. Although he was speaking of individual psychotherapy, his comment is no less true of family therapy approaches: "While every professional psychotherapist has deep commitments to some theoretical framework within which his therapeutic work is embedded, there is no evidence that one set of theoretical assumptions is more satisfactory than another—either in terms of what it permits the therapist to do or the outcomes to which it gives rise" (p. 282).

RESULTS OF FAMILY THERAPY

Research on the outcomes of family and marital therapy over the past decade has expanded exponentially, and there has been a parallel growth in the number of practitioners attracted to the field. When Wells, Dilkes, and Trivelli published one of the first reviews of family outcome studies in 1972, only 13 studies were available. Only 6 years later, when Gurman and Kniskern (1978) published one of the most recent and perhaps the most comprehensive review to date, over 200 studies reporting on results with almost 5,000 cases were available. The growth in family therapy outcome research is also reflected in the increase in the number of reviews that have become available. The first such review was published by Lebedun in 1970, and during the subsequent 10 years over 30 additional reviews appeared in the literature.

Since the substance of such a large body of research cannot be covered thoroughly here, this section will attempt to summarize some of the major findings and remaining problems that have been identified. Only a sample of the methodologically sound studies available are discussed in any detail. Those interested in more detailed information should consult excellent reviews by de Witt (1978), Gurman and Kniskern (1978), Jacobson (1979), and Wells and Dezen (1978), as well as a recent overview of the current state of the art in family therapy outcome research provided by Gurman and Kniskern (1981b).

Family therapy researchers face all the problems attendant on research in individual psychotherapy, together with other problems particular to this field:

1. The unit of study is larger and more complex.
2. Events that occur are often the result of many factors.
3. The identification and control of variables are complex and difficult.
4. The unit of study is in a state of continuous change.
5. Observers are often a part of the system they observe and may change with it.
6. The area of study is wider, encompassing intrapsychic, relationship, communication, and group variables as well as contextual variables such as community, cultural, and social pressures.

The familiar problems of all outcome research are also to be found here. There are no adequate criterion measures with which to assess change. There is no adequate diagnostic or classification system for the clinical conditions being studied. And no empirical method exists for comparing treatment methods. In short, outcome studies are plagued by major problems at every stage of the scientific enterprise, from specification of the important antecedent conditions in the participants, through precise delineation of the intervening treatment variables, to measures of specific results (Coché, 1978; Gurman & Kniskern, 1978). The best that can be said at present is that family therapy outcome studies enjoy the same inconclusive results as have characterized attempts to evaluate all other known forms of psychotherapeutic intervention. "Despite decades of persistent debate, the advent of new techniques, theoretical writings, and—alas—voluminous empirical studies, the basic issue concerning specific effects as a function of specific interventions remains as foggy as ever" (Strupp, 1973). This impression is discussed further in relation to the current status of outcome research in individual psychotherapy by Weiner and Bordin in Chapter 7.

Realizing that evidence for the efficacy of family therapy is short of overwhelming, let us look at the empirical studies that have been reported. If as suggested by Wells et al. (1972) one restricts oneself to those studies that report on at least three cases, clearly specify the outcome measures used, and include a control group, fewer than a dozen reports are available (Gurman & Kniskern, 1978).

Most of the uncontrolled, single-group studies that constitute the majority of the total number of research reports to date contain other methodological flaws, such as reliance on subjective reports as the sole outcome measure and failure to report pretherapy and/or follow-up measures. Nevertheless, there is some merit in many of these studies. The realities of clinical work being what they are, unwanted compromises are almost inevitable, and researchers must do the best possible job under the circumstances. The most common methodological flaw across all family therapy outcome studies is the lack of a control group. Although controlled treatment studies have a logical power that is undeniable, there are several important caveats to keep in mind (Gurman & Kniskern, 1971b): (a) The research ethics of placing families in need of help in a no-treatment control group has serious emotional, political, and social implications; (b) untreated controls often secure some sort of help for themselves, as has been well documented in individual psychotherapy research (Bergin and Lambert, 1978); and (c) the relevant variables on which control and experimental families should be matched are unknown.

Summarizing across all uncontrolled, single-group studies and the 12 controlled studies, it appears that the improvement rate is roughly two-thirds: 73% for family therapy and 65% for marital therapy (Gurman & Kniskern, 1978).

Two of the early studies with an adequate methodology (actually an early and a final report of the same project) remain among the most impressive reports to date (Langsley et al., 1968, 1969). In this project 150 families residing in the metropolitan Denver area for whom hospitalization had been recommended for one of its members were randomly assigned to a short-term, crisis-intervention treatment group. The control group comprised 150 similar families with a patient who was admitted for conventional psychiatric inpatient treatment. The criterion measures were hospitalization rates, days lost from functioning, and performance on two rating scales. The scales, which were called the Social Adjustment Inventory and the Personal Functioning Scale, were apparently devised by the research group for this study. Six-month follow-up data are available for 90% of the subjects.

All of the 150 family therapy cases were treated without admission to the hospital. Over the subsequent 6-month period following treatment, 13% were hospitalized. This result compared favorably with the 29% readmission rate among the hospitalized controls. Days lost from functioning had a median of 5 for the family therapy cases and 23 for the control group. Both groups showed improvement on the two rating scales used, but there were no significant differences between the groups. Thus patients treated by family therapy instead of being admitted to a hospital returned to functioning an average of 2 weeks earlier, were functioning as well 6 months later, and were less likely to have spent part of the 6 months since treatment in the hospital in comparison to similar patients who had been hospitalized initially.

It should be emphasized that basic tenets of sound research methodology were observed in this study. The families were randomly assigned to experimental and control groups, the groups were found to be statistically equal in all major respects, several outcome measures were utilized, and measures were obtained prior to and at the conclusion of treatment as well as at the end of a 6-month follow-up period.

The major shortcomings in the study are that the outcome measures employed are confounded with the short-term nature of the treatment, the crisis orientation of the approach, and the family therapy methods (Wells et al., 1972) and that the validity of the rating scales used is questionable. Nevertheless, the study is on the whole impressive. Averting hospitalization for 150 seriously disturbed individuals is no mean accomplishment, and the differential readmission rates following treatment indicate that hospitalization was averted rather than simply delayed.

A more recent report provides some striking results regarding the use of family interventions to prevent or avert the placement of a family member in a group or foster home or some other institutional care facility (Kinney et al., 1977). Therapists entered the homes of families in crisis for extended periods of time to help each family find suitable coping methods other than the outplacement of one of its members. Outside placement was prevented for 121 of 134 family members, resulting in an average saving of over $2300 per client compared to projected placement costs. These results are encouraging despite the fact that the intensity of therapeutic activity and availability was confounded with the location of intervention (Gurman & Kniskern, 1981b).

Further research will have to become more specific and less broad-gauged than has been the case thus far. The question of whether family therapy "works" is not only too general to be meaningful, but is also simply unanswerable. The real question for future research is which kind of therapy administered by which therapist is likely to lead to what specific result in specified types of families. Although we are obviously a long way from the achievement of this kind of precision, knowledge proceeds and increasingly sophisticated research is being done.

A few general statements concerning which of the myriad family therapies are most effective can be formulated:

1. For marital problem conjoint treatment seems clearly superior to either collaborative, concurrent, or individual treatment (Gurman & Kniskern, 1978).

2. Behavioral and nonbehavioral therapy seem to be equally effective for minimally to moderately distressed couples (Gurman & Kniskern, 1981b)

3. The lone treatment techniques that consistently have been shown to facilitate

positive outcomes (at least for marital approaches) are those that increase the communication skills of couples (Birchler, 1979).

4. Conjoint behaviorally oriented therapy for couples with sexual dysfunctions appears to be the treatment of choice for such problems, provided that severe nonsexual marital problems do not exist (Jacobson, 1978).

5. Many types of family therapy appear to be at least as effective as (and often more effective than) commonly used treatments such as individual psycho-therapy for problems that involve family conflict (Gurman & Kniskern, 1981b).

6. Behavioral family therapy appears to be very effective in decreasing the frequency of such selected intrafamily childhood behavior as aggressiveness (Patterson, 1976).

7. Some family therapies, notably the structural approach of Minuchin, appear to be highly effective in the treatment of childhood and adolescent psychoso-matic problems such as asthma (Minuchin et al., 1978) and anorexia (Min-uchin, 1974). In addition, Stanton and Todd (1978) have reported highly impressive results of well-controlled studies utilizing structural family ther-apy with adult drug addicts.

Although it is not an outcome study, a report by Minuchin (1974) provides an excellent example of the increasingly sophisticated research which is beginning to emerge in the family therapy literature. Both children in a family Minuchin studied were diabetic, but they presented very different medical problems. Dede, the older, was a superlabile diabetic who had been admitted to the hospital for treatment of ketoacidosis 23 times in 3 years. The younger sister, Violet, had some behavioral problems, but they were not severe and her diabetes was under good control. It was possible to demonstrate that the sisters responded differently to family stress by measuring the level of plasma-fatty acids (FFA) in the blood from samples drawn during structured interviews. Minuchin states that the blood samples were drawn from each family member in such a way that obtaining the samples did not interfere with ongoing interactions.

The sisters watched through a one-way screen while their parents were subjected to stress conditions. Even though they were not directly involved, each showed marked increases in FFA levels. When they were brought into the room with the parents, the levels rose still higher, but much more so for Dede than her younger sister. When with the parents, the more responsive girl, Dede, was seen to play a different role from that of her sister. Dede's support was frequently sought by each parent in such a way that she could not respond to one without seeming to side against the other. This was not true of the younger sister, whose support was not sought by either parent. After the interview with the parents, Violet's FFA level returned promptly to baseline, whereas Dede's remained elevated for the next 1½ hours. Significantly, both parents showed elevated FFA levels in the latter part of their stress interview, but these levels lowered when the children entered the room.

Apparently, interspouse conflict and stress were reduced when the conflict was detoured through the children and the usual parental roles were assumed.

ETHICAL ISSUES IN FAMILY THERAPY

In the opinion of many experts, family therapy raises unique ethical issues for therapists in addition to those that are present in individual settings (Fitzgerald, 1973; Hare-Mustin, 1980; Gurman, 1978; Gurman & Klein, 1980; Williams, 1967; Fox, 1967; Grosser & Paul, 1964; Woody & Woody, 1973; Wynne, 1971). Generally speaking, these ethical issues have broadly to do with (1) potential conflicts with prevailing social values, and (b) potential conflicts with traditional professional ethics.

The potential conflicts with prevailing social values mostly involve concerns that family therapy constitutes a threat to the family unit. The threat is seen in the encouragement of strong negative feelings and in the possibility of loss of parental authority and respect. Expression of strong hostility is specifically likely to be seen as a threat, since it may lead to unnecessary hurt through verbal acting out and, possibly, to physical violence when away from the therapist. In fact, however, negative feelings are not new to families, even though expressing such feelings in the presence of an outsider may be. Such feelings are a threat to the family unit only if they are poorly handled by the therapist (Charny, 1972). The therapist's task is to place such feelings in the context of realistic ambivalence and to neutralize harmful effects through establishing an atmosphere of empathy for the feelings of others. As negative affects are made less fearful and anxiety producing, positive affects become richer and the family unit is enhanced rather than weakened.

Similarly, concerns abut the loss of parental respect and authority are groundless if an appropriate therapeutic atmosphere is established. Empathy and support for others' failings, fears, and weaknesses lead to greater tolerance and recognition of personal worth. Parental authority based purely on social roles may be lost by admission of inadequacies but, if empathy and compassion are established, the need to see or be seen as omnipotent gives way to a relationship built on mutual tolerance and respect for each individual as a person. With families who place a high value on the traditional hierarchical system of family life, it is important for the therapist to prepare the family by focusing on the potential gains that can follow the abdication of the omnipotent position of the parents. Grosser and Paul (1964) have presented a comprehensive discussion of this issue.

With respect to the potential for violence between sessions as a result of the material raised in the therapy, Grosser and Paul (1964) feel that the therapist must explain what might be involved before family therapy is initiated, pointing out possible disagreeable situations and the potential rewards. This is good advice.

Fears have been expressed that family therapy threatens the integrity of the family unit, but some clinicians have argued that individual therapy is even more of a threat. Fitzgerald (1973), for example, points out that in individual therapy it is often noted that improvement in the patient is followed by deterioration in some other family member. I have reviewed several studies showing deleterious effects that individual therapy often has on other family members, particularly spouses (Fox, 1967). If the family members are all present, it is easier for the therapist to monitor changes in each and to work toward helping people effect changes that are not perceived as harmful by others. Similarly, Hurvitz (1967) has noted that individual therapy patients are able to criticize their spouses with impunity before a sympathetic therapist. In such contexts negative feelings often flourish, making the emergence of marital conflicts more likely and their resolution more difficult.

In all therapies personal values, social values, and conflicts between them arise of necessity. In family therapy, encompassing as it does man's oldest social institution, the conflicts are more pronounced. The women's rights movement of the 1970s and the sexual revolution of the 1960s are but two examples of social phenomena that have serious implications for traditional family values and that affect patients and therapists like. In a challenging but thought-provoking article Hare-Mustin (1980) argues that family therapy may not be in the best interest of individual family members in given instances. One example may occur when successfully disengaged offspring are required to attend family therapy sessions and thereby risk becoming reenmeshed in an unhealthy system. Another example can occur when, in an effort to restore family functioning, the therapist unwittingly encourages movement toward a traditional model of family life that encourages stereotyping, especially in sex-role task assignment. Similar concerns regarding the latter issue have been raised by Gurman (1979) and Gurman and Klein (1980), particularly with regard to some aspects of behavioral family therapy approaches. Although Wendorf (1981) has objected to Hare-Mustin's arguments by pointing out the risks of not including some members in particular circumstances and by calling attention to the apparently lower rate of negative effects for family therapy than for individual therapy (Gurman & Kniskern, 1981), her warnings remain well taken.

It is the responsibility of therapists to be aware of changing social standards, to explore their impact on their personal and professional roles. "The professional helper should recognize that values do get transmittd in therapy, and that this transmission must be an open and conscious process" (Woody & Woody, 1973).

The second broad category of ethical problems concerns issues that may place the family therapist in conflict with the professional ethics that have been developed for individual patient–therapist relationships. One such issue is confidentiality of information. In traditional psychotherapy this is a relatively straightforward matter. Any information the patient reveals in the context of the help-seeking relationship is privileged information and may not be divulged without the patient's consent. This is not only an ethical matter; in many states it is also a matter of law. Family therapists sometimes find themselves on the horns of a dilemma; one member of a family may reveal information that the therapist is instructed not to reveal to other family members. The therapist must, of course, honor such requests. However, doing so may conflict with another ethical–moral principle according to which the therapist must not withhold information from clients that would appear to be helpful to them. Thus the need to honor one person's right to privacy may conflict with another's right to know. Since both parties are patients of the same therapist, the therapist can get caught in the middle.

Generally, the therapist will do well to discuss this issue with the family beforehand. Some therapists frankly instruct people not to tell the therapist anything they do not wish others to know, since they feel that their responsibility is to the family as a whole and that they will therefore share any information given to them. Others bypass the issue by refusing to talk to any member alone. Yet it is almost impossible to avoid such issues at all times.

For example, the husband of a couple I once saw confessed an extramarital affair through a letter and asked that his wife not be told. It was my judgment that the confession was an attempt to alleviate his guilt and that a revelation of this long-past incident would do nothing more than upset his wife. I withheld the information. At other times the matters is not so simple. Generally, when people insist on telling me things they wish kept secret from the family, I follow the recommendation of Grosser and Paul (1964) and honor the request for silence while insisting that the person explore with me the reasons for secrecy. Typically, it is a maneuver to secure special status with the therapist through a shared secret or an attempt to block the emergence of certain material in the conjoint sessions. As these motives are revealed and discussed, patients generally decide to divulge the withheld information themselves.

Another example of the conflict between individual and family rights may occur when a not dangerous but mentally ill member of a family is unwilling to commit himself or herself for treatment. Caesar (1980) supports the constraints that have been placed on society to protect the rights of individuals in such cases but argues that these individual rights must be balanced by consideration of the family as a support system for the person concerned and the impact of nontreatment upon that family. While successfully blocking the warehousing of nondangerous patients, the author argues, "We have consigned many persons to live lives of quiet desperation, have destroyed the mental and emotional health of those who love and care for them, and destroyed families—to the ultimate detriment and even destruction of the disabled person" (Caesar, 1980).

A final ethical problem or group of problems centers around the question of who is to be regarded as the patient. Grosser and Paul (1964) think that the answer depends on the nature of the problem of the referral. when a disturbed individual comes to the attention of a therapist who then recommends that family members be included in the treatment in order to help the patient, the client is clearly the original patient. Grosser and Paul believe this is particularly true if a period of individual therapy has preceded the initiation of family sessions. There is some merit to this line of thought but it is not a clear-cut matter. Patients are often referred for family treatment while one member is in the hospital or is about to be released. Although one person may appear to be more disturbed by virtue of having been hospitalized, a new therapist beginning with the family can easily begin with its being clearly understood that the client is the family.. If the therapist who had been treating the individual in the hospital is to be the family therapist, some transition sessions will be necessary to resolve any feelings concerning a supposed patient–therapist alliance.

A number of issues too complex to discuss here arise when family clients begin divorce and/or custody proceedings. Whose interests should the therapist protect in such instances? Steinberg (1980) warns that a therapist working with only one spouse during divorce proceedings may easily widen the breach between the partners and increase the stress for all parties concerned. Steinberg suggests a team approach involving the family therapist and an attorney to help minimize the stress of divorce and proposes several creative forms of collaboration. Niochols (1980) provides some excellent advice for marital and family therapists whose clients become involved in separation and/or custody proceedings.

Finally, several authors have commented on the rich opportunities provided by family sessions for therapists to act out their own unresolved interpersonal difficulties (Williams, 1967; Grosser & Paul, 1964; Wynne, 1971). Different family members inevitably seek the therapist's support and sympathy. Without thorough understanding of their own needs, awareness of the effects of their families of origin on their current behavior, and an appreciation of the need-satisfaction system in their present families, the therapist will be hard put to avoid the many potentials for participation in covert alliances that will subvert the therapeutic process. Although it is generally a good idea to announce a policy of neutrality, I also make it clear that at any point in time I may very well side with one person against another. In the long run the family will discover that my allegiance shifts and is rather evenly distributed, but this even-handedness will not necessarily characterize each session.

Although there are potential problems, ethical conflicts, and more than enough opportunities for mistakes in this method of intervention, therapists should not be timid about working with families. Family units also have considerable cohesiveness and mutual support, which helps them to survive external stress, including many therapeutic errors. As Wynne (1971) somewhat ruefully puts it, "I have been far more impressed with the difficulty of bringing about genuine and lasting change in family patterns than in the dangers of unintentionally disorganizing them. . . . Indeed, *families have a staggering capacity to remain the same.*"

TRAINING IN FAMILY THERAPY

The essential ingredients in learning family therapy are basically the same as those in learning individual therapy: conceptual knowledge, observation, practice under supervision, and self-understanding. A training program that I initiated while at the Ohio State University Family Therapy Clinic is fairly typical of those in other settings. Trainees (psychology interns, psychiatry residents, graduate social work students, and graduate nursing students) are given the opportunity to participate in a course in family therapy that covers the major theoretical positions and uses role playing to illustrate specific techniques. Videotapes provide live material for discussion of clinical applications. (See Bodin, 1969, for a discussion of the use of videotapes in training family therapists.) Trainees unable to take the course are furnished with a reading list similar to the bibliography at the end of this chapter. They are encouraged initially to read broadly across differing theoretical positions and then to proceed in depth into those authors who seem particularly cogent to them. Thus the trainees are encouraged to learn one system well as a framework to guide their observations and interventions.

In the clinic trainees begin by observing sessions conducted by cotherapists and participating in the follow-up discussions. Often role playing is used in these "debriefing" sessions to expore other interventions that might have been used or to concretize the effect that might eventuate from a change in one of the family members. After experience in observing, the trainee is assigned to a case as a cotherapist with a member of the staff.

Finally, with regard to training, anyone seriously interested in becoming a therapist should sooner or later see the need for a personal therapy experience. I encourage, but do not require, personal therapy. In practice most of my trainees seek out personal therapy experiences, but I prefer to respect each person's judgment as to when it is appropriate to do so.

The training and supervision literature in family therapy has increased enormously, keeping pace with almost all other aspects of the rapidly growing field. Liddle and Halpern's (1978) comparative review of the training literature between 1961 and 1978 contains over 100 references. Despite the enormous investment of time and energy represented by these studies, Gurman and Kniskern's (1981) summary is correct: "We must acknowledge and underline the field's *empirical* ignorance about this domain. Indeed, there now exists no research evidence that training experiences in marital–family therapy in fact increase the effectiveness of clinicians."

For me, psychotherapy is not so much a set of techniques as it is a way of life—a method of living that is committed to open communication and the seeking out and fostering of mutually enhancing interpersonal relationships. Family therapy is a particularly fulfilling way for me to pursue such a way of life. The pace is fast, the feelings generated are intense, and the rewards are numerous. I have become so attuned to the pervasive effects of the family on each person's daily life that it is impossible for me to talk to individual patients without "seeing" their families beside them. In this sense individual therapy has become a special case of family therapy. There are persistent questions yet to be answered, and challenges to one's ingenuity abound; but for sheer professional and personal gratification, the various mental health professions offer no role that can compete with that of family therapist.

REFERENCES

Ackerman, N. W. *Psychodynamics of family life.* New York: Basic Books, 1958.
Ackerman, N. W. The growing edge of family therapy. In C. Sager and H. Kaplan (Eds.), *Progress in group and family therapy.* New York: Brunner/Mazel, 1972.

Andolfi, M. Prescribing the families own dysfunctional rules as a therapeutic strategy. *Journal of Marital and Family Therapy,* 1980, **6,** 29–36.

Bateson, G. Minimal requirements for a theory of schizophrenia. *Archives of General Psychiatry,* 1960, **2,** 477–491.

Bateson, G. Slippery theories. *International Journal of Psychiatry,* 1966, **2,** 415–417

Bateson, G., Jackson, D. D., Haley, J., & Weakland, J. H. Toward a theory of schizophrenia. *Behavioral Science,* 1956, **1,** 154–159.

Bateson, G., Jackson, D. D., Haley, J., & Weakland, J. H. A note on the double bind—1962. *Family Process,* 1966, **5,** 230–242.

Bauman, G., & Roman, M. Interaction testing in the study of marital dominance. *Family Process,* 1966, **5,** 230–242.

Bayley, N., & Schaefer, E. S. Relationship between socioeconomic variables and the behavior of mothers toward young children. *Journal of Genetic Psychology,* 1960, **96,** 61–77.

Beels, C., & Ferber, A. Family therapy: A review. *Family Process,* 1969, **8,** 280–318.

Behrens, M., Rosenthal, A., & Chodoff, P. Communication in lower-class families of schizophrenics: II. Observations and findings. *Archives of General Psychiatry,* 1968, **18,** 689–696.

Bell, J. E. *Family Group Therapy.* Washington, D.C.: Public Health Monograph No. 64, Department of Health, Education and Welfare, 1961.

Bell, J. E. *Promoting action through new insights: Some theoretical revisions from family group therapy.* Paper presented at the annual meeting, American Psychological Association, 1963.

Bellville, T., Raths, O. N., & Bellville, C. J. Conjoint marriage therapy with a husband and wife team. *American Journal of Orthopsychiatry,* 1969, **39,** 473–483.

Bergin, A. E., & Lambert, M. J. The evaluation of therapeutic outcomes. In S. L. Garfield & A. E. Bergin (Eds.), *Handbook of psychotherapy and behavior change* (2nd ed.). New York: Wiley, 1978.

Birchler, G. R. Communication skills in married couples. In A. S. Bellack & M. Hersen (Eds.), *Research and practice in social skills training.* New York: Plenum, 1979.

Birchler, G. R., & Spinks, S. H. Behavioral systems—marital and family therapy: Integration and clinical application. *American Journal of Family Therapy,* 1980, **8,** 6–28.

Blood, R. O., & Wolfe, D. M. Negro-white differences in blue-collar marriages in a northern metropolis. *Social Forces,* 1969, **48,** 59–64.

Bodin, A. Conjoint family assessment. In P. McReynolds (Ed.) *Advances in psychological assessment.* Palo Alto, Calif. Science and Behavior Books, 1968.

Bodin, A. Videotape applications in training family therapists. *Journal of Nervous and Mental Disease,* 1969, **148,** 251–261.

Bowen, M. Family relationships in schizophrenia. In A. Auerback (Ed.), *Schizophrenia.* New York: Ronald, 1959.

Bowen, M. A family concept of schizophrenia. In D. D. Jackson (Ed.), *Etiology of schizophrenia.* New York: Basic Books, 1960.

Bowen, M. The family as the unit of study and treatment. *American Journal of Orthopsychiatry,* 1961, **31,** 4–60.

Bowen, M. The use of family therapy in clinical practice. *Comprehensive Psychiatry,* 1966, **7,** 345–374.

Broderick, C. B., & Schrader, S. S. The history of professional marriage and family therapy. In A. Gurman & D. Kniskern (Eds.), *Handbook of family therapy*. New York: Brunner/Mazel, 1981.

Brodey, W. On family therapy—a poem. *Family Process*, 1963, **2**, 280–287.

Brodkin, A. M. Family therapy: The making of a mental health movement. *American Journal of Orthopsychiatry*, 1980, **50**, 4–17.

Buber, M. *I and thou*. New York: Scribner, 1958.

Caesar, B. Preserving the family: A brief for limited commitment of nondangerous mentally ill persons. *Journal of Marital and Family Therapy*, 1980, **6**, 309–317.

Carrol, E., Cambor, G. C., Leopold, J. V., Miller, M. D., & Reis, W. J. Psychotherapy of marital couples. *Family Process*, 1963, **2**, 25–33.

Carson, R. C. *Interaction concepts of personality*. Chicago: Aldine, 1969.

Castaneda, C.. *Journey to Ixtlan*. New York: Simon & Shuster, 1972.

Charny, I. *Marital love and hate*. New York: Macmillan, 1972.

Coche, J.M. *The uniqueness of family therapy outcome research: Critical research issues*. Paper presented at the society for Psychotherapy Research, Toronto, June 1978.

Coughlin, F., & Winberger, H. C. Group family therapy. *Family Process*, 1968, **7**, 37–50.

Davis, A., & Havinghurst, R. J. Social class and color differences in childrearing. *American Sociological Review*, 1946, **11**, 698–710.

Doar, D. Conjoint psychological testing in marriage therapy: New wives in old skins. *Professional Psychology*, 1981, **12**, 549–555.

Elbert, S., Rosman, B., Minuchin, S., & Guerney, B. A method for the clinical study of family interaction. Paper presented at the meeting of the American Orthopsychiatric Association, Chicago, March 1964.

Ely, A. L., Guerney, B. G., Jr., & Stover, L. Efficacy of the training phase of conjugal therapy. *Psychotherapy: Theory, research and practice*, 1973, **10**, 201–207.

Ewing, J. A., & Fox, R. E. Family therapy of alcoholism. In J. Masserman (Ed.), *Current psychiatric therapies* (Vol. 8). New York: Grune & Stratton, 1968.

Ferber, A., & Mendelson, M. Training for family therapy. *Family Process*, 1969, **8**, 25–32.

Ferreira, A. J. The "double-bind" and delinquent behavior. *Archives of General Psychiatry*, 1960, **3**, 359–367.

Ferreira, A. J. Family myth and homeostasis. *Archives of General Psychiatry*, 1963, **9**, 457–463.

Fisher, L. Dimensions of family assessment: A critical review. *Journal of Marriage and Family Counseling*, 1976, **2**, 367–382.

Fisher, S., & Mendell, D. The communication of neurotic patterns over two and three generations. *Psychiatry*, 1956, **19**, 41–46.

Fitzgerald, R. V. Conjoint marital psychotherapy: An outcome and follow-up study. *Family Process*, 1969, **8**, 260–271.

Fitzgerald, R. V. *Conjoint marital therapy*. New York: Aronson, 1973.

Fox, R. E. The effect of psychotherapy on the spouse. *Family Process*, 1967, **7**, 7–16.

Fox, R. E. . . . In love with an inch. *Voices: The Art and Science of Psychotherapy*, 1974, **10**, 32–34.

Framo, J. L. Systematic research on family dynamics. In I. Boszormenyi-Nagy & J. Framo

(Eds.), *Intensive family therapy: Theoretical and practical aspects*. New York: Hoeber/ Harper & Row, 1965.

Framo, J. L. Comment. *Family Process*, 1969, **8**, 319–322.

Framo, J. L. Review. *Contemporary Psychology*, 1973, **18**, 523–524.

Frank, E., Anderson, C., & Rubinstein, D. Marital role ideals and perception of marital role behavior in distressed and nondistressed couples. *Journal of Marital and Family Therapy*, 1980, **15**, 55–63.

Frank, J. *Persuasion and healing*. Baltimore: John Hopkins Press, 1961.

Freeman, V. J., Klein, A. F., Riehman, L. M., Lukoff, I. F., & Heisey, V. E. *Allegheny general hospital study project, final report*. Pittsburgh: Mimeographed, 1964.

Greer, S. E., & D'Zurilla, T. J. Behavioral approaches to marital discord and conflict. *Journal of Marriage and Family Counseling*, 1975, **1**, 299–315.

Grosser, G. H., & Paul, N. L. Ethical issues in family group therapy. *American Journal of Orthopsychiatry*, 1964, **34**, 875–885.

Grotjahn, M. Clinical illustrations from psychoanalytic family therapy. In B. Green (Ed.), *The psychotherapies of marital disharmony*. New York: Free Press, 1965.

Gurman, A. S. The effects and effectiveness of marital therapy: A review of outcome research. *Family Process*, 1973, **12**, 145–170.

Gurman, A. S. Contemporary marital therapies: A critique and comparative analysis of psychoanalytic, behavioral and systems theory approaches. In T. J. Paolino & B. S. McCrady (Eds.), *Marriage and marital therapy*, New York: Brunner/Mazel, 1978.

Gurman, A. S. Behavioral marriage therapy in the 1980's: The challenge of integration. *American Journal of Family Therapy*, 1980, **8**, 86–96.

Gurman, A. S. & Klein, M. H. Marital and family conflicts. In A. Brodsky & R. Hare-Mustin (Ed.), *Women and psychotherapy: An assessment of research and practice*. New York: Guilford Press, 1980.

Gurman, A. S., & Kniskern, D. P. (Eds.), *Handbook of family therapy*. New York: Brunner/ Mazel, 1981. (a)

Gurman, A. S., & Kniskern, D. P. Family therapy outcome research: Knowns and the unknowns. In A. S. Gurman & D. F. Kniskern (Eds.), *Handbook of family therapy*. New York: Brunner/Mazel, 1981. (b)

Gurman, A. S., & Kniskern, D. P. Research on marital and family therapy: Progress, perspective, and prospect. In S. L. Garfield & A. E. Bergin (Ed.), *Handbook of psychotherapy and behavior change: An emperical analysis* (2nd ed.). New York: Wiley, 1978.

Gurman, A. S., & Knudson, R. M. Behavioral marriage therapy: I. psychodynamic-systems analysis and critique. *Family Process*, 1978, **17**, 121–138.

Gurman, A. S., Knudson, R. M., & Kniskern, D. P. Behavioral marriage therapy: IV. Take two aspirin and call us in the morning. *Family Process*, 1978, **17**, 164–180.

Haley, J. Family of the schizophrenic: A model system. *Journal of Nervous and Mental Disease*, 1959, **129**, 357–374. (a)

Haley, J. An interactional description of schizophrenia. *Psychiatry*, 1959, **22**, 325–331. (b)

Haley, J. *Strategies of psychotherapy*. New York: Grune and Stratton, 1963.

Haley, J. A review of the family therapy field. In J. Haley (Ed.), *Changing families: A family therapy reader*. New York: Grune and Stratton, 1971.

Haley, J. *Problem solving therapy.* San Francisco: Jossey-Bass, 1976.

Handlon, J. H., & Parloff, M. B. Treatment of patient and family as a group: Is it group therapy? *International Journal of Group Psychotherapy,* 1962, **12,** 132–141.

Hare-Mustin, R. T. Family therapy may be dangerous for your health. *Professional Psychology,* 1980, **11,** 935–938.

Henggeler, S. W., Tavormina, J. B. Social class and race differences in family interaction: Pathological normative, or confounding methodological factors. *Journal of Genetic Psychology,* 1980, **137,** 211–222.

Hess, R. D., & Handel, G. The family as a psychosocial organization. In G. Handel (Ed.), *The psychosocial interior of the family.* Chicago: Aldine, 1967.

Hill, R. Methodological issues in family development research. *Family Process,* 1964, **3,** 186–194.

Hoffman, L. Deviation-amplifying processes in natural groups. In J. Haley (Ed.), *Changing families: A family therapy reader.* New York: Grune and Stratton, 1971.

Howells, J. G. *Theory and practice of family practice.* New York: Brunner/Mazel, 1971.

Hurvitz, N. Marital problems following psychotherapy with one spouse. *Journal of Consulting Psychology,* 1967, **31,** 38–47.

Jackson, D. D. The question of family homeostasis. *Psychiatric Quarterly Supplements,* 1957, **31,** 79–90.

Jackson, D. D. Family interaction, homeostasis and some implications for conjoint family psychotherapy. In J. Masserman (Ed.), *Individual and familial dynamics.* New York: Grune and Stratton, 1959.

Jackson, D. D. The monad, the dyad, and the family therapy of schizophrenics. In A. Burton (Ed.), *Psychotherapy of the psychosis,* New York: Basic Books, 1961.

Jackson, D. D., & Weakland, J. H. Conjoint family therapy: Some considerations on theory, technique, and results. *Psychiatry,* 1961, **24,** 30–45.

Jacob, T. Patterns of family conflict and dominance as a function of child age and social class. *Developmental Psychology,* 1974, **10,** 1–12.

Jacobson, N. S. A review of the research on the effectiveness of marital therapy. In T. L. Paolino & B. S. McCrady (Eds.), *Marriage and marital therapy.* New York: Brunner/Mazel, 1978.

Jacobson, N. S. Behavioral treatments for marital discord: A critical appraisal. In M. Hersen, R. M. Eisler, & P. M. Miller (Eds.), *Progress in behavioral modification.* New York: Academic Press, 1979.

Jacobson, N. S. Behavioral marital therapy. In A. S. Gurman & D. P. Kniskern (Eds.), *Handbook of family therapy.* New York: Brunner/Mazel, 1981.

Jacobson, N.S., & Margolin, G. *Marital therapy: strategies based on social learning theory and behavior exchange principles.* New York: Brunner/Mazel, 1979.

Jacobson, N. S., & Martin, B. Behavioral marriage therapy: Current status. *Psychological Bulletin,* 1976, **83,** 540–566.

Jacobson, N. S., & Weiss, R. L. Behavioral marriage therapy: III. The contents of Gurman et al. may be hazardous to our health. *Family Process,* 1978, **17,** 149–164.

Kaffman, M. Short term family therapy. *Family Process,* 1963, **2,** 216–234.

Kaplan, H. S. *The new sex therapy.* New York: Brunner/Mazel, 1974.

Kapleau, P. *The three pillars of zen.* Boston: Beacon Press, 1965.

Kempler, W. Experimental family therapy. *International Journal of Group Psychotherapy,* 1965, **15,** 57–71.

Kinney, J. M., Madsar, B., Fleming, T., & Haapola, D. A. Homebuilders: Keeping families together. *Journal of Clinical and Consulting Psychology,* 1977, **45,** 667–673.

Klein, M. H., Dittman, A. T., Parloff, M. B., & Gill, M. M. Behavior therapy: Observations and reflections. *Journal of Consulting and Clinical Psychology,* 1969, **33,** 259–266.

Kwiatkowska, H. Family are therapy. *Family Process,* 1967, **6,** 37–55.

L'Abate, L. *Understanding and helping the family.* Atlanta: Author (mimeographed), 1974.

Langsley, D. G., Flomenhaft, K., & Machotka, P. Follow-up evaluation of family crises therapy. *American Journal of Orthopsychiatry,* 1969, **39,** 753–760.

Langsley, D. G., Pittman, F. S., Machotka, P., & Flomenhaft, K. Family crisis—results and implications. *Family Process,* 1968, **7,** 145–158.

Laquer, H. P., Laburt, H. A., & Morong, E. Multiple family therapy: Further developments. *International Journal of Social Psychiatry,* 1964, Congress Issue, 70–80.

Lazarus, A. A. *Behavior therapy and beyond.* New York: McGraw-Hill, 1971.

Lebedun, M. Measuring movement in group marital counseling. *Social Casework,* 1970, **51,** 35–43.

Levant, R. E. A classification of the field of family therapy: A review of prior attempts and a new paradigmatic model. *American Journal of Family Therapy,* 1980, **8,** 3–16.

Levitt, E. E. The results of psychotherapy with children. *Journal of Consulting Psychology,* 1957, **21,** 189–196.

Levy, J., & Epstein, N. B. An application of the Rorschach test in family investigation. *Family Process,* 1964, **3,** 344–376.

Liberman, R. Behavioral approaches to family and couple therapy. *American Journal of Orthopsychiatry,* 1970, **40,** 106–118.

Liddle, H., & Halpern, R. Family therapy training and supervision: A comparative review. *Journal of Marriage and Family Counseling,* 1978, **4,** 77–98.

Lidz, T. *The family and human adaptation.* New York: International Universities Press, 1963.

Lidz, T, Cornelison, A., Fleck, S., & Terry, D. Intrafamilial environment of the schizophrenic patient. I: The father. *Psychiatry,* 1957a, **20,** 329–342.

Lidz, T., Cornelison, A., Fleck, S., & Terry, D. Intrafamilial environment of schizophrenic patients. II: Marital schism and marital skew. *American Journal of Psychiatry,* 1957b, **114,** 241–248.

Locke, H. J., & Wallace, K. M. Short-term marital adjustment and prediction tests: Their reliability and validity. *Journal of Marriage and Family Living,* 1959, **21,** 251–255.

Loveland, N. T., Wynne, L. C., & Singer, M. T. The family Rorschach: A new method for studying family interaction. *Family Process,* 1963, **2,** 187–215.

Lowman, J. Measurement of family affective structure. *Journal of Personality Assessment,* 1980, **44,** 130–141.

MacGregor, R. Multiple impact psychotherapy with families. *Family Process,* 1962, **1,** 15–29.

MacGregor, R., Ritchie, A., Serrano, A., & Shuster, F., Jr., *Multiple impact therapy with families.* New York: McGraw-Hill, 1964.

Masters, W. H., & Johnson, V. E. *Human sexual inadequacy*. Boston: Litttle, Brown, 1970.

Minuchin, S. *Families and family therapy*. Cambridge: Harvard University Press, 1974.

Minuchin, S., & Fishman, H. C. *Family therapy techniques*, Cambridge, Mass.: Harvard University Press, 1981.

Minuchin, S., & Montalvo, B. Techniques for working with disorganized low socio-economic families. *American Journal of Orthopsychiatry*, 1967, **37**, 880–887.

Minuchin, S., Montalvo, B., Guerney, B. G., Jr., Rosman, B. L., & Shumer, F. *Families of the slums*. New York: Basic Books, 1967.

Minuchin, S., Rosman, B. O., & Baker, L. *Psychosomatic Families*. Cambridge, Mass.: Howard University Press, 1978.

Mishler, E., & Waxler, N. Family interaction processes and schizophrenia: A review of current theories. *International Journal of Psychiatry*, 1966, **2**, 375–415.

Miyoshi, N., & Liebman, R. Training psychiatric residents in family therapy. *Family Process*, 1969, **8**, 97–105.

Nichols, J. F. The marital/family therapist as an expert witness: Some thoughts and suggestions. *Journal of Marital and Family Therapy*, 1980, **6**, 293–299.

Olson, D. H. Marital and family therapy: Integrative review and critique. *Journal of Marriage and the Family*, 1970, **32**, 501–538.

Olson, D., Sprenkle, D., & Russell, C. Circumplex model of marital and family system: I. Cohesion and adaptability dimensions, family types, and clinical application. *Family Process*, 1979, **18**, 3–28.

O'Rourke, J. F. Field and laboratory: The decision-making behavior of family groups in two experimental conditions. *Sociometry*, 1963, **26**, 422–435.

Palazzoli-Selvini, M., Boscolo, L., Cecchin, G., & Prata, G. *Paradox and counterparadox: A new model in the therapy of the family in schizophrenia transaction*. New York: Aronson, 1978.

Patterson, G. R. The aggressive child: Victim and architect of a coercive system. In E. J. Mash, L. A. Hamerlynck, & L. C. Handy (Eds.), *Behavior modification and families*. New York: Brunner/Mazel, 1976.

Perlmutter, M., Loeb, D., Gumpert, G., O'Hara F., & Higbie, I. Family diagnosis and therapy using video playback. *American Journal Orthopsychiatry*, 1967, **37**, 900–905.

Pittman, F. S., Langsley, D. G., & DeYoung, C. D. Work and social phobias: A family approach treatment. *American Journal of Psychiatry*, 1967–68, **124**, 1535–1541.

Pool, M., & Frazier, J. R. Family therapy: A review of the literature pertinent to children and adolescents. *Psychotherapy: Theory, research and practice*, 1973, **10**, 256–260.

Rabiner, E. L., Mokinski, H., & Gralnick, A. Conjoint family therapy in the inpatient setting. *American Journal of Psychotherapy*, 1962, **16**, 618–631.

Radine, N. Father-child interaction and the intellectual functioning of four-year-old boys. *Developmental Psychology*, 1972, **6**, 353–361.

Riesman, D. *The lonely crowd*. New Haven: Yale University Press, 1950.

Robinson, E., & Eyberg, S. The dyadic parent-child interaction coding system: Standardization and validation. *Journal of Consulting and Clinical Psychology*, 1981, **49**, 245–250.

Robinson, E. A., & Price, M. G. Pleasureable behavior in marital interaction: An observational study. *Journal of Consulting and Clinical Psychology*, 1980, **48**, 117–118.

Roman, M., & Bauman, G. Interaction testing: A technique for the psychological evaluation of small groups. In M. Harrower, et al. (Eds.), *Creative variations in the projective techniques*. Springfield Ill.: Thomas, 1960.

Ross, W. D. Group psychotherapy with patients' relatives. *American Journal of Psychiatry*, 1948, **104**, 623–626.

Safer, D. J. Family therapy for the children with behavior disorders. *Family Process*, 1966, **5**, 243–255.

Satir, V. The family as a treatment unit. *Confinia Psychiatrica*, 1965, **8**, 37–42.

Satir, V. *Conjoint Family Therapy*. Palo Alto, Calif.: Science and Behavior Books, 1964.

Schaffer, L., Wynne, L. C., Day, J., Ryckoff, I. M., & Halperin, A. On the nature and sources of the psychiatrist's experience with the family of the schizophrenic. *Psychiatry*, 1962, **25**, 32–45.

Shapiro, R. J., & Budman, S. H. Defection, termination, and continuation in family and individual therapy. *Family Process*, 1973, **12**, 55–68.

Sigal, J., Rakoff, V., & Epstein, N. Indicators of therapeutic outcome in conjoint family therapy. *Family Process*, 1967, **6**, 215–226.

Singer, M. T., & Wynne, L. C. Thought disorder and the family relations of schizophrenics: III. Projective test methodology. *Archives of General Psychiatry*, 1965, **12**, 187–201.

Sprankle, D. H., & Fisher, B. L. An empirical assessment of the goals of family therapy. *Journal of Marital and Family Therapy*, 1980, **6**, 131–139.

Snyder, D. K., Wills, R. M., & Keiser, T. W. Empirical validation of the marital satisfaction inventory: An actuarial approach. *Journal of Consulting and Clinical Psychology*, 1981, **49**, 262–268.

Stanton, M. D., & Todd, T. C. Some outcome results and aspects of structural family therapy with drug addicts. In D. Smith, S. Anderson, M. Buxton, T. Chung, N. Gottlieb, & W. Harvey (Eds.), *A multicultural view of drug abuse*. Cambridge, Mass.: Schenkman, 1978.

Steidl, J. H., Finkelstein, F., Wexler, J., Feigenbaum, H., Kitsen, J., Kliger, A., & Quinlan, D. Medical condition, adherence to treatment regimens, and family functioning. *Archives of General Psychiatry*, 1980, **37**, 1025–1027.

Steinberg, J. L. Towards an interdisciplinary commitment: A divorce lawyer proposes attorney-therapist marriages or, at least, an affair. *Journal, Marital and Family Therapy*, 1980, **6**, 259–268.

Steinglass, P. Assessing families in their homes. *American Journal of Psychiatry*, 1980, **137**, 1523–1529.

Straus, M. A., & Brown, B. W. *Family measurement techniques: Abstracts of published instruments, 1935–1974* (Rev. ed.), Minneapolis: University of Minnesota Press, 1978.

Strodtbeck, F. L. Husband-wife interaction over revealed differences. *American Sociological Review*, 1951, **16**, 468–473.

Strupp, H. H. Toward a reformulation of the psychotherapeutic influence. *International Journal of Psychiatry*, 1973, **11**, 263–365.

Stuart, R. B. Operant interpersonal treatment for marital discord. In D. H. L. Olson (Ed.), *Treating relationships*. Lake Mills, Iowa: Graphic Press, 1976.

Szasz, T. S. The communication of distance between child and parent. *British Journal of Medical Psychology*, 1959, **32**, 161–170.

Usandivaras, R., Issaharoff, E., Hammond, H., Ramanos, D., Moujan, O. F., & O'Farrel,

J. Un nuevo test para estudiar los pequenos gropos. *Revista de Psicologia y Psicho-therapia de Grupos*, 1963, Tomo II, No. 3.

Vincent, C. E. *Sexual and marital health: The physician as a consultant.* New York: McGraw-Hill, 1973.

Walters, J. A review of family research in 1959, 1960, and 1961. *Marriage and Family Living*, 1962, **24,** 158–169.

Watzlawick, P. A review of the double-bind theory. *Family Process*, 1963, **2,** 132–153.

Watzlawick, P. A structured family interview. *Family Process*, 1966, **5,** 256–271.

Watzlawick, P., Beavin, J., & Jackson, D. D. *Pragmatics of human communication*, New York: Norton, 1967.

Watzlawick, P., Weakland, J., & Fisch, R. *Change: Principles of problem formation and problem resolution.* New York: Norton, 1974.

Weiss, R. L., & Margolin, G. Marital conflict and accord. In A. R. Ciminero, M. S. Cal-horin, & H. E. Adams (Eds.), *Marriage and marital therapy.* New York: Brunner/Mazel, 1978.

Weiss, R. L., & Cerreto, M. *Marital status inventory.* Unpublished manuscript, University of Oregon, 1975.

Weiss, R. L., Hops, H., & Patterson, G. R. A framework for conceptualizing marital con-flict, technology of altering it, some data for evaluating it. In L. A. Hamerlynck, L. C. Hardy, & E. J. Mask (Eds.), *Behavior change: Methodology, concepts and practice.* Champaign, Ill.: Research Press, 1973.

Weiss, R. L., & Margolin, G. Marital conflict and accord. In A. R. Ciminero, M. S. Cal-horin, & H. E. Adams (Eds.), *Handbook for bvehavioral assessment.* New York: Wiley, 1977.

Weissman, S., & Montgomery, G. Techniques for group family enrichment. *Personnel and Guidance*, 1980, **59,** 113–116.

Wells, R. A. The use of joint field instructor-student participation as a teaching method in casework treatment. *Social Work Education Reporter*, 1971, **19,** 58–62.

Wells, R. A., & Dezen, A. E. The results of family therapy revisited: The nonbehavioral methods. *Family Process*, 1978, **17,** 251–274.

Wells, R. A., Dilkes, T. C., & Trivelli, N. The results of family therapy: A critical review of the literature. *Family Process*, 1972, **11,** 189–207.

Wendorf, D. J. A data-based reply to Hare-Mustin on family therapy perils. *Professional Psychology*, 1981, **12,** 665–667.

Williams, F. S. Family therapy: A critical assessment. *American Journal of Orthopsychiatry*, 1967, **37,** 912–919.

Winter, W. D., & Ferreira, A. J. (Eds.), *Research in family interaction: Reading and com-mentary.* Palo Alto, Calif.: Science and Behavior Books, 1969.

Winter, W D., Ferreira, A. J., & Olson, J. L. Story sequence analysis of family TAT's. *Journal of Projective Techniques and Personality Assessment*, 1965, **29,** 392–397.

Woody, R. H., & Woody, J. D. *Sexual, marital and familial relations: Therapeutic interven-tions for professional helping.* Springfield,: Ill. Thomas, 1973.

Wynne, L. C. Comment. *Family process*, 1969, **8,** 326–328.

Wyune, L. C. some guidelines for exploratory conjoint family therapy. In J. Haley (Ed.), *Changing families: A family therapy reader.* New York: Grune and Stratton, 1971.

Wynne, L., Ryckoff, I., Day, J., & Hirsch, S. Pseudomutuality in the family relations of schizophrenics. *Psychiatry,* 1958, **21,** 205–220.

Wynne, L., & Singer, M. *Thinking disorders and family transactions.* Paper presented at the annual meeting, American Psychiatric Association, 1964.

Zuk, G. H. Family therapy. *Archives of General Psychiatry,* 1967, **16,** 71–79.

Zuk, G. H. *Family therapy: A triadic-based approach.* New York: Behavioral, 1971.

Zuk, G. H., & Rubinstein, D. A review of concepts in the study and treatment of families of schizophrenics. In I. Boszormenyi-Nagy & J. Framo (Eds.), *Intensive family therapy.* New York: Hoeber, 1965.

CHAPTER 10

Behavior Therapy and Behavior Modification

PETER E. NATHAN, GEORGEANN WITTE, AND JAMES W. LANGENBUCHER

There is no commonly agreed upon definition of behavior therapy. Current definitions range from the very narrow to the all-encompassing. Erwin (1978) notes, helpfully, that much terminological confusion could be avoided by distinguishing between behavior therapy as a theoretical paradigm and behavior therapy as a collection of techniques more or less closely based on behavioral theory.

As a theoretical model, behavior therapy emphasizes learning-based explanations of psychopathology and behavior change. In this model psychopathology is viewed as maladaptive learned behavior shaped by environmental contingencies. The maladaptive behavior is seen as the fundamental problem, rather than as a symptom expressive of unconscious conflict or philosophical crisis. In their rejection of the traditional "disease" model of psychopathology, behavior therapists argued for the essential similarity of all behavior: Both normal and abnormal behavior are acquired—and modified—according to the same fundamental learning processes that relate behavior to environmental events in a lawful manner. As will be shown later, behavior therapists may disagree on the specific processes involved in this learning, but almost all agree on the common core of principles guiding their work. To most, behavior therapy is characterized by a commitment to empirical evaluation in both research and practice, including reliance on experimental, controlled observation of research subjects and empirical evaluation of treatment effects. A touchstone of the field has been its enduring respect for operationalized criteria: Behavior therapists seek overt, objective evidence for the effectiveness of their techniques.

Behavior therapy may also be seen as a set of techniques. Most behavior therapists would agree that systematic desensitization, modeling, operant conditioning, and aversive procedures all qualify as behavior therapy methods. Either because evidence of their effectiveness is limited or because of disagreements over their theoretical or empirical underpinnings, fewer behavior therapists would accept implosion, flooding or cognitive techniques such as covert sensitization, cognitive restructuring, and self-control procedures as standard behavior-therapy procedures. Regardless of degree of acceptance, the techniques listed above confront maladaptive behavior in the here and now rather than, as with most of the dynamic therapies, largely as it relates to long-past traumatic events.

Although there is considerable controversy, even within the field, over whether all behavior therapy techniques derive from laboratory research, or even whether the techniques are entirely consistent with the fundamental laws of learning, the close ties between behavior therapy and learning theory are indisputable and distinguish it from other forms of psychotherapy.

Controversy in the field extends to terminology. While *behavior therapy* is both the most general and most widely used term, *behavior modification, applied behavior analysis,* and *cognitive behavior modification* often appear in the literature as well. Although some have suggested that *behavior modification* be applied only to operant methods, the term is most frequently used interchangeably with *behavior therapy* (Kazdin, 1978a; Wilson, 1978). Proponents of applied behavior analysis, on the other hand, seek to distinguish themselves from behavior therapists. Applied behavior analysis stems almost entirely from Skinner's basic studies on operant schedules of reinforcement; accordingly, it focuses strictly on overt behavior and its control by environmental contingencies and excludes attention to thoughts and emotions. Its techniques are used extensively in institutional settings, where single-subject experimental treatment designs, as well as ward-wide token economies, can be implemented. In contrast, cognitive behavior modification is a mediational approach to psychopathology that emphasizes the importance of internal cognitive processes in maintaining (and modifying) problem behavior. Treatment seeks most often to change these covert processes as well as to alter external contingencies to bring about behavior change.

This contemporary factionalism reflects, in part, the diversity of influences on the historical development of behavior therapy. One important influence was the Russian physiologist, Pavlov, who established the principles of classical (respondent) conditioning responsible for much learning and the source of several therapeutic techniques. In a series of classic experiments on the salivary responses of dogs, Pavlov (1906) demonstrated that a previously neutral stimulus, when repeatedly presented just before a stimulus–involuntary response sequence, could acquire the capacity to elicit involuntary physiological responses, even in the absence of the original stimulus (Hersen, Eisler, & Miller, 1975; Kanfer & Phillips, 1970). Influenced by Pavlov, the American psychologist J.B. Watson investigated the relevance of these principles to human behavior. For example, Watson and Raynor (1920) explored the possibility that phobic reactions could be acquired through the process of classical conditioning. Generally considered the "father" of behavioral clinical psychology in this country, Watson was an early proponent of the use of the experimental method and operational criteria in psychological research and treatment.

Another important line of research from this period examined the impact of the consequences of a behavior (rather than that of its antecedents, as in classical conditioning) on the future probability of that behavior. First Thorndike (1931) and later Skinner (1938) conducted experiments that led to the formulation and refinement of the *law of effect:* If a behavior is followed by "a satisfying state of affairs" (e.g., positive reinforcement), then the organism will tend to emit the behavior more frequently, particularly in the presence of stimuli associated with the reinforcement; conversely, behavior repeatedly followed by an "annoying state of affairs" (e.g., punishment) is emitted less and less frequently. Experimental study of the operant (instrumental) conditioning model derived from the law of effect led to an understanding of behavioral variation as a function of different schedules of reinforcement, and set the stage for the development of numerous behavior modification techniques.

Although influential advances in learning theory continued to be made by Hull (1943), Guthrie (1935), and Tolman (1932) in the 1930s and 1940s, the application of these principles to the explanation and treatment of human psychopathology took longer to develop. With the exception of isolated efforts—Jones' (1924) treatment of a phobic boy, Mowrer and Mowrer's (1938) treatment of enuresis with electrical bell and pad conditioning, and Dollard and Miller's (1950) attempt to reformulate psychoanalytic theory in learning-theory terms—few clinical applications of learning theory appeared during this time. In part this was a function of the prominence of psychoanalysis and of general satisfaction with its role. In part it may also have been due to the stridency and provocativeness of Watson and other early behaviorists, whose earlier outspokenness and "radical behavioral" positions created few friends and many enemies among professionals and the lay public alike.

Behavior therapy as an applied behavioral science first began to emerge in earnest in the 1950s. Separate but related developments in several countries contributed to this emergence. The English psychologist, Eysenck (1959), drew on the learning theories of Pavlov, Hull, and Mowrer to propose conditioning treatments. Wolpe (1958), in South Africa and later the United States, pioneered the use of systematic desensitization, a technique presumed to be derived from classical conditioning, in the treatment of phobic and anxiety disorders. Lazarus (1958), a South African colleague of Wolpe's, expanded many of these treatments in innovative case applications that demonstrated their flexibility with different populations. The publication of Skinner's *Science and Human Behavior* in 1953 spurred the application of operant procedures to human problems at the same time that Lindsley, a student of Skinner's, evaluated the utility of techniques derived from operant conditioning principles with a clinical (schizophrenic) population. Unlike procedures derived from classical conditioning, operant-based procedures were first utilized only with institutionalized psychotics, prisoners, and the severely retarded.

The more recent development of the social learning model, which is a supplement—and in some instances an alternative—to the older models of learning, has spurred development of new intervention modes. Unlike the operant and classical learning models, the social learning model emphasizes the role of cognitive mediating processes in behavior (Bandura, 1969). Although external environmental stimuli and reinforcing behavioral consequences are assumed to exert control over behavior, according to this model, their influence is also assumed to be moderated by cognitive factors. Modeling therapies based on this theory attempt to foster observational or vicarious learning, which need not depend on motor responses or reinforcement for its effects.

During the 1950s and 1960s, the fledgling behavior-therapy movement had to justify its existence in the face of attacks from the prevailing therapeutic establishment. Doubtless the opposition would have prevailed had it not been for repeated demonstrations of the apparent effectiveness of behavior therapy, especially with clinical populations abandoned as incurable by others. Although reports of controlled studies of therapeutic outcome originated from the work of client-centered psychologist Carl Rogers, behavior therapists promoted this trend to their benefit. Armed with replicable and objective evidence, behavioral researchers and clinicians persistently argued for the efficacy of behavior therapy techniques. Gradually, the movement gained momentum—and converts. By the end of the 1960s, behavior therapy could boast two journals (*Behaviour Research and Therapy*, 1963; *Journal of Applied Behavior Analysis*, 1968), a flourishing professional society (The Association for the Advancement of Behavior Therapy, founded in 1966), several authoritative texts, and a foothold in several graduate psychology departments.

This trickle of institutional recognition increased to a torrent in the decade of the 1970s and the early years of the 1980s. The number of behavior therapy journals now stands at almost two dozen; all are amply supplied with material by behavioral authors. Graduate programs with specializations in behavior therapy have become routine; behavior therapists are now found in impressive numbers in diverse settings. Perhaps because it no longer must be preoccupied with defending itself from attack from traditional clinicians, the behavioral movement is now beset by dissension from within its ranks. One prime example is the rise of cognitive behavior modification theory and techniques and the controversy its development has touched off. Arguing that psychopathology results from faulty thought patterns, cognitive theorists propose treatment focused almost entirely on changing cognitions; they place far less emphasis on behavioral change as a central component of therapy. Recent speculations on the clinical significance of emotion and affect have also touched a nerve among "old-school" behavior therapists, who eschew mediating variables not linked directly to operational referents because they defy strict empirical validation. Our detailed review of behavioral theory and practice, which follows, will consider the significance of these controversies in greater detail.

THEORETICAL ISSUES IN BEHAVIOR THERAPY

The spread of behavior therapy applications to diverse populations and problems in the last two decades, and the growing sophistication of outcome and experimental behavioral research, have raised unforeseen questions that have led, in turn, to increasingly complex and divergent theoretical formulations within behavior therapy. Recent developments in applied behavior analysis, neobehavioristic (S-R) learning theory, social learning theory, and cognitive behavior modification illustrate the extent of current theoretical variety.

Applied Behavior Analysis

Perhaps more than any other area in behavior therapy, applied behavior analysis has remained largely untouched by theory and theoretical controversy (Baer, 1982). Following the example of Skinner, its practitioners eschew theory in favor of the demonstration of empirical control in unmistakable terms. Skinner's method, the experimental analysis of behavior, seeks to describe in purely empirical terms the relationship between behavior and environmental events (Ferster & Skinner, 1957; Kazdin, 1978a; Skinner, 1938). In practice, the method relies on the study of the individual organism over long periods of time, emphasizes environmental control, and values unequivocal effects. Models of behavior are not overtly formulated, but rather are supposed to emerge from cumulative records of data (Skinner, 1953). The heirs of this tradition have continued on this atheoretical, pragmatic course, with the result that applied behavior analysis remains more a commitment to a particular methodology than a model of behavior.

The program of research on operant learning begun by Skinner established the lawful relationship of various schedules of reinforcement, extinction, and punishment procedures to different classes of behavior. Applied behavior analysis adapted these methods and findings to techniques for treating clinical populations. These techniques were first successfully used in the management of chronic schizophrenia, mental retardation, and childhood disorders and later in the modification of behavior in other clinical and nonclinical settings. The impact of applied behavior analysis in educational settings has been particularly great, as has its effect on chronic institutional populations.

Despite these successes, however, applied behavior analysis has encountered some difficulties in demonstrating effective behavioral control. The failure to transfer treatment gains over settings (generalization) or time (maintenance) and the failure of some clients to respond to operant procedures remain persistent problems for applied behavior analysis. Kazdin refers to these as problems in the refinement of technology, thereby implying that the conceptual foundation is sound (Kazdin, 1978a, p. 303). And, indeed, perhaps too much has been made of its failures: even Skinner noted that the experimental history of the individual organism, characteristics of the response, rates of responding, and so forth all tend to make animal operant conditioning more complex than might be expected, and human conditioning appears vastly more intricate than this (Kazdin, 1978a).

Yet applied behavior analysis has also been subject to persistent criticism on conceptual grounds. Bandura (1977b) among others has repeatedly challenged the notion that behavior is solely a function of environmental determinants. Others have criticized applied behavior analysis for its neglect of such cognitive processes as thoughts and expectancies, which play an obvious role in human behavior (Kazdin & Wilson, 1978).

Neobehavioristic (S–R) Learning Theory

Although applied behavior analysis remains a steady source of productive research and effective techniques, the most lively activity in the field of behavior therapy comes from those who object to the operant model and favor more complex models of man. The neobehavioristic (S–R) theory of behavior therapy (Eysenck, 1982), derived principally from the classical conditioning model of Pavlov and the mediational models of Hull and Mowrer, has provoked considerable controversy and witnessed continual revision and expansion over the years. Neobehavioristic theory

and practice have focused primarily on the neurotic disorders. Since fear and anxiety are presumed to motivate most of these disorders, attention to these constructs
is central to the neobehavioristic model.

Mowrer's two-stage theory of fear and avoidance behavior (Mowrer, 1939)
shaped initial behavioral conceptions of fear (Kazdin, 1978a). Mowrer suggested
that the different types of learning investigated by Thorndike and Pavlov represented instances of sign learning and solution learning, respectively, and that both
processes were involved in fear-related behavior. The former refers to the classical
conditioning of involuntary reactions, including emotional ones, in which the conditioned stimulus comes to serve as a sign that either an aversive or a pleasant event
will follow. Over time this stimulus itself begins to elicit the conditioned response.
Solution learning, in contrast, results from the instrumental conditioning of trial-
and-error behavior, as, for example, when a random response such as lever pressing
terminates an aversive event and so is learned. Also central to Mowrer's account is
the notion that fear has motivating or drive properties. The first step in the sequence
of avoidance behavior comes when fear becomes conditioned to some neutral stimulus through involuntary conditioning or sign learning. Since fear is an unpleasant
stimulus, reduction of fear acts as a reinforcement. Thus any behavior that allows
escape from or avoidance of the fear is learned and strengthened by virtue of its
fear-reducing qualities (Kanfer & Phillips, 1970). Buttressed by abundant empirical
support for this two-stage process in animal learning, Mowrer proposed that human
neurosis was acquired and reinforced in much the same way: Behaviors maladaptive
in some larger sense were maintained by their instrumental value in reducing conditioned fears (Rachman, 1976; Kazdin, 1978).

The gradual accumulation of contradictory evidence has forced a change in
Mowrer's neobehavioristic account of fear and avoidance behavior. For example,
many laboratory studies have found that avoidance behavior is extraordinarily resistant to extinction, far more so than could be predicted from the two-stage theory.
Other experiments have indicated that avoidance behavior can be acquired without
fear being reduced or even involved in any way. The evidence also suggests that not
all fears are necessarily acquired by classical conditioning processes, but may instead be transmitted through vicarious or informational learning (Kazdin, 1978a).
Finally, the clinical observation of desynchrony, or independent responding in the
behavioral, physiological, and subjective components of fear, poses problems for a
theory that postulates a close correspondence between fear and avoidance behavior,
as the two-stage model does (Rachman, 1976, pp. 126–128).

Eysenck has attempted to account for some of these findings in his theory of the
neuroses. For example, Eysenck (1976, 1982) has proposed a modification of the
traditional theory of the neuroses that would account for the apparent enhancement
(rather than extinction) of the conditioned fear response. In the face of nonaversive
encounters with the feared stimulus, according to his argument, both duration of
exposure and strength of the unconditioned stimulus (UCS) are crucial to this *incubation* effect. If the UCS is intense or strong enough, the conditioned response
(CR) comes to acquire drive properties of its own through close association (contiguity) with the potent UCS–UCR sequence. When it has taken on motivating

properties, this CR can then serve to reinforce the CS–CR connection and can overcome the natural tendency toward extinction. Similarly, CS exposure can cause either extinction or incubation, depending on the length of exposure time. At very short durations of exposure, the CS elicits fear without having time to extinguish appreciably, and hence the response is augmented; with longer exposures, it habituates and is gradually extinguished. Thus the theory predicts that, with a very strong UCS and brief exposures of the CS, fear will increase rather than decrease with repeated exposure. However, in most cases extinction will occur as predicted by classical learning theory (Eysenck, 1976, 1982).

Eysenck's theory also incorporates the notion of *preparedness*. Originally proposed by Seligman (1971) to account for persistent anomalies in human and animal fear conditioning, *prepared* fears are *prepotent*, reflecting the effects of evolutionary selection pressures. The resistance to extinction of most phobias and their apparent ease of acquisition, even with delayed or degraded feedback, are explained by their value in contributing to the preservation of the species. By this line of reasoning, common phobias (fear of the dark, of snakes, of high places) can be seen to have an obvious adaptive function.

Together, preparedness and the incubation of fear are said to account for the observed patterning of human phobias, although both aspects of the theory have been subject to considerable criticism on both conceptual and empirical grounds.

Problems in both the two-stage and neobehavioristic accounts of fear and avoidance behavior have stimulated continuing research on these processes. A current conditioning alternative is the three-systems analysis suggested by Lang (1977). This approach has highlighted the complexities of the fear response by illuminating the complex determinants of desynchrony in the behavioral, physiological, and subjective components of fear. Following a more openly cognitive mediational line, these researchers have suggested that different cognitive structures and modes of conceptual processing may govern responding in each of the three systems; preliminary evidence suggests that this may be the case, though much more empirical data are required for confirmation of the theory.

As noted, learning theory conceptualizations of psychopathology and treatment have traditionally focused on overt behaviors and external reinforcement and conditioning contingencies; despite the admission of occasional mediating variables such as *fear*, recent revisions of these traditional theories have continued to ignore cognitive processes as explanatory possibilities. By contrast, other behavioral researchers have advanced theories in which explicitly cognitive mechanisms play the largest role in accounts of behavior. The swift rise in popularity of these theories attests both to the perceived inadequacies of traditional learning theory and to the appeal of models of behavior that admit the possibility of self-determination and self-directed behavior change.

Social Learning Theory

The most comprehensive of these new theories, Bandura's social learning theory, has exerted a pronounced impact on current clinical practice and theory. For many, the mention of this theory brings to mind the word *modeling*. This association is natural because most of the research in this tradition has involved social modeling procedures as independent variables (Rosenthal, 1982).

The work of Bandura and his colleagues has established that modeling may be a most important source of human learning. Modeling permits observers quickly to exhibit new patterns of behavior after watching similar responses being modeled only a few times. As Bandura notes, this observational learning offers great advantages over the laborious shaping of behavior through selective reinforcement of trial-and-error responses that behavioristic learning theory proposes as primary. Modeling allows integrated solutions to be grasped intact, greatly increasing the efficiency and safety of learning (Bandura, 1977b; Rosenthal & Bandura, 1978). Imagine, for example, having to learn to drive a car by the operant trial-and-error shaping of correct responses. Aside from its utility in teaching new response sequences, modeling may also have inhibitory or disinhibitory effects on responses already available in the observer's repertoire—as, for example, when observing a model perform a feared act without adverse consequences results in decreased fear and increased willingness to perform the same act.

For the most part, traditional theories of learning rely on the principles of contiguity (classical conditioning) and reinforcement (operant conditioning) to explain modeling effects. The acquisition of entire response sequences in observational learning is explained by reference to the action of the stimulus–response chaining and the discriminative cueing of particular sequence components. Learning without any reinforcement, or with only vicarious reinforcement (e.g., only the model is rewarded), is viewed as the end result of a conventional learning process in which one has been routinely reinforced in the past for imitative learning, and thus matching-to-standard serves as a generalized cue for extrinsic reinforcement, even though such reinforcement may not be apparent in a given trial (Gewirtz, 1971).

In contrast, Bandura proposes a cognitive model involving attentional, motivational, and retention processes to account for vicarious influence. Each component subprocess transforms the stimulus input; these transformations reflect active attempts to make sense of the world. For example, attending to a stimulus requires selective attention in order to filter out key events from other stimuli of negligible importance, not merely the passive reception of incoming data (Bandura, 1977b). Similarly, retention of a long sequence of modeled actions appears to depend on reductive and highly symbolic memory representations that abstract the essence, if not the particulars, of the behavior. To Bandura, "what seems clear is that learning results from cognitive processes and not sheer contiguity or classically conditioned bonds" (Rosenthal & Bandura, 1978, p. 627).

Of course, vicarious learning is not the only sort of learning: People learn from external operant reinforcement and classical conditioning as well. However, while not denying that nonmediational regulatory systems do affect behavior, Bandura emphasizes that the influence of environmental contingencies is primarily determined by cognitive processes. For example, simply repeated contiguity is not enough to ensure that an association is learned; people must recognize the correlation and the predictive function of the stimulus if it is to have any influence on behavior (Bandura, 1977b). Operant conditioning, according to this model, can also be explained through the operation of cognitive processes. Beliefs about reinforcement schedules can have a greater influence on behavior than the reinforcer itself. Whether a particular contingency increases, reduces, or has no impact on behavior depends primarily on expectations about the effects of the consequences, a finding at variance with the traditional operant position (Bandura, 1977b, p. 102).

Social learning theory also addresses the question of human agency very differently. Both the applied behavior analysis and neobehavioristic models implicitly endorse linear, unidirectional models of causal influence; behavior is a function of independent environmental and predetermined individual (e.g., genetic) factors and is always reactive to outside influence. In contrast, Bandura suggests that personal and environmental influences are interdependent. A person is not merely reactive to reinforcement, but can create changes in the external environment that may, in turn, alter future behavior, cognitions, or both. For example, hostile behavior generally elicits punitive or aggressive responses from the social environment, which in turn promote negative or deviant ideas about the self-aggressive counter-response, and so on (Bandura, 1977b, p. 198). Behavior is not determined by the environment; rather, each exerts concurrent control on the other. Through this model Bandura has also attempted to address keenly felt objections to the mechanistic determinism of behaviorism. By allowing for self-produced influences as a contributing factor in behavior, Bandura suggests that people may be considered at least partially free.

Bandura also presents a detailed theoretical model to account for the changes in behavior brought about by different clinical behavior change methods. He postulates a common cognitive mechanism underlying these effects: expectations of personal efficacy. According to Bandura, self-referential judgments mediate the relationship between knowledge and action, even in fairly routine performances. Effective performance requires not only knowing roughly what to do, but also a sense of confidence that one can adapt to meet the demands of new situations. Self-efficacy is this estimate of personal capabilities concerning future behavior in conditions that constitute a challenge to one's skill or ability (Bandura, 1977a, 1982).

Although self-efficacy is key to predicting performance, other influences on behavior are crucial as well, including situational constraints, appropriate skills, and incentives and motivation. However, given sufficient latitude in each of these areas, social learning theory predicts that variations of self-efficacy will serve as the most important predictor of behavior (Bandura, 1977a).

Four main sources of information contribute to efficacy judgments: performance attainments, vicarious experience, physiological states, and verbal persuasion. Because they are based on authentic mastery experiences, performance accomplishments provide the most influential source of efficacy information. Comparative studies attest to the superiority of treatments involving performance (Bandura, 1977a, p. 107). For example, performance (in vivo) desensitization consistently leads to greater behavior change in less time than does imaginal, symbolic desensitization (Bandura, 1977a). Whatever the source of efficacy information, however, behavioral outcome performance corresponds closely to antecedent levels of self-efficacy, and changes in efficacy judgments are reliably reflected in behavior. Indeed, self-efficacy appears to be a better predictor of behavior than past perform-ance of the same kind (Bandura & Adams, 1977; Bandura, 1982).

Social learning theory has not been without its critics, most of whom support more traditional, nonmediational learning theories. Observing that self-efficacy rep-resents a highly situation-specific expectancy, some have argued that a careful anal-ysis of past reinforcement histories would reveal efficacy judgments to be merely a reflection of prior learning (Borkovec, 1978; Poser, 1978). Even granting some construct validity to self-efficacy, moreover, it is not clear what additional explana-tory power the concept supplies; the theory seems to suggest that skill (competence) and motivation alone may be insufficient to predict performance, although how they can be assessed independently of self-efficacy is never indicated (Kazdin, 1978b). Still others have raised questions about the methods used to measure self-efficacy. The problem of having to rely on verbal report has come under special fire, given the well-known susceptibility of self-report to therapist expectations and situational demand characteristics (Borkovec, 1978; Poser, 1978).

Cognitive Behavior Modification

The most recent newcomer to the arena of behavioral theory and practice is cogni-tive behavior modification (CBM); its rapid ascendance reflects both a renewed surge of interest in cognitive processes in other areas of psychology and dissatisfac-tion with nonmediational clinical treatments. At present, this perspective encom-passes a variety of therapeutic procedures based on diverse conceptual models (Mahoney & Arnkoff, 1978; Meichenbaum & Cameron, 1982). Techniques as di-verse as self-control procedures, covert conditioning, cognitive restructuring, and coping skills and problem-solving therapies are currently included under the rubric of cognitive behavior modification. CBM models are based on the assumption that cognitive processes are responsible for most maladaptive behavior and that these cognitions must be modified in therapy. However, the actual procedures used are largely identical to those of behavior therapy, with a heavy reliance on perform-ance-based treatments. Although imagery, affect, and logical argument are used more extensively in CBM than in behavior therapy, there is no clear discontinuity between the two (Mahoney & Arnkoff, 1978; Meichenbaum & Cameron, 1982).

Both social learning theory and CBM make the important distinction between behavioral procedures as the agent of change and cognitive process as the mecha-nism, an assertion that separates mediational and nonmediational models of behav-ior. Rosenthal (1982) remarks, in fact, that most of the differences between the various cognitive positions and social learning theory appear to be more a matter of semantics and politics than of substance. Whether this will remain the case when the fledgling CBM theories are formalized and expanded into coherent models remains to be seen.

One emerging distinction involves the notion of "man-as-scientist" prevalent in CBM models of therapy. Mahoney, for example, has advanced a "personal science" approach to adjustment, in which the same general skills utilized by the research scientist are taught to clients as adaptive problem-solving skills (Mahoney, 1977; Mahoney & Arnkoff, 1978). Clients are trained to collect information reliably, to generate alternative explanations about their difficulties, and then to test them by conducting real-life experiments. This model assumes that affect and behavior are in large part determined by the individual's cognitive constructs and that, insofar as these constructs mirror reality, the self will generally prosper. Presumably, the more rational and accurate information obtained by these methods will further treatment and reinforce skill acquisition by providing veridical feedback about the self in the world. Another aspect of this approach is the concept of *metacognition*, which refers to "thinking about thinking," or reflecting on one's own cognitive strategies and processes (Meichenbaum & Cameron, 1982). Recent research suggests that a number of clinical populations may have metacognitive deficits, a fact that points to innovative cognitive interventions focusing on the self-regulatory components of control processes.

A number of CBM theorists have advanced theories of behavior and therapeutic change. Meichenbaum, for example, has suggested that changes in three domains are necessary—and perhaps even sufficient—to bring about enduring treatment results (Meichenbaum, 1977, Meichenbaum & Cameron, 1982). As with all behavioral therapies, first of all, the principal focus and chief outcome measure remains behavior change. Meichenbaum carefully notes the reciprocal nature of the change, as does Bandura: As the behavior of the client is modified, environmental reactions to the client are altered as well, resulting in further change. Second, successful therapy also alters the private speech and images of the client, the self-regulatory cognitions that influence affective response to behavioral productions and guide their execution. This notion is obviously very similar to Bandura's construct of self-efficacy. Third, effective treatment is also said to effect changes in clients' cognitive structures, that is, in their basic implicit assumptions about the world and habitual styles of thinking (Meichenbaum & Cameron, 1982, p. 327). Although the intuitive appeal of this model is great, empirical verification for it is currently lacking.

Meichenbaum has also developed an intriguing model of the clinical operations that will promote these changes (Meichenbaum, 1977; Meichenbaum & Cameron, 1982). Like the domains of change proposed earlier, these operations are thought to be invariant across different forms of therapeutic influence. A first step involves teaching clients to observe their own behavior more accurately. Whether this initially involves self-exploration or self-monitoring of behavior makes no real difference, according to Meichenbaum, because the benefits of the processes set in motion are not entirely dependent on "objective" results. Self-observation first helps clients gain a more clear and differentiated understanding of their problem as new data come to light. A process of translation is also said to occur at this time. Through selective reinforcement, explanation, or interpretation, therapists encourage clients, not always explicitly, to develop new formulations of the presenting problems. Meichenbaum and Cameron assert, "It is our belief that the therapist begins to impart to the client his or her own theoretical constructs, so that the client gradually comes to interpret events and experiences in terms of the theoretical constructs used by the therapist" (pp. 327–328). Whatever its form, the therapist's translation of the problem is likely to be more benign or "normalized" than the client's initial construal. The therapist's interpretation is also more likely to suggest a solution to the problem. Both of these operations give the client *hope*, which a number of observers (see Frank, 1974) have suggested is vital to therapy.

The second phase of therapy focuses on developing new adaptive thoughts and behaviors. Not only must the therapist be concerned with teaching skills and arranging contingencies to reinforce the new behavior, but he or she should also monitor the client's cognitions in response to the successes and failures of these learning trials. Meichenbaum cites Bandura (1977a) to illustrate the importance of self-referent judgments concerning competence and self-efficacy to treatment outcomes. He suggests that in vivo learning experiences arranged both to maximize the probability of success and to foster self-attributions of competence will lead to the most effective treatment (Meichenbaum & Cameron, 1982).

The final phase of therapy concentrates on consolidating the cognitive and behavioral changes begun earlier. Meichenbaum asserts that "the way in which clients interpret the changes they have made will influence the degree to which changes are generalized and maintained" (Meichenbaum & Cameron, 1982, p. 331). This requires that the client both recognize the change and attribute it to the self rather than to external forces. The importance of self-attributions for clinical success has been supported by a number of studies, all of which suggest that viewing the self or one's own effort as responsible for change is crucial for maintenance in both child and adult populations, across a wide range of disorders (Bandura, 1982).

Meichenbaum's model is typical in many respects of CBM theory: long on interesting assertion and short on hard evidence. Because of the newness of the field, the research that could either confirm or refute these theories is absent or still in progress. Until data begin to appear, CBM models must be viewed as little more than intriguing hypotheses. Despite its youth, however, CBM has attracted a cadre of loyal followers (and a no less committed group of detractors.) Learning theory critics charge that CBM, like social learning theory, incorrectly relies on introspective reports and on unparsimonious inferences about behavior. While a discussion of the controversy surrounding the use of first-person verbal reports as data would be tangential to this summary, suffice it to say that the issue has not been resolved within psychology as a whole or within the philosophy of science. Nor is the argument against inference proven: As many have demonstrated, all science is inferential to some degree and parsimony is more an esthetic than a logical requirement (Mahoney, 1977; Weimer, 1976).

However, CBM theory has been more prone than most to the dangers of unfounded speculation and tautologous inference, as its own proponents have warned (Mahoney, 1977b). Further, CBM models have made surprisingly little use of the findings of cognitive psychology, despite the clear potential for a fruitful exchange (Bower, 1978). One can only hope that these difficulties will be resolved as empirical research and theoretical refinement within the area proceed.

Concluding Remarks

A sampling of recent theoretical developments in behavior therapy has revealed considerable vitality. In response to criticism and in reaction to empirical anomalies, models of behavior have become increasingly oriented to cognitive processes. Nonmediational learning models have become increasingly sophisticated as well, as they have moved from animal conditioning to the complexities of human psychopathology. Despite these advances, however, many still regard the theory of behavior therapy as inadequate to the task of explaining behavior, therapeutic change, and even the results of its own powerful methods. The current models are notably silent on such factors as the role of emotion in therapeutic change, the client–therapist relationship, and the role of the therapist, although most behavior therapy practitioners have an uneasy sense of their importance. Whether behavior therapy will address these issues, and what it will develop into if it does, remain only guesses. Perhaps its greatest hope for resolving these and other problems lies in its methodology and commitment to empiricism which, finally, may be its most enduring legacy as well.

BEHAVIORAL TREATMENT

The Psychoses

The psychoses were the first syndromes to receive systematic behavioral attention. Before psychotics—most of them schizophrenics—were the objects of behavioral treatment, they were the subjects of basic empirical investigation in the middle 1950s by operant pioneer B. F. Skinner and his student, Ogden R. Lindsley.

The basic thrust of Skinner and Lindsley's research was to determine whether hospitalized chronic schizophrenics would demonstrate the same behavioral responses to operant reinforcement schedules that pigeons and rats had previously shown. Demonstrating equivalent operant responding across species, as Skinner and Lindsley (1956) did, helped show the universality of the operant laws of learning and their identity as basic building blocks of behavior. Although trained as a basic scientist, Lindsley also tried his hand at behavioral assessment and "therapy" (he and Skinner first coined the term *behavior therapy*). To this end, Lindsley categorized his schizophrenic subjects on the basis of operant response patterns. He also gave them access to an experimental situation in which they could cooperate or compete with an unseen partner with whom they could communicate only electronically, and he showed that it was possible to shape behavior from competitive to cooperative even in these severely regressed patients.

Lindsley and Skinner's work influenced a number of clinically trained persons who saw clinical significance in their research findings; its impact on theory was much less.

One of the first to develop a behavioral theory of schizophrenia was Albert Bandura (1969), who, on reading the work of Lidz (1957a, b) and others on family-based dynamic theories of schizophrenia, was impressed by the importance of the family in the development of psychopathology. Bandura concluded that most of the basic symptoms of schizophrenia, including delusions, suspiciousness, grandiosity, denial of reality, and hallucinations, could be learned by direct parental and sibling reinforcement as well as by parental modeling of deviance. Ullmann and Krasner (1969) also viewed schizophrenic behavior in the family context, seeing it as a consequence of "the failure of reinforcement for a sequence of behavior." According to Ullmann and Krasner, the schizophrenic patient learns to stop paying attention to environmental cues to reinforcement (to which nonschizophrenics do learn to attend) following repeated failure of reinforcement at the hands of his or her parents.

With many others, we find these conceptions of schizophrenia basically unsatisfying, since they fail to account for behavior that is as intense and chaotic as schizophrenic behavior often is. The field awaits a more compelling behavioral theory of the etiology of schizophrenia.

The impact of Skinner and Lindsley's work was greatest on those who first developed behavioral treatments for schizophrenia. One of the first of these applied behavior analysts was Teodoro Ayllon, author of the first report on the use of operant methods to shape the behavior of hospitalized schizophrenic patients (Ayllon & Michael, 1959). Individual operant procedures such as withdrawing a nurse's attention from a patient complaining of imaginary tormentors, increasing an aide's attention to the same patient when she spoke of her affection for her children or her wish to go for a walk in town, reinforcing behaviors incompatible with previously displayed assaultive behavior, and reinforcing appropriate eating behavior in a patient who had previously refused to feed herself all involved systematic reinforcement for appropriate behavior and punishment or withdrawal of reinforcement for inappropriate behavior. All resulted in positive behavioral changes in patients previously inaccessible to treatment.

Designed to bring the benefits of individual operant conditioning to larger numbers of patients without requiring concomitant increases in trained staff, the first token economy was developed on a ward for chronic schizophrenic patients at the Anna (Illinois) State Hospital in 1965 by Ayllon and fellow psychologist Nathan Azrin. Tokens earned for appropriate behavior could be used to purchase supplemental food, privacy, recreation, and time with a therapist. Since tokens assumed the behavior-shaping function in Ayllon and Azrin's token economy, they saved much staff time, which was devoted to planning more elaborate behavior-change programs for larger numbers of patients. Ward duties (cleaning, bed making, meal serving, etc.), off-ward work details, and individual "psychotic" behaviors all benefited from systematic giving and withholding of tokens. Many of the patients on the ward had not emitted normal prosocial behaviors for years, and the token economy succeeded in eliciting behaviors from them that were unimaginable before the system was instituted.

More sophisticated token economies evolved from the initial efforts of Ayllon and Azrin. One of the most influential was the token economy developed by Atthowe and Krasner (1968) on an 86-bed ward at the Palo Alto (California) Veterans Administration Hospital. Whereas tokens in this token economy could be redeemed for usual reinforcers like cigarettes, money, passes to leave the ward, and access to television, more effective were reinforcers of special attractiveness to individual patients, such as the chance to earn solitude on the ward while others were at work or the opportunity to feed milk to kittens. Since some patients hoarded tokens rather than spend them (in that way diminishing their immediate reinforcement value), Atthowe and Krasner chose to "devalue" all tokens at the end of each month, to encourage a "consumer" society that would accord maximal valuation to the tokens. Patients at a higher level of social and intellectual functioning were not "paid" for their work immediately; instead, they received their tokens once a week, on a regularly scheduled payday, just as in the outside, salaried world. A final group of patients, the most energetic and well functioning, became independent of the token system altogether with a "credit card," which permitted them access to all reinforcers in the token system, added privileges, special status, and the requirement that they work longer and harder at their jobs than any other patients on the ward. A 2-year evaluation of this innovative token economy revealed a marked increase in patient activity, in appropriate behavior, and in discharge from the ward to the world outside.

The 1970s witnessed a testing of the limits of comprehensive token economies for schizophrenics, along with an extension of operant behavior change methods to normal children at home and in school as well as to other groups of severely disturbed persons, including autistic children, juvenile delinquents, and mentally retarded children and adults. If the extraordinary early promise of operant technology as a cure for schizophrenia has not been realized, neither have the predictions of some that an Orwellian system of mind and body control would descend on all institutionalized psychotics if token economies were permitted to take root.

Hersen and Bellack's recent review of contemporary token economies (1981) convinced them that (a) token economies do elicit and reinforce a wide range of desirable patient behaviors, (b) the overall social functioning of chronic patients, some very regressed, can be markedly improved, some to the point of hospital discharge, in a token system, (c) token economies, as compared to ward milieu treatment for chronic patients, are associated with higher discharge rates, and (d) patients discharged from token economies have a better chance of remaining in the community than patients released from milieu treatment units.

Hersen and Bellack's conclusions were clearly influenced by the most thorough evaluation of a token economy done to date, reported late in the 1970s (Paul & Lentz, 1977). A comprehensive token economy in an Illinois state hospital ward was compared both to a milieu treatment unit and to a ward providing standard hospital treatment for similar patients. Among the notable strengths of the study were the program's 6-year tenure, which permitted the very lengthy follow-up period, the wide range of patient and staff characteristics assessed (in order to ensure comparability among patients and staff on all three treatment units), the strict rules that guaranteed the consistency and quality of treatment provided within each treatment unit, and the diversity of outcome data tapped for comparative purposes. Data on outcome showed the clear superiority of the token economy, in terms of both level of patient functioning within the hospital and rate of patient discharge from the hospital. Rehospitalization rates among treatment programs did not differ, although the token economy discharged significantly more patients to the community. The token economy was effective, interestingly enough, even though it provided patients significantly fewer psychotropic drugs than the two other programs.

Token economies have also begun to be used in outpatient and day-hospital settings, to manage and support the behavior of discharged chronic schizophrenics who still require partial institutional support. The partial hospitalization program at the Western Psychiatric Institute and Clinic in Pittsburgh, now 2 years old, enrolls 40 patients, half male and half female, whose mean number of previous hospitalizations is 3.38 (Turner & Luber, 1980). The program is a complex and sophisticated one that reinforces not simply basic housekeeping and personal-care behaviors but prosocial skills—behaviors designed to equip patients for their life in the community. An inquiry into the meaning of the tokens to the patients earning them revealed, interestingly, that their reinforcement value came not so much from their worth—what they could purchase—but from their indication of how well the patient was doing, as feedback on behavioral adequacy. Accordingly, Turner and Luber recommend that this important feedback function of tokens be heightened in day treatment settings since it is consonant with the prosocial aims of these programs.

Another recent review of behavioral approaches to schizophrenia (Salzinger, 1981) concludes that many of the behaviors modified by token economies are chosen for attention because they annoy staff and, hence, further isolate the patient from his or her environment. Salzinger suggests, accordingly, that individualized behavior therapy that focuses on other behaviors, those that are central to each person's disorder, may make more sense.

Adams, Brantley, Malatesta, and Turkat (1981) took this approach in an attempt to modify the disturbed cognitive processes of a 25-year-old schizophrenic man whose cognitive dysfunction was his most distressing symptom (although it was not as obvious to those around him as other symptoms of his disorder).

Newly released after 3 months of hospitalization, the patient complained of feeling "confused," "spaced out," and experiencing considerable difficulty understanding what his therapist and others were saying. During the first five treatment sessions a variety of behavioral techniques were employed to teach the patient to attend more effectively to appropriate external and internal stimuli and to ignore inappropriate ones. Four additional treatment sessions were spent "fine tuning Mr. O's skills and phasing out the therapist's involvement." Tangible evidence that these lessons in cognitive functioning had been learned came when the patient was offered a high-level part-time job at a local university.

The Anxiety, Phobic, and Obsessive–Compulsive Disorders

Because these three syndomes share a common feature, anxiety, they have been brought together in DSM-III (1980) under the major diagnostic heading of Anxiety Disorders; for the same reason, they share crucial behavioral treatment strategies.

Most observers date serious behavioral attention to the anxiety, phobic, and obsessive–compulsive disorders to the publication in 1950 of Dollard and Miller's *Personality and Psychotherapy*, a groundbreaking reinterpretation of neurotic behavior from the behavioral rather than the prevailing psychoanalytic perspective. Shortly thereafter, Eysenck insisted that neurosis could be described best according to two objective, empirically based behavioral dimensions (neuroticism/nonneuroticism and extroversion/introversion), rather than by the unvalidated psychoanalytic concepts by which it had previously been defined. Eysenck has continued to play an important role in behavioral reinterpretations of these disorders by virtue of his prolific writings on etiology, assessment, and theory. Of equal importance, Eysenck's early comparative reviews of dynamic and behavioral treatment of these disorders (reviewed elsewhere in this chapter) gave essential initial credibility to the applied efforts of behavioral clinicians.

Wolpe's important influence on methods of treatment for these disorders has largely been as the principal proponent of systematic desensitization and related treatments for the anxiety disorders; he has adopted a corresponding view of their etiology that attempts to account for the success of the counterconditioning treatment methods. Wolpe believes that human anxiety disorders and experimental neuroses in animals (which he studied early in his career) are comparable in three important ways: (a) Both are acquired by learning (primarily Pavlovian conditioning); (b) both are subject to primary stimulus generalization; and (c) both can be eliminated by unlearning (1952, 1958, 1969). Wolpe has maintained essentially the same theoretical position on etiology and treatment to this time (Wolpe, 1981a, b, c), despite criticism for unwarranted extrapolation from the laboratory to the consulting room and an unwillingness to consider other explanations for those phenomena than his own (Bandura, 1969; Eysenck, 1972; Lazarus, 1977; Kazdin & Hersen, 1980).

Prevailing behavioral opinion on the etiology of these disorders is probably closer to Bandura's broader view (1969, 1977 a,b) than to Wolpe's more narrow one. Modeling, classical conditioning, and operant conditioning all play roles in these behaviors, according to Bandura, as do response feedback processes (self-reinforcement, a cognitive variable) and internal symbolic central mediational processes (supplemental cognitive factors) that permit assessment of *self-efficacy*, Bandura's term for hypotheses about personal competence that determine much of what we do.

Treatment of Anxiety and Phobic Behavior. Based on his conviction that "if a response inhibitory of anxiety can be made to occur in the presence of anxiety-evoking stimuli it will weaken the bond between these stimuli and the anxiety" (Wolpe, 1969, p. 15), Wolpe developed *reciprocal inhibition therapy*, better known as systematic desensitization to generations of behavior therapists. Systematic desensitization has been and remains a treatment of choice for many anxiety and phobic disorders.

A variety of stimuli can be used to compete with—countercondition—fear or anxiety. Two of the most common are deep muscle relaxation and assertive behavior. Accordingly, behavior therapy for these disorders often combines relaxation training and assertive behavior training from its earliest stages.

The most common technique to induce deep muscle relaxation is Jacobson's

(1938) progressive relaxation method. As adapted by Wolpe and subsequently used by countless behavior therapists, progressive relaxation requires successive relaxation and contraction of the voluntary muscle groups, usually from head to toe, to teach necessary discriminations in muscle tension level and voluntary control of relaxation. The first of these exercises focuses on the hands and arms:

> I am now going to show you the essential activity that is involved in obtaining deep relaxation. I shall again ask you to resist my pull at your wrist so as to tighten your biceps. I want you to notice very carefully the sensations in that muscle. Then I shall ask you to let go gradually as I diminish the amount of force exerted against you. Notice, as your forearm descends, that there is decreasing sensation in the biceps muscle. Notice also that the letting go is an activity, but of a negative kind—it is an "uncontracting" of the muscle. In due course, your forearm will come to rest on the arm of the chair, and you may then think that you have gone as far as possible—that relaxation is complete. But although the biceps will indeed be partly and perhaps largely relaxed, a certain number of its fibers will still, in fact, be contracted. I shall therefore say to you, "Go on letting go. Try to extend the activity that went on in the biceps while your forearm was coming down." It is the act of relaxing these additional fibers that will bring about the emotional effects we want. Let's try and see what happens [Wolpe, 1969, p. 102].

Succeeding relaxation exercises move to the face and shoulders, trunk and abdomen, thighs, legs, and feet. The patient is to practice the exercises once or twice a day for 20 minutes at a time. Relaxation training typically occupies part of each of the first several anxiety or phobic behavior treatment sessions.

Training in assertive behavior is another component of the typical systematic desensitization package, largely because assertive behavior—self-expression, self-control, and/or self-assertion in interpersonal situations—is thought to inhibit anxiety and fearfulness as effectively as does relaxation. Assertive training is also of value—and is taught—to persons who are not fearful or anxious but are simply unable to exhibit properly forthright and assertive verbal behavior with others.

Assertive behavior is commonly taught by having the patient rehearse assertive responses he or she might make to the person with whom assertion is difficult, usually a parent, spouse, sibling, or boss (Kazdin, 1982). Alberti and Emmons (1974) have identified seven behavioral elements that together constitute successful assertive behavior: eye contact, body posture, gestures, facial expression, voice, timing, and verbal content. Identification of deficits in one or more of these assertion modalities helps to target remediation efforts.

Once relaxation and assertive training are under way, an anxiety or fear hierarchy is constructed. With the therapist's help, the patient arranges scenes associated with anxiety or fear in the order of their capacity to elicit it. Ten to 20 or more scenes typically make up a hierarchy. By the time the hierarchy is completed, relaxation training is usually far enough along to enable systematic desensitization to commence. Systematic desensitization involves induction of deep muscle relaxation followed by exposure to scenes from the anxiety or fear hierarchy long enough for the patient actually to feel immersed in the real situation. The aim is to couple the experience of relaxation with exposure to a scene previously capable of inducing fear or anxiety; this is the essence of counterconditioning. If relaxation is intense enough, the experience of anxiety or fear is presumably inhibited. Proceeding through the entire fear or anxiety hierarchy in this way, the patient is supposed to lose his fear or anxiety both to comparable scenes in the real world and to the imagined scenes.

Systematic desensitization, deep muscle relaxation, and assertive training have been studied intensively through the years, to determine the diagnostic groups for whom they are most useful, to establish their "active ingredients," and to assess the time and behavior change limits of this approach to treatment. The interested reader is referred to several recent comprehensive reviews of this literature for details on this research (Craighead, Kazdin, & Mahoney, 1981; Lutzker & Martin, 1981; Walker, Hedberg, Clement, & Wright, 1981).

A recent empirical study of the active ingredients of systematic desensitization reveals the extent of behavior therapy's current "cognitive revolution." The study (Anderson & Borkovec, 1980) tested Lang's (1977, 1978) bio-informational theory of emotional imagery, which requires that cognitive and somatic responses to fear be added to its behavioral components for a full account of the experience of fear or anxiety. The study explored the utility of a multicomponent analysis of counterconditioning by presenting either the feared stimulus alone (to speech-anxious subjects) or both the stimulus and the cognitive, somatic, and behavioral responses that accompanied it, to determine which information set provided the truest picture of the fear response. The multicomponent analysis yielded meaningful changes in cognitions, measures of physiologic arousal, and behavior, affirming that both stimulus and response dimensions are necessary for a complete picture of the fear response.

The cognitive revolution has also influenced treatment of phobic and anxious behavior. For example, Woodward and Jones (1980) recently compared three behavioral treatments for phobic disorders; all contained important cognitive elements. Cognitive restructuring (challenging a patient's irrational beliefs about situations or objects that cause fearful or anxious behavior), modified systematic desensitization with imaginal coping and mastery, and cognitive behavior modification (essentially, a combination of cognitive restructuring and modified systematic desensitization) were compared. Cognitive behavior modification yielded more improvement in anxious behavior in 27 outpatients complaining of nonspecific anxiety than the other two, more narrow treatments, leading the authors to recommend a multidimensional approach to fear reduction that undertakes to modify both cognitive and physiological correlates of anxiety rather than either one or the other.

Biran and Wilson (1981) compared the efficacy of cognitive restructuring and guided exposure for height, elevator, and darkness phobias. In the latter condition, called in vivo desensitization in years past, patients came in increasingly close contact with the feared situation, first with the therapist's help and then, if possible, alone. Guided exposure was more effective than cognitive restructuring in altering fear-related avoidance behaviors and enhancing patients' sense of self-efficacy (Bandura, 1977b). In other words, actual exposure to the feared objects both decreased fear-related responses and increased the patients' sense of cognitive mastery over the fears; cognitive restructuring may only have been capable of the latter behavior change.

A recent NIMH-sponsored conference that brought together leading clinical investigators interested in the anxiety, phobic, and obsessive–compulsive disorders (Barlow & Wolfe, 1981) concluded that (a) there does not appear to be further need for straightforward outcome studies of techniques for treating clinical phobias, since performance-based exposure procedures (e.g., Biran and Wilson's guided exposure) have been proved effective, (b) future research should be carried out with clinical populations rather than with groups of college students with mild phobic- or anxiety-based behavioral problems, since clinical populations present special problems that require techniques developed for them, (c) all future research on the anxiety disorders should assess the problem in each of the three response systems, subjective, behavioral, and physiological, (d) specific attention should be paid to answering the question of why exposure-based treatments work for the anxiety and phobic disorders, and (e) studies should examine the interaction of pharmacological (drug) and exposure-based treatments, since some patients respond best to drugs, others to psychological treatments, and others to a combination of the two.

Treatment of the Obsessive–Compulsive Disorders.   In contrast to the anxiety and phobic disorders, for which treatments ranging from systematic desensitization to in vivo desensitization have been proposed, only a single accepted behavioral treatment for the obsessive–compulsive disorders exists. In their definitive treatise on the behavioral treatment of these disorders, Rachman and Hodgson (1980) state that fact this way: "It is pleasing to record that during the past five to ten years significant advances have been made in coming to grips with the intractability of these disorders. For the first time psychologists are in possession of a treatment program— exposure and response prevention—that is demonstrably successful in reducing the difficulties of most, but by no means all, obsessional patients" (p. 299).

This bold statement is buttressed by data from a lengthy series of clinical investigations revealing that obsessions and compulsions, like anxious and phobic behaviors, are characterized not by a single symptom but by a complex of cognitive, physiological, and behavioral phenomena. Exposure and response prevention, supplemented when necessary by drugs (if the physiological experience of anxiety is too great) or by cognitive restructuring (if the cognitive elements of the disability are strong), successfully confront all three components of the syndrome. An illustration is helpful here.

> Our second illustration is of a 55-year-old man who complained of elaborate repetitive, prolonged stereotyped checking behavior that seriously interfered with his life and threatened to result in his dismissal from a job that he had held for many years. Before leaving his apartment each day, he had repeatedly to carry out hundreds of stereotyped checking rituals designed to ensure that the windows were securely shut, that the taps were not dripping, that the stove was off, that the front door was secure and so on. It took him up to four hours to complete these checks before leaving the apartment. Consequently, he had to rise very early on workdays and, because of the strain and effort involved, was extremely reluctant to leave the apartment on other days. As his

checking compulsions were confined mainly to his own home, the treatment was carried out on a domiciliary basis. The therapist made several visits to the apartment and repeatedly demonstrated how to prepare to leave in less than ten minutes, explaining each action and its rationale as she did it. The patient was then encouraged to model the therapist's behavior. After expressing surprise and even dismay at the therapist's style and speed, he gradually approximated the desired behavior. As usual, he was told to refrain from carrying out any ritualistic behavior after completing the necessary preparations for leaving. He made steady and rewarding progress and learned how to keep his checking to an acceptable minimum and how to leave his apartment within 15 minutes. However, during the closing stages of the treatment and in the follow-up period he needed a good deal of prompting, monitoring, and praise from the therapist. For practical reasons most of this was provided by conversations on the telephone. The general therapeutic outcome was good, and the patient was able to continue living an independent, productive life instead of requiring long-term institutional care. [Rachman & Hodgson, 1980, pp. 304–305]

Guided participation—prompted exposure to a compulsion- and obsession-inducing environment—and simultaneous prevention of the resultant compulsive responses combined to free this patient of a serious, potentially disabling behavioral pattern. Though deceptively simple and free from the complicated theory that has rationalized other psychological treatments for the obsessions and compulsions, the behavioral approach is effective with many patients and generally requires relatively brief intervention.

The Depressive Disorders

Since 1975 the research literature on the behavioral treatment of depression has burgeoned. This sudden growth in part reflects the unexpected success of behavioral treatments in comparison with pharmacotherapy in early studies, a success that challenged the virtual hegemony of antidepressant medications, long the treatment of choice for depression. The rise of behavioral research and treatments also reflects the variety and fertility of the behavioral formulations of depression, each of which has spawned new therapeutic procedures. Although the various theories overlap to a considerable degree, distinctions based on the processes thought to be central to behavioral change help clarify the differences among them (Hollon, 1981).

Based on the classical conditioning paradigm, affect-mediated theories of depression emphasize the role of conditioned anxiety in the formation of depression. For example, Wolpe (1979) outlined a theory of depression based on the model of experimental neurosis: Depression is consequent to the inhibition of normal behavior by conditioned anxiety. Treatments naturally seek to decondition this anxiety, through systematic desensitization, flooding, and implosion. The latter two treatment methods involve prolonged exposure, either in fantasy or reality, to anxiety- or fear-provoking aversive stimuli until the fear or anxiety is deconditioned. Drawing on his case files, Wolpe reports on 25 individuals treated in this fashion over a period of 30 years. Although almost 90% reported positive outcomes, sometimes with follow-ups of 20 years, the retrospective and uncontrolled nature of this study renders the conclusions only suggestive. Similarly, while other reports supporting the effectiveness of systematic desensitization, flooding, and implosion are encouraging, they are based on studies with inadequate controls or poor designs, preventing firm conclusions about the effectiveness of these procedures.

Operant approaches to depression view the syndrome as the result of a reduction in the frequency of positive reinforcement, particularly social reinforcement. This theory emphasizes the importance of environmental events, the range of potential reinforcers, and the social skills of the individual, which determine, respectively, the availability of reinforcers and whether or not they are elicited (Eastman, 1977; Kovacs, 1979). Treatment typically seeks to increase behaviors that will evoke reinforcement, either through contingency management or skills training. A few studies have utilized the Premack principle, in which a low-frequency behavior is repeatedly paired with a naturally occurring behavior, so that both are reinforced. This technique has not met with particular success. Self-monitoring of pleasant events has been shown to effect some changes, although again without consistency (Kovacs, 1979; Whitehead, 1979). Recent suggestions for improving responses to these procedures stress the importance of self-attributions and of treatments tailored to the individual (Blaney, 1981).

However, most outpatient studies have involved some behavioral skills training procedures, ranging from assertion training to marital therapy to social-skills training. The evidence concerning most of these interventions is mixed. In part this may be due to methodological inadequacies and the seemingly endless combinations of behavioral programs that make comparisons difficult (Blaney, 1981). However, some large and well-controlled group studies have found effects for behavioral therapy. For example, McLean and Hakstian (1979) found behavior therapy superior to traditional psychotherapy, drug treatment, and relaxation training, irrespective of the therapist's previous experience or the client's profile on a host of outcome-related variables. The results of this study and an earlier study by McLean also suggest that couples or marital therapy, when possible, contributes significantly to successful treatment outcome, although it is not clear if this improvement is related solely to control of the interpersonal environment or to an overall increase in adaptive behaviors (Hollon, 1981; Whitehead, 1979).

Drawing on Kanfer's self-control theory of behavior, Rehm (1977) developed a self-control model of depression that explicitly attempts to account for the distinctive cognitive and affective components of depression as well as its overt behavioral manifestations. This theory follows traditional behavioral theory in assuming that behavior is controlled by external reinforcement; however, covert self-control responses function to maintain behavioral consistency and bridge delay in the absence of immediate external support (Rehm, 1977, p. 791). Three processes are involved in self-control: self-monitoring, self-evaluation, and self-reinforcement. Deficits or failures in any or all of these components are seen as the basis for the specific signs of depression. For example, Rehm suggests that overly strict self-evaluative criteria, which would bias perceptions of success and failure, lead to the low self-esteem and sense of worthlessness found in the depressed. Therapy attempts to correct these deficiencies through specific procedures aimed at each component. Excessively harsh self-evaluative criteria might be treated by first having the client self-monitor positive activities and then using this information to specify behavioral goals with more realistic subgoals, which then become subject to overt and covert reinforcement to strengthen their influence (Rehm, 1977).

The empirical evidence has been fairly supportive of the self-control theory of depression. In an early study Fuchs and Rehm (1977) found self-control therapy superior to nonspecific therapy control and waiting-list conditions in a group treatment format. A recent study comparing the effectiveness of self-control therapy to a combination of self-control therapy and antidepressant medication again demonstrated the power of this approach: Both groups improved markedly and maintained these gains at a 3-month follow-up. The group combining pharmacological and behavioral treatments improved significantly more rapidly, suggesting promising interactions of the two treatments (Roth, Bielski, Jones, Parker, & Osborn, 1982).

The cognitive therapy of depression is based on the assumption that the affective and behavioral signs of depression are the result of shifts in underlying cognitive organization and processing. According to Beck, who first proposed this theory, depression may be triggered by a sudden loss or a chronic deprivation that, because of one or more cognitive distortions, is inappropriately attributed to the self. Overgeneralization, magnification, and arbitrary inference exemplify such distortions. New experiences are appraised in terms of these deficiencies, leading to a disruptive *cognitive triad*: a negative view of the world, a negative self-concept, and a negative appraisal of the future (Beck, 1976, p. 106).

Cognitive therapy attempts to correct these distortions by focusing on a variety of targets. The separate affective and behavioral components of depression are treated individually by testing the client's beliefs and attitudes through methods ranging from verbal persuasion to empirical demonstration. Typically, behavioral techniques are used to demonstrate the fallacies and distortions in one's thought and then to correct them. For example, graded task assignments with pleasant activities might be used to increase awareness of positive reinforcement and instill a sense of self-confidence and mastery. Other techniques such as distancing through "so what" statements, exaggeration, and cognitive rehearsal are also used to alter maladaptive thought patterns directly.

One of the earliest alternatives to traditional psychotherapy for depression, cognitive therapy has received considerable empirical validation. Numerous well-controlled studies have indicated that it tends to produce significantly better treatment outcomes than purely behavioral interventions, nonspecific controls, or pharmacotherapy, and that these gains generally are maintained over time (Hollon, 1981; Kovacs, 1979; Ruch, Beck, Kovacs & Hollon, 1977; Weissman, 1979). The available evidence also suggests that combining cognitive therapy with pharmacotherapy adds little to the benefits achieved from cognitive therapy alone, although some have questioned these studies on methodological grounds (Hollon, 1981).

Beck's cognitive therapy explicitly incorporates behavioral manipulations in addition to cognitive procedures. The successful self-control therapies also utilize both cognitive and behavioral techniques. Interestingly, many of the more successful "behavioral" treatments for depression also appear to contain cognitive therapy components, although their creators have not acknowledged them as such. For example, Azrin and Besalel (1981) evaluated an operant reinforcement program that included a number of cognitive exercises and found the program effective at the end of treatment and at a follow-up on both behavioral and subjective measures; Hersen, Bellack, and Himmelhoch (1980) found that a social-skills training program that included social perception instructions and practice with correct self-evaluation produced significant and durable improvements in nonpsychotic depressives.

Although converging evidence seems to favor a cognitive–behavioral approach to the treatment of depression, methodological problems limit the conclusions to be drawn. For example, the adequacy of the pharmacological interventions utilized in treatment comparison studies has been questioned. A massive literature attests to the effectiveness of drug treatment for depression; it remains the treatment of choice for many depressed patients today (Hollon, 1981). Accordingly, the more sophisticated outcome studies have pitted behavioral therapy against pharmacotherapy to judge its effectiveness against a proven standard. However, some have raised doubts that these studies provide a fair test for the drug treatments. For example, in perhaps the best-known study in the literature, by McLean and Hakstian (1979), the drug dosage was well below typical levels seen in outpatient therapy (Hollon, 1981). And Becker and Schuckit (1978) have argued that an important study that compared cognitive therapy and antidepressant medication (Rush et al., 1977) may have constituted an inadequate test of pharmacotherapy because the medication was tapered off *before* the outcome measures were taken, and the expected worsening in patients withdrawing from medication would thus skew the results against drug therapy.

On the other hand, both the pharmacological and psychological treatment literatures report a very high dropout rate for drug interventions, typically at 20 to 30%, while dropouts from behavioral interventions are vastly lower, on the order of 5%. Whether this argues for the greater acceptability of behavioral treatment is unclear from the design of studies comparing both. What is clear is that, when comparing pharmacological interventions with behavioral procedures to establish relative superiority, behavioral researchers must ensure that an optimal trial of drug therapy has been undertaken.

Inadequate diagnostic assessments in most treatment studies also prevent firm conclusions about the effectiveness of these therapies. Standardized diagnostic criteria such as those in DSM-III have not been consistently utilized (although their use appears to be growing). Instead, far too many studies rely solely on self-ratings and vague clinical impressions (Weissman, 1979; Whitehead, 1979).

Research on the treatment of depression has also been hindered by a failure to specify completely the nature of the outcome and by too narrow a breadth of measurement. Because depression is a syndrome encompassing distinctive behavioral, affective, and cognitive signs and symptoms, extensive assessments are necessary to determine the adequacy of treatment outcomes. Although combinations of treatments (for example, behavioral and pharmacological) may operate through independent processes, their interactions may not necessarily be additive, requiring assessment across all components in order to account for the potential range of outcomes (Hollon, 1981).

The relative scarcity of long-term outcome studies of behavioral treatment also represents a particular problem, given the recurrent, cyclical nature of depression. The true effectiveness of behavioral treatment for depression must remain in doubt until the results of extended follow-up assessments become known (Hollon, 1981; Whitehead, 1979). Finally, since the groups studied have consisted almost entirely of unipolar, moderately depressed outpatients, little is known about the effectiveness of behavioral treatment with bipolar or more severely depressed patients. Despite these qualifications, however, behavioral treatments for depression, particularly those involving both performance and cognitive elements, have shown remarkable promise, and their use with moderately depressed populations appears justified.

The Substance-Use Disorders

For many years alcoholism and drug dependence were conceptualized rather simple-mindedly as learned means to reduce conditioned anxiety. Based on laboratory findings that suggested that alcohol enabled rats to function more effectively in the face of stressful or frightening environments (Conger, 1956), this theory did not take into account the far greater cognitive and emotional complexity of the human being. More recent and more elaborate theories of etiology benefitting from research with humans indicate that, unlike lower animals, people do not deal more effectively with stress or become less anxious when they are intoxicated (Mendelson, 1964; Nathan & O'Brien, 1971). Furthermore, the determinants of substance abuse appear to depend on social and environmental influences as well as on individual organismic ones (Nathan & Lipscomb, 1979). Contemporary social learning models of alcoholism and drug dependence, Miller and Foy (1981) suggest, must take into account antecedents and consequences of abusive drinking that are *situational* (e.g., beer, wine, and whiskey advertisements); *social* (peer pressures to drink or use drugs); *emotional* (painful emotions like depression and anxiety can be altered by alcohol or drugs); and *physiological* (chronic pain or withdrawal symptoms can be prevented by alcohol or drugs). Finally, recent research by Marlatt and his colleagues suggests that expectancies about the effects of alcohol have powerful effects on the impact of alcohol on behavior; in other words, cognitions about the effects of the drug—what we tell ourselves the drug will do for us—are also influential in determining our pattern of use (Marlatt, 1978; Marlatt & Rohsenow, 1980).

Treatment for Alcoholism.   The first behavioral approaches to treatment of alcoholism employed electric shock and nausea-inducing drugs in the attempt to induce conditioned aversion to alcohol. Electrical aversion, which was first used more than 50 years ago (Kantorovich, 1929), is now rarely employed; extensive empirical research indicates that electrical aversion is ineffective as a treatment for alcoholism (MacCulloch et al., 1966; Miller & Hersen, 1972; Wilson, Leaf, & Nathan, 1975). By contrast, chemical aversion, whose use with alcoholics was first reported more than 40 years ago (Voegtlin, 1940), remains the centerpiece of comprehensive treatment programs for alcoholics offered by a number of private alcoholism hospitals located in the western United States. Early (e.g., Lemere & Voegtlin, 1950; Voegtlin & Lemere, 1942) and later (e.g., Neuburger et al., 1982; Wiens, Montague, Manaugh, & English, 1976) reports on the pairing of emetine, a nausea-inducing drug, with the sight, taste, and smell of a favorite alcoholic beverage over five or six hour-long conditioning sessions have been very positive. With notable consistency, between 45% and 60% of patients so treated have maintained abstinence for up to 1 year. These follow-up figures are high for alcoholism treatment.

More recently, microanalyses of the comprehensive treatment programs containing chemical aversion have been undertaken to "zero in" on the sources of the therapeutic success supporters of the method have claimed. Preliminary studies (Cannon & Baker, 1981; Cannon, Baker, & Wehl, 1981) suggest both that chemical aversion conditioning does lead to a pronounced conditioned aversion to alcohol (that fact had only been presumed by those who employed the method) and that chemical aversion is associated with more favorable outcome results 6 months after treatment than either a multifaceted inpatient treatment program without chemical aversion or electrical aversion. Although these date are preliminary, they do suggest that chemical aversion may be the active ingredient in the complex behavioral treatment programs in which it has been employed with notable success.

One of the most controversial alcoholism treatment efforts in recent years has been the attempt to induce controlled or non–problem drinking in chronic alcoholics. Most of the treatment programs with this aim have been behavioral in orientation; most have also been multidimensional, typically combining aversive conditioning, assertive training, and social-skills training to provide patients with renewed vocational, familial, and interpersonal skills and the motivation to employ these skills while drinking significantly reduced amounts of alcohol. Unique to the most widely reported and apparently most successful of these programs (Sobell & Sobell, 1973) was *alternatives training*, which was designed both to provide patients with the ability to refuse an invitation to drink with a friend and to give them sufficient training in behaviors inimical to drinking to allow choice of nondrinking over drinking situations.

The Sobells' individualized behavior therapy program is most widely cited by advocates of controlled-drinking training for alcoholics because, at the 2-year follow-up mark, patients provided the experimental treatment were drinking significantly less, were more likely to be abstinent, and were more likely to be maintaining a pattern of controlled drinking (Sobell & Sobell, 1976). A 3-year follow-up of the same patients (Caddy, Addington, & Perkins, 1978) was equally encouraging.

A recent published report on reinterviews of the Sobells' original 20 experimental controlled-drinking subjects (Pendery, Maltzman, & West, 1982) raises the explicit question of intentional experimenter deception in the initial random assignment of subjects to the study's experimental and control, and abstinence-oriented and controlled-drinking-oriented groups, as well as in the collection of data on treatment outcome. These allegations are being examined by a high-level independent investigating group asked by the Sobells' employers, the Addiction Research

Foundation in Toronto, to complete a thorough investigation of all data bearing on the study. Their report has not yet been submitted; until it has been made public, it is impossible to assess the validity of the charges made against these investigators. Suffice it to say, though, that the charges are both serious and troubling; allegations of intentional fraud shake the foundations of science in ways that simply shoddy or careless research cannot.

Ironically, since the Sobells' study was virtually the only investigation of con-trolled drinking to report strongly positive data in support of controlled-drinking treatment for chronic alcoholics, controlled-drinking treatment has not become a treatment of choice for chronic alcoholics, as some had predicted. In fact, there are few facilities in this country that now offer controlled-drinking treatment to chronic alcoholics, even though some individuals (see Miller & Caddy, 1977); Sanchez-Craig & Annis, 1982; Strickler, Bradlyn, & Maxwell, 1981) offer this "preventive" treatment to problem drinkers.

Controversies also surrounded publication of the Rand Corporation's reports on their follow-up of several thousand alcoholics treated at federally funded alcoholism treatment centers throughout the United States (Armor, Polich, & Stambul, 1976; Polich, Armor, & Braiker, 1980). Among the most controversial of their findings was that many chronic alcoholics appear to maintain periods of controlled non–problem drinking for long periods of time, before and after heavier drinking peri-ods. The 1980 report also concluded that non–problem drinking was associated with no greater risk of return to alcoholic drinking or of further social or physical deterio-ration than abstinence, a finding that generated a great deal of opposition from many supporters of the abstinence model of alcoholism treatment. What the Rand reports did not claim, although some of their readers mistakenly believed they did, was that treatment methods to induce controlled, non–problem drinking had been developed and should be encouraged.

Although efforts continue to develop and test multifaceted behavioral treatment programs for alcoholics, most of them combining standard behavioral treatment elements such as relaxation training, systematic desensitization, assertive and social-skills training, and training in alternative nondrinking behaviors (e.g., Olson, Devine, Ganley, & Dorsey, 1981), it seems clear that the treatment of choice for alcoholism from the behavioral perspective—or from any other, for that matter—remains to be found. One-year abstinence rates for the most successful treatments generally remain in the 30% to 50% range, a figure that does not encourage the view that a truly effective treatment for chronic alcoholism, the nation's number one public health problem (NIAAA, 1983), has been developed.

Smoking-Cessation Programs.   Smoking is now widely recognized as "the major preventable cause of death in America" (USDHEW, 1979, p. ii). It is the single most important environmental cause of cancer and cardiovascular disorder, both leading causes of death in the United States. For these reasons, smoking-cessation programs based on behavioral principles have proliferated during the past 2 dec-ades. Unfortunately, the decade of the 1960s yielded disappointing therapeutic out-comes: Only 15% to 25% of treated smokers stayed off cigarettes for as long as a year (Orleans, 1980), and only 20% to 30% of those achieving initial abstinence maintained it for a year (Hunt, Barnett, Branch, 1971).

The decade of the 1970s, however, has produced nearly a doubling in these long-term abstinence rates (Orleans et al., 1981). Among the newer, more effective behavioral approaches to treatment is Lichtenstein's aversive *rapid-smoking* procedure (Lichtenstein et al., 1973), in which smokers are required to puff on their cigarettes every few seconds and to smoke a number of cigarettes in a single session in an enclosed room, in order to heighten the aversiveness of the smoking situation and lead to development of an aversive response to cigarettes. A few toxic reactions to rapid smoking have led to safer variants of the technique, including normal-paced aversive smoking (Hackett & Horan, 1979) and smoke holding (Kopel & Suckerman, 1982).

A change in cardiac function during rapid-smoking treatment that requires careful monitoring, especially in those above the age of 40, may occur (Poole et al., 1980). When rapid smoking was compared to alternatives that do not stress the body (rapid smoking was compared to cue exposure, a stimulus control method, and simple support, a control procedure), no differences among the three methods in abstinence rate, which averaged 14% at a 1-year follow-up, were observed (Raw, 1978; Raw & Russell, 1980). We conclude, then, that rapid smoking may represent a health hazard to some persons and that initial claims for the success of rapid smoking have not been fully supported. One explanation for the limited success of rapid smoking with some smokers is provided by a recent study (Lando & McGovern, 1982) reporting that smokers for whom maintenance efforts were intensive (as against minimal) and whose initial treatment began with rapid-smoking treatment immediately (rather than with rapid-smoking treatment that followed an initial preparatory period) were more likely to abstain from smoking than others. In other words, differences in preparation for treatment and in maintenance also affect outcome figures for rapid smoking.

Brand fading—reducing smokers' consumption of tar and nicotine by requiring them to smoke cigarettes lower and lower in tar and nicotine—is associated with measurable reductions in smokers' carbon monoxide and thiocyanate levels and in rate of consumption, suggesting "decreased risk on both direct (alveolar carbon monoxide and saliva thiocyanate levels) and indirect (rate of consumption) measures of tobacco exposure" on a "majority" of subjects (Prue, Krapfl, & Martin, 1981). One problem with the nicotine-fading method, however, is the typical addicted smoker's tendency to smoke more cigarettes and to draw on them more deeply, often without awareness, in order to achieve the same intake of nicotine.

Treatment for Drug Dependence.   While there is voluminous literature on behavioral efforts to treat alcoholism and smoking, some of which is reviewed above, behavioral attempts to treat drug dependence have been few and far between—and, if anything, less effective. Among methods tried and generally discarded have been electrical and covert (imaginal) aversion conditioning (Gotestam & Melin, 1974; Liberman, 1968), desensitization and assertive training (O'Brien, Raynes, & Patch, 1972) and contingency (token) management (Boudin, 1972). More recent behavioral efforts include a theoretical/empirical understanding of drug self-administration behavior within the framework of reinforced operant behavior (Bigelow, Stitzer, Griffiths, & Liebson, 1981). Another recent paper reports on an attempt to increase employment by former heroin addicts in order to decrease the likelihood of their returning to the drug (Hall, Loeb, Coyne, & Cooper, 1981). Fifty-five probationers and parolees with histories of heroin abuse were randomly assigned to an 11-hour "Job Seekers' Workshop" (or to a 3-hour informational workshop as a control measure). At 3 months posttreatment, 86% of the experimental subjects had found jobs while only 54% of the controls had done so. In other words, the Job Seekers' Workshop apparently enhanced the ability of participants to interest employers in hiring them. To the extent that holding a job reduces the likelihood that a former heroin addict will return to the drug, the workshop idea seems to be an excellent one.

The Paraphilias and the Sexual Dysfunctions

Although a variety of behavioral theories of the paraphilias (DSM-III's new name for DSM-II's sexual deviations) have been put forth, Bandura's delineation of three social learning mechanisms seems most helpful. The first involves parents who model sexually deviant behavior for their children either openly or covertly. Modest experimental confirmation of this mechanism (Bandura cites Giffin, Johnson, & Litin, 1954) exists. Bandura also points to the experience of positive reinforcement for new and deviant sexual behavior as an additional etiologic mechanism; early deviant behaviors associated with or reinforced by parents or friends may become a regular part of the sexual repertoire. Bandura cites Stoller (1967), who reported that the wives and mothers of 32 male transvestites had reinforced the males' growing sexual deviance and "taught" them to dress as women in this regard. Bandura also concludes that, once sexually deviant behavior acquires stress-reducing properties and thereby becomes strongly self-reinforcing, it is likely to be maintained despite punishment for it by society.

Treatment of the Paraphilias. Aversion bulked large in the behavioral treatment of the paraphilias (primarily homosexuality) until the 1970s. Dating from 1935, when Max paired pictures of nude males with painful electric shock in the attempt to produce a conditioned aversion to homosexual stimuli in a male homosexual, aversion procedures have also included apomorphine, an emetic drug that induces nausea and vomiting, as an unconditioned aversive stimulus (Raymond, 1956; Freund, 1960), as well as the more familiar electric shock (Thorpe et al., 1964; Feldman & MacCulloch, 1965, 1971).

Aversive procedures to treat the paraphilias and homosexuality are rarely employed nowadays, both because their efficacy has not been supported empirically and because the ethics of treating homosexuals by trying to change them to heterosexuals have been questioned. In a presidential address to the annual convention of the Association for the Advancement of Behavior Therapy, Davison (1977) criticized the attempts of behavior therapists to reorient their homosexual clients to a life of heterosexuality and advocated refusal to treat homosexuals who wished sexual reorientation by behavior therapists. However, he did affirm that behavior therapy designed to help homosexuals derive greater happiness from their sexual orientation and/or more proficiency in their sexuality remained wholly appropriate. Although some observers continue to believe that aversive conditioning does have utility in the treatment of homosexuality (McConaghy, Armstrong, & Blaszczynski, 1981) and advocate its use—in the form of covert sensitization—to reduce deviant sexual arousal but not to reorient homosexuals to heterosexuality, most behavior therapists now choose other methods.

The two current paraphilias that have received most attention from behavior therapists are exhibitionism and pedophilia. In line with contemporary behavioral thinking, the deviant sexual behavior of the pedophile is rarely the only focus of behavioral treatment. Barlow (1974), for example, one of those most experienced in treating the disorder, lists four potentially modifiable components of pedophilia: heterosexual arousal, heterosocial skills, deviant arousal, and gender-role deviation.

In line with this conceptualization, Josiassen, Fantuzzo, and Rosen (1980) describe treatment of a self-referred 37-year-old white male complaining of actual pedophilia, obsessive ruminations on pedophilia, excessive masturbation, and clinical depression. During the initial stage of treatment, lasting for several months, the patient received aversion conditioning to pedophilic stimuli two and three times per week, as well as relaxation training and musical reinforcement in the presence of heterosexual stimuli. The aim of this intensive, lengthy conditioning process was to reinforce heterosexual behavior and thinking and punish pedophilic thinking and behavior. During a subsequent stage of treatment additional efforts to increase heterosexual awareness and accelerate development of social skills took place. Aversion conditioning continued and the patient was also asked to self-monitor in vivo sexual arousal. Heterosexual arousal was strongly reinforced by the therapist when it was reported. Social-skills training, motivated by the patient's self-reports of inadequate social behavior, was also instituted. In addition, therapist-selected male and female actors interacted with the patient once a month, to enable him to practice appropriate social skills. Results of this lengthy, intensive, and multifaceted treatment program were encouraging: The patient increased heterosexual arousal and behavior, decreased pedophilic arousal and behavior, increased successful social interactions of various kinds, and experienced more pleasure and less depression at home and on the job.

Aversive conditioning, most often with covert imagery, has been widely used in the behavioral treatment of exhibitionism. Maletzky (1974, 1977, 1980) employs what he calls assisted covert sensitization to treat exhibitionism. Employing 10 to 20 twice-weekly treatment sessions, Maletzky pairs a noxious odor (derived from valeric acid) with covert sensitization scenes; the patient progresses through a hierarchy of exhibitionistic scenes specific to him, imagining at the same time an array of punishing consequences for his exhibitionism. Although other behavioral treatment packages have been employed, covert sensitization is currently the behavioral treatment of choice for this sexual disorder (Blair & Lanyon, 1981). At the same time, the absence of controlled outcome studies, small sample sizes, and diverse procedures make any summary statements about these approaches to this disorder premature. For more detailed reviews of this literature, the interested reader is referred to Adams, Tollison, and Carson (1981) and Barlow and Abel (1981).

Treatment of the Sexual Dysfunctions. Sexual dysfunctions—including the most common male dysfunctions, premature ejaculation and impotence (renamed Inhibited Sexual Excitement in DSM-III), and the most common female dysfunction, frigidity (also renamed in DSM-III)—have been successfully treated by behavioral means. In fact, there are many who believe that Masters and Johnson, who were responsible both for calling attention to the widespread nature of these disorders and for developing effective treatment approaches to them, developed a largely behavioral treatment program. Systematic desensitization, to decrease the anxiety associated with previous sexual failure experiences, has also been used to treat inhibited sexual excitement and inhibited sexual desire, a related dysfunction, in both men and women. Assertive training has been employed as well to give patients the sense that they can assume control of those aspects of the sexual relationship that previously caused them distress (Nathan & Jackson, 1976).

A recent overview of behavioral therapy for male erectile dysfunctions (Reynolds, 1981) discusses several other behavioral techniques that have been used along with systematic desensitization. Among them are in vivo desensitization, couples sex therapy (the Masters and Johnson approach to treatment of sexual dysfunction), arousal reconditioning (masturbation and fantasized heterosexual contact are prescribed, in order to increase the sexual arousal experienced during actual heterosexual contact), thought stopping (active cessation of distracting recurrent negative thoughts during sexual intercourse), and cognitive restructuring (modification of erroneous beliefs about male and female sexuality that, because they cause fear or anxiety, may contribute to the erectile dysfunction). When employed, singly or in combination, depending on the circumstances, these behavioral approaches have been effective. In the absence of controlled studies and extended follow-ups, however, the superiority of these treatment methods to others, to active self-treatment, or to the passage of time remains uncertain.

Procedures that have been used to treat female sexual inhibition include systematic desensitization to reduce or eliminate the anxiety and fear that surround sexual involvement, in vivo desensitization to inhibit anxiety and fear while a more positive emotional and physical experience is experienced, and masturbatory training, which teaches orgasm via masturbation and then attempts substitution of a male partner (Segraves, 1981). As with the behavioral approaches to male sexual dysfunctions, proof of the efficacy of these methods awaits data from controlled studies.

Developmental Disorders: Autistic, Withdrawn, and Antisocial Behavior and Mental Retardation

People with these developmental disorders, each of which has been successfully alleviated through behavioral approaches, include autistic children, whose severe impairments offer little likelihood of their ever functioning outside of a sheltered institutional setting; isolated children who, although not psychotic, have formidable difficulties in relating to other people; children and adolescents whose antisocial behavior has resulted in their being adjudged juvenile delinquents; and young people and adults born with such serious intellectual limitations that they have had to spend much of their lives in institutions for the retarded. Autism is widely believed to be a biophysiological condition involving neurotransmitter dysfunction; in this respect it is similar to schizophrenia and the bipolar affective disorders. How autism develops and why it afflicts one child and not another, however, are questions that remain unanswered. Although Ferster (1961) posited a behavioral theory of autism (the autistic child suffers from the absence of consistent parental reinforcement necessary for the development of appropriate social behavior), that theory has not been influential. Central to behavioral views of less serious childhood disorders, including childhood social isolation and withdrawal and childhood phobic behavior, is the assumption that parents often unintentionally reward their children's most undesirable behavior by attending to it while ignoring behavior which is more appropriate and desirable; when obedience and cooperation are ignored and temper tantrums are reinforced, even with negative attention, the former will diminish and the latter increase. Modeling is thought to be an important mechanism by which antisocial behavior is instilled. Promiscuous sexual behavior by children or teenagers is frequently modeled by promiscuous parents, while antisocial behavior is often associated with peer pressures and the realization that antisocial behavior is admired by peers even while it is condemned by the adult society against which the child or adolescent may be rebelling.

Treatment of Autistic Children.   Infantile autism is a relatively uncommon childhood disorder that first manifests itself before 30 months of age. It is characterized by a pervasive lack of responsiveness to other people, gross deficits in language development, peculiar speech patterns, and bizarre behavior (e.g., resistance to change, peculiar interest in inanimate objects).

Behavioral treatment for autistic children can be provided by professional mental health workers, including psychologists and those trained by them in individual behavior change methods, or by parents trained in behavior modification, so that the autistic child can be kept at home rather than in an institution. Parent training is a relatively new development.

Individual behavioral treatment by trained therapists typically focuses on the child's inadequate or nonexistent speech and on his or her bizarre or disruptive social behavior. Modeling, successive approximation, and pacing, all reinforced typically with small bits of food, with social reinforcement (e.g., hugs or praise), or with small candies, are used to build in verbal behavior, beginning with its simplest units and then progressing to words, phrases, and sentences, and social behavior (acknowledging the presence of others in the room, saying hello, smiling). Various time-out or punishment techniques, including aversive techniques such as unpleasant-tasting foods (e.g., mustard) or, in extraordinary cases, painful electric shock, may be used to diminish behavioral excesses such as screaming and crying, head banging (which can be life threatening in serious cases), agitation and intense psychomotor behavior, and violence toward others. Although still controversial, aversive conditioning techniques to decrease or eliminate disruptive behavior so that other, more appropriate behavior can be reinforced are now well accepted among those who work with autistic children (Lovaas & Simmons, 1969; Schreibman, Koegel, Mills, & Burke, 1981).

An intriguing new approach to shaping social behavior in these children is to use normal peer models to demonstrate appropriate social and verbal behavior to them instead of depending on the adult teacher/clinician to do the modeling. In a recent study in which four autistic children were being taught color and shape discriminations to encourage interest in their environment, using three normal children and a high-functioning autistic child as models for correct discrimination led to rapid increases in correct discrimination responding, as against very slow progress when the models were adults (Egel, Richman, & Koegel, 1981).

Training parents to work with autistic children (Harris & Milch, 1981) extends the children's behavioral training program from just 6 hours a day to at least double that figure. Parents of autistic children can function both to extend the language acquisition efforts of in-school teachers by continuing reinforcement procedures designed to instill socially responsive speech in their children (Harris, 1975) and to reduce inappropriate and increase appropriate social behavior in the home (Harris & Romanczyk, 1976). Teaching parents how they might be reinforcing unwanted behavior (e.g., whining, clinging, acting out) and ignoring wanted behavior, and teaching them also how to shape new, more wanted behaviors can be accomplished readily with motivated parents of autistic children.

Treatment of Isolated and Withdrawn Children. Although the most extreme clinical examples of failure to develop adequate social relations—autism and childhood schizophrenia—are catastrophic disorders without peer among childhood disorders, poor academic performance, inadequate behavioral development, and social avoidance as a means of anxiety reduction are also examples of inadequate social behavior that require remediation. All can be serious childhood problems with ramifications that extend to adulthood (Conger & Keane, 1981). As a consequence, behavior therapists have directed considerable attention in recent years to these conditions.

Techniques used with success to instill social skills in these children and to diminish the fear they experience in close social interactions include filmed modeling, live modeling, peer pairing (same and different-aged peers socializing with withdrawn children), contingency management, coaching and instructional techniques (instructions on making friends, engaging in social interaction, emitting certain crucial social behaviors, etc.), and problem-solving approaches. In point of fact, behavioral treatment often combines two or more of these techniques, in line with the behavioral axiom that attacking a set of problem behaviors from more than one perspective is most often successful (Conger & Keane, 1981).

Treatment of Antisocial Children and Adolescents. The earliest of behavioral techniques with antisocial youths involved the use of contingency management procedures—token economies—to improve ward functioning and ward management (Braukmann et al., 1975). Tokens were given for ward tasks, for personal hygiene, for adequate social behavior, and for classroom attention. So successful have these procedures been in making it possible to manage large groups of troubled adolescents that token economies are now a feature of many or most institutions for antisocial youths. When possible, stratified token economies are employed; they reinforce adequate social and academic behavior not only with tokens but also with special privileges such as successively more desirable living environments that permit greater freedoms and comforts. For both management and treatment, token economy–contingency management methods for juvenile delinquents and antisocial children have proven their value (Nietzel, 1979).

Management of the Mentally Retarded.   Behavioral techniques resembling those for institutionalized schizophrenic adults are used to make the management of the institutionalized mentally retarded more orderly and efficient. Individual behavioral treatment techniques are used to teach social and cognitive skills, both to enable the retarded to function more successfully in the institutional environment and, in some cases, to prepare them to return to the outside community more successfully.

Matson, Ollendick, and Adkins (1980) report on a comprehensive dining program for 40 adult residents of a state institution for the mentally retarded in Pennsylvania. The experimenters selected 26 behaviors associated with eating, including those having to do with orderliness, eating, utensil usage, neatness, and table manners. The 3-month training period employed in vivo modeling, supervised practice, peer social reinforcement, self-evaluation, and monitoring to teach the residents the skills necessary to function more independently at mealtimes. These techniques were sparing of individual clinician time and thus highly cost-effective. Hence this management program met the goal both of enhanced ward management (fewer personnel were required to monitor resident mealtimes) and of enhanced resident independence.

Another recent report (Matson, Kazdin, & Esveldt-Dawson, 1980) describes individualized behavioral treatment programs to provide interpersonal skills for two moderately retarded boys who were also emotionally disturbed. Their social-skills deficits included inappropriate physical movements (rocking and other stereotypes) and facial mannerisms (tics, smiling at inappropriate times), insufficient eye contact, and inappropriate voice intonation and content of conversation. Instructions, performance feedback, social reinforcement, and modeling and role playing enabled the boys to make significant improvements in social skills, which brought them to the social-skills level of normal control children of the same age and gender. Presumably, these gains increased the possibility that these boys would lead more normal lives within the institution and, possibly, outside it.

Physical Disease, Behavioral Health, and Behavioral Medicine

Joseph D. Matarazzo, founding president of the American Psychological Association's new Division of Health Psychology, sees the emerging field of *behavioral medicine* as concerned with the "needs of actual patients—those who are ill and disabled and who are being treated by physicians in hospitals and in private offices.

This population of patients continues to provide excellent opportunities for licensed medical and clinical psychologists whose interests in health psychology are directed toward actual clinical application and research" (1982, p. 12). Matarazzo (1980) has also defined a related field, *behavioral health:* "Behavioral health is an interdisciplinary field dedicated to promoting a philosophy of health that stresses *individual responsibility* in the application of behavioral and biomedical science knowledge and techniques to the maintenance of health and the prevention of illness and dysfunction by a variety of self-initiated individual or shared activities" (p. 813).

Behavioral theory and behavior therapy methods predominate in the fields of behavioral medicine and behavioral health. Behavioral interventions to heighten compliance with medical treatment regimens, to help manage chronic pain, to treat physical disease, and to ease the burdens of the dying and those who care for them are all within the scope of behavioral medicine. By contrast, behavioral health activities center on the reduction of future health risks in currently healthy individuals. Since premature cardiovascular disease is the leading preventable cause of death in this country, behavioral health workers have developed programs to reduce or eliminate smoking, manage stress more effectively, increase exercise levels, and decrease overweight. Training programs for psychologists in behavioral health and behavioral medicine have proliferated; training in clinical psychology is often a precursor or concomitant, since psychological disorder and physical disease often coexist and, as important, the interviewing, assessment, and intervention skills acquired in clinical training serve importantly in the new applications, too.

Compliance.   Compliance with dental regimens is a particularly difficult problem (Melamed & Siegel, 1980), both because of the time and discomfort involved in complying with most regimens and because of our ambivalence at visits to the dentist, where the need for compliance is established. Lutzker and Claerhout (1981) describe the successful solution of one common dental compliance problem—getting children to floss and brush their teeth on a regular basis. Money, tokens worth money, and desirable "extras" were all made contingent on a group of four children's flossing and brushing regularly and in such a way as to pass two objective tests of dental hygiene. Another approach to dental compliance, fee reduction contingent on compliance, was explored by Iwata and Becksfort (1981). A portion of the dental fees of randomly selected adult patients enrolled in a program of preventive periodontal care was returned contingent on improvements in objective measures of dental plaque formation. Although subjects in both the contingency and noncontingency groups showed reductions in plaque—a sign of compliance with the regimen—those in the fee-reduction group showed greatest improvement in compliance. Six months later the fee-reduction patients had increased noncompliance somewhat—although they continued to comply better than the control group.

The worst-case consequence of noncompliance with a dental regimen is usually tooth loss. Noncompliance with some medical regimens, however, can mean an increase in life-threatening symptoms or, in some cases, premature death. Diabetes and renal (kidney) disease are serious medical conditions for which noncompliance with strict medical regimens can mean physical deterioration and death. Epstein and his colleagues (1981) report a successful compliance program designed to increase the percentage of negative urine tests (a measure of dietary compliance) in 19 children with insulin-dependent diabetes. Instructing the children and their parents in insulin adjustment and the importance of decreasing intake of simple sugars and saturated fats and increasing exercise, the investigators then made compliance pay off with points in a token economy and praise from parents. This arrangement produced significant increases in percentages of negative urines, which were maintained over a subsequent follow-up period.

Keane, Prue, and Collins (1981) describe an even more serious compliance situation—two patients with end-stage renal disease who were required to continue a painful, demanding, and limiting hemodialysis program that cleansed their blood of the toxins their own inoperative kidneys could not remove. Dialysis required these patients to restrict and control their diets and to limit fluid and food intake to compensate for lack of kidney function. A contract between medical staff and the two patients, as well as contingent praise from staff for meeting weight standards, led to a reduction in weight gain between dialysis sessions and better long-term maintenance of appropriate weight.

Pain Control.   Behavioral pain-management procedures—the use of behavioral methods to control pain without the necessity of using dependency- and tolerance-inducing drugs—are detailed by Melamed and Siegel (1980). The recognition that pain is often an operant—that family, friends, and nursing personnel may attend more to the patient when he or she complains of pain—is an essential starting point to full understanding of behavioral pain control. Fordyce (1971) developed a training program based on this operant conceptualization of pain. He also outlined a plan to reduce pain medication by gradually increasing the time between dosages so that ultimately the medication becomes unnecessary. Neither of these procedures is appropriate when intractable pain results from, for example, metastatic cancer. The pain for which these procedures are suggested is chronic pain that has become self-perpetuating in the face of equivocal physical findings. Other behavioral methods of pain control include cognitive strategies, which provide patients accurate descriptions of the physical sensations they should expect to experience during or after a painful diagnostic procedure or an operation; exposure to a realistic coping model, so that successful adaptation to the anticipated pain can be modeled; and the imposition of cognitive tasks that will occupy the patient with interesting activities so that he or she does not focus exclusively on the pain (Melamed & Siegel, 1980).

Varni (1981) describes the successful use of several self-regulation techniques by three adult hemophiliacs afflicted with the chronic arthritic joint pain that so often accompanies this disease. These patients learned progressive muscle relaxation and meditative breathing, and they developed guided imagery associated with past experiences of relief from the arthritic pain. The use of these techniques by these three young adults led to a clinically significant reduction in their perception of pain, which had persisted 12, 14, and 7 months at follow-up. More important, reduction in pain was associated with an improvement in physical condition, including a decrease in frequency of bleeding episodes. In other words, relief of severe pain led to changes beneficial to the underlying disease state.

Treatment of Physical Disease.   Although behavior therapists have treated a very wide range of physical disorders, our discussion here focuses on but two, for reasons of space limitations. The first, cardiovascular disease, is the leading cause of death in the United States; heart attack, stroke, angina, and cardiac insufficiency are all aspects of a disease process that alters the proper functioning of the heart and blood vessels. Although behavior therapy cannot restore a diseased heart to effective functioning, it can modify some consequences of the disorder, including high blood pressure, irregular or rapid heart rate, and irregular or rapid respiration, and it can also ameliorate some antecedents of heart disease: smoking, overweight, inadequate stress management, lack of exercise, and poor body tone (Yates, 1980). As well, behavioral clinicians have improved compliance with drug treatment for heart disease (Steptoe, 1981).

Steptoe (1981) has also reviewed recent efforts to modify what is called the Type A behavior pattern, characterized by impatience, time urgency, perfectionism, and irritability and frustration when progression toward a goal is impeded. The Type A behavior pattern has been implicated in premature heart disease. Its modification, by attempts to teach relaxation, to modify the need for perfect performance, and to reduce the perceived impact of time on behavior, is designed to prevent heart disease secondary to it. In fact, prevention of cardiovascular disease through the reduction of behavioral risk factors has become a major activity of behavioral clinicians, both with individual clients and, as detailed below, in the work site.

Anorexia nervosa (diagnosed in the presence of excessive weight loss, usually in adolescent girls, an irrational fear of becoming obese, compulsive overactivity, marked disturbance in body image, and amenorrhea) is a less common disorder that also can be treated by behavioral techniques. Behavioral techniques employed to treat two hospitalized 17-year-old women with anorexia nervosa (Mavissakalian, 1982) centered on operant reinforcement for weight gains. For appropriate eating behavior at mealtime, weight gains, and activity, patients were rewarded with free time outside their rooms and freedom from certain hospital rules. Weight gains in substantial amounts, which returned both patients to normal weight, were consequent to this treatment; normal weight was reported through and beyond a follow-up period of several months.

Behavioral Health Enhancement at the Work Site.   A natural bridge between the interests of industry (chief among them the profit motive and the concept of cost-effectiveness) and those of clinicians and behavioral theorists exists in programs designed to shed light on employee stress and its treatment. Industry has long been interested in stress because of its consequences for productivity and profit (Landy & Trumbo, 1976). Industry has also investigated task-induced stresses for their effects on worker well-being, such as the effects of shift work on the health and social relations of employees (Akerstedt, Patkai, & Dahlgren, 1977; Wedderburn, 1967). Behavior therapists, in turn, have been interested in stress both for its own health consequences and for its role in other clinical disorders (e.g., reactive disorders, substance abuse). Behavior therapy and industry have joined forces to study stress treatment methods.

For example, Peters, Benson, and Porter (1977) studied the effects of relaxation response breaks on employee well-being. One hundred twenty-six corporate personnel were assigned to treatment and control groups, and self-reports of worker health and social functioning were taken. Peters reported significant benefits to workers following from relaxation training and the opportunity to practice it at the work site. Alderman and Schoenbaum (1975) reported a program to control a correlate of stress, hypertension, in more than 300 employees of New York City's Gimbel's department store. The program, which involved screening, medication, and counseling in the work site, used behavioral methods to facilitate patient compliance with the medical regimen. At follow-up visits nurses and paraprofessional counselors monitored patients' blood pressure, reviewed the course of their therapy, identified complications and problem areas, and led the patients in problem solving to ensure program adherence. Over the course of 1 year the subject dropout rate was held to an amazing 3%. Two-thirds of those eligible for treatment chose to participate, and 80% of these experienced a decline in blood pressure either to normal limits, or by a factor of 10% at a per-patient cost per year of just $97.80. So far, though, no other studies have provided quality data on stress and its sequelae in the workplace, on the magnitude of the problem, on its most effective remedy or, most importantly, on the cost-effectiveness of work-site intervention.

Behavioral health methods are of potential value to industry in the area of smoking cessation programs, too (Danaher, 1977; Hackett & Horan, 1979; Lichtenstein & Danaher, 1976). For example, Live for Life (Johnson & Johnson's positive lifestyle change program) offered the rapid-smoking technique (Lichtenstein, Harris, Birchler, Wahl, & Schmahl, 1973) to employees in a quasi-experimental fashion. Nonrandomized treatment and control groups were distributed over four (treatment) and five (control) corporate sites in a nonequivalent control group design with some 4100 subjects. Results after 1 year of program implementation indicated a 15% decrease in the percentage of current smokers at the experimental sites and, perhaps through some carry-over effect, a 4% reduction in current smokers at the control sites.

The Speedcall Corporation (Shepard, 1980) chose an alternative approach. It offered contingent reinforcement (cash incentives) to employees to refrain from smoking, a policy now practiced by some 3% of American corporations and 6% of Canadian ones. With the exception of the Johnson & Johnson program, though, good experimental design and controls have not been observed, and information on the durability and cost-effectiveness of such programs has not been forthcoming.

Other challenges to behavioral medicine have been posed by the opportunities to provide employees with instruction in exercise and physical fitness (e.g., Bjurstrom & Alexiov, 1978; Cox, Shepard, & Corey, 1981), weight control (Stunkard & Brownell, 1980), and general health mangement (e.g., Rose, Heller, Pedoe, & Christie, 1980). Much of this work has been well controlled, with large sample sizes and comprehensive dependent measures. Shepard and associates (Cox, et al.,

1981; Shepard, Corey, Renzland, & Cox, 1982; Shepard, Cox, & Corey, 1981), for example, in a controlled longitudinal experiment, studied the effects of training and participation in physical exercise on absenteeism, turnover, health-care costs, and productivity. Only on the index of productivity did experimental subjects fail to show significant improvements over control subjects. Through a weight-control program based on the principles of self-monitoring of both eating (Mahoney, 1974) and physical activity (Stuart, 1971) combined with nutritional counseling, Johnson & Johnson's program has achieved a 1% decrease in the percentage of workers above their ideal weight at experimental work sites, while at the five control sites there was a 6% increase in percentage of the work force above their ideal weight. Experimental design was the same as that described above. Although evaluation of program effectiveness remains a weakness of behavioral medicine in industry, these and other efforts have encouraged corporate decision makers by producing a growing literature on tangible rewards to industry, including decreased costs, increased job satisfaction, and increased employee loyalty.

Behavior Therapy in Terminal Care.   In recent years psychologists have paid a great deal more attention to the elderly and to the sociopsychological phenomena associated with dying. A recent volume devoted to behavior therapy for the terminally ill (Sobel, 1981) defines this field as follows: "One general aim, therefore, of this emerging discipline is to help a patient or family manage their own adaptive responses. The goal is not to control death or to dictate a one-dimensional strategy of coping. On the contrary, behavioral thanatology seeks to educate the patient to facilitate self-control leading to an awareness of one's own instrumentality, 'coping potency,' and capacity to maintain self-worth in the face of death" (p.6). Among the behaviors to which behavioral thanatologists address themselves are the depression of the dying patient, the pain of terminally ill cancer patients, the experience of grief among the elderly, the destructive effect the approaching death of a loved one has on remaining family members, and the stress caused their care givers by the terminally ill. Behavioral thanatologists use many of the same behavioral techniques described above to treat depression, grief, pain, and family discord—with one crucial difference. Instead of treating emotional milestones along life's normal path, they are confronting the consequences of the very last steps of life. In doing so, these behavior therapists address issues that have long been ignored by psychologists and physicians. Now the dying are being accorded the same right to behavioral treatment—and the same respect—as the living.

ETHICAL ISSUES

The striking growth of behavior therapy has been paralleled by an equally spectacular growth in public criticism of the ethics of behavioral theory and practice. Proponents of the client-centered, humanistic branches of psychotherapy have consistently criticized behavior therapy for painting a sterile and mechanistic picture of human behavior. Behavior therapists, they say, view clients as objects for calculated manipulation, automatons incapable of free choice. According to the humanistic argument, this philosophy leads inevitably to treatment failure, because it simplifies the complex nature of human beings. The lay public, on the other hand, often shows an exaggerated respect for the behaviorists' power to control, and that respect is likely to be colored by fear. Such fears are increased by the popularity of movies such as *A Clockwork Orange*, which dramatize techniques of behavioral control and social domination. Nor has the public's perception been helped by the exaggerated claims and apocalyptic statements of prominent behaviorists (see Skinner, 1971) who announce the dawn of a new social order based on behavioral technology.

Although strenuous efforts on the part of spokespeople for the behavioral movement appear to have corrected some misconceptions—such as the classification of ECT (electroconvulsive shock therapy) as a behavioral technique—recent experimental evidence suggests that public attitudes toward behavior modification are still largely negative. For example, in a replication of an earlier study Woolfolk and Woolfolk (1979) again found strong negative effects for the behavior modification label, although this was moderated, in a naive audience, by claims for the efficacy of behavioral techniques.

A resolution of scientific and ethical questions might begin by distinguishing between the techniques, as derived from an experimental science, and the particular persons and situations involved in their application (Begelman, 1975; Erwin, 1978). As Begelman (1975) notes, "The significance of clarifying the confusion is that there is no meaningful ethical or legal argument against the use of 'positive reinforcement' or 'aversive control,' but only against the specific way in which techniques based on such principles may from time to time be employed" (p. 160).

Although the ethical application of behavioral techniques requires a case-by-case examination of moral issues, several classes of situations by their nature call for special concern. For example, because behavioral techniques such as contingent reinforcement can be applied against one's will, they have seemed ideal for use in prisons, schools, and mental institutions. Some have argued that one who is convicted of a crime or committed involuntarily forfeits the right to voluntary treatment and becomes subject to society's claim for rehabilitation and prevention. Thus the use of behavior therapy with captive populations, whether in prisons, schools, or mental institutions, has aroused justifiable protests against coercion and involuntary treatment. Both judges and legal philosophers have argued in turn that imprisonment does not strip one of constitutional protection, including the right to consent to treatment, and that involuntary treatment is thus tantamount to inflicting extra punishment, even if it is of "benefit" to the recipient (Erwin, 1978, p. 201). This suggests that behavioral practitioners in prisons ought to obtain the consent of prisoners themselves before giving treatment, unless the sentence specifically instructs its use. But even this principle may not afford ethical justification for behavior therapy. Subtle pressures generated by the institutional environment, such as the need to gain favor with powerful authorities, may preclude truly voluntary consent. Such problems indicate the need for additional safeguards to guarantee the ethical application of behavioral technology (Stolz et al., 1978).

Further difficulties arise in institutions such as schools or mental hospitals, in which the population served is presumed incapable of informed consent, by reason of age or incapacity. Although society arguably has the right to enforce treatment for the individual and social good, and although behavior modification has generally shown evidence for remarkable successes with these groups, behavioral techniques may also be used to promote a docility and conformity more conducive to smooth institutional functioning than to individual benefit. The danger of abuse in these settings suggests the need for external review and for involvement of the client's representatives or members of the community in the choice of treatment goals and procedures (Davison & Stuart, 1975; Erwin, 1978; Stolz et al., 1978). Whether the recently established constitutional right of involuntarily committed patients to refuse psychotropic medication will be extended to other forms of psychotherapy is unclear (White & White, 1981); in any case, safeguards would still be necessary in institutional settings with clients of diminished mental capacity.

Aversive procedures and token economies have also come under fire from those concerned with ethical accountability. Although some maintain that the use of pain to change behavior is wrong prima facie, few argue against using aversive techniques to stop the severely self-mutilative behavior of autistic children, when other methods have failed. Most cases are not so clear-cut, however, and despite an initial enthusiasm generated by their cost-effectiveness and expediency, most prominent behaviorists now argue against their use, unless they are demonstrably superior to other methods and the client freely consents to their application (Erwin, 1978).

Token economy programs have come in for particularly extensive criticisms on moral grounds. Detractors charge that these behavioral procedures produce a mercenary orientation and decrease intrinsic motivation through the use of potent external reinforcers. Demonstrations of the effectiveness of token economies as a tool for classroom management and educational development, and as a means of promoting the rehabilitation of chronic mental patients even after the programs have ended, have scarcely appeased these detractors. In a discussion of this controversy Bandura (1982) drew a distinction between incentives used to regulate performance and incentives used to develop competence. Controlled studies indicate that task-contingent incentives given under conditions of well-learned routine performance can enhance, lower, or leave unchanged interest in the activity, depending on a vast number of other factors. In contrast, rewards for task mastery, which both reinforce and provide information about developing competencies, reliably maintain or increase interest in the activity (Bandura, 1982, pp. 133–134). Inasmuch as most behavioral token economy programs are explicitly concerned with skill acquisition and the development of personal competence, their effects on interest in the activity and on intrinsic motivation are likely to be positive, although independent confirmation of this in every program remains an ethical obligation for the behavior therapist, particularly when captive populations are involved.

The treatment of social deviance has been another ethical issue of concern to behavioral practitioners. Behaviors that are not necessarily distressing in themselves, but are painful chiefly because of the negative reactions of others, as in the case of homosexuality, have been the cause of much controversy in the mental health establishment. Behavior therapists have been in the forefront of this debate. Many (see Begelman, 1975; Erwin, 1978) have raised questions about the use of behavior therapy with homosexuals, and others (Davison, 1977) have exhorted their colleagues to give up such treatment entirely. They question whether such treatment could ever be truly voluntary, given the extent and depth of antihomosexual sentiment. By trying to change the sexual orientation of homosexuals, they argue, one also tacitly defines homosexuality as a disease and thereby contributes to the maintenance of social prejudice. While this issue merits serious reflection, remedies such as an unconditional refusal to offer treatment seem to do an injustice to the *individual* client. In this situation general solutions often do not work. In cases in which the client has been pressured into treatment as a result of social concerns, the therapist might be justified in refusing to treat homosexuality, and instead offer to help the client recognize and resist the pressure. In other cases a rational and careful decision to alter one's sexual orientation must be respected; to do otherwise would by to deny the client's fundamental right to treatment and would betray a paternalism no less blind than the prevailing prejudice (Begelman, 1975).

Some areas of ethical concern are unique to behavior therapy. Others, however, like those posed by the treatment of social deviance and programs for captive populations, properly concern all clinicians, regardless of theoretical persuasion. Ethical dilemmas that arise in the course of ordinary practice for all therapists include protection of client rights, definition of the problem and selection of goals and intervention methods, and confidentiality and accountability. Behavior therapy, with its emphasis on clearly formulated goals, experimentally validated techniques, and objective outcome measures, would seem to lend itself particularly well to meaningful solutions to these problems. As psychotherapy moves toward client participation, behavior therapy may come to help rather than hinder a deepening consideration of the moral questions involved in every form of therapy.

EVALUATION

Asking the Questions

In the development of what Rachman and Wilson (1980) called conventional comparative outcome research, two critical questions were asked: (a) Is psychological treatment of human problems at all effective? and (b) Is one form of treatment superior to another? The first has been answered, satisfactorily and in the affirmative. The answer to the second remains ambiguous. This section reviews, briefly, reasons that these questions have been—and continue to be—asked.

First, the negative initial review (1952) and subsequent reviews of Eysenck and others, to the effect that clients treated by dynamic and humanistic therapists do not experience gains beyond those to be expected solely on the basis of chance, have thrown a very long shadow. One consequence was the enhanced effort to develop effective clinical strategies and to test those strategies in both the laboratory and the field. This "crisis of confidence" (Strupp, 1981) turned the attention of clinicians and researchers to alternative approaches, many of them behavioral; in a real sense, it empowered the development and testing of behavioral approaches to research and therapy (Rachman & Wilson, 1980).

Another motive for controlled research on clinical outcome proceeded directly from the rise of behavioral technology. At its core, behavior therapy is an applied science with an explicit emphasis on values conducive to empirical research, including (a) the precise and replicable delineation of therapeutic procedures, (b) testable concepts rooted in the traditions of the laboratory, and (c) dependence on experimentation to validate existing clinical methods and suggest new ones.

A third impetus to conventional comparative outcome research was the lively irreverence with which early behavior therapists (e.g., Eysenck, 1960; Lazarus, 1958, 1961; Wolpe, 1958) tried to debunk many of the assertions central to competing clinical approaches, notably, the concept of unconscious determinants of behavior and the development of theoretical elements and nosological schemas based on underlying disease processes. In this way behavior therapy separated itself from both traditional verbal therapies and somatic treatment methods, and, incidentally, extended the psychology/psychiatry feud that has waged for some decades (Cattell, in press). A related effect was overexuberance and, in some cases, self-aggrandizement: "In the early days, circa 1958–1968, many words but few data were dedicated to the edict that behavior therapy was 'superior.' Circumscribed studies were eagerly paraded to bolster the proclaimed advantages of behavior therapy" (Franks, in press, p. 1). Such unrealistic claims, which habitually accompany the debut of new procedures, can hinder as much as help the new approaches (Kazdin & Wilson, 1978a).

A final motive for the conduct of conventional comparative outcome research is the external threat to the financial viability of the mental health professions posed by third-party reimbursers—insurance carriers and public funding agencies (Cummings, 1977; Greenspan & Sharfstein, 1981; McSweeny, 1977):

> When society is being asked to pay for psychotherapy, it proposes to exercise its right and responsibility to determine how the terms *health* and *need for services* will be defined, who is qualified to provide such services, and how effective (they) are . . . . Particularly in a period when the costs of health care continue to soar, private and public health insurance planners will seek to impose clear and restrictive rules of eligibility on both patient and psychotherapist. [Parloff, 1979, p. 297]

Conventional Comparative Outcome Research

Many behavioral researchers would now support Kazdin and Wilson (1978a), who said:

> In our view, the excessive reliance on comparative outcome research has been unfortunate. In the first place most . . . has been premature. A rational approach to studying the comparative effects of therapy . . . requires first demonstrating the efficacy and validity of specific treatment approaches . . . . Once this is established, the *comparative* value of the methods can be investigated. In the second place, the majority of

studies . . . are conceptually flawed and lacking in methodological adequacy, so that it is difficult if not impossible to draw worthwhile conclusions from them. Premature and poorly designed, these . . . studies have fueled some fruitless controversies about what works better than what. [p. 230]

The outcome research that has been done, premature in the eyes of some, includes controlled experiments, in which the effects of two or more therapies are compared on compatible groups of clients, as well as so-called meta-analyses (Smith & Glass, 1977) of entire literatures, in which results from different studies are statistically combined.

At its simplest, the conventional comparative outcome study is familiar to all. A number of subjects are recruited and assigned randomly to two groups. Premeasures of dependent variables of interest are taken, and each group is given psychological treatment that varies between groups along one or more dimensions. After the conclusion of therapy postmeasures are taken. Mean group differences at posttest on the dependent measures are found, and inferential statistics are calculated to determine the statistical significance of the mean group differences at posttest. Though Rogers (Rogers & Dymond, 1954) pioneered the use of control groups in such research, many early studies (e.g., Gelder & Marks, 1966; Lazarus, 1961) and some more recent ones have abjured the inclusion of control subjects. An improvement on the waiting-list control group (Rogers & Dymond, 1954) was the so-called attention-control or placebo group (Paul, 1966, 1967), by which subjects' expectancy of improvement is fostered in the absence of a potent intervention just as in its presence. Most such studies have been conducted by behavior therapists, whose disregard for the clinical efficacy of nonbehavioral procedures has led them to employ individual psychotherapy (Gillan & Rachman, 1974), group psychotherapy (Townsend, House, & Addario, 1975), transactional analysis (Jesness, 1975), and interactional marital therapy (Liberman, Levine, Wheeler, Sanders, & Wallace, 1976) as inert controls. It is a delicious measure of justice that so cynical a motive should have produced so paradoxical an outcome: Some such studies have found equal effectiveness for both behavior therapy and the inert control at follow-up (e.g., Marks, 1971; Patterson, Levene, & Breger, 1971) or even the immediate posttest (e.g., Crighton & Jehu, 1969).

Behavioral techniques have been contrasted with a broad assortment of other strategies on most significant subgroups of the general clinical population, including persons with simple (Zitrin, Klein, & Woerner, 1976), multiple (Gillan & Rachman, 1974) and social phobias (DiLoreto, 1971; Lazarus, 1966; Paul, 1966), homosexual behavior (Feldman & MacCulloch, 1971), male impotence (Kockott, Dittmar, & Nusselt, 1975), obesity (Hall, Hall, DeBoer, & O'Kulitch, 1977; Stunkard, 1972), alcoholic (Hunt & Azrin, 1973) and nonalcoholic problem-drinking styles (Pomerleau, Pertschuk, Adkins, & Brady, 1976), and chronic adult (Hartlage, 1970) and childhood schizophrenia (Ney, Pavelsky, & Markely, 1971), among a variety of other disorders.

A recent and classic example of this kind of comparative outcome experiment, the book-length *Psychotherapy versus Behavior Therapy* (Sloane, Staples, Cristol,

Yorkston, & Whipple, 1975) has occasioned much comment (e.g., Garfield, 1976; Kazdin & Wilson, 1978a, b; Luborsky, Singer, & Luborsky, 1975; Strupp & Hadley, 1979; Wolpe, 1975). Most agree that Sloane et al. is the best-controlled and most extensively evaluated piece of comparative outcome research to enter the literature so far. One especially thoughtful review of this influential work is by Rachman and Wilson (1980, pp. 231–36), who note its following strengths: (a) the study of a large number (90) of clients, randomly assigned to experimental condition; (b) the matching of experimental groups on the indices of client sex and severity of complaint; (c) an independent variable of only three levels: behavior therapy, psychoanalytic therapy, and waiting-list control: (d) the use of expert therapists to administer each treatment; (e) extremely low subject attrition, and (f) the inclusion of 8-month follow-up data.

Critics of the study have lamented its authors' decision to "mix" personality disorder and neurotic patients in a single design (though others have pointed to the low reliability of these diagnoses to question the extent of mixing after all). Others have questioned the decision to exclude patients with disorders especially amenable to behavioral treatment (e.g., sexual dysfunction and substance abuse). A third criticism of the Sloan et al. study is more substantive, in our judgment. Woven into the study's design is the implicit assumption of what Kiesler (1966) called the therapy uniformity myth. The assumption that there is anything so generic as psychoanalytic therapy or behavior therapy is fallacious. Prominent behaviorist Nathan Azrin (1977) says it another way:

> Unlike the laboratory emphasis in isolating a single variable . . . clinical research has typically required a treatment program incorporating many component procedures . . . . The criticism is frequently made of such "package" programs that one cannot identify which variable(s) is effective. My strategy has been to use such programs unapologetically and to include as many component procedures as seem necessary to obtain, ideally, a total treatment success. Once a treatment program is found to be *extraordinarily* successful, analytic studies . . . will be useful. But little seems to be gained by limiting oneself to partial benefits *initially* in order to achieve conceptual purity. [p. 144]

In other words, perhaps Sloane and his colleagues should have permitted a comparison of the full range of behavioral and analytic procedures rather than the carefully delineated and circumscribed comparisons they allowed—though the resulting control and equivalence problems would have been formidable, to say the least!

Unfortunately, the results of Sloane et al. were not unambiguous. Indices of social, sexual and work adjustment, global improvement, and improvement in target symptoms were taken from four sources: clients, therapists, independent assessors, and "informants" or significant others. Poor interrater correlations were the rule. After 4 months of treatment, clients provided behavior therapy were superior to those given psychotherapy in work and social adjustment and global improvement, and both therapy groups were doing better than the control group in regulating target symptoms. By the 8-month follow-up virtually all between-group differences had been wiped out. Only a tentative superiority of the behavior therapy group over the control group in target symptoms remained, although the difference was dubiously recovered by the application of individual T-tests (in a study with three experimental groups!).

If psychotherapy outcome experiments, in fact, are "bound to be of limited value, leave little room for development, and are at times misleading," (Rachman & Wilson, 1980, p. 258), equal or greater discontent over so-called meta-analyses (Glass, 1976; Glass & Smith, 1976; Smith & Glass, 1977; Smith, Glass, & Miller, 1980) has been voiced. A secondary analysis of data, meta-analysis is an outgrowth of a tradition of combining independent tests of significance nearly half a century old (Birnbaum, 1954; Edgington, 1972a, b; Fisher, 1948; Jones & Fiske, 1953; Pearson, 1938; Rosenthal, 1978; Wallis, 1942). Smith and Glass (1977) combined effect sizes from 375 comparative outcome studies of behavior therapy, psychodynamic therapy, Adlerian, eclectic and gestalt therapy, RET, client-centered counseling, implosion, and transactional analysis. They found that "despite volumes devoted to the theoretical differences among different schools of psychotherapy, the results of research demonstrate negligible differences in the effects produced by different therapy types. Unconditional judgments of superiority of one type or another of psychotherapy . . . are unjustified." In contrast to Eysenck (1952), who found no therapy to be effective, Smith and Glass concluded that all are. "The average client receiving therapy was better off than 75% of the untreated controls" (p. 754). Systematic desensitization had consistently highest marks, with RET and behavior modification a distant second or third. But during a higher-order analysis, in which multidimensional scaling was used to combine therapies in behavioral and nonbehavioral "superclasses," even these differences disappeared.

Unfortunately, no meta-analyst has been able to overcome the burden imposed on meta-analysis by the imperfect quality of the studies on which it is based and the uncertain rules for their inclusion or exclusion in the analysis. For instance, only 26 of the 75 behavioral outcome studies reviewed by Kazdin and Wilson (1978a) were included in the Smith and Glass analysis; behavioral successes with depression, obsessive–compulsive disorders, marital problems, disorders of childhood, and a variety of conduct disorders were conspicuously absent. Present were studies with inadequate (Barendregt, 1957) or retrospective measures (Cooper, 1963), no control groups (e.g., Ashby, Ford, Guerney, & Guerney, 1957), and little relevance to clinical problems, for example, writing instruction (Beckstrand, 1973). Not only do Smith and Glass fall prey to the myth of therapy uniformity, but there is an implicit assumption of therapist, dependent measure, and client–group uniformity as well. "No attempt is made to distinguish between the effect of this medley of treatments on schizophrenics, or alcoholics or adolescent offenders . . . or patients suffering from migraine, or from asthma" (Rachman & Wilson, 1980, p. 254).

Their comprehensive review of conventional comparative outcome research, extending back through several decades of controlled research and including both the Sloane study and the Smith and Glass meta-analysis, led Rachman and Wilson (1980) to conclude that while consistent differences among different approaches to intervention were not found, the following can be said: (a) Not a single comparison showed behavior therapy to be inferior to psychotherapy; (b) no evidence of symptom substitution following behavior therapy was obtained; (c) behavior therapy is more broadly applicable to the full range of psychological disorders; and (d) behavior therapy is capable of producing broadly based treatment effects. It is important to note, however, that Rachman and Wilson's guarded optimism about behavior therapy is not shared by all, including all behavior therapists. Agras (1978), a leader in behavioral medicine, recently remarked on the "sense of hesitancy and undertainty (that) hangs over the field" (p. xiii). Marks, one of behavior therapy's pioneers, concluded in 1976 that it is very limited in its applicability, useful as the main strategy in no more than 10% of adult cases.

Asking Better Questions

As Paul (1967) noted in his landmark book, "The initial question posed, 'Does psychotherapy work?' is virtually meaningless." Moreover: "Narrowing the questions to specific schools of psychotherapy, such as 'Does client-centered therapy work?' or 'Does behavior therapy work?' is no more meaningful than the general question. . . . In all its complexity, the question toward which all outcome research should ultimately be directed is the following: '*What* treatment, by *whom*, is most effective for *this* individual with *that* specific problem, and under *which* set of circumstances?' " (p. 111).

The specificity with which questions have been formulated has been a steadily strengthened focus of behavioral methodology for a number of years. This focus is at the heart of behavior therapy's response to the present impasse.

Response Specificity.   A major flaw in conventional comparative outcome research is dependence on a unitary criterion of therapeutic change. To this end, Mintz reported in 1977 that the most widely used index of change from psychotherapy was a global rating made by the therapist. By contrast, behavioral researcher Peter Lang, (1969, 1970), focusing on measurement of the most clinically relevant response domains, recommended triple response modes (cognition, physiological arousal, and overt behavior) for the purpose. Originally derived from Lang's research on fears and phobias, the so-called three systems of fear have since added to a fresh understanding of anxiety (Rachman & Wilson, 1980), obsessive–compulsive disorders (Rachman & Hodgson, 1980), pain (Phillips, 1978), and even "craving" in alcoholics (Hodgson, Rankin, & Stockwell, 1979).

This development in the specificity with which the therapy outcome question may be addressed is of extreme significance, for the model of triple response modes allows experimenters to predict (a) an appropriate match between clinical technique and measure of outcome, (b) differential between-treatment effects on different response modalities, and (c) differential between-treatment latencies for these effects to occur. That is, the question is no longer "Does this procedure work?" but rather "What response mode does it affect first, and how quickly?"

Measure Specificity.   For the traditional psychotherapies verbal exchange is the fundamental medium of therapeutic change. It is not surprising, therefore, that clinical researchers have relied on verbal material (e.g., ratings of improvement in functioning by therapists, clients, or assessors) as measure (as well as means) of therapeutic improvement.

Unfortunately, several decades of clinical research suggest that exclusive reliance on the clinical judgment of therapists or assessors may be very unwise. Sherman, Trief, and Sprafkin (1975), for example, reported that patients instructed to "fake healthy" or "fake sick" could do so successfully during psychiatric interviews. As well, clients' behavior during interviews, and their resulting evaluation by clinicians, are measurably vulnerable both to the verbal behavior (Matarazzo & Wiens, 1972) and even the physical distance (Lassen, 1973) of the interviewer. Overall, "the accumulated findings give little support to the utility of clinical judgments. . . . [They] have not been able to predict behavior better than the person's own direct self-report, simple indices of . . . past behavior, or demographic variables" (Mischel, 1973, p. 254).

Practical extensions by behavior therapists of Lang's theoretical work on the triple response mode (1969, 1970) suggest instead that criteria of therapeutic change should canvass the three systems of human response—cognition, physiological arousal, and overt behavior. These samples should be taken, where possible, in the client's actual environment (Mischel, 1973; Rachman & Wilson, 1980; Wilson & Evans, 1976) and by means of standardized instruments (Teasdale, Walsh, Lancashire, & Mathews, 1977). Required are three measurement operations that correspond to the response domains—cognition, physiological arousal, and overt behavior—and are contiguous with them—self-reports, recordings of autonomic activity, and behavioral observations.

SELF-REPORTS. Mainstays of behavioral outcome research are clients' self-reports, gathered not from vulnerable clinical interviews but from formal instruments with known psychometric qualities. The oldest of these is the Fear Survey Schedule, various forms of which were developed by Akutagawa (1956), Geer (1965), Wolpe and Lang (1964, 1969), and Braun and Reynolds (1969). Other instruments to measure social anxiety, depression, and a variety of other phenomena have been used by behavior therapists for research purposes (see Barlow, 1981, and Ciminero, Calhoun, & Adams, 1977, for comprehensive reviews of self-report assessment instruments.

RECORDINGS OF AUTONOMIC ACTIVITY. Physiological arousal may be monitored by detecting either of two types of organismic events (Brown, 1972): (a) bioelectric potentials, such as galvanic skin response (GSR), in which the organism transforms a physical or chemical event into an electric impulse; or (b) a mechanical signal, such as blood pressure or pulse rate. Numerous statistics, such as amplitude, frequency, and latency, are recoverable from psychophysiological measures which have been developed to monitor the activity of the cardiovascular, electrodermal, nervous, gastric, and sexual systems of the human being. Assessment of autonomic arousal as part of treatment outcome research has been widely reported in the behavioral literature.

OVERT BEHAVIOR. Measures of overt behavioral change have been, more than any other, central to the development of behavioral outcome research. As Kazdin and Wilson (1978a) explained, behavioral measures are (a) consistent with the inter-actionist philosophy of social learning theory, (b) most sensitive to between-treatment clinical gains, (c) least vulnerable to both experimenter- and subject-centered sources of bias and response distortion, and (d) easily replicable by independent investigators. The work by Goldfried (1976) and others (e.g., Cone, 1977; Fixsen, Phillips, & Wolf, 1972; Hagen, Craighead, & Paul, 1975; Reid, 1970) on the validity, reliability, fakeability, and demand characteristics of behavioral observations has done much to further Bandura's (1978) trenchant vision that "the best measure of behavior is behavior, and not reports about it" (p. 91).

REFERENCES

Adams, H. E., Brantley, P. J., Malatesta, V., & Turkat, I. D. Modification of cognitive processes: A case study of schizophrenia. *Journal of Consulting & Clinical Psychology*, 1981, **49**, 460–474.

Adams, H. E., Tollison, C. D., & Carson, T. P. Behavior therapy with sexual deviations. In S. M. Turner, K. S. Calhoun, & H. E. Adams (Eds.), *Handbook of clinical behavior therapy*. New York: Wiley, 1981.

Agras, S. Foreward. In A. Kazdin and G. T. Wilson, *Evaluation of Behavior Therapy: Issues, Evidence, and Research Strategies*. Cambridge, MA: Ballinger, 1978.

Akerstedt, T., Patkai, P., & Dahlgren, K. Field studies of shiftwork: II. Temporal patterns in psychophysiological activation in workers alternating between night and day work. *Ergonomics*, 1977, **20**, 621–631.

Akutagawa, D. A. *A study in construct validity of the psychoanalytic concept of latent anxiety and a test of projection distance hypothesis*. Unpublished doctoral dissertation, University of Pittsburgh, 1956.

Alberti, R., & Emmons, M. *Your perfect right*. San Luis, Obispo, Calif.: Impact Press, 1974.

Alderman, M. H., & Schoenbaum, E. E. Detection and treatment of hypertension at the work-site. *New England Journal of Medicine*, 1975, **293**, 65–68.

American Psychiatric Association. *Diagnostic and statistical manual of mental disorders* (2nd Ed.). Washington, D.C.: APA, 1968.

American Psychiatric Association. *Diagnostic and statistical manual of mental disorders* (3rd Ed.) Washington, D.C.: APA, 1980.

Anderson, M. P., & Borkovec, T. D. Imagery processing and fear reduction during repeated exposure to two types of phobic imagery. *Behaviour Research and Therapy*, 1980, **18**, 537–540.

Armor, D. J., Polich, J. M., & Stambul, H. B. *Alcoholism and treatment*. Santa Monica, Calif.: Rand Corp., 1976.

Ashby, J., Ford, D. H., Guerney, B., & Guerney, L. Effects on clients of a reflective and a leading type of psychotherapy. *Psychological Monographs*, 1957, **71**, 1–32.

Atthowe, J. M., & Krasner, L. Preliminary report on the application of contingent reinforcement procedures (token economy) on a "chronic" psychiatric ward. *Journal of Abnormal Psychology*, 1968, **73**, 37–43.

Ayllon, T., & Azrin, N. H. The measurement and reinforcement of behavior of psychotics. *Journal of the Experimental Analysis of Behavior*, 1965, **8**, 357–383.

Ayllon, T., & Michael, J. The psychiatric nurse as a behavioral engineer. *Journal of the Experimental Analysis of Behavior*, 1959, **2**, 323–334.

Azrin, N. H. A strategy for applied research: Learning based but outcome oriented. *American Psychologist*, 1977, **32**, 140–149.

Azrin, N. H., & Besalel, V. A. An operant reinforcement method of treating depression. *Journal of Behavior Therapy and Experimental Psychiatry*, 1981, **12**, 145–151.

Baer, D. M. Applied behavior analysis. In G. T. Wilson & C. M. Franks (Eds.), *Contemporary behavior therapy*. New York: Guilford Press, 1982.

Bandura, A. *Principles of behavior modification*. New York: Holt, 1969.

Bandura, A. Self-efficacy: Toward a unifying theory of behavior change. *Psychological Review*, 1977, **89**, 191–215. (a)

Bandura, A. *Social learning theory*. Englewood Cliffs, N.J.: Prentice-Hall, 1977. (b)

Bandura, A. On paradigms and recycled ideologies. *Cognitive Therapy and Research*, 1978, **2**, 79–104.

Bandura, A. Self-efficacy mechanisms in human agency. *American Psychologist*, 1982, **37**, 122–147.

Bandura, A., & Adams, N. E. Analysis of self-efficacy theory of behavioral change. *Cognitive Therapy and Research*, 1977, **1**, 287–310.

Barendregt, J. T. A psychological investigation of the effect of group psychotherapy in patients with bronchial asthma. *Journal of Psychosomatic Research*, 1957, **2**, 115–119.

Barlow, D. H. The treatment of sexual deviation: Toward a comprehensive behavioral approach. In H. E. Adams & K. H. Mitchell (Eds.), *Innovative treatment methods in psychopathology*. New York: Wiley, 1974.

Barlow, D. H. (Ed.). *Behavioral assessment of adult disorders*. New York: Guilford Press, 1981.

Barlow, D. H., & Abel, G. G. Recent developments in assessment and treatment of paraphilias and gender-identity disorders. In W. E. Craighead, A. E. Kazdin, & M. J. Mahoney (Eds.), *Behavior modification: Principles, issues, and applications*. Boston: Houghton Mifflin, 1981.

Barlow, D. H., & Wolfe, B. E. Behavioral approaches to anxiety disorders: A report on the NIMH-SUNY, Albany, research conference. *Journal of Consulting and Clinical Psychology*, 1981, **49**, 448–454.

Beck, A. T. *Cognitive therapy and the emotional disorders*. New York: International Universities Press, 1976.

Becker, J., & Schuckit, M. A. The comparative efficacy of cognitive therapy and pharmacotherapy in the treatment of depression. *Cognitive Therapy and Research*, 1978, **2**, 193–197.

Beckstrand, P. TA as a means of teaching writing in high school. *Transactional Analysis Journal*, 1973, **3**, 161–163.

Begelman, D. A. Ethical and legal issues of behavior modification. In M. Hersen, R. M. Eisler, & P. M. Miller (Eds.), *Progress in behavior modification* (Vol. 1). New York: Academic Press, 1975.

Bigelow, G. E., Stitzer, M. L., Griffiths, R. R., & Liebson, I. A. Contingency management approaches to drug self-administration and drug abuse: Efficacy and limitations. *Addictive Behaviors*, 1981, **6**, 241–252.

Biran, M., & Wilson, G. T. Treatment of phobic disorders using cognitive and exposure methods: A self-efficacy analysis. *Journal of Consulting and Clinical Psychology*, 1981, **49**, 886–899.

Birnbaum, A. Combining independent tests of significance. *Journal of the American Statistical Association*, 1954, **49**, 559–574.

Bjurstrom, L., & Alexiov, N. A program of heart disease intervention for public employees. *Journal of Occupational Medicine*, 1978, **20**, 795–806.

Blair, C. D., & Lanyon, R. I. Exhibitionism: Etiology and treatment. *Psychological Bulletin*, 1981, **89**, 439–463.

Blaney, P. H. The effectiveness of cognitive and behavioral therapies. In L.P. Rehm (Ed.), *Behavior therapy for depression. Present status and future directions*. New York: Academic Press, 1981.

Borkovec, T. D. Self-efficacy: Cause or reflection of behavioral change? *Advances in Behaviour Research and Therapy*, 1978, **1**, 163–170.

Boudin, H. M. Contingency contracting as a therapeutic tool in the deceleration of amphetamine use. *Behavior Therapy*, 1972, **3**, 604–608.

Braukmann, C. J., Fixsen, D. L., Phillips, E. L., & Wolf, M. M. Behavioral approaches to treatment in the crime and delinquency field. *Criminology*, 1975, **13**, 299–331.

Braun, P. R., & Reynolds, D. N. A factor analysis of a 100-item fear survey inventory. *Behavior Research and Therapy*, 1969, **7**, 399–402.

Brown, C. C. Instruments in psychophysiology. In R. A. Greenfield & N. S. Sternbach (Eds.), *Handbook of psychophysiology*. New York: Holt, Rinehart & Winston, 1972.

Caddy, G. R., Addington, H. J., & Perkins, D. Individualized behavior therapy for alcoholics: A third-year independent double-blind follow-up. *Behaviour Research and Therapy*, 1978, **16**, 345–362.

Cannon, D. S., & Baker, T. B. Emetic and electric shock alcohol aversion therapy: Assessment of conditioning. *Journal of Consulting & Clinical Psychology*, 1981, **49**, 20–33.

Cannon, D. S., Baker, T. B., & Wehl, C. K. Emetic and electric shock alcohol aversion therapy: Six- and twelve-month follow-up. *Journal of Consulting and Clinical Psychology*, 1981, **49**, 360–368.

Cattell, R. B. Let's end the feud. *American Psychologist*, in press.

Ciminero, A. R., Calhoun, K. S., & Adams, H. E. *Handbook of behavioral assessment*. New York: Wiley, 1977.

Claerhout, S., & Lutzker, J. R. Increasing children's self-initiated compliance to dental regimens. *Behavior Therapy*, 1981, **12**, 165–176.

Cone, J. D. The relevance of reliability and validity for behavioral assessment. *Behavior Therapy*, 1977, **8**, 411–426.

Conger, J. C., & Keane, S. P. Social skills intervention in the treatment of isolated or withdrawn children. *Psychological Bulletin*, 1981, **90**, 478–495.

Conger, J. J. Reinforcement theory and the dynamics of alcoholism. *Quarterly Journal of Studies on Alcohol*, 1956, **17**, 296–305.

Cooper, J. E. A study of behavior therapy in 30 psychiatric patients. *Lancet*, 1963, **1**, 411.

Cox, M., Shephard, R. J., & Corey, P. Influence of an employee fitness programme upon fitness, productivity and absenteeism. *Ergonomics*, 1981, **24**, 795–806.

Craighead, W. E., Kazdin, A. E., & Mahoney, M. J. *Behavior modification: Principles, issues, and applications* (2nd Ed.). Boston: Houghton Mifflin, 1981.

Crighton, J., & Jehu, P. Treatment of examination anxiety by systematic desensitization or psychotherapy in groups. *Behaviour Research and Therapy*, 1969, **7**, 245–248.

Cummings, N. A. The anatomy of psychotherapy under national health insurance. *American Psychologist*, 1977, **32**, 711–718.

Danaher, B. G. Rapid smoking and self-control in the modification of smoking behavior. *Journal of Consulting and Clinical Psychology*, 1977, **45**, 1068–1075.

Davison, G. C. Homosexuality, the ethical challenge. *Journal of Homosexuality*, 1977, **2**, 79–81.

Davison, G. C., & Stuart, R. B. Behavior therapy and civil liberties. *American Psychologist*, 1975, **30**, 755–763.

DiLoreto, A. *Comparative psychotherapy*. New York: Aldine-Atherton, 1971.

Dollard, J., & Miller, N. E. *Personality and psychotherapy: An analysis in terms of learning, thinking, and culture*. New York: McGraw-Hill, 1950.

Eastman, C. Behavioral formulations of depression. In C. M. Franks & G. T. Wilson (Eds.), *Annual review of behavior therapy, theory and practice* (Vol. 5). New York: Brunner/Mazel, 1977.

Edgington, E. S. An additive method for combining probability values from independent experiments. *Journal of Psychology*, 1972, **80**, 351–363 (a).

Edgington, E. S. A normal curve method for combining probability values from independent experiments. *Journal of Psychology*, 1972, **82**, 85–89 (b).

Egel, A. L., Richman, G. S., & Koegel, R. L. Normal peer models and autistic children's learning. *Journal of Applied Behavior Analysis*, 1981, **14**, 3–12.

Epstein, L. H., Beck, S., Figueroa, J., Farkas, G., Kazdin, A. E., Daneman, D., & Becker, D. The effects of targeting improvements in urine glucose on metabolic control in children with insulin dependent diabetes. *Journal of Applied Behavior Analysis*, 1981, **14**, 365–375.

Erwin, E. *Behavior therapy: Scientific, philosophical and moral foundations*. Cambridge: Cambridge University Press, 1978.

Eysenck, H. J. The effects of psychotherapy: An evaluation. *Journal of Consulting Psychology*, 1952, **16**, 319–324.

Eysenck, H. J. *The dynamics of anxiety and hysteria*. London: Routledge & Kegan Paul, 1957.

Eysenck, H. J. Learning theory and behaviour theory. *Journal of Mental Science*, 1959, **105**, 61–75.

Eysenck, H. J. (Ed.). *Behaviour therapy and the neuroses*. Oxford: Pergamon Press, 1960.

Eysenck, H. J. Classification and the problems of diagnosis. In H. J. Eysenck (Ed.), *Handbook of abnormal psychology*. New York: Basic Books, 1961.

Eysenck, H. J. Behavior therapy is behavioristic. *Behavior Therapy*, 1972, **3**, 609–613.

Eysenck, H. J. The learning theory model of neurosis—a new approach. *Behaviour Research and Therapy*, 1976, **14**, 251–267.

Eysenck, H. J. Neobehavioristic (S-R) theory. In G. T. Wilson & C. M. Franks (Eds.), *Contemporary behavior therapy: Conceptual and empirical foundations*. New York: Guilford Press, 1982.

Feldman, M. P., & MacCulloch, M. J. The application of anticipatory avoidance learning to the treatment of homosexuality. 1. Theory, technique, and preliminary results. *Behaviour Research and Therapy*, 1965, **3**, 165–183.

Feldman, M. P., & MacCulloch, M. J. *Homosexual behaviour: Therapy and assessment*. Oxford: Pergamon Press, 1971.

Ferster, C. B. Positive reinforcement and behavioral deficits of autistic children. *Child Development*, 1961, **32**, 437–456.

Ferster, C. B., & Skinner, B. F. *Schedules of reinforcement*. New York: Appleton-Century-Crofts, 1957.

Fisher, R. A. Combining independent tests of significance. *American Statistician*, 1948, **2**, 30.

Fixsen, D. L., Phillips, E. L., & Wolf, M. M. Achievement place: The reliability of self-reporting and peer-reporting and their effects on behavior. *Journal of Applied Behavior Analysis*, 1972, **5**, 19–30.

Frank, J. *Persuasion and healing: A comparative study of psychotherapy* (Rev. ed.). Baltimore: Johns Hopkins University Press, 1974. (Originally published, 1961.)

Franks, C. M. On conceptual and technical integrity in psychoanalysis and behavior therapy, two fundamentally incompatible systems. In H. Arkowitz & S. Messer (Eds.), *Psychoanalytic and behavior therapy: Are they compatible?* New York: Plenum Press, in press.

Freund, K. Some problems in the treatment of homosexuality. In H. J. Eysenck (Ed.), *Behaviour therapy and the neuroses*. London: Pergamon Press, 1960.

Fuchs, C. Z., & Rehm, L. P. A self-control therapy program for depression. *Journal of Consulting and Clinical Psychology*, 1977, **45**, 206–215.

Garfield, S. L. Review of *Psychotherapy versus behavior therapy* by R. B. Sloane et al. *Contemporary Psychology*, 1976, **21**, 328–329.

Geer, J. A. The development of a scale to measure fear. *Behaviour Research and Therapy*, 1965, **3**, 45–53.

Gelder, M. G., & Marks, I. M. Severe agoraphobia: A controlled prospective trial of behaviour therapy. *British Journal of Psychiatry*, 1966, **112**, 309–319.

Gerwirtz, J. L. The roles of overt responding and extrinsic reinforcement in "self-" and "vicarious-reinforcement" phenomena and in "observational learning" and imitation. In R. Glaser (Ed.), *The Nature of Reinforcement*. New York: Academic Press, 1971.

Giffin, M. W., Johnson, A. M., & Litin, E. M. Antisocial acting out: 2. Specific factors determining antisocial acting out. *American Journal of Orthopsychiatry*, 1954, **24**, 668–684.

Gillan, P., & Rachman, S. An experimental investigation of desensitization in phobic patients. *British Journal of Psychiatry*, 1974, **124**, 392–401.

Glass, G. V. Primary, secondary, and meta-analysis of research. *Educational Research*, 1976, **5**, 3–8.

Glass, G. V., & Smith, M. L. *Meta-analysis of psychotherapy outcome studies*. Paper presented at the Society for Psychotherapy Research, San Diego, California, 1976.

Goldfried, M. R. Behavioral assessment. In I. B. Weiner (Ed.), *Clinical methods in psychology*. New York: Wiley-Interscience, 1976.

Gotestam, K. D. & Melin, L. Covert extinction of amphetamine addiction. *Behavior Therapy*, 1974, **5**, 90–92.

Greenspan, S. I., & Sharfstein, S. S. Efficacy of psychotherapy: Asking the right questions. *Archives of General Psychiatry*, 1981, **38**, 1213–1219.

Guthrie, E. R. *The psychology of learning*. New York: Harper, 1935.

Hackett, G., & Horan, J. J. Partial component analysis of a comprehensive smoking program. *Addictive Behaviors*, 1979, **4**, 259–262.

Hagen, R. L., Craighead, W. E., & Paul, G. L. Staff reactivity to evaluative behavioral observations. *Behavior Therapy*, 1975, **6**, 201–205.

Hall, S. M., Hall, R. G., DeBoer, G., & O'Kulitch, P. Self and external management compared with psychotherapy in the control of obesity. *Behaviour Research and Therapy*, 1977, **15**, 89–96.

Hall, S. M., Loeb, P., Coyne, K., & Cooper, J. Increasing employment in ex-heroin addicts: 1. Criminal justice sample. *Behavior Therapy*, 1981, **12**, 443–452.

Harris, S. L., & Romanczyk, R. G. Treating self-injurious behavior of a retarded child by overcorrection. *Behavior Therapy*, 1976, **7**, 235–239.

Harris, S. L., & Milch, R. E. Training parents as behavior therapists for their autistic children. *Clinical Psychology Review*, 1981, **1**, 49–64.

Harris, S. L., & Romanczyk, R. G. Treating self-injurious behavior of a retarded child by overcorrection. *Behavior Therapy*, 1976, **7**, 235–239.

Hartlage, L. C. Subprofessional therapists' use of reinforcement versus traditional psychotherapeutic techniques with schizophrenics. *Journal of Consulting and Clinical Psychology*, 1970, **34**, 181–183.

Hersen, M., & Bellack, A. S. Treatment of chronic mental patients. In W. E. Craighead, A. E. Kazdin, & M. J. Mahoney, (Eds.), *Behavior modification: Principles, issues, and applications* (2nd ed.). Boston: Houghton Mifflin, 1981.

Hersen, M., Bellack, A. S., & Himmelhoch, J. M. Treatment of unipolar depression with social skills training. *Behavior Modification*, 1980, **4**, 547–556.

Hersen, M., Eisler, R. M., & Miller, P. M. Historical perspectives in behavior modification: Introductory comments. In M. Hersen, R. M. Eisler, & P. M. Miller (Eds.), *Progress in behavior modification* (Vol. 1). New York: Academic Press, 1975.

Hodgson, R. J., Rankin, H. J., & Stockwell, T. R. Alcohol dependence and the priming effect. *Behaviour Research and Therapy*, 1979, **17**, 379–388.

Hollon, S. D. Comparisons and combinations with alternative approaches. In L. P. Rehm (Ed.), *Behavior therapy for depression: Present status and future directions*. New York: Academic Press, 1981.

Hull, C. L. *Principles of behavior: An introduction to behavior theory*. New York: Appleton-Century, 1943.

Hunt, G. H., & Azrin, N. H. The community-reinforcement approach to alcoholism. *Behaviour Research and Therapy*, 1973, **11**, 91–104.

Hunt, W. A., Barnett, L. W., & Branch, L. G. Relapse rates in addiction programs. *Journal of Clinical Psychology*, 1971, **27**, 455–456.

Iwata, B. A., & Becksfort, C. M. Behavioral research in preventive dentistry: Educational and contingency management approaches to the problem of patient compliance. *Journal of Applied Behavior Analysis*, 1981, **14**, 111–120.

Jacobson, E. *Progressive relaxation*. Chicago: University of Chicago Press, 1938.

Jesness, C. F. Comparative effectiveness of behavior modification and transactional analysis programs for delinquents. *Journal of Consulting and Clinical Psychology*, 1975, **43**, 758–779.

Jones, L. V., & Fiske, D. W. Models for testing the significance of combined results. *Psychological Bulletin*, 1953, **50**, 375–382.

Jones, M. C. The elimination of children's fears. *Journal of Experimental Psychology*, 1924, **7**, 382–390.

Josiassen, R. C., Fantuzzo, J., & Rosen, A. C. Treatment of pedophilia using multistage aversion therapy and social skills training. *Journal of Behavior Therapy & Experimental Psychiatry*, 1980, **11**, 55–61.

Kanfer, F. H., & Phillips, J. S. *Learning foundations of behavior therapy*. New York: Wiley, 1970.

Kantorovich, N. (An attempt at associative-reflex therapy in alcoholism.) *Nov. Reflexol. Fiziol. Nerv. Sist.*, 1929, **3**, 436–447. (*Psychological Abstracts*, 1930, **4**, 493.)

Kazdin, A. E. *History of behavior modification*. Baltimore: University Park Press, 1978. (a)

Kazdin, A. E. Conceptual and assessment issues raised by self-efficacy theory. *Advances in Behavior Research and Therapy*, 1978, **1**, 177–185. (b)

Kazdin, A. E. Symptom substitution, generalization, and response covariation: Implications for psychotherapy outcome. *Psychological Bulletin*, 1982, **91**, 349–365.

Kazdin, A. E., & Hersen, M. The current status of behavior therapy. *Behavior Modification*, 1980, **4**, 283, 302.

Kazdin, A. E., & Wilson, G. T. Criteria for evaluating psychotherapy. *Archives of General Psychiatry*, 1978, **35**, 407–418. (a)

Kazdin, A. E. & Wilson, G. T. *Evaluation of behavior therapy: Issues, evidence, and research strategies*. Cambridge, Mass.: Ballinger, 1978. (b)

Keane, T. M., Prue, D. M., & Collins, F. L., Jr. Behavioral contracting to improve dietary compliance in chronic renal dialysis patients. *Journal of Behavior Therapy and Experimental Psychiatry*, 1981, **12**, 63–67.

Kiesler, D. J. Some myths of psychotherapy research and the search for a paradigm. *Psychological Bulletin*, 1966, **65**, 110–136.

Kockott, G., Dittmar, F., & Nusselt, L. Systematic desensitization of erectile impotence: A controlled study. *Archives of Sexual Behavior*, 1975, **4**, 493–500.

Kopel, S. A., & Suckerman, K. Smoke holding: Summary of physiological data. Unpublished manuscript, Rutgers University, 1982.

Kovacs, M. Treating depressive disorders: The efficacy of behavior and cognitive therapies. *Behavior Modification*, 1979, **3**, 496–517.

Lando, H.A., & McGovern, P. G. Three-year data on a behavioral treatment for smoking: A follow-up note. *Addictive Behaviors*, 1982, **7**, 177–181.

Landy, F. J., & Trumbo, D. A. *Psychology of work behavior*. Homewood, Ill.: Dorsey Press, 1976.

Lang, P. J. The mechanics of desensitization and the laboratory study of fear. In C. M. Franks (Ed.), *Behavior therapy: Appraisal and status*. New York: McGraw-Hill, 1969.

Lang, P. J. Imagery in therapy: An informational processing analysis of fear. *Behavior Therapy*, 1977, **8**, 862–886.

Lang, P. J. *A bio-informational theory of emotional imagery.* Presidential address to the annual meeting of the Society for Psychophysiological Research, Madison, Wisconsin, 1978.

Land, P. J., Melamed, B. G., & Hart, J. A psychophysiological analysis of fear modification using an automated desensitization procedure. *Journal of Abnormal Psychology,* 1970, **76,** 220–234.

Lassen, C. L. Effect of proximity on anxiety and communication in the initial psychiatric interview. *Journal of Abnormal Psychology,* 1973, **81,** 226–232.

Lazarus, A. A. New methods in psychotherapy: A case study. *South African Medical Journal,* 1958, **32,** 660–664.

Lazarus, A. A. Group therapy of phobic disorders by systematic desensitization. *Journal of Abnormal and Social Psychology,* 1961, **63,** 504–510.

Lazarus, A. A. Broad spectrum behavior therapy and the treatment of agoraphobia. *Behaviour Research and Therapy,* 1966, **4,** 95–97.

Lazarus, A. A. Has behavior therapy outlived its usefulness? *American Psychologist,* 1977, **32,** 550–554.

Lemere, F., & Voegtlin, W. An evaluation of the aversion treatment of alcoholism. *Quarterly Journal of Studies on Alcohol,* 1950, **11,** 199–204.

Liberman, R. P. Aversive conditioning of drug addicts: A pilot study. *Behaviour Research and Therapy,* 1968, **6,** 229–231.

Liberman, R. P., Levine, J., Wheeler, E., Sanders, N., & Wallace, C. J. Marital therapy in groups: A comparative evaluation of behavioral and interactional formats. *Acta Psychiatrica Scandinavica,* 1976, Supplementum 266.

Lichtenstein, E., & Danaher, B. G. Modification of smoking behavior: A critical analysis of theory, research and practice. In M. Hersen, R. M. Eisler, & P. M. Miller (Eds.), *Progress in behavior modification* (Vol. 3). New York: Academic Press, 1976.

Lichtenstein, E., Harris, E., Birchler, G. R., Wahl, J. M., & Schmahl, D. P. Comparison of rapid smoking, warm, smoky air and attention placebo in the modification of smoking behavior. *Journal of Consulting and Clinical Psychology,* 1973, **40,** 92–98.

Lidz, T., Cornelison, A. R., Fleck, S., & Terry, D. The intrafamilial environment of the schizophrenić patient. 1. The father. *Psychiatry,* 1957, **20,** 329–342. (a)

Lidz, T., Cornelison, A. R., Fleck, S., & Terry, D. The intrafamilial environment of schizophrenic patients. 2. Marital schism and marital skew. *American Journal of Psychiatry,* 1957, **114,** 241–248. (b)

Lindsley, O. R. Operant conditioning methods applied to research in chronic schizophrenia. *Psychiatric Research Report,* 1956, **5,** 118–139.

Lovaas, O. I., & Simmons, J. Q. Manipulation of self-destruction in three retarded children. *Journal of Applied Behavior Analysis,* 1969, **2,** 143–157.

Luborsky, L., Singer, B., & Luborsky, L. Comparative studies of psychotherapy: Is it true that "Everyone has won and all must have prizes?" *Archives of General Psychiatry,* 1975, **32,** 995–1008.

Lutzker, J. R., & Martin, J. A. *Behavior change.* Monterey, Calif.: Brooks/Cole, 1981.

MacCulloch, M. J., Feldman, M. P., Orford, J. F., & MacCulloch, M. L. Anticipatory avoidance learning in the treatment of alcoholism: A record of therapeutic failure. *Behaviour Research and Therapy,* 1966, **4,** 187–196.

Mahoney, M. J. *Cognition and behavior modification.* Cambridge, Mass.: Balinger, 1974.

Mahoney, M. J. Reflections on the cognitive learning trend in psychotherapy. *American Psychologist*, 1977, **32**, 5–13.

Mahoney, M. J., & Arnkoff, D. Cognitive and self-control therapies. In S. L. Garfield & A. E. Bergin (Eds.), *Handbook of psychotherapy and behavior change* (2nd ed.). New York: Wiley, 1978.

Maletzky, B. M. "Assisted" covert sensitization in the treatment of exhibitionism. *Journal of Consulting and Clinical Psychology*, 1974, **42**, 34–40.

Maletzky, B. M. "Booster" sessions in aversion therapy: The permanency of treatment. *Behavior Therapy*, 1977, **8**, 460–463.

Maletzky, B. M. Assisted covert sensitization. In D. J. Cox & R. J. Daitzman (Eds.), *Exhibitionism: Description, assessment, and treatment.* New York: Garland, 1980.

Marks, I. M. Phobic disorders four years after treatment: A prospective follow-up. *British Journal of Psychiatry*, 1971, **118**, 683–688.

Marks, I. M. The current status of behavioral psychotherapy: Theory and practice. *American Journal of Psychiatry*, 1976, **133**, 253–261.

Marlatt, G. A. Craving for alcohol, loss of control, and relapse: A cognitive-behavioral analysis. In P. E. Nathan & G. A. Marlatt (Eds.), *Experimental and behavioral approaches to alcoholism.* New York: Plenum, 1978.

Marlatt, G. A., & Rohsenow, D. J. Cognitive processes in alcohol use: Expectancy and the balanced placebo design. In N. K. Mello (Ed.), *Advances in substance abuse: Behavioral and biological research* (Vol. 1). Greenwich, Conn.: JAI Press, 1980.

Matarazzo, J. D. Behavioral health and behavioral medicine: Frontiers for a new health psychology. *American Psychologist*, 1980, **35**, 807–817.

Matarazzo, J. D. Behavioral health's challenge to academic, scientific, and professional psychology. *American Psychologist*, 1982, **37**, 1–14.

Matarazzo, J. D., & Wiens, A. *The interview: Research on its anatomy and structure.* Chicago: Aldine-Atherton, 1972.

Matson, J. L., Kazdin, A. E., & Esveldt-Dawson, K. Training interpersonal skills among mentally retarded and socially dysfunctional children. *Behaviour Research and Therapy*, 1980, **18**, 419–427.

Matson, J. L., Ollendick, T. H., & Adkins, J. A comprehensive dining program for mentally retarded adults. *Journal of Applied Behavior Analysis*, 1980, **18**, 107–112.

Mavissakalian, M. Anorexia Nervosa treated whith response prevention and prolonged exposure. *Behaviour Research and Therapy*, 1982, **20**, 27–31.

McConaghy, N., Armstrong, M. S., & Blaszczynski, A. Controlled comparison of aversive therapy and covert sensitization in compulsive homosexuality. *Behaviour Research and Therapy*, 1981, **19**, 425–434.

McLean, P. D., & Hakstian, A. R. Clinical depression: Comparative efficacy of outpatient treatments. *Journal of Consulting and Clinical Psychology*, 1979, **47**, 818–836.

McSweeny, A. J. Including psychotherapy in national health insurance: Insurance guidelines and other proposed solutions. *American Psychologist*, 1977, **32**, 722–730.

Meichenbaum, D.J. *Cognitive behavior modification.* New York: Plenum, 1977.

Meichenbaum, D. J., & Cameron, R. Cognitive-behavior therapy. In G. T. Wilson & C. M. Franks (Eds.), *Contemporary behavior therapy.* New York: Guilford, 1982.

Melamed, B. G., & Siegel, L. J. Management of dental patients. In *Behavioral medicine: Practical applications in health care*. New York: Springer, 1980.

Mendelson, J. H. Experimentally induced chronic intoxication and withdrawal in alcoholics. *Quarterly Journal of Studies on Alcohol*, Supplement No. 2, 1964.

Miller, P. M., & Foy, D. W. Substance Abuse. In S. M. Turner, K. S. Calhoun, & H. E. Adams (Eds.), *Handbook of clinical behavior therapy*. New York: Wiley-Interscience, 1981.

Miller, P. M., & Hersen, M. Quantitative changes in alcohol consumption as a function of electrical aversive conditioning. *Journal of Clinical Psychology*, 1972, **28**, 590–593.

Miller, W. R., & Caddy, G. R. Abstinence and controlled drinking in the treatment of problem drinkers. *Journal of Studies on Alcohol*, 1977, **38**, 986–1003.

Mintz, J. The role of the therapist in assessing psychotherapy outcome. In A. Gurman & A. Razin (Eds.). *Effective Psychotherapy*. Oxford: Pergamon Press, 1977.

Mischel, W. Toward a cognitive social learning reconceptualization of personality. *Psychological Review*, 1973, **80**, 252–283.

Mowrer, O. H. A stimulus-response analysis of anxiety and its role as a reinforcing agent. *Psychological Review*, 1939. **46**, 553–564.

Mowrer, O. H., & Mowrer, W. M. Enuresis—A method for its study and treatment. *American Journal of Orthopsychiatry*, 1938, **8**, 436–459.

Nathan, P. E., & Jackson, A. D. Behavioral modification. In I. B. Weiner (Ed.), *Clinical methods in psychology*. New York: Wiley-Interscience, 1976, 517–590.

Nathan, P. E., & Lipscomb, T. R. Behavior therapy and behavior modification in the treatment of alcoholism. In J. H. Mendelson & N. K. Mello (Eds.), *Diagnosis and treatment of alcoholism*. New York: McGraw-Hill, 1979.

Nathan, P. E., & O'Brien, J. S. An experimental analysis of the behavior of alcoholics and nonalcoholics during prolonged experimental drinking: A necessary precursor of behavior therapy? *Behavior Therapy*, 1971, **2**, 455–476.

National Institute on Alcohol Abuse and Alcoholism. *Fifth Report to Congress on Alcohol and Health*. Washington, D.C.: U. S. Government Printing Office, 1983.

Neubuerger, O. W., Miller, S. I., Schmitz, R. E., Matarazzo, J. D., Pratt, H., & Hasha, N. Replicable abstinence rates in an alcoholism treatment program. *Journal of the American Medical Association*, 1982, **248**, 960–963.

Ney, P. G., Palvesky, A. E., & Markely, J. Relative effectiveness of operant conditioning and playtherapy in childhood schizophrenia. *Journal of Autism and Childhood Schizophrenia*. 1971, **1**, 337–349.

Nietzel, M. T. *Crime and its modification*. New York: Pergamon Press, 1979.

O'Brien, J. S., Raynes, A. E., & Patch, V. D. Treatment of heroin addiction with aversion therapy, relaxation training and systematic desensitization. *Behaviour Research and Therapy*, 1972, **10**, 77–80.

Olson, R. P., Devine, V. T., Ganley, R., & Dorsey, G. C. Long-term effects of behavioral versus insight-oriented therapy with inpatient alcoholics. *Journal of Consulting and Clinical Psychology*, 1981, **49**, 866–877.

Orleans, C. S. Quitting smoking: Overview and critical issues. In *Smoking and behavior*. Washington, D.C.: U.S. Government Printing Office, 1980.

Orleans, C. T., Shipley, R. H., Williams, C., & Haac, L. A. Behavioral approaches to smoking cessation—1. A decade of research progress 1969–1979. *Journal of Behavior Therapy and Experimental Psychiatry*, 1981, **12**, 125–129.

Parloff, M. B. Can psychotherapy research guide the policy-maker? A little knowledge may be a dangerous thing. *American Psychologist*, 1979, **34**, 296–306.

Patterson, V., Levene, H., & Breger, L. Treatment and training outcomes with two time-limited therapies. *Archives of General Psychiatry*, 1971, **25**, 161–167.

Paul, G. L. *Insight versus desensitization in psychotherapy*. Stanford, Calif. Stanford University Press, 1966.

Paul, G. L. Insight versus desensitization in psychotherapy two years after termination. *Journal of Consulting Psychology*, 1967, **31**, 333–345.

Paul, G. L., & Lentz, R. J. *Psychosocial treatment of chronic mental patients: Milieu versus social-learning programs*. Cambridge: Harvard University Press, 1977.

Pavlov, I. P. The scientific investigation of the psychical faculties or processes in the higher animals. *Science*, 1906, **24**, 613–619.

Pearson, E. S. The probability integral transformation for testing goodness of fit and combining independent tests of significance. *Biometrika*, 1938, **30**, 134–148.

Pendery, M. L., Maltzman, I. M., & West, L. J. Controlled drinking by alcoholics? New findings and a reevaluation of a major affirmative study. *Science*, 1982, **217**, 169–175.

Peters, R. K. Benson, H., & Porter, D. Daily relaxation response breaks in a working population: 1. Effects on self-reported measures of health, performance and well-being. *American Journal of Public Health*, 1977, **67**, 946–953.

Phillips, C. Tension headache: Theoretical problems. *Behaviour Research and Therapy*, 1978, **16**, 249–262.

Polich, M., Armor, D. J., & Braiker, H. B. *The course of alcoholism: Four years after treatment*. New York: Wiley, 1980.

Pomerleau, O. F., Pertschuk, M., Adkins, D., & Brady, J. P. *Comparison of behavioral and traditional treatment of problem drinking*. Paper presented at the Annual Meeting of the Association for the Advancement of Behavior Therapy, New York, 1976.

Poole, A. D., Sanson-Fisher, R. W., German, G. A., & Harker, J. The rapid-smoking technique: Some physiological effects. *Behaviour Research and Therapy*, 1980, **18**, 581–586.

Poser, E. G. The self-efficacy concept: Some theoretical, procedural and clinical implications. *Advances in Behaviour Research and Therapy*, 1978, **1**, 193–202.

Prue, D. M., Krapfl, J. E., & Martin, J. E. Brand fading: The effects of gradual changes to low tar and nicotine cigarettes on smoking rate, carbon monoxide, and thiocyanate levels. *Behavior Therapy*, 1981, **12**, 400–416.

Rachman, S. The passing of the two-stage theory of fear and avoidance: Fresh possibilities. *Behaviour Research and Therapy*, 1976, **14**, 125–131.

Rachman, S. J., & Hodgson, R. J. *Obsessions and compulsions*. Englewood Cliffs, N.J.: Prentice-Hall, 1980.

Rachman, S., & Wilson, G. T. *The Effects of Psychological Therapy* (2nd ed). Oxford: Pergamon Press, 1980.

Raw, M., Israel, Y., Glaser, F. B., Kalant, H., Popham, R. E., Schmidt, W., & Smart, R. G. The treatment of cigarette dependence. In Y. Israel (Ed.), *Research advances in alcohol and drug problems* (Vol. 4). New York: Plenum, 1978.

Raw, M., & Russell, M.A.H. Rapid smoking, cue exposure, and support in the modification of smoking. *Behaviour Research and Therapy*, 1980, **18**, 363–372.

Raymond, M. J. Case of fetishism treated by aversion therapy. *British Medical Journal*, 1956, **2**, 854–857.

Rehm, L. P. A self-control model of depression. *Behavior Therapy*, 1977, **8**, 787–804.

Reid, J. B. Reliability assessment of observation data: A possible methodological problem. *Child Development*, 1970, **41**, 1143–1150.

Reynolds, B. S. Erectile dysfunction: A review of behavioral treatment approaches. In R. J. Daitzman (Ed.), *Clinical behavior therapy and behavior modification* (Vol. 2). New York: Garland STPM Press, 1981.

Rogers, C. R., & Dymond, R. *Psychotherapy and personality change*. Chicago: Chicago University Press, 1954.

Rose, G., Heller, R., Pedoe, H., & Christie, D. Heart disease: A randomized controlled trial in industry. *British Medical Journal*, 1980, **280**, (6216) 747–751.

Rosenthal, R. Combining results of independent studies. *Psychological Bulletin*, 1978, **85**, 185–193.

Rosenthal, T. L. Social learning theory. In G. T. Wilson & C. M. Franks (Eds.), *Contemporary behavior therapy: Conceptual and empirical foundations*. New York: Guilford Press, 1982.

Rosenthal, T. L., & Bandura, A. Psychological modeling: Theory and practice. In S. L. Garfield & A. E. Bergin (Eds.), *Handbook of psychotherapy and behavior change* (2nd ed.) New York: Wiley, 1978.

Roth, D., Bielski, R., Jones, M., Parker, W., & Osborn, G. A comparison of self-control therapy and combined self-control therapy and antidepressant medication in the treatment of depression. *Behavior Therapy*, 1982, **13**, 133–144.

Rush, A. J., Beck, A. T., Kovacs, M., & Hollon, S. D. Comparative efficacy of cognitive therapy versus pharmaco-therapy in outpatient depressives. *Cognitive Therapy and Research*, 1977, **1**, 17–37.

Salzinger, K. Remedying schizophrenic behavior. In S. M. Turner, K. S. Calhoun, & H. E. Adams, (Eds.), New York: Wiley-Interscience, 1981.

Sanchez-Craig, M., & Annis, H. M. *Initial evaluation of a program for early-stage problem drinkers: Randomization to abstinence and controlled drinking*. Paper at American Psychological Association annual convention, Washington, D.C., 1982.

Schreibman, L., Koegel, R. L., Mills, J. I., & Burke, J. C. Social validation of behavior therapy with autistic children. *Behavior Therapy*, 1981, **12**, 610–624.

Segraves, R. T. Female sexual inhibition. In R. J. Daitzman (Ed.), *Clinical behavior therapy and behavior modification* (Vol. 2). New York: Garland STPM Press, 1981.

Seligman, M. E. P. Phobias and preparedness. *Behavior Therapy*, 1971, **2**, 307–320.

Shepard, D. Incentive for not smoking: Experience at the Speedcall Corporation. Unpublished manuscript, Harvard School of Public Health, 1980.

Shepard, R., Corey, P., Renzland, P., & Cox, M. Fitness program reduces health care costs. *Dimensions*, 1982 (Jan.), 14–15.

Shepard, R., Cox, M., & Corey, P. Fitness program participation: Its effects on worker performance. *Journal of Occupational Medicine*, 1981, **23**, 359–363.

Sherman, M., Trief, P., & Sprafkin, R. Impression management in the psychiatric interview:

Quality, style, and individual differences. *Journal of Consulting and Clinical Psychology*, 1975, **43**, 867–871.

Skinner, B. F. *The behavior of organisms: An experimental analysis*. New York: Appleton-Century, 1938.

Skinner, B. F. *Science and human behavior*. New York: Macmillan, 1953.

Skinner, B. F. *Beyond freedom and dignity*. New York: Bantam Books, 1971.

Sloane, R. B., Staples, F. R., Cristol, A. H., Yorkston, N. J., & Whipple, K. *Psychotherapy versus behavior therapy*. Cambridge, Mass.: Harvard University Press, 1975.

Smith, M. L., & Glass, G. V. Meta-analysis of psychotherapy outcome studies. *American Psychologist*, 1977, **32**, 752–760.

Smith, M. L., Glass, G. V., & Miller, T. I. *The benefits of psychotherapy*. Baltimore: Johns Hopkins University Press, 1980.

Sobel, H. J. (Ed.). *Behavior therapy in terminal care: A humanistic approach*. Cambridge, Mass.: Ballinger, 1981.

Sobell, M. B., & Sobell, L. C. Individualized behavior therapy for alcoholics. *Behavior Therapy*, 1973, **4**, 49–72.

Sobell, M. B., & Sobell, L. C. Second year treatment outcome of alcoholics treated by individualized behavior therapy. *Behaviour Research and Therapy*, 1976, **14**, 195–215.

Steptoe, A. *Psychological factors in cardiovascular disorders*. New York: Academic Press, 1981.

Stoller, R. J. Transvestites' women. *American Journal of Psychiatry*, 1967, **24**, 333–339.

Stolz, S. B., & Associates. *Ethical issues in behavior modification*. San Francisco: Jossey-Bass, 1978.

Strickler, D. P., Bradlyn, A. S., & Maxwell, W. A. Teaching moderate drinking behaviors to young adult heavy drinkers: The effects of three training procedures. *Addictive Behaviors*, 1981, **6**, 355–364.

Strupp, H. H. Clinical research, practice, and the crisis of confidence. *Journal of Consulting and Clinical Psychology*, 1981, **49**, 216–219.

Strupp, H. H., & Hadley, S. W. Specific versus nonspecific factors in psychotherapy: A controlled study of outcome. *Archives of General Psychiatry*, 1979, **36**, 1125–1136.

Stuart, R. B. A three-dimensional program for the treatment of obesity. *Behaviour Research and Therapy*, 1971, **9**, 177–186.

Stunkard, A. J. New therapies for the eating disorders. *Archives of General Psychiatry*, 1972, **26**, 391–398.

Stunkard, A. J., & Brownell, K. D. Work-site treatment for obesity. *American Journal of Psychiatry*, 1980, **137**, 252–253.

Teasdale, J. D., Walsh, P. A., Lancashire, M., & Mathews, A. M. Group exposure for agoraphobics: A replication study. *British Journal of Psychiatry*, 1977, **130**, 186–193.

Thorndike, E. L. *Human learning*. New York: Century, 1931.

Thorpe, J. G., Schmidt, E., Brown, P. T., & Castell, D. Aversion-relief therapy: A new method for general application. *Behaviour Research and Therapy*, 1964, **2**, 71–82.

Tolman, E. C. *Purposive behavior in animals and men*. New York: Century, 1932.

Townsend, R. E., House, J. F., & Addario, D. A comparison of biofeedback-mediated relaxation and group therapy in the treatment of chronic anxiety. *American Journal of Psychiatry*, 1975, **132**, 598–601.

Turner, S. M., & Luber, R. F. The token economy in day hospital settings: Contingency management or information feedback. *Journal of Behavior Therapy and Experimental Psychiatry*, 1980, **11**, 89–94.

Ullmann, L., & Krasner, L. *A psychological approach to abnormal behavior*. Englewood Cliffs, N.J.: Prentice-Hall, 1969.

United States Department of Health, Education, and Welfare (USDHEW). *Smoking and health: A report of the Surgeon General*. Washington, D.C.: U.S. Government Printing Office, 1979.

Varni, J. W. Self-regulation techniques in the management of chronic arthritic pain in hemophilia. *Behavior Therapy*, 1981, **12**, 185–194.

Voegtlin, W. The treatment of alcoholism by establishing a conditioned reflex. *American Journal of the Medical Sciences*, 1940, **199**, 802–810.

Voegtlin, W., & Lemere, F. The treatment of alcoholic addiction: A review of the literature. *Quarterly Journal of Studies on Alcohol*, 1942, **2**, 768–803.

Walker, C. E., Hedberg, A., Clement, P. W., & Wright, L. Clinical procedures for behavior therapy. Englewood Cliffs, N.J.: Prentice-Hall, 1981.

Wallis, W. A. Compounding probabilities from independent significance tests. *Econometrica*, 1942, **19**, 229–248.

Watson, J. B., & Raynor, R. Conditioned emotional reactions. *Journal of Experimental Psychology*, 1920, **3**, 1–14.

Wedderburn, A. A. Social factors in satisfaction with swiftly rotating shifts. *Occupational Psychology*, 1967, **41**, 85–107.

Weimer, W. B. *Psychology and the conceptual foundations of science*. Hillsdale, N.J.: Erlbaum, 1976.

Weins, A. N., Montague, J. R., Manaugh, T. S., & English, C. J. Pharmacological aversive counterconditioning to alcohol in a private hospital: One year follow-up. *Journal of Studies on Alcohol*, 1976, **37**, 1320–1324.

Weissman, M. M. The psychological treatment of depression. *Archives of General Psychiatry*, 1979, **36**, 1261–1269.

White, M. D., & White, C. A. Involuntarily committed patients' constitutional right to refuse treatment: A challenge to psychology. *American Psychologist*, 1981, **36**, 953–962.

Whitehead, A. Psychological treatment of depression: A review. *Behaviour Research and Therapy*, 1979, **17**, 495–509.

Wilson, G. T. On the much discussed nature of the term "behavior therapy." *Behavior Therapy*, 1978, **9**, 89–98.

Wilson, G. T., & Evans, I. M. Adult behavior therapy and the therapist-client relationship. In C. M. Franks & G. T. Wilson (Eds.), *Annual review of behavior therapy: Theory and practice* (Vol. IV). New York Brunner/Mazel, 1976.

Wilson, G. T., Leaf, R. C., & Nathan, P. E. The aversive control of excessive alcohol consumption by chronic alcoholics in the laboratory setting. *Journal of Applied Behavior Analysis*, 1975, **8**, 13–26.

Wolpe, J. Experimental neuroses as learning behavior. *British Journal of Psychology*, 1952, **43**, 243–268.

Wolpe, J. *Psychotherapy by reciprocal inhibition*. Stanford, Calif.: Stanford University Press, 1958.

Wolpe, J. *The practice of behavior therapy*. New York. Pergamon Press, 1969.

Wolpe, J. Foreword. In R. B. Sloane, *et al. Psychotherapy versus behavior therapy*. Cambridge: Harvard University Press, 1975.

Wolpe, J. The experimental model and treatment of neurotic depression. *Behaviour Research and Therapy*, 1979, **17**, 555–565.

Wolpe, J. The dichotomy between classical conditioning and cognitively learned anxiety. *Journal of Behavior Therapy and Experimental Psychiatry*. 1981, **12**, 35–42. (a)

Wolpe, J. Reciprocal inhibition and therapeutic change. *Journal of Behavior Therapy and Experimental Psychiatry*, 1981, **12**, 185–188. (b)

Wolpe, J. Behavior therapy versus psychoanalysis. *American Psychologist*, 1981, **36**, 159–164. (c)

Wolpe, J., & Lang, P. J. A fear survey schedule for use in behavior therapy. *Behaviour Research and Therapy*, 1964, **2**, 27–30.

Wolpe, J., & Land, P. J. *Fear Survey Schedule*. San Diego, Calif. Educational and Industrial Testing Service, 1969.

Woodward, R., & Jones, R. B. Cognitive restructuring treatment: A controlled trial with anxious patients. *Behaviour Research and Therapy*, 1980, **18**, 401–407.

Woolfolk, R. L., & Woolfolk, A. E. Modifying the effect of the behavior modification label. *Behavior Therapy*, 1979, **10**, 575–578.

Yates, A. J. *Biofeedback and the modification of behavior*. New York: Plenum, 1980.

Zitrin, C. M., Klein, D. F., & Woerner, M. G. Behavior therapy, supportive psychotherapy, imipramine and phobias. Unpublished manuscript, Long Island Jewish-Hillside Medical Center, Hillside Division, Glen Oaks, New York, 1976.

CHAPTER 11

Crisis Intervention and Emergency Psychotherapy

JAMES N. BUTCHER, ZIGFRIDS T. STELMACHERS, AND GAIL R. MAUDAL

Situational crises prompt many individuals to seek psychological attention, as the following cases illustrate:

Esther, a 63-year-old outpatient from a mental health clinic, presented herself one evening complaining that she had had a "breakdown" and could not continue working. She was very agitated, depressed, and mildly confused. She wanted to be hospitalized. She thought she had taken a large number of pills earlier in the evening.

Ellen, a 38-year-old housewife, learned that her husband had been injured in a motorcycle accident that morning and was not expected to live. She became quite frantic and was not able to take care of the children. She was brought to the mental health center by a neighbor who became quite concerned when she found the 2-year-old daughter wandering in the neighborhood unattended.

Tom, a 24-year-old medical student, became quite despondent and suicidal after learning of his failing performance on several major courses in his program. For several days he remained in his room and would not take telephone calls from his home. Finally friends persuaded him to go to the health center.

The critical nature of these situations is reflected in the immediacy and urgency of the real-life problems facing each individual, and in the apparent immobility or inability of the person to move toward a satisfactory resolution by himself or herself. A crisis situation is one in which an outcome of some sort is inevitable, and prompt corrective action is consequently important. An effective intervention, which is aimed at alleviating the crisis or better yet enabling the person to act decisively, may prevent further and perhaps more severe consequences from developing. A timely positive intervention at the point of crisis may prove more effective than many hours of therapy later on.

Justification for providing emergency psychological treatment or crisis intervention is not difficult to find. Many individuals who are faced with a psychological crisis may find traditional hospitals and clinics inaccessible to them when they are most needed—at the peak of the crisis. Situational crises frequently do not fit into the 9-to-5 workday of many mental health facilities. The past 15 years have witnessed a great deal of development in the provision of emergency mental health services; and crisis intervention services, once considered a stopgap measure, have become an important treatment of choice for many psychological problems. Crisis intervention programs originated as an attempt to serve unmet treatment needs of individuals, but now they have come into their own as an important treatment alternative. The first section of this chapter reviews briefly the origins of crisis intervention, and subsequent sections are devoted to theoretical formulations of crisis intervention, goals of crisis therapy, assessment in crisis intervention, the tactics of crisis therapy, evaluation in crisis intervention, and issues in the ongoing management of a crisis intervention center.

ORIGINS OF CRISIS INTERVENTION

Crisis intervention has several historical origins. In most instances in which emergency therapeutic interventions were initiated, the situation was such as to require immediate action or attention, usually for larger numbers of individuals than could be managed with typical therapeutic means, and generally with little opportunity for obtaining a great deal of personal historical information. Four major historical developments that have contributed to the present-day crisis intervention movement are the treatment of traumatic neuroses in World War II, attention to grief work, interest in suicide prevention, and the free clinic movement.

Treatment of Traumatic Neuroses in World War II

The upheaval in family relationships and the personally stressful situations brought about by World War II created a great need for expanded psychological services. In order to meet the treatment needs of large numbers of soldiers who experienced stress-related neuroses, new treatment approaches were developed. Short-term treatment of the individual was undertaken as soon as possible after breakdown had occurred, before newly acquired maladaptive patterns of behavior could be consolidated and incorporated into the soldier's total adjustment (Grinker & Spiegel, 1944, 1945; Kardiner, 1941).

In order to prevent a collapse of self-esteem, the individual was kept in his unit and given less stressful duties. These early forms of crisis intervention were highly effective in relieving the symptoms of neurosis and in preventing the individual from retreating into more maladaptive behavioral patterns. They served to underscore one of the tenets of crisis theory: that intervention at the time of disruption is not only effective, but in a sense preventive as well.

Grief Work and Development of Early Crisis Clinics

The work of Erich Lindemann (1944), in which he described treatment of grief reactions of families of people who died in the Coconut Grove nightclub fire in 1943, is a classic study in crisis intervention. Lindemann compared brief and prolonged grief reactions in individuals and concluded that the duration of the grief reaction was a function of the bereavement process, or how the individual handled the grief. He delineated phases of grief work through which a person must go to free himself or herself from the deceased and readjust to the environment without the presence of the deceased person.

Lindemann's contribution to understanding the normal process of grief and the demonstration that an individual may be helped during the process of grief work established the efficacy of crisis intervention treatment. One of Lindemann's most important formulations for crisis theory was that behavior in a crisis situation is unique—it is related to the crisis situation itself and not to the premorbid personality as postulated by traditional psychiatric practice (Kaplan, 1968). Lindemann described several characteristics associated with stress disorders: (a) They are usually acute in nature, with a specifiable onset and of relatively brief duration; (b) the number of alternative courses of action, whether adaptive or maladaptive, is limited; (c) the possible courses of action are usually identifiable and predictive of outcome; (d) the observable symptoms of stress are usually transitory features of the individual's struggles to overcome his or her problem situation rather than signs of mental disorder; and (e) characteristic psychological tasks posed by each situation are specifiable.

Since Lindemann's work other investigators have studied crises related to bereavement (Kraus & Lilienfeld, 1959; Madison, 1968; Parkes, 1964; Parkes, Benjamin, & Fitzgerald, 1969); transitional states (Tyhurst, 1958); and premature birth (Bibring, Dwyer, Huntington, & Valenstein, 1961; Caplan, 1964; Kaplan & Mason, 1965). These studies have supported Lindemann's theory of transitional pathology associated with crisis states.

The work of Lindemann and his collaborator, Caplan, not only contributed to the theoretical formulation of crisis work, but also influenced the development of the first crisis clinics. These were generally supported by and often attached to existing hospitals or clinics. Caplan began a project on the study of crisis at the Family Guidance Center at Harvard prior to 1954, and other crisis treatment facilities followed shortly in the early 1950s in Galveston (Ritchie, 1960); at Bellak's Trouble-Shooting Clinic in Elmhurst, New York (1958); at the Langley Porter Clinic in San Francisco (Kalis, 1961); at the Benjamin Rush Center in Los Angeles (Jacobson, Wilner, Morley, Schneider, Strickler, & Sommer, 1965); at Cincinnati General Hospital (MacLeod & Tinnin, 1966); and at Massachusetts General Hospital in Boston (Sifneos, 1964).

Suicide Prevention

The crisis of imminent suicide has for a long time been the most visible form of crisis state. Consequently much of the impetus for crisis intervention derived from the suicide prevention movement. In Britain, the "befrienders" or Samaritan Movement was organized in 1953. This group of concerned lay persons set forth the goal of preventing suicide by providing companionship to people who identified themselves as being in crisis (Bagley, 1971). In 1958 the first suicide prevention center was established in Los Angeles (Farberow & Schneidman, 1961). The successful management of suicide-related crises was made possible by some innovative *turning points* which were subsequently incorporated into the crisis intervention movement (Farberow, 1968). These included development of the telephone as the primary means of communicating with people who needed help, the initiation of an around-the-clock and weekend service, and the introduction of nonprofessional personnel into the role of providing direct patient contact (Helig, Farberow, Litman, & Shneidman, 1968).

The Free Clinic Movement

The development of free clinics represents the most recent contribution to the crisis intervention movement. During the late 1960s and early 1970s, the mental health field witnessed the growth of a large number of nontraditional treatment facilities. The focus of such helping agencies was to provide crisis management assistance to individuals who would otherwise have no place to go. In several large metropolitan areas a wide variety of agencies opened to serve a specific group or problem situation, for example, gay rights, draft counseling, suicide hot lines, drug-related emergencies, venereal disease, and emergency counseling programs. Whereas some of these treatment or referral facilities were initiated by professionals such as physicians, psychologists, and social workers, a large number of them were begun with the energies of concerned lay persons and students.

It was primarily the antiestablishment reaction accompanying the counterculture movement of the late 1960s that produced great diversity in free clinic innovations. This period of youth revolt against governmental policies in Vietnam and of wide utilization of and experimentation with drugs, particularly hallucinogens, produced not only a high level of tension and maladaptive life-style options, but also an acute mistrust for anything resembling authority or establishment. A large segment of the United States population was in the vulnerable position of being at high risk for developing psychological problems, but at the same time had no access to sources of help since establishment agencies were considered unsympathetic to their problems.

A primary value of the free clinics was to provide a nonestablishment staff who spoke the language and shared the values of the counselee (Freudenberger, 1972; Smith, Luce, & Dernburg, 1970). This situation fostered the development of several free clinics across the country, which revolutionized thinking about the treatment and delivery of mental health services. Free clinics introduced "rap sessions" in which "street people" came together at the facility without registering or otherwise identifying themselves. They became involved in group discussions which kept them together but did not make them "straight." Such self-treatment, at what was almost a mutual aid society for youth, was often all the help that was needed, but it sometimes served as a stepping stone into more systematic group or individual therapy.

The free clinics of the sixties served an important function: They provided crisis intervention counseling to individuals who, as a result of their antiestablishment attitudes, were alienated from available mental health resources. Over time, however, many "traditional" facilities began to offer emergency psychological services on a 24-hour basis.

Although many of the early free clinics vanished from the scene—some after only a few months—some clinics still exist and continue to provide psychological services to individuals in crisis. Some of the remaining free clinics have actually moved into the "traditional" mental health sector, receiving financial support from governmental agencies and providing psychological services to underserved populations.

In summary, the articulation of crisis intervention methods and theory has stemmed from various sources. It would be incorrect to assume that the evolution has been a smooth or natural one. Yet despite its diverse origins and the inherent difficulties with any novel approach to human problem solving, crisis intervention therapy has established itself as a viable, useful vehicle of intervention. What began as an expedient, pressed on us because of varying external circumstances, has generated unanticipated and gratifying benefits. Today crisis work is no longer seen as a last alternative, far inferior to reconstructive, uncovering long-term treatment; it is looked at instead as a legitimate treatment alternative and even as the treatment of choice for certain kinds of problems and certain types of patients: "Crisis intervention is not a second-class psychotherapy, but a unique form of intervention, based on its own unique assumptions." (Goldberg, 1973, p.350).*

THEORETICAL FORMULATIONS OF CRISIS INTERVENTION

The theoretical formulation of crisis intervention was primarily the contribution of Gerald Caplan and derived from his work with Erich Lindemann at the Community Mental Health Project in Cambridge, Massachusetts (Caplan, 1964). Crisis theory centers around the concept of a homeostatic equilibrium in which the individual is in a relative state of psychosocial balance. That is, the person's usual coping or adaptive techniques are operating sufficiently to handle his or her daily problems. When difficult problem situations present themselves, the individual calls into play the mechanisms that have worked successfully in previous situations. A crisis situation occurs, according to Caplan (1961), "when a person faces an obstacle to important life goals that is, for a time, insurmountable through the utilization of customary methods of problem solving." The obstacle may result in an emotionally hazardous situation when the individual perceives a potentially unmanageable threat surrounding it. The crisis is an internally experienced, acute disturbance resulting from the individual's inability to cope with ominous events encompassing him or her.

The crisis is usually followed by a period of disorganization and confusion, resulting in generally ineffective attempts at problem solution. In time, usually about 4 to 6 weeks, according to Caplan, some outcome to the crisis situation (for better or

---

* A number of recent publications highlight the extent of crisis intervention therapy in recent years: Hoff (1978); Butcher and Koss (1978); Butcher and Kolotkin (1979); Budman (1981); Calhoun, Selby, and King (1976); Mann (1978); Resnik, Ruben, and Ruben (1975); Rosenbaum and Beebe (1975); Puryear (1979); Weinstein (1979); Auerbach and Kilman (1977); Figley (1978); and Sifneos (1979).

worse) has been reached. This outcome can be positively directed with timely and effective crisis intervention techniques, and the individual at this point in a crisis situation is highly amenable to therapeutic intervention.

Caplan (1964) delineated four phases of a typical crisis situation. When the crisis begins to develop and the individual feels the emotional tension and disorganization, he or she attempts to manage the situation by his or her previously learned coping mechanisms. In the second phase these coping efforts fail to resolve the problem, and further disorganization ensues. The third phase is characterized by a greatly increased tension level and further mobilization of internal and outside resources. He or she may seek help or change his or her direction or goals. If these intensified efforts fail to resolve the crisis and lower the tension, then the fourth phase of crisis develops—extensive personality disorganization and perhaps emotional breakdown.

Crisis Intervention versus Crisis Therapy

One of the primary functions of many crisis centers has been to handle cases that do not readily fit into the more traditional mental health offerings. Although formal "treatment" of people in crisis is a relatively new professional endeavor, it has become apparent that not all emotional crises are of the same type and magnitude, and thus cannot be managed in the same way. Each situation requires careful evaluation to determine what form of intervention is needed and what kinds of outcomes can be expected.

Jacobson, Strickler, and Morley (1968) and Morley (1970) describe four levels of crisis intervention, all of which are considered effective. The first level is called *environmental manipulation*. At this level the helper serves as a referral source or puts the troubled person in touch with an appropriate resource. The second level, termed *general support*, involves working in a limited way with the troubled person—interested listening without threatening or challenging his or her statements. The third level, characteristic of Caplan's approach, Morley calls the *generic approach*. "This level requires that the helping agent have a thorough knowledge of crisis in general, specific crises in particular, and kinds of approaches which are particularly effective in resolving specific crises." The fourth level is called *individually tailored*, and it requires in addition to the specification of the first three levels that the crisis worker be trained in abnormal psychology and personality theory and have a thorough knowledge of psychodynamics. The intervention on this level assumes that the crisis is related to the individual's long-term personality dynamics.

For the purposes of this chapter, we distinguish between two types of crisis problems that appear at crisis centers or walk-in clinics: *dispositional crisis* cases and *crisis therapy* cases. This distinction will prove useful to the intake worker who is faced with the decision of evaluating for referral or further treatment. The following two cases illustrate some elements of the first general type of crisis problem.

Mary, a 31-year-old separated mother, called regarding a custody fight following an argument with her estranged husband. He refused to bring their 2-year-old child back after a visit. Following an interview, it became apparent that Mary was angry and frightened but generally well functioning. She did not desire or require counseling regarding her life situation. Instead, the conflict she was faced with was a legal one. She was referred to legal aid and a follow-up was conducted to assure that the referral was successful.

An elderly woman was brought to the center by the police after they found her sitting on a curb in −20° weather. She was pleasant and smiling, but couldn't supply any information about herself. Nearby nursing homes were contacted to determine if they had "lost" anyone. The home was located and the police returned her. Follow-up indicated that she was receiving medical attention.

These cases represent dispositional crises. They illustrate the point that not all crises are psychological in nature. Neither Mary nor the elderly woman required nor stood to gain from crisis therapy. However, well-timed intervention may have prevented these crises from developing into ones that would have had more serious consequences.

It is useful, then, to draw a distinction between what might be called *crisis intervention* and what is termed *crisis therapy*. This distinction somewhat parallels Bloom's (1963) distinction between a stressful situation and a crisis. Bloom notes that "crisis differs from stress in that there are time limits to a crisis, but, in general, acute stress is a crisis." The distinction is more clearly expressed through Klein and Lindemann's (1961) definitions of an *emotionally hazardous situation* and a *crisis*. They define an emotionally hazardous situation as "a situation in which a sudden change in the field of social forces causes a person's relations with others, or his expectations of himself to change." Crisis is "a term reserved for the acute, and often prolonged disturbance to an individual or to a social orbit as the result of an emotionally hazardous situation."

One theoretical consideration that helps clarify this distinction is the amount of ego investment a person has in a potential crisis situation. An individual's perceptions of events are "autistic," in the sense that they are highly influenced by his or her personal needs and values. If a person is "needy," requiring much outside support to sustain his or her quota of self-esteem, even a mildly stressful situation may plunge him or her into a crisis. Conversely, if a person is relatively need-free and has a healthy self-concept, even highly stressful situations may not represent a blow to his or her self-esteem. Strickler and Allgeyer (1967) view crises as occurring "only if the individual senses that he does not possess available means of coping with the hazard, which is seen consciously or unconsciously as a vital threat to his narcissistic, libidinal or dependency needs and supplies." In such cases crisis therapy is indicated. The person is encouraged to focus on the factors that precipitated the crisis and to explore new, potentially adaptive means of handling it. If a person's ability to cope is not threatened by a stressful situation, he or she is a candidate for crisis intervention, but not crisis therapy. The goal is not restoration of a psychic homeostasis, since the balance has not been upset. Instead the goal is that of adroit dispositional management, that is, meeting the nonpsychological needs of the situation. This can involve something as simple as locating a person a bed for the night, or something as complex as providing information about state commitment procedures.

The role of crisis interveners, although perhaps less glamorous than that of crisis therapists, should not be relegated to the status of second-class citizenship. Although the eventual disposition may be simple and clear-cut, the disposition results only after the crisis intervener has made a sufficiently thorough assessment of the stress situation to determine that the crisis is not psychological in nature, or that the stress is perceived as ego-alien in origin and not part of the person's own doing.

An assessment error illustrates this point. One crisis worker saw a 19-year-old male who complained that he suffered from flashbacks. He had taken LSD 9 months previously. Proceeding on the assumption that he was dealing with a typical flashback case, the crisis worker assured the youth that his symptoms were anxiety related and would soon dissipate. He sent him home after encouraging him to call if difficulties persisted. Only in later case supervision did the crisis worker indicate that the flashbacks were periods during which the patient heard voices telling him he was the devil. Additionally, the patient was unemployed and was a "culture dropout" who strongly identified with the "Jesus freak" movement. Although none of these facts is pathognomonic in itself, together they are at least cause for concern and adequate basis for further assessment, probably entailing something more than dispositional management. It is important to note that the role of astute assessment is not only the first phase of crisis therapy, but constitutes an important part of every case, whether the clinician's response is eventually designated crisis intervention or crisis therapy.

Is a crisis situation always easy to identify? Golan (1969) noted that, although a worker sometimes encounters patients with clear-cut presenting problems, more often he or she faces an "undifferentiated, multifaceted problem situation" which is difficult to conceptualize. The components of a crisis situation defined by Sifneos (1960) provide a useful framework for conceptualizing crisis situations. He identified four elements in an emotional crisis: the hazardous event, the vulnerable state, the precipating factor, and the state of crisis itself.

By what practical criteria might we distinguish between crisis intervention cases and crisis therapy cases? It is of course not possible to specify guidelines that would be applicable for every crisis intervention center, since particular staffing situations and typical presenting problems dictate treatment and referral policies. Nevertheless, it is important to recognize that there are factors that are relevant for deciding which cases should be seen in additional therapy sessions by a trained therapist and which cases may be terminated after an initial contact, with or without some provision for follow-up.

In most crisis intervention settings, time and staff resources limit the number of sessions an individual may be seen. However, the point we would like to make is that it is neither necessary nor desirable to see most cases for an extended period of time. Thus the prime consideration involves determining whether a limited, directive intervention, for example, finding the person a place to stay, getting a previously made decision crystallized, and the like, will restore the individual's adjustment to a previous satisfactory level. The essential consideration for continuing an individual in therapy is some determination that he or she may benefit from an extended number of sessions and the accompanying relationship with a therapist. This is a complex decision which must be made jointly by therapist and client on the basis of such factors as the following:

1. *Workability.* Are the problems such as to be manageable with the temporary aid of an outside opinion? That is, are the problems in large part internal and within the power of the individual to resolve?

2. *Capability of self-examination.* Does the individual have the ability to examine with the therapist the problem situation in the light of his or her own contribution to the crisis?

3. *Motivation.* Does the person have the motivation or personal resources to act on his or her own decision? Can he or she accept direction from a therapist? What action has he or she taken thus far to resolve the problems?

4. *Accessibility.* Is he or she presently in therapy elsewhere? In many instances a crisis patient may be in therapy elsewhere, which generally contraindicates setting up a new therapeutic contract.

5. *Advisability in terms of personality structure.* Would a therapeutic relationship (which is inherently directive in nature) be detrimental to the person's future adjustment? It may be that seeing the individual for a longer period of time would serve to define him or her as a "patient" who *needs* a lot of help from others—this may foster negative self-attitudes, which are an undesirable outcome of the intervention. Fostering dependency in a person who prides himself or herself on being "strong" may result in problems worse than those for which he or she originally sought help.

6. *Intrapsychic problems.* Perhaps the most essential characteristic for clients amenable to crisis therapy is that their problems are, to a significant degree, intrapsychic in nature and have resulted in some damage to their self-concept. Treatment calls for a psychodynamic understanding of the problems and an insight-oriented treatment approach.

7. *Treatment history.* It is important to explore the patient's past therapeutic experience, both qualitatively and quantitatively. This can be an especially useful variable in helping the therapist determine whether crisis therapy is indicated. If a patient reveals an extensive history of unsuccessful treatment attempts, one must entertain the hypothesis that he or she is dealing with a "doctor shopper" who terminates when therapy begins to look like work, or an obsessional intellectualizer who views therapy as an end in itself rather than a means which can be utilized to bring about a desired change. In such cases the therapist does well to scrutinize carefully what the patient's expectations of treatment were, what he or she tried to accomplish, what worked and did not work, and why. However, some patients may have legitimately, and in good faith, sought out therapy in the past, and it may be quite reason-

able for them to do so again. In these cases it is useful for the therapist to discern whether the current problem is similar in nature to the previous one, what factors helped the patient in the past, and what other resources were utilized to bring about problem resolution.

8. *Cost–benefit.* Would the benefit that might result from utilizing the available staff resources for this particular patient be worth the cost? This is a difficult question to answer (or even to ask ourselves). There are few clear-cut criteria to guide our judgment of potential "gain." More often the limited resources available restrict what we might like to recommend. The crisis therapist or intake interviewer may have to weigh the question before committing future staff time to a specific case.

Requirements of Capable Crisis Intervention

It is apparent that many crisis problems do not require the attention of highly specialized psychotherapists with advanced professional degrees. Many types of problems may be adroitly handled by an informed and attentive lay person. In some settings paraprofessionals have become increasingly involved in both traditional and nontraditional treatment activities. Part of the impetus for paraprofessional involvement arose from mental health manpower needs, but an equally important stimulus was the dissatisfaction lay people felt toward the traditional therapeutic options during the 60s and 70s. Paraprofessional mental health workers have been recruited from many ranks and strata of the population to perform a variety of therapeutic activities ranging from drug counseling to manning suicide telephones. This lay "therapist" movement has not been unique to the United States. Torrey (1971) reports on the development of emergency psychiatric ambulance services in the Soviet Union, and, in Britain, a far-reaching suicide prevention system, the Samaritan Movement, was founded in 1953 (Bagley, 1971). There has been a rapid development of Samaritan units in many cities since then. The Samaritans offer day or night service—advice, friendship, and other forms of help. The people operating these units usually have no professional training in therapy but are frequently members of the clergy or intelligent lay persons who have been given some training relevant to the Samaritan work. The goal of the Samaritan work is to help prevent suicide. An interesting feature of the Samaritan movement is its emphasis on befriending as opposed to the American preference for counseling. Befriending is what many socially isolated, suicidal individuals need, and befriending is exactly what most mental health professionals and counselors are not supposed to engage in because it is "unprofessional," because it represents "overinvolvement," and because it is generally incompatible with the therapist–client model. Sometimes counselors take their title too literally and use it as a license to advise people about how to live their lives with all the authority vested in the counselor's role. Or, perhaps even worse, the roles of friend and therapist may be mixed, causing confusion in the person seeking help, who is often incapable of differentiating between the two aspects of the interaction. The Samaritans keep the two roles clearly separated: Their volunteers befriend and their consultants provide the necessary professional treatment (Stelmachers, 1976).

In some settings in which paraprofessionals have been utilized as therapists, an almost paradoxical situation is found; paraprofessionals are now assuming the traditional therapy roles they once rejected as narrow or inappropriate. In many instances the paraprofessional steps into this therapist role with very little in the way of traditional training or supervision. It is unfortunate that many paraprofessional groups in the United States have not developed roles or expended their energies in exploring some very unique contributions they might make to mental health work. This is not to imply that paraprofessionals have no useful role in the area of crisis intervention, but rather to suggest that perhaps their full potential and most useful roles have not been fully realized.

In many crisis centers paraprofessionals can provide useful services as crisis interveners, providing they possess or can acquire some skills necessary to the demands of the situation. The following are seen as essential minimum requirements:

1.   The worker must possess an empathic ability which enables him or her to understand the problems being faced by the patient *as* they are being experienced.

2.   He or she must be able to listen attentively and selectively for material relevant to the problem at hand, and to elicit appropriate material from reluctant or verbally–emotionally incapacitated persons.

3.   He or she must be able to listen objectively without imposing his or her own needs, wishes, and values on the material.

4.   He or she must be able to assess the individual's problems, conflicts, assets, and resources in the context of the crisis situation surrounding him or her. This requirement is the most important and the least often met. Before the interview is even half over, the crisis worker must have a tentative formulation of the problem, which allows him or her to determine whether the client is in need of some immediate crisis intervention or perhaps in need of crisis therapy. He or she must be able to evaluate such things as premorbid level of functioning, mental status, suicidal potential, and change motivation. Although he or she need not be a trained psychiatric diagnostician, he or she must be well versed in the clinical significance of important behaviors or symptoms. Many paraprofessionals have not had sufficient training to conduct mental status examinations or to evaluate sufficiently the patient's premorbid level of functioning and should be closely supervised if these activities are required. Assessment in the initial interview is considered in greater detail in a later section.

5.   He or she must have up-to-date knowledge of the community resources that might be potential referral options, and be aware of various administrative/legal procedures that may be encountered (e.g., categorical assistance qualifications, child abuse legislation, commitment procedures for mental illness, and emancipation rights).

6.   One potentially valuable characteristic for the crisis worker is that he or she be a member of the particular subculture or counterculture group that might utilize the agency.

Distinctions between Crisis Therapy and Other Therapeutic Approaches

Crisis therapy can be distinguished from other forms of therapy, including psycho-analytic psychotherapy, client-centered therapy, and even many "short-term" thera-peutic approaches, on the basis of several variables such as time requirements, therapeutic goals, methods utilized, types of presenting problems, and characteris-tics of patients seen.*

Crisis therapy is generically a form of short-term therapy. Although it is still in the process of being defined and characterized, the broader issue of the legitimacy of short-term versus long-term, or traditional psychoanalytic, treatment is generally settled at this point. Several studies have found no support for the hypothesis that the number of treatment sessions is positively related to amount of therapeutic gain (Lorr, McNair, Michaux, & Raskin, 1962; Muench, 1965; Shlien, Mosak, & Drei-kurs, 1962). In a well-controlled study, Shlien, Mosak, and Dreikurs (1962), em-ploying the Q-sort technique, found that imposing time limits on two types of psychotherapy, client-centered and Adlerian, provided more immediate improve-ment than time-unlimited therapy. All three groups improved eventually, however, whereas no change was observed in a group of normals and a group of patients awaiting treatment. Shlien et al. found that time-limited therapy is not only as effec-tive, but twice as efficient (20 sessions vs. 37 sessions) as time-unlimited treatment. Their conclusion was that "time limits place emphasis where it belongs; on quality and process, rather than upon quantity."

Psychoanalytic and Short-Term Treatment

Crisis and short-term therapy can be readily distinguished from traditional psycho-analysis on the basis of time requirements, since the process of psychoanalysis is generally a lengthy, intrapsychically complicated, and generally nondirective treat-ment method.** Yet many of the principles of psychoanalysis have been applied to short-term therapy. In the late 1930s Alexander (Alexander & French, 1946) con-ducted several studies in an effort to abbreviate psychoanalytic treatment, that is, to develop techniques of treatment from psychoanalysis that could bring about desired therapeutic results in a shortened time span. He believed that the way for a patient to be relieved of his or her neurotic conflicts was for him or her to undergo new emotional experiences that could undo the punishing effects of early (usually child-hood) emotional experiences. He noted that emotional adjustment had become a problem for a large proportion of the population, and that "here lies the most vital function of psychotherapy: to give rational aid to all those who show early signs of

---

* For an extended discussion of the distinctions between short-term emergency therapy and other thera-peutic approaches, see Aguilera, Messick, and Farrell (1970); Butcher and Koss (1978).

** Interestingly, however, even Freud was not opposed to the idea of brief therapy and, in fact, suc-cessfully treated the noted conductor Bruno Walter for a neurotic reaction in six sessions (Sterba, 1951). Freud (1919) noted, "It is very probable, too, that the application of our therapy to numbers will compel us to alloy the pure gold of analysis plentifully with the copper of direct suggestion" (pp. 167–168).

maladjustment, a flexible approach based on sound principles of psychodynamics and adjustment to the great variety of those in need is therefore a pressing necessity of our day" (Alexander & French, 1946). He pointed out that psychodynamic principles can be used for therapeutic effect regardless of the duration of treatment, whether for just one or two interviews or for several years. More recently other psychoanalytically oriented but short-term approaches to psychotherapy have been published (e.g., Bellak & Small, 1965; Malan, 1976, 1979; Mann, 1973; Strupp, 1981).

There are other factors that differentiate crisis therapy from short-term and traditional psychoanalysis besides length of treatment. Crisis therapy can be distinguished from both according to the characteristics of the presenting problem and the manner in which the problem is treated. The person in crisis, regardless of what his or her adaptive potential may be, presents himself or herself at a time in life when his or her adaptive and creative capacities are inadequate to handle the change of input to his or her system. Phrased simply, something has changed with him or her so that he or she has lost a sense of mastery and in desperation is reaching out. He or she is different from the short-term or traditional long-term patient in that he or she is currently faced with a perceived (often reality-based) crisis that must be resolved. To understand the crisis and help the person resolve it, the therapist begins by actively developing a rapid and clear-cut understanding of the precipitating factor and the personal relevance of that factor for the patient. Strickler and LaSor (1970) note that "without a clear picture of all the elements leading to a crisis, utilization of the crisis intervention model is impossible and the sessions begin to resemble conventional short-term therapy with the focus on pathology, rather than on the crisis itself." Whereas the psychoanalytic and other traditional approaches often deemphasize the focal symptoms and precipitating factors and place major importance on exposing the unconscious conflicts underlying them (Frank, 1966), placing the treatment focus on the precipitating factor is the most salient characteristic of crisis therapy.

Another dimension that distinguishes crisis therapy from traditional short-term psychotherapy is the characteristics of at least part of the patient population. Undoubtedly there is some overlap between the crisis population and the short-term therapy population, in part because anyone can at some time experience a crisis, and also because some people enter other forms of therapy as a result of successful crisis treatment. However, there are subsegments of the crisis population whose only contact with mental health treatment is during periods of crisis. Parad (1966), perhaps provocatively, once suggested that crisis intervention may be most validly applicable for the very strong or the very weak, for those requiring only short periods of help and for those not motivated for continuing services. The "weak" are those who have severely limited adaptive capacities resulting from constitutional endowment or pervasive early-life experiences, such as the marginally compensated person who resists medication except for brief periods when he or she is overpowered by symptoms. The motivation for change in this group is limited, and the benefits received from longer contacts probably do not exceed the costs. The "strong" are those who have healthy adaptive potential, but who for a time are faced with nearly insurmountable real-life stress, such as death or financial setback.

Some authors have suggested that certain diagnostic types are particularly amenable or not amenable to crisis intervention therapy. Goldenberg (1973), for example, concludes that the following types are properly classified as psychiatric emergencies and are likely to require and benefit from crisis therapy: (a) severe depressive reactions; (b) acute psychotic states; (c) hyperactive excited states; (d) acute anxiety and panic reactions; (e) acute hysterical reactions; (f) miscellaneous groups of intoxications; (g) severe fear and hysterical manifestations as a result of sexual attack; (h) separation anxiety; (i) fire setting; and (j) grief and bereavement. Hoch (1965) recommends against brief intervention for patients who exhibit chronic psychiatric disorders for which they have never received treatment (e.g., long-standing obsessive–compulsive neuroses or chronic psychosomatic reactions), for patients with marked sexual aberrations, and for patients with primary depression; he recommends it as the treatment of choice for anxiety states, hysterical reactions, homosexual panic, and acute psychosomatic disorders. Castelnuovo-Tedesco (1966) indicates that brief treatment does not work if the patient is outspokenly self-centered, passive–dependent, masochistic, or self-destructive.

It should be emphasized that a crisis intervention approach should ideally be problem centered rather than diagnosis centered. To list several diagnostic types as particularly suitable for crisis therapy misses one essential point: that the suitability of this particular treatment mode does not depend on a given type of individual but rather on a given type of *situation*. In this sense, any diagnostic or personality type is suitable for crisis therapy, depending on what is happening to that individual at a given time. Thus, the same individual may appropriately require crisis intervention, crisis therapy, or even long-term reconstructive psychotherapy at different points in his or her life.

Wolberg (1965) advocates long-term treatment for patients in the following circumstances: (a) where extensive personality reconstruction is the prime objective; (b) where dependency is so entrenched that prolonged support is essential; (c) where there are persistent and uncontrollable acting-out tendencies, as in some homosexuals, psychopaths, drug addicts, alcoholics, and individuals driven by repressed infantile needs to involve themselves in self-destructive and dangerous activities; and (d) where there is constant and irrestrainable anxiety. However, he recommends short-term treatment for patients in whom the breakdown is of recent origin and whose personality structure and defenses have enabled them to function satisfactorily prior to the present illness; where the goal is a resolution of an acute upset in a chronic personality; and where the goal is reconstruction of personality in cases unsuited for, or who are unable to avail themselves of, long-term therapy, for example, persons who possess strong dependency drives but are able to operate with some degree of independence and may become infantilized by prolonged therapy, or persons with a fragile ego structure which may shatter through the use of probing techniques or because of violent transference reactions.

The first two groups of patients that Wolberg considers appropriate for short-term therapy resemble the types of patients we consider appropriate for crisis therapy. Space limitations prevent a more extensive and comprehensive listing of patient characteristics for crisis therapy. Those presented here should serve only as general support for the idea that crisis therapy is not for every patient. Specifically, however, the crisis worker is best advised not to restrict his or her services along too many predetermined lines. Progress in crisis therapy depends more on the individual's ability and motivation to return to his or her former level of functioning than on his or her diagnostic label. Treatment focuses on the crisis itself, rather than on long-standing pathology or well-ingrained character problems. It is also important to remember that channeling a patient into a suitable form of therapy is a proper and often profitable therapeutic endeavor in itself.

One last group for whom crisis therapy has proved useful and for whom it is often the only kind of treatment available includes patients from lower sociocultural groups. Several studies have documented that lower-class persons are less likely than others to be accepted as patients to receive treatment beyond diagnostic workup, and less likely to stay in treatment through the prescribed duration of the therapy. (Brill & Storrow, 1960; Hollingshead & Redlich, 1958; Hunt, 1960; Lief, Lief, Warren, & Heath, 1961; Lorion, 1973, 1974; Rosenthal & Frank, 1958). These studies suggest that even when cost of treatment is not a factor, problems such as bus fares, babysitters, clinic hours, and residential mobility militate against involvement. It has also been suggested that the lower-class person's time perspective is limited, that he or she has difficulty conceptualizing delay of treatment rewards for lengthy periods, that he or she encounters an intense transference distortion, and that he or she does not value (or is less able to engage in) psychotherapeutic contracts in which the principal element is "talk."

Jacobson (1965) makes the following observation in this latter regard:

> The situation is very different when patient and therapist agree to meet around a specific crisis which the patient experiences. Any successful approach to psychotherapy when the therapist and patient are psychosocial strangers must, at least at first, minimize the difference between the persons involved and maximize what unites them. Everyone beyond a certain age has personally experienced the major and minor crisis connected with childhood and adolescence. . . . Since crisis experiences cut across cultural lines, the therapist, on the basis of his own experiences, can achieve empathy with the patient. The patient in turn senses that the therapist is able to respond empathically. . . . In other words, the motivating forces in crisis ontogenetically precede cultural differentiation and thus have universal elements.

Jacobson points out that special advantages are to be gained from crisis therapy for this population because the patient's crisis becomes the deliberate focus of treatment, whereas in many traditional psychiatric clinics this is not the case. The circumscribed nature of the therapy, the major emphasis on action versus "talk cure," and the brevity of the treatment are also likely to decrease the possibility of difficult transference distortions. Empirical studies at the Benjamin Rush Center bear out these ideas (Jacobson, 1965). About 54% of the center's patient population falls into Classes IV and V, the two lowest classes in the Social Stratification System of Hollingshead and Redlich (1958). No relationship is found at the center between social class and either variables related to the therapeutic process or number of visits, percentages treated, and rating of improvement at termination. Furthermore, by meeting at first on the common ground of crisis, the therapist and client gradually work through the problems of their different backgrounds. One study (Chafetz, 1964) found that patients who are first seen on a walk-in basis are more motivated for longer-term treatment than those who are not.

GOALS OF CRISIS THERAPY

In crisis therapy it is of course necessary to work within the constraints of some essential compromises. Goals must usually be limited. However, we concur with Wolberg (1965) that "once a basic modification has been accomplished, irrespective of how tiny, the adaptive equation becomes unbalanced and more substantial alterations can continue." The following four goals, though not exhaustive, provide a useful framework in which the crisis therapist can direct his or her efforts.

1. *Symptom relief*. The word *symptom* refers to any complaint for which the patient seeks treatment (Battle, Imber, Hoehn-Saric, Stone, Nash, & Frank, 1966). These may include disturbances of performance or communicative behavior, or states of subjective distress.

Crisis therapy and other short-term therapies have often been characterized as directed at symptom relief, whereas long-term psychotherapy is seen as reconstructive, dealing with the uncovering of unconscious impulses and long-standing maladaptive trends. The conclusion that generally follows is that symptom relief is in itself a compromised goal. This distinction, however, is more apparent than real, and at best it represents an unfortunate dichotomy.

Wolberg (1965) maintains that it is time therapists overcame the "prejudice of depth," because "psychotherapy is no mining operation that depends for its yield exclusively on excavated psychic ore." He points out, "We have to accept the fact that no single form of therapy known today in psychiatry is anything but non-specific and hence is directed at symptoms." Furthermore, the empirical success using techniques of behavior modification (see Chapter 1) suggests that symptom removal can be a major stepping stone toward personality growth and reorganization. One might visualize, for example, a man who seeks help because he is virtually immobilized by anxiety attacks. The therapist is able to formulate a reasonable psychodynamic interpretation for his own understanding, but the patient is too immobilized to integrate it. Consequently the therapist provides the patient with medication, which perhaps is the purest form of symptom-relief treatment. Suppose, then, that the patient is now able to resume his job, take his place as a contributing family member, regain some confidence and, recognizing that he is back in control, perhaps even confront the conflict that initially produced his anxiety. The goal of symptom relief has been attained, but it has resulted in such intangibles as increments in self-esteem and perhaps even changes in self-concept. It is apparent, then, that symptom relief is not an inferior goal. One may address symptoms as a means to an end, or as an end in themselves, but the results may be the same.

2. *Aid in restoration of the individual's adjustment balance.* There are three restoration target goals the therapist might consider, depending on the complexity of the patient's problems and the resources at hand. The scope of the therapy sessions and the projected modifications depend on the sights that are taken. These three goals are (a) prevention of further decompensation, (b) restoration to the level of adjustment that existed prior to the crisis, and (c) restoration to an optimal level of functioning.

The appropriateness of goal (a) versus goal (b) or (c) depends in large part on the goals the patient brings to crisis therapy and on his or her availability and openness to intervention. We agree with Strickler and Allgeyer (1967) that the minimum "goal of crisis intervention is preventive, since the outcome can be affected significantly by the presence of timely help."

It is apparent that the third level, restoration to or achievement of the person's optimal level of functioning, represents the largest gain for the patient. The achievement of goal (b) versus goal (c) depends largely on the degree of skill of the therapist, specifically his or her ability to view the crisis as the culmination of maladaptive coping and to help the patient acquire a broader range of adaptive coping mechanisms.

3. *An understanding of the precipitating factors.* The doctrine of psychic determinism is one of the oldest principles of psychological thought. The applied psychologist proceeds from the assumption that behavior is caused. Similarly, crises are not random occurrences, but result from a particular interplay of forces in which the individual is a main character.

When people enter any form of therapy, there are usually precipitating factors that precede and influence their decision to seek help. However, the precipitating factor takes on added importance when a person is in crisis. It is imperative that the therapist discern very rapidly what the precipitants are, because this is where crisis therapy begins. The precipitating factor is often the proverbial "last straw." In a crisis, it *always* exists, although its exact form and meaning may be submerged and camouflaged. The veracity of this strong statement is upheld even with patients who have a "chronically" poor adjustment and generally poor prognosis.

Birley and Brown (1970), for example, studied 50 schizophrenic patients and discovered that 60% of them had experienced an event that would be considered potentially disturbing within 3 weeks of their most recent relapse. Oberleder (1970), examining 12 patients who were diagnosed as having senile psychosis or arteriosclerosis with psychosis and had an average age of 76.4, found that *all* of them had precipitating crises that preceded their hospitalization. In a well-controlled study comparing 185 depressed patients with normal controls, Paykel, Myers, Dienelt, Klerman, Lindenthal, and Pepper (1969) determined that depressed patients interviewed after substantial improvement reported almost three times as many life events in the 6 months immediately prior to the symptomatic onset of depression as did controls during a comparable 6-month period. Events generally regarded as undesirable and those involving losses or exits from the social field particularly distinguished the depressed patients from the controls. These included marital difficulties, deaths and illnesses, and work changes.

Bloom (1963) found that a crisis is usually defined clinically primarily in terms of knowledge of a precipitating event and secondarily in terms of a slow resolution. In an effort to determine how clinicians identify a crisis, he presented eight expert judges with 14 case histories constructed so that it was possible to study the differential effects of five variables: (a) knowledge or lack of knowledge of a precipitating event; (b) rapidity of onset of reactions; (c) awareness or lack of awareness on the part of the patient of inner discomfort; (d) evidence of behavioral disorganization; and (e) rapidity of resolution. He found that the judgment of crisis is made significantly more often when there is a known precipitating event than when the precipitating event is unknown.

4. *Knowledge of the origin of the crisis in past experiences and prevailing personality problems.* We have noted previously that the most desirable goal of crisis intervention is not only to prevent further decompensation or restore a person to a prior level of adjustment, but to assist him or her in achieving or regaining his or her optimal level of functioning. To achieve this goal, it is necessary for the therapist and patient to formulate not only what the crisis is, but "why" it is. One often finds in examining the precipitating factors that there is nothing inherently crisis-producing about a certain set of precipitating events. There is no one event that pathognomonically suggests crisis. Of course, there are some life events such as unexpected deaths, military combat, or natural disasters which would predictably result in crises for all but the most adaptable. But this type of crisis, with clear-cut, readily understood precipitants, represents only a fraction of the crises encountered. Psychological breakdown can occur on the basis of the accumulation of various stressors over time. This is a different concept from the specific reactivity of one person to a specific stress whose meaning derives from a very personal and individual interpretation made by that person. It is also different from the impact of an overwhelming stress, such as death of a spouse, which would probably be universally strong. It is more often the case that the precipitating factors can only be understood in terms of their dynamic, symbolic, and personal meaning to the patient. One must ask why it is that one executive reacts to a business failure with overwhelming feelings of guilt, failure, and loss of esteem, while another integrates such an event, chalks it up to experience, and goes on about the business of living. It becomes apparent, then, that simply identifying and isolating the factors that precipitate the request for help are only the beginning steps.

We believe that in many cases a successful resolution of an ego-invested problem cannot occur without an examination of the forces that produced the problem. Menninger (1954) comments in this regard that "the ego always does more than attempt to manage the immediate emergency. In spite of resistance implicit in the semistabilized emergency adjustment, the ego perennially endeavors to return to its original normal adjustment level." This is similar to the adaptational approach presented by Frank (1966). Frank explains that his adaptational approach can be best understood theoretically in terms of its relationship with the psychoanalytic and behavioral therapy models, which may be seen as occupying opposite ends of a continuum. In the psychoanalytic approach the focal symptom is seen as secondary to the unconscious conflicts underlying it. The goal of analysis is to produce insight and self-awareness, with the assumption that behavioral change will follow. At the other end of the continuum lie particular forms of behavior therapy that concentrate explicitly on the removal of focal symptoms by utilizing laws of learning.

The adaptational approach both resembles and differs from these two theoretical constructions. It assumes that symptoms—and we would add crises—are meaningful communications. Hence the therapeutic aim is not solely to remove the stress, but to understand the communication. The focus is on precipitating factors rather than historical intrapsychic causes of the crisis per se, but the emphasis is not completely ahistorical, because the therapist understands that behavior is multiply determined and actively seeks out any intrapsychic causes that give meaning to the currently encountered symptoms and precipitating factors. Harris, Kalis, and Freeman (1963) note, "The most apparent difference between this type of brief treatment and more traditional forms of psychotherapy is in the systematic focusing on the current situation, with historical material utilized only as it arises spontaneously and relates directly to the current problems."

This approach does not assume that there is any "basic" conflict that must be discovered before a crisis can be resolved. It suggests instead that, in order to understand and consequently deal with the personal nature of the precipitating factors, one must also look beyond them to potential antecedents such as child-rearing patterns, past traumas, or simply personality trait patterns and the other people with whom the patient interacts.

The Legitimacy of Single-Contact Therapy

Psychotherapeutic intervention need not entail a long series of contacts. Actually, most patients beginning psychotherapy expect the therapy to require only 5 to 10 sessions (Garfield, 1971), and several recent studies show that many patients do not remain in therapy beyond that. Rubenstein and Lorr (1956) reported that between 30% and 60% of patients accepted for therapy terminate within the first 6 sessions. Rogers (1960) reported that over half of the clinic populations he surveyed dropped out before the eighth session. A large-scale survey of 979,000 patients who had received some type of psychiatric treatment found an average of 4.7 contacts with the therapist (National Center for Health Statistics, reported in Lorion, 1974).

Two studies by Goin, Yamamoto, and Silverman (1965) and Yamamoto and Goin (1965) suggest that patients usually leave treatment at clearly defined points and not just in the middle of treatment. It seems to be the case not only that individuals expect a brief therapeutic experience and usually receive it, but also that they frequently leave when they have arrived at some subjectively defined end point. Many individuals seek short-term help because they feel less threatened in the relative anonymity of a brief therapeutic encounter; because they have worked through the problem situation, weighed all alternatives, and simply need an outside opinion and a boost to get started; or because they do not wish to reevaluate the long-gone past, but simply need an evaluation or opinion from an objective outsider. Many people seek reassurance that a decision they have made was the correct one.

Every crisis psychotherapy session should be conducted as though it may be the last contact with the patient. A large number of individuals do not return for additional sessions, even when the therapist asks them to return. Ideally, the crisis therapist should consider all cases as single contacts and assume that the individual will, after some redefinition of his or her situation and remotivation, be able to modify his or her life events without continued support of the therapist. It may be necessary for the therapist to schedule additional sessions (and the patient *may* return) to work on other problems or to do a follow-up; however, the therapist should not bank on having the person in for another session next week. In crisis therapy, next week is now.

What can be accomplished in a single session? A great deal if the therapist keeps his or her eye on the goal. The fact that single contacts with a therapeutic agent can be beneficial has been well documented in social work literature (Parad, 1971). Early social workers such as McCord (1931) and Reynolds (1932) noted that the "short contact" or the single-interview case can produce positive results by clearing up problems that are of immediate concern. Wayne (1966) stated, "We consider it significant, conceptually, if not statistically, that some patients undergoing crisis therapy show prompt and relatively lasting improvement as the result of a single interview" (p. 114). The philosophy of short-term clinical intervention in social casework was summed up nicely by Taft (1933): "If there is not therapeutic understanding and use of one interview, many interviews, equally barren, will not help. In the single interview . . . there is no time to hide behind material, no time to explore the past or future. I myself am the remedy at this moment, if there is any."

The Modus Operandi of the Crisis Therapist

People in crisis appearing for an initial interview at a crisis center may be emotionally distraught or blunted after having tried "everything else possible" and failed. They are usually desperate for help and hopeful that a solution can be provided. They arrive with preconceived ideas of what to expect from a crisis therapist, or may be so preoccupied with the situation that they are almost surprised when they find themselves discussing private matters with a stranger. What kind of a person do the patients find? How can they immediately and quite openly discuss often sensitive and usually painful matters? Are there definable attributes of a good crisis therapist that encourage "instant" rapport and trust? Or is the crisis situation itself usually so urgent and overwhelming that just *any* person will suffice in that role? We think not. Bellak and Small (1965) observe that, by definition, brief psychotherapy involves intervention within the shortest possible period of time, and thus it cannot be haphazard. Crisis therapy, by virtue of its fast-moving pace and very time-limited structure, requires a highly confident, skillful, and directive therapist.

The crisis therapist should present the image of one who has the capacity to understand the patient's problems. The therapist should appear human and concerned about the patient's felt conflict, but at the same time businesslike about the information he or she needs to acquire rather quickly. Traditional attitudes of therapists as objective (aloof), disinterested (noninvolved), and nondirective (inefficient) are not appropriate in the crisis context. Abroms (1968) comments correctly that a therapist is more than just a catalyst: "A catalyst influences only the rate of a process, not its end products." This underlines the importance of activity and direction pointing in crisis therapy. In Abrom's words, "We assume that all effective therapists are directive." The therapist must be in command all the time—thus there is no substitute for experience and the acquired ability to size up problems rapidly, to articulate the relevant dynamics, and to initiate affirmative action. It is necessary to obtain relevant background information quickly without being caustically intrusive. The crisis therapist, during the early phases of the first interview, is a diagnostician who, in Brantner's (1973) words, becomes a "sponge" and absorbs everything about the person. He or she may delay giving feedback until later in the interview, when a full picture of the individual in crisis is acquired, or it may be necessary to begin tentative therapeutic interventions, for example, support, before all the assessment information is in.

The crisis therapist must be flexible and sensitive to the roles he or she may be required to play to effect the desired cognitive and behavioral reorientation of the patient. Depending on the demands of the situation, he or she may need to be supportive or confronting, friendly or antagonistic, accepting or rejecting of the patient's ideas, and so forth. The therapist must be able to call forth the appropriate "stimulus conditions" (through his or her response to the patient's problems) from a variety of available roles or attitudes and bring them to bear on the patient's problem situation. One way in which the crisis therapist differs from other therapists is that he or she *is* involved in the session. As Seabolt (1973) states, "The crisis therapist is there to reflect reality, and reality does not sit passively and mirror feelings back to the client. The crisis therapist responds as a person giving pertinent feedback to the client as to how he comes across, is perceived and is responded to by others" (p. 69).

When the time comes to move toward an intervention (after a satisfactory assessment is obtained), the therapist must aggressively take hold of the session. Again in Seabolt's well-chosen words, the therapist "conveys an important message of being in command of the situation." The therapist must act positively and decisively toward the definite goal or goals he or she determines will alleviate the crisis situation. Whether the situation demands supporting the patient's present efforts, confronting his or her unrealistic expectations, exploring more workable options, or whatever, the therapist must call the plays. He or she may need to take a strong stand on an issue or an action. If he or she is right, it may reinforce a patient's basic learning; if he or she is wrong, it may help the patient clarify and crystallize an opposite though workable, acceptable alternative.

Throughout the session the crisis therapist operates as a goal setter, helping the patient chart new strategies, clarify previously unworkable adaptive mechanisms, and shelve or give up on unattainable goals. He or she may not only suggest new goals or strategies, but persuade the patient concerning what the only viable options are. It is usually valuable for the therapist to work through possible factors that could interfere with these plans and to develop rebuttals to such obstacles.

Many roles and requirements are placed on the crisis therapist. To work out an effective intervention in the brief time available, he or she must carry out several activities almost simultaneously: assessing the nature and extent of the problem and the individual's potential response; inquiring about relevant facts; offering encouragement and support if needed; and evaluating how the patient integrates feedback. The next two sections of the chapter deal in some detail with the two major activities of the crisis therapist: assessment of the individual in crisis and implementation of the tactics of crisis therapy. Isolating these activities out of the therapeutic process for separate discussion is artificial, since both processes are intertwined in the typical crisis therapy situation. Yet it is hoped that a separate exploration of assessment and intervention will provide the reader with an awareness of the range of skills required of a crisis therapist. The structure of the presentation that follows should not be taken as the suggested order for conducting crisis therapy.

ASSESSMENT IN CRISIS THERAPY

The critical nature of the situation, the time constraints, and the necessity for therapeutic intervention to begin almost immediately make it impossible for the therapist to conduct a detailed assessment apart from actual treatment.* Within the space of just the first interview, several objectives must be accomplished:

1. Establishing a relationship with the patient.
2. Gathering assessment information necessary for treatment planning.
3. Arriving at a tentative formulation of the problem incorporating the precipitating problem together with the personality structure. This involves arriving at a working hypothesis of the precipitant and its subsequent hazardous meaning to the individual.
4. Giving the patient some perspective on the problem, including an understanding of his or her adaptive and maladaptive coping mechanisms in relation to it.
5. Exploring new adaptive ways the patient can deal with the problem.
6. Arriving at a strategy for achieving the agreed-upon goals and making a therapeutic contract if additional sessions are planned.
7. Arranging for future visits.

The second of these objectives, the gathering of assessment information, is the one addressed in this section. The remaining objectives, which are less defined and

* A detailed discussion of assessment methods in crisis intervention can be found in Butcher and Herzog (1982).

more likely to vary with each individual situation, are addressed in the next section on tactics the therapist may choose to use.

In considering assessment in crisis therapy, it is first helpful to distinguish assessment from diagnosis. Formal psychiatric diagnosis is not particularly useful in crisis therapy and may in fact be detrimental, in that it may orient the therapist toward seeing and planning for "chronic pathology" and blind him or her to important and manageable critical events. Although a reaction to crisis is often seen as indicative of the person's prestress personality, evidence from studies that have attempted to predict the outcome of a stress situation solely on the basis of personality has tended to disconfirm this belief (Aita, 1949; Bibring, 1961; Glass, 1956; see also Kaplan, 1968).

It is important to keep in mind that the primary goal of crisis therapy is to restore the patient's functioning to the level of adjustment that existed prior to his or her recent decompensation. Consequently, the focus of treatment is not on whatever long-standing pathology may be present, but rather on "the patient's failure to cope in the here-and-now problem" (Jacobson et al., 1965). There is little relationship between diagnosis and the ability of a person to return to optimal level of functioning, although there is some relationship between diagnosis and the capacity for reconstructive change. As Kaplan (1968) noted, "The person's prestress personality is likely to influence his response to a crisis, but his personality alone does not determine the outcome, which is markedly affected by his current relationships." Outcome of crisis, of course, is determined not only by the prestress personality and the crisis itself, but by a host of mediating variables, such as extent and quality of social support and locus of control, in addition to other less systematically investigated attributes, such as faith, optimism, a sense of identity and purpose, and so forth. Crisis treatment assumes, then, that a crisis is distinct from a chronic condition, although it may be affected by it. This assumption indicates a need for thorough and accurate assessment rather than diagnosis in the traditional sense.

The importance of assessment in crisis treatment cannot be overemphasized. Klopfer (1964) has critically questioned the value of initiating any psychotherapy without first obtaining as much assessment information as possible, and DeCourcy (1971) has underscored the importance of adequate assessment by reporting a case in which a woman patient was being seen in a short-term directive counseling situation for problems centering around her husband's alleged homosexual practices. An incidental assessment study uncovered a severe paranoid schizophrenic reaction in the woman and a relatively problem-free husband. Other case excerpts vividly demonstrating the importance of adequate assessment in crisis intervention are reported by Lambley (1974) and Small (1972).

Compared to traditional psychotherapies, crisis therapy often occurs in settings that are relatively less traditional and that call for relatively more active and directive therapist roles. However, none of these factors gives the therapist license to disregard important therapeutic content. In spite of time pressures and apparent urgencies of the situation, one cannot afford to abandon guidelines that constitute part of any good clinical interview. The therapist should be as nonobtrusive as possible and allow the psychological content to be contributed by the patient and not by the therapist. Every attempt should be made to facilitate the flow of therapeutically relevant personal history information without the therapist's prematurely imposing a framework (perhaps an incorrect one) or structuring the interview in such a way that some types of important information are not divulged. For example, if the therapist initially comes across as a happy and cheerful extrovert, patients may feel reluctant to discuss their problems because "surely she wouldn't be interested." Sometimes the therapist needs to do nothing more than say, "Tell me about the problem that brings you in." If patients are withdrawn, frightened, or anxious, some additional responses may be necessary to bring them to a point where they are able to tell their story.

At the beginning of the first session the clinician should do no more than this, since superfluous activity at this stage serves only to contaminate needed clinical data. The initial interview is not the place for giving casual reassurance, making glib remarks on the patient's physical appearance, or even initiating a friendly handshake. All these perhaps socially appropriate behaviors have no place in the therapist's initial stimulus projection. The therapist should begin his or her observation of the patient immediately—noting, for example, whether the patient is seeking reassurance and whether he or she shakes hands in a friendly manner. Before the therapist can assist the patient in formulating his or her problem, he or she must be able to assess its important dimensions. One can generally gain most of the initially necessary assessment information by listening and briefly encouraging the patient to present the problem as he or she sees it. Especially in crisis therapy one should guard against the inclination to do or to say too much too soon. Astute listening and observation are absolutely necessary to formulating the problems adequately.

More specifically, adequate assessment for crisis therapy should include the following kinds of observation and data collection.

Determining Whether or Not the Patient Can Be Adequately Assessed at the Time

Some patients may have contributing features that augment or stimulate their crisis, but which also interfere with making an accurate assessment of it. Patients who are currently in toxic states due to drug or alcohol use often fall into this category, as do patients who have overdosed on barbiturates or tranquilizers. In this situation the foremost crisis that must be dealt with is the physical risk. To handle this type of crisis efficiently, some crisis centers cooperate with hospital emergency rooms or make arrangements for medical consultation on an on-call basis.

If an intoxicated patient does not require acute medical attention or hospitalization, it may still be necessary to provide the patient with a place where he or she can detoxify, pending assessment. This may be provided by working out arrangements with detoxification centers or drug treatment units. Some centers provide beds right at the center, to ensure that the patient is not lost or injured during the referral process.

A second set of patients for whom assessment may have to be deferred includes those who are currently and perhaps temporarily overcome by the crisis, and are consequently too agitated or physically exhausted to provide necessary assessment information, but for whom there are known factors that militate against immediate hospitalization. These might be people in severe anxiety states, people who have had previous psychiatric hospitalization without benefit, or people who are known to have fast recovery potential. Providing such people with medication and an opportunity to recuperate may be an important first step which can precede the actual full assessment of the crisis situation.

Gathering Essential Demographic Information

Essential demographic information includes such items as the patient's name, age, place of residence, marital status, occupation, and education, the names of key relatives or friends, and whether the patient is currently in treatment elsewhere. Many crisis centers use brief forms so that this information is readily available to the therapist before he or she begins the initial interview. As a result, some data-gathering questions may be separate from and not interfere with collecting the more "clinical" information.

The clinical utility of these demographic variables defies specific description; however, the astute clinician can formulate various hypotheses about factors such as intelligence, motivation, interpersonal relationships, and subcultural mores on the basis of a patient's name, place of residence, occupation, and education. A well-dressed and articulate surburban housewife who comes in to talk about her fear of dying probably requires a different strategy than does an inner-city welfare recipient who presents with the same problem. Needless to say, all hypotheses formed on the basis of such demographic information must be rigorously explored before they are presumed to represent fact.

Some agencies explicitly offer anonymity to their clients. This may be inviting to some clients who are reluctant to reveal their identities, but it makes collection of demographic data difficult. In some emergent situations it is important to be able to reach the client, and even nonemergent "regular" crisis clients benefit from one or several follow-up contacts, which are not possible with clients who remain anonymous. Weighing the advantages against the disadvantages of anonymity, it seems that it is more important for the clinician to have such identifying information available for decision making and timely intervention, even at the price of losing some clients who are reluctant to reveal who they are. The extent to which clients identify themselves depends largely on the staff's conviction that such information is essential and the resulting vigor applied by the agency to obtain the information.

Getting Information from Outside Sources

Clinicians tend to overvalue their personal observations and impressions made during the interview. They also give considerable weight to the client's verbal statements as opposed to other, perhaps more subtle, behavioral cues. In crisis situations such an emphasis may lead to an incomplete or even misleading assessment and intervention plan. Crisis patients, by the very nature of being in a crisis, are often very emotional, confused, perplexed, highly anxious, withdrawn, or agitated. These emotional states make them poor and unreliable informants. Data from such informants may be spotty, exaggerated, or otherwise distorted. In such situations information from outside sources, such as family members, friends, police officers, therapists, ministers, or landladies, is essential to arrive at a comprehensive formulation of the client's problem.

Not infrequently, there is a considerable difference between the psychological climate of the crisis center's office and that of the place where the crisis situation developed. Not surprisingly, clients are apt to be calmer, more relaxed, and in better emotional control in the supportive setting of a crisis center staffed with friendly and helpful counselors. Moreover, the interpersonal irritant that so often precipitates a crisis, such as the unfaithful wife or the drinking husband, is not present. It would be clinically inappropriate to conclude from the client's "normal" behavior that the crisis is minimal or nonexistent, and that it is safe to send the client back to the locus of crisis. Quite possibly the reappearance of a certain stimulus complex will again precipitate a crisis. One cannot afford to forget that the setting to a large extent determines how people behave, and that the agency setting is artificial and unrealistic for the purpose of predicting an individual's behavior in "real life." Therefore, it is unadvisable to minimize the observations of a "hysterical mother," an "overreactive therapist," or a "dumb cop" who lacks formal mental health training but has the considerable advantage of having observed the client during a domestic quarrel.

Finding the Precipitant

It is important to determine what final event brought the client to the crisis center. This is especially critical for persons with multiple problems who present them somewhat indiscriminately and without priorities attached to them. Chronic problems may be mixed with acute ones and serious ones with minor annoyances. This makes focused intervention difficult because time limitations make a broad-brush approach impossible, and because some of these problems may not require any intervention at all. Once the immediate precipitant is identified, it usually indicates the main problem area or the problem that is most responsible for the crisis and therefore the problem that should become the focus of intervention. This makes for effective and economical treatment.

If the client is unable to identify a precipitant, it may be profitable to ask him or her to describe the events of the day just before a decision was made to go to a crisis center. The astute clinician may be able to ferret out the precipitating event from the client's description.

Assessing the Current Level of Functioning

The patient's current level of functioning is most efficiently assessed by direct observations that follow a standard mental status examination format (see Wells & Ruesch, 1972) covering the following:

Appearance and behavior. Take note of apparent state of health, body type, manner of dress, care of appearance, facial expressions, and motor activity such as posture, gait, tremulousness, and clenching of fists. There is a wealth of information in the appearance and behavior of patients, which is useful in confirming or generating hypotheses about the individual. Do the inferences about the patient from the way he or she appears seem consistent with what the patient says about himself or herself?

Speech and verbal behavior. Verbal behavior and the structure of speech are important areas of assessment, because they may reveal disordered thinking or powerful feelings of which the patient is not aware. The structure and styles of verbal behavior are often rather subtle, and consequently difficult for an inexperienced crisis therapist to assess—especially when the content the patient presents is, itself, complex and difficult to organize. However, this is an important fund of information which should not be ignored.

The clinician should also note such things as the freedom with which the patient speaks. Some patients may be evasive, halting, noncommittal, monosyllabic, or even mute, whereas others may be spontaneous, garrulous, effusive, or display great pressure of speech. Qualitatively, speech may be coherent and precise, or it may be circumstantial, dissociated, and illogical. In this regard, one must be careful to note flight of ideas, perseveration, neologisms, "world salads," or bizarre statements.

Thought content. It is essential to determine the predominant ideas occupying the patient's mind. One should note in particular those ideas that the patient spontaneously relates to the therapist. More specific inquiry may be used to reveal the patient's thoughts about what he or she thinks the problem is and what is the cause of distress. The therapist should be aware that the thoughts, attitudes, and concerns carrying the most emotional significance are often not stated directly, but can be detected in the patient's illogical, irrational, unguarded, and loosely considered productions.

In order to evaluate the degree to which the client's daily functioning has been affected by the crisis, the clinician should strive to answer the following questions: (a) To what extent has the crisis disrupted the client's overall life pattern? (b) Is the patient able to go to work, school? (c) Has the crisis affected the client's sleep pattern, personal hygiene? (d) Has it begun to have an effect on the client's family and friends? (e) Is there an increase in drinking, drug use, or reckless behavior? (f) Is the client's perception of reality becoming distorted? (g) How ready is the client to accept help? And, most important: (h) Has the crisis damaged the client's feeling of self-worth, self-respect? As disturbed, sick, or deviant as the client's behavior may be, how different is it from the client's usual pattern of behavior?

Observing the Patient's Emotional State

In observing a patient's emotional state, one should consider both mood and affect. *Mood* refers to the individual's general, overall, more-or-less prolonged emotional tone, whereas *affect* refers to the client's momentary emotional responsiveness, which may vary during the interview in relation to changing thought content. It may be important to determine if the particular emotion the individual is expressing, for example, anger, is primarily a situationally induced and transitory state, or is rather a "sign" or representative instance of more persistent behavior trends, for example, chronic hostility. Further questioning may be required to make such determinations. One should note not only the person's direct statements regarding his or her feelings, but also any revealing indirect statements, facial expressions, and motor activity. Frequently, clients may express verbally a set of attitudes or feelings that do not correspond with the emotions they are actually experiencing. A therapist who detects such disparity in a client's manner of presentation may find fruitful therapeutic terrain. Finally, the therapist should to some extent monitor his or her own empathic feelings for clues to the patient's emotions.

When it comes to the accurate perception of emotional tone, clinical "hunches" and intuition play an important role. A state of explosiveness, for instance, is difficult to describe and is rarely expressed by the client by direct verbal statements. Many experienced crisis therapists come to sense it, to be able to hear with a third ear and see with a third eye. At times such soft signs are to be trusted more than direct verbal communication which is more subject to the client's own willful distortion and deception. A seasoned crisis intervention veteran's declaration that he or she feels uncomfortable in the presence of a client or that the client makes him or her nervous should be given as much credence and weight regarding management implications as a client's overt verbal threat to harm one of the staff members.

Observing the Patient's Manner of Relating

One should observe the manner in which the patient relates to the therapist and to others, as this provides important information about how he or she gets along with other people. Does he or she seem sullen, resentful, sarcastic, or uncooperative? Does he or she appear cool and distant, warm and friendly, flat, indifferent, ingratiating, or seductive? One can assume during the initial interview that any such attitudes and modes of behavior derive mainly from the patient's own personality style and way of relating to people, providing that the therapist's own inputs are minimal.

Assessing Premorbid Adjustment As Distinct from Current Stress

This assessment area is illustrated by Figure 11.1. As the model suggests, crises result from an interplay of stressful life experiences with congenital or acquired vulnerabilities. Some populations distinguish themselves as being particularly high on one or the other axis, and the probability of their confronting a crisis is consequently very high. For example, the genetic component in schizophrenia has now been well documented (Gottesman & Shields, 1972). Because many schizophrenics have genetic predispositions toward decompensation, it is probable that relatively innocuous life experiences may be perceived as crises—point A in the diagram.

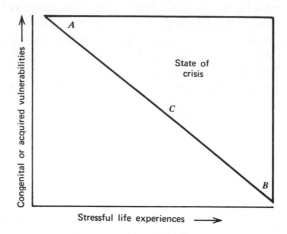

Figure 11.1.   A vulnerability/stress model of crisis.

Such is the case with a schizophrenic who came to a crisis center because she had left her keys to her apartment at work and did not know what to do.

On the other axis one finds relatively well-functioning people, depicted at point *B*, who are faced with threatening life experiences such as a marital crisis, unemployment, discrimination, or an unexpected death in the family.

The middle ground, point *C*, is occupied largely by people who have specific congenital or acquired vulnerabilities or "weak spots." These vulnerabilities are subject to being reactivated when the person confronts particular life experiences, as in the case of a woman reared by alcoholic parents who finds that her husband has an uncontrolled drinking problem. When a therapist begins to work with a patient in crisis, it is necessary for him or her to be able to assess accurately the particular combination of forces resulting in the crisis. The appropriate plan of action depends in large part on this assessment.

To assess the premorbid level of adjustment or adaptive potential, it is useful to explore the manner in which the patient has handled past crises and the current crisis before coming for treatment. Erikson (1953) focused in this regard on the difference between *accidental crises* and *developmental crises*. Patients are often able to describe past accidental crises in response to the question, "Has anything like this happened to you in the past?" or "What have you done when you felt like this in the past?" If there are no apparent accidental crises, one can explore standard developmental crises such as school entry and exit, marriage, first job, and the like. The methods in which crises were handled previously can then be analyzed according to their affective, perceptive–cognitive, behavioral, and biophysiological content, as suggested by Golan (1969).

As a result of her research Golan (1978) concluded that most responses to crises can be placed in the following eight categories:

1.   Carried on as usual: made no new effort

2. Expressed grief in words or actions or both (adopted depressive behavior)
3. Expressed anger by words or actions or both (adopted aggressive behavior)
4. Escaped reality by words or actions or both (slept excessively; fantasized; became psychotic, used alcohol or drugs)
5. Developed neurotic symptoms (adopted phobic behavior, compulsive rituals, hysteric manifestations)
6. Developed somatic symptoms (suffered from migraine, ulcers, dermatitis)
7. Engaged in reality-oriented efforts to deal with the situation (cut down expenses; looked for a job; returned to the parental home)
8. Mobilized energies for new, growth-producing activities (started training for a new career; innovated basic changes in the home)

Rapaport (1962) has suggested that it is also useful to classify the way in which a crisis is perceived, since this allows one to understand better the response, adaptive or maladaptive, that ensues. She notes that the "initial blow" may be seen as (a) a threat, either to basic needs or to the sense of physical or emotional integrity; (b) a loss, either of a person or of an ability or capacity; or (c) a challenge. Strickler and LaSor (1970) have further delineated her second category of loss into (a) loss of self-esteem, particularly in regard to the person's ability to function well in certain social roles or relationships; B) loss of sexual role mastery in terms of performance in vocational and heterosexual areas for males, and maternal and vocational areas for women; and (c) loss of nurturing by virtue of loss of nurturing objects or roles.

Rapaport's categories bear some resemblance to those of Pollack (1971), who classified crises in students as external stress, frustration, and conflict. Rapaport noted that threat calls forth a high level of anxiety, loss or deprivation is accompanied by depression or mourning, and challenge stimulates moderate anxiety, some hope, and a release of energy for problem solving.

It is also possible to assess the premorbid level of adjustment by relying in part on the personal history data already available. Work history, educational success, and marital and interpersonal relationships provide important clues to the premorbid level of adjustment. It is usually necessary to do more specific questioning in areas such as previous psychiatric history, medical history, medication, and use of drugs and alcohol. It is also useful, if possible, to talk with family members, friends, or professional colleagues who are directly familiar with the patient's previous level of adjustment. Information from these various sources can facilitate identifying the strengths and coping mechanisms the patient brings to the crisis situation, as well as understanding why he or she has not been able to cope adaptively with the current crisis.

Making Successive Assessments

Sometimes a single assessment episode is insufficient to provide a satisfactory formulation of problem and treatment. An obvious example is a patient whose current mental state prevents a complete assessment. A groggy patient with slurred speech following an overdose first has to be medically evaluated for possible danger to life and a psychological evaluation may not be possible until many hours later. At other times the symptom picture is confusing and leads to clinical indecision or conflicting opinions. Just how psychotic is a particular male patient, for example? Can he maintain himself on his own outside an institution? Does his condition make him exploitable or vulnerable to victimization? With such clients the final decision can only be made after a succession of assessment episodes separated in time and demonstrating either an increase or decrease in disturbance. Such clients keep reappearing at the crisis center or are brought to it again and again by some community "gatekeeper." While this is frustrating to the client, the community, and the clinician, it may still be preferable to choosing a more restrictive treatment option before it becomes clear that it is necessary.

Classification of Emotional Crises

It is important for the clinician to be able to evaluate the extent of emotional crisis the client is undergoing. Factors such as recency and severity of the crisis situation need to be evaluated and weighed before the therapist can determine the potential impact of the crisis upon the individual. Baldwin (1978) developed a framework for classifying emotional crises that can be very useful for clinicians to employ in their efforts to gain a perspective on the crisis situation. Figure 11.2 presents definitions and case illustrations of six crises he found to typify crisis situations facing the clinician.

Assessing the Patient's Level of Motivation

This area of assessment is concerned with determining the patient's expectations regarding his or her and the therapist's role in crisis therapy. Rado (1965) has described four motivational levels which are useful to keep in mind in making this assessment. The first and lowest level of motivation, which he calls *magic craving*, is illustrated by the completely discouraged and helpless man who retreats to the hope that the physician–parent will do miracles for him. Such motivation is exemplified by the thought, "The doctor must not only cure me, he must do everything for me, by magic." This regression is triggered by the distress and helplessness of the patient, and it is not adaptive.

The second level of motivation is called *parental invocations* and is exemplified by the thought, "What can the doctor do for me? The doctor should do everything for me. I want to be her favorite child." Although this kind of response suggests regression to the period of infantile reliance on parents, it is at least potentially an adaptive response compared to that of magic craving.

The third level, *cooperative striving,* is even more adaptive than reaching out for a parent or magician. It is exemplified in the thought, "I am ready to cooperate with the doctor. I must learn how to help myself and do this for myself."

The fourth and most adaptive level of motivation is *realistic self-reliance*. It is exemplified by the thought, "I will cooperate with the doctor. This is my opportunity to make full use of all my potential resources for adaptive growth."

CLASS 1: DISPOSITIONAL CRISES

Definition. Dispositional crises are defined by distress resulting from a problematic situation in which the therapist responds to the client in ways peripheral to a therapeutic role; the intervention is not primarily directed at the emotional level.

Examples. Making a *referral* to a medical facility for a young woman with a problem pregnancy following a realistic decision for an abortion; providing *information* to a family member about local treatment options for an alcoholic relative; granting a college student *administrative* release from an untenable living situation in a residence hall; providing psychological *education* to a young man about situational causes of impotence after he has experienced an episode of impotence while very intoxicated.

CLASS 2: CRISES OF ANTICIPATED LIFE TRANSITIONS

Definition. Crises that reflect anticipated, but usually normative, life transitions over which the client may or may not have substantial control. The client may present for help prior to, during, or after the life transition has taken place.

Examples. Mid-life career changes, retirement, getting married, becoming a parent, divorce/separation, terminal/chronic illness.

CLASS 3: CRISES RESULTING FROM TRAUMATIC STRESS

Definition. Emotional crises precipitated by externally imposed stressors or situations that are unexpected and uncontrolled, and that are emotionally overwhelming.

Examples. Sudden death of a family member or spouse, rape, assault, unexpected catastrophic illness, sudden loss of job or status.

CLASS 4: MATURATIONAL/DEVELOPMENTAL CRISES

Definition. Emotional crises resulting from attempts to deal with an interpersonal situation reflecting a struggle with a deeper (but usually circumscribed) issue that has not been resolved adaptively in the past and that represents an attempt to attain emotional maturity.

Examples. Crises with focal issues involving dependency, value conflicts, sexual identity, capacity for emotional intimacy, responses to authority, or attaining reasonable self-discipline.

CLASS 5: CRISES REFLECTING PSYCHOPATHOLOGY

Definition. Emotional crises in which pre-existing psychopathology has been instrumental in precipitating the crisis or in which psychopathology significantly impairs or complicates adaptive resolution.

Examples. Clients presenting with borderline adjustment, severe neuroses, characterological disorders, or schizophrenia.

CLASS 6: PSYCHIATRIC EMERGENCIES

Definition. Crisis situations in which general functioning has been severely impaired and the individual rendered incompetent or unable to assume personal responsibility.

Examples. Acutely suicidal clients, drug overdoses, reactions to hallucinogenic drugs, acute psychoses, uncontrollable anger, alcohol intoxication.

Figure 11.2. Definitions and examples of six types of crisis situations. From B.A. Baldwin, "A paradigm for the classification of emotional crises: Implications for crisis intervention," *American Journal of Orthopsychiatry,* 1978, *48* (3), 538–551.

Rado suggests that the utility of any particular level of motivation depends on the particular circumstances; however, only at the third and fourth levels can the therapist help the patient acquire new emotional skills which are likely to be self-perpetuating and independent of variations in the patient's feelings toward the therapist.

Assessing Current Life Stresses

While the therapist is assessing the aforementioned areas, the focus of the interview for the most part is in the area of the current life stresses precipitating the crisis. After being asked to state what the problem is that brings him or her in, the patient is encouraged to relate the current crisis to past problems or to particular personality styles he or she has. The interviewer should draw on this information to delineate as best he or she can the psychological hazards confronting the patient and the precipitating event that has brought him or her for help. At this point it is also necessary to determine whether the problem is a *chronic* one which has persisted for some time, a continuing situation which has existed for a long time but has only recently become a problem, or a psychological difficulty of entirely recent origin. The assessment made in this regard bears directly on decisions about referral, as is more fully elaborated in the previous section on goals of crisis therapy.

It is possible for the clinician to obtain a relatively objective appraisal of the stress an individual is currently experiencing by using one of the quantitative life events questionnaires that are available: the Schedule of Recent Experiences (SRE) developed by Rahe, Meyer, Smith, Kjaer, and Holmes (1967) to study the frequency of stressful life events among tuberculosis patients; the Social Readjustment Rating Questionnaire (SRRQ) developed by Holmes and Rahe (1967) to study the amount of readjustment required for individuals who had undergone a major life event; the Psychiatric Epidemiology Research Inventory (PERI) developed by Dohrenwend and Dohrenwend (1978) to sample a broader range of life events than the SRRQ; and the Life Experience Survey (LES) developed by Sarason, Johnson, and Siegel (1978) to measure both stressful life events and the impact they have on the individual.

Use of any of these life events forms will provide the clinician with some idea about the possibility that significant situational factors may be involved in the individual's case. One of these interview schedules, the PERI, was designed to provide information on recent events within the past year and allows for a rough diagnostic classification of symptoms. Most crisis intervention specialists do not employ these instruments in a strict psychometric way, however, but simply incorporate the concept of stressful life events in their initial interview and attempt to give appropriate weight to those factors that have appeared in the literature to have high stress weights.

Assessing Dangerousness

Any clinician working in a crisis intervention setting frequently faces the difficult situation of being expected to make assessments of dangerousness. It is imperative for the clinician to have a thorough understanding of the concept of dangerousness because of recent changes in laws regulating involuntary commitment and the precedent-setting court rulings concerning the duty of mental health specialists to warn prospective victims if their lives have been threatened. In general, commitment laws are becoming tighter, with greater emphasis on "police power" as the basis for involuntary intervention, for example, dangerousness to self or others as distinct from inability to care for oneself. Psychologists risk being sued if they fail to warn a victim of foreseeable danger posed by one of their clients (Knapp & Vandecreek, 1982).

In sharp contrast to society's implied confidence in our ability to make accurate predictions of dangerousness is the mental health professionals' woefully inadequate performance in this area. As a matter of fact, clinicians tend to overpredict dangerousness vastly—with false positives reportedly ranging from 60% to 90%. Why do we perform so poorly? One reason is that homicide and serious violence, like suicide, are statistically rare. Secondly, there is a difference between the assessment of dangerousness and the prediction of a particular violent act. Whether dangerousness as a potential results in an overt act of violence depends on various contextual or situational factors that are out of the clinician's control. A clinician may accurately assess the risk, but no assault will take place without the presence of a stimulus, a precipitant, an opportunity, and perhaps a weapon. Finally, society is particularly interested in the prediction of violence that is almost by definition unpredictable—for instance, the nice young man who suddenly kills all of his family members—because such violence cannot be readily understood and anticipated, and is therefore more frightening.

A pervasive methodological problem hinders our efforts to refine our dangerousness predictions. This is the absence of an adequate typology for violent persons. Different subclasses of individuals commit violent acts for very different reasons, and therefore the predictors for one type do not work for predicting another. To mention a few: the sociopathic killer, the young mother who kills her infant during a dissociative state, the schizophrenic who commits a sudden and bizarre murder, the dependent immature husband who kills in response to his wife's threat to leave, and the individual who commits violent acts against family members. A predictive instrument, in order to be maximally effective, would have to be aimed at both violence subtype and specific situation—a very difficult set of measurement problems.

The relationship of mental illness to dangerousness becomes an important issue because the legal definition of dangerousness includes mental illness as a necessary component. In practice, of course, this is often ignored. For example, the police often transport individuals who threaten suicide or homicide to a psychiatric institution before they have had any opportunity to make a judgment regarding the presence or absence of mental illness. The circular presumption is that such threats must be indicators of an underlying mental disturbance.

Contrary to earlier beliefs that there was not a significant relationship between crime and mental illness, the more recent and methodologically more sophisticated studies find a strong relationship between certain kinds of crime, especially crime involving violence against persons, and certain types of mental illness, especially psychosis and more specifically yet schizophrenia (Monahan, 1981; Zitrin, Hardesty & Burdick, 1976). The rates of murder, rape, and aggravated assault are all significantly higher for the mentally ill than the rates of the same crimes in the general population. One should hasten to add, however, that such findings do not warrant the maintenance of stereotypes of mentally ill persons as "mad killers." Most mentally ill individuals do not commit crimes of any sort, and the knowledge of their being at greater risk for violence, while significant, is not very useful for individual prediction. Perhaps the most useful clinical finding is that murder as a single, isolated, unplanned, purposeless episode of violent acting out with no profit or personal advantage is most typically committed by a young male schizophrenic.

What clues should a clinician look for in assessing dangerousness potential? Most risk factors reported in the literature are adequate for a general classification of persons into low-, medium-, and high-risk categories and for assessment of *chronic* risk. They are much less useful for individual prediction, especially in regard to *imminent* dangerousness (which is what most statutes call for). In this group belong such historical items as parental brutality and seduction, fire setting, cruelty to animals, and bed wetting above a certain age; also, such current stressors as job loss and business failures and such personality attributes as low frustration tolerance, prediction for motoric self-expression, intense self-centeredness, quick temper, paranoid mentation, low capacity for empathy and fantasy, and excessive sensitivity to having one's masculinity challenged. Other predictors, as already discussed above, have utility only for certain cubclasses of violence.

The best single predictor of future violence is a history of actual violence, but even that is quite inadequate for individual prediction because of extremely low recidivism rates (approximately 0.5% for homicide with a 20-year follow-up period). In a clinical setting, for the prediction of imminent risk of violence one should look for the following factors: previous violence, expressed fear of losing control (and evidence for the client seeking help to regain control), recent threats of violence or actual violence in absence of provocation, use of alcohol and drugs, especially in nonpsychotic individuals, a tendency to carry weapons for protection, presence of guns, and "suggestive actions," such as public handling of weapons and reckless driving. In the case of husband/wife relationships, one would look for victim provocation in close ambivalent relationships, frequent disturbance calls, and the threat of losing one's spouse.

As in the case of suicide, no rating scales, tests, or list of clues can replace a thorough evaluation, including psychiatric history, criminal record, history of violence, current mental status, general personality characteristics, current stresses, and recent threats.

When it comes to treatment of potentially violent individuals, the prospects are rather bleak. One author (Halleck, 1978) has this to say:

> The amount of actual prevention we can obtain by focusing on individuals is minimal. . . . Disillusionment with the possibility of predicting and preventing violence in individuals and desperation over the usefulness of rehabilitation have led most criminologists to advocate greater use of punishment as a deterrent and greater police protection and carefulness on the part of victims. . . . Psychodynamic formulations . . .

may be aesthetically pleasing but they have little value to society or the practicing physician . . . there is no pharmacotherapy for violence. The usefulness of psychotherapy in preventing the occurrence of violence in violence-prone individuals or in rehabilitating violent individuals is unproven. . . . At the present time, unless the clinician is dealing with high-risk groups who have a history of violence, our predictions are rarely good enough to justify involuntary intervention. [pp. 49–57]

THE TACTICS OF CRISIS THERAPY *

What does a crisis therapist do to bring about relief of emotional distress or behavioral change with an individual in crisis? The therapist has several effective tools ranging from attentive listening to complimenting or criticizing the patient's behavior, giving advice, enlisting environmental support, or interceding with concerned relatives. What power does a therapist have that enables him or her to aid in the resolution of problems that are out of the individual's control, that is, problems in which the patient is intimately involved and aware of the complexities but is unable to resolve himself or herself? Perhaps the treatment situation, in which the therapist is engaged as an interested but objective participant is itself the most valuable asset to the change-oriented relationship, since it allows the therapist to perceive what new directions are required without being bogged down with the futility and inactivity surrounding the patient.

An important factor in the therapist's ability to offer assistance lies in the authoritative nature of the role he or she fills. The therapist is viewed as an expert who has the knowledge or power to help, and the patient generally expects or at least hopes that the therapist will offer some relief. This expectation is in itself a powerful change agent, and placebo effects in bringing about patient changes have been well documented (see Chapter 7). Wolberg (1965) among others has pointed out that the placebo effect is rooted in the individual's expectation that the person whom he or she consults has the knowledge, the means, and the magic to bring his or her difficulties to a halt; in response to this expectation, Wolberg advises, "The therapist should neither exaggerate nor crush it, but accept it."

In this section we discuss some of the tactics that prove useful in the conduct of crisis therapy. It needs to be recognized, however, that these tactics vary in their effectiveness for treating different kinds of individuals who present in crisis situations. Hence the particular tactic to employ in a given situation cannot always be readily specified, and it is sometimes difficult for the crisis therapist to know precisely what to do. Because he or she intervenes initially on the basis of limited data,

---

* The reader will find the following sources relevant and useful for gaining additional familiarity with the tactics of crisis therapy: Aguilera, Messick, and Farrell (1970); Barten and Barten (1972); Barten (1971): Beck and Robbins (1946); Bellak and Small (1965); Bergin and Garfield (1971); Caplan (1961); Caplan (1964); Coleman (1960); Darbonne (1968); Frank (1961); Golann and Eisdorfer (1972); Haley (1963); Koegler and Brill (1967); Lerner (1972); Lewin (1970); Mann (1973); Massermann (1969); McGee (1974); Parad (1965); Phillips and Wiener (1966); Reid and Shyne (1969); Rothman (1970); Sifneos (1972); Small (1971); and Wolberg (1965).

he or she must often rely on an educated guess and hope that his or her tactics produce the desired effect. Sometimes the result is immediately apparent, at other times feedback from the patient provides some information about the adequacy of the intervention, and in still other instances a therapist may not know whether the tactics have been effective until a follow-up is conducted. The brief exposition of tactics below is by no means exhaustive, and it is difficult to extract therapeutic tactics out of the process itself without greatly oversimplifying the therapist's task. We can however, give the reader an idea of the more frequently used and useful procedures in crisis therapy.

Offering Emotional Support

An individual appearing for an initial crisis interview is often experiencing a heightened state of anxiety or depression and has almost always recently experienced failure at managing his or her own situation. He or she is probably preoccupied with the precipitating event and has difficulty focusing attention on anything else. Before the patient can begin to consider alternative strategies of problem resolution, he or she may need to receive some clear *emotional support* from the therapist. This support may range in degree from simply acknowledging the existence of the problem (with the implicit communication that the problem "can't be too bad, since we are at least able to talk about it") to offering strong verbal reassurance ("I am quite certain that you did the right thing in leaving").

Several theorists (e.g., Truax & Wargo, 1966; Wolpe, 1958) have pointed out that the essential ingredients for therapeutic effectiveness comprise (a) sensitivity and understanding of the patient's situation and a manner of communicating this awareness, (b) the communication of nonpossessive warmth and acceptance of the patient, and (c) the communication of therapist genuineness and authenticity to the patient (see also Chapter 7). These are necessary conditions for communicating emotional support to a patient, and in crisis therapy these "ingredients" are just as essential as in other forms of psychotherapy for bringing about desired change—although they may be more difficult to attain since the duration of treatment, especially if there is only a single contact with the patient, is all too brief.

The grief work involved in much of crisis therapy (Lindemann, 1944; Paul, 1966; Weinstein, 1979) is facilitated or, to be more exact, made possible by the therapist's providing strong emotional support to the patient. Having someone to rely on in times of severe stress encourages the patient to express overwhelming feelings he or she has been holding back. It is not a sign of weakness for individuals to utilize others in this way at such times, nor does it suggest that the therapist is encouraging dependency in the patient, since the time-bound structure, if correctly managed, helps to prevent this unwanted side effect.

In cases where clients have been victimized by the actions of others it is particularly necessary to deal with guilt *they* might experience by providing support to them. It is known from many studies that victims often end up blaming themselves for the victimization, and the crisis intervener can relieve such unwarranted and self-damaging guilt by conveying to victims strongly that they did nothing wrong to invite or provoke the attack.

Providing Opportunities for Catharsis

Several therapists have noted the *importance of catharsis* in successful psychotherapy (Breuer & Freud, 1895; Frank, 1961; Rosenzweig, 1936; Shoben, 1948). In some more recent behaviorally oriented therapeutic approaches as well, cathartic techniques are viewed as important procedures, for bringing about successful behavioral change (Hogan, 1968; Lazarus, 1968; Stampfl & Levis, 1967; Ullman & Krasner, 1965). It is especially important for individuals in crisis who may be experiencing a great deal of affect' (or perhaps are unable to express their emotions directly) to be offered an opportunity to discharge such feelings in the relative safety of a therapeutic situation. Thus the therapist must be aware of the high arousal state of most individuals in initial crisis therapy sessions, and be sensitive to their cathartic needs (Butcher and Kolotkin, 1979).

The therapist must accordingly set the stage for the free expression of emotion by the patient. He or she must strive to elicit strong feelings, and must give the patient permission to express intense emotions. With depressed patients who have difficulty letting their feelings out, even vicarious catharsis may help, since the patient may thereby be able to reverse the aggression and anger he or she has turned on himself or herself (Bellak & Small, 1965). A response from the therapist such as "Some part of you must have wished your father dead," for example, has the advantage of not requiring the patient to take full responsibility for the hostility expressed. As Paul (1966) notes, "The client must be encouraged to 'experience' his emotions, to examine them, to 'own up' to them, to feel them fully as emotion." The therapist must also be prepared for possibly uncontrollable waves of emotion which may appear in effective crisis therapy. After such storms of expressed emotion, patients are frequently at their most receptive point for therapeutic input. Work by Nichols (1974) has confirmed that emotive psychotherapy is effective in producing catharsis, and that catharsis in turn leads to therapeutic improvement.

Communicating Hope and Optimism

The communication of hope and optimism to the patient is an important ingredient of effective psychotherapy (Frank, 1968). An optimistic attitude on the part of the therapist is especially effective in dealing with individuals in crisis, since the loss of hope in solving one's problems usually accompanies deterioration of adjustment during a crisis. As Aldrich (1968) has pointed out, "If the therapist expects that the patient's capacity to respond favorably to short-term symptomatic treatment is evidence of his capacity to cope autonomously with residual unresolved conflicts, the therapist's optimistic expectations may cancel out the earlier expectations of failure the patient has perceived from others.

When the therapist *sincerely* communicates hope and the possibility of problem resolution to the patient, the individual may react positively and begin to view his or her options in a more flexible fashion. A "deadpan" therapist, or worse yet a pessimistic one, can do little to mobilize the action resources within the patient.

However, the crisis therapist must be cautious in committing himself or herself to any such attitudes routinely. An important assessment must be made first. Is there a ray of hope in the patient's life? If the therapist feels realistically hopeful, then some change leverage may be effected; if he or she is not sincere and provides superficial reassurance and false hope that the patient detects (and they usually do), then the outcome may be therapeutic failure. Few tactics provide greater credibility gaps between therapist and patient than reassurance when a therapist holds unrealistic expectations about outcome.

Being Interested and Actively Involved

To most patients in crisis, their problems are of the utmost importance at the moment. Consequently, *the therapist must be interested and actively involved* in the unfolding events, tedious though they might be to discuss. The therapist's "interest" in the patient's problem situation communicates positive feelings which may have the effect of mobilizing the individual to focus on particularly effective aspects of his or her life. One thing is fairly certain: The obverse—evident lack of interest in the patient—generally has undesirable and unwanted effects. This is not meant to imply that the therapist must be exuberant over every minute detail of every case. On the contrary, the therapist, listening selectively, may even need to inform the patient of the irrelevance of some types of information. What we are saying is that the therapist must be interested and involved in the patient's situation, regardless of the particular tactics he or she uses at the moment.

Listening Selectively

The crisis therapist must cultivate an ear for workable material and ignore aspects of the case that are irrelevant, unmanageable, or beyond any practical grasp. Not everything the patient brings to the session can be dealt with. For the therapy to be short term, only material that is immediately relevant can receive attention. Rusk (1971) notes in this regard that people in crisis are frequently unable to address the stress or conflict situation directly and may defensively launch into pseudocrises. These may take such forms as preoccupation with physical symptoms, reversion into explanation of long-standing difficulties, or focus on irrelevant concerns. *Selective listening is one of the most important tactics for a therapist to learn.* It is crucial for the therapist to sift out of the morass of multiplex trends and irrelevant material *only* that information that bears useful on bringing about desired change.

The concept of skillful or benign neglect suggested by Pumpian-Mindlin (1953) describes this therapeutic tactic nicely. It is important for the therapist to keep the session moving and not become preoccupied with defensive entanglements of the patient. Castelnuovo-Tedesco (1966) observes, "In the brief treatment of these depressive disorders, it is important to recognize early the major characterological defenses and, in the main, to respect them, to leave them alone, and not to become involved in premature attempts at character analysis which are not in keeping with the circumscribed goals of brief treatment" (p. 206). Rusk (1971) adds that anxiety too must be handled gently, leaving existing defenses intact unless others can be substituted.

Providing Factual Information

It is frequently necessary for the crisis therapist to provide *factual information* relevant to the patient's problem. It may be necessary to clear up misconceptions that cloud a session, as in the case of a patient who was fond of tossing out such "statistics" as, "I heard that 30% of all homosexuals have troubles with their sex glands." The myths that many people hold and sometimes use to sanction or excuse certain behaviors may need to be dispelled in order for the proper therapeutic focus to be obtained. A straightforward, nontechnical explanation which is both brief and authoritative works best for this purpose. The beginning therapist often falls into a habit of lecturing (frequently over the patient's head), rather than simply noting a fact. When the therapist provides any information, he or she runs the risk of interrupting the flow of the session to do so. Thus he or she should be judicious in interrupting, making sure that it is warranted and not just a self-serving display of the therapist's own knowledge and sophistication.

Formulating the Problem Situation

Therapy sessions, particularly those in which much factual information is first needed to make therapeutic decisions, are frequently cluttered with names, dates, facts, untruths, emotional discharges, and other unsorted things. The therapist must attempt to get a handle on all the material being presented and arrive at an agreement with the patient as to what problems are to be dealt with, what goals are to be attained, and what potential mechanisms for attaining these ends are available. A preliminary *formulation of the problem situation,* in the form of a synthesis of forces acting on the patient, his or her experienced resulting conflicts, and his or her ineffective mechanisms, can help bring order into the material and sharpen a workable focus for the therapy. A synthesis that includes a statement of essential facts and some observations and tentative hypotheses enables the patient to integrate the elements considered important by the therapist and to correct or provide addenda to the therapist's perceptions of the situation.

This formulation represents an important stage in the session, since it in effect defines the "work area" for the session and provides the material for forming therapeutic contracts later on. Additionally, the realization that if events can be explained they can be handled serves to diminish the patient's anxiety and fosters hope. As Rusk (1971) noted, verbalizing the circumstances, relationships, and feelings involved in a crisis situation externalizes them. Not only is a preliminary formulation essential, then, but subsequent formulations are useful in fostering the synthetic ability of the patient at various stages of therapy. Reviewing feelings and expressions manifested in earlier sessions is a helpful device for allowing the patient to devleop an understanding of how today's needs for action relate to events just past.

Being Emphatic and to the Point

The crisis therapist should strive to *be emphatic and to the point* in providing feedback or interpretations to the patient. Irrelevant comments and off-target interpretations should be avoided—it is better to say nothing at all than to fill the session with unimportant observations and pointless questions. The beginning therapist should consciously determine the proportion of content the patient contributes compared with his or her own comments. This of course varies with the patient, but a good rule of thumb is that during the early part of the session the therapist should limit verbal input to about 10% of the time, and to eliciting information from the patient only. During the latter part of the therapy session the inputs from both therapist and patient may appropriately become more equal in amount. It is also important for the therapist to be "straight" with the patient when he or she does comment, since only by being a model of openness can he or she create an atmosphere conducive to honest communication between patient and therapist.

Predicting Future Consequences

It is frequently useful, especially when the patient has a character disordered life style, to *predict what will happen if the patient follows his or her present course of action*—spelling out in detail the possible consequences of his or her behavior. This is a useful technique for focusing on workable courses of action in that it helps to clarify what the patient may expect to occur if his or her life style is not altered. The patient may be informed at the time that the purpose of the prediction is the hope of providing it false, as Bellak and Small (1965) recommend. Many individuals cannot or do not make such predictions about the outcomes of their own behavior; consequently they cannot weigh behavioral strategies to obtain desired outcomes. This ability to predict one's fate given a particular behavioral sequence is frequently impaired in individuals undergoing stress.

Giving Advice and Making Direct Suggestions

Giving advice and making direct suggestions are effective therapeutic tools if properly and sparingly used. These techniques are useful because people seek out and accept the formulations of authorities they respect. Many individuals in crisis go to a therapist to obtain an opinion about their situation and to seek advice or suggestions for remedying it. This is especially true when the patient is of low-income status (see Lorion, 1973). Auld and Myers (1954) report in this regard that low-income patients tend to see the therapist as a magician or mind reader and to view their problems as organic (nerves) and as requiring physical treatment. Redlich, Hollingshead, and Bellis (1955) similarly comment that lower-class patients are relatively likely to seek advice and guidance in psychotherapy and to be disappointed when it is not offered. A distinction should be made between the classes of advice: (a) advice regarding real-life circumstances (e.g. "You should get a divorce") and (b) advice regarding treatment issues (e.g. "You should consider medication"). It is usually much safer to be directive on the second type of advice than on the former. To give advice about real-life situations is more dangerous because it presumes not only the therapist's full understanding of the client's personality and life situation, but also superior wisdom on the therapist's part.

As we have seen, the therapist has a "given" authority which provides him or her leverage to bring about change. The power of direct suggestion accordingly works to mobilize many patients to attempt new behaviors. If successful, these attempts will not only begin to relieve the patient's problem situation and give confidence in his or her ability to change, but will also provide an impetus for the therapist to initiate additional and perhaps more substantial changes. Thus it is important to make suggestions that it is within the patient's power to carry out and that at the same time contribute toward problem resolution. The therapist who gives either bad advice or too many suggestions finds that the patient may quickly lose confidence in his or her therapeutic powers. Furthermore, some patients are fond of playing the "Yes, but I've tried that already" role, which tends to generate a nonproductive power struggle. If the therapist finds that his or her "sage" advice is being ignored or attacked, then he or she must reevaluate the effectiveness of this therapeutic tactic or the quality of the advice, or both. On the other hand, advice regarding treatment issues is not only quite appropriate but frequently necessary for ambivalent, passive, discouraged, paralyzed, or indecisive crisis patients. After all, treatment issues definitely fall within the area of professional expertise of the psychologist, and it is somewhat disconcerting to see how often therapists require clients to make treatment decisions that in no way can be "informed," basing this approach on the questionable assumption that they are being "nondirective" or "client-centered" or avoiding being "authoritarian."

Setting Limits

Sometimes it is not enough for the therapist just to be understanding and thoughtful in providing structure and advice to the patient. He or she may in addition have to be very *directive in setting limits* for the patient. Abroms (1968) describes several types of behavior that may require the therapist to set firm limits. These include destructive behavior, such as suicidal or homicidal threats; disorganized behavior, especially as found in regressed, psychotic individuals; acting-out or rule-breaking behavior; withdrawal; and excessive dependency. In such cases the therapist may need to establish explicit rules aimed at stopping the behavior and aiding the patient in placing these maladaptive behaviors under his or her own control.

Clarifying and Reinforcing Adaptive Mechanisms

It may be that all the elements for change are present within the experience and adaptive capacities of the patient, in which case the therapist needs merely to *clarify and reinforce these adaptive mechanisms.* This may involve determining what behaviors have worked in the past and strengthening them to meet the new adaptive requirements. Some patients come to a therapist with a good solution at hand; that is, they "really know what to do" but for some reason are reluctant or unable to do it. The therapist who recognizes this situation and believes that it is within the patient's power to carry out a reasonable plan of action may simply serve the patient by allowing him or her to adjust himself or herself to the task at hand and encouraging him or her to be less timid about the decision. In other cases the patient may have no clear options and must adapt in some specific and perhaps limited way. Then the preferred treatment strategy is not to develop new alternatives, but to focus on making the only available alternatives more acceptable to the patient. Recognizing when there is limited power for behavior change is important, since it facilitates spending the available time on the most potentially fruitful therapeutic task.

Confronting the Patient

With respect to limited power for change, the crisis therapist frequently finds himself or herself working with immobilized patients who have unrealistic goals or maladaptive life styles which require frank and direct examination. Often such patients rigidly attempt to maintain their life stance despite persistent failures and accompanying psychological pain. The appropriate therapeutic tactic may then be the *direct and aggressive confrontation of the patient's ideas or behavior.* For the immobilized individual who does not know where to begin, the confrontation therapeutic technique frequently initiates a critical reappraisal of the problem (Garner, 1970). The use of confrontation, from relatively mild but pointed questions aimed at drawing the patient's attention to neglected or denied problem areas to more blatant and accusatory "attacking" statements, is aimed at forcing the patient to appraise his or her situation realistically. The rational–emotive techniques detailed by Ellis (1962) are perhaps the most useful guidelines to confrontation for a therapist to follow. Another useful technique for challenging a patient's beliefs is *paradoxical intention* (Frankl, 1960), which attempts to make the individual assume attitudes or practices diametrically opposed to his or her accepted ones.

An inexperienced or timid therapist may be reluctant to confront or challenge in an aggressive fashion the belief systems of the patient. Many beginning therapists find confrontation awkward and unsettling, because their "natural" response to the patient is acceptance and "unconditional positive regard." Hence they are seen by the patient as "nice and understanding," but little else. In crisis therapy a "nice" person is not necessarily a "therapeutic" person. Very often the situation calls for the therapist's being critical of the behavior of the patient, and a therapist who cannot objectively and effectively confront patients when it is appropriate to do so is ineffective with many of the people in crisis he or she tries to help.

The crisis intervener should be careful not to deprive the client of the temporary cushion of denial during a time when the client is psychologically incapable of facing the full impact of reality. Confrontation is a powerful but also dangerous tool that in the hands of an inexperienced and eager counselor can lead to much damage. Denial is all too frequently viewed as an undesirable defense mechanism—its healthy and beneficial function is at times unrecognized and undervalued.

Terminating the Session Abruptly

A somewhat extreme form of confrontation is sometimes necessary to make an impact on certain patients. It occasionally happens that the patient's situation is such that *abrupt termination of the session* is not only necessary but in the long range therapeutic. Individuals who for various reasons (unwillingness, defensiveness, etc.) are not at the point of working on their problems may be best handled by an abrupt termination with an explanation such as this from the therapist: "It is evident that you are not able to work on these problems at this time, even though I believe that you know what is necessary to make your situation better; if you decide to work on your problems, you may schedule another appointment." This tactic communicates to the patient that, although the therapist is interested in his or her welfare and wishes to be of help, it is necessary for the patient to come to terms with his or her immobility in the situation. For some types of patients this indicates that their present frame of mind does not facilitate problem resolution, and it may produce a prompt increase in their level of cooperation and participation in the session.

Making Concrete Demands

In the event that additional therapy sessions are planned or a follow-up is scheduled, it is usually a good idea to *place some concrete demands or requirements on the patient* before the next meeting or contact. This expectation should be something that emerges naturally out of the material as a task to be done and is, in both the therapist's and patient's judgment, a manageable request. The task, even if small, will communicate to the patient that if treatment continues the therapist will expect him or her to work on his or her problems outside of the therapy sessions. The patient may experience some feelings of immediate improvement if he or she is able to perform the task successfully, and the therapist will obtain an assessment of the patient's motivation for change from the way he or she manages the assignment.

Working Out a Contract

Implicit in the previous point is the idea of working out a *therapeutic contract* or set of concrete goals for the treatment program. A *change plan* (Phillips & Wiener, 1966) should be formulated in which there is a clear "statement of what behavior has to change, how the change may be brought about, by whom the change can be wrought" (p. 68). In time-bound psychotherapy a contract between the patient and therapist is essential for a number of reasons. The patient should have a clear idea of the number of sessions that will be involved and what, explicitly, is to be accomplished in this time. The behaviors to be changed or the environmental conditions to be manipulated need to be charted, and the means for achieving these ends need to be clearly delineated.

Enlisting the Aid of Others

The crisis therapist often finds that the patient is so embroiled in and bound to his or her situation that little progress can be attained until significant environmental factors are alleviated or unless other persons, close to the patient, are involved, Lorion (1973) warns that "to ignore the social reality of a patient's existence while attempting to implement change in therapy may be self-defeating." The patient's economic, social, and family situation must be tied in with individual treatment plans. Parad (1961) considers crisis therapy distinct from traditional short-term therapy precisely in that it views work with significant others as very important. Hence the crisis therapist may do well to *enlist the aid of others in an effort to change* the pressures impinging on the patient. He may encourage the significant others in the patient's life to come in for a meeting or allow a home visit by the therapist. Employers may be contacted to work out more satisfactory work arrangements for some patients. Outside contacts should of course be worked out in detail with the patient.

FOLLOW-UP AND EVALUATION IN CRISIS THERAPY

Follow-up of the patient's progress after termination of treatment constitutes an important function of any therapeutic offering. It is especially important for crisis therapy to be guided by knowledge for results from follow-up studies, because the therapist's input in a case is usually great and the consequences of perseverating "errors" over future cases are profound. Brief crisis therapy lends itself particularly well to follow-up, since the therapeutic contracts that are arranged are usually concrete enough to allow the therapist to ascertain if the behavioral change strategies have been followed through.

The role of the therapist here is viewed in an entirely different light than in the therapeutic teachings of a few years ago. Psychologists have relinquished some of their cherished ideals such as "The therapist is a mirror," or "A therapist never initiates contact with a patient." It is likely that the benefits of these ideals always existed more in the mind of the therapist than of the patient anyway. One effect of this shift is that crisis workers can feel quite comfortable doing fairly aggressive follow-ups. One can readily see that the same factors that call for therapist directiveness also call for directiveness and aggressiveness in follow-up. In crisis work follow-up can be broadly defined as any activity, other than the therapy sessions themselves that enables the crisis worker to determine if he or she has mobilized all resources that might be instrumental in insuring a successful resolution of the crisis. Follow-up should not be limited to contacts made after therapy is successfully terminated. If this were the case, it is likely that at least half of the crisis population would never be followed up, since many fail to return for scheduled visits after their initial contact.

It is worth reiterating that some of the personality characteristics that cause people to find themselves in the midst of a crisis operate in preventing them from successfully resolving the crisis. For example, a passive–dependent woman drops in with the complaint that her alcoholic husband beats her. The base rate expectations lead one to speculate that that same dependency and passivity may prevent her from confronting and handling this situation, in spite of the fact that she sincerely asserts at the moment that this is what she wants to do and knows she should do. If she fails to return for her next appointment, a well-timed follow-up may communicate to her that it is understandable why this is such a difficult step for her, and may present her with an opportunity to discuss and work through some of her feelings which have prevented her from dealing with her presenting crisis adaptively.

Follow-up can also be utilized to ensure that referrals are successfully completed. As we have previously mentioned, crisis intervention often involves directing clients to already existing agencies and services. For example, one comprehensive crisis center found that nearly 50% of its contacts required referral as part of the final disposition (Stelmachers, 1972). Follow-up at this point ensures that the referral contact is successfully made and communicates to the patient that the therapist, in making the referral, was not just "passing the buck." The concern expressed through this follow-up contact opens the door for further intervention if the referral is unsatisfactory or unsuccessful.

An important group of patients who need close follow-up are people who have attempted suicide. It has been well documented that those patients who successfully commit suicide do so within 3 months after treatment termination, and most of them have made unsuccessful attempts previously. Although follow-up may not prevent suicide, it may communicate to the patient that his or her welfare is important and that immediate treatment options do exist. Despite the obvious importance of follow-up in crisis work, surveys indicate that most crisis centers are lax, if not negligent, in this respect (Bloomfield et al., 1971).

The follow-up of individual patients is closely related to the broader goal of evaluating the work accomplished by the crisis center itself. The necessity for evaluation of the therapeutic offerings is probably given as much lip service as is the necessity for follow-up; however, in most settings the actual yield is paltry, since few centers utilize a formal evaluation procedure that allows for quantitative analysis.

We would like to underscore the importance of follow-up in individual treatment and the necessity for evaluation of treatment programs by describing one extensive approach to implementing these ideals.

Butcher and Kolotkin (1979) pointed out that follow-up is particularly crucial to the success of brief psychotherapy since this type of treatment is perhaps more vulnerable to deterioration effects than is long-term therapy. Often brief therapy is terminated prior to the gain of maximum benefit and the client is expected to "consolidate gains" in the weeks following termination. Follow-up in crisis-oriented or brief psychotherapy is often an integral part of the treatment itself—not an afterthought.

A brief description of one center that has engaged in extensive follow-up research and the evaluation of treatment programs (Kiresuk & Sherman, 1968) is presented as a model. The Crisis Intervention Center has been in existence since July of 1971. It is located within Hennepin County General Hospital, near the inner-city neighborhoods of Minneapolis, Minnesota. It is open 24 hours a day, 7 days a week, and offers assistance without regard to eligibility to any individual in need. Telephone, walk-in, and home-visit services are available, and the center has direct access to medical and inpatient psychiatric facilities. The clinic is directed by a clinical psychologist. The staff of 25 consists of psychiatric nurses, psychiatric social workers, psychologists, community mental health workers, and on-call psychiatrists. Students of varying disciplines and volunteers are also utilized. The center emphasizes immediate crisis resolution through direct intervention and appropriate follow-up. Services include brief, reality-oriented therapy, medication, and appropriate referrals. During the first year of operation it sustained 14,000 telephone and 7,000 walk-in contacts (Lund, 1974).

The clinical effectiveness of the center has been measured by utilized a set of procedures, consisting of goal attainment scaling and consumer satisfaction interviews, developed by Kiresuk and Sherman (1968). In goal attainment scaling, appropriate treatment goals are selected and scaled as a negotiated contract between client and clinician. If a client is unwilling or unable to participate in the negotiation, the clinician completes the follow-up guide alone. Clinicians specify behaviorally the expected level of treatment sucess, as well as degrees of "less than expected success" and "more than expected success." An example of some of the treatment goals is shown in Table 11.1 (Stelmachers, Lund, & Meade, 1972). The actual follow-up interviews to determine whether the goals have been achieved are made by independent workers, often over the phone. Consumer satisfaction is assessed by the follow-up workers, who ask brief additional questions such as "How satisfied were you with the services you received at the Crisis Intervention Center?" and "Would you return again?" Feedback is immediately made available to individual clinicians.

An evaluation of results of the first 109 clients followed up revealed a mean goal attainment score of 51.69 (a goal attainment score of 50 represents the "expected" level of goal attainment for a single client; the mean score represents a summary of goal attainment success across the various scales constructed). The mean scores for various staff disciplines were quite similar, the range being from 49.25 to 52.20. Of the follow-up guides constructed in the Hennepin County Crisis Intervention Center, 67.0% contained only one or two scales. This illustrates the fact that many crisis contacts are of a rather limited nature, which results in limited goal setting. Some preliminary data indicate that clients who actually receive crisis treatment have a larger number of scale goals (2.33) than clients who are referred for treatment elsewhere (1.54).

The client satisfaction survey, included as part of the follow-up, revealed that 79% of the crisis patients were either "very satisfied" or "satisfied" with the services they received. Only 10.3% of clients showed evidence of new mental or physical problems since the time of their contact.

The goal attainment scaling procedure can be further utilized in research by al-

Table 11.1. Sample of Goal Attainment Scales[a]

Level of Outcome	Attitude toward Treatment	Success of Referral	Depression	Manipulation
Most unfavorable treatment outcome thought likely	Patient does not keep intake appointment and refuses new appointment at follow-up	Detoxification center refuses to accept patient	Patient is immobilized by depression and apathy over death of husband and is unable to care for self; perhaps in an institution	Patient makes rounds of community service agencies demanding medication and refuses other forms of treatment
Less than expected success with treatment	Patient keeps intake appointment, but refuses further treatment	Detoxification center accepts patient but complains at follow-up that the referral was not appropriate	Patient is chronically depressed, but is able to function at a level necessary to continue living	Patient no longer visits CIC with demands for medication but continues with other community agencies and still refuses other forms of treatment
Expected level of treatment success	Patient keeps intake appointment and accepts treatment, but reports that he does not expect it to help him	Detoxification center accepts patient and comments at follow-up that, although the patient was difficult to handle, the referral was probably appropriate	Patient is still depressed and apathetic but reports periods of up to a day when she does not think of husband	Patient no longer attempts to manipulate for drugs at community service agencies but will not accept another form of treatment
More than expected success with treatment	Patient keeps intake appointment and accepts treatment, and makes some positive comments about his expectations (i.e., "I don't know, I suppose it might help")	Detoxification center accepts patient and comments at follow-up that the referral was definitely appropriate	Patient reports severe depression only on occasions which evoke special memories	Patient accepts nonmedication treatment at some community agency
Best anticipated success with treatment	Patient accepts treatment and expresses enthusiasm concerning his treatment expectations (i.e., "I think this really might help me")	Detoxification center accepts patient and comments at follow-up that the referral was definitely appropriate and compliments CIC unit's handling of case	Patient reports she is no longer depressed over death of husband, and realizes she must go on living without him	Patient accepts nonmedication treatment, and by his own report shows signs of improvement

[a] Adapted from Steimachers, Lund, and Meade (1972, p. 63).

lowing a quantitative assessment of whether or not particular groups of patients attain the goals that have been worked out or whether specific therapists or therapeutic approaches are more or less successful at bringing about desired goals.

ORGANIZATION AND OPERATION OF CRISIS INTERVENTION PROGRAMS

Many crisis intervention–oriented psychologists, in addition to applying crisis strategies in their clinical practice, will become involved in the development and administration of crisis intervention programs. Therefore, it may be useful for us to provide some background and organizational and programmatic information as to how to organize and operate a crisis intervention service. The translation of the *concept* of crisis intervention into practice depends very much on the guiding philosophy of the program, its comprehensiveness, its mission, the physical facilities, the staffing pattern, the target population, and sources of funding. Actually, from the viewpoint of the practicing clinician, crisis theory in the abstract is rather unsatisfactory because, unlike psychoanalysis, for instance, it is less well defined and influential in determining its actual step-by-step application. In Korchin's (1976) opinion crisis intervention is more an orientation and way of thinking than a systematic body of theory, knowledge, and practice. Factors other than the declaration of a problem as "crisis" dictate the professional response to an urgent situation. And these forces are often in conflict with each other. For example, a father's, a landlady's or a police officer's notion of what is an emergency may be vastly different from that of the identified patient, and the complexity of definition increases when the various opinions are added. Not uncommonly, one finds the concerned person who accompanied the client to the clinic to be experiencing a greater crisis than the client, who may view the concern as grossly exaggerated and unwarranted. All this means is that various agents with different perspectives end up with different conceptualizations and different expectations with regard to the type of intervention needed in a given case. For a crisis program to be responsive to such diverse expectations, it has to be able to accommodate a wide range of problem situations, from highly emergent and life-threatening ones to situations that could quite comfortably wait until regular office hours the next morning. To consider some such nonemergent contacts as a misuse or abuse of crisis services because they don't fit the theoretical definition of crisis is not helpful, because much of the crisis program's business will consist of such "unwelcome" contacts. The only truly unifying concept in all this that distinguishes crisis services from others is that they are *unscheduled*.

Program Components

Most crisis services will have several components, whether they are organizationally identified or not. Some of them may represent services offered in the community as separate programs. Nevertheless, the staff of a relatively comprehensive crisis center should have some expertise in as many of these areas as possible.

Otherwise, especially in communities with many crisis-oriented agencies, clients may get a succession of referrals instead of decisive intervention.

Besides providing crisis intervention proper, the staff should be prepared to deal with an occasional psychiatric emergency. One definition of a psychiatric emergency proposed by the American Psychiatric Association is the following: "a situation that includes an acute disturbance of thought, behavior, mood, or social relationship which requires immediate intervention as defined by the client for family or social unit" (Barton, 1978). A significant portion of a crisis center's client population will have psychiatric histories and/or be currently in psychiatric treatment. They will present themselves with a wide variety of psychiatric symptoms exacerbated by a crisis situation. For such a population, the crisis program should have the trained staff to conduct mental status examinations and diagnostic interviews, to administer psychotropic medications, and, if necessary, to seclude, restrain, or hospitalize.

The crisis intervention service will also serve at times as a walk-in clinic or drop-in center for nonemergent clients requiring evaluation. For clients with dispositional problems or those needing food, clothing, or shelter, emergency social services would be appropriate, or the facility may sometimes be in the ludicrous position of providing services that are available instead of those that are needed, for example, offering brief psychotherapy to a client who is mildly depressed because he can't afford to buy shoes for his children.

For immediate accessibility, it is mandatory for the crisis service to have one or several hot lines, preferably identified by target population, such as suicide, rape, child abuse, and the like. Because there are clients who are unwilling or unable to come to the center, home visits and other outreach services can be valuable additional service elements. Some crisis programs are entirely based on outreach (McGee, 1974). Some crisis programs have even extended the concept of outreach to placing acutely disturbed clients in private homes, called crisis homes or safe houses, for short periods of time (Brook, 1980). Such homes offer a safe temporary shelter and avoid unnecessary and costly hospitalization by providing treatment in a less restricted environment resembling more normal living.

Finally, some crisis programs offer prepetition screening to clients considered for involuntary commitment.

Unlike a regular clinic or mental health center, a crisis program has less freedom to reject clients who don't fit the program's main stated purpose or advertised emphasis. Clients, especially those with multiple problems, often choose services in a rather indiscriminate fashion, ignoring the typical administrator's tendency to categorize. Whenever the claim is made by someone that a crisis exists, it is difficult to reject those who are chronic, "inappropriate," nonemergent, too psychiatric, or intoxicated.

Target Symptoms, Problems, and Populations

Ideally, staff in a crisis program should not only be familiar with general crisis theory, principles, and techniques, but should also have specific knowledge about the characteristics and particular needs of various target populations: clients who are homicidal or violent, clients whose potential for dangerousness is an issue, suicidal individuals, victims of crime and natural disasters, clients who are dying or grieving or have experienced a significant loss, persons whose crisis is related to alcoholism or substance abuse, and probably many others. A substantial research and clinical literature exists about each of these content areas, and some familiarity with them is mandatory for the crisis intervention specialist to be maximally effective. Just as in the case of the already discussed program components of crisis intervention, the community may offer specialized services for some of these target problems. Some of these programs may lack professional staff, but they provide focused commitment and advocacy, something that general crisis intervention centers cannot accomplish. Therefore, a comprehensive crisis center should not attempt to compete with these programs but should instead complement them by offering professional backup and consultation. One side contributes concentrated dedication to a select group of clients, and the other side contributes a broad mental health expertise and more specialized services (such as psychotropic medications, psychotherapy, mental status examinations, medical examination of rape victims, etc.). Such a collaboration represents a very desirable arrangement, because neither side can accomplish the task alone (Stelmachers, 1982).

Setting

Crisis programs work out of hospital emergency rooms or psychiatry departments, or are part of a mental health center, or are basically free standing and administratively independent. Typically the first two are staffed by professionals, and the last by volunteers with professional backup or consultation available as needed. There are obvious advantages and disadvantages to each of these three settings. The free-standing center is probably least encumbered by bureaucratic constraints and best accommodates clients who feel unwelcome or uncomfortable in establishment agencies. However, the reliance on volunteers can seriously limit the scope of the program, and volunteer recruitment, training, supervision, and retention present an ongoig problem for the agency.

Federally funded community mental health centers are mandated to offer emergency services. Mental health professionals are readily available and, at least in the eyes of some clients, there is less stigma attached to visiting a mental health center than to visiting a hospital-based psychiatric service. On the other hand, a survey of 99 mental health centers in 43 states selected at random revealed that 32 of the centers failed to answer their advertised emergency phone numbers, and half of the centers that did answer had no staff on hand; also, half of the people who answered the phone had no training in mental health (*Psychiatric News*, 1977). Mental health services may have improved since 1977; however, many mental health centers still lack adequate medical/psychiatric personnel. The physical facilities of most such mental health centers do not lend themselves to the safe and efficient treatment of many behavioral emergencies.

While a hospital-based crisis program may have an overly medical orientation that is inappropriate for a large number of crisis clients and may suffer from lower accessibility and acceptability due to bureaucratic hurdles characteristic of large institutions, it nevertheless offers many important advantages lacking in other settings (Resnik & Ruben, 1975; Stelmachers, 1980). More and more hospitals are being used as primary care providers, and deinstitutionalization of the mentally ill has shifted the clinical burden from state hospitals to public and private general hospitals and their emergency departments. Police and other community gatekeepers readily bring troubled and troublesome persons to the local emergency rooms, which are open around the clock and are typically equipped to handle behavioral disturbances. Ambulances are readily available for transportation, and medical treatment can be easily obtained for such emergencies as overdoses and other suicide attempts. Hospitalization can be readily arranged in medical and psychiatric wards, and psychotropic medications can be dispensed to clients needing them. In larger hospitals the presence of security guards makes it possible to enforce legal emergency holds for involuntary evaluation and hospitalization.

Staffing

Crisis intervention programs employ every conceivable mix of mental health professionals, paraprofessionals, and volunteers. Who is selected seems to depend on the administrative setting, the available budget, or the program director's preference. Most of the staff, regardless of their professional affiliations, act as mental health generalists much of the time, and no one has convincingly demonstrated that one staffing pattern or one particular professional discipline is to be preferred over the others. The only possible exception may be nurses, who are probably indispensable if the crisis center is located in a hospital. One note of caution, however. Although some professional mental health background and experience in psychotherapy is necessary for at least some of the staff, a degree in social work or clinical psychology should not be taken as sufficient evidence of competence in crisis intervention and treatment of behavioral emergencies. Specialized training is needed for crisis management.

In terms of the overall skill level or professional training, it is advisable to have a wide range of levels present to meet the equally wide range of client problems. At various times the staff will have to offer, singly or in combination, support reassurance, information, advocacy, facilitation, opportunity for ventilation, active listening, and even temporary friendship, as well as technically demanding crisis therapy. For best results—and also for cost-effectiveness—the level and type of intervention should be matched with the level and type of training of staff. Thus the best crisis intervention staff should be multilevel and multidisciplinary, selected on the basis of both general mental health background and specialized experience and skills with behavioral emergencies and particular target populations.

Program Evaluation

Program evaluation of crisis intervention and behavioral emergency centers leaves much to be desired. Aside from inertia and a general reluctance to submit one's practice to scrutiny, there are several reasons for the difficulty of assessing the quality of care provided by crisis services. Many such services permit or encourage anonymity of clients, which makes follow-up problematic. A large number of crisis clients are transients or otherwise mobile individuals with unstable life patterns who are difficult to locate. In a follow-up study there is a larger sample loss in the transient population of the crisis center as compared with regular mental health clients. The clinical interaction is very brief, so that the effects of such an intervention can be expected to be rather circumscribed and to be strongly influenced by factors outside the crisis intervention. This makes attribution of changes to treatment more difficult. As one writer puts it, "The cases whose outcomes are most susceptible to measurement often undergo rather long and complex courses of care, of which the emergent portion is only the beginning. It is necessary, then, either to control for the influence of the care received after the patient leaves the emergency department, or to estimate 'outcome' on the basis of data available at the point when the emergency care ends—'approximate outcome' '' (Walker, 1980).

Another difficulty with evaluating crisis clients is that they are frequently too disturbed, psychotic, or confused to participate meaningfully in goal setting and treatment planning. Some of them cannot even remember the contact and therefore cannot provide any feedback regarding their view of the intervention. Client satisfaction measures also become questionable indicators of treatment quality, because a substantial number of crisis clients are involuntary, resistive, and uncooperative. Finally, program evaluation, even at a primitive level, may be too costly an enterprise for many of the free-standing centers that rely on volunter help and private funding.

The above problems have not kept investigators from trying. Many attempts have been made to evaluate crisis services, and some of them show encouraging results. Some research has questioned specific treatment effects of crisis intervention (Gottschalk, Fox, & Bates, 1973; Maris & Connor, 1973).

For the most part, crisis services have concentrated on process variables, such as therapist characteristics, but many have conducted outcome studies involving real-life measures, such as hospitalization and suicide rates, patient saisfaction measures, symptom improvement, acceptance of treatment recommendations and referral success, interprogram comparisons, peer review and quality-of-care audit, and, finally, structural evaluation of program impact of an entire center.

In summary, there is no doubt that significant improvement takes place following crisis intervention, but this improvement may be largely due to a variety of nonspecific treatment effects. As one writer states it rather pessimistically, "In many instances, the conditions are self-limiting, and the likelihood of a really bad or really good outcome does not depend on the quality of care. The truly serious conditions, in which outcomes can be readily measured in terms of survival or meaningful reduction of morbidity, are relatively infrequent" (Walker, 1980). It is, of course, possible that the nonspecific effects would not occur outside the context of a convincing crisis intervention scheme. For these effects to take place, they may have to be imbedded in a setting that conforms to clients' expectations about who is competent to deliver what services for what problems within what kind of structure. At the very minimum, we can say that even if people were well off without crisis intervention, once they receive it they are satisfied with it and show improvement that they themselves are willing to attribute to intervention (Stelmachers, 1977).

Standards of Care

It is a sign of professional maturity that official guidelines have been established that dictate clinical practice in crisis intervention. Some of them, such as the standards adopted by the American Association of Suicidology, actually govern practice to the extent that a center chooses to be certified by AAS (McGee, 1976). When it comes to psychiatric emergency care, there are several sets of standards by such national organizations as the Joint Commission on Accreditation of Hospitals, the National Institute of Mental Health, the American Medical Association, and Blue Cross/Blue Shield. The rather serious flaws in these standards have been discussed by Barton (1982). Some of these standards offer very little reference to emergency services per se, do not specify what professional disciplines should be involved in crisis intervention, consider outreach and consultation services optional, and in general are, in the words of Barton, "extremely vague and not too helpful in clinical programming, facility planning, or staff training and qualifications" (p. 336).

A few years ago the American Psychiatric Assciation Task Force on Emergency Care Issues in collaboration with other national organizations drafted proposed standards for psychiatric emergency services in general hospitals, mental health centers, and state hospitals. The guidelines for psychiatric emergency care in hospital emergency departments consist of 37 standards, ranging in content from specifying the need for an outreach team to requiring that there be a policy and procedures manual and documented evidence of staff training in psychiatric emergency care. Among the standards' demands are that no emergency evaluation take longer than 18 hours, and that the basic needs of family and significant others be considered. Once adopted, these standards will help crisis services to evaluate themselves against national norms.

The same APA task force has also developed a scheme for categorizing emergency services: horizontal categorization (comprehensiveness of the services), vertical categorization (specialty care capability and resources in selected critical care areas), and circular categorization (capability of a region to coordinate its emergency services). Furthermore, protocols and algorithms have been developed for handling certain behavioral emergencies, such as child abuse, drug intoxication, violence, restraints, and involuntary commitment.

Barton (1982) concludes her review by emphasizing the need for "more precise, appropriate, and comprehensive standards in psychiatric emergency care." Unless these standards can be somehow enforced, "the inertia in a ponderous health care system already plodding along providing a mediocre to poor level of care to a vulnerable population may persist" (p. 343).

REFERENCES

Abroms, G. M. Setting limits. *Archives of General Psychiatry,* 1968, **19,** 113–119.

Aguilera, D. C., Messick, J. M., & Farrell, S. M. *Crisis intervention: Theory and methodology.* St. Louis: Mosby, 1970.

Aita, J. A. Efficacy of the brief clinical method in predicting adjustments. *Archives of Neurology and Psychiatry,* 1949, **61,** 170–176.

Aldrich, C. K. Brief psychotherapy: A reappraisal of some theoretical assumptions. *American Journal of Psychiatry,* 1968, **125,** 585–592.

Alexander, F., & French, T. *Psychoanalytic therapy.* New York: Ronald Press, 1946.

Auerbach, S. M., & Kilmann, P. R. Crisis intervention: A review of outcome research. *Psychological Bulletin,* 1977, **84,** 1189–1217.

Auld, F., & Myers, J. Contributions to a theory for selecting psychotherapy patients. *Journal of Clinical Psychology,* 1954, **10,** 56–60.

Bagley, C. An evaluation of suicide prevention agencies. *Life-threatening Behavior,* 1971, **1,** 245–259.

Baldwin, B. A. A paradigm for the classification of emotional crises: Implications for crisis intervention. *American Journal of Orthopsychiatry,* 1978, **48** (3), 538–551.

Barten, H. H. (Ed.). *Brief therapies.* New York: Behavioral Publications, 1972.

Barten, H. H., & Barten, S. S. (Eds.) *Children and their parents in brief therapy.* New York: Behavioral Publication, 1972.

Barton, G. *Categorization scheme proposal for psychiatric emergency care settings.* Draft developed with the Task Force on Emergency Care Issues for the Amerian Psychiatric Association, Washington, D.C., 1979.

Barton, G. M. Standards of care. In J. Gorton & R. Partridge (Eds.), *Practice and management of psychiatric emergency care.* St. Louis: Mosby, 1982.

Battle, C. C., Imber, S. D., Hoehn-Saric, R., Stone, A. R., Nash, E. H., & , Frank, J. D. Target complaints as criteria of improvement. *American Journal of Psychotherapy,* 1966, **20,** 184–192.

Beck, B. M., & Robbins, L. L. *Short-term therapy in an authoritative setting.* New York: Family Service Association, 1946.

Bellak, L., & Small, L. *Emergency psychotherapy and brief psychotherapy.* New York: Grune & Stratton, 1965.

Bergin, A. E., & Garfield, S. L. (Eds.). *Handbook of psychotherapy and behavior change: An empirical analysis.* New York: Wiley, 1971.

Bibring, G. L., Dwyer, T. F., Huntington, D. S., & Valenstein. F. A study of the psychological processes in pregnancy and of the earliest mother-child relationship. *Psychoanalytic Study of the Child,* 1961, **16,** 25–72.

Birley, J. L., & Brown, G. W. Crises and life changes preceding the onset or relapse of acute schizophrenia: Clinical aspects. *British Journal of Psychiatry,* 1970, **116,** 327–333.

Bloom, B. L. Definitional aspects of the crisis concept. *Journal of Consulting Psychology,* 1963, **27,** 498–502.

Brantner, J. The first interview. In J. Butcher, J. Ayers, & I. Benoist. *Role of assessment in crisis intervention: A video taped discussion.* Clinical Psychology Program, University of Minnesota, 1973

Breuer, J., & Freud, S. (1893–1895) *Studies on hysteria. Standard Edition.* (Vol. II). London: Hogarth Press, 1955.

Brill, N. Q., & Storrow, H. A. Social class and psychiatric treatment. *Archives of General Psychiatry,* 1960, **3,** 340–344.

Brook, B. D. Community families: A seven-year program perspective. *Community Psychology,* 1980, **8,** 147–151.

Budman, S. H. (Ed.). *Forms of brief therapy.* New York: Plenum, 1981.

Butcher, J. N., & Herzog, J. Individual assessment in crisis intervention: Observation, life history, and personality approaches. In C. D. Spielberger & J. N. Butcher (Eds.), *Advances in personality assessment* (Vol. 1). New York: LEA Publishing, 1982.

Butcher, J. N.., & Kolotkin, R. L. Evaluation of outcome in brief psychotherapy. *Psychiatric clinics of America,* 1979, **2** (1), 157–169.

Butcher, J. N., & Koss, M. P. Research on brief and crisis-oriented psychotherapies. In S. L. Garfield & A. E. Bergin (Eds.), *Handbook of psychotherapy and behavior change.* New York: Wiley, 1978.

Calhoun, L. G., Selby, J. W., & King, H. E. *Dealing with crisis.* New York: Prentice-Hall, 1976.

Caplan, G. *An approach to community mental health.* New York: Grune & Stratton, 1961.

Caplan, G. *Principles of preventive psychiatry.* New York: Basic Books, 1964.

Castelnuovo-Tedesco, P. Brief psychotherapeutic treatment of the depressive reactions. In G. J. Wayne & R. R. Koegler (Eds.), *Emergency psychiatry and brief therapy.* Boston: Little, Brown, 1966.

Chafetz, M. E. *The effect of an emergency psychiatric service on motivation for treatment.* Paper presented at the annual meeting of the American Psychiatric Association, Los Angeles, May 1964.

Coleman, M. D. Emergency psychotherapy. In J. H. Masserman & J. L. Moreno (Eds.), *Progress in psychotherapy* (Vol. V). New York: Grune & Stratton, 1960.

Darbonne, A. Crisis: A review of theory, practice and research. *International Journal of Psychiatry,* 1968, **6,** 371–379.

DeCourcy, P. The hazard of short-term psychotherapy without assessment: A case history. *Journal of Personality Assessment,* 1971, **35,** 285–288.

Dohrenwend, B. S., & Dohrenwend, B. P. Some issues in research on stressful life events. *Journal of Nervous and Mental Diseases,* 1978, **166,** 7–15.

Ellis, A. *Reason and emotion in psychotherapy.* New York: Lyle Stuart, 1962.

Erikson, E. Growth and crisis of the healthy personality. In C. Kluckholn & H. Murray (Eds.), *Personality in nature, society and culture.* New York: Knopf, 1953.

Farberow, N. L. Suicide prevention: A view from the bridge. *Community Mental Health Journal,* 1968, **4,** 469–474.

Farberow, N. L., & Schneidman, E. S. (Eds.). *The cry for help.* New York: McGraw-Hill, 1961.

Figley, C. R. *Stress disorders among Vietnam veterans: Theory, research and treatment.* New York: Bruner/Mazel, 1978.

Frank. J. D. *Persuasion and healing: A comparative study of psychotherapy.* New York: Schocken, 1961.

Frank, J. D. Treatment of the focal system: An adaptational approach. *American Journal of Psychotherapy,* 1966, **20,** 565–575.

Frank, J. D. The role of hope in psychotherapy. *International Journal of Psychiatry*, 1968, **5,** 383–395.

Frankl, V. E. Paradoxical intention: A logotherapeutic technique. *American Journal of Psychotherapy*, 1960, **14,** 520–535.

Freud, S. (1919) Lines of advance in psycho-analytic therapy. *Standard Edition* (Vol. XVII). London: Hogarth Press, 1955.

Freudenberger, H. J. The free clinic concept. *International Journal of Offender Therapy*, 1972, **15,** 121–125.

Garner, H. H. Brief psychotherapy and the confrontation approach. *Psychosomatics*, 1970, **11,** 319–325.

Garfield, S. L. Research on client variables in psychotherapy. In A. E. Bergin & S. L. Garfield (Eds.), *Handbook of psychotherapy and behavior change.* New York: Wiley, 1971.

Glass, A. J. *Psychiatric prediction and military effectiveness. Research Report WRAIR-64-65.* Washington, D.C.: Walter Reed Army Institute of Research, 1956.

Goin, M. Yamamoto, J., & Silverman, J. Therapy congruent wih class-linked expectations. *Archives of General Psychiatry*, 1965, **13,** 133–137.

Golan, N. When is a client in crisis? *Social Casework,* July 1969, 389–394.

Golan, N. *Treatment in crisis situations.* New York: Free Press, 1978.

Golann, S., & Eisdorfer, c. (Eds.). *Handbook of community mental health.* New York: Appleton-Century-Crofts, 1972.

Goldenberg, H. *Contemporary clinical psychology.* Monterey, Calf.:Brooks/Cole, 1973.

Gottesman, I. I., & Shields, J. *Schizophrenia and genetics.* New York: Academic Press, 1972.

Gottschalk, A. L., Fox, R. A., & Bates, D. E. A study of prediction and outcome in a mental health crisis clinic. *American Journal of Psychiatry*, 1973, **130** (10), 1107–1111.

Grinker, R. R., & Spiegel, J. P. Brief psychotherapy in war neuroses. *Psychosomatic Medicine*, 1944, **6,** 123–131.

Grinker, R. R., & Spiegel, J. P. *Men under stress.* Philadelphia: Blakiston, 1945.

Haley, J. *Strategies of psychotherapy.* New York: Grune & Stratton, 1963.

Halleck, S. L. Psychodynamic aspects of violence. In R. L. Sadoff (Ed.), *Violence and responsibility.* New York: Spectrum Publications, 1978.

Harris, M. R., Kallis, B. L., & Freeman, E. H. Precipitation stress: An approach to brief therapy. *American Journal of Psychotherapy*, 1963, **17,** 465–471.

Helig, S. M., Farberow, N. L., Litman, R. E., & Schneidman, E. S. The role of nonprofessional volunteers in a suicide prevention center. *Community Mental Health Journal*, 1968, **4,** 287–295.

Hoch, P. H. Short-term versus long-term therapy. In L. R. Wolberg (Ed.), *Short-term psychotherapy.* New York: Grune & Stratton, 1965.

Hoff, L. A. *People in crisis: Understanding and helping.* Menlo Park, Calif. Addison-Wesley, 1978.

Hogan, R. The implosive technique. *Behavior Research and Therapy*, 1969, **6,** 423–431.

Hollingshead, A. B., & Redlich, F. C. *Social class and mental illness: A community study.* New York: Wiley, 1958.

Holmes, T. H., & Rahe, R. H. The Social Adjustment Rating Scale. *Journal of Psychosomatic Research*, 1967, **11**, 213–218.

Hunt, R. G. Social class and mental illness: Some implications for clinical theory and practice. *American Journal of Psychiatry*, 1960, **116**, 1065–1069.

Jacobson, G., Strickler, M., & Morley, W. Generic and individual approaches to crisis intervention. *American Journal of Public Health*, 1968, **58**, 339–343.

Jacobson, G., Wilner, D., Morley, W., Schneider, S., Strickler, M., & Sommer, G. The scope and practice of an early-access brief treatment psychiatric center. *American Journal of Psychiatry*, 1965, **121**, 1176–1182.

Jacobson, G. F. Crisis theory and treatment strategy: Some socio-cultural and psychodynamic considerations. *Journal of Nervous and Mental Disease*, 1965, **141**, 209–218.

Kalis, G. L., Harris, M. R., Prestwood, A. R., & Freeman, E. H. Precipitating stress as a focus in psychotherapy. *Archives of General Psychiatry*, 1961, **5**, 219–226.

Kaplan, D. M. Observations on crisis theory and practice. *Social Casework*, 1968, **49**, 151–155.

Kaplan, D. M., & Mason, F. A. Maternal reactions to premature birth viewed as an acute emotional disorder. In H. J. Parad (Ed.), *Crisis intervention: Selected readings*. New York: Family Service Association of America, 1965.

Kardiner, A. *The traumatic neuroses of war*. New York: Hoeber, 1941.

Kiresuk, T. J., & Sherman, R. E. Goal attainment scaling: A general method for evaluating comprehensive community mental health programs. *Community Mental Health Journal*, 1968, **1** (1), 443–454.

Klein, D., & Lindemann, E. Preventive intervention in individual and family crisis situations. In G. Caplan (Ed.), *Prevention of mental disorders in children*. New York: Basic Books, 1961.

Klopfer, W. G. The blind leading the blind: Psychotherapy without assessment. *Journal of Projective Techniques and Personality Assessment*, 1964, **28**, 387–392.

Knapp, S., & Vandecreek, L. Tarasoff: five years later. *Professional Psychology*, 1982, **13** (4), 511–521.

Koegler, R. R., & Brill, N. Q. *Treatment of psychiatric out patients*. New York: Appleton-Century-Crofts, 1967.

Korchin, S. *Modern clinical psychology: Principles of intervention in the clinic and community*. New York: Basic Books, 1976.

Kraus, A. S., & Lilienfeld, A. M. Some epidemiological aspects of the high mortality rate in the young widowed group. *Journal of Chronic Diseases*, 1959, **10**, 207–217.

Lambley, P. The dangers of therapy without assessment: A case study. *Journal of Personality Assessment*, 1974, **38**, 263–265.

Lazarus, A. A. Learning theory and treatment of depression. *Behavior Research and Therapy*, 1968, **6**, 83–89.

Lerner, B. *Therapy in the ghetto*. Baltimore: Johns Hopkins University Press, 1972.

Lewin, K. K. *Brief encounters: Brief psychotherapy*. St. Louis: Warren H. Green, 1970.

Lief, H. I., Lief, U. F., Warren, C. O., & Heath, R. C. Low dropout rate in a psychiatric clinic. *Archives of General Psychiatry*, 1961, **5**, 200–211.

Lindemann, E. Symptomatology and management of acute grief. *American Journal of Psychiatry*, 1944, **101**, 141–148.

Lorion, R. P. Socioeconomic status and traditional treatment approaches reconsidered. *Psychological Bulletin,* 1973, **79,** 263–270.

Lorion, R. P. Patient and therapist variables in the treatment of low income patients. *Psychological Bulletin,* 1974, **81,** 344–354.

Lorr, M., McNair, D., Michaux, W., & Raskin, A. Frequency of treatment and change in psychotherapy. *Journal of Abnormal and Social Psychology,* 1962, **64,** 281–292.

Lund, S. H. Program evaluation project report, 1969–1973. Program Evaluation Project Report—NIMH Grant #5 R01 1678904. 1974.

Macleod, J. A., & Tinnin, L. W. Special service project: A solution to problems of early access and brief psychotherapy. *Archives of General Psychiatry,* 1966, **15,** 190–197.

Madison, D. The relevance of conjugal bereavement for preventive psychiatry. *British Journal of Medical Psychology,* 1968, **41,** 223–233.

Malan, D. H. *The frontier of brief psychotherapy.* New York: Plenum, 1976.

Malan, D. H. *Individual psychotherapy and the science of psychodynamics.* London: Butterworth, 1979.

Mann, J. *Time limited psychotherapy.* Cambridge, Mass.: Harvard University Press, 1973.

Mann, P. A. *Community psychology: Concepts and applications.* New York: Free Press, 1978.

Maris, R., & Connor, H. E. Do crisis services work? A follow-up of a psychiatric outpatient sample. *Journal of Health and Social Behavior,* 1973, **12,** 14.

Masserman, J. H. (Ed.). *Current psychiatric therapies* (Vol. 9). New York: Grune & Stratton, 1969.

McCord, E. Treatment in short-time contacts. *The Family,* 1931, **12,** 191–193.

McGee, R. K. *Crisis intervention in the community.* Baltimore: University Park Press, 1974.

McGee, R. K. (Ed.). *Evaluation criteria for the certification of suicide prevention and crisis intervention programs.* American Association of Suicidology, 1976.

Menninger, K. Psychological aspects of the organism under stress. *Journal of the American Psychoanalytic Association,* 1954, **2,** 280–310.

Mitchell, J. T., & Resnik, H. L. P. *Emergency response to crisis.* Bowie, Md.: Robert J. Brady, 1981.

Monahan, J. *Predicting violent behavior: An assessment of clinical techniques.* Beverly Hills, Calif.: Sage Publications, 1981.

Morley, W. E. Theory of crisis intervention. *Pastoral Psychology,* 1970, **21,** 14–20.

Muench, G. A. An investigation of time limited psychotherapy. *Journal of Counseling Psychology,* 1965, **12,** 294–299.

National Clearing House for Drug Abuse Information. *Free Clinics,* March 1974, Series 27, No. 1.

Nichols, M. P. Outcome of brief cathartic psychotherapy. *Journal of Consulting and Clinical Psychology,* 1974, **42,** 403–411.

Oberleder, M. Crisis therapy in mental breakdown of the aging. *The Gerontologist,* 1970, **10,** 111–114.

Parad, H. J. Preventive casework: Problems and implications. *The social welfare forum, 1961.* Papers from the National Conference on Social Welfare. New York: Columbia University Press, 1961.

Parad, H. J. (Ed.). *Crisis intervention: Selected readings.* New York: Family Service Association of America, 1965.

Parad, H. J. The use of time limited crisis intervention on community mental health programming. *Social Service Review,* 1966, **40,** 275–282.

Parad, L. Short term treatment: An overview of historical trends, issues and potentials. *Smith College Studies in Social Work,* 1971, **61,** 119–147.

Parkes, C., Benjamin, B., & Fitzgerald, R. Broken heart: A statistical study of increased mortality among widowers. 1969, **1,** 740–743.

Parkes, C. M. Effects of bereavement on physical and mental health—A study of the medical records of widows. *British Medical Journal,* 1964, **2,** 274–279.

Paul, L.Crisis intervention. *Mental Hygiene,* 1966, **50,** 141–145.

Paykel, E. S., Myers, J. K., Dienelt, M. N., Klerman, G. L., Lindenthal, J. J., & Pepper, M. P. Life events and depression: A controlled study. *Archives of General Psychiatry,* 1969, **21,** 753–760.

Phillips, E. L., & Wiener, D. N. *Short-term psychotherapy and structured behavior change.* New York: McGraw-Hill, 1966.

Polak, P. R., Kirby, M. W., & Deitchman, W. S. Treating acutely psychotic patients in private homes. *New Directions for Mental Health Services,* 1979, **1,** 49–64.

Pollack, D. Crisis and response in college students. *Journal of Abnormal Psychology,* 1971, **78,** 49–51.

New CMHC survey shows better emergency service. *Psychiatric News,* August 19, 1977, **12** (16).

Pumpian-Mindlin, E. Consideration in selection of patients for short-term therapy. *American Journal of Psychotherapy,* 1953, **7,** 641–652.

Puryear, D. A. *Helping people in crisis.* San Francisco: Jossey-Bass, 1979.

Rado, S. Relationship of short-term psychotherapy to developmental stages of maturation and stages of treatment behavior. In L. R. Wolberg (Ed.), *Short-term psychotherapy.* New York: Grune & Stratton, 1965.

Rahe, R. H., Meyer, M., Smith, M., Kjaer, G., & Holmes, T. H. Social stress and illness onset. *Journal of Psychosomatic Research,* 1964, **8,** 35–44.

Rapaport, L. The state of crisis: Some theoretical considerations. *Social Service Review,* 1962, **36,** 211–217.

Redlich, F., Hollingshead, A., & Bellis, E. Social class differences in attitudes toward psychiatry. *American Journal of Orthopsychiatry,* 1955, **25,** 60–70.

Reid, W., & Shyne, A. *A brief and extended casework.* New York: Columbia University Press, 1969.

Resnik, H. L. P., & Ruben, H. L. *Emergency psychiatric care.* Sponsored by the National Institute of Mental Health. Bowie, Md.: Charles Press, 1975.

Reynolds, B. An experiment in short-contact interviewing. *Smith College Studies in Social Work,* 1932, **3,** 3–107.

Ritchie, A. Multiple impact therapy: An experiment. *Social Work,* 1960, **5,** 16–21.

Rogers, L. S. Drop-out rates of psychotherapy in government aided mental hygiene clinics. *Journal of Clinical Psychology,* 1960, **16,** 89–92.

Rosenbaum, C. P., & Beebe, J. E. *Psychiatric treatment: Crisis, clinic and consultation.* New York: McGraw-Hill, 1975.

Rosenthal, D., & Frank, J. The fate of psychiatric clinic outpatients assigned to psychotherapy. *Journal of Nervous Mental Disease*, 1958, **127**, 330–343.

Rosenzweig, S. Some implicit common factors in diverse methods of psychotherapy. *American Journal of Orthopsychiatry*, 1936, **6**, 412–415.

Rothman, T. (Ed.). *Changing patterns in psychiatric care*. New York: Crown, 1970.

Rubenstein, E., & Lorr, M. A comparison of terminators and remainers in outpatient psychotherapy. *Journal of Clinical Psychology*, 1956, **12**, 345–349.

Rusk, T. N. Opportunity and technique in crisis psychiatry. *Comprehensive Psychiatry*, 191, **12**, 249–263.

Sarason, I. G., Johnson, J. H., & Siegel, J. M. Assessing the impact of life changes: Development of the Life Experience Survey. *Journal of Consulting and Clinical Psychology*, 1978, **46**, 932–946.

Shlien, J., Mosak, H., & Dreikurs, R. Effects of time limits: A comparison of two psychotherapies. *Journal of Counseling Psychology*, 1962, **9**, 31–34.

Shoben, E. J., Jr. A learning theory interpretation of psychotherapy. *Harvard Educational Review*, 1948, **18**, 129–145.

Sifneos, P. E. A concept of "emotional crisis." *Mental Hygiene*, 1960, **44**, 169–179.

Sifneos, P. E. Seven years experience wth short term dynamic psychotherapy. *Proceedings of the Sixth International Congress of Psychotherapy*, London, 1964.

Sifneos, P. E. *Short-term psychotherapy and emotional crisis*. Cambridge, Mass.: Harvard University Press, 1972.

Sifneos, P. E. *Short-term psychotherapy: Evaluation and technique*. New York: Plenum, 1979.

Small, L. *The briefer psychotherapies*. New York: Brunner/Mazel, 1971.

Small, L. The uncommon importance of psychodiagnosis. *Professional Psychology*, 1972, **3**, 111–119.

Smith, D., Luce, J., & Dernberg, E. The health of Haight-Ashbury. *Transaction*. April 1970, 35–45.

Stampfl, T. G., & Levis, D. J. Essentials of implosive therapy: A learning theory based psychodynamic behavioral therapy. *Journal of Abnormal Psychology*, 1967, **72**, 496–503.

Stelmachers, Z. T. Crisis Intervention Center: An interim report. *Program Evaluation Project Newsletter*, January 1972.

Stelmachers, Z. T. Mental health crisis intervention programs. In M. M. Melum (Ed.), *The changing role of the hospital: Options for the future*. American Hospital Association, 1980.

Stelmachers, Z. T. Unit management. In J. Gorton & R. Partridge (Eds.), *Practice and management of psychiatric emergency care*. St. Louis: Mosby, 1982.

Stelmachers, Z. T., Ellenson, G. M., & Baxter, J. *Quality control system of a crisis center: Method and outcome results*. Unpublished paper, 1977.

Stelmachers, Z. T., Lund, S. H., & Meade, C. J. Hennepin County Crisis Intervention Center: Evaluation of its effectiveness. *Evaluation*, Fall 1972, 61–65.

Strickler, M., & Allgeyer, J. The crisis group: A new application of crisis theory. *Social Work*, 1967, **12**, 28–32.

Strickler, M., & LaSor, B. The concept of loss in crisis intervention. *Mental Hygiene,* 1970, **51,** 301–305.

Strupp, H. H. Toward the refinement of time-limited dynamic psychotherapy. In S. H. Budman (Ed.), *Forms of brief therapy.* New York: Guilford Press, 1981.

Taft, J. *The dynamics of therapy in a controlled relationship.* New York: Macmillan, 1933.

Tapp, J., & Spanier, D. Personal characteristics of volunteer counselors. *Journal of Consulting Psychology,* 1973, **41,** 245–250.

Torrey, E. F. Emergency psychiatric ambulance services in the USSR. *American Journal of Psychiatry,* 1971, **128,** 45–49.

Truax, C. B., & Wargo, D. G. Psychotherapeutic encounters that change behavior: For better or for worse. *American Journal of Psychotherapy,* 1966, **20,** 499–520.

Tyhurst, J. S. *The role of transitional states—including disaster—in mental illness.* Symposium on Preventive and Social Psychiatry. Walter Reed Army Institute of Research. Washington, D.C.: U. S. Government Printing Office, 1958.

Ullman, L., & Krasner, L. (Eds.). *Case studies in behavior modification.* New York: Holt, Rinehart & Winston, 1965.

Umana, R. F., Gross, S. J., & McConville, M. T. *Crisis in the family.* New York: Gardner Press, 1980.

Walker, E. *Research on behavioral emergencies in medical settings.* Unpublished manuscript, July 1980.

Wayne, G. J. The psychiatric emergency: An overview. In G. J. Wayne & R. R. Koegler (Eds.), *Emergency psychiatry and brief therapy.* Boston: Little, Brown, 1966.

Weinstein, S. E. *Mental health issues in grief counseling.* U. S. Department of Health, Education and Welfare, 1979.

Wells, F., & Ruesch, J. *The mental examiners handbook* (Rev. ed.). New York: Psychological Corporation, 1972.

Wolberg, L. R. The technique of short-term psychotherapy. In L. R. Wolberg (Ed.), *Short-term psychotherapy.* New York: Grune & Stratton, 1965.

Wolpe, J. *Psychotherapy by reciprocal inhibition.* Stanford, Calif.: Stanford University Press, 1958.

Yamamoto, J., & Goin, M. On the treatment of the poor. *American Journal of Psychiatry,* 1965, **122,** 267–271.

Zitrin, A., Hardesty, A. D., & Burdock, E. I. Crime and violence among mental patients. *American Journal of Psychiatry,* 1976, **133** (2), 142–149.

CHAPTER 12

Community Mental Health and Primary Prevention

EMORY L. COWEN

The emergence of the fields of community mental health and primary prevention in mental health is relatively recent. Because the two fields share common elements of (a) protest against perceived insufficiencies of past mental health practices and (b) striving to identify new and more effective ways to strengthen psychological adjustment, they tend to fuse in the outsider's view into an amorphous "blob" of change. In fact, however, the two approaches differ substantially in their assumptions, the populations they serve, and the nature and timing of their defining practices. This chapter considers why and how these two domains have evolved and illustrates their main activities.

EMERGENCE OF THE TWO FIELDS

Astute observers of today's rapidly changing mental health scene (Rappaport, 1977; Sarason, 1981) stress the importance of a historical perspective in understanding current dilemmas and identifying promising future alternatives. To ignore history is to invite repetition of past errors.

Measured against all of recorded history, the formal mental health field is very young. Concern about "adjustment," however, is hardly new. Humankind's first interest was in behavior that went awry—the more florid the deviance, the greater the concern (Zax & Cowen, 1976). Significant vestiges of that view remain today to shape mental health's focuses and activities. Thus as recently as 2 decades ago the influential Joint Commission on Mental Illness and Health (1961) concluded that "major mental illness is the core problem and unfinished business of the mental health movement and . . . the intensive treatment of patients with critical and prolonged mental breakdowns should have first call on fully trained members of the mental health professions" (p. xiv). Measured over time, it can thus be said that mental health's first goal has been to solve the riddle of profound psychological disorder. Schizophrenia is a fine case in point (Cowen, 1982d).

Extreme psychological deviance is nonrepressible, frightening, and threatening.

These attributes mobilize social and professional conscience and thus time and resources in a search for effective solutions. While practitioners do their heroic best to contain or minimize residual effects of profound disorder, competent and highly motivated workers pursue energetically on many fronts a time- and resource-absorbing quest to identify new understandings and "cures." All such efforts notwithstanding, the conditions continue to exact staggering human and social costs.

Over the ages many understandings of the nature of profound psychological disorder have been advanced. The earliest supernatural and religious explanations assumed that deviance reflected possession by spirits or demons. Those views eventually yielded to more rational, scientific explanations—biological, environmental, and combinations of the two (Zax & Cowen, 1976). These "advances" notwithstanding, few would argue even today that the mysteries of profound psychological disorder have been unraveled (Paul, 1969). Although methods for assessing disorder have become more sophisticated, and we now have a more substantial data base, basic assumptions about profound disorders and the search for "Dr. Ehrlich's magic bullet" to cure them have remained largely constant.

For centuries extreme psychological deviance was the only form recognized by society. Slowly, however, as a byproduct of social evolution and change, views of dysfunction broadened—both at the "entity" level, to include conditions such as the symptom and character neuroses, psychosomatic disorders, antisocial personality, and, more recently, the so-called existential or philosophical neuroses, and with respect to concerns of people in general about ineffective functioning, unsatisfying interpersonal relationships, lack of fulfillment, unhappiness, and internal suffering. These changes vastly expanded mental health's purview and increased pressures for help on its delivery system.

At some point in this slow evolutionary process a distinct field called mental health surfaced as an entity. The field's implicit mandate was to do something about the ravages of human psychological dysfunction. Less clear, however, were the specific means to be used in pursuing that sacred charge. Fortified by the wisdom of hindsight, we can *now* identify a variety of different pathways that mental health *might* have taken in exercising its mandate. But it took only *one*—the one that best mirrored the beliefs, concepts, pressure points, and knowledge bases of the time. Each of these was significantly shaped by then-current views and by successes in the field of physical medicine from which the mental health field was spawned. Simply put, physical medicine was responsible for failings of the body, and mental health was analogously to be sovereign over twistings of the mind.

Although the mental health field has never truly challenged that overarching restorative thrust, it has gone through important internal transformations. Some call these changes revolutions; others call them paradigm shifts (Kuhn, 1970). They are periods of major theoretical churning, accompanied by significant modifications in practice, that occur when current knowledge and ways can no longer solve existing problems or problems as redefined (Kuhn, 1970; Rappaport, 1977; Zax & Cowen, 1976).

The wellspring for the first mental health revolution, starting with Phillipe Pinel's efforts in the late eighteenth century, was the shock and revulsion that caring professionals came to feel about the inhumane treatment of the mentally ill (Boc-koven, 1963). The leitmotif of that revolution was the transofrmation from "mad-house to hospital" (i.e., bringing about sweeping humanitarian reform in hospital care for the profoundly sick). The revolution was not limited to a single person or to a brief moment in time. (Indeed, vestiges of it remain in evidence today.) Other early influential figures included William Tuke in England and Benjamin Rush in the United States. Later key figures such as Dorothea Dix and Clifford Beers helped to bring it to the attention and enlist the support of a wide general public. Basically, however, this revolution neither reconceptualized disordered behavior nor brought about major advances in amelioration. It focused exclusively on problems of ex-treme deviance. It was a humanitarian revolution. Behind its immediate goal of providing better living conditions and more humane care for the profoundly ill—people earlier consigned through ignorance, disdain, and indifference to a "snake pit"—was the implicit but perhaps illusory long-term goal of improved recovery rates.

Like the first revolution, the second (the so-called psychodynamic revolution) unfolded slowly. Sigmund Freud was the giant of that revolution. Freud's interests centered on a group of less-than-profound psychological disorders that had pre-viously either been ignored or been of concern only to *non*–mental health groups such as physicians, neurologists, faith healers, or, indeed, charlatans. His pioneer-ing efforts in identifying and developing remedies for a cluster of conditions called neuroses significantly expanded prevalent views of mental health's proper domain in ways that shaped the field's everyday practices for a century. As that revolution unfolded, its scope expanded. Many more psychological dysfunctions came to be included under mental health's umbrella, and many new ways to deal with that expanded family of disorders were developed and explored as variations on major themes that Freud first set down. The quantum leaps of the second revolution, to be sure, vastly expanded mental health's scope and activities. But again they did *not* materially affect its basic definition of mandate. Different problems, yes! Many more, and more subtle maladaptations, yes! New, perhaps more promising cures, yes! But the guiding focus remained to identify psychological problems and deal with them to the best of our ability.

For many years, indeed decades, the second revolution was fueled by the excite-ment of the new challenges it posed and by the progress made in meeting those challenges. New helping approaches were developed that meaningfully addressed real problems in real people. Those reinforcements powered efforts toward further refinements and extensions. Yet a constraining force slowly came into clearer focus, that is, the important problems that the second revolution had *not* solved or perhaps not even raised. In brief overview, these included the following:

1.   Dramatic expansion of mental health's scope and society's growing sen-sitivity to people's psychological well-being (Rieff, 1959) converged to create a situation in which mental health resources were insufficient to meet demand as spontaneously defined, much less underlying need. Albee (1959), who reviewed professional personnel resources in mental health for the original Joint Commission

on Mental Illness and Health (1961), concluded that there were serious shortages that would continue indefinitely. Later statements (Albee, 1966; Apter, 1982; Sarason, 1976) warned that if we followed the pathways set down by the second revolution, there would *never* be sufficient professional personnel in mental health.

2.   Despite dedicated and persistent efforts by able, highly motivated mental health professionals, satisfactory solutions had not been found for the vexing problems of major mental illness such as schizophrenia (Paul, 1969; Scheff, 1966). Those conditions remained more than just a challenge; they were a costly social blight.

3.   Key mental health technologies such as psychotherapy, seen early in the second mental health revolution as saviors to lead us out of a wilderness, had not lived up to that promise. Early evaluations of psychotherapy rested primarily on direct clinical experience and observations. So assessed, it was (and still is) found to be a helpful procedure. However, the cumulation of formal outcome research data both for adults (Eysenck, 1952, 1961) and children (Levitt, 1957, 1971) raised serious cautionary signs. Recent searching analyses of psychotherapy's effectiveness, based on large bodies of data (Bergin & Lambert, 1978; Bergin & Suinn, 1975; Gomez-Schwartz, Hadley, & Strupp, 1978), concluded that the approach, though useful in many instances and moderately effective overall, was inexact and not a fully satisfactory social answer. Weiner and Bordin review these analyses in Chapter 7 of this book.

4.   There was also a broader social question of which people had access to mental health services. Compelling evidence was amassed showing that less well-placed people in society did not have equal access to such services (Hollingshead & Redlich, 1958; Lorion, 1973, 1974; Ryan, 1969; Sanua, 1966). Schofield (1964) caricatured that reality by coining the achronym YAVIS (Young, Attractive, Verbal, Intelligent, Successful) to describe those who had preferential access to mental health services such as psychotherapy. The implication of Schofield's argument was that prestigious and costly mental health services were least available where they were most needed—a point also reflected in the catchy call-to-arms of the recent President's Commission on Mental Health (1978): "services for the unserved and underserved." Whereas those words were first linked specifically to disadvantaged minority groups, the commission's usage was broader. It included rural dwellers, the chronically ill, retired people, and children, all of whom, it was argued, had been shortchanged with respect to mental health services.

5.   Because mental health services had developed within a predominantly white middle-class tradition, they were for the most part packaged in the frills and ribbons of that tradition, including fixed, prescheduled, 50-minute sessions held in well-appointed offices staffed by efficient, verbally facile reception personnel. Unfortunately, since such trappings are unnatural or even alien to major segments of society, they turned many people off prospective services before those services could ever take hold (Bredemeier, 1964; Lorion, 1973; Reiff, 1966; Reiff & Riessman, 1965). Moreover, many mental health professionals had been reluctant to take on clients whose characteristic ways of thinking and acting, use of language, and economic status differed markedly from their own background and experience. The

belief of some clinicians that such differences presaged negative outcomes all too easily led to self-fulfilling prophecies. Despite serious recent effort to identify new approaches better attuned to the needs and styles of the poor (e.g., Lerner, 1972), mental health services today are still tailored for and disproportionately allocated to well-educated, white middle-class clientele.

6.   The mental health field had not responded to a range of destructive, non-repressible social problems such as racism, urban violence, addiction, prison riots, and delinquency. Whether that aloofness was due to lack of interest, inadequate technology, or active separation of such problems from mental health's definition of proper domain, the field had contributed little to their resolution.

The preceding summary identifies significant problems *not* solved by or emerging from the second revolution. Many are more than just problems of the larger house of mental health—they are also endemic to its subdomains, such as school mental health (Cowen & Lorion, 1976).

Three key threads run through these diverse problems: (a) Modern society's mental health resources are insufficient to meet need and are inequitably distributed; (b) the time-consuming, costly, culture-bound nature of mental health's technology creates pressures to find more useful, parsimonious, flexible ways; and (c) the field's past unswerving emphasis on serious disturbance and its limited success in dealing with those conditions put into bold relief the question of whether psychological damage can truly be undone after it passes a certain critical stage.

Elsewhere (Cowen, 1973, 1977; Zax & Cowen, 1976) the term *end-state* mentality has been used to describe mental health's historical bias. We have defined ourselves and are seen as doctors of the mind. Our assessments seek to understand deficit. Our interventions start when rooted problems are brought forcibly to our attention. We have been reactive, not proactive. Unwittingly, mental health's most honored and best developed methods have come into play at the poorest possible times, that is, with conditions that most resist constructive change. Ironically, in a period of major worldwide concern about energy shortages and the need for energy conservation, one of mental health's most compelling dilemmas can be put in exactly those terms: To what extent, planfully or otherwise, has the mental health field engineered a delivery system that offers the *fewest* possible miles per gallon? The collective weight of the problem cited is staggering. Even though more than $17 billion, 12% of the nation's total health expenditures, were allocated to mental health in 1978, the President's Commission on Mental Health (1978) was obliged to conclude that the sum was inadequate to meet the nation's mental health ends.

The preceding storm clouds were noted in part by three recent presidential commissions appointed to study such matters (Joint Commission on Mental Health, 1961; Joint Commission on the Mental Health of Children, 1969; President's Commission on Mental Health, 1978). The second revolution had unfolded. Society had changed. Problems had changed (Sarason, 1981). Again, existing knowledge and technology could no longer address psychological problems as defined. Pressures were moving us toward another major paradigm shift, perhaps a third mental health revolution. Indeed, Hobbs (1964) heralded just such a revolution, the community mental health revolution—an active, systematic search for better, more efficient ways to reach many more people in need of help.

Although the community mental health movement had important early antecedents (R. Caplan, 1969; Levine & Levine, 1970), its recent accelerated growth reflects mounting discontent with the shortcomings of an existing order. The movement has been operationalized by significant developments in early detection and screening, mental health consultation, crisis intervention, using flexible new settings and delivery modes, and introducing new breeds of service personnel into an expanded cadre of help givers. Each of those changes is based on perceived insufficiencies of past ways; each seeks a meaningful resolution.

CMH developments, to use value terms, have no doubt been important, helpful, and liberalizing. As a result, today's total mental health delivery system is surely more flexible and effective than that of several decades ago. Even so, the sum of those salutary changes has not been enough to overcome the foreboding problems they were designed to address. At its core, the CMH development does less to challenge past guiding assumptions in mental health than it does to question whether the practices that vivified those assumptions were the only or best ways to do so. Accordingly, future historians, who can profit from the spectacles of distance and time perspective, may come to see the CMH revolution, the one that Hobbs called the third revolution, as little more than a last-gasp phase of the second.

Whereas the CMH thrust represents a strong and needed protest against the identified biases, tunnel vision, and ineffectuality of past ways, another qualitatively different and more basic set of alternatives now gestating may come to epitomize better a true third mental health revolution. Rather than just questioning past mental health practices, these evolving approaches challenge its pivotal assumptions, much as years before epidemiology and public health medicine offered conceptual alternatives to a then-dominant disease-containment model of physical medicine. The link, in this case, is the realization that no disordered condition, physical or psychological, has ever been overcome by treating its victims (Bloom, 1979; Goldston, 1977a). An alternative view is that it may be more realistic, humane, and cost-effective in the long run to prevent dysfunction and/or to build health, than to struggle, however skillfully or compassionately, to minimize its costly, devastating residuals.

That notion is the quintessential kernel of primary prevention in mental health. Its basic concepts and practices and the skills and training it requires differ qualitatively from prior thinking and practice in mental health. Primary prevention seeks to prevent dysfunction before it occurs and to promote health, not to counterpunch after things have already gone sour. It rests on a strategy known to many military generals and football coaches that a good offense is the best defense. Primary prevention is directed impersonally to large numbers of individuals before the fact of disorder. Eschewing diagnosis and treatment, its main tools are mental health education, competence training, social system modification, reducing sources of stress on people, and training people to cope more effectively with stress when it occurs.

Only in retrospect can it be seen that an emphasis on primary prevention approaches *might* have been one legitimate way for the mental health field to have construed its original mandate—a latent option in a never fully articulated universe of alternatives (Sarason, 1971). The social fabric of that time, indeed of later history, did not favor such an outcome. Yet as we look anew today at mental health's needs and pressure points in the light of the field's history of accomplishments (and *non*accomplishments), we can see both that primary prevention work is sorely needed and that it offers mental health the most genuine set of alternatives it has ever had.

We have thus far reviewed the historical evolution of the mental health field, considered its major current problems, and outlined in global approximate shorthand several major strategies that hold promise for addressing those problems. Table 12.1 summarizes those strategies schematically. Beginning with a main-effects distinction among (a) classical human services, (b) community mental health approaches, and (c) primary prevention approaches in mental health, it identifies the global objectives, specific targets, and mechanisms and approaches associated with each strategy. Three clarifications are in order. First, the term "classic human services" is used panprofessionally to include psychiatry, clinical psychology, and social work. Second, although all three approaches seek *ultimately* at some level to optimize psychological well-being, they differ in terms of when, how, and with whom interventions are undertaken, as can be seen in the columns labeled Specific Targets and Mechanisms and Approaches. Prime targets in both classical human service and CMH approaches are individuals experiencing psychological problems. Within the CMH approach, community is seen as the means for providing earlier, more flexible, and more effective services, packaged and delivered at better times in more appropriate settings and by an expanded cadre of helping personnel. Primary prevention is directed before the fact to well people—including people known epidemiologically to be at risk for becoming disturbed. The technologies listed in the table's last column are natural derivatives of each approach's goals, target groups, and time constraints. Third, both *community mental health* and *primary prevention,* it should be stressed, are "family" names; each subsumes a broad network of conceptually related but operationally diverse approaches. The rest of this chapter describes and illustrates some of the more important of these approaches.

COMMUNITY MENTAL HEALTH APPROACHES

The domain of CMH has been the topic of many recent books (e.g., Bloom, 1977; Heller & Monahan, 1977; Rappaport, 1977; Zax & Specter, 1974). The movement's main push, as already noted, came from concerns about perceived mechanical shortcomings of past mental health repair strategies. Legislation establishing CMHCs in 1963 was designed to remedy one such problem; that is, that profound mental disorder was characteristically engaged so late in its unfolding that options for dealing effectively with it were restricted. As a buffer between people and mental hospitals the CMHC was conceived as a force to short-circuit serious disorder.

There were other unresolved problems as well, however, and the CMH move-

Table 12.1. Similarities and Differences in Mental Health Strategies

Basic Strategy	Global Objectives	Specific Targets	Mechanisms and Approaches
Classic approaches	Minimize or correct problems of adjustment, unhappiness, self-image, ineffectuality	Individuals with problems	Restorative and repair techniques such as diagnosis and psychotherapy
Community mental health approaches	Same as above	Individuals with problems	More efficient, far-reaching repair techniques such as consultation, crisis intervention, early detection and intervention and the flexible use of new types of settings and personnel
Primary prevention in mental health	Prevent occurrence of problems and/or build psychological strengths	People in general including those at risk but not yet ill	Health building approaches such as mental health education and competence training, stress reduction and inoculation, social systems analysis and modification, intervention around critical life events, developing networks and support systems

ment, without truly abandoning a casualty-repair orientation, became broader in concept and practice than just CMHCs. Other of its important action areas include the following:

1. Developing new, community-based interventions for psychological conditions that have historically eluded classic approches.

2. Identifying psychological problems sooner, when less time-consuming and more promising interventions can be tried. *Sooner* in this case refers both to (a) the cross-sectional unfolding of given episodes of disorder and (b) the person's life history, when relatively parsimonious interventions can yield greater long-term benefit.

3. Developing a more flexible repertoire of approaches attuned to the life styles and needs of those in society who cannot or do not avail themselves of traditional services.

4. Extending mental health's sphere of operation to more natural settings than hospitals or clinics, such as schools, churches, and inner-city storefronts, in order both to access dysfunction sooner and to reach more people in need. Many CMH programs thus bypass mental health's passive–receptive mode of waiting for upset people to seek out professional help in offices and clinics in favor of an active, outreaching mode.

5. Recognizing that crises and stressful life events disproportionly influence people's psychological well-being and developing programs to minimize their negative consequences. This area is a particular focus of Butcher et al. in Chapter 11 of this volume.

6. Fostering developments such as mental health consultation that can help to expand helping services geometrically.

7. Understanding and buttressing society's natural sources of interpersonal help and support.

8. Training and using new types of personnel, including nonprofessionals, as direct help agents to extend flexibly the reach of the helping arm.

The preceding activities account for much of the variance of the CMH thrust. They are linked structurally by their community roots and by the fact that they break away from the constraining features of the previously dominant one-to-one helping model within the consulting suite. This new combination expands considerably the potential array of solutions to old problems. The sections to follow cite examples of work illustrating these subareas.

Alternatives for End-State Conditions

Profound Psychological Maladjustment.   Earlier we spoke of the unremitting nature of serious mental illness and the problems that it creates for individuals, families, and society at large. The functional psychoses offer a clear example. Zax and

Cowen (1976) suggest an analogy between terminal schizophrenia and terminal cancer, namely, that once either condition reaches a certain point of morbidity, there is no return. The profundity and tenacity of that problem have led to the exploration of diverse community-based, potential resolutions. Early concepts such as the day and night hospital, each predicated on matching patient needs and community resources, exemplify that effort.

The halfway house (Clark & Yeomans, 1969; Colarelli & Siegel, 1967) is a related approach. Work by Fairweather and his colleagues (Faithweather, 1967; Fairweather, Sanders, Maynard, & Cressler, 1969; Fairweather, Sanders, & Tornatzky, 1974; Fairweather & Tornatzky, 1977) bears centrally on that development. Early on, Fairweather demonstrated that a hospital-based program that provided chronic patients opportunities for autonomy and self-governance significantly improved their discharge rates. However, recidivism (readmission to the hospital because of relapse) was high, due perhaps to the fact that the program did not provide the specific skills or resources patients needed for effective community living. Hence an autonomous communal living setting (the "lodge") was conceived of and implemented, emphasizing the acquisition of such skills and experiences; for example, patients were trained to assume administrative responsibilities and run a business. The lodge structure was based on assumptions and practices that differed from those typically used with chronic patients. At its core the program sought to provide a framework to enable socially marginal expatients to develop adaptive skills, with the help of supporting resources.

Compared to matched control patients in standard aftercare programs, lodge residents spent significantly more time in the community and had better employment records, with lower per capita costs. Even so, the lodge experiment was less than completely successful. Lodge alumni, after discharge, did not *maintain* good employment records, and they showed the same recidivism rate as controls. The program's main accomplishments were unstigmatizing patients and strengthening their autonomy; the ever-elusive goal of permanent cure was *not* realized.

This important limitation notwithstanding, the program's way-station gains should not be dismissed casually. Although some, to be sure, were less than enduring, the program modeled intriguing community concepts and structures that helped to carry chronic patients some way down a difficult path. The question is whether meaningful, enduring resolutions can be built on that base. Later dissemination work by this group (Fairweather et al., 1974; Fairweather & Tornatzky, 1977) trained other groups to adopt the lodge model for chronic mental patients and studied that social innovation process experimentally.

Structurally related models based on imaginative uses of community resources and living arrangements have also been reported for severely disturbed children. Hobbs (1966) observed that roughly 1.5 million American children were too upset psychologically to be able to make progress in their natural home, community, and school environments. Under normal living conditions such youngsters languish and fail to develop commensurate with their potentials. For them, traditional treatment is not an approach of choice. During his work with the original Joint Commission (1961), Hobbs identified an appealing community-based alternative for engaging the problems of severely disturbed children, in countries with fewer resources than ours. The alternative rested on two key assumptions about such children: (a) that behavioral adaptation to a community setting is more important than psycho-dynamic uncovering or understanding, and (b) that round-the-clock education in a caring context is more helpful for them than several hours of individual treatment per week.

Based on these observations and assumptions Hobbs and his colleagues (Hobbs, 1966, 1967, 1975; Lewis, 1967) began Project Re-Ed, a communal educational setting in which young (ages 6 to 12) disturbed children live 5 days a week. Home and community ties are maintained during the residence period, and precipitous separations are avoided. Re-Ed's front-line help agent, exemplifying a new breed of worker (Apter, 1982), is the teacher–counselor. Teacher–counselors are selected from among competent, experienced teachers who demonstrate interest in and seeming talent for the challenging role of living closely (24 hours a day) and work-ing intensively with seriously disturbed youngsters. After selection they receive intensive training.

Re-Ed strives to create a minicommunity characterized by a climate of mutual trust. It encourages appropriate expression of feelings and uses constructive limit setting to help youngsters to manage impulses better. Educational approaches are used to impart requisite skills. The child's moment-to-moment behavior, not under-lying dynamics, is always the prime focus. Evaluations of Re-Ed (Hobbs, 1966; Weinstein, 1969) report an impressive 80% success rate with this difficult group of children. Specifically, Re-Ed children showed decreases in negative symptoms such as aggressiveness, tantrums, and bed wetting and improvements in school and so-cial adjustment and overall competence. They also appeared better adjusted than controls on formal test measures and behavior ratings by parents, teachers, and community agents. Given the fact that Re-Ed stays averaged only 5 months, another mark of the program's success was that all alumni were found to be functioning adequately in regular schools 18 months after discharge. Per capita Re-Ed costs were far less than those of prior alternatives such as private therapy, state hospital placement, and residential treatment.

A program conducted in Elmont, New York (Donahue, 1967; Donahue & Nich-tern, 1965) for young, severely disturbed (e.g, schizophrenic) children illustrates another way to broaden intervention options through judicious use of community settings and resources. Although Elmont, like Re-Ed, assumes that education is a better and more natural vehicle for child growth than therapy, it used a day-care rather than a residential approach. Elmont's goal, which was to provide a rich indi-vidualized educational program for profoundly disturbed children who were candi-dates for school exclusion, was clear from the start. Given severe fiscal and personnel shortages, however, the real question was how to *achieve* that goal. Inge-nious use of an amalgam of community resources provided the answer. A syn-agogue contributed the space for the program, and a small donation by the local Kiwanis purchased equipment, materials, and supplies. The program's key direct-help agents were nonprofessional "teacher-moms," women selected for their warm, caring qualities and a strong interest in working with disturbed children. The program's limited professional time was heavily invested in recruiting, training, and supervising the teacher-moms. These women worked intensively in one-to-one interactions with program children, based on individually developed study plans. Evaluation of the first wave of Elmont children showed that more than half, earlier destined to frustrating nonproductive careers, had returned to normal classes and were functioning well, both educationally and interpersonally. Thanks to major community inputs—both material elements and services—the Elmont program was remarkably inexpensive.

Mental Deficiency.   Mental deficiency, a difficult problem for individuals, families, and communities, is another condition often seen as an immutable end state. However, strong legitimate concerns have been raised about labeling and categorizing such individuals (Mercer, 1973; Sarason & Doris, 1979), and interest has grown in the questions of (a) a community's responsibility for problems of mental deficiency and (b) how community resources can be used to modify views about, and approaches used with, such individuals.

Past planning for mental defectives has often started with buildings, as if a building would per se solve the problem. Perhaps it can in terms of removing affected individuals from society's view and matrix of perceived responsibilities. At the same time, important questions have been posed about what that means for well-being and optimal development of affected individuals (Sarason, Zitnay, & Grossman, 1971). Based on both extensive experience in settings for mental defectives and involvements as a consultant to a state planning agency, Sarason et al. (1971) wrote a provocative essay, from a community perspective, urging reconsideration of assumptions and practices in the care and treatment of mental defectives. They argued that new buildings create as many problems as they solve by isolating children geographically and psychologically from their natural homes and, inadvertently, absolving communities of responsibility for the problems that mental deficiency poses.

Sarason's concern was that decisions (e.g., buildings to house defectives) are often etched prematurely in bronze and that such thinking blinds us to a potentially sizable and rich universe of alternatives (Sarason, 1971). Sarason's point in this case was that a new building for defectives, however well planned and elegant, would have sharply restricted the universe of alternatives (certainly community-based ones) for addressing real problems experienced by that group. Implicit was his conviction that settings are created and shaped long before they are built.

Sarason uses the "what-if" approach to orient people's thinking to the universe of alternatives. What-if questions start by ruling out prior "unquestionable" givens (e.g.,   What if Congress passed a law making the practice of psychotherapy illegal?), thereby forcing people to contemplate alternatives that might not otherwise occur. Although Sarason is not necessarily invested in the specific action that the what-if question suggests, he believes that optimally rational plans best follow full, open consideration of a rich universe of alternatives. The question for mental deficiency was: What if you had to develop residential facilities for defectives with the following constraints? (a) They may not be on institutional land, (b) they may not house more than 12 people, and (c) *no* new buildings could be erected (Sarason et al., 1971). The question was obviously designed to force people's thinking toward community care alternatives. It led to the formulation of a three-pronged community-based program that included (a) a day-care center run by the parents' association, (b) an independent living unit for youth working in the community, and (c) a family involvement program to house young retardates with difficult family situations 5 days a week. Parents of program youth had to agree beforehand to (a) a time-limited stay for the youth and (b) spending time in the unit observing their offspring's behavior and interactions and how they were handled (mostly with behavior modification approaches). Individual problems that could not be accommodated within the framework of those three components were referred to other community agencies and settings.

All three aspects of the new program, each reflecting new assumptions and practices, had deep community roots. Together they offered a community solution to what was seen fundamentally as a community problem. Interestingly, in a recent autobiographical account, Sarason (1982) notes that the awareness developed early in his career of the importance of the social geographical surrounds (i.e., historico-community contexts) that so significantly shaped his thinking about mental deficiency later powerfully influenced in community directions his ways of viewing and adddressing a variety of mental health issues and problems that, on the surface, seemed very different from those of mental deficiency.

Delinquent and Hard-Core Youth.   Most communities experience reactions such as embarrassment or indignation over the problems posed by chronically jobless and delinquent youth. Such problems have been around for a long time and have resisted orthodox clinical approaches. Many clinicians see people in this group categorically as untreatable and give them short shrift. As part of the CMH thrust, however, several community-based programs bypassing prior assumptions have been conceptualized and successfully implemented for such youth. Several examples follow.

The New Careers program in the 1960s was a social movement with important shaping impact (Pearl & Riessman, 1965; Riessman & Popper, 1968). Based on the assumption that degrading living conditions and lack of jobs and life opportunities on the one side were intimately intertwined with disaffection and/or mental health problems on the other, the movement assumed that providing skill training and jobs for the poor, particularly poor youth, was more important for their mental health than orthodox clinical interventions. The program sought to provide training for positions that could meaningfully extend needed human services to the poor.

One early influential New Careers program was conducted at the Howard University Institute of Youth Studies (IYS) (Fishman, Denham, Levine, & Shatz, 1969; Klein, 1967; MacLennan, 1969) to address the problems of hard-core, inner-city delinquent youth in Washington, D. C. The program was built on skill training, establishing competencies, and placing trainees productively in jobs. Training had two major components: (a) imparting generic skills such as learning more about oneself, the community, and the world at large, observing and recording information, using supervision effectively, and becoming familiar with community settings and services; and (b) specific job-related training. Program youth were trained for a dozen different human-service positions, including day-care worker, welfare worker, recreation aide, geriatric assistant, school aide, and counselor. Training was sufficiently flexible to permit trainees to change areas if job opportunities in specific areas dried up.

The IYS program trained more than 100 youth, all of whom had histories of chronic dropping out of school, delinquency, and unemployment. Virtually all were black inner-city residents under age 21. Comprehensive evaluation, based on interviews with former trainees and their supervisors 2½ years after the program ended, provided many indications of the program's effectiveness. For example, whereas 90% of the IYS trainees were unemployed when they entered the program, 87% were employed 2 ½ years later. Many had either furthered their education or had plans to do so. The frequency of delinquent acts had fallen off sharply.

Goldenberg (1968, 1971) developed a conceptually related community-based program for hard-core inner-city youth in New Haven, Conn., called the Residential Youth Center (RYC). He also believed that individual treatment had less promise for such youth than the creation of situationally realistic settings designed to foster positive change in them. The RYC, a short-term residential facility reflecting that view, bypassed several key assumptions of prior work with hard-core youth: (a) that their problems are best addressed in settings geographically removed from their natural turf; (b) that mental health professionals are best qualified to work with them; and (c) that youth settings should be conceived in the images of mental health professionals' values and technologgies.

The RYC was set up in the heart of New Haven's inner city. Its staff consisted mostly of young people who had grown up in the area. Staff responsibilities were defined "horizontally"; that is, all staff members—cooks, secretaries, custodians, *not* just professionals—had prime across-the-board responsibility for some residents. Conversely, all staff members, including professionals, shared responsibility for such program maintenance activities as cooking, cleaning, and building upkeep. The RYC had a homey atmosphere with fluid communication channels and open access to the surrounding community. The program emphasized vocational and educational training heavily and also provided formal and informal counseling.

Residents (all voluntary admissions) were youth between ages 16 and 21, who had an average stay of 5 months in the program. All participated actively in the center's governance and operation, with assigned daily responsibilities. Evaluation of RYC, which included a nonprogram control group, showed that residents gained importantly in employment rates, work attendance, and income and dropped significantly in arrests and incarcerations. Attitude and personality measures also yielded positive findings. The average cost of stay ($3000 per resident) compared favorably with the then-estimated cost of $4000 just for processing a single youth through the juvenile court system (Duggan, 1965).

Rappaport, Seidman, and Davidson (1979) described a progam in which college students were paired with referred adolescents for whom formal court action was about to be initiated. The program was designed as an alternative to the juvenile justice system for adolescents in legal jeopardy. It was not a therapy program. It stressed the development of meaningful relationships between students and target youth in which the students' main roles were social advocacy and behavioral contracting. Interactions were intended to develop existing strengths in target youth and to keep them out of legal troubles. For several separate year-cohorts, project participants compared to controls had fewer and less serious police contacts or petitions filed. These important gains held up over a 2-year follow-up period.

The effectiveness of these programs for delinquent youth suggests that imaginative community-based programs, well beyond the Procrustean bed of orthodox clinical practice, offer promising entrees to a troublesome set of social and human problems. Indeed, that is the larger message of this entire subsection. Although the issues and programs explored range widely in content, they share significant structural communalities. Each addresses a complex end-state condition that has heretofore eluded resolution. Each starts by reconceptualizing the issue, that is, by carefully reexamining prior unquestionable givens. Each uses the community as a means; in other words, as part of the reconceptualization process, attractive new community structures, resources, settings, and/or personnel usages are developed. The promising programs that have resulted, though less than 100% effective, light a path toward useful options that community contexts harbor—options that can help to overcome mechanical shortcomings of previously dominant mental health practices.

Early Detection and Intervention

The core goal of secondary prevention is to stop relatively mild disorders from becoming more serious and prolonged. That worthy objective can be construed in two qualitatively different ways (Zax & Cowen, 1976). The first, a key to the operating strategies of CMHCs, is to identify and deal effectively with episodes of disorder early in their unfolding. If, for example, prodromal signs of an acute schizophrenic reaction can be detected, perhaps steps can be taken to avert the draining human and social costs of a prolonged full-blown episode. Secondary prevention can also be viewed ontongenetically. Identifying signs of dysfunction early in a person's life history, before the dysfunction becomes rooted and fans out, creates opportunities for less time-consuming, more promising preventive interventions. That longitudinal emphasis necessarily puts the young child on center stage, and is an emphasis that some have long urged (Smith & Hobbs, 1966).

Mental health's present child-serving system has been described as passive–receptive (Cowen & Gesten, 1978). It does not go out and look for problems, because more than enough problems, relative to available resources, find the system spontaneously. Since that has always been "nature's way," early problems often fester and spill over into new areas. Not infrequently, later aggravated forms of earlier neglected problems express themselves as demands on the mental health or related (e.g., criminal justice, welfare) systems. The community offers attractive options for shifting mental health's classic passive–receptive stance to a more active, seeking mode. In that mode community settings and resources are used to detect problems early and more systematically and to introduce prompt, less costly, and less time-consuming correctives.

The family and the school are the two social systems that most influence children's early development. These systems shape self-images and coping and adaptive mechanisms, and they offer high-impact identification models. Although early detection can in principle be done within either system, parsimony favors schools. In Western society at least, schools are the principal system that communally affects all children during their formative years (Bardon, 1968). Moreover, for programmatic purposes, large numbers of children can be assessed and tracked in schools by virtue of their being under a single roof and administrative structure.

School children must ultimately conform to two sets of standards. They must acquire increasingly complex bodies of knowledge (they must *learn*) within specific frameworks of rules and regulations (they must *adapt*). Educators have become aware of the important interfaces between these two sets of demands. Chronic inability to meet either augurs failure in the system (Glidewell & Swallow, 1969). And children who do not "cut it" in school are at grave risk for failing to achieve important later-life goals. For all those reasons, schools have come to be seen as important community sites for developing programs in systematic early detection, remediation, and prevention of children's adaptive problems.

The St. Louis County Project, which started in 1947, was among the first large-scale early detection–prevention programs (Gildea, 1959; Gildea, Glidewell, & Kantor, 1967; Glidewell, Gildea, & Kaufman, 1973; Rae-Grant & Stringer, 1969). The project first developed teacher observation and rating measures, sociometric techniques, and semiprojective devices to assess children's school adjustment. Based on data obtained from these measures, professionally led therapy groups were set up for parents of young children with school adjustment problems. Positive early findings and a wish to expand the program led to the recruitment and training of lay leaders to run similar groups. Teacher estimates of current school behavior showed improvement for 80% of the children of parents seen in the new groups, compared to 80% judged nonimproved among control children whose parents were not in groups. As the project evolved, procedures to evaluate children's school adjustment were extended and further objectified. One product was the Academic Progress Chart (APC), a grid that depicts a child's academic and psychological development graphically within a matrix of chronological age expectancies. Retrospective application of the APC showed that 60% of the youngsters ultimately referred to school mental health services could have been identified 1 to 8 years earlier—a discovery that again spotlights the fact that many early unattended problems intensify over the years.

The St. Louis project later used their sophisticated assessment battery in a large-scale study comparing the efficacy of different types of interventions: the volunteer lay education program alone versus that program plus in-school professional counseling, and training and consultation services versus no-treatment controls. The project was based on 830 youngsters from 30 classrooms in 15 schools. Both interventions showed positive effects over a 2½-year follow-up period, more so for boys than for girls. These effects appeared immediately for middle-class families, but only after some delay for low-income families (Glidewell et al., 1973).

A group within the California State Department of Education pioneered the development of an in-school screening approach in the late 1950s and early 1960s (Bower, 1969; Bower & Lambert, 1961). Their battery included self-concept and sociometric measures and the AML, which is a quick screening device used by teachers. Based on screening data collected for 5500 youngsters in 75 California school districts, these investigators found substantial (87%) overlap in children identified as maladjusted by teachers and clinicians. Identified children had lower peer ratings and poorer self-concepts than nonidentified peers and did less well on intelligence and reading and arithmetic achievement tests. The importance of this approach, in Bower's (1969) view, was that it provided tools for identifying vulnerable children "before the problem is one for the mental institution, court, or hospital." He recognized that early identification is not an end in itself, but rather sets the stage for informed intervention using secondary prevention approaches. Without the latter kind of effective help, even the finest screening program may be little more than a source of frustration and irritation for school personnel.

Important later programmatic efforts in California rest on the base established by Bower et al. An example is the comprehensive intervention developed by the Pace I.D. Center for 6000 first- to fourth-graders in San Mateo County (Van Vleet & Kannegieter, 1969). That project focused on K-2 youngsters with maladjusted AML scores. Program children, their teachers and families, and key community people had the benefit of intensive social work services both for (a) planning and expediting help for target children and (b) coordinating efforts among home, school, and community service agencies. Several child psychiatrists served as consultants to project staff.

A 3-year program evaluation showed that the PACER group improved. For example their A (aggression) scores on the AML decreased significantly more than the scores of control subjects. The improvement was uneven, however. It was greater on emotional than on educational measures, and greater for girls than for boys. Indeed, some of the differences among groups were due primarily to less slippage, rather than greater gain, by intervention compared to control subjects. In other words, on some dimensions the program's main contribution was to hold the line against base-rate deterioration shown by controls.

Another important early detection and prevention program was conducted in a predominantly black, urban ghetto environment (Chicago-Woodlawn)—an area with documented rampant school adjustment problems (Kellam & Schiff, 1967). Problem detection was based on a composite of information including interviews, a self-concept measure, direct observation, parent responses on a symptom checklist, and, importantly, teacher ratings of child behavior. Even though 80% of Woodlawn's teachers were black, 70% of the primary graders were judged to have school adjustment problems compared to the national base rate of 30% (Glidewell & Swallow, 1969). Those stark findings were the basis for establishing a preventively oriented intervention program (Kellam, Branch, Agrawal, & Ensminger, 1975; Kellam, Branch, Agrawal, & Grabill, 1972) in which 6 of Woodlawn's 12 schools became experimental (program) settings and 6 became control settings. The program's main component was a set of weekly first-grade classroom meetings, led jointly by the teacher and a mental health staff person. (Teachers took greater responsibility as the program proceeded.) The meetings sought to bolster children's confidence and to catalyze group identity and sense of belonging. Staff and parent meetings were held to support and provide information about the classroom program. Although little immediate program gain was found, 3-year follow-up showed that program children exceeded controls in social adaptation and intellectual development.

The Rochester Primary Mental Health Project (PMHP) (Cowen, 1980b; Cowen, Trost, Lorion, Dorr, Izzo, & Isaacson, 1975) has been continuously involved for 26 years in school-based early detection and prevention programming. PMHP's screening battery includes group tests for assessing intellectual and personality status, social work interviews with parents of primary graders, and teachers' objective ratings of children's classroom problems (Lorion, Cowen, & Caldwell, 1975) and competencies (Gesten, 1976). PMHP found that about one in three children had moderate to serious school adjustment problems (Cowen et al., 1975; Cowen, Zax, Izzo, & Trost, 1966). PMHP uses screening data both to identify children who need help and to establish specific intervention goals and strategies for them. The project has developed quasi-mathematical (computer-based) procedures to describe the predominant nature of a child's school adjustment problems (Lorion, Cowen, & Caldwell, 1974). This "pure-types" approach identifies aggressive acting-out, shy-anxious, and learning problems as the three most frequent clusters of school adjustment difficulties.

The project uses carefully selected, trained, nonprofessional child-aides, working under professional supervision, as the prime direct help agents with referred children (Cowen et al., 1975). Aides are selected for interpersonal and life-experience qualities, rather than for the usual criteria of education and advanced degrees. Both research data (Sandler, 1972) and clinical judgments (Cowen, Dorr, & Pokracki, 1972) show them to be warm, caring people who are natural help agents. Initial PMHP aide training is focused and time limited. Although the project provides further on-the-job training and supervision, it depends heavily on selecting aides with natural facilitating qualities.

The professional's role in PMHP has changed drastically over time. He or she is now heavily involved in recruiting, training, and supervising aides and in educative, resource, and consultative activities with school personnel. The professional thus functions as a mental health "quarterback," directing a team of help agents, which significantly expands the reach of early effective, preventively oriented services (Cowen, Lorion, Kraus, & Dorr, 1974). A single half-time aide can provide extensive services to 12 to 14 maladapting youngsters during the school year. Hence, PMHP's delivery system reaches 10% to 15% of the primary-grade population—those youngsters who most need early help to profit from the school experience.

PMHP has been involved since its inception in program evaluation research. The PMHP volume (Cowen et al., 1975) summarizes program effectiveness data based on some 15 outcome studies. PMHP's most recent outcome study (Weissberg,

Cowen, Lotyczewski, & Gesten, 1983), based on data for seven consecutive independent year-cohorts of referred children, provides further systematic evidence of the program's effectiveness. PMHP is also cost-effective. A report by Dorr (1972) shows that an approximate 40% cost increment in PMHP extends the reach of effective services by 1000%. A single PMHP aide-child contact session costs only 10% to 20% of what private professional services cost. As with Fairweather et al.'s lodge model for chronic patients, after PMHP's effectiveness was established, the project emphasized dissemination activities. A recent survey (Cowen, Spinell, Wright, & Weissberg, 1983) found that similar programs have been established in some 350 schools in nearly 100 school districts around the world. Moreover, several states have passed legislation establishing within-state networks of school-based PMHP programs.

Although this section has emphasized early detection and prevention programs for young, school-aged children, such programming is not intrinsically yoked to that specific age group or setting. Head-Start, a massive social program for preschoolers, is also predicated on the view that early intervention has significant preventive potential. Although Head-Start projects have been diverse, many have included components designed to foster emotional as well as cognitive growth. Much the same can be said for a host of early-detection and stimulation programs that have been developed with even younger age groups, particularly disadvantaged ghetto infants in the first 2 years of life (Cowen, 1973; Gottfried, 1973; Jason, 1975). Given the fact that assessment of such infants often identifies weaknesses in specific cognitive and social skills that are important for later school success, systematic early detection provides a base on which to build constructive interventions. A recent comprehensive review (Kornberg & Caplan, 1980) describes many programs, including those for the poor, based on principles of systematic early detection and prevention.

The programs that have been cited are illustrative. They suggest that early detection with young children offers a vista-expanding, community-grounded alternative to traditional passive–receptive clinical modes that are limited to a small fraction of society's most visible casualties. Technology now available permits this active, outreaching approach to identify large numbers of youngsters from all social strata early on, before problems root and fan out. Early screening data provide a concrete index of reality that planners cannot afford to ignore. If the extent of children's early adjustment problems dwarfs a system's resources for dealing with those problems, alternative, scope-expanding, helping alternatives must be developed. In any such process, it is imperative that community options be considered.

Community-Based Approaches for the Poor

Three major presidential commissions in the last 2 decades have underscored the fact that the inner-city poor are shortchanged in terms of mental health services. Recent years have witnessed important changes in American cities. Today, more than one-sixth of the nation's population lives in a dozen or so urban centers. The proportion of minority group members, particularly blacks, has nearly trebled in the past 50 years. Most urban school districts now have more minority pupils than whites. In the District of Columbia, for example, minority enrollment exceeds 95% (Zax & Cowen, 1976).

Alongside these dramatic population shifts, mounting forces such as the conviction that all people are entitled to a square deal in life and commitments to black identity, pride, and activism have raised questions about the nature and extent of resources and services, including mental health services, to which the poor have access. The consistent answer is that neither enough nor the right kinds of services have been available (Ramey, 1978; Rappaport, 1977; Reiff, 1968; Riessman, Cohen, & Pearl, 1964; Ryan, 1969). Beginning with Faris and Dunham's (1939) classic sociological survey nearly half a century ago and continuing with many later reports (Hollingshead & Redlich, 1958; Lorion, 1973, 1974; Ramey, 1978; Sanua, 1966; Srole, Langner, Michael, Opler, & Rennie, 1972) two main conclusions recur: (a) the incidence and diagnosed severity of most psychological disorders increase as one moves from the periphery to the center of a city; and (b) the poor have last and weakest call on mental health's most prestigious, valued services and on its most skilled, experienced practitioners. The advent of a nationwide network of CMHCs has not, as was hoped, overcome that imbalance (Balch, 1974; Ramey, 1978).

Although the first of the above two conclusions describes a surface reality, it would be a mistake to accept it uncritically. Among the factors it fails to take into account are: (a) how mental illness or psychological problems are defined and how different groups use labels in those spheres; (b) cultural, linguistic, and attitude differences among groups; and (c) the appropriateness of mental health services as conceived and packaged for various segments of society (Balch & Miller, 1974). Simply put, mental health services have evolved in middle-class traditions and formats that have neither adequately reached nor effectively served the poor. Bredemeier (1964) has identified certain factors that turn the poor away from traditional mental health services and others that prompt mental health professionals to shy away from work with the poor.

Although professionals in the past have been wedded to the view that psychological disorder is a problem of the individual, consistent cooccurrences between so-called mental health problems and squalor, poverty, and lack of opportunity make it difficult to defend that position. Efforts to address the psychological problems of the poor cannot be oblivious either to their oppressive real-life problems or to their characteristic ways of defining and engaging those problems. Rather, such efforts must be mindful of the possibilities that (a) social change may have more to offer the poor than all of mental health's combined technology and resources and (b) if mental health is to contribute meaningfully, it must do so via formats, settings, and interventions that heed the realities of inner-city living. Ramey (1978) has reported that most black people avoid classic mental health services, including those provided by CMHCs; that 60% of the relatively few who do explore such services are lost at intake; and that many of those who get past a first contact drop out before treatment can really be implemented.

Such concerns prompted active exploration in the 50s and 60s of new service structures better attuned to the needs and realities of the poor. The New Careers movement cited earlier, for example, sought to find simultaneous resolutions to two then- (and still) rampant problems of the inner-city poor: low employment rates and lack of availability of a variety of needed human services, including mental health services. One high-impact program within that framework was the Neighborhood Service Center (NSC) (Peck & Kaplan, 1969; Riessman, 1967), which was set in the slum-blighted South Bronx ghetto. At that time the South Bronx had very high rates of poverty, unemployment, delinquency, homicide, and disease. Income and education levels were well below average, housing conditions were substandard, and mental health services were virtually nonexistent. The NSC's prime goals were to meet low-income clientele on their own turf, provide services compatible with their needs and life styles, and harness existing strengths in people.

Individual NSCs were set up to serve 50,000 people within densely populated geographic areas. The NSC concept rested on an understanding of relationships between a subcommunity's organization and the psychological makeup of its inhabitants, including knowledge of people's characteristic ways of engaging psychological problems. The NSC tried first to find ways to attract clientele and then to provide services that were consistent with their needs and life styles. It also sought to strengthen neighborhood cohesion by promoting activities and groups that increased people's involvement and minimized their sense of powerlessness.

Two structural steps were taken to address the troublesome problem of perceived inappropriateness of services. First, nonprofessionals were recruited and trained as NSC's prime direct service agents (Reiff & Riessman, 1965). These were neighborhood people whose cultural backgrounds, language, and life experiences and styles were much like those of prospective clients. Having been reared in the same ghetto, they well understood its profile and problems. They were also at ease in the NSC's informal neighborhood storefront setting, a setting unencumbered by middle-class formats and trappings. Consumers saw them as trustworthy people, that is, as "us" rather than "them." Second, the NSC packaged services, including mental health services such as psychosocial first aid and/or counseling, in concrete, practical, problem-oriented ways that corresponded to residents' natural ways of perceiving and defining problems.

Although objective frameworks for evaluating the effectiveness of New Careers programs have since been developed (Blanton & Alley, 1977), it was difficult at the time to evaluate the NSC's mental health service component. This was because it was embedded in a nontraditional, multipurpose program package and in a broader thrust (e.g., in improving housing, upgrading neighborhoods, and creating employment opportunities) designed to strengthen the community, its institutions, and its service agencies. The overall success of that broad approach is ultimately reflected in the sociodemographic marker variables such as those noted above in describing the South Bronx. Short-term efforts to evaluate specific programs weigh heavily on utilization, cost, and impressionistic clinical data. The NSC's services were indeed widely used by a group of people who had not previously had access to mental health services. Its per capita costs were low; the annual budget of $50,000 for a population area of 50,000 people yielded a cost estimate of $1 per person. Moreover, those closest to the development saw it clinically as an effective, realistic approach to a heretofore underserved group, many of whom are beset with serious living and/or psychological problems. The NSC illustrates another innovative way to use community settings, resources, and personnel to develop promising new approaches to longstanding, difficult social and mental health problems.

New Personnel Uses

For many years mental health services were provided within a narrow structural framework. The modal format used was a two-person dyad in which the help agent was a trained, credentialed mental health worker and the client an individual experiencing psychological difficulties. That format is not inappropriate in any absolute sense. Indeed, one important thing we learned from the second mental health revolution was that it often worked well and meaningfully. At the same time, battle-line experiences raised serious questions about the model's *sufficiency* for meeting the nation's mental health needs: Do people in need have uniform access to that delivery system? Is the system equally sensible and workable across social strata? Does the system field problems at optimal, natural times? Are there sufficient personnel to meet the need for help as defined within the system's framework? As evidence mounted suggesting that the answer to each of those questions was "no," explorations of new alternatives accelerated. Mental health consultation, involvement of natural, informal care givers, and the planned use of nonprofessional help agents, each reflecting that exploration process, are considered in the next sections.

Consultation.   Among the important emphases of the original Joint Commission on Mental Illness and Health (1961) were the recognition of existing professional personnel shortages (Albee, 1959) and a more liberal, inclusive view of who was qualified to provide mental health services. One task force of that commission reported data with powerful shaping value for the field of mental health consultation. That task force (Gurin, Veroff, & Feld, 1960) surveyed the de facto help-seeking behaviors of people with emotional problems and came up with some eye-opening findings (recently updated by Gourash, 1978; Veroff, Kulka, & Douvan, 1981). They established that 25% of the population at some time reported the need for formal psychological help and that about 15% actually sought such help. However, only a small fraction (18%) of the latter went to a mental health professional. By contrast, 42% took their problems to clergypersons and 29% to family physicians. These compelling findings doused cold water on the image of indispensability long held by many mental health professionals. They were not the only priests.

A new reality had been established, and there were many ways to react (e.g., fight it, join it, ignore it). Different people have reacted differently. Some chose to join it. That meant first recognizing that people package and deal with psychological problems in personal idiosyncratic ways and then identifying mechanisms for informing and supporting non–mental health personnel who are called on daily to engage those problems. The gut questions raised by that view are (a) which groups field systematic appeals for help with psychological problems and (b) what specific mental health activities and inputs can promote the most beneficial outcomes in such situations.

Gurin et al.'s (1960) finding that most psychological problems come first to the attention of people who lack mental health background or training spotlighted one important subgroup from that amorphous mass, namely, surrogate professionals such as physicians, the clergy, lawyers, nurses, and educators, who are known to carry a heavy load of such traffic. The latter fact, by the way, is not all bad. Indeed, such contacts offer the advantages of spontaneity and/or occurrence *because* the troubled person knows, trusts, and respects the competence and natural wisdom of the care giver (Caplan, 1964). Sometimes, however, the people whose help is sought feel overtaxed, a reality that provides one key raison d'être for consultation. Precisely because the approach respects early, natural, and important lines of interpersonal help seeking, it has potential for being a first-line bulwark against the development of later, more serious psychological problems.

There is by now a voluminous literature on consultation. One volume (Mannino, MacLennan, & Shore, 1975) catalogued 1200 citations in the area prior to 1973. A more recent compilation (Grady, Gibson, & Trickett, 1980) added 900 new citations for 1973 to 1978. Many other volumes (e.g., Caplan, 1970; Goodstein, 1978) have been written exclusively on the topic. Those writings identify several different types of consultation. Perhaps the oldest and best known is clinical case consultation, which provides information to broaden the consultee's understanding of psychological problems, considers specific handling and responding strategies, and suggests alternatives that go beyond a consultee's background and training. Clinical case consultation seeks to strengthen the caregiver's hand and to provide resources and backstopping that help him or her deal more effectively with the problems of clientele in psychological distress.

But consultation is broader than just clinical case consultation. It can, for example, be targeted structurally to individuals, groups, or agency settings. It can deal with client or consultee problems and can stress either clinical or process issues. Whatever its specifics, the aim is to share mental health knowledge and expertise and thus to address the psychological problems of more people, earlier in their natural unfolding processes. The ultimate goal is to increase mental health's wallop geometrically. If, for example, as has been said, one-third to one-half of the problems brought to pediatricians are basically psychological, a mental health consultation program with 10 to 12 pediatricians can potentially reach thousands of people at psychologically meaningful, helpful times. Similarly, large segments (e.g., rural and low-density population areas) of this vast country are largely without formal mental health services (Robinson, DeMarche, & Wagle, 1961). In those regions people must necessarily take their psychological problems to whoever among available caregivers will listen and try to help. When people not so trained must act as de facto mental health help agents, consultation can offer much in upgrading skills and providing support (Griffith & Libo, 1968; Huessy, 1966; Spielberger, 1967).

Mental health consultation is, above all, an approach born of hard realities, including the following: (a) mental health resources are insufficient to meet need; (b) early intervention is more promising than late intervention for psychological problems; (c) promoting health is conceptually preferable to struggling against rooted disorder; (d) psychological problems are often interwoven naturally with other complex problems of living; and (e) many problems are brought spontaneously to people who are not trained to deal with them. Thus consultation as an approach well illustrates how changing times and views of psychological problems favor the generation of community-based alternatives.

Although consultation has significantly modified the total mental health delivery system, it is not an easy development to evaluate. On the plus side, it offers the important advantages of early, aggressive outreach to problems, including many that would otherwise elude the mental health system; capitalizing on early entry points and natural relationships of trust; and expanding the reach of mental health services to heretofore unreachable sectors of society. One difficulty in evaluating consultation, however, is that it is an indirect service, in that its ultimate intended targets are people served by intermediaries. The feedback and data most readily available to the consultant include such things as *consultees'* gain in knowledge and sophistication and their attitudes toward the consultation experience. However gratifying and reinforcing positive change on these dimensions can be, it does not guarantee parallel change in the feelings and behavior of the ultimate target people, the clients of the consultees—an area often bypassed in consultation outcome research (Cowen, 1978; Kelly, 1971). Although several recent reviews have reported positive findings based on consultation outcome research studies (Mannino & Shore, 1975; Medway, 1982), more information is needed on its effects with ultimate intended targets before consultation's place in the mental health armamentarium can be fixed.

Informal Caregivers   Consultation's first strong push was toward visible, recognized professional caregiver groups. The seeming good sense and success of that approach led to expansion of its focus. A next logical step was to turn attention to other groups such as welfare workers, police officers, and health and child care workers, whose job roles also bring them into frequent contact with emotional distress. Although the official concerns of these groups are with other than psychological matters, people's wholeness and the specific, often pressing, nature of their problems create situations in which significant psychological components cannot be ignored. Hence consultation's role broadened to include such groups and to embrace a modified family of situations and activities. That expansion in scope is overviewed in Gershon and Biller's (1977) volume; separate articles consider some of its specific manifestations, such as police consultation (Bard, 1970).

The preceding ferment and change in practice called attention to an even broader issue: Just how *do* psychologically troubled individuals go about seeking to reduce their tensions and upsets? All people at one time or another experience stress and psychological problems and feel a need to lean on others for help, support, and resolution. Fortunately, many people have ready access to good, natural social supports and ties (e.g., friends, neighbors, relatives, co-workers) that offer wisdom and comfort in difficult moments. Thank goodness for that! Indeed, if everyone had truly solid first lines of defense, there would be less need for mental health professionals. But for large numbers, interpersonal help is either not available at all or not available when needed. Under these circumstances people seek help wherever and however they can find it. Hence many individuals with no formal mental health background whatsoever are inevitably cast in helping roles by virtue of either their social position or their compassion and interest in others. That fact was formally noted long ago (Caplan, 1974; Cowen, 1967; Duhl, 1963; Kelly, 1964). Generic terms such as *informal caregivers* or *urban agents* were used to describe those invisible help agents. They were recognized to play different roles in different cultures and social strata. Contacts with them were known to be informal and spontaneous, rather than preplanned. Such help giving, though real and widespread, is more difficult to track than the activities of professional caregivers, precisely because it is more scattered and unpredictable.

Collins (1973) made the point that informal caregivers and natural neighborhood helpers are the prime de facto source of interpersonal help across broad bands of urban society. Specifically, Collins and Pancoast (1976) estimated that less than 15% of the urban poor, in contrast to the 70% of the middle-class sample studied by Gurin et al. (1960), took their personal problems to the clergy or physicians. For the poor, natural neighbor helpers and community gatekeepers were sought out when personal problems came up.

Caplan (1974), who perceived the compelling nature of that reality, sounded the following challenge: "How can we made contact with [informal care givers] and how can we educate them so that they give wise counsel to those in crisis who seek them out?" One strategy has been to extend training and consultation frameworks to include informal caregivers (Doane & Cowen, 1981; Verdone, 1975; Weisenfeld & Weis, 1980). Another even more basic strategy has been to chart the actual nature and extent of interpersonal helping being done by informal caregivers. Cowen (1982e), for example, summarized a series of studies of the interpersonal helping activities of four such groups: hairdressers (Cowen, Gesten, Boike, Norton, Wilson, & DeStefano, 1979; Cowen, Gesten, Davidson, & Wilson, 1981; Searcy-Miller, 1980); divorce lawyers (Doane & Cowen, 1981); industrial foremen (Kaplan & Cowen, 1981); and bartenders (Cowen, McKim, & Weissberg, 1981). These studies were guided by simple questions such as: How much time did the groups actually spend engaging people's moderate to serious psychological problems? What kinds of problems, specifically? What methods did they use to deal with those problems? How did they feel about being called on to serve in that role? How good a job did they think they were doing?

Answers to these questions have helped to chart an important though heretofore poorly understood reality. Although the findings, to be sure, differed somewhat from group to group, several common denominators emerged. It is very common for people to discuss personal problems with informal caregivers. Hairdressers and lawyers who were studied, for example, spent up to 40% of their contact time with clients doing exactly that. In the aggregate, the problems raised with informal helpers were much like those brought to mental health professionals. Reported handling strategies varied across groups; they included techniques often used by mental health professionals (e.g., listening, presenting alternatives) and some that most professionals would frown upon (e.g., recounting personal experiences, changing the topic). Most helpers felt good about the help-giving role and believed that they were reasonably effective. But they also felt that they were sometimes over their heads and could profit from professional inputs. Among the studies' more specific findings were the facts that groups "pulled" for somewhat different types of problems and that the ecology of the helper–helpee interaction, particularly with bartenders, influenced the form, content, and depth of exploration of problems. A comparative study of black and white beauty shops (Searcy-Miller, 1980) confirmed the special place and importance of the informal help-giving process in inner-city contexts.

These studies were designed to illuminate and not to place a value judgment on an important reality. The four informal care-giver groups studied represent only a small fraction of what is undoubtedly a far more extensive social phenomenon. What the studies failed to establish—and it is very important—is just how *effective* informal help givers are (Lieberman & Mullan, 1978). Answers to that critical question would structure ways in which the mental health fields could best support, perhaps even learn from, the pervasive process of informal interpersonal helping. Although the professional's first imperialistic reflex may be to extend mental health consultation to informal helpers to upgrade their skills and improve their efficacy, skepticism has been voiced about that prospect (Gottlieb, 1974; Rappaport, 1977). The legitimate question raised is the extent to which any such benevolently intended intervention might throw out the baby with the bath water; that is, it might impose rigid mental health truths in situations where they do not fit and ignore hard-won, albeit nontextual, street wisdom. A recent volume by Froland, Pancoast, Chapman, and Kimboko (1981) offers pertinent thoughts about resolving this dilemma through meaningful new partnerships between mental health professionals and informal caregivers.

Nonprofessional Help Agents.   Today most people take nonprofessional mental health workers for granted. That wasn't always so. To the contrary, until very recently the mental health professions were a tightly locked guild system. That began to change as mental health's scope expanded late in the second revolution and pressures for service thus increased greatly. The existing system simply could not meet demand, much less need. But that was not the only reason. Over time it also became apparent that there were contexts and circumstances in which nonprofessionals might be able to provide more appealing, indeed more appropriate, services than professionals.

Many volumes have been written about the unfolding of the nonprofessional movement in this country (see Arnhoff, Rubenstein, & Speisman, 1969; Gartner, 1971; Gershon & Biller, 1977; Grosser, Henry, & Kelly, 1969; Sobey, 1970). Although a few example were cited earlier in this chapter, they barely scratch the surface of this important development. Other, varied examples are considered in the next sections.

Several early programs that challenged a then-dominant temper of the times had a disproportionately high impact in shaping the nonprofessional movement in mental health. One such model used volunteer college undergraduates as companions with chronic mental patients, as part of an exploration of a liberalized treatment concept with that group. The Harvard Project (Umbarger, Dalsimer, Morrison, & Breggin, 1962) and the Connecticut Valley State Hospital Program (Holzberg, Knapp, & Turner, 1967) exemplify that pioneering thrust. Recent surveys show that variants of the basic model established by these early programs are not operating out of more than 1000 campus or clinic settings.

A second high-impact early development was the paradigmatic work by Rioch (1967) at NIMH to train housewives as psychotherapists. Predicated on the assumptions that (a) all communities harbor sizable pools of potential helping power and (b) personal and experiential qualities are as important as professional training and degrees in preparing helpers or more so, that pilot program had considerable modeling and heuristic value. Many later programs, such as PMHP's a child-aide program discussed earlier, are based on Rioch's structural model, even though the specific roles and activities of the helpers have broadened.

The important point to stress, however, is the remarkable burgeoning, that some (Sobey, 1970) call a revolution, of the nonprofessional movement in mental health. This growth is reflected in the diversity of the people who have functioned as help agents, the target populations they have served, the settings they have worked in, and the activities in which they have been involved. Nonprofessionals have worked as volunteers and paid employees; they have varied markedly in age, education, sociodemographic status, and social position. Mental health programs have been reported in which the prime help agents are college, high school or elementary students, housewives, indigenous neighborhood workers, retired people, delinquents and exoffenders, and members of community service organizations. Service recipients in those programs have been equally diverse, including classic mental health patients, the elderly, school children, hard-core or delinquent youth, clinic patients, inner-city residents, women seen through pregnancy or well-baby clinics, medical patients in hospitals, individuals who have entered the criminal justice or corrections systems, and people who have experienced recent crises. Similarly, diverse roles are played in many programs: the roles of friend, companion, or support agent; counselor or therapist; as expediter or facilitator of services; and imparter of educational or life skills. Some of those roles, as suggested earlier, are highly innovative; they do not at all follow mental health's traditional ways of defining problems or rendering services. The indigenous inner-city nonprofessional is a good illustration. Such workers' street wisdom and know-how, the trust that users have in them, and felicitous matches in style and cultural background often win access to clientele and create a basis for rapport not typically available through professionals.

The willingness to use nonprofessional workers reflects a decision to go with the variables of life history, personal style, and prior experience rather than traditional educational or degree criteria. Even so, extensive guides have been written (e.g., Carkhuff & Pierce, 1975; Danish, D'Augelli, & Hauer, 1980) about nonprofessional training. Such training varies in nature and extent across programs, reflecting the biases and belief systems of those who run the program, trainers' resources and know-how, and workers' actual job functions. Some of the latter are conceived in the image of established professional roles, as when the nonporfessional is trained to perform less demanding or rewarding professional functions. In other cases, especially with indigenous nonprofessionals, the role is new and differs qualitatively from prior professional roles. For some nonprofessionals the active, generic work element is the committed human relationship; for others experience and know-how acquired in specific environments significantly shape their roles; and for still others particular skills such as behavior modification, play therapy, or counseling must be mastered to do an effective job.

The wealth of experience gathered with programs that have used nonprofessionals helps to identify some of the movement's obvious pluses and minuses. One clear virtue is that it expands services dramatically. A second is the access it provides to unserved or underserved groups. A third is the harnessing of excitement and enthusiasm that offer a pleasant contrast in otherwise gloomy institutional settings such as mental hospitals. A fourth is the optimism that such workers often have and the fact that they are more flexible and less constrained by so called tried-and-true ways. There may well be things for professionals to learn from the naive but natural ways of nonprofessionals.

But there are concerns as well, such as key skills that nonprofessionals may lack or the anxiety that some clients have about the possibility of receiving services seen as second best. Too, mechanical or administrative headaches are associated with programs that use nonprofessionals, such as creating new roles, overhauling tables of organization, establishing career ladders and advancement opportunities based on competence rather than degree criteria (Danish, 1977), and finding durable budgetary bases for those programs. Moreover, this type of programming sometimes threatens vested professional interest.

Given the extent of this movement's emphases on program development and implementation, hard-nosed research evaluation of its effects has not kept pace (Gershon & Biller, 1977). Although it is unlikely that the development could have grown as it has unless it both addressed socially significant issues and was seen to be clinically effective, it has remained aloof from systematic research scrutiny. Several reviews of program outcome studies in the area (Durlak, 1979; Gershon & Biller, 1977; Gruver, 1971) emphasize both their paucity and their methodological insufficiencies, even though they conclude on positive notes.

The nonprofessional thrust, strongly responsive to perceived social need, is a development with deep community roots (Kalafat & Boroto, 1977). Although many mental health professionals have tuned out on it and have gone about business as usual, those closest to it have learned that it can significantly modify a prior delicate "balance of nature" in professional roles. Within the framework of such programs less professional time goes into direct services of assessment and therapy and much more into "quarterbacking" roles (Cowen, 1967) such as recruitment, training, and supervision of nonprofessionals. Nonprofessionals do *not* replace professionals; rather, their use creates new and, it is hoped, more socially utilitarian roles for them. The pot of gold at the end of that rainbow is to reach many more people than before with needed, effective services.

PRIMARY PREVENTION IN MENTAL HEALTH

Community mental health and primary prevention in mental health are very different approaches, even though each is in its own way a protest against the perceived insufficiencies of existing practice. Without significantly challenging mental health's historic credo of curing the sick, the multipronged CMH movement seeks by changes in method, timing, locus, and person to deal more effectively with some of its most stubborn problems. Primary prevention in mental health, by contrast, directly challenges mental health's basic mind sets and pivotal assumptions. Its goal is to cut down the flow of psychological problems, rather than to counterpunch against established disorder.

Although several recent volumes have been written on primary prevention in mental health (see Felner, Jason, Moritsugu, & Farber, 1983; Kent & Rolf, 1979; Price, Ketterer, Bader, & Monahan, 1980), the literature and research in this area are sparser and more scattered than in CMH. One reason for this, notwithstanding convergence among primary prevention's abstract definitions (Caplan, 1964; Cowen, 1980s; Goldston, 1977a), is that the term is not yet well understood concretely (Cowen, 1977). In practice, the field has been plagued by sloppy terminological usage and applications involving very different concepts such as *prevention, prevention in mental health, primary prevention,* and *primary prevention in mental health* (Cowen, 1983a).

Prevention is an extremely broad, inclusive, and nearly meaningless term. It is broad enough to embrace the goal of preventing virtually any adverse condition, physical or psychological, by virtually any method. *Prevention in mental health* at least narrows the focus to conditions that are relevant to the mental health fields, though it is still loose enough to include three qualitatively different strategies: (a) tertiary prevention—minimizing further negative consequences of established, serious disorder; (b) secondary prevention—keeping less severe disorders from becoming prolonged and debilitating; and (c) primary prevention—preventing the occurrence of disorder, and/or building psychological health. The generic term *primary prevention*, still very broad, describes procedures to promote many different types of wellness—physical or psychological—and/or to forestall dysfunctions in any area. *Primary prevention in mental health,* the most specific of the four terms and the focus of the sections to follow, narrows those worthy general goals to adjustment outcomes.

The preceding important distinctions, particularly those among primary, secondary, and tertiary prevention in mental health, are neither clearly understood nor fully respected (Cowen, 1980a, 1983a). And as people seek for whatever reasons to join a primary prevention bandwagon, the term's definitional limits are sorely stretched. In the end, many things that have little or nothing to do with primary prevention in mental health are nonetheless coded with that label (Cowen, 1982a). Such practice retards the field's development by blurring vital distinctions in assumption and practice between that concept and established mental health approaches. Of the four terms considered, only *primary prevention in mental health* offers that clear, sharp contrast.

Mounting dissatisfaction with past ways, serious current unresolved problems, and the common-sense appeal of primary prevention in mental health have all contributed to its recent ascent (President's Commission Report, 1978). Growing interest is evident in several ways: (a) The concept has been cited with increasing frequency in talks, books, and journals (indeed, several new journals are, in principle, devoted exclusively to that topic); (b) it has been appearing more frequently in the reports and recommendations of influential mental health planning troups; (c) it has become a more important concept in graduate training in mental health; and (d) more primary prevention offices have been established at the federal, state, and municipal levels, and, even in fiscally troubled times, some of those offices have had funds to plan and develop new programs.

Both readiness and rhetoric for primary prevention in mental health are growing. These ingredients will not be well nourished by fuzzy, elasticized definitions of the concept. Rather, they require a narrow, exacting definition of the term to maximize contrast with prior options. Since primary prevention's main goals are to forestall the development of psychological problems and to enhance people's psychological health, the backbone of the approach is the development of fruitful interventions (programs) or manipulations with the following *structural* qualities. They must be (a) group or mass oriented, *not* targeted to individuals; (b) designed for well, not already sick, people (though they can include or even feature people known by virtue of life circumstances or recent events to be at risk for psychological difficulties); and (c) intentional in the sense of resting on a knowledge base that suggests potential for the program to reduce maladjustment or promote psychological health (Cowen, 1980a, 1982b). Although those structural requirements are harsh and restrictive, they do not limit a program's content, methodology, or target groups. Indeed, in all of the latter respects, program diversity is desirable. Programs that meet the preceding requirements can be seen as legitimate, aspiring primary prevention programs in mental health. To actually *be* such a program also requires that intended, positive (adjustment) outcomes be shown empirically. Some authors (Cowen, 1977; Kelly, 1977) have gone one step further, arguing that short-term gains from such programs must also be shown to endure over time.

Most programs that are labeled *primary prevention in mental health* fail to meet one or more of the preceding requirements; for example, they are targeted to already disturbed people, or their thrust has little to do with adjustment, or they involved some variant of individual therapy with upset people. Were the present exacting definitional framework taken seriously, only a small fraction of programs that journal compilations or abstracting services cite as examples of primary prevention in mental health would qualify (Cowen, 1982a).

Primary prevention in mental health can be seen as a two-stage process. First, rational decisions must be made about promising programmatic steps that can be taken in seeking to prevent maladjustment or promote psychological health. Then programs vivifying those decisions must be mounted, conducted, and evaluated. Those two components have been called primary prevention's *generative* and *executive* strands, respectively (Cowen, 1980a). The generative base needed to fuel sound programs consists of knowledge of relationships between qualities of people, structures, processes, events, and experiences, on the one side, and adjustment outcomes (good or bad) on the other.

A hand-in-glove relationship between generation and execution can be illustrated by some concrete examples. Spivack, Platt, and Shure (1976) summarized numerous studies showing that clinical and/or maladjusted groups are deficient in a family of interpersonal problem-solving skills. Such data led to the conclusion that these skills mediate adjustment and then to the development of programs designed to impart them to young children as yet nonaffected (Shure & Spivack, 1982). Bloom, Asher, and White (1978) marshaled compelling epidemiological data demonstrating that divorced adults show higher rates of maladjustment or pathology than married adults on diverse indicators. These facts formed a generative foundation on which was built a successful primary prevention program, based on social support and skill training, for currently divorcing adults (Bloom, Hodges & Caldwell, 1982).

A generative base for primary prevention in mental health comes about either intentionally or serendipitously. *Intentional* describes the situation in which investigators do basic research designed to inform the shape of a later specific primary prevention intervention. An example might be a study of relationships between properties of primary-grade class environments and young children's school adjustment with the later goal in mind of strengthening programmatically environmental qualities associated with adjustment and reducing those associated with maladjustment. *Serendipitous* applies to many existing studies in many areas, with no primary prevention connection or intent when they were done, which nevertheless identify important relationships between personal qualities, situations, or events and adjustment outcomes. For example, children from high- compared to low-noise-level dwellings may be found to be underachieving academically and also, incidentally, to be more maladjusted.

Only a small fraction of primary prevention's current generative base is intentional; most of that base is to be found in work done for diverse other purposes. It can thus be seen, metaphorically, as ore to be mined as soon as the veins are discovered. This is no easy task, however, since the sources are almost sure to be scattered, not only in many of psychology's traditional areas but, more importantly, in fields as diverse as family relationships, education, sociology, child development, political science, epidemiology, social ecology, economics, architecture, and environmental engineering. Strange bedfellows indeed, yet bedfellows that portray realistically a complex pattern of interfaces ultimately needed to shape a sound generative base for primary prevention in mental health. Among the obvious implications of this view are that (a) primary prevention specialists will need be trained in ways different from the ways in which mental health professionals have been trained up to now (Cowen, 1983b) and (b) they will interact with new clusters of disciplines heretofore seen as orthogonal to mental health.

Although forming a generative base for primary prevention programs in mental health and actually conducting such programs are two qualitatively different processes, they are linked symbiotically. A program built on a weak or ill-reasoned generative base will intrinsically be limited. Both sound generation and execution must happen for primary prevention in mental health to develop properly. We attach no value judgments (such as seeing one as "better" or "more important" than the other) to these two processes. Rather, what seems clear is that primary prevention's current knowledge-base exists more through happenstance than planning. Strengthening that base is a never-ending challenge. When and how it is strengthened are important keys to future executive programming. Intentional generation is one way to accelerate the pacing of that process. But even though the current generative base for primary prevention in mental health is still spotty and scattered, enough of it exists to warrant undertaking a variety of programs at this time.

Primary prevention in mental health directs attention to types of variables and outcomes different from those that have traditionally concerned mental health. It focuses more on (a) people who appear invulnerable to psychological disorder (Garmezy, 1976; Garmezy, Masten, Nordstrom, & Ferrarese, 1979) than on those who seem vulnerable, (b) effectance motivation (Harter, 1978; White, 1959) than on motivational deficit; (c) health-producing experiences (Finkel, 1974; Hollister, 1967) than on traumas; (d) competence (Anderson & Messick, 1974; Gesten, 1976; Kent & Rolf, 1979) than on incompetence; and (e) improving the quality of life (Zautra & Goodhart, 1979) than on defects in living conditions. Two molar strategies that it follows in advancing those new focuses are strengthening people's competencies, resources, and coping skills through direct training or constructive environmental change and reducing sources of stress on people. These guiding orientations, however, have been implemented in different ways. The sections to follow illustrate some of these ways.

Mental Health Education

Because primary prevention in mental health is a mass-oriented building approach, education should in principle be its most natural and powerful tool. Within that frame of reference mental health education (MHE) is a well-rooted, theoretically attractive option designed to help people to acquire attitudes, specific knowledge, and behavior strategies that promote and maintain psychological wellness. The approach is appealing because it is proactive, it has fine potential for reaching many people, especially through the use of the mass media (Schanie & Sundel, 1978), and it has much flexibility in terms of target groups, topical focuses, formats, and timing. These many hypotthetical virtues notwithstanding, MHE in practice has been a mixed bag (Bloom, 1980) that includes colossal failures (Cumming & Cumming, 1957) and occasional highs (Hereford, 1963; Johnson & Breckenridge, 1982; Maccoby & Alexander, 1979; Muñoz, Glish, Soo-Hoo, & Robertson, 1982).

It is hard to know for sure why MHE has failed to live up to its promise. One problem is that the term is very broad and amorphous and encompasses many different kinds of activities. It is, in other words, a structural approach, with a near infinity of potential contents and formats. The latter are probably not equipotential in their before-the-fact justifiability (i.e., the soundness of their generative bases), their relevance to prospective consumers, or their effectiveness. When some years ago Davis (1965) argued that the main reason for MHE's lack of success was that the mental health fields did not have useful, practical bodies of information to pass along to the general public, he was not indicting so much the method as the soundness of its generative base.

MHE programs have also suffered from inadequate or improper evaluation. The judgmental word *improper* bears clarification. Many if not most MHE programs are provided for intermediaries (e.g., parents, family members, teachers) in the hope that positive changes in them will lead to adjustive gain (primary prevention effects) in the program's ultimate targets, such as the children with whom they interact. Without program evaluation such positive effects can of course not be shown. Evaluations that focus exclusively on intermediaries are most likely to provide information about the extent to which they enjoyed and profited from the program, the new knowledge they acquired, and how their attitudes and behaviors changed. Although such data are interesting in their own right and often reinforcing, they do not guarantee that adjustment gain has taken place in the program's ultimate intended targets. The latter is primary prevention's first goal. If the MHE development is to have a richer fruition, future programs must be built on sounder generative bases, and their evaluations must show psychological growth or prevention of maladjustment in ultimate targets.

Competence Training

Skill or competence training is another conceptually attractive educational approach to primary prevention in mental health. It differs from MHE in having a narrower focus and being more firmly grounded on a sound, well-developed generative base. The approach starts with the assumption that certain pivotal skills or competencies, different perhaps for different age and sociodemographic groups, mediate positive adjustment. A discipline's generative base indentifies these key competencies.

The development by Ojemann (1961) of a program to teach children "causal" thinking is an early example of this approach. By casual thinking, Ojemann meant an orientation to causes, understandings, and analytic processes, in contrast to more traditional "surface" approaches that emphasize acquisition of facts. Ojemann believed that acquiring casual thinking skills would generalize to help a child cope better with adaptive demands. Early studies comparing children trained in the causal and in the traditional mode showed greater cognitive gain for the former in areas such as generalization of knowledge, weighing alternatives, and sensitivity to factors underlying behavior. Later studies probed the generality of those findings to the sphere of personal adjustment. Bruce (1958), for example, found that sixth-graders taught causally had lower anxiety and higher security scores than nonprogram peers. Muuss (1960) reported similar findings, including healthier overall adjustment profiles for a causally trained sample of fifth- and sixth-graders. With fourth- and fifth-graders Griggs and Bonney (1970) found that causally trained subjects had higher self-concept, sociometric, and overall adjustment scores than controls. Thus acquiring a set of cognitive, analytic, problem-engaging skills rooted basal competencies that appeared to radiate positively to adjustment.

Work already cited by a research team at the Hahnemann Medical Center has more recently shown that clinical or maladjusted groups of children, adolescents, and adults across sociodemographic strata and settings were consistently deficient in an interrelated family of interpersonal cognitive problem-solving (ICPS) skills, including abilities to recognize other people's feelings, generate alternative solutions to problems, take the role of the other, identify behavioral consequences, and read means–end relationships (Spivack et al., 1976). These workers reasoned that if young children could be taught those ICPS skills the new knowledge would generalize positively to adjustment. A relevant curriculum was developed for inner-city preschoolers both in the classroom and at home (Shure & Spivack, 1978, 1982; Spivack & Shure, 1974). The program's findings were impressive. For one thing, the teaching "took"; that is, trained children exceeded nonprogram controls in acquiring the ICPS skills. They, particularly youngsters seen initially as inhibited and maladjusted, were also judged by teachers to be significantly better adjusted. Both cognitive and adjustive gains endured over a year's time and generalized to new classroom settings. Importantly from the standpoint of primary prevention theory, direct linkages were shown between ICPS and adjustment gains. Thus a program represented and conducted as a cognitive–educational program yielded significant adjustment gain. Without ever being directly engaged, problems and symptoms were reduced by rooting critical cognitive competencies. The question that this demonstration spotlights is the extent to which a broad competence-training approach can help to alter mental health's past unswerving reactive stance.

The Hahnemann group's promising findings stimulated many replications, extensions, and program adaptations for a range of age and sociodemographic groups (e.g., Allen, Chinksy, Larcen, Lochman, & Selinger, 1976; Elardo & Caldwell, 1979; Gesten, Flores de Apodaca, Rains, Weissberg, & Cowen, 1979; Gesten, Rains, Rapkin, Weissberg, Flores de Apodaca, Cowen, & Bowen, 1982; Weissberg, Gesten, Carnrike, Toro, Rapkin, Davidson, & Cowen, 1981; Weissberg, Gesten, Rapkin, Cowen, Davidson, Flores de Apodaca, & McKim, 1981; Winer, Hilpert, Gesten, Cowen, & Schubin, 1982). That surge produced enough information to warrant a recent comprehensive literature review (Urbain & Kendall, 1980). Although this and other reviews (Weissberg & Gesten, 1982) cite positive findings from the newer ICPS training programs, such data have been less robust and less internally consistent than the original Hahnemann findings. These differences may reflect changes in program formats, content, and evaluation methodology as well as issues involved in applying the program to different age and sociodemographic groups.

The ICPS approach is one significant competence training approach for primary prevention in mental health. It has the virtues of meeting the concept's stringent definitional criteria and producing empirical data showing that focal program skills can be acquired and that, when this happens, adjustment also improves. The approach's greatest value, however, is not as a literal sine qua non, but rather as a structural paradigm for primary prevention in mental health. It is instructive to note that a related approach, which includes developing specific social skills training programs and/or "coaching" programs for young children with early, mild social adjustment problems, has also attracted recent attention and reported positive findings (Hartup, 1979; LaGreca & Santagrossi, 1980; Oden, 1980; Wanlass & Prinz, 1982).

Conceptually related programs have also been developed to promote other competencies believed to undergird adjustment. Stamps (1975), for example, developed a program based on self-reinforcement principles to teach inner-city fourth-graders realistic goal-setting behaviors. As such behaviors were acquired, children's achievement scores improved, and they gained on measures of locus of control, responsibility, openness and self-awareness, and acceptance. The latter again reflect positive radiation to the adjustment sphere. Similar positive demonstrations have been reported based on strengthening children's curiosity behaviors (Susskind, 1979), sharing behaviors (Jason, Robin, & Lipshutz, 1980), and relationship formation (Vogelsong, Most, & Yanchko, 1979).

Although the latter developments are embryonic, they are important to note because they highlight a significant issue. Although the ICPS development has been important and has illuminated an attractive structural pathway, it is conceivable that the early positive ICPS findings were fixed upon so literally that they restricted exploration of *other* significant competencies that also mediate adjustment. The following questions should structure a *generalized* competence training approach: (a) What are the gut competencies that mediate adjustment for different age and sociodemographic groups? (b) How can situationally appropriate training programs to impart those skills best be developed? (c) What linkages can be shown between competence acquisition and adjustive gain? (Cowen, 1977)

The goal of fostering competence can also be pursued at a molar level, as for example with communities (Iscoe, 1974; Rappaport, 1977; Rhoads & Raymond, 1981). This view is reflected in Rappaport, Davidson, Wilson, and Mitchell's (1975) work developing the Community Psychology Action Center (CPAC), an inner-city setting designed to identify and strengthen existing community competencies. CPAC worked against what Ryan (1971) decried as a "blaming-the-victim" approach to the poor. Instead of molding people within an existing system, it accepted the values and styles of inner-city people as they were and sought to amplify an existing culture by broadening its known competence bases. CPAC made no attempt to deal with psychological problems as typically defined. Another example of the same approach was reported by Hodgson (1979), who developed a setting to encourage the formation of support systems in a community characterized by isolation, fragmentation, anomic reactions, and depression. These programs sought to foster independence and positive behaviors, based on the assumption that developing people's strengths is the best of all ways to engage problems.

Stressful Life Events

Both life stresses and specific adverse events have been found consistently to relate to negative psychological outcome (Dohrenwend, 1978; Dohrenwend & Dohrenwend, 1969; Felner, Farber, & Primavera, 1980; Felner, Stolberg, & Cowen, 1975; Holmes & Masuda, 1974), though the extent and form of such outcomes are known to be mediated by personal, situational, and stylistic variables (Dohrenwend, 1978; Sandler, 1980). Examples of critical life events with known negative consequences include divorce (Bloom et al., 1978; Felner et al., 1980; Hetherington, Cox, & Cox, 1978), bereavement (Silverman, 1976) school transition (Bogat, Jones, & Jason, 1980; Felner, Ginter, & Primavera, 1982), sudden infant death (Goldston, 1977b), economic decline and job loss (Dooley & Catalano, 1980; Monahan & Vaux, 1980), and natural disaster (Baisden & Quarantelli, 1981). Crises, including critical life events, have been viewed as times of exaggerated danger or opportunity. Ineffectively handled, they leave potentially serious, enduring psychological scars; constructively resolved, they strengthen a person's ability to cope with future problems (Caplan, 1964). This reality structures another important challenge for primary prevention in mental health: developing effective interventions to short-circuit the negative outcomes to which critical life events often lead.

To pursue this goal calls for an important paradigm shift in mental health (Bloom, 1979). Instead of waiting for evolved problems to insinuate themselves on an existing formal delivery system (the passive–receptive mode), an alternative, more active, three-stage model is implicated: (a) Identify, epidemiologically, correlationally, or however, critical events with unfortuate outcomes (many of which are already well known or suspected); (b) assess comparatively groups of people currently experiencing or not experiencing these events and establish their short- and long-term sequelae; (c) based on such generative data, mount and evaluate programs designed explicitly both to enhance such people's skills and resources and to forestall otherwise anticipated negative psychological outcomes.

Examples can be cited of program models based on this structural paradigm. Bloom et al. (1982), in the light of generative data pointing to widespread negative psychological sequelae of divorce, developed a 6-month intervention program for newly divorcing adults that both provided significant supports and trained relevant skills and competencies. Program subjects exceeded controls in overall adjustment and in specific adjustment areas; in other words, the program succeeded in preventing some of the negative psychological fallout that typically follows divorce. Felner et al. (1982), addressing the negative psychological consequences of school transition, developed a program for entering high school students that combined environmental engineering (that is, minimizing environmental complexity and flux) and strengthening peer and teacher support. Program subjects exceeded controls on grades and attendance and had less negative self-concepts and perceptions of the school environment. Roskin (1982) identified a group of people who had experienced multiple recent critical life events. His preventive intervention, which was based on mental health education, fostering mutual support, and teaching specific competencies, resulted in significant reductions in somatic concerns, depression, and anxiety for program subjects. Similarly, Tableman, Marciniak, Johnson, and Rodgers (1982), working with stressed low-income mothers known to be susceptible to psychological difficulties, developed a preventive program teaching life skills and management approaches, providing support, and strengthening self-esteem. Participants compared to controls improved in overall adjustment and ego strength and decreased in feelings of depression, anxiety, and inadequacy.

A different, somewhat narrower application of the same principles can also be cited. Most children at one time or another must face anxiety-producing dental, medical, or surgical experiences. Prior generative findings suggested that these experiences are often followed by short- or long-term negative psychological outcomes. Later it was shown that certain interventions based on expressive and/or modeling procedures at critical juncture points help children better to cope with and adjust to such critical events (Graziano, DeGiovanni, & Garcia, 1979; Melamed & Siegel, 1975; Thelen, Fry, Fehrenbach, & Frautschi, 1979). Indeed, Graziano et al. (1979) state explicitly that stress inoculation training and training in coping and mastery skills have much to offer in the primary prevention of psychological problems created by medical and dental procedures—a point made earlier, and in a more generalized context, by Cumming and Cumming (1966).

Findings from this important cluster of studies suggest that constructive intervention following critical life events can help to short-circuit psychological problems that often follow them. In this domain an ounce of prevention may well be worth a pound of cure.

Social Systems Analysis and Change

A hallmark of the second mental health revolution was the extent to which it formulated, promulgated, and later rooted a psychodynamic view of psychological problems. However timely and useful that emphasis was during its moment in history, as the later revolution's scenario unfolded, it became an Achilles heel (Mitchell & Trickett, 1980). Striking associations between impoverished living conditions, poor nourishment, restricted job and life opportunities, demeaning attitudes by others, and "ghettoism," on the one side and indicants of maladaptation on the other (Dohrenwend & Dohrenwend, 1981) led some observers to conclude that rectification in that sphere was primary prevention's first challenge (Rappaport, 1977; Reiff, 1968). Although there is much truth in that observation, it is not an easy challenge to meet. Imaginable solutions call for more power, resources, knowledge, and technology and better access lines than the combined mental health fields have. Even so, it is important that the connection be stressed: Society's most basic structures and systems powerfully affect people's adjustment.

Well short of the macrosociety, concepts and practices of system modification can be applied to specific institutional structures such as churches and schools and even in planning new communities (Klein, 1978; Lemkau, 1969; Murrell, 1971). Like the macrosociety, such subsystems have significant impact on the well-being of their inhabitants, for better or worse. The choice is either to accept such effects as they fall or to understand and try to shape them constructively. The ultimate question is how to engineer environments that optimize people's psychological well-being and development, a key objective for primary prevention in mental health. This question energizes a complex, three-step (two generative and one executive) process: (a) developing frameworks that accurately describe key dimensions of social environments and reflect differences among individual settings; (b) understanding relationships between specific setting qualities and person outcomes, both main effects and interaction effects such as optimal person–environment (ecological) matches; and (c) harnessing information derived from (b) to engineer environments that strengthen inhabitants' adjustment. Examples of work done at those three levels are cited in the next sections.

Attempts to describe dimensions of high-impact social environments have mushroomed in recent years. These efforts reflect diverse environments ranging from communities (Barker & Schoggen, 1973; Price & Blashfield, 1975) to schools (Barker & Gump, 1964; Moos, 1979a) to families (Jacob, 1975; Lennard & Bernstein, 1969). They also vary in molecularity of description. Stallings' (1975) framework for describing primary-grade class environments, for example, has more than 600 observational categories. Among the pioneering efforts in this domain is the long-term effort by Moos and his colleagues (Insel & Moos, 1974; Moos, 1973, 1974, 1976, 1979a, 1979b) to develop instruments to assess the basic properties of nine different types of social environments, including mental hospital wards, therapy groups, work settings, military companies, and educational environments. In that work several key dimensional clusters were found to recur repeatedly in describing inhabitants' perceptions of diverse environments. Virtually all environments studied could be categorized according to their standing on *relational* clusters, reflecting people's patterns of affiliation and involvement; *goal orientation* qualities, such as the environment's task orientation or competitiveness, and *maintenance* dimensions, including orderliness and rule clarity (Moos, 1974, 1979b).

Additional work has been done relating qualities of social environments to a broad range of inhabitant behaviors and adaptations. Educational environments, which significantly influence children's psychological development, well exemplify that thrust. In an early classic study Barker and Gump (1964) found that children from small (undermanned) schools, compared to thsoe from large (overmanned) schools, became involved in more and more varied activities, developed clearer identities, and had greater visibility to others. In like manner, Kelly (1979) explored the adaptation of students to high school environments characterized by high or low pupil turnover rates. Also at a molar level, the Bank Street group (Minuchin, Biber, Shapiro, & Zimiles, 1967; Zimiles, 1967) found that children educated in "modern" (thought- and process-oriented) compared to traditional educational environments had more highly differentiated self-concepts, greater acceptance of negative impulses, heavier investments in their status as children, and greater openness about their sex-role images. Similarly, Reiss and Martell (1974) found that children educated in open classes were more fluent, persistent, and imaginative than peers educated in contained classes.

Whereas the preceding studies were based on molar, often binary, descriptions of environment, other investigations have used more fully articulated frameworks to depict qualities of the school's social environment. Stallings' (1975) observations of 273 first- and third-grade Follow Through classes were based on an elaborately differentiated framework for coding class environment variables and events. She found important relationships between specific classroom qualities and variables such as child cooperation, persistence, and curiosity. Moos' recent (1979a) volume, based primarily on high school students' perceptions of class environments, is a gold mine for such information. For example, students from less compared to more structured classes reported greater satisfaction with the teacher, a greater sense of well-being, and less alienation. Relationship- and innovation-oriented classes are associated with greater student satisfaction and interest in content and enhanced social and personal growth; high perceived control classes are much the opposite. Although classes high in competition and task orientation augment achievement, they are associated with lower student morale, creativity, and interest.

Trickett and Moos (1974) reported in this regard that student satisfaction and positive mood were highest in classes perceived as high in involvement and as having close student–teacher relationships. Downward extensions of this approach to the elementary level have shown that fourth- and fifth-grade youngsters who saw their classes as high in order and organization, affiliation, and involvement, compared to age-mates who did not, had more positive moods and greater peer acceptance, received higher teacher ratings of adjustment, and had more self-control (Humphrey, 1981; Wright & Cowen, 1982).

Most of the data reported above are simple main-effects findings. In practice, however, things don't always work out the same way for all students. A study by Harpin and Sandler (1979), for example, found that externally compared to internally oriented seventh-grade boys were judged to have more serious adjustment problems in high-control classrooms; by contrast, internals had poorer grades than externals in high- as opposed to low-control classrooms. O'Neill (1976) reported that divergent-thinking children had significant higher self-esteem scores in open than in self-contained classes, and Reiss and Dyhdalo (1975) found that nonpersistent (distractible) boys had higher educational achievement scores in contained compared to open classes. Similar interactive findings at the college level were reported by Stern (1970). The point to stress is that the important person–environment interaction must be taken into account in planning optimal educational experiences (Kelly, 1979; Trickett, Kelly, & Todd, 1972).

The type of thinking thus far applied to school environments can be extended to other social contexts, as illustrated by Jacob's (1975) review of differential interaction patterns in normal and pathological families. Lennard and Bernstein's (1969) earlier research in that same area showed that normal families exceeded schizophrenic families in (a) their emphasis on self-initiated versus responsive behaviors; (b) age-appropriate socialization; (c) openness of communication lines; (d) parent support; and (e) harmonious interactions.

Describing a system's qualities accurately and understanding relationships between those qualities and person outcomes are the critical generative steps needed to inform interventions and/or manipulations (e.g., consultation, new teaching formats, structural change) designed to improve their effects on inhabitants' adjustment. This last difficult step operationalizes primary prevention's executive component. Several heuristic examples can be cited. Susskind (1979) was concerned with children's curiosity behavior, which is highly valued by educators as an abstraction. Curiosity behavior is reflected in the questions children ask in class. Susskind's empirical study of question asking in third- and sixth-grade social studies classrooms yielded paradoxical findings. In an average 30-minute class period, the entire class posed only 2 questions; by contrast teachers posed more than 50, most of which were factual. These data differed subtantially from the teachers' before-the-fact "guestimates" of the frequency of both their and children's questions. Teachers, in fact, asked many more questions than they themselves had earlier judged to be ideal. There was, in other words, a serious discrepancy between theory and practice with regard to question-asking behavior in the class. A system that greatly valued the abstract principle of children's curiosity failed to produce such behavior concretely. Identifying that unintended but important system quality helped Susskind (1979) to develop a program designed to align behavior more closely with expressed values. After presenting baseline question-asking data to teachers, he provided them with technology to stimulate student participation and curiosity. After the training, student question asking increased, teacher question asking decreased, and teachers asked a higher proportion of questions that led to student discussion. A system flaw was detected, and correctives were introduced that increased curiosity behavior.

Moos' framework provides useful entrees to environment change and has been so used successfully in several contexts (Moos, 1976, 1979a, 1979b). The key steps in the change cycle are to assess views of environment systematically based on relevant perspectives and sets, provide feedback to participants, plan specific environment changes based on that information, implement the changes (the executive step), and reassess. Moos (1979a) summarizes several such interventions, including ones designed to strengthen treatment programs for alcoholics, acute schizophrenics, and correctional inmates; change the milieu of an adolescent residential center; and modify classroom learning environments constructively.

Another way to approach the challenge of environment change is to modify teaching formats and practices in ways that can strengthen children's adjustment. If, as has been shown, high student-perceived affiliation and involvement relate consistently to positive teacher ratings of children's adjustment, then the goal of developing effective formats for strengthening those qualities is appealing conceptually. The literature on the effects of cooperative learning (Gump, 1980; Slavin, 1977) offers some suggestions. Recent advances, for example, have been reported in the development and application of the "jigsaw" (peer) teaching method (Aronson, Blaney, Stephan, Sikes, & Snapp, 1978; Blaney, Stephan, Rosenfield, Aronson, & Sikes, 1977).

This small-group approach, predicated on cooperation among pupils in mastering bodies of knowledge, was developed and evaluated in fifth-grade classrooms in Austin, Texas, over a 6-year period (Aronson et al., 1978). The vexing social issues behind the program's development were heightened racial tension and violence in schools following mandated busing. The program team decided to alter the structure of social studies classes to foster cooperation rather than competition. Students were organized into five-person jigsaw groups that cut across racial and academic ability lines. Each student had to master a segment of the day's assignment and teach it to group-mates. Without effective collaboration an assignment could not be completed satisfactorily. The program ran three to four times a week for 6 weeks. Not only did it help to address the problems of tension and violence for which it was developed, but jigsaw students did just as well academically as traditionally taught peers (Luckner, Rosenfield, Sikes, & Aronson, 1976). They also improved more in self-esteem and liking of peers. A later separate test of the approach, based on a 10-week social studies program for fifth-graders (Wright & Cowen, 1983), showed that jigsaw pupils came to see their classes as more orderly, organized, involved, and competitive than did no-program comparison students. Their teachers also rated them lower on problem behaviors and higher on competence behaviors. Finally, jigsaw subjects exceeded comparison subjects in academic performance, and the greatest gains were made by those with relatively *low* initial academic standing.

The above demonstrations suggest that the yoked strategies of establishing linkages between environmental properties and outcomes and introducing system change designed to improve outcomes offer a sensible, workable pathway to primary prevention in mental health.

Social Support Groups and Networks

The formal mental health system, as suggested, engages only a small fraction of people's appeals for psychological help. A large fraction is engaged less formally by caregivers, urban agents, and natural helpers. Even more basically, forces within natural environments operate to maintain and promote mental psychological health (Gottlieb, 1981). Social support groups and networks exemplify these forces. Caplan (1964) was among the first to stress the importance of social support. Since then, much has been written about this emergent area (Caplan & Killilea, 1976; Collins & Pancoast, 1976; Froland et al., 1981; Sarason, Carroll, Maton, Cohen, & Lorentz, 1977; Silverman, 1980). Support groups can be seen as patternings of attachments among individuals that develop out of basic human needs to share common concerns and problems and to identify ways to cope with them. One of their most important characterizing features is mutuality (Silverman, 1980). Both Heller (1979) and Gottlieb and Todd (1979) argue that they are very important for primary prevention in mental health because they capitalize on natural ties among people in ways that strengthen well-being. Support groups are made up of adults who get together to exchange words and ideas periodically around an area of shared concern. More specifically, they seek to promote emotional mastery of upsetting situations, to provide information, guidance, or skills bearing on their mutual concerns, and to offer members feedback and support with respect to their feelings and actions in ways designed to enhance self-images and behavior.

Because many people who get involved in support groups believe that certain problems and situations are understood best or perhaps only by those who have experienced them, the movement has largely been a "grass-roots" development, without major professional inputs. More strongly put, professional involvements are often actively *avoided.* Although several early classic programs (e.g., Alcoholics Anonymous, Synanon, Recovery Inc., and Parents Without Partners) drew heavily on support principles, support groups have truly mushroomed in number and type in the past decade. Examples include groups for parents of handicapped or retarded children, families of mental hospital patients, Vietnam veterans, gays, couples experiencing chronic infertility, bereaved people, and people with specific diseases or handicapping conditions, to mention but a few. Sarason et al. (1977), using social network concepts, describe a resource network program in which people exchange knowledge and services to meet multiple goals, including human service goals. Both Lenrow (1978) and Mitchell and Trickett (1980), following a similar conceptual approach, emphasize the importance of networks to psychological adaptation and the vital role they play in human help-seeking behavior.

The rapid growth of the support-group movement was cited prominently in the recent President's Commission Report (1978). Indeed, the report's first set of recommendations dealt with community supports—a term used broadly to include family, friends, and neighbors; organized community groups in churches, civic clubs, and voluntary organizations; and a broad range of volunteer programs. With its strong emphasis on meeting the mental health needs of the unserved and underserved, the Commission stressed that in many sections of modern society natural support systems are the prime if not the only de facto source of interpersonal helping (Collins & Pancoast, 1976; D'Augelli, Vallance, Danish, Young, & Gerdes, 1981).

Support group is a generic term for many different types of group interactions that share some common goals and procedures. In practice such groups vary along many dimensions, including obvious ones such as the specific mutual concern on which they focus and the extent to which they are self-starting, and less obvious ones, including how they proceed formally (e.g., with or without a leader), how planned versus spontaneous they are, reciprocity lines among and proximity of members, and the extent to which adjustment issues are focal. Relatively little is known about relationships among variations on those dimensions and outcomes.

Descriptions of support groups and how they are run far outnumber empirical evaluations of such programs. But there are some evaluations. Indeed, earlier in this chapter positive outcome data were reported based on several interventions featuring support components for divorcing adults, people experiencing multiple recent life events, and welfare mothers. Gottlieb (1981) summarizes other positive outcome data for several different types of support groups, including ones for adults about to enter "blended" marriages, recently widowed women, parents of newly born premature infants, cancer patients and their families, and couples going through the transition to initial parenthood. Thus encouragng early returns justify further investments to develop the area.

An intriguing variant of the support group approach, the so-called helper-therapy principle (Riessman, 1965), also bears mention. The fact that many low-status, disenfranchised social groups such as inner-city residents, retired people, and tuned-out junior and senior high school students are susceptible to emotional problems highlighted the challenge of finding ways to prevent such maladjustment. In developing an innovative mental health program for the inner-city poor, Riessman (see above) used indigenous neighborhood helpers as prime service providers, in the belief that the arrangement would bring realistic, effective services to people who sorely needed them and would also genuinely benefit the helpers. The essence of the helper-therapy principle is the conviction that for alienated, disenfranchised groups, whatever their age levels, socioeconomic status, or the reason for their disenfranchisement, the very process of bringing needed help to others can enhance their *own* mental health.

An entirely independent set of "academic" findings offers support and empirical footings for that principle. Staub's (1978) comprehensive review concludes that successful, real-life experience in helping others is a powerful force in shaping prosocial behavior in children. Riessman and Staub's conclusions reflect markedly different contexts, settings, methods, problem orientations, and data bases. That they accord so well encourages the systematic development of support programs based on the helper-therapy concept. Such programs embody mutually enhancing solutions to pressing social problems by yoking primary prevention strategies for helpers with secondary prevention approaches for those who need help. Available evidence suggests that that approach works well. Twinned adjustment gains in help agents and target persons have been reported in studies in which retirees (Cowen, Liebowitz, & Liebowitz, 1968; Matefy, 1978) and tuned-out high school students (Tefft & Kloba, 1980) functioned as help agents with young maladapting children in the schools and in which indigenous retirees worked as resource persons, expediters, and facilitators for other retirees in the same community (Gatz, Barbarin, Tyler, Mitchell, Moran, Wirzbicki, Crawford, & Engelman, 1982).

Support groups and networks have probably been around in one form or another for as long as people have. Their special qualities include their naturalness, spontaneity, and mutuallity, not to mention the empathy and esprit de corps that bedfellows in common adversity develop. Because such groups often form at or shortly after the time of an adverse experience, they can help to avert later, negative, outcomes. Support groups differ in significant ways, including cost, accessibility, and participants' sense of psychological comfort, from standard mental health services. A modest amount of positive program outcome data suggests that they may have special potential for primary prevention in mental health.

Although professionals have become more aware of the support-group movement in recent years and have done much research to clarify the nature and importance of support in human adaptation, the actual movement has deep, homeostatic roots that antedate professionalism. There are, no doubt, important roles (e.g., brokerage and expediting roles, program evaluation roles, and perhaps, in some cases, consultation and training roles) that professionals can play in the future of this development. At the same time stern warnings have been sounded about dangers of throwing out the baby with the bath water that may be inherent in overprofessionalizing it (Collins & Pancoast, 1976; Mitchell & Hurley, 1980; Rappaport, 1977). Such discussions stress the need for new professional roles based on collaborative relationships (Froland et al., 1981) and remind us that professionals may have as much to learn in this area as they can contribute (Mitchell & Hurley, 1980; Silverman, 1980).

SUMMARY AND OVERVIEW

Just as we have been warned not to think of the larger society in once-and-forever ways (Sarason, 1981), it would be a mistake to think of the mental health field in such terms. Seemingly elemental (yet, in reality, complex) questions such as What *is* a psychological problem? or What *is* a mental health service? are answered differently today than they were answered 100 or 500 years ago. Such answers cannot be separated from society's evolution, including major changes in living conditions and values and advances in knowledge and technology. What is called the mental health field at any point in time is embedded in a much broader context that reflects preceding realities.

The mental health field, as any other, seeks to understand and resolve the important problems of its mandated area. But concepts, conditions, and problems change, formerly satisfactory ways become inadequate, and effective new ways must be found to address new issues. What is now happening in community mental health and primary prevention in mental health should be seen in exactly those terms.

Structurally, the second mental health revolution, now almost a century old, was itself an attempt to find new, workable answers to the vexing problems of *its* time. That revolution occurred during a period of rapid social change and though it forged significant advances in many areas, it by no means solved all of mental health's many problems. Moreover, the major expansion that it brought about in the field's scope helped to identify new problems, such as the limited effectiveness of some of its pivotal approaches and the inequitable distribution and lack of reach of services for large segments of society. Awareness of those problems was hardly instanteous; but as they became clear more attention was directed to the challenges of adapting long-regnant concepts and ways to a significantly changed social context.

Before summarizing these concepts and practices, we shall present an oversimplified view of the paradigmatic intervention model spawned by the second mental health revolution. A person experiences psychological problems that cannot be satisfactorily resolved via the contact lines and person resources in his or her natural environment. The person seeks the help of a trained mental health professional through a clinic, hospital, community mental health center, or private practice. The professional undertakes some form of assessment of the problem (by interview, formal or informal testing, etc.)—enough to decide whether his or her services are appropriate and which are the optimal formats for rendering such services. Arrangements are made for regular meetings to take place between the professional and the client. The meetings are scheduled for a particular location and for fixed, predetermined time periods. Their ultimate purpose is to help clients to understand themselves better, feel better about themselves and their life situations, and/or be able to function more effectively. Sometimes, perhaps often, the approach works. But there are many instances in which it does not, and many other instances that for various reasons fall beyond the system's scope.

Although both the community mental health thrust and primary prevention in mental health are concerned about the mechanical defects and practical insufficiencies of prior approaches, they read those problems differently. They have different assumptions and concepts and therefore have qualitatively different defining practices. Both in rationale and in fact, differences between those two approaches are greater than the differences between community mental health approaches and past mental health orthodoxy. Simply put, community mental health approaches offer alternatives to past ways in the locus, timing, formats, and agents of mental health services in hopes that such modifications will yield more, and more effective, services. In this context the word *community* in the phrase *community mental health* should be seen as a potential means for achieving these objectives, not as an end in itself.

Community mental health approaches, like their orthodox predecessors, are targeted first to people experiencing problems, although through the judicious use of community settings they can offer earlier access to problems. Such approaches often have an aggressive outreaching quality, in contrast with mental health's past passive–receptive mode. It is hoped that by reaching problems sooner, before they accumulate, more effective interventions can be mounted. Community sites have also facilitated development of diverse, flexible formats that make services available and more attractive to large, heretofore functionally unreached segments of the population. Such approaches also pay greater heed to the realities of when and how people experience and express emotional problems. Consultation work with caregivers and urban agents, for example, is based on the awareness that these people inevitably engage psychological problems. Finally, the movement has stimulated active, imaginative uses of many new breeds of person-power in ways that broaden the nature of services and significantly expand their reach. On balance, the movement can be seen as a healthy, constructive development that rests on a clear view of many of mental health's important unresolved problems and a commitment to try to overcome them. It has unquestionably broadened mental health's armamentarium and provided fruitful starts toward solving longstanding, vexing problems. Among the issues that the approach has not yet well resolved are these two: (a) Since the development is rooted in the clinical tradition. Many of its key elements are not yet sufficiently or adequately evaluated. (b) However much the CMH approach can further evolve and develop, does its basic (conceptual) focus on *problems* restrict its ultimate potential?

Primary prevention in mental health comes from yet another ionosphere. It challenges the gut premises on which the mental health field has been built. Its paramount goals, to promote psychological health and prevent dysfunction from occurring in the first place, contrast sharply with mental health's historic emphases on understanding and doing one's best to contain or minimize psychological dysfunction. As a psychology of wellness, primary prevention in principle offers the mental health field the most attractive and far-reaching set of alternatives it has had since its inception. In this sense it is more than just a fine-tuning of advances from the second revolution; it has potential for becoming a true third mental health revolution.

Primary prevention in mental health includes a broad family of programs, manipulations, and interventions designed to prevent maladjustment or to promote psychological well-being. Properly conceived, its programs should rest on a sound, generative knowledge base demonstrating relationships among characteristics of people, settings, environments, life events and experiences, and positive or negative psychological outcomes. Programs for primary prevention in mental health must be set within the framework of several exacting structural requirements. They must be mass oriented to groups of people and before the fact of maladjustment, although they can be targeted to groups known epidemiologically to be at risk. They must also be intentional, in the sense of resting on a knowledge base suggesting that program operations can reasonably be expected either to short-circuit maladjustment or to promote psychological health. Finally, they must eventually provide data demonstrating that the preceding key goal has been met. One reason it is important to insist on those harsh definitional criteria is that they maximize the contrast between primary prevention and other mental health approaches. The stated definitional constraints, however, are all *structural;* they do not restrict either the target groups or the methodologies of primary prevention programs in mental health. Examples of such programs have been cited that are directed to very diverse groups, sociodemographically and according to age, and are based on a range of methodologies including mental health education, specific competence training, intervention around critical life events, social system analysis and modification, and support groups.

Primary prevention's current concepts and rhetoric are both far ahead of its firm demonstrations. The field's development has been hampered by extrinsic factors such as negative attitudes to the concept, protection of vested interest, and competition for scarce funds, as well as intrinsic factors that can be addressed by actions under our immediate control (Cowen, 1980a). Prominent among the latter is the need to adhere to a clear, discriminating definition of the concept, so that true primary prevention programs, as opposed to pseudoprograms so labeled by fiat, can be developed and assessed. A second intrinsic deterrent is that primary prevention's knowledge base and defining methodologies are very different from those on which the mental health field has always rested. Accordingly, different types of training (Cowen, 1983b) are needed to prepare primary prevention specialists in mental health. Such people are likely to have different identifications, patterns of professional interest, and interactions and work arenas from past mental health professionals. Also, to date, primary prevention has been insufficiently and inadequately researched. Although some steps have been taken to redress that imbalance (Cowen, 1982c), the field remains deficient both in heuristic program models and in empirical documentation.

Sarason (1971) inveighs against oversimplified interpretations based on "good guys" versus "bad guys" views of people and concepts. In the spirit of that observation, it is not the intent of this chapter to polarize the complex world of mental health into good versus bad approaches and to champion the former. The field of mental health emerged and evolved as it did for good and sufficient reasons. Many of its bedrock practices are good, important, and useful in the absolute sense. Some of these, with continuing refinement and additions to our knowledge base, can become even better in the future. But the world in which those ways came about has changed substantially in terms of living conditions, communication patterns, threats and dangers, and ways of perceiving and defining problems. One inevitable by-product of that change, which will doubtless also be a byproduct of as yet unknown and unknowable future social change, is that old answers no longer suffice, and new problems, for which there are no answers, have been identified.

Community mental health approaches and primary prevention approaches in mental health are addressed to the inevitable problems of a changing reality. One approach basically accepts past assumptions but seeks to develop more effective far-reaching practices; the other is based on a qualitatively different base of premises and programming. Both approaches show encouraging early clinical and empirical returns. Both can help to forge a richer, more utilitarian future mental health delivery system. Those of the old ways that are viable will continue to have a prominent place in that system. This chapter's main thesis is that humankind's psychological well-being can be well served by significant shifts in the allocation of society's limited mental health resources to nourish these two important families of emerging alternatives.

REFERENCES

Albee, G. W. *Mental health manpower trends.* New York: Basic Books, 1959.

Albee, G. W. Give us a place to stand and we will move the earth. In J. C. Harris (Ed.), *Mental health manpower needs in psychology.* Lexington, Ky.: University of Kentucky Press,1966.

Allen, G. J., Chinksy, J. M., Larcen, S. W., Lochman, J. E., & Selinger, H. V. *Community psychology and the schools: A behaviorally oriented multi-level preventive approach.* Hillsdale, N.J.: Lawrence Erlbaum Associates, 1976.

Anderson, S., & Messick, S. Social competence in young children. *Delopmental Psychology,* 1974, **10,** 282–293.

Apter, S. J. *Troubled children, troubled systems.* New York: Pergamon Press, 1982.

Arnhoff, F. N., Rubenstein, E. A., & Speisman, J. C. *Manpower for mental health.* Chicago: Aldine, 1969.

Aronson, E., Blaney, N., Stephan, C., Sikes, J., & Snapp, M. *The jigsaw classroom.* Beverly Hills, Calif.: Sage Publications, 1978.

Baisden, B., & Quarantelli, E. L. The delivery of mental health services in community disasters: An outline of research findings. *Journal of Community Psychology,* 1981, **9,** 195–203.

Balch, P. Social class and pathways to treatment at a community mental health center. *American Journal of Community Psychology,* 1974, **2,** 365–371.

Balch, P., & Miller, K. Social class and the community mental health center. *American Journal of Community Psychology,* 1974, **2,** 243–253.

Bard, M. *Training police as specialists in family crisis intervention.* Washington, D.C.: U.S. Government Printing Office, 1970.

Bardon, J. I. School psychology and school psychologists. *American Psychologist,* 1968, **23,** 187–194.

Barker, R. G., & Gump, P. *Big school, small school.* Stanford, Calif.: Stanford University Press, 1964.

Barker R. G., & Schoggen, P. *Qualities of community life.* San Francisco: Jossey-Bass, 1973.

Bergin, A. E., & Lambert, M. J. The evaluation of therapeutic outcomes, In S. L. Garfield, & A. E. Bergin (Eds.), *Handbook of psychotherapy and behavior change: An empirical analysis* (2nd ed.). New York: Wiley, 1978.

Bergin, A. E., & Suinn, R. M. Individual psychotherapy and behavior therapy. In M. R. Rosenzweig & L. C. Porter (Eds.), *Annual Review of Psychology,* 1975, **26,** 509–556.

Blaney, N. T., Stephan, C., Rosenfeld, D., Aronson, E., & Sikes, J. Interdependence in the classroom: A field study. *Journal of Educational Psychology,* 1977, **69,** 121–128.

Blanton, J., & Alley, S. Models of program success in New Careers programs. *Journal of Community Psychology,* 1977, **5,** 359–371.

Bloom, B. L. *Community mental health: A general introduction.* Monterey, Calif.: Brooks-Cole, 1977.

Bloom, B. L. Prevention of mental disorders: Recent advances in theory and practice. *Community Mental Health Journal,* 1979, **15,** 179–191.

Bloom, B. L. Social and community interventions. *Annual Review of Psychology,* 1980, **31,** 111–142.

Bloom, B. L., Asher, S. J., & White, S. W. Marital disruption as a stressor: A review and analysis. *Psychological Bulletin,* 1978, **85,** 867–894.

Bloom, B. L., Hodges, W. F., & Caldwell, R. A. A preventive program for the newly separated. *American Journal of Community Psychology,* 1982, **10,** 251–264.

Bockoven, J. S. *Moral treatment in American psychiatry.* New York: Springer, 1963.

Bogat, G. A., Jones, J. W., & Jason, L. A. School transitions: Preventive intervention following an elementary school closing. *Journal of Community Psychology,* 1980, **8,** 343–352.

Bower, E. M. *Early identification of emotionally handicapped children in school* (2nd ed.). Springfield, Ill.: C. C. Thomas, 1969.

Bower, E. M., & Lambert, N. M. *A process for in-school screening of children with emotional handicaps.* Sacramento, Calif.: California State Department of Education, 1961.

Bredemier, H. C. The socially handicapped and the agencies: A market analysis. In F. Riessman, J. Cohen, & A. Pearl (Eds.), *Mental health of the poor.* New York: Free Press, 1964.

Bruce, P. Relationship of self-acceptance to other variables with sixth-grade children oriented in self-understanding. *Journal of Educational Psychology,* 1958, **49,** 229–238.

Butcher, J. (1983). This volume.

Caplan, G. *Principles of preventive psychiatry.* New York: Basic Books, 1964.

Caplan, G. *Theories of mental health consultation.* New York: Basic Books, 1970.

Caplan, G. *Support systems and community mental health.* New York: Basic Books, 1974.

Caplan, G., & Killilea, M. (Eds.). *Support systems and mutual help: Multidisciplinary explorations.* New York: Grune & Stratton, 1976.

Caplan, R. *Psychiatry and community in 19th century America: The recurring concern with the environment in the prevention and treatment of mental disorder.* New York: Basic Books, 1969.

Carkhuff, R. R., & Pierce, R. M. *Trainer's guide in the art of helping: An introduction to life skills*. Amherst, Mass.: Human Resource Development Press, 1975.

Clark, A. W., & Yeomans, N. T. *Fraser House: Theory, practice and evaluation of a therapeutic community*. New York: Springer, 1969.

Colarelli, N. J., & Siegel, S. M. *Ward H: An adventure in innovation*. Princeton, N. J.: Van Nostrand, 1966.

Collins, A. H. Natural delivery systems: Accessible sources of power for mental health. *American Journal of Orthopsychiatry*, 1973, **43**, 46–52.

Collins, A. H., & Pancoast, D. L. *Natural helping networks: A strategy for prevention*. Washington, D.C.: National Association of Social Workers, 1976.

Cowen, E. L. Emergent approaches to mental health problems: An overview and directions for future work. In E. L. Cowen, E. A. Gardener, & M. Zax (Eds.), *Emergent approaches to mental health problems*. New York: Appleton-Century-Crofts, 1967.

Cowen, E. L. Social and community interventions. In P. Mussen & M. Rosenzweig (Eds.), *Annual Review of Psychology*, 1973, **24**, 423–472.

Cowen, E. L. Baby-steps toward primary prevention. *American Journal of Community Psychology*, 1977, **5**, 1–22.

Cowen, E. L. Some problems in community program evaluation research. *Journal of Consulting and Clinical Psychology*, 1978, **46**, 792–805.

Cowen, E. L. The wooing of primary prevention. *American Journal of Community Psychology*, 1980, **8**, 258–284.(a)

Cowen, E. L. The Primary Mental Health Project: Yesterday, today and tomorrow. *Journal of Special Education*, 1980, **14**, 133–154.(b)

Cowen, E. L. Primary prevention research: Barriers, needs and opportunities. *Journal of Primary Prevention*, 1982, **2**, 131–137.(a)

Cowen, E. L. The special number: A compleat roadmap. In E. L. Cowen (Ed.), Research in primary prevention in mental health. *American Journal of Community Psychology*, 1982, **10**, 239–250.(b)

Cowen, E. L. (Ed.). Research in primary prevention in mental health. *American Journal of Community Psychology*, 1982, **10**, 239–367.(c)

Cowen, E. L. Choices and alternatives for primary prevention in mental health. In M. P. Goldstein (Ed.), *Preventive intervention in schizophrenia: Are we ready?* Washington, D.C.: NIMH Primary Prevention Series, Government Printing Office, 1982.(d)

Cowen, E. L. Help is where you find it: Four informal helpgiving groups. *American Psychologist*, 1982, **37**, 385–395.(e)

Cowen, E. L. Primary prevention in mental health: Past, present and future. In R. D. Felner, L. A. Jason, J. Moritsugu, & S. S. Farber (Eds.), *Preventive psychology: Theory, research and practice in community interventions*. New York: Pergamon Press, 1983. (a)

Cowen, E. L. Training for primary prevention in mental health. *American Journal of Community Psychology*, 1983, **11**. In press (b)

Cowen, E. L., Dorr, D., & Pokracki, F. Selection of nonprofessional child-aides for a school mental health project. *Community Mental Health Journal*, 1972, **8**, 220–226.

Cowen, E. L., & Gesten, E. L. Community approaches to intervention with young children. In B. B. Wolman, J. Egan, & A. O. Ross (Eds.), *Handbook of treatment of mental disorders in childhood and adolescence*. Englewood Cliffs, N.J.: Prentice-Hall, 1978.

Cowen, E. L., Gesten, E. L., Boike, M., Norton, P., Wilson, A. B., & DeStefano, M. A. Hairdressers as caregivers: I: A descriptive profile of interpersonal help-giving involvements. *American Journal of Community Psychology,* 1979, **7,** 633–648.

Cowen, E. L., Gesten, E. L., Davidson, E. R., & Wilson, A. B. Hairdressers as caregivers: II. Relationships between helper-characteristics and help-giving behavior and feelings. *Journal of Prevention,* 1981, **1,** 225–239.

Cowen, E. L., Leibowitz, E., & Leibowitz, G. The utilization of retired people as mental health aides in the schools. *American Journal of Orthopsychiatry,* 1968, **38,** 900–909.

Cowen, E. L., & Lorion, R. P. Changing roles for the school mental health professional. *Journal of School Psychology,* 1976, **14,** 131–137.

Cowen, E. L., Lorion R. P., Kraus, R. M., & Dorr, D. Geometric expansion of helping resources. *Journal of School Psychology,* 1974, **12,** 288–295.

Cowen, E. L., McKim, B. J., & Weissberg, R. P. Bartenders as informal interpersonal help-agents. *American Journal of Community Psychology,* 1981, **9,** 715–729.

Cowen, E. L., Spinell, A., Wright, S., & Weissberg, R. P. Continuing dissemination of a school-based early detection and prevention model. *Professional Psychology,* 1983, **14,** 118–127.

Cowen, E. L., Trost, M. A., Lorion, R. P., Dorr, D., Izzo, L. D., & Isaacson, R. V. *New ways in school mental health: Early detection and prevention of school maladaptation.* New York: Human Sciences Press, 1975.

Cowen, E. L., Zax, M., Izzo, L. D., & Trost, M. A. The prevention of emotional disorders in the school setting: A further investigation. *Journal of Consulting Psychology,* 1966, **30,** 381–387.

Cumming, E., & Cumming, J. *Closed ranks: An experiment in mental health education.* Cambridge, Mass.: Harvard University Press, 1957.

Cumming, J., & Cumming, E. *Ego and milieu: Theory and practice of environmental therapy.* New York: Atherton, 1966.

Danish, S. J. Human development and human services: A marriage proposal. In I. Iscoe, B. L. Bloom, & C. D. Spielberger (Eds.), *Community psychology in transition.* Washington, D.C.: Hemisphere Publishing, 1977.

Danish, S. J., D'Augelli, A. R., & Hauer, A. L. *Helping skills: A basic training program* (2nd ed.) New York: Human Sciences Press, 1980.

D'Augelli, A. R., Vallance, T. R., Danish, S. J., Young, C. E., & Gerdes, J. L. The community helpers project: A description of a prevention strategy for rural communities. *Journal of Prevention,* 1981, **1,** 209–224.

Davis, J. A. *Education for positive mental health.* Chicago: Aldine, 1965.

Doane, J. A., & Cowen E. L. Interpersonal helpgiving among family practice lawyers. *American Journal of Community Psychology,* 1981, **9,** 547–558.

Dohrenwend, B. P., & Dohrenwend, B. S. *Social status and psychiatric disorder: A causal inquiry.* New York: Wiley-Interscience, 1969.

Dohrenwend, B. P., & Dohrenwend, B. S. Social and cultural influences on psychopathology. *Annual Review of Psychology,* 1974, **25,** 417–452.

Dohrenwend, B. P., & Dohrenwend, B. S. Socioenvironmental factors, stress and psychopathology. *American Journal of Community Psychology,* 1981, **9,** 128–164.

Dohrenwend, B. S. Social stress and community psychology. *American Journal of Community Psychology,* 1978, **6,** 1–14.

Donahue, G. T. A school district program for schizophrenic, organic and seriously disturbed children. In E. L. Cowen, E. A. Gardner, & M. Zax (Eds.), *Emergent approaches to mental health problems.* New York: Appleton-Century-Crofts, 1967.

Donahue, G. T., & Nichtern, S. *Teaching the troubled child.* New York: Free Press, 1965.

Dooley, D., & Catalano, R. Economic change as a cause of behavior disorder *Psychological Bulletin,* 1980, **87,** 450–468.

Dorr, D. An ounce of prevention. *Mental Hygiene,* 1972, **56,** 25–27.

Duggan, J. N. An example of secondary prevention activities in the schools: Talent searching in a culturally deprived population. In N. M. Lambert (Ed.), *The protection and promotion of mental health in schools.* Bethesda, Md.: U. S. Department of Health, Education and Welfare, Public Health Service Publication No. 1226, 1965.

Duhl, L. J. The changing face of mental health. In L. J. Duhl (Ed.), *The urban condition: People and policy in the metropolis.* New York: Basic Books, 1963.

Durlak, J. A. Comparative effectiveness of professional and nonprofessional helpers. *Psychological Bulletin,* 1979, **86,** 80–92.

Elardo, P. T., & Caldwell, B. M. The effects of an experimental social development program on children in the middle childhood period. *Psychology in the Schools,* 1979, **16,** 93–100.

Eysenck, H. J. The effects of psychotherapy: An evaluation. *Journal of Consulting Psychology,* 1952, **16,** 319–324.

Eysenck, H. J. The effects of psychotherapy. In H. J. Eysenck (Ed.), *Handbook of abnormal psychology.* New York: Basic Book, 1961.

Fairweather, G. W. *Methods for experimental social innovation.* New York: Wiley, 1967.

Fairweather, G. W., Sanders, D. H., Maynard, H., & Cressler, D. L. *Community life for the mentally ill: An alternative to institutional care.* Chicago: Aldine, 1969.

Fairweather, G. W., Sanders, D. H., & Tornatzky, L. *Creating change in mental health organizations.* New York: Pergamon Press, 1974.

Fairweather, G. W., & Tornatzky, L. G. *Experimental methods for social policy research.* New York: Pergamon Press, 1977.

Faris, R. E. L., & Dunham, H. W. *Mental disorders in urban areas.* Chicago: University of Chicago Press, 1939.

Felner, R. D., Farber, S. S., & Primavera, J. Children of divorce, stressful life events and transitions: A framework for preventive efforts. In R. H. Price, R. F. Ketterer, B. C. Bader, & J. Monahan (eds.), *Prevention in mental health: Research, policy and practice.* Beverly Hills, Calif.: Sage Publications, 1980.

Felner, R. D., Ginter, M., & Primavera, J. Primary prevention and school transitions: Social support and environmental structure. *American Journal of Commuty Psychology,* 1982, **10,** 277–290.

Felner, R. D., Jason, L. A., Moritsugu, J., & Farber, S. S. (Eds.). *Preventive psychology: Theory, research and practice in community interventions.* New York: Pergamon Press, 1983.

Felner, R. D., Stolberg, A. L., & Cowen, E. L. Crisis events and school mental health referral patterns of young children. *Journal of Consulting and Clinical Psychology,* 1975, **43,** 305–310.

Finkel, N. J. Strens and traumas: An attempt at categorization. *American Journal of Community Psychology,* 1974, **2,** 265–275.

Fishman, J. R., Denham, W. H., Levine, M., & Shatz, E. O. *New careers for the disadvantaged in human services: Report of a social experiment.* Washington, D. C.: Howard University Institute for Youth Studies, 1969.

Froland, C., Pancoast, D. L., Chapman, N. J., & Kimboko, P. J. *Helping networks and human services.* Beverly Hills, Calif.: Sage Publications, 1981.

Garmezy, N. *Vulnerable and invulnerable children: Theory, research and intervention.* Washington, D.C.: American Psychological Association, 1976.

Garmezy, N., Masten, A., Nordstrom, L., & Ferrarese, M. The nature of competence in normal and deviant children. In M. W. Kent & J. E. Rolf (Eds.), *The primary prevention of psychopathology (Vol. 3): Social competence in children.* Hanover, N.H.: University Press of New England, 1979.

Gartner, A. *Paraprofessionals and their performance.* New York. Praeger, 1971.

Gatz, M., Barbarin, O. A., Tyler, F. B., Mitchell, R. E., Moran, R. A., Wirzbicki, P. J., Crawford, J., & Engleman, A. Enhancement of individual and community competence: The older adult as community worker. *American Journal of Community Psychology,* 1982, **10,** 291–303.

Gershon, M., & Biller, H. B. *The other helpers: Paraprofessionals and nonprofessionals in mental health.* Lexington, Mass.: Lexington Books, 1977.

Gesten, E. L. A Health Resources Inventory: The development of a measure of the personal and social competence of primary grade children. *Journal of Consulting and Clinical Psychology,* 1976, **44,** 775–786.

Gesten, E. L., Flores de Apodaca, R., Rains, M. H., Weissberg, R. P., & Cowen, E. L. Promoting peer related social competence in young children. In M. W. Kent & J. E. Rolf (Eds.), *The primary prevention of psychopathology (Vol. 3): Social competence in children.* Hanover, N.H.: University Press of New England, 1979.

Gesten, E. L. Rains, M. H., Rapkin, B. D., Weissberg, R. P., Flores de Apodaca, R., Cowen, E. L., & Bowen, R. Training children in social problem-solving competencies: A first and second look. *American Journal of Community Psychology,* 1982, **10,** 95–115.

Gildea, M. C.-L. *Community mental health.* Springfield, Ill.: Thomas, 1959.

Gildea, M. C.-L., Glidewell, J. C., & Kantor, M. B. The St. Louis school mental health project: History and evaluation. In E. L. Cowen, E. A. Gardener, & M. Zax (Eds.), *Emergent approaches to mental health problems.* New York: Appleton-Century-Crofts, 1967.

Glidewell, J. C., Gildea, M. C.-L., & Kaufman, M. K. The preventive and therapeutic effects of two school mental health programs. *American Journal of Community Psychology,* 1973, **1,** 295–329.

Glidewell, J. C., & Swallow, C. S. *The prevalence of maladjustment in elementary schools: A report prepared for the Joint Commission on the mental health of children.* Chicago: University of Chicago Press, 1969.

Goldenberg, I. I. The Residential Youth Center: The creation of an assumptions-questioning rehabilitative setting. In *Criminal corrections in Connecticut: Perspectives and Progress.* West Hartford, Conn.: Connecticut Planning Committee on Criminal Administration, 1968.

Goldenberg, I. I. *Build me a mountain: Youth, poverty and the creation of new settings.* Cambridge, Mass.: M.I.T. Press, 1971.

Goldston, S. E. An overview of primary prevention programming. In D. C. Klein & S. E.

Goldston (Eds.), *Primary prevention: An idea whose time has come.* (DHEW Publication No. (ADM) 77-447). Washington, D.C.: U. S. Government Printing Office, 1977. (a)

Goldston, S. E. Primary prevention: A view from the federal level. In G. W. Albee & J. M. Joffe (Eds.), *Primary prevention of psychopathology, Vol. 1: The issues.* Hanover, N.H.: University Press of New England, 1977. (b)

Gomes-Schwartz, B., Hadley, S. H., & Strupp, H. H. Individual psychotherapy and behavior therapy. In M. R. Rosenzweig & L. W. Porter (Eds.), *Annual Review of Psychology,* 1978, **29,** 435–471.

Goodstein, L. D. *Consulting with human service systems.* Reading, Mass.: Addison-Wesley.

Gottfried, N. W. Effects of early intervention programs. In K. S. Miller & R. M. Dreger (Eds.), *Comparative studies of Blacks and Whites in the United States: Quantitative studies in social relations.* New York: Seminar Press, 1973.

Gottlieb, B. H. Reexamining the preventive potential of mental health consultation. *Canada's Mental Health,* 1974, **22,** 4–6.

Gottlieb, B. H. Preventive interventions involving social networks and social support. In B. H. Gottlieb (Ed.), *Social networks and social support.* Beverly Hills, Calif.: Sage Publications, 1981.

Gottlieb, B. H., & Todd, D. Characterizing and promoting social support in natural settings. In R. F. Muñoz, L. R. Snowden, & J. G. Kelly (Eds.), *Social and psychological research in community settings.* San Francisco: Jossey-Bass, 1979.

Gourash, N. Help-seeking: A review of the literature. *American Journal of Community Psychology,* 1978, **6,** 413–423.

Grady, M. A., Gibson, M. J. S., & Trickett, E. J. *Mental health consultation theory, practice and research: An annotated bibliography.* College Park, Md.: University of Maryland, 1980.

Graziano, A. M., DeGiovanni, I. S., & Garcia, K. A. Behavioral treatment of children's fears: A review. *Psychological Bulletin,* 1979, **86,** 804–830.

Griffith, C. R., & Libo, L. M. *Mental health consultants: Agents of community change.* San Francisco: Jossey-Bass, 1968.

Griggs, J. W., & Bonney, M. E. Relationship between "causal" orientation and acceptance of others, "self-ideal self" congruence, and mental health changes for fourth- and fifth-grade children. *Journal of Educational Research,* 1970, **63,** 471–477.

Grosser, C., Henry, W. E., & Kelly, J. G. (Eds.). *Nonprofessionals in the human services.* San Francisco: Jossey-Bass, 1969.

Gruver, G. G. College students as therapeutic agents. *Psychological Bulletin,* 1971, **76,** 111–127.

Gump, P. V. Intro-setting analysis: The third grade classroom as a special but instructive case. In E. P. Willems & H. L. Raush (Eds.), *Naturalistic viewpoints in psychological research.* New York: Holt, Rinehart & Winston, 1969.

Gump, P. V. The school as a social situation. In M. R. Rosenzweig & L. W. Porter (Eds.), *Annual Review of Psychology,* 1980, **31,** 553–582.

Gurin, G., Veroff, J., & Feld, S. *Americans view their mental health: A nationwide interview survey.* New York: Basic Books, 1960.

Harpin, P. M., & Sandler, I. N. Interactions of sex, locus of control and teacher control: Toward a student-classroom match. *American Journal of Community Psychology,* 1979, **7,** 621–632.

Harter, S. Effectance motivation reconsidered: Toward a developmental model. *Human Development*, 1978, **21**, 34–64.

Hartup, W. W. Peer relations and the growth of social competence. In M. W. Kent & J. E. Rolf (Eds.), *Primary prevention of psychopathology (Vol. 3): Social competence in children*. Hanover, N.H.: University Press of New England, 1979.

Heller, K. The effects of social support: Prevention and treatment implications. In A. P. Goldstein & F. H. Kanfer (Eds.), *Maximizing treatment in psychotherapy*. New York: Academic Press, 1979.

Heller, K., & Monahan, J. *Psychology and community change*. Homewood, Ill.: Dorsey, 1977.

Hereford, C. F. *Changing parental attitudes through group discussion*. Austin: University of Texas Press, 1963.

Hetherington, E. M., Cox, M., & Cox, R. The aftermath of divorce. In J. H. Stevens & M. Mathews (Eds.), *Mother-child, father-child relationships*. Washington, D.C.: National Association for Education of Young Children, 1978.

Hobbs, N. Mental health's third revolution. *American Journal of Orthopsychiatry*, 1964, **34**, 822–833.

Hobbs, N. Helping disturbed children: Psychological and ecological strategies. *American Psychologist*, 1966, **21**, 1105–1115.

Hobbs, N. The reeduction of emotionally disturbed children. In E. M. Bower & W. G. Hollister (Eds.), *Behavior science frontiers in education*. New York: Wiley, 1967.

Hobbs, N. *The futures of children*. San Francisco, Calif.: Jossey-Bass, 1975.

Hodgson, S. *Intervening to support high risk populations*. Toronto, Canada: University of Toronto Press, 1979.

Hollingshead, A. B., & Redlich, F. C. *Social class and mental illness: A community study*. New York: Wiley, 1958.

Hollister, W. G. Concept of strens in education: A challenge to curriculum development. In E. M. Bower & W. G. Hollister (Eds.), *Behavioral science frontiers in education*. New York: Wiley, 1967.

Holmes, T. A., & Masuda, M. Life change and illness susceptibility. In B. S. Dohrenwend & B. P. Dohrenwend (Eds.), *Stressful life events: Their nature and effects*. New York: Wiley, 1974.

Holzberg, J. D., Knapp, R. H., & Turner, J. L. College students as companions to the mentally ill. In E. L. Cowen, E. A. Gardner, & M. Zax (Eds.), *Emergent approaches to mental health problems*. New York: Appleton-Century-Crofts, 1967.

Huessy, H. R. (Ed.). *Mental health with limited resources: Yankee ingenuity in low-cost programs*. New York: Grune & Stratton, 1966.

Humphrey, L. L. Children's self-control in relation to perceived social environment: A naturalistic investigation. Unpublished doctoral dissertation, University of Rochester, 1981.

Insel, P. M., & Moos, R. H. Psychosocial environments: Expanding the scope of human ecology. *American Psychologist*, 1974, **29**, 179–188.

Iscoe, I. Community psychology and the competent community. *American Psychologist*, 1974, **29**, 607–613.

Jacob, T. Family interaction in disturbed and normal families. *Psychological Bulletin*, 1975, **82**, 33–65.

Jason, L. A. Early secondary prevention with disadvantaged preschool children. *American Journal of Community Psychology*, 1975, **3**, 33–46.

Jason, L. A., Robson, S. D., & Lipshutz, S. A. Enhancing sharing behaviors through the use of naturalistic contingencies. *Journal of Community Psychology,* 1980, **8,** 237–244.

Johnson, D. L., & Breckenridge, J. N. The Houston Parent-Child Development Center and the primary prevention of behavior problems in young children. *American Journal of Community Psychology,* 1982, **10,** 305–316.

Joint Commission on Mental Health of Children. *Crisis in child mental health: Challenge for the 1970's.* New York: Harper & Row, 1969.

Joint Commission on Mental Illness and Health. *Action for mental health.* New York: Basic Books, 1961.

Kalafat, J., & Boroto, D. R. The paraprofessional movement as a paradigm community psychology endeavor. *Journal of Community Psychology,* 1977, **5,** 3–12.

Kaplan, E. M., & Cowen, E. L. The interpersonal helpgiving behaviors of industrial foremen. *Journal of Applied Psychology,* 1981, **66,** 633–638.

Kellam, S. G., Branch, J. D., Agrawal, K. C., & Ensminger, M. E. *Mental health and going to school: The Woodlawn program of assessment, early intervention, and evaluation.* Chicago: University of Chicago Press, 1975.

Kellam, S. G., Branch, J. D., Agrawal, K. C., & Grabill, M. E. Woodlawn Mental Health Center: An evolving strategy for planning community mental health. In S. E. Golann & C. Eisdorfer (Eds.), *Handbook of community mental health.* New York: Appleton-Century-Crofts, 1972.

Kellam, S. G., & Schiff, S. K. Adaptation and mental illness in the first grade classroom of an urban community. American Psychiatric Association, *Psychiatric Research Reports,* 1967, **21,** 79–91.

Kelly, J. G. The mental health agent in the urban community. In Symposium No. 10, *Urban America and the planning of mental health services.* New York: Group for Advancement of Psychiatry, 1964.

Kelly, J. G. The quest for valid preventive interventions. In G. Rosenblum (Ed.), *Issues in community psychology and preventive mental health.* New York: Behavioral Publications, 1971.

Kelly, J. G. The search for ideas and deeds that work. In G. W. Albee & J. M. Joffe (Eds.), *Primary prevention of psychopathology (Vol. 1): The issues.* Hanover, N.H.: University Press of New England, 1977.

Kelly, J. G. (Ed.). *Adolescent boys in high school: A psychological study of coping and adaptation.* Hillsdale, N.J.: Lawrence Erlbaum Associates, 1979.

Kent, M. W., & Rolf, J. E. (Eds.). *Primary prevention of psychopathology (Vol. 3): Social competence in children.* Hanover, N.H.: University Press of New England, 1979.

Klein, D. C. (Ed.). *Psychology of the planned community: The New Town experience.* New York: Human Sciences Press, 1978.

Klein, D. C., & Goldston, S. E. (Eds.). *Primary prevention: An idea whose time has come.* Washington, D.C.: U.S. Department of Health, Education and Welfare, 1977.

Klein, W. L. The training of human service aides. In E. L. Cowen, E. A. Gardner, & M. Zax (Eds.), *Emergent approaches to mental health problems.* New York: Appleton-Century-Crofts, 1967.

Kornberg, M. S., & Caplan, G. Risk factors and preventive intervention in child therapy: A review. *Journal of Prevention,* 1980, **1,** 71–133.

Kuhn, T. S. *The structure of scientific revolutions* (2nd ed.). Chicago: University of Chicago Press, 1970.

LaGreca, A. M., & Santagrossi, D. A. Social skills training with elementary school students: A behavioral group approach. *Journal of Consulting and Clinical Psychology,* 1980, **48,** 220–227.

Lemkau, P. V. The planning project for Columbia. In M. F. Shore & F. V. Mannino (Eds.), *Mental health and the community: Problems, programs and strategies.* New York: Behavioral Publications, 1969.

Lennard, H. L., & Bernstein, A. *Patterns in human interactions.* San Francisco: Jossey-Bass, 1969.

Lenrow, P. B. The work of helping strangers. *American Journal of Community Psychology,* 1978, **6,** 555–571.

Lerner, B. *Therapy in the ghetto: Political importance and personal disintegration.* Baltimore: Johns Hopkins University Press, 1972.

Levine, M., & Levine, A. *A social history of helping services: Clinic, court, school and community.* New York: Appleton-Century-Crofts, 1970.

Levitt, E. E. The results of psychotherapy with children: An evaluation. *Journal of Consulting Psychology,* 1957, **21,** 189–204.

Levitt, E. E. Research on psychotherapy with children. In A. E. Bergin & S. L. Garfield (Eds.), *Handbook of psychotherapy and behavior change: An empirical analysis.* New York: Wiley, 1971.

Lieberman, M. A., & Mullan, J. T. Does help help? The adaptive consequences of obtaining help from professionals and social networks. *American Journal of Community Psychology,* 1978, **6,** 499–517.

Lorion, R. P. Socioeconomioc status and traditional treatment approaches reconsidered. *Psychological Bulletin,* 1973, **79,** 263–270.

Lorion, R. P. Patient and therapist variables in the treatment of low-income patients. *Psychological Bulletin,* 1974, **81,** 344–354.

Lorion, R. P., Cowen, E. L., & Caldwell, R. A. Problem types of children referred to a school based mental health program. *Journal of Consulting and Clinical Psychology,* 1974, **42,** 491–496.

Lorion, R. P., Cowen, E. L., & Caldwell, R. A. Normative and parametric analyses of school maladjustment. *American Journal of Community Psychology,* 1975, **3,** 293–301.

Luckner, G. W., Rosenfeld, D., Sikes, J., & Aronson, E. Performance in interdependent classrooms: A field study. *American Educational Research Journal,* 1976, **13,** 115–123.

Maccoby, N., & Alexander, J. Reducing heart disease risk using the mass media: Comparing the effects on three communities. In R. F. Muñoz, L. R. Snowden, & J. G. Kelly (Eds.) *Social and psychological research in community settings.* San Francisco: Jossey-Bass, 1979.

MacLennan, B. W. New Careers: Program development and the process of institutional change. In M. F. Shore & F. V. Mannino (Eds.), *Mental health and the community: Problems, programs and strategies.* New York: Behavioral Publications, 1969.

Mannino, F. V., MacLennan, B. W., & Shore, M. W. *The practice of mental health consultation.* New York: Gardner Press, 1975.

Mannino, F. V., & Shore, M. F. The effects of consultation: A review of the literature. *American Journal of Community Psychology,* 1975, **3,** 1–21.

Matefy, R. E. Evaluation of a remediation program using senior citizens as psychoeducational agents. *Community Mental Health Journal,* 1978, **14,** 327–336.

Medway, F. J. School consultation research: Past trends and future directions. *Professional Psychology,* 1982, **13,** 422–430.

Melamed, B. G., & Siegel, L. J. Reduction of anxiety in children facing hospitalization and surgery, by use of filmed modeling. *Journal of Consulting and Clinical Psychology,* 1975, **43,** 511–521.

Mercer, J. R. *Labeling the mentally retarded.* Berkeley, Calif.: University of California Press, 1973.

Minuchin, P., Biber, B., Shapiro, E., & Zimiles, H. *The psychological impact of school experience.* New York: Basic Books, 1969.

Mitchell, R. E., & Hurley, D. J. Collaboration with natural helping networks: Lessons from studying paraprofessionals. In B. H. Gottlieb (Ed.), *Social networks and social support.* Beverly Hills, Calif.: Sage Publications, 1981.

Mitchell, R. E., & Trickett, E. J. Task force report: Social networks as mediators of social support: An analysis of effects and determinants of social networks. *Community Mental Health Journal,* 1980, **16,** 27–44.

Monahan, J., & Vaux, A. Task force report: The macroenvironment and community mental health. *Community Mental Health Journal,* 1980, **16,** 14–26.

Moos, R. H. Conceptualizations of human environments. *American Psychologist,* 1973, **28,** 652–665.

Moos, R. H. *Evaluating treatment environments: A social ecological approach.* New York: Wiley, 1974.

Moos, R. H. Evaluating and changing community settings. *American Journal of Community Psychology,* 1976, **4,** 313–326.

Moos, R. H. *Evaluating educational environments.* San Francisco: Jossey-Bass, 1979. (a)

Moos, R. H. Improving social settings by social climate measurement and feedback, In R. F. Muñoz, L. R. Snowden, & J. G. Kelly (eds.), *Social and psychological research in community settings.* San Francisco: Jossey-Bass, 1979. (b)

Muñoz, R. F., Glish, M., Soo-Hoo, T., & Robertson, J. The San Francisco Mood Survey Project: Preliminary work toward the prevention of depression. *American Journal of Community Psychology,* 1982, **10,** 317–329.

Murrell, S. A. (Ed.). *Newcom: The psychosocial environment* (Vol. 2). Louisville, Ky.: University of Louisville Urban Studies Center, 1971.

Muuss, R. E. The effects of a one and two year causal learning program. *Journal of Personality,* 1960, **28,** 479–491.

Oden, S. L. A child's social isolation: Origins, prevention, intervention. In G. Cartledge & J. F. Milburn (Eds.), *Teaching social skills to children.* New York: Pergamon Press, 1980.

Ojemann, R. H. Investigations on the effects of teacher understanding and appreciation of behavior dynamics. In G. Caplan (Ed.), *Prevention of mental disorders in children.* New York: Basic Books, 1961.

O'Neill, P. Educating divergent thinkers: An ecological investigation. *American Journal of Community Psychology,* 1976, **4,** 99–107.

Paul, G. L. Chronic mental patient: Current status—future directions. *Psychological Bulletin,* 1969, **71,** 81–94.

Pearl, A., & Riessman, F. *New careers for the poor.* New York: Free Press, 1965.

Peck, H. B., & Kaplan, S. R. A mental health program for the urban multi-service center. In

M. F. Shore & F. V. Mannino (Eds.), *Mental health and the community: Problems, programs and strategies*. New York: Behavioral Publications, 1969.

President's Commission on Mental Health. *Report to the President* (Vol. I). Washington, D.C.: U. S. Government Printing Office, Stock No. 040-000-00390-8, 1978.

Price, R. H., & Blashfield, R. K. Explorations in the taxonomy of behavior settings: Analysis of dimensions and classification of settings. *American Journal of Community Psychology*, 1975, **3**, 335–357.

Price, R. H., Ketterer, R. F. Bader, B. C., & Monahan, J. (Eds.). *Prevention in mental health: Research, policy and practice*. Beverly Hills, Calif.: Sage Publications, 1980.

Rae-Grant, Q., & Stringer, L. A. Mental health programs in schools. In M. F. Shore & F. V. Mannino (Eds.), *Mental health and the community: Problems, programs, and strategies*. New York: Behavioral Publications, 1969.

Ramey, L. A. (Ed.). *Issues in Black mental health*. Atlanta, Ga.: Southern Regional Education Board, 1978.

Rappaport, J. *Community psychology: Values, research, and action*. New York: Holt, Rinehart & Winston, 1977.

Rappaport, J., Davidson, W. S., Wilson, M. N., & Mitchell, A. Alternatives to blaming the victim or the environment: Our places to stand have not moved the earth. *American Psychologist*, 1975, **30**, 525–528.

Rappaport, J., Seidman, E., & Davidson, W. S. Demonstration research and manifest versus true adaptation: The natural history of a research project to divert adolescents from the legal system. In R. F. Muñoz, L. R. Snowden & J. G. Kelly (Eds.), *Social and psychological research in community settings*. San Francisco, Calif.: Jossey-Bass, 1979.

Reiff, R. Mental health manpower and institutional change. *American Psychologist*, 1966, **21**, 540–548.

Reiff, R. Social interventions and the problem of psychological analysis. *American Psychologist*, 1968, **23**, 534–541.

Reiff, R., & Riessman, F. The indigenous nonprofessional: A strategy of change in community action and community mental health programs. *Community Mental Health Journal*, Monograph No. 1, 1965.

Reiss, S., & Dyhdalo, N. Persistence, achievement and open-space environments. *Journal of Educational Psychology*, 1975, **67**, 506–513.

Reiss, S., & Martell, R. *Educational and psychological effects of open space education in Oak Park, Illinois*. Final Report to Board of Education, District 97, Oak Park, Illinois, 1974.

Rhoads, D. L., & Raymond, J. S. Quality of life and the competent community. *American Journal of Community Psychology*, 1981, **9**, 293–301.

Rieff, P. *Freud: The mind of the moralist*. New York: Viking Press, 1959.

Riessman, F. The "helper" therapy principle. *Social Work*, 1965, **10**, 27–32.

Riessman, F. A neighborhood-based mental health approach. In E. L. Cowen, E. A. Gardner, & M. Zax (Eds.), *Emergent approaches to mental health problems*. New York: Appleton-Century-Crofts, 1967.

Riessman, F., Cohen, J., & Pearl, A. (Eds.). *Mental health of the poor*. New York: Free Press, 1964.

Riessman, F., & Popper, H. I. *Up from poverty: New career ladders for nonprofessionals.* New York: Harper & Row, 1968.

Rioch, M. J. Pilot projects in training mental health counselors. In E. L. Cowen, E. A. Gardner, & M. Zax (Eds.), *Emergent approaches to mental health problems.* New York: Appleton-Century-Crofts, 1967.

Robinson, R., DeMarche, D. F., & Wagle, M. K. *Community resources in mental health.* New York: Basic Books, 1961.

Roskin, M. Coping with life changes: A preventive social work approach. *American Journal of Community Psychology,* 1982, **10,** 331–340.

Ryan, W. (Ed.). *Distress in the city: Essays on the design and administration of urban mental health services.* Cleveland: Case-Western Reserve University Press, 1969.

Ryan, W. *Blaming the victim.* New York: Random House, 1971.

Sandler, I. N. Characteristics of women working as child-aides in a school based preventive mental health program. *Journal of Consulting and Clinical Psychology,* 1972, **36,** 56–61.

Sandler, I. N. Social support measures, stress and maladjustment of poor children. *American Journal of Community Psychology,* 1980, **8,** 41–52.

Sanua, V. D. Sociocultural aspects of psychotherapy and treatment: A review of the literature. In L. E. Abt & L. Bellak (Eds.), *Progress in clinical psychology* (Vol. VIII). New York: Grune & Stratton, 1966.

Sarason, S. B. *The culture of the school and the problem of change.* Boston: Allyn-Bacon, 1971.

Sarason, S. B. Community psychology, networks and Mr. Everyman. *American Psychologist,* 1976, **31,** 317–328.

Sarason, S. B. *Psychology misdirected.* New York: Free Press, 1981.

Sarason, S. B. *Psychology and social action: Selected papers.* New York: Praeger, 1982.

Sarason, S. B., Carroll, C., Maton, K., Cohen, S., & Lorentz, E. *Human services and resource networks.* San Francisco: Jossey-Bass, 1977.

Sarason, S. B., & Doris, J. *Educational handicap, public policy, and social history: A broadened perspective on mental retardation.* New York: Free Press, 1979.

Sarason, S. B., Zitnay, G., & Grossman, F. K. *The creation of a community setting.* Syracuse, N.Y.: Syracuse University Press, 1971.

Schanie, G. F., & Sundel, M. A community mental health innovation in mass media prevention evaluation: The Alternatives Project. *American Journal of Community Psychology,* 1978, **6,** 573–581.

Scheff, T. J. *Being mentally ill: A sociological theory.* Chicago: Aldine, 1966.

Schofield, W. *Psychotherapy: The purchase of friendship.* Englewood Cliffs, N.J.: Prentice-Hall, 1964.

Searcy-Miller, M. L. An investigation of the interpersonal helpgiving involvements of black and white beauticians. Unpublished doctoral dissertation, University of Rochester, 1980.

Shure, M. B., & Spivack, G. Interpersonal problem-solving in young children: A cognitive approach to prevention. *American Journal of Community Psychology,* 1982, **10,** 341–356.

Silverman, P. R. The widow as a caregiver in a program of preentive intervention with other widows. In G. Caplan & M. Killilea (Eds.), *Support systems and mutual help: Multidisciplinary explorations.* New York: Grune & Stratton, 1976.

Silverman, P. R. *Mutual help groups: Organization and development.* Beverly Hills, Calif.: Sage Publications, 1980.

Slavin, R. Classroom reward structure: An analytical and practical review. *Review of Educational Research,* 1977, **44,** 633–650.

Smith, M. B., & Hobbs, N. The community and the community mental health center. *American Psychologist,* 1966, **21,** 499–509.

Sobey, F. *The nonprofessional revolution in mental health.* New York: Columbia University Press, 1970.

Spielberger, C. D. A mental health consultation program in a small community with limited professional mental health resources. In E. L. Cowen, E. A. Gardner, & M. Zax (Eds.), *Emergent approaches to mental health problems.* New York: Appleton-Century-Crofts, 1967.

Spivack, G., Platt, J. J., & Shure, M. B. *The problem-solving approach to adjustment.* San Francisco: Jossey-Bass, 1976.

Spivack, G., & Shure, M. B. *Social adjustment of young children.* San Francisco: Jossey-Bass, 1974.

Srole, L., Langner, T. S., Michael, S. T., Opler, M. K., & Rennie, T. A. C. *Mental health in the metropolis.* New York: McGraw-Hill, 1962.

Stallings, J. Implementation and child effects of teaching practices in Follow Through classrooms. *Monographs of the Society for Research on Child Development,* 1975, **40** (Serial No. 163).

Stamps, L. W. *Enhancing success in school for deprived children by teaching realistic goal setting.* Paper presented at Society for Research in Child Development, Denver, 1975.

Staub, E. *Positive social behavior and morality (Vol. 1): Social and interpersonal influences.* New York: Academic Press, 1978.

Stern, G. *People in context.* New York: Wiley, 1970.

Susskind, E. Encouraging teachers to encourage children's curiosity: A pivotal competence. *Journal of Clinical Child Psychology,* 1979, **8,** 101–106.

Tableman, B., Marciniak, D., Johnson, D., & Rodgers, R. Stress management training for women on public assistance. *American Journal of Community Psychology,* 1982, **10,** 359–367.

Tefft, B. M., & Kloba, J. A. Underachieving high-school students as mental health aides with maladapting primary grade children. *American Journal of Community Psychology,* 1981, **9,** 303–319.

Thelen, M. H., Fry, R. A., Fehrenbach, P. A., & Frautschi, N. M. Therapeutic videotape modeling: A review. *Psychological Bulletin,* 1979, **86,** 701–720.

Trickett, E. J., Kelly, J. G., & Todd, D. M. The social environment of the high school: Guidelines for individual change and organizational redevelopment. In S. E. Golann & C. Eisdorfer (Eds.), *Handbook of community psychology.* New York: Appleton-Century-Crofts, 1971.

Trickett, E. J., & Moos, R. H. Personal correlates of contrasting environments: Student satisfaction in high school classrooms. *American Journal of Community Psychology,* 1974, **2,** 1–12.

Umbarger, C. D., Dalsimer, J. S., Morrison, A. P., & Breggin, P. R. *College students in a mental hospital*. New York: Grune & Stratton, 1962.

Urbain, E. S., & Kendall, P. C. Review of social-cognitive problem solving interactions with children. *Psychological Bulletin*, 1980, **88**, 109–143.

Van Vleet, P., & Kannegieter, S. (Eds.). *Investments in prevention: The prevention of learning and behavior problems in young children*. San Francisco: Pace ID Center, 1969.

Verdone, P. *Early identification, referral, and treatment of bar patrons in crisis*. Symposium presented at the meeting of the American Psychological Association, Chicago, 1975.

Veroff, J., Kulka, R. A., & Douvan, E. *Mental health in America: Patterns of help-seeking from 1957–1976*. New York: Basic Books, 1981.

Vogelsong, E. L., Most, R. K., & Yanchko, A. Relationship enhancement training for preadolescents in public schools. *Journal of Clinical Child Psychology*, 1979, **8**, 97–100.

Wanlass, R. L., & Prinz, R. J. Methodological issues in conceptualizing and treating childhood social isolation. *Psychological Bulletin*, 1982, **92**, 39–55.

Weinstein, L. Project Re-Ed schools for emotionally disturbed children: Effectiveness as viewed by referring agencies, parents and teachers. *Exceptional Children*, 1969, **35**, 703–711.

Weisenfeld, A. R., & Weis, H. M. A mental health consultation program for beauticians. *Professional Psychology*, 1979, **10**, 786–792.

Weissberg, R. P., Cowen, E. L., Lotyczewski, B. S., & Gesten, E. L. The Primary Mental Health Project: Seven consecutive years of program outcome research. *Journal of Consulting and Clinical Psychology*, 1983, **51**, 100–107.

Weissberg, R. P., & Gesten, E. L. Considerations for developing effective school-based social problem-solving programs. *School Psychology Review*, 1982, **11**, 56–63.

Weissberg, R. P., Gesten, E. L., Carnrike, C. L., Toro, P. A., Rapkin, B. D., Davidson, E., & Cowen E. L. Social problem-solving skills training: A competence building intervention with 2nd–4th grade children. *American Journal of Community Psychology*, 1981, **9**, 411–424.

Weissberg, R. P., Gesten, E. L., Rapkin, B. D., Cowen, E. L., Davidson, E., Flores de Apodaca, R., & McKim, B. J. The evaluation of a social problem-solving training program for suburban and inner-city third grade children. *Journal of Consulting and Clinical Psychology*, 1981, **49**, 251–261.

White, R. W. Motivation reconsidered: The concept of competence. *Psychological Review*, 1959, **66**, 297–333.

Winer, J. I., Hilpert, P. L., Gesten, E. L., Cowen, E. L., & Schubin, W. E. The evaluation of a kindergarten social problem-solving program. *Journal of Primary Prevention*, 1982, **2**, 205–216.

Wright, S., & Cowen, E. L. Student perception of school environment and its relationship to mood, achievement, popularity and adjustment. *American Journal of Community Psychology*, 1982, **10**, 687–703.

Wright, S., & Cowen, E. L. The effects of peer teaching on student perceptions of class environment, adjustment and academic performance. *Journal of Community Psychology*, 1983, **11**. (In press.)

Zautra, A., & Goodbart, D. Quality of life indicators: A review of the literature. *Community Mental Health Review*, 1979, **4**, 1–10.

Zax, M., & Cowen, E. L. *Abnormal psychology: Changing conceptions.* (2nd ed). New York: Holt, Rinehart & Winston, 1976.

Zax, M., & Specter, G. A. *An introduction to community psychology.* New York: Wiley, 1974.

Zimiles, H. Preventive aspects of school experience. In E. L. Cowen, E. A.Gardner, & M. Zax (Eds.), *Emergent approaches to mental health problems.* New York: Appleton-Century-Crofts, 1967.

Author Index

Subject Index

Psychology and Psychiatry in Courts and Corrections: Controversy and Change
  by Ellsworth A. Fersch, Jr.
Restricted Environmental Stimulation: Research and Clinical Applications
  by Peter Suedfeld
Personal Construct Psychology: Psychotherapy and Personality
  edited by Alvin W. Landfield and Larry M. Leitner
Mothers, Grandmothers, and Daughters: Personality and Child Care in
Three-Generation Families
  by Bertram J. Cohler and Henry U. Grunebaum
Further Explorations in Personality
  edited by A. I. Rabin, Joel Aronoff, Andrew M. Barclay, and Robert A. Zucker
Hypnosis and Relaxation: Modern Verification of an Old Equation
  by William E. Edmonston, Jr.
Handbook of Clinical Behavior Therapy
  edited by Samuel M. Turner, Karen S. Calhoun, and Henry E. Adams
Handbook of Clinical Neuropsychology
  edited by Susan B. Filskov and Thomas J. Boll
The Course of Alcoholism: Four Years After Treatment
  by J. Michael Polich, David J. Armor, and Harriet B. Braiker
Handbook of Innovative Psychotherapies
  edited by Raymond J. Corsini
The Role of the Father in Child Development (Second Edition)
  edited by Michael E. Lamb
Behavioral Medicine: Clinical Applications
  by Susan S. Pinkerton, Howard Hughes, and W. W. Wenrich
Handbook for the Practice of Pediatric Psychology
  edited by June M. Tuma
Change Through Interaction: Social Psychological Processes of Counseling and
Psychotherapy
  by Stanley R. Strong and Charles D. Claiborn
Drugs and Behavior (Second Edition)
  by Fred Leavitt
Handbook of Research Methods in Clinical Psychology
  edited by Philip C. Kendall and James N. Butcher
A Social Psychology of Developing Adults
  by Thomas O. Blank
Women in the Middle Years: Current Knowledge and Directions for Research and Policy
  edited by Janet Zollinger Giele
Loneliness: A Sourcebook of Current Theory, Research and Therapy
  edited by Letitia Anne Peplau and Daniel Perlman
Hyperactivity: Current Issues, Research, and Theory (Second Edition)
  by Dorothea M. Ross and Sheila A. Ross
Review of Human Development
  edited by Tiffany M. Field, Aletha Huston, Herbert C. Quay, Lillian Troll,
  and Gordon E. Finley
Agoraphobia: Multiple Perspectives on Theory and Treatment
  edited by Dianne L. Chambless and Alan J. Goldstein
The Rorschach: A Comprehensive System, Volume III: Assessment of Children and Adolescents
  by John E. Exner, Jr. and Irving B. Weiner
Handbook of Play Therapy
  edited by Charles E. Schaefer and Kevin J. O'Connor
Adolescent Sexuality in a Changing American Society: Social and Psychological Perspectives
for the Human Service Professions (Second Edition)
  by Catherine S. Chilman
Failures in Behavior Therapy
  edited by Edna B. Foa and Paul M.G. Emmelkamp